CHESHIRE'S MODERN LAW

OF

REAL PROPERTY

TWELFTH EDITION

BY

E. H. BURN

B.C.L., M.A.

of Lincoln's Inn, Barrister, Student of Christ Church, Oxford,
Lecturer in the Law of Land in the Inns of Court

LONDON

BUTTERWORTHS

1976

ENGLAND:	BUTTERWORTH & CO. (PUBLISHERS) LTD. LONDON: 88 Kingsway, WC2B 6AB
AUSTRALIA:	BUTTERWORTH & CO. (AUSTRALIA) LTD. SYDNEY: 586 Pacific Highway, Chatswood, NSW 2067 Also at Melbourne, Brisbane, Adelaide and Perth
CANADA:	BUTTERWORTH & CO. (CANADA) LTD. TORONTO: 14 Curity Avenue, 374
NEW ZEALAND:	BUTTERWORTH & CO. (NEW ZEALAND) LTD. WELLINGTON: 26–28 Waring Taylor Street, 1
SOUTH AFRICA:	BUTTERWORTH & CO. (SOUTH AFRICA) (PTY.) LTD. DURBAN: 152–154 Gale Street

©

BUTTERWORTH & CO. (PUBLISHERS) LTD.
1976

ISBN Casebound: 0 406 56543 0
Limp: 0 406 56544 9

PREFACE TO THE TWELFTH EDITION

Professor Cheshire was born ninety years ago, on June 27th, 1886. The editor presents to its nonagenarian author his second edition of *Modern Law of Real Property*, and he does so with the affection and respect in which Professor Cheshire is held by many lawyers of many generations. It is again entirely due to his encouragement and approval that it has been possible to prepare this edition.

Further changes have been made in layout and treatment. In particular, the passages which deal with contract have been gathered from the various parts of the book and penned in a new section in the introduction; and the chapter on concurrent interests now follows that on settlements and trusts for sale, with the addition of a section on the matrimonial home. Other chapters have been further recast; the short chapter on trusts has been omitted and references where necessary given to the standard works on the subject; and some obsolete material excised.

Apart from the substantial number of new decisions, statutes have come thick and fast, and more and more are promised. This has involved the rewriting of much of the text to include, for example, the Land Charges Act 1972 and the Local Land Charges Act 1975, which replace the Land Charges Act 1925; the Defective Premises Act 1972; the Consumer Credit Act 1974, in so far as it relates to mortgages; the Inheritance (Provision for Family and Dependants) Act 1975, which is substituted for the Inheritance (Family Provision) Act 1938; and three controversial statutes: the Rent Act 1974, the Finance Act 1975, which introduced capital transfer tax in lieu of estate duty, and the Community Land Act 1975. Each of the three has created its own problems, and they may well be clarified, amended, or even repealed before the next edition of this book appears. The Law Commission has likewise been active and its Reports heralding yet further legislation have been incorporated. Statutory change proceeds at a pace disconcerting to layman and lawyer alike.

I am most grateful to all those friends and critics (and these are not mutually exclusive categories) who have given me their help and advice. I would particularly like to thank Mr. L. H. Hoffmann, of Lincoln's Inn, for preparing the chapter on Security of Tenure and Control of Rent; Mr. K. Davies, Reader in Law in the University of Reading, for preparing that on Public Planning; Mr. S. M. Cretney, Fellow of Exeter College, Oxford, Mr. A. E.

Farwell, of Her Majesty's Land Registry, Mr. M. P. Furmston, Fellow of Lincoln College, Oxford, Mr. N. J. Patten, of Lincoln's Inn (who also compiled the Index), and Dr. B. A. Rudden, Fellow of Oriel College, Oxford, for their help on particular matters; and Professor R. H. Maudsley, of King's College, London, for his invaluable advice which has sustained me throughout.

Finally, I wish to thank the publishers for undertaking the compilation of the List of Cases and Tables of Statutes and Statutory Instruments, and for their ready and expert help at all times.

This edition purports to state the law as it was on the fiftieth anniversary of the 1925 Legislation, but more recent developments have been incorporated where space permitted.

E. H. B.

CHRIST CHURCH, OXFORD.

March, 1976

PREFACE TO THE FIRST EDITION

My classical friends assure me that the principles which every author should observe were laid down for all time by Horace. Compose, submit the result line by line to Maecius, consult the judgment of two friends, and preserve to yourself a *locus poenitentiae* by withholding publication for nine years. Such rules are no doubt of inestimable value, but unfortunately the real property legislation of the last few years has been too rapid to permit of an author profiting by the wisdom of Horace in the particular matter of delay. Despite his awful warning,

nescit vox missa reverti,

which never seemed so impressive to me as it does now on the eve of publication, I felt, in view of the representations of colleagues and pupils, that some attempt should be made to publish with as little delay as possible an account of the new system of real property law.

As the lack of adequate time is the only excuse that I can offer for the shortcomings of this book, it may be in point to indicate why I have thought it advisable to publish as soon as possible. The old system of real property law was described with such lucidity and fullness in several works of repute that it would have been presumptuous to offer another book had the law remained unaltered. It is, however, to be profoundly modified on January 1st, 1926. The process of modification was begun by the Law of Property Act, 1922. This was originally designed to come into operation on January 1st, 1925, but a closer examination of the Act showed that it would not lead to a simplification of the law, especially in the matter of accessibility, unless it were cast into a different form. Its greatest defect was that while it introduced a number of new rules and brought about a number of abolitions, both in the existing common law and the existing statutes, it did not repeal and re-enact the latter in a manner calculated to render the search for the law the simple task it should be. To avoid, therefore, what might have been chaos, the legislature set to work in 1924 to consolidate a great part of the statute law bearing on real property, and to incorporate the principles and alteration of the Act of 1922 in the consolidating statutes. Such of the provisions of the Act of 1922 as were not of a merely transitional character were repealed and re-enacted in the consolidating statutes, while the date at which the transitional provisions were to come into operation was postponed to January 1st, 1926. Six consolidating bills were drafted and

appeared in print during the late summer of 1924, but it was
not until April, 1925, that they were passed by Parliament.

The position was, then, that only in April, 1925, did the new
legal rules which, for the moment at any rate, are destined to
regulate rights of property in the land, become known, and
though they were postponed from coming into operation until
January 1st, 1926, the result was that a student had but eight
months within which to master the new system. Examinations
wait for no man, and when it is remembered that the King's
Printer's copies of the new Acts cover more than six hundred
pages, it will be realised that the prospect with which a student
was faced was not a happy one.

When it was known in January, 1924, what the intentions of
the legislature were, I therefore felt justified in attempting to
prepare a book which would not merely record the changes, but
would present the law as a composite whole. Despite the short
time available, I felt that something was required, before the new
era dawned in January, 1926, to enable students to envisage a
legal system which is, in many respects, widely different from
that described in existing books. The present book represents
an attempt to supply the want. It has many defects, but it is
hoped that they are defects which can be readily eradicated should
sufficient support be forthcoming to justify the publication of a
second edition.

One of these defects is a somewhat excessive length, though
something may be said in palliation of what, to a student, is
perhaps the worst vice known to the law. In the first place the
number of pages has been greatly increased owing to the manner
in which the text has been set out. The subject is complicated,
and the design has been to space the text out and to add numerous
headings and indentations, so that the subject matter may easily
catch the eye of a reader. Secondly, the book contains a number
of repetitions which are due partly to the speed at which it has
been written and partly to the intervals which, owing to other
calls upon my time, have separated the composition of its various
parts. Thirdly, it must be admitted that the bulk of real property
law is greater now than it formerly was. At the beginning of
my labours I was imbued with the idea that the task of a student
had been lightened. So much had disappeared. The old rules
relating to remainders, the old canons of descent, the rule in
Shelley's Case, copyholds, gavelkind—they were all gone, and
one's first impression was that the amount of law which a book
on real property need deal with had been diminished. This will
be true in twenty or thirty years' time, but unfortunately it is far
from the truth at the present moment. Quite apart from the
fact that a knowledge of the old law remains necessary for the
purpose of investigating title, it is also a fact that a great many
of the new rules can neither be understood nor explained unless

the former rules are known. The Administration Act, 1925, for instance, abolishes curtesy, but the Law of Property Act, 1925, retains it in the case of entailed interests.

So much may be said by way of excuse. The Horatian requirement of time has been lacking, but not the other essentials. The rôle of Maecius has been filled by Mr. T. K. Brighouse, M.A., a former colleague of mine in the University College of Wales, Aberystwyth, who, though not a lawyer, has been an experienced and valuable critic on the literary side. Despite what must be a distinctly repellent subject to a layman, he has read every word of this book at least twice, and has not only saved me from some of the worst mistakes of a naturally defective style, but has advised and procured alterations in many passages where my proposed treatment would have obscured the lucidity of statement. The extent of my obligation to him is immeasurable.

On the legal side, the help I have received has been equally considerable. The main task has fallen on Mr. P. H. L. Brough of the Equity Bar, who has sacrificed a great deal of his time to reading and advising on the manuscript before it has been submitted to others. Moreover, he has given me the benefit of his practical experience in the initial stages of the book by helping to arrange the form in which some of the more difficult parts of the new legislation might be set out. His clearness of vision and his natural aptitude for realising the object of an obscure enactment have been of inestimable value to me.

I owe a debt of deep gratitude to Sir John Miles, B.C.L., M.A., Fellow and Tutor of Merton College, Oxford, who, besides encouraging me to begin the preparation of this book, has always been anxious at the sacrifice of his own time to afford me the benefit of his mature knowledge and sound advice.

To Professor J. D. I. Hughes, B.C.L., M.A., of Leeds University, to Mr. Ernest A. Steele, LL.B., of Halifax, and to Mr. L. E. Salt, M.A., Fellow and Bursar of Pembroke College, Oxford, I am under a deep obligation. They have each done me the honour of reading the whole of the book in proof form, and when I recall the number of their suggestions and criticisms to which I have paid heed, I realise the extent of my indebtedness to them. Their unselfish labours have prevented the appearance of innumerable sins, both of omission and commission, and their judgment has frequently kept me from straying into an unwise method of treatment.

Mr. Harold Potter, LL.B., of Birmingham University, and Mr. John Snow, M.A., of New College, Oxford, have very kindly read the chapter on conveyancing and have suggested several practical improvements which have been of the utmost value to me. It is, however, only fair to Mr. Potter to say that he would have elaborated the introductory note to Book III in a manner which would have greatly increased its usefulness and value, had not his proposals unfortunately reached me too late to permit of their inclusion.

The above is an inadequate acknowledgment of the services which have been rendered to me, but at the same time it must be recorded that none of the gentlemen who have so willingly extended me their aid is responsible in the slightest degree for the mistakes and failings which no doubt will be found to characterise this book. For these I am wholly responsible, while only partially responsible for anything which may be worthy of approval.

Lastly, I must acknowledge the help, of a different character, but no less valuable, which I have received from my wife. From the moment when this book was begun she abandoned a great part of her leisure and, having mastered for the occasion the unattractive art of typing, converted an almost illegible manuscript into a form which made the task of all those who had to deal with it a task of ease instead of a burden.

G. C. C.

OXFORD,
Sept. 1925.

TABLE OF CONTENTS

BOOK I

INTRODUCTION TO THE STUDY OF THE MODERN LAW

BOOK II

ESTATES AND INTERESTS IN LAND

PART I

THE ESTATE IN FEE SIMPLE ABSOLUTE IN POSSESSION

PART II

INTERESTS ARISING UNDER A STRICT SETTLEMENT OR TRUST FOR SALE

PART III

COMMERCIAL INTERESTS

A. INTERESTS CONFERRING A RIGHT TO THE LAND ITSELF

B. INTERESTS CONFERRING A RIGHT ENFORCEABLE AGAINST THE LAND OF ANOTHER

BOOK III

THE TRANSFER AND EXTINCTION OF ESTATES AND INTERESTS

PART I

PART II
TRANSFER *INTER VIVOS* BY ESTATE OWNERS

PART III
TRANSFER BY OPERATION OF LAW

PART IV
TRANSFER ON DEATH

PART V
EXTINCTION OF ESTATES AND INTERESTS

PART VI
INCAPACITIES AND DISABILITIES WITH REGARD TO THE HOLDING AND TRANSFER OF ESTATES AND INTERESTS

BOOK IV
PLANNING LAW

INDEX

LIST OF CASES

A.

H.

TABLE OF STATUTES

References in this Table to "*Statutes*" are to Halsbury's Statutes of England (Third Edition) showing the volume and page at which the annotated text of the Act will be found.

TABLE OF STATUTORY INSTRUMENTS

ABBREVIATIONS

STATUTES AND RULES

A.E.A.	Administration of Estates Act
A.J.A.	Administration of Justice Act
C.P.A.	Compulsory Purchase Act
F.A.	Finance Act
I.E.A.	Intestates' Estates Act
J.A.	Judicature Act
L.C.A.	Land Charges Act
L.P.A.	Law of Property Act
L.P.(A.)A.	Law of Property (Amendment) Act
L.R.A.	Land Registration Act
L.R.R.	Land Registration Rules
P.&A.A.	Perpetuities and Accumulations Act
R.S.C.	Rules of the Supreme Court
S.I.	Statutory Instrument
S.L.A.	Settled Land Act
T.A.	Trustee Act
T.C.P.A.	Town and Country Planning Act

PERIODICALS

A.S.C.L.	Annual Survey of Commonwealth Law
C.L.J.	Cambridge Law Journal
C.L.P.	Current Legal Problems
C.L.Y.	Current Law Year Book
Conv. (N.S.)	Conveyancer (New Series)
E.G.	Estates Gazette
H.L.R.	Harvard Law Review
J.P.L.	Journal of Planning and Property Law
	Journal of Planning and Environment Law
Jurid. Soc.	Juridical Society's Papers
L.G.C.	Local Government Chronicle
L.J. News	Law Journal
L.Q.R.	Law Quarterly Review
L.S.G.	Law Society Gazette
L.T.	Law Times
M.L.R.	Modern Law Review
New L.J.	New Law Journal
N.I.L.Q.	Northern Ireland Legal Quarterly
Sol. Jo.	Solicitor's Journal

BOOKS

Ashburner	*Ashburner's Principles of Equity*, 2nd ed., by D. Browne (1933)
Bacon	*Bacon's New Abridgement of the Law*, 7th ed., by Sir Henry Gwillim and C. E. Dodd (1832)
Bailey	*The Law of Wills*, by S. J. Bailey, 7th ed. (1973)
Barnsley	*Conveyancing Law and Practice*, by D. G. Barnsley (1973)
Behan	*The Use of Land as Affected by Covenants*, by J. C. V. Behan (1924)
Blackstone	*Commentaries on the Laws of England*, by Sir William Blackstone, 15th ed., by E. Christian (1809)
Bromley	*Family Law*, by P. M. Bromley, 4th ed. (1971)
Brunyate	*Limitation of Actions in Equity*, by J. B. Brunyate (1932)

Bullen and Leake and Jacob — *Precedents of Pleadings*, 12th ed., by I. H. Jacob (1975)

Burnett — *The Elements of Conveyancing*, by J. F. R. Burnett, 8th ed. (1952)

Burton — *An Elementary Compendium of the Law of Real Property*, by W. H. Burton, 8th ed., by E. F. Cooper (1856)

Campbell — *A Guide to the Law of Commons*, by I. Campbell, 2nd ed. (1973)

Challis — *Challis's Law of Real Property*, 3rd ed., by C. Sweet (1911)

Chapman — *Capital Transfer Tax*, by A. L. Chapman (1975)

Cheshire and Fifoot — *The Law of Contract*, 8th ed., by G. C. Cheshire, C. H. S. Fifoot and M. P. Furmston (1973)

Co. Litt. — *Coke's Commentary upon Littleton*, 19th ed., with notes by F. Hargrave and C. Butler (1832)

Coote — *Coote's Treatise on the Law of Mortgages*, 9th ed., by R. L. Ramsbotham (1927)

Cretney — *Principles of Family Law*, by S. M. Cretney (1974)

Cruise — *Cruise's Digest of the Laws of England*, 4th ed., by H. H. White (1835)

Dart — *Dart's Vendors and Purchasers of Real Estate*, 8th ed., by E. P. Hewitt and M. R. C. Overton (1929)

Davies — *Compulsory Purchase and Compensation*, by K. Davies, 2nd ed. (1975)

Digby — *An Introduction to the History of the Law of Real Property*, 5th ed., by K. E. Digby and W. M. Harrison (1897)

Easton — *The Law of Rentcharges (commonly called chief rents) mainly from a conveyancing standpoint*, 2nd ed., by H. C. Easton (1931)

Elphinstone — *Introduction to Conveyancing*, by Sir Howard Elphinstone, 7th ed., by F. T. Maw (1918)

Elphinstone — *Covenants affecting Land*, by Sir Lancelot Elphinstone (1946)

Emmet — *Emmet's Notes on Perusing Titles and on Practical Conveyancing*, 16th ed., by J. T. Farrand and J. Gilchrist Smith (1974)

Evans — *The Law of Landlord and Tenant*, by D. L. Evans (1974)

Fairest — *Mortgages*, by P. B. Fairest (1975)

Farrand — *Contract and Conveyance*, 2nd ed., by J. T. Farrand (1973)
The Rent Act 1974, by J. T. Farrand (1975)

Farwell — *Farwell on Powers*, 3rd ed., by C. J. W. Farwell and F. K. Archer (1916)

Fearne — *An Essay on the Learning of Contingent Remainders and Executory Devises*, by Charles Fearne, 10th ed., with notes by C. Butler, with *An Original View of Executory Interests in Real and Personal Property*, by Josiah W. Smith (1844)

Fisher and Lightwood — *Fisher and Lightwood's Law of Mortgage*, 8th ed., by E. L. G. Tyler (1969)

Foa — *Foa's General Law of Landlord and Tenant*, 8th ed., by H. Heathcote-Williams (1957)

Fry — *A Treatise on the Specific Performance of Contracts*, by Sir Charles Fry, 6th ed., by G. R. Northcote (1921)

Gale — *Gale's Law of Easements*, 14th ed., by S. G. Maurice and R. Wakefield (1972)

Garner — *Local Land Charges*, by J. F. Garner (1974)

George — *The Sale of Flats*, 3rd ed., by E. F. George and A. George (1970)

Gibson — *Gibson's Conveyancing*, 20th ed., by R. H. Kersley (1970)

Gilbert	*Gilbert on Uses and Trusts*, 3rd ed., by E. B. Sugden (1811)
Goode	*Introduction to the Consumer Credit Act 1974*, by R. M. Goode (1974)
Gray	*The Rule against Perpetuities*, by J. C. Gray, 4th ed., by R. Gray (1942)
Guest and Lloyd	*The Consumer Credit Act 1974*, by A. G. Guest and M. G. Lloyd (1975)
Hague	*Leasehold Enfranchisement*, by N. T. Hague (1967)
Hall	*A Treatise of the Law relating to Profits à prendre and Rights of Common*, by J. E. Hall (1871)
Halsbury	*Halsbury's Laws of England*, 3rd ed. (1952–1963); 4th ed. (1973–).
Hanbury	*Hanbury's Modern Equity*, 9th ed., by R. H. Maudsley (1969)
Hargreaves	*An Introduction to the Principles of Land Law*, 4th ed., by G. A. Grove and J. F. Garner (1963)
Harris	*Variation of Trusts*, by J. W. Harris (1975)
Harris and Ryan	*An Outline of the Law Relating to Common Land and Public Access to the Countryside*, by B. Harris and G. Ryan (1967)
Harvey	*Settlements of Land*, by B. W. Harvey (1973)
Hawkins and Ryder	*Hawkins and Ryder on the Construction of Wills*, ed. by E. C. Ryder (1965)
Hayes	*An Introduction to Conveyancing*, by William Hayes, 5th ed. (1840).
Hayton	*Registered Land*, by D. J. Hayton (1973)
Hayton and Tiley	*Elements of Capital Transfer Tax*, by D. J. Hayton and J. Tiley (1975)
Heap	*An Outline of Planning Law*, by Sir Desmond Heap, 6th ed. (1973)
Hill and Redman	*Hill and Redman's Landlord and Tenant*, 16th ed., by M. Barnes, L. A. Dennis, C. Lockhart-Mummery and J. R. Gaunt (1976)
Holdsworth	*A History of English Law*, by Sir William Holdsworth
Ing	*Bona Vacantia*, by N. D. Ing (1971)
Jarman	*Jarman on Wills*, 8th ed., by R. W. Jennings and J. C. Harper (1951)
Lawson	*The Law of Property*, by F. H. Lawson (1958)
Leake	*A Digest of the Law of Uses and Profits of Land*, by S. M. Leake (1888)
Lightwood	*Treatise on Possession of Land*, by J. M. Lightwood (1894)
McAuslan	*Land, Law and Planning: Cases, Materials and Text*, by P. McAuslan (1975)
McNair	*The Law of the Air*, by Sir Arnold McNair, 3rd ed., by M. R. E. Kerr and A. H. M. Evans (1964)
Maitland	*The Collected Papers of Frederick William Maitland*, ed. H. A. L. Fisher (1911)
	The Constitutional History of England, by F. W. Maitland (1908)
	Equity, by F. W. Maitland, revised by John Brunyate (1936)
	Forms of Action at Common Law, by F. W. Maitland, ed. by A. H. Chaytor and W. J. Whittaker (1936)
M. & B.	*Land Law: Cases and Materials*, by R. H. Maudsley and E. H. Burn, 3rd ed. (1975)
	Trusts and Trustees: Cases and Materials, by R. H. Maudsley and E. H. Burn (1972)
Megarry	*The Rent Acts*, by Sir Robert Megarry, 10th ed. (1967–1970)
Megarry and Wade	*The Law of Real Property*, by Sir Robert Megarry and H. W. R. Wade, 4th ed. (1975)
Mellows	*The Law of Succession*, by A. R. Mellows, 2nd ed. (1973)

Sugden	*A Practical Treatise of Powers*, by Edward Sugden, 8th ed. (1861)
	The Law of Vendors and Purchasers of Estates, by Edward Sugden, 14th ed. (1862)
Telling	*Planning Law and Procedure*, by A. E. Telling, 4th ed. (1973)
Theobald	*Theobald on Wills*, 13th ed., by S. Cretney and G. Dworkin (1971)
Tudor	*Tudor's Leading Cases on Real Property, Conveyancing, and the Construction of Wills and Deeds*, 4th ed., by T. H. Carson and H. B. Bompas (1898)
Vaizey	*A Treatise on the Law of Settlements of Property*, by J. S. Vaizey (1887)
Viner	*A General Abridgment of Law and Equity*, by Charles Viner, 2nd ed. (1791)
Vinogradoff	*Villainage in England*, by P. Vinogradoff (1892)
Waldock	*The Law of Mortgages*, by C. H. M. Waldock, 2nd ed. (1950)
Wheatcroft and Hewson	*Capital Transfer Tax*, by G. S. A. Wheatcroft and G. D. Hewson (1975)
White and Tudor	*White and Tudor's Leading Cases in Equity*, 9th ed., by E. P. Hewitt and J. B. Richardson (1928)
Wilkinson	*The Standard Conditions of Sale of Land*, by H. W. Wilkinson, 2nd ed. (1974)
Williams	*A Treatise on the Law of Vendor and Purchaser of Real Estate and Chattels Real*, 4th ed., by T. Cyprian Williams and J. M. Lightwood (1936)
	The Contract of Sale of Land as affected by the Legislation of 1925, by T. Cyprian Williams (1930)
Williams	*Williams' Law and Practice in Bankruptcy*, 18th ed., by M. Hunter and D. Graham (1968)
Williams and Mortimer	*Williams and Mortimer on Executors, Administrators and Probate*, ed. by J. H. G. Sunnucks and R. L. Bayne-Powell (1970) (being the 15th ed. of *Williams on Executors* and the 3rd ed. of *Mortimer on Probate*)
Wisdom	*Water Rights, including Fishing Rights*, by A. S. Wisdom (1969)
Wolstenholme and Cherry	*Wolstenholme and Cherry's Conveyancing Statutes*, 13th ed., by J. T. Farrand (1972)
Wontner	*Wontner's Guide to Land Registry Practice*, 12th ed., by F. Quickfall (1975)
Woodfall	*Woodfall's Law of Landlord and Tenant*, 27th ed., by L. A. Blundell and V. G. Wellings (1968)
Wurtzburg and Mills	*Wurtzburg and Mills Building Society Law*, 13th ed., by John Mills (1970)

BOOK I

INTRODUCTION TO
THE MODERN LAW

SUMMARY

INTRODUCTION TO THE STUDY
OF THE MODERN LAW

SECTION I. INTRODUCTORY NOTE

Merits of
English
land law.

    The early editions of this work suggested that the English
land law offers no intellectual entertainment and that it is scarcely
a subject worthy of study for its own sake.   Further reflection
and the rebukes of critics, however, show that this lament,
momentarily justifiable though it may have been in 1925 (the
date of the first edition), after trying conclusions with some seven
hundred pages of new legislation, is less than fair and that it
underrates the virtues and accomplishments of this department of
English law.   It may, indeed, be difficult to agree with the Real
Property Commissioners of 1829 that it is a department which
" appears to come almost as near to perfection as can be expected
in any human institutions,"[1] but, nevertheless, whether it is regarded as a mirror of one aspect of English life over a period of
nearly a thousand years or as a body of law that has adapted itself
without undue strain to a succession of political and social up-
heavals, culminating in the welfare state, it is no mean contribution to the legal thought of the world.

    It would not be wise in the opening pages of the book to
develop this theme fully, but three illustrations may be given, the
force of which should become clearer in the course of reading.

    Perhaps the most vivid is the invention and development by the
common law of the doctrine of an estate in the land as something
distinct from the land itself, a distinction which has enabled
proprietary rights to be moulded with a flexibility wholly unknown
to the legal systems that derive from Rome.   One learned com-
mentator, indeed, has gone so far as to say that :—

> " Our law of property is, on this side at least, far richer, far more
> practical, and at the same time far more generalised and more logical
> than any other."[2]

---

[1] First Report p. 6.
[2] Lawson, *Rational Strength of English Law*, p. 97.

4

Moreover, the development of the doctrine was accompanied by a precision of technical language that made it possible to reduce the most intricate set of dispositions to comparative simplicity. The old rules that governed future interests, for instance, were not unlike a series of mathematical formulæ. Superficially they seemed shrouded in mystery and they brought little pleasure to the average student, but to one who applied them in the light of the technical vocabulary no problem presented undue difficulty.

Another outstanding contribution to legal institutions, described by Maitland as the most distinctive feature of English law, has been the conception of the trust, a conception that not only attained the object for which it was introduced—the modification of the feudal land law—but which in the course of its development has become the axis round which revolve so many activities of the English-speaking people.

Nevertheless, the public importance of the land law in the feudal society of its origin eventually brought its troubles. When the country settled down after the upheaval of the Norman Conquest, the social bond which, both on the public and on the private side of life, united men together in a political whole was the land. Broadly speaking, land constituted the sole form of wealth, and it was through its agency that the everyday needs of the governing and the governed classes were satisfied. The result of this was that from an early date a complicated system of law, founded on custom and developed by the decisions of the courts, began to grow up, and we may call it for convenience the common law system.

In its origin this system was eminently suitable for a society that was based and centred on the land, and appropriate to the simple notions prevailing in a feudal population, but in several respects it gradually came to outlive the reason for its existence. It tended to become static. Rules that were in harmony with their early environment lived on long after they had become anachronisms. Law will wither unless it expands to keep pace with the progressive ideas of an advancing community, but in this particular context the rigidity and formalism of the common lawyers retarded the process, and, though equity intervened to great effect in several directions, the few reforms attempted by the legislation before the first quarter of the nineteenth century served to complicate rather than to simplify the law. Statutory reform, however, began in earnest after the report of the Real Property Commissioners in 1829. Though lavishing, as we have seen, extravagant praise upon the substantive rules of law, the commissioners went on to express their opinion that the modes by which interests in land were created, transferred and secured had become unnecessarily defective and that they demanded substantial alteration. The result of this view was that on their

Tendency of the law to become static.

Legislative reforms of early nineteenth century.

recommendation a number of statutes were passed between 1833 and 1837 which swept away many impediments to the smooth operation of the law.   The chief of these were :—

> Prescription Act 1832 ;
> Fines and Recoveries Act 1833 ;
> Real Property Limitation Act 1833 ;
> Dower Act 1833 ;.
> Inheritance Act 1833 ;
> Wills Act 1837.

Tendency towards simplification of conveyancing.

Between 1837 and 1922 the legislature became more and more active in the sphere of real property law, but most of the enactments were directed towards the simplification of conveyancing and the extension of the landowners' powers of enjoyment.   No comprehensive effort was made to smooth the path by abolishing the substantive defects that had settled on the main body of the law like barnacles on the hull of a ship.   Then came the war of 1914, and with it a general desire to set the social life of the nation in order.   One of the results of this desire was to give an impetus to land legislation, and it will be as well to state at the outset the main idea which lay at the back of the legislation that resulted.   It was nothing more than a desire to render the sale of land as rapid and simple a matter as is the sale of goods or of shares.   A layman knows that if he desires to transfer to another the ownership of a chattel, such as a motor car or a picture, the normal requirement is the making of a contract which names the parties, records their intention, describes the article to be sold and states the price to be paid.   The moment that such a contract is concluded, the ownership of the article, in the absence of a contrary intention, passes to the buyer.   At first sight it is difficult to appreciate why the same simple expedient cannot be adopted in the case of land, and not unnaturally a layman grows impatient of the long and expensive investigation attendant upon the conveyance of a piece of land.

Main object of legislation of 1925.

Contrast between land and goods.

But the difference is inevitable, and the reason is that in the great majority of. cases the possessor of personal goods is their absolute owner, and therefore able to pass a title which will confer upon their deliveree an equally full and unincumbered ownership. If A. is in possession of a piano, it is probable that he is its owner, and in most cases a buyer is safe in paying its value and taking delivery of possession.   No doubt the maxim of the law is *nemo dat quod non habet*, and if it should happen that A., instead of being the owner, is a thief or is merely holding the piano under a hire purchase agreement, then a buyer from him will not acquire ownership.   But the fact remains that despite risks of this nature a buyer is generally justified in assuming that the possessor of goods is also the owner, and as a rule there is no need to go to trouble and expense in order to ascertain whether some person other than the possessor has any interest in them.

It is a legitimate risk to take. But for a purchaser of land to be content with the word of the vendor and with the appearance of ownership that flows from his possession would be an act of sheer folly.

Land and goods are and must ever be on a different plane. Land is fixed, permanent and vital to the needs of society, and a subject-matter in which rights may be granted to persons other than the ostensible owner. A. is in possession of land and is obviously exercising all the powers of enjoyment and management which amount to the popular idea of ownership, but none the less it is by no means certain that he is in fact entitled to dispose of the interest that he may have agreed to sell. He may be merely in possession under a lease for any period from one to 999 years or more, or he may be a mere life tenant holding under a family settlement ; and even though he holds the fee simple—the largest interest known to the law and one that approximates to the absolute ownership of goods—it is likely that he or his predecessors have granted to third parties rights, such as mortgages, restrictive covenants and rights of way, which continue to be enforceable against the land regardless of any transfer to which it may have been subjected. So long as third parties can in this way have legally enforceable rights against land which outwardly appears to belong absolutely to the possessor, it is difficult, in the absence of compulsory registration of title, to devise a system under which conveyances of land can be conducted with the facility of sales of goods, and it will always be incumbent on a purchaser to make careful searches and inquiries in order to see that the land is unburdened.

Permanence of land causes multiplicity of rights.

We may start, then, with the assumption that no effort of legislative genius can, from the point of view of simplicity and rapidity, put conveyances of land on an equal footing with sales of goods. But when the question of reforming the law came before Parliament in 1922, the result of 600 years of development from a feudal origin was that the law of real property contained so many antiquated rules and useless technicalities that additional and· unnecessary impediments had arisen to hinder the facile transfer of land. The real property law as it existed in 1922 might justly be described as an archaic feudalistic system which, though originally evolved to satisfy the needs of a society based and centred on the land, had by considerable ingenuity been twisted and distorted into a shape more or less suitable to a commercial society dominated by money. The movement of progressive societies has been from land to money, or rather to trade, and a legal system which acquired its main features at a time when land constituted the major part of the country's wealth can scarcely be described as suitable to an industrial community. To borrow the words of Bagehot directed to a different subject, the 1922 real property law might be likened to " an old man who

Difficulties attending reform of English land law.

still wears with attached fondness clothes in the fashion of his youth ; what you see of him is the same ; what you do not see is wholly altered."

To take any structure, whether it be a system of law, a constitution or a house, and for a period of 600 years to patch it here and there in order to adapt it to new conditions, cannot fail to lead to complications of a bewildering character.

Simplification of law of real property.

The Legislation of 1925. Confirmed in the views just mentioned, the legislature began in 1922 to reform the law on a far more ambitious scale than had been attempted in the earlier legislative changes, for, though the main purpose was to simplify conveyancing, yet this was pursued not merely by a simplification of the machinery of land transfer, but also by a free use of the pruning knife. In the official view, reforms were needed as a prelude to the simplification and extension of the system of registration of title.[1]

Law of Property Act 1922.

The first Act to be passed was the Law of Property Act 1922, which was described in its preamble as

" An Act to assimilate and amend the law of Real and Personal Estate, to abolish copyhold and other special tenures, to amend the law relating to commonable lands and of intestacy, and to amend the Wills Act, 1837, the Settled Land Acts, 1882 to 1890, the Conveyancing Acts, 1881 to 1911, the Trustee Act, 1893 and the Land Transfer Acts, 1875 and 1897."

The all-important fact that emerges from this descriptive title is that one main object was to " assimilate . . . the law of real and personal estate."

Assimilation of real and personal property by the Act of 1922.

We shall see as we proceed that a comparison of the law relating to real and personal property respectively is, from the point of view of convenience and reason, very much to the advantage of the latter. Part I of the Act therefore put the two forms of property as nearly as possible upon the same footing, a result which was obtained partly by abolishing the chief differences that formerly existed between the two, and partly by eliminating many of the technical anachronisms that had grown up in the land laws. In addition, the law of personal property, which thus became the dominating system, was itself amended in several particulars.

Necessity for further legislation.

The date at which the Act of 1922 was appointed to come into operation, however, was postponed, for the changes it made were sufficiently drastic to necessitate the re-drafting and consolidation of the real property statute law from the year 1285. The Law of Property (Amendment) Act 1924 was therefore passed to facilitate the task of consolidation, and then all but the

---

[1] Wolstenholme and Cherry, *Conveyancing Statutes* (12th Edn.), vol. i. p. clxvi.

transitional provisions of this Act and of the Act of 1922 were absorbed into the following seven statutes, passed in 1925.[1]

Settled Land Act ;
Trustee Act ;
Law of Property Act ;
Land Registration Act ;
Land Charges Act ;
Administration of Estates Act ;
Universities and College Estates Act.[2]

1925 legislation.

The practical result at the present day is that the whole law of real property is contained partly in these statutes, partly in older statutes, partly in subsequent legislation, such as the various Landlord and Tenant Acts, the Town and Country Planning Acts and the Rent Acts, and partly in the mass of judge-made rules so far as these, which still form the bulk of the law, have not been abolished or modified by statute.

Practical results of the legislation.

Real property law, like most of the other branches of our jurisprudence, falls into three divisions, which are due to the order of its historical development :—

Three-fold historical division of Real Property Law.

First of all we get the purely common law system, which was designed to meet the needs of a feudal society.

Secondly in order of time we have the equitable system which, though not comprehensive, was gradually evolved in certain directions with a view to adapting the common law rules to a society moved by different ideals and possessing a more commercial outlook on life.

And finally we come to the various legislative enactments by which the judge-made law of land was rendered more adequate to the needs of society.

We will now sketch in its barest outline the common law system, then describe at somewhat greater length certain conceptions that were introduced into the law by the Chancellor in the exercise of his equitable jurisdiction, and finally discuss the legislative changes of 1925.

---

[1] For a detailed commentary see the six volumes of Wolstenholme and Cherry, *Conveyancing Statutes* (13th Edn. 1972, edited by J. T. Farrand). Previous editions are valuable, as these contain the commentaries of Wolstenholme (who was responsible for drafting C.A. 1881 and S.L.A. 1882) and Cherry (the property statutes of 1922 and 1925).

[2] These Acts are all consolidating Acts. Where the Acts of 1922 and 1924 make no changes in the old law, there is a presumption that the Acts of 1925 did not change it. *Beswick* v. *Beswick*, [1968] A. C. 58 ; [1967] 2 All E. R. 1197 *cf. Maunsell* v. *Olins*, [1975] A. C. 373, at pp. 392–3. But where they do, there is only a presumption that the Acts of 1925 did not change the changes made by those Acts. See *Grey* v. *I. R. C.* [1960] A. C. 1 ; [1959] 3 All E. R. 603 ; *Lloyds Bank, Ltd.* v. *Marcan* [1973] 1 W. L. R. 339, at p. 344 ; affirmed [1973] 1 W. L. R. 1387 ; Wolstenholme and Cherry, vol. 1, p. 31 ; (1959) 75 L. Q. R. 307 (R.E.M.).

SECTION II.   THE COMMON LAW SYSTEM

(1) THE DOCTRINE OF TENURE[1]

Feudalism.

Feudalism in Europe. The outstanding feature of the English land law and one that explains many of its peculiarities is that, at least from the time of the Norman Conquest, it fell into line with the continental systems and became and remained for several centuries intensely feudalistic. *Feudalism* itself is a word of some vagueness and ambiguity, and one that was certainly unknown to the peoples to whom it is applied. It is often expected to represent the history of Western Europe from the eighth to the fourteenth century,[2] and, like the modern use of the word *capitalism*, to describe the social characteristics of the period.[3] To a lawyer, however, it represents :—

> "A state of society in which the main social bond is the relation between lord and man, a relation implying on the lord's part protection and defence ; on the man's part protection, service and reverence, the service including service in arms. This personal relation is inseparably involved in a proprietary relation, the tenure of land— the man holds of the lord, the man's service is a burden on the land, the lord has important rights in the land."[4]

Thus it is the negation of independence. It implies subordination, it means that one man is deliberately made inferior to another.

Reason for introduction of feudalism.

In pre-feudal days the land of Europe was owned absolutely, though subject to custom, by persons who were grouped together in village communities, and it therefore becomes a matter of interest to discover why it was that a great part of the world lapsed from a state of comparative freedom into one of servility, why landowner-ship disappeared and land tenure took its place. The change represented a retrogressive step in the history of man, but in Europe it was one of the necessary consequences of the disruption of the Roman Empire by the Barbarian invaders. The overthrow of that Empire caused chaos and disorganization in Europe and produced conditions in which it was necessary for private persons to procure for themselves a higher degree of protection than could be furnished by their own unaided efforts. In those days interfer-ence with personal freedom or with the ownership of property might come from several different quarters, such as a revolt of peasants, the arrogance of a powerful neighbour, the extortion of a government or the hostility of some tribe. The only method of obtaining security was mutual support, and so it came to pass that men deliberately subordinated themselves to the strong hand of some magnate versed in the arts of war, and were compensated for

Disruption of Roman Empire.

Feudalism resorted to for security.

---

[1] For the history of this doctrine, see Simpson, *Introduction to the History of Land Law*, pp. 1 *et seq.*
[2] Pollock and Maitland, *History of English Law* (2nd Edn.), vol. i. p. 67.
[3] Plucknett, *Concise History of the Common Law* (5th Edn.), p. 506.
[4] Maitland, *Constitutional History of England*, p. 143.

the diminution of personal independence and the loss of land-ownership by acquiring the protection afforded by the forces of which he disposed. This process involved both a personal and a proprietary subordination, but it is only on the latter that we need dwell.

One of the effects of the feudalization of Europe was that from a legal aspect land became the exclusive bond of union between men. Individual or communal landownership was destroyed. The ownership of the whole of the land in any given district was vested in the overlord, and the persons who had formerly owned it in their own right now held it from the overlord. In return for the land which they held they were bound to render services, chiefly of a military nature, to the overlord, while the latter in his turn was bound to protect his tenants. Feudalism implied a reciprocity of rights and duties. The lord gained in dignity and consequence and became entitled to personal services, while the tenant obtained security.

Growth of feudalism on Continent.

This conversion from ownership to tenure began in the lower ranks of society, but quickly spread upwards until it finally embraced the greater part of the land of Western Europe. Various reasons contributed to this extension. The general anarchy of the times, the lack of a central government sufficiently strong to ensure a well-ordered and peaceful existence, and the natural ambition of magnates to increase the extent of their possessions induced even the large landowners to put themselves and their land under the protection of someone greater than themselves.

Reasons for spread of feudalism.

This development took place under the Franks, and in the time of the Carolingians a still further impetus was given to the movement, for the government itself—if such a term can be applied to those times—was obliged to resort to the principle of feudalism. Administration had to be carried on somehow and taxes were difficult to collect. The solution was to farm out Crown lands to great men who paid a sum of money to the government and who in return became lords of the lands (which were called benefices) and of the persons who dwelt thereon. A little later, when military pressure from the east and the south made it imperative that society should be organized on a basis that would afford protection to the State, the device of granting benefices in return for military services, a device that was gradually failing owing to the scarcity of Crown lands, was widened in scope by an act of confiscation.

Government based on feudalism.

The Church had become the greatest landowner in Europe. Charles Martel, who was Mayor of the Frankish Empire in the first part of the eighth century, deliberately carried out wholesale seizures of Church property, but in A.D. 751 some sort of amicable arrangement was made whereby vast tracts of Church lands were granted by the ecclesiastical corporations to laymen at the request of the King. The Church ownership of the lands was recognized

Church lands feudalized.

by the payment of an uneconomic rent to the corporations, while the tenants—and this was the significance of the transaction—became liable by virtue of their holdings to render services to the King.[1] Thus did the net of feudalism spread everywhere. In this way life and government were made to depend upon the land.[2]

Social and administrative unit.

The Manor. This can be seen by an examination of that unit of society which is called the Manor. The grant of benefices led to the creation of great estates or manors vested in the grantees from the Crown. Topographically a manor denoted a certain area of land consisting of a number of houses, strips of arable and pasture land and waste lands, all of which were within the domain of the lord of the manor. The waste, in proportion to the cultivated land, formed by far the greater part of the manor, a fact which serves to explain the inclosures of later centuries. But we shall miss the significance of this system unless we realize that the manor was both a social and an administrative unit through the agency of which a whole country was governed. Each manor was, as it were, a small government in itself.

The central government required soldiers and money, but instead of approaching its subjects directly it looked no further than the lord of the manor. His obligation *vis-à-vis* the government was to supply a fully equipped fighting force, and the right which he obtained in return was that of holding his manor or group of manors immune from the legal and administrative control of the government. Thus, when the power of a central government was on the wane, it became customary to grant immunities to powerful men, which meant nothing more nor less than that the functions of government were handed over to feudal lords.

VINOGRADOFF has said :—

> " As in the later Empire, the government is obliged to have recourse to great landlords in order to carry out its functions of police, justice, military and fiscal authority. Great estates had become extra-territorial already under Roman rule in the fourth and fifth centuries, and it would be superfluous to point out how much more the governments of the barbarians stood in need of the help of great landowners."[3]

Lord's right of jurisdiction.

One of the most important features of the administrative side of a Continental manor was the lord's right of jurisdiction. As the royal writ did not run within the territorial limits of a manor, the lord set up local courts of his own, and it was only in the manorial court of the defendant that a plaintiff was entitled to sue. Thus, to use the expressive language of STUBBS,[4] there was

> " a graduated system of jurisdiction based on land tenure, in which every lord judged, taxed, and commanded the class next below

---

[1] Vinogradoff, *Cambridge Medieval History*, vol. ii. p. 646.
[2] See generally, *Encyclopædia Britannica, sub nom.* Feudalism.
[3] Vinogradoff, *op. cit.* p. 651.
[4] *Constitutional History*, vol. i. p. 292.

him, . . . in which private war, private coinage, private prisons took the place of the imperial institutions of government."

Summary. By way of summary we may say that the characteristics of feudalism are the relation of lord and vassal; the principle that every person interested in land is a mere holder thereof, a tenant and not an owner ; the condition that this tenure shall continue to exist only so long as the tenant performs the particular services imposed upon him at the beginning of the tenure ; and lastly the recognition of a reciprocity of rights and duties. The foundation of the whole system is the fief—that is to say, the land which the inferior holds as tenant of the superior. The word *fief* becomes *feudum* in Latin, and *feud*, and later *fee* in English.

Characteristics of feudalism.

Feudalism in England. We now come to consider the effect which this Continental feudalism had upon the land law of England. As the scope of this book makes it undesirable to elaborate particular questions of legal history, it is not proposed to discuss the extent to which feudalism existed in England prior to the Conquest. That a system was in vogue which bore similarities to Continental feudalism cannot be doubted, but the only fact that we need notice here is that the Normans applied their own ideas to the conditions prevalent in this country, and succeeded in establishing an English variety of feudalism which, though differing in many respects from that of the Continent, became a striking and universal feature of the land law. The policy of William left England, whatever it may have been before, a highly feudalized state. He took the line that, since the English landowners had denied his right to the Crown of England and had compelled him to assert it by force, their landed possessions became his to dispose of as he chose.[1] What he did was not so much to seize land and parcel it out among his Norman followers, as to allow all Englishmen who recognized him as King to redeem by money payments the estates which by right of conquest had momentarily passed to him.

Feudalism established in England.

This process of confiscation and redistribution flowed on evenly, and though it cannot be said that the redistributions amounted to direct feudal grants, there is no doubt that they came to be regarded as such when the idea of Norman feudalism took hold of men's minds. As STUBBS says :—

" After each effort the royal hand was laid on more heavily ; more and more land changed owners, and with the change of owners the title changed. The complicated and unintelligible irregularities of the Anglo-Saxon tenures were exchanged for the simple and uniform feudal theory. The 1500 tenants in chief of Domesday take the place of the countless landowners of King Edward's day. . . . It is enough for our purpose to ascertain that a universal assimilation of

---

[1] Stenton, *William the Conqueror*, pp. 494-5.

title followed the general changes of ownership. The king of
Domesday is the supreme landlord ; all t^ land ^f the nation, the
old folkland, has become the King's, and all private land is held
mediately or immediately of him ; all holders are bound to their
lords by homage and fealty, either actually demanded or understood
to be demandable, in every case of transfer by inheritance or
otherwise."[1]

**English
feudalism
different
from
continental
type.**

This English feudalism differed from the Continental variety
in that all freemen were bound by the Salisbury Oath of 1086 to
swear allegiance directly to the King instead of to the immediate
lord from whom they held their lands ; and again in the fact that
William, instead of setting up great territorial jurisdictions,
organized administration in such a way that he governed the
country through sheriffs who were directly responsible to him.
Though the Frankish system of tenure displaced the Anglo-Saxon
system, the establishment of a feudal mode of government was
deliberately avoided. But in respect of tenure the result was
much the same as on the Continent. By a certain date, which we
need not attempt to define, the doctrine of land tenure became
universal in England.

Every acre of land in the country was held of the King. As
POLLOCK and MAITLAND have said :—

" The person whom we may call the owner, the person who has the
right to use and abuse the land, to cultivate it or leave it uncultivated,
to keep all others off it, holds the land of the King either immediately
or mediately." [2]

Seignories.

If a tenant held immediately of the King, he was said to
hold of him in chief or *in capite*. But the position might be less
simple. Instead of a tenant holding directly of the King he
might hold mediately, as for instance where C. held of B. who
held of A. who held of the King. C., who stood at the bottom of
the scale, and who to a layman would look more like an owner
than anybody else, was called the *tenant in demesne—tenet terram
in dominico suo*. The persons between him and the King were
called *mesne lords*, and their lordships were called *seignories*. A.
held the land, not *in demesne* but in service, since he was entitled to
the services of B., and B. was in a similar position, since he was
entitled to the services of C. The services due from these tenants
would not necessarily be of the same nature, for A. might hold of
the King by military service, B. of A. in return for a money rent,
and C. of B. in return for some personal service. In such a case
each grantee owed to his immediate grantor the service that he had
agreed to render, and from this point of view the service was called
intrinsec. Services were not merely personal, but charged on the
tenement, so that if A. failed in the performance of his military
duties the King could distrain upon the land in the hands of C., as

---

[1] Stubbs, *Constitutional History*, vol. i. pp. 296–7.
[2] *History of English Law* (2nd Edn.), vol. ii. p. 232.

could A. if B. fell into arrear with the rent. B. could agree to perform the military service in place of A., but no private arrangement of this kind could free the land from the burden. From this point of view the service was called *forinsec*, *i.e.* foreign to any bargain between other parties.[1] Of course, if, for example, A. failed to perform his military service and the King proceeded against the land in C.'s occupation, the latter had a remedy against A., called the writ of *mesne*. A tenant came under an obligation, confirmed by the oath of fealty, to serve his lord faithfully, and the price of infidelity in this respect was the forfeiture of his fief. In particular, forfeiture ensued if he did anything to the disinherison of his lord, as, for example, if he deliberately failed to defend an action for the recovery of land brought against him by a third party.[2]

Perhaps the most striking fact about English feudalism was the universality of this doctrine of land tenure. On the Continent tenure applied only to those who held lands in return for military services,[3] but in England it applied to every holder whatever the nature of the duties that he had agreed to perform might be. Moreover a movement began by which the number of mesne lordships was increased to a bewildering extent. As each year passed, more and more sub-tenancies were created. A., who held of the King, would transfer his land or part of it to B., and B. to C., and so on, but each transfer, instead of being an out and out grant by which the transferor got rid of his entire interest, would operate as a grant of land to be held by each transferee as tenant of his immediate transferor. As a result " innumerable petty lords sprang up between the great barons and the immediate tenant of the soil." [4]

Universality of tenure in England.

This process, which was termed subinfeudation, was carried to such lengths that Maitland was able to discover a case where there were as many as eight sub-tenancies in the same piece of land. One explanation of this reluctance to part with one's entire interest was the economic significance of land in the centuries immediately succeeding the Conquest. Apart from cattle, land was practically the only form of wealth. Money was scarce, and something had to take its place as a medium of exchange. This can be illustrated by the recompense usually given for services rendered.

Subinfeudation.

Subinfeudation spreads because land was main form of wealth.

Domestic servants in a manor were paid by a crude method of profit-sharing. As Vinogradoff has stated, " The swine-herd of Glastonbury Abbey, for instance, received one sucking-pig a year, the interior parts of the best pig and the tails of all the

---

[1] **Pollock and Maitland,** *History of English Law* (2nd Edn.), vol. i. p. 237.

[2] For a discussion of this defunct principle, see the judgment of DENNING, L.J., in *Warner* v. *Sampson*, [1959] 1 Q. B. 297, 312–6 ; [1959] 1 All E. R. 120, 123–6.

[3] Holdsworth, *History of English Law*, vol. ii. p. 199.

[4] Hayes, *Introduction to Conveyancing*, vol. i. p. 9.

others which were slaughtered in the abbey.   The chief scullion had a right to all remnants of viands—but not of game—to the feathers and the bowels of geese." [1]

But the form which payment took in the case of labourers on the manorial estate, and also in the case of servants who rendered non-domestic services for a great lord, was a grant of land to be held only so long as the services were properly performed.   Thus **it was through one of the forms of tenure, known as tenure by sergeanty, that most of the wants of men were satisfied.   The** persons who severally acted as president of a lord's court, carried his letters, fed his hounds, cared for his horses and found him in bows and arrows, generally held land as tenants in sergeanty of the lord.[2]   They would continue to hold the land as long as they served faithfully and no longer.

In other words, the importance of land as a means of payment made it advisable for tenants to keep as tenacious a hold upon it as possible, and, when a transfer was contemplated, to sub-infeudate rather than dispose of it outright.   But for reasons into which we need not enter,[3] the practice of subinfeudation was obnoxious to the great lords, and was finally stopped in 1290 by the Statute *Quia Emptores*.[4]

Sub-infeudation stopped by *Quia Emptores*.

This important statute altered the law in two respects.

First, it set at rest a controversy by enacting that every free man should be at liberty to alienate the whole or part of his land without the consent of his lord.   If part only were conveyed, the services were to be apportioned.

Secondly, it enacted that every alienee should hold the land of the same lord of whom the alienor previously held.   The effect of this was to prevent the creation of new tenancies. The alienor dropped out, the alienee stepped into his shoes for all purposes, and thus instead of a new sub-tenancy there was the substitution of one tenant for another.   If, therefore, the existence of a mesne lordship is proved at the present day, it follows that it must have been created before 1290.   The statute, however, extended only to land held for a fee simple estate, *i.e.* the largest interest known to the law,[5] and it has never prevented the creation of a new tenure by the grant of a lesser estate, such as a fee tail or a life interest.

Crown not bound by *Quia Emptores*.

The statute did not bind the Crown.   This had two consequences.

In the first place, the privilege of unrestricted alienation did not avail tenants *in capite*.   In their case the consent of the Crown

---

[1] Vinogradoff, *Villainage in England*, pp. 321–2.
[2] Pollock and Maitland, *History of English Law* (2nd Edn.), vol. i. p. 285.
[3] See Challis, *Law of Real Property* (3rd Edn.), pp. 18–19.
[4] Holdsworth, *History of English Law*, vol. iii. p. 79.
[5] The meaning of " fee simple " will appear later ; *infra*, pp. 34 ; 148.

remained necessary and in practice this was given only on the payment of a fine.[1]

Secondly, the Crown was unaffected by the abolition of sub-infeudation and was therefore still able to create new tenancies in respect of the fee simple.

Quia Emptores was indeed a landmark in the history of real property. Its chief virtue was that it led to the gradual disappearance of the numerous petty lordships that had arisen between the Crown and the tenant *in demesne*. Blackacre might no doubt have been held before 1290 by B. of A., but if in course of time it passed into the hands of a succession of alienees, each one being substituted for his predecessor, it would ultimately become extremely difficult to prove the existence of A.'s original lordship. Thus, there was a constant tendency for seignories to become vested in the Crown, and to this extent the law was simplified.

Importance of Quia Emptores.

Forms of Tenure. A feature of English feudalism, and one that complicated the law of land, was that there was not one common kind of tenure. We have seen how in early days, if a man wanted work of a regular nature done for him, he would generally get it done in exchange for land granted by him to the workman. Considering the diversity of personal needs which require to be satisfied, it is obvious that the services due from tenants would vary considerably in nature, importance and dignity. One tenant had to fight; another to look after a household, or to provide arms, or to pray for the soul of his overlord, or to do such agricultural work as might be demanded of him. There were vast differences between the possible services. It was considered an honourable thing to fight, but not to plough, and thus it came to pass that there gradually arose different forms of tenure based upon the differences in the nature of the services. The following table shows the state of affairs in the time of Edward I, when the tenures had become stabilized.

Plurality of forms of tenure.

Variety of services.

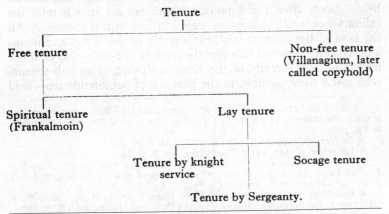

Tenure

Free tenure — Non-free tenure (Villanagium, later called copyhold)

Spiritual tenure (Frankalmoin) — Lay tenure

Tenure by knight service — Socage tenure

Tenure by Sergeanty.

---

[1] Challis, *op. cit.*, pp. 14, 15. Such fines were abolished by the Tenures Abolition Act 1660.

Divergent
methods of
land holding.

In addition to these regular tenures there also existed in certain districts a few customary methods of landholding under which land was subject in various respects to a number of abnormal incidents.   Instances are gavelkind, borough-English and ancient demesne.

Gavelkind is a word which denotes the customs that have applied since the Conquest to socage land situated in Kent.[1] Such land was in certain particulars subject to different legal rules from those obtaining in other parts of the country.   Thus,

(a) the land descended upon intestacy to all the sons equally ;
(b) a husband who survived his wife was entitled until his re-marriage to a life estate in one-half of her land although issue of the marriage might not have been born [2] ;
(c) a widow was entitled until her re-marriage to dower in one-half of her husband's land ;
(d) an infant could alienate his land by the form of conveyance known as a feoffment when he reached 15 years of age ; and
(e) the land was devisable.

Borough-English was a custom, found in certain parts of the country, under which the land descended to the youngest son to the exclusion of all the other children.[3]

Ancient demesne land was land held by freehold tenants in any manor which had belonged to the Crown in the time of Edward the Confessor or William the Conqueror.[4]   The tenants in ancient demesne were subject to certain restraints and entitled to certain immunities.[5]

Nature of
knight
service.

Knight Service.[6]   The most important of the regular tenures in early days was knight service, or the tenure by which a man was obliged to render military services in return for the land that he held.   Soon after the Conquest a process set in whereby the military needs of the country were satisfied in this manner.   All the land of the country was held directly of the King, and it was a practically universal rule that the tenants in chief—that is, those men who held directly of the King as distinct from sub-tenants who owed their position to the practice of subinfeudation—held

---

[1] Pollock and Maitland, *History of English Law* (2nd Edn.), vol. ii. pp. 271 *et seq.* ;   Blackstone, vol. ii. p. 84 ;   Challis, *Law of Real Property* (3rd Edn.), p. 14.
[2] *Re Howlett*, [1949] Ch. 767 ;   [1949] 2 All E.R. 490.
[3] Littleton, ss. 165, 211 ;   Blackstone, vol. ii. p. 83.
[4] Co. Fourth Inst. 269 ;   Blackstone, vol. ii. p. 99 ;   Holdsworth, *History of English Law*, vol. iii. pp. 263–9 ;   Challis, *Law of Real Property* (3rd Edn.), p. 29 ;   *Merttens* v. *Hill*, [1901] 1 Ch. 842.
[5] Real Property Commissioners' Third Report, pp. 12 *et seq.   Merttens* v. *Hill, supra; Earl Iveagh* v. *Martin*, [1961] 1 Q. B. 232 ; [1960] 2 All E. R. 668.
[6] See Holdsworth, *History of English Law*, vol. iii. pp. 37–46.

by knight service. Each tenant in chief had to produce for forty days in each year a definite number of fully armed horsemen. The number required in any particular case did not depend upon the extent of the tenant's land, but was arbitrarily fixed when the grant of the land was made, and, as the unit of the feudal host was a constabularia consisting of ten knights, it appears always to have been some multiple of 5 or 10.[1] For about a hundred years after the Conquest the army—to the strength of about 5000 knights—was actually raised in this way, but it was soon discovered that such a short service as forty days scarcely promoted the success of military operations, and the King began about 1166 to exact money payments called scutage from the tenants in chief instead of requiring the production of the fixed quota of knights. But by the time of Edward I even scutage had become useless as a means of providing an army, and it can be said that thenceforth the tenure ceased to be military in the sense that it no longer served to supply forces for the defence of the realm.[2]

Scutage.

What at first sight seems remarkable is that knight service, instead of falling into oblivion after it had ceased to fulfil its original function, continued to develop, and ended by hardening into a legal system far stricter and more onerous than it had hitherto been. The explanation of this inopportune survival was that, quite apart from the duty of military service, the tenure carried with it certain feudal incidents which had such a high financial value for the lords of whom the lands were held that to foster and develop it became a matter of great personal interest. Subinfeudation led to the extension of knight service, and though the military sub-tenant had neither to fight nor to pay scutage, yet, being a military tenant, he was subject to a number of onerous claims from which he would have been free had his tenure been one of the other forms. As the matter is now merely of antiquarian interest, we must confine ourselves to the barest statement of the most valuable of the rights enforceable against a military tenant, namely :—

Survival of tenure by knight service.

1. RELIEF. The lord was entitled to the payment of a certain sum, called a relief, when a new tenant succeeded to the land on the death of the old tenant. Payment of the relief entitled the heir to immediate possession, but this was not so where the land was held of the King. In this case the official escheator took possession and held an inquest as to who was next heir. It was only when the heir had done homage and paid the relief that he was entitled to enter the land. This royal privilege of first possession was called *primer seisin*.[3]

Incidents of knight service.

2. AIDS. The lord was entitled to demand in three special cases that his tenants should pay him a certain sum of money called

[1] Round, *Feudal England*, pp. 259–60.
[2] Pollock and Maitland, *History of English Law* (2nd Edn.), vol. i. p. 252.
[3] *Ibid.*, vol. i. p. 311.

an aid. The three cases arose when the lord was imprisoned and required a ransom ; when he desired to make his eldest son a knight ; and when he was obliged to supply his eldest daughter with a dowry on her marriage.

3. ESCHEAT *PROPTER DELICTUM TENENTIS.* The commission by the tenant of a felony caused the land to escheat, that is to pass to the lord of whom it was held. Felony originally meant a breach of that faith and trust which ought to exist between lord and vassal, *e.g.* where the tenant laid violent hands on his lord. At an early date, however, felony lost its exclusively feudal signification and came to mean in effect any serious crime such as murder. The result of this was to benefit the lords, and though it would seem incompatible with the interests of the Crown as custodian of the public peace that the land of a murderer or a thief should pass to a subject, the right of escheat was expressly confirmed by Magna Carta in 1215, subject to the proviso that the land should be held by the Crown for a year and a day. Forfeiture of the land was now said to occur because the felon's blood was attainted or corrupted.[1]

4. WARDSHIP. The most profitable right of the lord was that of wardship. If an existing tenant died leaving as his heir a male under 21 or a female under 14, the lord was entitled to the wardship of the heir, and as a consequence was free to make what use he liked of the lands during the minority without any obligation to render an account of his stewardship. Upon reaching the prescribed age the ward might sue for *livery* or *ousterlemain, i.e.* might enforce delivery of the land. For this privilege half a year's profits had to be paid, though relief was not exigible.

5. MARRIAGE. Another privilege which the lord enjoyed in respect of infant tenants was the right of marriage. As Blackstone has said :

" While the infant was in ward, the guardian had the power of tendering him or her a suitable match, without disparagement or inequality ; which if the infants refused, they forfeited the value of the marriage, *valorem maritagii*, to their guardian ; that is, so much as a jury would assess, or anyone would *bona fide* give to the guardian for such an alliance ; and if the infants married themselves without the guardian's consent, they forfeited double the value, *duplicem valorem maritagii*."[2]

Sergeanty services essentially personal.

Tenure by Sergeanty [3] was in early times, and from an economic point of view, of considerable importance, but it soon ceased to be anything more than a peculiarly dignified method of holding land. All tenures imply service of one kind or another, but the characteristic of sergeanty was that it required the tenant to perform services of an essentially personal nature. It was that

---

[1] Pollock and Maitland, (2nd Edn.), vol. i. p. 303 ; Digby, *History of the Law of Real Property*, p. 132 ; Holdsworth, *History of English Law*, vol. iii. p. 67.

[2] Blackstone, vol. ii. p. 70.

[3] Holdsworth, *op. cit.*, vol. iii. pp. 46 *et seq.*

particular form of landholding which was designed to supply the necessities of life. In the first place the great officials of the realm were sergeants, and as such might be required " to carry the banner of the king, or his lance, or to lead his army, or to be his marshall, or to carry his sword before him at his coronation, or to be his sewer at his coronation or his carver or his butler, or to be one of his chamberlains at the receipt of his exchequer or to do other like services."[1]

Duties of this nature came to be regarded as conferring honour and dignity, and for this reason outlasted the tenure itself, but they did not exhaust the forms of personal services that might be demanded from sergeants. A great lord would require that his accounts should be kept, his letters carried, his estates managed, armour provided, his food cooked, and so on, and he would in most cases grant lands to various sergeants to be held by them so long as the duties were faithfully performed. However, as time went on, it was realized that this was scarcely a convenient method of supplying the needs of life, and tenure by sergeanty began to decay as early as the fourteenth century. It died out altogether except in the case of those great men who performed honourable services for the King, or of humbler persons whose duty it might be to perform some small military duty, such as to supply transport. Moreover, the idea took root, and was fixed law by Littleton's day, that the tenure could exist only between the King and his immediate tenants in chief. The tenure of the great men who performed what were regarded as honourable services came to be called *grand sergeanty*, while that of the lesser military tenants was termed *petit sergeanty*. Grand sergeanty came to be similar to knight service, while petit sergeanty, after the time of Littleton, was practically equivalent to socage.[2]

Decay of sergeanty.

Abolition of Military Tenures. It is not necessary to describe these tenures further, because in 1660 a considerable simplification of the forms of landholding was effected by the legislature. The Statute for the abolition of Military Tenures,[3] which was passed in that year, practically destroyed all the *free* lay tenures except socage. Tenure by knight service was destroyed altogether, and sergeanty was allowed to continue only in an emasculated form. Formerly it had rendered the tenant liable to onerous duties similar to those that might be exacted from a knight service tenant, but the effect of the Act was to abolish it as a separate tenure, and, where it existed, only to leave the privilege of performing those honorary services which, as we have seen, were peculiar to the higher ranks of sergeants. In

Conversion of military tenures into Socage.

---

[1] Littleton, s. 153.
[2] Holdsworth, *History of English Law*, vol. iii. p. 51.
[3] Tenures Abolition Act 1660.

other words, sergeanty was converted into socage,[1] the exceptional feature of the converted land being that the tenant might in some cases substantiate his right to perform certain honorary and dignified services.

**Frank-
almoin.**

Frankalmoin was the tenure by which a man made provision for the repose of his soul, and it arose where lands were granted to an ecclesiastical body on the implied understanding that as tenant it would say prayers and masses for the souls of the grantor and his heirs.   For various reasons the tenure fell into desuetude, and, though it was not formally abolished by the Act of 1660, it was seldom encountered in practice.[2]

**1660 Act
simplified
landholding.**

The Act of 1660 was, then, a move in the right direction, since it simplified the system of landholding by practically reducing the former tenures to two, that is to say, to socage and copyhold, though the simplification was not quite so complete as this, owing to the retention of those divergent customary methods of holding land known as gavelkind, ancient demesne and borough-English.[3] Yet even apart from these peculiar cases it is obvious that the existence from 1660 to 1925 of two separate and quite different methods by which a man might hold land, tended to increase the complexities of conveyancing and to render real property law unnecessarily difficult.

We must now briefly describe the two tenures of socage and copyhold which held the field until the legislation of 1925 abolished the latter.

**Socage
a non-
military
tenure.**

Socage.[4] As distinguished from knight service, socage was that species of tenure which represented the new aspect that the economic life of the country gradually assumed. It was essentially non-military and free from the worst features of knight service. At first it could not be defined in positive terms, but was described negatively as being that form of tenure which was neither spiritual, military, sergeanty nor villeinage.

**Early
history.**

In early days the services due in respect of the land varied considerably. The tenant might pay a nominal rent sufficient to record the fact that the lands were held of the lord, or a substantial rent equal to the economic value of the land, while sometimes his obligation would extend to the performance of agricultural

---

[1] Challis, *Law of Real Property* (3rd Edn.), p. 9.
[2] The chief reason for the decline of frankalmoin tenure was that upon alienation of the land, even to another ecclesiastical body, or upon escheat of the lordship to a superior lord, the tenure was converted into socage. Moreover, no fresh grant in frankalmoin, except by the Crown, has been possible since *Quia Emptores ;* Challis, *Law of Real Property* (3rd Edn.), p. 11.   Ecclesiastical bodies more frequently held land by one of the other tenures; Maitland, *Constitutional History of England*, p. 25.
[3] *Supra*, p. 18.
[4] Holdsworth, *History of English Law*, vol. iii. pp. 51 *et seq.*

services. Originally, no doubt, the socmanni, as they were called, belonged to the lower orders of society, but the tendency was for this mode of landholding to extend upwards, since it was free from the worst of the feudal burdens incidental to knight service, and to escape those even the greater landowners were willing to sacrifice something of their dignity.

The next step was that it became usual to commute services, whatever these might have been, into money payments, and though these, when they were originally fixed, no doubt represented the economic value of the land, yet with the gradual fall in the value of money they became in course of time so insignificant in amount as scarcely to merit the trouble of collection.[1] Thus at the present day it is practically impossible to prove that A. holds of B. in socage tenure, for the payment of rent which would have revealed the existence of the tenure has in most cases not been made for centuries. B. does not lose much, for the rent is generally of little pecuniary value, and the only other event which might have benefited him before the doctrine of escheat was abolished as from January 1st, 1926—namely, the death of the tenant intestate and without heirs, whereby the land would pass to B. by escheat—is normally of rare occurrence. Of course the land must be held of somebody, and the rule is that, where no private person can prove his lordship, it is deemed to be held of the Crown.

Commutation of services.

So socage became the great residuary tenure. It included every tenure which was not knight service, sergeanty, frankalmoin or villeinage, and its outstanding characteristic came to be that it involved some service which was absolutely certain and fixed, and which in the vast majority of cases took the form of a money payment.[2] Though subject to aids and to relief, it was free from the obnoxious rights of wardship and marriage that characterized knight service. The guardian of an infant socage tenant was the nearest relative who was incapable of inheriting the land. It was enacted by the Statute of Marlborough 1267 that a guardian in socage must account for the profits of the land at the end of his stewardship, and must not give or sell the ward in marriage.

Copyhold Tenure.[3] The other tenure to which as late as 1925 English land might be subject was copyhold, the modern name for the old villeinage. Although this tenure was abolished as from January 1st, 1926, something must be said about its origin and peculiar characteristics.

Copyhold tenure.

We see in this tenure a system of land holding which represented in modern times customs far older than feudalism, and

Origin of copyholds.

---

[1] Pollock and Maitland, *History of English Law* (2nd Edn.), vol. i. p. 291.
[2] Littleton, s. 117.
[3] Holdsworth, *History of English Law*, vol. iii. pp. 491 *et seq.*; vol. vii. pp. 296 *et seq*; Simpson, *Introduction to the History of Land Law*, pp. 145 *et seq.*

which dated back to the primitive method of agriculture called the open field system. In remote days the actual tillers of the English soil were almost certainly members of free village communities who owned in common the land that they farmed; but after the Conquest, although they still continued to follow those precepts and habits of agriculture that had been customary for generations, they were gradually absorbed into the feudal system. An overlord had appeared, a new concept in the shape of the manor had been established, and by imperceptible degrees the humble tillers found themselves part of the manorial organization; no longer free owners, but instead subservient to an overlord upon whose will, according to the strict letter of the law, they were absolutely dependent. BLACKSTONE thought that the modern copyholders were merely serfs who by continual encroachments on their superiors had gradually established a customary right to estates which strictly speaking had always been held at the will of the lords,[1] but in fact the truth is the exact reverse, for the lords had gradually induced the belief that only by their will were these ancient owners permitted to enjoy their customary rights and estates.[2]

Importance of the manor.

To understand the character of copyhold tenure we must refer once more to the feudal manor which was the unit of society in mediaeval England.

A typical manor consisted of

> (*a*) the land belonging to the lord, which was called his demesne,
>
> (*b*) the land held of the lord by free tenants whether in socage or knight service,
>
> (*c*) the land held of the lord by persons called villein tenants,
>
> (*d*) rights of jurisdiction exercisable by the lord over the free tenants in the Court Baron, and over the villeins in the Court Customary,
>
> (*e*) waste land on which the tenants were entitled to pasture their cattle.

Farm system.

The first point that emerges about the villeins is that it was they who cultivated the lord's demesne, a practice which originated in what has been termed the farm system. " Farm " in Anglo-Saxon times meant food, and the system in vogue was for the tenant, in return for his holding, to produce a farm—that is, enough food to sustain his lord for some given period, say a night, a week or a fortnight.[3]

Labour service system.

In the thirteenth century this primitive system gave way to the labour service system,[4] which meant that the villein tenant

---

[1] Blackstone, vol. ii. p. 95.
[2] See Pollock, *The Land Laws*, pp. 43–52 ; and Appendix, Note D.
[3] Vinogradoff, *Villainage in England*, pp. 301–2.
[4] *Ibid.*, p. 304.

came under an obligation, often specified in the greatest detail,[1] to cultivate by his own labour his lord's demesne. But the mere obligation to perform agricultural services does not alone suffice to distinguish a villein from a socage tenant, since it was by no means impossible for a socage tenant to be subject to the same liability. What, then, was the test of villein tenure ?

One fact which might be thought at first sight to provide this test is that the villeins received no protection in the King's courts. If they were unjustifiably ejected by the lord, they could recover neither possession nor damages in the royal courts, for in the view of the latter they were nothing more than tenants at the will of the lord.[2] But though superficially the tenure seemed precarious to the last degree, it was saved from being so in actual fact because the tenants were entitled to protection from the lord's manorial court, where those rules which had been hallowed by immemorial custom within the manor were recognized and enforced. These manorial customs gradually grew into legal systems under which the rights and the duties of the tenants were defined, and the everyday events of marriage, succession, alienation and the like were regulated.[3] But the lack of a remedy in the royal courts was not a sufficient test of villeinage or no villeinage since it also affected an ordinary tenant for years.

That test is to be found, however, in the nature of the services rendered by a tenant. If a man was bound to perform agricultural services it could not be said that he was necessarily a villein tenant, but if he did not know from day to day *what* kind of work would be assigned to him, then he was looked upon as a villein tenant. In other words, the test was the uncertainty of the nature of the work. As POLLOCK and MAITLAND have said :—

> " When they go to bed on Sunday night they do not know what Monday's work will be ; it may be threshing, ditching, carrying ; they cannot tell. This seems the point that is seized by law and that general opinion of which law is the exponent : any considerable uncertainty as to the amount or the kind of the agricultural services makes the tenure unfree. The tenure is unfree, not because the tenant holds at the will of the lord, in the sense of being removable at a moment's notice, but because his services, though in many respects minutely defined by custom, cannot be altogether defined without frequent reference to the lord's will."[4]

So then in the thirteenth century villeinage was that tenure in which the return made by the tenant for his holding was the performance on his lord's demesne of agricultural services uncertain in nature.

Marginal notes:

Test of villein tenure.

Test of villein tenure found in nature of services.

---

[1] See, for example, Pollock and Maitland, *History of English Law* (2nd Edn.) vol. i. p. 366.

[2] *Ibid.*, p. 360.

[3] Vinogradoff, *Villainage in England*, p. 172.

[4] *Op. cit.*, vol. i. p. 371.

Money payment system.

But in the fourteenth and fifteenth centuries this labour service system gave way to a money payment system under which the tenant in villeinage paid a rent to his lord instead of giving personal services, and the lord cultivated his demesne by hired labour.[1] This was an example of the general movement from natural husbandry to the money system, which was fostered in England by several causes, such as the growth of the woollen trade with Flanders and the great increase of trade with the Continent as a result of the English occupation of Normandy and Aquitaine.[2]

Villeinage becomes copyhold.

The result of the change as regards villeinage was to benefit the tenant, because the rents remained stabilized despite the gradual fall in monetary values. This transition from labour services to money payments corresponded with the transition in nomenclature from villeinage to copyhold tenure.

" With the completion of the transition from praedial services to money rents, tenure in villeinage may be said to have come to an end. . . . The essence of villein tenure had consisted in the uncertainty of the tenant's services, and when the old agricultural services were commuted for a fixed money payment, this uncertainty passed away."[3]

Meaning of term " copyhold."

The derivation of the word " copyhold " is this : the copyhold tenant, like his predecessor the villein, held at the will of the lord; but yet at the same time he held on the conditions which had become fixed by the customs of his particular manor. The lord's will could not be exercised capriciously, but only in conformity with custom. He still held a court, and that court kept records of all transactions affecting the lands. These records were called the rolls of the court. When, for instance, a tenant sold his interest to a third party, the circumstances of the sale would be recorded, and the buyer would receive a copy of the court rolls in so far as they affected his holding. Inasmuch as he held his estate by copy of court roll, he came to be called a copyholder.

Importance of change to tenant.

The change from villeinage to copyhold was of far-reaching importance to the tenant. He was rid of all traces of servility; he acquired an interest which in essentials was on all-fours with interests in land held by socage tenure, and above all he obtained recognition and protection from the King's courts. This protection was assured by the end of the fifteenth century. Coke summed up the position in expressive language :—

" But now copyholders stand upon a sure ground, now they weigh not their lord's displeasure, they shake not at every sudden blast of wind, they eat, drink and sleep securely ; only having a special care of the main chance, viz., to perform carefully what duties and services

---

[1] Holdsworth, *History of English Law*, vol. iii. p. 204.
[2] Vinogradoff, *Villainage, in England*, p. 180.
[3] Page, *The End of Villeinage*, p. 83, cited Holdsworth, vol. iii. p. 206.

soever their tenure doth exact, and custom doth require : then let lord frown, the copyholder cares not, knowing himself safe, and not within any danger. For if the lord's anger grow to expulsion, the law hath provided several weapons of remedy ; for it is at his election, either to sue a *subpoena* or an action of trespass against the lord. Time hath dealt very favourably with copyholders in divers respects." [1]

Despite the possibility of enfranchisement, a process by which copyhold might be converted into socage tenure, a great proportion of English land, even in 1925, was still copyhold. The tenure was distinguished by several defects. For instance, the customs, which represented the local law governing land of this tenure, varied considerably from manor to manor, so that it was impossible to determine the law applicable to a disputed matter without an examination of the manorial records ; the form of conveyance was far different from that required in the case of socage ; copyhold and socage lands were often intermixed in so confusing a fashion as to make it difficult to discriminate between them, a dilemma from which the only escape in the event of a sale was the execution of two conveyances, one appropriate for copyhold, the other for a socage holding ; certain rights of the land were so burdensome to the tenant that they caused strife and ill-will ; and finally, it was impossible for either the lord or the tenant, without the assent of the other, to exploit the minerals under the land.

Defects of copyhold tenure.

This bare summary of the history of copyhold tenure should be enough to show that from about the beginning of the seventeenth century it was nothing more nor less than an outmoded and exceedingly inconvenient form of ordinary tenure. It served no particular social need and it certainly impeded a simplified system of conveyancing because of its frequent diversity from socage tenure. It has been rightly described as " an anachronism and a nuisance." [2]

Summary of Tenures in 1925. If we now take stock of the feudal tenures as they existed in 1925 we shall find the position to have been as follows : the greater part of English land was held by socage tenure, a considerable part was subject to copyhold tenure, while the remainder was held either in grand sergeanty or in frankalmoin, or was affected by the peculiar customs of gavelkind, borough-English or ancient demesne. Here was room for at least one form of simplification, and we shall see later [3] that the Law of Property Acts 1922 and 1925 seized the opportunity. They converted copyhold and ancient demesne into socage tenure ; they abolished gavelkind, borough-English, and all other customary modes of descent ; and they purported to abolish frankalmoin. [4] The honorary services incident to sergeanty were

Abolition of all tenures except socage.

---

[1] *Compleat Copyholder*, s. 9.
[2] Underhill, *Century of Law Reform*, p. 310.   [3] *Infra*, p. 84.
[4] As to frankalmoin, see *infra*, p. 86.

retained. Escheat *propter defectum sanguinis*, which was the right of a lord to take the land of his tenant who had died intestate without leaving heirs, was abolished and replaced by a right in the Crown to take the land as *bona vacantia* in the same way that it takes goods.

Present position of doctrine of tenure.

The result is that though the general theory of tenure is still a part of English law in the sense that all land is held of a superior and is incapable of absolute ownership, yet the law of tenure is both simpler and of less significance than it was before 1926. It is simpler because there is now only one form of tenure—namely, socage. It is of less significance because all the tenurial incidents (including escheat) which might in exceptional cases have brought profit to a mesne lord have been abolished, so that there is no inducement for a private person to prove that he is the lord of land. We can, in fact, now describe the theory of tenure, despite the great part that it has played in the history of English law, as a conception of merely academic interest. It no longer restricts the tenant in his free enjoyment of the land.

(2) THE DOCTRINE OF THE ESTATE[1]

What is the nature of the tenant's interest?

Tenure signifies the relation between lord and tenant, and what it implies is that the person whom we should naturally call the owner does not own the land, but merely holds it as tenant of the Crown or of some other feudal superior. But if he is not owner of the land, what is the nature of the interest that he holds? In statutes, in judicial decisions and in common speech he is always described as a " landowner," but we may well ask what it is that he owns.

It may be said at once that the doctrine of tenure as developed in England made it difficult, if not impossible, to regard either him or his lord as the owner of the land itself. The land could not be owned by the tenant, since it was recoverable by the lord if the tenurial services were not faithfully performed; it could not be owned by the lord, since he had no claim to it as long as the tenant fulfilled his duties.[2]

No doctrine of ownership in English land law.

Quite apart from this practical difficulty, however, the truth is that English law has never applied the conception of ownership to land. " Ownership " is a word of many meanings, but in the present context we can take it to signify a title to a subject-matter, whether movable or immovable, that is good against the whole world. The holder of the title, such as the owner of a motor-car,

---

[1] Holdsworth, *History of English Law*, vol. iii. pp. 101–37 ; Pollock and Maitland, *History of English Law*, (2nd Edn.), vol. ii. pp. 2–29 ; Hargreaves, *Introduction to Land Law* (4th Edn.), pp. 19–25 ; 42–54 ; Simpson, *Introduction to the History of Land Law*, pp. 44 *et seq.*

[2] Hargreaves, *op. cit.*, p. 44.

has a real as opposed to a personal right—he is the absolute owner. This position is illustrated by the Roman doctrine of *dominium*, under which the *dominus* was entitled to the absolute and exclusive right of property in the land. Nothing less in the way of ownership was recognized. A man had either absolute ownership or no ownership at all. Possession was regarded as fundamentally different—*nihil commune habet proprietas cum possessione*—and, though it was adequately protected, the remedies available were personal, not real.

In sharp contrast to this attitude, English law, in analysing the relation of the tenant to the land, has directed its attention not to ownership, but to possession, or, as it is called in the case of land, *seisin*. All titles to land are ultimately based upon possession in the sense that the title of the man seised prevails against all who can show no better right to seisin. Seisin is a root of title, and it may be said without undue exaggeration that so far as land is concerned there is in England no law of ownership, but only a law of possession.

> " . . . ' seisin ' . . . is an enjoyment of property based upon title, and is not essentially distinguishable from right. In other words, the sharp distinction between property and possession made in Roman law did not obtain in English law ; seisin is not the Roman possession and right is not the Roman ownership. Both of these conceptions are represented in English law only by seisin, and it was the essence of the conception of seisin that some seisins might be better than others." [1]

This unfailing emphasis upon the concrete and obvious fact of possession will be apparent if we consider for a moment the following three topics :—the remedies that lie for the recovery of land, the position of a tenant who is wrongfully dispossessed, and the long established mechanism of conveyancing.

The English actions for the recovery of land, called in early days *real actions*, have consistently and continuously turned upon the right to possession. Moreover, their object throughout has been not to enquire whether the title to possession set up by the defendant is an absolute title good against all persons, but whether it is relatively better than any title that the plaintiff can establish. English land law is committed to the doctrine of relative titles to possession. Thus, the issue raised in the most ancient and solemn remedy, the *writ of right*, was not whether the demandant (plaintiff) could prove an absolute title good against third parties, but whether he or the defendant could establish the earlier and therefore the better seisin.[2] Similarly, the possessory assizes, simpler remedies introduced by Henry II to supplement the writ

[marginal note:] English law concentrates on possession, not on ownership.

[marginal note:] Possessory nature of early actions for the recovery of land.

---

[1] Plucknett, *Concise History of the Common Law* (5th Edn.), p. 358.
[2] Lightwood, *Possession of Land*, pp. 73–4 ; Plucknett, *Concise History of the Common Law* (5th Edn.), p. 358 ; Simpson, *Introduction to the History of Land Law*, pp. 34 *et seq.*

of right and to rectify a recent invasion of possession, merely considered the specific question whether the demandant or his ancestor had been unjustly disseised of his free tenement by the defendant. The assize of *novel disseisin, i.e.* recent dispossession, enabled A. to recover land from B. on proof that he had been ejected by B. The assize of *mort d'ancestor* availed him if he could show that he was the heir of his deceased ancestor, X., and that X.'s seisin had been usurped by the defendant.

The sole question in these actions was one of fact relating to seisin. Did B. disseise A.? Did B. take the seisin held by A.'s ancestor?[1] If so, the court ordered restoration of the seisin, but it did not adjudge that A. held an absolute title good against all adversaries. If the defendant wished to agitate the question of title further, he would be driven to issue a writ of right.[2]

At a later date the various *writs of entry* met the case where the disseisin of which the demandant complained was not so immediate, as, for example, where B., after disseising the demandant, had granted the land to Y., who had granted it to the defendant. These actions, no less than the possessory assizes, merely decided whether the better right to seisin lay in the demandant or in the defendant.

Possessory nature of modern action for recovery of land.

Finally, it must be observed that this mediaeval principle of relativity of titles dominated the later action of ejectment and still dominates the modern action for the recovery of land as it is now called.[3] All that the plaintiff need do is to prove that he has a better right to possession than the defendant, not that he has a better right than anybody else. If, for instance, he is ejected by the defendant, he will recover by virtue of his prior possession, notwithstanding that a still better right may reside in some third person.[4]

Effect of loss of seisin on proprietary rights.

The effects that flow from a disseisin of the tenant afford a further illustration of the crucial part played by possession in English law. It was established at an early date that the seisin wrongfully taken by the disseisor was the commencement of a fresh title and that it gave him a real though tortious interest, valid against all but the disseisee and his successors in title.

" Possession being once admitted to be a root of title, every possession must create a title which, as against all subsequent intruders, has all the incidents and advantages of a true title."[5]

The disseisor has full beneficial rights over the land. He holds a fee simple estate which is transmissible either *inter vivos* or by

---

[1] Holdsworth, *History of English Law* vol. iii. p. 90 ; Maitland, *Forms of Action*, p. 28.

[2] Plucknett, *Concise History of the Common Law* (5th Edn.), p. 359.

[3] (1940), 56 *L. Q. R.* 376 (A. D. Hargreaves), replied to by Holdsworth in 56 *L. Q. R.* 479–82.

[4] *Asher* v. *Whitlock* (1865), L. R. 1 Q B. 1 ; M. & B. p. 161.

[5] Pollock and Wright, *Possession in the Common Law*, p. 95.

will, and which the disseisee cannot defeat unless he takes proceedings within twelve years after the wrongful entry.[1] Moreover, although the disseisee had a right of action to recover the land, for a long period in our legal history his lack of possession confronted him with serious and ever-increasing difficulties as against the disseisor and his successors in title. In mediaeval days and for long afterwards, the effect of the disseisin was to deprive him of most of his beneficial rights over the land until he had vindicated his claim to seisin in the appropriate real action. His former rights were reduced to a right of entry, a reduction that entailed certain important consequences.

> Thus, he lost the power of alienation, for, being dispossessed, he was unable to make the delivery of seisin essential for a conveyance of land, and a right of entry could neither be devised until 1837,[2] nor conveyed *inter vivos* until 1845.[3]
>
> Circumstances might well occur which would deprive him of his right of entry and leave him with a mere right of action—a *chose in action* that was equally inalienable, though it would descend to his heirs.[4] For instance, where the disseisor died while still in possession, the land passed to his heir by operation of law with the result that the interest held by him was no longer regarded as tortious. The right of entry was said to be "tolled," *i.e.* taken away, by descent cast.[5]
>
> Again, if the disseisee failed to recover seisin, his widow had no right to dower ;[6] if he died heirless, the land did not in all cases escheat to his lord ;[7] and if he died leaving an infant heir, his lord was not entitled to wardship.[8]

The position may be summarized in the words of HOLDSWORTH : "The person seised has all the rights of an owner ; the person disseised has the right to get seisin by entry or action ; but, till he has got it, he has none of the rights as an owner. In other words, the common law recognizes, not *dominium* and *possessio*, but seisin only."[9]

The third illustration of the emphasis laid by English land law upon possession, not upon ownership, is afforded by the practice of conveyancers. A vendor must prove to the satisfaction of the purchaser, not only that he is entitled to the land which he has agreed to sell, but also that his title is not subject to adverse claims vested in third parties. He can scarcely be expected to prove that he has a title good against the whole world, for, since land is permanent and indestructible, it may well be that there

Possession is a root of title for conveyancing purposes.

---

[1] Limitation Act 1939, *infra*, pp. 883 *et seq.*
[2] Wills Act 1837, s. 3. [3] Real Property Act 1845, s. 6.
[4] Hayes, *Introduction to Conveyancing*, vol. i. p. 231.
[5] The doctrine of descent cast was abolished by the Real Property Limitation Act 1833, s. 39.
[6] Maitland, *Collected Papers*, vol. i. p. 366. [7] *Ibid.*, pp. 368–9.
[8] *Ibid.*, p. 369. On the subject generally, see Holdsworth, *History of English Law*, vol. iii. pp. 91–2.
[9] *Ibid.*, p. 95.

exists a competing and better title created many years ago and still existing.

English land law has no doctrine akin to that of Roman law by which possession for a definite but short period had the positive effect of investing the possessor with *dominium*. As one writer has observed, the absolute ownership of a perishable chattel, such as a motor-car, is a comparatively easy matter to prove, but " if we were to insist upon the same fulness of ownership with regard to land we should have to trace back our title to the original grant of Paradise to Adam." [1] What the vendor can do, however, and what he does in practice is to rely upon the fundamental principle that seisin is evidence of his title to the land.

> " With very few exceptions, there is only one way in which an apparent owner of English land who is minded to deal with it can show his right so to do ; and that way is to show that he and those through whom he claims have possessed the land for a time sufficient to exclude any reasonable probability of a superior adverse claim." [2]

Only subject-matter of ownership is an estate in the land.

What, then, emerges so far is that land cannot be the subject-matter of ownership, though the person in whom its seisin is vested is entitled to exercise proprietary rights in respect of it. But again the question recurs—what is the nature of the interest held by the person seised ? Is there nothing that he can be said to own ? The answer made by English law is unique. The person entitled to seisin owns an abstract entity, called an *estate*, which is interposed between him and the land.[3] " The English lawyer . . . first detaches the ownership from the land itself, and then attaches it to an imaginary thing which he calls an estate." [4]

The estate represents the extent of his right to seisin. Thus the correct description of a tenant entitled to immediate seisin for his life is that he is *seised of Blackacre for an estate for life*. This estate entitles its owner to exercise proprietary rights over the land for the prescribed period, subject to observance of the tenurial duties, and it may be disposed of as freely as any other subject-matter of ownership. This doctrine, as will be explained later,[5] is not confined to the case where a man is entitled to immediate seisin. If he is definitely entitled to it at some future time, he is equally the owner of an estate.

Features of the doctrine of the estate.

Two phenomena of great significance have emerged during the development of this doctrine by the common law.

First, estates vary in size according to the time for which they are to endure. On this basis they are classified as estates of freehold and estates less than freehold.

---

[1] Hargreaves, *Introduction to Land Law* (4th Edn.), p. 42.
[2] Pollock and Wright, *Possession in the Common Law*, pp. 94-5.
[3] Lawson, *Rational Strength of English Law*, p. 87.
[4] Markby, *Elements of English Law*, s. 330.
[5] *Infra*, p. 36.

Secondly, several different persons may simultaneously own distinct and separate estates in the same piece of land.

These matters will now be discussed in more detail.

The main classification of estates depends upon their quantification and their quantification depends upon their duration. The estate will vary in size according to the time for which it is to continue. " Proprietary rights in land are, we may say, projected upon the plane of time."[1] Thus a person may be entitled to seisin for ever or for a lesser period.

Estates are sub-classified into those of freehold and those less than freehold. Into which of these categories they fell depended in the earliest days upon the quality of the tenure by which the estate owner held his land. A tenant in knight service, sergeanty, socage or frankalmoin was called a " freeholder," since the services due from him were free from servile incidents. He was said to have a frank tenement or freehold estate to distinguish him from a villein tenant.[2] Such was the original meaning of the expression " freehold estate."

But one of the characteristics of these free tenants was that the time for which they were entitled to hold the land was not fixed and certain. They invariably held either for life or for some other space of time dependent upon an event that might not happen within a lifetime, and it was this uncertainty of duration, not the quality of the services to be rendered, that gradually came to be regarded as the essential feature of a freehold estate.[3] Thus, even at the present day, an estate is freehold if its duration is uncertain; it is less than freehold if the time of its termination is fixed or capable of being fixed. The life tenant is a freeholder, but not so the tenant holding under a lease for a definite period, even though he holds for as long a period as 999 years.[4]

Freehold and non-freehold estates were further distinguished in respect of seisin. At first the word " seisin " was used to denote possession both of land and of chattels, but this usage did not last long and by the fifteenth century a man was said to be seised of land, but possessed of chattels. Later the subject-matter of seisin became even further restricted. The real actions that lay for the recovery of land, the possessory assizes and the writs of entry, were available only to freeholders, *i.e.* to tenants

Estates classified according to their duration.

Meaning of freehold estate.

Freeholds and non-freeholds distinguished in respect of seisin.

---

[1] Pollock and Maitland, *History of English Law* (2nd Edn.), vol. ii. p. 10. Compare the language used in the course of argument in *Walsingham's Case* (1579), 2 Plowd. 547, at p. 555 : " The land itself is one thing, and the estate in the land is another thing, for an estate in the land is a time in the land, or land for a time, and there are diversities of estates, which are no more than diversities of time, for he who has a fee simple in land has a time in the land without end or the land for time without end."

[2] Pollock and Maitland, *op. cit.*, vol. ii. p. 78 ; Holdsworth, *History of English Law*, vol. ii. p. 351.

[3] Co. Litt. 43*b*.

[4] See, generally, *Preston on Estates*, vol. i. c. 1.

in fee simple, in tail and for life. These actions, as we have seen, were based entirely upon seisin and since they availed only freeholders it is not unnatural that the word " seisin " was reserved exclusively to describe the possession of a freehold estate. Since mediaeval days it has been correct, for instance, to describe a tenant for life as seised, but a tenant for years as possessed, of the land.

On the basis of duration common law has classified estates in the manner set out in the following table.

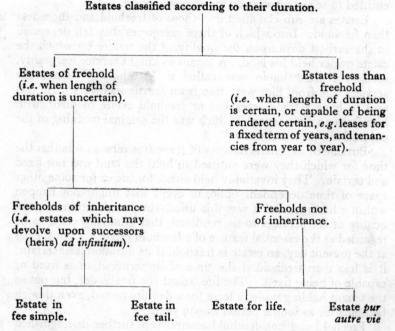

Estates classified according to their duration.

Estates of freehold (*i.e.* when length of duration is uncertain).

Estates less than freehold (*i.e.* when length of duration is certain, or capable of being rendered certain, *e.g.* leases for a fixed term of years, and tenancies from year to year).

Freeholds of inheritance (*i.e.* estates which may devolve upon successors (heirs) *ad infinitum*).

Freeholds not of inheritance.

Estate in fee simple.   **Estate in fee tail.**   **Estate for life.**   **Estate *pur autre vie***

As regards duration, the three freehold estates may be distinguished as follows :

The fee simple is the largest estate in point of duration, for, being one that is granted to a man *and his heirs*, it will last as long as the person entitled to it for the time being dies leaving an heir, and therefore it may last for ever in the sense that it may never pass to the Crown for want of an heir. The word *fee* denotes its inheritability, and the word *simple* indicates that it is inheritable by the general heirs of the owner for the time being whether they be ascendants, descendants or collateral.

The estate tail, which is the only other estate of inheritance, is less in quantum than the fee simple since it is inheritable only by the specified descendants of the original grantee and never by his ascendants, and also because it is descendible only to his lineal issue and not to his collateral relatives.

Thus it is inferior to the fee simple in the sense that it has not as great a capacity for perpetual existence. The classic formula for its creation is—to A. and the *heirs of his body*.

Life estates include an estate which A. holds for his own life and also one that he holds during the lifetime of B., this second species being called an estate *pur autre vie*.

The second phenomenon mentioned above is that the fee simple, which entitles the tenant to use the land for an infinite time, is regarded by English law as an aggregate out of which any number of smaller *and simultaneous* estates may be carved.[1] The entire subject-matter of enjoyment is apportionable among a number of persons, each of whom is the present owner of his individual portion. *[Apportionment of fee simple allowed by English law.]*

> By way of illustration let us suppose that a fee simple owner desires that A. shall enjoy Blackacre for life, that on A.'s death the right of enjoyment shall pass to B. for life and that subject to these life interests the fee simple shall be vested in C.

Every legal system that permits dispositions of this kind must necessarily particularize the legal nature of the rights, if any, vested in the successive beneficiaries, and the solution reached must depend upon whether or not the land itself is capable of ownership. It is obvious that any system of law which admits this capacity cannot regard A., B. and C. as simultaneous owners, for, in so far as ownership imports the right of immediate user, B. and C. cannot use the land at the same time as A., unless, of course, they are made joint, not as in our example successive, owners. The jurisprudential solution, therefore, if the land itself is the subject of ownership, is to insist that it can be the subject only of absolute ownership, and that where, as in the above example, there is a limitation to a succession of persons the entire and absolute ownership shall pass from one beneficiary to another upon the happening of the prescribed events. This is what is called *substitution*. Under this doctrine, if land is limited to A., then to B. and then to C., the legal result is that these persons in their turn become owners of the property, each taking by substitution for the one who preceded him ; each in his turn being complete owner ; but each taking nothing until his turn comes.[2] *[No apportionment possible if land itself capable of ownership.]*

B., for instance, is not even a limited owner of the land during the life of A., but on the death of the latter he becomes the absolute owner of the land for a limited time. Until his turn comes he has no proprietary interest that he can alienate or other-wise dispose of.

This is the solution of Roman law and of certain modern *[The rule in Roman law.]*

---

[1] Digby, *History of the Law of Real Property*, p. 270.
[2] See Markby, *Elements of Law*, s. 330.

legal systems which regard *dominium* as the exclusive and unlimited right to the land itself, not merely to its user.

By Roman law, A., the owner, might indeed let the land to X. by *locatio conductio* or grant it to him for life by way of *usufruct*, but his ownership was affected by neither transaction. In the former case, X., if evicted, had merely a contractual right enforceable against A. alone ; in the latter, he acquired only a *jus in re aliena*, *i.e.* a right to use for his life land the ownership of which remained vested in A.

Why apportionment possible in English law.

English law, however, having divorced ownership from the land itself and attached it to an imaginary thing called an *estate*, which entitles the owner to use the land for a longer or a shorter period of time, has been able to take a bolder course. Having decided that estates may vary in size according to their duration, it goes a step further and concedes that any estate, whether its duration is long or short and whether it confers a right to immediate or to future seisin, is capable of a present existing ownership.

Two results flow from this view.

English law recognizes different degrees of ownership.

First, there may be different degrees or gradations of estate ownership. The tenant in tail and the tenant for life, no less than the tenant in fee simple, are owners of their estates. As compared with the tenant in fee simple, they must, indeed, be described as *limited* owners, since their estates have not the same capacity of infinite duration. None the less they are owners, and their ownership differs from that of the tenant in fee simple only in degree—in quantity. There is no difference in kind or quality.[1]

The same remedies for the recovery of the land and the same powers of dealing with the estate by way of alienation are available, irrespective of the size of the estate. The different freehold estates, in other words, represent various grades in the hierarchy of ownership.

Futurity of right to seisin not incompatible with present ownership.

The second result of the English doctrine is that an estate may be the subject of a present existing ownership, even though the right of the owner to seisin is postponed to a future time. This is explicable in elementary terms.

> An estate is the right to possess and use the land for the period of time for which it has been granted. In the case of the fee simple the period is infinite, since the estate is capable of perpetual existence. The entire ownership, in other words, resides in the person holding the fee simple, since he and his successors are entitled to use the land for ever. But time is divisible, and this right of perpetual user may be divided into successive periods of limited duration or, as one writer put it, into successive intervals of time.[2] One slice of the perpetual time, one slice of the entire ownership, may be given to A., another to B., and so on.

---

[1] Pollock and Maitland, *History of English Law* (2nd Edn.), vol. ii. p. 7.
[2] (1857), 1 *Jurid. Soc.* p. 537 (S. M. Leake).

Therefore, if the fee simple owner makes a grant

to A. for life, then to B. for life and then to C. in tail,

each grantee receives at once a portion of the one uniform subject-matter, namely the right to use the land. A., B. and C. each hold a distinct and separate share of the identical thing. The only difference between them lies in the periods for which the user is to be enjoyed. Moreover, there is no futurity about the *ownership* of B. and C. Upon the execution of the grant they become the immediate and absolute owners of an estate. It is not the right of ownership, but the right to actual seisin of the land that is future. Indeed, by virtue of their power of disposition they may exchange their property for money and so make it immediately available.[1]

In conclusion, it may be said that this doctrine of the estate has given an elasticity to the English law of land that is not found in countries outside the area of the common law.[2] This is particularly true in respect of settlements, *i.e.* dispositions of property designed to provide for a succession of persons, such as the present and future members of a family. The desire to do this has dominated English real property law throughout its long history; for land, with its virtue of permanency, is an ideal source of endowment and its use for this purpose has been favoured by the courts. The aims of a settlor will be more effectively attained if he is permitted to vest a definite right of ownership in certain persons upon the occurrence of certain prescribed events in the future, as for example by directing that if a son is born to the present tenant of Blackacre, he shall, on reaching his majority, immediately acquire a definite proprietary interest, even though the present tenant is still alive. If the land itself is the subject-matter of ownership, the simultaneous existence of two or more owners, unless they are to take jointly, is, as we have seen, impossible, and therefore in countries where that concept of ownership prevails the power to create successive interests stretching into the future is necessarily restricted. But once admit that what is owned is an imaginary thing called an estate, then it immediately becomes possible to frame elaborate and subtle schemes for the passing of the beneficial enjoyment of the land to one person after another in certain prescribed eventualities. There is room " to deal with ownership in a more fanciful way than if it were attached to the soil." [3]

Advantages of the English doctrine.

We will now conclude with a short description of the term of years which, quantitatively considered, is the smallest proprietary interest recognised by English law.

---

[1] 1 *Jurid. Soc.* p. 538.

[2] It has been described by a distinguished writer as " one of the most brilliant feats of the English mind " ; Lawson, *Rational Strength of English Law*, p. 97.

[3] Markby, *The Elements of Law*, s. 330.

Term of years not a freehold interest.

Leasehold Interest.[1] This interest, generally referred to as a term of years, arises where land has been demised, *i.e.* leased, to a man for a definite number of years. It thus lacks the requirement of an uncertain duration, and though the period for which it is to last may be very great, as for instance 999 years, yet it is not a freehold estate, and in the eye of the law is a smaller interest than a life estate.

Meaning of " Real Property ".

Moreover it is not even real property. At an early period English law arrived at the general principle that, while land could be recovered specifically by a dispossessed tenant from a man who had ejected him, yet a person who was deprived of personal chattels could not enforce their actual recovery, but had to content himself with compensation in the shape of pecuniary damages. Broadly speaking, actions fell into two classes. The *real actions* lay for the restitution of some object, and the *personal actions* for the recovery of damages. As land was the only object of which restitution *in specie* could be enforced, it followed that it formed the only subject matter of a real action, and it is not surprising to find the ancient lawyers seizing upon this fact and defining land as real property. Property which could be recovered in a real action was itself called real property, and thus it resulted that real property consisted solely of interests in land.

Leasehold not real property.

But not every interest in land could be specifically recovered, for, as we have seen, the real actions were available only to freeholders, *i.e.* only to tenants who were seised of the land. A tenant for years was possessed, not seised, and if dispossessed he could originally bring only a personal action for the recovery of damages. It is true that by the close of the Middle Ages a remedy had been introduced whereby he might recover the term itself, but nevertheless he was still regarded, and has ever since been regarded, as a non-freeholder. The doctrine of seisin was never extended to his interest, and the *possessory assizes* and the *writ of right*, which were the real actions properly so called, were never made available to him. He continued to hold merely personal property because originally his sole remedy was to bring a personal action.

Reason why terms of years not freehold.

At first sight this refusal of the law to regard a leaseholder's interest as real property is curious. It was not due to the unimportance or insignificance of terms of years. Such interests were on the contrary exceedingly valuable. The cause of their segregation, the reason why they were dissociated from the real actions and from feudal doctrine, was probably none other than economic pressure.[2]

At a time when investments in the modern sense of the term

---

[1] Holdsworth, *History of English Law*, vol. iii. 213–7; vol. vii. 238–96; Simpson, *Introduction to the History of Land Law*, pp. 68–73 ; 87–9 ; 229–38.
[2] Pollock and Maitland, *History of English Law* (2nd Edn.), vol. ii. pp. 113 *et seq.*; Plucknett, *Concise History of the Common Law* (5th Edn.), pp. 571–3.

were unknown, one of the few methods by which a man might increase his income was to purchase a beneficial lease and take the profits of the land as interest on the money expended. Again, one of the ordinary methods of exacting security for a debt was for the debtor to lease his lands at a nominal rent to the creditor, so that the latter could obtain interest at the agreed rate out of the profits of the land without coming into conflict with the usury laws.[1] Another familiar form of investment was to purchase a wardship, which was the right to administer for one's own benefit the lands of an infant tenant in knight service. But if terms of years and wardships were to be effective investments, it was necessary that they should not be regarded as freehold estates in land carrying seisin, or, in more general terms, it was convenient to exclude them from the domain of strict real property law. There were several considerations that made this line of action advisable, but none more potent than the fact that freehold estates as distinct from chattels could not be left by will. It may have been a matter of sound policy that an estate in lands should inevitably descend to the heir of the deceased tenant, but it would be poor comfort to tell a man who had invested his money in the purchase of a term of years that he had lost the right of bequeathing his money because he had converted it into land. After showing that as early as 1200 there was a large speculative traffic in wardships, MAITLAND says :—

> " And then as to the term of years, we believe that in the twelfth century and later, this stands often, if not generally, in the same economic category. It is a beneficial lease bought for a sum of ready money ; it is an investment of capital, and therefore for testamentary purposes it is *quasi catallum*."[2]

Original advantages of leaseholds.

Thus the position reached by the common law was that estates of freehold represented real property law in the strict sense of that term, and as such were subject to all the consequences of feudal tenure ; while on the other hand leaseholds (together with some other rights in land) were not so subject, and for this reason were neither affected by the incidents of feudalism, nor governed by the same legal rules as freeholds.

Chattels classified as real and personal.

This position soon gave rise to a difficulty, for a term of years, no· matter how it might be treated by the technique of the law, was obviously a valuable interest in land, and one which it was appropriate to bring within the province of the land laws. To sever its connection with the law of land merely because it was outside the scope of the real actions would have been absurd, and so the law was obliged to surmount the difficulty by the invention of a new terminology.

It was already a commonplace that the subject-matter of proprietary interests was either real property or chattels. Chattels

---

[1] Holdsworth, *History of English Law*, vol. iii. pp. 128, 215.
[2] Pollock and Maitland, *History of English Law* (2nd Edn.), vol. ii. p. 117.

were personal property, since they were not specifically recoverable in a real action. Leaseholds were thus subject to the law of chattels, but since they lacked the attribute of movability the obvious solution was to regard them as a *tertium quid*—interests partly real and partly personal. Thus it was that personal property was sub-divided into chattels real and chattels personal.

Chattels real.

" Chattels real, saith Sir Edward Coke, are such as concern or savour of the realty ; as terms for years of land, wardships in chivalry, . . . the next presentation to a church, estates by statute merchant, statute staple,[1] *elegit*[2] or the like. And these are called real chattels, as being interests issuing out of or annexed to real estates ; of which they have one quality, viz. immobility, which denominates them *real*, but want the other, viz. a sufficient legal indeterminate duration, and this want it is that constitutes them *chattels*."[3]

Chattels personal.

Thus there are two classes of chattels known to English law— chattels real as described by COKE, and chattels personal, which originally were confined to movable things, but which are now taken to comprise many forms of wealth, such as negotiable instruments, copyright, patents, trade marks, shares in a company and so on.

The Law of Property classified.

We see, therefore, that the Law of Property as a whole falls into the following three divisions :

The *law of real property* strictly so called, *i.e.* the rules that govern freehold interests in land—the fee simple, the entailed interest and the life interest.

The *law of chattels real, i.e.* the rules that govern leaseholds.

The *law of pure personalty*.

Of these three departments of law the first and the last stand furthest apart, for the law of real property has been constructed on feudal principles, while the law of pure personalty has drawn its inspiration from a variety of non-feudal sources, such as Roman and Canon law and the customs of merchants. Midway between the two comes the law of chattels real, which BLACKSTONE describes as having a " mongrel amphibious nature," since it has derived its rules partly from real property law and partly from the law of pure personalty. The tendency, however, for several centuries has been to bring freeholds into conformity with chattels real, and the process of assimilation has been carried to such lengths, especially by the legislation of 1925, that we now have substantially a common and uniform system of law for real property and chattels real.[4]

---

[1] A tenancy by statute merchant or statute staple arose when a merchant creditor by taking advantage of the Statutes Merchant and Staple (Edward I and III) obtained seisin of his debtor's lands ; see Digby, *History of the Law of Real Property*, p. 282.

[2] *Infra*, pp. 804–5. [3] Blackstone, vol. ii. p. 386.

[4] *Infra*, pp. 88 *et seq*.

SECTION III. MODIFICATION OF THE COMMON LAW BY EQUITY

SUMMARY

Introductory Note. Our next task is to show how equity modified and tempered the feudal principles of the common law by its introduction of the " use " and the consequent establishment of the trust concept, which is probably the most outstanding characteristic of English law. It is this concept that has produced the peculiarly English distinction between the legal and the equitable estate that forms the basis of modern conveyancing.

(1) DISADVANTAGES INCIDENTAL TO THE COMMON LAW TENURES

To understand the origin of uses it is necessary to examine the position of a tenant of land under the common law. That his position was not without its troubles can be realized by a glance at some of the disabilities and burdens which weighed upon him, several of which were due to the important part played by seisin in the feudal system. The feature of that system was its immaturity, as regards both the interests which might be created in land and the methods by which the interests could be dealt with. Possession is an obvious fact, and in early days it was the dominating fact upon which most of the repressive rules that came into being were founded.

Stagnating effect of doctrine of seisin.

Two fundamental principles which in themselves were sufficient to establish the importance of seisin were that the feudal services which in the early history of tenure were of such consequence to the lord were enforceable against the person seised

Importance of seisin.

and only against him; and again that it was only against the same
person that an action for the recovery of land could be brought.
It was necessary that there should always be some person capable
of meeting adverse claims and preserving the seisin for successors.[1]
The effect of not knowing who was actually seised of land would
be the loss of public and private rights therein,[2] and therefore two
inviolable rules that became established were that there must
never be an abeyance of seisin, or in other words that there must be
an uninterrupted tenancy of the freehold ; and that every transfer
of a freehold estate must be effected by an open and public delivery
of seisin.   Any disposition that would cloud the title to the seisin
was forbidden at common law.

The following were some of the fetters laid on the free enjoyment of a freehold estate at common law :—

(A) Conveyances were required to be public and formal

Conveyances made cumbrous.

In a feudal society it was imperative that there should be
no uncertainty as to the identity of the freehold tenant of any
piece of land.   A question might arise regarding the title to the
land or the right of a lord to enforce the feudal dues to which
he was entitled, and as both these matters could be settled
only if it was known who was seised, common law ordained
that every transfer of a freehold estate must be effected by
an open and public delivery of seisin, either upon or within
view of the land conveyed.   The merit of this was that in the
event of a dispute the actual freehold tenant would be well
known to the neighbourhood.   The method itself was called

Feoffment with livery of seisin.

feoffment with livery of seisin, but the operative part of the transaction was the delivery, and a charter of feoffment, which
only served to authenticate the transaction, was not strictly
necessary.[3]

There were other kinds of common law assurances, but it may
be said of them all that they were open and notorious, though,
when the feudal vigour began to abate, they gradually ceased to
bear this characteristic.[4]   It often happens that a man, instead
of publishing his dealings with land to the world at large, prefers
to resort to some transaction which is secret and free from
ceremony, but at common law this was a desire that was unattainable, at any rate in the early days.

---

[1] See Co. Litt. 342*b*, Butler's note (1).
[2] Challis, *Law of Real Property* (3rd Edn.), p. 100.
[3] Co. Litt., 271*b*, note 1.
[4] Hayes, *Introduction to Conveyancing*, vol. i. pp. 29–30.   For the history
of the subject see Holdsworth, *History of English Law*, vol. iii. pp. 220–46 ;
vol. vii. pp. 353 *et seq.*

(B) The Types of Interests were strictly Limited

As it was essential that the seisin should not be in abeyance for an instant, but should always be vested in a freehold tenant, it followed that every conveyance of freehold had to be made to take immediate effect, so that the seisin passed at once to the grantee. This meant that many dispositions which a tenant might legitimately desire to make were rendered impossible. For instance, a gift of a freehold interest which was to vest in the donee if and when he attained 21 years of age was void, since such a gift had to be completed by delivery of seisin, and if seisin were delivered at once, it would, having been parted with by the donor, be vested in nobody until the donee attained 21. If a grant were made to A. for life and after his death to B. when he attained 21, the grant to the latter failed unless he had reached that age at the death of A., because otherwise an abeyance of seisin would have occurred. Again, under a grant to A. for life and after his death to the future children of B., only children who were in existence at A.'s death could take, for to allow later children to come in would have broken still another general principle, namely, that a transfer of a freehold interest had to be carried out by a public transaction.

Thus it is clear that the concentration of the common law upon the simple fact of possession led to extreme simplicity in the interests that might be created, and restricted within narrow bounds the limitation of future interests.[1]

Power of disposition restricted.

(C) A Tenant at Common Law could not Devise his Freehold Estate

Whatever may have been the rule in Anglo-Saxon days, one of the effects of the introduction of feudal tenures into this country was to abolish the right of leaving freeholds by will, except in a few particular localities and boroughs. To have allowed such wills would not only have diminished the lord's right of taking the land by escheat and have been a hardship to the heir, but it would have run counter to a feudal policy which demanded that every transfer should be notorious and public.[2]

No wills of freeholds.

(D) A Tenant at Common Law was Liable to certain Onerous Feudal Incidents[3]

This is no place to elaborate the burdensome nature of the tenurial dues that have already been briefly described. It must

---

[1] *Infra*, pp. 296 *et seq.*
[2] Holdsworth, *History of English Law*, vol. iii. pp. 75–6.
[3] See *supra*, pp. 19–20.

Blackstone's
account of
military
tenures.

suffice to cite an expressive passage in which BLACKSTONE sums up the position of one who held his lands in knight service :—

" In the meantime the families of all our nobility and gentry groaned under the intolerable burthens, which (in consequence of the fiction adopted after the Conquest) were introduced and laid upon them by the subtlety and finesse of the Norman lawyers. For, besides the scutages to which they were liable in defect of personal attendance, which however were assessed by themselves in parliament, they might be called upon by the king or lord paramount for aids, whenever his eldest son was to be knighted or his eldest daughter married ; not to forget the ransom of his own person. The heir, on the death of his ancestor, if of full age, was plundered of the first emoluments arising from his inheritance, by the way of relief and primer seisin ; and, if under age, of the whole of his estate during infancy. And then, as Sir Thomas Smith very feelingly complains, ' when he came to his own, after he was out of wardship, his woods decayed, houses fallen down, stock wasted and gone, lands let forth and ploughed to be barren,' to reduce him still farther, he was yet to pay half a year's profit as a fine for suing out his livery ; and also the price or value of his marriage, if he refused such wife as his lord and guardian had bartered for, and imposed upon him ; or twice that value, if he married another woman. Add to this, the untimely and expensive honour of Knighthood, to make his poverty more completely splendid. And when by these deductions his fortune was so shattered and ruined that perhaps he was obliged to sell his patrimony, he had not even that poor privilege allowed him, without paying an exorbitant fine for a licence of alienation." [1]

Grants in
Mortmain
forbidden.

There were additional disadvantages that resulted directly from the important part played by the feudal services. Thus, for instance, several of the feudal dues consisted of payments which were made by the newcomer upon the death of a tenant, and, as these would never be enforceable if the lands were granted to a body which never died, the rule soon became established that lands, granted to an association such as a monastery without the licence of the King and the lord paramount, were forfeited. Such a grant was called a *grant in mortmain*, and statutes were passed from time to time maintaining the rule as to forfeiture.[2]

Rigidity
of common
law.

Enough has now been said to show that the position of a freehold tenant at common law, as regards freedom of disposition, was not enviable.

" Large deductions must, therefore, be made from the praise lavished on the ancient common law, when its provisions are said to have promoted security of enjoyment, simplicity of title and notoriety of transfer. As civilization advanced, it proved less and less sufficient to attain those favourite objects of its founders, while it was manifestly ill-adapted to meet the growing demands of freedom and commerce. The rules of ownership and modes of assurance which we have endeavoured to explain, composed an unbending and oppressive code, utterly inadequate to the extended view and

---

[1] Blackstone, vol. ii. p. 76.
[2] *Ibid.*, vol. ii. p. 268 ; *infra*, p. 931.

complicated interests of an intelligent and wealthy community. The progress of society called for a more pliant and liberal policy." [1]

(2) DISADVANTAGES OF COMMON LAW TENURES AVOIDED BY THE DEVICE OF PUTTING LANDS IN USE

History shows us that whenever a grievance presses hardly on the greater part of the population, it is not long before a remedy is discovered, and it was certainly not long before a " more pliant and liberal policy " was introduced with regard to the rights and powers of landowners in general. But the new policy did not come from the common law. It was the sole work of the Chancellor, who made it possible by means of the protection which he gave in his court of equity to the new conception called the *use* of lands. It was due to this alone that a tenant was enabled to retain the ordinary advantages of landholding which were assured to him by the common law while escaping some of the worst disabilities of that system.

Influence of the Chancellor.

(A) Origin and Effect of Putting Lands in Use

Origin. The word " use " is derived not from the Latin *usus* but from *opus*.[2] Maitland has shown us that before Domesday it was a common practice for one man to deal with land *ad opus*—on behalf of—another, as, for instance, where the sheriff seized lands *ad opus domini Regis*, where a knight about to go to the Crusades conveyed his property to a friend on behalf of his wife and children, or where the vendor of an unfree tenement surrendered it to the lord to hold on behalf of the purchaser.[3] The word *opus*, which was in such connections commonly adopted, became gradually transformed into *oes*, *ues*, and thence into *use*. Now, if one person could deal with land on behalf of or to the use of another for a particular purpose, the question that inevitably occurred to men was why one person should not in a *general* way be allowed to hold land to the use of another. This, as a matter of fact, is exactly what was done in course of time. The tenant A. would transfer his land by a common law conveyance to B., who undertook to hold it on behalf of, or, adopting the correct expression, to the use of, A. In such a case B. was called the *feoffee to uses*, that is, the person to whom the feoffment had on certain conditions been made; while A. went by the name

Derivation of word " use."

---

[1] Hayes, *Introduction to Conveyancing*, vol. i. pp. 30–1.
[2] Maitland, *Collected Papers*, vol. ii. p. 403 ; Pollock and Maitland, *History of English Law* (2nd Edn.), vol. ii. p. 228. For the origin and history of uses, see Holdsworth, *History of English Law*, vol. iv. pp. 407 *et seq.* ; (1965), 81 *L. Q. R.* 562 *et seq.* (J. L. Barton) ; Simpson, *Introduction to the History of Land Law*, pp. 163 *et seq.*
[3] Maitland, *supra*.

of the *cestui que use*, which meant the person on whose behalf the land was held.

The practice did not spring into life all at once, and Maitland believed that 1230 was the earliest time at which one man was holding land permanently and generally to the use of another.

> " In the second quarter of the thirteenth century came hither the Franciscan friars.   The rule of their order prescribes the most perfect poverty : they are not to have any wealth at all. . . . Still, despite this high ideal, it becomes plain that they must have at least some dormitory to sleep in.   They have come as missionaries to the towns. The device is adopted of having land conveyed to the borough community to the use of the friars." [1]

By the fourteenth century this device had become more extensive and there is evidence that it was a common practice for a land-holder to convey his land to two or more friends *ad opus suum*— to his own use[2]—or to the use of a third person.

Cestui que
use lost his
rights in the
eye of com-
mon law.

Legal Effect of putting Lands in Use. The important point to observe is the legal effect of this practice.   It was to cut off the *cestui que use* in the eyes of *the common law* from all connection with the land.   By an assurance operating at common law he had conveyed his estate to the feoffees to uses, and was therefore deprived of all common law rights over the land. He was nothing, the feoffees were everything ; he had exchanged an actual estate for an intangible right, for instead of keeping seisin he had decided to rely upon the confidence that he had reposed in the feoffees.

> " If, therefore, B. (the feoffee) refused to account to his *cestui que use* A. for the profits, or wrongfully conveyed the estate to another, this was merely a breach of confidence on the part of B., for which the common law gave no redress ; much less did that law acknowledge any right in A. to the possession or enjoyment of the land.   The ordinary judicature knew no other proprietor than B. ; to him, and to him alone, attached the privileges and liabilities of a landholder ; for he it was, to whom the possession was legally delivered.   To have regarded A. in any other light than that of a mere stranger to the soil would have been to subvert a system raised upon in-vestiture and tenure.   It was accordingly decided at a very early period[3] that the common law judges had no jurisdiction whatever in regard to the use." [4]

If the feoffees failed or refused to carry out the directions im-posed upon them,[5] or if they deliberately alienated the land for their

---

[1] Maitland, *Equity*, p. 25 ; and see *Collected Papers*, vol. ii. p. 408.   A Papal Bull ordained in 1279 that a use was not property.
[2] Maitland, *Equity*, pp. 25–6.
[3] 4 Edw. 4.
[4] Hayes, *Introduction to Conveyancing*, vol. i. p. 33.
[5] 3 Rot. Parl. 511, No. 112, cited Ames ; 21 *H.L.R.*, p. 265 ; *Select Essays in Anglo-American Legal History*, vol. ii. p. 741.

own purposes,[1] there was no common law action by which they
could be rendered liable, and as a *cestui que use* who was let into
possession of the land was regarded as a mere tenant at will of
the feoffees to uses, he could be turned out by the latter at
any moment, and in the event of contumacy could be sued in
trespass.[2]

This absence of all remedy seems at first sight to stultify
the practice of putting lands in use, and it would have been
fatal had no alternative means been discovered for protecting the
cestui que use. But an adequate form of protection was ready to
hand. From about the year 1400 the Chancellor, in the first blush
of his growing jurisdiction, stepped in and interceded on behalf of
the *cestui que use*. He could not interfere with the jurisdiction
of the common law courts by proceeding in a direct fashion
against the land itself, because the absolute title to the land was
vested in the feoffees by operation of the immutable principles
enforced in those courts, but his role was to see that men acted
honestly according to the precepts of good morality, and, in
accordance with the principle that equity acts *in personam*, he did
not hesitate to proceed against feoffees who disregarded the moral
rights of the *cestui que use*. He was in a stronger position than the
common law courts, for not only could he order a person to
perform some definite act under pain of attachment, but his
power of *viva voce* examination enabled him to discover breaches
of good faith.

Uses protected by Chancellor.

> " The spectacle of feoffees retaining for themselves land which they
> had received upon the faith of their dealing with it for the benefit of
> others was too repugnant to the sense of justice of the community
> to be endured. The common law could give no remedy, for by
> its principles the feoffee was the absolute owner of the land. A
> statute might have vested, as the Statute of Uses a century later did
> vest, the legal title in the *cestui que use*. But in the absence of a
> statute the only remedy for the injustice of disloyal feoffees to uses was
> to compel them to convey the title to the *cestui que use* or hold it for
> his benefit. Accordingly the right of the *cestui que use* was worked
> out by enforcing the doctrine of personal obedience."[3]

Basis of protection.

In other words, the wrong which an unfaithful feoffee committed was breach of contract, but it was a breach for which at
that time no remedy lay in the ordinary courts, since the general
principle of the enforceability of contracts was still undeveloped.
Further, it was common for a use to be declared in favour of a
third party, and even if the modern doctrine of contract had been
perfected, the rules as to privity of contract would have precluded
the grant of a remedy to the *cestui que use*.

---

[1] Sanders, *Uses and Trusts*, vol. i. p. 67.
[2] Preston on Estates, vol. i. p. 145.
[3] Ames, *Select Essays in Anglo-American Legal History*, vol. ii. p. 741.

(B) CREATION OF THE DISTINCTION BETWEEN THE LEGAL AND THE EQUITABLE ESTATE

Attitude of
equity.

Thus we find that from the year 1400 the Chancellor began to build up a comprehensive jurisdiction over uses, but it is especially important to observe that his intervention in this field led to the introduction into English law of what is generally described as a duality of landownership. He did not deny that the *feoffee* was entitled at common law to the exclusion of the *cestui que use*, since the land had been conveyed to him by a conveyance effective at common law. That fact was inescapable, but what the Chancellor insisted upon was that the *feoffee* should scrupulously observe the directions imposed upon him by the *feoffor*. The feoffment had not been made to him for his own benefit.

Duality of
ownership.

In other words, while the feoffee was regarded as owner by the common law, the *cestui que use* was considered to be the true owner by equity : the former had the legal ownership, the latter the equitable ownership of the same piece of land. Thus we get the essentially English distinction between the legal and the equitable estate—the legal estate recognized and protected by the common law courts, and the equitable estate recognized and protected only by the Chancellor. This is what is meant by duality of ownership. Starting with the assumption that A. had conveyed land to B. to be held to the use of A., or to the use of C., HAYES, writing in 1840, described the position that arose, in a passage the lucidity of which justifies citation [1] :—

> " But, under the auspices of an ecclesiastical chancellor, the use, though alien to the soil, took root in our civil jurisprudence, and attained to a degree of influence and importance which at length almost superseded the ancient polity. Means were soon devised for compelling B., the owner in point of law, to keep good faith towards A. or C., the owner in point of conscience. The king, in his Court of Chancery, assumed jurisdiction to extort a disclosure upon oath of the nature and extent of the confidence reposed in B., and to enforce a strict discharge of the duties of his trust. Hence EQUITY arose. From this period, when the right of A. (or C.) became cognizable in the Court of Chancery, we may speak of him as the equitable or beneficial owner, and of B. as the legal owner. But in order to preserve a clear perception of the twofold character of the system, we must keep steadily in view the fact that B. had still the *real* right, to be enforced, on one side of Westminster Hall, by judgment of law *in rem*, which went at once to the possession of the land itself ; while A. (or C.) had nothing more than a mere right *in personam*, to be enforced on the other side of the Hall, by subpœna, directed against the individual trustee. The Chancery, in assuming jurisdiction over the use, left untouched and inviolate the ownership at the common law. It exercised no direct control over the land, but only coerced

---

[1] Hayes, *Introduction to Conveyancing*, vol. i. pp. 33–4.

and imprisoned the person of the legal owner who obstinately resisted its authority. It usurped none of the powers or functions of a court of law, but, leaving to the latter the redress of wrongs done to the realty, confined its jurisdiction to matters of trust and confidence, which could not be reached by the arm of ordinary justice."

Advantages of putting Lands in Use. Before we proceed any further it is desirable to notice how some of the worst burdens incidental to tenure at common law might be avoided by the device of a use. *Tenurial burdens avoided by uses.*

There were at least six substantial advantages that might accrue to the *cestui que use*.

(i) Lands became Devisable

The very natural desire that the power of testamentary disposition, which already applied to goods and chattels, should be extended to land, contributed more largely than any other factor to the rapid establishment of the use. The obligation of the feoffees to administer the legal estate according to the wishes of the *cestui que use* was not confined to the lifetime of the latter, and from an early date it was the usual practice for the beneficial owner to specify what the destination of the use should be after his death. In this indirect way, by making a testamentary disposition of the equitable as distinct from the legal estate, men were accustomed to provide for their younger sons, daughters and other relatives, to ensure the payment of their debts and to make charitable gifts.[1]

(ii) Conveyances of Land Facilitated[2]

The common law principle that a conveyance should be open and notorious could easily be evaded by means of the use, for just as the *cestui que use* could direct what dispositions of the land should be made after his death, so he could give similar directions that would be operative during his life. A transfer of the use required no formality ; the one essential was that the intention of its owner should be clearly manifested. Moreover, the system of conveyancing was radically affected as the result of an equitable doctrine which applied even where land had not deliberately been put in use. This was that a mere contract to sell a legal estate raised a use in favour of the purchaser immediately on payment of the purchase money. Such a contract was called a *bargain and sale*, and though at first it passed merely an equitable estate to the purchaser, it gained a far wider operation after the Statute

---

[1] Holdsworth, *History of English Law*, vol. iv. pp. 438–9.
[2] *Ibid.*, pp. 424–7.

of Uses in 1535 and developed into the normal method of conveying *legal* estates.[1]

(iii) SETTLEMENTS OF LAND FACILITATED

We have already mentioned,[2] and indeed shall have occasion to explain more fully later,[3] that the power of a landowner at common law to create future interests was so severely restricted that only the simplest forms of settlements of a legal estate were possible. This stringency was relaxed upon the introduction of uses. The use, to which the restrictive rules of common law were wholly inapplicable, conferred upon its owner an almost unrestrained liberty to specify who the future beneficiaries should be, upon what events their interests should arise, and in what order the interests should take effect. The equitable estate was, in fact, a pliable instrument, a subject-matter that could be moulded by its owner into such forms as might appear desirable to him. Thus arose what were called shifting and springing uses. [4]

(iv) AVOIDANCE OF FEUDAL BURDENS

The most oppressive of the feudal burdens to which a tenant was liable at common law[5] were those that became exigible at his death, namely, wardship, marriage, reliefs and primer seisin. No relief from these would be gained by the appointment of a sole feoffee to uses, for the latter, in his capacity as tenant at law,

---

[1] For the history of the matter, see Holdsworth, *History of English Law*, vol. vii. pp. 356–60. The process of development may be briefly described as follows :

(1) A., having bargained and sold land to B. for a fee simple estate and having received the purchase money, was implicitly seised to the use of B.

(2) The Statute of Uses provided that when A. stood seised to the use of B., the latter should acquire the *legal* estate (*infra*, p. 54). Had this been the only enactment, therefore, a bargain and sale after the statute would have provided a secret method of conveying *legal* estates.

(3) The Statute of Enrolments, however, passed at the same time, enacted that no estate of *inheritance or freehold* should pass, nor should any use be raised, by a bargain and sale, unless the bargain and sale was made by deed and enrolled in one of the King's Courts of Record.

(4) The last statute applied only to sales of freehold or inheritable estates. Therefore a bargain and sale of a leasehold might be made privately without enrolment. This fact was quickly appreciated (certainly before 1620), and it became usual to transfer a fee simple as follows : A. bargained and sold Blackacre to B. *for one year*. On payment of the purchase money A. became seised to the use of B. The Statute of Uses operated upon this state of affairs and passed the legal possession to B., leaving the reversion in A. Next day A. executed a deed of *release* which extinguished his reversion and consequently enlarged B.'s leasehold into the fee simple. This form of conveyance, which was called a *lease and release*, remained the normal method of conveyance until 1841, when it was enacted that a release alone should be as effectual as a lease and release. A simple deed of grant was substituted for a release in 1845.

[2] *Supra*, p. 43.
[4] *Infra*, pp. 301 *et seq.*
[3] *Infra*, pp. 296 *et seq.*
[5] *Supra*, pp. 19–20.

would be caught in the feudal net and *his* death would entitle the lord to exact such dues as might be demandable. The usual practice, therefore, was to enfeoff, not one, but several, persons as joint tenants. The rule of joint tenancy is that the share of a tenant who dies does not pass to his heir but accrues to the surviving tenants.[1] He leaves nothing for which his heir can be made to pay a relief, he leaves nobody over whom the lord can claim the right of wardship or of marriage. The one essential, therefore, was to ensure that the number of feoffees never fell below two. The death of the *cestui que use* himself, despite his position as the true beneficial owner, created no right to feudal dues, since they were the consequence of tenure, and the use " being the creature of conscience, the offspring of moral obligation, could not be the subject of tenure."[2] " The lord could not look behind the feoffees ; they were his tenants : it was nothing to him that they were allowing another person to enjoy land which by law was theirs."[3]

(v) Avoidance of Forfeiture and Escheat

Land held by tenure at common law was forfeited to the Crown if the tenant committed high treason, and upon his conviction or outlawry for felony it passed to the Crown for a year and a day and then escheated to the lord.[4] These unpleasant consequences, however, were avoided, if a tenant, before embarking upon some doubtful enterprise, had the prescience to vest his lands in a few confidential friends. The delinquent might possibly suffer the extreme penalty, but at least his family would not be destitute.

(vi) Evasion of the Mortmain Statutes

We have noticed that, since those feudal dues that became exigible at the death of a tenant would be lost to the lord if land came into the hands of a body that might never die, such as a corporation, a series of Acts, generally called the Mortmain Statutes, were passed from an early date providing that land granted to a corporation without the licence of the King and lord paramount should be forfeited.[5] Uses, however, provided an obvious means of evading this prohibition, and, until the practice was finally stopped in 1392,[6] it was a common plan for a donor to enfeoff a number of persons to hold to the use of a monastery or other corporation.

---

[1] *Infra*, p. 212.
[2] Hayes, *Introduction to Conveyancing*, vol. i. p. 34.
[3] Maitland, *Equity*, p. 27.
[4] See Challis, *Law of Real Property* (3rd Edn.), pp. 33 *et seq.*
[5] *Infra*, p. 931.   [6] 15 Ric. 2, c. 5.

Influence of common law doctrines on the use. We should next notice how the Chancellor dealt with this new form of ownership called the use or equitable estate. It was his own creation. He had invented something hitherto unknown to the law. He was free to do what he liked with his own. In the quaint language of an old judge, the use was as clay in the hands of the potter,[1] and, as the owner of a use was in theory allowed to give any imaginable directions as to its enjoyment, the Chancellor might have allowed it to be moulded into forms entirely subversive of common law principles. There were, in fact, several forms of landed interests, unattainable at common law, which he did permit to be carved out of the use, but they were mostly confined to the realm of future interests. Thus, for instance, the dispositions mentioned on page 43, which would have been void at common law, were open to a landowner if he was content to create them by way of use.

It may be said in general, indeed, that in framing rules for the governance of the use the Chancellor refused to be bound, or to let the development of the use be hampered, by any of the common law rules connected with tenure. And yet it was certainly not his policy to encourage wide deviations from the established tenets of law. The exact contrary was the case. Having begun by affording an adequate protection to the use, he then to some extent allowed the fact that its basis rested on personal confidence to fade into the background, and proceeded to regard it as a kind of interest in land, " a sort of immaterialized piece of land," in which actual estates might be created just as they might be created at common law.[2]

In other words, the general policy of the Chancellor in his development of the use was to adopt the accepted rules of common law. When necessary he was prepared to depart from those rules on the ground of convenience, but he usually took them as his guide. It can, indeed, be said " that there scarcely is a rule of law or equity of more ancient origin, or which admits of fewer exceptions, than the rule that Equity followeth the law."[3]

Thus upon the death of the *cestui que use*, Equity applied the common law rules of descent ; the common law rights of a husband to the wife's property after her death were extended to the equitable interest, though a wife was not dowable out of her husband's equitable estates until 1833 ; and estates, similar in extent to those possible at law, might be created in the use. " There is the same division in Equity as there is at law, of estates of freehold and inheritance, of estates of freeholds only, and of estates less than freehold ; of estates in possession, remainder or reversion ; and of estates several and of estates undivided."[4]

---

[1] *Brent's Case* (1575), 2 Leon. 14, 16.   [2] Maitland, *Equity*, p. 31.
[3] Butler's note to Co. Litt., 250b, xvi.
[4] *Ibid.*

Summary. To sum up this part of the discussion we may say that a use of lands existed where the legal estate was vested in A. in such circumstances that he was subject to a trust enforceable in Equity to convey the legal estate to such persons, and in the meantime to apply the rents and profits in such manner, as the *cestui que use* should direct; and, failing directions, should hold the land and pay the profits to the use of the *cestui que use* himself.[1]

[margin: Definition of use.*]*

(C) The Later History of Uses and the Rise of the Modern Trust Estate

What, then, is the essential difference between the legal and the equitable estate ? It is clear at first sight that the legal estate carries the bare technical ownership, while its equitable counterpart gives the *cestui que use* beneficial ownership. One is the nut the other the kernel. If land is conveyed to

[margin: Later history of uses.*]*

A. and his heirs to the use of B. and his heirs,

there is no doubt that A. is the true *legal* owner. But it is an unprofitable ownership, for unless he succeeds in some fraudulent enterprise he will be compelled to deal with the land as B. desires. In truth, the difference goes much deeper than this, but before stating wherein it lies we should say something of the subsequent history of uses.

Statute of Uses 1535. The equitable estate, which was the greatest achievement of the Chancellor, was not allowed to pursue its course of development undisturbed. It was assailed by the legislature under Henry VIII, who, with a view to the " extirping and extinguishment of all such subtle practised feoffments, fines, recoveries, abuses," procured the passing of the Statute of Uses in 1535.[2] Many reasons were alleged in justification of this statute, but the real object of the King's action was to restore to something like their ancient buoyancy and dimensions those feudal dues of which the collection had been rendered so much less fruitful by the practice of conveying land to uses. The simplest remedy was to abolish uses altogether, and this the King essayed to do. Holdsworth has shown how Henry, pursued by the spectre of poverty, made his grand attack on this popular institution.[3] The feudal revenues had undoubtedly declined, and whatever indulgence Parliament showed the King in other respects, it refused to vote him a permanent and adequate income. For

[margin: Object of Statute of Uses.*]*

---

[1] Sugden's *Gilbert on Uses*, p. 1 ; Fearne, *Contingent Remainders*, p. 291, note *h*.

[2] 27 Hen. 8, c. 10.

[3] 26 *H.L.R.*, pp. 108–27 ; Holdsworth, *History of English Law*, vol. iv. pp. 450–61.

some six years Henry was engaged upon his design. In 1529 a Bill was drafted so drastic in its proposals that, had it ever become a statute, it would have changed the face of the land law and struck a death-blow at uses. But opposition arose from two quarters : from the majority of landowners, who saw themselves deprived of the power to make family settlements, secret conveyances and wills, and from the lawyers, who dreaded the loss of profitable business. In no way daunted Henry set to work on a new scheme, and proceeded to remove the opposition of the legal profession by threatening to institute a stringent inquiry into the abuses of the common law, an inquiry which was pretty certain to be fruitful in disclosures, and one which was to be followed by a reform of those abuses. In 1535 there were three draft bills before Parliament, and out of these the final Act, the Statute of Uses, emerged.

Opposition to Statute.

The Act contained a very long preamble, the general object of which was to denigrate as grievances the advantages which uses conferred upon the landowning class as a whole, while keeping in the background the real purpose of the statute, which was to replenish the royal coffers. The preamble made the Statute look as if it were a highly popular measure, but MAITLAND put the matter in its true historical setting when he said :—

Final draft.

> "A long preamble states the evil effects of the system [of uses], and legal writers of a later day have regarded the words of this preamble as though they stated a generally admitted evil. As a matter of historical fact this is not true. The Statute of Uses was forced upon an extremely unwilling parliament by an extremely strong-willed King. It was very unpopular and was one of the excuses, if not one of the causes, of the great Catholic Rebellion known as the Pilgrimage of Grace. It was at once seen that it would deprive men of that testamentary power, that power of purchasing the repose of their souls, which they had long enjoyed. The King was the one person who had all to gain and nothing to lose by the abolition of uses."[1]

Effect of the Statute of Uses. The statute was passed, however, and its effect was to abolish the distinction between the legal and the equitable estate in the case of the passive use, that is to say where the feoffees stood seised to the use of B. and were the mere passive instruments for carrying out the directions of B. A conveyance to

The temporary abolition of Uses.

A. and his heirs to the use of B. and his heirs,

which before the statute would have carried only the equitable estate to B., operated after 1535 to pass the legal estate to him. This was so because the statute provided in effect that, when any person was seised of lands to the use of any other person, the *cestui*

---

[1] Maitland, *Equity*, p. 34 ; and see Froude, *History of England*, vol. iii. pp. 91, 105, 158.

que use should be deemed to have lawful seisin of the land to the extent of his interest in the use, and the seisin, that prior to the statute would have been in the feoffee to uses, A., should be deemed to be in the *cestui qui use* B. In other words, the statute brought about two results :—

First, to adopt a technical expression, it executed the use, that is to say, it turned B.'s former equitable estate into a legal estate carrying common law seisin ; and

Secondly, the common law seisin, which would normally have been vested in A. as a consequence of the conveyance, was taken away from him entirely.[1]

A. was a mere nonentity, and as a general rule nothing was to be gained by conveying to A. to the use of B. instead of making a direct conveyance at common law to B., since in both cases B. was seised of the legal estate, and by reason of that fact was in both cases subject to the dues, burdens and incapacities that had always affected an estate at common law.

The advantages of the statute lay with the common lawyers and with the King, its disadvantages with the general class of land-owners. The common lawyers profited because not only did they escape from the far-reaching scheme of law reform with which they had been threatened six years earlier, but they also acquired a profitable jurisdiction over the uses that had been turned into legal estates. The King profited because the conversion of uses into legal estates involved the abolition of the power to devise lands, and this, in itself, increased very considerably the value of the tenurial incidents.[2]

Advantages and disadvantages of the statute.

The statute was a real grievance in many ways. For one thing the common belief was that it prevented wills of land, and, though this was a misapprehension,[3] it caused such irritation [4] that it was found necessary in 1540 to pass the Statute of Wills which permitted a tenant to devise all his socage lands and two-thirds of his lands held in knight service.

Unpopularity of the statute.

It would seem then, if we proceeded no further with the history of uses, as if Lord COKE was right when he said that

" the makers of the statute at last resolved, that uses were so subtle and perverse, that they could by no policy or provision be governed or reformed ; and therefore, as a skilful gardener will not cut away the leaves of the weeds, but extirpate them by the roots, and as a wise householder will not cover or stir up the fire which is secretly kindled in his house, but utterly put it out ; so the makers of the said statute did not intend to provide a remedy and reformation by the continuance or preservation, but by the extinction and ex-

---

[1] Fearne, *Contingent Remainders*, p. 273, Butler's note.
[2] Holdsworth, *History of English Law*, vol. iv. pp. 463–4.
[3] See (1944), 7 *C. L. J.* 354 (R. E. Megarry).
[4] Froude, *History of England*, iii. p. 89.

tirpation of uses ; and because uses were so subtle and ungovern-
able, they have with an indissoluble knot coupled and married them
to the land, which of all the elements is the most ponderous and
immovable." [1]

This, however, was to go too far, for the Act did not entirely
abolish uses. There were at least two cases in which the grantees
to uses retained the legal estate and were still compelled by the
Chancellor to fulfil the intention of the grantor.

First, since the statute applied only where a feoffee was seised
to the use of another, it was necessarily inoperative where a term
of years, as distinct from a freehold estate, was given to A. to the
use of B., for A. was possessed, not seised, of the subject-matter.

Secondly, the exclusion of the statute was admitted where an
active duty was imposed upon the feoffees to uses, as for instance
where they were directed to collect the rents and profits and to
pay them to B. In these circumstances it was recognized that the
legal estate must remain with the feoffees, for otherwise they
could not justify their right to the rents.

In both these instances, the conscience of the feoffees to uses
was affected and they came under a moral duty to deal with the
legal estate on behalf of the beneficiary—in the one case to transfer
the term to him, in the other to secure the rents for him—and it
was a duty that was enforceable only by the Chancellor. As
regards terminology, however, it became usual to describe the
person whose conscience was affected in these cases as being
under a *trust* to carry out the directions of the grantor. [2] The
uses were not those which the statute could execute, yet they
were trusts which in conscience ought to be performed. [3] The
statutory abolition of the passive use, of course, was in no way
affected by this exercise of the Chancellor's jurisdiction. It long
remained true that if the fee simple were granted to A. to the use
of B., A. was divested of the legal estate and deprived of his
former functions. Nevertheless, the principle that a moral duty
must be performed was developed with such insistence that the
passive use was ultimately restored in the shape of the passive
trust, for the courts of equity gradually extended the circumstances in which the person upon whom the statute conferred
the legal estate was bound in conscience to hold it in trust for
some other person in accordance with the intention of the grantor. [4]

A striking example of this enduring concern of Chancery with
the problem of conscience is furnished by the ancient rule that
there could be no use upon a use. The rule established before
the statute was that if land were conveyed to

---

[1] *Chudleigh's Case* (1595), 1 Co. Rep. 124a.
[2] Plucknett, *Concise History of the Common Law* (5th Edn.), pp. 598–9.
[3] Blackstone, vol. ii. p. 336.
[4] Plucknett, *op. cit.*, p. 599.

A. and his heirs to the use of B. and his heirs to the use of C. and
his heirs,

it was only the use in favour of B. that took effect. He acquired
the equitable estate, and the second use in favour of C. was ruled
out as being repugnant to the first.[1] This was confirmed at
common law soon after the statute in *Jane Tyrrel's Case*,[2] the
result of which was that B., not A., acquired the legal estate and
the limitation in favour of C. was still nugatory. The repugnancy
of his use with that of B. was, of course, apparent, for as was said
in another case,

" The use is only a liberty to take the profits, but two cannot severally
take the profits of the same land, therefore there cannot be an use
upon an use."[3]

Although it was equally obvious, as Blackstone remarks,[4] that B.
was never intended by the parties to have any beneficial interest
in the land, the Chancery court at first came to the same conclusion
and repudiated the second use.[5] Ultimately, however, and
certainly by 1700, it reversed this view and restored the passive
use by holding that B. must be regarded as holding the legal
estate in trust for C. It was against conscience for one man to
retain what was clearly intended for another. The exact stages by
which this result was reached are not discernible. It was long
thought that *Sambach* v. *Dalston* (or *Daston*)[6] in 1634 was the
decisive authority, but recent researches have shown that this is
to go too far.[7] The importance of that decision was the refusal of
the court to ignore the grantor's intention. In the actual circumstances of the case he intended to benefit not only C., but also an
infant after the death of C. and therefore the court directed B. to
make such dispositions of the land as would fulfil the whole of
the grantor's design. This direction, however, did not involve

Passive use finally restored.

---

[1] (1532), Bro. Ab., Feoff. al Uses, 40 ; cited Ames, *Select Essays in Anglo-American Legal History*, vol. ii. p. 748.
[2] (1557), 2 Dyer, 155a ; Digby, *History of the Law of Real Property*, p. 375.
Jane bargained and sold land (*supra*, p. 49) to her son, G. and his heirs,
upon the understanding that G. was to hold to the use of Jane for life and
thereafter to the use of himself in tail. The purchase money was paid, and
therefore by implication of law (*supra*, p. 50) Jane was seised to the use of
G. The statute operated upon this use, and gave G. the legal fee simple.
But further uses had been declared, namely, to Jane for life and then to G.
in tail, and the question was whether these were valid or not. It was held
that they were void.
[3] *Daw* v. *Newborough* (1716), 1 Comyns 243 ; cited Ames, *op. cit.*, vol. ii.
p. 748.
[4] Vol. ii. p. 336.
[5] *Girland* v. *Sharp* (1595), Cro. Eliz. 382 ; Digby, *History of the Law of
Real Property*, p. 375.
[6] Tothill, 188 ; Nelson 30, *sub. nom. Morris, Lambeth et Margery* v.
Darston.
[7] (1958), 74 *L. Q. R.* 550 (J. E. Strathdene) ; Simpson, *Introduction to the
History of Land Law*, p. 180 ; see further (1966), 82 *L. Q. R.* 215 (J. L. Barton).

the restoration of the passive use or any recognition of the modern passive trust, for B.'s obligation was to divest himself of the legal estate, not to retain it and hold it on behalf of C.[1]

Rise of the modern passive trust.

Eventually, however, a change in the political situation facilitated the restoration of the passive use. The passive use had been abolished in 1535 for the sole reason that the King laid the loss of his feudal revenue at its door. But towards the end of the seventeenth century a complete revolution had occurred in the political sphere. Owing to the abolition of the military tenures in 1660 and to the gradual fall in the value of money, the feudal dues had become of little consequence and, indeed, the royal finances had been put on a more satisfactory footing. This fact, coupled with an almost universal desire for the old liberty of action, enabled the Chancellor once more to recognize the former distinction between the legal and the equitable estate whenever the intention was that B. should hold land on behalf of C. The device eventually adopted by conveyancers to make this intention effective was merely to limit a use upon a use.[2]

> If it was desired to create an equitable estate in favour of C., instead of adopting the pre-statute method of a conveyance to A. to the use of C., all that was necessary was to add a second use and make the conveyance run to A. to the use of B. to the use of C.

The effect of this was that the statute divested A. of his interest and passed the legal estate to B., with the result that, since the second use was not executed by the statute, C. was left with a mere equitable estate corresponding with the equitable estate that existed in the pre-statute days under the name of the use.

The trust.

Thus the old distinction was retained in spite of the statute, but both the method of creating the distinction and the terminology adopted to describe it were changed. The first use in favour of B., which was executed by the statute, was still called a use, but the second one in favour of C., on which the statute did not operate, was for greater clearness always designated a " trust."[3]

The practice ultimately adopted was to leave A. out altogether and to create the equitable estate by conveying the land

> *unto and to the use* of B. and his heirs in trust for C. and his heirs.

The effect of this was that B., called the *trustee*, acquired the legal estate by virtue of the common law ; but he also obtained the use, and though he was deemed to take the legal estate at common law and not under the statute, for there was no other person seised

---

[1] Plucknett, *Concise History of the Common Law* (5th Edn.), pp. 601–2.
[2] *Ibid.*, p. 602.
[3] Hayes, *Introduction to Conveyancing*, vol. i. p. 54. See Holdsworth, *History of English Law*, vol. v. pp. 307–9 ; vol. vi. pp. 641–4.

to his use,[1] yet, since a use had been declared in his favour, the rule that there could be no use upon a use prevented the statute from operating upon the second use and passing the legal estate to C.[2]

Thus, despite the complacent optimism of Lord COKE, the old distinction between the legal and the equitable estate was fully restored by at any rate the early eighteenth century. In 1738, Lord HARDWICKE stated the position in these words :—

> " Yet [after 1535] the judges still adhered to the doctrine, that there could be no such thing as *an use upon an use*, but where the first use was declared, there it was executed, and must rest for that estate : therefore, on a limitation to A. and his heirs, to the use of B. and his heirs, in trust for D., B.'s estate was held there to be executed by the statute, and D. took nothing.
> " Of this construction equity took hold, and said that the intention was to be supported. It is plain B. was not intended to take, his conscience was affected. To this the reason of mankind assented, and it has stood on this foot ever since, and by this means a statute made upon great consideration, introduced in a solemn and pompous manner, by this strict construction, has had no other effect than to add at most three words to a conveyance."[3]

The last remark of the Lord Chancellor, however, though picturesque and arresting, was scarcely accurate, for, as we shall see, the statute had a vital and a lasting effect in so far as it enabled a class of future interests (springing and shifting uses), hitherto unknown to the common law, to be carved out of the legal estate.[4]

(D) THE ESSENTIAL DIFFERENCE BETWEEN THE LEGAL AND THE EQUITABLE ESTATE

The position with regard to equitable estates remained as indicated above until January 1st, 1926. If, that is to say, it was desired to create a trust estate, all that was necessary was to convey land *unto and to the use of* trustees in fee simple, in trust for the *cestui que trust*—or beneficiary, as we will designate him in future.

Nature of the trust estate.

The questions that now require answering are :—

1. What is the nature of trust estates, and
2. What is the exact point of difference between them and legal estates ?

---

[1] " The statute ought to be expounded that when the party seised to the use and the *cestui que use* is one person, he never taketh by the statute, except there be a direct impossibility for the use to take effect by the common law " : Bacon, *Uses*, 47.

[2] *Samme's Case* (1609), 13 Co. Rep. 54 ; *Doe d. Lloyd* v. *Passingham* (1827), 6 B. & C. 305 ; *Orme's Case* (1872), L. R. 8 C. P. 281 ; *Hadfield's Case* (1872), L. R. 8 C. P. 306 ; *Cooper* v. *Kynoch* (1872), 7 Ch. App. 398 ; *Sanders on Uses and Trusts*, (5th Edn.), vol. i. p. 89 ; Hargreaves, *Introduction to Land Law* (4th Edn.), pp. 96–8.

[3] *Hopkins* v. *Hopkins* (1738), 1 Atk. 581, at p. 591.

[4] *Infra*, pp. 300–5.

Trusts more
highly
developed
than Uses.

1. In the first place it may be said in a general way that the old uses which continued, after and in spite of the statute, to have their old effect were simply the same original uses appearing under the different name of trusts.[1] But this is not the whole story. As Lord MANSFIELD said in *Burgess v. Wheate*[2] :—

> "An use and a trust may essentially be looked upon as two names for the same thing ; but the opposition consists in the difference of the practice of the Court of Chancery."

As is inevitable in the development of any legal conception equitable interests became much more elaborate and were adapted to many more purposes than in the days before the Statute of Uses. Lord Keeper HENLEY said in the same case[3] :—

> "Geometry was the same in the time of Euclid as in that of Sir Isaac Newton, though he applied the principles and rules to effect greater discoveries and more important demonstrations. . . . An use, say the older books, was neither *jus in re*, nor *ad rem*, but a confidence resting in privity of person and estate, without remedy but in a court of equity. What else is a trust ? what other definition can be given of it ? No other is attempted. But it is said since the existence of trusts (since the statute), equity has modelled them into the shape and quality of real estates, much more than it did in earlier times when they were called uses. It has made tenants by the curtesy, permitted tenants in tail to suffer common recoveries etc. And why ? Because equity follows the law. And between *cestui que trust* and those claiming by, from and under him, it is equity that he should be considered as formally possessed of that estate of which he is and appears substantial owner. But this is only the effect of the equitable jurisdiction's growing to maturity, and was an accident that to a degree accompanied uses as well as trusts. Lord Bacon observes that they grew to strength and credit by degrees and as the Chancery grew more eminent."

Expansion
of subject-
matter of
trusts.

Thus uses required that the feoffee to uses should have the fee simple estate, but trusts could be declared upon the estates of tenants in tail, for life or years ; uses were generally passive, that is, the feoffee was a dormant instrument compelled by equity to obey the directions of the *cestui que use*, but later development allowed the creation of special trusts under which the trustee might be directed to perform such duties as the sale of land, the accumulation of profits, the managements of estates and so on. Again, the use applied only to land, but the subject-matter of trusts has expanded to such a degree that at the present day it includes, not only every conceivable kind of property, but even objects unconnected with property. The

---

[1] *Lloyd* v. *Spillet* (1740), 2 Atk. 150, *per* Lord HARDWICKE.
[2] (1757–9), 1 Eden 177, at p. 217.
[3] *Ibid.*, at p. 248.

trust, for instance, has enabled unincorporated associations, such as clubs, trade unions and nonconformist bodies, which, owing to the indefinite and fluctuating character of their personnel, are not persons in the legal sense, both to own property and to fulfil the objects of their formation. The ownership of premises cannot reside in an unincorporated club, but it may be vested in a few persons, who, in the capacity of trustees, will not only have a legally protected ownership but will be amenable to the jurisdiction of the court if they fail to administer the property on behalf of the members and in accordance with the rules.[1] Then again the trust is not the only form of equitable interest known to the law. The interest that arises in favour of a person who has made a valid contract for the purchase of land or a valid contract for a lease ; the right which an owner possesses to enforce certain restrictive covenants ; the interest in land retained by a person before 1926 who mortgaged the land in return for a loan of money—these are all equitable interests and exhibit the one great characteristic that distinguishes trust from legal estates.

2. That brings us to the second point. What is that charac- Difference teristic, or, in other words, what is the difference between between legal and the legal and the equitable estate ? equitable estates.

As we have said, the difference is not adequately defined by the statement that the legal estate confers an empty title, while the equitable estate amounts to beneficial ownership of the land. The fundamental distinction is this :—

> A legal estate is a right *in rem*, an equitable estate a right *in personam*, that is to say, the former confers a right enforceable against the whole world, the latter one which can be enforced only against a limited number of persons.

If A. is entitled to the legal estate in Blackacre, then as a general rule it is true to say that, apart from some voluntary act of his own, he cannot be deprived of his rights in the land by the fraud of some third person. If, for instance, the owner of a fee simple grants a term of years in the land to A. and then sells and conveys the fee simple to X., fraudulently concealing the existence of the lease, the rights of A. as the owner of a legal estate are entirely unaffected by the transaction. Legal estate a right *in rem*.

Exactly the same principle applies to all legal as distinct from equitable interests. For instance, a landowner may allow his neighbour to enjoy some right over his land such as a right of way. If the right which is so enjoyed exhibits

---

1 See Maitland, *Collected Papers*, vol. iii. *The Unincorporate Body*, pp. 271–84 ; *Trust and Corporation*, pp. 321–404.

certain characteristics (to be described in a later chapter),[1] it is known as an easement, and an easement is capable of being a legal interest, and, if so, is permanently enforceable against all subsequent owners of the land over which it is exercisable. That land may very well be bought by a person who does not know of the right and has no reason to know of it, but nevertheless it will be binding upon him. The person entitled to enjoy the right has a legal interest which can be enforced against all persons whether they know of it or not.

Equitable estate a *jus in personam*.

So then the legal estate, or in fact any legal interest however small, is binding against all people, no matter how they have obtained what seem to be absolute and unrestricted rights over the land. But the rights conferred upon the owner of an equitable estate are not and never have been so extensive as this, though they are enforceable against so many people that they come to look very like *jura in rem*. The general principle is that they are enforceable only against those persons who, owing to the circumstances in which they have acquired the land, ought in conscience to be held responsible. This principle derives from the consistent refusal of the Chancellor to enforce the use against a person who acquired the land from the feoffee to uses unless he was affected by the confidence that had been reposed in the original feoffee.

> " As the use had its beginning in personal confidence, so its continuance, as a binding obligation on the legal owner of the land, was measured by the continuance of that confidence."[2]

The number of persons who were deemed to be affected by this confidence gradually grew in number.

Enforceability of equitable estates gradually extended.

The starting point was of course that the trustee himself, or the *feoffee to uses* as he was originally called, was permanently bound to observe the trust. The first extension of this was made in 1465, when it was held that a person who bought the land from the trustee with notice of the conditions upon which the land was held was bound by the trust.[3] The next stage, reached in 1522, was that all those who came to the trustee's estate by way of succession, such as his heir or doweress, were held responsible for carrying out the trust.[4]

---

[1] *Infra*, pp. 513 *et seq.*
[2] Hayes, *Introduction to Conveyancing*, vol. i. p. 42. See also Sanders, *Uses and Trusts*, vol. i. pp. 55–6.
[3] Y.B. 5 Ed. IV, Mich. pl. 16, fo. 7. For the whole of this subject see the account given by Jenks in his *Modern Land Law*, pp. 141 *et seq.*
[4] Y.B. 14 Hen. VIII, Mich. pl. 5, fo. 8, cited Jenks, *op. cit.*; Maitland, *Equity*, p. 117.

The law, which had reached this point at the time when the Statute of Uses was passed, was adopted and carried further by the courts when equitable estates reappeared under the name of trusts. Thus it was decided by *Chudleigh's Case* in 1595 [1] that a voluntary alienee from the trustee, that is to say, a person who had acquired the estate without giving valuable consideration for it, was bound by the trust even though he had no notice of its existence. Therefore a trust was enforceable both against a man who bought the land *with notice* of the trust, and against one who received it by way of gift but without notice. Again, at some date after 1660 [2] trusts were made enforceable against creditors of the trustee who had seized the trust estate with a view to obtaining satisfaction for the debts due to them.

The one person, therefore, whose conscience was unaffected and against whom the equitable estate became unenforceable was the purchaser for value of the legal estate *without notice* of the rights of the *cestui que use*. If the feoffee to uses fraudulently sold and conveyed the land to an unsuspecting purchaser, the equity of the *cestui que use* was gone so far as the land was concerned and he could not claim relief against the purchaser. Nevertheless his equity remained in full force against the fraudulent trustee.

> "The *very* land was irrecoverably gone, but the use remained; and while the conscience of the person *to* whom the possession had passed was unaffected, the person *from* whom it had passed was still liable, as before, to fulfil the equities tacitly included in the use."[3]

Doctrine of Notice. The only other point to observe is the policy adopted by the court with regard to the vital question of notice. A purchaser of the land for valuable consideration from the trustee was not liable to carry out the trusts provided that he had no notice of them when he acquired the legal estate, but it is obvious that, unless a careful watch had been kept on the conduct of such a purchaser, he would have taken care not to have notice. The definition of notice was therefore made elastic. If a purchaser was diligent enough and acted in a reasonable and sensible manner, making all those investigations which the purchaser of land normally did make, then he was affected only by actual notice of trusts. If, however, he omitted to make the usual investigations then he might be affected by constructive notice.

Equitable doctrine of notice.

---

[1] 1 Co. Rep at 122*b*; *Mansell* v. *Mansell* (1732), 2 P. Wms. 678.
[2] See Maitland, *Equity*, p. 112.
[3] Hayes, *Introduction to Conveyancing*, vol. i. p. 43.

Constructive notice.

Constructive Notice. It has always been regarded as difficult to frame a satisfactory definition of constructive notice,[1] but it is generally taken to include two different things[2]:—

1. The notice which is implied when a purchaser omits to investigate the vendor's title properly or to make reasonable inquiries as to deeds or facts which come to his knowledge.

2. The notice which is imputed to a purchaser by reason of the fact that his solicitor or other legal agent has actual or implied notice of some fact. This is generally called " imputed notice."

Now the question is : what ought a prudent, careful man to do when he is purchasing an estate ? The answer will afford us an insight into the equitable doctrine of notice, and at the same time will show us in what circumstances a purchaser takes an estate free from any trust or other equitable interests to which it may be subject.

It is not necessary to go back further than the Conveyancing Act 1882 (now re-enacted by the Law of Property Act 1925[3]), which contained a section designed to protect purchasers against a doctrine that had been refined to the point of unfairness. The Act provides that no purchaser is to be affected by notice of any instrument, fact or thing unless he actually knows of it, or unless he would have known of it had such inquiries and inspections been made, as ought reasonably to have been made by him, or unless his solicitor, while carrying out that particular transaction, actually obtains knowledge of that instrument, etc., or would have obtained it had he made reasonable inquiries and inspections. What it comes to, then, is that a purchaser is deemed to have notice of anything which he has failed to discover either because he did not investigate the title properly, or because he did not inquire for deeds relating to the land, or because he did not inspect it.

We will take these three cases separately :—

Nature of investigation of title.

(i) Notice from not Investigating Title. For centuries it has been regarded as essential that a man who is purchasing land should investigate the title of his vendor, that is to say, should require the vendor to " prove his title " by producing evidence to show that the interest which he has contracted to sell is vested in him, and that it is unincumbered by rights and interests enforceable against the land by third parties. Under the system of unregistered conveyancing,[4] proof of the title[5] takes the form of requiring the vendor to set out the history of the land in what is called an *abstract of title* with a view to showing how the

---

[1] Sugden, *Law of Vendors and Purchasers*, p. 755.
[2] White and Tudor, *Leading Cases in Equity* (9th Edn.), vol. ii. p. 172.
[3] S. 199 (1) (ii).
[4] For registered conveyancing, see *infra*, pp. 103, 766 *et seq.*
[5] For a fuller account of investigation of title see *infra*, pp. 730 *et seq.*

interest he has contracted to sell became vested in him, so as to prove that for a given number of years he and his predecessors have rightfully exercised dominion over the land consistent with that interest. The old rule both at law and in equity was that, if a vendor could adduce evidence of acts of ownership for a period of not less than sixty years, he had satisfied the obligation which lay upon him, and, unless anything appeared to the contrary, had proved a title which the purchaser was bound to accept. But there was no rigid rule about the length of this period, for it was useless to trace the title for sixty years unless the result was to show that the vendor was entitled to convey that interest which he had agreed to sell.[1] For instance, a vendor might very well show sixty years' possession in himself, but if this possession was held under a long lease, something more was obviously required to substantiate a right to sell the fee simple. The vendor's proof must always begin with a " good root of title," *i.e.* with some instrument transferring the interest that the purchaser now seeks to obtain.

The Vendor and Purchaser Act 1874 provided that in an open contract of sale, that is, where no express stipulation had been entered into fixing a precise date from which title should be traced, forty years should be substituted for the old period of sixty years. Thus under the law as it existed in 1925 a vendor who failed to persuade the purchaser to accept a shorter title was obliged to adduce evidence of acts of ownership stretching over a period of at least forty years. This obligation was satisfied by the vendor showing what conveyances of the estate—whether *inter vivos* or as a result of death—had been effected, for, to take a simple illustration, if documents could be produced showing that forty-five years earlier X. had bought the estate for valuable consideration and then left it by will to the vendor, it was pretty clear that the latter could make a good title.

> " If, then, on the sale of a freehold in fee, the vendor produces the title-deeds for the last 40 years, and these show that the fee simple in the land sold has been conveyed to him, free from incumbrances, and if there be satisfactory evidence that the deeds produced relate to the land sold, and the vendor be in possession of the lands and of the deeds, he has shown a good title to the land."[2]

The general obligations of a vendor are the same under the modern law, except that the period for which title must be traced under an open contract, reduced from forty to thirty years in 1925,[3] has been further reduced to fifteen years.[4]

---

[1] Williams, *Vendor and Purchaser* (1st Edn.), p. 76.
[2] *Ibid.*, p. 84.
[3] L.P.A. 1925, s. 44 (1).
[4] L.P.A. 1969, s. 23 in respect of contracts made on or after January 1st, 1970. See Law Commission Interim Report on Root of Title to Freehold Land (1967) (Law Com. No. 9).

Abstract of title.

The first duty of the vendor is to prepare an abstract of title, that is, a statement of the material parts of all deeds and other instruments by which the property has been disposed of during the period in question, and also of all facts, such as births, deaths and marriages, which affect the ownership of the land. But in addition to producing this abstract the vendor is required to verify its contents by producing either the actual documents abstracted or the best possible evidence of the contents of those which he is not in a position to produce, and by proving facts, such as births and deaths, which are material to the title.

Connection between notice and investigation of title.

We can now understand what is meant by constructive notice. One object of investigating title is to discover whether the land is subject to rights vested in persons other than the vendor, and the equitable doctrine of notice ordains that a purchaser is bound by any right which he would have discovered had he made the ordinary investigations as sketched above. Moreover, if the vendor has imposed conditions requiring a purchaser to accept a title shorter than the statutory period, the doctrine of notice is extended to rights which would have been disclosed had title been shown for the full period.[1]

In general, then, it may be said that a purchaser will be bound by equitable interests of which he may in fact be ignorant but whose existence he would have discovered had he acted as a prudent man of business, placed in similar circumstances, would have acted.[2]

Omission to inquire for deeds may constitute notice.

(ii) Notice from not inquiring for Deeds. As we have just seen, the system of unregistered conveyancing requires that a person who is buying land should examine the vendor's deeds, in order both to ascertain whether a good title can be made and to ensure that no third person possesses rights enforceable against the land. It follows from this that, if a purchaser makes no inquiries for the title-deeds, and allows them to remain in the possession of a third person, he will be deemed to have notice of any equitable claims which the possessor of the deeds may have against the land.[3] If, however, he makes inquiry but fails to secure their production, his liability for any equity that they would have disclosed depends upon whether or not his failure was due to his own gross negligence. If he is satisfied with an unreasonable excuse for their non-production, he is liable[4] ; but if the excuse is reasonable, he may successfully shelter behind the plea of purchaser of the legal estate for valuable consideration without notice.[5]

---

[1] *Re Cox and Neve's Contract*, [1891] 2 Ch. 109, at pp. 117–8.
[2] *Bailey* v. *Barnes*, [1894] 1 Ch. 25, at p. 35.
[3] *Walker* v. *Linom*, [1907] 2 Ch. 104.
[4] *Oliver* v. *Hinton*, [1899] 2 Ch. 264, at p. 274.
[5] *Hewitt* v. *Loosemore* (1851), 9 Hart 449 ; on the subject generally see *infra*, pp. 688 *et seq.*, especially p. 689, n. 5.

(iii) NOTICE FROM NOT INSPECTING LAND. A purchaser should also make inquiries of any tenant or other person in occupation of the land, since the occupation of a person is notice to a purchaser of the interest of that person ; not only indeed of this interest, but of his other rights.[1] " A tenant's occupation is notice of all that tenant's rights,[2] but not of his lessor's title or rights."[3] This is known as the rule in *Hunt* v. *Luck* and it was further elaborated in that case by VAUGHAN WILLIAMS, L.J., as follows[4] :—

Failure to inspect land may also constitute notice.

> " If a purchaser or a mortgagee has notice that the vendor or mortgagor is not in possession of the property, he must make inquiries of the person in possession—of the tenant who is in possession—and find out from him what his rights are, and, if he does not choose to do that, then whatever title he acquires as purchaser or mortgagee will be subject to the title or right of the tenant in possession."

It is not clear how far the rule operates to give a purchaser or mortgagee constructive notice of the interest of a person in occupation, if the vendor or mortgagor is also in occupation.[5]

Legal and Equitable Estate finally contrasted. We are now in a position to return to our explanation of the essential difference between the legal and the equitable estate. We have said that a legal interest is enforceable against all the world, while an equitable interest can be enforced only against a limited number of persons. To be more precise, if an equitable interest in Blackacre is created in favour of X., the following are the persons who, if they subsequently acquire an interest in the land, will take that interest subject to X.'s right :

Who is bound by equitable interests.

1. a person who acquires Blackacre as the heir, devisee or personal representative of the trustee ;
2. a person who has acquired the legal estate in Blackacre *without the payment of valuable consideration*, even though he has no actual or constructive notice of the equitable interest ;
3. a creditor of the trustee, whether with or without notice of the trust ; or
4. a person who has given valuable consideration for the legal estate in Blackacre, but who is affected by actual or constructive notice of the equitable interest.

---

[1] *Barnhart* v. *Greenshields* (1853), 9 Moo. P. C. 18. But not of an equity to rectification of a tenancy agreement which the tenant may have against the vendor, *Smith* v. *Jones*, [1954] 1 W. L. R. 1089 ; [1954] 2 All E. R. 823; M. & B. p. 47.

[2] *E.g.*, an option to purchase. *Daniels* v. *Davison* (1809), 16 Ves. 249.

[3] *Hunt* v. *Luck*, [1901] 1 Ch. 45, at p 51 *per* FARWELL, J. ; approved by C.A. [1902] 1 Ch. 428, 432.

[4] *Hunt* v. *Luck*, *supra*, at p. 433.

[5] *Caunce* v. *Caunce*, [1969] 1 W. L. R. 286 ; [1969] 1 All E. R. 722 ; *cf.* *Hodgson* v. *Marks*, [1971] Ch. 892, at pp. 934–5 ; [1971] 2 All E. R. 684, *infra*, p. 774. See Barnsley, *Conveyancing Law and Practice*, pp. 333–4.

Enforce-
ability of
equitable
interest.

An equitable interest such as a trust is, then, if we put the matter with strict regard to historical accuracy, one that can be enforced only against those particular persons, but a definition which is almost equally accurate [1] is that an equitable interest is one that is enforceable against the whole world *except a purchaser for valuable consideration of the legal estate which is subject to the equitable interest, provided that, when the purchaser acquired the legal estate, he had no notice, either actual or constructive, of the equitable interest.* In the case of such a person there is no reason why equity should not allow the common law to run its normal course. Equity follows the law, and will not interfere with law unless there is some very strong equitable ground for doing so. Where a person has paid for the interest which is secure at law, and more-over has acted honestly and diligently, there is no equitable reason for postponing him to somebody who from the point of view of equity is in no stronger position, and from the point of view of law is in a far inferior position.

Pilcher v.
Rawlins.

The position was put very forcibly by James, L.J., in *Pilcher v. Rawlins* [2] :—

> " I propose simply to apply myself to the case of a purchaser for valuable consideration, without notice, obtaining, upon the occasion of his purchase, and by means of his purchase deed, some legal estate, some legal right, some legal advantage ; and, according to my view of the established law of this court, such a purchaser's plea of a purchase for valuable consideration without notice is an absolute, unqualified, unanswerable defence, and an unanswerable plea to the jurisdiction of this court. Such a purchaser, when he has once put in that plea, may be interrogated and tested to any extent as to the valuable consideration which he has given in order to shew the *bona fides* or *mala fides* of his purchase, and also the presence or the absence of notice ; but when once he has gone through that ordeal, and has satisfied the terms of the plea of purchase for valuable consideration without notice, then this court has no jurisdiction whatever to do anything more than to let him depart in possession of that legal estate, that legal right, that legal advantage which he has obtained whatever it may be. In such a case the purchaser is entitled to hold that which, without breach of duty, he has had conveyed to him."

Apparently, the only exception to this immunity enjoyed by the purchaser for value without notice arises where in fact the vendor's only title to convey the fee simple is that he is tenant for life under a settlement, but he fraudulently conceals the existence of the settlement. [3]

In brief, then, an equitable estate is not so safe as a legal estate. An equitable owner may find himself, without any fault or negligence on his part, postponed to a third person who has obtained the legal estate in the same lands, and his remedy will be reduced to that of recovering the value of the estate from the

---

[1] But see Maitland, *Equity*, pp. 120–21.

[2] (1871), L. R. 7 Ch. App. 259, at p. 268; M. & B. p. 27.

[3] *Weston* v. *Henshaw*, [1950] Ch. 510 ; See, however, *Re Morgan's Lease*, [1972] Ch. 1 ; [1971] 2 All E. R. 235 ; see *infra*, p. 795.

fraudulent or negligent trustee. The facts of *Pilcher* v. *Rawlins* will serve to illustrate this proposition.

Pilcher, who was the sole surviving trustee of £8,373, which he held in trust for X. for life and after his death for X.'s children, lent the money to Rawlins on a legal mortgage of Blackacre. This was a perfectly legitimate transaction, the effect of which was to vest the legal estate of Blackacre in Pilcher as trustee on the same trusts for X., so that until the mortgage was redeemed by Rawlins, Picher acquired the legal and X. the equitable estate in the lands.

Rawlins then arranged to grant a legal mortgage of Blackacre to Z. in return for a loan of £10,000. As things stood this was impossible because a legal mortgage before 1926 necessitated the transfer to the lender of the legal fee simple, and this was vested in Pilcher. Pilcher, however, decided to abet Rawlins in the fraudulent scheme. First of all Rawlins (who was a solicitor) prepared an abstract of title to Blackacre which stopped short of and excluded the mortgage to Pilcher and thus made it appear that the legal fee simple was still vested in himself. Of course it was not, but at this point Pilcher came into the plot by re-conveying his legal estate in Blackacre to Rawlins in consideration of a repayment of X.'s trust moneys. This repayment was never in fact made, but Rawlins, having thus attained the legal estate, was enabled to transfer it to Z., who paid over the £10,000. The deed of re-conveyance was suppressed. When the fraud was discovered, the question was, which of the two innocent parties, X. or Z., had the better right to Blackacre.

It was held that, as Z. had acted reasonably and honestly, the legal interest which had passed to him must prevail over the mere equitable interest vested in X. Pilcher was the sole trustee and as such had the legal estate and the title-deeds. That being so, the effect of his reconveyance was to give the legal estate to Rawlins, and, as the whole mortgage transaction was concealed, there was no document to put Z. on inquiry.

Throughout the preceding account we have principally considered one form of equitable interest, the trust, but though this is the most important species, we must observe that it is not the only one. The trust, already described, is an interest which corresponds with a legal interest in the sense that just as there may be a legal fee simple, entailed interest or life interest, so also may there be equitable counterparts possessing the same incidents, for equity follows the law.[1] But other equitable interests may exist which have no analogy at common law. The more important of these, which will require a more detailed discussion later, are the following:— *Other forms of equitable interests.*

1. **The Estate Contract.** This arises where the owner of a legal estate either agrees to convey it to the other contracting party or to create a legal estate out of it in favour of that other. Thus, if A., the owner of the fee simple absolute in Blackacre, agrees to sell it to B. or to create a term of years absolute out of it in favour of B., the equitable interest in the land as

---

[1] We shall see later (*infra*, pp. 97–8) that by the legislation of 1925 it is now impossible for entailed and life interests to subsist as *legal* as distinct from equitable estates.

measured by the terms of the contract passes at once to B., although the legal estate remains with A. until an actual conveyance or lease has been executed.[1]

2. **The Restrictive Covenant**, *i.e.* a covenant by which the use of the covenantor's land is restricted for the benefit of the covenantee's adjoining land, *e.g.* where it is agreed that it shall not be used for the purposes of trade. The effect of such a covenant, if the necessary conditions are satisfied,[2] is that the covenantee acquires an equitable interest in the burdened land in the sense that he is entitled to an injunction preventing a breach of the agreement by the covenantor or by his successors in title except a purchaser for value of the legal estate without notice of the covenant.

3. **The Equity of Redemption**, *i.e.* the right of a mortgagor to redeem the mortgaged property upon payment of all that is due by way of capital or interest.[3]

4. **The Equitable Charge**, which arises where, without the transfer of any definite estate, land is designated as security for the payment of a sum of money.[4] In such a case, the chargee acquires an equitable interest that entitles him to take judicial proceedings for the sale of the land.[5]

5. **The Equitable Lien.** This is similar in effect to the equitable charge, and most generally arises when the vendor conveys the land to the purchaser before he has been paid. If so, he becomes entitled by operation of law to an equitable lien on the land for the amount of the unpaid purchase money which is enforceable by a sale under the direction of the court.[6]

Equitable interest distinguished from a "mere equity."

An equitable interest is distinguishable from what is generally called an *equity* or a *mere equity*. This is a concept that defies precise definition, but it includes a right to enforce an equitable remedy, such as specific performance, or to set aside or rectify a conveyance for fraud, undue influence, mistake and similar reasons.[7]

The distinction between such an equity and an equitable interest emerges if we consider their binding effect upon third parties. The purchaser[8] for value[9] of a legal estate, as we have

---

[1] *Infra*, p. 742.   [2] *Infra*, pp. 597 *et seq.*   [3] *Infra*, p. 638.
[4] Land can be similarly charged at law. See *infra*, pp. 647, 651.
[5] *Infra*, p. 686.   [6] *Infra*, p. 127.
[7] *Phillips* v. *Phillips* (1862), 4 De G. F. & J. at p. 218, *per* Lord WESTBURY; *National Provincial Bank Ltd.* v. *Ainsworth*, [1965] A. C. at pp. 1238, *per* Lord UPJOHN ; at 1252–3, *per* Lord WILBERFORCE ; (1955), 71 *L. Q. R.* 480 (R. E. Megarry). *Shiloh Spinners, Ltd.* v. *Harding*, [1973] A. C. 691, at p. 721, *per* Lord WILBERFORCE. See generally Hanbury's *Modern Equity* (9th Edn.), pp. 695 *et seq.*
[8] Including a lessee or mortgagee. *Caunce* v. *Caunce*, [1969] 1 W. L. R. 286 ; [1969] 1 All E. R. 722.
[9] Including money, money's worth, or the consideration of marriage *i.e.* a future marriage.

seen, takes it free from equitable interests of which he had no notice.[1] But the purchaser of an equitable interest in land takes it subject to existing equitable interests in the same land whether he has notice of them or not. The reason is that every conveyance of an equitable interest is an innocent conveyance in the sense that it conveys only that which the assignor is entitled to convey. Hence, the purchaser of an equitable interest is bound by an earlier equitable interest whether he has notice of it or not.[2] *Qui prior est tempore potior est jure.*[3] On the other hand, the purchaser of an equitable interest is not bound by a mere equity, though prior in point of time, unless he had notice of it when he took his assignment.[4]

To state the distinction in another way: the defence of purchaser for value without notice avails the purchaser of an equitable interest against the owner of an earlier equity, but not against the owner of an earlier equitable interest.

SECTION IV. SETTLEMENTS[5]

The desire of the upper classes to order the future destiny of their land and to prevent its sale out of the family, which has been a feature of English social life for many centuries, requires attention in any historical survey, since it has decisively affected the form and substance of real property law. The inclination of a fee simple owner, an inclination deeply rooted in parental anxiety and distrust, is to make what is called a *settlement* by which he retains the benefit of ownership during his own life, but withholds the entire ownership in the shape of the fee simple from his descendants for as long as possible by reducing them, one after the other, to the position of mere limited owners. The English doctrine of estates is ideally adapted to the achievement of this object. The fee simple of infinite duration is divisible into shorter periods of time each of which may be allotted successively to a number of persons, with the result that while these periods are running there is no person able to dispose of the entire ownership.

Historical importance of settlements.

---

[1] Such a purchaser can pass a title free from the equitable interest to a successor in title, even though the latter has notice. *Wilkes* v. *Spooner*, [1911] 2 K. B. 473; M. & B. p. 29.

[2] It has, however, been held that, if B, an equitable incumbrancer for value without notice of A's prior equitable incumbrance, gets in the legal estate, he takes precedence over A, even if he then has notice. *Bailey* v. *Barnes*, [1894] , 1 Ch. 25 ; *cf. McCarthy & Stone, Ltd.* v. *Julian S. Hodge & Co. Ltd.*, [1971] 1 W. L. R. 1547; [1971] 2 All E. R. 973.

[3] *Phillips* v. *Phillips*, (1862), 4 De G. F. & J., at p. 215; *Cave* v. *Cave* (1880), 15 Ch.D. 639. But see *infra* pp. 711–13, for the modification of this principle by L.P.A. 1925, s. 137 (1).

[4] *Garrard* v. *Frankel* (1862), 30 Beav. 445.

[5] Simpson, *Introduction to the History of Land Law*, pp. 218–24.

The strict settlement.

Settlements in one form or another have been common since at any rate the early thirteenth century,[1] and indeed for some 200 years after the statute *De Donis Conditionalibus* in 1285,[2] it was possible to grant an estate tail that would perforce descend from heir to heir and would permanently remain inconvertible into a fee simple. Although by the end of the fifteenth century means had been contrived to cut short such an impolitic tying-up of the land, by allowing any tenant in tail in possession and of full age to bar the entail and so to acquire the fee simple,[3] the urge to keep the land in the family for as long as the law would permit still persisted, and by the time of the Restoration the general form of the *strict settlement* had been established. It is desirable to appreciate its general design even at this early stage in the book if the significance of much of the existing legislation is to be grasped. Suppose, for instance, that a fee simple owner, A., a widower, has decided to use the land as a source of endowment for his only son B., who is about to be married, and for B.'s issue. In such a case the practice for several centuries has been for A. to execute a deed of settlement by which he limits the land

> to himself for life, then to B. for life and then, after making provision for B.'s widow and younger children, to the first and every other son of B. successively in tail.

Under such a settlement the desire of A. to keep the land in the family is at least partly achieved, for no one will be able to acquire complete control over the land before the eldest son of B., who may bar the entail and so convert it into a fee simple as soon as he attains his majority. To create a fee simple absolute, however, the disentailment must either be effected by him after he has become entitled in possession on the deaths of A. and B. or, if he desires to act earlier, it must be effected with the collaboration of the present possessor. There is no difficulty, therefore, if he waits until the successive life tenants, A. and B., are dead, for in that case he is tenant in tail in possession and free to act independently. But even while, say, B. is tenant for life in possession, he may join as party to the disentailment and thus enable his son to acquire the fee simple absolute.

The device of a re-settlement.

This collaboration of life tenant in possession and tenant in tail in remainder—usually of father and son—has consistently been utilized by conveyancers as part of the scheme to prolong the retention of the land in the family. That scheme will, of course, succeed automatically if the eldest son or other heir in each generation refrains throughout his life from barring the entail, for in that event the entailed interest will descend in due

---

[1] *Infra*, p. 237, gifts to a person and a special class of heirs.
[2] *Infra*, p. 238. For the effect of this statute, see Plucknett, *Legislation of Edward I*, pp. 125–35.
[3] *Infra*, p. 240, common recovery.

course to his own heir. But the danger is that he will bar the entail when he becomes entitled in possession and will then acquire and sell the fee simple. Hence the long established practice of making what is called a *resettlement* by which the eldest son, on the attainment of his majority, is in most cases persuaded to bar the entail with the concurrence of his father and then voluntarily to settle the fee simple thus acquired upon himself for a mere life interest with a further limitation in favour of his own sons successively in tail. This ensures that the land will remain in the family for yet another generation. If, therefore, a resettlement is effected in each generation, the land is held by a succession of limited owners and there is nobody who can claim to be owner of the fee simple.[1]

Settlements, as we have said, are of respectable antiquity, but at common law the opportunities of carving up the *legal* fee simple so as to anticipate events that might affect the family in the future were severely restricted, for limitations only of the simplest nature were allowed. The Chancellor, on the other hand, had never imposed restrictions upon limitations of the *equitable* estate. The use might be moulded into any form congenial to its creator and adapted to solve the riddles of the future. The Statute of Uses, therefore, played an important part in the evolution of the strict settlement, an evolution that was complete towards the end of the seventeenth century. The flexibility of the use was imparted to the legal estate by the statute. What was impossible at common law might now be achieved by a single assurance, either a grant to uses or a will. The simple expedient of vesting the legal estate in feoffees with a declaration of the uses to which they were to hold, entitled the beneficiaries to legal interests in the land, as and when their rights matured. The opportunities of a settlor were now greater.

Importance of the Statute of Uses.

> For instance, common law did not permit a man to convey a freehold estate to himself, nor did it recognize any estate limited to take effect after the grant of a fee simple.[2]

Grant of fee simple defeasible by later events.

Neither of these rules affected the use and they ceased to affect the legal estate into which the use was converted by the Statute of Uses, if the limitation were made by a grant to uses or by will. The normal method of creating a marriage settlement was for the settlor to grant his fee simple to feoffees to the use of himself in fee simple until the intended marriage, and thereafter to the use of himself for life with remainder to such uses in favour of his wife and issue as his fancy might dictate. Thus, after the statute he acquired a determinable fee simple during the interval between the settlement and the marriage, but on his marriage it was displaced in favour of the subsequent limitations, which were themselves legal.[3]

---

[1] For a clear account see Elphinstone (7th Edn.), *Introduction to Conveyancing*, pp. 638 *et seq.*
[2] *Infra*, p. 300. [3] Digby, *History of the Law of Real Property*, pp. 357-8.

Springing
and shifting
uses.

Again, at common law a freehold estate could not be given to a man to begin at some future date,[1] nor was it permissible to annex to a grant a condition that the freehold should shift from the donee to another person upon the happening of a prescribed event.[2]

Yet, the Chancellor had always protected such limitations of the equitable estate and therefore when uses were statutorily converted into legal estates, a limitation to feoffees to the use of X. when he married (springing use) or to the use of Y. for life, but if he became insolvent then to the use of Z. for life (shifting use), operated to vest a legal estate in X. and Z. upon the occurrence of the prescribed events.

Importance
of powers
of appoint-
ment.

Another innovation of the Chancellor that greatly increased the pliability of settlements was the *power of appointment*. The normal procedure upon the creation of a use was for the feoffor to declare then and there the exact uses to which the land should be held. But such a definitive declaration was not essential. The feoffor might reserve to himself or to a third person a power to declare in the future what uses should arise or to revoke existing uses and substitute new ones in their place. The donee of such a power, who might be a stranger having no proprietary interest, present or future, in the land, was thus enabled before the Statute of Uses to give fresh directions as to the enjoyment of the equitable estate. If, for example, in place of an existing use in favour of A. for life, he *appointed* to the use of B. in tail, the original feoffees immediately stood seised to the use of B. who consequently acquired an equitable estate tail. If the appointment were made after the statute, B. would take a legal estate tail.

Thus, through the machinery of powers, an appointor was able to dispose of an estate that he did not own, and the legal ownership might at his instance be freely shifted and modified to suit exigencies occurring after the date of the settlement.

Disadvan-
tages of
settlements.

A settlement of land, though it afforded a convenient means of providing for descendants and, when followed by periodic re-settlements, of keeping the land in the family, suffered from three particular disadvantages. It tended to render land inalienable, it might have an adverse effect upon the prosperity of the family and it complicated conveyancing.

(i) Might
render land
inalienable.

Inalienability of Land.—The first of these dangers was inherent in the pliability that the legal estate had inherited from the use. It soon became obvious that, unless some limit of time was imposed upon the power to create future interests, an astute employment of a series of springing and shifting clauses might well render the fee simple inalienable for an unreasonable period. Thus, the general employment in settlements of such devices to create a series of merely limited interests, enduring far into the future, would have starved the market of land to the detriment of

---

[1] *Infra*, pp. 297–8.   [2] *Infra*, p. 299.

the community. The courts have always fought against the creation of inalienable interests and have held them void.[1] Further, they have developed what is now called the *rule against perpetuities*, which looks to the date at which a contingent interest will vest, if it vests at all, and holds it to be void as a perpetuity if the date is too remote. This rule, which will require detailed treatment later,[2] allows a settlor to provide that an estate shall shift to a person or spring up in his favour upon the occurrence of a prescribed contingency, but it ordains that the estate shall be void unless the contingency, if it ever happens at all, will necessarily happen not later than twenty-one years from the death of some person or persons alive when the settlement takes effect.

Settlements Tended to Impoverish Families. The chief defect inherent in a system of strict settlements and of periodic re-settlements is that at no point of time is there any beneficiary competent to exercise many of the powers of a fee simple owner, unless indeed a right to do so is reserved by the settlement or granted by some statute. The person who under this system has every appearance of being owner is the life tenant in possession, but since his beneficial interest must necessarily determine with his death it follows that any interest granted by him must also determine at that moment. A conveyance by him purporting to pass the fee simple will at common law pass to the grantee nothing more than an estate *pur autre vie*, and a lease for any number of years will automatically determine on his death unless saved by statute or permitted by the settlement. The grave effects resulting from this limited power of alienation in the days when the strict settlement was the foundation of landed society can easily be realized. Given a system whereby it is usual for a fee simple owner, in view of his approaching marriage, to limit the land to himself for life and then to his eldest son in tail, and given further the inclination to re-settle the land in each generation on the eldest son for life, with remainder in tail to *his* eldest son, a moment's reflection will show what a prejudicial effect such a perpetual series of life tenants, each devoid of the power to convey the fee simple estate, must have not only on the supply of land available for purposes of trade, but also on the prosperity of the settled land itself.

The common practice, by which the eldest son under a strict settlement was persuaded on reaching his majority to convert his estate tail into a fee simple and then to re-settle the fee simple upon himself for a mere life estate with remainder to his own issue in tail, was stigmatized as follows by a critic some hundred years ago.[3]

Effect of settlement upon power of alienation.

(ii) Adverse effect on the prosperity of the land.

---

[1] *Infra*, p. 371.   [2] *Infra*, p. 312 *et seq.*
[3] Cliffe Leslie, *Fraser's Magazine*, Feb. 1867, cited Scrutton, *Land in Fetters*, p. 135.

" It is commonly supposed that a son acts with his eyes open and with a special eye to the contingencies of the future and of family life. But what are the real facts of the case ? Before the future owner of the land has come into possession, before he has any experience of his property, or of what is best to be done, or what he can do with regard to it, before the exigencies of the future or his own real position are known to him, before the character, number and wants of his children are learned, or the claims of parental affection and duty can make themselves felt, while still very much at the mercy of a predecessor desirous of posthumous greatness and power, he enters into an irrevocable disposition by which he parts with the rights of a proprietor over his future property for ever, and settles its devolution, burdened with charges, upon an unborn heir."

No absolute owner under a system of settlement and re-settlement.

Under such a system there never exists, apart from statute, a beneficial owner capable of selling or dealing with the fee simple.   In the words of Sir FREDERICK POLLOCK :—

" The lord of this mansion is named by all men its owner ; it is said to belong to him ; the park, the demesne, the farms are called his. But we shall be almost safe in assuming that he is not the full and free owner of any part of it. He is a ' limited owner,' having an interest only for his own life. He might have become the full owner . . . if he had possessed the means of waiting, the independence of thought and will to break with the tradition of his order and the bias of his education, and the energy to persevere in his dissent against the counsels and feelings of his family. But he had every inducement to let things go their accustomed way. Those whom he had always trusted told him, and probably with sincere belief, that the accustomed way was the best for the family, for the land, for the tenants and for the country. And there could be no doubt that it was at the time the most agreeable to himself."[1]

It is clear, in fact, that an uncontrolled system of settlements and re-settlements is an evil—both social and economic—to any country which tolerates it, though it was not one that was apparent to the lawyers of the early nineteenth century. Thus we find the Real Property Commissioners in their report of 1829 stating:

" The owner of the soil is, we think, vested with exactly the dominion and power of disposition over it required for the public good, and landed property in England is admirably made to answer all the purposes to which it is applicable. Settlements bestow on the present possessor of an estate the benefits of ownership, and secure the property to his posterity. . . . In England families are preserved and purchasers always find a supply of land in the market."

Disadvantages of settling and re-settling land.

This language is specious. It is true in the sense that settled land could usually be sold in fee simple, because a settlement might contain, and a well-drawn settlement would contain, powers enabling the tenant for life to deal with the land by way of sale, lease, mortgage and so on.[2] If he took advantage of such a power and for instance sold the land to X., the fact that he was a mere

---

[1] *Land Laws*, p. 9.
[2] For a seventeenth-century precedent, see Holdsworth, *History of English Law*, vol. vii. p. 547.

life tenant was no obstacle to the transfer of the fee simple, for the feoffees had been directed by the settlement to hold to such uses as might be appointed by the donee of the power and therefore they now held to the use of the appointee X. Thus under the Statute of Uses, X. acquired a legal fee simple. But although the land could be rendered manageable and saleable by this device, it happened only too often that powers were either omitted altogether or were too restricted in character. Speaking broadly, land was kept in families only at the expense of removing it from commerce and too often starving it of money necessary for its development and improvement. No doubt the evil was not so great under the rural conditions prevalent until the early nineteenth century, but it became urgent when the vast spread of industrialism produced a demand for coal and other minerals, and converted England from an agricultural to a trading community. To appreciate the nature of the problem it is only necessary to examine the position of a life tenant of settled land in, say, 1835. This was admirably summed up by UNDERHILL[1] :—

" Unless the will or settlement . . . contained express powers (which was frequently not the case) a tenant for life could neither sell, exchange, nor partition the settled property, however desirable it might be. If the estate consisted of a large tract of poor country, fruitful in dignity but scanty in rent, and specially if the portions of younger children charged on it were heavy, he too often found it a *damnosa hereditas* ; the rents, after payment of interest on the portions, leaving a mere pittance for the unfortunate life tenant to live on, and quite disabling him from making improvements, or even keeping the property in a decent state of repair. Nay more, if he did spend money in improvements, the money was sunk in the estate to the detriment of his younger children. He could not pull down the mansion-house, however old or inconvenient it might be, nor even, strictly, make any substantial alteration in it. Unless expressly made unimpeachable for waste, he could not open new mines. But in addition to these disabilities, what pressed still more hardly upon him, and on the development of the estate generally, was his inability to make long leases.[2] Consequently when valuable minerals lay beneath a settled property, or the growth of the neighbouring town made it ripe for building sites (the rents for which would greatly exceed the agricultural rent) nothing could lawfully be done. The tenant for life could not open mines himself, even if he had the necessary capital for working them ; nor, even if unimpeachable for waste, could he grant leases of them to others for a term which would repay the lessees for the necessary expenditure in pits and plant ; nor could he grant building leases or sell for building purposes at fee farm rents. In some settlements powers were expressly inserted, enabling the trustees to grant such leases and to sell, exchange and partition. But frequently, especially in wills, such powers were omitted, and in such cases the only means of doing justice to the land was to apply for a private Act of Parliament authorizing the trustees or life tenant to sell, exchange, partition or lease. But such Acts were expensive luxuries, only open to the

---

[1] *Century of Law Reform*, pp. 284–5.
[2] A tenant *in tail*, however, was empowered by the Fines and Recoveries Act 1833, s. 41, to grant a lease for a term not exceeding 21 years.

rich, and beyond the means of most country gentlemen of moderate means."

Statutory Reform.   When, however, the modern industrial era set in, the legislature took the matter in hand, and in a tentative manner began to pass a series of public Acts of Parliament which enabled settled land to be dealt with in a manner likely to enhance its prosperity.   A start was made in the 1840s with statutes which empowered tenants for life to borrow money for the purpose of carrying out permanent drainage improvements and to charge the loan on the inheritance.   Then the Improvement of Land Act 1864 enabled a tenant for life to raise money with the consent of the Ministry of Agriculture in order to execute certain specified improvements, and to charge the loan on the corpus of the property.[1]   Further examples were the Limited Owners Residences Acts 1870 and 1871, which allowed money to be raised for completing or adding to a mansion-house ; and the Limited Owners Reservoirs Act 1877, which sanctioned the same method for the construction of permanent waterworks.

But in 1856 the much more important Settled Estates Act had been passed which contained the germ of all the future legislation on the subject.   Its object was to facilitate leases and sales of settled estates, and after being amended by several statutes in the succeeding generation, it was replaced in 1877 by the Settled Estates Act of that year.   This allowed the Chancery Division of the High Court to sanction the sale, exchange or partition of the settled land, and the grant of leases of 21 years for an agricultural or occupation lease, 40 years for a mining lease, and 99 years for a building lease.   It also allowed the tenant for life without resorting to the court to make a valid lease up to a period of 21 years.   So this Act made great strides towards permitting all opportunities for the proper development of the land to be seized, but its weakness was that, except in the case of short leases, its enabling powers could not be exercised without an order of the court.   It had in truth facilitated dealings, since it substituted an order of the court for a private Act of Parliament, but it stopped short of placing the powers unreservedly in the hands of the tenant for life.

About this time an agitation sprang up for the total abolition of life estates and the restriction of grants to the creation of a fee simple, the argument being that settlements, besides making conveyances difficult and costly, deprived a father of a much-needed power of control over his eldest son, and prevented an estate from being thrown on the market when its poverty made such a course desirable.   For better or for worse the argument did not prevail.   It was realized that settlements enabled a fair and reasonable provision to be made for all the members of a

Marginal notes:
Disadvantages gradually eliminated by statute.

Early Acts.

Settled Estates Act 1877.

Agitation to abolish settlements.

---

[1] *Infra,* p. 628.

family, and therefore, while the general features of the time-honoured system were retained, a plan was evolved to prevent settled land from becoming an inert mass through lack of capital or of adequate powers of management.[1]

The Settled Land Act 1882. The principle adopted by Lord Cairns and incorporated in the famous Settled Land Act of 1882 was to put the entire management of the land into the hands of the tenant for life for the time being, and to give him, at his own sole discretion and without asking the permission of the court or the trustees of the settlement, wide powers of selling, leasing, mortgaging and otherwise dealing with the property. These powers were independent of, and could not be restrained by, the settlement itself, but they were subject to certain statutory provisions designed to protect the interests of all persons entitled under the settlement, and to prevent the tenant for life from acquiring more than a life interest in the income or profits.

New era opened with Settled Land Act 1882.

The objects of the Act were lucidly explained by CHITTY, L.J., in the following words [2] :—

" The object is to render land a marketable article, notwithstanding the settlement. Its main purpose is the welfare of the land itself, and of all interested therein, including the tenants and not merely the persons taking under the settlement. The Act of 1882 had a much wider scope than the Settled Estates Acts. The scheme adopted is to facilitate the striking off from the land of the fetters imposed by settlement ; and this is accomplished by conferring on *tenants for life in possession*, and others considered to stand in a like relation to the land, large powers of dealing with the land by way of sale, exchange, lease and otherwise, and by jealously guarding those powers from attempts to defeat them or to hamper their exercise. At the same time the rights of persons claiming under the settlement are carefully preserved in the case of a sale by shifting the settlement from the land to the purchase money which has to be paid into court or into the hands of trustees."

The Act of 1882 was amended in small particulars by further statutes passed in 1884, 1887, 1889, and 1890, but its policy has stood the test of time, and though it has now been repealed and replaced by the Settled Land Act 1925, its general principles still continue to govern the rights and the liabilities of a tenant for life under a strict settlement.

Complication of Conveyancing. The third disadvantage of a settlement—its aggravation of the complexity of conveyancing —became evident when a tenant for life, by virtue of a power conferred upon him, had agreed to sell the fee simple to a purchaser. In this event, he would prove the title down to the date of the settlement in the normal fashion by tracing the history of

(iii) Settlements raised a conveyancing difficulty.

---

[1] *Century of Law Reform*, pp. 287–90.
[2] *Re Mundy and Roper's Contract*, [1899] 1 Ch. 275, at p. 288.

the land back to a good root of title, in order to show that the fee
simple was owned by the original settlor. So far there was nothing
abnormal, but at this point arose the difficulty that the vendor
himself did not own the estate that he had contracted to sell. His
case would be, of course, that as tenant for life under a settlement
he possessed a power, conferred upon him either by the settlement itself or after 1882 by the Settled Land Act, to convey the
fee simple. The general rule on this matter is that the exercise
of a power, whether it is given by act of parties or by statute, is
void unless all the conditions imposed by the instrument or statute
from which it derives are literally observed. If attention is concentrated on a sale after 1882, the governing factors in this
respect were that the Act of that year empowered a tenant for
life under a settlement to convey a good title to the fee simple,
provided that the purchase money was paid to the trustees. In
other words, before the statutory power of sale or any other
statutory power was validly exercisable, it was essential that, *within
the meaning of the Act,*

> the instrument under which the vendor held was a " settlement " ;
> the vendor himself was a " tenant for life " or one of the persons to
> whom the statutory powers were given ;
> the trustees were properly constituted.

In order, therefore, to verify that these conditions were
satisfied, it was necessary for the original deed of settlement and,
in fact, several further deeds if there had been one or more
re-settlements, to be abstracted by the vendor and investigated by
the purchaser. Thus, in order to satisfy himself that a good title
would be made, the purchaser was confronted with the formidable
task of scrutinizing a series of transactions and documents stretching
back perhaps for very many years.

The doctrine
of
overreaching.
In contrast to this complication which beset a purchaser of
settled land, his position vis-à-vis the beneficial interests under the
settlement was simple. This was due to the doctrine of overreaching : it originated in conveyancing practice and was adopted
by the Settled Land Act 1882. The Act provides that if the purchaser pays the purchase money to at least two trustees or into
Court (and *not* to the tenant for life) the interests of the beneficiaries
under the settlement shall be transferred from the land to the
purchase money.[1] Thus the purchaser by virtue of the Act
takes the land free from the beneficial interests ; and he does this
even though he has notice of them and even though the interests
may be legal. The conveyancing advantage to the purchaser is
obvious. So far as the beneficiaries are concerned, they lose their
opportunity of enjoying the land qua land, but, instead, they
have equivalent interests in the purchase money. A beneficial
interest in a fund of £50,000 is just as valuable as the same interest

---

[1] S.L.A. 1882, ss. 20, 22 (5), 39 (1).

in land worth £50,000 ; more valuable, if the money is invested more profitably ; less valuable if the land was a better investment. The question is of one of choice of investment of the family capital.

Trust for Sale.—So far we have concentrated attention upon the strict settlement. An entirely different way of applying the principle of the settlement to land was by means of a trust for sale, a method that has been common in wills for some 500 years and in deeds since the early nineteenth century.[1] This transaction, which has now almost supplanted the strict settlement, falls into two parts and, though not strictly necessary, it is usually effected by two separate deeds. If, for instance, it precedes the marriage of the settlor: *The trust for sale.*

> The first deed in its opening clause conveys the fee simple to the trustees upon trust (with the consent of the husband until the intended marriage, and after the marriage with the consent of the husband and wife, or of the survivor, and after the death of the survivor at the discretion of the trustees), to sell the said fee simple. *Conveyance to the trustees.*
>
> The second clause of the deed directs the trustees to hold the money arising from the sale and the rents and profits accruing prior to the sale upon such trusts as are declared by a deed already engrossed and made between the same parties and on the same date as the present deed.[2]

According to the equitable doctrine of conversion the effect of the execution of this deed is that in the eyes of equity the land is notionally converted into money, for that doctrine, based on the principle that equity looks on that as done which ought to be done, insists that an imperative direction to turn land into money shall impress the land with the quality of money no matter how long the sale may be postponed.[3] The important point to notice, therefore, is that a trust for sale relating to the fee simple and containing a succession of beneficial limitations is a settlement of personalty, not of realty.

> The second deed sets out the beneficial trusts of the personalty into which the realty has already been notionally converted. It will usually provide in the first place that the income, whether arising from the invested purchase money or from the rents and profits prior to the sale, shall be held in trust for the husband during his life and after his death in trust for his wife if she survives him. Secondly, it will provide that after the death of the husband and wife the capital shall be divided among the children or remoter issue of the marriage in such shares as the husband and wife or the survivor shall appoint, and, failing appointment, among the children equally.[4] *Declaration of the beneficial interests.*

The investigation of title upon a sale by the trustees raises none of the difficulties that, as we have already seen, formerly attended

---

[1] (1929), 3 *C. L. J.*, p. 63 (J. M. Lightwood).
[2] See Burnett, *Elements of Conveyancing* (8th Edn.), pp. 455–6.
[3] *Fletcher* v. *Ashburner* (1779), 1 Bro. C. C. 497. The reverse is also true.
[4] Burnett, *op. cit.*, pp. 456–8.

a sale by a tenant for life under a strict settlement. The legal fee simple is vested in the trustees for sale and it is from them that the purchaser takes his title. His main concern is to ascertain that the settlor was entitled to the fee simple that was conveyed to the trustees for sale. As far as the interests of the beneficiaries are concerned, the purchaser takes free from them if he pays the purchase money to at least two trustees.[1] In contrast to the position under the strict settlement, overreaching under the trust for sale is automatic : no statutory intervention is necessary. " The legal estate is held by the trustees for sale on trust to sell and the beneficial interests are imposed upon the proceeds of sale or upon the rents and profits until sale. They are not upon the land. The only trust upon the land is the trust to sell. Where therefore the trustees for sale sell the land in performance of their duty to sell, the land which the purchaser takes is unaffected by any trusts ; the trusts are and always have been imposed upon the purchase money."[2] Nevertheless, section 2 (1) of the Law of Property Act 1925 makes statutory provision for overreaching.

Furthermore, the purchaser is not responsible for the proper application of the money, provided that he pays it to at least two trustees. The beneficiaries must now look to the trustees and to them alone. This was not always so. In earlier days it was considered that the purchaser, since he had notice of the existence of beneficial limitations, was bound to see that the money was applied in accordance with the trust,[3] and it therefore became the usual practice to insert a clause in the first deed authorizing the trustees to give the purchaser a receipt exonerating him from liability in this respect. This has been made unnecessary, however, by a series of statutes dating from 1859,[4] which are now represented by the following :

> The receipt in writing of a trustee for any money . . . payable to him under any trust or power shall be a sufficient discharge to the person paying . . . the same and shall effectually exonerate him from seeing to the application or being answerable for any loss or misapplication thereof.[5]

The two methods of settling land.

Summary. Before 1926 there had been evolved two methods of settling land ; the strict settlement, in which the purchaser takes his title from the tenant for life under the Settled Land Act 1882, and the trust for sale in which he takes it from the trustees for sale. In both he may overreach the interests of the beneficiaries, even though he has notice of them. As to which was used depended on the object of the settlor. The strict settlement was

---

[1] Or to a trust corporation. L.P.A. 1925, ss. 2 (1) (ii), 27 (2) ; L.P.(A.)A. 1926, Sched.

[2] Hanbury's *Modern Equity* (9th Edn.), p. 26.

[3] Vaizey, *The Law of Settlements of Property*, pp. 1409–12.

[4] L.P.(A.)A. 1859, s. 23 ; Conveyancing Act 1881, s. 36 ; Trustee Act 1893, s. 20.

[5] Trustee Act 1925, s. 14 (1).

appropriate where " land was settled with the object of founding a family or continuing the possession of family estates in the line of primogeniture "[1] ; here the tenant for life would reside on the land and himself exercise control over it.   On the other hand the trust for sale was convenient where the property settled was not to be kept in the family, but was to be treated as an investment and as a source of income for the beneficiaries.   It was especially useful where the fund settled was a mixture of personalty and realty and where the ultimate object was the division of land among children equally.   As we shall see the dominant factor today has become that of taxation.[2]

Finally we may notice that in 1925, the legislature, impressed by the advantages that the trust for sale imparted to the practice of conveyancing, made it the basis of several of the reforms introduced in that year.   In particular, it was by extending the machinery and principle of the trust for sale that the law relating to concurrent interests[3] was strikingly simplified.

Device of trust for sale extended in 1925.

SECTION V. THE SIMPLIFICATION OF THE LAW IN 1925

SUMMARY

Introductory Note.—Even as late as the conclusion of the war of 1914 there were many features of the land law which seemed unnecessarily cumbrous and antiquated to a generation that, for the moment at any rate, considered itself destined to effect a general simplification of life.   There was certainly much in the fundamentals of the subject that would seem strange to an impartial critic.   Thus land was the subject of tenure, not of ownership, but instead of there being one common form of tenure with incidents of universal application, there were the two distinct forms of socage and copyhold, with various divergent offshoots such as gavelkind and borough-English.   This division of tenures, which led to differences in the ordinary incidents of

Complications resulting from tenures.

---

[1] 3 *C. L. J.* at p. 63.   [2] *Infra*, pp. 204 *et seq.*   [3] *Infra*, p. 220.

ownership and in the modes of conveyance, was complicated by a cross-division under which estates were classified as being either freehold or leasehold. The main object of the legislation of 1925 was the simplification of conveyancing, and the committee that was appointed to suggest alterations was instructed by its terms of reference " to consider the present position of land transfer, and to advise what action should be taken to *facilitate and cheapen the transfer of land.*" It was found, however, that a necessary pre-liminary to the attainment of this object was the simplification of the law of real property. It is scarcely possible to modernize a system of transfer if the subject-matter of the transfer is itself governed by effete and antiquated rules. An analysis of the legislation of 1925, therefore, requires us to consider how it simplified, first the law of real property, and then the system of conveyancing.

(1) SIMPLIFICATION OF THE LAW OF REAL PROPERTY

Three systems of land law before 1926.

In 1925 land was subject, not to one system, but to three systems of law. This surprising result was caused by the dis-tinction between freeholds and chattels real,[1] and by the existence of two forms of tenure—socage and copyhold. The law of real property strictly so-called, which governed freehold interests in land, was still different in several respects from that which governed chattels real. Furthermore, whether the interest enjoyed by a proprietor were a freehold or a chattel real, the land affected would be held either by socage or by copyhold tenure. This was an added complication, since in several important respects the rules governing socage and copyhold lands were divergent. There was thus a law of freeholds, a law of leaseholds and a law of copyholds. The obvious solution, therefore, and the one adopted by the legislature, was first to institute one common form of tenure by the abolition of copyhold ; then to assimilate as far as practicable the law of real property and of chattels real ; finally, to abolish certain anachronisms of the common law—irritating survivals that were inimical to a simplified legal system. We will consider these three improvements separately.

(A) THE REDUCTION OF TENURES TO ONE COMMON FORM

Classes of tenure gradually reduced.

History of Simplification of Tenures.—The account that we have already given of tenure shows that for a long period there has been a gradual but continuous reduction in the number of possible tenures. This process was far advanced before 1926, but in that year uniformity was at last attained.

Six hundred years ago the law on this subject was complicated. In the time of Edward I there were four distinct and important

---

[1] *Supra*, pp. 38-40.

varieties of tenure, distinguished from each other by the different kinds of services due and each exhibiting fundamental differences in the substantive rule of law to which they were subject.[1] This led to the growth of a mass of confused and intricate law, and it was only by slow degrees that simplification began to emerge. The Statute *Quia Emptores* 1290, though it was not concerned with the actual reduction of the several varieties, at least stemmed the increasing confusion, since it forbade the creation of any further tenures within each variety. The introduction of the doctrine of *uses* led indirectly to a decline in the importance of tenures, for the relationship of lord and tenant would lose much of its value and significance if it was freed from those tenurial incidents the avoidance of which was one of the chief inducements to put land in use. *Statute Quia Emptores.*

The Statute of Uses, on the other hand, was a retrograde step in the process of simplification, though it was only for a time that it restored the importance of tenures. Before another century had passed the King no longer looked to the feudal incidents for a revenue, while the country as a whole evinced a desire to regain the advantages which had disappeared with the abolition of uses, and to be rid of the burdensome incidents that were a feature of the law of tenures. *Statute of Uses.*

In fact, even before the ultimate re-establishment of uses in the seventeenth century the first direct simplification of tenures was effected by the Statute for the Abolition of Military Tenures in 1660. The effect of this Act was the reduction of tenures to socage, copyhold and frankalmoin, though the honorary incidents of grand sergeanty were retained, and various customary modes of holding land, such as gavelkind, borough-English and ancient demesne, continued to exist in certain parts of the country. In effect only two important tenures remained—namely, socage and copyhold. *Statute 12 Car. II, c. 24.*

The position, then, long before 1925, showed a vast improvement upon that of the time of Edward I, but, as we have already seen, the continued existence of copyhold as a distinct tenure not only disturbed the simplicity of conveyancing, but also tended to embarrass the full exploitation of the land.[2] Not only did the form of conveyance vary according as the land was socage or copyhold, but, what was a far more serious blemish, such legal incidents as the mode of descent and the types of interest creatable often differed from those recognized by the general law. In this respect, indeed, there was not even a system of law common to all copyholds, for the actual customs upon which the legal incidents were dependent frequently varied from manor to manor. There was thus room for reform in this particular field of law, and the opportunity was seized by the legislature. *Copyhold tenure a hindrance to conveyancing.*

---

[1] *Supra*, pp.   *et seq.*   [2] *Supra*, p. 27.

Abolition
of all
tenures
except
socage.

All previous modes of descent, whether operating by the general law or by the custom of gavelkind or borough-English or by any other custom of any county, locality or manor, were abrogated.[1] Escheat[2] *propter defectum sanguinis* was discarded and replaced by the right of the Crown to take as *bona vacantia* the interest of a tenant who died intestate and heirless.[3] The honorary services incident to tenure by sergeanty, where they still existed, were expressly reserved, but the tenure itself had already disappeared.[4] An attempt was also made to abolish frankalmoin, though whether it succeeded is doubtful. The Statute of 1660, which by its first section abolished knight service, provided in s. 7 that nothing in the first section was to affect frankalmoin. The Administration of Estates Act 1925, instead of abolishing frankalmoin by express language, merely repealed s. 7 of the Statute of 1660.[5] This repeal, however, would appear to be fruitless, for even if the seventh section had been omitted from the Statute, frankalmoin would have been unaffected by an enactment that merely abolished knight service. The matter is indeed of little importance, for no land can be held by frankalmoin at the present day unless it has been continuously so held by the same ecclesiastical tenant since before *Quia Emptores* 1290.[6] Finally and at long last, the decisive step was taken of abolishing copyhold tenure. As from January 1st, 1926, every parcel of copyhold land was enfranchised and converted into freehold land held by socage tenure.[7]

Features
of old
law of
copyholds.

Manorial
incidents.

Extinguishment of Manorial Incidents. It was realized, of course, that copyhold tenure could not be dismissed in this peremptory manner, for certain manorial incidents had long been associated with it, and to extinguish without compensation such of those as possessed a money value would obviously be unjust to the beneficiary, whether lord or copyholder. The solution adopted was based upon a tripartite classification of these incidents.

The first class, consisting of those that had become anachronisms were extinguished immediately subject to a single payment of compensation.[8]

Manorial
incidents of
pecuniary
value.

The second class consisted of those incidents that still possessed a money value. These were temporarily saved,[9] but it was

---

[1] A.E.A. 1925, s. 45 (1) (a).   [2] *Supra*, p. 28.
[3] A.E.A. 1925, s. 45 (1) (d).   [4] L.P.A. 1922, s. 136.
[5] 2nd Sched.   [6] *Supra*, p. 22, note 2.
[7] L.P.A. 1922, Part V, ss. 128–137, and 12th Sched. as amended by L.P.(A.)A. 1924, s. 2 and 2nd Sched. ; L.P.A. 1922, s. 189.
[8] L.P.A. 1922, 12th Sched (1) ; forfeiture for an alienation without the lord's licence ; liability of the copyholder to customary suits and to do fealty ; customary modes of descent or any custom relating to dower (*infra*, p. 870), curtesy (*infra*, p. 244) or freebench (Blackstone, vol. ii. p. 337).
[9] L.P.A. 1922, s. 128 (2) : *rents* ; *fines* payable to the lord in certain circumstances, *reliefs* payable to the lord upon descent of the land ; *heriots*, the right of the lord to seize the best beast or best chattel upon the tenant's decease ; *forfeitures* for a variety of acts by the tenant ; the right of the lord to fell *timber* trees.

provided that they should be extinguished upon the payment of compensation, the amount of which was to be determined either by agreement or by the Minister of Agriculture and Fisheries at the instance of either party. The final date of extinction was to be December 31st, 1935, though if by then no agreement upon the amount of compensation had been reached either party might apply to the Minister requiring the amount to be determined, provided that the application was made before December 31st, 1940. Owing to the war, this was later extended to November 1st, 1950.[1]

The following incidents, falling within the third class, were permanently saved and they continue to attach to the land, unless the parties agree to their extinction upon payment of compensation.[2]

Manorial incidents that still continue.

(*a*) Any commonable rights to which the tenant is entitled.[3]

(*b*) Any right of the lord or the tenant to mines, minerals, gravel, pits or quarries, whether in or under the land.[4]

(*c*) Any rights of the lord in respect of fairs, markets or sporting.[4]

(*d*) Any liability for the construction, maintenance, cleansing or repair of any dykes, ditches, canals, sea or river walls, bridges, levels, ways, etc.[5]

Thus, after some 800 years of development the doctrine of tenure still characterizes the English law of real property. Land is still incapable of ownership by a subject. Every acre is held by a tenant, not owned, though by a gradual process of elimination the various forms of tenure that complicated the law in former days have at last been reduced to the one type—socage. But what are the practical effects of the doctrine? Are the rights that the English tenant in fee simple enjoys any less valuable, for instance, than those of an absolute owner of land in the State of New York where all feudal tenures have been expressly abolished? Is tenure a mere name, a reminder only of the pomp and splendour of former days? The truth is, of course, that it is a mere historical survival that now has little practical effect. To have styled the tenant a landowner some centuries ago would have been inaccurate, since his very right to retain the land was conditioned on his performance of the tenurial liabilities. But in course of time these liabilities have almost entirely disappeared, and it is only on the rarest occasion that anything of value can now be claimed by virtue of tenure. Until 1926, indeed, a lord, if he were still able to establish his lordship, might be fortunate enough to derive an unearned increment under the doctrine of

Unimportance of doctrine of tenure.

Few living results of tenure.

---

[1] S.I. 1949, No. 836.
[2] L.P.A. 1922, s. 138 (12).   [3] *Ibid.*, 12th Sched. (4) *infra.* p. 561.
[4] *Ibid.*, 12th Sched. (5).   [5] *Ibid.*, 12th Sched. (6).

escheat, but he lost even this vague *spes successionis* when the Administration of Estates Act 1925 provided that the land of a tenant who dies intestate without leaving near relatives shall pass to the State.[1] Even in such a non-feudal State as New York it is difficult to see to whom else it can pass.   The feudal doctrine of tenure has no doubt impressed an indelible mark upon the framework of the law, but it no longer affects the tenant's rights of enjoyment, though the modern tendency to stress the rights of the community at large has resulted in the imposition of restrictions upon him that were unknown to earlier ages.   The living results of feudalism must be sought, not in the realm of tenures, but in that classification of estates which is a peculiarity of English law.   Apart from this " wonderful calculus of estates," as Maitland expressed it, perhaps the sole feudal incident that is a living force at the present day consists of those rights of common which the successors of the copyhold lord and tenant may still hold in the manorial waste. To quote Maitland again :—

> " Everyone knows that this doctrine [of tenure], however indispensable as an explanation for some of the subtleties of real property law, is, in fact, untrue. ' The first thing the student has to do is to get rid of the idea of absolute ownership.'   So says Mr. Williams[2] ; but we may add, with equal truth, that the second thing he has to do is to learn how, by slow degrees, the statement that there is no absolute ownership of land has been deprived of most of its important consequences."[3]

If this was true in 1880 when Maitland wrote, how unsubstantial must the doctrine of tenure be after the abolition of copyholds.[4]

(B) THE ASSIMILATION OF REAL AND PERSONAL PROPERTY LAW

Tendency to unify law of realty and personalty.

Originally, as we have seen, there were wide distinctions between the law of real and of personal property, but there has been a tendency ever since an early age to make both these departments of the law subject to the same legal rules, and in the main

---

[1] Ss. 45, 46 (1) (vi).   Escheat may, however, still exist if a trustee in bankruptcy of a landowner disclaims the land (*British General Insurance Co., Ltd.*, v. *A.G.*, [1945] L. J. N. C. C. R. 113; (1946), 62 *L. Q. R.* 223 (R. E. Megarry), or if a corporation (other than a company incorporated under the Companies Acts) holding real property is dissolved.   *Re Sir Thomas Spencer Wells*, [1933], Ch. 29, at p. 54 ; *Re Strathblaine Estates Ltd.*, [1948] Ch. 228.   See too (1954), 70 *L. Q. R.* 25 (D. W. Elliott) ; *Re Lowes' Will Trusts*, [1973] 1 W. L. R. 882 (" By a happy chance [escheat to the Crown of realty propter defectum sanguinis] has arisen from the past in connection with the Phoenix Inn in Stratford-on-Avon ", *per* RUSSELL, L.J., at p. 884).
[2] Williams, *The Law of Real Property* (12th Edn.), p. 17.
[3] Maitland, *Collected Papers*, vol. i. p. 196.   See also Challis, *Law of Real Property* (3rd Edn.), p. 3.
[4] " Hundreds of . . . phrases and concepts which permeate our law will have to be remembered if reforming zeal ever proposes to sweep away the theoretical structure of tenures and estates upon which English land law rests".   *Lowe (Inspector of Taxes)* v. *J. W. Ashmore, Ltd.*, [1971] Ch. 545, at p. 554, *per* MEGARRY, J.

the rules that have been adopted are those that govern personal property. Thus the legislation of 1925 essayed to complete a process of assimilation that was already far advanced. We shall perhaps gain a greater clearness of view if we first consider in what particulars a common body of legal rules had been created before 1926, and then review the contents of the statutes designed to procure as complete a unification as possible.

(i) Matters in which Assimilation had been effected prior to 1926

(*a*) **Remedies for Dispossession.** The original rule that leaseholds, unlike freeholds, were not specifically recoverable [1] ceased to be true towards the middle of the fifteenth century, by which time the action *ejectione firmae* was available to the termor. The actions that lay for recovery were still, indeed, different according as the demandant's interest was freehold or leasehold, but complete assimilation in this particular was attained in the seventeenth century, by which time the *ejectione firmae* had been borrowed from the law of chattels real and, under the name of the action of ejectment, had been adapted to the recovery of freeholds.[2]

Remedies assimilated in 17th century.

(*b*) **The Power of Testamentary Disposition.** It was always possible to bequeath leaseholds and other forms of personal property, but the feudal law would not admit a will of freeholds. A partial power of testamentary disposition over real property was obtained, however, in 1540, when the Statute of Wills permitted tenants to devise all their socage lands and two-thirds of their land held in knight service. This testamentary power was completed by the Statute for the Abolition of Military Tenures in 1660,[3] which converted knight service tenure into free and common socage.

Assimilation in 1660.

(*c*) **Availability of Property for Creditors.** The history of this is given below,[4] but we may state here that while at an early date leaseholds and other forms of personal property belonging to a deceased debtor constituted assets available for all creditors, the general rule was that a fee simple estate passed directly to the heir or devisee of a deceased tenant and could not be seized by his creditors. Gradual inroads upon this immunity of real property were, however, made by statute and by equity, and assimilation was almost attained in 1833, when the Adminis-

Original immunity of realty.

Deceased debtor.

---

[1] *Supra,* p. 38.
[2] Holdsworth, *History of English Law,* vol. vii. pp. 4 *et seq.*
[3] 12 Car. II, c. 24.   [4] *Infra,* pp. 816–21.

tration of Estates Act made all land belonging to a deceased debtor available as assets for the one class of creditors—namely, simple contract creditors—who had not already obtained a remedy against freeholds. There was, however, still a difference in respect of remedies, for to render personal property available a creditor had to proceed against the personal representatives, while to satisfy his claim against real property, which did not vest in the personal representatives, he had to bring a suit in equity for administration. Assimilation on this point came with the Land Transfer Act 1897, which provided that realty should vest in the personal representatives, as had always been the practice with personalty.

Living debtor.

The law that regulated the right of a creditor to seize the land of his *living* debtor was also assimilated before 1926. At common law all the chattels, real and personal, of a judgment debtor might be seized, but there was no right to satisfaction out of his freeholds. The Statute of Westminster 1285 made half the debtor's land available for creditors, and this was extended to the whole of the land by the Judgments Act of 1838.[1]

(ii) **Matters in which Assimilation was effected by the Legislation of 1925**

The process of assimilation was carried further by the legislation of 1925 in the following respects.

(a) The Size and Nature of Estates and Interests. Before 1926 there was a fundamental distinction between realty and personalty with regard to the interests that might be created.

Interests in real property.

In the case of real property it has been possible for many centuries to create not only legal and equitable estates of different sizes—namely, the fee simple, the estate tail and the life estate— but also to split the full fee simple up into a series of partial and successive legal or equitable interests, as for example by a grant to A. for life, then to B. in tail, and then to C. in fee simple.

Interests in personal property at common law.

The position with regard to personal property was different. Pure personalty (goods and money) and chattels real (such as an unexpired lease for 20 years) were *at common law* the subjects of absolute ownership only. They were outside the doctrine of estates altogether and they could not be divided into successive interests. A grant of an existing term of years to A. for life or in tail made A. at common law the owner of the entire term. A gift for an hour was a gift for ever. The position *in equity* was slightly

Interests in personal property in equity.

---

[1] *Infra*, pp. 804–5.

different, for to a limited extent equity did permit successive interests to be created in personalty if the device of a grant to trustees was adopted. If the owner of a leasehold for 30 years granted it to trustees

> upon trust for A. for life and then upon trust for B. for life,

A. did not become absolute owner of the whole term as he would have done at common law, but held merely for life, while on his death B. similarly became entitled to a life estate. The interests both of A. and of B. were of course equitable. There was one method, however, though it was seldom used, by which even at common law an effective life estate might be given in personalty— namely, by will. Without adopting the instrument of a trust a testator might make a direct bequest of a leasehold

> to A. for life with a further gift to B. for life,

and the bequests would be upheld. But it is important to observe that under the old law it was impossible to create an estate tail in leaseholds either by a direct bequest or through the instrumentality of trustees. A term of years, not being an estate of inheritance, could not be entailed.[1]

A summary of the old law of the subject is, then, that in real property there might be legal or equitable fees simple, estates tail or life interests, either alone or in succession, but that in personal property there was normally only absolute ownership, though there might be equitable and, exceptionally, legal life interests. **Summary of old law.**

Assimilation, as regards both the size of the interests creatable and their nature when created, was, however, effected as from January 1st 1926 by the Law of Property Act 1925. In the first place, this provides that personalty may be entailed.[2] The result is that the nature of the subject-matter no longer affects the quantitative interest that may be carved out of it. In realty there may be a fee simple estate, in personalty absolute ownership ; while in both cases either entailed interests or life interests may validly be created. Secondly, as we shall see later,[3] entailed and life interests, whether in real or in personal property, can no longer exist as legal estates, but must always be equitable. Moreover, it is no longer possible to have a future *legal* estate in freeholds. **Assimilation in 1926.**

(*b*) **Descent on Intestacy.** Perhaps the most striking difference between realty and personalty in 1925 lay in the rules that regulated their descent or distribution upon the death of **Realty and personalty subject to different intestacy rules.**

---

[1] *Leventhorpe* v. *Ashbie* (1635), 1 Roll. Abr. 831.
[2] L.P.A. s. 130 (1) ; *infra*, p. 255.
[3] *Ibid.*, s. 1 (1), (2), (3), *infra*, p. 97.

the owner intestate. The old canons of descent, based upon feudal doctrines as amended by statute, governed the descent of fee simple and entailed estates, while the Statutes of Distribution contained a different set of rules prescribing what relatives were entitled to share the leaseholds and personal chattels of the deceased. Both these systems, together with various customary modes of descent, have been abolished and new distributive rules have been introduced which apply to both real and personal property.[1] The old canons of descent have, however, been retained for entailed interests.

(*c*) **The Order in which Assets were applied in payment of debts.** It is essential that definite rules shall prescribe the order in which the beneficiaries under a will must be deprived of their interests for the benefit of the unpaid creditors of the testator. The old rules on this matter represented another difference between real and personal property, for they required the exhaustion of the general personal estate before recourse was had to the realty. The old rules have now been replaced by fresh statutory provisions which, from this point of view, have put realty and personalty on the same footing.[2]

(*d*) **The Necessity for Words of Limitation.** A conveyance which was intended to pass the whole fee simple had under the old law to contain technical words of limitation, namely, to A. *and his heirs* or to A. *in fee simple*, otherwise it operated to pass only a life estate. Such words were not necessary in the case of a transfer of leaseholds ; a simple grant to A., without more, was sufficient to transfer the whole interest of the grantor. Assimilation on this point, however, was effected by the Law of Property Act 1925,[3] which provides that a conveyance of freehold land without words of limitation shall pass the whole interest held by the grantor unless a contrary intention appears in the conveyance.

(*e*) **The Method of creating Legal Mortgages.** The method of creating a legal mortgage of the fee simple before 1926 was by a conveyance of the legal fee simple to the mortgagee with a proviso that he should re-convey the estate upon repayment of the loan ; but where the subject-matter of the mortgage was a leasehold interest, the almost universal practice was for the mortgagor to grant a sub-lease of the property to the mortgagee.

---

[1] A.E.A. 1925, ss. 45, 46, as amended by I.E.A. 1952 and Family Provision Act 1966 ; *infra*, pp. 871 *et seq.*
[2] *Ibid.*, s. 34 (3) ; 1st Sched., Part II ; *infra*, pp. 824 *et seq.*
[3] S. 60 (1) ; *infra*, p. 153.

This particular difference between freeholds and leaseholds has now disappeared, for the practice of conveying the fee simple is forbidden, and it is enacted that a legal mortgage of freeholds must be made by the grant of a lease or its equivalent.[1]

(f) The Application of the Rule in Dearle v. Hall. If successive assignments or mortgages of an *equitable* interest in property were made before 1926, the order in which the several assignees or mortgagees were entitled to repayment out of the property depended upon the nature of the property. If it was land, whether freehold or leasehold, they ranked for payment according to the order of time in which they had taken their assignment or mortgage; but if it was pure personalty, the rule in *Dearle* v. *Hall* [2] applied, and the priorities were governed by the order of time in which the assignments or mortgages had been notified to the trustees of the personalty. This rule now applies to equitable interests in land, so that a later assignee who is the first to notify the estate owner of the land affected ranks prior to an earlier assignment of which he had no notice when he took his own assignment.[3]

Rule in Dearle v. Hall.

Conclusion. The above review of those differences between realty and personalty that were eradicated by the legislation of 1925 shows that the law relating to the two forms of property has been assimilated as far as is possible. Certain differences must, of course, inevitably persist. For instance, easements and profits may subsist in land, but not in pure personalty ; time under the Limitation Act varies according as the subject-matter is realty or personalty ; the forms of alienation are different ; so is the procedure on alienation, for investigation of title, though not usual in the case of personalty, is essential upon the transfer of an interest in land ; but it would seem that most of the divergences must always in the nature of things continue to exist, since they result inevitably from the physical difference between the two forms of property.

Remaining differences between realty and personalty.

(C) The Abolition of Certain Anachronisms

A subsidiary part of the simplification of land transfer was the abolition of certain real property rules and doctrines which, though they had originally been introduced to preserve principles of importance in feudal days, were nothing more than obstructive anachronisms in 1925. The abolitions and alterations of this

Anachronisms abolished.

---

[1] *Infra*, pp. 642 *et seq.*
[2] *Dearle* v. *Hall* (1828), 3 Russ. 1.
[3] L.P.A. 1925, s. 137 ; *infra*, pp. 711 *et seq.*

character effected by the various Acts will be described later, and we shall therefore content ourselves for the moment with a mere enumeration of those that are the most important.

(i) The abolition of the rule in *Shelley's Case*.[1]

(ii) The indirect abolition of the old contingent remainder rules.[2]

(iii) The abolition of the rule in *Whitby* v. *Mitchell*.[3]

(iv) The almost complete abolition of the old canons of descent.[4]

(v) The final abolition of the doctrine of *Dumpor's Case* so far as it related to leases.[5]

(vi) The reversal of the rule that husband and wife were not always two persons for the purposes of the acquisition of land.[6]

(vii) The abolition of special occupancy.[7]

(2) SIMPLIFICATION OF CONVEYANCING : THE CULT OF THE ESTATE OWNER

(A) Unregistered Conveyancing

Under the system of unregistered conveyancing, a purchaser must make inquiries and bear the responsibility of satisfying himself on two matters—first, that the vendor is entitled to convey the estate which he has contracted to sell, secondly, that there are no incumbrances in favour of third parties that will continue to affect the land after the conveyance.

The legislation of 1925 made no fundamental alteration in the practice relating to the former matter, but devoted its main attention to the question of incumbrances. In the normal case there will be no undisclosed incumbrances, but nevertheless the doctrine of constructive notice exists and a purchaser dare not do otherwise than institute an expensive inquiry. His danger is obvious. Land is different from such subjects of ownership as goods, since more often than not it is affected by rights vested in parties other than the ostensible owner.

Peter may appear to be absolute unincumbered tenant in fee simple of Blackacre, but investigation may disclose that James has an easement of way over the land, that John is

---

[1] *Infra*, p. 252.
[3] *Infra*, pp. 314–5 ; 317–8.
[5] *Infra*, pp. 425–6.
[7] *Infra*, p. 266, note 1.

[2] *Infra*, p. 310.
[4] *Infra*, pp. 866–7.
[6] *Infra*, pp. 923–4.

entitled to a yearly rentcharge of £50 out of it, that Matthew has a right to prevent the erection of buildings upon it, or that Paul, having lent £500 to Peter, has taken an equitable charge upon Blackacre as security for repayment of the loan.

The power to create rights of this description in favour of third parties, and enforceable primarily against the land itself rather than against its owner, is a valuable, in fact an inevitable, feature of our social life. For the sake of brevity, we will describe them in future as third party rights.

In some cases (as for instance in the case of easements, profits and restrictive covenants), third party rights are a necessary local complement of landownership ; in others they originate in the financial requirements of owners ; while in others (as for instance in the rights given to children by a settlement), they are due to the social traditions of family life. They may be conveniently divided into two classes— *Classification of third party rights.*

first, those arising either under a settlement or a trust for sale, as for instance financial provisions made for children by a marriage settlement ;

secondly, those arising under some other transaction connected with the landowner's activities as a landowner or business man. Examples of this second class are easements, profits, restrictive covenants, estate contracts, mortgages, annuities, rentcharges, pending actions and deeds of arrangement.

But whatever their origin or character, it is obvious that the possibility of their existence and the risk that they may continue to bind the land after its sale, must cause a purchaser to walk warily and with no undue haste.

" None of these things," says an expert writer, referring to a number of liabilities not imposed by deed, such as orders of court, pending actions, rent charges and easements, " may appear in the abstract of title presented by a vendor to a purchaser, yet they may cause the purchaser to be ejected from the land he has paid for, or, if he remains in possession, thrust payments or other liabilities on him, of which had he known, he would not have bought the land." [1]

The extent to which a purchaser is affected by them depends upon the fundamental distinction between the legal and the equitable estate.[2] A purchaser for value of the legal fee simple which is subject to third party rights is absolutely bound by them if they amount to legal estates or interests, the question of his actual knowledge or ignorance of their existence being irrelevant. *Extent to which purchaser bound by third party rights.*

---

[1] (1925), 41 *L. Q. R.* (J. S. Stewart Wallace), pp. 176–7.
[2] *Supra,* pp. 61 *et seq.*

On the other hand, he is not bound by rights that are merely equitable in nature, unless he has actual or constructive notice of their existence. Thus:

> An easement or a profit in perpetuity, a rentcharge or a lease for a definite number of years will be enforceable against an innocent purchaser because each is a legal interest, *i.e.* a right *in rem* enforceable against the whole world. On the other hand, if a fee simple owner has made an estate contract with X. (*e.g.* has agreed to grant him a lease or to sell him the legal fee simple), or if he has subjected the land to a restrictive covenant in favour of Y. (as for instance by covenanting that he will erect no business premises), the rights thus vested in X. and Y. since they are merely equitable in nature, will not bind a subsequent purchaser who takes a conveyance of the legal estate from the fee simple owner, unless he is affected with notice.

The outstanding facts then, are that a purchaser has more to fear from legal than from equitable third party rights, and conversely that the third party himself is less secure with an equitable than a legal right.

Outline of statutory alterations in 1925.

The following is a bare sketch of how the legislation attempted to simplify the problem of third party rights.

1. It drastically curtailed the category of legal estates and legal third party rights. The result is that under the modern law most of the latter are equitable.

2. It made the legal estate the basis of conveyancing. The principal effect of this is that the legal estate can be conveyed only by its owner, not as frequently occurred under the former law by a person[1] who had no estate in the land at all.

3. The existing system by which in certain circumstances the conveyance of a legal estate by way of sale overreached equitable third party rights, *i.e.* encumbered the purchase money instead of the land with their payment and relieved the purchaser of the duty to investigate them, was extended. In the result,

> (a) these rights are cleared off the land altogether if they can equally well be satisfied out of the purchase money ; but

> (b) if this is not possible, then they can be registered as *land charges* in a public register, so that their owners are protected and a purchaser is warned.

This sketch now requires a little elaboration.

---

[1] *Supra*, p. 79.

1. **Reduction in the number of Legal Estates.** Before 1926 any recognized interest in land, regarded quantitatively, might be either legal or equitable. The Law of Property Act 1925, however, reduces the possible legal estates to the fee simple absolute in possession in the case of freeholds, and the term of years absolute in the case of leaseholds.

The person in whom such an estate is vested is called the *estate owner*. All other estates, interests and charges in or over the land can exist only as equitable interests,[1] with the exception of those interests permitted to exist at law by section 1 (2) of the Act.[2]

In the case of freeholds, for instance, the

determinable fee simple,[3]
entailed interest,[4]
life interest,[5]
future interest of whatever size,[6]

can subsist only in equity, not at law. Each one must be created behind a trust, *i.e.* the legal estate in the land affected must be held by an *estate owner* whose function it is to give effect to the equitable interest. The very terminology, indeed, is changed. The correct expression now, for instance, is " entailed interest " not " estate tail," and " life interest " instead of " life estate."

Section 1 of the Law of Property Act runs as follows :

(1) The only estates in land which are capable of subsisting or of being conveyed or created at law are—

(a) An estate in fee simple absolute in possession ;

(b) A term of years absolute.

(2) The only interests or charges in or over land which are capable of subsisting or of being conveyed or created at law are—

(a) An easement, right, or privilege in or over land for an interest equivalent to an estate in fee simple absolute in possession or a term of years absolute ;

(b) A rentcharge in possession issuing out of or charged on land being either perpetual or for a term of years absolute ;

(c) A charge by way of legal mortgage ;

(d) Land tax,[7] tithe rentcharge,[8] and any other similar charge on land which is not created by an instrument ;

(e) Rights of entry exercisable over or in respect of a legal term of years absolute, or annexed, for any purpose, to a legal rentcharge.

(3) All other estates, interests, and charges in or over land take effect as equitable interests.

---

[1] S. 1 (1), (2), (3).   [2] *Infra.*   [3] *Infra*, p. 363.
[4] *Infra*, p. 237.   [5] *Infra*, p. 263.   [6] *Infra*, p. 310.
[7] Abolished by the Finance Act 1963, s. 73, Sched. 14, Pt. vi.
[8] Extinguished by the Tithe Act 1936, s. 48, Sched. 9 and replaced by a sixty years' redemption annuity payable to the Crown. This is a legal interest within the meaning of " any other similar charge . . . " of para. (d).

It will be observed that in referring in the first sub-section to *estates* and in the second to *interests* the Act invented a new terminology that depends upon the difference between a right to the land itself and a right to some claim against the land of another person.

To be entitled to a legal as distinct from an equitable interest in the land itself it is necessary to hold an estate, and the only estate that qualifies for this purpose is either the fee simple absolute in possession or the term of years absolute according as the subject-matter is freehold or leasehold.[1]

On the other hand, a claim against the land of another, if falling within the five items in sub-section (2) is termed an *interest* in that land, but to constitute a *legal* interest it must correspond in duration to one of the two legal estates. A person entitled in perpetuity or for 21 years to an easement, such as a right of way over Blackacre, owns a legal interest in Blackacre. If he is entitled to it for life, he is a mere equitable owner.

Thus, the ancient doctrine of estates under which the fee simple, the entail and the life interest were recognized as estates at common law, has been drastically abridged. There is only the one freehold estate at law—the fee simple absolute in possession. The doctrine, however, has only been " as it were, pushed back into equity"[2] in the sense that the interests that were formerly estates at law still subsist with equal vigour as equitable interests.

Powers of appointment now equitable.

2. **The Legal Estate as the Basis of Conveyancing.** This may be illustrated by two observations. First, we have seen that it was a common practice before 1926 to limit land to A. and B. in fee simple to such uses as X. might appoint, with the result that if X., who had no proprietary interest in the land, " appointed " to the use of Y. and his heirs, A. and B. thereupon stood seised to the use of Y. and he took a *legal* fee simple under the Statute of Uses.[3] This is no longer possible. The Statute of Uses has been repealed[4] and, though land may still be limited to A. and B. upon such trusts as X. shall appoint, this merely empowers X. to dispose of the equitable interest. With very few exceptions powers are now equitable.[5]

Title to legal estate alone investigated.

Secondly, if a legal estate that is held in trust for beneficiaries is offered for sale, the purchaser's sole concern in the normal case is to trace the title of the vendors to the legal estate. He is

[1] Rivington, *Law of Property in Land* (5th Edn.), p. 24.
[2] Lawson, *Rational Strength of English Law*, p. 94.
[3] *Supra*, p. 74.
[4] L.P.A. 1922, s. 207, Sched. 7.
[5] *Infra*, pp. 281.

entirely unaffected by the beneficial interests, for these are over-reached and are no longer binding on the land once the legal estate has been conveyed.[1]

3. **Overreaching and Investigation of Title.** The policy of freeing the title to the legal estate from beneficial interests to which it may be subject, had begun in 1882 in the case of settled land. This was continued by the 1925 legislation. Furthermore the conveyancing machinery was greatly simplified. Before 1926 a settlement was created by a single deed which conferred legal estates and interests upon the successive beneficiaries, so that for instance the husband acquired a legal estate for life and the eldest son a legal estate tail.[2] When the tenant for life exercised, say, his statutory power of sale under the Settled Land Act 1882, his conveyance did, indeed, overreach these legal interests, but, as we have seen, the conveyancing difficulties were not in-considerable.[3] These derived mainly from the fact that, since the fee simple was not vested in the tenant for life, his right to convey it rested solely upon the statutory powers. The whole settlement required investigation, and before the purchaser was relieved from liability in respect of the beneficial limitations, it was incumbent upon him to make sure that the statutory conditions for the exercise of the power had been satisfied.

Former difficulties attending conveyance of settled land.

These difficulties, however, were removed by the Settled Land Act 1925. Owing to the reduction in the number of legal estates, the limited and beneficial interests arising under a settle-ment are now necessarily equitable, and the legal fee simple out of which they have been carved must, in accordance with the statutory provisions, be vested in the first tenant for life and be transferred to each subsequent tenant for life as and when he becomes entitled to possession.[4]

Difficulties removed in 1925.

Thus the tenant for life occupies a dual position. Although he is a mere tenant for life as regards beneficial enjoyment, he is the owner of the legal fee simple for conveyancing purposes. This means that within the scope of his statutory powers he can dispose of the legal estate, whether it be the fee simple absolute in possession or the term of years absolute, so as to pass to the purchaser a title free from the rights under the settlement ; but it does not mean that he becomes entitled to the capital money arising from the transaction. It is, in fact, a condition of the purchaser's immunity that the money should be paid to the trustees.

Dual position of tenant for life.

---

[1] *Infra*, pp. 792–3, 796–7.
[2] These interests could also be equitable. After the re-introduction of the use in the form of the trust (*supra*, pp. 56–59) it was, of course, possible to create a strict settlement by the alternative method of a grant unto and to the use of trustees to hold the legal estate upon the requisite trusts, in which case the beneficiaries would be entitled to equitable interests.
[3] *Supra*, pp. 79–81.
[4] *Infra*, pp. 170–4 ; 789–90.

Modern method of creating a settlement.

In order to emphasize this separation of the legal estate from the beneficial and equitable interests and to facilitate conveyancing, a new method of creating a settlement, framed on the pattern of the trust for sale, was introduced by the Settled Land Act 1925. Every settlement *inter vivos* must now be made by two deeds. One (the *vesting deed*) vests the legal fee simple in the tenant for life, describes the property and names the trustees ; the other (the *trust instrument*) declares the beneficial interests of the tenant for life and the other persons entitled under the settlement.[1]

Over-reaching of equitable interests.

The effect of a conveyance made by the tenant for life in his capacity as estate owner is to overreach the equitable interests of the beneficiaries, *i.e.* it clears them off the title to the legal fee simple and converts them into equivalent interests in the purchase money. Their fate is of no concern to the purchaser, provided that he pays the purchase money to the trustees, not to the tenant for life. His sole object is to investigate the title to the *legal* estate. He must, therefore, trace that title down to the first vesting deed, *i.e.* he must require the vendor to show that the person who purported to vest the legal estate in the first tenant for life was in fact entitled to do so. He does not see, nor in general may he demand to see, the trust instrument. That instrument is the sole charter of the beneficiaries. The rights that it grants to the beneficiaries are still intact, still secure, but they are now transferred to the purchase money. The whole operation set in motion upon a conveyance by the tenant for life is an illustration of what is called the *curtain* principle. The vesting deed is, as it were, a curtain that masks the equitable interests.[2]

Rights incapable of attaching to money protected by registration.

In the case, then, of a trust for sale and strict settlement, the beneficial interests are cleared altogether off the title to the legal estate and, since they are transferred to the purchase money, no harm is done to their owners. Family rights and incumbrances in the nature of pecuniary claims do not impede a conveyance of the legal estate. There are, however, other equitable third party rights to which the doctrine of overreaching is necessarily inapplicable, since they are incapable of being attached to money. For instance, an estate contract or a restrictive covenant of which a purchaser has had notice must continue to affect the land after conveyance to him of the legal estate. In such cases the obvious method of simplifying the task of the purchaser and at the same time of protecting the equitable owner is to require rights of this nature to be publicly recorded if they are to remain binding against purchasers. This was the policy adopted by the legislature in 1925.

---

[1] S.L.A. 1925, s. 4 ; *infra*, pp. 170–4. In the case of a settlement made by a testator, the legal estate devolves upon his executors who hold it upon trust to convey it to the tenant for life. The will itself constitutes the trust instrument and the executors make a *vesting assent*, corresponding to the vesting deed, in favour of the tenant for life ; *infra*, p. 790.

[2] For a more detailed account of these matters, see *infra*, pp. 165 *et seq.*

Legislation enabling rights against land to be registered has long been in force, but it has appeared in successive and somewhat slow stages. Thus life annuities charged upon land were made registrable as far back as 1777, and the system was extended to judgments in 1838, to pending land actions in 1839, to deeds of arrangement in 1887, and to what are called land charges in 1888. These several topics are the subject of full discussion later,[1] but what should be observed at once is that a great extension of the system of registration was made by the Land Charges Act 1925. Without going into details, it may be said that practically all equitable rights against land, except those which arise under a trust for sale or a settlement, may be entered in one of the registers kept at the Land Charges Department of the Land Registry in Plymouth. Registration of a registrable right constitutes notice of it to the whole world ; failure to register it carries the penalty that it is void against a purchaser[2] ; and this is so even if the purchaser has actual notice of the unregistered right. Therefore in the case of a third party right that falls within the provisions of the Act, all now turns on registration ; its owner can secure complete protection for himself by registration, while a purchaser need do no more than search at the Land Registry to discover whether the land is incumbered or not. An examination of section 2 (2) of the Land Charges Act 1972[3] will show that most of the charges which are registrable are equitable. The important exception is the puisne mortgage, that is to say, any legal mortgage not being a mortgage protected by a deposit of documents relating to the legal estate affected.[4] A puisne mortgage, although a legal interest, does not therefore bind a purchaser for value unless registered. It is made registrable, as will be seen later, in order to comply with the post 1925 scheme for the priority of mortgages.[5]

By way of summary, it may be said, then, that one of the principal objects of the 1925 legislation was to simplify and clear the title to the legal fee simple, which is the estate that the majority of purchasers wish to obtain. As a result of the legislation the general position is now as follows :

The only legal freehold estate in Blackacre is the fee simple absolute in possession.

Extension of system of registration.

Summary of alterations made in 1925.

---

[1] *Infra*, pp. 737 *et seq.*
[2] Some unregistered charges are void against a purchaser for value of any estate, legal or equitable ; others are void only against a purchaser of a legal estate for money or money's worth. L.C.A. 1972, s. 4 (5), (6), *infra*, p. 743.
[3] L.C.A. 1925 has been replaced by L.C.A. 1972 and Local Land Charges Act 1975.
[4] Class C (i), *infra*, p. 741.
[5] *Infra*, p. 698. The Matrimonial Homes Act 1967 added a new Class F land charge which does not owe its origin to equity or to common law. *Infra*, p. 233.

In all cases this will be vested in a definite person or body of persons called the *estate owner*.

According to the circumstances the estate owner will be one of the following :

A beneficial owner entitled in his own right.
Trustees for sale.
The tenant for life or " statutory owners " [1] in the case of settled land.
Personal representatives.
A mortgagor. [2]
A bare trustee. [3]

A conveyance of the legal fee simple must be made by or in the name of the estate owner, not by anybody else. Thus the exercise of a power of appointment can no longer affect the legal estate, [4] and in the case of a settlement the tenant for life conveys the legal fee simple because the Settled Land Act 1925 requires that it shall be vested in him, not as formerly because he was statutorily entitled to convey what he had not got. The conveyance of a legal fee simple that is subject to equitable third party rights is considerably simplified :

Rights which arise under a settlement or a trust for sale continue to be overreached by the conveyance[5] and cleared off the title, for no injury is done to their owners by converting them into rights against the purchase money.

If the rights do not arise in that way but are nevertheless convertible into rights against the money, the estate owner may clear them off the title by creating a settlement or a trust for sale for that particular purpose, called an *ad hoc* settlement or an *ad hoc* trust for sale. [6]

If the rights do not arise under a settlement or a trust for sale and are not convertible into money rights, such as an estate contract or a restrictive covenant, their continued enforcement depends in general on their registration as land charges.

---

[1] These are the persons who take the legal fee simple in settled land when there is no person entitled to take it as tenant for life, *infra*, p. 176.

[2] In a mortgage of a legal fee simple, the mortgagor remains the estate owner of the legal fee simple, but nevertheless the mortgagee is entitled by virtue of his power of sale to convey it to a purchaser.

[3] A bare or naked trustee is one who holds property for the absolute benefit of a beneficiary of full age, and who himself has no beneficial interest in the property and no duty except to transfer it to its owner ; *Christie* v. *Ovington* (1875), 1 Ch. D. 279. See Halsbury's *Laws of England* (3rd Edn.), vol. 38. para. 1495 ; Pettit, *Equity and the Law of Trusts* (3rd Edn.), pp. 47–8.

[4] Save in a few exceptional cases, *infra*, pp. 280–1.

[5] *Supra*, p. 99.

[6] *Infra*, pp. 797–9.

The extension of this system of registration of land charges has dramatically curtailed the operation of the doctrine of notice. In the case of registrable third party rights, their enforceability no longer depends on the state of the purchaser's mind ; it is the state of the register which is crucial.

The old rules concerning notice,[1] however, continue to apply to a residual category of equitable third party rights which are neither overreachable nor registrable. Here a purchaser is bound unless he is a bona fide purchaser of the legal estate for value without actual or constructive notice. This category is necessarily limited, because most equitable third party rights are in practice susceptible to overreaching or registration. Certain situations where the old rules concerning notice continue to apply were contemplated by the draftsmen of the 1925 legislation, for instance, a restrictive covenant entered into before 1926.[2] But in recent years the old rules have been applied in a number of situations which were presumably not foreseen.[3]

Old rules concerning notice may still apply.

One aspect of the clear-cut distinction between the legal estate and the equitable interest deserves attention. Land is employed to satisfy at least two requirements, one affecting the family of its owner, the other affecting its commercial exploitation. It must be subject to rules that facilitate its employment as a continuing source of income for the present and future members of a family, but at the same time it must be under effective administration and above all be readily transferable by way of sale, lease, mortgage and similar transactions if good estate management so demands. These two requirements, at first sight contradictory, have been reconciled by English law. The estate owner, despite the existence of family trusts, is given full powers of management and disposal in respect of the land, but he holds them as trustee for such equitable beneficiaries as may exist. In this way the well-being of the land, the needs of the market and the prosperity of the family are harmonized.[4]

Reconciliation of family and commercial needs.

(B) Registered Conveyancing[5]

So far we have discussed the changes made by the 1925 legislation which were intended to simplify the law of real property

---

[1] *Supra,* pp. 63–67.   [2] *Infra,* p. 605.

[3] *Ives (E. R.) Investment, Ltd.* v. *High,* [1967] 2 Q. B. 379 ; [1967] 1 All E. R. 504 ; M. & B. p. 478 (licence by estoppel), *infra,* p. 586 ; *Poster* v. *Slough Estates,* [1968] 1 W. L. R. 1515 ; [1968] 3 All E. R. 257 ; M. & B. p. 504 (right of entry to remove a fixture on termination of lease), *infra,* p. 527 ; *Caunce* v. *Caunce,* [1969] 1 W. L. R. 286 ; [1967] 1 All E. R. 722 ; M. & B. p. 221, *infra,* p. 796 (beneficial interest of wife who had contributed towards purchase price) ; *Shiloh Spinners, Ltd.* v. *Harding,* [1973] A. C. 691, especially at pp. 720–721 *per* Lord WILBERFORCE ; [1973] 1 All E. R. 90 ; M. & B. p. 34 (equitable right of re-entry on breach of covenant).

[4] Lawson, *Rational Strength of English Law,* pp. 91–2.

[5] The authoritative account is Ruoff and Roper (prior and present Chief Land Registrars respectively), *Law and Practice of Registered Conveyancing*

within the framework of the system of unregistered conveyancing. The intention was that the unregistered system should be replaced by a simplified system of registered conveyancing. This is now in the process of being extended on a compulsory basis over the **Extension** whole of England and Wales, a process which will be completed **of** as rapidly as available resources permit.[1] The system now **registered** handles about 65% of all conveyancing.
con-
veyancing.
Registration of title was introduced into England as long ago as 1862.[2] At first it was voluntary and then in 1897 provision was made to extend it to areas to be defined from time to time by Orders in Council.[3] The revised system is contained in the Land Registration Acts 1925 to 1971[4] which are supplemented by the Land Registration Rules 1925 as amended by subsequent rules.[5] An area is declared to be an area of compulsory registration by Order in Council, and responsibility for extension is vested in the central government.[6] Until January 13th, 1967 it was possible for any title to land in England and Wales to be registered voluntarily, but this practice was then suspended so as to concentrate on the extension of compulsory registration to all built-up areas.[7]

Contrast The object of the system is to replace the cumbrous method of **with** unregistered conveyancing by one whereby a registered title is **unregistered**
conveyanc-
ing.

(3rd Edn., 1972). See also Ruoff, *Concise Land Registration Practice* (2nd Edn., 1967) ; Ruoff, *Land Registration Forms* (2nd Edn., 1973) ; *Encyclopaedia of Forms and Precedents* (4th Edn., 1970), vol. xvii. pp. 112–270 (R. B. Roper). Wolstenholme and Cherry, *Conveyancing Statutes* (13th Edn., 1972), vol. 6. Barnsley, *Conveyancing Law and Practice* (1973), chaps. 2, 3, 4, 12, 16.   Hayton, *Registered Land* (1973).   Wontner's *Guide to Land Registry Practice* (12th Edn., 1975).   The Land Registry issues Practice Notes in conjunction with the Law Society (1972), and the Chief Land Registrar an Annual Report on H.M. Land Registry.   The Law Commission is revising registered conveyancing.   It has so far published three Working papers ; No. 32 (leaseholds), No. 37 (overriding interests) and No. 45 (identity and boundaries ; and rectification and indemnity).   And a fourth is promised on methods of protection of interests in land, including mortgages and charges.   Law Com. No. 64, Ninth Annual Report 1973–1974, para. 12.
   [1] (1976) 120 Sol. Jo. 61.   For compulsory registration areas see Registration of Title Order (S.I. 1975, No. 160) ; M. & B. p. 88.   There were 4,670,990 separate titles on the register at March 31st, 1975.   Report for 1974–1975, para. 2.
   [2] Land Registry Act 1862.
   [3] Registered conveyancing must be distinguished from the system of registration of assurances practised in parts of Yorkshire which merely recorded conveyances and devises in a public register.   These deeds registries are now closed.   L.P.A. 1969, ss. 16–22.
   [4] *I.e.* L.R.A. 1925, 1936, 1966 and Land Registration and Land Charges Act 1971, Parts I and II.
   [5] See L.R.R. 1956, 1964 and 1967 ; L.R. (Matrimonial Homes) R. 1967, L.R. (Official Searches) R. 1969, L.R. (Powers of Attorney) R. 1971; L.R. Fee Orders 1970, 1971 and 1975 ; L.R. (Souvenir Land) R. 1972, and L.R. (Capital Transfer Tax) R. 1975.
   [6] L.R.A. 1925, ss. 120–125 as amended by L.R.A. 1936, s. 1 and L.R.A. 1966, s. 1 (1).   Until 1966 this was done on the application of the county or county borough concerned.
   [7] L.R.A. 1966, s. 1 (2).   Voluntary registration is still possible in classes of cases specified by the Registrar *e.g.* certain large building developments, or certain cases of lost or destroyed deeds.   See (1967), 31 Conv. (N.S.) 7 and Ruoff and Roper, pp. 204–6 ; Practice Leaflet No. 12.

guaranteed by the state. We have seen that the conveyancing of unregistered land depends upon the production by a vendor of a series of documents which recount previous transactions affecting the land and demonstrate to a purchaser the ability of a vendor to convey what he has agreed to convey. " Title " to the interest to be conveyed is thus something deduced from evidence. It has to be proved afresh each time a disposition of land is made. The conveyancing of registered land is different in principle and in practice. Once the title to land is registered, its past history is irrelevant. The title thenceforth is guaranteed by the state, and a purchaser can do no other than rely on it. " Title " has now become something more than evidence. In a sense, it is itself the subject matter of the conveyance. Transfer of land becomes the substitution of one person's name for another's in a registry. That transfer necessarily shifts the whole title registered in the former proprietor's name.

Registered conveyancing is not, however, a new system of land law. It is based on the familiar concepts of estates and interests, settlements, leases, mortgages, covenants etc., and is an integral part of the 1925 Legislation. As we have seen, the only two legal estates which can exist at law are the fee simple absolute in possession and the term of years absolute,[1] and these are the only two legal estates which can be registered under separate titles.[2] Not all leases are so registrable, but the general effect of the legislation is that only leases with more than 21 years to run can be registered.[3] Other interests are dealt with in one of two ways

Based on existing land law.

(*a*) as overriding interests, in which case they bind a registered proprietor and his transferees whether or not they are entered on the register.[4]

(*b*) as minor interests, in which case they must be entered on the register of the land affected if they are not to be overridden by a subsequent registered disposition of the land for value.[5]

Registration and Entry on Register. It is important to grasp the distinction between interests which may be *registered* and interests which may be *entered on the register*. The former

Distinction between registration and entry.

---

[1] *Supra*, p. 97.
[2] L.R.A. 1925, s. 2 (1). For the suggestion that the Act creates a statutory estate, distinct from the fee simple or term of years at common law, see *infra*, p. 154. Legal interests which may be registered in addition to those in corporeal land, are those in manors, mines and minerals, advowsons and rents. L.R.R. 1925, r. 50. But legal easements may only be registered as appurtenant to the registered title of the dominant tenement. L.R.R. 1925, r. 257. *Infra*, p. 586. In practice, rents mean rent charges only. Undivided shares cannot be registered.
[3] *Ibid.*, s. 8. The question as to when a lease must be registered and when it may be registered is complex and is discussed, *infra*, pp. 509 *et seq.*
[4] *Infra*, p. 109.   [5] *Infra*, pp. 109–10.

are confined to the two legal estates,[1] the titles to which are substantively registered under their own separate title numbers. Minor interests, as the name implies, are interests lesser than registered interests and may be protected by the entry of a notice, caution, inhibition, or restriction[2] on the register of the title affected. The entry is made on the proprietorship or charges register[3] of that title, and operates by way of an incumbrance against it. It follows too that in the case of a strict settlement, the tenant for life, and, in the case of a trust for sale, the trustees for sale, will be registered proprietors, and, as will be seen,[4] warning is given to a purchaser by the entry of a restriction on the registered title that the settlement or trust for sale exists, without however telling him what the individual beneficial interests are. Thus the doctrine of overreaching applies to the interests of the beneficiaries and the curtain principle is retained. " References to trusts shall, so far as is possible, be excluded from the register."[5] Registered conveyancing is thus not a new system of land law. It is, however, more than just a new system of conveyancing, and, as we shall see, has important effects on the substance of the land law.

Nature of powers and title under the Act.

The Land Registration Act 1925 lays down precise rules for dealings in the land, and attempts an enumeration of the powers of an owner under the Act.[6]

" The powers of disposition possessed by a registered proprietor are those expressly conferred on him by the Land Registration Act, 1925, and he has no others."[7]

This rule affects not only the land itself, but also the creation of other rights over it, such as easements and mortgages. But there remains a residual power[8] to negotiate and bring into existence equitable rights,[9] though these are minor interests and need protection through entry on the register. Obviously, then, a rule of fundamental importance is that the legal title can be affected only by observing the proper requirements.

In order to be effectual at law a disposition of registered land must be completed by registration. Thus a transfer for value of registered freehold or leasehold land must be completed by the Registrar entering on the register the transferee as the registered proprietor and until he has done this the transferor is deemed to

---

[1] *Supra.*   [2] *Infra*, pp. 779 *et seq.*
[3] *Infra*, p. 108.   [4] *Infra*, pp. 196, 203.
[5] L.R.A. 1925, s. 74 ; *cf.* s. 88 (1) and *Abigail* v. *Lapin*, [1934] A. C. 491, at p. 500.
[6] *Ibid.*, ss. 18, 21, 25, 40, 69 (4), 101, 106, 107, 109 ; L.R.R. 1925, r. 74.
[7] Ruoff and Roper, p. 126.
[8] L.R.A. 1925, ss. 101, 107. A contract of sale is an obvious example.
[9] Leases for 21 years or less, although legal estates, cannot be registered substantively, and are usually overriding interests not requiring protection on the register. *Infra*, p. 509.

remain the proprietor.[1] As soon as he has done this, however, the legal estate will pass at once to the transferee.[2]

Registration of a title need not be effected immediately the area in which it lies is made an area of compulsory registration. Title to freehold land must be registered on its first *sale* after the relevant date, while for registrable leaseholds the rule is that every *grant* of a leasehold for forty years or more, and every assignment on *sale* of a lease with forty or more years still to run, must be registered.[3] If registration is not applied for within two months,[4] the legal estate will not be regarded as vesting in the transferee.[5]

First registration.

The Register.[6] The register is divided into three parts, a property register, a proprietorship register, and a charges register.[7] It was intended that the register should " mirror " the title, though, as we shall see, it does so in only a qualified manner. The register is kept on a card index system, and each of its three parts relating to any given title is filed on a separate card or part of a card. The register is a register of title, so that where there is more than one legal title subsisting in one piece of land (the obvious case is that of a registered reversion subject to a registered lease) there will be one register for each title. A copy of the various entries on the register and of the filed plan of the title, called a Land Certificate,[8] is given to the registered proprietor of a title, and can be retained by him or deposited in the registry. It is not the certificate but the register retained in the registry which is the title.

Form of the register.

The property register describes and identifies the land, and the

Property register.

---

[1] L.R.A. 1925, ss. 19 (1), 22 (1). A prescribed form must be used L.R.R. 1925 rr. 98, 115. In practice the use of forms prescribed by r. 98 for freeholds is accepted by the Land Registry in the case of leasehold titles also.

[2] *Ibid.*, ss. 20 (1), 23 (1) as amended by F. A. 1975, s. 52, Sched. 12, para. 5, which set out in detail what appurtenances pass to the transferee, and also the matters subject to which his title subsists. See also L.R.R. 1925, r. 251.

[3] Compulsory registration does not extend to any area of land declared by the Registrar to be subject to a souvenir land scheme. Land Registration and Land Charges Act 1971, s. 4 ; L.R. (Souvenir Land) R. 1972 (S.I. 1972, No. 985). See (1971) 35 Conv. (N.S.) 390, at p. 397 (T. B. F. Ruoff and P. Meehan).

[4] This may be extended on application being made to the Registrar or to the Court of Appeal.

[5] L.R.A. 1925, s. 123. For the consequences of failure to register see Ruoff and Roper, pp. 197–9. Section 123 applies only to corporeal land, so that rentcharges are not thereby required to be registered. However, if land out of which a perpetual or terminable rentcharge is granted is itself registered, the title to the rentcharge must also be substantively registered, even in a voluntary area, and no matter how short the term of a terminable rentcharge. See Ruoff, *Rentcharges in Registered Conveyancing*, (1960), chaps. 1 and 2. *Infra*, p. 634.

[6] Registers of title are kept at ten District Registries. L.R. (District Registries) (No. 2) Order 1974 (S.I. 1974, No. 1304). The Headquarters of the Land Registry is at Lincoln's Inn Fields, London.

[7] L.R.R. 1925, r. 2. The register is not as a general rule open to the public L.R.A. 1925, s. 112 ; L.R.R. 1925, rr. 12, 287, 288 ; but it is always possible to discover whether or not a particular plot of land has been registered, rr. 12, 286. See Law Commission Working Paper No. 32 (1970), paras. 70–94.

[8] For a specimen Land Certificate, see M. & B. pp. 94–6.

interest in the land, which is the subject matter of the title, whether it be freehold or leasehold.   The interest must, as we have said already, be a legal one.   There may also appear on this register mention of specific benefits capable of subsisting as legal interests, such as legal easements, and the effect will be to create a registered title of the same nature in them.   There may also be a reference to other benefits, for instance to the freedom of the land from specific overriding interests.[1]

Proprietor-
ship and
changes
registers.

The proprietorship register states the nature of the title, *i.e.* absolute, good leasehold, possessory or qualified, the name, address and description of the proprietor, and also any entries that affect his right of disposing of the land.[2]   The charges register contains entries of incumbrances which burden the land, *e.g.* restrictive covenants and mortgages.

Classes of
title.

Classes of title.   There are four different classes of title, absolute title, good leasehold title (for a lessee only), possessory title, and, finally, qualified title, where an application for one of the other titles cannot be substantiated.

An absolute title is the most frequent.[3]   It cannot be registered until it has been approved by the Registrar,[4] who will carry out a full investigation of the title and who can compel the production of deeds and other evidence of title.[5]   An applicant who has a title which professional opinion would regard as good under unregistered conveyancing may expect to be registered with an absolute title, for the Registrar seems " to occupy the position of a willing but prudent purchaser ",[6] and is willing to overlook technical defects in a title if he is satisfied that there is no-one who can impugn it.   A title registered in this way is actually improved by registration.   The technical defect is cured, for no-one can subsequently raise it, save in the exceptional case of a rectification action.[7]

In the case of a leasehold,[8] an absolute title may be registered only if the Registrar approves not only the title to the lease-hold itself, but also the titles to the freehold and to any intermediate leaseholds that may exist.   If an absolute title to a lease-hold is registered, it vests the leasehold in the first proprietor subject to the same rights, interests and incumbrances as in the case

---

[1] L.R.R. 1925, r. 197.   *Re Dances Way, West Town, Hayling Island,* [1962] Ch. 490, [1962] 2 All E. R. 42.

[2] *Infra,* p. 780.

[3] For the inferior titles see *infra,* p. 768.

[4] L.R.A. 1925, s. 4.

[5] L.R.A. 1925, s. 15.

[6] Hargreaves in *Stephens' Commentaries* (21st Edn.), vol. i, p. 624.   See also Ruoff and Roper, at pp. 69–70 and (1963) *Law Society Gazette* 345, and (1954), 18 Conv. (N.S.) 130 (T. B. F. Ruoff).   The registrar relies on the language of L.R.A. 1925, s. 13, proviso (c).

[7] *Infra,* p. 770.

[8] The provisions relating to leaseholds are contained in L.R.A. 1925, ss. 8–12.   Lease includes underlease: L. R. A. s. 3 (x).   *Infra,* p. 509.

of a freehold registered with an absolute title, but subject to all implied and express covenants, obligations and liabilities incident to the registered land, including those arising under the lease.

Rectification and Indemnity. Once the title to the land has been registered, it vests in the registered proprietor,[1] and is thenceforth guaranteed by the state. But, as in unregistered conveyancing, the title is still less than absolute. Section 82 of the Land Registration Act 1925 gives to the court and to the Registrar wide powers to rectify the register where there is any error or omission. Section 83[2] however provides for an indemnity for those who have suffered loss in certain cases by reason of such rectification or by refusal of rectification. So the system of registered conveyancing is to some extent an insurance system.[3]

[margin: Rectification and Indemnity.]

Protection of Third Party Rights. We must now consider how third party rights are protected and how they affect a purchaser from the proprietor of registered land. We have seen that they are of two kinds, overriding interests and minor interests. The basic idea is simple enough. Some interests require protection on the register ; others do not. Overriding interests are those interests that bind a registered proprietor and his transferees, irrespective of entry on the register.[4] They are mostly listed in section 70 (1) of the Land Registration Act 1925. The main examples are profits à prendre, legal easements, leases for not more than 21 years, local land charges, rights acquired or being acquired under the Limitation Act and in paragraph (g) of section 70 (1), the

[margin: Protection of third party rights.]

[margin: Overriding interests.]

> " rights of every person in actual occupation of the land or in receipt of the rents and profits thereof, save where enquiry is made of such person and the rights are not disclosed."[5]

Minor interests, on the other hand, are interests needing protection by entry on the register.[6] Some of them are incapable of binding a purchaser even if protected by entry, but nevertheless affect the method of disposing of land. Thus, in the case of

[margin: Minor interests.]

---

[1] L.R.A. 1925, s. 69 (1).

[2] As amended by Land Registration Act 1966 and Part I of the Land Registration and Land Charges Act 1971.

[3] *Infra,* p. 770. The indemnity is payable by the Registrar out of moneys provided by Parliament. Land Registration and Land Charges Act 1971, s. 1. In 1974–1975, 60 claims resulted in the payment of £7,350, as against 40 claims amounting to £17,000 in 1973–1974. Report of Chief Land Registrar for 1974–1975, para. 20. Viewed against a fee revenue of about £13 million for the year 1974–1975, the sums paid by way of indemnity " fade almost into insignificance ".

[4] L.R.A. 1925, ss. 3 (xvi), 70. *Infra,* pp. 772 *et seq.*

[5] For a fuller discussion of this most important category see *infra,* p. 773.

[6] L.R.A. 1925, ss. 3 (xv), 59 (6) as amended by F. A. 1975, s. 52, Sched. 12, para. 5, 101. For the methods of protection see *infra,* pp. 779 *et seq.*

beneficial interests under a settlement or trust for sale that will be overreached on a sale of the land, a restriction will be entered on the proprietorship register indicating that the proprietor of the legal title is limited in his powers, but, if the terms of the restriction are complied with, a purchaser for value is not concerned with such beneficial interests.   But other minor interests such as restrictive covenants, equitable easements, legal and equitable rentcharges, and estate contracts do bind purchasers for valuable consideration, if protected by entry on the register.   Conversely, a purchaser will take free from them if they are not so protected by entry ; and, as in unregistered conveyancing, this is so, even if he has actual notice of their existence.[1] A donee, however, will be bound by minor interests even if they are not protected by entry.

It is the former category of overriding interests which has attracted criticism.[2] Overriding interests, which do not appear on the register (they may do, in which case they cease to be overriding interests),[3] detract from the principle that the register should be a mirror of the vendor's title.   Their existence will only be discovered by a purchaser if he resorts to the older methods of investigation, and this is particularly so where paragraph (g) applies.   As Lord DENNING, M.R., said in *Strand Securities Ltd.* v. *Caswell.*[4]

> " Section 70 (1) (g) is an important provision.   Fundamentally, its object is to protect a person in actual occupation of land from having his rights lost in the welter of registration.   He can stay there and do nothing.   Yet he will be protected.   No one can buy the land over his head and thereby take away or diminish his rights.   It is up to every purchaser before he buys to make inquiry on the premises. If he fails to do so, it is at his own risk.   He must take subject to whatever rights the occupier may have.   Such is the doctrine of *Hunt* v. *Luck*,[5] for unregistered land.   Section 70 (1) (g) carries the same doctrine forward into registered land . . . ".

(C) COMPARISON OF UNREGISTERED AND REGISTERED SYSTEMS

Position of purchaser under unregistered and registered conveyancing compared.

We may now compare the position of a purchaser of the legal fee simple of Blackacre under the two systems of conveyancing. Under both systems he must satisfy himself on two separate matters ; firstly, that the vendor is entitled to convey the fee simple, and, secondly, that there are no incumbrances in favour of third parties which will continue to bind the land after the conveyance.

---

[1] *Hodges* v. *Jones*, [1935] Ch. 657, at p. 671, *per* LUXMOORE, J.   *De Lusignan* v. *Johnson* (1973), 230 Estates Gazette 499 ; L.R.A. 1925, s. 59 (6).

[2] (1961) 24 *M. L. R.* 136 (G. Dworkin).   Farrand, *Contract and Conveyance* (2nd Edn.) pp. 184–209.   Barnsley, *Conveyancing Law and Practice*, pp. 53–55.   See *infra*, pp. 776–7.

[3] L.R.A. 1925, s. 3 (xvi).   The relevant statutory protections then apply.

[4] [1965] Ch. 968 at pp. 979–80 ; see also *per* RUSSELL, L.J., at p. 984 ; [1965] 1 All E. R. 820.

[5] [1902] 1 Ch. 428.   See *supra*, p. 67, and *infra*, pp. 774–5.

As far as the first matter is concerned, the task of a purchaser is clearly simplified under the registered system. An investigation of the vendor's title deeds is replaced by a search of the register at the Land Registry. There is, however, no such clear-cut difference in the matter of third party rights. Under the unregistered system since 1925, a purchaser must first search the Land Charges Register. He is bound by any registrable interests which have been registered at the time when he takes his conveyance from the vendor : if a registrable interest is not so registered, he takes free from it, even though he actually knows of its existence. Further, if the vendor is a tenant for life under a strict settlement or if the vendors are trustees for sale under a trust for sale, the purchaser takes free from the equitable interests of the beneficiaries under the doctrine of overreaching. Thirdly, under the unregistered system, a vendor is bound by certain rights which are neither registrable nor over-reachable but which in the last resort can only be discovered by his own inquiries and inspection of Blackacre. These include (*a*) legal third party rights, whether he knows about them or not *e.g.* a legal estate, such as a lease, or a legal interest, such as a legal easement[1] (*b*) a residual category of equitable interests, unless he is a bona fide purchaser for value of the legal estate in Blackacre without actual or constructive notice *e.g.* a pre-1926 restrictive covenant or a licence by estoppel.[2]

Under the registered system the position of a purchaser of Blackacre is different. On the one hand he is bound by minor interests which are entered on the register : if such an interest is not so entered, he takes free from it even though he actually knows of its existence. In this context an entry on the register has the same function that registration in the Land Charges Register has in unregistered conveyancing.[3] If, however, the vendor is a tenant for life or if the vendors are trustees for sale, the interests of the beneficiaries are also minor interests, but in these situations they will not bind a purchaser even when they have been protected by an entry on the register, because they will be overreached. On the other hand a purchaser is bound by overriding interests, even though he has no knowledge of them and even though they are not entered on the register. If they are entered, they cease to be over-riding interests and take effect as minor interests. The statutory list in section 70 of the Land Registration Act 1925 is a collection of interests which it is held desirable should be binding on a purchaser but which, for some reason or another, do not fit into the pattern

---

[1] He is not bound by a puisne mortgage (any legal mortgage not being a mortgage protected by a deposit of documents relating to the legal estate affected) unless it is registered as a land charge ; *supra,* p. 101.

[2] *Supra,* p. 103, n. 3.

[3] The provisions of the Land Charges Act 1972 are excluded from registered conveyancing. L.R.A. 1925, s. 59 ; see also *Webb* v. *Pollmount, Ltd.,* [1966] Ch. 584, at p. 599 ; [1966] 1 All E. R. 481, at p. 487, *per* UNGOED-THOMAS, J.

of the register.   They are discoverable by, but only by, the purchaser's inspection of Blackacre and by inquiries which he ought reasonably to have to make without assistance from the register. As we have seen, they not only include legal rights which are familiar in unregistered conveyancing *e.g.* legal easements and certain leases, but they also include the " rights of every person in actual occupation of the land or in receipt of the rents and profits thereof." It is this last category which may cause the kind of difficulty which was removed from unregistered conveyancing by the Land Charges Act 1925.

Thus in registered conveyancing there is no residual category of equitable interests to which the doctrine of the bona fide purchaser is applicable ;   that doctrine has been replaced by the provisions of the Land Registration Act 1925 for minor and overriding interests.   Thus PLOWMAN, J., in *Parkash* v. *Irani Finance Ltd.*, found a plaintiff's reliance on the doctrine " a little surprising, since one of the essential features of registration of title is to substitute a system of registration of rights for the doctrine of notice."[1]   The residual category of equitable interests, however, can exist under registered conveyancing, but any such interests which are not overriding interests must appear on the register if they are to bind a purchaser.[2]

Third party rights are treated differently under the two systems of conveyancing, and it is this different treatment that gives rise to differences in the substance of the land law ; and these differences we shall consider under the various topics in which they occur.

SECTION VI.   CONTRACT BEFORE CONVEYANCE[3]

SUMMARY

A contract for the sale of land usually precedes the conveyance of the legal estate to the purchaser;   and this is so whether the

---

[1] [1970] Ch. 101, at p. 109 ; [1969] 1 All E. R. 930 ;   *Hodgson* v. *Marks* [1971] Ch. 892 ; [1971] 2 All E. R. 684.   But *cf. Barclays Bank, Ltd.* v. *Taylor,* [1974] Ch. 137 ; [1973] 1 All E. R. 752 ; (1974) 124 N.L.J. 634 (S. Robinson). See also CROSS, J., in *National Provincial Bank, Ltd.* v. *Hastings Car Mart, Ltd.,* [1964] Ch. 9, at p. 16.
[2] *Infra,* pp. 764 *et seq.*
[3] See generally Barnsley, *Conveyancing Law and Practice ;   Emmet on Title* (16th Edn.) ;   Farrand, *Contract and Conveyance* (2nd Edn.) ;   *Gibson's Conveyancing* (20th Edn.).

land is registered[1] or unregistered. Similarly, a contract for a lease may be made first, and then followed at a later date by a formal grant of the legal term of years absolute.[2] There are thus two distinct stages to be considered, the contract and the conveyance, and in this section we are concerned with the contract.

(1) FORMATION OF CONTRACT

A contract for the sale or any other disposition of land is created in the same way as any other contract. There must be a final and complete agreement between the parties on its essential terms,[3] that is to say, the parties, the property, the consideration and, in the case of a lease, the commencement and the period of the tenancy.[4] The contract is then valid, even if made orally, but, as we shall see, it will only be enforceable by action if there is a signed memorandum in writing which complies with s. 40 of the Law of Property Act 1925, or, failing that, if there is a sufficient act of part performance.

If a contract for the sale of land specifies merely the names of the parties, a description of the property and a statement of the price, it is called an *open contract*. When this form of contract is made, the parties are bound by certain obligations implied by the law. These implied obligations, as we shall see, impose a burdensome duty of proof of title upon the vendor, and in the majority of cases the vendor is anxious to procure the insertion in the written agreement of special stipulations, in order that his strict legal liability may be modified. The parties may incorporate into their contract such terms as they think fit, subject only to the rule that certain stipulations contrary to the policy of the law are void. Thus a stipulation that the conveyance shall be prepared at the expense of the purchaser by a solicitor appointed by the vendor is void.[5] In practice contracts for the sale of land are generally in standard form. The Law Society's Conditions of Sale and the National Conditions of Sale,[6] contain standard forms of conditions and these are usually employed with such alterations as the parties may make to fit the particular transaction. Further, if the contract is made by correspondence, the Statutory Form of Conditions of Sale 1925 applies, except in so far as there is

Open contract.

---

[1] Ruoff and Roper, p. 327 ; Barnsley *op. cit.*, p. 109.

[2] *Infra*, p. 389.

[3] *Rossiter* v. *Miller* (1878), 3 App. Cas. 1124, at p. 1151, *per* Lord BLACKBURN.

[4] *Harvey* v. *Pratt*, [1965] 1 W.L.R. 1025, at p. 1027, *per* Lord DENNING, M.R. ; [1965] 2 All E. R. 786.

[5] L.P.A. 1925, s. 48 (1). See also s. 42.

[6] The latest editions of these two publications appeared in 1973 and 1969 (18th Edn.) respectively. For a critical commentary, see Wilkinson, *Standard Conditions of Sale of Land* (2nd Edn., 1974).

any modification or intention to the contrary expressed in the correspondence.[1]

DANCKWERTS, L.J. has referred to " the long-standing practice which has arisen among conveyances of referring to the provisions in a contract for the sale of land as ' conditions of sale ', whether special or general (such as those provided by the common forms produced under the name of the National Conditions of Sale, or those produced by the Law Society). The word ' condition ' is traditional rather than appropriate, and these provisions are not so much concerned with the validity of the contract of sale as with the production of the title and the performance of the vendor's and purchaser's obligations leading up to completion by conveyance. Shortly, they are no more than the terms of the contract."[2]

Subject to contract.   It is common practice in sales of land for the parties to agree a price " subject to contract ". The object of this procedure, " though it has drawbacks and is capable of being abused in certain circumstances, is based on a sound concept, namely, that the buyer should be free from binding commitment until he has had the opportunity of obtaining legal and other advice, arranging his finance and making the necessary inspections, searches and enquiries ".[3] In 1975 the Law Commission recommended that there should be no change in this practice, even though one consequence is that the purchaser may be " gazumped " (*i.e.,* the vendor may withdraw from the bargain or threaten to do so, in the expectation of receiving a higher price).

The effect of such phrases as " subject to contract ",[4] or " subject to a formal contract to be drawn up by our solicitors " is that there is no contract, unless there are some very exceptional circumstances necessitating a different construction.[5] Either party is free to repudiate the bargain until a formal contract has been made.

Thus in *Winn* v. *Bull,*[6]

> a written agreement was entered into whereby the defendant agreed to take from the plaintiff a lease of a house for a certain time at a certain rent, " subject to the preparation and approval of a formal contract." No formal or other contract was ever entered into between the parties. It was held that there was no contract.

---

[1] L.P.A. 1925, s. 46 ; S. R. & O. 1925 No. 779. See (1974) 90 L. Q. R. 55 (A. M. Prichard).

[2] *Property and Bloodstock, Ltd.* v. *Emerton,* [1968] Ch. 94, at p. 118 ; [1967] 3 All E. R. 321.

[3] Law Commission Report on " Subject to Contract " Agreements (Law Com. No. 65, 1975), para. 13.

[4] *Tiverton Estates, Ltd.* v. *Wearwell, Ltd.,* [1975] Ch. 146 ; [1974] 1 All E. R. 209.

[5] *Chillingworth* v. *Esche,* [1924] 1 Ch. 97. See Wilkinson, *Standard Conditions of Sale of Land* (2nd Edn.), chap. 5 for a useful summary of standard conditional phrases. Barnsley, *Conveyancing Law and Practice,* pp. 101–4. (1975) 39 Conv. (N.S.) 229–36, 311–13.

[6] (1877), 7 Ch. D. 29.

The parties may, however, be bound at once, although they intend to make a more formal contract later on. In *Branca* v. *Cobarro*,[1] for example.

> a written agreement to sell the lease and goodwill of a mushroom farm ended as follows : " This is a provisional agreement until a fully legalised agreement, drawn up by a solicitor and embodying all the conditions herewith stated, is signed ". It was held by the Court of Appeal[2] that the parties, by using the word " provisional " had intended the document to be immediately binding and to remain so until superseded by a more formal document.

Where a formal contract is drawn up, two copies are usually made, and each of the parties signs one of them. There is no binding contract until the copies have been physically exchanged.[3]

(2) ENFORCEABILITY OF CONTRACT

(A) MEMORANDUM IN WRITING

Section 40 of the Law of Property Act 1925[4] provides that :—

> " (1) No action may be brought upon any contract for the sale or other disposition of land or any interest in land, unless the agreement upon which such action is brought, or some memorandum or note thereof, is in writing and signed by the party to be charged or by some other person thereunto by him lawfully authorized.
> (2) This section . . . does not affect the law relating to part performance."

Sufficient memorandum.

It follows, therefore, that even when the parties are in complete accord upon all the terms of their agreement it will not be enforceable by either side in the absence of a sufficient memorandum or of an act of part performance as described later.[5]

The section applies to any contract for the sale or other disposition of land or any interest in land. This covers not only a

Contracts within the section.

---

[1] [1947] K. B. 854 ; [1947] 2 All E. R. 101.
[2] Reversing DENNING, J., who construed " provisional " as equivalent to " tentative ".
[3] *Trollope & Sons* v. *Martyn Bros.*, [1934] 2 K. B. 436, 455 ; *Eccles* v. *Bryant and Pollock*, [1948] Ch. 93 ; [1947] 2 All E. R. 865. If the exchange takes place by post the earliest date at which the contract is concluded is the date when the later of the two documents is posted ; *ibid. Harrison* v. *Battye*, [1975] 1 W. L. R. 58 ; [1974] 3 All E. R. 830 ; *cf. Smith* v. *Mansi* [1963] 1 W. L. R. 26 ; [1962] 3 All E. R. 857 (exchange unnecessary where there is only one document and the same solicitor acts for both vendor and purchaser) ; *Storer* v. *Manchester City Council*, [1974] 1 W. L. R. 1405 ; [1974] 3 All E. R. 824 ; (1974) 38 Conv. (N.S.) 385, 392.
[4] Replacing Statute of Frauds 1677, s. 4. For a detailed commentary, see Farrand, *Contract and Conveyance* (2nd Edn.), pp. 28 *et seq.* ; Barnsley, *Conveyancing Law and Practice*, pp. 82 *et seq.* For judicial criticism of the section, see *Wakeham* v. *Mackenzie*, [1968] 1 W. L. R. 1175, at p. 1178, *per* STAMP, J. ; (1967) 31 Conv. (N.S.) 182, 254 (H. W. Wilkinson). And for its relationship with part performance *Steadman* v. *Steadman*, [1974] Q. B. 161, at p. 184, *per* SCARMAN, L.J.
[5] *Infra*, pp. 121.

contract for the sale of freehold land, but also includes a contract for the grant of a lease,[1] mortgage, easement or profit. It applies to a contract for the creation of a new interest in land as well as to a contract for the disposition of an existing interest. Land is given a very wide definition in the Law of Property Act,[2] and has been held to include an interest in the proceeds of sale under a trust for sale of land.[3]

Contents of memorandum.

The contract itself need not be in writing. All that is required is that before an action is brought, there should be a written memorandum containing not only the terms of the contract, but also an express or implied recognition that a contract was actually entered into. Thus, if an oral contract is followed by a writing which is expressed to be " subject to contract ", there is no sufficient memorandum. As Lord DENNING, M.R. said in *Tiverton Estates, Ltd.* v. *Wearwell, Ltd.*[4] :

" I cannot myself see any difference between a writing which— (i) denies there was any contract ; (ii) does not admit there was any contract ; (iii) says that the parties are in negotiation ; or (iv) says that there was an agreement ' subject to contract ', for that comes to the same thing. The reason why none of those writings satisfies the statute is because none of them contains any recognition or admission of the existence of a contract."

The memorandum may come into existence after the contract has been formed, and in *Barkworth* v. *Young*[5] it was held that a memorandum made over fourteen years after the contract sufficed. It may even be made before the contract, where a written offer is accepted orally but unconditionally.[6]

The memorandum must contain not only the essential terms of the contract, that is to say, the names or adequate description of the parties, a description of the property and the nature of the consideration, but also any other special terms deemed to be essential by the parties.[7]

---

[1] *Cf.* L.P.A. 1925, s. 54 (2) for the creation by parol of leases for a term not exceeding three years.

[2] L.P.A. 1925, s. 205 (1) (ix) ; *infra*, p. 138.

[3] *Cooper* v. *Critchley*, [1955] Ch. 431 ; [1955] 1 All E. R. 520 ; M. & B. p. 228 ; *Steadman* v. *Steadman* [1974] Q. B. 161 ; [1973] 3 All E. R. 977, followed on this point without argument [1974] 3 W.L.R. 56 ; [1974] 2 All E. R. 977 ; *Thompson's Trustee in Bankruptcy* v. *Heaton*, [1974] 1 W. L. R. 605, at p. 610.

[4] [1975] Ch. 146, at p. 160 ; [1974] 1 All E. R. 209 ; M. & B. p. 55. The Court of Appeal did not follow its own previous decision in *Law* v. *Jones* [1974] Ch. 112 ; [1973] 2 All E. R. 437 (holding that " subject to contract " was a suspensive condition capable of subsequent oral waiver) ; see also *Griffiths* v. *Young* [1970] Ch. 675 ; [1970] 3 All E. R. 601. (1974) 38 Conv. (N.S.) 127 (F. R. Crane) ; *Emmet on Title* (16th Edn.), pp. 35–8.

[5] (1856), 4 Drew 1.

[6] *Reuss* v. *Picksley* (1866), L. R. 1 Exch. 342 ; *Parker* v. *Clark*, [1960] 1 W. L. R. 286 ; [1960] All E. R. 93 ; *Tiverton Estates, Ltd.* v. *Wearwell, Ltd.*, *supra*, at p. 166.

[7] *Tiverton Estates Ltd.* v. *Wearwell, Ltd.*, *supra*, at p. 161 ; *Tweddell* v. *Henderson*, [1975] 1 W. L. R. 1496 ; [1975] 2 All E. R. 1096.

There is this qualification, however, that

> " if a term is exclusively for the benefit of one party, that party may
> sometimes waive the benefit of it and sue on the contract for en-
> forcement, even though the memorandum contain no evidence of
> that term." [1]

Further, if the oral term omitted from the memorandum is
beneficial to the defendant, the plaintiff may submit to perform it
and thus cure its omission from the memorandum. [2]

The memorandum must either name the parties or describe
them in such a manner that they can be identified without fair
and reasonable dispute, and without resorting to parol evidence
directly connected with the contract. If, for instance, the
intending vendor is not named, but is referred to in the memorandum as the " proprietor " of the premises,[3] or as " executor "[4]
or " trustee "[5] or " personal representative," [6] such description
will suffice to satisfy the statute, since the identity of the person
described can be easily ascertained ; but if he were merely
described as " the vendor,"[7] or " landlord,"[8] the memorandum
would be useless, for the court would be driven to require parol
evidence on the very point on which the statute requires written
evidence.[9]

Evidence of terms necessary.

Parties.

The same principle applies to the description of the property,
which is the second point upon which the memorandum must
furnish evidence. It is impossible to lay down beforehand what
is a sufficient description of property, for, however detailed the
expressions and even the plans may be, there is more often than
not room for controversy,[10] but the general principle is—*id certum
est quod certum reddi potest*,[11] and, provided that the memorandum
furnishes something definite to go on, extrinsic evidence will be
admitted to explain such descriptions as

Property.

" Mr. Ogilvie's house," [12]

---

[1] *Hawkins* v. *Price*, [1947] Ch. 645, at p. 659 ; [1947] 1 All E. R. 689, at
p. 690, *per* EVERSHED, J. The learned judge advisedly said " may *sometimes*,"
since it has been suggested (Fry, *Specific Performance* (6th Edn.), p. 243)
that to be capable of waiver a term must be " of no great importance." If
this vague test represents the law the result will surely be chaotic uncertainty.
See also *Heron Garage Properties, Ltd.* v. *Moss*, [1974] 1 W. L. R. 148 ; [1974]
1 All E. R. 421.
[2] *Martin* v. *Pycroft* (1852), 2 De G. M. & G. 785 ; followed in *Scott* v. *Bradley*,
[1971] Ch. 850 ; [1971] 1 All E. R. 583, by PLOWMAN, J. in preference to *Burgess*
v. *Cox*, [1951] Ch. 383 ; [1950] 2 All E. R. 1212 ; (1951) 67 L. Q. R. 300
(R.E.M.).
[3] *Rossiter* v. *Miller* (1878), 3 App. Cas. 1124, at p. 1140.
[4] *Hood* v. *Lord Barrington* (1868), L. R. 6 Eq. 218.
[5] *Catling* v. *King* (1877), 5 Ch. D. 660.
[6] *Fay* v. *Miller, Wilkins & Co.*, [1941] Ch. 360 ; [1941] 2 All E. R. 18.
[7] *Potter* v. *Duffield* (1874), L. R. 18 Eq. 4.
[8] *Coombs* v. *Wilkes*, [1891] 3 Ch. 77.
[9] See *Sale* v. *Lambert* (1874), L. R. 18 Eq. 1 ; *Potter* v. *Duffield* (1874),
L. R. 18 Eq. 4.
[10] *Shardlow* v. *Cotterell* (1881), 20 Ch. D. 90, at p. 93, JESSEL, M.R.
[11] *Plant* v. *Bourne*, [1897] 2 Ch. 281, at p. 288.
[12] *Ogilvie* v. *Foljambe* (1817), 3 Mer. 53.

or

> " 24 acres of land, freehold . . . at Totmonslow in the parish of Draycott, in the county of Stafford." [1]

**Considera-
tion.**

Thirdly, the memorandum must contain the consideration. This too must be stated with reasonable precision. Thus an option to purchase land " at a reasonable valuation " has been upheld as being sufficiently certain.[2]

**Contract
for lease.**

Finally, in the case of a contract for a lease, the dates at which the tenancy is to begin and to end must appear in writing.

> " It is settled beyond question that, in order for there to be a valid agreement for a lease, the essentials are not only for the parties to be determined, the property to be determined, the length of the term and the rent, but also the date of its commencement." [3]

The courts will not infer a stipulation that it is to commence within a reasonable time after the agreement.

**Form of
memoran-
dum.**

The memorandum need not be in any particular form, but may, for example, consist of a letter written by one of the parties to the other or to a third person, or of an affidavit or a will[4] ; and it may also consist of a document that has been drawn up with the express intention of repudiating the parol agreement.[5] In fact any kind of signed document which contains all the essential terms that have been agreed between the parties will satisfy the statute.

Signature.

The signature must be that of "the party to be charged" or his agent, or, in other words, of the defendant in the action. If, therefore, in an agreement between A. and B. the memorandum is signed by A. only, it follows that B. can enforce the contract, but that A. cannot.[6] The signature need not be a subscription written at the foot of the agreement, but may appear anywhere, provided that it was written with the view of governing the whole instrument.[7] Indeed, the signature may consist merely of the defendant's initials[8] or of his printed name,[9] provided that the intention clearly is to authenticate the document.[10]

---

[1] *Plant* v. *Bourne, supra*; *Auerbach* v. *Nelson,* [1919] 2 Ch. 383.
[2] *Talbot* v. *Talbot* [1968] Ch. 1.   See also *Smith* v. *Morgan* [1971] 1 W. L. R. 803 ; [1971] 2 All E. R. 1500 (a right of first refusal " at a price to be agreed upon " held to mean lowest price at which vendor willing to sell), and the analysis by MEGARRY, J. in *Brown* v. *Gould* [1972] Ch. 53 ; [1971] 2 All E. R. 1505.
[3] *Harvey* v. *Pratt,* [1965] 1 W.L.R. 1025, at p. 1027, *per* Lord DENNING, M. R.; [1965] 2 All E. R. 786.
[4] *Re Holland,* [1902] 2 Ch. 360, at p. 383.
[5] *Bailey* v. *Sweeting* (1861), 9 C. B. (N. S.) 859 ; *Dewar* v. *Mintoft,* [1912] 2 K. B. 373.
[6] *Laythoarp* v. *Bryant* (1836), 2 Bing. NC. 735.
[7] *Cf. Johnson* v. *Dodgson* (1837), 2 M. & W. 653 ; distinguish *Caton* v. *Caton* (1867), L. R. 2 H. L. 127.
[8] *Hill* v. *Hill,* [1947] Ch. 231 ; [1947] 1 All E. R. 54.
[9] *Cf. Cohen* v. *Roche,* [1927] 1 K. B. 169; *Leeman* v. *Stocks,* [1951] Ch. 941; 1951] 1 All E. R. 1043.
[10] A further signature may be necessary if the memorandum is altered after the original signature.   See *New Hart Builders, Ltd.* v. *Brindley,* [1975] Ch. 342 ; [1975] 1 All E. R. 1007 ; (1975) 39 Conv. (N.S.), 376 (C. T. Emery).

An agent is "lawfully authorized" to sign the memorandum on behalf of his principal if his authority to do so has been conferred upon him in writing or orally, or if it is reasonably inferable from the attendant circumstances[1] and especially from his instructions. For instance, Authority of agent to sign.

> " the mere appointment by an owner of an estate agent to dispose of a house confers no authority to make a contract ; the agent is solely employed to find persons to negotiate with the owner ; but, if the agent is definitely instructed to sell at a defined price, those instructions involve authority to make a binding contract and to sign an agreement." [2]

Where there is a sale by auction, the auctioneer becomes the agent of both parties upon the fall of the hammer. He derives his authority to act for the vendor from his instructions to sell, while his authority to sign on behalf of the purchaser is implied from the bid.[3] If, therefore, he signs a memorandum, either at the time of the sale or so soon afterwards that his signature can reasonably be regarded as part of the transaction of sale, the memorandum is binding upon both parties.[4]

When the terms of the agreement are contained not in one, but in several documents, the difficult question often arises whether parol evidence is admissible to connect one document with another. Suppose, for instance, that Memorandum contained in several documents.

> an intending lessee A. has signed a document containing all the terms of the agreement and has paid a quarter's rent in advance. The other party, B., has not signed the written agreement, but has signed a receipt for the rent in the following terms :
>
> " Received of A. £30, being payment of one quarter's rent in respect of the house at Hammersmith."
>
> A. cannot sue on the first document alone since it does not contain B.'s signature ; nor on the receipt, because for one reason, though implicitly referring to a lease, it does not state when it is to begin and end.[5] But if A. is allowed to adduce parol evidence with a view to showing that the receipt is connected with and should be read with the memorandum, then taking the two together he will have a complete memorandum containing all that the statute requires.

In such a case, it has long been established that, if one document expressly refers to another, the latter can be put in evidence, When parol evidence admitted to connect documents.

---

[1] *Davies* v. *Sweet*, [1962] 2 Q. B. 300, at p. 305; [1962] 1 All E. R. 92.
[2] *Keen* v. *Mear*, [1920] 2 Ch. 574, at p. 579, *per* ROMER, J.
[3] *Emmerson* v. *Heelis* (1808), 2 Taunt. 38.
[4] *Bell* v. *Balls*, [1897] 1 Ch. 663 ; *Chaney* v. *Maclow* [1929] 1 Ch. 461 ; *Phillips* v. *Butler*, [1945] Ch. 358 ; [1945] 2 All E. R. 258.
[5] *Cf. Long* v. *Millar* (1879), 4 C. P. D. 450.

but as the authorities now stand an implicit reference is also regarded as sufficient.[1]

The present law was stated by JENKINS, L.J., in *Timmins* v. *Moreland Street Property Co., Ltd.*[2] :

> " I think it is still indispensably necessary, in order to justify the reading of documents together for this purpose, that there should be a document signed by the party to be charged, which, while not containing in itself all the necessary ingredients of the required memorandum, does contain some reference, express or implied, to some other document or transaction.   Where any such reference can be spelt out of a document so signed, then parol evidence may be given to identify the other document referred to, or, as the case may be, to explain the other transaction, and to identify any document relating to it.   If by this process a document is brought to light which contains in writing all the terms of the bargain so far as not contained in the document signed by the party to be charged, then the two documents can be read together so as to constitute a sufficient memorandum for the purposes of section 40."

Suppose, for instance, that two parties to an agreement for a lease insert a carbon paper into a typewriter and type the following :

> " I agree to take a lease of 50 High Street for five years at £100 a year from December 25, 1975, and to pay £25 by way of rent in advance."

" I," *i.e.* the tenant, signs the top paper ; the landlord signs the carbon copy and also signs a receipt for £25.   If, now, the tenant sues for specific performance he is met by a difficulty, for he cannot rely upon the carbon copy signed by the defendant, since it contains no description of " I."   If, however, there is an implicit reference in the carbon copy to some document which describes " I," there is sufficient written evidence of the necessary terms.   It is clear that the implicit reference exists in at least two forms, since the carbon copy indicates that there is (*a*) the original writing of which the carbon is a duplicate, and (*b*) a transaction connected with the payment of £25.   This transaction may be represented by a document, *e.g.* a cheque signed by the plaintiff, and it is open to the plaintiff to show that it is so in fact.[3]

Under this rule the hypothetical agreement suggested above would be enforceable by the tenant against the landlord.

---

[1] *Baumann* v. *James* (1868), 3 Ch. App. 508 ; *Hill* v. *Hill*, [1947] Ch. 231 ; [1947] 1 All E. R. 54.

[2] [1958] Ch. 110, at p. 130 ; [1957] 3 All E. R. 265.

[3] This hypothetical case is based upon *Stokes* v. *Whicher*, [1920] 1 Ch. 411, which was distinguished in *Timmins* v. *Moreland Street Property Co., Ltd.*, [1958] Ch. 110 ; [1957] 3 All E. R. 265.   See too *Fowler* v. *Bratt*, [1950] 2 K. B. 96 ; [1950] 1 All E. R. 662 ; *L. D. Turner Ltd.* v. *R. S. Hatton (Bradford) Ltd.* ; [1952] 1 All E. R. 1286.

Effect of Non-compliance. The effect of non-compliance with s. 40 is not to invalidate the contract, but merely to prevent a party from bringing an action for damages or a claim for specific performance. The contract is valid, but unenforecable by action.[1] It may however be indirectly enforced. Thus if a purchaser defaults, the vendor may forfeit, or keep, a deposit which has been paid under an oral contract.[2] Conversely, if a vendor defaults, the purchaser can recover his deposit by a claim in quasi-contract on a total failure of consideration.[3]

(B) ACT OF PART PERFORMANCE

It now remains to be noticed that even though there is no memorandum under the Law of Property Act 1925, yet, if there has been an oral contract followed by a sufficient act of part performance, the result in equity is in effect to exclude the operation of the statute. The attitude adopted by equity is that it would be fraudulent for a defendant to take advantage of the absence of a signed memorandum if he has stood by and allowed the plaintiff to alter his position for the worse by carrying out acts in performance of the contract. *[Basis of the doctrine of part performance.]*

If, for instance, B. has orally agreed to let premises to A., and if A. goes into actual possession of and improves the premises, it would be fraudulent, or at least inequitable, for B. to refuse to implement his bargain on the ground that a sufficient memorandum was lacking.[5] Equity therefore grants a decree of specific performance of the contract against B. In doing this, however, it does not charge him on the contract itself, but holds him liable upon the equities arising from the changed position in which A. finds himself.[6] A. has prejudiced himself by acting on the assumption that B. would carry out the bargain, and the fact that he has been allowed to do this gives him an undoubted equity against B. Upon proof of his act of part performance, therefore, he is allowed by equity to give parol evidence of an agreement that would otherwise require written evidence. If he satisfies the court in these two respects, he is entitled to a decree ordering the other party to execute a formal lease to include the terms which have been agreed upon.

The crucial question is—What is an act of part performance? Although one of the parties may have done several things towards performing his side of the agreement, it does not at all follow that *[What acts amount to part performance.]*

---

[1] *Leroux* v. *Brown* (1852), 12 C. B. 801 ; *Maddison* v. *Alderson* (1883), 8 App. Cas. 467, at p. 474 *per* Lord SELBORNE, L.C. ; *Delaney* v. *T. P. Smith, Ltd.*, [1946] K. B. 393 ; [1946] 2 All E. R. 23.
[2] *Monnickendam* v. *Leanse* (1923), 39 T. L. R. 445.
[3] *Pulbrook* v. *Lawes* (1876), 1 Q. B. D. 284.
[4] The doctrine is recognised and preserved by L. P. A. 1925, ss. 40 (2), 55 (d).
[5] *Caton* v. *Caton* (1866), 1 Ch. App. 137, at p. 148, Lord CRANWORTH.
[6] *Maddison* v. *Alderson* (1883), 8 App. Cas. 467 at p. 475, *per* Lord SELBORNE.

they will amount to part performance. The act must of itself on a balance of probability[1] establish the existence of the oral contract. It must be an act which is intelligible only on the assumption that some such contract as that alleged has been made, and if it is explicable on some other equally good ground, it does not satisfy the test. Further, there may be more than one act, and the acts when joined together " may throw light on each other; and there is no reason to exclude light ".[2] The flexibility of this approach is enhanced when even " spoken words may themselves be part performance of a contract ".[3]

A change of possession is, in the majority of cases, associated with the doctrine. Entry into possession is clearly sufficient. If, for instance, A. is found to be in actual possession of land which has hitherto been owned and occupied by B., the only reasonable **explanation of this change of possession is that the parties have entered into some contract, either of sale or lease, with regard to the land. Entry into possession, therefore, is an act of part performance, and if B. resists a suit for specific performance by relying upon the absence of a written memorandum, A. will be permitted to show by parol evidence what the actual contract was.**[4]

On the other hand, remaining in possession, unless there are additional circumstances, is not sufficient.

Distinction
between
entering
into and
remaining in
possession.

If A. is tenant in possession of lands under a lease which expires on December 25th, the mere fact that he is still in possession on January 1st is not sufficiently unequivocal to found a suit for specific performance of a parol agreement to grant him a new lease.

The possibility that the landlord has entered into a new contract relating to the land is certainly one explanation of A.'s continuance in possession, but it is not the only explanation. There are others equally good, as, for instance, that he refuses to go or that he has been given a few days' grace. But if, in addition to remaining in possession after the proper date, A. begins to pay rent at a higher rate than under the old lease,[5] or if he spends money with the approval of the landlord on the improvement of the premises,[6] the requirement of part performance is satisfied, for what he has done is explicable only on the assumption that the landlord has agreed to grant a new lease. If the act relied upon by the plaintiff clearly refers to the type of contract that he

---

[1] *Steadman* v. *Steadman*, [1974] 3 W. L. R. 56 ; at pp. 81–82, *per* Lord SIMON OF GLAISDALE and at p. 61, *per* Lord REID.
[2] *Ibid.*, at p. 82, *per* Lord SIMON OF GLAISDALE.
[3] *Ibid.*, at p. 82.
[4] *Morphett* v. *Jones* (1818), 1 Swan. 172 ; *Brough* v. *Nettleton*, [1921] 2 Ch. 25. *Kingswood Estate Co., Ltd.* v. *Anderson*, [1963] 2 Q. B. 169; [1962] 3 All E. R. 593.
[5] *Miller and Aldworth* v. *Sharp*, [1899] 1 Ch. 622.
[6] *Nunn* v. *Fabian* (1865), L. R. 1 Ch. App. 35.

seeks to prove, the fact that some ingenious mind might suggest a different explanation will not avail the defendant.[1]

Although possession generally forms the basis of a claim under the doctrine, this is not necessarily so. Thus in *Rawlinson v. Ames*,[2]

> the defendant entered into an oral contract with the plaintiff to take a lease of a flat, part of the contract being that certain alterations should be made by the plaintiff. During the progress of the alterations the defendant frequently visited the flat and made suggestions as to the manner in which the work should be done. Her suggestions were carried out, and when, on the completion of the work, she repudiated the contract, she was adjudged liable in a suit for specific performance. The submission of the plaintiff to interference by the defendant and the adoption of her suggestions were plainly referable to a contract relating to the premises.

Part performance not inseparable from possession.

A number of further questions arise from the recent decision of the House of Lords in *Steadman v. Steadman*.[3] In that case

Steadman v. Steadman.

> a husband and wife, whose marriage had broken down, entered into an " oral package deal " by way of compromise. The wife would surrender to the husband her half interest in the matrimonial home for £1,500 ; the husband would pay £100 in respect of arrears of maintenance, and the maintenance order in favour of the wife would be discharged. This oral contract was made the subject of an order by the magistrates. The husband paid the £100, and his solicitor prepared and sent a deed of transfer of the wife's interest to her for signature. The wife then refused to complete and relied upon the fact that the contract was oral and therefore unenforceable under s. 40. The House of Lords held by a majority of four to one that both the payment of the £100 and the preparation and sending of the deed of transfer were sufficient acts of part performance, and, accordingly, ordered specific performance of the contract against the wife.

(a) Referability to the Contract

Referability to contract.

It will be seen that the acts performed by the husband did not of themselves prove the precise terms of the contract. It used to be said that the acts must be unequivocally referable to the contract. This strict rule was modified in *Kingswood Estate Co., Ltd. v. Anderson*, and there was unanimous approval in *Steadman v. Steadman* of UPJOHN, L.J.'s statement[4] in that case :

> " The true rule is in my view stated in Fry on Specific Performance, 6th ed., p. 278, section 582 : ' The true principle, however, of the operation of acts of part performance seems only to require that the acts in question be such as must be referred to some contract,

---

[1] Cf. *Broughton v. Snook*, [1938] Ch. 505 ; [1938] 1 All E. R. 411. See also *Liddell v. Hopkinson*, (1974), 233 Estates Gazette 512 (*leaving* of possession held to be sufficient act).

[2] [1925] 1 Ch. 96 ; *Dickinson v. Barrow*, [1904] 2 Ch. 339.

[3] [1974] 3 W. L. R. 56 ; [1974] 2 All E. R. 997 ; M. & B. p. 61 ; *Re Windle*, [1975] 1 W. L. R. 1628.

[4] [1963] 2 Q. B. 169 at p. 189 ; [1962] 3 All E. R. 593 ; *Wakeham v. Mackenzie*, [1968] 1 W. L. R. 1175 ; [1968] 2 All E. R. 783 ; *New Hart Builders, Ltd. v. Brindley*, [1975] Ch. 342 ; [1975] 1 All E. R. 1007.

and may be referred to the alleged one ; that they prove the existence of some contract, and are consistent with the contract alleged.' "

Accordingly, no act done in furtherance of an oral contract
will satisfy the requirements of part performance unless it is one
which demonstrates that *some* contract has been made.   It need
not refer to the precise terms of the contract upon which the
plaintiff relies.

Reference
to land.

(b) *Reference to Land*

Even though it may not be necessary for the act of part performance to indicate the terms of the contract, it was argued in
Steadman v. *Steadman* that the act must at least be such as to
show that there was a contract relating to land ; and, in particular,
the question arose whether if an oral contract contains several
terms, but only one of which deals with an interest in land, it is
sufficient that there has been part performance only of one or more
of the *other* terms.   Various opinions were expressed.   Lord
SALMON and Lord MORRIS OF BORTH-Y-GEST said that the act
must indicate the term of the contract which concerns the disposition of an interest in land ;[1] Lord REID and Viscount DIL-
HORNE took the opposite view ;[2] and Lord SIMON OF GLAISDALE
found it unnecessary to determine the point because there were
acts of part performance which specifically indicated the land
in question.[3]

Payment
of money.

(c) *Payment of Money*

Before *Steadman* v. *Steadman* it was sometimes said that
payment of money could never be a sufficient act of part performance.[4] This view, however, was decisively rejected by a
majority of the House of Lords in that case.[5]

There may be many cases where the payment of money is an
equivocal act.   The *mere* payment of money without any admissible
evidence of the surrounding circumstances need not imply a
pre-existing oral contract ; the payment is equally consistent
with other hypotheses.   But as *Steadman* v. *Steadman* shows,
such evidence may be admissible.   Lord SALMON said[6]

> " The circumstances surrounding a payment may be such that the
> payment becomes evidence not only of the existence of the contract
> under which it was made but also of the nature of the contract . . .
> There is no rule of law which excludes evidence of the relevant
> circumstances surrounding the payment—save parol evidence of
> the contract on behalf of the person seeking to enforce the contract
> under which the payment is alleged to have been made . . .   The

---

[1] *Steadman* v. *Steadman*, [1974] 3 W. L. R. 56, at pp. 86–8, and 66 respectively.   Lord MORRIS OF BORTH-Y-GEST dissented.
[2] *Ibid.*, at pp. 60–1, and 72 respectively.
[3] *Ibid.*, pp. 80–1.
[4] *Thursby* v. *Eccles* (1900), 49 W. R. 281 ; *Chaprionere* v. *Lambert* [1917] 2
Ch. 356.
[5] [1974] 3 W. L. R. 56 ; [1974] 2 All E. R. 977 ; (1974) 38 Conv. (N.S.)
354 (F. R. Crane) ; 90 L. Q. R. 433 (H. W. R. Wade).
[6] *Steadman* v. *Steadman*, [1974] 3 W. L. R. 56, at pp. 88, 90.   See the two
examples given at pp. 88–9 ; and Lord SIMON OF GLAISDALE at p. 83.

wife's admission in open court plainly connected the payment of the £100 with the parol agreement relating to the disposition of an interest in land and showed that the payment was in part performance of that agreement. She has not repaid or ever offered to repay any part of the £100. This payment, in my opinion, bars the wife from relying on the statute and she is accordingly bound to perform her part of the agreement."

In summary, it is clear that the payment of money is not *per se* an act of part performance. But it would seem that, if it is paid in such circumstances that the payee is unwilling or unable to restore it (as, for instance, if he is insolvent), the mischief aimed at by the statute disappears, and the payment may be a sufficient act.

Since the basis of the doctrine of part performance is that the plaintiff, having altered his position on the faith of the contract, acquires an equity against the defendant, it follows that the part performance must be by the plaintiff. *(Party who has acted can alone sue.)*

It is important to observe that a person who is compelled to base his action on part performance is not in such a favourable position as one who can produce a memorandum satisfying all the requirements of the statute. If the plaintiff relies on a memorandum and proves his case, he is entitled as of right to an award of damages at common law : he may also be able to obtain a decree of specific performance in equity, but, if for some reason, such as undue delay in seeking relief, he cannot obtain one, then he is limited to the recovery of damages only. On the other hand if he relies solely on part performance, he must show that the contract is one for which the court has jurisdiction to grant specific performance ;[1] otherwise he is remediless, common law damages not being available. That is not to say that a plaintiff who relies on part performance will never recover damages. For Lord Cairns' Act 1858[2] gave to the Court of Chancery power to award damages either in addition to[3] or in substitution for specific performance. This includes a situation where no damages would be available at common law, as where the plaintiff relies on part performance, and is available even where a decree of specific performance would be refused on some discretionary ground.[4] The damages are not necessarily assessed on the same basis as common law damages ; and may be more beneficial.[4] *(Distinction between contract enforceable at law and one enforceable in equity.)*

(3) EFFECT OF ENFORCEABLE CONTRACT[5]

If a contract for sale is capable of specific performance, an immediate equitable interest in the land passes to the purchaser. *(Vendor in a fiduciary position.)*

---

[1] See *Lavery* v. *Purcell* (1888), 39 Ch. D. 508, at p. 519.
[2] Chancery Amendment Act 1858 s. 2 ; Statute Law Revision and Civil Procedure Act 1883, s. 5. (1975) 34 C. L. J. 224 (J. A. Jolowicz).
[3] *Grant* v. *Dawkins*, [1973] 1 W. L. R. 1406 ; [1973] 3 All E. R. 897.
[4] *Wroth* v. *Tyler*, [1974] Ch. 30 ; [1973] 1 All E. R. 897 ; *infra*, p. 131.
[5] See Hanbury's *Modern Equity* (9th Edn.), pp. 233–4 ; Farrand, *Contract and Conveyance* (2nd Edn.), pp. 225–31, Barnsley, *Conveyancing Law and Practice*, pp. 223–37.

The legal estate remains in the vendor until the conveyance has been executed, but meanwhile equity regards the vendor as a trustee for the purchaser, and is prepared to decree specific performance at the instance of the latter.[1]   In the words of JESSEL, M.R. [2]

> " The moment you have a valid contract for sale the vendor becomes in equity a trustee for the purchaser of the estate sold, and the beneficial ownership passes to the purchaser, the vendor having a right to the purchase money, a charge or lien on the estate for the security of that purchase money, and a right to retain possession of the estate until the purchase money is paid, in the absence of express contract as to the time of delivering possession."

Thus, for instance, pending completion

> the purchaser may dispose of his equitable interest by sale or otherwise ;   he becomes owner of the rents and profits which fall due after the time fixed for completion ;   and he can demand an occupation rent if the vendor remains in possession after that time.

On the other hand, as from the date of the contract, the purchaser must bear the risk of any loss or damage suffered by the property, as, for instance, from an accidental fire or from a fall in prices ;   and from the date fixed for completion he must meet the cost of all necessary outgoings.

Vendor's rights.   Pending the completion of the sale, the vendor occupies a fiduciary position, and therefore he must manage and preserve the property with the same care as a trustee must show with regard to trust property.   He must, for instance, relet the premises if an existing lease runs out, but before doing so he must consult the purchaser.[3]   Nevertheless, the vendor is not an ordinary trustee, since he possesses certain personal rights of a valuable nature in the land, which he is entitled to protect on his own behalf.   Thus :

> 1. he has a right to remain in possession until the purchase money is paid, and to protect that possession, if necessary, by the maintenance of an action, though while in possession he is under a duty to maintain the property in a reasonable state of preservation and so far as may be in the state in which it was when the contract was made ; [4]

---

[1] *Shaw* v. *Foster* (1872), L. R. 5 H. L. 321, at pp. 333, 338 ; *Howard* v. *Miller*, [1915] A. C. 318, at p. 326. There may be a decree, even though, between contract and completion, a compulsory purchase order has been made by a local authority. *Hillingdon Estates Co.* v. *Stonefield Estates, Ltd.*, [1952] Ch. 627 ; [1952] 1 All E. R. 85.

[2] *Lysaght* v. *Edwards* (1876), 2 Ch. D. 449, at p. 506 ; *Lake* v. *Bayliss* [1974] 1 W. L. R. 1073 ; [1974] 2 All E. R. 1114.

[3] *Egmont (Earl of)* v. *Smith* (1877), 6 Ch. D. 469; *Abdulla* v. *Shah*, [1959] A.C. 124.

[4] *Clarke* v. *Ramus*, [1891] 2 Q. B. 456; *Phillips* v. *Lamdin*, [1949] 2 K. B. 33 ; [1949] 1 All E. R. 770.

2. he is entitled to take the rents and profits until the time fixed for completion ; and
3. he possesses an equitable lien on the property for the amount of the purchase money. An equitable lien is in the nature of a charge on land and entitles the person in whom it resides to apply to the court for a sale of the property in satisfaction of his claim. Unlike a common law lien, it is not dependent on possession.[1]

Although the equitable ownership has passed to the purchaser, the vendor retains a substantial interest in the land, and for that reason is generally called a qualified trustee.[2] Lord CAIRNS, dealing with a case where a valid contract had been made for the sale of a London theatre, said[3] :— *(Vendor a qualified trustee.)*

> " There cannot be the slightest doubt of the relation subsisting in the eye of a Court of Equity between the vendor and the purchaser. The vendor was a trustee of the property for the purchaser ; the purchaser was the real beneficial owner in the eye of a Court of Equity of the property, subject only to this observation, that the vendor, whom I have called the trustee, was not a mere dormant trustee, he was a trustee having a personal and substantial interest in the property, a right to protect that interest, and an active right to assert that interest if anything should be done in derogation of it. The relation, therefore, of trustee and *cestui que trust* subsisted, but subsisted subject to the paramount right of the vendor and trustee to protect his own interest as vendor of the property."

Thus, the trusteeship relates only to the property sold, which, failing express agreement, is confined to vacant possession of the land together with any physical accretions thereto. Therefore the vendor is entitled to retain compensation money payable in respect of the requisitioning of the property and falling due between the date of the contract and the date of the conveyance.[4]

Likewise, if between these dates the premises are damaged by fire, the former rule was that the money paid by the insurance company in respect of the loss belonged to the vendor, not to the purchaser, for the policy of insurance was no part of the property sold.[5] This particular aspect of the principle, however, has been reversed by the Law of Property Act 1925, which provides [6] that where, after the date of any contract for sale or exchange of land, money becomes payable under any policy maintained by the vendor in respect of any damage to, or destruction of, property included in the contract, the money shall on completion of the

---

[1] White and Tudor, *Leading Cases in Equity* (9th Edn.), vol. ii., p. 857. See *Uziell-Hamilton* v. *Keen* (1971), 22 P. & C. R. 655.
[2] *Rayner* v. *Preston* (1881) 18 Ch. D. 1, at p. 6, *per* COTTON, L.J.
[3] *Shaw* v. *Foster* (1872), L. R. 5 H. L. 321, at p. 338.
[4] *Hamilton–Snowball's Conveyance*, [1959] Ch. 308 ; [1958] 2 All E. R. 319.
[5] *Rayner* v. *Preston*, *supra*. See also *Re Watford Corpn. and Ware's Contract*, [1943] 1 Ch. 82 ; [1943] 1 All E. R. 54.
[6] L. P. A. 1925, s. 47.

contract be paid by the vendor to the purchaser. This obligation may be varied by the contract, it is subject to the liability of the purchaser to pay the premiums falling due after the date of the contract, and is also subject to any requisite consents of the insurers.[1]

Registration of the contract.

A binding contract for the sale of land is registrable as an *estate contract* under the Land Charges Act 1972.[2] If not registered it is void against later purchasers for money or money's worth of the legal estate in the land.[3] In the case of registered land, a notice, caution or restriction may be entered on the register ; if no such entry is made, the contract will be overridden by a registered disposition made for valuable consideration. The purchaser may, however, have an overriding interest by virtue of his actual occupation of the land, in which case his rights will bind a subsequent purchaser whether he has notice or not.[4]

Options. Finally we must consider two special cases, an option to purchase and a right of pre-emption (*i.e.*, a right of first refusal).

An option to purchase is an offer to sell which " the grantor is contractually precluded from withdrawing so long as the option remains exercisable ".[5] A contract to purchase is formed when the notice exercising the option is given to the grantor. Although the option does not itself form a contract, it does create an immediate equitable interest in favour of the grantee as soon as it is granted. The grantee's right to call for a conveyance of the land is an equitable interest ; as far as the grantor is concerned, " his estate or interest is taken away from him without his consent, and the right to take it away being vested in another, the covenant giving the option must give that other an interest in the land ".[6]

---

[1] This would appear to put the purchaser in a doubtful position. If the house which is the subject of the sale is burnt down, the purchaser is nevertheless obliged to pay the purchase money, and if the insurance company refuses to give the requisite consent to the transfer of the insurance money, he will be unable to obtain payment of that money under the section. On the other hand, having regard to the nature of fire insurance, it seems clear that the vendor is not entitled both to the insurance money and to the purchase money. A purchaser is well advised to insure the property himself immediately after the contract and not to rely on this section.

[2] S. 2 (4), Class (iv).

[3] *Ibid.*, s. 4 (6) ; *infra*, pp. 744.

[4] L.R.A. 1925, s. 70 (1) (g), *infra*, p. 773.

[5] *Beesly* v. *Hallwood Estates, Ltd.*, [1960] 1 W. L. R. 549, at p. 556 *per* BUCKLEY, J. See generally (1974) 38 Conv. (N.S.) 8 (A. Prichard).

[6] *London and South Western Rail Co.* v. *Gomm* (1882), 20 Ch. D. 562, at p. 581, *per* JESSEL, M.R. ; *Griffith* v. *Pelton*, [1958] Ch. 205, at p. 225 ; *Webb* v. *Polmount*, [1966] Ch. 584, at p. 597 ; *Mountford* v. *Scott* [1975] Ch. 258; [1975] 1 All E. R. 198 ; *George Wimpey & Co., Ltd.*, v. *I.R. Comrs.* [1974] 1 W. L. R. 975, at p. 980 ; [1974] 2 All E. R. 602 ; affirmed [1975] 1 W. L. R. 995 ; [1975] 2 All E. R. 45. For the application of the rule against perpetuities, see *infra*, pp. 338, 356.

In *Brown* v. *Gould*, MEGARRY, J. distinguished an option from a right of pre-emption as follows :[1]

> " Under an option, only one step is normally needed to constitute a contract, namely, the exercise of the option. Under a right of pre-emption, two steps will usually be necessary, the making of the offer in accordance with the right of pre-emption, and the acceptance of that offer."

The effect of a right of pre-emption is uncertain. It has been held that it does not create an equitable interest in the land ;[2] on the other hand, there are statutory provisions which assume that it does,[3] and there is authority in favour.[4]

(4) REMEDIES OF PARTIES FOR BREACH OF CONTRACT

The remedies which are available to either party in the event of a breach of a contract for sale are :[5]

1. Action for damages,
2. Specific performance,
3. Rescission,
4. Rectification.

1. **Action for Damages.** In the event of a breach of any contract the rule of law that governs remoteness of damage limits the liability of the defendant to the actual loss caused, provided that having regard to the knowledge, actual or constructive, possessed by him at the time of the contract he ought reasonably to have contemplated that such such loss was likely to occur.[6] The only duty cast upon a party in this respect is to foresee the loss that will occur in the usual course of things, unless he knows of exceptional circumstances by which it may be increased.[7]

Remoteness of damage.

---

[1] [1972] Ch. 53, at p. 58.

[2] *Manchester Ship Canal Co.* v. *Manchester Racecourse Co.*, [1901] 2 Ch. 37 ; *Murray* v. *Two Strokes, Ltd.* [1973] 1 W. L. R. 823 ; [1973] 3 All E. R. 357. See (1973) 89 L. Q. R. 462 (M. J. Albery). *First National Securities, Ltd.* v. *Chiltern District Council* [1975] 1 W. L. R. 1075 ; [1975] 2 All E. R. 766.

[3] L.C.A. 1972, s. 2 (4), where it is registrable as an estate contract ; L.P.A. 1925, s. 186 ; P. & A. A. 1964, s. 9 (2).

[4] *Birmingham Canal Co.* v. *Cartwright* (1879), 11 Ch. D. 421, cited in 89 L. Q. R. at p. 463.

[5] For liability in tort for negligent misstatement during pre-contract negotiations see *Esso Petroleum Co., Ltd.* v. *Mardon,* [1975] Q.B. 819 ; [1975] 1 All E. R. 203.

[6] *Hadley* v. *Baxendale* (1854), 9 Ex. 341 ; *Victoria Laundry (Windsor). Ltd.* v. *Newman Industries, Ltd.,* [1949] 2 K. B. 528 ; [1949] 1 All E. R. 997. *Koufos* v. *C. Czarnikow, Ltd. The Heron II,* [1969] 1 A. C. 350 ; [1967] 3 All E. R. 686 ; Cheshire and Fifoot, *Law of Contract,* (8th Edn.), pp. 582 *et seq.*

[7] *Cottrill* v. *Steyning and Littlehampton Building Society* [1966] 1 W. L. R. 753 ; [1966] 2 All E. R. 295 ; dist. *Diamond* v. *Campbell-Jones,* [1961] Ch. 22 ; [1960] 1 All E. R. 583.

Damages recoverable by vendor.

In the case of a contract for the sale of land this rule applies when it is the vendor who brings the action. The loss caused to the vendor in the usual course of things by the failure of the purchaser to complete is the deprivation of the purchase price diminished by the value of the land that he still holds, and he is therefore entitled to recover by way of damages the difference, if any, between the value of the land which remains in his possession and the price he would have got had the contract been completed.[1] Thus, if he re-sells, he is entitled to recover both the difference in price and the expenses attending the re-sale.[2]

Damages recoverable by purchaser.

When it is the purchaser who sues for breach, the measure of damages depends upon whether the breach was due

(i) merely to the vendor's inability to make a good title, or

(ii) to his failure to do all that he could to complete the conveyance.

(i) Where the vendor is unable to complete the conveyance owing to a defect in his title, and is not personally at fault, the general rule is excluded by the rule in *Bain* v. *Fothergill*; the purchaser cannot recover damages for the loss of his bargain, but is limited to the recovery of his deposit, if any, and of the expenses incurred by him in investigating the title.[3] The justification for this anomalous departure from the general rule is said to be the extreme difficulty that attends the making of a good title to English land.[4] Thus if the owner of leaseholds agrees to sell them without stating that his lessor's licence is necessary, and if the licence is refused, the purchaser will not be entitled to recover general damages.[5] But the anomaly is less compelling where the title to land is registered, and it will not be extended.[6]

The vendor may be liable in damages for fraudulent or innocent misrepresentation under the Misrepresentation Act 1967, unless he can prove that he had reasonable grounds to believe and did believe up to the

---

[1] *Laird* v. *Pim* (1841), 7 M. & W. 474 ; *Harold Wood Brick Co., Ltd.* v. *Ferris*, [1935] 1 K. B. 613 ; affd., [1935] 2 K. B. 198.

[2] *Noble* v. *Edwardes* (1877), 5 Ch. D. 378 ; *Keck* v. *Faber* (1916), 60 Sol. Jo. 253.

[3] *Flureau* v. *Thornhill* (1776), 2 Wm. Bl. 1078.

[4] *Bain* v. *Fothergill* (1874), L. R. 7 H. L. 158 ; *Barnes* v. *Cadogan Developments, Ltd.*, [1930] 1 Ch. 479, at p. 488 ; *J. W. Café's, Ltd.* v. *Brownlow Trust*, [1950] 1 All E. R. 894.

[5] *Bain* v. *Fothergill*, supra.

[6] *Wroth* v. *Tyler* [1974] Ch. 30, at pp. 52–6 ; [1973] 1 All E. R. 897 ; (full damages recovered by purchaser against vendor unable to complete because after contract his wife entered a caution in respect of her right of occupation under Matrimonial Homes Act 1967 ; *infra*, p. 233). See (1973) 123 N.L.J. 393 (H. W. Wilkinson).

time the contract was made that the facts represented were true.[1] The effect of the Act is thus to restrict the operation of the rule to cases where the vendor knows that he has no title to the land and has made no representation.[2]

(ii) But a vendor who fails or refuses to take the steps which are necessary to complete the title and which are within his power is liable in damages.[3] So if he has not acted honestly, or has refused or neglected to make a good title,[4] as for instance where a vendor of leaseholds induces his lessor to withhold the necessary licence,[5] or declines to carry out the contract, or fails to clear the land of a mortgage,[6] or if his agreement to sell is unlawful,[7] he is liable to pay substantial damages. If the value of the property is greater than the purchase price, the plaintiff recovers the difference, though in this case he cannot recover his conveyancing costs.[8] If the value of the property is less than the purchase price, he is entitled to a return of the deposit with interest and also to damages in respect of the cost of investigating the title.[9] Where damages are awarded to the purchaser in substitution for specific performance,[10] they are based on the value of the land at the date of the judgment and not at the date of the breach of contract.[11] Damages awarded in substitution for specific performance are thus a true substitute.

2. **Specific Performance.** The most effective remedy available to either party is to sue for specific performance, *i.e.* to demand that the contract be completed according to its

Specific performance where damages not adequate remedy.

---

[1] S. 2 (1).

[2] *Watts* v. *Spence*, [1975] 2 W. L. R. 1039 ; [1975] 2 All E. R. 528 ; criticized in (1975) 91 L.Q.R. 307.

[3] *Williams* v. *Glenton* (1866), L. R. 1 Ch. 200, at p. 209 ; *Phillips* v. *Lamdin*, [1949] 2 K. B. 33 ; [1949] 1 All E. R. 770.

[4] *Wallington* v. *Townsend*, [1939] Ch. 588 ; [1939] 2 All E. R. 225.

[5] *Day* v. *Singleton*, [1899] 2 Ch. 320.

[6] *Thomas* v. *Kensington*, [1942] 2 K. B. 181.

[7] *Milner* v. *Staffordshire Congregational Union (Incorporated)*, [1956] Ch. 275 ; [1956] 1 All E. R. 494.

[8] *Re Daniel*, [1917] 2 Ch. 405. The loss for which compensation is recoverable is the difference between the purchase price and the value of the property if it had been conveyed in accordance with the contract. But if the property had in fact been so conveyed, the conveyancing costs would have fallen on the purchaser, and therefore he cannot recover both the difference and the costs ; *ibid.*, at p. 412, *per* SARGANT, J.

[9] *Wallington* v. *Townsend, supra*; see also *Lloyd* v. *Stanbury*, [1971] 1 W. L. R., 535; [1971] 2 All E. R. 267.

[10] See *supra*, p. 125.

[11] *Wroth* v. *Tyler*, [1974] Ch. 30 ; [1973] 1 All E. R. 897 ; *Grant* v. *Dawkins*, [1973] 1 W. L. R. 1406 ; [1973] 3 All E. R. 897 ; *cf. Horsler* v. *Zorro*, [1975] Ch. 302 ; [1975] 1 All E. R. 584 ; criticized in (1975) 91 L. Q. R. 337 (Michael Albery).

terms.   One of the general principles established by equity
is that this relief should be given only where damages do not
afford an adequate remedy.   But the subject matter of a
contract for the sale of land is of unique value, so that specific
performance of the contract is available to a purchaser as a
matter of course.   Furthermore, even though a vendor could
be adequately compensated by damages for the failure of a
purchaser to complete, yet, in pursuance of the doctrine that
remedies should be mutual, equity grants specific performance to a vendor as well as to a purchaser.[1]

An adequate discussion of specific performance is outside
the scope of this book,[2] but it may be noticed that the remedy
is discretionary, though the discretion is not exercised in an
arbitrary or capricious manner, but according to the rules
that have been established by the judges.   If the defendant
can show any circumstances independent of the written
contract which make it inequitable to decree specific performance, as for instance where the terms are ambiguous, and
are understood by the parties in different senses, or where the
vendor or the purchaser has not acted fairly, or where the
completion of the contract would cause hardship to an
innocent vendor or purchaser, the court will not grant the
remedy.

Specific performance with compensation.

In certain circumstances the court will decree specific
performance in favour of the plaintiff subject to the condition
that he pays compensation in respect of some term of the
contract which he has not literally fulfilled.

" Where for instance, some steps towards the completion of the
contract have not been taken or . . . the contract itself has not
been completed at the time agreed upon between the parties,
or where the vendor has not the same interest in the estate as
that which he had contracted to sell, or there was some deficiency in the quality or quantity of it, the party not able
strictly to perform the contract on his part formerly, at law, had
no remedy by way of damages against the other ; but, in equity,
in many cases he would be able to obtain specific performance
if adequate compensation could be made for the non-literal
performance of the contract." [3]

Specific performance when completion delayed.

The most important case in which equity grants specific
performance with compensation is where a contract for the
sale of land is not completed upon the date fixed in the contract.[4]   *At law* time was always considered to be of the essence
of the contract, and a party who failed to complete upon the

---

[1] *Kenney* v. *Wexham* (1822), 6 Madd. 355, at p. 357 ; LEACH, V.-C.
[2] See generally Hanbury's *Modern Equity* (9th Edn.), pp. 34 *et seq.* ; Snell,
Equity (27th Edn.) pp. 573 *et seq.*   White and Tudor, *Leading Cases in Equity*
(9th Edn.), vol. ii, pp. 372 *et seq.*
[3] White and Tudor, vol. ii. p. 434.
[4] See generally Farrand, *Contract and Conveyance*, (2nd Edn.), pp. 238–
250, Barnsley, *Conveyancing Law and Practice*, pp. 365–70.

agreed date was remediless. Thus, if the vendor failed to complete, the purchaser could repudiate the contract and recover the deposit and the costs of investigating the title. Equity, however, taking a different view that now prevails in all courts,[1] has always been prepared to decree specific performance notwithstanding failure to observe the exact date fixed for completion, *provided that this will not cause injustice to either party.* Equity looks

> " not at the letter but at the substance of the agreement, to ascertain whether the parties, notwithstanding that they named a specific time within which completion was to take place, really and in substance intended no more than that it should take place within a reasonable time."[2]

Thus specific performance will not be decreed if the parties have expressly stipulated that time shall be essential, or if there is something in the nature of the property or in the surrounding circumstances which renders it inequitable to treat the appointed date as non-essential.[3]

> So, if the nature of the property is such as to make its conveyance at the agreed date imperative, *e.g.* when the contract is for the sale of licensed premises,[4] or of a shop as a going concern, specific performance, even with compensation, will not be decreed ; but if there is nothing special in the nature of the property or in the purposes for which it is required and if there has been no unreasonable or negligent conduct, the court will decree specific performance, subject to the condition that the defaulting party gives compensation for the delay.

A new contract cannot be made at the will of one of the parties and therefore, where time is not initially essential, one party cannot make it so of his own volition.[5] Nevertheless, there must be some limit to delaying tactics, and it is established that after the date fixed for completion has passed one party may serve a notice on the other requiring completion within a specified time.[6] The notice will be valueless unless the time allowed is reasonable,[7] but if satisfactory in this respect it will bind both parties.[8]

---

[1] L.P.A. 1925, s. 41, re-enacting Judicature Act 1873, s. 25 (7).
[2] *Jamshed Khodaram Irani* v. *Burjorji Dhunjibhai* (1915), 32 T. L. R. 156, at p. 157, *per* Lord HALDANE.
[3] *Stickney* v. *Keeble*, [1915] A. C. 386, at pp. 415–6 ; *per* LORD PARKER. See also *Rightside Properties, Ltd.* v. *Gray*, [1975] Ch. 72 ; [1974] 2 All E. R. 1169.
[4] *Lock* v. *Bell*, [1931] 1 Ch. 35.
[5] *Green* v. *Sevin* (1879), 13 Ch. D. 589, at p. 599.
[6] *Finkielkraut* v. *Monohan*, [1949] 2 All E. R. 234.
[7] *Smith* v. *Hamilton*, [1951] Ch. 174 ; [1950] 2 All E. R. 928 ; *Re Barr's Contract*, [1956] Ch. 551 ; [1956] 2 All E. R. 853 ; *Ajit* v. *Sammy*, [1967] 1 A. C. 255.
[8] *Finkielkraut* v. *Monohan*, *supra* ; *Quadrangle Development and Construction Co., Ltd.* v. *Jenner*, [1974] 1 W. L. R. 68 ; [1974] 1 All E. R. 729.

Discharge
of contract.

Rescission.

Forfeiture
of deposit.

3. **Rescission.** A breach of contract in every case gives the innocent party a right to sue for damages, but if it is a breach of some term which is a condition precedent to his liability (*e.g.* failure of the vendor to show a good title or to deliver the actual land or interest described in the contract), he may treat the contract as discharged, and elect either to rescind the contract altogether,[1] or to hold the defaulting party to it and recover damages.

If the vendor elects to rescind, he may re-sell the property as owner, but he cannot recover damages in addition, for if this were allowed he would enjoy a double remedy.[2] He is entitled, however, to retain any deposit that the purchaser may have paid. Thus in *Howe* v. *Smith*,[3]

> £500 was paid as deposit and part payment of the purchase money. The purchaser, who was in default in completing the contract, sued to recover the £500, but it was held that, since it was the intention of the parties that this sum should be deposited as a guarantee for the due performance of his obligations, it must be forfeited to the vendor.

A vendor who elects to rescind, however, may not insist on the performance of the contract so as to claim recovery of part of the deposit not yet paid by the purchaser.[4] But whether the rule as to retention of the deposit applies or not is in each case a matter of construction, and if the terms show that the money has not been paid as a guarantee of performance, but solely by way of part payment, it is recoverable by the purchaser even though the contract is rescinded owing to his own default.[5]

A purchaser may be able to secure the return of his deposit under section 49 (2) of the Law of Property Act 1925, which provides that

> " Where the court refuses to grant specific performance of a contract, or in any action for the return of a deposit, the court may, if it thinks fit, order the repayment of any deposit."

In considering this provision VAISEY, J., said :—

> " In my judgment the primary purpose of the provision was to remove the difficulty which had stood in the way of a pur-

---

[1] *Myton, Ltd.* v. *Schwab-Morris*, [1974] 1 W. L. R. 331 ; [1974] 1 All E. R. 326.

[2] *Barber* v. *Wolfe*, [1945] Ch. 187 ; [1945] 1 All E. R. 399.

[3] (1884), 27 Ch. D. 89. On deposits generally see Farrand, *Contract and Conveyance* (2nd Edn.), pp. 262–70, Barnsley, *Conveyancing Law and Practice*, pp. 218–23. For an analysis of the situation where an estate agent holds the pre-contract deposit of a prospective purchaser, see *Burt* v. *Claude Cousins & Co., Ltd.*, [1971] 2 Q. B. 426 ; [1971] 2 All E. R. 611 ; *Barrington* v. *Lee*, [1972] 1 Q. B. 326 ; [1971] 3 All E. R. 1231 ; *Sorrell* v. *Finch* (1975), *Times*, June 13th. See the dissenting judgments of Lord DENNING, M.R. in all three cases. (1972) 88 L. Q. R. 184 (F. M. B. Reynolds).

[4] *Lowe* v. *Hope*, [1970] Ch. 94 ; [1969] 3 All E. R. 605.

[5] *Mayson* v. *Clouet*, [1924] A. C. 980.

chaser who, though in a position successfully to resist specific performance in equity, was at law precluded from recovering his deposit.[1] Possibly this was not only the primary object of the provision, but its sole object, for it should be noticed that while the court may order the return of the whole of the deposit, it is not, at any rate in terms, authorised to order the return of less than the whole."[2]

Rescission may also be available in two further situations. First, where one party has been induced to enter into the contract as the result of a misrepresentation by the other party.[3] Second, where a right to rescind is one of the express terms of the contract.[4] There is commonly found in a contract of sale a condition that allows the vendor to rescind if the purchaser should insist on any requisition which the vendor is unable or unwilling to comply with.[5] But " a vendor, in seeking to rescind, must not act arbitrarily, or capriciously, or unreasonably. Much less can he act in bad faith... Above all, perhaps, he must not be guilty of ' recklessness' in entering into his contract."[6] Thus, in *Baines* v. *Tweddle*,[7] a vendor was unable to exercise a contractual right to rescind because he had failed to seek the concurrence of his mortgagees before contracting to sell free from the mortgage.

Misrepresentation.
Contractual right to rescind.

4. **Rectification.** If, as the result of a mistake common to both parties, the written evidence omits some material term and therefore does not express the true bargain between the parties, the court has jurisdiction to rectify the contract.[8] In such a case it first rectifies the written contract by adding the oral omission or variation, and then decrees specific performance of

Oral terms excluded from writing by mistake.

---

[1] *Re Scott and Alvarez's Contract*, [1895] 2 Ch. 603.
[2] *James Macara, Ltd.* v. *Barclay*, [1944] 2 All E. R. 31 at p. 32 : affd. on other grounds [1945] K.B. 148 ; [1944] 2 All E. R. 589 ; *Hunt Ltd.* v. *Palmer*, [1931] 2 Ch. 287 ; *Finkielkraut* v. *Monohan*, [1949] 2 All E. R. 234 ; *Schindler* v. *Pigault*, (1975), 30 P. & C. R. 328. See also Law Commission Working Paper No. 61 Penalty clauses and forfeiture of moneys paid (1975), para. 66, where it is suggested that a defaulting purchaser should be able to challenge the forfeiture of a deposit exceeding a statutory percentage of the purchase price (say 5%). On the principles governing relief against forfeiture of deposit, see *Stockloser* v. *Johnson* [1954] 1 Q. B. 476 ; [1954] 1 All E. R. 630 ; *Linggi Plantations, Ltd.* v. *Jagatheesan* [1972] 1 M. L. J. 89, P. C. ; *Windsor Securities, Ltd.* v. *Loreldal, Ltd. and Lester*, (1975), *Times*, September 10th.
[3] See Cheshire and Fifoot *Law of Contract* (8th Edn.), pp. 242 *et seq.*
[4] Emmet on *Title* (16th Edn.), pp. 221–3.
[5] See *e.g.* Condition 18 of the Law Society's Contract and Conditions of Sale 1973.
[6] *Selkirk* v. *Romar Investments, Ltd.*, [1963] 1 W. L. R. 1415, at p. 1422 ; [1963] 3 All E. R. 994, *per* Lord RADCLIFFE.
[7] [1959] Ch. 679. [1959] 2 All E. R. 724 ; *Re Des Reaux and Setchfield's Contract*, [1926] Ch. 178.
[8] *United States* v. *Motor Trucks Ltd.*, [1924] A. C. 196 ; *Joscelyne* v. *Nissen*, [1970] 2 Q. B. 86 ; [1970] 1 All E. R. 1213.

the contract as rectified. At one and the same time it reforms and enforces the contract.[1] This remedy will be
granted even where the mistake is embodied in the final deed
of conveyance.[2]

Object and scope of summons.

Vendor and Purchaser Summons. The Vendor and
Purchaser Act 1874 introduced a new method whereby parties
to a contract of sale, whose disagreement upon some matter prevents the completion of the contract, may apply in a summary
way to a judge in Chambers, and obtain such an order as may
appear just. This summary proceeding is termed a vendor and
purchaser summons, and is now governed by the Law of Property
Act 1925.[3] Typical questions which lead to a summons are the
sufficiency of the title shown by the vendor, the sufficiency of an
answer made to a requisition, the construction of the contract,
and the question whether a vendor is entitled to rescind.

The Act expressly excludes the possibility of raising any
question that affects the existence or the validity of the contract
in its inception, as for instance, the question whether there is a
sufficient memorandum.

Not only may the court decide the question submitted to it,
but it may also grant consequential relief, that is, may order such
things to be done as are the natural consequence of the decision.
For instance, it may order rescission in favour of a purchaser,
together with the return of his deposit.

SECTION VII. THE DEFINITION OF LAND

As we are about to discuss the interests that may subsist in
land, it is obviously appropriate that we should first gain a clear
idea of the meaning attributed by law to the word " land."

Distinction between corporeal and incorporeal here-ditaments.

Law is at one with the layman in agreeing that " land "
includes the surface of the earth, together with all the sub-jacent
and super-jacent things of a physical nature such as buildings,
trees and minerals,[4] but it also gives the word a far wider meaning, and one which would not occur to those unversed in legal
terminology. Using the word " hereditament " to signify a right
that is heritable, *i.e.* capable of passing by way of descent to heirs,
our legal ancestors reached the remarkable[5] conclusion that

---

[1] *Ibid.*, p. 201 ; *per* Lord BIRKENHEAD.
[2] *Craddock Bros., Ltd.* v. *Hunt*, [1923] 2 Ch. 136. On the subject generally
see Cheshire and Fifoot, *Law of Contract* (8th Edn.), pp. 217–19. *Riverlate
Properties, Ltd.* v. *Paul*, [1975] Ch. 133 ; [1974] 2 All E. R. 656.
[3] L.P.A. 1925, s. 49(1).
[4] As to waste products dumped on land, see *Rogers (Inspector of Taxes)* v.
Longsdon, [1967] Ch. 93 ; [1966] 2 All E. R. 49.
[5] Co. Litt. 6a ; *Lloyd* v. *Jones* (1848), 6 C. B. 81, 90.

hereditaments are either corporeal or incorporeal. As BLACK-
STONE said :

> " Hereditaments, then, to use the largest expression, are of two
> kinds, corporeal and incorporeal. Corporeal consist of such as
> affect the senses ; such as may be seen and handled by the body ;
> incorporeal are not the object of sensation, can neither be seen nor
> handled, are creatures of the mind and exist only in contemplation.
> Corporeal hereditaments consist of substantial and permanent
> objects." [1]

What this comes to is that the subject-matter of estate ownership may consist either of corporeities or of incorporeities.
There is nothing remarkable in this, for it is obvious that an
incorporeity such as a right of way may, equally with a house or
a piece of land, be held in fee simple or for life. What is remarkable, however, is a terminology which declares that an
interest in a corporeity, *i.e.* a physical thing capable of carrying
seisin, is itself a corporeal *interest*, but that an interest in an
incorporeity is an incorporeal *interest*. This nomenclature will
not bear a moment's examination, for no proprietary interest can
be other than a mere *right* of ownership, and no matter what the
nature of its subject-matter may be, it must always be incorporeal.

The distinction is unwarranted.

> " All property, of whatever kind, is an *incorporeal* right to the *cor-
> poreal* use and profit of some *corporeal* thing." [2]

It is difficult to answer the following criticism of AUSTIN :

> " With us *all* rights and obligations are not *incorporeal things* ; but
> certain rights are styled *incorporeal hereditaments*, and are opposed
> by that name to *hereditaments corporeal*. That is to say, *rights of*
> a certain species . . . are absurdly opposed to the *things* (strictly
> so called) which are the *subjects* or *matter* of rights of another species.
> The word *hereditaments* is evidently taken in two senses in the two
> phrases which stand to denote the species of hereditaments. A
> corporeal hereditament is the thing itself which is the subject of the
> right ; an incorporeal hereditament is not the subject of the right, but
> the right itself." [3]

The continued use to the present day of this unscientific
terminology need not, however, disturb us. The two facts to
bear in mind are: first, that whether an interest, such as a fee
simple estate, exists in a corporeity or an incorporeity, it is an
interest in *land* ; secondly, that the number of incorporeities
recognized by English law is considerable. BLACKSTONE described

Land has an extensive meaning in law.

---

[1] *Commentaries*, vol. ii. p. 17.
[2] (1857), 1 *Jurid. Soc.*, p. 542 (S. M. Leake).
[3] *Jurisprudence* (5th Edn.), vol. i. p. 362. ; but see Sweet's answer in Challis,
Law of Real Property (3rd Edn.), pp. 48–58. L.P.A. 1925, s. 1 (2), *supra*, p. 97,
perpetuates the confusion in describing a right to, for instance, an easement
as an interest in land, notwithstanding that in s. 205 (1) (ix) it includes an easement in the definition of " land." The truth is that an incorporeity, such as
an easement, is neither an estate nor an interest, but something in which an
estate or an interest can exist.

no fewer than ten *incorporeal hereditaments* some of which are no longer of practical importance.[1] The most important now are easements,[2] profits[3] and rents.

Statutory
definition
of land.

The following is the definition of *land* for the purposes of the Law of Property Act 1925 :—

> " ' Land ' includes land of any tenure, and mines and minerals, whether or not held apart from the surface, buildings or parts of buildings (whether the division is horizontal, vertical or made in any other way) and other corporeal hereditaments ; also a manor, an advowson, and a rent and other incorporeal hereditaments, and an easement, right, privilege, or benefit in, over, or derived from land ; but not an undivided share in land . . . " [4]

Land
includes
fixtures.

There is one class of corporeal things, namely *fixtures*, which are regarded as " land " and which are sufficiently important to merit a somewhat extensive treatment.

FIXTURES

Meaning of
fixtures.

The primary meaning from a historical point of view of " fixtures " is chattels which are so affixed to land or to a building on land as to become in fact part thereof.[5] Such chattels lose the character of chattels and pass with the ownership of the land, for the maxim of the law is, *quicquid plantatur solo, solo cedit*.

The legal
test.

This question whether a chattel has been so affixed to land as to become part of it is sometimes exceedingly difficult to answer. It is a question of law for the judge,[6] but the decision in one case is no sure guide in another, for everything turns upon the circumstances and mainly, though not decisively, upon two particular circumstances, namely, the *degree of annexation* and the *object of annexation*.[7] We will take these considerations separately.

Degree of an-
nexation an
important
element.

1. **Degree of Annexation.** The general rule is that a chattel is not deemed to be a fixture unless it is actually fastened to or

---

[1] *Commentaries*, vol. ii. c. iii. The list is: advowsons, tithes, commons, ways, offices, dignities, franchises, corodies, (a right to receive victuals for one's maintenance), annuities and rents. " Whether the benefit of a restrictive covenant can be described as an incorporeal hereditament is a very doubtful question ". *Earl of Leicester* v. *Wells-next-the-Sea U.D.C.*, [1973] Ch. 110, at p. 119, *per* PLOWMAN, J.

[2] *Infra*, p. 514.   [3] *Infra*, p. 558.

[4] Section 205 (1) (ix); *cf.* the definitions in S.L.A. 1925, s. 117 (1) (ix) ; T.A. 1925, s. 68 (6) ; L.C.A. 1925, s. 20 (6). See also Interpretation Act 1889, s. 3. As to whether land includes an interest under a trust for sale, see *infra*, p. 222, n. 4.

[5] **Leake, *Uses and Profits of Land*, p. 103.**

[6] *Reynolds* v. *Ashby*, [1904] A. C. 466.

[7] *Holland* v. *Hodgson* (1872), L. R. 7 C. P. 327, at p. 334 ; *per* BLACKBURN, J. ; M. & B. p. 81.

connected with the land or building. Mere juxtaposition or the laying of an article, however heavy, upon the land does not *prima facie* make it a fixture, even though it subsequently sinks into the ground. If a superstructure can be removed without losing its identity, it will not in general be regarded as a fixture. Examples are a Dutch barn, consisting of a roof resting upon wooden uprights, the uprights being made to lie upon brick columns let into the ground[1]; or a printing machine weighing several tons, standing on the floor and secured by its own weight.[2] The case is the same if the posts that support the roof of a corrugated iron building are not embedded in the concrete floor, but are held in position by iron strips fixed into the floor. The concrete foundation, which is of course a fixture, is regarded as a separate unit from the superstructure.[3] Again, a printing machine that stands by its own weight upon the floor is not a fixture, even though the driving apparatus is attached to the building at certain points.[4] On the other hand a chattel that is attached to land, however slightly, is *prima facie* to be deemed a fixture. Thus, a verandah connected with a house is a fixture,[5] as also are doors, windows, chimneypieces, ovens and other similar things.

Nevertheless the extent of annexation is not a decisive test.

" Perhaps the true rule is, that articles not otherwise attached to the land than by their own weight are not to be considered as part of the land, unless the circumstances are such as to shew that they were intended to be part of the land, the onus of showing that they were so intended lying on those who assert that they have ceased to be chattels; and that, on the contrary, an article which is affixed to the land even slightly is to be considered as part of the land, unless the circumstances are such as to shew that it was intended all along to continue a chattel, the onus lying on those who contend that it is a chattel."[6]

It is for this reason that the second consideration mentioned above is material, namely, the:

2. Object of Annexation. The test here is to ascertain whether the chattel has been fixed for its more convenient

Purpose of
annexation
an important
element.

---

[1] *Elwes* v. *Maw* (1802), 3 East, 38, at p. 55; *Wiltshear* v. *Cottrell* (1853), 1 E. & B. 674.

[2] *Hulme* v. *Brigham*, [1943] K. B. 152; [1943] 1 All E.R. 204.

[3] *Webb* v. *Bevis, Ltd.*, [1940] 1 All E. R. 247; distinguish *Jordan* v. *May*, [1947] K. B. 427; [1947] 1 All E. R. 231; M. & B. p. 84 (electric lighting engine and dynamo bolted to a concrete bed. These were held to be fixtures, *aliter* the batteries). The degree of affixation is not necessarily the same in every type of case; see, *e.g.*, *London County Council* v. *Wilkins*, [1955] 2 Q. B. 653; [1955] 2 All E. R. 180; affd. [1957] A. C. 362; [1956] 3 All E. R. 38 (whether a wooden sectional hut is exempt from rateability).

[4] *Hulme* v. *Brigham*, [1943] K. B. 152; [1943] 1 All E. R. 204.

[5] *Buckland* v. *Butterfield* (1820), 2 Brod. & Bing. 54.

[6] *Holland* v. *Hodgson* (1872), L. R. 7 C. P. 328, at p. 335, *per* BLACKBURN, J.; *Bradshaw* v. *Davey*, [1952] 1 All E. R. 350 (yacht mooring in the Hamble River held intended to be a chattel).

use as a chattel, or for the more convenient use of the land or building.[1]

> For example, stones laid one upon another without any mortar for the purpose of forming a wall become fixtures, but if stones are deposited in a builder's yard and for the sake of convenience stacked one on top of another they are not fixtures.[2]

Again, a comparatively durable method of affixation will not render a chattel a fixture, if the method of annexation is necessary to its proper enjoyment as a chattel. Thus in the well-known case of *Leigh* v. *Taylor* : [3]

> A tenant for life, the owner of some valuable tapestry, laid strips of wood over the drawing-room paper and fixed them to the walls with two-inch nails. Canvas was stretched over these strips, and the tapestry was fastened by tacks to the strips. It was held that the tapestry had not become a fixture.

VAUGHAN WILLIAMS, L.J., said :

> " In my judgment it is obvious that everything which was done here can be accounted for as being absolutely necessary for the enjoyment of the tapestry, and when one arrives at that conclusion there is an end of the case." [4]

The principle of this decision was adopted where a lessee had erected some oak and pine panelling and a chimney-piece.[5]

On the other hand, chattels may be annexed to or placed on land in circumstances which show an obvious intention to benefit the use of the land, and if this is so they become fixtures. Examples are, seats secured to the floor of a cinema hall,[6] and such objects as statues, stone seats and ornamental vases, held in position merely by their own weight, which are part of the architectural design of a house and its grounds.[7]

Persons between whom a question of fixtures may arise.
It is useful to note even at this early stage the principal transactions in which the question whether particular chattels are fixtures or not requires decision. The question arises as between the following parties.[8]

---

[1] *Wake* v. *Hall* (1883), L. R. 8 App. Cas 195, at p. 204.
[2] *Holland* v. *Hodgson*, (1872), L. R. 7 C. P. 328, at p. 335.
[3] [1902] A. C. 157 ; M. & B. p. 84.
[4] See the same case in C. A. *sub. nom. Re De Falbe*, [1901] 1 Ch. 523, 537.
[5] *Spyer* v. *Phillipson*, [1931] 2 Ch. 183.
[6] *Vaudeville Electric Cinema Ltd.* v. *Muriset*, [1923] 2 Ch. 74. *Cf. Lyon & Co.* v. *London City and Midland Bank*, [1903] 2 K. B. 135.
[7] *D'Eyncourt* v. *Gregory* (1866), L. R. 3 Eq. 382.
[8] See too *Simmons* v. *Midford*, [1969] 2 Ch. 415 ; [1969] 2 All E. R. 1269 (drainpipe under roadway held to be chattel with which neighbour claiming an easement of drainage could not interfere) ; *cf. Montague* v. *Long* (1972), 24 P. & C. R. 240.

(1) As between Landlord and Tenant

In the course of time, the rule that an article becomes part of the land to which it has been affixed has been relaxed in favour of the tenant for years, and he is now allowed to remove three particular classes of articles notwithstanding that they are fixtures in the strict sense of the term. *Certain fixtures removable.*

First, it has long been the rule that during the term the tenant may remove fixtures that have been attached to the land for the purpose of carrying on his particular trade, since it is in the public interest that industry should be encouraged. Thus in *Poole's Case*[1] in 1703 it was held by Lord Holt " that during the term the soap-boiler might well remove the vats he set up in relation to trade, and that he might do it by the common law (and not by virtue of any special custom), in favour of trade and to encourage industry. But after the term they become a gift in law to him in reversion, and are not removeable." *Trade fixtures.*

Engines for working collieries,[2] salt pans,[3] coppers and pipes erected by a brewing tenant,[4] the fittings of a public house[5] and petrol pumps installed at a wayside garage[6] have been held to come within the description of trade fixtures.

Secondly, it is now well established that during the term a tenant may remove such chattels as he has affixed to a house for the sake either of ornament or of convenience, but this relaxation of the strict rule is not supported by such strong reasons as apply in the case of trade fixtures and it will not be extended. Examples of objects which have been held removable on this ground are ornamental chimney-pieces, wainscot fixed to the wall by screws, fixed water-tubs, stoves and grates, ranges and ovens.[7] *Ornamental and domestic fixtures.*

But any fixture which partakes of the nature of a permanent improvement and which cannot be removed without substantial damage to the house, such as a conservatory connected by a door with one of the living rooms, does not come within the exception of an ornamental fixture.[8]

Trade, ornamental and domestic fixtures must be removed before the end of the tenancy, otherwise they become a gift in law to the reversioner,[9] but a further period of grace is allowed when the tenant continues in possession after the term under a reasonable supposition of consent on the part of the landlord.[10]

---

[1] (1703) 1 Salk. 368.
[2] *Lawton* v. *Lawton* (1743), 3 Atk. 13.
[3] *Mansfield* v. *Blackburne* (1840), 6 Bing. N. C. 426.
[4] *Lawton* v. *Lawton, supra.*
[5] *Elliott* v. *Bishop* (1854), 10 Ex. 496.
[6] *Smith* v. *City Petroleum Co.*, [1940] 1 All E. R. 260.
[7] See Woodfall, *Landlord and Tenant* (27th Edn.), pp. 704–705.
[8] *Buckland* v. *Butterfield* (1820), 2 Brod. & B. 54.
[9] *Poole's Case* (1703), 1 Salk. 368, *supra.*
[10] *Ex parte Brook* (1878), 10 Ch. D. 100, at p. 109 ; *Leschallas* v. *Woolf,* [1908] Ch. 641.

Agricultural
fixtures.

The third exception relates to agricultural fixtures. Formerly, a farmer was in an unfavourable position with regard to chattels that he had fixed to his holding, for it was held in *Elwes* v. *Maw* [1] in 1803 that, though the sole purpose of their affixation was to further and improve his agricultural operations, yet they could not be regarded as trade fixtures. In that case, the tenant farmer had built at his own cost a beast-house, a carpenter's shed, a fuel house, a wagon-house and a fold-yard, each of which he removed before the end of the lease, leaving the premises in the same state as when he first became tenant. He was held liable to pay damages to the landlord.

The only mitigation at common law of this rigour came in 1901, when it was decided that, though buildings put up by a farmer are not trade fixtures, yet glasshouses built by a market-gardener for the purposes of his trade do come within this description and may be removed before the end of the tenancy against the will of the landlord. [2]

This particular matter has, however been put upon a more equitable footing by a succession of statutes and the position now is as follows :—

Any engine, machinery, fencing *or other fixture* affixed to an agricultural holding by a tenant and any building erected by him thereon, for which he is not otherwise entitled to compensation, becomes his property and is removable by him during the tenancy or within two months after its termination. After the expiration of this period the property in fixtures is no longer vested in him. [3]

Within at least a month before the termination of the tenancy notice of removal must be given to the landlord, who thereupon acquires an option to purchase the fixture. [4] There is no right of removal until the tenant has paid all rent and satisfied his other obligations under the tenancy.

The result of these developments is that if a landlord disputes the right of his tenant to remove a certain chattel from the premises, there are two separate questions to be answered. First, has the chattel become a fixture by reason of its affixation to the land ? If not, *cadit quaestio*. If, however, the answer is in the affirmative, the further question arises whether it is a landlord's or a tenant's fixture, and this of course depends upon whether the chattel falls within one of the three categories already described. [5]

(2) As between Mortgagor and Mortgagee

Fixtures
belong to
mortgagee.

Fixtures pass with the land to the mortgagee even though not mentioned in the deed, [6] as also do those which are added later

---

[1] (1802), 3 East, 38 ; Smith's *Leading Cases* (13th Edn.), vol. ii. p. 193.
[2] *Mears* v. *Callender*, [1901] 2 Ch. 388.
[3] Agricultural Holdings Act 1948, s. 13 (1).   [4] *Ibid.*, s. 13 (2), (3).
[5] *Bain* v. *Brand* (1876), 1 App. Cas. 762, at p. 767, *per* Lord Cairns.
[6] *Vaudeville Electric Cinema, Ltd.* v. *Muriset*, [1923] 2 Ch. 74. L.P.A. 1925, ss. 62 (1) ; 205 (1) (ii).

by the mortgagor himself while in possession. Moreover, a mortgagor in possession is not entitled to remove " tenant's " fixtures, whether they have been annexed to the land before or after the mortgage transaction.[1] These rules apply whether the mortgage is legal or equitable, and whether it affects freehold or leasehold premises. Where, however, fixtures have been annexed to land by a *third party* under an agreement between him and the mortgagor which permits him to remove them in certain circumstances, his right of removal cannot in general be defeated by the mortgagee. The mortgagee, by allowing the mortgagor to remain in possession, implicitly authorizes him to make agreements usual and proper in his particular trade.[2]

(3) As between Vendor and Purchaser

A conveyance of land, in the absence of express reservation, passes fixtures, but not chattels[3] to the purchaser without special mention,[4] and they cannot be removed by a vendor who remains in possession between the contract of sale and the completion of the transaction, even though they consist of articles which, as between landlord and tenant, would be " tenant's fixtures."[5] The fixtures are deemed to have been paid for by the price fixed for the land, and if the vendor desires to remove them or to receive an additional sum in respect of them a clause to that effect must be inserted in the contract.[6]

Fixtures belong to purchaser.

(4) As between Tenant for Life and Reversioner or Remainderman

The general rule obtains that chattels annexed by a tenant for life so as to become part of the land belong to the owner of the fee simple. Nevertheless the personal representatives of a deceased tenant for life are entitled to remove " such fixtures as are removable by a tenant for years," *i.e.* objects affixed for purposes of trade, ornamentation or domestic use.[7]

---

[1] *Longbottom* v. *Berry* (1869), L. R. 5 Q. B. 137.
[2] *Gough* v. *Wood & Co.*, [1894] 1 Q. B. 713.
[3] *Moffatt* v. *Kazana*, [1969] 2 Q. B. 152 ; [1968] 3 All E. R. 271 ; *H. E. Dibble, Ltd.* v. *Moore*, [1970] 2 Q. B. 181 ; [1969] 3 All E. R. 1465.
[4] L.P.A. 1925, s. 62 (1). The section is set out, *infra*, p. 530.
[5] *Gibson* v. *Hammersmith Ry. Co.* (1863), 32 L. J. Ch 337. *Phillips* v. *Lamdin*, [1949] 2 K. B. 33 ; [1949] 1 All E. R. 770.
[6] On hire-purchase agreements and fixtures see (1963), 27 Conv. (N. S.) 30 (A. G. Guest and J. Lever).
[7] *Lawton* v. *Lawton* (1743), 3 Atk. 13 ; *supra*, p. 115. There is some question whether the power of removal by the personal representative is not more restricted than in the case of a tenant for years.

(5) As between the Executor of a Fee Simple Owner and a Devisee

If A., the tenant in fee simple of Blackacre, devises Blackacre to B., it might be argued that A.'s executors are entitled to remove, at any rate, "tenant's fixtures." The rule, however, is well established that all fixtures, no matter of what description, pass with the land to the devisee.[1]

---

[1] *Re Whaley*, [1908] 1 Ch. 615.

BOOK II

ESTATES AND INTERESTS IN LAND

SUMMARY

After this brief introductory survey, the next task is to describe the estates and interests that may subsist in land. The general arrangement of the following account of this matter is based upon the distinction between family interests arising under a settlement or a trust for sale and what, for want of a better title, are called " commercial interests," *i.e.* interests such as leaseholds, mortgages and easements, that arise in the ordinary routine of business and for the most part are not inevitable parts of family endowment schemes. What deserves to be emphasized is that the propensity of landowners to distribute portions of the fee simple among a succession of descendants or other relatives, a propensity that has been a feature of English social life for many centuries, though far less pronounced now in this age of crippling taxation, has left an indelible mark upon the law of real property. To this sentiment is due the occurrence in conveyancing practice of entailed, life and future interests and of powers of appointment, interests that are never found except as cogs in the wheel of a settlement.

Before the proposed dichotomy of interests can be elaborated, however, it is necessary to describe the fee simple absolute in possession. This is the axis round which any account of landed interests must revolve, for it represents the subject-matter out of which lesser proprietary rights, whether family or commercial, may be carved.

PART I

THE ESTATE IN FEE SIMPLE ABSOLUTE IN POSSESSION

SUMMARY

SECTION I. DEFINITION

Meaning of "fee simple." The first essential is to investigate the precise meaning of the statutory expression fee simple absolute in possession, which as we have seen is the only *freehold* interest capable of existing as a legal estate.[1] The word *fee* had by Littleton's day come to denote that the estate was inheritable, that is to say, that it would endure until the person entitled to it *for the time being*—whether the original donee or some subsequent alienee—died intestate and left no heir.[2] The word *simple* showed that the fee was one which was capable of passing to the heirs *general* and was not restricted to passing to a particular class of heirs.[3] This last fact therefore distinguishes a fee simple from another kind of fee which used to be called a fee tail and is now called an entailed interest, for this is a freehold that passes, on the intestacy of its owner, only to the particular class of lineal descendants specified in the instrument of creation.[4]

Thus

if a tenant in fee simple died intestate before 1926, his estate passed to his nearest heir, who according to the circumstances might be a descendant or an ascendant, a lineal or a collateral relative.[5]

---

[1] L.P.A. 1925, s. 1 (1) (a) ; *supra*, pp. 97–8.
[2] Pollock and Maitland, *History of English Law* (2nd Edn.), vol. ii. p. 14.
[3] Co. Litt. 1a, b, 18a ; Blackstone, vol. ii. 105.
[4] *Infra*, pp. 243–4.   [5] *Infra*, pp. 867–70.

An entailed interest, on the other hand (and this is still the law), was capable of passing only to lineal descendants, and these might, according to the terms of the instrument of gift, be either lineal descendants in general or a restricted class of descendants, such as male heirs or the issue of the tenant by a specified wife. The characteristic of general inheritability is still the attribute of a fee simple, but the significance of this is now modified, as will be explained later, by the abolition of the doctrine of heirship on intestacy except in the case of the entailed interest. The land itself no longer passes to the nearest heir but upon the death of the owner intestate is held by the administrators on trust for sale, for distribution among the nearest relatives according to a scheme introduced by the Administration of Estates Act 1925, as amended by subsequent legislation.[1] The relatives specified by the Act, however, comprise descendants and ascendants, both lineal and collateral, and it is therefore still true to say that a fee simple is an estate which is the subject of general inheritability.

Fee simple distinguished from fee tail.

But it is not every fee simple that is a legal estate, for the Law of Property Act 1925 confines that attribute to a fee simple absolute in possession. Postponing for the moment the consideration of the last two words, we must inquire what is meant by the word " absolute." This is not defined in the Act, but it clearly excludes an estate that is defeasible either by the breach of a condition or by the possibility that it may pass to some new owner upon the happening of a specified event. More than a hundred years ago Preston explained the purport of *absolute* in the following words [2] :—

Meaning of " absolute."

> " The epithet *absolute* is used to distinguish an estate extended to any given time, without any condition to defeat, or collateral limitation to determine the estate in the mean time, from an estate subject to a condition or collateral limitation. The term absolute is of the same signification with the word pure, or *simple*, a word which expresses that the estate is not determinable by any event besides the event marked by the clause of limitation."

Thus a fee simple absolute is distinguished from a *determinable* fee simple, *i.e.* one which according to the express terms of its limitation may determine by some event before the completion of the full period for which it may possibly continue.[3]

Determinable fee simple.

If, for instance, premises are limited in fee simple to an incorporated golf club "so long as the premises are used for the purposes of the Club," the interest is a fee simple because it may possibly continue for ever, but it is not a fee simple absolute since it will cease and will return to the grantor or his successors if at some time in the future the premises are used for other purposes.

---

[1] *Infra*, p. 871.
[2] Preston on *Estates*, vol. i. pp. 125–6.
[3] See "Determinable Interests," *infra*, pp. 362–5.

Fee simple liable to be divested.

Again, the limitation of a fee simple may be accompanied by an executory limitation over which provides that if a certain event happens the estate shall pass from the grantee to another person. As, for instance, where there is a grant of Whiteacre,

> to A. in fee simple, but if he becomes entitled to Blackacre, then to B. in fee simple.

Here the fee simple given to A. is not absolute, since it is liable to be divested from him on the occurrence of the specified event. There is one exception to this rule, for it is provided that a fee simple which is liable to be divested under the provisions of the "Lands Clauses Acts, the Schools Sites Acts or any similar statute" shall nevertheless be a fee simple *absolute*.[1] Statutes of this type, which enable land to be acquired compulsorily by a local authority for certain public purposes, generally provide expressly that if the purpose fails or is not carried out the land shall revert to the original owner or shall vest in some other person. An express provision to this effect is not, however, essential to bring a statute within the exception. It is sufficient if the implication is that the local authority shall be divested of its interest upon the fulfilment or failure of the purpose for which the land was acquired.[2]

Fee simple vested in corporation.

The Law of Property Act 1925 also provides that a fee simple vested in a corporation shall be regarded as absolute notwithstanding its liability to determine upon the dissolution of the corporate body.[3]

Fee simple on condition.

If a condition is annexed to the limitation of a fee simple providing that the grantor shall be entitled to re-enter and recover his interest if a certain event happens or does not happen, it is equally clear on general principles that the estate is not a fee simple absolute within the meaning of the description given by Preston.

Fee simple liable to be defeated on non-payment of perpetual rent.

Nevertheless the provision of the Law of Property Act 1925, which denied the character of a legal estate to an interest of this nature, caused considerable difficulty. In certain parts of England and especially in Manchester, Bristol and Bath it has been a common practice for a purchaser of a fee simple, instead of paying the purchase money in a lump sum, to enter into a covenant to pay a

---

[1] L.P.A., 1925, s. 7 (1).

[2] *Tithe Redemption Commission* v. *Runcorn Urban District Council*, [1954] Ch. 383 ; [1954] 1 All E. R. 653 (highway vested in the local highway authority).

[3] S. 7 (2). As to whether the lands of a corporation upon its dissolution reverted to the donor or escheated to the lord, see Co. Litt. 13b ; **Gray**, *Rule against Perpetuities*, (4th Edn.), ss. 44–52 ; Challis, *Law of Real Property* (3rd Edn.) pp. 35–6, 467–8 ; *Hastings Corporation* v. *Letton*, [1908] 1 K. B. 378 ; *Re Woking U.D.C.*, [1914] 1 Ch. 500 ; *Re Sir Thomas Spencer Wells*, [1933] 1 Ch. 29 ; (1933), 49 L. Q. R. 240 ; (1934), 50 L. Q. R. 33 (F. E. Farrer) ; (1935), 51 L. Q. R. 347 (M. W. Hughes), 361 (F. E. Farrer).

perpetual annual rentcharge, often called a fee farm rent.[1] The payment of the rent is secured to the vendor and his successors by the reservation of either a right of entry or a right of re-entry. The former permits the vendor and his successors to enter the land at any time in the future if the annual payment falls into arrear and to hold the land *as a leasehold interest* until the arrears are paid.[2] The right of re-entry (which is more common in the case of a lease[3]) arises where the conveyance contains a condition that the purchaser and his successors will pay the rent and that the vendor shall be entitled to re-enter if this condition is broken. In this case the person entitled to the rent may either re-enter upon the land or bring proceedings for its recovery, whereupon the interest of the purchaser is forfeited and the vendor *re-acquires his old estate.*[4]

The fact that a fee simple liable to interruption in either of these ways was not a legal estate within the meaning of the Law of Property Act 1925 operated to the prejudice of a landowner, for not only did it seem to make the land subject to the Settled Land Act and thus to require the execution of a vesting deed, but it made it difficult to discover where the legal estate resided.[5]

In view of this inconvenience it was later enacted that

" a fee simple subject to a legal or equitable right of entry or re-entry is for the purposes of this Act a fee simple absolute." [6]

The word " absolute " does not imply freedom from incumbrances. Thus a fee simple, though subject to a lien or a mortgage, whether legal or equitable, or to a mere charge, is none the less absolute.

Estate absolute though incumbered

Finally, to have the character of a legal estate, a fee simple absolute must be *in possession.* " Possession " is not here confined to its popular meaning, for it includes receipt of rents and profits or the right to receive the same.[7] Therefore a tenant in fee simple who has leased the land to a tenant for years is the owner of a legal estate even though he is not in physical possession of the land. If, however, he is entitled to the fee simple only at some time in the future, as for instance in the case of a limitation

Meaning of " in possession.'

to A. for life and then to B. in fee simple,

B has an equitable fee simple. The land is settled land under the Settled Land Act 1925, unless the limitation takes effect under a trust for sale.[8]

---

[1] *Infra*, pp. 624 *et seq.* In the British area 80% of owner-occupied residential property may be subject to rentcharges. Law Commission Report on Rentcharges 1975 (Law Com. No. 68) para. 16.

[2] Litt, s. 327; Co. Litt. 202*b*; *ibid.*, note 93 by Hargrave and Butler.

[3] *Infra*, pp. 435 ; 441.   [4] Litt, s. 325.

[5] (1926), 61 *L. J. News* 49 (F. E. Farrer).

[6] L.P.(A.)A. 1926, Sched. The rentcharge, being perpetual, is a *legal* interest under L.P.A. 1925, s. 1 (2) (b), *supra*, p. 97 ; and under *ibid.*, s. 1 (2) (e), the right of entry, being " annexed to a legal rentcharge," is also a *legal* interest. See also M. & B., p. 5 n. 3.

[7] L.P.A. 1925, ss. 205 (1) (xix) ; 95 (4); *District Bank, Ltd.* v. *Webb*, [1958] 1 W. L. R. 148 ; [1958] 1 All E. R. 126.

[8] *Infra*, p. 167.

SECTION II.   MODE OF CREATION

Quantum of
an estate
shown by
words of
limitation.

Position
before 1882
in deeds.

Words of Limitation. Whether a fee simple passes to a grantee or a devisee of land depends upon the words of limitation contained in the deed or will. Words of limitation are those whose purpose it is to indicate the exact estate that is to pass.[1] In the case of deeds the law was in former times exceedingly strict upon this point. If certain expressions were adopted the effect was to create a fee simple; if others, a fee tail or life estate. Thus before 1882 the only way of creating a fee simple by a direct grant *inter vivos* was by a limitation to the grantee *and his heirs*. This expression has been common form since the birth of English law, and perhaps its original implication was that the tenant could not alienate his interest without first consulting the apparent heirs. In the thirteenth century, however, all restraints of that kind on alienation disappeared and it became settled that the expression did not confer rights of any sort upon the heir, but was used merely to show that the tenant had an estate that would endure at least as long as his heirs endured.[2]

If in a *deed* there was for instance a grant to

" A. and his assignees,"
" A. for ever,"
" A. and his descendants,"
" A. and his successors," [3]

then, however untechnical the expression might be, and however obvious the intention of the parties might be to convey the fee

Position
after Con-
veyancing
Act 1881.

simple, the only effect was to pass a life estate to A. This strictness was mitigated and an alternative form of words was permitted by the Conveyancing Act 1881, which provided that in deeds executed after December 31st, 1881, the fee simple should pass if the expression " in fee simple " was adopted.

Devises of
land.

In the case of land *devised by will* the law was more liberal in its definition of words of limitation than it was in the case of deeds. Thus in addition to the technical expression " and his heirs," any informal words which clearly showed that the testator intended to give the fee simple were allowed to have that effect,[4] but notwithstanding this more lenient attitude the fact remained that laxity in the use of words of limitation frequently defeated

Wills Act
1837.

intention. The Wills Act 1837 therefore provided that

" where any real estate shall be devised to any person without any words of limitation, such devise shall be construed to pass the fee simple, or other the whole estate or interest which the testator had power to dispose of by will in such real estate, unless a contrary intention shall appear by the will." [5]

---

[1] For comparison with words of purchase see *infra*, p. 253.
[2] Pollock and Maitland, *History of English Law* (2nd Edn.), vol. ii. p. 13.
[3] *Bankes* v. *Salisbury Diocesan Council of Education Incorporated*, [1960] Ch. 631 ; [1960] 2 All E. R. 372.
[4] *Jarman on Wills* (8th Edn.), p. 1802.   [5] S. 28.

The effect of this enactment was to reverse the former law.

Before 1837 the effect of using a non-technical expression was to pass only a life estate, unless an intention to pass the whole fee simple could be clearly deduced ; but since 1837 the effect is to pass the entire interest which the testator happens to have in the lands, unless his intention clearly is to give some smaller interest. The burden of proving that a smaller interest passes lies on those who maintain that hypothesis.

The rule thus introduced for wills by the Act of 1837 was extended to deeds by the Law of Property Act 1925. It provides that [1] *Present position for deeds and wills.*

> " a conveyance of freehold land to any person without words of limitation, or any equivalent expression, shall pass to the grantee the fee simple or other the whole interest which the grantor had power to convey in such land, unless a contrary intention appears in the conveyance."

It will be noticed that the language of this section corresponds closely with that of the Wills Act 1837.

The position, then, at the present day, both for deeds and for wills, is that, if it is desired to confer a fee simple upon X., the wisest plan is to limit the land to "X. in fee simple" or to "X. and his heirs"; but that, if any other expression is used, as for instance "to X.", or "to X. for ever," the fee simple, if owned by the alienor, will pass unless the instrument clearly shows that there was no such intention.[2]

A limitation before 1926, not *to A. and his heirs*, but *Rule in Shelley's Case.*

to A. for life, remainder to his heirs

would have conferred a fee simple estate upon A. under the rule known as the *Rule in Shelley's Case*. This rule, which is described below at page 252, has, however, been abolished, and the effect of such a limitation now is to give a life interest to A. and a fee simple estate to his heir.

Where it was desired to grant a fee simple to a corporation sole,[3] *i.e.* a body politic having perpetual succession and consisting of a single person, such as a bishop, a parson, the Crown or the Public Trustee, the old law was that the grant must be made to the person in question *and his successors*, otherwise it merely operated to confer an estate for life on the actual holder of the office.[4] This rule has, however, been altered,[5] and a conveyance of freehold land in which the word " successors " has been omitted passes to the corporation the fee simple or other the whole interest which the grantor has, unless a contrary intention appears in the conveyance. *Corporation sole.*

---

[1] L.P.A. 1925, s. 60 (1).
[2] See, for example, *Quarm* v. *Quarm*, [1892] 1 Q. B. 184.
[3] *Infra*, p. 929.
[4] Co. Litt. 8*b*, 94*b*.
[5] L.P.A. 1925, s. 60 (2).

Corporation aggregate.
In the case of a corporation aggregate,[1] *i.e.* a collection of several persons united into one body under a special name and having perpetual existence, such as a limited liability company incorporated under the Companies Act 1948, it is sufficient to grant to the corporation under its corporate name.[2]

Voluntary conveyances.
If a feoffment were made before the Statute of Uses to a stranger in blood without the receipt of a money consideration (*i.e.* a voluntary conveyance), and *without declaring a use* in favour of the feoffee, the rule was that the land must be held by the feoffee to the use of the feoffor.[3] The equitable interest that thus returned by implication to the feoffor was called a resulting use. The effect of the enactment by the Statute of Uses that a *cestui que use* should have the legal estate was, of course, that the legal estate resulted to the feoffor.[4] In order to prevent this it became the practice in the case of such a conveyance to declare in the *habendum*[5] of the deed that the land was granted " unto and to the use of " the grantee. The repeal of the Statute of Uses by the legislation of 1925 would, in the absence of a further enactment, have restored the original rule, and it might have led practitioners to believe that the expression " to the use of " was still necessary in order to render a voluntary conveyance effective. It is, however, enacted that

> " in a voluntary conveyance a resulting trust for the grantor shall not be implied merely by reason that the property is not expressed to be conveyed for the use or benefit of the grantee "[6]

Registered Land.
In registered land there are two points to notice about the fee simple absolute in possession. First, where the registered proprietor transfers it *inter vivos*, no words of limitation are required in the transfer.[7] Secondly, as we have seen, the legal estate will not pass to the transferee until the transfer is completed by registration.[8] For this reason it has been suggested[9] that the Land Registration Act 1925 really provides a new statutory title to land, one that is not the fee simple, but a new fee based on it. But the argument is really a verbal one as to how the consequences of registration affect the character of what is registered. Sections 5 and 69 (1) of the Act refer to a registered proprietor as having a fee simple absolute in possession vested in him and it seems only a complication to depart from this terminology.[10]

---

[1] *Infra*, p. 928.
[2] Co. Litt. 94*b*.
[3] Sanders, *Uses and Trusts*, (5th Edn.), vol. i. p. 60.
[4] *Ibid.*, p. 97 ; *Beckwith's Case* (1589), 2 Co. Rep. 56*b*.
[5] *Infra*, p. 764.
[6] L.P.A. 1925, s. 60 (3).
[7] *Infra*, p. 767.
[8] L.R.A. 1925, s. 19 (1), 20 (1). *Supra*, p. 107.
[9] Ruoff and Roper, pp. 72–3, referring to " a great deal of learned and hypothetical argument ". See (1949), 12 *M. L. R.* 139, 477 (A. D. Hargreaves) ; 205 (H. Potter). (1947), 11 Conv. (N. S.) 184, 232 (R. C. Connell). Farrand, *Contract and Conveyance* (2nd Edn.), pp. 178–80 ; Barnsley, *Conveyancing Law and Practice*, pp. 30–2.   [10] See also ss. 18, 20.

SECTION III. THE LEGAL POSITION OF A TENANT IN FEE SIMPLE

Extent of Ownership. The legal position of a tenant in fee simple may be considered from two points of view—the subject-matter of his interest and the proprietary rights exercisable by him in that subject-matter.

The fee simple is the largest estate in *quantum* known to the law, since it may continue for ever. Moreover, a comprehensive meaning is given by the law to the expression *corporeal hereditaments* as used in the definition of land. In accordance with the maxim *cujus est solum, ejus est usque ad coelum et ad inferos*, the common law principle is that a tenant in fee is owner of everything attached to or lying below the surface.[1] But this has been eroded by statute. Thus, at common law all mines and minerals that lie beneath the soil belong absolutely to the tenant in fee but by statute all interests in coal are vested in the National Coal Board,[2] and petroleum existing in its natural condition in strata is vested in the Crown.[3] Further, the Crown is entitled to all gold and silver in gold and silver mines.[4] Although the tenant does not acquire the ownership of anything that overhangs his land, such as a cornice, an illuminated advertisement, telephone wires or the bough of a tree, he can maintain an action of nuisance or of trespass against the person who allows it to be there,[5] unless it has been acquired by that person as an easement.[6] Moreover, in the absence of trustworthy evidence of ownership, there is a legal presumption that the fee simple owner, if in possession, is *prima facie* owner of chattels found on the land.[7]

The proprietary rights of the tenant, however, do not extend to treasure trove.

" Treasure trove is, where any gold or silver in coin, plate, or bullion is found concealed in a house, or in the earth, or other private place,

Marginal notes:
Subject-matter of his interest.
Things on or below the land.
Treasure trove.

---

[1] For the history of " this brocard " see *Commissioner for Railways* v. *Valuer-General* [1974] A. C. 328, at pp. 351–2, *per* Lord WILBERFORCE. See also *Grigsby* v. *Melville*, [1974] 1 W. L. R. 80 ; [1973] 3 All E. R. 455.

[2] Coal Act 1938 : Coal Industry Nationalisation Act 1946.

[3] Petroleum (Production) Act 1934.

[4] *The Case of Mines* (1567), 1 Plowd. 310. Royal Mines Acts 1688, 1693.

[5] *Wandsworth Board of Works* v. *United Telephone Co.* (1884), 13 Q. B. D. 904 ; *Lemmon* v. *Webb*, [1895] A. C. 1 ; *Gifford* v. *Dent*, [1926] W. N. 336; *Kelsen* v. *Imperial Tobacco Co. (of Great Britain and Ireland)*, *Ltd.*, [1957], 2 Q. B. 334 ; [1957] 2 All E. R. 343 ; *Woollerton and Wilson, Ltd.* v. *Richard Costain Ltd.*, [1971] 1 W. L. R. 411 ; [1970] 1 All E. R. 483. No such action arises from the mere fact that an aeroplane passes through the air over land ; Civil Aviation Act 1949, s. 40 (1). See McNair *Law of the Air* (3rd Edn., 1964), pp. 31 *et seq.*

[6] *Simpson* v. *Weber* (1925), 541 T. L. R. 302.

[7] *South Staffordshire Water Co.* v. *Sharman*, [1896] 2 Q. B. 44 ; *Hannah* v. *Peel*, [1945] K. B. 509 ; *Hibbert* v. *McKiernan*, [1948] K. B. 142 ; *Re Cohen*, [1953] Ch. 88; [1953] 1 All E. R. 378; *City of London Corporation* v. *Appleyard* [1963] 1 W. L. R. 982 ; [1963] 2 All E. R. 834; *Moffatt* v. *Kazana*, [1969] 2 Q. B. 152 ; [1968] 3 All E. R. 271. See Goodhart, *Essays in Jurisprudence and the Common Law*, pp. 75–90 ; Harris, *Oxford Essays in Jurisprudence* (ed. Guest), pp. 69–106.

the owner thereof being unknown, in which case the treasure belongs
to the King or his grantee having the franchise of treasure trove ; but
if he that laid it be known or afterwards discovered, the owner and
not the King is entitled to it ; this prerogative right only applying in
the absence of an owner to claim the property.　If the owner, instead
of hiding the treasure, casually lost it, or purposely parted with it,[1] in
such a manner that it is evident he intended to abandon the property
altogether, and did not purpose to resume it on another occasion, as
if he threw it on the ground, or other public place, or in the sea, the
first finder is entitled to the property as against every one but the
owner, and the King's prerogative does not in this respect obtain.　So
that it is the hiding, and not the abandonment, of the property that
entitles the King to it." [2]

**Wild
creatures.**
The owner's rights in respect of wild animals, such as game,
depend upon the circumstances.　Such animals are not within
the absolute ownership of any particular person.　There are two
exceptions, for wild animals which have been tamed belong to
the person who has tamed them, and animals too young to escape
belong to the occupier of the land on which they are until they gain
their natural liberty.[3]　In other cases the tenant in fee or, indeed,
the occupier of the land, has not an absolute, but a qualified, right
of ownership over the animals within the confines of his property
in the sense that the exclusive right to catch and appropriate them
belongs to him *ratione soli*.[4]　Thus, game which is killed by a
trespasser belongs to the occupier of the land on which it is killed.
The only exception to this principle and one not altogether free
from doubt is that if A. starts game on the land of B., and hunts it
on to the ground of C. and kills it there, the ownership of the
game belongs to A. the hunter, though of course he is liable in
trespass both to B. and to C.[5]

Rights over Water.　A landowner has certain valuable rights
over water that may run through or be situated on his land.

The right of abstraction at common law, however, has been
substantially modified by statute, in particular by the Water
Resources Act 1963.[6]　England and Wales is divided into ten

---

[1] *Quaere*, however, whether a possessor can divest himself of possession of
a thing by its deliberate abandonment ; Pollock and Wright, *Possession in the
Common Law*, p. 124 ; *Haynes' Case* (1613), 12 Co. Rep. 113 ; *Arrow Shipping
Co.* v. *Tyne Improvement Commissioners*, [1894] A. C. 508, at p. 532.

[2] Chitty on the Prerogative, p. 152, cited *A.-G.* v. *Moore*, [1893] 1 Ch.
676, 683 ; *A.-G.* v. *Trustees of British Museum*, [1903] 2 Ch. 598.

[3] *Case of Swans* (1592), 7 Co. Rep. 15b.

[4] *Blades* v. *Higgs* (1865), 11 H. L. Cas. 621, *per* Westbury, L. C.　The
Crown has a prerogative right to swans, and royal fish, *i.e.* whales and sturgeon.
Any such right to other wild creatures was abolished by the Wild Creatures and
Forest Laws Act 1971, s. 1 (1) (a).

[5] *Sutton* v. *Moody* (1697), 1 Ld. Raym. 250, criticized by Lord Chelmsford
in *Blades* v. *Higgs* (1865), 10 H. L. Cas., at p. 639.

[6] As amended by the Water Resources Acts 1968, 1971, Water Act 1973.
See generally (1969), 33 Conv. (N. S.) 14 (M. Harwood) ; Wisdom, *Water
Rights* (1969).

areas, each administered by a regional water authority[1] which runs a compulsory system of licensing for the abstraction of water.

Water standing upon his land in a lake or pond is part of the land and belongs to him. If it stands partly upon his land and partly upon that of another, each is probably entitled to such part as lies opposite his own bank, but only up to a point half way between his and the opposite bank.[2] Water may be abstracted from such lakes and ponds without a licence under the Act.[3] *Ponds and lakes.*

Water percolating underneath the land and not contained in a defined and contracted channel is a common supply in which nobody has any property, but at common law it becomes the absolute property of any occupier by whom it is appropriated.[4] Thus if an occupier abstracts percolating water, he becomes the owner of it and will not be liable to his neighbours, though the effect may have been to dry up a spring or a well on their land.[5] Under the Act, however, a license is normally required unless the water is taken for the domestic purposes of the occupier's household.[6] *Percolating water.*

The next type of case is where a river or stream runs in a *definite channel*, whether above or below the surface, though it must be noted that an underground stream does not come within this category until it is established that it follows a definite course.[7] Underground water, the course of which cannot be ascertained without excavation, ranks as percolating water. Two questions arise where a stream follows a definite course ; first, the rights of the riparian owner or owners in the *bed*, secondly, their rights in the *water*. *Streams and rivers.*

The bed of a *non-tidal* river belongs, when there is no evidence of acts of ownership to the contrary, to the owner of the land through which it flows, but when the lands of two owners are separated by a running stream, each owner is *prima facie* owner of the soil of the bed of the river *ad medium filum aquae*. The soil of the bed is not the common property of the two owners, but the share of each belongs to him separately, so that, if from any cause the stream becomes diverted, each owner may use his share of the bed in any way he chooses.[8] On the other *Rights in the bed.*

---

[1] Water Act 1973, s. 2. These replace the river authorities set up under the Water Resources Act 1963.

[2] See *Mackenzie* v. *Bankes* (1878), L. R. 3 App. Cas. 1324.

[3] Water Resources Act 1963, s. 2 (3).

[4] *Ballard* v. *Tomlinson* (1885), L. R. 29 Ch. D. 115, at p. 121, *per* BRETT, M. R.

[5] *Acton* v. *Blundell* (1843), 12 M. & W. 324 ; *Chasemore* v. *Richards* (1859), 7 H. L. Cas. 349 ; *Rugby Joint Water Board* v. *Walters* [1967] Ch. 397 ; [1966] 3 All E. R. 497 ; *Langbrook Properties, Ltd.* v. *Surrey County Council*, [1970] 1 W. L. R. 161 ; [1969] 3 All E. R. 1424. See too *Bradford Corpn.* v. *Pickles*, [1895] A. C. 587.

[6] Water Resources Act 1963, ss. 23, 24 (3).

[7] *Bleachers' Assocn. Ltd.* v. *Chapel-en-le-Frith Rural Council*, [1933] Ch. 356.

[8] *Bickett* v. *Morris* (1866), L. R. 1 Sc. & Div. 47 (especially at p. 58).

hand, the bed of a *tidal* river, up to a point where the water flows
and reflows regularly, belongs to the Crown unless it has been
granted to a subject.[1]

**Rights in
the water.**

But the water as distinct from the bed of a river is not the
subject of absolute ownership, and, though subject to certain
rights exercisable by the owners of the lands through which it
flows, it does not belong to them in the ordinary sense of the
term. Such a riparian owner has at common law, as a natural
incident of his ownership, certain riparian rights, which have been
authoritatively described as follows :—

> "A riparian proprietor is entitled to have the water of the stream
> on the banks of which his property lies, flow down as it has been
> accustomed to flow down to his property, subject to the ordinary
> use of the flowing water by upper proprietors, and to such further
> use, if any, on their part in connection with their property as may
> be reasonable under the circumstances." [2]

The common law, as thus stated, may be elaborated into three
propositions [3] :—

**Riparian
rights at
common
law.**

1. A riparian owner may take and use the water for ordinary
   purposes connected with his riparian tenement (such as
   domestic purposes or the watering of his cattle),[4] even though
   the result may be to exhaust the water altogether.

2. A riparian owner may take the water for extraordinary purposes,
   provided, first that such user is connected with the riparian
   land, and secondly that he restores the water substantially
   undiminished in volume and unaltered in character. Common
   examples are where water is employed in the irrigation of
   the adjoining land or the working of a mill, for in such cases
   practically the same amount of water ultimately returns to
   the stream.[5] Manufacture, in the present connection, is
   prima facie an extraordinary purpose, though the ultimate
   solution of this question depends upon local trading conditions,
   and on the use to which the water of rivers is put in the
   adjoining district.[6]

3. A riparian owner has no right whatever to take the water for
   purposes unconnected with the riparian tenement.[7] Thus
   it has been held that the mere possession of a mill on the
   bank of a stream does not entitle a waterworks company to

---

[1] *A.-G.* v. *Lonsdale* (1868), L. R. 7 Eq. 377, at p. 388.
[2] *John Young & Co.* v. *Bankier Distillery Co.*, [1893] A. C. 691, at p. 698,
per Lord MACNAGHTEN ; *Provender Millers (Winchester), Ltd.* v. *Southampton
C.C.*, [1940] Ch. 131 ; [1939] 4 All E. R. 157.
[3] *Attwood* v. *Llay Main Collieries*, [1926] Ch. 444, at p. 458.
[4] But not spray irrigation. *Rugby Joint Water Board* v. *Walters*, [1967]
Ch. 397 ; [1966] 3 All E. R. 497.
[5] *Embrey* v. *Owen* (1851), 6 Ex. 353; Dist. *Rugby Joint Water Board* v.
Walters, *supra*.
[6] *Ormerod* v. *Todmorden Mill Co.* (1883), 11 Q. B. D. 155, at p. 168, *per*
Lord ESHER ; see (1959) 22 *M.L.R.* 35 (A. H. Hudson).
[7] *McCartney* v. *Londonderry and Lough Swilly Ry. Co.*, [1904] A. C. 301 ;
Attwood v. *Llay Main Collieries, supra*.

collect the water in a reservoir for the benefit of a neighbouring town.[1]

Under section 23 (1) of the Water Resources Act 1963[2]

Water Resources Act 1963.

" no person shall abstract water from any source of supply in a water authority area, or cause or permit any other person so to abstract any water, except in pursuance of a licence under this act granted by the water authority and in accordance with the provisions of that licence."

The main exceptions to this are the abstraction of

(i) up to 1,000 gallons of water, if it does not form part of a continuous operation, or of a series of operations, whereby in the aggregate more than 1,000 gallons are abstracted.[3]

(ii) water for the domestic purposes of the occupier's household and agricultural purposes other than spray irrigation. In both these cases the water must be taken for use on a holding consisting of the riparian land and any other land held therewith.[4]

The public have a common law right to navigation in a tidal river up to the point where the tide ebbs and flows,[5] but the non-tidal part of a river is analagous to a road running between two properties, and though the public may by dedication acquire the right of navigation thereon, it must be proved in case of dispute that this has been established by long enjoyment or by Act of Parliament.[6] Such a right of navigation if once established prevails over the ordinary rights of a riparian owner, and he cannot make any use of the bed of the river or of its water which will prejudice enjoyment by the public ; he is not, for instance, entitled to erect a wharf or other building on the bed so as to obstruct to the smallest extent the passage of boats.[7]

Public rights in a river.

An owner of lands adjoining the sea is also entitled to the sea-shore[8] down to a point which is reached by an ordinary high tide, but all the shore below that is vested in the Crown or its grantee.[9]

Land adjoining sea.

---

[1] *Swindon Waterworks Co.* v. *Wilts. and Berks. Canal Navigation Co.* (1875), L. R. 7 H. L. 697.

[2] As amended by Water Act 1973, s. 9.

[3] Water Resources Act 1963, s. 24 (1).

[4] *Ibid.*, ss. 24 (2), 135 (1).

[5] *A.-G.* v. *Tomline* (1880), 14 Ch. D. 58. See *Iveagh* v. *Martin*, [1961] 1 Q. B. 232 ; [1960] 2 All E. R. 668 ; *Evans* v. *Godber*, [1974] 1 W. L. R. 137 ; [1974] 3 All E. R. 341.

[6] *Orr-Ewing* v. *Colquhoun* (1877), L. R. 2 App. Cas. 839.

[7] *A.-G.* v. *Terry* (1874), L. R. 9 Ch. App. 423.

[8] See *Government of Penang* v. *Beng Hong Oon* [1972] A. C. 425, at pp. 435, 439.

[9] *Lowe* v. *Govett* (1832), 3 B. & Ad. 863 ; *Blundell* v. *Cotterall* (1821), 5 B. & Ald. 268 ; *Alfred F. Beckett, Ltd.* v. *Lyons*, [1967] Ch. 449 ; [1967] 1 All E. R. 833. For the rights of the public over the sea-shore, see (1974) J.P.L. 705 (A. Wharam).

No right to
fish in
non-tidal
river.

Rights over Fish. As regards the person who possesses the right of fishing in a river, a distinction must again be drawn between tidal and non-tidal rivers, for, while all members of the public are entitled to fish in the former up to the point where the tide ebbs and flows, the right in the case of a non-tidal river belongs to the owner of the bed of the stream, or to any person who has acquired a right from or against him. It is often thought that if a river is navigable the public have a right to fish in it, but this is not true in respect of that part of a river which lies above the flow of the tide, for the privilege of navigation no more confers a right to fish than the right to pass along a public highway entitles a member of the public to shoot upon it.[1] Bowen, L.J., said :—

> " There is another most important matter to be recollected as regards such streams as the Thames, viz. that although the public have been in the habit, as long as we can recollect, and as long as our fathers can recollect, of fishing in the Thames, the public have no right to fish there—I mean they have no right as members of the public to fish there. That is certain law. Of course they may fish by the licence of the lord or the owner of a particular part of the bed of the river, or they may fish by the indulgence, or owing to the carelessness or good nature, of the person who is entitled to the soil, but right to fish themselves as the public they have none, and whenever the case is tried the jury ought to be told this by the judge in the most emphatic way, so as to prevent them from doing injustice under the idea that they are establishing a public right. There is no such right in law . . ."[2]

Fishing
right as an
incorporeal
right.

The position is, then, that the owner of the bed of a river is presumptively entitled to the fishing, and if, for instance, the opposite banks are in different hands, each proprietor is owner of the fishing *usque ad medium filum aquae*.[3] But this fishing may become separated from the ownership of the bed and be vested as an incorporeal right in the hands of another person, and when this has been done it exists either as a several fishery or as a common of fishery. Both these rights are instances of what is called a *profit à prendre*. A several fishery is, as was said by Lord Coleridge,

> " a right to take fish *in alieno solo*, and to exclude the owner of the soil from the right of taking fish himself." [4]

A right to fish in the river of another in common with the owner, or in common with others to whom the same right has

---

[1] *Smith* v. *Andrews*, [1891] 2 Ch. 678, at p. 696. It is an offence to fish in such a river even though the fish are returned alive to the water; *Wells* v. *Hardy*, [1964] 1 Q. B. 477 ; [1964] 1 All E. R. 953.
[2] *Blount* v. *Layard*, [1891] 2 Cn. 681 note, at p. 689.
[3] *Hanbury* v. *Jenkins*, [1901] 2 Ch. 401. It seems that he has a right to cast a fly over the mid-line or to follow a fish, hooked on his side, which swims across to the other side. *Welsh National Water Development Authority* v. *Burgess* (1974), 28 P. & C. R. 378, at p. 383.
[4] *Foster* v. *Wright* (1878), L. R. 4 C. P. D. 438, at p. 449.

been granted, is called a " common of fishery," or " common of piscary." [1]

Restrictions on Ownership.

Restrictions on Ownership. In his account of the fee simple estate, written in 1885, Challis was able to give a comforting description of the extensive powers of enjoyment available to its owner. *(marginal note: Restrictions to which a landowner is subject.)*

> " It confers," he said, " and since the beginning of legal history it always has conferred, the lawful right to exercise over, upon, and in respect, to the land, every act of ownership which can enter into the imagination, including the right to commit unlimited waste." [2]

Challis would, no doubt, have agreed with Samuel Johnson that a man cannot be allowed by society to be complete master of what he calls his own, and that he must submit to the restrictions placed by the law upon the exercise of his proprietary rights. [3] There is little doubt, however, that the restrictions now imposed by statute upon a landowner's right to enjoy what at common law is his own would have passed the understanding of both those writers. Even in Challis' time, of course, statutory interference with the freedom of a landowner was not unknown. He was obliged, for instance, to erect new buildings in conformity with local by-laws, and he might be compelled to demolish houses that were unfit for habitation. Later he became subject to legislation passed in the interests of the poorer sections of the community, such as the Housing Acts [4] and the Rent Acts, [5] which further increased his burdens and circumscribed his proprietary rights.

But the most vigorous attack upon the right of a man to do what he likes with his own has been made by the various Town and Country Planning Acts, which seek to prevent the evils that inevitably arise if no public control is placed upon the development of land. That building operations need to be controlled in the interests of the community is, of course, obvious. Land is scarce, the demand for houses increases with a rapidly rising population, the profit instinct is no weaker than formerly, and unless something is done to curb the activities of the speculative builder certain unfortunate results must inevitably ensue. Too often, uncontrolled development sacrifices agricultural land and places of natural beauty, defaces the countryside with unco-ordinated buildings sprawling along the main roads and causing embarrassment to the sanitary and educational authorities, and in general it is effected with little thought for the amenities of the neighbourhood or for the problems that it will raise in the future. Nevertheless, there is a need to preserve a just balance between the rights of landowners and the interests of the community. *(marginal note: Planning Control.)*

---

[1] Leake, *Uses and Profits of Land.* p. 176. *Infra*, pp. 563.
[2] *The Law of Real Property* (3rd Edn.), p. 218.
[3] In a letter to Boswell, February 3rd, 1776.
[4] *Infra*, pp. 407-9.   [5] *Infra*, pp. 468 *et seq.*

Community
Land Act
1975.

1975 saw the passing of the Community Land Act. This makes the carrying out of development (except for projects of minor importance) a procedure which is not, as hitherto, merely subject to regulation by local planning authorities, but which will be under their control in the more direct sense that they have first call on the " development land " themselves. They are empowered to acquire it and to decide whether or not to dispose of it to private developers and, if so, to choose which developers are to have it, and when. While they are considering this question, any available planning permissions remain in suspense. Moreover land is to be acquired by public bodies at a price *exclusive* of prospective development value, but disposed of by them *inclusive* of such value. This system comes near to nationalizing prospective development value in land. That goal is likely to be brought even nearer in 1976 by an Act to impose an 80% tax on such value in those remaining cases (again, except for projects of minor importance) in which the authorities allow land to be privately developed without first passing through their hands. Private ownership will then be virtually confined to land in its existing use.

To give an adequate account of these matters in the present chapter would upset the balance of the book and divert the attention of the reader from fundamental principles, but they are of such importance in the modern law that they are dealt with in a separate account and at a later stage.[1]

---

[1] *Infra*, pp. 937 *et seq.*

BOOK II

ESTATES AND INTERESTS IN LAND

PART II

INTERESTS ARISING UNDER A STRICT SETTLEMENT OR TRUST FOR SALE

SUMMARY

CHAPTER I

THE STRICT SETTLEMENT AND
THE TRUST FOR SALE

SUMMARY

Introduction. The evolution of the strict settlement and the trust for sale have already been described in the historical introduction.[1]

The general idea of a settlement is to create, either by deed or will, out of real or personal property, a series of beneficial interests in favour of a succession of persons. The two methods by which

Meaning of a settlement

---

[1] Supra, pp. 71 *et seq.*

land may be settled today are either by strict settlement under the Settled Land Act 1925, or by trust for sale under the Law of Property Act 1925.[1] They are mutually exclusive. Indeed it is expressly enacted that the statutory definition of a settlement contained in the Settled Land Act 1925 shall not apply to land held upon trust for sale.[2]

Importance of distinction between settlement and trust for sale.

It is vital to distinguish the two methods of settlement. The chief practical importance of the distinction is that upon the occasion of a conveyance title to settled land must be made by the tenant for life, since the legal estate is vested in him, while title to land held upon trust for sale must be made by the trustees for sale. The result of a mistake in this regard is troublesome and expensive, for a purchaser who takes a conveyance from the trustees when the instrument is a settlement or from the tenant for life in the reverse case, does not thereby acquire the legal estate. We must also reiterate at the outset of the discussion that a purchaser, who takes a conveyance from the correct vendor, takes the land free from the interests of the beneficiaries under the settlement, provided that he pays the purchase money to at least two trustees or to a trust corporation. The interests of the beneficiaries are transferred from the land to the purchase money and are overreached.[3]

Decline of the strict settlement.

Of these two methods of settling land we shall discuss first the strict settlement under the Settled Land Act 1925. In recent years however, mainly due to considerations of estate duty and taxation, the strict settlement has become less widely used. In particular, the classic strict settlement, which was created on the occasion of a marriage so as to provide for all members of the family and thereby to keep the land as far as possible within the family,[4] is most unlikely to be created to-day. It is the trust for sale which is mainly used for family settlements, whether created *inter vivos* or by will ; and furthermore its conveyancing machinery has been extended by the 1925 legislation to concurrent interests [5] and intestacy.[6]

SECTION I.   THE STRICT SETTLEMENT

(1) THE DEFINITION OF A SETTLEMENT UNDER THE SETTLED LAND ACT 1925

Extended meaning of settlement.

The word *settlement* properly so called connotes succession. Its normal meaning is any instrument or series of instruments by

---

[1] See Harvey, *Settlements of Land* (1973).
[2] S.L.A. 1925, s. 1 (7).
[3] *Supra*, pp. 80–82.   For a full discussion of overreaching see *infra*, pp. 792–3, 796–7.
[4] *Supra*, pp. 72–3. For a detailed account see Cheshire, *Modern Real Property* (10th Edn.), pp. 126–31.
[5] *Infra*, pp. 210 *et seq*.   [6] *Infra*, pp. 862 *et seq*.

which successive interests are carved out of realty or personalty and under which, in the case of land, there will usually be at any given time some person entitled in possession to a beneficial interest for life. But the Settled Land Act 1925 is not content to stop short at cases where there is a succession properly so called. Its further aim is to facilitate dealings wherever the disposition of the land is retarded or obstructed by some impediment affecting its title. Infancy affords a simple illustration.

If a favourable offer has been made for the purchase of land to which an infant is entitled in fee simple, the rule that no person under 18 years of age[1] can execute a valid conveyance will cause the loss of a profitable bargain, unless some way out of the impasse can be contrived. But all difficulty disappears if the will is regarded as a " settlement " and if some person of full age is designated to exercise the statutory power of sale.

In a case of this nature there is, of course, no settlement and no tenant for life as usually understood, but any device which renders the statutory powers exercisable in respect of the infant's land is an undoubted advantage to all concerned. What the Act does, therefore, with the object of rendering an absolute title easily transferable despite the existence of what would normally be inhibitory factors, is to define " settlement " in broad terms so as to include a number of cases where there is no succession in the ordinary sense, and also, where necessary, to grant the statutory powers to a person who according to ordinary language is not a tenant for life. In fact, not only is the statutory definition of a " settlement " very wide, but wherever there is a settlement within the meaning of the Act and no tenant for life properly so called, and therefore no person normally competent to exercise the statutory powers, one of two things will occur, namely, either

some person will be designated by the Act as entitled to exercise the powers ; or

the powers will be exercisable by trustees, who in this context are called " statutory owners."[2]

A settlement for the purposes of the Act exists in each of the following cases [3] :

Definition of a " settlement."

(i) Where land stands limited in trust for any persons *by way of succession.*

This refers to the normal case where land is limited to a

---

[1] *Infra*, p. 915.   [2] *Infra* pp. 176–7.   [3] S.L.A. 1925, s. 1.

series of persons by way of succession, as for instance to A. for life, remainder to B. for life, remainder to C. in fee simple.[1]

We now come to the cases where instruments are deemed to be settlements.

(ii) Where land stands limited in trust for any person *in possession*—

    (*a*) for an entailed interest whether or not capable of being barred or defeated ;

    (*b*) for an estate in fee simple or for a term of years absolute subject to an executory gift over on failure of issue or in any other event ;

    (*c*) for a base or determinable fee[2] or any corresponding interest in leasehold land ;

    (*d*) for an estate in fee simple or for a term of years absolute in favour of an infant.

We have here several examples of the extended meaning given to the term " settlement." Thus :

Entailed interests.

where the possessor is a tenant in tail or tenant of a base fee, the instrument of creation is a settlement, and the tenant is deemed to hold the land under a settlement.

Limitation subject to gift over.

The same position arises where property is vested in a possessor, subject, however, to a gift over to somebody else on the happening of a certain event, as for instance:

where a house is devised to A. in fee simple subject to a condition that he resides and provides a home for X. there, and if he breaks this condition, then devise over to B. in fee simple.

In such a case the will is a settlement and A. is tenant for life within the meaning of the Act.[3]   Lastly,

Infant as beneficial owner.

a conveyance which purports to grant a fee simple absolute to an infant cannot take effect according to its terms, for an infant is incapable of holding a legal estate. Instead, the conveyance operates as an agreement by the grantor to execute a settlement by means of a vesting deed in favour of trustees (statutory owners),[4] and a trust instrument in favour of the infant.

---

[1] It need not be expressly limited.   The trust may arise by operation of law, as, for instance, where there is a resulting or constructive trust following a life interest : *Bannister* v. *Bannister*, [1948] 2 All E. R. 133 ; M. & B. p. 460 ; *Binions* v. *Evans*, [1972] Ch. 359 ; [1972] 2 All E. R. 70 ; M. & B. p. 467 (Lord DENNING, M.R. dissented at p. 366) ; *infra*, p. 585 ; *cf. Ivory* v. *Palmer*, [1975] I. C. R. 340, *infra*. p. 583.   See Harvey, *op. cit.*, pp. 54, 82 *et seq. Emmet on Title* (16th Edn.), pp. 666–8.

[2] Including a fee determinable by condition, S.L.A. 1925, s. 117 (1) (iv).

[3] *Re Richardson*, [1904] 2 Ch. 777.

[4] S.L.A. 1925, s. 27 (1) ; *infra*, p. 177.

(iii) Where land stands limited in trust for any person to take effect as a fee simple or term of years absolute on the happening of some event.

If, for instance, a fee simple estate is limited in trust for the two sons of X, who attain the age of eighteen years, the first son to reach that age becomes absolutely entitled to a half share, but also entitled to the fee simple in the entirety of the land contingent on the death of his brother during infancy.[1] This is one of the cases where, pending the occurrence of the contingency, the powers are exercisable by the statutory owners.[2]

(iv) Where land stands charged *voluntarily*,[3] *or in consideration of marriage or by way of family arrangement*[4] with the payment of any rentcharge or capital sums for the portions, advancement, maintenance or otherwise for the benefit of any persons.[5]

If, for example, A. charges his fee simple absolute with an annuity for his wife and capital sums for his children, the instrument which creates the charge is a " settlement," and, although the rentchargor, A., is not a tenant for life, yet by s. 20 (1) (ix) of the Act he is given the powers of a tenant for life. Strictly speaking, therefore, he should execute a vesting deed and appoint trustees. If he does so, he may sell the fee simple under the Act, and overreach the rentcharges so as to make them recoverable from the trustees to whom payment will have been made. If, however, the purchaser is willing to buy subject to the charges, A. is permitted by a later statute to sell as absolute owner without the necessity of executing a vesting deed. This statute provides as follows :—

Nothing in the Settled Land Act 1925 shall prevent a person on whom the powers of a tenant for life are conferred by s. 20 (1) (ix) from conveying or creating a legal estate subject to a prior interest as if the land had not been settled land.[6]

What emerges from the account given above is that a settlement may consist of a number of instruments. This will occur, for instance :

where lands, which in the first place have been settled on A.

---

[1] *Re Bird*, [1927] 1 Ch. 210.
[2] S.L.A., 1925, s. 23.
[3] *I.e.*, not for valuable consideration.
[4] Presumably " family arrangement " in this context includes an arrangement made not voluntarily, but for valuable consideration, *cf. Williams* v. *Williams* (1867), 2 Ch. App. 294 at p. 301.
[5] S.L.A. 1925, s. 1 (1) (v); *Re Austen*, [1929] 2 Ch. 155.
[6] L.P.(A.)A. 1926, s. 1 (1).

for life with remainder in tail to his eldest son, are resettled on A. for life, remainder (subject to the charges created by the original settlement) to the eldest son for life, with remainder over.

In this case the two settlements may be read as one, being together called a *compound settlement*,[1] and the Act provides that the word *settlement* shall be construed as referring to such compound settlement where it exists.[2]

Creation of settlement requires two deeds.

(2) THE MACHINERY OF A SETTLEMENT AFTER 1925

We have already seen that in order to emphasize the separation of the legal estate from the equitable interests of the beneficiaries and also to facilitate a conveyance of the former, the Settled Land Act 1925 introduced a new method for the creation of a settlement by enacting as follows [3] :—

" Every settlement of a legal estate in land *inter vivos* shall, save as in this Act otherwise provided, be effected by two deeds, namely, a *vesting deed* and a *trust instrument* and if effected in any other way shall not operate to transfer or create a legal estate." [4]

This method must now be examined in more detail.

Function of vesting deed.

1. **The Vesting Deed.** The function of the vesting deed is to vest the legal fee simple in the person who for the time being is to have the actual enjoyment of the land, or, if he is an infant or otherwise legally incapable, then to vest it in some other person who is denominated a *statutory owner*.[5] The virtue of thus passing the legal fee simple to a person who is beneficially entitled to some lesser interest is that, should he later desire, in the interests of the beneficiaries generally, to dispose of the fee simple by way of sale, lease or otherwise under one of the powers conferred upon him by the Settled Land Act 1925, he can produce a document which not only shows that the legal estate is vested in him, but also certifies the facts essential to a valid exercise of the statutory power.

Contents of vesting deed.

This vesting deed, then,—called the *principal vesting deed*—conveys to the tenant for life or the statutory owner the whole legal estate which is held upon trust for persons by way of succession. It is a short document and must contain the following statements and particulars [6] :

    (*a*) a description, either specific or general, of the settled land ;

    (*b*) a statement that the settled land is vested in the person

---

[1] *Re Ogle's Settled Estates*, [1927] I Ch. 229, at pp. 232–33.
[2] S.L.A. 1925, s. I (I) (i), proviso.   [3] *Supra*, p. 100.
[4] S.L.A., 1925, s. 4 (I).   [5] *Ibid.*, ss. 23, 26, 117 (I) (xxvi).
[6] *Ibid.*, s. 5 (I).

or persons to whom it is conveyed or in whom it is declared to be vested upon the trusts from time to time affecting the settled land ;

(c) the names of the trustees of the settlement ;

(d) a statement of any powers, over and above those conferred upon every tenant for life by the Act, which it is desired to give to the tenant for life under the settlement ;

(e) the name of any person entitled to appoint new trustees of the settlement.

If after the execution of a principal vesting deed more land is acquired which is to become subject to the settlement, it is conveyed to the tenant for life by what is called a *subsidiary vesting deed*.[1]

Subsidiary vesting deed.

The following is a precedent of a principal vesting deed :—

Precedent of vesting deed.

THIS VESTING DEED made (&c.) between JOHN H. of (&c.) of the first part, JANE W. of (&c.) of the second part and X. of (&c.), Y. of (&c.), and Z. of (&c.) (hereinafter called the trustees) of the third part.

WITNESSETH and it is hereby declared as follows :—

1. In consideration of the intended marriage between John H. and Jane W. the said John H. as Settlor hereby declares that :

ALL THAT (*setting out the parcels by reference to a schedule or otherwise*) are vested in John H. in fee simple (*or in the case of leaseholds refer to the terms*).

UPON THE TRUSTS declared concerning the same by a Trust Instrument bearing even date with but intended to be executed contemporaneously with these presents and made between the same parties and in the same order as these presents or upon such other trusts as the same ought to be held from time to time.

2. The trustees are the trustees of the settlement for all the purposes of the Settled Land Act, 1925.

3. The following additional or larger powers are conferred by the said trust instrument in relation to the settled land and by virtue of the Settled Land Act, 1925, operate and are exercisable as if conferred by that Act on a tenant for life. (*Here insert the additional powers.*)

4. The power of appointing a new trustee or new trustees of the settlement is vested in the said John H. during his life.

IN WITNESS (&c.) [2]

2. The Trust Instrument. At the same time a second deed, called the trust instrument, is executed which

Function of trust instrument.

(a) declares the trusts affecting the settled land ;

(b) appoints trustees of the settlement ;

---

[1] S.L.A. 1925, s. 10. [2] *Ibid.*, 1st Sched., Form No. 2.

(c) contains the power, if any, to appoint new trustees of the settlement ;

(d) sets out, either expressly or by reference, any powers intended to be conferred by the settlement in extension of those conferred by the Act ;

(e) bears any ad valorem stamp duty which may be payable in respect of the settlement.[1]

Thus it is the trust investment which declares the trusts upon which the legal estate is to be held.   If we look at the vesting deed alone, the tenant for life seems to be fully entitled to sell the fee simple.   So he is.   An intending purchaser need not look beyond the deed, but at the same time such a person is told in the vesting deed that the land is held upon trust and that there are trustees, and this knowledge throws upon him the obligation to pay the purchase money, not to the tenant for life, but to the trustees.   If he does this, his obligations are at an end, and it is no concern of his what is done with the money. But what we need to look at for the moment is the trust instrument, since it records the equitable interests which it is the object of the settlement to confer upon the beneficiaries. The property comprised in the settlement, whether it remains in the form of land or is sold and converted into money, is **actually enjoyed by the persons who are described in, and upon the conditions which are prescribed by, the trust instrument. We must not be misled by the vesting deed** into thinking that the tenant for life, who is thereby declared to be the fee simple owner, can sell the whole estate and pocket the proceeds.

The following is a precedent of a trust instrument[2] which is the counter-part to that of the vesting deed set out above [3] :

This Trust Instrument is made [&c.] between *John H.* of [&c.] (hereinafter called the Settlor) of the first part, *Jane W.* of [&c.] of the second part, and *X.* of [&c.], *Y.* of [&c.], and *Z.* of [&c.] (hereinafter called the trustees) of the third part.

Whereas by a deed (hereinafter called the Vesting Deed) bearing even date with but executed contemporaneously with these presents, and made between the same parties and in the same order as these presents, certain hereditaments situated at   in the county of   were vested in the Settlor Upon the trusts declared concerning the same by a trust instrument of even date therein referred to (meaning these presents).

Now in consideration of the intended marriage between the Settlor and *Jane W.*, this Deed witnesseth as follows :—

1. The Settlor hereby agrees that he will hold the hereditaments and property comprised in the Vesting Deed   In trust for himself until the solemnisation of the said marriage and thereafter   Upon the trusts following, that is to say :—

---

[1] S.L.A. 1925, s. 4 (3).   [2] *Ibid.*, 1st Sched. Form No. 3.
[3] *Supra*, p. 171.

2. Upon trust for the Settlor during his life without impeachment of waste with remainder Upon trust if *Jane W.* survives him that she shall receive out of the premises during the residue of her life a yearly jointure rentcharge of [&c.] and subject thereto Upon trust for the trustees for a term of 800 years from the date of the death of the Settlor without impeachment of waste Upon the trusts hereinafter declared concerning the same. And subject to the said term and the trusts thereof Upon trust for the first and other sons of the said intended marriage successively according to seniority in tail male with remainder [&c.] *with an ultimate remainder in trust for the Settlor in fee simple.*

[*Here add the requisite trusts of the portions term, and any other proper provisions including the appointment of the trustees to be trustees of the settlement for the purposes of the Settled Land Act, 1925, extension of Settled Land Act powers, and a power for the tenant for life for the time being of full age to appoint new trustees of the settlement.*]

In witness [&c.].

The rule that an *inter vivos* settlement must be created by two contemporaneous deeds called the principal vesting deed and the trust instrument, applies differently to a settlement by will. In this case the legal estate devolves upon the personal representatives of the settlor, who hold it upon trust to convey it to the person entitled to the tenancy for life under the will.[1] This conveyance may be made by a *vesting assent, i.e.* by an assent in writing but not under seal.[2] The position then is, that the vesting assent corresponds to the vesting deed that forms part of a settlement *inter vivos*, and the will itself is deemed to be the trust instrument.

[margin: Settlement by will.]

Thus the legal estate conveyed to the tenant for life by the vesting deed is kept rigorously separate from the equitable interests of the beneficiaries which are created by and contained in the trust instrument. Throughout the duration of the settlement and however long that duration may be, the legal estate must and will be vested in a person or persons competent to deal with it as permitted by the Act. If no vesting deed has been executed, the tenant for life or statutory owner[3] can require the trustees of the settlement to repair the omission.[4] Normally, the legal estate will remain with the first tenant for life until his death, though in certain exceptional circumstances, as for example where his equitable life interest is forfeited under the terms of the settlement, it will pass to the trustees. On his death it will devolve on the trustees who will as soon as practicable convey it by a vesting assent to the person next entitled.[5]

[margin: Legal estate kept separate from equitable interests.]

The evasion of the statutory requirement of a vesting deed is prevented by section 13 of the Settled Land Act 1925.[6] This provides that where a tenant for life or statutory owner has become

[margin: Evasion of Act prevented.]

---

[1] S.L.A. 1925, s. 6.
[2] *Ibid.*, s. 8 (1).
[3] *Infra*, pp. 174-7.
[4] S.L.A. 1925, s. 9 (2).
[5] *Infra*, p. 790.
[6] S.L.A. 1925, s. 13, as amended by L.P.(A.)A. 1926, Sched.

entitled to have a vesting deed or assent executed in his favour, then, until such an instrument has in fact been executed, no disposition of the land made *inter vivos* by any person shall operate to pass a legal estate, unless it is made in favour of a purchaser having no notice that the tenant for life or statutory owner has become so entitled. Such a purported disposition operates as a contract to convey the legal estate as soon as the vesting deed has been executed, and it is a contract that is registrable as a land charge.[1]

There is an exception, however, in favour of personal representatives, for they are allowed to sell settled land in the ordinary course of administration even though no vesting deed has been executed when their title accrues.[2]

Cases where vesting deed not necessary.

Moreover, there are three cases in which there is no necessity for a vesting deed :—

(i) Where the land ceases to be settled.

If, for instance, a tenant in tail in possession of settled land, free from any trusts or incumbrances, bars the entail before a vesting deed is executed in his favour, he thereby terminates the settlement, and can make title as a fee simple owner.[3]

(ii) Where the beneficiaries terminate the settlement.

Beneficiaries, if of full age, may terminate the settlement and so avoid the necessity for a vesting deed. If, for instance, an owner devises his residence to his wife for life with remainder to his children in fee simple, the widow becomes tenant for life on his death and as such is entitled to a vesting deed. Instead, however, she may surrender her life interest to the remaindermen in fee, and then all the parties can create a trust for sale, with themselves as trustees, the income until sale and the ultimate proceeds to be held on trusts corresponding to those of the settlement.

(iii) If the land has become settled merely because it has been voluntarily subjected to family charges,[4] the tenant for life, as we have seen, is allowed by the Law of Property (Amendment) Act 1926 to convey a legal estate subject to the charges without being required to procure the execution of a vesting deed.[5]

(3) THE DEFINITION OF THE TENANT FOR LIFE

Definition of tenant for life

A tenant for life, is defined as follows in section 19 (1) of the Settled Land Act 1925 :

---

[1] *Infra,* pp. 742.
[3] *Re Alefounder's Will Trusts* [1927] 1 Ch. 360.
[5] *Supra,* p. 169.

[2] S.L.A. 1925, s. 13.
[4] S.L.A. 1925, s. 20 (1) (ix).

" The person of full age who is for the time being beneficially entitled under a settlement to possession of settled land for his life is for the purposes of this Act the tenant for life of that land and the tenant for life under that settlement."

He is deemed to be such, notwithstanding that the land or his estate therein is charged with the payment of incumbrances.[1] If two or more persons are jointly entitled to possession, they together constitute the tenant for life.[2]

Persons with the Powers of a Tenant for Life. Obviously however there are several cases where land is settled in the sense that it is subject to a " settlement " within the statutory meaning of that word,[3] and yet where there is no tenant for life as defined in section 19. A tenant in tail in possession is a simple example of the situation.[4] The Act, therefore, takes care to ensure that wherever there is a " settlement " there shall always be some person with the powers of a tenant for life. In the first place it provides that the following persons shall have the powers of a tenant for life [5] and shall be included in the expression " tenant for life." [6]

Persons
having the
powers of a
tenant for
life.

(i) A tenant in tail, including both a tenant after possibility [7] and one who is by statute restrained from barring his estate tail, but excluding a tenant in tail whose land has been bought with money provided by Parliament in consideration of public services.

(ii) A person entitled to a legal estate subject to a gift over on failure of issue or in any other event.[8]

(iii) A person entitled to a base[9] or a determinable fee[10] or a similar interest in leaseholds.

(iv) A tenant for years determinable on life, not holding merely under a lease at a rent.

> We shall see that leases *at a rent* for a term of years determinable at the death of the tenant are now converted into terms for 90 years,[11] and that such a person cannot have the powers of a tenant for life,[12] but this conversion does not operate where such a term takes effect under a settlement. For instance, a devisee to whom lands are given for 30 years if he should so long live has the powers of a tenant for life.

(v) A tenant *pur autre vie* not holding merely under a lease at a rent.[13]

---

[1] S.L.A. 1925, s. 19 (4).
[2] *Ibid.*, s. 19 (2).
[3] *Supra*, pp. 166-9.
[4] *Supra*, p. 168.
[5] S.L.A. 1925, s. 20.
[6] *Ibid.*, s. 117 (1) (xxviii).
[7] *Infra*, pp. 246-7.
[8] But a gift over on failure of issue becomes incapable of taking effect as soon as there is any issue who attains 18; L.P.A. 1925, s. 134 (1), as amended by Family Law Reform Act 1969, s. 1 (3), Sched. 1.
[9] *Infra*, pp. 259-60.
[10] *Infra*, pp. 362 *et seq.*
[11] *Infra*, p. 384.
[12] *Re Catling*, [1931] 2 Ch. 359.
[13] *Re Johnson*, [1914] 2 Ch. 194.

(vi) A tenant for his own or any other life, or for years determinable on life, whose interest is liable to cease in any event during that life, or is subject to a trust for accumulation of income.

> For instance, a devise to A. so long as he shall live on the estate for at least three months in each year, with a gift over to B. upon failure to observe this condition, makes A. tenant for life within the present section.[1]

(vii) A tenant by the curtesy.[2]

(viii) A person entitled to the *income* of land under a trust for payment thereof to him during his own or any other life,[3] or until sale of the land, or until some event (*e.g.* bankruptcy) terminates his interest. But if the land is subject to an immediate binding trust for sale, the person so entitled is not to be deemed tenant for life.

(ix) A person beneficially entitled to land for an estate in fee simple or for a term of years absolute subject to any estates, interests, charges or powers of charging, subsisting or capable of being exercised under a settlement.

> If, for instance, lands are settled on A. for life with remainder in fee simple to his eldest son B., with powers for A. to charge the land with portions for his younger children, B., on the death of A., will hold the fee simple subject to any such charges that may have been created. He is tenant for life under the above clause and as such can deal with the estate, notwithstanding the charge to which it is subject.[4]

Position where there is no person having powers of tenant for life.

Statutory Owners. Comprehensive though this list is, it still fails to provide for the case of every settlement. For instance, a settlement within the meaning of the Act exists if land is limited in trust for any person in fee simple contingently upon the happening of some event,[5] or when the person entitled in possession is entitled only to a *part* of the income from the trust [6] or where no person is entitled to any of its income at all as in the case of a discretionary strict settlement where the trustees are directed to pay the income to such members of a class of persons as they may think fit.[7] In none of these cases is the beneficiary a tenant for life or a person who has the powers of a tenant for life. The Act, therefore,

---

[1] *Re Paget* (1885), 30 Ch. D. 161. See also *Bannister* v. *Bannister*, [1948] 2 All E. R. 133 ; M. & B. p. 460 ; *Binions* v. *Evans*, [1972] Ch. 359 ; [1972] 2 All E. R. 70 ; M. & B. p. 467 ; *infra.*, p. 585 ; *cf. Ivory* v. *Palmer*, [1975] I. C. R. 340, *infra*, p. 583.
[2] *Infra*, pp. 244.
[3] *Re Llanover Settled Estates*, [1926] Ch. 626.
[4] He also has the option under L.P.(A.)A. 1926, s. 1 (1), *supra*, p. 169, of conveying the legal estate to a purchaser subject to the charge, provided that the purchaser is agreeable.
[5] *Re Bird*, [1927] 1 Ch. 210. *Supra*, p. 169.
[6] *Re Frewen*, [1926] Ch. 580.
[7] *Re Gallenga Will Trusts*, [1938] 1 All E. R. 106.

provides that where such a situation arises the legal estate shall be vested in statutory owners—that is to say,

(a) any person of full age upon whom they are conferred by the settlement, and

(b) **in any other case the trustees of the settlement.**[1]

Further, where the person who would otherwise be a tenant for life is an infant, the legal estate and statutory powers are vested during the minority of the infant in

(a) a personal representative, if the land is vested in him and no vesting instrument has yet been executed

(b) in every other case, the trustees of the settlement.[2]

(4) THE POWERS OF THE TENANT FOR LIFE

In accordance with the policy that has prevailed since the Settled Land Act 1882, the person vested with the legal estate, normally the tenant for life in actual possession, is empowered by the Settled Land Act of 1925 to manage and even to dispose of the fee simple, an aspect of his position that must now be developed in some detail. The general policy is that he shall have many of the powers of dealing with the land that are available to an estate owner entitled beneficially in his own right, but subject to this overriding proviso, that any gain accruing from the exercise of a power shall be held on trust for the equitable beneficiaries according to the limitations of the settlement. To this end the Act confers upon the tenant for life the right to exercise any of the following powers:— *Tenant for life as manager of the land.*

(A) **Power to Sell or Exchange.** The tenant for life may sell the settled land, or any part thereof, or any easement, right or privilege of any kind over or in relation to the land.[3] Every sale must be made for the best consideration in money that can reasonably be obtained,[4] but instead of being made in return for a lump sum it may be made in consideration, wholly or partly, of a rent payable yearly or half-yearly and secured upon the land sold. Such a rent may be perpetual or terminable, and in the latter case—that is to say, when it will cease to be payable after a certain number of years—it must be treated partly as principal and partly as interest, and the part constituting principal must be dealt with as capital money. The interest accruing on the principal sum must be accumulated by way of compound interest and added each year to capital.[5] The rent must be the best that can reasonably be obtained, though for a period not exceeding five years from the sale it may be nominal.[6] The statutory remedies *Rent as consideration.*

---

[1] S.L.A. 1925, ss. 23, 117 (1) (xxvi).   [2] *Ibid.*, s. 26.   *Infra*, pp. 916–9.
[3] *Ibid.*, s. 38 (i).
[4] *Ibid.*, s. 39 (1).   *Wheelwright* v. *Walker (No. 2)*. (1883), 31 W. R. 912.
[5] *Ibid.*, s. 39 (2).   [6] *Ibid.*, s. 39 (3).

for the recovery of a rentcharge given by the Law of Property Act 1925[1] lie for recovery of the rent.[2]

Fully-paid securities as consideration. It is also provided that where the land is sold to any company incorporated by special Act of Parliament or by any order having the force of an Act of Parliament, the purchase money may consist, either wholly or partially, of fully-paid securities of any description of the purchasing company.[3]

Exchange. The tenant for life may make an exchange of the whole or part of the land, or of any easement, right, or privilege over it, for other land or for an easement, right, or privilege over other land, and he may pay or accept money in order to render the exchanges equal in value.[4]

Exception of mines and minerals. When a sale or exchange is made, the tenant for life is permitted to except the mines and minerals, and in such a case to reserve for the settled land all proper rights and powers incidental to mining purposes.[5]

Mansion-house. The powers of sale and exchange are exercisable with regard to any principal mansion-house which stands on the settled land, but in two cases mere notice to the trustees of the proposed transaction[6] does not suffice, and the tenant for life must first obtain either the consent of the trustees or an order of the court, namely :

(i) where the settlement existed before 1926, and does not expressly dispense with the necessity for such consent or order ; and

(ii) where the settlement came into operation after 1925, but contains a provision that such consent or order is necessary.

The court must determine as a fact whether any particular house is a principal mansion-house,[7] but it is enacted that a house which is usually occupied as a farmhouse, or which, together with its pleasure-grounds and park and lands, does not exceed 25 acres in extent, is not a principal mansion-house within the meaning of the Act and can in all cases be disposed of without the consent of the trustees.[8]

Leasing powers. (B) **Power to Grant Leases.** The tenant for life may lease the whole or part of the land or any easement, right, or privilege incidental thereto for any purpose whatever, whether involving waste or not, for any of the following maximum periods :—

(a) 999 years for a building lease,
(b) 100 years for a mining lease,

---

[1] S. 121 ; *infra*, p. 629.   [2] L.P.(A.)A. 1926, Sched.
[3] S.L.A. 1925, s. 39 (5).   [4] *Ibid.*, ss. 38 (iii), 40.
[5] *Ibid.*, s. 50.   [6] *Infra*, p. 184.
[7] *Re Feversham Settled Estate*, [1938] 2 All E. R. 210.
[8] S.L.A. 1925, s. 65.

(c) 999 years for a forestry lease,

(d) 50 years for any other kind of lease.[1]

When any of the above leases is made,

(i) the tenant for life must give one month's notice in writing to the trustees,[2]

(ii) he must procure the best rent reasonably obtainable,[3] and

(iii) the lease must be by deed[3] and must contain a covenant by the lessee for payment of the rent, and a condition allowing the tenant for life to re-enter if the rent is not paid within a specific time not exceeding thirty days.

Duties of tenant in granting leases.

The deed must be so framed that the lessee will take possession within twelve months, but if the land is already leased to a third person, then, provided that such existing lease has no more than seven years to run, it is lawful to grant what is called a reversionary lease to take effect in possession when the existing one determines.[4]

Without any notice to the trustees, a lease may be granted for a term not exceeding twenty-one years at the best rent that can reasonably be obtained without a fine, provided that the lessee is made impeachable for waste.[5] If the lease does not exceed three years, it may be made by writing without a deed, but the lessee must enter into a written agreement to pay the rent.[6]

Lease without notice to trustees.

As in the case of the power of sale, the tenant for life may lease the land and reserve the minerals,[7] and if he desires to lease the principal mansion-house, he must obtain the consent of the trustees in the cases which have been specified above.[8]

Special provisions are inserted in the Act with regard to building, mining and forestry leases:—

(i) A building lease[9] must be made partly in consideration of the lessee or some other person erecting new or additional buildings or improving or repairing buildings, and partly in consideration of the payment of rent. A peppercorn or nominal rent may be reserved for the first five years of the term.[10] A lease is valid although it does not specify a definite time within which the building or rebuilding shall begin.[11]

Building leases.

---

[1] S.L.A. 1925, s. 41.   [2] *Ibid.*, s. 101.
[3] *Re Morgan's Lease*, [1972] Ch. 1 ; [1971] 2 All E. R. 235 ; (1971), 87 L. Q. R. 338 (D. W. Elliott).
[4] S.L.A. 1925, s. 42 (1) (i).
[5] For the meaning of waste, see *infra*, p. 267.
[6] S.L.A. 1925, s. 42 (5).   [7] *Ibid.*, s. 50.
[8] *Ibid.*, s. 65, *supra*, p. 178.
[9] *Infra*, p. 490.   [10] S.L.A. 1925, s. 44.
[11] *Re Grosvenor Settled Estates*, [1933] Ch. 97.

Mining
leases.

(ii) As regards minerals the rule at common law is that a tenant for life unimpeachable for waste[1] can *open* and work mines and retain the whole profits, though this right can no longer be exercised without the permission of the local planning authority, since it involves a material change in the user of land within the meaning of the Town and Country Planning Act 1971. A tenant for life impeachable cannot *open* mines, but he can continue to work to his own profit those that have already been

Part of rent
is capital.

lawfully opened by a predecessor.[2] These rules have been varied by statute. If the tenant for life is impeachable for waste in respect of minerals, three-quarters of the rent arising from a mining lease becomes capital ; if unimpeachable, one-quarter becomes capital and the residue goes to him as income.[3] A tenant for life who is impeachable for waste under the settlement is not impeachable in respect of mines that have been lawfully opened by a predecessor, and therefore he is entitled to three-fourths of the rents.[4] These rules with regard to minerals have lost much of their importance since the passing of the Coal Industry Nationalization Act 1946, but they are still material, for " minerals " include " all substances in, on or under the land, obtainable by underground or by surface working."[5]

Forestry
lease.

(iii) A forestry lease is defined by the Act as a " lease to the Forestry Commissioners for any purpose for which they are authorized to acquire land by the Forestry Act, 1919," [6] but this is now to be construed as a reference to the Minister of Agriculture, Fisheries and Food, in whom the former powers of the Commissioners to acquire land are now vested.[7] In a forestry lease the rent may be nominal for any period not exceeding the first ten years or may be made to vary according to the value of the timber cut in any one year, and any other provisions may be made for the sharing of the profits of the user of the land between the tenant for life and the Minister.[8]

Power to
borrow
money.

(C) **Power to raise Money by the Grant of a Legal Mortgage of the Settled Land.** A capital sum of money may be raised by mortgage in order to meet some expense that is connected with the settled land or desirable in the interests of its prosperity. There are nine different purposes specified by the Act for which a tenant for life may raise money in this manner, but

---

[1] For the meaning of waste, see *infra*, p. 267.
[2] *Re Hall* [1916] 2 Ch. 488.
[3] S.L.A. 1925, s. 47. These provisions may be displaced by the settlement ; s. 48.
[4] *Re Chaytor*, [1900] 2 Ch. 804 ; *Re Fitzwalter* [1943] Ch. 285 ; [1943] 2 All E. R. 328.
[5] S.L.A. 1925, s. 117 (1) (xv).   [6] *Ibid.*, s. 117 (x).
[7] Forestry Act 1967 s. 50 ; Sched. 6, para. 5.
[8] S.L.A. 1925, s. 48.

as five of these are connected with the conversion of copyhold into socage and of perpetually renewable leases into long terms, it is only necessary to notice that a mortgage of the legal estate is permissible when the object is[1] :

(i) The discharge of an incumbrance on the settled land.

Purposes for which money may be borrowed.

> If, for instance, different parts of the land are subject to three separate mortgages, the tenant for life may grant a new mortgage of the entire land to another mortgagee and use the money to pay off the three original debts.[2]
> The incumbrance must be permanent, thus excluding any annual sum payable only during a life or for a term of years.[3]

(ii) Payment for any improvement authorized by the Settled Land Act 1925 or by the settlement.

> This is a valuable power that was introduced in 1925. A tenant for life may spend existing capital money on carrying out any of the improvements authorized by the Act,[4] but he had no power under the old Settled Land Acts to borrow new money on mortgage for the purpose, though he could raise a loan under the Improvement of Land Acts with the approval of the Ministry of Agriculture and Fisheries.

(iii) Equality of exchange.

(iv) Payment of the costs of any transaction effected under (i) to (iii) above.

A legal mortgage by the tenant for life may take the form either of a charge by deed by way of legal mortgage or of a long lease,[5] and a tenant for life who grants a mortgage term for any of the above four purposes is not subject to those provisions of the Settled Land Act[6] which in a normal case restrict the length of lease that may be made.[7] This must be distinguished from the case where the tenant for life borrows money for his own purposes by mortgaging his beneficial interest, as for instance his equitable life interest.[8]

(D) Power to effect improvements. The tenant for life is empowered to effect certain authorized improvements on the land and to have the cost defrayed out of capital.[9] Moreover, his right to this payment, unlike the practice prevailing before 1926, is no longer conditional on his submitting a scheme of operations to the trustees or to the Court before the work is done.[10]

---

[1] S.L.A. 1925, s. 71.   See too Leasehold Reform Act 1967, s. 6 (5).
[2] *Re Clifford* [1902] 1 Ch. 87.
[3] S.L.A. 1925, s. 71 (2).
[4] *Ibid.*, s. 83 ; *infra.*
[5] *Infra*, pp. 642 *et seq.*   [6] *Supra*, pp. 178–9.
[7] S.L.A. 1925, s. 71 (3).   [8] *Infra*, p. 651.
[9] S.L.A. 1925, s. 83.   [10] *Ibid.*, s. 84 (1).

The Act authorizes thirty-four specific improvements which are classified into three categories according to the permanence or impermanence of their results.[1]

Part I improvements comprise twenty-five different works that clearly increase the permanent capital value of the land, such as drainage, irrigation, bridges, defences against water, the provision of farmhouses and cottages for labourers and the rebuilding of the mansion house.

Part II improvements are those, the lasting value of which is more doubtful, such as the erection of houses for land agents, the repair of damage due to dry rot or boring for water.

Part III improvements are those whose value is transitory, as, for example, the installation of a heating or electric power apparatus for buildings, the wiring of a house for electricity or the purchase of moveable machinery for farming or other purposes.

Power to accept leases.

(E) **Power to accept Leases of other Land.** A new power was introduced by the Act of 1925 allowing the tenant for life to accept a lease of any other land[2] or of mines and minerals, or of any easement, right or privilege, " convenient to be held or worked with or annexed in enjoyment to the settled land," and there is no limit to the length of the term which he may so accept.[3]

Miscellaneous powers.

(F) **Miscellaneous Powers.** There are several miscellaneous powers which the tenant for life is entitled to exercise, and of these the following may be mentioned :—

Power to contract to make dispositions.

(i) power to contract to make any sale, exchange, mortgage, charge or other disposition authorized by the Act.[4] The transaction must be in conformity with the Act at the time of the performance of the contract. Thus in the case of a contract for a lease the lease must satisfy the requirement that the rent must be the best reasonably obtainable when the lease is granted.[5] Such contracts are enforceable by and against every successor in title of the tenant for life.[6]

Power to grant options.

(ii) power to grant, by writing, with or without consideration, an option to purchase or take a lease of settled land, or any easement, right, or privilege over it.[7] The price or rent must be the best reasonably obtainable and must

---

[1] S.L.A. 1925, 3rd Sched. For the significance of this classification, see *infra*, p. 195.

[2] This includes a power to accept an extended lease under Leasehold Reform Act 1967, s. 6 (2) (a), *infra*, p. 491.

[3] S.L.A. 1925, s. 53.   [4] *Ibid.*, s. 90.

[5] *Re Rycroft's Settlement*, [1962] Ch. 263 ; [1961] 3 All E. R. 581.

[6] S.L.A. 1925, s. 90 (2).   [7] *Ibid.*, s. 51.

be fixed when the *option* is granted.[1] The option must be made exercisable within an agreed number of years not exceeding ten.

(iii) power to accept, with or without consideration, a surrender of any lease of settled land ; [2]

Surrender of leases.

(iv) power, if the result will be for the general benefit of the settled land, to make grants or leases at a nominal price or rent for certain public and charitable purposes, *e.g.* the grant of land not exceeding one acre for a village institute or a public library.[3]

Powers for benefit of public.

(v) power to grant or lease a restricted amount of land at a nominal price or rent for the purpose of providing allotments or dwellings for the working classes ; [4]

Allotments, etc.

(vi) power *with the consent of the trustees* or *under an order of the court* for a tenant for life who is impeachable for waste to sell timber that is ripe and fit for cutting, provided, however, that three-quarters of the net proceeds become capital money and one-quarter becomes income ; [5]

Timber.

(vii) power *under an order of the court* to sell heirlooms, but in such a case the money arising from the sale becomes capital money, which in this case may be spent on the purchase of other heirlooms.[6]

Heirlooms.

(G) Power to effect any Transaction under an Order of the Court.

" Any transaction " within the powers of an absolute owner may be sanctioned by the court if this will be for the benefit of the settled land or the beneficiaries, even though it is a transaction not otherwise authorized by the Act or the settlement.[7] Thus approval was given to a scheme to raise money out of capital to enable the tenant for life to continue to reside in the mansion house.[8] Moreover the width of the definition of " transaction " enables the court to alter the beneficial interests under the settlement. This was commonly done for the purpose of saving estate duty on the death of beneficiaries, and the jurisdiction was largely superseded by that given to the court under the Variation of Trusts Act 1958.[9] Both jurisdictions still remain, but the fiscal attractions are much reduced since the determination of an

---

[1] *Re Morgan's Lease*, [1972] Ch. 1 ; [1971] 2 All E. R. 235.
[2] S.L.A. 1925, s. 52.
[3] *Ibid.*, s. 55.   [4] *Ibid.*, s. 57 (2).
[5] *Ibid.*, s. 66.   [6] *Ibid.*, s. 67.
[7] *Ibid.*, s. 64 (1). " Transaction " is defined in s. 64 (2) as amended by Settled Land and Trustee Acts (Court's General Powers) Act 1943, s. 2. *Re White-Popham Settled Estates*, [1936] Ch. 725 ; [1936] 2 All E. R. 1486 ; *Re Mount Edgcumbe (Earl of)*, [1950] Ch. 615 ; [1950] 2 All E. R. 242 ; *Re Simmons*, [1956] Ch. 125 ; *Re Rycroft's Settlement*, [1962] Ch. 263 ; [1961] 3 All E. R. 581.
[8] *Re Scarisbrick Re-Settlement Estates*, [1944] Ch. 229 ; [1944] 1 All E. R. 404.
[9] See generally Hanbury's *Modern Equity* (9th Edn.) Ch. 21 ; Harris, *Variation of Trusts* (1975).

interest in possession under a trust is now a chargeable transfer for capital transfer tax purposes.[1]

Cases where more than notice is required. As a general rule a tenant for life need not obtain the consent of the trustees to his exercise of a power, but if he intends to sell, exchange, mortgage or charge the land, to make a lease exceeding twenty-one years or to grant an option to purchase or to take a lease of the land, he must notify the trustees of his intention at least one month before he completes the transaction.[2]   Except in the case of a proposed mortgage or charge, it is permissible, indeed usual, to give a general notice, *i.e.* one which states his intention to grant, for example, leases from time to time, without mentioning any specific lease already arranged.[3]   There are, however, as we have seen, several cases in which something more than notice is required, and it may be helpful to restate these in summary form :

Powers
requiring
order of
court.

First, an order of the court must be obtained before the tenant for life may :

    (*a*) grant more than the amount of land specified in the Act for providing allotments or dwellings for the working classes ;[4]

    (*b*) buy or sell heirlooms ;[5]

    (*c*) grant building or mining leases for terms longer than those specified in the Act.[6]

Powers
requiring
order of
court or
consent of
trustees.

Secondly, *either* an order of the court *or* the consent of the trustees must be obtained before the tenant for life may :

    (*a*) sell or lease the principal mansion-house in the cases specified above ;[7]

    (*b*) sell the timber in the event of his being impeachable for waste.[8]

Powers
requiring
consent of
trustees.

Thirdly, there are two cases in which the tenant for life must obtain the consent in writing of the trustees, namely, before he

    (*a*) compromises or otherwise settles any claim or dispute relating to the settled land ;[9]

    (*b*) releases, waives or modifies a right imposed on other land for the benefit of the settled land, as, for instance, an easement or a covenant.[10]

Settlement
may grant
additional
powers.

Additional Powers and Restriction of Powers. Such, then, are the powers conferred upon the tenant for life by the Act, but it must be remembered that there is nothing to prevent

---

[1] F.A. 1975, s. 21, Sched. 5., paras. 3, 4 ; *infra* p. 206.
[2] S.L.A. 1925, s. 101 (1).
[3] *Ibid.*, s. 101 (2).
[4] *Ibid.*, s. 57 (2).
[5] *Ibid.*, s. 67.
[6] *Ibid.*, s. 46.   [7] *Ibid.*, s. 65, *supra*, p. 178.   [8] *Ibid.*, s. 66.
[9] *Ibid.*, s. 58 (1).   [10] *Ibid.*, s. 58 (2).

additional powers being given to him by the settlement, for it is expressly provided[1] that when a settlor authorizes the exercise of any powers additional to or larger than those enumerated above, they shall operate in exactly the same manner and with the same results as if they had been permitted by the Act. Thus a settlement may allow the tenant for life:

1. to grant a lease to take effect in possession not later than three years after its date.[2]

2. to use as income the whole of the rent reserved on a mining lease,[3] or

3. to raise money on mortgage for the purchase of a dwelling-house.[4]

In fact all the powers given by a settlement are expressly preserved, for it is provided that nothing in the Act shall take away, abridge or prejudicially affect any power under the settlement which is exercisable by the tenant for life or by the trustees with the consent of the tenant for life.[5] If however, there is any conflict between the Act and the settlement, the Act prevails, and any power (not being a mere power of revocation or appointment[6]) conferred on the trustees becomes exercisable by the tenant for life as an additional power.[7]

Such a conflict occurs, for instance, if the settlement empowers the tenant for life to sell with the consent of a third person, for such a conditional power is inconsistent with the unfettered power of sale given by the Act.[8]

But though a settlor is allowed to confer upon the tenant for life the right to exercise powers additional to those permissible under the statute, it is enacted in no uncertain terms that any provisions inserted in the settlement with a view to cutting down the statutory powers shall be void. Section 106 of the Settled Land Act 1925 runs as follows :— *Prohibition against exercise of powers void.*

" If in a settlement, will, assurance, or other instrument . . . a provision is inserted—

(*a*) purporting or attempting, by way of direction, declaration, or otherwise, to forbid a tenant for life or statutory owner to exercise any power under this Act, or his right to require the settled land to be vested in him ; or

(*b*) attempting, or tending, or intended, by a limitation, gift, or

---

1 S.L.A. 1925, s. 109.
2 *Encyclopaedia of Forms and Precedents* (4th Edn.), vol. 20. p. 700.
3 *Ibid.*, p. 699.
4 *Ibid.*, p. 702.
5 S.L.A. 1925, s. 108 (1).
6 As, for example, where land is limited upon such trusts as T. shall appoint, and subject thereto to A. for life. Here, T.'s power to revoke the life interest and to appoint new interests remains exercisable by him : Wolstenholme and Cherry, vol. 3, p. 222.
7 S.L.A. 1925, s. 108 (2).
8 *Re Jefferys*, [1939] Ch. 205 ; (1939), 55 *L. Q. R.* 22 (H.P.).

> disposition over of settled land, or by a limitation, gift, or disposition of *other* real or any personal property, or by the imposition of any condition, or by forfeiture, or in any other manner whatever, to prohibit or prevent him from exercising, or to induce him to abstain from exercising, or to put him into a position inconsistent with his exercising, any power under this Act, or his right to require the settled land to be vested in him ;

> that provision, as far as it purports, or attempts, or tends, or is intended to have, or would or might have, the operation aforesaid, shall be deemed to be void." [1]

Exemplified by conditions as to residence.
A condition, that is sometimes inserted in settlements requiring the tenant for life to reside on the settled land will serve to illustrate the application of this section.

> Suppose that land is settled on X. for life with a proviso that if he does not reside on the settled land for at least three months in each year he shall forfeit his interest.

Such a clause is void so far as it " tends " to hinder or obstruct the exercise by X. of his statutory powers. This, of course is its natural tendency, for if he sells or leases the estate he must necessarily infringe the condition as to residence. It is a deterrent of this nature that is within the mischief of the section, and the rule therefore is that, notwithstanding a disposition of the land under his statutory powers, his life interest in the income remains intact. [2] If, on the other hand, there is no question of the exercise of the powers, his failure to satisfy the condition operates as a forfeiture of his interest. [3] If it has never been his intention to exercise the powers, it cannot be said that the condition has in any way hampered his freedom of action.

Another example of the operation of the section is this :—

> If the settlor vests a fund of money in the trustees, with authority to apply the income thereof upon the maintenance of the estate and to pay any surplus not required for that purpose to the tenant for life, X., the prospect of losing this income might tend to dissuade X. from exercising his power of sale. As a general rule, therefore, if X. sells the land he still remains entitled to the income for life. [4]

Powers not assignable.
Again, as long as the land remains settled, the powers of a tenant for life are indestructible in the sense that they are not capable of assignment or release, but remain exercisable by him notwithstanding any assignment by operation of law or otherwise of his beneficial interest under the settlement. [5] Thus :

---

[1] *Re Aberconway's Settlement Trusts*, [1953] Ch. 647 ; [1953] 2 All E. R. 350.
[2] *Re Paget's Settled Estates* (1885), 30 Ch. D. 161 ; *Re Patten*, [1929] 2 Ch. 276. (An excellent example of the principle) ; *Re Orlebar*, [1936] Ch. 147.
[3] *Re Acklom*, [1929] 1 Ch. 195 ; M. & B. p. 256. *Re Haynes*, [1887] 37 Ch. D. 306 ; *Re Trenchard*, [1902] 1 Ch. 378.
[4] *Re Ames*, [1893] 2 Ch. 479 ; *Re Herbert*, [1946] 1 All E. R. 421 ; dist. *Re Burden*, [1948] Ch. 160 ; [1948] 1 All E. R. 31 ; *Re Aberconway's Settlement Trusts, supra* ; (1954) C.L.J. 60 (R. N. Gooderson).
[5] S.L.A. 1925, s. 104 (1).

If land stands settled on A. for life, remainder to B. for life with remainder over, and B. sells his reversionary life interest for value to X., the statutory power to grant leases after the death of A. is exercisable by B., for the design of the Act is to enable a tenant for life to exercise his powers whether he has disposed of his beneficial interest or not.[1]

In such a case as this the former rule was that B. could not exercise his powers without the consent of his assignee for value, X., but the necessity for such consent has now been removed by the Act.[2] The rights of the assignee are, however, protected, for whatever interest he had in the property originally assigned to him he has a corresponding interest in any money, securities or land into which that property may have been converted as a result of the exercise of some power.[3] Moreover, notice of an intended transaction must be given to him.[4]

If, however, it is shown to the satisfaction of the court that a tenant for life has by reason of bankruptcy, assignment, incumbrance, or otherwise ceased to have a substantial interest in the settled land, and has unreasonably *refused* to exercise the statutory powers, an order may be made authorizing the trustees of the settlement to exercise the powers in his name.[5] The mere fact that he has grossly neglected the land and has allowed it to become derelict does not justify the making of an order. The court must be satisfied that there has been an unreasonable refusal to exercise the powers.[6]

Position where tenant for life has no substantial interest in the settled land.

Although any attempted assignment of the powers by the tenant for life is void, it is provided that if the life interest, with the intention of causing its extinction, is surrendered to the remainderman or reversioner next entitled under the settlement, the statutory powers shall cease to be available to the tenant for life and shall be exercisable as if he were dead.[7] For instance :

Effect of a surrender of a life interest.

> if a tenant for life becomes bankrupt and the trustee sells his life interest to the tenant in tail in remainder,[8] or if a father surrenders his life interest to the tenant in tail in remainder, the statutory powers become exercisable by the tenant in tail.

Exercise of the Powers of a Tenant for Life in Favour of Himself. When a tenant for life exercises his statutory

Provisions enabling dealings with tenant for life.

---

[1] *Re Barlow's Contract*, [1903] 1 Ch. 382 ; *Earl of Lonsdale* v. *Lowther*, [1900] 2 Ch. 687.
[2] S.L.A. 1925, s. 104 (4).
[3] *Ibid.*, s. 104 (4) (*a*).
[4] *Ibid.*, s. 104 (4) (*c*).
[5] *Ibid.*, s. 24 (1). This section does not apply to a statutory owner, *Re Craven Settled Estates*, [1926] Ch. 985.
[6] *Re Thornhill's Settlement.* [1940] 4 All E. R. 83 ; affirmed, [1941] Ch. 24 ; [1940] 4 All E. R. 249 ; M. & B. p. 260.
[7] S.L.A. 1925, s. 105 (1). L.P.(A.)A. 1926, Sched. A remainderman or reversioner does not qualify if there is an intervening limitation which may take effect. *Re Maryon-Wilson's Instruments*, [1971] Ch. 789 ; [1969] 3 All E. R. 558.
[8] *Re Shawdon Estates Settlement*, [1930] 1 Ch. 217 ; affirmed, [1930] 2 Ch. 1.

powers, he is normally dealing with persons who have no connection with the estate, but it may happen that in his private capacity and not as tenant for life he wishes to exercise one of the powers in favour of himself. The possibility of such a dealing between him and the settled estate was first allowed to a restricted extent by the Settled Land Act 1890, but his freedom in this respect has been extended by the Act of 1925, and it is now provided that any disposition of the settled land may be made to him, that capital money may be advanced on mortgage to him, and that land may be bought from or exchanged with him.[1]

Since a person can scarcely negotiate a transaction with himself, it is provided that in all such cases the trustees shall have all the powers of a tenant for life in reference to negotiating and completing the transaction, and the right to enforce any covenants entered into by the tenant for life.[2] Where the tenant for life is himself one of the trustees, he should be a conveying party as well as the person in whose favour the conveyance is made.[3]

Position of tenant for life as trustee.

Tenant for Life is Trustee for the Beneficiaries. Finally, it must be observed that the tenant for life, though he is given an almost unfettered liberty to exercise the statutory powers, is at the same time constituted trustee for all interested parties. The Act provides that :

> " A tenant for life or statutory owner shall, in exercising any power under this Act, have regard to the interests of all parties entitled under the settlement, and shall, in relation to the exercise thereof by him, be deemed to be in the position and to have the duties and liabilities of a trustee for those parties."[4]

Several judicial pronouncements have placed those duties on a high level. It has been said that the duty to " have regard to the interests of all parties " requires the tenant for life to consider all the interests in the widest sense, not merely pecuniary interests, but even the aspirations and sentiments of the family.[5]

> " He must " [said Lord Esher] " take all the circumstances of the family, and of each member of the family who may be affected by what he is about to do ; he must consider them all carefully, and must consider them in the way that an honest outside trustee would consider them ; then he must come to what, in his judgment, is the right thing to do under the circumstances—not the best thing, but the right thing to do."[6]

---

[1] S.L.A. 1925, s. 68 (1).   [2] *Ibid.*, s. 68 (2).

[3] *Re Pennant's Will Trusts*, [1970] Ch. 75 ; [1969] 2 All E. R. 862.

[4] S.L.A. 1925, s. 107 (1) re-enacting s. 53 of the 1882 Act. *Re Pelly's Will Trusts*, [1957] Ch. 1, at p. 18 ; [1956] 2 All E. R. 326.

[5] *Re Marquis of Ailesbury's Settled Estates*, [1892] 1 Ch. 506, at p. 536 ; *per* LINDLEY, L.J. ; and see BOWEN, L.J., *passim.* " He must act as an upright, independent and righteous man would act in dealing with the affairs of others," *per* FRY, L.J., at p. 546.

[6] *Re Earl of Radnor's Will Trusts* (1890), 45 Ch. D. 402, 417.

Nevertheless, having regard to the deliberate policy of the Act in conferring upon the tenant for life virtually the status of absolute owner, this superimposed trusteeship is somewhat abnormal, for in the nature of things it must inevitably be " a highly interested trusteeship." [1] The mere imposition of a trust is insufficient to ensure that powers, so freely confided to the judgment of the tenant for life, will not be exercised from motives of selfishness and personal aggrandizement. A tenant for life, who, with the object of securing a larger income wherewith to meet his debts or to indulge expensive tastes, or in order to relieve himself from the cares of management, or because he is hostile to the remainderman, sells land that will obviously be of far greater value in a few years' time, owing perhaps to rapidly changing conditions in the neighbourhood, can scarcely be described as acting " as an upright, independent and righteous man would act in dealing with the affairs of others," [2] and yet none of these facts alone is sufficient to render him liable, provided that he obtains the best price reasonably obtainable and otherwise observes the requirements of the Act. [3]

The Court may, however, intervene upon clear proof that the tenant for life has exercised a power with the sole object of conferring some benefit upon himself or upon some relative other than the remainderman, as, for example, where he accepts a bribe from a lessee, [4] where he makes an unsuitable investment, [5] or where a widow entitled for life *durante viduitate* makes a lease to her second intended husband in order to ensure her continued occupation of the premises. [6]

(5) THE TRUSTEES OF THE SETTLEMENT

The Settled Land Act 1925 gives a list of five different classes of persons competent to act as trustees of the settlement and arranges them in a binding order of priority as follows [7] :— *Who are trustees.*

    (i) The persons, who under the settlement are trustees with power of sale of the settled land.

        A power given to trustees to sell settled land is in fact abortive, since the Act provides that it shall be exercisable not by them, but by the tenant for life. [8] The

---

[1] *Re Stamford and Warrington*, [1916] 1 Ch. 404, at p. 420, YOUNGER, J.
[2] See p. 188, note 5.
[3] Cp. the remarks of PEARSON, J., in *Wheelwright* v. *Walker* (1883), 23 Ch. D. 752, at pp. 761–2 ; M. & B. p. 262. See too *England* v. *Public Trustee* (1967), 205 *Estates Gazette* 651 when SELLERS, L.J., suggested that S.L.A. 1925 should be amended to provide that notice of an intended sale by the tenant for life should be given to the other beneficiaries under the settlement.
[4] *Chandler* v. *Bradley*, [1897] 1 Ch. 315.
[5] *Re Hunt's Settled Estates*, [1906] 2 Ch. 11.
[6] *Middlemas* v. *Stevens*, [1901] 1 Ch. 574 ; M. & B. p. 263.
[7] S.L.A. 1925, s. 30 (1) (i)–(v).   [8] *Ibid*,. s. 108 (2).

only effect is to make the persons to whom it is given trustees *ex necessitate* of the settlement.

(ii) The persons who are declared by the settlement to be trustees thereof for the purposes of the Settled Land Act.

These persons will normally constitute the trustees, for an express reservation of the power of sale contemplated by the first paragraph will rarely occur in practice.

(iii) The persons, who under the settlement are trustees with power of sale of any *other* land comprised in the settlement which is subject to the same limitations as the land that is being dealt with.

(iv) The persons who, under the settlement, are trustees with a future power of sale.

If, for example, a testator devises his land to his wife for life and after her death to X. and Y. upon trust to sell the fee simple, then, failing persons qualified under the first three paragraphs, X. and Y. will be the trustees of the settlement during the wife's life.

(v) The persons appointed by deed by the beneficiaries, provided that the beneficiaries are of full capacity and entitled to dispose of the whole settled estate.

Where a settlement is created by will, or has arisen by reason of an intestacy, and there are no trustees, the personal representatives of the deceased are trustees of the settlement until others are appointed; but if there is only one personal representative, not being a trust corporation, he must appoint an additional trustee to act with him.[1]

If at any time there are no trustees as defined above, or if for any reason it is expedient that new trustees should be appointed, the court may appoint fit persons to hold the office.[2]

Compound Settlement.

Compound Trustees. Where land is settled by a series of separate instruments, the instruments together form one settlement which is called a *compound settlement*.[3] The commonest example of this occurs in the case of a re-settlement, which, as we have seen, involves three instruments, *i.e.* the original settlement, the disentailment and the re-settlement.[4] The principle that the several instruments may be regarded as constituting one settlement becomes important when the tenant for life, in excercise of his statutory power of sale, desires to convey the fee simple to the purchaser free from the limitations of the various instruments.

---

[1] S.L.A. 1925, s. 30 (3).   [2] *Ibid.*, s. 34.
[3] *Re Ogle's Settled Estates*, [1927] 1 Ch. 229, 233–4, per Romer, J. ; M. & B. p. 23
[4] *Supra*, pp. 72–3.

If, after a re-settlement, a sale has been effected by the father as first tenant for life he can execute the conveyance in any one of three capacities : Conveyance of settled land.

(a) He may convey as tenant for life under the original settlement.

> The merit of this is that his conveyance overreaches the limitations of both settlements, and if the purchase money is paid to the trustees of the original settlement the purchaser acquires a title free from the rights of the beneficiaries. The disadvantage is that the tenant for life, since he is acting under the original settlement, cannot avail himself of any additional powers which may have been reserved by the deed of re-settlement.

(b) He may convey as tenant for life under the re-settlement.

> The position here is reversed, for although he can exercise any additional powers, he cannot convey a title free from rights of beneficiaries, that have been created by the original settlement. Conveyancers sought before 1926 to overcome this difficulty by reciting in the re-settlement that the life interest re-settled upon the father was " in restoration and by way of confirmation of " his life interest under the original settlement, but it was only on the eve of a statutory amendment of the law[1] that this device was held to be effective.[2] It had previously been held that " when once conveyancers have in fact " transmuted the old body into a new body, they cannot claim to have retained the old body, whatever incantations they may use in the process." [3]

(c) He may convey as tenant for life under the compound settlement.

> This plan combines the advantages of the two preceding methods, since the tenant for life can exercise additional powers given by the re-settlement and can overreach, within the statutory limits,[4] the limitations of both settlements. Under the old law, however, this method was often open to a fatal objection, for its efficacy depends upon the existence of compound trustees, and before the legislation of 1925, it frequently happened that there were no such trustees. If compound trustees had not been appointed in the original settlement it was impossible to rectify the omission in the re-settlement, and unless all the beneficiaries were of full

---

[1] *Infra*, p. 192.

[2] *Parr* v. *A.-G.*, [1926] A. C. 239 (December 18th, 1925).

[3] *A.-G.* v. *Parr*, [1924] 1 K. B. 916, at p. 931, *per* ATKIN, L. J.; *Re Constable's Settled Estates*, [1919] 1 Ch. 178.   [4] *Infra*, pp. 792–3.

age (an improbable event), it was necessary to incur the expense of making an application to the court.

Compound trustees.

The difficulty that there may be no compound trustees has been avoided by the legislation of 1925 which is retrospective and is as follows :—

(i) trustees under an instrument which is a settlement are trustees also of a settlement constituted by that instrument and any subsequent instruments, *i.e.* the original trustees are trustees of any compound settlement which later comes into being ; [1]

(ii) trustees under a re-settlement, where there are no trustees under the original settlement, are trustees of the compound settlement ; [2]

(iii) where a re-settlement states that a life interest limited to a tenant for life is *in restoration or confirmation* of his interest under the original settlement, he is entitled as of his former interest, and can exercise the statutory powers both under the original settlement and under the re-settlement. [3]

Protection of trustees.

Protection of Trustees. It is not the policy of the legislature to subject the trustees of the settlement to a strict liability for the acts of the estate owner. Provisions are therefore inserted in the Settled Land Act 1925 designed to protect them in certain circumstances, and they now enjoy a greater measure of immunity than under the Act of 1882. Thus they are not liable for giving any consent or for not bringing any action which they might have brought, and, in the case of a purchase of land with capital money or in the case of a lease of the settled land by the tenant for life, they are not bound to investigate the propriety of the disposition. [4] Again, where the tenant for life directs capital money to be invested in any authorized security, the trustees are not liable for the acts of an agent employed by him or for failing to obtain a valuation of the proposed security [5]; neither are they liable for having delivered documents of title to the tenant for life, though they are responsible for securities representing capital money. [6] Each trustee is answerable only for what he actually receives, notwithstanding his signing any receipt for conformity, and he is not answerable for the acts and defaults of his co-trustees or for any loss not due to his own wilful default. [7] In short, the role of the trustees is to manage and protect the money that is paid to them.

---

[1] S.L.A. 1925, s. 31.
[2] *Ibid.*, as added by L.P.(A.)A. 1926, Sched.
[3] *Ibid.*, 1925, s. 22 (2) ; *Re Cradock's Settled Estates*, [1926] Ch. 944.
[4] *Ibid.*, 1925, s. 97.   [5] *Ibid.*, s. 98 (1).   [6] *Ibid.*, s. 98 (3).
[7] *Ibid.*, s. 96. This is a rule applicable to trustees generally : T.A. 1925, s. 30 (1).

(6) CAPITAL MONEY

It is obvious that in several cases the exercise of a statutory power will result in the payment of money to the trustees ; this is called capital *money*. Thus, for instance, *What is capital money.*

1. money which becomes due on the sale of the land or of heirlooms ; [1]

2. fines paid by lessees in consideration of obtaining a tenancy ; [2]

3. three-quarters or one-quarter (as the case may be) of a mining rent ; [3]

4. three-quarters of the money arising from the sale of timber by a tenant for life who is impeachable for waste ; [4]

5. consideration paid for an option to purchase or take a lease of the settled land ; [5]

6. damages or compensation received by the tenant for life in respect of a breach of covenant by his lessee or grantee, [6] and

7. money raised by a mortgage of the land for the purposes authorized by the Act [7]

are all examples of capital money. [8] The expression also covers money arising otherwise than under the Act which ought to be treated as capital, [9] as for example money paid under a fire insurance policy which the tenant for life was under an obligation to maintain.

As regards the manner in which capital money must be disposed of, the first point is that if raised for some particular purpose, it must be applied accordingly. Thus, money that has been borrowed on mortgage in order to carry out some specific improvement on the land must be so spent. If, however, the money has not been raised for some particular object, but is due, for instance, to the sale of the land, it must be applied in one or more of the modes set out in the Settled Land Act 1925. [10] In addition to any special mode permitted by the settlement itself there are twenty-one different modes indicated by the Act. [11] It would be inappropriate in a book of this nature to set out the whole list, but a few of the more important methods will be noted :— *Application of capital money.*

(a) The most usual destination of capital money is investment in what are called *trustee securities*—that is to say, invest- *Investment.*

---

[1] S.L.A. 1925, s. 67 (2).   [2] *Ibid.*, s. 42 (4).
[3] *Ibid.*, s. 47 ; *supra*, p. 180.   [4] *Ibid.*, s. 66 (2).
[5] *Ibid.*, s. 51 (5).   [6] *Ibid.*, s. 80 (1).
[7] *Ibid.*, s. 71 ; *supra*, pp. 180–1.
[8] And see S.L.A. 1925, ss. 52 ; 54 (4) ; 55 (2) ; 56 (4) ; 57 (3) ; 58–61.
[9] S.L.A. 1925, s. 81.   [10] *Ibid.*, s. 73.
[11] See too Leasehold Reform Act 1967, s. 6 (5).

ments in which the Trustee Investments Act 1961[1] authorizes trustees to invest trust funds. Money which is thus required to be invested is paid to the trustees or into court at the option of the tenant for life, and the investment is made according to his direction. It cannot afterwards be altered without his consent. The money, either before or after investment, represents the land from which it originated, and it is held in trust for the same persons for whom the land was held under the settlement and for the same interests, so that, for instance, the income arising from the investments is paid to the tenant for life in the same way as the annual profits of the land would have been paid prior to its sale.[2]

Loan on mortgage.

(b) Provided that " proper advice " is taken, capital money may be lent on mortgage of " freehold property " in England and Wales or Northern Ireland and of " leasehold property in those countries " if the lease has at least 60 years to run ;[3] further, a report of the value of the property must be obtained and not more than two-thirds of the value of any suitable property may be lent :[4] and when the settled land is sold in fee simple or for a term having at least 500 years to run, it is now enacted that a sum not exceeding two-thirds of the purchase money may be allowed to remain on mortgage of the land sold.[5]

Purchase of land.

(c) Capital money may also be expended in the purchase of land or of mines or minerals convenient to be worked with the settled land, provided that the interest so bought is either the fee simple or a leasehold having at least sixty more years to run.[6] Again, it may be used to finance a person who has agreed to take a lease or grant for building purposes of the settled land, advances being made to him on the security of an equitable mortgage of his building agreement.[7]

Expenditure on improvements.

(d) Lastly capital money may be used in payment for any improvement authorized by the Settled Land Act 1925.

Where capital money is with trustees.

The procedure that governs payment varies according as the capital money is in the hands of the trustees or in court. In the former case the trustees, unless ordered by the court, must not pay for the improvement until

---

[1] See generally *Hanbury's Modern Equity* (9th Edn.), pp. 313 *et seq.* ; Snell, *Equity* (27th Edn.), pp. 206, *et seq.*

[2] S.L.A. 1925, s. 75.

[3] Trustee Investments Act 1961, s. 1, Sched. I, Part II, para. 13. It appears that money should only be lent on a first legal mortgage. Hanbury *op. cit.*, p. 323 ; Snell, *op. cit.*, p. 211.

[4] T.A. 1925 , s. 8.   [5] *Ibid.*, s. 10 (2).

[6] S.L.A. 1925, s. 73 (1) (xi) and (xii).   [7] *Ibid.*, s. 73 (1) (xviii).

they have obtained from a competent engineer or able practical surveyor, employed independently of the tenant for life, a certificate certifying that the improvement has been properly executed and declaring the amount that ought to be paid.[1] Where the capital money is in court, the court may, on a report or certificate of the Minister of Agriculture, Fisheries and Food, or of a competent engineer or able practical surveyor, approved by it, or on such other evidence as it may think sufficient, make what order it thinks fit for the application of the money in payment of the improvement.[2]

Where capital money is in court.

In cases where the work done is not of lasting value it is economically sound that the tenant for life should ultimately restore the amount expended to capital by the creation of a sinking fund out of income, and it is with this object in view that the Act classifies the authorized improvements into the three categories that have already been mentioned.[3] The position is this :—

Rules to repayment of cost.

Part I improvements. The tenant for life cannot be required to set up a sinking fund.

Part II improvements. Before meeting the cost out of capital, the trustees *may* if they think fit, and must if so directed by the court, require that the money shall be repaid to them out of the income of the settled land by not more than fifty half-yearly instalments.[4]

Part III improvements. The trustees *must* require the whole cost to be paid out of income in the manner mentioned above.[5]

The court, when in possession of the capital money, is in the same position as the trustees with regard to requiring repayment of the money, except that it is not bound to require repayment in twenty-five years.

The effect of an order requiring repayment by instalments is that the settled land becomes subject to a yearly rentcharge which takes effect as if it were limited by the settlement prior to the estate of the tenant for life.[6] If, however, the subject-matter of the settlement is agricultural land used as such for the purposes of a trade or business,[7] capital money may be applied in the execution of any improvements specified in the Agricultural Holdings Act 1948,[8] without any provision being made for the replacement of the cost out of income.[9] How prejudicial this may be to remaindermen is evident from the inclusion in the specified

---

[1] S.L.A., 1925 s. 84 (2).   [2] *Ibid.,* s. 84 (3).
[3] *Ibid.,* Sched. III ; *supra,* p. 182.   [4] *Ibid.,* s. 84. (2) (*a*)
[5] *Ibid.,* s. 84 (2) (*b*).   [6] *Ibid.,* s. 85.
[7] Agricultural Holdings Act 1948, s. 1, (2).
[8] *Ibid.,* Third Sched.   [9] *Ibid.,* s. 81 (1) ; 94 (1).

improvements of the execution of running repairs other than those which the tenant is under an obligation to carry out.[1] This power to pay for improvements out of capital, however, is not available to trustees holding land under a trust for sale.[2]

(7) REGISTERED LAND

The provisions of the Settled Land Act 1925 apply to registered land but take effect subject to the provisions of the Land Registration Act 1925.[3] The legal estate in the settled land is registered in the name of the tenant for life or statutory owner.[4] The beneficial interests under the settlement are included in the definition of minor interests[5] and " take effect as minor interests and not otherwise."[6] These interests are protected by restrictions entered on the proprietorship register[7] and are binding on the registered proprietor for his life but do not affect a disposition by his personal representative.[8]

Thus, if X. is the tenant for life and Y. and Z. are the trustees of a settlement, X. will be the registered proprietor of the fee simple of the settled land and the register will contain a dual restriction, first preventing the registration of any disposition under which capital money arises unless the money is paid to Y. and Z. or into court[9] and then preventing the registration of any disposition not authorized by the Settled Land Act 1925. By this means, the beneficial interests of a strict settlement are protected without their details being brought onto the register. There is still a curtain, and a purchaser who complies with the restrictions will override the beneficial interests in the same way that he would overreach them in the case of unregistered land.

SECTION II. THE TRUST FOR SALE

An alternative method of settling land is to adopt the device of a trust for sale.

---

[1] *Re Duke of Northumberland,* [1951] Ch. 202 ; [1950] 2 All E. R. 1181 ; *Re Sutherland Settlement Trusts,* [1953] Ch. 792 ; *Re Lord Brougham and Vaux's Settled Estates,* [1954] Ch. 24.
[2] *Re Wynn,* [1955] 1 W. L. R. 940 ; [1955] 2 All E. R. 865 ; *Re Boston's Will Trusts,* [1956] Ch. 395 ; [1965] 1 All E. R. 593.
[3] S.L.A. 1925, s. 119 (3). See generally Ruoff and Roper, pp. 382 *et seq.* For settled land during a minority see *infra,* p. 922.
[4] L.R.A. 1925, s. 86 (1).
[5] *Ibid.,* s. 3 (xv) (b).
[6] S. 86 (2). See (1958), 22 Conv. (N. S.) 14, at pp. 23-4 (F. R. Crane) where it is suggested that, if no restrictions are entered, a beneficiary in possession of settled land cannot claim an overriding interest under L.R.A. 1925, s. 70 (1) (g). *Infra,* p. 773.
[7] L.R.R. 1925, rr. 56–58, 104, and Forms 9–11. See Ruoff, pp. 163–4.
[8] L.R.A. 1925, s. 86 (3).
[9] Or to at least two trustees or to a trust corporation.

In general this arises where land is transferred by deed or will to trustees with an imperative direction that they are to effect a sale and to hold the proceeds thereof upon certain specified trusts. The manner of its formation has already been sufficiently described,[1] though it should be recalled that owing to the doctrine of conversion in equity, the land notionally becomes money, with the result that the interests of the beneficiaries are in the proceeds of sale and not in the land,[2] and are automatically overreached on a sale of the land by the trustees for sale.[3]

It is essential to define a trust for sale. As we have seen, the strict settlement and the trust for sale are mutually exclusive and successive or limited interests in land create a settlement under the Settled Land Act 1925, unless the land is held upon trust for sale.[4]

(1) THE DEFINITION OF A TRUST FOR SALE

The definition in section 205 (1) (xxix) of the Law of Property Act 1925 reads as follows :

"Trust for sale, " in relation to land, means an immediate binding trust for sale, whether or not exercisable at the request or with the consent of any person, and with or without a power at discretion to postpone the sale.

We must now consider the meaning of the words "trust," "immediate," and "binding ."

(A) TRUST

An instrument does not create a trust for sale unless it contains a peremptory direction imposing a duty upon the trustees to sell. A *trust* to sell must always be distinguished from a *power* to sell. A trust is obligatory upon the trustee, a power leaves it to his discretion whether he will sell or not. It has, indeed, been enacted that a disposition coming into operation after 1925 which directs that the trustees shall *either retain or sell* land shall constitute a trust for sale with power to postpone the sale,[5] but, apart from this statutory provision, whether an instrument creates a trust or confers a power is a question that can be answered only by construing its terms. What is in form a trust for sale may be nothing more than a discretionary power ; what is in form a power may, when properly construed, be an imperative trust.[6] The distinction is of great importance in conveyancing, for if what is given to the trustees is a mere power of sale, it is exercisable not

---

[1] *Supra*, pp. 81–2.

[2] See *Irani Finance, Ltd.* v. *Singh*, [1971] Ch. 59, at p. 80 ; [1970] 3 All E. R. 199, *per* CROSS, L.J. ; and *infra*, p. 222, note 4.

[3] *Supra*, p. 82, *infra*, p. 796.

[4] S.L.A. 1925, s. 1 (7). *Supra*, p. 166.

[5] L.P.A. 1925, s. 25 (4).

[6] *Re Newbould*, (1913), 110 L. T. 6, *per* SWINFEN EADY, L.J. ; compare *Re White's Settlement*, [1930] 1 Ch. 179. For the distinction between a power and a trust, see *infra*, pp. 276–8.

by them but by the tenant for life.[1]   The trustees become trustees
within the Settled Land Act 1925, the land is settled land within
the meaning of the same Act and is not subject to a trust for sale,
and the proper person to make title is the tenant for life.[2]

(B) IMMEDIATE

Must be
" immedi-
ate."

The word " immediate " does not mean that the land must be
sold at once, for power to postpone the sale is implied in every
case, unless a contrary intention appears.[3]   Its significance is
to distinguish a trust for sale from a *future* trust for sale.   A
future trust is not immediately effective, and it is enacted that where
it is imposed upon land, the trustees are to be trustees for the
purposes of the Settled Land Act, not trustees for sale.[4]   Thus,
if land is devised to a wife for life and after her death upon trust for
sale, the land *during her life* is settled land and is governed by the
Settled Land Act.[5]

(C) BINDING

Must be
" binding."

In its natural meaning " binding trust " is tautologous.   A
trust is different from a power because it is obligatory, not discretionary : the trustees are bound to sell the land ultimately,
though the actual time of the sale is left to their discretion.   A trust
which imposes a duty upon the trustees as distinct from one which
gives them a mere power may rightly be described as binding.
Yet the word has been inserted in a statutory definition and the
courts have searched for a secondary meaning.   ROMER, J.,
suggested that, if it was not surplusage, the object of its insertion
might be to emphasize the exclusion of a revocable trust for sale.[6]
The cases in which the word has been discussed are concerned with
the situation where settled land has been re-settled by way of
trust for sale before the Settled Land Act settlement has been
exhausted, and the judges have sought to find a solution in the
word binding to the problem whether the unexhausted settlement
has precedence over the trust for sale or vice versa.

Thus in *Re Leigh's Settled Estates (No. 1)*[7] X. was tenant in tail
of settled land which was subject to an equitable jointure rentcharge in favour of her mother.   In 1923 X. disentailed and con-

---

[1] S.L.A. 1925, s. 108 (2).
[2] *Ibid.*, ss. 30 (1) (i), 108, 109 ; *supra*, p. 189. The position before 1926
involved a conflict of powers, since the tenant for life had a statutory, the
trustees an express, power of sale.   S.L.A. 1882, s. 56, provided that in such a
case the tenant for life should be unfettered in the exercise of the power, and
that the trustees should not sell without his consent.
[3] L.P.A. 1925, s. 25 (1).
[4] S.L.A. 1925, s. 30 (1) (iv).
[5] *Re Jackson's Settled Estate,* [1902] 1 Ch. 258 ; *Re Hanson,* [1928] Ch. 96 ;
Re Herklot's Will Trusts, [1964] 1 W. L. R. 159; [1964] 2 All E. R. 66 ; M. & B.
p. 183.
[6] *Re Parker's Settled Estates,* [1928] Ch. 247, at p. 261.
[7] [1926] Ch. 852; M. & B. p. 186.

veyed the fee simple, still subject to the charge, to trustees upon trust for sale The question arose whether in 1926 the land was settled land or whether it was held upon trust for sale.

It was clearly settled land[1] unless the conveyance made by X. in 1923 was an " immediate binding trust for sale " within the meaning of the Law of Property Act 1925. TOMLIN, J., held that the land remained settled land and was not subject to a binding trust for sale, since in his opinion the word " binding " is not used to indicate that the trustees for sale are bound to sell sooner or later but refers to the interests that will be bound, *i.e.* overreached, when the trustees convey. To be " binding," the trust must enable the trustees to execute a conveyance which will bind the whole subject-matter of the settlement, *i.e.* interests prior to the trust as well as those arising under its provisions. This test was not satisfied in the present case, for a conveyance in 1923 could not overreach the widow's prior equitable charge. To do this it would be necessary to obtain the additional powers of overreaching by creating an ad hoc trust for sale,[2] and this could only be done by replacing the trustees by a trust corporation or by having them approved by the court.[3]

This restricted view of the scope of the ordinary trust for sale has been implicitly[4] and expressly rejected.[5] In *Re Parker's Settled Estates*[6] ROMER, J., came to the conclusion that there can be a binding trust for sale notwithstanding that the trustees for sale are unable to overreach all charges having, under the settlement, priority to the trust for sale. He, however, then held that land cannot be described as held upon trust for sale so as to take it out of the Settled Land Act unless the *whole legal estate* is vested in the trustees. He was of opinion that if there are prior *equitable* interests the trust for sale excludes the Settled Land Act, since the whole legal estate is in the trustees ; but if there are prior *legal* estates or interests then the trust for sale is not sufficient to exclude that Act, since the *whole* legal estate is not in the trustees. In *Re Parker's Settled Estates* there was a prior legal term of years to secure portions and accordingly the land remained settled land.[7]

---

[1] S.L.A. 1925, s. 1 (1) (v). [2] L.P.A. 1925, s. 2 (2), *infra*, pp. 797 *et seq.*
[3] After the trustees had been approved by the court TOMLIN, J., upheld the trust for sale. *Re Leigh's Settled Estates (No. 2)*, [1927] 2 Ch. 13.
[4] *Re Ryder and Steadman's Contract*, [1927] 2 Ch. 62. Land vested in X., Y. and Z. as tenants in common subject to an equitable jointure rent charge in favour of A. C.A. held that after 1925 X. Y. and Z. held on a *statutory* trust for sale although they could not overreach A's prior equitable interest. *Infra*, p. 222.
[5] *Re Parker's Settled Estates*, [1928] Ch. 247 ; M. & B. p. 186 ; see (1928), 65 L. J. Newsp. 248, at pp. 272, 293.
[6] *Supra.*
[7] See too *Re Norton*, [1929] 1 Ch. 84 ; M. & B. p. 188 ; (1929), 67 L. J. Newsp. 24, at p. 44 (J. M. L.) (ROMER, J., held that there was no binding trust for sale since the trustees could not call for the legal estate from personal representatives due to a prior *equitable* charge, S.L.A. 1925, s. 7 (5)) ; *Re Beaumont's Settled Estates*, [1937] 2 All E. R. 353 ; *Re Sharpe's Deed of Release*, [1939] Ch. 51 ; [1938] 3 All E. R. 449.

(2) THE POWERS OF THE TRUSTEES FOR SALE

Provisions affecting postponement of sale.

The powers of the trustees for sale are set out in the Law of Property Act 1925. Under section 25 a power to postpone a sale is implied in every trust for sale unless a contrary intention appears, and the trustees are not liable for an indefinite postponement in the absence of an express direction to the contrary.[1] A disregard of such an express direction, however, does not prejudice a purchaser of a legal estate, for it is enacted that he shall not be concerned with directions that relate to postponement.[2] The power to postpone must, like any other power given to trustees, be exercised unanimously by them;[3] if there is disagreement between the trustees for sale, the court may at its discretion direct them to carry out the sale.[4]

Powers of trustees pending sale.

The power of postponement may lead to the land remaining unsold for a considerable period, and it is essential that during the interval between the creation of the trust and the actual sale, the trustees should possess powers of disposition and management. These are given to them in abundance by the Law of Property Act 1925.

Despite the fundamental distinction between a settlement and a trust for sale, it is provided by section 28 of the Law of Property Act 1925 that the trustees for sale, in relation to the land and the proceeds of sale, shall have all the powers both of a tenant for life and of trustees of a settlement under the Settled Land Act 1925.[5] Thus, for example, they may grant leases, raise money on mortgage for improvements and, so long as they retain some land, may invest the proceeds of sale in the purchase of other land.[6] It is further provided by the same section that they shall have the powers of management that are exercisable by trustees under section 102 of the Settled Land Act 1925 during the minority of a tenant for life of *settled* land.[7]

Although, in the case of settled land these powers given by

---

[1] L.P.A. 1925, s. 25 (1) (2) : *Re Rooke*, [1953] Ch. 716 ; [1953] 2 All E. R. 110 (direction by testator to sell farm " as soon as possible after my death " held to be contrary intention) ; *Re Atkins' Will Trusts*, [1974] 1 W. L. R. 761 ; [1974] 2 All E. R. 1.   [2] *Ibid.*, s. 25 (2).

[3] A power to act by a majority may be given in the Trust Deed. *Re Butlin's Settlement Trusts* (1974), 118 Sol. Jo. 757.

[4] *Ibid.*, s. 30, *infra*, pp. 202, 227, *Re Roth* (1896) 74 L. T. 50 ; *Re Hilton*, [1909] 2 Ch. 548 ; *Re Mayo*, [1943] Ch. 302 ; [1943] 2 All E. R. 440 ; M. & B. p. 190 ; *Re Buchanan-Wollaston's Conveyance*, [1939] Ch. 738 ; [1939] 2 All E. R. 302. See also *Bull* v. *Bull* [1955] 1 Q. B. 234 ; [1955] 1 All E. R. 253 ; *Jones* v. *Challenger* [1961] 1. Q. B. 176, 1960 1 All E. R. 785 ; M. & B. p. 200 ; *Rawlings* v. *Rawlings*, [1964] P. 398 ; [1964] 2 All E. R. 804 ; *Barclay* v. *Barclay* [1970] 2 Q. B. 677 ; [1970] 2 All E. R. 676. *cf. Re* 90 *Thornhill Rd, Tolworth, Surrey*, [1970] Ch. 261 ; [1969] 3 All E. R. 685 (sale not ordered under S.L.A. 1925, s. 93 when joint tenants for life disagreed as to the exercise of the power of sale).

[5] *Ibid.*, s. 28 (1), as amended by L.P.(A.)A. 1926, s. 7.

[6] *Re Wakeman* [1947] Ch. 607 ; [1947] 2 All E. R. 47 ; *Re Wellsted's Will Trusts*, [1949] Ch. 296 ; [1949] 1 All E. R. 577 ; M. & B. p. 198.

[7] *Infra*, p. 921.

section 102 are exercisable only during the minority of the tenant for life, they may be exercised by trustees for sale whether there is a minority or not.[1]

In many cases the trustees for sale will not wish themselves to exercise the powers that have been given to them by section 28. Section 29 (1), therefore, provides that while the land remains unsold they may revocably and in writing delegate from time to time the *powers of leasing, of accepting surrenders of leases, and of management* to any person of full age (not merely being an annuitant), who is beneficially entitled in possession to the net rents and profits for his life or for any less period.[2] He must exercise the powers so delegated only in the names and on behalf of the trustees.[3] They are not liable for his acts or defaults. He alone is personally liable and in relation to the exercise of a power is deemed to be in the position of a trustee.[4] Thus, pending sale, the welfare of the land may be entrusted to the person most anxious to promote it. It must be noticed, however, that only those powers that are set out in section 29 may be delegated. The legal estate remains in the trustees for sale, and only they can convey the fee simple. This is the basis of their trust.

Right of trustees to delegate certain powers.

The exercise of their powers by the trustees for sale, including that of sale itself, may be made subject the consent of any persons.[5]

Provisions affecting consents.

If the consent of not more than two persons is required, a purchaser[6] must ascertain that the requirement has been satisfied. If, however, the consent of more than two persons is required his obligation is satisfied if any two of the persons specified give their consent.[7] If the person whose consent is required is not sui juris or becomes subject to a disability, his consent, in favour of a purchaser, shall not be deemed to be required. But in the case of an infant the trustees should obtain the consent of his parent or guardian, and in the case of a mental patient that of the receiver.[8]

As we have seen, the powers of a tenant for life under the Settled Land Act 1925 cannot be cut down by any provisions inserted in the settlement.[9] There is no similar provision in the Law of Property Act 1925 for the curtailment of the powers of trustees for sale. Indeed their power of sale can be restricted by

---

[1] *Re Gray*, [1927] 1 Ch. 242.

[2] L.P.A. 1925, s. 29 (1). *Stratford* v. *Syrett* [1958] 1 Q. B. 107 ; *Napier* v. *Light* (1975) 236 Estates Gazette 273. Formerly, the law was different. While the land remained unsold the powers of leasing and of management were not possessed by the trustees. Instead, they were given to the person beneficially entitled to the income (S.L.A. 1882, s. 63), though they were not exercisable by him without the leave of the court (S.L.A. 1884, s. 7). If the powers are now delegated to him, he is in the same position as if before 1926 he had obtained the above leave.

[3] L.P.A. 1925, s. 29 (2).   [4] *Ibid.*, s. 29 (3).

[5] If they refuse to give it any person interested may apply to the court for an order of sale. L.P.A. 1925, s. 30. *Re Beale's Settlement Trusts*, [1932] 2 Ch. 15.

[6] As defined by L.P.A. 1925, s. 205 (1) (xxi).   [7] *Ibid.*, s. 26 (1).

[8] *Ibid.*, s. 26 (2) as amended by the Mental Health Act 1959, s. 149, Sched. 7.

[9] S.L.A. 1925, s. 106, *supra*, p. 184.

the imposition of a requirement of consent and the power to postpone sale may be excluded by a contrary intention. Apart from these cases, however, it would appear that the powers of trustees for sale, like those of a tenant for life, are irreducible.[1]

Consultation with beneficiaries.

We must now consider how far the trustees for sale must observe the wishes of the beneficiaries. Under a statutory trust for sale[2] it is their duty, so far as practicable, to consult the persons of full age for the time being beneficially interested in possession in the rents and profits of the land until sale, and, so far as is consistent with the general interest of the trust, to give effect to the wishes of such persons, or, in the case of dispute, of the majority according to the value of their combined interests. A purchaser is not, however, concerned to see that this provision has been complied with.[3] It does not apply to express trusts for sale, unless a contrary intention appears in the instrument creating the trust. Thus a settlor or testator may either give the trustees for sale complete freedom of discretion or compel them to consult the beneficiaries ; but in the case of a statutory trust for sale there must be consultation.

Any person interested may apply to court.

Finally, if the trustees for sale refuse to sell or to exercise any of the powers conferred on them by sections 28 and 29 of the Law of Property Act 1925 or if any requisite consent cannot be obtained, any person interested[4] may apply to the court under section 30 for an order directing the trustees to act accordingly, and the court may make such order as it thinks fit.[5] The court has the widest possible discretion under this section, and will take into account all the circumstances of the case.[6]

---

[1] See *Re Davies Will Trusts*, [1932] 1 Ch. 530 (life interest to nephew " so long as he shall reside upon and assist in the management of the farm " held not forfeitable by exercise of powers inconsistent with such condition. The decision related to statutory trusts for sale under L.P.A. 1925, s. 35, but the principle would appear to apply to express trusts for sale as well.

[2] *Infra.*

[3] L.P.A. 1925, s. 26 (3), as amended by L.P.(A.)A. 1926, Sched. ; (1973), 117 Sol. Jo. 518 (A. M. Prichard).

[4] *Stevens v. Hutchinson*, [1953] Ch. 299, 305 ; [1953] 1 All E. R. 699 ("a person interested in some proprietory right under the trust for sale," *per* UPJOHN, J.). *Re Solomon*, [1967] Ch. 573 ; [1966] 3 All E. R. 255.

[5] L.P.A. 1925, s. 30 :   *Re Buchanan-Wollaston's Conveyance*, [1939] Ch. 738 ; [1939] 2 All E. R. 302 ; *Re Mayo*, [1943] Ch. 302 ; [1943] 2 All E. R. 440, *supra*, p. 200 ; *Re Hyde's Conveyance*, (1952), 102 Law Jo. 58 ; *Bull* v. *Bull*, [1955] 1 Q. B. 234 ; [1955] 1 All E. R. 253 ; *Jones v. Challenger*, [1961] 1 Q. B. 176 ; [1960] 1 All E. R. 785 ; M. & B. p. 200 ; *Rawlings v. Rawlings*, [1964] P. 398 ; [1964] 2 All E. R. 804 ; *Re Solomon*, [1967] Ch. 573 ; [1966] 3 All E. R. 255 ; *Barclay v. Barclay*, [1970] 2 Q. B. 677 ; [1970] 2 All E. R. 676 ; *Re Hardy's Trust* (1970), 114 S. J. 864 ; *Jackson v. Jackson*, [1971] 1 W. L. R. 1539 ; [1971] 3 All E. R. 774 ; (1971), 87 *L. Q. R.* 153 (P. V. Baker). *Burke* v. *Burke*, [1974] 1 W. L. R. 1063 ; [1974] 2 All E. R. 944 ; *Re Turner*, [1975] 1 W. L. R. 1556 ; [1975] 1 All E. R. 5 ; *Re McCarthy*, [1975] 1 W. L. R. 807 ; [1975] 2 All E. R. 857 ; *Re Densham*, [1975] 1 W. L. R. 1519. See *infra*, p. 227.

[6] See Wolstenholme and Cherry, Vol. 1, p. 89 ; M. & B. p. 204 ; (1972) 36 Conv. (N. S.) 99 ; (1975) 119 Sol. Jo. 582 (J. G. Miller).

(3) STATUTORY TRUSTS FOR SALE

A trust for sale may either be created expressly by act of parties or imposed by statute. The following is a summary of the circumstances in which a statutory trust for sale is imposed by the 1925 legislation in pursuance of its policy to simplify conveyancing by separating the legal estate from the equitable interests :

(a) Where an estate owner dies intestate.[1]

(b) Where property vested in trustees by way of security becomes discharged from the debtor's right of redemption.[2]

If, for example, trust money has been invested in a mortgage of a legal estate and the right of the mortgagor to redeem the land has been extinguished under the Limitation Act 1939[3] or by a foreclosure order,[4] the land, being thus subjected to a trust for sale, is regarded as converted into money and it will pass as such under a beneficiary's will.

In the following cases an express trust for sale is usually created, but if not a statutory trust arises automatically.

(c) Where land is devised or conveyed to two or more persons as tenants in common.[5]

(d) Where land is devised or conveyed beneficially to two or more persons as joint tenants.[6]

(e) Where a legal estate is conveyed to an infant jointly with one or more persons of full age other than trustees or mortgagees.[7]

(f) Where the trustees of a *personalty* settlement or trustees for sale of land purchase land in virtue of a power contained in the settlement.[8] The effect of this, having regard to the doctrine of conversion, is that the land remains money in the eyes of equity and thus the original character of the settlement is preserved.

(4) REGISTERED LAND

Where registered land is subject to a trust for sale, whether express or statutory,[9] the legal title to the land is registered in the names of the trustees for sale, not exceeding four in number.[10] As in the case of settled land, the interests of the beneficiaries are minor interests whether or not they are protected by restrictions entered on the proprietorship register. Where an express or statutory trust for sale appears on the title the Registrar will enter a restriction restraining a disposition, except by his order or

---

[1] A.E.A. 1925, s. 33 (1) ; *infra*, pp. 864, 871.
[2] L.P.A. 1925, s. 31 (1). [3] *Infra*, p. 662. [4] *Infra*, p. 673.
[5] L.P.A. 1925, s. 34 (2), (3) ; *infra*, pp. 222-4.
[6] *Ibid.*, s. 36 (1) ; *infra*, pp. 226-8. [7] *Ibid.*, s. 19 (2) ; *infra*, p. 916.
[8] *Ibid.*, s. 32 (1). The statutory trust may be excluded by a contrary intention.
[9] See further *infra*, p. 235, and generally Ruoff and Roper, chs. 20 and 37.
[10] L.R.A. 1925, ss. 94, 95.

that of the court, unless the proprietors are entitled for their own benefit, or can give valid receipts for the capital money, or unless one of them is a trust corporation.[1]

A purchaser who complies with the restriction will override the beneficial interests in the same way that he would overreach them in the case of unregistered land.

SECTION III. MODERN SETTLEMENTS

We have seen that there are at present two methods open to a landowner who desires to provide for a succession of beneficiaries. He may create a settlement under the Settled Land Act 1925 or a trust for sale. Before, however, we attempt to discuss them as alternative methods of settling property, we must notice the fiscal problems that affect any form of settlement under which successive limited interests are given to members of a family.

One factor of crucial importance in the development of the law of settlements in modern times has been the fiscal implication of particular forms of the use of property. Income tax, estate duty (now replaced by capital transfer tax) and capital gains tax have all played their part in developing the modern law. Under the estate duty system, which was in force from 1894 to 1974, duty was payable upon the value of property which passed on a death, and this included not only the assets which the deceased owned absolutely, but also the capital value of a trust in which he had a limited interest, such as a life interest. In this situation, the classical form of strict settlement containing a series of successive interests in the land was particularly unsuitable from a fiscal point of view.

Estate duty.

The most suitable ways of dividing up family capital were either to share it among members of the family, or to create a discretionary trust in their favour. No tax was payable, until 1974, on a transfer made not less than seven years before the donor's death. The donor may not wish to give blocks of capital to beneficiaries, for they may waste or squander it. And if the capital is in the form of land, such a division would involve the breaking up of the estate. A discretionary trust, in which the trustees held the property upon trust for such of the beneficiaries as they should in their absolute discretion think fit, gave no interest to any individual beneficiary, and no property thus passed on death. Until 1969, it was possible therefore for the owner of capital to place it in a discretionary trust at least seven years before he died, and for no estate duty to be payable on his death, or on the death of any of the beneficiaries. Such a trust could be made to continue for the period of perpetuity, with a gift made to vest in identifiable individuals immediately before the

---

[1] *Ibid.*, s. 58 (3) ; L.R.R. 1925, r. 213, Form 62 (as amended by the Registrar) ; Ruoff and Roper, p. 408.

expiration of the period. Much land in England was of course the subject of a strict settlement when the impact of estate duty became serious and there was no one therefore who was able to create such a trust. This problem was solved by the Variation of Trusts Act 1958[1] which gave power to the court to approve, on behalf of persons unable to consent on their own behalf, the variation of a settlement where this was for the benefit of such persons.

The fiscal advantages of discretionary trusts were greatly reduced by the Finance Act 1969, under which estate duty was payable, when a beneficiary died, upon the portion of the capital equivalent to the share of income received by that beneficiary during (generally speaking) the previous seven years. This liability could be avoided or reduced by paying the income to young and fit beneficiaries, and, so long as all the income had been distributed, capital could be paid to the older beneficiaries without incurring liability. Also, the Act had no effect upon the freedom from liability of a settlor who set up the trust seven years before he died.

Finance Act 1969.

The whole situation has been changed by the abolition of estate duty and the imposition of capital transfer tax by the Finance Act 1975. The Act must be examined for the details of the system.[2] In outline, all gratuitous transfers,[3] whether *inter vivos* or on death, are subject to the tax. The rates are contained in section 37 of the Act, which provides two tables, Table 1 applying to transfers on or at any time within three years of death, and Table 2 applying to other *inter vivos* transfers. Table 2 provides lower rates than Table 1 at levels up to £300,000, and the rates up to £100,000 are half those of Table 1. Each is lower than the estate duty rate was. The object is to ensure that capital is taxed once every generation, whether given away during the donor's lifetime or on his death. There are some exemptions,[4] such as transfers *inter vivos* or on death between spouses ; £1,000 per annum per donor, and £100 per annum per donee ; gifts in consideration of marriage (up to £5,000 in the case of the donor's children) ; and gifts to charities,[5] political parties[6] and national heritage gifts.[7]

Capital transfer tax.

Rates of tax.

Exemptions.

Exemptions apart, a transfer is taxable according to the appropriate table. A second gift is taxed as an addition to the previous gift, the rate starting at that applicable on the table to the amount of the previous gift. Thus it is necessary for a donor

Aggregation of successive gifts.

---

[1] *Supra,* p. 183.
[2] See generally Wheatcroft and Hewson, *Capital Transfer Tax* ; Chapman, *Capital Transfer Tax* ; Hayton and Tiley, *Elements of Capital Transfer Tax* ; Morcom and Parry on *Capital Transfer Tax.*
[3] Including the element of bounty in a sale at an undervalue.
[4] F.A. 1975, s. 29, Sched. 6.
[5] Unlimited, if made more than one year before death ; up to £100,000, if made in that year and on death.
[6] As for charities.
[7] Unlimited, whenever made.

to keep a lifetime " score " of his gifts. If the tax is paid under Table 2 and the donor dies within three years, a further sum will be due. The testamentary transfer is necessarily the last one.

Grossing up.   A further complication is added by the fact that the transferor is liable for the tax unless the transferee pays it. The transfer is thus a transfer of the net ; if the transferor, for example, writes a cheque for £100,000 in favour of X (disregarding the exempt £1,000), and he is taxable upon the net gift of £100,000. Assuming this to be his first gift, he will be treated as giving £119,483, for the tax on that sum under Table 2 will be £19,483. A further chargeable gift of £100,000 would count as a gross gift of £190,205, for, on the higher rates then applicable, the tax would be £90,205. This grossing up is not necessary if the transferee pays the tax. But there is no real saving, for the transferee receives less. The transferee would pay £14,125, on the first transfer of £100,000 gross, and £37,250 on the second ; but he would receive only £148,625 instead of £200,000.[1]

Settlements.   The greatest complexities come with the taxation of settlements.[2] Settlements are divided into two types for tax purposes ; depending on whether or not there is an interest in possession under the settlement. Obviously there is such an interest in the case of a strict settlement ; but not in the case of a discretionary trust. With settlements which have an interest in possession, tax is payable on the capital value of the settlement, as would be expected, when the tenant for life dies, and also when his interest comes to an end, for example, by sale, assignment, surrender etc., except in the case where he obtains the reversionary interest in the property. This is because the acquisition of the reversion does not affect tax liability. Thus, if a tenant for life and remainderman split up the capital of the trust between them, tax is payable upon the share taken by the remainderman, because the life interest has terminated in it, but not upon that taken by the tenant for life because his life interest terminated by the acquisition of the reversionary interest in that part. The rate of tax on the death of a tenant for life is determined by his personal score. It is treated as a transfer on death by him. All in all the tax implications upon settlements with interests in possession are not noticeably more severe that they were with estate duty, except that a termination *inter vivos* is immediately taxable. Again the pattern is to ensure that the capital is taxed once every generation. Successive limited interests will cause unnecessary tax liability ; but reversionary interests, other than those which have at any time been acquired for a consideration, are excluded property, and can be dealt with, without attracting tax liability, before the tenant for life's death.

Discretionary trusts.

---

[1] See Wheatcroft and Hewson, para. 1–26.
[2] *Ibid.*, ch. 6.

As might again have been expected, discretionary trusts have been severely affected by the legislation. Tax is charged when capital is paid out of the trust. The rates vary, and are more severe and more complex, in the case of settlements created after March 26th, 1974.[1] Even if nothing is paid out, tax is charged every tenth year upon the capital, on the assumption of a distribution, but charged at only 30% of the rate which would have been chargeable if a distribution payment had been made. Tax so paid is a credit against that due on a later actual distribution payment. Again, the pattern is to ensure the payment of tax once every generation.

Thus it seems that discretionary trusts have lost all their fiscal advantages. But they cannot be changed into fixed trusts or maintenance and accumulation trusts without paying tax on the capital at the time of the change. Much pressure was brought upon the Government to give some relief against the impact of this measure upon existing discretionary trusts, many of which had for years been free of estate duty liability. In response to this pressure, a " cheap " measure of distribution is permitted, under which distribution payments may be made to beneficiaries at lower rates prior to 1986, the charge being only 10% of the rates on which the tax would ordinarily be chargeable in the case of distributions prior to April 1st, 1976, rising to 20% in the case of distributions made before April 1st, 1980. It is thought that many trustees will take advantage of this opportunity.[2]

It is difficult to foresee how these alterations will affect the practice of settling land.[3] Clearly, they take away the fiscal advantages of discretionary trusts. They affect very little a settlement with an interest in possession, except that the tenant for life cannot avoid the capital being taxable if his interest determines. Successive life interests, such as were common in classical strict settlements, are disadvantageous, as they were under estate duty. There will be some attraction in splitting up estates in order to avoid tax liability. But the transferor of land will either have to pay the tax due on the transfer, or to arrange with the transferee to pay it. There is no difference for tax purposes between settled land and land held under a trust for sale.

With the general warning that fiscal considerations dominate advice to be given on the creation of a settlement, we may now discuss the strict settlement and trust for sale as methods of settling property.

Strict settlement and trust for sale compared.

Except in one respect, it is now possible to reproduce by way of trust for sale the situation that obtains under a strict settlement. As we have seen, it was the deliberate policy of the 1925 legislation to extend the use of the trust for sale. Trustees for sale are given

---

[1] The date on which this tax was announced in the House of Commons.
[2] See (1975) 125 New L.J. 1135 (V. Chapman).
[3] *Ibid.*, ch. 12.

all the powers of a tenant for life and the trustees of a settlement under the Settled Land Act 1925,[1] they may revocably delegate the powers of leasing and management to any person of full age for the time being beneficially entitled to the net rents and profits of the land during his life;[2] and entailed interests may be created in personalty.[3]   Thus, to-day, a settlement, the object of which is to keep the land or the capital money representing it in the family, may be achieved through a trust for sale.   Paradoxically, it is easier to prevent the land from being sold if it is settled by way of trust for sale.[4]   Not only may the trustees retain the land under their power to postpone sale indefinitely,[5] but they may be restrained from selling it unless they obtain the consent of certain persons,[6] and the settlor may choose as one of these the person beneficially entitled to the income for his life.   The exception to the achievement of this similarity is that under the Settled Land Act 1925 the tenant for life is master in his own house ;[7] he may exercise himself as of right all the powers given to him by that Act ; and those powers are indefeasible.[8]   Under a trust for sale, on the other hand, his counterpart can only exercise powers of leasing and management by way of revocable delegation from the trustees for sale ; and the duty to sell may not be delegated.[9]

Flexibility of trust for sale.

Furthermore there are two ways in which the trust for sale is more flexible than the strict settlement.   The strict settlement applies only to land, whereas the trust for sale may include all kinds of property, including land.   Thus two separate trusts are required if a settlor desires to create a family trust of mixed property and insists on creating a strict settlement of the land.   Secondly, a trust for sale is more convenient where the settlor desires to make provision for his children equally.   They can be given concurrent interests in the land, and, as we shall see, this is one of the occasions in which a statutory trust for sale is imposed by the Law of Property Act 1925.[10]

Trust for sale might be made the one mode of settlement.

Thus, if it were enacted that all settlements of land must be created by way of trust for sale, nothing of value would be lost. Any ambition to keep the land in the family could still be satisfied, in fact even more effectively than by employing a strict settlement. Admittedly the powers of management and the decision concerning sale would not be given as of right to the head of the family, who would have to rely on the revocable delegation of the powers by the

---

[1] L.P.A. 1925, s. 28 ; *supra*, p. 200.
[2] *Ibid.*, s. 29 ; *supra*, p. 201.
[3] *Ibid.*, s. 130 (1) ; *infra*, p. 255.
[4] See in particular *Re Inns*, [1947] Ch. 576 ; [1947] 2 All E. R. 308 ; M. & B. p. 198.
[5] L.P.A. 1925, s. 25 ; *supra*, p. 200.
[6] *Ibid.*, s. 26 ; *supra*, p. 201.
[7] (1944), 8 Conv. (N.S.) 147 (H. Potter).
[8] S.L.A. 1925, s. 106 ; *supra*, pp. 184–7.
[9] *Supra*, p. 201.
[10] *Infra*, p. 222.

trustees for sale. On the other hand, this loss would be outweighed by the further simplification of conveyancing, if all settlements of land had to be created by way of trust for sale. For one thing, the occasional difficulty of deciding whether land is settled or held on trust for sale would no longer arise.[1] It would never be doubtful whether the trustees or the tenant for life were the appropriate parties to make title. It would always be made by the trustees. Furthermore under a trust for sale there is less complication and expense involved when the holder of the life interest dies. As we shall see, under the Settled Land Act the legal title to the settled land passes to the trustees of the settlement as special personal representatives, who must take out special letters of probate to the settled land and then by a vesting assent vest the legal title in the new tenant for life.[2] The cost of the special probate and the vesting instrument has to be borne by the trust. In the case of the trust for sale, however, on death the legal title remains in the trustees for sale, and if the powers of management have been delegated, the delegation automatically ceases. All the trustees for sale have to do is to make a new delegation to the next holder of the life interest.

Finally we must remember that under the present system of duality of settlement, the two forms are mutually exclusive.[3] In order to create a trust for sale, it is essential to use the appropriate technical language, such as " upon trust to sell " ; failing that the settlement falls automatically under the Settled Land Act 1925. Thus, a testator who makes a home-made will, leaving his house to his widow for life and then to his children, unwittingly sets in motion the complicated machinery of that Act.[4] It would seem, indeed, that the task of the conveyancer would be facilitated and unnecessary expense avoided if the Settled Land Act were repealed and replaced by a short statute amplifying the provisions of the Law of Property Act with regard to trusts for sale.[5]

---

[1] *Supra*, pp. 197–9.

[2] *Infra*, p. 790.

[3] S.L.A. 1925, s. 1 (7) ; *supra*, p. 166.

[4] See Law Reform Committee Report on Interpretation of Wills (1973 Cmnd. 5301), paras. 60–62, 65(9).

[5] See Hanbury's *Modern Equity* (9th Edn), pp. 523–7 ; (1928), 166 L. T. 45 ; (1938), 85 *L. J. News* 353 (J. M .L.) ; (1938), 54 *L. Q. R.* 576 (M. M. Lewis) ; (1944), 8 Conv. (N. S.) 147 (H. Potter) ; (1957), *C. L. P.* 152 (E. H. Scamell) ; (1961) 24 M. L. R. 123 (G. A. Grove) ; (1962), *C.L.P.* 104 (E. C. Ryder) ; Survey of the Land Law of Northern Ireland (1971) paras. 88–100.

CHAPTER II

CONCURRENT INTERESTS

SUMMARY

Distinction between several and concurrent ownership.

Introductory. As we have already observed, the 1925 legislation used the statutory trust for sale to solve the conveyancing problems which arose from the holding of concurrent interests before 1926.[1] We must now examine this in some detail.

Several and concurrent ownership must first be distinguished. The owner of an interest in land may be entitled to possession either alone or in conjunction with other persons, and in both cases he may be entitled to take possession either now or at some time in the future. If he is entitled in his own right without having any other person joined with him in point of interest, he is said to hold in severalty ; but where he and other persons have simultaneous interests in the land, they are said to hold concurrently, or in co-ownership, and to have concurrent interests. In other words, land may be the subject of several, that is, separate ownership, or of co-ownership.

---

[1] *Supra*, pp. 166, 203.

SECTION I. THE LAW BEFORE 1926

Such a fundamental change in the principles applicable to concurrent interests was effected by the legislation of 1925 that we need do little more than enumerate the various forms that such interests might take before 1926, and the methods by which they might be converted into several interests. At common law there are four possible forms of co-ownership, one of which, tenancy by entireties, is now defunct;[1] while another, coparcenary, seldom arises.[2] The two found in practice are joint tenancy and tenancy in common.

(A) JOINT TENANCY

A joint tenancy arises whenever land is conveyed or devised to two or more persons without any words to show that they are to take distinct and separate shares, or, to use technical language, without words of severance.[3] If an estate is given, for instance, to

A. and B. in fee simple, *[margin: Definition of joint tenancy.]*

without the addition of any restrictive, exclusive or explanatory words, the law feels bound to give effect to the whole of the grant, and this it can do only by creating an equal estate in them both.[4] From the point of view of their interest in the land they are united in every respect. But if the grant contains words of severance showing an intention that A. and B. are to take separate and distinct interests, as for instance where there is a grant to

A. and B. equally,

the result is the creation not of a joint tenancy, but of a tenancy in common.

The two essential attributes of joint tenancy which must be kept in mind if the true meaning of the legislation of 1925 is to be grasped are the absolute unity which exists between joint tenants, and the right of survivorship. *[margin: Characteristics.]*

(1) There is, to use the language of Blackstone,[5] a thorough and intimate union between joint tenants. Together they form one person. This unity is fourfold, consisting of unity of title, time, interest and possession. All the titles are derived from the same grant and become vested at the same time;[6] *[margin: Unity between joint tenants.]*

---

[1] For a discussion, see 11th Edn. of this book, p. 338.
[2] *Infra*, p. 219.
[3] Litt. s. 277; Blackstone, vol. ii. p. 179.
[4] *Ibid.*, p. 180.   [5] *Ibid.*, p. 182.
[6] In the case of a grant to uses, the fact that the interests vested at different times did not prevent the creation of a joint tenancy, *e.g.* under a grant to X. and Y. to the use of all the sons of A. born within the lifetime of the settlor, sons born after the time of the grant became joint tenants with those alive at the time of its execution.

all the interests are identical in size; and there is unity of possession, since each tenant *totum tenet et nihil tenet*. Each, holds the whole in the sense that in conjunction with his co-tenants he is entitled to present possession and enjoyment of the whole; yet he holds nothing in the sense that he is not entitled to the exclusive possession of any individual part of the whole.[1] Unity of possession is a feature of all forms of co-ownership.

For this reason one joint tenant cannot, as a general rule, maintain an action of trespass against the other or others, but can do so only if the act complained of amounts either to an actual ouster, or to a destruction of the subject matter of the tenancy.[2]

Right of survivorship.

(2) The other characteristic that distinguishes a joint tenancy is the right of survivorship, or *jus accrescendi*, by which, if one joint tenant dies without having obtained a separate share in his lifetime, his interest is extinguished and accrues to the surviving tenants whose interests are correspondingly enlarged.[3] For example:

A. and B. may be joint tenants in fee simple, but the result of the death of B. is that his interest totally disappears and A. becomes owner in severalty of the land.

There are cases, however, where the right of survivorship does not benefit both tenants equally, for if there is (say) a grant to

A. and B. during the life of A.

and A. dies first, there is nothing that can accrue to B.[4]

Cases where a tenancy in common is preferred to a joint tenancy.

Preference of equity for tenancy in common.

From early times the right of survivorship caused a divergence of views between common law and equity. Common law favoured joint tenancies because they inevitably led to the vesting of the property in one person through the operation of the doctrine of survivorship, and thus facilitated the performance of those feudal dues that were incident to the tenure of land. But a tenancy

---

[1] By Littleton's time the expression *totum tenet et nihil tenet* had become *per my et per tout*, which in Blackstone's view (vol. ii, p. 182) meant that each tenant was seised " by the half or moiety and by all." *My*, however, did not mean half, but was an early form of the French word *mie*.

[2] Blackstone, vol. ii, p. 183 ; *Martyn* v. *Knowllys* (1799), 8 Term Rep. 145 ; *Murray* v. *Hall* (1849), 7 C. B. 441 ; *Stedman* v. *Smith* (1857), 8 E. & B. 1 ; *Wilkinson* v. *Haygarth* (1847), 12 Q. B. 837.

[3] Litt. s. 280.   Co. Litt. 181*a* ; Blackstone, vol. ii. p. 183.

[4] Co. Litt. 181*b*.

in common never involved this right of survivorship, and equity, which was not over-careful of the rights of the lord, soon showed a marked inclination, in the interests of convenience and justice, to construe a joint tenancy as a tenancy in common.[1]

Equity aims at equality, a feature that is conspicuous for its absence if the survivor becomes the absolute owner of the land. This preference of equity for a tenancy in common has been shown in three cases :—

(a) **Where money is advanced on mortgage by two or more persons.** Where two or more persons advance money, either in equal or in unequal shares, and take a mortgage of land from the borrower to themselves jointly, the rule *at law* is that they are joint tenants, so that the land and the right to the money belong absolutely to the survivor. The rule *in equity*, however, which prevails over the rule at law, is that they are tenants in common, and that the survivor is a trustee for the personal representatives of the deceased mortgagees.[2]

Joint loan on mortgage.

This equitable rule caused difficulty in those cases where trustees advanced trust money on mortgage. In practice a conveyance of land to trustees is always made to them as joint tenants, for the very nature of their office requires that the death of one shall not disturb the administration of the trust or deprive the survivor of power to execute conveyances and to give binding receipts for money. These advantages, however, will be lost if the trustees are to be regarded as tenants in common, for in that case each of them is entitled to a separate, though at present an unidentifiable, share of the land that passes on his death to his personal representatives. To avoid this inconvenience, it soon became the practice to insert a *joint account clause* in a mortgage to trustees. This declares that upon the death of one of the mortgagees the receipt of the survivor shall be a sufficient discharge for the money, and that the survivor shall be able to re-convey the land without the concurrence of the personal representatives of the deceased trustee.

Loans on mortgage by trustees.

Joint account clause.

The position has been made clearer by the Law of Property Act 1925,[3] which (re-enacting the Conveyancing Act 1881) provides that where there is a mortgage for the payment of money and either the sum advanced is expressly stated to be advanced by more persons than one on a joint account, or a mortgage is *made to them jointly and not in*

---

[1] Burton, *Real Property*, para. 165.

[2] *Petty* v. *Styward* (1632), 1 Eq. Cas. Abr. 290 ; *Steeds* v. *Steeds* (1889), 22 Q. B. D. 537 ; White and Tudor, *Leading Cases in Equity* (9th Edn.), vol. ii. pp. 882–5.

[3] L.P.A. 1925, s. 111.

shares, the money lent shall, *as between the mortgagees and the mortgagor*, be deemed to belong to the mortgagees on a joint account, and the survivor shall be able to give a complete discharge for the money. Trustees always advance money on a joint account, and the fact that they are trustees is never disclosed in the mortgage.[1]

It will be noticed that the Act is not confined to loans of money made by trustees, but applies generally to all joint mortgages coming within the provisions of the section ; and in a case where there is no question of trustees, it is important to remember that the joint account rule just stated applies only as between the mortgagor and the mortgagees, and not even between them if a contrary intention is shown in the deeds. As between the mortgagees themselves evidence is admissible to show that, despite the presence of a joint account clause, it was intended that the money should belong to them as tenants in common.[2]

Joint purchase of land.

(b) Where joint purchasers of land provide the purchase money in unequal shares. The invariable rule *at law* is that when purchasers take a conveyance to themselves in fee simple, they become joint tenants, and upon the death of one of them the whole estate passes to the survivor. Equity adopts the same attitude and does not treat the purchasers as being tenants in common, unless it can be inferred that they did not intend to take jointly.[3]

Money contributed in unequal shares.

Thus, though this is not the only circumstance that will raise the inference, it is established that purchasers who contribute the money in unequal proportions are to be regarded as tenants in common of the land conveyed.[4]

Partnership land.

(c) Where land is bought by partners. In the leading case of *Lake v. Craddock*,[5] where five persons joined in buying some waterlogged land with a view to its improvement by drainage, the court laid down the general rule that persons who make a joint purchase for the purposes of a joint undertaking or partnership, either in trade or in any other dealing, are to be treated in equity as tenants in common. The right of survivorship is incompatible with a commercial undertaking—*jus accrescendi inter mercatores pro beneficio commercii locum non habet*.[6] Thus :

---

[1] *Encyclopædia of Forms and Precedents* (4th Edn.), vol. 14. p. 201.
[2] *Re Jackson* (1887), 34 Ch. D. 732.
[3] *Lake* v. *Gibson* (1729), Eq. Cas. Ab. 294, *pl.* 3 ; *Lake* v. *Craddock* (1732), 3 P. W. 158 ; White and Tudor, *Leading Cases in Equity* (9th Edn.), vol. ii. p. 881.
[4] *Robinson* v. *Preston* (1858), 4 K. & J. 505; *Lake* v. *Craddock*, *supra*; White and Tudor *op. cit.*, vol. ii. p. 882.
[5] *Supra*.
[6] Co. Litt. 182a.

> If two partners take a grant or a lease of a farm and one dies, the survivor will be a trustee not only of the stock, but also of the land, for the personal representatives of the deceased partner.[1]

When once it is clear that property is partnership property, the rule in equity is that it is held by the partners as tenants in common, and it has been enacted by the Partnership Act 1890,[2] that all property brought into the business, or subsequently bought for the purposes of the business, or bought with money belonging to the business, is *prima facie* partnership property.

Despite these exceptional cases, the fundamental rule is that whenever land is granted or devised to two or more persons simply and without words of severance, the donees become joint tenants holding a single title, interest and possession, and when one dies his interest is extinguished and passes to the survivor or survivors.

Nature of joint tenancy summarized.

Determination of Joint Tenancy.

Since " each joint tenant stands, in all respects, in exactly the same position as each of the others,"[3] it follows that anything which creates a distinction between them severs the tenancy and converts it into a tenancy in common. Stated in more detail, its determination may be effected by,

   (i) alienation by one joint tenant ;

  (ii) acquisition by one tenant of a greater interest than that held by his co-tenants ;

 (iii) partition ;

 (iv) sale ;

  (v) mutual agreement ;[4] and

 (vi) " any course of dealing sufficient to intimate that the interests of all were mutually treated as constituting a tenancy in common ".[5]

These methods require some discussion.

(i) Although during the continuance of the tenancy one joint tenant holds nothing separately from his fellows, there is a general rule to the effect that *alienatio rei praefertur juri accrescendi*[6] and in accordance with this doctrine it has long been the law that one joint tenant can alienate his share to a stranger. The effect of such alienation, whether by way

Alienation by a joint tenant.

---

[1] *Elliot* v. *Brown* (1791), 3 Swan. 489.
[2] Sections 20, 21.
[3] Challis, *Law of Real Property* (3rd Edn.), p. 367.
[4] *Williams* v. *Hensman* (1861), 1 John & H. 546, 557 ; *Burgess* v. *Rawnsley*, [1975] Ch. 429 ; [1975] 3 All E. R. 142 ; *infra*, p. 230.
[5] *Ibid.*, at p. 557, *per* PAGE WOOD, V.-C.
[6] Co. Litt. 185 a.

of sale or mortgage, is to convert the joint tenancy into a tenancy in common, since the alienee and the remaining tenant or tenants hold by virtue of different titles and not under that one common title which is essential to the existence of a joint tenancy.

If A. and B. are joint tenants in fee simple and A. makes a grant in fee simple to X., the result is that B. and X. hold the lands as tenants in common, in equal undivided shares. If A., B. and C. are joint tenants in fee simple and A. makes a grant to X. in fee simple, X. is tenant in common with B. and C., though as between themselves the latter continue to hold as joint tenants.[1]

Again, the effect of the bankruptcy of a joint tenant is to sever the tenancy and to pass his interest to his trustee in bankruptcy.[2]

Owing to the doctrine of survivorship, no severance results from a disposition by will—*jus accrescendi praefertur ultimae voluntati.*[3]

Acquisition of a larger interest by a joint tenant.

(ii) A joint tenancy is also severed if one of the joint tenants subsequently acquires an interest greater in quantum than that held by his co-tenants. This destruction of the unity of interest may result from the act of the parties or by operation of law. As an instance of the former :

If A. and B. are joint tenants for life and A. purchases the fee simple in reversion, the jointure is severed; A. holding an undivided half in fee simple and B. an undivided half for life. When B. dies, the fee simple in the entirety of the land vests in A.[4]

Again, A. may release his interest to B. and so terminate the tenancy by vesting the whole ownership in B.[5]

A case in which a greater interest than that held by his co-tenants is cast upon a joint tenant by operation of law occurs where the reversion in fee descends to one of the joint tenants.[6]

If the joint tenants agree deliberately to put an end to the

---

[1] Litt. s. 292.

[2] *Bedson* v. *Bedson*, [1965] 2 Q. B. 666, at p. 690; [1965] 3 All E. R. 307, at p. 319, *per* RUSSELL, L.J. *Re Rushton*, [1972] Ch. 197 ; [1971] 2 All E. R. 937.

[3] Blackstone, vol. ii. pp. 185–6.

[4] Co. Litt. s. 182b ; *Wiscot's Case* (1599), 2 Co. Rep. 60b.

[5] *Re Schär*, [1951] Ch. 280 ; [1950] 2 All E. R. 1069.

[6] Cruise, *Digest*, Tit. xviii. c. ii. s. 7. Contrary to the view of the majority of the Court of Appeal, it is submitted that the two methods of severance already discussed avail a husband or wife in respect of the matrimonial home; *Bedson* v. *Bedson*, [1965] 2 Q. B. 666, at p. 688–91; [1965] 3 All E. R. 307, at pp. 318–20, *per* RUSSELL, L.J., *dissenting.* In *Re Draper's Conveyance*, [1969] 1 Ch. 486, at p. 494 ; [1967] 3 All E. R. 853 ; M. & B. p. 212, PLOWMAN, J., preferred the view of RUSSELL, L.J.

tenancy, the two methods open to them, in addition to a mutual agreement that henceforth they shall hold as tenants in common, are (iii) partition and (iv) sale.

(iii) Partition is a method whereby the joint *possession* is disunited, and its effect is to make each former co-tenant separate owner of a specific portion of the land, and thus to terminate the co-ownership for ever. Instead of holding an undivided share in the whole, each person will hold a divided share in severalty. If 50 acres are held by A. and B. as joint tenants in fee simple, the effect of the destruction of the unities of title or interest is, as we have seen, to create a tenancy in common ; but the effect of partition is that each becomes absolute owner of 25 acres. *Partition.*

Before 1926, partition was either voluntary or compulsory. Compulsory partition was abolished in 1925.[1] Accordingly, co-owners may agree between themselves to divide the property into separate shares to be held in individual ownership. The actual amount or position of the land that is to be allotted to each party may be settled by the co-owners themselves, or by an arbitrator selected by them, or even by the drawing of lots.[2] The usual practice is first to enter into a preliminary agreement whereby the co-owners consent to the land being partitioned into allotments convenient to be held in separate ownership and as nearly as possible of equal values, provision being made for the payment of a sum of money to secure equality of partition where it is impossible to give each party land of equal value.[3] When the division has been settled, the last step is for the co-owners to execute that form of conveyance which is appropriate to the interest involved. A deed is necessary in the case of land, but joint tenants must execute a deed of release, while the proper form for tenants in common is a deed of grant. *How voluntary partition effected.*

(iv) The normal and the simplest method of bringing a joint tenancy to an end is by sale. If all the joint tenants agree to sell, the joint title can be passed to the purchaser and the land will vest in him as single owner. Prior to 1926, if one joint tenant was obstructive, the others could compel a sale by the indirect method of bringing a partition action. *Sale of entire land.*

---

[1] *I.e.* by the repeal of the Partition Acts ; L.P.A. 1925, 7th Sched.
[2] Litt. ss. 55, 243–6.
[3] For a precedent see *Encyclopaedia of Forms and Precedents* (4th Edn.), vol. 15. p. 856.

(v) The mutual agreement need not be specifically enforceable. The significance of the agreement is not that it binds the parties, but that it serves as an indication of a common intention to sever.[1]

(vi) It may be possible to infer from the particular facts of a case a common intention to sever, as where one joint tenant negotiates with another for some rearrangement of interest, even though the negotiations break down.[2]

(B) TENANCY IN COMMON

A tenancy in common arises

Creation of tenancy in common.

(i) where land is limited to two or more persons with words of severance showing an intention, even in the slightest degree,[3] that the donees are to take separate shares, or

(ii) where equity reads what is at law a joint tenancy as a tenancy in common,[4] or

(iii) where one joint tenant disposes of his interest to a stranger, or acquires an interest greater than that of his co-tenants.[5]

Limitation with words of severance.

The following expressions have at one time and another been construed as words of severance sufficient to create a tenancy in common :

" equally to be divided " ;
" to be divided " ;
" in equal moieties " ;
" equally " ;
" amongst " ;
" share and share alike."

So also, if land is devised to A. and B. on condition that they pay in equal shares ten shillings a week to X. during his life, this imposition of an equal burden on both donees shows that what would normally be a joint tenancy is to be a tenancy in common.[6]

Differences between joint tenancy and tenancy in common.

(i) Unity

There is a fundamental distinction between tenancy in common and joint tenancy.

In the first place, that intimate union which exists between joint tenants does not necessarily exist in a tenancy in common. In the latter case the one point in which the tenants are united is the right to possession.[7] They all occupy promiscuously, and

---

[1] *Burgess* v. *Rawnsley*, [1975] Ch. 429, at p. 448, *per* Sir JOHN PENNY-CUICK.

[2] *Burgess* v. *Rawnsley*, *supra*. See also *Re Draper's Conveyance* [1969] 1 Ch. 486 ; [1967] 3 All E. R. 853, *infra*, p. 230.

[3] *Robertson* v. *Fraser* (1871), 6 Ch. App. 696, 699.

[4] *Supra*, pp. 213-5.

[5] *Supra*, pp. 216-7.

[6] *Re North*, [1952] Ch. 397 ; [1952] 1 All E. R. 609.

[7] **Co. Litt.** 189 *a*.

if there are two tenants in common, A. and B., A. has an equal right with B. to the possession of the whole land. But their union may stop at that point, for they may each hold different interests, as where one has a fee simple, the other a life interest ; and they may each hold under different titles, as for instance where one has bought and the other has succeeded to his share.[1] Each has a *share* in the ordinary meaning of that word. His share is undivided in the sense that its boundary is not yet demarcated, but nevertheless his right to a definite share exists.

The second characteristic, and it is really the complement of the first, is that the *jus accrescendi* has no application to tenancies in common, so that, when one tenant dies, his share passes to his personal representatives, and not to the surviving tenant.[2]

(ii) Survivorship.

> " A tenancy in common, though it is an ownership only of an undivided share, is, for all practical purposes, a sole and several tenancy or ownership ; and each tenant in common stands, towards his own undivided share, in the same relation that, if he were sole owner of the whole, he would bear towards the whole."[3]

Although the tenancy thus possesses certain advantages over a joint tenancy, it suffers from this disadvantage that, since the shares are distinct, it becomes necessary on a sale of the whole land to make a separate title to each separate share.

The three methods by which a tenancy in common is determined and converted into separate ownership are (i) partition, (ii) sale, and (iii) the acquisition by one tenant, whether by grant or by operation of law, of the shares vested in his co-tenants.

Determination of tenancy in common.

(C) COPARCENARY

Coparcenary arose at common law wherever land descended to two or more persons who together constituted the heir. This occurred if a tenant in fee simple or a tenant in tail died intestate leaving only female heirs. In each case the females succeeded jointly to the estate and were called coparceners. Coparcenary also arose under the custom of gavelkind, according to which the land descended to all the sons equally, failing them to all the daughters equally, and failing them to all the brothers equally.[4] Gavelkind, however, has been abolished ; the rules regulating the disposition of a fee simple estate upon the intestacy of its owner have been altered by the Administration of Estates Act 1925 ;[5] and coparcenary can now arise only in the case of entailed interests.

If the owner of an entailed interest (other than an interest in tail male) dies without having either barred the entail or disposed

Coparcenary confined to entails.

---

[1] Blackstone, vol. ii. p. 191.
[2] *Ibid.*, p. 194.
[3] Challis, *Law of Real Property* (3rd Edn.), p. 368.
[4] *Supra*, p. 18. [5] *Infra*, pp. 871 *et seq.*

of the interest by will, and if he leaves no male heirs who are entitled to succeed *per formam doni*, the interest passes to the female heirs of the appropriate class.[1] For instance:

> Where the owner of an entailed interest general dies intestate leaving no sons, but three daughters, the interest descends to all the daughters jointly.[2] The daughters are called coparceners because, in the words of Littleton,
>
> > " by the writ, which is called *breve de participatione facienda*, the law will constrain them that partition shall be made among them."[3]

Distinction between coparcenary and other concurrent interests.

Coparceners constitute a single heir, and they occupy a position intermediate between joint tenants and tenants in common.[4] Like joint tenants they have unity of title, interest and possession ; like tenants in common their estate is unaffected by the doctrine of survivorship, and if there are three coparceners and one dies, her share passes separately to her heirs or devisee, not to the survivors, though the unity of possession continues. It follows that unity of time is not necessary to constitute coparcenary, for if a man has two daughters to whom his estate descends and one dies leaving a son, such son and the surviving daughter will be coparceners.[5]

Determination of coparcenary.

Coparcenary is converted into separate ownership (i) by partition, or (ii) by the union in one coparcener of all the shares ; and it is converted into a tenancy in common if one coparcener transfers her share to a stranger.[6]

Coparcenary after 1925.

The present position with regard to coparcenary is that interests held by coparceners are necessarily equitable, since for the most part they consist of entailed interests,[7] and these arise only under a settlement or a trust for sale. Therefore, it would seem that when a tenant in tail dies intestate, leaving female heirs, the legal fee simple vests in the trustees in the case of a settlement and is held by them on trust for sale and to give effect to the equitable rights of the coparceners.[8]

Pre-1926 law of concurrent interests hindered conveyancing.

SECTION II. THE LAW AFTER 1925

The object of the legislation of 1925 was to simplify conveyances of land, and where this simplicity could not otherwise be

---

[1] On entailed interests, see *infra*, pp. 237 *et seq.*

[2] Litt., ss. 55, 241, 254, 265 ; Blackstone, vol. ii. p. 187.

[3] Litt. s. 241. As distinct from the case of joint tenancy and tenancy in common, partition may be compelled at common law, since the co-tenancy arises, not by act of parties, but by operation of law.

[4] Challis, *Law of Real Property* (3rd Edn.), p. 374.

[5] Co. Litt. s. 164a.   [6] Litt. s. 309.

[7] If a person who was a lunatic on January 1st, 1926, and was therefore incapable of making a will, dies without recovering his testamentary capacity, his beneficial interest in land devolves according to the old canons of descent— A.E.A. 1925, s. 51 (2). Coparcenary, therefore, may still arise under this provision in the case of a fee simple estate.

[8] S.L.A. 1925, s. 36 (1) (2).

attained, to make radical alterations in the pre-1926 law. The law relating to concurrent interests was a subject that called for considerable alteration. If conveyancing is to be a simple matter, one primary essential is that the legal estate to be acquired by a purchaser should be vested in an easily ascertainable person and not distributed among a number of persons whose titles will each require to be investigated.

Joint tenancy. Joint tenancy does not raise difficulties in this respect, for although several persons are interested in the land, yet there is but one title to be deduced, and if the purchaser is satisfied as to the validity of the deed or the will under which the tenancy stands limited, he is not concerned further with the tenants except to see that they are all parties to the deed of sale.

Tenancy in common. In tenancy in common, however, the case is different, for the existence of a number of persons interested in the land, each of whom, as we have seen, is entitled to a separate share, raises a serious hindrance to simplicity of transfer. An analogous difficulty occurs in the case of a settlement where the beneficial title is distributed among a number of persons *in succession*, but we have seen that this plurality of interests is not allowed to hinder conveyancing, since the tenant for life is treated as the fee simple owner for purposes of transmission, and the interests of the various beneficiaries are not allowed to affect a purchaser. The conveyancing problem raised by a number of successive interests is in fact comparatively simple, because the tenant for life is obviously marked out as the person to act as an intermediary for passing the legal estate.

Especially tenancy in common.

But where land is held by tenants in common, there is no one person in whom the legal estate can appropriately be vested, for all the tenants have the equal right to present enjoyment, so that tenancy in common is a greater hindrance to simplicity of transfer than a settlement. The complication here is that the separate title of each tenant must be investigated.

" Lastly, all this confusion is ' worse confounded ' by concurrent ownership in tenancy in common. Here is an example which recently came before me in my official capacity. A man by his will devised his freeholds to the use of his wife for life, and after her death to the use of his children in fee simple. He had ten children ; one of them died during the widow's life, leaving a similar will, seven children, and a widow. This is quite a simple example ; yet the result is that a house worth about £150 per annum is (the widow being dead) now vested (not merely in equity but at law) in seventeen persons in the following proportions :

Each of the nine living children of testator or their assigns .. $\frac{7}{70}$

Each of the seven children of the deceased child, subject to the prior life interest of their mother .. .. .. $\frac{1}{70}$

Moreover, several of the parties have mortgaged their shares, and in the result when the great expense of proving the title of each of the seventeen has been paid, a very small balance will remain for distribution.   Thus, tenancy in common is (having regard to the Settled Land Acts) a far greater detriment to the proper management of land than settlements (which are popularly debited with this sin), and introduces infinitely greater difficulty with regard to its sale, as not only must the parties be unanimous, but the title of each of them has to be deduced."[1]

Tenancies in common of *legal* estate abolished.

To end all such confusion the Law of Property Act 1925 revolutionized the law relating to tenancies in common.

The object was to enable land which is subject to such tenancies to be sold without casting upon the purchaser any obligation to consider the titles or the beneficial rights of the tenants.   The first step in the attainment of this object is the enactment that

" a *legal* estate is not capable of subsisting or of being created in an undivided share in land."[2]

What this particular enactment means is that there can never again be a *legal* tenancy in common, *i.e.* a tenancy in common of a legal estate.

Trust for sale now arises in all cases.

It is then enacted that an undivided share in land shall not be created except behind a trust for sale.[3]   This involves two consequences :—

First, the legal estate must be held by trustees holding as *joint* tenants upon trust for sale.

Secondly, the subject-matter of the tenancy in common is converted from land to money, for, as we have already seen land directed to be sold is regarded by equity as having already been sold.[4]

---

[1] Sir Arthur Underhill in Fourth Report, 1919. p 30.

[2] L.P.A. 1925, s. 1 (6).   The 1925 legislation refers to "undivided share" not to "tenancy in common."

[3] S.L.A. 1925, s. 36 (4).

[4] Nevertheless, this principle that the equitable tenants in common hold interests in personalty, not in the land, is not free from exceptions.   Thus, (a) pending the sale, they have the same right to possession of the land as legal tenants in common had before 1926, *Bull* v. *Bull*, [1955] 1 Q. B. 234 ; [1955] 1 All E. R. 253 ; *cf. Barclay* v. *Barclay*, [1970] 2 Q. B. 677 ; [1970] 2 All E. R. 676 ; (b) an agreement by one tenant to sell his share to the other or others is a contract for the sale of land within the meaning of the Law of Property Act 1925, s. 40 (*supra*, p. 115), and therefore requires a note or memorandum signed by the vendor ; *Cooper* v. *Critchley*, [1955] Ch. 431 ; [1955] 1 All E. R. 520. See (1955), 18 *M. L. R.* 408 (H. R. Gay) ; 1955 *C. L. J.* 156 (H. W. R. Wade); (c) the interests of co-owners may be interests in land within the meaning of Administration of Justice Act 1956, s. 35, and a charging order may be made against any property which they jointly own, *National Westminster Bank Ltd.* v. *Allen*, [1972] Q. B. 718 ; [1971] 3 All E. R. 201 ; *infra*, p. 805.   Cf. *Irani Finance Ltd.* v. *Singh* [1971] Ch. 59 ; [1970] 3 All E. R. 199 ; (1971) 34 M.L.R. 441 (S. M. Cretney) ; (d) a tenant in common may be a " person interested in land " within L.R.A. 1925, s. 54(1), and so entitled to register a caution in respect of his minor interest.   *Elias* v. *Mitchell*, [1972] Ch. 652 ; [1972] 2 All E. R. 153.   *Infra*, p. 782.   See generally M. & B. pp. 225 *et seq.*

The doctrine of conversion proved troublesome where a legal estate had been granted before 1926 to tenants in common in tail.   The effect of the 1925 legislation was to make them equitable tenants in common of personalty,

The corner stone of this new edifice is the vesting of the legal estate in joint tenants as trustees upon trust for sale, and since it is essential to the success of the scheme that this legal joint tenancy should remain invulnerable until terminated by sale, the old rules as to severance[1] have been abolished for *legal* joint tenancies. It is enacted that

Joint tenancy of legal estate cannot be severed.

> " no severance of a joint tenancy of a *legal* estate, so as to create a tenancy in common in land, shall be permissible."[2]

If, therefore, it is desired to vest a fee simple absolute in possession or a term of years absolute in tenants in common, the correct method is to create an express trust for sale by conveying the legal estate to trustees upon trust to sell the land and to hold the rents and profits until sale and the ultimate proceeds of sale upon such trusts as the grantor may see fit to create.[3] He may provide, for instance, that the beneficiaries shall be entitled to the proceeds in unequal shares, in which case they become equitable tenants in common.

An alternative method is merely to convey the legal estate to trustees upon *the statutory trusts*, an expression which is defined by the Act to mean,

> upon trust to sell the land, with power to postpone the sale, and to hold the net rents and profits until sale and the ultimate proceeds of sale upon trust to give effect to the beneficial and equitable rights of the persons to whom the land was limited. [4]

If the correct method of a conveyance upon trust for sale is not adopted, the Law of Property Act 1925 contains a number of provisions designed to ensure that, no matter what form the transaction may have taken, the effect shall be exactly the same as if the tenancy in common had been properly limited behind a trust for sale. There appear to be three normal cases, namely:

Effect of failure to create a trust for sale.

> a direct conveyance of the legal estate to tenants in common ;
> a devise to tenants in common ;
> a contract to convey an undivided share.

With regard to a conveyance, section 34 (2) of the Law of Property Act 1925 provides that

(i) Conveyance.

> where [after 1925] land is expressed to be conveyed to any persons in undivided shares and those persons are of full age, the conveyance shall operate as if the land had been expressed to be conveyed to the

---

but as a result of this they became absolute owners, since before 1926 personalty could not be entailed and the new rule making this possible (*infra*, p. 255) applied only to instruments executed after 1925. Hence the Law of Property (Entailed Interests) Act 1932, s. 1, overruling *Re Price*, [1928] Ch. 579, provides that in such a case the entail shall continue to exist in the personalty arising under the trust for sale.

[1] *Supra*, pp. 215–6.
[2] L.P.A. 1925, s. 36 (2).
[3] See *Encyclopaedia of Forms and Precedents* (4th Edn.), vol. 19, p. 1036.
[4] L.P.A. 1925, s. 35 (1).

grantees, or, if there are more than four grantees, then to the first four named in the conveyance, as joint tenants upon the statutory trusts.

Thus, if land is conveyed in fee simple to A., B., C., D. and E. in equal shares, A., B., C. and D. become joint tenants of the legal estate, while all five are entitled under the statutory trusts as equitable tenants in common to the proceeds of sale and the rents and profits until sale.

(ii) Devise.

A devise to two or more persons in undivided shares operates to vest the legal estate in the trustees (if any) of the will for the purposes of the Settled Land Act 1925, or, if there is none, in the personal representatives, but in either case the land is held on the statutory trusts and not as settled land.[1]

(iii) Contract to convey.

A contract to convey an undivided share in land is deemed to be fully performed by a conveyance of a corresponding share in the proceeds of sale arising under a trust for sale.[2]

Settlement.

As regards settlements, section 36 (4) of the Settled Land Act 1925 provides that a tenancy in common shall not be capable of creation except under a trust instrument or under the above provisions of the Law of Property Act 1925, and shall then take effect under a trust for sale.   Thus if it is desired to settle land on A. and B. for their lives in equal shares, with remainder to C. in fee simple, the legal estate must be vested in the trustees upon trust for sale, and the disposition merely operates to give the beneficiaries a corresponding share of the net proceeds of sale and the rents and profits until sale.

If beneficiaries under an existing settlement become entitled in possession to the land, *e.g.* where in a

> devise to X. for life, remainder to X.'s children equally during their lives,

X. dies leaving three children, the legal fee simple that was formerly held by X. as tenant for life must be vested in the trustees of the settlement and held by them upon the statutory trusts.[3] The settlement within the meaning of the Settled Land Act 1925 comes to an end and is replaced by a trust for sale.

Quaere whether the legislation embraces all tenancies in common.

The policy of the Law of Property Act 1925 is clearly to subject all forms of co-ownership to a trust for sale, except those which are within the Settled Land Act 1925.   It seems doubtful, however, whether the language of these enactments covers all cases in which a tenancy in common may arise, as for example when two

---

[1] L.P.A. 1925, 2. 34 (3).   For an example, see *Re House*, [1929] 2 Ch. 166.
[2] *Ibid.*, s. 42 (6).   Elaborate provisions are made in L.P.A. 1925, 1st Sched. Part IV, for the conversion into equitable interests of tenancies in common that were in existence on December 31st, 1925.   These transitional provisions have given rise to a number of important decisions, but owing to the necessity of keeping this book within reasonable limits they are not dealt with here : See further : *Gibson's Conveyancing* (20th Edn.), pp. 817–824.
[3] S.L.A. 1925, s. 36 (1), (2), (3).

persons buy land and contribute the purchase price in unequal shares.[1] This was the position in *Bull* v. *Bull*,[2] where a mother and son bought a house as a dwelling place for themselves, the conveyance being made to the son only, who had provided the greater part of the purchase price. In an action in which the issue was the validity of a notice to quit served on the mother, the Court of Appeal, citing s. 36(4) of the Settled Land Act 1925, held that the parties were tenants in common in equity, and that the legal estate vested in the son upon the statutory trusts for sale.

This decision, though expedient, is difficult to fit into the words of the legislation. There was nothing that could constitute a trust instrument within the meaning of the Settled Land Act 1925 ; and the land was not " expressed to be conveyed " to persons in undivided shares as required by the Law of Property Act 1925. It would seem, then, that the courts will readily impose a trust for sale if this will fulfil the intention of the parties.

Let us examine the effect of the statutory trust for sale that arises in these various cases from the point of view, first, of a purchaser of the land, secondly, of the beneficiaries. *(Advantage of new scheme.)*

The advantage to the purchaser is that he is no longer compelled to investigate the title of each tenant in common. He is concerned only with the legal estate held by the joint tenants upon trust for sale, since the rights of the persons beneficially entitled exist merely as equitable interests behind the trust for sale, and they are overreached upon a conveyance of the land by the trustees for sale, provided that the purchase money is paid to at least two trustees or to a trust corporation. It is a matter of indifference, therefore, that some of the tenants in common are infants, or that some of them are unwilling to acquiesce in the sale. Although it is true that in the case of a statutory, as distinct from an express, trust for sale the trustees are required, so far as practicable, to consult, and give effect to the wishes of the beneficiaries entitled in possession, or in the case of a dispute, of the majority in terms of value, yet it is expressly enacted that it shall be no concern of a purchaser to see that this requirement has been complied with.[3] *(Advantage to purchaser.)*

The advantage to the tenants in common is that, no matter how numerous they may be, a sale of the land affected is always possible without difficulty or undue expense. Neither are they prejudiced by the loss of their rights in the land itself, for they have corresponding rights in the money arising from the sale. *(Advantage to tenants in common.)*

---

[1] *Supra*, p. 214.

[2] [1955] 1 Q. B. 234; [1955] 1 All E. R. 253 followed in *Cook* v. *Cook*, [1962] P. 181; [1962] 2 All E. R. 262; affd. [1962] P. 235; [1962] 2 All E. R. 811. See too *Re Buchanan-Wollaston's Conveyance*, [1939] Ch. 217 ; affd. [1939] Ch. 738, where a conveyance to purchasers as joint tenants (who contributed unequally) was treated as coming within L.P.A. 1925, s. 36 (1).

[3] L.P.A. 1925, s. 26 (3) ; as amended by L.P.(A.)A. 1926, Sched.

Thus if A. is entitled under the tenancy in common to a half share in the land, and B. and C. are entitled to a quarter share each, the duty of the trustees is to ensure that A., B. and C. receive the purchase money in the same proportions. They need not sell at once, nor indeed at any time, for they are statutorily empowered to postpone the sale,[1] or, instead of selling, to partition the land among the persons beneficially entitled.[2] The tenants in common can still deal with their equitable interests as freely as they could formerly have dealt with their legal interests. If A., B. and C. are tenants in common and C. sells his equitable interest to D., the legal joint tenancy remains vested in the trustees upon the statutory trusts for A., B. and D.

Changes in joint tenancies.

Joint Tenancies. Certain consequential changes have also been effected in joint tenancies, and the law relating to this matter varies according as the land is, or is not, settled within the meaning of the Settled Land Act 1925.

Settled land.

The position with regard to settled land is what it was before 1926. If two or more persons are beneficially entitled for their lives under a settlement, as for example where land is devised to X. and Y. for their lives with remainder to Z. in fee simple,[3] they together constitute the tenant for life within the meaning of the Settled Land Act and there is no question of any trust for sale.[4] They are invested with the legal estate, and it is their function to make title upon a sale or other disposition of the land.

Joint tenants beneficially entitled.

In the second case, however, where the land is not settled, but is *beneficially* limited for a legal estate to joint tenants, *e.g.*

> where a father conveys Blackacre to his two sons in fee simple without words of severance,

it is enacted that the *legal* estate shall be held upon trust for sale in like manner as if the persons beneficially entitled were tenants in common.[5] This means, not that they become equitable tenants in common, but equitable joint tenants of the proceeds of sale and of the income until sale. Thus if land is granted to A., B. and C. jointly in fee simple, A., B. and C. become joint tenants of the legal estate upon trust for sale for themselves as equitable joint tenants. A legal and an equitable joint tenancy are automatically and inescapably brought into existence. A., B. and C. are trustees for sale of the legal estate and can therefore make title with facility, but they are joint beneficiaries with regard to the equitable interest. They may postpone the sale of the land,

---

[1] L.P.A. 1925, s. 25.

[2] *Ibid.*, s. 28 (3).

[3] See also *Re Gaul and Houlston's Contract*, [1928] 1 Ch. 689, devise to X. and Y. in fee simple, subject to a charge, created voluntarily, of £1,000 in favour of Z. Thus, the land was settled by virtue of S.L.A. 1925, s. 1 (1) (v) ; *supra*, p. 169, note 4.

[4] S.L.A. 1925, s. 19 (2).

[5] L.P.A. 1925, s. 36 (1).

indefinitely, but if the date at which it should be effected becomes a matter of dispute, any one of them may apply under section 30 of the Law of Property Act 1925 to the court which may make such order as it thinks fit. We have already seen that while it is the primary duty of the trustees for sale to sell, they have nevertheless a power to postpone sale.[1] Unless, therefore, A., B. and C. unanimously agree to exercise the power of postponement, the land must be sold.[2] The court, however, will not order a sale on an application by A. if he had covenanted to sell only with the consents of B. and C.[3] Nor will the court order a sale where land has been acquired with some particular purpose in mind, as for instance, the joint occupation of a house and that purpose still subsists.[4]

> " Thus, if the purpose was that the house should be the matrimonial home, then so long as that purpose is still alive, the court will not allow the husband or the wife arbitrarily to insist on a sale. But if the parties are divorced and in consequence the contemplated purpose is dead, then the trust for sale will take effect, subject always to the discretion of the court to postpone it."[5]

The number of persons holding the legal estate must not exceed four.[6]

This change in the law is unintelligible unless we remember that a *legal* joint tenancy can no longer be severed. It is essential to the success of the new rules for tenancies *in common* that the legal joint tenancy which must necessarily arise should continue undisturbed and should not be convertible into a tenancy in common by some transaction or event amounting to a severance, for otherwise the legal title would be split up into a number of separate titles and the old troubles incidental to a conveyance of the legal estate would return. Hence the new rule that a *legal* joint tenancy cannot be severed.[7] The object of the introduction of an equitable tenancy is to preserve to each tenant his right to sever his interest and thus to avoid the danger of his premature death and the consequent operation of the *jus accrescendi*. Why trusts for sale necessary.

We have already considered the methods by which a joint tenancy may be severed and converted into a tenancy in common,[8] Modern position of beneficial joint tenant.

---

[1] *Supra*, p. 200. [2] *Re Mayo*, [1943] Ch. 302 ; [1943] 2 All E. R. 440.
[3] *Re Buchanan-Wollaston's Conveyance*, [1939] Ch. 378 ; [1939] 2 All E. R. 302.
[4] *Bull* v. *Bull*, [1955] 1 Q.B. 234; [1955] 1 All E.R. 253; *Jones* v. *Challenger*, [1961] 1 Q.B. 176, [1960] 1 All E.R. 785; M. & B. p. 200; *Rawlings* v. *Rawlings*, [1964] p. 398; [1964] 2 All E.R. 804; *Re Solomon*, [1967] Ch. 573; [1966] 3 All E.R. 255; *Barclay* v. *Barclay*, [1970] 2 Q.B. 677; [1970] 2 All E.R. 676; *Jackson* v. *Jackson*, [1971] 1 W.L.R. 1539; [1971] 3 All E.R. 774; *Burke* v. *Burke*, [1974] 1 W.L.R. 1063; [1974] 2 All E.R. 944; *Re Turner*, [1974] 1 W.L.R. 1556; [1975] *Re McCarthy*, [1975] 1 W.L.R. 807; [1975] 2 All E.R. 857; *Re Densham*, [1975] 1 W.L.R. 1519, 1531. See Wostenholme and Cherry, vol. I, p. 89; M. & B. p. 204; (1972) 36 Conv. (N.S.) 99, (1975) 119 Sol. Jo. 582 (J.G. Miller).
[5] *Bedson* v. *Bedson*, [1965] 2 Q.B. 666, at p. 678; [1965] 3 All E.R. 307, *per* Lord Denning, M.R.
[6] L.P.A. 1925, s. 34 (2). [7] *Ibid.*, s. 36 (2), *supra*, p. 223.
[8] *Supra*, pp. 215–8.

but it is important to notice with some particularity the course open to a beneficial joint tenant who desires to prevent the survivorship of his equitable interest to the other tenants.

> If land has been conveyed to A. and B. as joint tenants, what is the effect upon A.'s beneficial interest if he predeceases B. ? The answer, of course, is that it survives absolutely to B. to the detriment of A.'s successors. The further question then arises, what can A. do in his lifetime to avoid this possible loss ? In other words, how can the legal or the equitable joint tenancy, or both, be determined ?

The solution is, either to determine the joint tenancy altogether, or, while retaining the legal joint tenancy, to sever it on its equitable side. Let us consider the two cases separately.

(1) A joint tenancy is determined altogether by any one of the following methods :

Determination of the legal and the equitable joint tenancies.

(*a*) **Sale of the Legal Estate.** If A. and B. sell in their capacity as trustees for sale, their conveyance passes the legal fee simple to the purchaser freed from their rights as joint tenants. The purchaser is not concerned with these rights, since they exist behind the trust for sale and are merely equitable in nature.

A trust for sale cannot be exercised unless there are at least two trustees, but it is enacted by the Law of Property (Amendment) Act 1926 that a surviving joint tenant, who is solely and *beneficially* entitled to the land, may deal with the legal estate as if it were not held on a trust for sale.[1] Thus if land is devised in fee simple to a husband and wife jointly, the wife, on the death of her husband, can pass a good title to a purchaser of the legal estate without appointing another trustee in place of her husband.[2]

Law of Property (Joint Tenants) Act 1964.

Such a conveyance, however, is not without its dangers, for a deceased tenant, without the knowledge of the survivor, may have severed his interest, a fact that will not appear on the vendor's abstract of title to the legal estate. It was formerly felt, therefore, that the only sure method of overreaching the equitable interest arising by virtue of the severance was for the survivor to reconstitute the trust for sale by appointing a new trustee. But this is no longer necessary. The Law of Property (Joint Tenants) Act 1964,[3] which is retrospective to January 1st, 1926, provides that

> the survivor of two or more joint tenants shall, in favour of a purchaser of the legal estate, be deemed to be solely and

---

[1] Sched. amending L.P.A. 1925, s. 36.
[2] According to *Re Cook*, [1948] Ch. 212 ; [1948] 1 All E. R. 231 ; M. & B. p. 223 ; this would be the position apart from the Act of 1926, since, on the death of the husband the entire interest in the land, both legal and equitable, vests in the wife. The trust for sale ceases, since she is now owner and cannot be trustee for herself.
[3] See Wolstenholme and Cherry, vol. 2, pp. 149–151 ; (1964) 28 Conv. (N.S.) 329 ; (1966) 30 Conv. (N.S.) 27 (P. Jackson).

beneficially interested if he conveys as beneficial owner[1] or the conveyance includes a statement that he is so interested.[2]

This provision, however, is not to apply if a memorandum of severance has been endorsed on or annexed on the conveyance by which the legal estate was vested in the joint tenants; or if a receiving order, or a petition for such an order, has been registered under the Land Charges Act 1972.[3]

(*b*) **Partition.** If all the joint tenants are of full age it is clear that as beneficial owners they may partition the land between themselves, whereupon the legal joint tenancy will be converted into separate ownership. Apart from this, however, the Law of Property Act 1925 provides, as we have seen, that where a legal estate is beneficially limited to persons as joint tenants it shall be held on trust for sale *in like manner as if the persons beneficially entitled were tenants in common.*[4] Then, another section provides that where the proceeds of sale have become absolutely vested in tenants in common of full age, the trustees may, with the consent of the persons (if any) of full age interested in possession in the profits of the land until sale,

(i) partition the land in whole or in part, and

(ii) provide by way of mortgage or otherwise for the payment of any equality money.[5]

(*c*) **Release.** Where land is held by A. and B. as joint tenants it is open to either of them to release his interest to the other, whereupon the alienee will become sole and several owner.[6] An agreement for such a release is unenforceable by action unless it is evidenced by a written memorandum signed by the vendor or his agent.[7]

(2) **Severance.** It remains to be seen how it is possible to sever the equitable joint tenancy between A. and B. without disturbing the joint tenancy of the legal estate. This result is achieved if either of the tenants enters into any transaction which severs the tenancy and converts it into a tenancy in common, as for example where he alienates his

Determination of the equitable joint tenancy only.

---

[1] As to the effect of conveying as beneficial owner, see *infra*, p. 761.

[2] S. 1 (1). The Act does not apply if the title to the land has been registered; *ibid.*, s. 3.

[3] *Ibid.*, s. 1 (1), proviso. Registration constitutes notice of the order or petition to the purchaser.

[4] Section 36 (1), *supra*, p. 226.

[5] L.P.A. 1925, s. 28 (3). See *Re Gorringe and Brayton's Contract*, [1934] Ch. 614n ; *Re Brooker*, [1934] Ch. 610.

[6] *Ibid.*, s. 36 (2).

[7] *Cooper* v. *Critchley*, [1955] Ch. 431 ; [1955] 1 All E. R. 520 ; M. & B. p. 228.

share to a stranger [1] ; or if one of the tenants acquires an interest greater in quantum than that held by the other[2] ; or where there is an agreement between the joint tenants that one of them will purchase the interest of the other, even though that agreement is not in writing and not specifically enforceable.[3]

Notice of desire to sever.

The Law of Property Act 1925 added a new and very useful method of severance.

Section 36(2) provides in effect that :

If any tenant desires to sever the joint tenancy in equity, he may give to the other joint tenants a written notice[4] of such desire, whereupon he becomes entitled as tenant in common to his share of the profits of the land and of the purchase money after the land is sold.[5]

Suppose, for instance, that land is limited to A., B. and C. as joint tenants.

We know that this creates both a legal and an equitable joint tenancy. If C. dies without having dealt with his interest, A. and B. retain the legal estate as trustees for sale, and hold the equitable interest under the doctrine of survivorship, freed from the interest of C. But if in his lifetime C. gives notice in writing of his desire to sever, his equitable joint tenancy becomes an equitable tenancy in common, and A. and B. hold the legal estate upon trust to sell and to divide the proceeds between themselves as equitable joint tenants and the personal representatives of C. The equitable tenancy in common will continue to exist until either the sale is carried out, or the shares become vested in one person, or partition is effected.

Meaning of "party-wall."

Party-Walls. We must finally examine the effect of the legislation of 1925 upon party-walls. According to Fry, J., the term " party-wall " may mean [6] :

(*a*) a wall of which two adjoining owners are tenants in common ; or

(*b*) a wall divided vertically into two strips, one half of the

---

[1] *Supra*, p. 215.   [2] *Supra*, p. 216.

[3] *Burgess* v. *Rawnsley*, [1975] Ch. 429 ; [1975] 3 All E. R. 142 ; M. & B. p. 216.

[4] *Re 88 Berkeley Road, London N.W.9*, [1971] Ch. 648 ; [1971] 1 All E. R. 254 (notice properly served if sent by recorded delivery, even if not received by addressee. L.P.A. 1925, s. 196 (4).).

[5] *Re Draper's Conveyance* [1969] 1 Ch. 486 ; [1967] 3 All E. R. 853 ; M. & B. p. 212 (issue of summons held to amount to notice in writing under s. 36(2).) ; (1968) 84 L. Q. R. 462 (P. V. B.). Whether a unilateral act not amounting to notice under s. 36(2) can effect severance is a matter of dispute. *Burgess* v. *Rawnsley, supra*, at p. 215.

[6] *Watson* v. *Gray* (1880), 14 Ch. D. 192, 194–5.

thickness belonging to each of the neighbouring owners ; or

(c) a wall belonging entirely to one owner, but subject to an easement in the other to have it maintained as a dividing wall ; or

(d) a wall divided vertically into two equal strips, each strip being subject to a cross easement in favour of the owner of the other.

It may be said that *most* of the party-walls in this country come within the first class, that is, are held by the adjoining owners as tenants in common, and in view of this it is clear that the effect of the statutory alterations relating to concurrent interests would have been absurd had special provisions for party-walls not been added. The effect would have been to render the majority of such walls subject to a trust for sale !

It is therefore enacted [1] that a wall which under the old law would have been held by tenants in common shall be regarded as severed vertically as between the respective owners, and that the owner of each part shall have such rights to support and user over the other part as he would have had *qua* tenant in common under the old law. In other words, most party-walls now fall within the last class enumerated by FRY, J.[2]

SECTION III. THE MATRIMONIAL HOME
(A) OWNERSHIP

The matrimonial home occupies a most important part in family property law,[3] and in many cases it is the only substantial asset of the family.[4] If a husband and wife wish to own a home jointly, they may do so by creating an express trust for sale, under which it is conveyed to trustees (who may be themselves), who become joint tenants of the legal estate upon trust for sale for themselves, as either equitable joint tenants or equitable tenants in common. The terms of the trust may declare not only the nature of the equitable beneficial interests, but also the quantum of the interest which each spouse is to own.[5] This is an

---

[1] L.P.A. 1925, s. 38, Sched. I, Part V, see also s. 187 (2).

[2] For statutory modification of these rules see *e.g.* London Building Acts (Amendment) Act 1939, Part VI.

[3] See generally Bromley, *Family Law* (4th Edn.), pp. 375 *et. seq.* ; Cretney, *Principles of Family Law* (1974), pp. 144 *et seq.* ; Law Commission Working Paper, Family Property Law (Law Com. No. 42 1971), especially the review of the present law at pp. 52 *et seq.*

[4] 52% of married couples are owner occupiers. Todd and Jones, *Matrimonial Property* (1972), p. 9, cited Law Commission Family Law, First Paper on Family Property (Law Com. No. 52 1973).

[5] Fraud or mistake apart, this is conclusive *Wilson* v. *Wilson*, [1963] 1 W. L. R. 601 ; *Leake* v. *Bruzzi*, [1974] 2 All E. R. 1196, [1974] 1 W. L. R. 1528.

application of the machinery invented by the 1925 legislation for concurrent interests. But in some cases it may not be so simple. The quantum may not be declared. Further, the legal estate in the property may be conveyed to *one* spouse only (usually the husband), but the beneficial interest is shared between husband and wife. The first question to decide in this type of case is whether, according to the strict principles of trust law,[1] each of the spouses has an interest in equity ; if so, then the superstructure of the trust for sale is erected, and a statutory trust for sale comes into operation.

If husband and wife have made no express provision, there are two main situations in which a spouse may obtain a beneficial interest.

Contribution. If, say, the wife contributes part of the purchase money, then, unless there is evidence of a contrary intention, there is a resulting trust in equity under which the husband, as purchaser, holds the property in trust for himself and his wife to the extent of their respective contributions.[2] The contribution of the wife is not limited to a direct cash payment towards the purchase price. It may also be towards the initial deposit when the house is bought with the aid of a mortgage, or, in some circumstances, towards the payment of the mortgage instalments themselves.[3] The contribution may even be indirect, provided that it can be regarded as money's worth,[4] as, for instance, where a wife gave unpaid help in her husband's greengrocery business thereby saving the wages which he would have had to pay to an assistant.[5] Her services in running the home do not, however, suffice.

---

[1] *Gissing* v. *Gissing*, [1971] A.C. 886 ; [1970] 2 All E. R. 780 ; *Cowcher* v. *Cowcher* [1972] 1 W. L. R. 425 ; [1972] 1 All E. R. 943. *Cf. Eves* v. *Eves*, [1975] 1 W. L. R. 1338 ; [1975] 3 All E. R. 768 ; *Re Densham*, [1975] 1 W. L. R. 1519, which favour a constructive trust as a solution. See generally Snell, *Principles of Equity* (27th Edn.), pp. 175–179, 520–530. These rules apply to property disputes between parties who have broken off their engagement to marry. Law Reform (Miscellaneous Provisions) Act 1970, s. 2(1).

[2] See e.g. *Gissing* v. *Gissing*, *supra* ; *Cowcher* v. *Cowcher*, *supra* ; *Heseltine* v. *Heseltine*, [1972] 1 W. L. R. 342 ; [1971] 1 All E. R. 952. The presumption of the resulting trust may also be rebutted by the presumption of advancement that a beneficial gift was intended. This presumption is applicable where the *husband* provides the purchase-money, and is itself rebuttable. The presumption of advancement appears to be of little weight to-day. *Pettitt* v. *Pettitt*, [1970] A.C. 777 ; [1969] 2 All E. R. 385 ; *Falconer* v. *Falconer*, [1970] 1 W. L. R. 1333 ; [1970] 3 All E. R. 449.

[3] See Cretney *op. cit.*, pp. 156–157.

[4] *Wachtel* v. *Wachtel* [1973] Fam. 72, at p. 92 *per* Lord DENNING, M.R.

[5] *Nixon* v. *Nixon*, [1969] 1 W. L. R. 1676 ; [1969] 3 All E. R. 1133. See also *Muetzel* v. *Muetzel*, [1970] 1 W. L. R. 188 ; [1970] 1 All E. R. 443 ; *Falconer*, *supra* ; *Davis* v. *Vale*, [1971] 1 W. L. R. 1022 ; [1971] 2 All E. R. 1021 ; *Hargrave* v. *Newton*, [1971] 1 W. L. R. 161 ; [1971] 3 All E. R. 886 ; *Hazell* v. *Hazell*, [1972] 1 W. L. R. 301 ; [1972] 1 All E. R. 923 ; *Cowcher* v. *Cowcher*, *supra* ; *Farquharson* v. *Farquharson* (1971), 115 Sol. Jo. 444. For mistresses, see *Richards* v. *Dove*, [1974] 1 All E. R. 883 ; *Eves* v. *Eves*, *supra*, 119 ; *cf. Cooke* v. *Head*, [1972] 1 W. L. R. 518 ; [1972] 2 All E. R. 38 ; *Tanner* v. *Tanner*, [1975] 1 W. L. R. 1346 ; [1975] 3 All E. R. 776.

Improvements. Section 37 of the Matrimonial Proceedings and Property Act 1970 declares that a husband or wife who has made a substantial contribution in money or money's worth to the improvement of real or personal property in which either or both of them has a beneficial interest, will be treated as having a share (or an enlarged share) in that beneficial interest.[1] This is subject to any express or implied agreement to the contrary. The contributor is entitled to any share agreed, or in default as may seem in all the circumstances just.

Finally, it must be emphasized that a wife cannot claim any property interest in the matrimonial home during the marriage or on the death of her husband, unless she has made a financial contribution which entitles her to rely on the strict principles of trust law. However, if the marriage breaks down, and there is a decree of divorce, nullity of marriage or judicial separation, the court is given the widest discretionary powers under the Matrimonial Causes Act 1973 to order a distribution of the spouses' property.[2] In particular, section 25 (1) (f) of the Act requires the court to have regard to

" the contributions made by each of the parties to the welfare of the family, including any contributions made by looking after the home or caring for the family."

(B) OCCUPATION

Separate from any beneficial interest which a spouse may own is the right of occupation given by the Matrimonial Homes Act 1967.[3] This gives to one spouse, A, a right of occupation of a dwelling-house which the other spouse, B, " is entitled to occupy by virtue of any estate or interest or contract or by virtue of any enactment[4] giving him or her the right to remain in occupation." [5] More specifically, if in occupation, A has a right not to be evicted or excluded by B without the leave of the court ; if not in occupation, A has a right with the leave of the court to enter and occupy

---

[1] *Davis* v. *Vale, supra* ; *Harnett* v. *Harnett*, [1973] Fam. 156, at p. 167 ; affirmed [1974] 1 W. L. R. 219 ; [1974] 1 All E. R. 764 ; *Kowalczuk* v. *Kowalczuk*, [1973] 1 W. L. R. 930 ; [1973] 2 All E. R. 1042 ; *Griffiths* v. *Griffiths*, [1974] 1 W. L. R. 1350 ; [1974] 1 All E. R. 932 ; *Samuels (WA)'s Trustee* v. *Samuels*, (1975) 233 Estates Gazette 148.   See (1975) 125 N. L. J. 20 (V. Chapman).

[2] Replacing Matrimonial Proceedings and Property Act 1970.   Where this Act applies, it is inappropriate to make a separate award for improvements under s. 37.   *Griffiths* v. *Griffiths, supra*.   For the relationship between the two jurisdictions generally, see (1974), 118 Sol. Jo. 431 (S. M. Cretney).

[3] See generally the discussion of the Act by MEGARRY, J. in *Wroth* v. *Tyler*, [1974] Ch. 30 ; [1973] 1 All E. R. 897 ; (1968), 32 *Conv.* (N.S.) 85 (F. R. Crane) ; Bromley. *Family Law*, pp. 386 *et seq.* ; Cretney, *Principles of Family Law* (1974), pp. 168–177 ; M. & B. pp. 38–41.

[4] *E.g.* Rent Act 1968.   *Penn* v. *Dunn*, [1970] 2 Q. B. 686 ; [1970] 2 All E. R. 858.

[5] S. 1 (1).

the house.[1]   The right is only available to A, where A is " not so entitled," or has merely an equitable interest in the dwelling-house or in its proceeds of sale.[2]   As we have seen, such an interest may arise from A's contribution to its acquisition or improvement.[3] The court is given wide discretionary powers to make such order as it thinks just and reasonable.[4]   The right is a charge on B's estate, and has priority, as if it were an equitable interest, from the date of B's acquisition of his estate, or of the marriage or of the Act,[5] whichever is the latest.[6]   It ends on the death of B or on the termination of the marriage, unless the court makes an order to the contrary during the marriage.[7]

This right is registrable as a Class F land charge,[8] or, in the case of registered land, by means of a notice or caution.[9]   It is not an overriding interest, even if the spouse is in actual occupation.[10]

A may register his charge without notifying B of the registration, and thus cause difficulty where B later enters into a contract to sell the dwelling-house in ignorance of the registration.   Further may register after B has contracted to sell and thus make it impossible for B to perform the contract, at the cost of substantial damages for its breach.[11]

(C) LAW COMMISSION FIRST REPORT ON FAMILY PROPERTY (1973)[12]

The report recommends the introduction of a principle of co-ownership under which, in the absence of agreement to the contrary, a matrimonial home would be shared equally between husband and wife.[13]   " There would be great advantages. . . . It would reflect the realities of family life, in which husband and wife regard the home as ' theirs ' without considering the legal title or the principles of trust law.   It would apply during the subsistence

---

[1] S. 1 (1) (*a*), (*b*).   *Rutherford* v. *Rutherford*, [1970] 1 W. L. R. 1479; [1970] 3 All E. R. 422 (husband not in occupation may not register a charge until he has obtained leave of court under s. 1 (1) (*b*)).

[2] S. (1), (9).   Matrimonial Proceedings and Property Act 1970, s. 38, reversing *Gurasz* v. *Gurasz*, [1970] P. 11 ; [1969] 3 All E. R. 822.

[3] See Law Commission Report on Family Provision in Matrimonial Proceedings, 1969 (Law Com. No. 25), para. 59.

[4] S. 1 (3).   For the power of the court to regulate the occupational rights of a spouse under s. 1 (2), see *Tarr* v. *Tarr*, [1973] A. C. 254.

[5] January 1st, 1968.

[6] S. 2 (1).

[7] S. 2 (2).

[8] L.C.A. 1972, s. 2 (7).   In 1973–1974 these averaged 252 a week.

[9] Matrimonial Homes Act 1967, s. 2 (7).   The corresponding average was 125.   Report on H.M. Land Registry 1974–1975, para. 13.

[10] *Ibid.*

[11] *Watts* v. *Waller*, [1973] Q. B. 153 ; [1972] 3 All E. R. 257 ; *Wroth* v. *Tyler*, *supra* ; (1974) 38 Conv. N.S. 110, (1975) 39 Conv. N.S. 78 (D. J. Hayton) ; (1974) C. L. P. 76 (D. G. Barnsley).

[12] Law Com. No. 52.

[13] *Ibid.*, para. 30.

of the marriage and would give security of ownership to the spouse who is now considered by law as having no proprietary interest in the home. It would recognise that each spouse contributes to the marriage and to the family and that the joint efforts of both make possible the purchase and maintenance of the home. It would eliminate the uncertainties of litigation in which ownership rights are established by proof of financial contribution." [1]

SECTION IV. REGISTERED LAND

Where the trust for sale machinery of the Law of Property Act 1925 is used for the creation of concurrent interests, the restriction procedure operates, and there is no difficulty. [2] But, as we have seen, a sole registered proprietor may nevertheless be a trustee, as where a husband and wife both contribute towards the purchase price of the matrimonial home, and the transfer is taken in the name of the husband who becomes the sole proprietor. [3] In this case, the husband should apply for a restriction to be entered on the register. If he does not, the wife may do so, if the land certificate is produced at the Registry or is already on deposit there, for instance, because there is a registered charge [4]; otherwise she may enter a caution. [5] Failing an entry on the register, a purchaser takes free from the interests of the beneficiaries under the trust, unless they are overriding under section 70 (1) (*g*). [6] It would seem that an interest in possession under a settlement or a trust for sale would come within paragraph (*g*). Such an interest under a settlement, however, is expressly excluded by the Act. [7] There is no such provision in the case of an interest under a trust for sale. It would seem therefore that this would qualify[8]; but to make a distinction between these two interests is surprising, and has been described as an anomalous and probably accidental result. [9]

As we have seen, a spouse's right of occupation under the

---

[1] *Ibid.*, para. 25. The Law Commission will publish a further report with detailed recommendations and a draft bill. Eighth Annual Report 1973–1974 (Law Com. No. 64) para. 25. See Law Commission Working Paper No. 42 (1971) Part I for details of this suggested matrimonial home trust.

[2] *Supra*, p. 203.

[3] *Supra*, p. 232. See Ruoff and Roper, ch. 37, especially pp. 790–791. For the effect in unregistered land, see *Caunce* v. *Caunce*, [1969] 1 W. L. R. 286; [1969] 1 All E. R. 722. *Infra*, p. 796.

[4] *Infra*, p. 713.

[5] *Elias* v. *Mitchell*, [1972] Ch. 652; [1972] 2 All E. R. 153; (1973) 117 Sol. Jo. 115, 136 (G. Miller). L.R.A. 1925, s. 54 (1) proviso. See *infra*, p. 782.

[6] *Infra*, p. 773.

[7] L.R.A. 1921, s. 86 (2); *supra*, p. 196, n. 6.

[8] The occupation of a wife, however, may be not her occupation, but that of her husband. See *Hodgson* v. *Marks*, [1971] Ch. 892, at p. 934; *Caunce* v. *Caunce*, *Supra*.

[9] (1958) 22 Conv. (N.S.) 14, at p. 24 (F. R. Crane). See also Barnsley, pp. 48, 50, 316; M. & B. pp. 221–222.

Matrimonial Homes Act 1967[1] may be protected by the entry of a notice or caution. This right of occupation is not an over-riding interest.[2]

---

[1] Matrimonial Homes Act 1967, s. 2 (7).
[2] *Supra*, p. 234.

CHAPTER III

ENTAILED INTERESTS

SUMMARY

SECTION I. HISTORY

Introductory Note. The estate known to the common law as a conditional fee was the precursor of the estate tail. About the year 1200 it was becoming a common practice to limit lands to a man and a special or restricted class of his heirs, as for instance :— *Conditional fee precursor of estate tail.*

1. to a man and " the heirs of his body " ; or
2. to a husband and wife and the heirs springing from their marriage ; or
3. to a woman and the heirs of her body—a form of gift that was called a *maritagium*.[1]

Meaning of conditional fee.

As the object of such a gift was to provide for a man's descendants, it was an understood thing that if the donee or one of his issue to whom the land descended died without leaving any heirs of the class specified in the instrument of creation, the estate, being no longer required for the maintenance of the family, should revert to the donor, and should not, like a fee simple, pass to the general heirs of the donee.[2]   The courts, however, animated probably by a desire to render land freely alienable and to this end to prevent it from being irrevocably ear-marked for a particular family, took an entirely different view of the matter, for they held that if a grant were made to A. and the heirs of his body, or to him and any similarly restricted class of heirs, A. could make an out-and-out alienation of his estate, binding on his own heirs and on the donor, as soon as a child of the class indicated was born to him.   They said that the effect of such a gift was to confer upon A. a conditional fee, that is to say, an absolute fee simple, conditional however upon the birth of issue capable of inheriting the estate according to the terms of the original gift.   When once that condition was satisfied, even though the child died the next minute, A. was in as favourable a position as if the lands had originally been granted to him in fee simple, for at common law a condition once performed is utterly gone; but if the condition was not fulfilled by the birth of issue, then on A.'s death the estate reverted to the donor and his heirs.[3]

Statute De Donis.

Statute *De Donis*.   But this rule, which meant in effect that the donee could alienate the land and thus defeat both the right of his issue to succeed to the estate and the right of the donor to take the estate back if issue already born became extinct, was not popular.   As early as 1258 there was an outcry against a doctrine that ran so contrary to the expressed intention of donors, and the result of this feeling was the passing in 1285 of the famous statute *De Donis Conditionalibus*.[4]   This enacted that the intention of the donor according as it was manifestly expressed in the original gift, should thenceforth be

---

[1] Holdsworth, *History of English Law*, vol. iii. pp. 74, 111; Plucknett, *Legislation of Edward I*, pp. 125–131.

[2] If the gift took the form of what was called *liberum maritagium*, the rule was that after the land had descended three times there should no longer be any reverter to the donor and his heirs.   Thus, the third heir became entitled in fee simple ; Plucknett, *op cit.*, pp. 126–9.

[3] Pollock and Maitland, *History of English Law* (2nd Edn.), vol. ii, pp. 16–19 ; Co. Litt. 19a ; Challis, *Law of Real Property* (3rd Edn.), pp. 263–8.

[4] Statute of Westminster II. (1285), set out in full, Digby, *History of the Law of Real Property*, p. 226.

observed, so that those to whom the land was given should have no power to alienate it, but that it should pass to their issue, or to the giver or his heirs if such issue failed, either by an absolute default of issue or, after the birth of issue, by its subsequent extinction.[1]

The result of this statute was the appearance of a new kind of fee or inheritable estate, called a fee tail, or in Latin *feodum talliatum*, and so called because the quantum of the estate was " cut down " in the sense that, unlike the case of the fee simple, the right to inherit was restricted to the class of heirs specially mentioned in the gift, and was not available to the heirs-general of the donee.[2]

> Origin of fee tail.

The land could not be disposed of by the tenant in tail, it could not be seized in satisfaction of his debts after it had come into the hands of his successors, and it was not forfeitable for treason or felony—a fact which, in those disturbed times, was regarded by the Crown as a serious defect.[3]

Special remedies were given to the issue and to the donor for the recovery of the land in case the form of the original gift was not observed, and these were called respectively the *writ of formedon* in the descender and the *writ of formedon* in the reverter.[4]

> Remedies of donor and issue.

There was thus set up an entailed interest in the true and proper sense of that term, that is to say, an interest in land that was bound to descend from one generation to another to the issue of the tenant, and which could not by any means whatsoever be removed from the family so long as any lineal heirs of the class specified were in existence. It was an unbarrable entail, since neither the right of the issue to succeed, nor the right of the donor and his heirs to take on failure of issue, could be barred or taken away.[5] This state of affairs continued for some 200 years after the Statute *De Donis*, but the statute, instead of being a blessing calculated to ensure the stability of families, proved to be one of the most mischievous institutions in the realm. In a famous passage Blackstone has described some of its effects :[6]

" Children grew disobedient when they knew they could not be set aside ; farmers were ousted of their leases made by tenants in tail ; for, if such leases had been valid, then, under colour of long leases, the issue might have been virtually disinherited ; creditors were defrauded of their debts, for if tenant in tail could have charged his estate with their payment, he might also have defeated his issue, by mortgaging

> Blackstone on the evils of unbarrable entails.

---

[1] See Challis, *Law of Real Property* (3rd Edn.), p. 228.
[2] Litt., s. 18 ; Challis, *op. cit.* (3rd Edn.), p. 60.
[3] First Report of Real Property Commission, 1829, p. 22.
[4] Holdsworth, *History of English Law*, vol. ii. p. 350.
[5] This apparently was not the intention of the draftsman of the statute. What was intended was that the land should be inalienable only until the third heir had entered, after which it could be alienated out of the family ; Plucknett, *Legislation of Edward I*, pp. 131–5.
[6] *Commentaries*, vol. ii., p. 116.

it for as much as it was worth ; innumerable latent entails were produced to deprive purchasers of the lands they had fairly bought, of suits in consequence of which our ancient books are full ; and treasons were encouraged, as estates tail were not liable to forfeiture longer than for the tenant's life. So that they were justly branded as the source of new contentions and mischiefs unknown to the common law, and almost universally considered as the common grievance of the realm. But as the nobility were always fond of this statute, because it preserved their family estates from forfeiture, there was little hope of procuring repeal by the legislature . . .''

Statute evaded.

Methods of barring Estates Tail. Although the legislature did not step in to remedy a grievance that appears to have borne so heavily upon the community, the ingenuity of lawyers finally—and at least as early as 1472—contrived to discover means whereby estates tail could be barred and converted into estates in fee simple, free from the succession rights of heirs and from the rights of those persons who were entitled to take upon a failure or extinction of heirs. The actual methods invented are now a matter of ancient history, and it must suffice here to state their names and their general effect.

Evasion by common recovery.

1. **Common Recovery.** The most usual method was *to suffer a common recovery.* In the earliest days of its history a common recovery was a collusive real action which a collaborator (called the *demandant*) brought against the tenant in tail for the recovery of the land entailed. The tenant in tail did not raise a substantial plea to the claim preferred against him, but stated, contrary to the truth, that he had obtained the land by conveyance from one X., who, at the time of the conveyance, had warranted for himself and his heirs that the title granted to the tenant in tail was a good one. X., who was an accomplice of the parties, admitted the warranty by disappearing from court. The court thereupon proceeded to deliver judgment, that on the one hand the demandant should recover the entailed lands for an estate in fee simple, and that on the other the tenant in tail should recover lands of equal value from X.

Effect of common recovery.

Now the effect of this collusive action was to defeat the rights both of the tenant's issue and of the persons entitled on failure of issue, because if lands of equal value had actually been recovered from X., which they never were, they would have replaced the original entailed estate and would have descended in the same manner. Ostensibly this was so, but none of the untrue allegations made in the course of the proceedings was traversable, and therefore all that the persons entitled after the death of the tenant acquired was a judgment enforceable against a man of straw. The court was not prepared to tolerate a plea that a judgment, solemnly pronounced, was in effect nugatory.[1]

After delivery of judgment the demandant would convey either the fee simple or its value to the former tenant in tail.

2. **Levy of a Fine.** The second method was to levy a fine. A fine, which from the earliest times had been regarded as the most sacred and efficacious form of conveyance known to the law,[2] was in substance a conveyance of land but in form an action.[3] It was an amicable composition or agreement of an action, made with the leave of the court, whereby the lands in question were acknowledged to belong to one of the parties, and it derived its name from the fact that it put an end (Lat. *finis*) to the action.[4] One of the purposes for which it was used was to bar an estate tail. The tenant in tail covenanted to sell the fee simple to a collaborator, and when he was sued by the latter in an action of covenant he decided to capitulate, and with the leave of the court a concord was drawn up acknowledging that the lands belonged to the plaintiff. *Evasion by fine.*

From one point of view the levying of a fine was not so effective as the suffering of a recovery, since it barred the rights only of the tenant's issue (thus setting up what is called a " base fee "), while a recovery barred not only the issue, but also everybody who became entitled to the estate on failure of issue. On the other hand, a fine, which was a personal action, enabled a tenant in tail who was not for the moment tenant in possession, *e.g.* *Difference between fine and common recovery.*

> where there was a grant to A. for life and after his death to B. in tail,

to bar his own issue without the necessity of obtaining the possessor's collaboration. In such circumstances, a *common recovery* was impossible unless the aid of the tenant for life, A., was obtained, because the proceedings reproduced the stages of a genuine action, and one of the fundamental rules of procedure was that a real action could be brought only against the person actually seised of the land.

Recoveries and fines, which even in their origin were collusive actions, gradually became wholly fictitious. Only formal matters *Abolition of recoveries and fines.*

---

[1] For a full account see Blackstone, vol. ii, pp. 357 *et seq.* ; Cruise, *Digest* Tit. xxxvi ; Burton, *Real Property* (8th Edn.), paras. 682–697 ; Pollock, *The Land Laws,* pp. 80–9 ; Digby, *History of the Law of Real Property,* pp. 251–4 ; First Report of Real Property Commission, 1829, pp. 21–3 ; Holdsworth, *History of English Law,* vol. iii, pp. 118 *et seq.* ; Simpson, *Introduction to the History of Land Law,* pp. 118 *et seq.*

[2] Holdsworth, *History of English Law,* vol. iii. p. 239.

[3] Pollock and Maitland, *History of English Law* (2nd Edn.), vol. ii. p. 94.

[4] Blackstone, vol. ii. p. 349; Challis, *Law of Real Property* (3rd Edn.), p. 304.

were transacted in court. If a tenant in tail desired to bar his entail, all that he did was to instruct his solicitor to suffer a common recovery. But the solicitor, in carrying out the instructions, did not simply frame a deed expressing the tenant's intention, but was obliged to prepare a long and complicated document that recited all the stages and events of an action which was supposed, contrary to fact, to have been litigated. Moreover, the fees that would have been payable had the action been actually brought were still payable. The result was that to convert a fee tail into a fee simple was a tedious and expensive transaction, and one which, owing to the complicated and exceedingly difficult state of the law, required an expert for its completion, and even then often failed to produce a sound title. The Real Property Commissioners, in their Report issued in 1829, stated :

" there is no object, however complicated, that could not be effected by a simple instrument, expressing in clear and intelligible language the intentions of the parties."

and the result of their recommendations was the passing of the Fines and Recoveries Act 1833, which abolished both recoveries and fines, and introduced a simple and straightforward method by which an estate tail might be barred.[1]

SECTION II. DIFFERENT CLASSES OF ENTAILED INTERESTS

SUMMARY

Introductory Note. We have already seen that an entailed interest is one that is given to a person and after his death to a specified class of that person's heirs. The different classes of entailed interests depend upon the terms of the instrument of gift and vary according as the estate is descendible to the heirs of the donee by any spouse or by a particular spouse, and also according as the heirs are restricted as to sex or not.

---

[1] *Infra*, p. 262.

There are two main classes of entailed interests.

 (1) Interests in tail general.
 (2) Interests in tail special.

We will deal with each of these separately.

(1) INTERESTS IN TAIL GENERAL

How they arise. An interest in tail general is the widest Estate tail type of entailed interest. Such an interest arises when land is general. limited to

 A. and the heirs of his body begotten,

without any restriction either as to the wife upon whose body the heirs are to be begotten, or as to the sex of the heirs who are to take.[1] It matters not how many times A. marries, for any child by any wife is eligible to succeed. If the entailed interest is not barred by the tenant during his lifetime nor disposed of by his will it still descends according to the old canons of descent which were formerly applicable to all inheritable fees,[2] but which were abolished by the Administration of Estates Act 1925, so far as regards the fee simple.

 The canons of descent that concern an entailed interest are Subject the following[3] :— to old
                           canons of
                           descent.

 1. DESCENT IS TRACED FROM THE LAST PURCHASER, *i.e.* from the original donee in tail.[4] *Purchaser* in this context denotes anyone who acquires an estate by act of parties as distinct from act of law.[5] In this sense of the word an owner of land is a purchaser unless he has inherited it—or, in other words, unless it has descended upon him as a result of the last owner's intestacy. Practically the one and only way in which a person acquires an entailed interest nowadays is by virtue of a family settlement, and if by deed or will lands are settled upon X. for life and after his death on his son and the heirs of his body, the son is a purchaser with regard to the entailed interest. When the son (A.) dies intestate, this first rule of descent requires us to look for *his* nearest lineal heir:

---

 [1] Litt., ss. 14, 15 ; Blackstone, vol. ii. p. 113.
 [2] L.P.A. 1925, s. 130 (4).
 [3] The canons are those that affected the descent of a fee simple before 1926 (*infra*, pp. 867–70), except those that relate to ancestors and collaterals.
 [4] Blackstone. vol. ii. p. 222.
 [5] It is a term, however, that has no uniform meaning ; see *I. R. Comrs.* v. v. *Gribble*, [1913] 3 K. B. 212, where at p. 218, Buckley, L. J., said : " ' Purchaser,' as it seems to me, may mean any one of four things. First, it may bear what has been called the vulgar or commercial meaning ; purchaser may mean a buyer for money. Secondly, it may also include a person who becomes a purchaser, for money's worth, which would include the case of an exchange. Thirdly, it may mean a purchaser for valuable consideration, which need not be money or money's worth, but may be, say, a covenant on the consideration of marriage. Fourthly it may bear that which in the language of real property lawyers is its technical meaning, namely a person who does not take by descent." See *infra*, p. 253.

and if A.'s eldest son B. takes the estate by descent and then him-self dies intestate, the rule demands that we should look for the nearest heir not of B., but of A., because B., having himself taken by descent, is not a purchaser. Of course the son of B., if he has one, will be entitled as heir.

2. PRIORITY OF MALES. An entailed interest must descend to the lineal issue of the last purchaser, and the males of this issue rank before females of equal degree.[1]

3. PRIMOGENITURE. Where there are two or more males of the same degree, the eldest takes the entire interest to the ex-clusion of the rest ; but if there are no males, but two or more females of the same degree, all the females inherit together and are called coparceners.[2]

4. REPRESENTATION. Lineal descendants, *ad infinitum*, of any person deceased represent their ancestor, that is, occupy the same position as he himself would have occupied had he been living. Suppose, for instance, that A., who is tenant in tail, has two sons, X. the elder and Y. the younger, and X. dies before A., but leaves a son Z. On the death of A. the interest will pass to the grandson Z. and not to the son Y.[3]

So where there is an interest in tail general limited to

A. and the heirs of his body,

and A. dies intestate having failed to bar the entail, his eldest son by his first wife will take first. If the eldest son has predeceased A. leaving no children, the second son of A., or such son's repre-sentative if he is dead, will take, and so on through the sons in the order of their seniority. Failing sons or children of sons, the daughters of A. will share equally as coparceners.

Curtesy still applies to entailed interests.

Curtesy. Before 1926 a husband was entitled in certain circumstances to a life interest in the whole of the land of which the wife died seised in fee simple or in tail. He became what was called a " tenant by the curtesy."[4] Curtesy has been abolished with regard to all interests except an entailed interest,[5] and there-fore the subject can only now be of importance when a female *tenant in tail* dies intestate.

Position after 1925.

The pre-requisites of this life interest are that the wife should have been actually[6] and solely[7] seised of the entailed interest, and that issue of the marriage capable of inheriting the land should

---

[1] Blackstone, vol. ii. pp. 212–14.
[2] *Ibid.*, vol. ii. p. 214. As to coparceners see *supra*, pp. 219–220.
[3] *Ibid.*, vol. ii, pp. 216–20.
[4] Or more particularly, by the Curtesie of England. Co. Litt. 35.
[5] A.E.A. 1925, s. 45 (1) (*b*) ; L.P.A. 1925, s. 130 (4). But curtesy in respect of a fee simple may still, though rarely, arise under the A.E.A. 1925, s. 51 (2). This provides that the old rules of descent shall apply to realty (excluding chattels real), to which a lunatic, living on January 1st, 1926 and dying after that date without having recovered testamentary capacity, is entitled.
[6] *I.e.* by actual occupation or by receipt of rents and profits. This was seisin in deed as distinct from seisin in law. *Parks* v. *Hegan*, [1903] 2 I. R.643.
[7] Co. Litt. 29*a* ; *Doe d. Neville* v. *Rivers* (1797), 7 Term Rep. 276.

have been born alive within her lifetime.[1] To satisfy the last requirement it is sufficient that a child should have been actually born alive though it may have died the next moment,[2] but it is essential that the child should be a person capable of succeeding to the land. Thus if there is a limitation to a woman and the heirs male of her body, and she bears a daughter only, her husband cannot take by curtesy.[3]

At common law once the requirements had been satisfied and an estate by the curtesy had vested in the husband, it could not be divested without his concurrence, for a wife could not alienate her freeholds except by a fine to which her husband was a party. The recognition, first by equity and in 1883 by statute, that a married woman could freely dispose of what was called her *separate property*,[4] revolutionized the position, for curtesy could be claimed only in non-separate property or in separate property that had not been alienated. At the present day non-separate property is extinct, and a new power of disposing of entailed interests by will was introduced by the Law of Property Act 1925. Hence it is only in the one case where a married woman dies intestate in respect of an entailed interest that her husband will become tenant by the curtesy.[5]

Interests in tail male general. This arises where lands are limited to

> A. and the heirs *male* of his body begotten,

the factor in which this species of estate differs from an interest in tail general being that only male heirs are to succeed.[6] Sons by any wife are capable of inheriting, and so are any other male issue claiming continuously through male issue, but daughters and their issue, whether male or female, can never inherit.

Interests in tail female general. This is analogous to the last interest except that the only heirs entitled to take are females. Though this is a possible form of limitation, it never arises in practice.[7]

(2) INTERESTS IN TAIL SPECIAL.

The characteristic of the remaining entailed interests is that by the words of the instrument of creation their descent is restricted to the heirs of the body of two specified persons, and not

[margin: Characteristic of special entails.*]*

---

[1] Litt. ss 35–52.

[2] Blackstone, vol. ii. p. 127.

[3] Co. Litt. 19a. As to curtesy in general, see Blackstone, vol. ii. pp. 126 *et seq.*; (1927) 43 L. Q. R. 87 (F. E. Farrer).

[4] *Infra*, pp. 923–4.

[5] *Hope* v. *Hope*, [1892] 2 Ch. 336. Law Reform (Married Women and Tortfeasors) Act, 1935, s. 4 (1) (a).

[6] Litt. s. 2 ; Blackstone, vol. ii. p. 114.

[7] Co. Litt. 25a. ; Hargrave's note.

to the heirs of one, as in the cases described above. Such an estate may be limited either to one donee, *e.g.* :

> to H. and the heirs begotten by him on the body of W.,

or to two donees, *e.g.* :

> to H. and W. and the heirs of their two bodies begotten.[1]

In both cases it will be seen that it is not the heirs of H. by any wife who are capable of inheriting the interest, but only the children and their issue who can trace their descent from the particular wife W. If the limitation is to

> H. and the heirs begotten by him on the body of his wife W.,

H. has an interest in tail special and the wife has nothing.[2] But the effect of a limitation to H. and W. and the heirs of their two bodies begotten varies according to the relative positions of H. and W. If W. is the wife of H. or a person whom he may lawfully marry, the effect is to vest a joint interest in tail special in H. and W. ;[3] but if H. and W. are persons who may not lawfully intermarry, by reason, for instance, of consanguinity, the limitation makes them joint tenants for life with separate inheritances.[4] That means that if H. dies first and has issue, W. becomes sole tenant for life, but that on the death of W. the issue of H. take one half and the issue of W. the other half as tenants in common in tail.[5] The result will be the same if, though capable of intermarrying, H. and W. do not actually intermarry.

After what has been said it will be sufficient to give the appropriate words of limitation for granting the remaining species of entailed interests :—

Interests in tail male special. Grant to

> A. and his heirs male which he shall beget on the body of his wife X. ;

or to

> A. and X. and the heirs male of their two bodies begotten.[6]

Interests in tail female special. This arises from the same limitation as that just described, with the substitution of female for male.[7]

Tenant in tail after possibility.

Interest in tail after possibility of issue extinct. An entailed interest special may by implication of law give rise to what is called an entailed interest after possibility of issue extinct. If lands are given to a man and his wife, or to the man or to the

---

[1] Litt. s. 16 ; Preston on Estates, vol. ii. p. 413.
[2] Litt. s. 29.   [3] Co. Litt. 20*b* ; 25*b*.
[4] Litt. 283 ; Preston, vol. ii. p. 417.   [5] Co. Litt. 182*a*.
[6] Litt. 25.
[7] For the whole of this section see Challis, *Law of Real Property* (3rd Edn.), pp. 290–5.

wife solely, in special tail, and one of them, or the designated spouse, dies before issue has been born, the survivor is termed a *tenant in tail after possibility*; and likewise if one dies leaving issue, but the other survives the issue.[1] In both these cases it will be seen that, owing to the premature death of one of the persons from whose body the appropriate heirs are to proceed, it is impossible that any person should become entitled to succeed to the interest in accordance with the terms of the original gift. The possibility of the right class of heirs coming into being no longer exists, and therefore the survivor is said to be a tenant after possibility. Such a person is virtually in the position of a tenant for life and he is not entitled to bar the entail.[2] He is given the statutory powers of a tenant for life by the Settled Land Act 1925.[3]

(3) WORDS OF LIMITATION

We have now to consider what words of limitation must be used in order to create an entailed interest. Owing to the way in which the matter was dealt with by the Law of Property Act 1925, it is unfortunately necessary to discuss the rules which obtained under the previous law. The examples that have been given above of the various classes of entailed interests indicate the general nature of the proper words of limitation, and a short treatment of the subject will suffice here.

(A) CREATION BY DEED BEFORE 1926

The first point is to ascertain the proper words of limitation necessary before 1926 for the creation of an entailed interest by deed. *(margin: Deeds before 1926.)*

1. The requirement of common law here was that the word *heirs* must be used and not such analogous expressions as *seed, offspring, descendants, issue* and so on.[4] The effect of a grant, for example, to " A. and his issue " was to confer upon A. a mere life estate. *(margin: Word "heirs" essential.)*

2. The next requirement was that some expression denoting that the inheritance was to pass to the direct descendants of A. should be used, and the surest phrase for this purpose was *of his body*. A grant to " A. and the heirs of his body " always conferred an entailed interest on A., but common law, though insisting upon the use of the word *heirs*, was not so exacting with regard to this second requirement, and was *(margin: Lineal heirs.)*

---

[1] Litt. 32.
[2] Fines and Recoveries Act 1833, s. 18 ; see *infra*, p. 261.
[3] S.L.A. 1925, s. 20 (1) (i).
[4] Co. Litt. 20 *a, b* ; Blackstone, vol. ii. p. 115.

satisfied with any words which expressly or by implication showed that the heirs were to issue from the body of A. Thus such expressions as

" of his flesh,"
" from him proceeding," or
" which he shall beget of his wife "

were sufficient for the purpose.[1]

Before January 1st, 1882, if the appropriate words of limitation as set out above were not adopted in a deed, the result was to confer a life estate upon the grantee, but the Conveyancing Act of 1881 [2] provided that in deeds executed after that date it should be sufficient to use the words *in tail* instead of *heirs of the body*, and the words *in tail male* or *in tail female* instead of *heirs male* or *heirs female* of the body.[3]

(B) CREATION BY WILL BEFORE 1926

Wills before
1926.

Greater latitude

allowed.

Greater latitude of terminology was, however, open to testators. It is more difficult to lay down hard and fast rules as to what words would, and what words would not, have created a certain interest when they were used in a testamentary as distinct from an *inter vivos* instrument, because the general principle of construction for wills is that the intention of the testator must be ascertained and given effect to, no matter what language he may have adopted, and as the *indicia* of intention vary infinitely and do not always impress judges in an equal degree, it is often dangerous to dogmatize that this or that expression will raise any particular estate. But at any rate we are on sure ground in saying that less formal language would create an entailed interest in a will than in a deed, and in fact any expressions that indicated an intention to give the devisee an estate of inheritance, descendible to his lineal as distinct from his collateral heirs, conferred an entailed interest upon him.[4]

Thus devises to

" A. and his seed," [5]
" A. and his offspring," [6]
" A. and his family according to seniority " [7]
" A. and his issue," [8]
" A. and his posterity " [9]

---

[1] Co. Litt. 20*b*.   [2] S. 51.
[3] For criticism see Challis, *Law of Real Property* (3rd Edn.), pp. 297–8.
[4] *Jarman on Wills* (8th Edn.), p. 1825.
[5] Co. Litt. 9*b*.
[6] *Young* v. *Davies* (1863), 2 Dr. & Sm. 167.
[7] *Lucas* v. *Goldsmid* (1861), 29 Beav. 657.
[8] *Oxford University* v. *Clifton* (1759), 1 Eden 473.
[9] *Wild's Case* (1599), 6 Co. Rep. 17*a*.

have all, at one time and another, been held capable of passing an entailed interest when such a construction was consistent with the intention of the testator.

The same rule of construction was applied in the case of executory instruments *inter vivos*, that is, in instruments which do not finally express the limitations in technical language, but indicate their general nature and leave the settlor's intention to be carried out by apt phraseology. What are called " marriage articles " form the commonest example of an executory instrument. They constitute a contract by which an intending husband and wife specify in general the terms upon which they are willing to enter into a marriage settlement. Thus, if marriage articles provide for the limitation of an interest to the " issue " of the husband and wife, the presumed intention will be carried out in the formal settlement by the grant of an entailed interest to the first son of the marriage, with remainders in tail to the other children.[1]

Executory instruments.

A devise " to A. and his children," requires particular attention because of the *Rule in Wild's Case*[2] laid down in 1599.[3] The rule was that

The rule in Wild's Case.

> where realty was devised to 'A. and his children', and A. had no child *at the time of the devise*, the word children was *prima facie* construed as a word of limitation, with the result that A. acquired an estate tail.

There was some justification for this. The testator clearly intended children to take in any event, but since they were not in existence they could take nothing except through A. and he could transmit to them nothing unless he was given an estate of inheritance.[4]

The rule, however, was not inflexible and it was disregarded by the courts where it would operate to defeat the intention of the testator as gathered from other passages in the will.[5]

(C) Words of Limitation After 1925

We are now left with this question :—what words are necessary and sufficient to create an entailed interest in the case of a deed or will that comes into operation after 1925. Section 130 (1) of the Law of Property Act 1925 enacts as follows :

Law of Property Act 1925.

> An interest in tail . . . (in this Act referred to as " an entailed interest ") may be created by way of trust in any property, real or personal, but only by the like expressions as those by which before [1926], a similar estate tail could have been created *by deed* (not being an executory instrument) in freehold land.

---

[1] *A.-G.* v. *Bamfield* (1703), 2 Freeman 268.   [2] (1599), 6 Co. 17*a*.
[3] See *infra*, p. 252, n. 4.
[4] *Radcliffe* v. *Buckley* (1804), 10 Ves. 195, at p. 202, *per* Sir William Grant, M.R.
[5] *Byng* v. *Byng* (1862), 10 H. L. Cas, 171, at p. 178 ; *Grieve* v. *Grieve* (1867), L. R. 4 Eq. 180.

Effect of
the Act.

The result is that the law on the subject is more inflexible now than it was before 1926. The strict requirements of the common law applicable to deeds have been extended to wills. Thus, in both instruments the limitation must be to "A. in tail," or to "A. and the heirs of his body," except that in the last case any expressions will suffice that without expressly saying "of the body" indicate that the heirs are to issue from the body of A. The only exception to this rule is that a direction that personal property shall be enjoyed with land in which an entailed interest has already been created is sufficient to create a corresponding entailed interest in the personal property.[1]

On the other hand, informal expressions contained in the instrument which would not have been sufficient in a deed before 1926 to create an entailed interest, though they would have been sufficient in a will or executory instrument, no longer suffice to create an entailed interest.[2] If, for instance, a testator who dies after 1925 devises land to " A. and his issue," an interest in tail does not pass to A.

Effect of
instrument
not con-
taining
formal words
of limitation.

The question that then arises is—what interest does pass to A. when informal expressions such as " issue," " seed," " descendants " or " children " are contained in a conveyance or in a devise of land ?[3] The Act purports to provide an answer in section 130 (2) :—

> Expressions contained in an instrument coming into operation after [1925], which, in a will, or executory instrument coming into operation, before [1926], would have created an entailed interest in freehold land, but would not have been effectual for that purpose in a deed not being an executory instrument, shall ... operate in equity, in regard to property real or personal, to create absolute, fee simple or other interests corresponding to those which, if the property affected had been personal estate, would have been created therein by similar expressions before [1926].

Effect is
what it
would be if
the subject
matter were
personalty.

The first point to notice is that this sub-section is not concerned with those formal expressions that would have been effectual in a deed before 1926 to create an estate tail in land. A gift of personalty to A. and the heirs of his body or to A. in tail formerly gave A. the absolute ownership of the property,[4] but now, by virtue of section 130 (1),[5] it gives him an entailed interest. What we are concerned with here are informal expressions, and we are told that if they appear in a grant or a devise of land operating after 1925, the donee is to acquire in the land the interest that he would have acquired in personalty had the same expression been contained in a gift of personalty. The question then is, what

---

[1] L.P.A. 1925, s. 130 (3).
[2] *Re Brownlie*, [1938] 4 All E. R. 54.
[3] See (1938), 6 *C. L. J.* 67 (S. J. Bailey) ; (1947), 9 *C. L. J.* 46 (R. E. Megarry); 185 (S. J. Bailey), 190 (J. H. C. Morris).
[4] *Chatham* v. *Tothill* (1771), 7 Bro. P. C. 453 ; *Portman* v. *Portman* (*Viscount*), [1922] 2 A. C. 472 ; Hawkins and Ryder, *Construction of Wills*, pp. 254-5.
[5] *Supra*, p. 249.

interest passes under a gift, for instance, of £5,000 Consolidated 4 per cent. Stock, in the following typical cases :

To A. and his issue.
To A. for life and then to his issue.
To A. and his descendants.
To A. and his children.

Find this and we know what interest is taken if the same expressions are adopted in a grant or devise of land.

The primary difficulty is that, since the effect of such informal expressions has always varied according as they appear in deeds or in wills, it is not obvious whether the rules for deeds or for wills are to be adopted. Presumably the solution is that a devise containing informal expressions is to have the effect that has always been allowed to a bequest containing the like expressions, and that a grant *inter vivos* is to have the effect that has always been attributed to a corresponding gift by deed of personalty.

Let us examine only *bequests* of personalty, for it is unlikely in practice that any but formal expressions will be found in a conveyance *inter vivos* of land.[1] It must be realized at once, however, that no unqualified rule can be laid down with regard to the *quantum* of interest that passes under this or that expression, for since the object in each case is to ascertain and to implement the intention of the testator, what always has to be done is to construe the will as a whole. Strictly speaking, the only correct answer to make to the question, " What interest is taken under a gift of personalty to A. and his issue ? " is, " That interest which the testator intended to give." Certain canons of construction have, however, become established that cover most of the expressions found in practice.

The effect is that which the testator intended.

The primary canon of construction is that a gift of personalty *to A. and his issue* shows an intention on the part of the testator that the issue alive when the will comes into operation shall take the property jointly with A.[2]

Gift to A. and his issue.

" Thus, if the gift be immediate, A. and his issue (if any) living at the testator's death would take in joint tenancy ; and if the gift be deferred, issue subsequently born before the period of distribution would be admitted along with them ; and if no issue had come into existence before the period of distribution, A. would take the whole."[3]

---

[1] For the effect of gifts by deed containing informal expressions, see (1938), 6 *C. L. J.*, p. 81.
[2] *Re Hammond*, [1924] 2 Ch. 276.
[3] *Hawkins on Wills* (3rd Edn.), pp. 241-2 ; the words quoted are those of **Hawkins** himself.

Gift to A. for life and then to his issue.

Again, if there is a bequest to A. for life and after his death to his issue, A. takes merely a life interest and the property is ultimately divided among the issue born during his life.[1]

Nevertheless this principle of construction which admits issue as beneficiaries in the instances given is displaced if it appears from the will as a whole that the testator meant to make A. sole and absolute owner.

Gift to A. and his descendants.

The word "issue" has consistently been held to mean *prima facie* descendants of every degree,[2] and it therefore seems to follow that a gift of personalty *to A. and his descendants* is construed, in the absence of a contrary intention, in the same way as a gift to A. and his issue.[3] The descendants alive at the death of the testator take the absolute ownership jointly with A.

Gift to A. and his children.

A gift of personalty *to A. and his children* is *prima facie* regarded as a gift to A. and the children concurrently, so that A. and his children alive at the testator's death take the property as joint tenants, or, if there are no children living at that time, A. takes the whole absolutely.[4]

Rule in Shelley's Case.[5]

—Finally, we must mention briefly the *Rule in Shelley's Case*,[6] which, though it has been abolished by the Law of Property Act 1925,[7] still applies to instruments coming into operation before 1926.[8]

Statement of the Rule.

This rule, which was a rule of law applicable to deeds and to wills, ordained that if in the same instrument an estate of *freehold* was limited to A., with remainder, either immediately or after the limitation of an intervening estate, to *the heirs* or to the *heirs of the body* of A., the remainder, though importing an independent gift to the heirs as original takers, conferred the fee simple in the first case, and the fee tail in the second case, upon A.. the ancestor.[9] Thus the effect of a grant

> to A for life, remainder to his heirs,

was to give A. the fee simple ; and the effect of a grant

> to A. for life, remainder to the heirs of his body,

was to give A. an estate tail.

---

[1] *Knight* v. *Ellis* (1789), 2 Bro C. C. 570 ; *Jarman on Wills* (6th Edn.), p. 1200.

[2] Hawkins and Ryder, *Construction of Wills*, p. 148.

[3] (1938) 6 *C. L. J.*, p. 75.

[4] Hawkins and Ryder *op cit.*, pp. 260–2. The rule in *Wild's Case* as stated above, *supra*, p. 195, never applied to personalty.

[5] See Challis, *Law of Real Property* (3rd Edn.), pp. 52 *et seq.* ; Cheshire, 11th Edn. of this book, pp. 198–202.

[6] (1581), 1 Co. Rep. 93*b*.   [7] S. 131.

[8] *Re Routledge*, [1942] Ch. 457 ; [1942] 2 All E. R. 418 (testator died in 1874) ; *Re Williams*, [1952] Ch. 828 ; [1952] 2 All E. R. 502 (testator died in 1921).

[9] Hayes, *Introduction to Conveyancing*, vol. i. p. 542 ; *Preston on Estates*, vol. i. pp. 263–4.

The interest which in terms was given to the heirs and which in most cases the donor, especially when he was a testator, meant the heirs to have, was in the eye of the law given to A. So A. could dispose of the estate and thereby defeat his heir, who would take only if A. died intestate still owning the estate.

Thus the operation of the rule was two-fold : it denied to a remainder the effect of a gift to the " heirs," and it attributed to the remainder the effect of a gift to A.[1] In fact, the legal effect of such a limitation was the direct opposite of what would naturally be expected, and it nearly always operated to defeat the intention of a testator.[2]

Another and more technical way of stating the rule is as follows :

> Where the ancestor by any gift or conveyance takes an estate of freehold, and in the same gift or conveyance an estate is limited, either mediately or immediately to his heirs, in fee or in tail, in such cases " the heirs " are words of limitation of the estate and not words of purchase.

This requires us to distinguish words of purchase from words of limitation. Words of purchase (*perquisitio*) point out, by name or description, the person who is to acquire (*perquirit*) an interest in land ; words of limitation indicate the size of the interest given by some instrument. A " purchaser " in this technical sense does not denote a person who buys land, but one to whom land is expressly transferred by *act of parties*, as for instance by conveyance on sale, by gift or by will. If land is given " to A. and his heirs," A. is a purchaser since he is personally designated as the transferee, but the words " and his heirs " are words of limitation. They merely indicate the *quantum* of interest that A. is to take, and give the heirs nothing by direct gift. The lands may, of course, descend to them as heirs if A. dies intestate, but they will not be purchasers since the land comes to them by operation of law and not by act of parties.[3] Thus, if land was given

Words of purchase and words of limitation distinguished.

---

[1] Hayes, *Introduction to Conveyancing*, vol. i. p. 534.

[2] For the feudal reasons for this rule, see *Van Grutten* v. *Foxwell*, [1897] A.C. 658, at p. 668.

[3] " Words of purchase are those which designate the first purchaser or person who is to take, and which cause an interest to attach in him originally. Words of limitation are words which serve to mark out the limits or quantity of an estate, and its course of devolution, and under which, in the case of an estate in fee or in tail, the heirs do not take originally but derivatively by descent from their ancestor "—Smith, *An Original View of Executory Interests* (1844), sections 403–4. Fearne, *Contingent Remainders*, pp. 79–80. " The word purchase (*perquisitio*) is applied in law to any lawful mode of acquiring property by the person's own act or agreement, as distinguished from acquisition by act of law, as descent, escheat and the like. A purchase in the above sense includes acquisition, not only under contract of sale for a valuable consideration, but also by gift or without consideration, and by devise."— Leake, *Property in Land*, p. 117. See also, *supra*, p. 243, note 5.

to A. for life, remainder to the heirs of his body,

what the *Rule in Shelley's Case* declared was that the words "heirs of his body" were not words of purchase pointing out the heir as a person entitled to a definite interest in the land, but were words of limitation employed to mark out the extent of the interest given to A.   Had the words "heirs of his body" been regarded as words of purchase, they would have indicated that the estate was given to the person who was found to be heir on the death of A.   In other words, this person would have claimed the estate as having been given to him by the original conveyance. The result, in fact, was the same as if the grant had been

to A. and the heirs of his body,

but it is essential to notice that the *Rule in Shelley's Case* operated only where there were in terms two estates given, *i.e.* a freehold to the ancestor, A., and then a remainder to the heirs, *e.g.*

to A. for life and after his death to the heirs of his body.

It is true that a limitation *to A. and his heirs* or *to A. and the heirs of his body* gives A. a fee simple in the first case and a fee tail in the second case, but these results do not ensue from *Shelley's Case*.   The law had been so established at a far earlier date.[1]

Abolition
of the Rule.

The *Rule in Shelley's Case* was abolished by section 131 of the Law of Property Act 1925 for all instruments coming into operation after 1925.   Accordingly, where there is a limitation to

A. for life and then to his heirs ; or to
A. for life and then to the heirs of his body.

Ancestor
takes a life
interest.

Heir takes
by purchase

the effect is to restrict A.'s interest to a life interest, and to appropriate a definite interest to the heir or to the heir of the body of A.   The heir is ascertained in accordance with the canons of descent that obtained before 1926,[2] and he takes the interest by way of purchase.   What interest he takes is perhaps a little doubtful, but presumably in all cases he takes the fee simple or other the whole interest which the donor had power to convey, unless a contrary intention appears in the deed or will.[3]

The result, then, of the abolition of the *Rule in Shelley's Case* upon the expressions which are now essential to create an entailed interest, seems to be this :—

---

[1] If, for example, lands had been given " to W. and her heirs for her and their use and benefit absolutely and for ever," the *Rule in Shelley's Case* would not have applied, *Re McElligott*, [1944] Ch. 216 ; [1944] 1 All E. R. 441 ; (1938), 54 *L. Q. R.* 70 (A. D. Hargreaves).

[2] *Infra*, pp. 867–70.

[3] L.P.A. 1925, s. 60 (1) ; Wills Act 1837, s. 28 ; *supra*, pp. 152–3.   The rule before the Wills Act 1837 was that a devise to the *heirs of the body* of a person conferred an estate tail (*Mandeville's Case* (undated), Co. Litt. 26*b*), and the question whether the fee simple could pass under s. 28 of the Wills Act does not seem to have arisen.

(*a*) A gift to A. for life, remainder to the heirs of his body will no longer vest an entailed interest in A., despite the enactment that such an interest may be created by the like expressions as those by which before January 1st, 1926, a similar estate tail could have been created by deed.[1]

(*b*) A gift to A. for life, remainder to the heirs of his body will be effectual to vest a definite interest in the *heir*, although such would not have been the result of a similar conveyance by deed under the old law.

SECTION III. ENTAILED INTERESTS AFTER 1925

SUMMARY

An entailed interest cannot subsist as a legal estate. It is necessarily an equitable interest[2] and the only possible methods by which it can be created are (1) a settlement by deed or will, and (2) an agreement for a settlement in which the trusts upon which the land is to be held are sufficiently declared.[3]

Entailed interest must be created by settlement.

(1) ENTAILED INTERESTS MAY BE CREATED IN ANY FORM OF PROPERTY

One of the radical changes introduced by the Law of Property Act 1925 is that any form of property, whether real or personal, may be limited in tail. At common law an estate tail could not be carved out of chattels or other personal property, but it appeared to the Legislature that there was no reason why entailed interests should not be allowed in the case of such forms of property as stocks and shares and long leaseholds. Section 130 (1), therefore, provided that :

Personalty can now be entailed.

" an interest in tail or in tail male or in tail female or in tail special

---

[1] *Supra*, p. 249.   [2] L.P.A. 1925, ss. 1, 130.
[3] *Ibid.*, s. 130 (6).

(in this Act referred to as ' an entailed interest ') may be created by way of trust in any property, *real or personal*, but only by the like expressions as those by which before the commencement of this Act a similar estate tail could have been created by deed (not being an executory instrument) in freehold land, and with the like results, including the right to bar the entail either absolutely or so as to create an interest equivalent to a base fee, and accordingly all statutory provisions relating to estates tail in real property shall apply to entailed interests in personal property." [1]

One important effect of this subsection is that beneficial interests under a trust for sale, which, as we have seen, by the doctrine of conversion, are interests in personalty, may now be entailed. [2]   Further an entail becomes subject to all rules, whether at common law or in equity, which governed and still govern estates tail in realty. [3]

Heirlooms settled to go with land.

Before the Act it sometimes happened that when freeholds were limited by settlement to a series of legal tenants for life and in tail, it was desired to give the persons who for the time being were entitled to the land the enjoyment of certain family heirlooms such as valuable pictures and the like. As the heirlooms, being chattels, could not be carved into estates in the same way as the land, the only mode of carrying out the intention was to vest them in trustees upon trust that they should go along with the land so far as the rules of law and equity would permit. [4] In such a case law and equity permitted any legal tenant for life of the land for the time being to have an equitable life interest in the heirlooms, but required that the absolute ownership should vest in the first person to get an estate tail in the land. The Act now provides that when personal estate is directed to be held upon trusts corresponding with the trusts of land in which an entailed interest has been created, such direction shall create a corresponding entailed interest in the personal property. [5]

(2) ENTAILED INTERESTS MAY BE BARRED

Indefeasible right of tenant to bar interest.

The Fines and Recoveries Act 1833, in a general enabling section, provides that every " actual tenant in tail," *i.e.* the tenant of an entailed interest that has not been barred, [6] whether entitled in possession, remainder, contingency [7] or otherwise shall have full power to dispose of the land for an estate in fee simple or for any lesser estate. [8] This right of the tenant to disentail and so enlarge

---

[1] L.P.A. 1925, s. 130 (1).   A will is not within this section unless it takes effect after 1925 ;   *Re Hope's Will Trust*, [1929] 2 Ch. 136.
[2] *Supra*, p. 197.
[3] *Re Crossley's Settlement Trusts*, [1955] Ch. 627 ;   [1955] 2 All E. R. 801.
[4] See *Re Morrison's Settlement*, [1974] Ch. 326 ;   [1973] 3 All E. R. 1094.
[5] L.P.A. 1925, s. 130 (3).
[6] Fines and Recoveries Act 1833, s. 1.
[7] See, for example, *Re St. Albans Will Trusts*, [1963] Ch. 365 ;   [1962] 2 All E. R. 402.   *Cf. Re Midleton's Will Trusts*, [1969] 1 Ch. 600 ;   [1967] 2 All E. R. 402.
[8] S. 15.

his equitable interest into a legal fee simple is absolute, and it cannot be restricted by any device on the part of the grantor; so, for instance, a clause inserted in the instrument of creation providing that the interest shall not be barred, or that it shall pass from the owner upon disentailment, is null and void.[1] The present mode of disentailment, however, falls to be considered under two heads according as the tenant is or is not entitled to actual possession.

(A) Mode of Disentailment where the Tenant is Entitled in Possession

Disentailing Assurance. A tenant in tail in possession and of full age may, without the concurrence of any other person, effectually bar the entailed interest and thereby enlarge it into a legal fee simple by adopting any form of conveyance which is sufficient to dispose of a fee simple estate in lands, provided, however, that in the case of an *inter vivos* disentailment the conveyance is effected by deed.[2] So the estate must be barred by a deed, called a disentailing assurance, and no disentailment can be effected by contract.[3]

Interest must be barred by deed.

The effect of a disentailing assurance which enlarges the entailed interest into a fee simple is to defeat entirely the rights both of the tenant's issue and of the persons whose estates are to take effect after the determination or in defeasance of the entailed interest. Suppose, for instance, that :

Effect of disentailing assurance.

> There is a grant of Blackacre to A. in tail, remainder to B. in tail, with a proviso that, if A. becomes entitled to Whiteacre, his entailed interest in Blackacre shall cease and shall vest in C. If A., before he becomes entitled to Whiteacre, executes a disentailing deed of Blackacre for an estate in fee simple, the result is that he takes a fee simple estate which defeats,
>> first, his own issue.
>> secondly, B., who was entitled to take on the determination of the entailed interest, and
>> finally, C., whose estate was in defeasance of A.'s entailed interest [4]

But, on the other hand, no disentailment can defeat interests that rank prior to the entailed interest [5]

(B) Mode of Disentailment where the Tenant is not Entitled in Possession

Under the normal strict settlement, by which land is limited to A. for life and then to his sons successively in tail, the eldest

Old law.

---

1 *Dawkins* v. *Lord Penrhyn* (1878), 4 App. Cas. 51, at p. 64.
2 Fines and Recoveries Act 1833, ss. 15, 40.
3 Registration of the deed is no longer required ; L.P.A. 1925, s. 133.
4 See *Milbank* v. *Vane*, [1893] 3 Ch. 79.
5 Fines and Recoveries Act 1833, ss. 15, 19.

son upon birth becomes entitled to an entailed interest in remainder. During the lifetime of his father he is not entitled to possession. The only method under the law prior to the Fines and Recoveries Act by which a tenant placed in this situation could effect a complete disentailment was to suffer a common recovery. If he adopted this course, he obtained an absolute fee simple in remainder which defeated the rights both of his own issue and of the persons who were entitled to take on failure of issue. But the difficulty from his point of view was that a recovery could be suffered only if the collaboration of the tenant in actual possession of the land—that is, in the case of settled land, his father—were obtained. This was a beneficial rule of law, since it enabled the father to influence his son and gave him considerable power to check a disentailment that might be undesirable. The son, however, if he failed to obtain the collaboration of his father, was free to levy a fine, and though this did not, like a recovery, convert the entailed interest into an absolute fee simple, it did produce the effect of creating in its place what is called a base fee that was unassailable by the issue, but of no avail against the remainderman and reversioner if the issue became extinct. The base fee is described below.[1] When fines and recoveries were abolished in 1833, it seemed desirable to the legislature to retain in a different form this doctrine of the old law of recoveries, and thus to empower the father to check an ill-advised disentailment. To this end a new functionary called the Protector of the Settlement was instituted, in order to prevent a tenant in tail who was entitled only in remainder from effecting a complete disentailment.

Protector of the Settlement.

The distinction between a tenant in tail *in possession* and a tenant in tail *in remainder*, therefore, is that the former can effect a complete bar without anyone's concurrence, while the latter can effect only a partial disentailment unless he obtains the consent of the Protector.

Present position.

The position at the present day is as follows :—

Disentailment with protector's consent.

(i) **A tenant in tail in remainder can effect a complete bar by executing a disentailing deed with the consent of the Protector.** The protector of a settlement functions only where there is an entailed interest in remainder, preceded by one or more beneficial life interests. In this case, the Fines and Recoveries Act 1833 provides in effect that the protector shall be the owner of the prior life interest or of the first of several life interests, or who would have been the owner had he not disposed of his beneficial interest.[2] Until there has been a resettlement,

---

[1] *Infra*, pp. 259–61.

[2] Fines and Recoveries Act 1833, s. 22. The Act in s. 32, however, allowed a settlor to appoint any persons up to the number of three to act as protector in place of the person described in the text above. This power of nominating

there is usually only one life interest under a marriage settlement, namely that given to the husband.

> Thus, if there is a limitation to H. for life with remainder to his eldest son in tail, the father, H., is the protector, and the son will not be able to acquire a fee simple in remainder, valid against persons whose interests are to take effect after the determination or in defeasance of the entailed interest, unless the consent of his father is expressed in the disentailing assurance itself or in a separate deed executed on or before the day on which the assurance is executed.[1]

The effect of a resettlement, however, is that life interests stand limited first to the father, then to the son, with the result that the son succeeds to the protectorship on the death of his father.

If there is no resettlement, the office of protector ceases on the death of the father, and the son, as tenant in tail in possession, can dispose of the land as his fancy dictates.

(ii) **A tenant in tail in remainder can effect a partial bar by executing a disentailing deed without the consent of the Protector.** When lands are subject to a strict settlement, family dissension may cause the eldest son to bar his entailed interest in remainder against the wishes of his father. The father may be niggardly or the son contumacious, and in that unfortunate event the probability is that the son will effect the partial disentailment that is within his power and will then dispose of the resultant base fee upon the best terms obtainable. The Fines and Recoveries Act [2] specifically enacts that a tenant in tail who is not for the moment entitled to actual possession of the land may execute a disentailing deed without the consent of the Protector, but that the effect of such a disentailment shall be merely to set up a base fee—that is to say, a fee simple that will defeat the tenant's own issue, but will not defeat persons who are entitled to take estates in the land upon the determination of the entailed interest by failure of issue or otherwise. Suppose, for instance, that:

> Lands stand limited to A. for life, remainder to A.'s eldest son in tail, remainder to A.'s second son in tail, and so on. If the eldest son of A. disentails during his father's life and without his father's consent, he

Margin note: Disentailment without protector's consent creates base fee.

---

a special protector has been abolished as regards settlements made after 1925; L.P.A. 1925, 7th Sched., repealing Fines and Recoveries Act, s. 32. If there is no protector under s. 22, the Court may be protector (s. 33), or the tenant in tail in remainder may disentail without consent. *Re Darnley's Will Trusts*, [1970] 1 W. L. R. 405 ; [1970] 1 All E. R. 319.

[1] *Ibid.*, ss. 34, 42. [2] S. 34.

will acquire a fee simple which cannot be defeated by any of his own issue, but which nevertheless will go over to his brother's family if at any time in the future his own issue fails. In other words, the eldest son acquires a fee simple that will not fail, *i.e.* will not pass to somebody else, unless and until his descendants fail.

There may be other base fees than the one now under consideration,[1] but these are beside the present point, and as regards entailed interests the Fines and Recoveries Act provides that :

> " The expression ' base fee ' shall mean exclusively that estate in fee simple into which an estate tail is converted where the issue in tail are barred, but persons claiming estates by way of remainder or otherwise are not barred." [2]

It is a less valuable fee simple than a fee simple absolute, since it will last only as long as there are in existence descendants who would have inherited the entailed interest had it never been barred; while a fee simple absolute continues as long as there exist any persons who are heirs, whether lineal or collateral, of the owner. In the example given above, if the eldest son of A., having barred the entail in his father's lifetime, conveys the interest so acquired to X. and then dies without having issue, the base fee held by X. ceases, and passes to the second son by way of remainder. On the other hand, had the interest conveyed to X. been a fee simple absolute, the death of the eldest son without issue would have made no difference to the perpetual nature of X.'s interest.

Conversion of base fee into fee simple absolute.

A base fee, however, may be converted, or will automatically become enlarged, into a fee simple absolute in any one of the following ways :—

Union of base fee with remainder in fee.

(*a*) UNION OF BASE FEE WITH REMAINDER OR REVERSION IN FEE. Suppose there is a limitation to

A. for life, remainder to B. in tail, remainder to C. in tail, remainder to B. in fee simple.

B. creates a base fee in himself by executing a disentailing deed during the life of A. and without his consent. The remainderman C. dies in the lifetime of B. without having issue. The position now is that both the base fee and the fee simple absolute in remainder are united in B. without there being any intermediate estate between them,

---

[1] Challis, *Law of Real Property* (3rd Edn.), pp. 325 *et seq.*   [2] S. 1.

and whenever this occurs the Fines and Recoveries Act enacts that the base fee shall be enlarged into as great an estate as the tenant in tail could have created had he been in possession at the time of disentailment.[1] In plain language, it is enlarged into a fee simple absolute.

(*b*) FRESH DISENTAILING DEED. If a tenant in tail in remainder creates a base fee, he can convert it into a fee simple absolute by executing a fresh disentailing deed with the consent of the Protector.[2] But if the Protector no longer exists, as for instance where the tenant for life under a strict settlement dies, the tenant can enlarge the base fee, whether he has parted with it or not, by himself executing a fresh disentailing deed.[3]

[margin: Fresh disentailment assurance.]

(*c*) LAPSE OF TIME. A base fee becomes valid against remaindermen and reversioners if any person takes possession under the disentailing assurance, and if he or any other person remains in possession by virtue of that assurance[4] for twelve years from the time when the tenant in tail would have been entitled to possession and therefore free to effect a complete bar of his own accord.[5]

[margin: Lapse of time.]

(*d*) DEVISE. The owner of a base fee *in possession* is now permitted to enlarge the base fee into a fee simple absolute by will.[6]

Tenants unable to disentail. Two classes of tenants in tail are unable to disentail their estates namely a tenant in tail after possibility[7] and a tenant in tail to whom or to whose ancestors an estate has been granted by Parliament as a reward for services rendered, if the statute by which the grant is made has expressly prohibited the right of disentailment. Examples are the Bolton, the Marlborough and the Wellington estates.[8]

[margin: Some entailed interests unbarrable.]

---

[1] Fines and Recoveries Act 1833, s. 39.
[2] *Ibid.* s. 35.
[3] *Ibid.*, s. 19 ; *Bankes* v. *Small* (1887), 36 Ch. D. 716.
[4] *Mills* v. *Capel* (1875), L. R. 20 Eq. 692.
[5] Limitation Act 1939, s. 11; replacing and extending the Real Property Limitation Act 1833, s. 23, and the Real Property Limitation Act 1874, s. 6. This section also applies to a disentailing assurance which, owing to some defect such as the lack of a deed, fails to bar the tenant's *issue*.
[6] L.P.A. 1925, s. 176 (1), (3) ; *infra.*
[7] Fines and Recoveries Act 1833, s. 18 ; *supra*, p. 246.
[8] Former examples were the Abergavenny, Shrewsbury and Arundel estates, but these have now been statutorily freed from restraints upon alienation. See also S.L.A. 1925, s. 23 (2).

(3) ENTAILED INTERESTS MAY BE DISPOSED OF BY WILL

Entailed
interests
may now
be devised.

Prior to 1926 a tenant in tail could not devise his estate, and if he died without having disentailed, it passed by descent to the appropriate class of heirs. The Law of Property Act 1925, however, provides that in a will *executed* on or after January 1st, 1926, a testator of full age may devise or bequeath all property of which he is tenant in tail *in possession* at the time of his death, and all money subject to be invested in the purchase of property, of which if it had been so invested he would have been tenant in tail in possession at his death.

The tenant has power to dispose of the estate

" in like manner as if, after barring the entail, he had been tenant in fee simple or absolute owner thereof for an equitable interest at his death," [1]

Effect of
devise.

and therefore the effect produced by the will is similar to that produced by a disentailing deed. But to guard against a disentailment by inadvertence, it is enacted that no will shall be sufficient to dispose of the estate unless it refers specifically either to the property entailed, or to the instrument creating the entail or to entailed property generally, and therefore a mere general devise or bequest is useless for the purpose. [2]

Base fee.

This power of disposition is also conferred by the Act [3] upon the owner of a base fee *in possession* provided that he is in a position to enlarge the base fee into a fee simple absolute. This position arises where a tenant in tail in remainder, having barred the entail without the consent of the tenant for life as Protector, becomes entitled to possession upon the death of the tenant for life. In such a case, as we have already seen, the owner of the base fee may bar the entail and enlarge the base fee into a fee simple absolute in possession by executing a fresh disentailing assurance. The extension of this principle made by the Law of Property Act 1925 is that the owner may *devise* the base fee so as to pass a fee simple absolute to the devisee provided that the will refers specifically either to the base fee or to the instrument by which it was acquired. But he has no such testamentary power unless he is in possession of the base fee or of its rents and profits. [4] It will thus be seen that the power to execute a fresh disentailing assurance given by the Fines and Recoveries Act is wider than the power of testamentary disposition given by the Law of Property Act, for the former can be exercised by the tenant in tail even after he has conveyed the base fee to a purchaser and has lost all right to possession of the land. [5]

---

[1] L.P.A. 1925, s. 176 (1).
[2] *Ibid.*, s. 176 (1). The word *specifically* was interpreted in a liberal sense by VAISEY, J., in *Acheson* v. *Russell*, [1951] Ch. 67 ; [1950] 2 All E. R. 572. For a criticism of the decision, see (1950), 66 *L. Q. R.*, 449 (R. E. M.).
[3] S. 176 (3).   [4] L.P.A. 1925, s. 176 (3).
[5] *Bankes* v. *Small* (1887), L. R. 36 Ch. D. 716.

CHAPTER IV

LIFE INTERESTS

SUMMARY

SECTION I. THE GENERAL NATURE OF LIFE INTERESTS

History of Life Interests. The modern life interest differs fundamentally from that found in the days of feudalism. In those days, when lands were granted not in return for a rent nor by way of settlement, but on the condition that the tenant should render services of a military nature to the grantor, the tenant was given an interest merely for his life, because, although he was known to the lord and was presumably a man upon whose fidelity and courage reliance might be placed, yet the character of his eldest son was an unknown factor, and it would have been folly for a grantor to have tied his hands by pledging himself in advance to accept the son as a new tenant on his father's death. So in the twelfth century the life estate was the greatest interest that any one could have in land, and it arose when a feudal grant was made by a lord to a tenant. At first the grantee of such a feud did not possess the free power of alienation, for to have permitted this would have prejudiced the lord's right to make the new tenant on the death of the old pay a fine (or relief, as it was called), for the privilege of obtaining the feud ; and again, a tenant possessed of a free power of alienation might cause irreparable injury by granting the land to a personal enemy of the lord. But the restraints on alienation gradually disappeared, and it was recognized by the Statute *Quia Emptores* 1290 that a feudal tenant could

Distinction between the ancient and modern life interest.

263

grant his interest to whom he pleased.[1] By degrees it was also recognized that the feud was an inheritable interest that would descend to the heirs-general of the tenant, and which therefore would endure as long as there were any such heirs in existence. It thus came to pass that an estate greater than a life estate became known to the law, and an interest which could endure only for life, as distinguished from a fee simple which might endure for ever, was added to the list of possible estates. In the words of HAYES :—

" Some time elapsed after the feudal relation began to be known in Europe, before the right of inheritable succession was fully conceded. In its primitive state the possession was held at pleasure, or for a short term only : afterwards, the tenure was for life, the lord resuming the land on the death of the tenant, and granting it out anew. But at length the son of the tenant was permitted to succeed : an indulgence which was followed by the extension of the grant, first to the tenant and his issue (*i.e.* in fee tail) and finally to him and his heirs (*i.e.* in fee simple, expressed in legal phraseology by the word fee, without more), the law marking out a course of descent, which, enlarging by degrees, embraced his relations, lineal and collateral, male and female."[2]

But though after the establishment of the fee simple it became possible and indeed common to create a life estate with peculiar incidents of its own, the object of this practice was materially different from that which underlies the life interest found in present-day conveyancing. The estate in those days was granted, generally by the rich ecclesiastical corporations, in return for an annual rent, and was the result of a purely business transaction analogous to the modern lease for a term of years. The tenant resembled the modern tenant farmer, except that he held for life instead of from year to year or for a fixed number of years, and although he was said to have a *lease*, the interest vested in him was a freehold interest and not a term of years. But in modern times the life interest is, as we have seen, created within the framework of a strict settlement or a trust for sale as an integral part of the beneficial interests thereunder.[3] This aspect of the nature of a life interest became more important in the nineteenth century, when the Settled Land Act 1882 gave to a tenant for life powers which extended beyond those that he had as the owner of a mere life interest.[4] The crucial question in a grant of land at the present day therefore is not whether a claimant may enjoy the land for his life, but whether he has the powers of a tenant for life under the Settled Land Act 1925.[5]

Modern life interest under a settlement.

---

[1] For the growth of the power of alienation, see Holdsworth, *History of English Law*, vol. iii. pp. 73 *et seq.* ; Plucknett, *Concise History of the Common Law*, pp. 523 *et seq.*; Simpson, *An Introduction to the History of Land Law*, pp. 48–53.   [2] *Introduction to Conveyancing*, vol. i. pp. 7–8.
[3] *Supra*, p. 167.   [4] *Supra*, p. 151.
[5] *Bannister* v. *Bannister*, [1948] 2 All E. R. 133 ; M. & B. p. 460 ; *Binions* v. *Evans*, [1972] Ch. 359 ; [1972] 2 All E. R. 70 ; M. & B. p. 467 ; *Dodsworth* v. *Dodsworth* (1973), 228 Estates Gazette 1115 ; M. & B. p. 458 ; *Ivory* v. *Palmer*, [1975] I. C. R. 340 ; *infra*, pp. 583, 585.

A life interest is a freehold interest—generally called a *mere freehold* to distinguish it from fees simple and entails, which are estates of inheritance—and under the modern law it is necessarily equitable in nature. It may be limited to endure for the life either of the tenant himself or of some other person, in which latter case it is called an interest *pur autre vie*.

An interest for the life of the tenant himself, though normally created expressly by a settlement, made either by deed or by will, may also arise by implication of law in the case of the tenant in tail after possibility,[1] or by operation of law where a husband becomes tenant by the curtesy in the entailed lands of his deceased wife.[2]

The interest *pur autre vie* is the lowest estate of freehold known to the law, and is not so great as an interest for the life of the tenant himself. It arises in two ways :

The first is where there is an express limitation to A. for the life of B. Such a limitation may be made, like an ordinary lease for years, in return for a rent, or as part of a settlement of land. A. is called the tenant *pur autre vie*, and B. the *cestui que vie*.[3]

Secondly, if a person, B., who is entitled to an estate for his own life assigns his interest to A., the effect is that A. becomes the tenant *pur autre vie*.[4]

From the point of view of rights and liabilities a tenant *pur autre vie* is in the same position as an ordinary tenant for life.

Thus, at common law, he is entitled to the rents and profits of the land during the continuance of his interest and to cut timber within the limits of estovers, while on the negative side he is liable for waste to the same extent as if he were holding for his own life.[5] Unless holding merely under a lease at a rent, he may exercise any of the wide powers conferred by the Settled Land Act 1925.[6] No matter how the interest arises, he possesses an absolute power of alienation during his life,[7] and after his death his alienee is entitled to hold for the rest of the *cestui que vie's* life.[8] In the absence of such alienation the interest passes on the death of the tenant to his devisee,[9] or, if he has made no will, to the persons who are entitled to take his property under the rules that govern intestacy.[10] Prior

Marginal notes: Classes of life interests. Interest for the life of the tenant himself. Tenant *pur autre vie.* Rights and liabilities of tenant *pur autre vie.*

---

[1] *Supra*, p. 246.
[2] *Supra*, p. 244.
[3] Litt., 56; Co. Litt., 41*b*.
[4] *Ibid.*, 41*b*.
[5] *Infra*, p. 267 (waste); p. 269 (estovers).
[6] S.L.A. 1925, s. 20 (1) (v) ; he is not so entitled if he is the assignee of a tenant for life holding under a settlement, *supra*, p. 186.
[7] Co. Litt., 41*b*.
[8] *Utty Dale's Case* (1590), Cro. Eliz. 182.
[9] Wills Act 1837, s. 3.
[10] A.E.A. 1925, s. 46.

to the legislation of 1925 there were certain peculiar rules which governed the devolution of an interest *pur autre vie*, but these have been abolished.[1]

Cestui que Vie Act 1707.

In view of the danger that a tenant *pur autre vie* may be tempted to conceal the death of the *cestui que vie*, the *Cestui que Vie Act* 1707 provides that a person entitled to the land upon the termination of the life interest may, after swearing an affidavit that he believes the *cestui que vie* to be dead, obtain an order from the High Court for the production of the *cestui que vie*. If the order is not complied with, the *cestui que vie* is taken to be dead and the person next entitled to possession may enter upon the lands.

SECTION II. THE RIGHTS AND OBLIGATIONS OF A TENANT FOR LIFE AT COMMON LAW

Rights in general of a tenant for life.

The rights and obligations at common law of a tenant for life entitled in possession may be summed up by saying that he may take the annual profits, but must not take or destroy anything that is a permanent part of the inheritance.[2] He is entitled to fruits of all kinds, but must leave unimpaired the source of the fruits. He has certain positive rights, and one negative duty which is prescribed by the doctrine of *waste*.

Emblements.

There is little that need be said of his positive rights. The profits that arise from the land, whether they arise continuously, periodically or occasionally, belong to him. A particular hazard, however, that confronts him is that after he has sown crops his

---

[1] A.E.A. 1925, s. 45 (1) (a) ; for the old law, see Challis, *Law of Real Property*, (3rd Edn.), pp. 358 *et seq*. A tenant *pur autre vie* could not at common law devise his interest, and the question that arose was—what was to happen to the land if he died in the lifetime of the *cestui que vie* ? This depended upon the form of the grant. If it were *to B. during the life of A.*, the land went on the death of B. to the person who first took possession. This person was called the *general occupant* (Blackstone, vol. ii. p. 259). Neither the general occupant nor the land that he held was liable for the debts of B. If the grant were *to B. and his heirs during the life of A.*, the land went on the death of B. to his heir, who took, not by descent, for title by descent can arise only in the case of an estate of inheritance, but as an occupant specially marked out and appointed by the original grant. He was called a *special occupant*, and again neither he nor the land was liable for the debts of B.

The Statute of Frauds 1677 (s. 3) made estates *pur autre vie* devisable and liable for debts. This section was repealed and re-enacted by the Wills Act 1837, after which the position was as follows : (a) an *estate pur autre vie* was devisable ; (b) if it was not devised and if there was no special occupant (*i.e.* if the grant was merely " to B. during the life of A."), the estate passed to the personal representatives of B. and was treated as personalty as regards its liability for the debts of B. ; (c) if it was not devised and if there was a special occupant (*i.e.* if the grant was " to B. and his heirs during the life of A."), the estate went to the heirs and was treated as realty as regards liability for debts. General and special occupancy were abolished by A.E.A. 1925, s. 45, and if B. dies in the lifetime of A. his interest in all cases passes to his personal representatives.

[2] For the position of a tenant for life under the Settled Land Act 1925, see *supra*, pp. 177 *et seq*.

tenancy may end unexpectedly before they are ripe as, for instance, by the death of a *cestui que vie*. In this event, he is entitled to re-enter the land at harvest time and to reap what he has sown. This is known as the right to *emblements*.[1] It is enforceable, however, only in respect of crops such as corn, hemp, flax and potatoes, which bear an annual fruit.[2] One crop only can be taken,[3] and the right does not extend to seeds that do not produce a crop within a year of sowing, such as young fruit-trees or the second crop of clover.[4]

The right can be exercised only if the estate comes to an end unexpectedly without any fault on the part of the tenant for life, and therefore, if it is forfeited in his lifetime owing to the breach of some condition, or if, being a determinable interest, it is brought to an end by the happening of the terminating event—as for instance by the re-marriage of a woman who is tenant *durante viduitate*—the crops belong to the reversioner.[5]

The position of the tenant for life on the negative side is governed by the common law doctrine of waste as enlarged by statute and equity, a doctrine that also affects a tenant for years.[6] Waste means in general such damage to houses or land as tends to the permanent and lasting loss of the person entitled to the inheritance, and it falls into two main classes :— *Liability for waste.* *Definition of waste.*

(i) **Voluntary Waste.** This is a wrong of commission consisting of a positive act of injury to the inheritance. It generally takes one of the following forms :— *Voluntary waste.*

1. PULLING DOWN OR ALTERING HOUSES.[7] Thus if glass windows be broken or carried away, it is waste, though they may have been put in by the tenant himself, and so also in the case of benches, doors, furnaces and other things fixed to the land.

2. OPENING PITS OR MINES.[8] It is waste to dig for gravel, lime, clay, stone and the like, unless for the reparation of buildings ; also to open a new mine, but not to work one that is already open.

3. CHANGING THE COURSE OF HUSBANDRY. To convert wood, meadow or pasture into arable land, or to turn arable or woodland into meadow or pasture, is technically waste. The old writers state that such acts are waste, not only because

---

[1] Co. Litt. 55*b*. The right of the tenant for years to emblements has been replaced by a statutory right, *infra*, p. 411.

[2] Co. Litt. 55*b* ; Blackstone, vol. ii. p. 122.

[3] *Graves* v. *Weld* (1833), 5 B. & Ad. 105.

[4] *Graves* v. *Weld*, *supra*.

[5] Co. Litt. 55*b* ; *Oland's Case* (1602), 5 Co. Rep. 116*a*.

[6] *Infra*, p. 410. For the history of " waste," see Holdsworth, *History of English Law*, vol. ii. pp. 248–9 ; vol. iii. pp. 121–3 ; vol. vii. pp. 275–81. For a fuller account of the substantive law, see Leake, *Uses and Profits of Land*, pp. 18 *et seq.*

[7] Co. Litt. 53*a*. *Marsden* v. *Edward Heyes, Ltd.*, [1927] 2 K. B. 1.

[8] Co. Litt. 53*b*, 54*b*.

they change the course of husbandry, but also because they destroy the owner's evidence of title, for if an estate which had been conveyed as pasture were found on the next conveyance to be arable, it might cause confusion.[1] This, of course, is no longer in itself a reason for regarding such an act of conversion as waste. In fact it is obvious that to change the system of husbandry must often have the effect of enhancing the value of land, as, for example, where a farm situated near a large town is tilled intensively as a market garden, and though such conversion is technically waste, the rule, established since at least 1833,[2] is that it will not entitle the owner of the inheritance to recover damages unless it causes an injury to the inheritance.[3] This kind of waste is known as ameliorating waste. In *Doherty* v. *Allman*,[4]

Ameliorating waste.

> a tenant for 999 years of land and buildings was proceeding to convert some dilapidated store buildings into dwelling houses when the lessor filed a bill for an injunction.

The injunction was refused on the ground that acts which improve the inheritance cannot constitute actionable waste. A similiar decision was reached where the tenant of an agricultural lease for 21 years converted part of the land into a market garden and erected glass-houses thereon for the cultivation of hot-house produce for the London market.[5]

What trees are timber.

4. CUTTING TIMBER. Timber trees are regarded as part of the inheritance and not part of the annual produce, and therefore it is waste to cut them, even though they are blown down by accident and have thus become what are called *windfalls*.[6] Sir GEORGE JESSEL, M.R., furnishes us with a definition of the term " timber " [7] :

> " The question of what timber is depends, first on general law, that is, the law of England ; and secondly, on the special custom of a locality. By the general rule of England, oak, ash and elm are timber, provided they are of the age of 20 years and upwards, provided also they are not so old as not to have a reasonable quantity of useable wood in them, sufficient . . . to make a good post. Timber, that is, the kind of tree which may be called timber, may be varied by local custom. There is what is called the custom of the country, that is, of a particular county or division of a county, and it varies in two ways. First of all, you may have trees called timber by the custom of the country—beech in some counties, hornbeam in others, and even whitethorn and blackthorn, and many other trees, are considered timber in peculiar localities—in addition to the ordinary timber trees.[8] Then again, in certain localities, arising probably from

---

[1] Blackstone, vol. ii. p. 282.
[2] *Doe d. Grubb* v. *Burlington (Earl)* (1833), 5 B. & Ad. 507.
[3] *Jones* v. *Chappell* (1875), L. R. 20 Eq. 539, at p. 541.
[4] (1877), 3 App. Cas. 709; M. & B. p. 22.
[5] *Meux* v. *Cobley*, [1892] 2 Ch. 253. Although this case and that referred to in the previous note concerned a tenant for years, there would be even stronger reasons for adopting the same attitude towards a tenant for life.
[6] *Garth* v. *Cotton* (1753), 3 Atk. 751.
[7] *Honywood* v. *Honywood* (1874), L. R. 18 Eq. 306, at p. 309.
[8] *E.g.* beech in Buckinghamshire, *Dashwood* v. *Magniac*, [1891] 3 Ch. 306 ; M. & B. p. 20 ; birch in Yorkshire, *Countess of Cumberland's Case* (1610), Moore, 812 ; willows in Hampshire, *Layfield* v. *Cowper* (1694), 1 Wood, 330.

the nature of the soil, the trees of even 20 years old are not necessarily timber, but may go to 24 years, or even to a later period, I suppose, if necessary ; and in other places the test of when a tree becomes timber is not its age but its girth." [1]

A tenant, whether for years or life, may cut and keep trees that do not fall within this definition of timber, such as larch, willows and chestnut, provided that they are ripe for felling and have not been planted for ornament, shelter or shade.[2] But only in three cases may he fell timber trees:— *When timber may be cut.*

First, where the land is a timber estate, that is, where it is cultivated merely for the produce of saleable timber and where the timber is cut periodically.[3] In such a case it is obvious that to cut the trees does not injure the inheritance, because the total value of the timber on the estate remains, roughly speaking, the same throughout, though new trees take the place of old.[4]

Secondly, where there is a local custom to cut timber periodically according to the normal and ordinary course of husbandry practised in the neighbourhood.[5]

Thirdly, every tenant for life is entitled to cut timber or other trees for three specific purposes, namely, for the fuelling or repair of a house (*housebote*), for making and repairing agricultural implements (*ploughbote*) and for repairing existing walls, fences and ditches (*haybote*). These are called *estovers*.[6] He will be liable for waste, however, if he exercises these rights in an unreasonable manner, as for instance if he fells growing trees for fuel when there is dead wood sufficient for the purpose.

(ii) **Permissive Waste.** Permissive waste arises from a mere act of omission, not of commission, and it is generally the result of allowing the buildings on an estate to fall into a state of decay.[7] *Permissive waste.*

Extent of Liability for Waste. At common law, tenants for life or years whose tenancies arose by operation of law, such as the doweress or tenant by the curtesy, were liable for waste; but no liability arose in the case of tenancies, whether for life or years, created by act of parties, for the courts were disinclined to excuse the folly of the lessor in not imposing an express restraint *Distinction between tenant impeachable and tenant unimpeachable.*

---

[1] If timber trees are blown down, they belong to the owner of the inheritance, but if they are dotards, *i.e.* decayed, they may be appropriated by the tenant, Co. Litt. 53*a* ; *Herlakenden's Case* (1589), 4 Co. Rep. 62, at p. 63*b* ; *Newcastle (Duke) v. Vane* (undated), 2 P. Wms. 241.

[2] *Re Harker's Will Trusts*, [1938] Ch. 323 ; [1938] 1 All E. R. 145.

[3] *Honywood v. Honywood* (1874), L. R. 18 Eq. 306, at p. 309.

[4] *Lloyd-Jones v. Clark-Lloyd*, [1919] 1 Ch. 426, at p. 436.

[5] *Dashwood v. Magniac*, [1891] 3 Ch. 306 ; M. & p. 20 ; *Re Trevor-Batye's Settlement*, [1912] 2 Ch. 339.

[6] Co. Litt. 41*b*.

[7] Co. Litt. 53*a*, 54*b*.

upon the tenant.[1] This, however, was altered by the Statute of Marlborough [2] 1267, which provided as follows :—

> " Fermors, during their terms, shall not make waste, sale, nor exile of house, woods, nor of anything belonging to the tenements that they have to ferm, without special licence had by writing of covenant, making mention that they may do it." [3]

This reference to a " special licence " recognized therefore, that a tenant for life might be expressly permitted to do acts that would normally constitute waste without incurring liability,[4] and from this point of view it led to the emergence of two classes of tenants for life, namely those impeachable for waste, and those unimpeachable for waste.

Tenant impeachable.

(i) A tenant who is impeachable is liable for the commission of voluntary waste,[5] but is not liable for permissive waste [6] unless the settlor has imposed upon him an obligation to keep the property in repair.[7]

Where such an obligation is imposed, an action lies against the tenant or against his personal representative, on the general equitable principle that a person who accepts a benefit must take the benefit *cum onere*.[8]

Where, however, the property which is settled upon the tenant consists of leaseholds, he is bound to perform any covenants, such as a covenant to repair, contained in the lease under which the property is held. Thus, if a house which is held by a testator on a long lease is bequeathed to A. for life, A. must take the *onus* with the *commodum*, and instead of throwing the financial burden upon the testator's estate must meet the cost of performing the covenants out of his own pocket.[9]

Tenant un-impeachable.

(ii) If, as is nearly always the case under a settlement, a tenant for life is unimpeachable, he is not liable either for voluntary or for permissive waste, and at common law may fell timber or open new mines and deal with the produce as absolute owner.[10]

Equitable waste.

Equity, however, has consistently set its face against an abuse of this immunity and the rule has long been that any tenant who commits wanton or extravagant acts of

---

[1] *Shrewsbury's (Countess) Case* (1600), 4 Co. Rep. 13b.
[2] 52 Hen. 3. c. 23.   Also called Marlbridge.
[3] " Fermor " includes everybody holding for life or years.
[4] *Woodhouse* v. *Walker* (1880), 5 Q. B. D. 404, at p. 406–7; M. & B. 19.
[5] Co. Litt. 53a.
[6] *Re Cartwright* (1889), 41 Ch. D. 532 ; *Re Parry and Hopkins*, [1900] 1 Ch. 160 ; *Woodhouse* v. *Walker, supra*.
[7] *Woodhouse* v. *Walker, supra*.
[8] *Jay* v. *Jay*, [1924] 1 K. B. 826.
[9] *Re Betty*, [1899] 1 Ch. 821; *Woodhouse* v. *Walker* (1880), 5 Q. B. D. 404.
[10] *Lewis Bowles's Case* (1615), 11 Co. Rep. 79b ; Tudor, *Leading Cases on Real Property* (4th Edn.), p. 153.

destruction, will be restrained by injunction and ordered to rehabilitate the premises. Examples of the application of this rule occur where the tenant dismantles a mansion or other house,[1] cuts saplings at unseasonable times,[2] or fells timber that has been planted for the ornament or shelter of the mansion-house and its grounds.[3] It is obviously difficult to decide whether timber is ornamental or not, but the question depends upon whether the person who carried out the planting intended the trees to be ornamental and not upon the personal opinion of the court or anybody else.[4]

Wanton acts of destruction of the kinds specified are said to constitute equitable waste because prior to the Judicature Act 1873 they could be remedied only in a court of equity ; but it is now expressly enacted that a tenant for life has no right to commit equitable waste unless an intention to confer such right appears in the instrument of creation.[5]

A tenant *pur autre vie* is liable for waste to the same extent as a tenant for his own life,[6] but a tenant in tail after possibility of issue extinct incurs no liability by the commission of voluntary or of permissive waste.[7]

Tenant after possibility.

Where an act of waste has been committed, the remainder-man or reversioner may sue for an account in the Chancery Division, or bring an action in the Queen's Bench Division, either for trover in respect of any things that may have been severed,[8] or for money had and received as a result of their sale,[8] or for the recovery of damages ; and he may sue in either Division for an injunction.

Rights of remainder-man or reversioner.

---

[1] *Vane* v. *Barnard* (1716), 2 Vern. 738; M. & B. p. 23.
[2] *Brydges* v. *Stephens* (1821), 6 Madd. 279.
[3] *Downshire* v. *Sandys* (1801), 6 Ves. 107.
[4] *Weld-Blundell* v. *Wolseley*, [1903] 2 Ch. 664.
[5] L.P.A. 1925, s. 135.
[6] Co. Litt. 41*b*, *Seymor's Case* (1612), 10 Co. Rep. 95*b*, 98*a*.
[7] *Williams* v. *Williams* (1810), 12 East, 209.
[8] *Seagram* v. *Knight* (1867), 2 Ch. App. 628, at p. 632.   See generally Tudor, *Leading Cases on Real Property* (4th Edn.), p. 156.

CHAPTER V

EQUITABLE POWERS[1]

SUMMARY

SECTION I. NATURE AND CLASSIFICATION

Definition.

The principal object of this chapter is to describe the doctrine of powers under which the right of alienation may be divorced from the ownership of the estate or interest to which it relates. In this sense a power may be defined as an authority given by one person called the donor to another person called the donee entitling the latter to deal with or dispose of realty or personalty, either absolutely or partially and either for his own benefit or for the benefit of others, and whether or not he is already beneficially interested in the subject-matter before he exercises the authority.

Classification of powers.

Powers are of various classes, but they can conveniently be divided as follows, namely, according to

(1) the purposes for which they are created;

---

[1] See Holdsworth, *History of English Law*, vol. vii. pp. 149–93 ; *Farwell on Powers* (3rd Edn.) ; *Hanbury's Modern Equity* (9th Edn.), pp. 103 *et seq.*

(2) the relation of the donee to the land ;

(3) the nature of the interests which their exercise creates.

(1) Powers Classified according to the Purposes for which they are Created

The purpose and object of a power may be to authorize the donee either to manage and administer the property within certain limits, or to dispose of its ownership by the creation of interests. A familiar example of an administrative power is furnished by the Settled Land Act 1925, which authorizes a tenant for life to manage the settled land in the interests of all concerned, as for instance by compromising claims, varying leases, modifying restrictive covenants or cutting timber. The same Act, by permitting the tenant for life to lease the land, also affords an example of the second class of powers whereby a person is enabled to dispose of an interest to which he is not beneficially entitled.

But the most important example of a dispositive, as distinct from an administrative, power arises where a person is authorized to appoint or to create actual interests in the land for the benefit, in some cases of himself, and in others of third persons. This is best illustrated from a settlement. A settlor, instead of declaring with finality what persons shall take interests in the land, what the extent of those interests shall be and in what circumstances they shall arise, may prefer to wait upon events and either to reserve to himself or to confer upon another a *power of appointment*, i.e. a power to make final dispositions at some time in the future. *Power of appointment.*

Such a power of appointing future interests was unknown to the common law. *Powers of appointment unknown at common law.*

" Simplicity was the striking feature of the common law, in regard as well to the estates which might be created, as to the modes by which they might be raised." [1]

If a feoffment of land was once made, it was impossible to provide at common law that the feoffor might revoke the conveyance and make a new disposition of the land, for the essence of the feoffment was that it transferred his whole interest and right of disposal.[2] It was indeed possible to annex a condition to a feoffment providing that the estate delivered should cease on a given event, but the efficacy and usefulness of this was diminished by the rule that only the feoffor and his heirs could re-enter upon the happening of the event, and that the effect of such entry was to render nugatory all estates passing under the feoffment.[3]

But upon the establishment of uses there was, according to the view of equity, no repugnancy in reserving to oneself or to *Originated with uses.*

---

[1] Sugden's *Gilbert on Uses*, p. xxxix.
[2] Co. Litt. 237a ; Sugden's *Gilbert on Uses*, p. 158, note.
[3] *Infra*, p. 370.

somebody else a power to revoke the uses that had been raised in the first instance and to replace them by the declaration of new uses. Thus :

> A. might convey to B. to such uses as A. the grantor, or as C. a stranger, should appoint, and in default of appointment to the use of D.

In other words, equity allowed the power of alienation to be detached from the ownership of the estate granted to B. and to be either retained by the grantor himself or vested in a stranger.[1] Under such a power the use might be appointed to E. subject to a right of revocation, and if this right of revocation were exercised, the use already given to E. might be withdrawn and superseded by one granted to F.[2] Originally the interests taken by E. and F. upon the exercise of the power were equitable, but they acquired the status of legal estates when the Statute of Uses 1535 enacted that where B. stood seised to the use of E., the latter was to have the legal estate.

Suppose for instance that :

Example of exercise of power of appointment.

In contemplation of a marriage to be solemnized between H. and W. land is given by a settlement to H. for life with remainder to W. for life, and after the death of the survivor to such one or more of the children of the said H. and W. for such estates and in such shares and subject to such restrictions as H. and W. shall at any time by a deed revocable or irrevocable jointly appoint.

H. and W., having two children—a son and a daughter—appoint the fee simple to the son subject to their own life interests. When exercising the power, however, they expressly reserve to themselves authority during their lives to vary or absolutely to revoke the estate so given, and to replace it by another estate granted under the power of appointment. For some reason or other H. and W. have decided to deprive the son of the fee simple already appointed in his favour, and therefore they first of all revoke and make void that estate, and then, still subject to their own life interests, limit and appoint the fee simple to the daughter.

Thus the fee simple that had been appointed in favour of the son, subject to the life interests of his parents, is destroyed and is replaced by a similar interest in favour of the daughter.

Terminology.

As regards terminology, when X. gives B. the right to exercise a power of appointment, X. is called the *donor* ; B. the *donee* or *appointor* ; the person in whose favour the appointment is made

---

[1] Markby, *Elements of Law*, p. 170.
[2] Hayes, *Introduction to Conveyancing*, vol. i. p. 70.

is termed the *appointee* ; and when the donee exercises the power he is said to make an appointment.

These powers of appointment may be either general, or special.

If the appointor is authorized to appoint the interest in favour of anybody in the world, including himself, without being required to obtain the consent of another person, he is said to have a *general power*, but if he may appoint only to the members of a restricted class, as for instance, "amongst the children of A.," he has a *special power*, and the persons whom he may select to take the property are called the *objects* of the power. Thus, the outstanding feature of a general, as distinct from a special power, is that the donee is the virtual owner of the property affected since he can appoint to himself at any moment during his life. Indeed, it is treated by the law as equivalent to ownership for certain defined purposes. For instance, property over which a testator has a general power passes under a general devise or bequest, as when the words of the will are:— *General and special powers.*

" I devise and bequeath all my real and personal estate, except what I otherwise dispose of by this my will, to X." [1]

In such a case the property is distributable among the donee's creditors in the event of his bankruptcy ; it is liable for capital transfer tax on his death ; and for the purposes of the rule against perpetuities it is treated as being at his free disposal.[2]

Nevertheless, the two conceptions of power and property are fundamentally distinct, and save in exceptional cases an un-exercised power is in no sense the " property " of the donee of the power.[3] Thus, a covenant to settle after-acquired property does not bind property over which the covenantor acquires a general power of appointment unless, of course, he exercises it in his own favour.[4]

The classification of powers into two classes, however, is not exhaustive, for there is an intermediate class consisting of powers that are hybrid in the sense that they are congruous neither with special nor with general powers.[5] They are treated by the courts as general for some purposes, but special for others.[6] The following are examples of this class:— *Hybrid powers.*

---

[1] Wills Act, 1837, s. 27; *infra*, p. 850.

[2] *Infra*, p. 329.

[3] *Re Armstrong* (1886), 17 Q. B. D. 521 ; see especially at p. 531, *per* FRY, L. J. See also (1942), 58 *L. Q. R.*, p. 404, note 19 (J. Gold).

[4] *Tremayne* v. *Rashleigh*, [1908] 1 Ch. 681. Again the exercise of a general power of appointment by a person who later becomes bankrupt is not a settlement of property within the meaning of the Bankruptcy Act 1914, s. 42; *infra*, p. 811; *Re Mathieson*, [1927] 1 Ch. 288.

[5] For an account, see Morris and Leach, *The Rule against Perpetuities* (2nd Edn.) pp. 136–8 ; Fourth Report of Law Reform Committee, 1956, Cmnd. 18, paras 44–6. See *Re Lawrence's Will Trusts*, [1972] Ch. 418 ; [1971] 3 All E. R. 433 where that category is discussed by MEGARRY, J.

[6] So far as concerns the rule against perpetuities, the Perpetuities and Accumulations Act 1964, s. 7 has now imposed a test for determining which of these hybrid powers are general, which special; *infra*, p. 354.

(i) A power given to X. to appoint to anybody in the world except himself.

This is neither general, since X. himself is excluded; nor special, since no restricted class of objects has been designated.[1]

(ii) A power given to X. to appoint to any person or persons alive at his death.[2]

This is not general, since X. cannot appoint to himself or to persons who predecease him; yet it is not special in the normal sense, since the objects include the whole human race living at his death.

(iii) A general power given to X. to be exercised with the consent of Y.[3]

Although not restricted in respect of objects, this is not properly speaking a general power, for X.'s right of alienation is not unrestricted and therefore he is not in the position of an absolute owner.

(iv) A general power exercisable jointly by two or more persons.[4]

Again, although the objects are not restricted, there is no person who can be regarded as absolute owner of the property to which the appointment relates.

(v) A general power exercisable only by will.

This, though traditionally called a *general testamentary power*, is more akin to a special power, for the donee cannot appoint to himself and is therefore far from being the absolute owner of the property affected.[5]

Power and Trust.

Power and Trust. It is crucial to distinguish between a power and a trust.[6] A trust exists wherever a person comes under an obligation to deal with property in a specified manner : a power exists where a person is authorized to dispose of property. The former involves an obligation, the latter a discretion. The distinction has important consequences. The court will itself perform a trust that the trustees have failed to carry out. The beneficiaries have rights and can insist that the trustees do their duty. But the court will never compel the exercise of a power. It will not interfere in a matter that is left to the free will of a party.[7]

---

[1] *Re Park*, [1932] 1 Ch. 580, where it was held to be valid.
[2] *Re Jones*, [1945] Ch. 105.
[3] *Re Watts*, [1931] 2 Ch. 302.
[4] *Re Churston Settled Estates*, [1954] Ch. 334, [1954] 1 All E. R. 725.
[5] Gray, *Perpetuities*, s. 526 (*b*) ; Morris and Leach, *op. cit.* pp. 147-9 ; *infra*, p. 330.
[6] Hanbury's *Modern Equity* (9th Edn.), pp. 95 *et seq.*
[7] *Brown* v. *Higgs* (1803), 8 Ves. 561, at p. 574 ; see generally White and Tudor, *Leading Cases in Equity*, vol. ii. p. 261.

If the donee fails to exercise the power of appointment, the property subject to the power passes to those who take in default of appointment. They may be specified in the instrument creating the power, but, if not, there is a resulting trust for the grantor.

In some cases, however, that which on the surface appears to be a mere power is construed to be a trust, and in this event, it is generally called " a power in the nature of a trust " or " a trust power ".[1]

Lord ELDON in *Brown* v. *Higgs*[2] said :—

> " There are not only a mere trust and a mere power, but there is also known to this court a power, which the party, to whom it is given is entrusted and required to execute ; and with regard to that species of power the court considers it as partaking so much of the nature and qualities of a trust, that if the person, who has that duty imposed upon him, does not discharge it, the court will, to a certain extent, discharge the duty in his room and place."

Whether a trust has been created depends upon the intention of the donor of the power as gathered from the terms of the relevant instrument. If he has specified an ascertainable class of persons, such as children and grandchildren, and if it is clear that he intended the members of that class to take the property in any event, though he has left to the donee the selection of the particular beneficiaries, then the inference is that he intended to create a trust.

> " When there appears a general intention in favour of a class, and a particular intention in favour of individuals of a class to be selected by another person, and the particular intention fails from that selection not being made, the court will carry into effect the general intention in favour of the class."[3]

The court will distribute the property equally among the members of the class as appropriate, and usually *per capita*.[4] If the donor has provided that in default of appointment the property shall go over to other persons, it is clearly impossible to infer that he intended to benefit the class in any event.[5] Even though there is no gift over in default of appointment, however, there is no hard and fast rule that a trust must be implied. It is imperative that the general intention in favour of the class should be disclosed by

---

[1] (1949), 13 Conv. (N. S.) 20 (J. G. Fleming) ; (1957) 35 *Can. B. R.* 1060 (O. R. Marshall) ; (1971) *C. L. J.* 68 (J. Hopkins).

[2] (1803), 8 Ves. 561, at p. 570.

[3] *Burrough* v. *Philcox* (1840), 5 My. & Cr. 72, at p. 92, *per* Lord COTTENHAM.

[4] *Re Llewellyn's Settlement*, [1921] 2 Ch. 281 ; *Re Arnold*, [1947] Ch. 131 ; [1946] 2 All E. R. 579.

[5] *Goldring* v. *Inwood* (1861), 3 Giff. 139.

the terms of the instrument.[1]   This test was satisfied in *Harding* v. *Glyn*[2] upon the following facts :

> A testator gave his leasehold house, furniture and goods to his wife but " *did desire her* " at her death to give the same " *unto and amongst such of his own relations as she should think most deserving and approve of.*" The wife gave the furniture and goods to a person who was not a relative of her husband, and it was held that the court must distribute that property among the statutory next-of-kin, since the will imposed upon the wife a trust " *by way of power of naming and apportioning.*"

An illustration to the opposite effect is afforded by *Re Weeke's Settlement*,[3] where a testatrix devised to her husband a life interest in certain real property and gave him " *power to dispose of such property by will amongst our children,*" and there was no gift over in default of appointment. It was held that the power conferred upon the husband was a mere power and not one coupled with a trust.[4] There were no words in the will which could possibly justify the inference that the testatrix intended the children to take if her husband made no appointment.

Until 1970, a trust to distribute property among a class of persons was held void for uncertainty, unless all the possible beneficiaries are ascertainable. A power, however, is valid so long as it can be said with certainty that any given individual is or is not a member of the class. In *McPhail* v. *Doulton*[5] the House of Lords held that the test previously applicable to powers should apply also to trust powers.

Distinction between trusts and powers still remains.
The assimilation by the House of Lords in *McPhail* v. *Doulton* of the test for certainty of objects in the case of trust powers and powers does not mean that the distinction between trusts and powers no longer exists. First, it should be noted that the new rule applies to powers and not to fixed trusts. Further the basic distinction still remains. A trust remains obligatory, a power discretionary. In the case of a trust power, a beneficiary has no interest in property until the trustees or donees of the power exercise it in his favour. Until then they have only a duty to consider the claim of a potential beneficiary, rather than a duty to make a distribution in his favour.

Finally, as we have seen,[6] land cannot be settled land, if it is subject to an immediate binding *trust* for sale ; if, however, trustees are given a mere *power* to sell, then there will be a settlement under the Settled Land Act 1925.

---

[1] *Re Weekes' Settlement*, [1897] Ch. 289.   [2] (1739), 1 Atk. 469.
[3] [1897] Ch. 289. See also *Re Combe*, [1925] Ch. 210 ; *Re Perowne*, [1951] Ch. 785 ; [1951] 2 All E. R. 201.
[4] *Cf. Re Llewelyn's Settlement*, [1921] 2 Ch. 289.
[5] [1971] A. C. 424 ; [1970] 2 All E. R. 228 ; *Re Baden's Deed Trusts (No. 2)*, [1973] Ch. 9 ; [1972] 3 All E. R. 1304. See M. & B. *Trusts and Trustees*, pp. 43 *et seq.* ; *Hanbury's Modern Equity* (9th Edn., Supplement 1971), to p. 125.
[6] *Supra*, p. 197.

(2) POWERS CLASSIFIED ACCORDING TO THE POSITION OF THE DONEE WITH REGARD TO THE LAND

Powers may be appendant, in gross, or simply collateral.

(1) *A power appendant* or, as it is sometimes called, *appurtenant*, is one reserved to a person who already has an interest in the land to which the power relates, so that, when he exercises it his enjoyment of the interest will be affected. An example is where a tenant for life is authorized to grant leases in possession, or where land is conveyed to a person in fee simple with power to revoke such interest and make a new appointment.[1] *Power appendant.*

(2) If the owner of a power has an interest in the land, but one that will not be affected when the authority is exercised, the power is *in gross*. Thus : *Power in gross.*

> if a tenant for life under a settlement is authorized to appoint a jointure to his widow or to allocate portions to his children, the interests which arise upon exercise of the power take effect upon the determination of his interest and do not affect its enjoyment.

(3) *A power simply collateral* is a bare power reserved to a stranger who has no interest in the property affected, and which he can exercise only on behalf of others, as for instance where an executor is authorized to pay to such friends as the testator's wife may nominate a sum not exceeding £25 in each case.[2] *Power simply collateral.*

This particular classification will be of importance when we consider the extinction of powers.[3]

(3) POWERS CLASSIFIED ACCORDING TO THE NATURE OF THE INTERESTS WHICH THEIR EXERCISE CREATES

Under the old law one of the classifications of powers was into :

(1) common law powers,
(2) statutory powers,
(3) equitable powers, and
(4) powers to appoint uses.

The significance of a common law power was that it enabled the donee to convey or create the legal estate, so that if for instance a testator authorized his executors to sell his land, but did not actually devise the land to them, they acquired the right at *Common law powers.*

---

[1] *Re Mills*, [1930] 1 Ch. 654.
[2] *Re Coates*, [1955] Ch. 495 ; [1955] 1 All E. R. 26.
[3] *Infra*, pp. 289 *et seq.*

common law to pass the *legal* estate to a purchaser.[1]   Likewise, a power of attorney may confer a common law power.[2]

Statutory powers.

A statutory power is a power given by a statute to convey or create a legal estate, as, for instance, where the Law of Property Act 1925 gives to a mortgagee power to convey the legal estate vested in the mortgagor.[3]

Equitable powers.

An equitable power on the other hand, permits the creation only of equitable interests.   It was and still is the commonest example of a power found in practice, and it arises, for instance, where personal property is vested in trustees with a power reserved to some person to appoint among the children of a marriage.

Powers to appoint interests in land.

But the powers that concern us most are the old powers to appoint uses.   We have seen that where A. stood seised to the use of B., the Statute of Uses 1535 operated to pass the legal estate to B.; and further that it was possible, not only to make a final declaration of the uses binding upon A., but also to reserve a power permitting the grantor or some other person to replace these by a fresh use that would carry the legal estate to the appointee.   The donee of a power was thus enabled to dispose of a *legal* estate held by another person.   But the legislation of 1925 shifted the basis of conveyancing from powers to estates.   The legal estate must now be conveyed only by the person in whom it is vested.   The Law of Property Act 1925 provides, therefore, that with a few exceptions an appointor shall be restricted to the disposition of the equitable interest in the land affected.

Now, in general, lead to creation of equitable interests.

The Statute of Uses has been repealed and it is now enacted that the provisions in any statute or other instrument requiring land to be conveyed to uses shall take effect as directions that the land shall be conveyed to a person of full age *upon the requisite trusts*.[4]

In short all powers, with a few exceptions, are now equitable in the sense that they affect and dispose of the equitable interest only, and therefore they do not concern, nor do the interests arising under them concern, a purchaser who takes a conveyance from the estate owner.   Thus in the very forefront of the Law of Property Act 1925 it is provided that :—

> " Every power of appointment over, or power to convey or charge land or any interest therein, whether created by a statute or other instrument or implied by law, and whether created before or after the commencement of this Act (not being a power vested in a legal mortgagee or an estate owner in right of his estate and exercisable by him or by another person in his name and on his behalf), operates only in equity." [5]

Distinction between legal and equitable powers.

In the next sub-section the Act distinguishes between *legal* and *equitable* powers, and later defines the two types in this way :

---

[1] Holdsworth, *History of English Law*, vol. vii. pp. 153 *et seq.*
[2] See now Powers of Attorney Act 1971.
[3] L.P.A. 1925, ss. 89 (1), 104 (1) ; *infra*, p. 671.
[4] *Ibid.*, s. 1 (9).   [5] *Ibid.*, s. 1 (7).

" Legal powers " include the powers vested in a chargee by way of legal mortgage or in an estate owner under which a legal estate can be transferred or created, and " equitable powers " mean all the powers in or over land under which equitable interests or powers only can be transferred or created.[1]

There are also provisions which compel the owner of the legal estate concerned to give effect to equitable interests created by the exercise of the power.[2]

So the essential classification of powers after 1925 is into legal and equitable powers, and the following are the only legal powers that exist :—

(a) the powers of sale and leasing etc. possessed by a legal mortgagee or chargee ;[3]

List of legal powers.

(b) the powers vested in an estate owner in right of his estate, *e.g.* the powers of a tenant for life under the Settled Land Act 1925;

(c) certain powers of a miscellaneous nature. Examples are :

the power of attorney, under which one person may dispose of a legal estate vested in another ;[4] the power of a receiver to dispose of a legal estate vested in a person suffering from mental disorder, if authorized to do so by a nominated judge or the Court of Protection.[5] the power of a public utility company, if compulsorily acquiring land, to vest the legal estate in itself in certain circumstances, *e.g.* where the owner refuses or is unable to execute the necessary deed.[6]

SECTION II. EXECUTION OF POWERS

Subject to section 27 of the Wills Act 1837[7] a power of appointment, " whether special, general or hybrid, is exercised if, and only if, the purported exercise, first, complies with any requirements of the power,[8] and second, sufficiently indicates an intention to exercise it."[9]

(A) OBSERVANCE OF FORMALITIES

The instrument that creates a power may require that its exercise shall be attended by special formalities, and the general rule on this matter is that all such formalities, no matter how

Specified formalities must be observed.

---

[1] L.P.A. 1925, ss. 3, 205 (1) (xi).
[2] *Ibid.*, s. 3 ; S.L.A., 1925, s. 16.
[3] *Infra*, pp. 669 ; 679.
[4] See L.P.A. 1925, ss. 1 (7), 7 (4) ; Powers of Attorney Act 1971.
[5] Mental Health Act 1959, Sched. 7.
[6] L.P.A. 1925, s. 7 (3) ; Lands Clauses Consolidation Act 1845, s. 77.
[7] *Infra*. p. 850.
[8] *Re Lane*, [1908] 2 Ch. 581 ; *Re Waterhouse* (1907), 77 L. J. Ch. 30 ; *Re Priestley's Will Trusts*, [1971] Ch. 562 ; [1971] 2 All E. R. 817.
[9] *Re Lawrence's Will Trusts*, [1972] Ch. 418, at p. 430, *per* MEGARRY, J.

trivial and unessential, must be strictly observed.[1] Thus in the case of *Hawkins* v. *Kemp* [2]

> It was required by the settlor that the appointment should be made by deed or instrument in writing, executed in the presence of and attested by three credible witnesses, enrolled in one of the courts at Westminster, and executed with the consent of the donee's wife, father, and father-in-law, and also of several trustees. It was held that all these arbitrary demands must be literally performed.

Statutory exceptions.

Not unnaturally, this led to the frequent failure of appointments, and therefore the legislature has provided that in three cases an execution shall not be defective owing to the breach of a technicality. The three cases are as follows :

Leasing powers.

(a) **Leasing powers.**[3] It is provided by the Law of Property Act 1925 that where in the intended exercise of a power of leasing, whether given by an Act of Parliament or by some instrument, a lease is actually granted, but is not binding upon the reversioners by reason of some deviation from the terms of the power, such lease shall, if it has been made in good faith and if the lessee has entered, take effect in equity as a contract for the grant of a valid lease. The effect is that the lessee can require the reversioners either to grant a new lease which complies with the requisite formalities, or to confirm the void lease, and it is provided that a confirmation may be either by memorandum signed by each of the parties or by memorandum signed by the party who accepts rent from the lessee. Such is the effect, for instance, where a mortgagor makes an oral lease under his statutory power of leasing, but omits to reserve a power of re-entry on non-payment of rent as required by the Law of Property Act 1925.[4]

The lessee under such a void lease is bound on his side to accept a confirmation if the reversioner is willing to give one.

Powers exercised by will.

(b) **Powers exercised by will.** In the case of powers to be exercised by will, trouble frequently arose through donors requiring the will to be attested by a given number of witnesses. The Wills Act of 1837, therefore enacts, first, that no testamentary appointment shall be valid unless the will is in writing and signed by the testator ; and unless the signature is acknowledged by the testator in the presence of two or more witnesses present at the same time ; and unless the witnesses attest and subscribe the will in the presence of the testator. These are the necessary formalities

---

[1] *Sugden on Powers* (8th Edn.), p. 206.
[2] (1803), 3 East 410. [3] S. 152.
[4] *Pawson* v. *Revell*, [1958] 2 Q. B. 360 ; [1958] 3 All E. R. 233. As for the reservation of a power of re-entry, see L.P.A. 1925, s. 99 ; *infra*, pp. 666–7.

for all ordinary wills. Secondly, the Act provides that every will executed in the above manner shall, so far as respects the *execution and attestation* thereof, be a valid execution of a testamentary power of appointment, notwithstanding any express requirement that the will should be executed with some additional or different form of execution or solemnity.[1]

(c) **Powers exercised by deed.** A similar provision was made for deeds by Lord St. Leonards Act 1859, in a section that is now incorporated in the Law of Property Act 1925.[2] This provides that a deed executed in the presence of and attested by two or more witnesses and signed by the person by whom it is executed[3] shall, so far as respects the *execution and attestation* thereof, be a valid execution of a power of appointment, provided that the donee has not been required by the donor to make the appointment by will. It is expressly enacted that such an execution is valid even though the donor required that the deed should be executed or attested with some additional or other form of execution or solemnity. On the other hand nothing in the Act is to relieve the donee from obtaining any consent or from doing anything having no relation to the mode of execution and attestation which may have been prescribed by the donor. Moreover, unlike the rule laid down in the Wills Act, there is no provision that an appointment *inter vivos* must be made by deed, and therefore a direction by the donor that the power shall be exercisable by a mere written instrument is effective.

Powers exercised by deed.

It should be stressed that the operation of these two statutory rules is restricted to the mode of executing and attesting the instrument. The rule *at law* still is that any other act which the donor of the power may have specified must be performed. Thus if a deed is required, the power cannot be exercised either by mere writing or by will, and if a will is required a deed is not sufficient.

Formalities, apart from statutory exceptions, must be observed at law.

But at this point equity intervenes, and although it will not compel a donee to exercise a power[4] (except one which is coupled with a trust),[5] it is prepared to aid a defective execution in favour of the following persons—charities, creditors of the donee, purchasers for value from him, and his wife and legitimate children.[6] The court, however, will not grant its aid unless the donee has shown a clear intention to exercise the power and has indicated

Rule in equity.

Non-execution.

Defective execution.

---

[1] Wills Act 1837, ss. 9, 10.
[2] S. 159. [3] S. 73.
[4] *Tollet* v. *Tollet* (1728), 2 P. Wms. 489 ; White and Tudor's *Leading Cases in Equity* (9th Edn.), vol. ii. p. 249.
[5] *Supra*, p. 277.
[6] For a discussion of the whole subject see White and Tudor, *supra*, vol. ii. pp. 255–9.

the proposed beneficiaries and the extent of their interests.[1]
Further, it must be clear that the defect is of a formal character,
not the failure to comply with what the donor regarded as essential.

Thus relief will be given,

> if a power exercisable by deed or will is in fact exercised by a signed
> but unattested paper,[2] or
>
> if a power exercisable by deed is exercised by will,[3] unless the
> formality of a deed was regarded as essential by the donor.[4]

But relief will not be given,

> if a power exercisable by will is exercised by an irrevocable deed,
> for the donor intended that the donee should be free throughout his
> life to revoke an appointment should he so desire.[5]

(B) Excessive Execution

Forms of excessive appointments.
If in the exercise of a special power the appointor transgresses
the limits that have been imposed upon him, he acts in excess of
the power and is said to make an excessive appointment. Such
an excess may take any one of three forms, for if the appointor :

(1) appoints to persons who are not objects of the power,
that is, who are not within the class of appointees designated by the donor [6] ; or

(2) grants interests larger than those permitted by the power ;
or

(3) annexes to the appointed interest, conditions and qualifications not authorized by the power,

in each case he makes an excessive execution.

Excess alone generally void.
The principle of law applicable to any kind of excessive
appointment is that where there is a proper and complete execution followed by an improper excess, the execution is valid and
the excess void ; but where it is impossible to distinguish between
what is proper and what is improper, then the whole appointment falls to the ground.[7]

Thus, to take an example of excess in the objects :

> if the donee is authorized to appoint among *the children of A.*, he is
> not permitted to appoint in favour of A.'s grandchildren, and there-
> fore, if he makes a grant to a child for life with a gift over to the issue
> of the child, the first gift is valid and the second void.[8]

---

[1] *Garth* v. *Townsend* (1869), L. R. 7 Eq. 220.

[2] *Kennard* v. *Kennard* (1872), 8 Ch. App. 227.

[3] *Tollet* v. *Tollet* (1728), 2 P. Wms. 489.

[4] *Cooper* v. *Martin* (1867), 3 Ch. App. 47, 57–8 ; *Re Hambro's Marriage
Settlements*, [1949] Ch. 484.

[5] *Coffin* v. *Cooper* (1865,) 13 W. R. 571 ; *Re Parkin*, [1892] 3 Ch. 510, at p.
517.

[6] *Re Boulton's Settlement Trust*, [1928] Ch. 703.

[7] *Alexander* v. *Alexander* (1755), 2 Ves. Sen. 640, at p. 644 ; *Re Cohen*,
[1911] 1 Ch. 37 ; *Re Farncombe's Trusts* (1878), 9 Ch. D. 652 ; *Farwell on
Powers* (3rd Edn.), p. 343 ; *Re Holland*, [1914] 2 Ch. 595.

[8] *Brudenell* v. *Elwes* (1801), 1 East 442.

In other words, if it is possible to separate the good from the bad, the separation will be made.[1] So, for instance :

> When property is appointed equally to an object and a stranger, the object will take one-half, but the other half, instead of going to the stranger, is divided among the persons who are entitled in default of appointment.
>
> But if a donee has a power of appointment among the children of A., and appoints to A.'s son X. and to X.'s wife and children (without specifying any shares), the whole gift fails, for it is quite impossible to sever the gifts and say what share is to go to the object X., and what to the strangers, the wife and children.[2]

(C) Fraud upon a Power

An appointment is bad as being a fraud on the power unless it is made *bona fide* and in order to carry out the design intended by the donor.[3] But fraud in this connection is used in a technical sense and is not necessarily confined to moral turpitude.

Meaning of " fraud " in connection with powers.

Lord PARKER said in *Vatcher* v. *Paull* [4]:—

> " The term fraud in connection with frauds on a power does not necessarily denote any conduct on the part of the appointor amounting to fraud in the common law meaning of the term or any conduct which could be properly termed dishonest or immoral. It merely means that the power has been exercised for a purpose, or with an intention, beyond the scope of or not justified by the instrument creating the power. Perhaps the most common instance of this is where the exercise is due to some bargain between the appointor and appointee, whereby the appointor, or some other person not an object of the power, is to derive a benefit. But such a bargain is not essential. It is enough that the appointor's purpose and intention is to secure a benefit for himself, or some other person not an object of the power. In such a case the appointment is invalid, unless the Court can clearly distinguish between the quantum of the benefit *bona fide* intended to be conferred on the appointee and the quantum of the benefit intended to be derived by the appointor or to be conferred on a stranger. " [5]

It is clear, of course, that an appointment is vitiated if it is made upon a bargain or understanding which fetters the appointed interest in the appointee's hands in favour either of the appointor himself or some stranger, or which is intended to benefit the appointor or a stranger.[6]

Bargain between appointor and appointee.

---

[1] *Re Kerr's Trusts* (1877), 4 Ch. D. 600, at p. 604.

[2] *Re Brown's Trust* (1865), L. R. 1 Eq. 74.

[3] *Portland* v. *Topham* (1864), 11 H. L. C. 32, *per* WESTBURY, L. C. See generally Hanbury, *Modern Equity* (9th Edn.), pp. 109 *et seq.*

[4] [1915] A. C. 372, at p. 378.

[5] The revocation of an appointment already made is not within the doctrine of fraud, since it cannot injure those who are entitled in default of appointment ; *Re Greaves*, [1954] Ch. 434 ; [1954] 1 All E. R. 771.

[6] *Duggan* v. *Duggan* (1880), 8 L. R. Ir. 152 ; White and Tudor, p. 269. *Re Nicholson's Settlement*, [1939] Ch. 11, at p. 18 *per cur.* ; [1938] 3 All E. R. 532, at p. 534.

Thus in the leading case of *Aleyn* v. *Belchier* [1] :

> a power of jointuring which was executed in favour of a wife with an agreement that the wife should receive only part of the appointed fund, and that the residue should go to pay the husband's debts, was held to be a fraud on the power

The benefit, however, is not limited to a financial one, as, for instance, in *Cochrane* v. *Cochrane*,[2] where :

> A wife obtained against her husband, who was the donee of a special power to appoint £50,000 among his children or remoter issue, a decree nisi for the dissolution of their marriage. The husband, being desperately anxious that the decree should be made absolute in order that he might marry again, settled his wife's demands respecting alimony and so induced her to press the divorce proceedings to a conclusion, by agreeing, *inter alia*, to appoint more than half of the £50,000 to the only child of the marriage. It was held, ten years later, that this appointment was void as a fraud on the power since it was made for the purpose of securing freedom to re-marry. If allowed to stand it would have meant that he could appoint less than £25,000 among the children of his second marriage, of whom there were three.

Power to select.

But an appointment may be stigmatized as fraudulent even though no actual bargain has been struck. Thus, in the case of a power to select from a class of persons, such as children, the duty of the appointor is to make a *bona fide* and fair distribution among the objects, and he obviously fails in this respect if his appointment is directed to the achievement of some collateral purpose. The true test is whether he exercised the power *bona fide* for the end designed.[3] What was his purpose ? If it was merely to select the appropriate beneficiaries, his decision, however capricious, stands. If it was to benefit, directly or indirectly, a non-object, the purpose is foreign to the power, and the appointment will be set aside as fraudulent, irrespective of whether his design succeeds or whether it was known to the appointee. In *Re Marsden's Trusts*,[4] for instance :

> A married woman appointed the whole property to her daughter to the exclusion of the other children, but an arrangement made between her and her husband, to which the daughter was not a party, showed that her motive was to benefit him, not to act fairly towards the children. According to the arrangement the hope of the wife that some provision out of the appointed property should be made for the husband, in the event of his survival, was discreetly to be conveyed to the daughter. Although the daughter was not privy to the scheme the appointment was held to be void.

---

[1] (1758), 1 Eden, 132 ; White and Tudor, *Leading Cases in Equity* (9th Edn.), vol. ii. p. 263 ; which see generally.
[2] [1922] 2 Ch. 230.
[3] *Re Wright*, [1920] 1 Ch. 108, at p. 119, *per* P. O. LAWRENCE, J.
[4] (1859), 4 Drew 594 ; *Topham* v. *Duke of Portland* (1869), 5 Ch. App. 40 ; *Re Crawshay*, [1948] Ch. 123 ; [1948] 1 All E. R. 107 ; *Re Dick*, [1953] Ch. 343 ; [1953] 1 All E. R. 559 ; (1948), 64 *L. Q. R.* 221 (H. G. Hanbury).

As COHEN, L. J., said in another case of family pressure[1] :

" If [the appointor] makes the appointment to an object with the belief that the object will be subject to strong moral suasion to benefit a non-object, which suasion the object would, in the appointor's opinion, be unable to resist, the appointment would, we think, be invalid as a fraud on the power."

An appointment made subject to an unauthorized condition affords a good example of the attitude adopted by the courts.

Position where unauthorized condition annexed.

Suppose that a testator, X., having a power exercisable in favour of his children, appoints the property to his daughter, but subject to the condition that she settles it on her own children.

This condition is excessive and must in any event be struck out, for otherwise non-objects would benefit, but whether the whole appointment is void as being fraudulent depends upon the true purpose and intention of the appointor.

If X. genuinely intended to benefit his daughter, the appointment stands good, freed from the condition.[2] If, on the other hand, what prevailed with him was not a genuine desire to benefit his daughter, but a determination to accomplish some object beyond the purpose of the power, the whole appointment is rejected as fraudulent.[3]

The position is different where the power is to appoint in favour of one person only, as for instance a wife or husband. Here, if there is no bargain between the appointor and appointee which fetters the enjoyment of the appointed property, the fact that the appointor hoped to achieve a collateral purpose is immaterial and does not invalidate the appointment. The reason is that no detriment is caused to other possible beneficiaries, for there are no other objects of the power. The terms of the power are that the appointee shall be benefited if the appointor so decides, and, there being no bargain to fetter him, he is free to enjoy the property as he thinks fit.[4]

The general rule is that an appointment made in fraud of a power is void *in toto*, and that the property goes as in default of appointment, unless indeed a new and valid appointment

Effect of fraud.

---

[1] *Re Crawshay*, [1948] Ch. 123, at p. 135.
[2] *Re Holland*, [1914] 2 Ch. 595. If the condition is annexed not to the appointed share, but to the appointor's own property, as, for example, where he bequeaths £5,000 to his daughter, an object of the power, with a condition attached that she shall forfeit this unless she settles her appointed share on a non-object, the condition is not treated either as excessive or fraudulent. The daughter is put to her election, *i.e.* she can either retain the appointed share free from the condition and forfeit the £5,000, or retain the £5,000 upon the terms of settling the appointed share ; *Re Burton's Settlements*, [1955] Ch. 82 ; [1954] 3 All E. R. 193.
[3] *Re Dick*, [1953] Ch. 343 ; [1953] 1 All E. R. 559 ; *Re Burton's Settlements, supra*, where the whole question is reviewed at pp. 96–101 ; 201–204 respectively,
[4] *Re Nicholson's Settlement*, [1939] Ch. 11, [1938] 3 All E. R. 532.

is made. Nevertheless, if the honest and dishonest parts can be severed, effect may be given to that which is lawful.[1]

Thus in the case of a power to appoint to children, the fraudulent exercise in favour of one child does not disturb the shares that have properly been appointed to the others.[2]

Protection of purchasers claiming under void appointments.

An important question, that has received attention from the legislature, arises when a purchaser takes a conveyance of property from an appointee whose title depends upon a fraudulent appointment. The question is whether such a purchaser acquires a good title.

The law before 1926.

The answer to this question under the law in force before 1926 depended upon the nature of the interest taken by the purchaser, that is to say, upon whether he obtained the legal or the equitable estate. A fraudulent appointment made under a common law power, or a power operating under the Statute of Uses, so that the legal estate passed to the appointee (as for instance where there was a grant to A. to such uses as B. should appoint and B. appointed to C.) was not void, but voidable, and a purchaser who could show that he had given value and had had no notice of the fraud on the power obtained a good and indefeasible title. On the other hand an appointment in fraud of an equitable power, that is, a power the exercise of which passed only the equitable estate, was void, and a person who took from the appointee could not avail himself of the plea that he was purchaser for value without notice. The exercise of an equitable power has no direct effect upon the legal ownership. The legal estate in the property is vested in some other person, and that person must convey the legal estate to the appointee in order to give legal effect to the appointment.[3]

The law after 1925.

When, therefore, most powers became equitable under the legislation of 1925 new provisions for the protection of purchasers were required. The Law of Property Act 1925 enacts that :

" An instrument purporting to exercise a power of appointment over property, which, in default of and subject to any appointment, is held in trust for a class or number of persons *of whom the appointee is one*, shall not be void on the ground of fraud on the power as against a purchaser in good faith." [4]

In the present context, however, a *purchaser in good faith* is defined as a person dealing with an appointee not less than 25 years old, for valuable consideration in money or money's worth, and without notice of the fraud or of any circumstances from which the fraud might with reasonable care have been discovered.[5] Even so, the protection is not complete, for if the appointee's interest

---

[1] *Whelan* v. *Palmer* (1888), 39 Ch. D. 648. See White and Tudor, *Leading Cases in Equity,* (9th Edn.), vol. ii. p. 274.
[2] *Harrison* v. *Randall* (1852), 9 Hare 397.
[3] *Cloutte* v. *Storey,* [1911] 1 Ch. 18.
[4] S. 157 (1).   [5] S. 157 (2).

exceeds what he would have got had no appointment been made, the title of the purchaser in good faith does not extend to the excess.[1]

To illustrate the rule and the qualification :

Suppose that there is power to appoint, subject to a life interest, a fund of £1000 among the children of A., and that in default of appointment the fund is to be divided equally among the children. If there are four children and a fraudulent appointment during the life interest is made to one of the children, a purchaser of this appointed interest will be unable to claim the protection of the Act unless he can prove that he had no notice of the fraud, and that the child was over 25 at the time of the purchase, and even then his right will not extend to more than £250.

SECTION III. DETERMINATION OF POWERS[2]

The normal way in which a power is determined is for the donee to execute a deed of release. It has always been the law that powers appendant and powers in gross can be released,[3] but it was not until 1882 [4] that the same procedure was made applicable to powers simply collateral.[5] It is now enacted [6] that all powers, except those in the nature of or coupled with a trust,[7] may be released either by deed or by a contract not to exercise the power. Thus, although the donee of a power exercisable only by will cannot make a valid appointment by an irrevocable deed, yet a release under seal of the power, or a covenant not to exercise it, is binding.[8]

Release.

Apart from express release the rule is that any dealing with the estate by the donee of the power which is inconsistent with its further exercise puts an end to the power, so that if a husband appoints one-fourth of the property to his wife and the residue to his children, and the wife dies, he cannot appoint her fourth to a second wife.[9]

Inconsistent dealing.

A power appendant, such as the power of leasing enjoyed by a tenant for life under the Settled Land Act 1925, is not extinguished

Settled Land Act powers.

---

[1] S. 157 (1), proviso.
[2] See generally (1968), 84 *L. Q. R.* 64 (A. J. Hawkins).
[3] *Re Radcliffe*, [1892] 1 Ch. 227, 231. *Re Mills*, [1930] 1 Ch. 654.
[4] Conveyancing Act 1881, s. 52.
[5] For definition, see *supra*, p. 279.
[6] L.P.A. 1925, s. 155.
[7] *Re Somes*, [1896] 1 Ch. 250. *Re Wills' Trust Deeds*, [1964] Ch. 219 ; [1963] 1 All E. R. 390.
[8] *Re Brown's Settlement*, [1939] Ch. 944 ; [1939] 3 All E. R. 391.
[9] *Re Hancock*, [1896] 2 Ch. 173 ; *Foakes v. Jackson*, [1900] 1 Ch. 807 ; *Re Wills' Trust Deeds*, *supra* ; *cf. Muir v. I. R. Comrs.*, [1966] 1 W. L. R. 1269 ; [1966] 3 All E. R. 38 ; *Re Courtauld's Settlement*, [1965] 1 W. L. R. 1385 ; [1965] 2 All E. R. 544.

by being exercised, and as we have seen, a tenant for life under that Act cannot release his statutory powers.[1]

Disclaimer.

Any power other than a Settled Land Act power or one coupled with a trust can be disclaimed by deed, and can then be exercised by the other person or the survivor of the other persons to whom it was given.[2]

---

[1] *Supra*, p. 186.
[2] L.P.A. 1925, s. 156.

CHAPTER VI

FUTURE INTERESTS[1]

SUMMARY

---

[1] For the history of this subject see Holdsworth, *History of English Law,* vol. vii. pp. 81 *et seq.*; and generally, see Gray, *The Rule against Perpetuities* (4th Edn.) ; Morris and Leach, *The Rule against Perpetuities* (2nd Edn. 1962 and Supplement 1964).

SECTION I.   THE POSITION BEFORE 1926

Pre-1926 law simplified.

The law affecting future interests was greatly simplified by the legislation of 1925, though this simplification was incidental rather than due to any direct enactment.   There is now in consequence less justification for Blackstone's dictum that " the doctrine of estates in expectancy contains some of the nicest and most abstruse learning of the English law."[1]   But we cannot appreciate the extent or the effect of the simplification unless we know something of the law before 1926, and we must therefore attempt in the following pages to give a short account of the difficulties that formerly beset the subject.   The historical stages in the evolution of the law have been described with great particularity and clearness by Holdsworth,[2] but in the present brief account, in order to diminish the complexity of the subject as far as possible, we shall not keep to the strictly historical method, but attempt merely to bring into relief the various classes

Knowledge of pre-1926 law still necessary.

---

[1] Blackstone, vol. ii. p. 163.
[2] *History of English Law,* vol. vii. pp. 81–149.

of future interests that might subsist under the old law. The arrangement we shall adopt, then, will be to describe, first, the future legal interests called *remainders*, secondly, the future legal interests called *executory interests*, and thirdly, the future equitable interests which might correspond either to remainders or to executory interests.

Types of future interests under the old law.

Before an explanation is given of these three classes it is advisable to develop a theme that pervades the whole of the present subject, namely, the meaning given by the law to the words " vested " and " contingent." Estates are either vested or contingent. The former may be vested either in possession or in interest.

Meaning of " vested " and " contingent."

An estate is vested in possession when its owner is entitled to present possession; it is vested in interest when there is a present unqualified right of taking possession as soon as it becomes vacant. If, for example, there is a limitation :

Vested in possession and vested in interest.

To A. for life and after his death to B. for life,

A. has an estate which is vested in possession, B. one which is vested in interest.[1] As Preston demonstrated over a hundred years ago, an estate vested in interest is always a present right in the sense that the owner is clothed with an immediate power of alienation, though it is not always present in the sense that he is entitled to the actual physical enjoyment of the land at the moment.[2] There is nothing conditional about it, *i.e.* there is nothing that must happen before the owner can establish his title. The test is always the same—is the owner absolutely entitled at the present moment to assume possession whenever it may fall vacant ? If so, he owns a vested interest—he is invested with a portion of the fee simple—even though in fact he may never obtain possession. In the example given above, for instance, it is obvious that B. may predecease A. and therefore may never enjoy the fruits of ownership, but this does not alter the fact that during his lifetime he continues to have an absolute and unqualified right to take possession upon the determination of the preceding estate. In the words of Fearne :

> " The present capacity of taking effect in possession, if the possession were to become vacant, and not the certainty that the possession will become vacant before the estate limited in remainder determines, universally distinguishes a vested remainder from one that is contingent." [3]

An estate is contingent if the accrual of the owner's title depends upon the occurrence of some event. If, for instance, there is a limitation :

Contingent interests.

---

[1] Hawkins and Ryder, *Construction of Wills* (1965), pp. 282–5 ; Hayes, *Introduction to Conveyancing*, vol. i. p. 17 ; Gray, *op. cit.*, s. 794.

[2] *Preston on Estates*, vol. i. p. 65.

[3] Fearne, *Contingent Remainders*, p. 216.

To X. and Y. for their lives, and then to the survivor of them in fee simple,[1]

the fee simple stands contingently limited while X. and Y. are still alive, for during that period neither of them can establish his claim to the estate. It is only the survivor who will be entitled, and at the moment it is dubious which of them will be the first to die. Again, if there is a gift

To A. for life and then to B. at 21,

B., if still under 21, has a mere contingent interest, for he has not yet satisfied the condition upon which the acquisition of a definite interest depends. He is not yet qualified to take possession whenever it falls vacant.[2]

Before it can be said that a beneficiary is entitled to a vested interest, two things must concur :

(*a*) his identity must be established ;
(*b*) his right to the interest (as distinguished from his right to possession) must not depend upon the occurrence of some event.

Until conditions (*a*) and (*b*) are satisfied he has nothing more than a contingent interest. We must notice, however, that, except in the context of the rule against perpetuities,[3] it is not necessary that the size of the interest should be ascertained. Thus where there is a limitation

To the children of A. who shall attain 21

the moment that A.'s eldest child becomes 21 he takes a vested interest. Yet the size of his share cannot be ascertained until 21 years after A.'s death. Until then it will diminish whenever further children qualify as members of the class.

We will now consider the three types of future interest that existed before 1926.

Remainders.

Legal Remainders. Common law permitted future interests, called remainders, to be carved out of a legal estate, though, as we shall see presently, there were several restrictive rules which had to be observed. If a settlor decided to create two or more successive estates in his land, and drafted the desired limitations in one instrument, as for instance by a feoffment

to A. for life and then to B. for life and then to C. in fee simple,

the first estate which preceded the next following remainder was

---

[1] *Whitby* v. *Von Luedecke*, [1906] 1 Ch. 783 ; *Re Legh's Settlement Trusts*, [1938] Ch. 39 ; [1937] 3 All E. R. 823.

[2] On the distinction between " vested " and " contingent " see Fearne, *Contingent Remainders*, p. 74 ; Gray, s. 9 and chapter iii ; Morris and Leach, ch. 2 ; *Theobald on Wills* (13th Edn.), ch. 41. In construing limitations, the court leans in favour of vested interests, sometimes in spite of language which at first sight appears to be contingent. See *Duffield* v. *Duffield* (1829), 3 Bl. N.S. 260, at p. 331, *per* BEST, C. J.

[3] *Infra*, pp. 320–1, 326–7.

called the "particular estate"[1] and those which followed were
denominated " remainders."

Such an estate was called a remainder, not because it was the
remnant that was left after the grant of the particular estate,
but because the land was to stand over or continue for the remainderman after the particular estate had determined.[2]

A remainder should not be confused with a reversion, which
is an interest that arises by operation of law, as distinct from act
of parties, whenever the owner of an estate grants a particular
estate, but does not dispose of the whole of his interest. If, for
instance, a tenant in fee simple makes a conveyance of the land in
tail, for life or for a term of years, there continues in him an estate
which is called a reversion because the land will revert into his
possession upon the determination of the particular estate.

Reversions distin-guished.

" A reversion is where the residue of the estate always doth continue
in him that made the particular estate." [3]

Remainders fall into two classes, being either vested or contingent. It follows from what has already been said that a person
has a vested remainder if he or his representatives are continually
entitled and ready to take actual possession of the land whenever
the particular estate ends. This implies that he must be a living
ascertained person and that his title as owner does not depend
upon the happening of some uncertain event. A simple example
is a grant

Vested remainder.

to A. for life, remainder to B. in fee simple.

As opposed to this, a remainder is contingent if the grantee
is not an ascertained person, or if, though ascertained, his title
awaits the occurrence of some event, for in neither case is there a
person ready to enter the land as soon as it is vacant. Grants

Contingent remainder.

to a bachelor for life, remainder to his son ; and
to A. for life, remainder in tail to his first son to attain 21,

are examples of contingent remainders.

A contingent remainder becomes a vested remainder when the
person to whom it is limited is ascertained, or when the
event upon which it is dependent happens. A contingent
remainder may be so limited that it can vest only *eo instanti*
with the determination of the particular estate, as for instance
where the grant is to A. during the life of B., remainder to
the heirs of B. In this case the death of B. terminates the
particular estate and at the same time enables the person who
is heir of B. to be ascertained,[4] for *nemo heres est viventis*.

Vesting of contingent remainder.

The result of the distinction between vested and contingent
interests is that reversions and vested remainders, despite the

Vested remainders are present estates.

---

[1] So called because it is a *particula*, or small part, of the estate of inheritance.

[2] Pollock and Maitland (2nd Edn.), *History of English Law*, vol. ii. p. 21 ;
(1890), 6 *L. Q. R.* 22, 25 (F. W. Maitland). [3] Co. Litt. 22*b*.

[4] Co. Litt. 298*a* ; see *Boraston's Case* (1587), 3 Co. Rep. 19 ; Fearne,
Contingent Remainders, p. 5, note (*d*).

element of futurity of possessory enjoyment that characterizes them, have always been regarded as *estates* in the true sense of the word, though, with the reduction in 1925 of legal estates to the fee simple absolute in possession and the term of years absolute, the more appropriate word is now "interests." Moreover, they are present, not future, interests. A future interest properly so called is one which cannot be the subject-matter of ownership until something happens that may never happen. This is not the position with regard to reversions and vested remainders, for although they may be described as future *interests* inasmuch as they do not at the moment carry immediate possession of the land, they are nevertheless present existing interests in the sense that they confer upon their holders a portion of the actual ownership of the land.

> "The fee simple being supposed to be carved out into parts or divisions by the creation of particular estates, a grant to any person of one of these portions of the fee vested him with, or vested him in, an estate in the land." [1]

Aliter contingent remainders.

They are classified as future interests merely because the right of possessory enjoyment is postponed, but they are present in the sense that they may be disposed of as freely as an estate carrying a right to immediate possession. On the other hand, a contingent remainder does not become an estate, but continues as a mere possibility of acquiring an estate, until the contingency upon which it depends has occurred. [2]

Rules for remainders before 1926.

After this preliminary description of remainders we are in a position to examine those restrictive rules of the common law that furnished the limits within which a settlor could create interests of this type, though we may note that they were not finally established until the beginning of the seventeenth century. [3] The exceeding strictness of these rules indicates the reluctance with which common law permitted the existence of future interests, and it is well at the outset of our inquiry to realize the main object which the law had in view. That object was to preserve the continuity of seisin. Seisin meant the possession of land by a freeholder, *i.e.* by a tenant in fee simple, in fee tail or for life, and it was a feudal rule of the greatest antiquity that there should be an uninterrupted tenancy of the freehold, or, in more technical language, that the seisin should always be full. Every feoffment had to convey an estate that would at once carry the freehold to the feoffee. [4] This rule was required in the early days of the law for two distinct reasons. In the first place, those profitable feudal incidents which, as we have seen, [5] explained the survival of the military tenures, were due from the person who was seised of the land

Importance of seisin.

---

[1] Hawkins on Wills (3rd Edn.), p. 263.
[2] Hargreaves, *Introduction to Land Law* (4th Edn.), pp. 47–50 ; 103–4.
[3] Holdsworth, *History of English Law*, vol. vii. pp. 81 *et seq.*
[4] *Preston on Estates*, vol. i. pp. 217, 249.   [5] *Supra*, pp. 19 *et seq.*

in question, and therefore it was of the utmost importance that an estate of freehold should never be without a known owner, for otherwise a lord might be prejudiced in the enforcement of his rights. Secondly, it was a rule of procedure that a real action lay only against the actual freeholder, so that if the identity of the person seised was in any way doubtful, a dispossessed owner of land might be prevented from taking proceedings for its recovery. For these reasons, therefore, it was an inviolable principle of the common law that any disposition of land calculated to produce an abeyance of the seisin was void.[1]

By way of preface it is well to appreciate that the following restrictive rules imposed upon the creation of legal remainders constituted the whole foundation of the old law relating to future interests, and that unless they are constantly kept in mind it is impossible to arrive at a correct understanding of that law. On the other hand, if they are thoroughly grasped, the abstruseness asserted by Blackstone need occasion no fear to the reader. *Importance of the rules.*

(a) **The limitation of a remainder was void unless it was preceded by the limitation of a particular estate of freehold.**

It was impossible at common law to limit a freehold remainder in such a way that it would arise of its own strength at some time in the future. A feoffment, for instance made *No freehold in futuro.*

> to B. for life when he attains the age of 21 years

was void. The rule which forbade a limitation of this nature depended upon two principles, viz.: that the seisin must not be in abeyance, and that a conveyance which divested the freehold from the feoffor must at the same time vest it in the feoffee.[2]

The classic conveyance of the old law was the feoffment with livery of seisin, and as the operative part of this assurance was the actual delivery of possession and not the charter of feoffment,[3] it was clear that the seisin must pass from the feoffor. If, however, the seisin departed from him, it must of necessity vest in some definite person, for otherwise an abeyance of seisin would ensue. An alienor, therefore, who desired to confer a life estate upon B. at 21 was confronted with a difficulty. There could be no immediate delivery to B., for he was to take an interest in the land only if he attained 21, and that event would remain uncertain for some time. Again, the feoffment could not be made at one date to take effect later, for it was essential that the feoffor should immediately be divested of the seisin.[4] *Reason for the rule.*

---

[1] Co. Litt. 342*b*; *Freeman d. Vernon v. West* (1763), 2 Wils. 165; Hayes, *Introduction to Conveyancing*, vol. i. p. 14; Challis, *Law of Real Property* (3rd Edn.), p. 100. [2] Fearne, *Contingent Remainders*, p. 281.
[3] Co. Litt. 271*b*, note. [4] *Per curiam, Barwick's Case* (1597), 5 Co. Rep. 93*b*.

Supporting estate of freehold.

The only method, then, of making an effective feoffment and of providing for continuity of seisin when it was desired to give B. a freehold estate at 21 was immediately to vest the seisin in some other person (called the particular tenant), who could answer the feudal requirements of the common law. Thus it came to be a rule that every freehold remainder which was to take effect upon the happening of a future contingency had to be supported by a particular estate of freehold,[1] so that the limitation which we are considering, instead of merely being to B. for life at 21, would be

to A. for life, remainder to B. for life when he attains 21.

This feudal rule outlived its reasons, but it continued to affect the limitation of remainders at common law until 1926, long after the feoffment had given way to other methods of conveyance.[2] It was a legacy of the Middle Ages which ceased to operate only with the inauguration of the new system on January 1st, 1926.

(b) A contingent remainder had to be so limited as to be capable of vesting either during the continuance of the particular estate or *eo instanti* that it determined[3]

No abeyance of seisin after termination of particular estate.

The particular estate of freehold that was required by the first rule to support all freehold contingent remainders had to be one which was capable of enduring until the contingency happened. Thus a limitation which contemplated an interval of time between the termination of the particular estate and the vesting of the remainder rendered the remainder void. If, for example, there was a grant

to A. for life and one year after A.'s death to B. for life ; or
to A. for life, remainder to such of his children as either before *or after* his death attained 21,[4]

the remainder was in the first example void, and in the second void *as regards the children attaining* 21 *after A.'s death*. If the first limitation had been allowed to stand, the effect would obviously have been to cause an abeyance of the seisin for one year; and a like result might have ensued in the second case, since the very terms of the limitation contemplated the accrual of an estate to the remaindermen even if they, or any of them, did not reach the age of 21 until after the particular estate had determined.

---

[1] Blackstone, vol. i. p. 118 ; *Buckler's Case* (1597), 2 Co. Rep. 55*a*. *Barwick's Case, supra* ; Fearne, *Contingent Remainders*, p. 281 ; Sanders on *Uses and Trusts* (5th Edn.), vol. i. p. 141 ; Holdsworth, *History of English Law*, vol. vii. p. 84 ; Challis, *Law of Real Property* (3rd Edn.), p. 104.
[2] *Savill* v. *Bethell*, [1902] 2 Ch. 523. 540.
[3] Fearne, *op cit.*, p. 307.
[4] *Re Lechmere and Lloyd* (1881), 18 Ch. D. 524 ; *Dean* v. *Dean*, [1891] 3 Ch. 150 ; *Miles* v. *Jarvis* (1883), 24 Ch. D. 633.

It followed as a logical result of this requirement that, even though a contingent remainder had been so limited as to be capable of becoming vested at the latest when the particular estate determined, yet it would fail unless it did actually vest (*i.e.* unless the contingency had actually happened) at the time of that determination. Thus, the weakness of contingent remainders at common law was their liability to destruction by reason of the premature determination of the particular estate. In the case, for instance, of a limitation to

Remainder must have vested when particular estate ended.

A. for life, remainder to the first son of B. to attain 21,

the remainder failed unless B.'s son had attained his majority at the time of A.'s death,[1] while in a limitation to

X. for life, remainder to his children at 21,

those children who attained 21 in X.'s lifetime took estates to the exclusion of children who reached the prescribed age afterwards.[2] We shall see later that remainders might also fail owing to the artificial destruction of the particular estate before the occurrence of the contingency.[3]

(c) A contingent remainder was void if it was limited to take effect by cutting short the particular estate[4]

Common law required that a contingent remainder should be so limited that it would take effect upon the natural determination of the particular estate of freehold, and not by breaking in upon it or by bringing it to an abrupt termination. There could be no remainder by proviso, *i.e.* it was impossible to terminate an estate by a proviso so as to make the estate which was to arise after the occurrence of the proviso a remainder.[5] Thus if the limitation was

No remainder by proviso.

to a widow for life, but if she re-married, to X. for life; or to B. for life on condition that when Y. married, B.'s estate should cease and remain to Y.,

the interests limited to X. and to Y. were void.

A limitation of this kind which attempted to defeat a prior estate was in effect a limitation upon condition, and had it been permitted it would have infringed the common law maxim that no one could take advantage of a condition (*i.e.* no one could enter and terminate the estate to which the condition was attached), except the grantor and his heirs, executors or administrators.[6]

---

[1] *White* v. *Summers*, [1908] 2 Ch. 256.
[2] *Festing* v. *Allen* (1843), 12 M. & W. 279.
[3] *Infra*, p. 308.
[4] Fearne, *Contingent Remainders*, p. 10, note (*h*), 261 ; *Cogan* v. *Cogan* (1596), Cro. Eliz. 360 ; Holdsworth, *History of English Law*, vol. vii. p. 84.
[5] *Blackman* v. *Fysh*, [1892] 3 Ch. 209, at p. 220.
[6] Fearne, *op. cit.* p. 261 ; Challis, *Law of Real Property* (3rd Edn.), p. 81. It would also have infringed the maxim that an entry for condition broken destroyed all the estates given by the original limitation ; *infra*, p. 370.

(d) No remainder could be limited after a fee simple estate[1]

A fee could not be mounted on a fee.

Since a fee simple estate is the largest interest that can be enjoyed in land, it was a rule of the common law that a future estate could not be limited to take effect as a remainder expectant upon the determination of a preceding fee simple. A fee could not be mounted on a fee. Thus

if a grant had been made in fee simple with a proviso that it should determine upon the payment of a certain sum or upon failure of the grantee to do a certain act, and go over to a stranger,

the gift over was void.

Definition of "remainder."

Summary. To summarize the law that has been stated above, we see that one class of future *legal* interests permitted by the common law consisted of remainders, which may be defined briefly as interests so limited as to be immediately expectant upon the natural determination of a particular freehold estate less in quantum than a fee simple. Only the simplest kinds of future interests could be created by way of remainder because, for various feudal reasons, their validity depended upon the observance of the four strict rules that we have specified.

Inadequacy of Common Law. It is evident from what has been said that in the matter of future limitations the common law fell short of what was required by society. In the nature of things there are three possible classes of future interests :

First, one that is to take effect in possession upon the determination of a previously limited estate, *e.g.* to A. for life and then to B. for life.

Secondly, one that is to take effect in possession by cutting short a previously limited estate, *e.g.* to A. for life, but as soon as B. is called to the Bar, then to B. for life.

Thirdly, one that arises of its own strength and has no support from or connection with a previously limited estate, *e.g.* to A. for life at 21.

Common law admitted the first class, but the overriding importance that it ascribed to seisin, together with its rules concerning feoffments and conditions, precluded altogether the recognition of the last two classes. Yet, feudal doctrines apart, there is no reason why these prohibited classes should not be available to a settlor, and we now have to see how they came to be recognized under the name of *executory interests* through the medium of equity.

---

[1] Fearne, *op. cit.* p. 12 ; Co. Litt. 18a ; *Musgrave* v. *Brooke* (1884), 26 Ch. D. 792.

Executory Interests. Executory interests were formerly purely equitable in nature, and their origin is to be found in the protection which the Chancellor afforded to the *use* of lands. The governor of the use was the intention of its owner, and though the Chancellor generally followed the rules of common law in regulating the equitable estate, his chief object was to give effect to the wishes of the owner. In the sphere of future interests, he attained the object by refusing to extend to limitations of the use those restrictions that common law imposed in the case of the legal estate. His general policy was to permit a man to create any form of future interest that seemed desirable to him provided that he was content to carve the interest out of the equitable estate and not out of the legal estate. In other words, a settlor had liberty of action if he took advantage of the machinery of uses. A grant to A. at 21 was void, but a grant to X. and his heirs *to the use of* A. at 21 was valid, for the common law rule requiring the support of a particular estate had no application to the equitable interest to which alone A. was entitled, and the Chancellor saw no reason why he should not compel X. to hold the land in favour of A. when the latter reached 21. The use in the hands of its owner was as clay in the hands of the potter,[1] and though in the case of the legal estate a fee could not be mounted on a fee, and though a freehold could not be made to spring up in the future nor to shift to another before its regular termination, there was no objection in principle to these dispositions being made of the equitable estate.

Thus even before the Statute of Uses 1535 it became possible, though not indeed common, to create future equitable interests of a kind that would have been impossible at common law. In course of time, when these interests were firmly established in our jurisprudence, they were classified either as *shifting* or as *springing uses* according as they displaced a prior estate or not.

A springing use was an interest limited by way of use to take effect at a future time without affecting any previously limited freehold estate.[2] Simple illustrations would be :

> feoffment to A. and his heirs to the use in fee simple of any wife whom B. may marry, or
> feoffment to A. and his heirs to the use in fee simple of C. at 21.

In the former case, the wife, and, in the latter, C. became entitled to the equitable estate as soon as the respective events occurred. Until then the use " resulted ", or returned to the feoffor and his heirs.

A shifting use was an interest limited by way of use to take effect at some time in the future, in defeasance of and by way of substitution for some prior freehold interest, and before such

Marginal notes: Executory interests equitable in origin. Equitable future interests free from restrictions. Springing uses. Shifting uses.

---

[1] *Brent's Case* (1575), 2 Leonard 14, 16, *per* MANWOOD, J.
[2] Smith, *An Original View of Executory Interests* (1844), s. 117; Sugden's *Gilbert on Uses.*, pp. 152–3.

prior interest had lasted its full measure of duration.[1] Examples
would be

> feoffment to F. and his heirs to the use of A. and his heirs, but if A
> becomes entitled to Blackacre, to the use of B. and his heirs ; or,
> feoffment to F. and his heirs to the use of C. and his heirs, but if
> C. marries D., to the use of E. and his heirs.

It will be observed that the limitations in favour of B. and of
E., if they had been contained in a direct feoffment instead of in
a feoffment to uses, would have been in conflict with the third
rule for remainders [2] and would therefore have been void.[3]

Effect of the Statute of Uses.   The critical event in the history of executory interests was the
Statute of Uses. The statute had converted most uses into
legal estates, and it therefore fell to the common law courts to
decide what effect it had upon these equitable springing and
shifting uses. There were two possible courses, either to hold
them void altogether or to permit their continued existence, but
to adopt the second course would require fortitude, since it would
enable future *legal* estates to be created of a kind quite impossible
of creation by way of remainder. As we have seen, a feoffment
to B. for life at 21 was void as a remainder, though a feoffment
to A. and his heirs to the use of B. for life at 21 was valid in equity
as a springing use. If this latter form of limitation were still to
be permissible, then it would be the *legal* estate, not as formerly
the equitable estate, that would spring up in B. at 21, for the
statute had enacted in effect that when A. was seised to the use
of B., the latter was to have the legal estate.[4] In other words, by
adopting the machinery of a feoffment to uses future limitations
of the legal estate could be framed without regard to the rules
laid down for remainders.

Executory interests became legal interests.   Fortunately for the development of settlements it was the
latter course that was adopted. It was held as early as 1538 that
springing and shifting interests, if contained in a feoffment to
uses, vested in the beneficiaries as legal estates upon the happening
of the specified events, and about 1555 the same conclusion was
reached with regard to similar interests limited by will.[5] If, for
instance,

> A. conveyed land *before the statute* to B. and his heirs to the use of
> X. and his heirs, but unless X. adopted the name and arms of A.
> within two years, then to the use of Y. and his heirs,

it was out of the equitable, not out of the legal, estate that a
future interest had been created in favour of Y. The legal estate

---

[1] Smith, *op. cit.*, s. 149.
[2] *Supra*, p. 299.
[3] It was said in the argument in *Hopkins* v. *Hopkins* (1734), Cas. *temp.*
Talbot, 45, at p. 51, that " springing uses are as old as uses themselves." For a
case between 1417 and 1424 in which the aid of the Chancellor was supplicated,
see (1896), 10 Selden Society, *Select Cases in Chancery*, 1364–1471, p. 114.
[4] *Supra*, pp. 54–5.
[5] Holdsworth, *History of English Law*, vol. vii. pp. 122 *et seq.*

was throughout vested in B. But *after the statute* the legal estate would shift from X. to Y. if there were no compliance with the name and arms clause, for in that event the terms of the original grant required B. to stand seised to the use of Y. Thus the use was allowed to retain its mercurial attributes despite its statutory transformation into the legal estate.

Thus side by side with legal remainders there grew up legal springing and shifting uses, the two last differing from the first in the fact that they could be limited without regard to those four rules that restricted the limitation of remainders. It must, however, be observed—for this was a technical rule that obtained until 1925—that the one way by which a grantor could create a valid executory interest by an instrument *inter vivos* was to adopt the expression *to the use of*, or some other expression contained in the statute. A grant to B. at 21 was void ; a grant to A. to the use of B. at 21 was valid.

Executory uses required technical words.

On the other hand, a *testator* was not subject to the same restriction. He could, by a direct devise, and without adopting the expression *to the use of*, create exactly the same springing and shifting dispositions as he might have created by a grant *inter vivos* to uses.

Executory devises required no technical words.

The subject of springing and shifting interests created by will, which came to be called *executory devises*, requires a little elaboration. The position before the Statute of Uses was that though the power of testamentary disposition was for feudal reasons withheld from the tenant of the *legal* estate, it was exercisable in respect of the equitable estate. A landowner who put his land in use could specify the persons who were to fill the position of *cestuis que use* after his death. The immediate effect of the Statute of Uses, which converted the equitable into the legal estate, was to abolish this indirect power of will making, but the abolition was felt to be such a grievance that in 1540 the Statute of Wills partially restored the power of testamentary disposition by enacting that all land held in socage and two-thirds of land held in knight service should be devisable. In 1660 tenure in knight service was abolished, so that from that time an owner enjoyed complete power of devising all his land by a direct will and was not compelled to employ the machinery of a devise to uses. In other words, the power of testamentary disposition was for the first time extended to the legal estate. The question that arose after the Statute of Wills was whether a testator could employ this power to create future interests analogous to the springing and shifting uses created by a grant *inter vivos* to uses, or whether he was obliged to limit the future interests in conformity with the rules that had been laid down for remainders. This question of the applicability of the Statute of Uses to a devise to express uses was much debated, since it was difficult to see how the earlier statute could affect a form of disposition that was not introduced until a later date. But though the subject roused

Executory devises.

many learned controversies,[1] no decision was ever given on the point, and it soon came to be considered a matter of no importance, for either by virtue of the Statute of Uses or with a view to carrying out the intention of testators, the courts consistently held that future limitations contained in wills were capable of producing exactly the same effect as if they had been made in a deed by a grant to uses. When once it was clear that a testator intended to create springing and shifting interests analogous to the interests that might be created by a grant to uses, then, despite the lack of the technical expression " to the use of," effect was given to that intention. Thus :

> a grant by deed to A. at 21

was void ;

> a grant to X. and his heirs to the use of A. at 21

was valid ; and

> a devise to A. at 21

was valid.

Executory interests distinguished from remainders. We see, then, that after the Statute of Uses a second class of future *legal* interests was added to the older class which consisted of remainders. The second class comprised springing and shifting uses created by an instrument *inter vivos*, called generically *executory uses*, and springing and shifting interests limited by will, called *executory devises*. *Executory interests* was an expression which included both executory uses and executory devises. A remainder, as we have seen, was a future estate so limited as to be immediately expectant upon the natural determination of a particular freehold estate less than a fee simple. An executory interest was a future estate which, inasmuch as it infringed one or more of the rules laid down by the original common law for remainders, would have been invalid if it had been contained in an assurance at common law, but which was valid *provided that it was limited either by will or by a conveyance to uses*.[2] If a settlor desired to travel outside the remainder rules, that is to say, if he desired to

> create a freehold *in futuro* unsupported by a particular estate,[3] or to
>
> enable beneficiaries to take, although their rights became vested after the termination of the particular estate,[4] or to
>
> make the particular estate shift on a given event to another donee,[5] or to

---

[1] See opinion of Booth, Collect. Jur., V. i. 427 ; Sanders, *Uses and Trusts*, vol. i. p. 250, and note ; Co. Litt. 272a, note (1) VIII. i ; Cruise, *Digest* Tit. xi. c. 4. ss. 15–18 ; Challis, *Law of Real Property* (3rd Edn.), p. 169.

[2] Challis, *op. cit.*, p. 172.

[3] *E.g.*, grant to X. and his heirs to the use of A. at 21 ; or devise to A. at 21.

[4] *E.g.*, grant to X. and his heirs to the use of A. for life and then to the use of such of A.'s children as before or after his death attain 21.

[5] *E.g.*, grant to X. and his heirs to the use of A. for life, but immediately B. is called to the Bar, then to the use of B. and his heirs.

add a shifting clause to the limitation of the fee simple,[1]

he was at liberty to do so, but he must have made the limitation either in a will or in a conveyance to uses.

Relation between Contingent Remainders and Executory Interests.

We must now consider the relation between contingent remainders and executory interests. The law as sketched above appears at first sight to be shrouded in mystery. There were two types of future legal interests,

Difficulties caused by existence of two types of future interests.

> one (the remainder), subject to strict rules which might operate to defeat the interest contrary to the settlor's intention,
> the other free from such rules and free from that liability to destruction which attended remainders.

The question that this dichotomy naturally suggests is whether a remainder could always be saved from destruction by framing it as an executory interest.

> Suppose, for example, that a feoffment were made to X. and his heirs *to the use of* A. for life and then *to the use of* B. and his heirs at 21, and that A. died before B. became 21.

As a remainder B.'s interest failed altogether, since, although it was capable of vesting at the determination of the particular estate, it had not in fact done so.[2] It would, however, be saved from destruction if it could be construed as an executory interest.

But in reality such questions did not admit of any reasonable doubt, for there was a sacred rule of common law, later known as the *Rule in Purefoy* v. *Rogers*, dating back to the sixteenth century and finally established in 1671,[3] which directed that a limitation that was capable of taking effect as a remainder must never be treated as an executory interest. The justification for this rule was that contingent remainders, unlike executory interests, were destructible, and therefore did not tend to a perpetuity, *i.e.* they did not so easily enable a settlor to create a succession of limited interests that would render the land inalienable for an unduly long period.

Rule in Purefoy v. Rogers.

Thus, the maxim was *once a remainder always a remainder*. This meant that if the future limitation, whether contained in a direct grant or in a grant to uses or in a will, was framed in accordance with the rules for remainders, it had to be treated as a remainder, even though subsequently it might be destroyed by the premature determination of the particular estate. Thus, if there

---

[1] *E.g.*, grant to X. and his heirs to the use of A. and his heirs; but if he does not adopt the name and arms of the settlor within six months, then to the use of B. and his heirs.

[2] Rule (b), *supra*, pp. 298-9.

[3] *Purefoy* v. *Rogers* (1671), 2 Wms. Saunders, 380.

were a grant to the use of A. for life and then to the use of B. in fee simple at 21, the gift to B. would fail if he were under 21 when A. died.[1]   The fact that the incantation " to the use of " had been adopted did not alter the nature of what in essence was a remainder. This remained the law until it was altered by the Contingent Remainders Act 1877.[2]

Importance of the common law rules for remainders.

The common law rules for remainders, therefore, were of vital importance whenever the validity of a future limitation was questioned.   No interest could be treated as an executory interest unless its limitation infringed one or more of those rules, as for instance by providing that a fee simple should shift from X. to Y. on a given contingency; and even so it would not be valid unless contained either in a grant to uses or in a will.

Equitable future interests still possible after Statute of Uses.

Equitable Future Interests before 1926.   We have seen that prior to the Statute of Uses equity allowed a settlor who carved future interests out of the equitable estate to disregard the rules which common law was in process of building up for remainders. We have also seen that the springing and shifting uses thus established, which were at that time purely equitable in nature, were converted into legal estates by operation of the statute, and that they came to occupy a position side by side with those other future legal interests called remainders.   But the role played by equity in this department of the law was not exhausted, for in the first place there were from the start certain limitations to which the Statute of Uses did not apply (uses of chattels real and personal, uses of copyholds, uses where the grantee to uses was obliged to perform active duties) ; and secondly, the old equitable estate (called the use), despite its formal abolition by the statute, was ultimately restored under the new name of " trust " to its old position of an equitable estate.[3]   From at least as early a date as 1700 Equity resumed the part that she had played in the realm of future interests before the Statute of Uses, and permitted settlors to carve out of trust estates future interests which were analogous to the contingent remainders and executory interests that might be carved out of the legal estate.   There thus emerged a third and distinct class of future interests, which we may denominate *future*

Future trusts.

trusts, differing from legal contingent remainders and legal executory interests in the fact that they entitled the beneficiaries to call for an equitable instead of a legal estate.

In order to create future trusts it was necessary to vest the legal estate in trustees and then to declare the future trusts upon which the land was to be held.   Suppose for instance that a settlor desired to vest the fee simple in A. as soon as the latter

---

[1] *Purefoy* v. *Rogers* (1671), 2 Wms. Saunders, 380 ; *Goodright* v. *Cornish* (1694), 4 Mod. Rep. 255 ; *Brackenbury* v. *Gibbons* (1876), 2 Ch. D. 417, 419 ; *White* v. *Summers*, [1908] 2 Ch. 256.
[2] *Infra*, p. 308.   [3] *Supra*, pp. 56–9.

attained the age of 21 years. If, before the Statute of Uses, he made a feoffment

> to X. and his heirs *to the use of* A. and his heirs at 21,

the *equitable* estate sprang up in favour of A. when he reached the necessary age. If a similar limitation were made after the statute, then, as we have seen, the *legal* estate would spring up in A. But if after the re-establishment of the use under the new name of trust, a settlor granted land

> *unto and to the use of* X. and his heirs in trust for A. and his heirs at 21,

the position was just what it was before the Statute of Uses, in that A. was entitled to the equitable estate as soon as he became 21, and until then there was a resulting trust for the grantor and his heirs.

These future trusts might correspond either to legal contingent remainders or to legal executory interests. Thus if, after vesting the legal estate in trustees, a settlor granted a future equitable interest which was to take effect upon the natural determination of a particular freehold estate also equitable in nature, as for instance by a limitation

Future trusts corresponding to legal contingent remainders.

> unto and to the use of T.₁ and T.₂ and their heirs in trust for A. for life and then in trust for the eldest son of A. at 21,

the interest given to the eldest son was termed an equitable contingent remainder. But though an interest of this kind corresponded to a legal contingent remainder in the sense that it was made to await the termination of a prior estate, it differed from its legal counterpart in a most important respect. This was that the rule requiring a legal contingent remainder to be vested by the time at which the particular estate ended did not apply to the limitation of an equitable contingent remainder.[1] In short, the *Rule in Purefoy* v. *Rogers* did not apply to future trusts. The reason for this immunity was that, as the legal estate in the trustees fulfilled all feudal necessities concerning seisin, there was no reason why the interest should fail merely because the contingency was not satisfied until after the determination of the preceding interest.[2]

Not affected by termination of prior estate.

Finally, a future trust shared to the full the mercurial attributes that had always been a feature of the future use. Springing and shifting trusts were just as free from the restrictive rules of the common law as were springing and shifting uses.

Future trusts corresponding to legal executory interests.

---

[1] Fearne, *Contingent Remainders*, p. 304 ; *Berry* v. *Berry* (1878), 7 Ch. D. 657 ; *Re Finch* (1881), 17 Ch. D. 211 ; *Astley* v. *Micklethwait* (1880), 15 Ch. D. 59.

[2] *Re Finch, supra, per* Jessel, M.R.

Differences
between
legal
contingent
remainders
and
executory
interests.

We will conclude this account of the law before 1926 with a short statement of the characteristics by which legal contingent remainders differed from executory interests.

(i) **Mode of Creation.** Executory interests, unlike contingent remainders, required either a grant to uses or a devise.

(ii) **Type of Interest that could be created.** By means of a will or a grant to uses it was possible to disregard the restrictive rules applicable to legal contingent remainders.

(iii) **Destructibility.** An executory interest was indestructible in the sense that it took effect when it was ready to do so, being entirely unaffected by the destruction of any precedent estate after which it was limited. On the other hand a legal contingent remainder failed altogether unless it became vested during the continuance of the particular estate. This premature determination of the particular estate might occur naturally by the death of the particular tenant before the specified contingency had been fulfilled, as where in a limitation

to A. for life, remainder to B. at 21,

A. died before B. became 21. In addition, there were certain methods by which it might be deliberately and artificially brought about.[1] Without going into details,[2] it is enough to say that this artificial destruction of the particular estate was usually avoided in settlements by a conveyancing device invented during the time of the Commonwealth,[3] and was finally rendered ineffective by the Real Property Act 1845. Moreover, the Contingent Remainders Act 1877 enacted that a contingent remainder should take effect despite even the natural and premature determination of the particular estate, provided that it had been limited in conformity with the rule against perpetuities. There were, indeed, a few cases in which this Act would not operate, but it is sufficiently accurate to say that after 1877 contingent remainders were just as indestructible as executory interests.

(iv) **Subject Matter.** Neither remainders nor executory *uses* could be carved out of chattels real or personal, but it was possible to create executory interests in such chattels by will. These gifts were called executory bequests.

" The third sort of executory devises, comprising all that relates to chattels, is where a term for years, or any personal estate, is devised (more properly bequeathed) to one for life, or otherwise; and after the decease of the devisee or legatee for life, or some other contingency or period, is given over to somebody else." [4]

---

[1] *I.e.* by the forfeiture, surrender or merger of the particular estate.
[2] For a full account, see 7th edition of this book, pp. 254–9.
[3] *I.e.* by the appointment of trustees to preserve contingent remainders.
[4] Fearne, *Contingent Remainders*, p. 402.

(v) Rules relating to Remoteness of Limitations. One of the most urgent problems that agitated the courts was whether any restriction as to the time within which contingent interests must become vested should be imposed upon settlors. If no check were imposed, it would be possible for a settlor to " tie up " the land, *i.e.* to prevent there being a vested estate, for an indefinite period. The modern rule on this subject is described in detail below.[1] The following is a summary of the law as it stood in 1925 :

(A) *Legal* contingent remainders were subject to the following separate rules :

(*a*) The rule, already noticed, that the remainder must have vested at the time when the particular estate ended, except after 1877 in those cases where the limitation was saved by the Contingent Remainders Act of that year.[2]

(*b*) The rule in *Whitby* v. *Mitchell.*[3]

(*c*) The rule against perpetuities.[4] There was seldom room for the application of this rule to legal contingent remainders, since at common law such remainders had to vest at the expiration of the particular estate, *i.e.* within a period that was shorter than that permitted by the rule. But a legal contingent remainder might be limited after another legal contingent remainder in such terms that the second remainder, though innocuous under (*a*) and (*b*) above, was an infringement of the rule against perpetuities. It was in such cases as these that the rule was held to be applicable.

(B) *Executory interests* were subject only to the rule against perpetuities.

(C) *Future trusts*, if they corresponded to legal contingent remainders, *e.g.*

> unto and to the use of T.$_1$ and T.$_2$ in fee simple in trust for A. for life and then in trust for such of the children as attain 25,

were subject both to the rule in *Whitby* v. *Mitchell* and to the rule against perpetuities[5] ; while if they corresponded to legal executory interests, *e.g.*

> unto and to the use of T.$_1$ and T.$_2$ in fee simple in trust for A. at 25,

they were subject only to the rule against perpetuities.

---

[1] *Infra*, pp. 315 *et seq.*
[3] *Infra*, pp. 314–5.
[5] *Re Finch* (1881), 17 Ch. D. 211.
[2] *Supra*, pp. 305–6 ; 308.
[4] *Re Nash*, [1910] 1 Ch. 1.

SECTION II. FUTURE INTERESTS AFTER 1925

(1) ALL FUTURE FREEHOLD INTERESTS ARE EQUITABLE, AND CORRESPOND TO THE OLD EQUITABLE REMAINDERS AND EXECUTORY INTERESTS

All future
interests
now
equitable.

Introductory Note. The radical alteration resulting from the legislation of 1925 was that future freehold interests were reduced in all cases to an equitable status. This was the inevitable result of the new rule that the only *legal* freehold estate is the fee simple absolute in possession. Entailed and life interests cannot subsist as legal estates, whether limited *in praesenti* or *in futuro* ; a fee simple absolute cannot subsist as a legal estate unless it carries the right to present possession.

Repeal of
Statute of
Uses.

Furthermore the Statute of Uses has been repealed, and therefore those future limitations to uses under which the *legal* estate could be made to spring up in a person, or to pass from one person to another on the occurrence of a future event, are no longer possible. Executory interests, as *legal* interests, vanished with the repeal of the statute upon which their validity depended, but the purposes they were formerly designed to serve can still be attained through the medium of a trust.

Let us now see how these changes have simplified the law relating to future interests.

Limitations
formerly
possible by
way of
future trusts
still possible.

Present position of Future Interests. Before the legislation of 1925, it was possible, as we have seen, for a future interest to be either a legal remainder, an executory interest, or a future trust. The first two have ceased to exist in the sense that they no longer give the beneficiary a legal estate. We are left, therefore, with what may be called future trusts, *i.e.* future equitable interests which before 1926 might correspond either to legal remainders or to executory interests. It was always possible, by a limitation operating on the equitable estate, to create the same types of future interests as could be created by way of legal remainder, but such equitable remainders had this advantage over their legal counterparts, that they were free from the restrictive rules of the common law. It was likewise possible to create springing and shifting interests which, except that they were equitable, were on all fours with executory interests.

What could be done before 1926 by means of these future trusts represents exactly the position after 1925. A settlor can create those future interests which it was possible to create in equity before 1926, but he cannot so frame his limitations as to confer legal estates or interests upon the future beneficiaries. In this latter respect the law is more stringent than formerly. In other respects, however, a settlor possesses complete freedom.

Future trusts were, indeed, subject to the rule against perpetuities and in exceptional circumstances to the rule in *Whitby* v. *Mitchell*; but the creation both of legal remainders and of executory interests was subject to technical rules which were of rigid application. Thus there were certain limitations which were outside the scope of a legal remainder, such as a grant to A. for life at 21, while the adoption of the expression " to the use of," or its equivalent was necessary to the validity of an executory use. But these technical rules have disappeared as a necessary consequence of the new principle that all future freehold interests must be equitable. Furthermore, the rule in *Whitby* v. *Mitchell* has been abolished.

Latitude under the post 1925 Law. Under the law after 1925 then, a person who keeps within the limits prescribed by the rule against perpetuities has complete liberty of action in the creation of future interests, both as regards the kinds of interests he can grant and the manner in which he can frame their limitation. It was indeed, possible before 1926 to create what estates were required, but, unless the originating instrument was a will, certain particular kinds, such as springing and shifting limitations, could be effectually created only by a grant to uses. But now, whatever estates a settlor creates and whatever expressions he adopts, the legal fee simple must vest in an estate owner, who will hold such legal estate upon trust to give effect to the future equitable interests. If a settlor desires to create a series of future interests, the land must be either settled, and or be subject to a trust for sale. As we have seen,[1] in the former case, the legal fee simple is vested in the tenant for life as estate owner, and, in the latter, in the trustees for sale. The rights of the beneficiaries, which are of necessity equitable, are overreached on a sale by the estate owner. *[margin: Abolition of technicalties.]*

As one distinguished writer said :

" Just the same interests can be created in future as have hitherto been possible—just the same life estates,[1] and remainders, and shifting and springing interests—but they will be equitable. The legal estate is one and indivisible, and is in the estate owner. To the world he represents the property ; all other interests are behind his estate, and upon a sale are shifted to the purchase money." [2]

We have said that all future freehold interests are necessarily equitable in nature at the present day. This is strictly true, but the qualifying effect of the word *freehold* must be noticed, for, if the future interest which is limited to the donee is not a fee simple, an entailed interest or a life interest, but consists of a term of years absolute, it will vest in the donee as a legal estate. The Law of Property Act 1925 provides that a term of years *[margin: Reversionary terms.]*

---

[1] *Supra*, p. 166.
[2] (1925) 60 *L. J. News.* 319 (J. M. L.).

absolute shall be capable of subsisting *at law*,[1] and it defines such a term as meaning one that takes effect either in possession or in reversion.[2]

Thus,

if land is leased to A. on March 1st for seven years dating from September 29th, this is a term of years absolute, and A. acquires a future legal estate which will become effective on the day fixed for its commencement.

On the other hand, a future leasehold interest *may* be equitable, as,

when A., possessing a term of 99 years, assigns it to trustees to hold on trust for B. when the latter attains the age of 21 years.

(2) RULES RELATING TO REMOTENESS

The consistent policy of the law has been to prevent land from being unnecessarily tied up and so removed from commerce. There are two ways in which a settlor may offend this policy, viz. either by imposing a restraint upon its future alienation, or by creating a succession of future interests and so postponing to a remote period the time when the land will vest in somebody for an absolute interest.   The law has attacked the first evil by invalidating most conditions against alienation,[3] and it has restrained the power of creating future interests by providing in the rule against perpetuities that such interests must arise within certain limits. It is with this rule that we are for the moment solely concerned.

(A) THE RULE AGAINST PERPETUITIES[4]

(i) General Nature and History of the Rule[5]

Desire of
owners to
restrain
future
generations.

The history of the rules whereby settlors have been prevented from limiting remote interests, is the history of a conflict between two antagonistic ideas.   On the one hand there is the desire of the man of means to regulate the future enjoyment of his property for as long a period as possible.   The right of making a settlement or a will is a potent weapon in the hands of a declining man, and unless human nature is transformed, the opportunity it offers of fixing the pecuniary destinies of the coming generations will not

---

[1] L.P.A. 1925, s. 1.
[2] *Ibid.*, s. 205 (1) (xxvii).   But see L.P.A. 1925, s. 149 (3), *infra*, p. 386, which provides that a term limited to take effect more than 21 years from the date of the instrument of creation shall be void.
[3] *Infra*, pp. 371-2.
[4] See the authoritative account of this difficult subject in Morris and Leach, *The Rule against Perpetuities* (2nd Edn. 1962), with supplement (1964) on P. & A. A. 1964.   See also *Theobald on Wills* (13th Edn.), chap. 42.
[5] See Simpson, *Introduction to the History of Land Law*, pp. 195 *et seq.*

be neglected. A landowner, unless he gives thought to the fiscal consequences, is not always content to leave a large estate at the free disposal of a son. Old age especially, satisfied with its own achievements and often irritated by the apparent follies of a degenerate time, is inclined to restrain each generation of beneficiaries within close limits, and to provide for a series of limited interests. A landowner views the free power of alienation with complacency when it resides in his own hand, but he does not feel the same equanimity with regard to its transfer to others.

" But this freedom of alienation and devise was not congenial to the spirit in which great landowners viewed their land. To preserve their family name and position, ' to keep the land in the family,' seemed to them a desirable and even laudable object ; to restrain any individual holder of the land from dealing with it so as to interfere with the interest of subsequent generations of the family in the family land was a necessary means to this end. To contrive restraints on alienation and succession which the law would enforce, to ascertain the furthest limits up to which the law would allow the grasp of the dead hand to be kept on the hand of the living, was the task set by the great landowners before their legal advisers." [1]

This aspiration, however, soon aroused the antagonism of the courts. The law is moved, and from the earliest times always has been moved, by a deep-seated antipathy to this human love of power. It is one thing to permit the free power of alienation, another to allow it to be exercised to its own destruction. The view of the law is that no disposition should be allowed which tends to withdraw land from commerce, and in pursuance of this policy two rules have emerged which have successfully prevented the particular evil of " perpetuities," though they are essentially different from each other in nature. The first, directed against inalienable interests and often called the *old rule against perpetuities*, forbids the creation of any form of unbarrable entail; the second, the *modern rule against perpetuities*, invalidates an interest that may vest at too remote a date in the future. *Desire of law to remove restraints.*

The Old Rule against Perpetuities. The antagonism of the law to an unbarrable entail became apparent at an early date in its doctrine of the conditional fee.[2] The purpose of a grant to a man and a specified class of heirs of his body was that the land should serve the necessities of each generation and pass from heir to heir ; but, as we have seen, the common law held that the grantee obtained a fee simple with an absolute power of alienation as soon as an heir of the prescribed class was born.[3] Irritated by such a decisive defeat of their intention, the great landowners procured the passing of the Statute *De Donis* 1285, which enacted in *Conditional fee.* *Statute De Donis.*

---

[1] Scrutton, *Land in Fetters*, p. 108.
[2] *Supra*, p. 237. For the history of the old and new rules, see Holdsworth, *History of English Law*, vol. vii. pp. 81–144 ; 193–238.
[3] *Supra*, p. 238.

effect that the intention of a donor was to prevail, and that an estate given to a man and the heirs of his body was perpetually to be reserved to the appropriate class of heir. Thus for the moment the power to grant an inalienable interest in the shape of an unbarrable entail came within the powers of a grantor, but the right was soon lost, for at any rate by the fifteenth century the law had recognized recoveries as methods by which entails could be barred and converted into fees simple absolute by tenants in tail in possession.

Estates tail become barrable.

Attempts to create unbarrable entails.

When it had thus become impossible to ensure the maintenance of land in a family by the simple means of a grant to a man and the heirs of his body, settlors began to cast about for some device whereby they could attain their desire by a more indirect but equally effectual means. One plan was to insert in settlements a *clause of perpetuity*, that is, a condition to the effect that the interest of any tenant in tail who attempted to bar his entail should be forfeited. Such conditions were, however, held void in three cases decided between 1600 and 1613.[1]

Clause of perpetuity.

For the next series of attempts contingent remainders were pressed into service. At first, probably about 1556,[2] it became usual to prolong the period during which the land should be inalienable by making a grant to a son for life with contingent remainders to his unborn children, instead of granting him an immediate estate tail. This form of settlement, however, did not fulfil even the limited purpose for which it was designed, since, owing to the common law rules relating to seisin, it was possible for the life tenant to deal with his estate in such a way as to cause the destruction of the contingent remainder to the children before their birth.[3] Such a premature destruction was, however, prevented at a later date by the appointment of trustees to preserve contingent remainders. Another attempt took the form of the limitation of a perpetual freehold, by which successive estates for life were granted to the unborn issue of a person *ad infinitum*. A settlor, A., would limit the land to his son for life, remainder to every person that should be his heir one after the other for the life of such heir; but it was held by the courts that all the contingent remainders after the life estate to the first unborn heir (*i.e.* A.'s son) were void.[4] This particular rule was generally, though incorrectly,[5] described as the rule against double possibilities, for it was said that the law

Successive contingent remainders.

---

[1] *Corbet's Case* (1600), 1 Co. Rep. 83*b*; *Mildmay's Case* (1605), 6 Co. Rep. 40*a*; *Mary Portington's Case* (1613), 10 Co. Rep. 35*b*.

[2] (1855), 1 Jurid. Soc. 47 (Joshua Williams); cited Scrutton, *Land in Fetters*, pp. 116–17.

[3] *Supra*, p. 308.

[4] Fearne, *Contingent Remainders*, p. 502.

[5] Challis, *Law of Real Property* (3rd Edn.), pp. 116–18; *Jarman on Wills* (8th Edn.), p. 293; Holdsworth, *Historical Introduction to Land Law*, p. 222, note 6.

would never countenance a possibility upon a possibility,[1] and in the limitation indicated one possibility was that A. would not have a son, another that the son, if born, would himself not have a son. The rule enforced by the courts was not, however, based on any such narrow ground. It was really a particular application of the parent rule that the grant of an unbarrable entail is void, and it was reaffirmed in 1890 in the case of *Whitby* v. *Mitchell*,[2] where the Court of Appeal decided once more that where lands were limited to a living person, and then to his unborn child, and then to the child of such unborn child, the last remainder was absolutely void. A settlor could exercise control up to a point but not beyond. He could withhold the fee simple from the grasp of his son by granting him a mere life estate, and he could, by the grant of an estate tail to his son's heir, prevent the acquisition of a fee simple until his son's son attained 21 ; but nothing that he could do could prevent his son and grandson from collaborating to bar the entail when the grandson attained 21.

Whitby v. *Mitchell*.

Still another device adopted by settlors was to carve a species of estate tail out of a term of years by the bequest of a long term to a person and his heirs one after the other *ad infinitum*. But such a limitation after the term to the first unborn heir was held void.[3]

Bequests of long terms.

Pausing here for a moment we see that the attempts which were constantly being made by settlors to keep their land within the family, although they varied in details, all had one object in common, namely, by a combination of estates tail and contingent remainders or executory bequests to set up unbarrable entails, and it was this particular species of inalienable estate that was regarded by the lawyers of the seventeenth century as a perpetuity.

Early meaning of " perpetuity."

" A perpetuity is the settlement of an estate or interest in tail, with such remainders expectant upon it as are in no sort in the power of the tenant in tail in possession to dock by any recovery or assignment." [4]

Thus at an early date contingent remainders ceased to endanger the free alienability of land, for they failed altogether unless they had vested when the particular tenant died ; they were easily destructible ; and, if they were nothing more than unbarrable entails in disguise, they were void on the ground that virtually they created an inalienable interest.

The Modern Rule against Perpetuities. What ultimately led to the emergence of a new rule against perpetuities was the decision in the early seventeenth century that executory interests,

Inadequacy of Old Rule against Perpetuities.

---

[1] Co. Litt. 184a.
[2] (1890), 44 Ch. D. 85.
[3] *Sanders* v. *Cornish* (1630), Cro. Car. 230 ; Jarman (8th Edn.), p. 291.
[4] *Duke of Norfolk's Case* (1681), 3 Ch. Ca., *per* Lord Nottingham.

Emergence
of modern
rule.

unlike contingent remainders, were indestructible,[1] for this meant that land might be tied up to an almost indefinite extent by the adoption of a number of shifting uses under which the land would pass from one person to another on the occurrence of given events. If, for instance, there were a devise :

> to A. and his heirs, but if the heirs ever fail then over to B and his heirs,

the successive occupants of the land under the first limitation would have been continually liable to lose their interest upon the occurrence of a contingency that might never happen or might not happen for generations. The courts, therefore, unaided by the legislature, undertook and succeeded in the task of finding some rule which would confine these executory interests within reasonable limits, and the principle upon which they proceeded was to restrict the remoteness of the date at which the executory interest might be made to vest.[2] They specified the latest moment at which this kind of future interest might be made to begin; or, to put it in another way, they said that though a settlor might fix a contingency upon which a vested interest was to spring up or to shift to a person, yet the contingency chosen must be one which, if it ever happened at all, would necessarily happen within a defined period of time. They ultimately held that no interest was to be valid unless it was bound to vest, if at all, within the compass of existing lives and twenty-one years after the extinction of the last life.

The two
rules
concerning
perpetuities.

Thus, English law has evolved two rules concerning perpetuities. Their common object is to promote the free circulation of property,[3] but they accomplish this purpose by different means. The first and older rule, already discussed, looks to the character of the limitations and holds them to be void as constituting a perpetuity if their effect would be to set up an unbarrable entail ; the later and modern rule looks to the date at which the contingent interests will vest, if they vest at all, and holds them to be void as a perpetuity if this date is too remote.[4] Though invariably called the "rule against perpetuities," a better name would be the "rule against remoteness of vesting."[5]

History of
modern rule

The modern rule began to emerge about 1660,[6] and it was finally completed by the House of Lords in *Cadell* v. *Palmer* in 1833.[7] The main stages in its development may be shortly

---

[1] *Pells* v. *Brown* (1620), 1 Cro. Jac. 590.
[2] Holdsworth, *History of English Law*, vol. vii. p. 225.
[3] See Simes, *Public Policy and the Dead Hand*, pp. 55 *et seq.*
[4] Gray, *The Rule against Perpetuities*, (4th Edn.), ss. 2, 118 ; Fearne, *Contingent Remainders*, p. 429 ; Challis, *Law of Real Property* (3rd Edn.), pp. 205–7.
[5] Gray, *op. cit.*, s. 2.
[6] *Snows* v. *Cuttler* (1664), 1 Lev. 135 ; *Wood* v. *Saunders* (1669), 1 Ch. Cas. 131 ; Holdsworth, *History of English Law*, vol. vii. pp. 222 *et seq.*
[7] (1833), 1 Cl. & F. 372.

stated.[1] In *The Duke of Norfolk's Case*, 1681-85,[2] there was a

> grant of a term of 200 years to trustees upon trust for the grantor's second son Henry and the heirs male of his body, but if his eldest son Thomas died without issue male *in Henry's lifetime*, then in trust for Charles, his third son.

Lord NOTTINGHAM held that the last limitation was good, since the shifting to Charles must take place, if it ever took place at all, upon the dropping of a life in being, namely that of Thomas. Thus the case did not fix the maximum period during which vesting might be suspended, but decided that an interest that must vest if ever within lives in being was valid. *Stephens* v. *Stephens*,[3] 1736, held that an executory devise to the unborn child of a living person upon attaining twenty-one was good, and thereby in effect extended the maximum period to lives in being plus a further twenty-one years. In *Thellusson* v. *Woodford*,[4] 1805, Lord ELDON was of opinion that the persons whose lives were chosen need have no connection with the settled property, but might be strangers chosen at random. This opinion was endorsed by *Cadell* v. *Palmer*,[5] which also decided that a term of twenty-one years without any reference to minorities might be added to existing lives, *e.g.* devise in fee simple to my eldest descendant alive twenty-one years after the death of my son Peter. This case, which finally settled the law, had to consider the following limitations :

> Land was devised to trustees for 120 years from the testator's death, *if* twenty-eight *persons named in the will should so long live*, and for twenty years from the determination of the term or from the death of the last life, whichever was the shorter.   *Cadell* v. *Palmer.*
>
> The House of Lords held that the limitation of the long term was valid, since, though it suspended the vesting of a fee simple absolute for a considerable period, yet the period, being confined to existing lives and a further space of twenty years, was not obnoxious as a perpetuity.

Position after 1925. Under the law as it stood prior to January 1st, 1926, the rule in. *Whitby* v. *Mitchell* applied to all future estates limited by way of contingent remainders, whether legal or equitable. The rule against perpetuities applied to executory interests and to equitable contingent remainders, and in certain cases it had been extended by the courts, though without any historical or doctrinal justification, to legal contingent remainders.[6]   *Abolition of old rule.*

Section 161 of the Law of Property Act 1925, however, abolished the rule in *Whitby* v. *Mitchell* in the following words :

---

[1] Pollock, *Land Laws*, Appendix Note G ; Gray, *op. cit.*, ss. 123 *et seq.* ; Holdsworth, *Historical Introduction to Land Law*, p. 224 ; Morris and Leach, *op. cit.*, pp. 8–11.
[2] (1681–85), 3 Ch. Cas. 1.   [3] (1736), Ca. *temp.* Talbot, 228.
[4] (1798), 4 Ves. Jun. 227 ; (1805), 11 Ves. Jun. 112.
[5] (1833), 1 Cl. & F. 372 ; M. & B. p. 287.   [6] *Supra*, p. 309.

' (1) The rule of law prohibiting the limitation, after a life interest to an unborn person, of an interest in land to the unborn child or other issue of an unborn person is hereby abolished, but without prejudice to any other rule relating to perpetuities.

(2) This section only applies to limitations or trusts created by an instrument coming into operation after the commencement of this Act."[1]

Thus the rule against perpetuities, fortified by the rules against accumulations,[2] is now the sole determinant of whether an interest is too remote. It applies both to realty and personalty out of which future contingent interests have been carved.

Amendment of the rule in 1964. In the course of its development the rule against perpetuities as laid down in *Cadell* v. *Palmer*, though based on sound policy and designed to be flexible, gradually became encumbered with complex and at times absurd interpretations that provided dangerous traps for the unwary practitioner.[3] Most of the anomalies, however, by which it was disfigured were removed for the future by the Perpetuities and Accumulations Act 1964, which gave substantial effect to the recommendations of the Law Reform Committee made in 1956.[4] The Act came into operation on July 16th, 1964, and it applies only to instruments taking effect on or after that date. In giving the details of the rule, therefore, it will be simpler to deal first with the position at common law and then under a separate heading to show in what respects that position has been altered for instruments taking effect after the commencement of the Act.

(ii) The Rule Applicable to Instruments taking Effect before July 16th, 1964.

(a) Statement of the Rule.

Length of the period. ### (1) The perpetuity period.

At common law, the vesting of an interest may be postponed during the lives of persons in being at the time when the instrument of creation takes effect, plus a further period of twenty-one years after the extinction of the last life.[5] Any interest so limited that it may possibly vest after the expiration of this period is totally void.

---

[1] A limitation to the unborn issue of an unborn taker is of course void under the modern rule, unless it is expressly confined within due limits as in *Re Nash*, [1910] 1 Ch. 1. As to the meaning of " coming into operation after " the Act, see *Re Leigh's Marriage Settlement*, [1952] 2 All E. R. 57.

[2] *Infra*, p. 357.

[3] For a devastating exposure of the " superfluous technicalities and complexities of the rule," see (1952), 68 *L. Q. R.* 35 (W. B. Leach).

[4] Fourth Report, 1956 (Cmnd. 18).

[5] The lives must be those of human beings, not those of corporations or animals. See *Re Kelly*, [1932] I. R. 255 ; M. & B. p. 291.

For the purposes of the rule, conception is treated as equivalent to birth.[1] Thus a child, whether a beneficiary or not, who is *en ventre sa mère* at the time when the instrument of gift takes effect may constitute a life in being;[2] and a child *en ventre sa mère* at the end of the perpetuity period may qualify as a beneficiary under the limitation.[3]

Conception treated as equivalent to birth.

A settlor need not choose persons who have interests in the settled property or a connexion with the family, and he has full liberty of action with regard to the number of persons he may select.[4] If it is substantially practicable to ascertain the extinction of the last life, the gift is good, although the lives may be so numerous that it may be a difficult and expensive matter to ascertain the date of the survivor's death. Thus a not uncommon practice is to prolong the period to the utmost limit by the use of a *royal lives clause*, which selects the living descendants of some modern English sovereign as the lives in being.[5] In one case, for instance, a will that took effect in 1925 directed that the distribution of certain shares among the beneficiaries should be postponed until the expiration of twenty-one years (less the last two days thereof) from the death of the last survivor of the descendants of her late Majesty Queen Victoria alive at the testator's death. Since there were 134 descendants scattered among at least ten countries in Europe alone, it was obvious that the difficulty of proving the fact and date of death of each descendant might be almost insuperable. Nevertheless, the direction was held to be valid.[6]

No restriction on number of lives.

If, however, the number of the selected lives is so great as to render it impossible to ascertain the death of the survivor, as for instance where a testator defined the period as "twenty-one years from the death of the last survivor of all persons who shall be living at my death,"[7] the gift, though not an infringement of the rule against perpetuities, is void for uncertainty.[8]

The lives in being must be designated either expressly, as in *Cadell* v. *Palmer*,[9] or by implication. Lives are designated by implication only if, according to the terms of the instrument of gift, they serve to measure the time within which the vesting contingency must occur. They must form a possible part of the

What constitutes a life in being.

---

[1] *Re Stern*, [1962] Ch. 732, at p. 737 ; [1961] 3 All E. R. 1129, at p. 1132.

[2] *Long* v. *Blackall* (1797), 7 Term Rep. 100 ; *Re Wilmer's Trusts*, [1903] 2 Ch. 411.

[3] Gray, *op. cit.* s. 220; Challis, *op. cit.* p. 182.

[4] *Cadell* v. *Palmer* (1833), 1 Cl. & Fin. F. 372.

[5] *Re Villar*, [1928] 1 Ch. 471 ; [1929] 1 Ch. 243 ; M. & B. p. 289.

[6] *Re Leverhulme (No. 2)*, [1943] 2 All E. R. 274, where Morton, J., added a warning against " using the formula in the case of a testator who dies in the year 1943 or at any later date : See, however, *Re Warren's Will Trusts* (1961), 105 Sol. Jo. 511 where a testatrix died in 1964 and Cross, J., upheld the will.

[7] *Re Moore*, [1901] 1 Ch. 936.

[8] And not even valid for 21 years. *E.g. Muir* v. *I. R. Comrs.*, [1966] I.W. L. R. 1269, at p. 1282 ; [1966] 3 All E. R. 38, at p. 44.

[9] *Supra*, p. 317.

apparatus for determining the moment at which the interest is to vest.

> " No lives can be of the slightest use unless they somehow restrict the period of time within which the gift is to be capable of vesting according to the conditions laid down by the donor."[1]

If, for instance, there is a

> bequest to A. for life, remainder to the children of B. alive at B's death,

B. is implicitly a life in being, for, though not himself a beneficiary, the time of his death forms part of the vesting contingency. Again, if a testator bequeaths a fund to such of his grandchildren as attain the age of twenty-one years, the children who survive him are effective lives in being, since the ascertainment of the beneficiaries requires a reference to their parents. The gift, therefore, is good, for the grandchildren "must all become of age within twenty-one years after the death of their parents (the testator's children), and the parents must all have been born (or begotten) in the testator's lifetime."[2]

Period where no lives chosen. If there are no lives in being, express or implied, by which to measure the perpetuity period, an absolute period of twenty-one years, and no longer is allowed.[3]

(2) The Rule affects only contingent gifts.

The rule forbids remote vesting. It must be emphasized that the object of the rule is to prevent the vesting of an interest from being suspended for an excessive period. It strikes only at contingent limitations. Thus it has been epitomized as follows by the leading authority on the subject:

> "No interest is good, unless it must vest, if at all, not later than twenty-one years after some life in being at the creation of the interest."[4]

" Vested," means vested in interest, and, as we have already seen, a person has such an interest when his identity is established and his right to the interest does not depend upon the occurrence of some event ; and, in a further requirement, peculiar to the rule against perpetuities, the size of this interest is known.[5] Speaking generally, *the three essentials of vesting for the purposes of the rule*

The three essentials of vesting.

---

[1] (1964) 80 *L. Q. R.* 496 (J. H. C. Morris and H. W. R. Wade). For a contrary view, see (1965) 81 *L. Q. R.* 105 (D. E. Allan) ; (1970) 86 *L. Q. R.* 357 (R. H. Maudsley.)

[2] Gray, *op cit.*, s. 370.

[3] *Palmer* v. *Holford* (1828), 4 Russ 403. See also *Re Hooper*, [1932] 1 Ch. 38 (gift for upkeep of certain monuments " so far as the trustees legally can do so" upheld for a period of 21 years).

[4] Gray, *op cit.*, s. 201.

[5] For its application to class gifts see *infra*, p. 326 : and to fluctuating payments see *Re Whiteford*, [1915] 1 Ch. 347 ; *Re Cassel*, [1926] Ch. 358 ; *Re Johnson's Settlement Trusts*, [1943] Ch. 341 ; *Beachway Management Ltd.* v. *Wisewell*, [1971] Ch. 610 ; [1971] 1 All E. R. 1 ; see (1971), 87 *L. Q. R.* 154 (P. V. B.).

are ascertained beneficiaries, interests definitely fixed from the point of view of quantum, and the occurrence of what may perhaps be called qualifying events.

By *qualifying events* are meant all those events and conditions that must happen before a beneficiary becomes entitled to take possession of property when the preceding interest in it terminates. If, for instance, there is a grant

to A. for life, remainder to B. in fee simple when B. marries,

an event, namely marriage, must happen before B. obtains an indestructible right to take possession.

The vesting of an interest must not, however, be confused with its duration, for the rule deals with the *commencement* of ·interests, not with their duration.[1] This means that an interest is validly limited if it begins within the period though it may terminate after the period has ended, for otherwise, as Gray remarks, all fee simple estates would be bad.[2] Thus, a devise to the unborn son of A. for life is valid, though obviously it may continue for longer than 21 years after the death of A., the life in being.[3] Equally valid is a further gift in fee simple to take effect on the determination of such life interest, provided that the donee will be ascertained within the perpetuity period.[4] Again, in *Wainwright* v. *Miller*,[5]

The rule is directed against remoteness of commencement, not of determination.

a settlement limited land in 1847 to W. for life with remainder to such of her children as she should appoint. She appointed to her daughter X., for life *until she should become a member of the Roman Catholic Church.*

The validity of this gift was contested on the ground that the event of X.'s conversion to Roman Catholicism might not occur within 21 years from the death of W., the life in being. It was held, however, that X.'s life interest was valid, since it was limited to begin within the perpetuity period.

So the rule against perpetuities may be re-stated in this way:

Re-statement of rule in connexion with vesting.

The limitation of future interests must be so framed that the beneficiaries and the quantum of their interests will necessarily be ascertained, and all qualifying events will necessarily have happened, within the perpetuity period.

All limitations void for remoteness will be found to be void because there is a chance either of the beneficiaries remaining

---

[1] *Re Chardon*, [1928] Ch. 464 ; *Re Cassel*, [1926] Ch. 358 ; dist. *Re Johnson's Settlement Trusts*, [1943] Ch. 341 ; [1943] 2 All E. R. 499 ; Morris and Leach, *op. cit.*, pp. 95–100.

[2] Gray, *op. cit.*, s. 232.

[3] *Stuart* v. *Cockerell* (1869), L. R. 7 Eq. 363.

[4] *Evans* v. *Walker* (1876), 3 Ch. D. 211.

[5] [1897] 2 Ch. 255.

unascertained, or of their interests being still unfixed or of certain events not having occurred, when the perpetuity period is exhausted.

(3) The facts upon which the question of remoteness depends.

Whether limitation void depends upon the facts existing when it took effect.

At common law, whether these pre-requisites of vesting are satisfied is settled in the light of the facts existing at the time when the instrument of gift took effect. The relevant time is the date of the testator's death in the case of a testamentary gift; but the date of the execution of the deed if the limitations are made *inter vivos*.[1]

Limitation void if it could possibly have vested beyond the perpetuity period.

In estimating whether a limitation is too remote, the common law applies a ruthless test. No matter when the question arises, the mind must be cast back to the time when the instrument of creation took effect, and if at that time it would have been possible to have conceived of circumstances in which the vesting of the property would be postponed for longer than the perpetuity period, the gift is void.

> "Unless it is created in such terms that it *cannot* vest after the expiration of a life or lives in being, and twenty-one years, and the period allowed for gestation, it is not valid, and subsequent events cannot make it so."[2]

Thus, at the time when the instrument of gift takes effect it must be clear that the beneficiaries will necessarily be ascertained, if at all, within the perpetuity period; and that any vesting contingency specified by the donor will necessarily be satisfied, if at all, within the same period.

According to this test, it is obvious, for instance, that a gift is too remote if made to take effect

> when a candidate for the priesthood "comes forward from St. Saviour's Church, St. Albans;"[3]

or,

> when a house ceases to be maintained as a dwelling place.[4]

---

[1] *Vanderplank* v. *King* (1843), 3 Hare 1.
[2] *Lord Dungannon* v. *Smith* (1846), 12 Cl. & Fin. 546, at p. 563.
[3] *Re Mander*, [1950] Ch. 547 ; [1950] 2 All E. R. 191.
[4] *Kennedy* v. *Kennedy*, [1914] A. C. 215. Other examples of remote contingencies are: *Re Lord Stratheden and Campbell*, [1894] 3 Ch. 265 ("on the appointment of the next lieutenant-colonel" of a volunteer corps) ; *Edwards* v. *Edwards*, [1900] A. C. 274 (when the coal under certain land is exhausted); *Re Wood*, [1894] 3 Ch. 381 (when a gravel pit is worked out) ; *Re Engels*, [1943] 1 All E. R. 506 (after termination of the present war with Germany) ; *Re Fry*, [1945] Ch. 348, at p. 352 ; [1945] 2 All E. R. 205, at pp. 206, 207 (when an unborn person, ascertainable within the perpetuity period, takes the testator's surname); *Re Flavel's Will Trusts*, [1969] 1 W. L. R. 444 ; [1969] 2 All E. R. 232.

The rule that a limitation is void *ab initio* unless it is clear at the time when the instrument of gift takes effect that it cannot vest beyond the perpetuity period, precludes any question of waiting to see what will probably happen in the future or even what in fact has happened since the gift was made. Attention must be concentrated solely on possibilities.

Thus a bequest to take effect "upon the realization of my foreign estate" is void, though it may be a confident assumption that the executors will have accomplished their task within a few years of the testator's death.[1]

Again, a limitation that might possibly have been too remote is not saved by the fact that in the events which have happened since the instrument of gift became effective the perpetuity period cannot now be exceeded.[2] Thus in *Proctor* v. *Bishop of Bath and Wells*:[3]

> An advowson was devised in fee simple to the first or other son of A. that should be bred a clergyman, and be in Holy Orders, but in case A. should have no such son, then the advowson was given over to B. in fee simple. A. died without ever having a son.

The first limitation failed, for at the time of the testator's death, it could not be said that if any son became a clergyman he would necessarily do so within twenty-one years from the death of A., the life in being. The gift over to B. also failed. Had the facts occurring after the testator's death been relevant, B. would have vindicated his right to the fee simple. He could have shown that the contingency upon which his interest was to vest had in fact occurred within the perpetuity period, for at the death of the life in being it was established that A. could never have a clerical son.[4]

A particular limitation upon which the rule that possible, not actual, events must be considered, occurs in what the Law Reform Committee has called the case of the *possibly unborn spouse*.[5] Suppose, for instance, that there is a limitation

> To John, a bachelor, for life, remainder for life to the first wife he may marry, remainder in fee simple to the children of the marriage who reach the age of twenty-one years and who are alive at the death of the survivor of John and such wife.

If this limitation is contained in a deed, the gift to the children is void. John is the only life in being; it is possible that he may marry a woman not yet born; if so, it is possible that she may

Marginal notes:

Not permissible to wait and see whether perpetuity period in fact exceeded.

Possibilities alone considered: example of possibly unborn spouse.

---

[1] *Re Jones*, [1950] 2 All E. R. 239.
[2] *Re Wilmer's Trusts*, [1903] 2 Ch. 411 at p. 422.
[3] (1794), 2 Hy. Bl. 358.
[4] In the case of instruments taking effect after July 15th, 1964, the facts occurring since the instrument of creation took effect are relevant; *infra*, pp. 344–50.
[5] *Re Frost* (1889), 43 Ch. D. 303 ; M. & B. p. 303 ; *Re Garnham*, [1916] 2 Ch. 413 ; M. & B. p. 304 ; *Re Deloitte*, [1926] Ch. 56 ; (1949), 13 *Conv.* (N.S.) 289 (J. H. C. Morris).

survive him for longer than twenty-one years and the interests of the children will therefore not vest until more than twenty-one years after the dropping of the life in being. It is immaterial that he may later marry a woman alive at the time when the deed took effect, for since she did not then answer to the description of his wife she cannot constitute a life in being for the purposes of the limitation.

If the same limitation is contained in a will, it is necessary to investigate the state of affairs at the testator's death. If John is not then married, the gift to the children is void for the reasons given above; but if he is married to Jane, the gift is valid, since Jane is a life in being, and therefore the children qualified to take must be ascertained within the perpetuity period.[1]

Presumption of fertility a further example. In applying the rule that possible, not actual, events must be considered, the common law courts have been perversely indifferent to the facts of nature. They have established a presumption that no person, male or female, is too old to beget children. The effect of this is well illustrated by *Re Dawson*.[2] In that case there was in effect a devise by T. in trust for his daughter D. for life, then for such of her children as should attain twenty-one, and for such of her grandchildren attaining twenty-one as should be born of any of her children dying under twenty-one.

The gifts to D. and to her *children* did not infringe the rule, but if we put a hypothetical case, and consider what might have happened, we shall see how the limitation to the *grandchildren* might have taken effect after the perpetuity period.

D. might have had an only child X. born after T.'s death, and X. might himself have died under 21 leaving a child Z. The will directed that Z. was to take only if he attained 21; the rule against perpetuities required that he must necessarily attain that age, if at all, within 21 years from the dropping of the last life in being. Clearly, Z. might not have satisfied this condition. X. was not a life in being when the will took effect; D., the only remaining life in being might have died before the birth of Z. and if so the latter could not attain the required age within the perpetuity period. It was therefore held that the limitations subsequent to D.'s life interest were void for remoteness.[3]

But the interest of the case lies in the fact that when T. died, D. was over 60 years of age, and all her children had attained 21; and with a view to upholding the will it was argued that as she was past child-bearing, and consequently could have no child born after T.'s death, all grandchildren would in fact be ready to take within 21 years after the dropping of the last life in being. That was true, but it was equally true that the rule against perpetuities is applied in accordance with what might happen, and since in the eyes of the law men and

---

[1] The principle applicable to this type of case has been amended so far as concerns instruments taking effect after July 15th, 1964; see *infra*, pp. 350–1.

[2] (1888), 39 Ch. D. 155; M. & B. p. 316.

[3] It might be thought that despite the invalidity of the limitation to the grandchildren, the gift to the children should have been allowed to stand. The limitations in this case, however, constituted a " class gift," and we shall see (pp. 326–7) that a class gift cannot be partly good and partly bad.

women are capable of having children, no matter how great their age may be, the devise to the grandchildren was held void.[1]

Logically, the presumption of fertility attributed to the old should equally affect the young. Whether it must be presumed that no person can be too young to beget children was indeed canvassed in *Re Gaite's Will Trusts*,[2] but was not determined. On the facts of that case, the argument in favour of such a presumption rested upon the possibility that within the short space of five years after the settlor's death a child might be born to his widow, already sixty-five years of age, and might then marry and have issue. The judge evaded the question of physical impossibility by holding that such a hypothetical marriage, contracted by a person under sixteen years of age contrary to the Age of Marriage Act 1929[3] was a legal impossibility.[4] And the court will not take into account an event which presupposes a contravention of statute or a breach of trust.[5]

Fertility of young persons.

(4) Statutory modification of age contingencies.

Prior to 1926, probably the commonest example of a gift that failed for remoteness and which in its downfall destroyed ulterior gifts was one that postponed the vesting of the beneficiary's interest until he reached an age greater than twenty-one years. Section 163 of the Law of Property Act 1925, however, met this situation by providing that where a limitation makes the absolute vesting of capital or income, or the ascertainment of a beneficiary or class of beneficiaries, dependent upon the attainment by the beneficiary or members of the class of an age exceeding twenty-one years, with the result that the gift or any gift over is rendered void for remoteness, the limitation shall take effect for the purposes of such gift or ulterior gift as if it had specified the age of twenty-one years.[6]

Statutory reduction of age specified in limitation.

Thus, if there is a

devise for life to the first son of X. (a bachelor at the time of the testator's death) to attain the age of thirty years

the first son to reach twenty-one is entitled to take under the devise, and any further interests dependent upon his death and not themselves obnoxious to the perpetuity rule take effect according to their limitation.

---

[1] See also *Jee* v. *Audley* (1787), 1 Cox, Eq. Cas. 324 ; M. & B. p. 297 ; *Ward* v. *Van der Loeff*, [1924] A. C. 653 ; M. & B. p. 297.

[2] [1949] 1 All E. R. 459 ; M. & B. p. 295. For its full discussion see Morris and Leach, *op. cit.*, pp. 84–6.

[3] Now the Marriage Act 1949, s. 2.

[4] As to the new statutory rule concerning fertility, see *infra*, pp. 343–4.

[5] *Re Atkins' Will Trusts*, [1974] 1 W.L.R. 761 ; [1974] 2 All E.R. 1 ; M. & B. p. 305.

[6] The section applies to any instrument executed after 1925 and to any testamentary appointment, devise or bequest contained in the will of a testator dying after 1925. But it has been repealed and replaced by a new provision in the case of wills or instruments *inter vivos* that became effective after July 15th, 1964 ; P. & A. A. 1964, s. 4 ; *infra*, pp. 351–3.

The section applies only where the gift would be too remote at common law.   Thus, if there is a devise

> to the first son of X. to attain thirty

and if, when the testator dies, X. is also dead leaving sons, the sons are lives in being and the limitation is valid at common law.   If a son satisfies the vesting contingency he must do so within his own lifetime[1].

Moreover, the statute applies only where the vesting contingency is the *attainment* by a beneficiary of a given age.   It will not, for instance, save a bequest

> to the eldest of my issue living thirty years after my death.

(b) Application of the Rule to class gifts

Meaning of "class gift."

" A gift is said to be to a class of persons when it is to all those who shall come within a certain category or description defined by a general or collective formula, and who, if they take at all, are to take one divisible subject in certain proportionate shares."[2]   There is a gift to a class if the limitation is

> to all the children of A. who shall attain 21,

On the other hand, a gift of

> £2,000 to each of the daughters of B.

is not a class gift.[3]

Meaning of vested in connection with class gifts.

We have seen that,[4] for the purpose of determining whether an individual member of a class has a vested interest, each member of the class obtains a vested interest on satisfying the necessary qualifications.   Thus in a gift

> to A. for life and after his death to such of his children as shall attain 25.

each child of A. obtains a vested interest on reaching that age. The significance of this vesting is that the child's interest is then indefeasible.   If his interest vests and he then dies before A., the child's estate will claim.   If however he dies at the age of 24, it will have no claim.   The interest of a child of A. who attains 25 is said to be vested " subject to open " ; that is to say, subject to open and admit future born children of A.

> Thus if A. has three children and all have attained 25, they all have vested interests.   But if A. then has three more children, the interest of the three eldest will be reduced from one third each to one sixth ; and will increase again if any of the younger children dies under the age of 25.

However, for the purpose of determining the validity of a gift on the ground of remoteness, the rule is that the gift to a class is

---

[1] The gift would also be valid if, at the time of the testator's death, X. were still alive, and a son of X. had already attained 30.   This would be an immediate gift to an ascertained person.

[2] *Pearks* v. *Moseley* (1880), 5 App. Cas. 714, at p. 723, *per* Lord Selborne.

[3] *Wilkinson* v. *Duncan* (1861), 30 Beav. 111 ; M. & B. p. 328.

[4] *Supra*, pp. 294 ; 320-1

only valid if the interest of every possible member of the class must vest, if at all, within the perpetuity period. If the interest of even one potential member could possibly vest outside the period, the *whole* gift fails. Those whose interests have already vested take nothing.[1] " The vice of remoteness affects the class as a whole, if it may affect an unascertained number of its members."[2] In other words, a class gift cannot be partially good, partially bad.

> Class gift cannot be partially good partially bad.

Suppose, for instance, that a testator leaves his residuary estate " to such of the children of A. who shall marry." If A. survives the testator, the whole gift is void. Even if, when the testator dies, A. already has children who must therefore marry, if at all, within their own lifetimes, there is no certainty that all his children who marry will do so within the perpetuity period. For A. may have a future born child who marries more than 21 years after the death of lives in being. The whole gift, however, would be valid if it were expressed to be to the *living* children of A. who marry ; or if, when the testator dies, A. were dead and therefore unable to have further children.[3]

Class Closing Rules.[4] Rules of construction, sometimes known as the rule in *Andrews* v. *Partington*,[5] have developed, which have the effect of determining which members of a class can take. They have the effect of artificially closing the class, and of excluding members who would otherwise have taken. They are rules of construction only, and defer to a contrary intention ; and the courts in recent years, it seems, are more ready than previously to find that intention.[6]

> Rule in *Andrews* v. *Partington*.

A class is artificially closed under these rules in order to allow the trustees to make a distribution[7] when one member of the class attains a vested interest and is entitled to be paid. Let us consider the position of trustees where there is a gift " to the children of A. who shall attain 21 " ; and when A.'s eldest child, X., becomes 21,

---

[1] *Leake* v. *Robinson* (1817), 2 Mer. 363.

[2] *Pearks* v. *Moseley, supra,* at p. 723, per Lord SELBORNE.

[3] The gift would also be saved if one of the children of A. were married when the testator dies. This would have the effect of bringing into operation the class-closing rules, and of artificially closing the class at the date of the gift, to include only those children of A. who were alive at that time. They must marry, if at all, within their own lifetimes. For these rules and the inter-relation between them and the rule against perpetuities, see *infra*.

[4] For a full discussion of these rules see (1954), 70 *L. Q. R.* 61 (J. H. C. Morris) ; (1958), *C. L. J.* 39 (S. J. Bailey) ; Morris and Leach, *op cit.,* pp. 109–125 ; Theobald on *Wills* (13th Edn.), Chap. 30. *Infra,* p. 855.

[5] (1791), 3 Bro. C. C. 401.

[6] *Re Bleckly,* [1951] Ch. 740; [1951] 1 All E. R. 1064; *Re Cockle's Will Trusts,* [1967] Ch. 690 ; [1967] 1 All E. R. 391 ; *Re Kebty-Fletcher's Will Trusts,* [1969] 1 Ch. 339 ; [1967] 3 All E. R. 1076 ; *Re Harker's Will Trusts,* [1969] 1 W. L. R. 1124 [1969] 3 All E. R. 1 ; *Re Henderson's Trusts,* [1969] 1 W. L. R. 651 ; [1969] 3 All E. R. 769 ; *Re Edmondson's Will Trusts,* [1972] 1 W. L. R. 183 ; [1972] 1 All E. R. 444 ; *Re Deeley's Settlement,* [1974] Ch. 454 ; [1973] 3 All E. R. 1127. See (1970), 34 *Conv.* (N.S.) 393 (J. G. Riddall).

[7] The rules apply to all forms of property, and to settlements as well as to wills.

there is a brother, Y., aged 11 and a sister, Z., aged 1.   X. asks the trustees for payment ; what are they to pay to him ?   If A. is still alive, there is danger in paying to X. a one-third share, because future born children of A. would reduce X.'s entitlement.   So the class closing rules, for the convenience of the administration of the trust, say that the trustees may calculate X.'s share by providing for only those children of A. who have been born.   His future born children are excluded.   Y. and Z. can claim their shares when they attain 21.   This is very convenient for the trustees and for X., Y. and Z. ; but inconvenient for any future born children of A.

The key to understanding when the class closes is to appreciate that it closes when the time for distribution arises ; when, that is, the first claimant becomes entitled to be paid.   Thus, in an immediate gift to a class, such as " to the children of A.", that class closes to include those alive at the date of the gift.   If vesting is postponed, for example, " to the children of A. who shall attain 21", the class closes when the first child of A. becomes 21.   If it is an interest in remainder, for example, " to X. for life, remainder to the children of A. who shall attain 21", the class closes when X. has died and when the first child of A. has attained 21, whichever event happens last, because that is the time at which the first member of the class becomes entitled to be paid.   There is an exception to these rules where there is an immediate gift and no existing claimant.   Thus if there is a gift to the children of A. and A. has no children, the class remains open to include all A.'s children.[1]

Inter-
relation of
class-closing
and
perpetuity
rules.

We have seen that the purpose of the class-closing rules is to simplify the administration of a trust by enabling the trustees to make payment to beneficiaries as soon as they have become entitled.   Essentially the rules have nothing to do with the rule against perpetuities. But it will be appreciated that there may be situations in which the rules interact, as for instance where there is a gift to a class in which the interests of some of the members must vest within the perpetuity period, but there is a possibility that those of others may vest outside it, with the result that the whole gift is void under the rule against perpetuities.   But if, as it were by a fluke, the class-closing rules exclude all the members whose interests would invalidate the gift, then it will be valid.   Thus if there is a gift before 1926 " to the children of A. who shall attain 25", that is void. But, if at the date of the gift there is a child of A. who is already 25, the class-closing rules operate to include only those children of A. who are alive at the date of the gift ; and they will clearly attain 25, if at all, within their own lifetimes.   The gift is therefore valid.   Further, to return to our earlier example[2] of a gift " to such of the children of A. who shall marry."   We saw

---

[1] *Weld* v. *Bradbury* (1715), 2 Vern. 705 ; *Re Ransome*, [1957] Ch. 348, at p. 359, *per* Upjohn, J.
[2] *Supra*, p. 327.

that this is void, if A. is alive at the date of the gift. If, however, one of the children of A. is then married, the gift is valid.

(c) *Application of the Rule to powers of appointment.*

A power of appointment may offend the rule against perpetuities in two respects, for either its *creation* or its *exercise* may be too remote. Before stating the law on these two matters, however, it is useful to stress once more the significance of the distinction between general and special powers.

Distinction between general and special powers.

To give a person a general power is in effect to give him the absolute fee, for it entitles him to vest the whole fee in any person in the world, including himself, and therefore it does not tend to the creation of remote interests.

> " He has an absolute disposing power over the estate, and may bring it into the market whenever his necessities or wishes may lead him to do so. . . . The donee may sell the estate the next moment."[1]

On the other hand, the grant of a special power has an immediate tendency to be a perpetuity, for, since the objects in whose favour it is exercisable are restricted, it imposes from the moment of its creation a fetter upon the free disposability of the land.[2] It is important to notice, however, that a general power exercisable jointly by two or more persons or by one person with the consent of another is a special power for the purposes of the rule against perpetuities, the view taken by the law being that a power which cannot be exercised without the concurrence of two minds is not equivalent to property.[3]

General powers. A general power to appoint by deed, or either by deed or will, is void unless it will become effectively exercisable, if at all, within the perpetuity period. At the date when the instrument of creation takes effect, it must be possible to say that within that period the donee will be ascertainable, the event upon which the power is to arise will have occurred and any condition precedent to the right of exercise will have been satisfied.

Validity of creation. Power to appoint by deed, or either by deed or will.

On this basis, each of the following powers is void:

A power given to the survivor of two living persons and their children.[4]

A power to arise upon the general failure of the issue of a marriage.[5]

A power given to an unborn person upon his marriage.[6]

---

[1] Sugden, *Powers* (8th Edn.), pp. 395–6, cited Morris and Leach, *op. cit.*, p. 148.   [2] Co. Litt. 272a, Butler's note.

[3] *Re Churston, Settled Estates*, [1954] Ch. 334; [1954] 1 All E. R. 725; *Re Earl of Coventry's Indentures* [1974] Ch. 77 ; [1973] 3 All E. R. 1. See also *supra*, pp. 275–6.

[4] *Re Hargreaves* (1889), 43 Ch. D. 401.

[5] *Bristow* v. *Boothby* (1826), 2 Sim. & St. 465. *Prima facie*, "Issue" includes descendants of every degree. See *Theobald on Wills* (13th Edn.), paras. 956–9.

[6] *Morgan* v. *Gronow* (1873), L. R. 16 Eq. 1 (in the case of the original appointment).

If a general power to appoint by deed, or either by deed or will, is exercisable within the perpetuity period, it is not rendered objectionable by the fact that it may possibly be exercised after the period has expired, as may well happen, for instance, if it is given to the unborn child of a living person. By virtue of the power, such a donee ascertained within due limits acquires an unrestricted right of alienation, and as in the case of any absolute owner he is free to decide when he will exercise that right.[1]

General testamentary power.

On the other hand, a general testamentary power, *i.e.* one that is exercisable only by will, though it will vest in the donee, if at all, within the perpetuity period, is void if it may be exercised beyond that period. The reason is that the property is tied up during the lifetime of the donee in the sense that he possesses no right of alienation until his death. Therefore, such a power is void if, as in the case of one given to the unborn child of a living person, it may be exercisable at too remote a time.[2]

Validity of appointment.

The donee of a general power, since he can appoint to anybody in the world, including himself, has complete and absolute freedom of disposition, and therefore for the purpose of testing the validity of his appointments the perpetuity period is reckoned from the exercise of the power, not from its creation.

Moreover, the irrational rule has prevailed that this is so even in the case of a general testamentary power,[3] though here, as we have just seen, the donee is not in the position of an absolute owner.

Validity of creation.

Special powers. As regards the validity of its creation, a special power is subject to the following rule:

" A special power which, according to the true construction of the instrument creating it, is capable of being exercised beyond lives in being and twenty-one years afterwards is, by reason of the rule against perpetuities, absolutely void."[4]

As in the case of a general power, a special power is too remote in its creation if the donee may not be ascertained or if the condition precedent to its exercise may not have occurred within lives in being and twenty-one years afterwards. But in the case of a special power there is the further requirement that the objects must be ascertainable within the same period. The difference in this respect between the two classes of powers may be illustrated by a power, to be exercised by deed, given to an unborn person.

Example of power given to unborn person.

A special power to this effect, as for instance, one conferred by settlement upon the eldest son of X., a bachelor, to appoint to his

---

[1] *Re Fane*, [1913] 1 Ch. 404 at p. 413.
[2] *Wollaston* v. *King* (1868), L. R. 8 Eq. 165; *Morgan* v. *Gronow* (1873), L. R. 16 Eq. 1.
[3] *Rous* v. *Jackson* (1885), 29 Ch. D. 521. See *infra*, pp. 354–5.
[4] *Re De Sommery*, [1912] 2 Ch. 622, at p. 630, *per* Parker, J. ; M. & B. p. 325.

children, is void *ab initio*.[1] At the time of the settlement, it can no doubt be said that the appointor will be ascertained, if at all, within twenty-one years from the death of the life in being, X; but it cannot be said that the children in whose favour alone the appointment may be made will be ascertainable, if at all, within the same period. In other words, the occasion upon which the power is to become operative may be too remote.[2]

On the other hand, as we have seen, a general power to the same effect exercisable by deed is valid. The donee, being ascertainable within the perpetuity period has complete control over the property, and once ascertained is in the same position as if he were already its absolute owner.[3]

Provided that a special power is so limited that it cannot be *exercised* beyond the perpetuity period, it is immaterial that under its terms an appointment may possibly be made that will be too remote, as in the case, for instance, of a devise

> to X. for life, remainder to such of his issue as he shall by will appoint.[4]

At the date of such a devise, it is impossible to say whether the perpetuity rule will be transgressed or not, but this uncertainty does not invalidate the power. The appointments will fail only if in fact they are too remote.[5] The question is not what may be done, but what in fact is done. In other words this is an exceptional case at common law where it is necessary to wait and see what happens.

Presuming now, that the power itself is valid in the sense that it is exercisable only within the perpetuity period, it remains to consider the test that governs the validity of appointments in fact made. It differs radically from that applicable to a general power, a fact that has been clearly explained by Lord ROMER in the following passage:—

> " If a person be given a general power of appointment over certain property he is virtually the owner of that property. If and when he exercises the power the interests of his appointees come to them by virtue of and are created by the deed of appointment. In the case of a special power it is very different. If, for example, property be settled on trust for A. for life and after his death on trust for such of A.'s children or remoter issue and in such proportions as B. shall by deed appoint, B. has no interest in the property whatsoever. He has merely been given the power of saying on behalf of the settlor which of the issue of A. shall take the property under the settlement

Marginal notes:

Power validly created not void merely because admits of remote appointments.

Test of validity of appointment.

---

[1] *Wollaston* v. *King* (1868), L. R. 8 Eq. 165.
[2] Gray, *op. cit.*, ss. 475, 477.
[3] *Bray* v. *Hammersley* (1830), 3 Sim. 513; S. C. *sub. nom. Bray* v. *Bree* (1834), 2 Cl. & Fin. 353.
[4] *Slark* v. *Dakyns* (1874), 10 Ch. App. 35. *Re Vaux*, [1939] Ch. 465, at p. 472 ; [1938] 4 All E. R. 297, at p. 302.
[5] *Re Fane*, [1913] 1 Ch. 404, at pp. 413–4.

and in what proportions.   It is as though the settlor had left a blank in the settlement which B. fills up for him if and when the power of appointment is exercised.   The appointees' interests come to them under the settlement alone and by virtue of that document."[1]

Perpetuity period reckoned from the date of the instrument of creation.

It follows from this that the limitations made in pursuance of the power must only be such as would have been valid in point of perpetuity had they been contained in the instrument that created the power.[2]   In short, the perpetuity period is reckoned from the time when that instrument came into operation.

Thus in one case:

A settlement made in 1844, upon the marriage of H. and W., limited land to W. for life and after her death to such of her children as she should appoint.   The terms of her appointment were that the income of the land should be divided equally between her two daughters, X. and Y., during their respective lives, but that upon the death of one it should pass in its entirety to the survivor.

It was held that the gift to the survivor was void.   It was a contingent gift, and the event upon which it was to vest—the death of one of the daughters—would not necessarily occur within twenty-one years from the deaths of H. and W. who constituted the sole lives in being when the special power was created in 1844.[3]

Re Brown and Sibly's Contract.

A further example of the rule is afforded by *Re Brown and Sibly's Contract*,[4] in which the facts were as follows:

By a marriage settlement made in 1821 land was limited to the use of W. M. for life, and after his death to the use of all or any exclusively of the children, grandchildren or other issue of W. M. (to be born before the appointment was made), as he should by deed or will appoint.

By his will, which took effect in 1868, W. M. appointed to his son W. E. M. in fee, but in case W. E. M. had no child who should attain 21, then in fee simple to W. M. B., who was the grandson of W. M.

If these limitations are set out in the 1821 deed, the position is this:—

W. M. for life (alive in 1821);
W. E. M. in fee (not a life in being in 1821);
W. M. B. in fee (not a life in being in 1821).

When viewed in this manner the invalidity of the last limitation is apparent, for whether any child of W. E. M. failed to attain

---

[1] *Muir (or Williams)* v. *Muir*, [1943] A. C. 468, at p. 483.
[2] *Ibid.*, at p. 481 ;   *Farwell on Powers* (3rd Edn.), p. 325.
[3] *Whitby* v. *Von Luedecke*, [1906] 1 Ch. 783 ;   *Re Legh's Settlement Trusts*, [1938] Ch. 39 ; [1937] 3 All E. R. 823.   W., however, might have achieved her object by making the interest in the entire income vested instead of contingent.   An appointment of one-half to X. for life with remainder to Y. for life, and of one-half to Y. for life with remainder to X. for life, would have been valid.   The rule against perpetuities is, indeed, of a highly technical nature, see (1952), 68 *L. Q. R.*, pp. 47–9 (W. B. Leach).
[4] (1876), 3 Ch. D. 156; M. & B. p. 327.

21 years, which was the condition precedent to the vesting of a
title in W. M. B., would not necessarily be known within 21 years
from the death of the life in being, W. M.

The rule, that the appointment ultimately made must be
regarded as having been made in the original instrument of creation, merely ensures that the donee of the power shall not grant
interests that the donor himself could not have granted. It is
permitted, however, to read and construe the appointments in the
light of the circumstances existing at the time when they are intended
to take effect, not at the time when the power was created.[1]

Facts existing at date of appointment relevant to its validity.

> Suppose that a deed of settlement, executed in 1941, limits
> land to A., a bachelor, for life, remainder to such of his issue
> as he shall by will appoint. A. makes a will appointing to his
> eldest daughter, X. *on her marriage.* A. dies in 1961.

If X. is unmarried when the will takes effect in 1961, the gift to her
is void, for she might not marry until more than twenty-one years
after the death of A., the only life in being at the time of the deed
of creation.

> The settlor in 1941 could not have validly limited land to A.,
> a bachelor, for life remainder to A.'s eldest daughter on her
> marriage.

If, in the other hand, X. is already married in 1961, the gift to her
is valid.[2]

> The settlor in 1941 could have validly limited land to A., a
> bachelor, for life, remainder to A.'s eldest daughter, *on condi-
> tion that she was married at the time of her father's death.*

What is read into the instrument of creation is not the precise
language of the appointment, but the precise appointment.[3]

(d) Effect of an infringement of the Rule upon subsequent interests[4]

A future interest dependent upon a vesting contingency that is
too remote is struck out of the disposition, together with all
subsequent interests that depend upon the same contingency.
Thus, in *Proctor* v. *Bishop of Bath and Wells*,[5] a

Remote interest, and later interests dependent thereon, extinguished.

> devise in fee simple to the first or other son of A. that should
> be bred a clergyman, and be in Holy Orders,

---

[1] Gray, *op. cit.*, s. 523; *Wilkinson* v. *Duncan* (1861), 30 Beav. 111; *Von Brockdorff* v. *Malcolm* (1885), 30 Ch. D. 172 ; *Re Thompson*, [1906] 2 Ch. 199 ; *Re Paul*, [1921] 2 Ch. 1 ; M. & B. p. 328.
[2] *Morgan* v. *Gronow* (1873), L. R. 16 Eq. 1.
[3] *Re Thompson, supra*, at p. 205, *per* Joyce J.
[4] See (1950), 10 *C. L. J.* 392 (J. H. C. Morris) ; (1950), 14 *Conv.* (N.S.) 148 (A. K. R. Kiralfy).
[5] (1794), 2 Hy. Bl. 358; *supra*, p. 323.

was void, since this contingency might not occur, if it ever occurred at all, until more than twenty-one years after the death of A. Moreover, the subsequent gift

in case A. should have no such son, then to B. in fee simple

was equally void, since its vesting depended upon precisely the same event that had invalidated the prior limitation. Its vesting hinged upon the identical remote contingency. Where such is the position, the subsequent limitation is aptly described as intrinsically void.[1]

Position where subsequent interest is intrinsically valid.

The difficulty arises where the subsequent limitation is not associated with the prior contingency, but is intrinsically valid in the sense that it is already vested in interest, though not in possession, or will necessarily become so, if at all, within the perpetuity period. That a valid interest should be adversely affected by the remoteness of a prior interest is a strange suggestion, but it is implicit in the prevailing doctrine, which is that any limitation that is *dependent or expectant* upon a prior remote limitation is itself invalid, since it is not intended to take effect until the prior limitation has been exhausted.[2] The range of this doctrine and the exact meaning of the vague expression "dependent and expectant" have never been judicially defined, and whether a limitation is affected by an earlier limitation contained in the same instrument is a question of some obscurity.[3] That the doctrine may defeat a settlor's intention is evident from the decision of EVE, J. in *Re Backhouse*[4] where a testator bequeathed a picture

to his son Jonathan for life; next
to his second son Charles for life; next
to his daughter Millicent for life; next
after her death to the first and every other
son then living of Jonathan, successively for
their respective lives according to seniority ; next
on similar trusts to the first and every other son of
Charles *then living*; next
on similar trusts to the sons of Millicent,
but not restricted to those then living; lastly
to the testator's own right heirs.

The first four limitations were valid, but the fifth—to the sons of Charles *then living*—was too remote. It was restricted to those living after all the sons of Jonathan were dead, and therefore whether the sons of Charles, some of whom might be born after

---

[1] Morris and Leach, *op. cit.* p. 173.
[2] *Re Abbott*, [1893] 1 Ch. 54, at p. 57.
[3] Sir John Romilly, for instance, said that a testamentary limitation was void if it was *ulterior* to remote limitations, even though made in favour of a person living at the testator's death ; *Re Thatcher's Trusts* (1859), 26 Beav. 365, at p. 370.
[4] [1921] 2 Ch. 51.

the will took effect, would satisfy this condition would not necessarily be ascertained within the perpetuity period.

Moreover, the learned judge held that this remote gift broke the chain of limitations and invalidated the gifts to the sons of Millicent and the ultimate gift to the testator's right heirs, though each of these was vested.

It is a question of construction in each case whether, according to the intention of the settlor, a limitation is dependent on a prior remote limitation, as in *Re Backhouse*, or is independent and valid, presuming that taken by itself it satisfies the rule against perpetuities. The relevant decisions do not make easy reading, but they have been reduced by BUCKLEY, J. to the following three categories:[1]

Question of construction whether a limitation is intended to be dependent or independent.

(1) If a series of successive interests is created, each intended to take effect upon and only upon the exhaustion or termination of all antecedent interests in the chain, and one of them is void for remoteness, every subsequent interest fails, even a life interest given to a living person which would necessarily vest within the perpetuity period.[2]

(2) Where an interest is created which will not take effect in possession until a future date, but must vest in interest within the perpetuity period, and its possessory enjoyment is not dependent on the exhaustion of the precedent interests, it will be unaffected by remoteness in any of the antecedent interests.[3] This is illustrated by *Re Coleman*.[4]

> A testator left his residuary estate on discretionary trusts to H. for life; after H.'s death upon similar discretionary trusts for any widow who might survive him; and after the death of such widow upon trust (not discretionary) for the children of H. at 21 in equal shares.

By virtue of the discretionary trusts, the trustees were empowered to confer an interest in any part of the income upon H. or his widow. But this trust in the widow's case was void, for H. might marry a woman born after the testator's death, and if so the discretion of the trustees, which was a condition precedent to her right to an interest, might be exercisable beyond the perpetuity period. Nevertheless, it was held that the limitation to the children was valid. By the terms of the will, they were to acquire shares in the residuary estate that were to vest both in interest and in possession on

---

[1] *Re Hubbard's Will Trusts*, [1963] Ch. 275 at pp. 284–8; M. & B. p. 330.

[2] *Beard* v. *Westcott* (1822), 5 B. & Ald. 801; *Re Buckton's Settlement Trusts*, [1964] Ch. 497 ; [1964] 2 All E. R. 487.

[3] *Re Hubbard's Will Trusts, supra*, at pp. 285–7. *Re Backhouse, supra*, p. 334, however, is inconsistent with this proposition.

[4] [1936] Ch. 528 ; followed in *Re Allan*, [1958] 1 W. L. R. 220 ; [1958] 1 All E. R. 401.

the death of H.'s widow, an event that would not be too remote. The will did not direct that the right to possession should be deferred until the discretionary trusts failed or were exhausted.

(3) The third category is, in the words of BUCKLEY, J.:

> " Where a testator or settlor gives property to A. either immediately or at some future date which is not too remote, but so frames his trusts that the interest of A. may be displaced by the exercise of some power or discretion, the interest of A. will be unaffected by any invalidity of that power or discretion on the ground of remoteness."[1]

In one case, for instance, a testator allocated a fund to be used at the discretion of trustees upon the maintenance of a mansion house so long as any person entitled to the house under a strict settlement shall be under twenty-one years of age, "and subject thereto" upon trust for A. absolutely. The discretionary trust for the maintenance of the house was admittedly too remote, but it was held that the trust in favour of A. was an independent limitation and was valid.[2]

Destination of property remotely limited.   The destination of the property affected by a remote limitation differs according as the disposition is made by deed or by will. In the former case it results to the settlor. In the case of a will, it goes to the residuary legatee or devisee, but to the persons entitled as on an intestacy of the testator if there is no residuary gift or if the residue itself is the subject matter of the limitation. If the void limitation is effected by the exercise of a special power of appointment, the property concerned passes to the persons entitled in default of appointment.

(e) Alternative limitations

Contingencies with a double aspect.   Where a settlor makes the vesting of a future gift dependent upon two alternative events, one of which is too remote and the other not, the gift is allowed to take effect if the event which is not too remote is the one that actually happens.[3] This doctrine provides an exception to the rule that possible, not actual, events are alone considered, for the court waits to see which of the two events in fact occurs.[4] Thus in the early case of *Longhead* v. *Phelps*[5] a marriage settlement declared that certain trusts should arise

---

[1] *Re Hubbard's Will Trusts*, [1963] Ch. 275 at p. 287, *per* BUCKLEY, J.

[2] *Re Canning's Will Trusts*, [1936] Ch. 309; see also *Re Abbott*, [1893] 1 Ch. 54.   The difficulties arising from this doctrine of dependency no longer affect instruments taking effect after July 15th, 1964 ; P. & A.A. 1964, s. 6 ; *infra*, pp. 355–6.

[3] *Longhead* v. *Phelps* (1770), 2 Wm. Bl. 704; *Leake* v. *Robinson* (1817), 2 Mer. 363; *Re Curryer's Will Trusts*, [1938] Ch. 952; [1938] 3 All E. R. 574; Gray, *op. cit.*, Chap. ix.

[4] Morris and Leach, *op. cit.*, pp. 181–4.   [5] *Supra.*

if H. should die without issue male *or* if such issue male should die without issue.

The latter contingency was obviously too remote, for whether H.'s male issue died without themselves leaving issue would not necessarily be known within 21 years from his death, but in fact he died without male issue and it was held that the trusts were valid. In a more recent case a testator created a trust to take effect

" upon the decease of my last surviving child *or* the death of the last surviving widow or widower of my children as the case may be whichever shall last happen."

Here again the last contingency was too remote, since one or more of the children might marry a person born after the testator's death, but it was held that the trust would be valid if the first contingency in fact happened, *i.e.* if all the widows and widowers were dead when the last surviving child died.[1]

The courts, however, have consistently held that this indulgence will not be shown to the valid gift unless the settlor has himself expressly and distinctly designated the two alternative contingencies.[2] If vesting is in terms made dependent upon a single event which in fact includes two contingencies, one too remote the other not too remote, the future gift is void, although the contingency which actually happens is the one that satisfies the perpetuity rule. The court will not split the expression used by the settlor, *i.e.* will not separate and state in an alternative form the two events that the expression in fact includes. By way of illustration we may refer once more to *Proctor* v. *Bishop of Bath and Wells*.[3] In that case the fee simple was devised

Alternative contingencies must be expressed.

to the first or other son of A. that should be bred a clergyman, and be in Holy Orders, but in case he should have no such son, then to B. in fee simple.

It is clear on analysis that the event upon which the gift to B. was dependent included two contingencies, namely,

(a) failure of A. to leave sons;
(b) failure of any son to take Holy Orders.

A gift to B. to take effect if A. left no sons would obviously be valid, but though A. did in fact die childless, it was held that B. was not entitled to the fee simple. If the description of the event had been alternative, instead of single, in point of expression, all would have been well; *i.e.* if the testator had expressly stated that the fee simple was to vest in B.,

if A. had no son *or* if he had no son who should take Holy Orders,

---

[1] *Re Curryer's Will Trusts*, [1938] Ch. 952 ; [1938] 3 All E. R. 574.
[2] *Re Bence*, [1891] 3 Ch. 242 ; *Miles* v. *Harford* (1879), 12 Ch. D. 691, at p. 702, *per* JESSEL, M.R.
[3] (1794), 2 Hy. Bl. 358; *supra*, pp. 323 ; 333.

B.'s claim would have been upheld, since it was the first contingency that in fact happened. What the court refused to do was to redraft in an alternative form the single expression appearing in the will. In cases of this kind the court does not concentrate upon implementing the testator's intention, for a man who says that an estate is to go over to B. if none of A.'s sons becomes a clergyman obviously means it to go over if A. never has a son. Whether the intention will prevail is purely a question of words.

> "You are bound to take the expression as you find it, and if, giving the proper interpretation to that expression, the event may transgress the limit, then the gift over is void."[1]

(f) *Exceptions to the Rule against Perpetuities*
(1) **Limitations after entailed interests**

Limitations after entailed interests.

A tenant in tail can bar his own and all subsequent interests. The rule, therefore, is that no limitation after an entailed interest is void for remoteness, provided that the subsequent limitation must vest, if at all, at or before the end of the perpetuity period. There is in fact no perpetuity.[2]

(2) **Contracts and Options**

Personal contracts not affected.

"It is settled beyond argument that an agreement merely personal, not creating any interest in land, is not within the rule against perpetuities."[3] Therefore, it is not void simply because the obligation it creates may last for an indefinite time.[4] For instance, in *Walsh* v. *Secretary of State for India*,[5]

> the East India Company entered into a covenant in 1770 whereby they promised to pay a certain sum of money if, at any time after 1794, they should cease to have a military force in their pay and service in the East Indies. It might have been centuries before such a state of things occurred, and in point of fact it was nearly a century, but nevertheless the court upheld the validity of the obligation.

Privity of contract excludes the rule.

It is equally well settled at common law that even a contract which creates an interest in land remains binding upon the parties themselves, notwithstanding that it may be enforceable beyond the perpetuity period. So long as privity of contract exists, there is no room for the rule against perpetuities. Thus in *Hutton* v. *Watling*[6]:—

> A written agreement by which X. sold his business to Y. stipulated that Y. should have the option, exercisable at any time in the future, to purchase the premises in which the business was carried on.

---

[1] *Miles* v. *Harford* (1879), 12 Ch. D. 691 at p. 703, *per* JESSEL, M.R.
[2] *Nicolls* v. *Sheffield* (1787), 2 Bro. C.C. 215; *Heasman* v. *Pearse* (1871), 7 Ch. App. 275.
[3] *South Eastern Rail. Co* v. *Associated Portland Cement Manufacturers,* (1900) *Ltd.,* [1910] 1 Ch. 12, at p. 33, *per* FARWELL J.
[4] *Witham* v. *Vane* (1883), Challis, *Law of Real Property* (3rd Edn.), p. 440.
[5] (1863), 10 H.L. Cas. 376.
[6] [1948] Ch. 26 ; [1947] 2 All E. R. 641 : affirmed on other grounds ; [1948] Ch. 398 ; [1948] 1 All E. R. 803.

An action by Y. for specific performance brought seven years later was met by the plea that the stipulation was void for remoteness. The plea failed. In such a case, Y. is entitled not only to recover damages from X.,[1] but also to a decree of specific performance if the land is still retained by X., for "specific performance is merely an equitable mode of enforcing a personal obligation with which the rule against perpetuities has nothing to do."[2]

But once the promisee seeks to enforce the promise against a third person, the position is changed. We now pass from the law of contract to the law of property, with the result that such an option as that in *Hutton* v. *Watling* or an option given to a lessee to purchase the reversion, since it creates an executory interest in land, cannot be enforced against third persons who later acquire the promisor's land unless it is confined within the perpetuity period.[3] Thus where a railway company sold land to one Powell subject to a right of repurchase if at any time thereafter the land was required for the railway, it was held that the right was unenforceable against the appellant, to whom Powell's heir had sold the land.[4]

Rule affects contracts binding land, if no privity of contract.

Jessel, M.R. said:

"If then the rule as to remoteness applies to a covenant of this nature, this covenant clearly is bad as extending beyond the period allowed by the rule. Whether the rule applies or not depends upon this as it appears to me—does or does not the covenant give an interest in the land ? If it is a bare or mere personal contract it is of course not obnoxious to the rule, but in that case it is impossible to see how the present appellant can be bound. He did not enter into the contract, but is only a purchaser from Powell who did. If it is a mere personal contract it cannot be enforced against the assignee. Therefore the company must admit that it somehow binds the land. But if it binds the land it creates an equitable interest in the land. The right to call for a conveyance of the land is an equitable interest or equitable estate."

Thus, an option to call for a lease of land exemplifies this principle and is void if it is exercisable beyond the perpetuity period, but it has long been recognized that an option given to a tenant to *renew* his existing lease is entirely unaffected by the rule against perpetuities.[5]

---

[1] *Worthing Corpn.* v. *Heather*, [1906] 2 Ch. 532.
[2] *Hutton* v. *Watling*, [1948] Ch. 26, at p. 36, *per* Jenkins, J. This rule has been reversed in the case of instruments taking effect after July 15th 1964 ; *infra*, p. 355.
[3] *Woodall* v. *Clifton*, [1905] 2 Ch. 257 ; M. & B. p. 334 ; *London and South Western Rail Co.* v. *Gomm* (1882), 20 Ch. D. 562 ; M. & B. p. 335 ; *Griffith* v. *Pelton*, [1958] Ch. 205 ; [1957] 3 All E. R. 75.
[4] *London and South Western Rail. Co.* v. *Gomm, supra*.
[5] *Woodall* v. *Clifton, supra*, at pp. 265, 268 ; *Weg Motors, Ltd.* v. *Hales*, [1961] Ch. 176 ; [1960] 3 All E. R. 762 ; *affirmed*, [1962] Ch. 49; [1961] 3 All E. R. 181.

(3) Certain easements and mortgages.

A further illustration of the principles laid down by JESSEL, M.R., is that the grant of an easement to arise *in futuro* may be void on the ground of remoteness, as for example where it entitles the grantee to use the drains and sewers "now passing *or hereafter to pass*" under a private road.[1]

Mortgages outside the rule. The rule against perpetuities has no application to mortgages, and therefore a postponement of the right of redemption for longer than the perpetuity period is not void for remoteness,[2] though it may be void on other grounds[3]

(4) Certain rights of entry

The rule affects certain rights of entry, but not others.

Proviso for forfeiture in lease. First, the right usually reserved to a lessor to enter upon the land and to terminate the lease if the tenant commits a breach of covenant[4] is not subject to the rule.[5]

Right of entry in respect of rentcharge. Secondly, the owner of a rentcharge, *i.e.* a person, other than a reversioner, entitled to the payment of an annual sum of money out of land,[6] is empowered by the Law of Property Act 1925,[7] in the event of non-payment to enter upon the land and to recover the money due either by levying distress or by leasing the land to a trustee until all arrears have been paid. The Act puts this right of entry, together with its attendant remedies, outside the rule against perpetuities.[8]

If the instrument creating the charge expressly empowers the creditor to enter the land and to determine the fee simple estate of the debtor for non-payment of rent, or to enter and enforce some covenant other than that to pay the sum due, it is doubtful whether such a power is excluded from the perpetuity rule by virtue of the Act.[9]

Right of entry in respect of indemnity rentcharge. Thirdly, a rentcharge is sometimes created merely by way of indemnity against another rentcharge.[10] If, for instance, an estate which as a whole is subject to a rentcharge is being sold off in lots, it is a common practice to throw the burden of the charge entirely upon one lot. In practice the purchaser of that lot then

---

[1] *Dunn* v. *Blackdown Properties Ltd.*, [1961] Ch. 433 ; [1961] 2 All E. R. 62 ; (1961), 25 *Conv.* (N.S.) 415 (G. Battersby) ; *Newham* v. *Lawson* (1971), 22 P. & C. R. 852.

[2] *Knightsbridge Estates Trust Ltd.* v. *Byrne*, [1939] Ch. 441, at p. 463 ; affd., [1940] A.C. 613 ; [1940] 2 All E. R. 401.

[3] *Infra*, pp. 655–6.   [4] *Infra*, pp. 435 ; 441.

[5] *Re Tyrrell's Estate*, [1907] 1 I.R. 292 at p. 298, *per* WALKER L.C.

[6] *Infra*, p. 629.

[7] L.P.A. 1925, s. 121.

[8] *Ibid.*, s. 121 (6).

[9] See Morris and Leach, *op. cit.* p. 218. The doubt has been removed by P. & A.A. 1964, s. 11, which, however, is not retrospective ; see *infra*, p. 357.

[10] *Infra*, p. 630.

gives the purchasers of the other lots an indemnity rentcharge issuing out of his land, so that if they as purchasers of parts of the whole land are compelled by the rent-owner to pay the charge, they will have a right to reimburse themselves out of the lot on which it has been thrown.

The former doubt whether the law of remoteness applied to such cases was dispelled by the Law of Property Act 1925, which provides that rentcharges created only by way of indemnity against other rentcharges, and powers to distrain or to take possession of land affected by such rentcharges, shall be excluded from the operation of the rule against perpetuities.[1]

Fourthly, a right of entry for condition broken attached to a fee simple is void if it is exercisable beyond the perpetuity period.[2] *Right of entry for condition broken.*

Fifthly, if a fee simple is sold in return for a perpetual annual rentcharge, the right of entry or re-entry that accrues to the vendor in the event of non-payment,[3] although exercisable for an unlimited period, does not withdraw the land from commerce and therefore is unaffected by the rule against perpetuities.[4] *Right of entry in case of fee farm rent.*

(5) Accumulative trust of income for the purpose of paying debts

The rule does not apply to a trust directing that income shall be accumulated with a view to the payment of the settlor's debts, or for the discharge of incumbrances charged upon the land, for such a trust, though capable of enduring for an indefinite time, may be determined at any moment either by the beneficiaries paying the debts and freeing the land, or by the creditors enforcing their claims by the seizure of the land.[5] Neither does the rule apply to a trust under which money is to be accumulated for the reduction of the National Debt[6] nor to trusts of registered pension funds for employees.[7] *Provision for payment of debts.*

(6) Administrative powers of trustees

The former rule was that administrative powers given to trustees, such as a power to sell or lease land, or to receive remuneration for their services, were void if they were capable of being exercised at too remote a time, notwithstanding that they were attached to a trust which itself was not too remote. This may be illustrated by *Re Allott*.[8] *Administrative powers of trustees.*

A testator left his mines to trustees upon trust to pay annuities to his daughters out of the profits. He directed that if a daughter

---

[1] L.P.A. 1925, s. 162 (1) (*a*).
[2] *Re Hollis' Hospital Trustees and Hague's Contract*, [1899] 2 Ch. 540 ; L.P.A. 1925, s. 4 (3) *infra*, p. 369.
[3] *Supra*, pp. 150–1.
[4] Compare the remarks of Lord Brougham in *Keppell* v. *Bailey* (1834), 2 My. & K. 517, at pp. 528–9.
[5] *Tewart* v. *Lawson* (1874), L. R. 18 Eq. 490; *Lord Southampton* v. *Marquis of Hertford* (1813), 2 Ves. & B. 54.
[6] Superannuation and other Trust Funds (Validation) Act 1927, s. 9.
[7] *Ibid.*, ss. 1, 2.   [8] [1924] 2 Ch. 498.

married, and was survived by her husband, such survivor should be entitled for his life to her annuity.

After the testator's death, a deed of family arrangement was entered into which incorporated the trusts of the will and which *inter alia* gave the trustees powers to grant leases not exceeding 99 years.

The life interest given to any surviving husband was valid despite the fact that he might be a person not born at the date of the execution of the deed. His life interest would necessarily arise, if it ever arose at all, immediately on the death of his wife. Nevertheless, the power of leasing was void, since it might be exercised, and so create a fresh interest, more than twenty-one years after the dropping of the lives in being if the husband lived so long.

The effect of administrative powers is not to tie up the property, but to facilitate its management, and therefore the Law Reform Committee recommended that they should be excluded from the perpetuity rule provided that the trusts to which they are ancillary are valid and subsisting. This recommendation has been accepted by the Perpetuities and Accumulations Act 1964, in the only section that is retrospective. It provides that:—

> The rule against perpetuities shall not operate to invalidate a power conferred on trustees or other persons to sell, lease, exchange or otherwise dispose of property for full consideration, or to do any other act in the administration (as opposed to the distribution) of any property, and shall not prevent the payment to trustees or other persons of reasonable remuneration for their services.[1]

It should be noticed that it is only *administrative* powers that are exempt from the rule against perpetuities. The rule applies to beneficial powers such as powers of appointment,[2] powers of distribution under a discretionary trust and powers of maintenance and advancement.[3]

(6) Certain limitations to charities

Charities.

An interest given to a charity, like any other gift, is void unless it will vest within the perpetuity period.[4] On the other hand, a limitation transferring property from one charity to another upon a certain contingency is valid, although the contingency may not occur until some indefinite time in the future. Provided that the interest of the first charity will begin within the perpetuity period, it is immaterial that the second charity may not take until a remote date. Thus in one case, where

> a testator bequeathed £42,000 to the London Missionary Society with a gift over to the Blue Coat School if the Society failed to keep his family vault in repair,

---

[1] Section 8 (1). If a power has been created before the commencement of the Act, *i.e.* July 16th, 1964, this section is applicable, provided that the exercise is effected after that date : s. 8 (2).   [2] *Supra*, p. 329.

[3] *Pilkington* v. *I. R. Comrs.* [1964] A. C. 612 ; [1962] 3 All E. R. 622 ; *Re Hastings-Bass*, [1975] Ch. 25 ; [1974] 2 All E. R. 193 (the statutory power of advancement under T. A. 1925, s. 32).

[4] *Chamberlayne* v. *Brockett* (1872), 8 Ch. App. 206; *Re Lord Stratheden and Campbell*, [1894] 3 Ch. 265 ; *Re Mander*, [1950] Ch. 547 ; [1950] 2 All E. R. 191.

it was held that the gift over was valid.[1] Had the gift over been, not to another charity, but to private persons, it would have been void.[2]

A gift to a charity is not void as a perpetuity merely because it creates an interest that may remain subject to the charitable trust for an indefinite period.[3]

(iii) The Rule Applicable to Instruments that take Effect after July 15th, 1964

In the case of a disposition[4] contained in an instrument[5] that takes effect after July 15th, 1964, the rules obtaining at common law with regard to remoteness have been modified and rationalized as follows by the Perpetuities and Accumulations Act 1964.[6]

Statutory modifications of the common law.

(a) The perpetuity period

As an alternative to the common law period during which it is permissible to suspend the vesting of interests, a settlor is empowered by the Act to specify a fixed period of years not exceeding eighty.[7] This is an alternative choice that may perhaps lead to the disappearance of royal lives clauses,[8] but to be effective the fixed period must be expressly designated as the perpetuity period. A limitation, for instance, to such of the issue of X. as may be living at the expiration of eighty years after his death, would not satisfy this requirement.

A fixed period of years may be chosen.

The donor of a special power may provide that the perpetuity period applicable to the limitations shall be a fixed number of years not exceeding eighty. Such period will, of course, begin to run from the effective creation of the power, and it cannot be extended by the donee when he makes an appointment.[9]

Special powers of appointment.

(b) Presumptions as to fertility

The rule at common law that a person of whatever age must be regarded as capable of having children[10] has been abolished in the case of instruments taking effect after July 15th, 1964.

Presumed ages of parenthood.

---

[1] *Re Tyler*, [1891] 3 Ch. 252 ; following *Christ's Hospital* v. *Grainger* (1849), 1 Mac. & G. 460. For a criticism of this decision see Gray, *op. cit.*, s. 603.

[2] *Re Talbot*, [1933] Ch. 895 ; *Re Bland-Sutton's Will Trusts*, [1951] Ch. 485 ; [1951] 1 All E. R. 494 ; reversed in part, [1952] A. C. 631 ; [1952] 1 All E. R. 984.

[3] *Chamberlayne* v. *Brockett* (1872), 8 Ch. App. 206, at p. 211; *Goodman* v. *Saltash Corpn.* (1882), 7 App. Cas. 633, at pp. 650, 651 ; *Re Bowen*, [1893] 2 Ch. 491, at p. 494.

[4] *Re Thomas Meadows & Co., Ltd.*, [1971] Ch. 278 ; [1971] 1 All E. R. 239.

[5] *Re Holt's Settlement*, [1969] 1 Ch. 100 ; [1968] 1 All E. R. 470 (court order approving an arrangement under the Variation of Trusts Act 1958 constitutes an instrument).

[6] The following account owes much to the article, *Perpetuities Reform at Last* by J. H. C. Morris and H. W. R. Wade, in (1964), 80 *L. Q. R.* pp. 486–534. See also Morris and Leach *op. cit.*, Supplement (1964) ; Wolstenholme and Cherry, vol. 2. pp. 135 *et seq.*

[7] P. & A.A. 1964, s. 1 (1). This provision does not apply to certain options to acquire an interest in land ; s. 9 (2), *infra*, p. 348.

[8] *Supra*, p. 319.

[9] P. & A.A. 1964, s. 1 (2).   [10] *Supra*, pp. 324–5.

Under the Act it is to be presumed in any proceedings that a male can beget a child at, but not under, the age of fourteen years; and that a female can have a child at, but not over, the age of fifty-five years.[1] In the case of a living person, however, evidence may be given to rebut these presumptions, by showing that he or she will not be able to have a child at the time in question.[2]

Whether adopted or legitimated child takes under gift to " children ".

The Act extends these presumptions to the possibility that a person will at any time have a child by adoption, legitimation or other means.[3] If a person is adopted or legitimated, the question arises whether or not he will take as a " child " of an adopting or legitimating parent under a gift to that person's " children ". The rule prior to the coming into force of the Children Act 1975 was that an adopted or legitimated child took under such a disposition if he had been adopted or legitimated *before* the instrument came into effect.[4] Under the Children Act 1975, which applies to instruments coming into effect after January 1, 1976, such a person can take whether or not the adoption or legitimation was before or after the date of the instrument.[5]

Effect of adoption or legitimation at advanced age.

A further question arises in relation to the presumption in the Perpetuities and Accumulations Act 1964, section 2, to the effect that a woman over the age of fifty-five is incapable of giving birth to a child. A woman over that age might, of course, adopt or legitimate a child.[6] For the purpose of the perpetuity rule, however, the presumption remains.[7] If property has been distributed on the basis of the presumption, and a woman does give birth to, or adopt, or legitimate, a child inconsistently with it, the High Court is empowered to make such order, " so far as may be just ", for placing the beneficiaries in the position they would have held had the presumption not been applied.[8]

(c) Uncertainty as to remoteness

Position at common law.

We have already seen that at common law a limitation is void if, in the light of the circumstances existing at the time of its effective creation, it may conceivably fail to vest within the perpetuity period. Its fate depends upon possible events in the future, not upon what in fact happens.[9] The Law Reform Committee recommended that the validity of a limitation should no longer be tested *ab initio* by reference to what may be within the bounds of

---

[1] P. & A.A. 1964, s. 2 (1) (*a*).
[2] *Ibid.*, 2 (1) (*b*).
[3] See also the effect of the Family Law Reform Act 1969, s. 15, *infra*, p. 854.
[4] Adoption Act 1958, s. 16; Legitimacy Act 1926, s. 3.
[5] S. 8, Sched. 1, paras. 1 (5), 3 (1), 5 (1), 12 (1) (3) ; *infra*, p. 856.
[6] Or even give birth to a child.
[7] P. & A. A. 1964, s. 2 (4). As it does also in relation to an adoption after the date of the instrument. Children Act 1975, s. 8, Sched. 1, para. 6 (5).
[8] *Ibid.*, s. 2 (2).
[9] *Supra*, pp. 322–5.

possibility, but that instead a "wait and see" principle should be adopted under which validity would be determined on the basis of actual events.[1] This recommendation has been accepted and in the case of instruments taking effect after July 15th, 1964, the "wait and see" principle applies to three distinct situations.

Statutory amendments.

(1) Interests capable of vesting beyond the perpetuity period

A disposition that is capable of vesting beyond the perpetuity period (*i.e.* the common law period or the fixed period not exceeding eighty years if this has been expressly specified) is to be treated as valid until such time as it becomes established that its vesting must occur, if at all, after the end of that period.[2] As soon as events show that it can never vest within the period, it becomes void; as soon as events show that it can never vest outside the period, it becomes immune from the doctrine of remoteness.[3]

The effect of this amendment may be illustrated by the old case of *Proctor* v. *Bishop of Bath and Wells*,[4] where there was

> a devise in fee simple to the first son of X. that should be bred a clergyman and be in Holy Orders. X. had no son born at the time of the testator's death.

The devise was void at common law. If a son were born he might not take Holy Orders, if at all, within twenty-one years from the death of X., the only life in being when the will took effect. But, under the Act of 1964, the devise is presumptively valid, not void *ab initio*. There must be a pause to see what happens. The gift will be valid if in fact a son is born who satisfies the vesting contingency within twenty-one years after X.'s death.

In the application of this "wait and see" principle, each distinct part of a limitation is treated by the Act as a separate disposition. For instance:

Waiting period differs for different parts of a disposition.

> A testator devises land to A. for life, remainder to his widow for life, remainder to such of the children of A. as are alive at the death of the widow; but if there be no such children, then to the first son of X. to marry.

In such a case, the gift to the children of A. and the gift to the first son of X. to marry are distinct dispositions subject to different waiting periods.

The "wait and see" principle applies equally to the validity of appointments made by the exercise of a special power.

Exercise of special power of appointment.

> Suppose that a testator, who dies in 1965, devises land to A., a bachelor, for life, remainder to such of his issue as he shall by will appoint. A. appoints in favour of his infant daughter, X. *on her marriage*. A. dies in 1975.

---

[1] Para. 10 (3) (1965 Cmnd. 18).   [2] P. & A. A. 1964, s. 3 (1).
[3] Para. 17 (1956 Cmnd. 18).   [4] (1794), 2 Hy. Bl. 358.

At common law the appointment is too remote.[1] Under the Act, it is valid provided that the daughter marries within twenty-one years after A's death.

Inter-
mediate
income.

One problem raised by these provisions is the destination of the intermediate income during the waiting period.[2] The general rule, subject to certain exceptions, is that a contingent gift carries the income arising from the corpus although the vesting contingency may ultimately never be satisfied, except so far as such income has been otherwise disposed of by the donor.[3] Suppose, for example, that a testator bequeaths the residue of his estate to his grandchild, X., upon her marriage and that she is an infant and unmarried at the time of the testator's death. In these circumstances, the income is accumulated during her infancy and the trustees may use it for her maintenance and education,[4] and may make advances to her out of capital,[5] but at her majority the income becomes and remains payable to her even though she may never marry.[6]

The rights of the beneficiaries in such a case, however, are subject to the perpetuity rule, the effect of which varies according as the disposition falls to be determined by the common law or by the Act of 1964.

> Suppose, for instance, that a will bequeaths the residue of the estate to the daughters of X. when they marry, and that X. is childless at the time of the testator's death.

At common law the bequest is void *ab initio*. It is impossible to say at the time when the will takes effect that if any children born to X. marry, they will do so within twenty-one years from her death.

Payments
out of
income
permitted
during
waiting
period.

But under the statutory "wait and see" provisions the gift is not void *ab initio*. It is void only if at the end of twenty-one years from X.'s death none of his daughters, if any, has married. The destination of the income of the corpus during this waiting period therefore presents a problem. If a daughter is born to X., is she to receive the benefit of the income although the bequest may ultimately become void for remoteness? The recommendation of the Law Reform Committee that such should be the rule[7] is accepted by the Act of 1964, which provides that when it becomes established that the vesting of a gift must occur, if at all, after the end of the perpetuity period, " the validity of anything previously done in relation to the interest disposed of by way of advancement,

---

[1] Compare the example discussed *supra*, p. 333.
[2] See Morris and Leach, *op. cit.*, pp. 93–5.
[3] See, *e.g.* L.P.A. 1925, s. 175 (2).
[4] Trustee Act 1925, s. 31 (1) (i) ; 31 (2). For dispositions taking effect after 1969 the age of majority has been reduced to 18. Family Law Reform Act 1969, s. 1. Scheds. 1, 3, para. 5.
[5] *Ibid.*, s. 32.
[6] *Ibid.*, s. 31 (1) (ii).
[7] Para. 22 (1956 Cmnd. 18).

application of intermediate income or otherwise" shall not be affected.[1]

(2) General powers capable of exercise beyond the perpetuity period

A general power of appointment that may possibly be exercised beyond the perpetuity period and which is therefore void at common law,[2] is to be treated as valid until it is established that it will not in fact be exercised at too remote a time.[3] If, for instance, it is exercisable only by will and is given to the unborn child of X., it will be valid if the donee is born and dies within twenty-one years after X.'s death; if it is exercisable by deed, or either by deed or will, but only on the marriage of the unborn child, it will be valid if the marriage occurs within the same period.

(3) "Any power, option or other right" capable of exercise beyond the perpetuity period

In a more comprehensive section, the Act deals separately with the remote exercise of "any power, option or other right". It provides that a power, option or other right is no longer to be rendered void merely because it may possibly be exercised at too remote a time. It will be void only if it is not in fact fully exercised within the perpetuity period.[4]

> For instance, a special power granted by a deed of settlement to the eldest son of X., a bachelor, is void *ab initio* at common law;[5] but under the Act it is not void unless exercised beyond the perpetuity period calculated from the date of the settlement.

On the other hand, if the exercise of a special power satisfies the test of remoteness prescribed by this sub-section, the question whether the appointed interests are too remote is governed, as we have seen, by an earlier subsection.[6]

The reference in this enactment to an "option" means *inter alia*, that a right conferred by contract upon one person to purchase the land of another at some unspecified time in the future is no longer void *ab initio*,[7] but void only if it is not in fact exercised within the perpetuity period.

Option to purchase land.

---

[1] P. & A.A. 1964, s. 3 (1).
[2] *Supra*, p. 329.
[3] P. & A.A. 1964, s. 3 (2).
[4] *Ibid.*, s. 3 (3). It will be noticed that a general power is caught by this sub-section as well as by sub-section (2).
[5] *Supra.*, pp. 330–1.
[6] P. & A.A. 1964, s. 3 (1) ; see the example given *supra*, pp. 345–6.
[7] As under the common law, *London and South Western Rail Co.* v. *Gomm* (1882), 20 Ch. D. 562; *supra*, p. 339; *Dunn* v. *Blackdown Properties Ltd.*, [1961] Ch. 433; [1961] 2 All E. R. 62; *supra*, p. 340.

But, except where the option is one that entitles a tenant to purchase his landlord's reversion, which is exercisable throughout the continuance of the lease however long this may be,[1] the only period applicable to an option to acquire for valuable consideration any interest in land is twenty-one years.[2]

Duration of the waiting period. In considering whether the wait and see provisions are applicable, the first step is to ascertain whether the disposition satisfies the common law rule against perpetuities. If the contingent interests that it grants must vest, if at all, within the period fixed by that rule, there is no need to invoke the statutory provisions. The Act of 1964 operates only where the vesting contingency may possibly occur after that period has expired. Where this is the case, the Act prescribes the period during which it is permissible to wait and see whether in the light of future events the limitations are or are not too remote. In the result the waiting period is as follows:—

Permissible time of waiting.

> The period of years not exceeding eighty if this has been specified by the settlor.
> Failing such a specification, a period based on the common law formula of lives plus twenty-one years, but restricted so far as lives are concerned to the individual persons defined by the Act itself. These, which may conveniently be called the "statutory lives", must be in being[3] and ascertainable at the time when the disposition takes effect.[4]

It is important to realize the consequence of this last requirement. If, for instance, the limitations of a will include a gift "to the widow of X.," she becomes a statutory life only if X. has predeceased the testator. If he survives the testator, his widow will not be ascertainable when the will takes effect. If there are no statutory lives and no specified term of years, the period of waiting is twenty-one years.[5]

"Statutory lives"
(a) Creator of the disposition.
(b) Certain beneficiaries.

The statutory lives are defined as follows:[6]

(a) The person by whom the disposition is made, if made by deed, even though he himself takes no interest in the property.[7]

(b) Any of the following persons in whose favour the disposition is made, namely—

---

[1] P. & A.A. 1964, s. 9 (1) ; *infra*, p. 356.
[2] *Ibid.*, s. 9 (2).
[3] Including children *en ventre sa mère*. P. & A.A. 1964, s. 15 (2).
[4] *Ibid.*, 1964, s. 3 (4) (*a*). The object of this sub-s. is merely to qualify the common law period so far as the relevant lives are concerned. It implies the retention of the additional twenty-one years.
[5] *Ibid.*, s. 3 (4) (*b*).
[6] *Ibid.*, s. 3 (5). The introduction of a statutory definition has been criticised in (1964), 80 *L. Q. R.* pp. 495–508 (J. H. C. Morris and H. W. R. Wade), and supported in (1970), 86 *L. Q. R.* 357 (R. H. Maudsley). See also (1965), 81 *L. Q. R.* 106 (D. E. Allan).
[7] *Ibid.*, s. 3 (5) (*a*).

(i) In the case of a class gift, any member or potential member of the class.[1]

A person is a member of the class if he has satisfied all the conditions that entitle him to an interest; he is a potential member if he has satisfied only some of the conditions but may in time satisfy the remainder.[2] If, for instance, there is a gift by will to such of the daughters of X. as may marry and if at the time of the testator's death X. has an unmarried daughter, she constitutes a life in being. She has satisfied the condition relating to birth and there is a possibility that she may later marry.

(ii) In the case of an individual disposition to a person subject to certain conditions, any person as to whom some of the conditions are satisfied and the remainder may in time be satisfied.[3]

This would be the position, for instance, if in the last illustration the gift had been to the first granddaughter of X. to marry, and if at the time of the testator's death a granddaughter had been born but was not yet married.

(iii) The above two provisions apply equally to special powers of appointment.[4]

If, for instance, the power is conferred by will and is exercisable in favour of any of the issue of X., descendants of X. alive at the testator's death constitute statutory lives.

(iv) The person on whom any power, option or other right is conferred.[5]

Trustees who possess a special power of appointment, for instance, fall within this category.

(c) In certain circumstances, the parents and grandparents of the designated beneficiaries also constitute persons whose lives are relevant in the present context. The Act provides that: *(c) Parents and grandparents of certain beneficiaries.*

The persons capable of ranking as "statutory lives" shall include a person having a child or grandchild who would be a life in being under the rules (b) (i to iv) given above ; and also a person any of whose children or grandchildren, if subsequently born, would by virtue of descent be a life in being under the same rules.[6]

Suppose, for instance, that a bequest is made to such of X.'s daughters as may marry, and that at the testator's death a daughter has been born to X. but has not yet married. In these circumstances, as we have seen in dealing with rule (b) (i),[7] the daughter ranks as

---

[1] P. & A.A. 1964, s. 3 (5) (b) (i).   [2] *Ibid.*, s. 15 (3).
[3] *Ibid.*, s. 3 (5) (b) (ii).   [4] *Ibid.*, s. 3 (5) (b) (iii) and (iv).
[5] *Ibid.*, s. 3 (5) (b) (v).   [6] *Ibid.*, s. 3 (5) (c).
[7] *Supra.*

a life in being. Under the instant rule, therefore, X. is equally qualified in that respect, and so also are such of X's parents and grandparents who are alive at the testator's death.[1]

Again, suppose that there is a bequest to the first granddaughter of X. to marry, and that at the testator's death X. has one unmarried son. In these circumstances, X., X.'s wife and X.'s unmarried son are lives in being under the instant rule, because, if a daughter is subsequently born to X.'s son, she would qualify under rule (*b*) (ii). If X.'s son were married after the testator's death, his wife would also qualify.

It is enacted, however, that the lives of the persons designated in (*b*) and (*c*) above shall be disregarded if their number is such as to render it impracticable to ascertain the death of the survivor.[2]

(*d*) Owner of precedent interest.

(*d*) Any person on the failure or determination of whose prior interest the disposition is limited to take effect constitutes a life being.[3]

A simple illustration of this is that under a limitation to A. for life remainder to the first grandchild of X. to marry, A. ranks as a life in being. It would seem, however, that he will not qualify as such under a limitation to A. for life, remainder to B. for life, remainder to the first grandchild of X. to marry, for it is on the determination of B.'s interest that the gift to the grandchild is to take effect.[4] It is this subsection which shows most clearly how the duration of the "wait and see" periods varies for different parts of one disposition.[5]

(*d*) *Special provisions designed to save remote interests*

The Act of 1964 contains three additional provisions designed to cure the vice of remoteness, but it is essential to bear in mind that these are not to be invoked until it has become clear that the limitations in question will not be saved by the "wait and see" rule.[6] The provisions are as follows:

(1) Provisions concerning the death of a surviving spouse

The case of the possibly unborn spouse.

This deals with the case of the possibly unborn spouse. Suppose for instance that the limitations contained in a will are

---

[1] See (1969) C. L. J. 284 (M. J. Prichard).
[2] P. & A.A. 1964, s. 3 (4) (*a*).
[3] *Ibid.*, s. 3 (5) (*d*). *Re Thomas Meadows & Co., Ltd. etc.*, [1971] Ch. 278 ; [1971] 1 All E. R. 239.
[4] See (1964), 80 *L. Q. R.*, p. 505 (J. H. C. Morris and H. W. R. Wade).
[5] *Supra.*, p. 344.
[6] Because s. 3, which introduces the "wait and see" rule is expressed to operate "apart" from ss. 4 and 5 which contain these three additional provisions.

to X., a bachelor, for life, remainder to his future wife for life, remainder to such of his children as are living at the death of the survivor of X. and such wife.

As we have seen, the limitation to the children is void at common law.[1] It is possible that X. may marry a woman not yet born, and therefore it cannot be affirmed at the time of the testator's death that the vesting contingency will necessarily occur within the perpetuity period.

Position at common law.

If X. marries a woman who is alive at the date of the will, the gift to the children will not be saved by the "wait and see" rule unless she dies not later than twenty-one years after X.'s death. The wife cannot qualify as a "statutory life", though possibly and most probably she is alive at the date of the testator's death, for under the Act of 1964 lives in being for the purposes of the "wait and see" rule must be ascertainable at the commencement of the perpetuity period.[2]

Wait and see provisions not a complete remedy.

It is therefore provided by the Act of 1964 that a disposition such as that given above, which fails for remoteness, shall be treated for all purposes as if it had been limited to take effect immediately before the end of the perpetuity period, if to do so will save it from being void for remoteness.[3]

Position under the Act of 1964.

If, then, in the case of the above example, X. marries, and his wife dies within twenty-one years of his death, the limitation to the children is saved under the "wait and see" rule. If she survives beyond that time, the "wait and see" rule is impotent, but the limitation is none the less saved, since by virtue of the above enactment it vests at the end of twenty-one years from X.'s death in the children then living and will take effect in possession on the death of the wife.

(2) Age reduction provisions.

An interest whose vesting is postponed until the attainment by the beneficiary of an age exceeding twenty-one years is void *ab initio* at common law, but as we have already seen it was provided by section 163 of the Law of Property Act 1925 that in such a case the age of twenty-one years should be substituted for that specified by the donor.[4]

Former law.

Such a disposition contained in an instrument taking effect after July 15th, 1964, may well be saved by the "wait and see" provisions of the Act of 1964.

Effect of "wait and see" provisions.

Suppose, for instance, that a gift is made by will to the first son of X., a bachelor, to attain the age of thirty years; and that X. is survived by a son aged ten.

---

[1] *Supra*, pp. 323–4.
[2] P. & A.A. 1964, s. 3 (4) (*a*) ; *supra*, p. 348.
[3] *Ibid.*, s. 5.
[4] *Supra*, pp. 325–6.

If the son satisfies the prescribed contingency, he will have done so within twenty-one years from the death of X., the life in being.

On the other hand, the wait and see rule may be ineffective. If, for instance, in the example just given the eldest son is only five years of age at X.'s death, the vesting contingency cannot be satisfied within the perpetuity period, though if section 163 were applicable the gift to him would be saved by the reduction of the vesting age from thirty to twenty-one years.

Extent of reduction under Act of 1964. It was felt, however, that instead of mechanically reducing the age to twenty-one years in every case, it would be preferable to conform more closely with the donor's wishes and to reduce it only to whatever age would suffice to prevent the limitation from being too remote. The Act of 1964, therefore, repeals section 163 of the Law of Property Act 1925,[1] though not retrospectively,[2] and replaces it by the following provision:—

> " Where a disposition is limited by reference to the attainment by any person or persons of a specified age exceeding twenty-one years, and it is apparent at the time the disposition is made or becomes apparent at a subsequent time—
>
> (a) that the disposition would, apart from this section, be void for remoteness, but
>
> (b) that it would not be so void if the specified age had been twenty-one years,
>
> the disposition shall be treated for all purposes as if, instead of being limited by reference to the age in fact specified, it had been limited by reference to the age nearest to that age which would, if specified instead, have prevented the disposition from being so void."[3]

Let us suppose once more that a will limits land to the first son of X., a bachelor, to attain thirty years of age and that at X.'s death his only son is four years old. In these circumstances it has become apparent that the "wait and see" rule cannot save the ultimate limitation. The son cannot attain the prescribed age within the perpetuity period. Hence the above section operates, and the qualifying age is reduced from thirty to twenty-five years.

Disposition in favour of two or more persons. If the disposition is in favour of two or more persons, as for example to the children of X. at 30 years of age, and if at X.'s death his son is four, his daughter five years old, the reduction of the specified age to twenty-five, necessary to save the son's interest, affects the daughter also.[4]

---

[1] P. & A.A. 1964, s. 4 (6), (7) as added by Children Act 1975, s. 108, Sched. 3, para. 43.   See (1965), 81 *L. Q. R.* 346 (J. D. Davies) which had argued that the repeal of s. 163 by s. 4 (6) was defective.

[2] *Ibid.*, s. 15 (5).

[3] *Ibid.*, s. 4 (1).

[4] The reason is that there is only one "disposition", not several "dispositions " to cover all members of the class ; (1964), 80 *L. Q. R.* p. 509 (J. H. C. Morris and H. W. R. Wade).   See (1969) C. L. J. 284, at pp. 286–91 (M. J. Prichard).

If the disposition specifies different ages for distinct classes of beneficiaries, as for instance thirty for sons and twenty-five for daughters, the classes are segregated for the purpose of estimating the extent of the reduction. The reduction must be such as is necessary in each separate class.[1]

Two or more different ages.

(3) Class exclusion provisions

We have already seen that at common law a class gift cannot be partly good, partly bad. If some members of the class may possibly fail to satisfy the vesting contingency within the perpetuity period, the whole gift fails even in respect of those members whose interests are already vested.[2]

Modification of rule that class gift cannot be partly good, partly bad.

The Act however abolishes this rule and in its place provides that the disposition shall take effect in favour of those members who acquire vested interests within the perpetuity period to the exclusion of those who fail to qualify within that time. This policy applies to two distinct cases.

First, where the only cause of failure at common law is that some members of the class may not be ascertainable within the perpetuity period.

(i) Where no question of age reduction.

In such a case, the Act provides that, unless their interests are saved by virtue of the "wait and see" provision, those members shall be excluded from the class.[3]

> Suppose, for instance, that a disposition is made by will to X., a bachelor, for life, remainder to such of his children as may marry. Suppose further that X. dies leaving a married son and an unmarried daughter.

If the daughter marries within twenty-one years after X.'s death, her interest is saved by the "wait and see" provisions; if she is still a spinster at the expiry of that time, she is excluded from the class. In the latter event, the gift, which would have been wholly void at common law, takes effect in favour of the son.

The second case is where neither the "wait and see" principle nor the age reduction provisions will save the gift, as may occur if the attainment by the members of the class of an age exceeding twenty-one years is part of the vesting contingency. The following is an example of such a case.

(ii) Question of age reduction arises.

> Bequest to X., a bachelor, for life, remainder to such of his children as marry and attain the age of twenty-five years.
> X. dies leaving a married daughter aged nineteen and a son aged three.

The inability of the son to reach the prescribed age within the perpetuity period which ends twenty-one years from the death of

---

[1] P. & A.A. 1964, s. 4 (2).   [2] *Supra*, pp. 326–7.
[3] P. & A.A. 1964, s. 4 (4).

X., the only life in being, may no doubt be rectified under the age reduction provisions.[1] But the marriage contingency remains, for whether this is satisfied may not be established until too remote a time. If in fact he marries within twenty-one years of X.'s death, the "wait and see" rule will operate to validate the whole gift. If not, then the daughter becomes the sole beneficiary, for the effect of the Act of 1964 is to exclude the son from the class of designated beneficiaries.[2]

(e) General and special powers of appointment.

Statutory definition of "special power."   We have already discussed the importance of the distinction between general and special powers of appointment in the context of the doctrine of remoteness.[3] We have also seen that it is sometimes difficult to determine whether a so-called "hybrid" power is to be classed as general or special.[4] This difficulty is removed by the Act of 1964 which defines what powers shall be treated as special powers for the purposes of the rule against perpetuities, but only for those purposes. By virtue of this enactment a power is to be treated as a special power, unless:—

> "(a) in the instrument creating the power it is expressed to be exercisable by one person only, and
> (b) it could, at all times during its currency when that person is of full age and capacity, be exercised by him so as immediately to transfer to himself the whole of the interest governed by the power without the consent of any other person or compliance with any other condition, not being a formal condition relating to the mode of exercise of the power."[5]

The result is that the only general power is one under which "there is a sole donee who is at all times free without the concurrence of any other person to appoint to himself."[6]

Hybrid powers.   Thus, for instance a power is to be regarded as a special power if it is exercisable by the donee jointly with other persons or only with the consent of other persons; or exercisable in favour of any persons alive at the donee's death; or exercisable in favour of any person except the donee. On the other hand, a power to appoint to any person in the world except X. should be classified as general.[7]

General testamentary power.   But the general testamentary power, *i.e.* one unrestricted in respect of objects but exercisable only by will,[8] is treated as exceptional by the Act.

Under the existing case law, such a power is regarded as special so far as the validity of its creation is concerned;[9] but as general

---

[1] *Supra*, pp. 351–3.   [2] P. & A.A. 1964, s. 4 (3).
[3] *Supra*, pp. 329 *et seq.*   [4] *Supra*, pp. 275–6.
[5] P. & A.A. 1964, s. 7.
[6] Fourth report of Law Reform Committee, para. 47 (1956 Cmnd. 18).
[7] Morris and Leach, *op cit.* p. 137.
[8] *Supra*, pp. 276 ; 330.
[9] *Wollaston* v. *King* (1868), L. R. 8, Eq. 165; *Morgan* v. *Gronow* (1873), L. R. 16 Eq 1; *supra*, p. 330.

when the question is whether an appointment is too remote.[1] The perpetuity period runs from the date of the instrument of creation in the former case, in the latter from the date of the appointment. To classify such a power as general in respect of the appointments is illogical for, unlike the case where exercise by deed is permissible, the donee is in no sense the virtual owner of the property. Any transfer of the ownership to himself is necessarily ineffective until after his death. Nevertheless, it was felt to be unwise to revise a rule that has obtained for some seventy years, and one upon which conveyancing precedents in constant use have been based. Therefore, the distinction between the validity of the power itself and the validity of appointments is retained by the Act.[2]

The expression "power of appointment" includes any discretionary power to transfer a beneficial interest in property without the furnishing of consideration.[3] It ranks as a special power.

Discretionary trusts.

(f) Extended scope of the Rule

The scope of the rule against perpetuities is enlarged in two respects by the Act of 1964. It is extended to possibilities of reverter and analogous possibilities, a matter that is dealt with in a later chapter;[4] and its effect upon certain contracts for the purchase of land is expanded.

Possibilities of reverter.

We have seen that at common law a contract for the purchase of land, since it creates an equitable interest in favour of the promisee, is not enforceable by or against third parties if it is too remote; but that it remains enforceable without any limit of time between the parties themselves, since the rule against perpetuities is not concerned with personal obligations.[5]

Contract for purchase of land, if too remote, no longer binding upon the parties.

The second limb of the common law rule, however, is now abolished. The Act provides in effect that:

> where a disposition, made *inter vivos* and creating proprietary rights capable of transfer, would be void for remoteness as between persons other than the original parties, it shall be void as between the person by whom it was made and the person in whose favour it was made or any successor of his.[6]

(g) Effect of an infringement of the Rule upon subsequent interests

The Law Reform Committee, after castigating the doctrine of dependency, recommended that

Common law doctrine of dependency abolished.

> " no limitation which itself complies with the rule should be invalidated solely by reason of being preceded by one or more invalid

---

[1] *Rous* v. *Jackson* (1885), 29 Ch.D. 521.
[2] P. & A.A., s. 7, proviso.   [3] *Ibid.*, s. 15 (2).
[4] *Infra*, pp. 369–70.   [5] *Supra*, pp. 338–9.
[6] S. 10. See (1964), 80 *L. Q. R.* pp. 524–5 (J. H. C. Morris and H. W. R. Wade).

limitations, whether or not it expressly or by implication takes effect after or subject to, or is dependent upon, any such invalid limitations." [1]

The Act of 1964 deals with this recommendation in the following terms:

"A disposition shall not be treated as void for remoteness by reason only that the interest disposed of is ulterior to and dependent upon an interest under a disposition which is so void, and the vesting of an interest shall not be prevented from being accelerated on the failure of a prior interest by reason only that the failure arises because of remoteness." [2]

Thus each limitation in a chain of limitations must be considered separately according to its own intrinsic validity and without regard to the remoteness of its predecessors. An interest which is already vested or which will necessarily vest, if at all, within the perpetuity period takes effect according to its individual terms. If, for instance, the facts of *Re Backhouse*[3] were to recur in a modern instrument, the gifts to the sons of Millicent and the ultimate gift to the testator's heirs would be accelerated by the elimination of the gift to the sons of Charles. The chain of limitations would be shortened, not broken as it was held to be in that case.

On the other hand, if the facts of *Proctor* v. *Bishop of Bath and Wells*[4] were to recur, the ultimate gift to B. in fee simple would still fail as being itself intrinsically void.

Acceleration.   It will be noticed that the concluding words of the enactment do not direct that the ulterior interest *shall* be accelerated, *i.e.* allowed to take effect immediately upon the failure for remoteness of the prior interest, but that such failure shall not prevent acceleration. The reason for this negative approach is that there may be other obstacles to acceleration. If, for example, the interest that fails is followed by a contingent interest, which in turn is followed by a vested interest, the latter is not accelerated until it is established whether, or not, the contingent interest will take effect.[5]

(h) *Exceptions to the Rule*

The exceptions to the rule recognized by the common law have been affected in three respects.

Administrative powers.   First, as we have already seen, the administrative powers of trustees are excluded from the rule even in respect of instruments taking effect before July 16th, 1964.[6]

Option to buy leasehold reversion.   Secondly, an option to acquire for valuable consideration the freehold interest expectant upon a lease, is wholly exempted from the rule regardless of the length of the lease, provided that it is

---

[1] Para. 33 (1956 Cmnd. 18).   [2] S. 6.
[3] *Supra*, p. 334.   [4] *Supra*, pp. 333–4.
[5] *Re Townsend's Estate*, (1886), 34 Ch. D. 357.
[6] P. & A.A. 1964, s. 8 (1) ; *supra*, pp. 341–2.

exercisable only by the lessee or his successors in title, and provided that it is not exercisable later than one year after the end of the lease.[1]

Thirdly, the former doubt as to the ambit of section 121 of the Law of Property Act 1925[2] has been removed. It is provided by the 1964 Act that the perpetuity rule shall not apply to any powers or remedies for recovering or compelling the payment of an annual sum to which that section relates, or otherwise becoming exercisable or enforceable on the breach of any condition or other requirement relating to that sum.[3]

Remedies for the recovery of a rentcharge.

(B) The Rules Against Accumulations of Income[4]

At common law, the rule against perpetuities governs not only the right to suspend the vesting of an estate, but also the right to direct the accumulation of income arising from an estate. Therefore, before the law was altered by statute in 1800 it was held that a direction for the accumulation of income for a period which did not exceed the perpetuity period was valid.[5] This was decided in the famous case of *Thellusson* v. *Woodford*,[6] where the facts were these:—

At the end of the eighteenth century a certain Peter Thellusson, a man of great wealth, took advantage of the rule and made a will the object of which was to accumulate an enormous fortune for the benefit of certain future and unascertained members of his family. He directed that the income arising from his land should be accumulated at compound interest during the lives of all his sons, grandsons and great-grandsons living at his death or born in due time afterwards, and that, on the death of the survivor, the capital sum so produced should be divided amongst the male representatives of his sons' families. At the time of the controversy engendered by this will it was calculated that the accumulation would endure for about 80 years, and produce an amount of approximately 100 million pounds.[7] It was held that these trusts for accumulation were valid, but a statute generally called the Thellusson Act,[8] was subsequently passed in order to prevent further examples of what has been called posthumous avarice.

Thellusson v. Woodford

---

[1] P. & A.A. 1964, s. 9 (1).

[2] *Supra*, p. 340.

[3] P. & A.A. 1964, s. 11 (1).

[4] See Morris and Leach, *The Rule against Perpetuities* (2nd Edn.), pp. 266–306; *Theobald on Wills* (13th Edn.), paras. 1544–1556.

[5] Fearne, *Contingent Remainders*, p. 537, note.

[6] (1790), 4 Ves. 227; affirmed (1805), 11 Ves. 112; M. & B. p. 341.

[7] Challis, *Law of Real Property* (3rd Edn.), p. 201. Holdsworth, *History of English Law*, vol. vii, pp. 228 *et seq.*; Morris and Leach *op. cit.*, 267 n. 5; (1970) 2 N. I. L. Q. 131 (G. W. Keeton). "On the death of the last surviving grandson in 1856, the estate was divided (not without more litigation) between the two male representatives of two of Peter Thellusson's sons who had left issue. But owing to mismanagement and costs of litigation, the estate realised a comparatively small amount." Holdsworth, at p. 230.

[8] Accumulations Act 1800.

Modern
law.

This statute has been re-enacted and amended by the Law of
Property Act 1925,[1] as well as by the Perpetuities and Accumulations Act 1964[2], and the position now is that a person who desires
the income of his property to be accumulated is restricted to
choosing *one* only[3] of the following periods for the duration of the
accumulation:

(1) the life of the grantor or settlor ;

(2) a term of 21 years from the death of the grantor, settlor or
testator ;

(3) the minority[4] or respective minorities of any person or
persons living or *en ventre sa mère* at the death of the
grantor, settlor or testator ;

(4) the minority or respective minorities only of any person
or persons who, under the limitations of the instrument
directing the accumulations, would for the time being, if
of full age, be entitled to the income directed to be accumulated ;[5]

(5) a term of twenty-one years from the date of the making of
the disposition;

(6) the minority or respective minorities of any person or
persons in being at that date.[6]

The last two periods were added by the Act of 1964 with the
object of giving a wider choice to persons who make an *inter vivos*
settlement. They apply only to instruments taking effect after
July 15th, 1964.

Difference
between (3)
and (4).

The difference between the third and fourth periods is that
while the third period is for the minority of a person living at the
death of the settlor or testator, the fourth includes the minority of
any person who may *afterwards* become entitled to an interest in
the land.[7] Thus by the choice of the fourth period an accumulation
may lawfully be directed for the minorities of persons who are not
alive at a testator's death. This is illustrated by the case of *Re
Cattell*,[8] where

> a testator vested property in trustees upon trust for the children of
> his sons and daughters. He directed that the income of the property
> should be accumulated during the minorities of any of the children.

---

[1] Ss. 164–6. The Act affects not only an express direction to accumulate
income, but also a power of accumulation, *Re Robb*, [1953], Ch. 459 ; [1953] 1
All E. R. 920 ; see also P. &. A.A. 1964, s. 13 (2).

[2] See Law Reform Committee, Fourth Report, Section C (1956 Cmnd. 18).

[3] *Jagger* v. *Jagger* (1883), 25 Ch. D. 729.

[4] In the case of dispositions taking effect after 1969, minority ends at the
age of 18. Family Law Reform Act 1969, s. 1. There are transitional provisions so that the change from 21 to 18 shall not invalidate any direction for
accumulation in a settlement or other disposition made by a deed, will or other
instrument which was made before 1970. *Ibid.*, s. 1 (4) Sched. 3, para. 7.

[5] L.P.A. 1925, s. 164 (1) (*a*), (*b*), (*c*), (*d*).

[6] P. &. A.A. 1964, s. 13 (1).

[7] Fearne, 537, Butler's note citing Preston.

[8] [1914] 1 Ch. 177; M. & B. p. 345.

The testator died in 1880. Gladys was born to one of his sons in 1885 and Frederick to another of his sons in 1912. It was argued that it was inadmissible to accumulate the income during these minorities, since the infants were not alive at the testator's death.

The Court of Appeal held that accumulation during both minorities was warranted by the statute. Lord PARKER said:

" In my opinion the fourth alternative period covers not only children who are born or *en ventre sa mère* at the death of the settlor, but children who are subsequently born, and I think that the fact that the fourth alternative comes immediately after, and in contrast with, the third alternative, which refers only to born children, and children *en ventre sa mère*, at the time of the death of the settlor, points strongly to this conclusion."[1]

This interpretation necessarily admits of accumulations during successive minorities, and is open to the objection that income may be withdrawn from use for a very considerable time; but, as Challis points out,[2] this latitude of choice is set off by the fact that the minorities chosen must be those of persons who are prospectively entitled to the income.

A settlor sometimes directs an accumulation of income to be made, not for the purpose of dividing the capital among children, but for the purchase of land. It is provided by section 106 of the Law of Property Act 1925,[3] that an accumulation for this particular purpose may be made to endure only for the fourth statutory period. *Accumulations for purpose of buying land.*

Where an excessive accumulation has been directed, the effect differs according as the direction violates the general perpetuity period or one of the six statutory periods. A direction for accumulation which transgresses the rule against perpetuities, by designating a period longer than a life or lives in being and 21 years afterwards, is void *in toto* and no income can be accumulated;[4] but a direction which, while it exceeds the statutory periods yet keeps within the general perpetuity period, is good *pro tanto*, and is void only in so far as it exceeds the appropriate statutory period.[5] The excess alone is void.[6] So if accumulation is ordered for the life of a person other than the settlor (which is not one of the statutory periods), it will be good for 21 years.[7] *Effect of excessive accumulation.*

---

[1] *Per* Lord PARKER, [1914] 1 Ch. 177, at p. 188.
[2] *Op. cit.*, p. 202.
[3] Re-enacting Accumulations Act 1892.
[4] *Curtis* v. *Lukin* (1842), 5 Beav. 147.
[5] What is the appropriate period raises a difficult question of construction that must be determined according to the language of the instrument and the facts of the case ; *Re Watt's Will Trusts*, [1936] 2 All E. R. 1555, at p. 1562, a test described by UPJOHN, J. as "artificial and difficult" ; *Re Ransome*, [1957] Ch. 348, at p. 361 ; [1957] 1 All E. R. 690, at p. 696.
[6] For the destination of the excessive accumulation, see *e.g. Green* v. *Gascoyne* (1864), 4 De G. J. & Sm. 565 ; M. & B. p. 348 ; *Theobald on Wills* (13th Edn.), para. 1555.
[7] *Longden* v. *Simson* (1806), 12 Ves. 295 ; *Griffiths* v. *Vere* (1803), 9 Ves. 127. See also *Re Ransome, supra.*

Accumulations during minorities.

If the person entitled to property under a trust is an infant, there is a statutory power given to the trustees to maintain the infant out of the income, and to accumulate any surplus income during the remainder of the minority.[1] Where, in accordance with the directions of a settlor, income has been accumulated for one of the statutory periods, and at the termination of that period the beneficiary is an infant, so that a further accumulation may be necessary, it is enacted that the two accumulations shall not be counted together and so held to amount to an infringement of the Act.[2]

The rule in *Saunders* v. *Vautier*.

The right to stop accumulations. In the case of instruments taking effect after July 15th, 1964, the presumption that no woman over fifty-five years of age can have a child, introduced by the Act of 1964,[3] applies to the right of beneficiaries to put an end to accumulations.[4] That right is defined in *Saunders* v. *Vautier*[5] and later cases and is as follows: Where there is a gift of capital and income to a beneficiary absolutely, but subject to a trust that the income is to be accumulated beyond the time of his majority, he may, on reaching it, stop the accumulation and insist that the capital and accumulated income be paid to him forthwith. Once the property belongs to him absolutely, his free enjoyment of it cannot be fettered. This right, however, will not avail existing beneficiaries if it is possible that further beneficiaries may come into existence, and before July 16th, 1964 the possibility that a woman over fifty-five years of age might have children sufficed to exclude the rule in *Saunders* v. *Vautier*. [6]

Exceptions to rule against accumulations

Exceptions. Section 164 of the Law of Property Act 1925 sets out certain exceptions to the rule against accumulations.[7] If a settlor directs income to be accumulated for any of the following purposes, the direction will be valid although it may exceed the statutory periods:

Provisions for payment of debts.

(a) **Accumulations for payment of debts.** Provisions for the payment of the debts of any person need not be confined within one of the six periods.[8]

Portion provisions.

(b) **Accumulation for raising portions.** Provisions for raising portions for any children or remoter issue of the grantor, settlor or testator, or for any children or remoter issue of a person taking any interest under the settlement,

---

[1] Trustee Act, 1925, s. 31; *infra*, p. 921.
[2] L.P.A. 1925, s. 165.   *Re Maber*, [1928] Ch. 88.
[3] *Supra*, pp. 350–1.   [4] P. & A. A. 1964, s. 14.
[5] (1841), 4 Beav. 115; *Wharton* v. *Masterman*, [1895] A. C. 186.   Morris and Leach, *op. cit.*, pp. 289–95; Fourth Report of Law Reform Committee, para. 14 (1956) Cmnd. 18).
[6] *Re Deloitte*, [1926] Ch. 56.
[7] Re-enacting Accumulations Act 1800, s. 2.
[8] L.P.A. 1925, s. 164 (2) (i).

or of a person to whom any interest is thereby limited,[1] are excepted from the Act. [2]

The reason appears to be that unless such accumulations were permissible, it would be necessary for large owners to sell part of their estates in order to make provision for their younger children; but at the same time it must be recognized that this particular exception admits of a latitude that may be productive, in a great degree, of all the inconveniences that were felt or apprehended under the rules of the common law, because, by a will artfully prepared, every purpose aimed at by Mr. Thellusson may be accomplished. [3]

But on the whole the courts have construed this enactment (which repeats the corresponding section of the Thellusson Act) in such a way as to render a flagrant evasion of the spirit of the statute impossible. Thus, an accumulation for the purpose of creating a fund out of which it would be possible to pay portions is not within the exception.[4] Again, an accumulation of the whole of a testator's property with a view to swelling a portions fund has been held void.[5]

Meaning of "portion."

As Lord CRANWORTH said, in *Edwards* v. *Tuck*,[6]

" a direction to accumulate all a person's property to be handed over to some child or children when they attain twenty-one can never be said to be a direction for raising portions for the child or children; it is not raising a portion at all, it is giving everything. ' Portion ' ordinarily means a part or a share, and though I do not know that a gift of a whole might not, in some circumstances, come under the term of a gift of a portion, yet I do not think it comes within the meaning of a portion in this clause of the Act which points to the raising of something out of something else for the benefit of some children or class of children. . . . If every direction for accumulation for a child was a portion, the intention of the Legislature, which was to prevent accumulations, such accumulations being most frequently directed for the benefit of children, would be entirely defeated."

(*c*) **Accumulation of timber.** The Act does not apply to any provision respecting the accumulation of the produce of timber or wood. [7]

Timber accumulation.

The probable explanation of this exception is that timber is not usually regarded as annual income, but merely as a resource for some particular occasion, so that a direction concerning its accumulation, provided that it conforms to the rule against perpetuities,[8] does not in effect withdraw income from the owner of the estate.[9]

---

[1] *I.e.*, the interest need not be carved out of the precise property the income of which is to be accumulated.
[2] L.P.A. 1925, s. 164 (2) (ii).
[3] Fearne, *Contingent Remainders*, p. 541, note by Preston.
[4] *Re Bourne's Settlement Trusts*, [1946] 1 All E. R. 411.
[5] *Wildes* v. *Davies* (1853), 1 Sm. & G. 475.
[6] (1853), 3 De G.M. & G. 40, at p. 58.   [7] L.P.A. 1925, s. 164 (1) (iii).
[8] *Ferrand* v. *Wilson* (1845), 4 Hare, 344.
[9] Fearne, *Contingent Remainders*, p. 537, Butler's note.

CHAPTER VII

DETERMINABLE INTERESTS

Definition
of deter-
minable
interest. A DETERMINABLE interest is one that may come to an end before
the completion of the maximum period designated by the grantor.
For instance, the first clause in a deed of strict settlement, made
by a man in view of his approaching marriage, provides that the
settlor shall hold the land in trust for himself in fee simple *until
the solemnization of the intended marriage*.[1] In such a case the
maximum interest taken by the settlor is a fee simple, but it is a
modified, not an absolute fee, since it will not run its full course
if the terminating event—the marriage—supervenes.

> " A *direct* limitation marks the duration of estate by the life of a
> person ; by the continuance of heirs ; by a space of precise and
> measured time ; making the death of the person in the first example ;
> the continuance of heirs in the second example ; and the length of the
> given space in the third example, the boundary of the estate or the
> period of duration.
>
> A *collateral* [*i.e.* determinable] limitation, at the same time that
> it gives an interest which may have continuance for one of the times,
> in a direct limitation, may, on some event which it describes, put an
> end to the right of enjoyment *during the continuance of that time*." [2]

Terminology. Much confusion of terminology is apparent among the writers
on this subject. Thus Preston, in the above quotation, speaks of
collateral limitations ; Littleton describes the terminating event
as a *condition in law*, while most of the other early writers adopt
the expression *conditional limitations*. The words *collateral* and
conditional, however, besides being obscure, are used in many
different senses, and the modern practice is to describe this particular species of modified interest as a determinable interest, and
the limitation by which it is created as a determinable limitation.[3]

Dwindling
importance
of deter-
minable
interests. The older writers deal fully with determinable fees simple,
and the classic example is that given by Blackstone, who states
that the effect of a grant to A. and his heirs, *tenants of the manor of*

---

[1] See the precedent of a trust instrument, *supra*, p. 172.
[2] *Preston on Estates*, vol. i. p. 42, cited Challis, *Law of Real Property* (3rd
Edn.), pp. 252–3.
[3] Challis, *op. cit.*, pp. 253–4.

Dale, is to give A. and his heirs a fee simple which will be defeated as soon as they cease to be tenants of that manor.

In such a case there resides in the grantor and his heirs what is called a *possibility of reverter*,[1] since there is a possibility that the terminating event will occur and so cause the estate to revert.[2]

Another example of a determinable fee is afforded by *Re Leach*,[3] where freeholds were devised

> upon trust to pay the rents to Robert until he should assign, charge or otherwise dispose of the same, or become bankrupt.

It was held that Robert took an equitable fee simple which would determine if one of the specified events occurred in his lifetime, but which would become absolute if he died without their having occurred.

Determinable fees, however, disappeared from practical conveyancing (and gave way to shifting future estates operating under the Statute of Uses) when it was once decided that the fee simple in the case of a determinable limitation could not be made to pass to a stranger on the occurrence of the terminating event. The common law has never allowed a fee to be limited after a fee simple. As was said by Lord CAIRNS in *The Buckhurst Peerage Case*[4]:

> " There is no instance in the books that we are aware of in which a fee simple, or a fee tail qualified in the way that I have mentioned, as by the addition of the words ' lords of the manor of Dale,' is followed by a remainder to other persons upon the first takers ceasing to be lords of the manor."

Thus at the present day, if it is desired to make a fee simple pass from the grantee to some other person when a given event does or does not happen, the limitation will take the form of the grant of an equitable future interest.

The uncertain duration of a determinable fee does not impede its effective disposition, for the instrument by which it is limited constitutes a settlement for the purposes of the Settled Land Act 1925.[5] The person entitled to possession is a tenant for life within the meaning of the same Act, and as such he may convey the land by way of sale, mortgage or lease under his statutory powers.[6] *Determinable fee is settled land.*

The matter aroused considerable controversy, but, in one case it was decided that the possibility of reverter arising on the grant of a determinable fee simple was subject to the rule against perpetuities.[7] This view has now been adopted by the *Possibility of reverter subject to rule against perpetuities.*

---

[1] Blackstone, vol. ii. p. 109.
[2] Co. Litt. 18*a*.
[3] [1912] 2 Ch. 422.
[4] (1876), 2 App. Cas 1, at p. 23.
[5] S. 1. (1) (ii) (*c*); *supra*, p. 168.
[6] *Supra*, pp. 177 *et seq.*
[7] *Hopper* v. *Liverpool Corporation* (1944), 88 Sol. Jo. 213 (limitation of a house in fee simple so long as it shall be used as a news room and coffee room). On the subject generally, see Morris and Leach, *Rule against Perpetuities* (2nd Edn.), pp. 209–18.

Perpetuities and Accumulations Act 1964.[1] Thus, if the terminating event in fact occurs within the perpetuity period (*i.e.* twenty-one years, unless the instrument of creation refers to lives in being or specifies a fixed period of years not exceeding eighty), the reverter will take effect by virtue of the "wait and see" provisions of the Act. Otherwise, it will be void and the determinable fee will become absolute.[2]

Resulting trust also subject to the rule.

An interest analogous to a possibility of reverter arises where a testator gives personalty to trustees upon trust to pay the income to a corporation or other body until some event occurs that may not occur within the perpetuity period. In such a case, the occurrence of the event raises a resulting trust in favour of the person entitled to the undisposed residue of the testator's estate. Formerly, a resulting trust of this nature was exempt from the rule against perpetuities,[3] but it has been subjected to the rule by the Act of 1964.[4]

Determinable life interests.

There may be a limitation of a determinable *life* interest.

> "If a man grant an estate to a woman *dum sola fuit*, or *durante viduitate*, or *quamdiu se bene gesserit*, or to a man and a woman during the coverture, or so long as such a grantee dwell in such a house, . . . or for any like incertaine time, which time as Bracton saith, is *tempus indeterminatum* : in all these cases if it be of lands or tenements, the lessee hath in judgment of law an estate for life determinable." [5]

The *protective trust* is a common example of a determinable life interest. Its basis is a life interest subject to an executory gift over upon the happening of a certain event such as bankruptcy or attempted alienation. The gift over may be in favour of other members of the family, but to-day it is more commonly in favour of trustees to hold upon discretionary trusts for a class which includes the tenant for life and members of his family ; and the latter is the basis of the protective trust adopted by section 33 of the Trustee Act 1925. Thus in a marriage settlement it is a common practice

Protective trust.

to attach a *protective* trust to the property brought into the settlement by the wife, by which the husband is given, not an absolute life interest, but an interest determinable on his bankruptcy. This is called a *protected life interest*. It is followed by discretionary trusts stating how the trustees may deal with the income of the property if the interest of the husband is determined by his bankruptcy. These trusts were formerly set out in detail, but this is no longer necessary for section 33 enacts that a mere declaration directing income to be held on *protective trusts* shall confer certain

---

[1] S.12 (1) (a).
[2] Law Reform Committee Fourth Report, 1956 (Cmnd. 18) para. 39.
[3] *Re Randall* (1888), 38 Ch. D. 213 ; *Re Blunt's Trusts*, [1904] 2 Ch. 767 ; *Re Chardon*, [1928] Ch. 464 ; *Re Chambers' Will Trusts*, [1950] Ch. 267.
[4] S.12 (1) (b).
[5] Co. Litt. 42a.

discretionary powers upon the trustees.[1] The statutory effect of using the expression is that the interest of the husband automatically determines if he attempts to alienate or charge it or if he becomes bankrupt,[2] and the trustees at their discretion may apply the income during the rest of his life for the maintenance or support, or otherwise for the benefit, of any one or more of the following persons :

> The husband,[3] the wife and the issue of the marriage, or, if there is no wife or issue, the persons who, if the husband were dead, would be entitled to the settled property or its income.

In cases of a determinable life interest the grantee takes an interest that may endure for life, or may determine sooner by the occurrence of the terminating event. It differs from a determinable fee in that it may be followed by a gift over to a third party which may validly take effect when the event occurs.[4]

A tenant for life whose estate is liable to cease on some event during that life has the powers of a tenant for life under the Settled Land Act 1925.[5]

Lastly, a *term of years* may be made determinable upon some event liable to occur before the period of the term has expired, as for instance where there is a lease for 50 years if A. shall so long live, or a lease for 20 years until B. marries. Such leases are now converted into leases for 90 years.[6]

Term of years.

---

[1] See generally Hanbury's *Modern Equity* (9th Edn.), pp. 171 *et seq.*, Snell's *Equity*, (27th Edn.), pp. 135 *et seq.* ; (1957) 21 *Conv.* (N.S.) 110 ; 323 (L. A. Sheridan).

[2] If, by virtue of a power contained in the settlement, the husband makes an advancement to an infant beneficary, this is not a disposition that will cause his life interest to be forfeited, *Re Shaw's Settlement*, [1951] Ch. 833 ; [1951] 1 All E. R. 656.

[3] In most cases the income will be paid to the husband. This is not an infringement of the bankruptcy law, for the income, since the husband has no *right* to it, is not property belonging to him that must pass to the trustee in bankruptcy; *infra*, pp. 372-3.

[4] Blackstone, vol. ii. p. 155.   [5] S.L.A., 1925, s. 20 (1) (vi) ; *supra*, p. 176.

[6] *Ibid.*, s. 149 (6). *Infra*, p. 384.

CHAPTER VIII

INTERESTS UPON CONDITION

SUMMARY

SECTION I. GENERAL NATURE AND EFFECT

Definition.

Conditions subsequent. An interest upon condition subsequent arises where a qualification is annexed to a conveyance, whereby it is provided that, in case a particular event does or does not happen, or in case the grantor or the grantee does or omits to do a particular act, the interest shall be defeated.[1] Examples of such interests taken from the Law Reports are :

> Grant to trustees in fee simple on condition that, if the land granted shall ever be used for other than hospital purposes, it shall revert to the heirs of the grantor ;[2]
> devise in fee simple to the council of a school on condition that the council shall publish annually a statement of payments and receipts ;[3]
> devise of land to J. " on condition that he never sells out of the family " ;[4]
> devise to A. for life provided that he makes the mansion-house his usual common place of abode and residence ;[5]

---

[1] Litt. s. 325 ; Cruise, *Digest*, Tit. xiii. c. 1. *Cf.* condition precedent where the qualification provides that the interest will not commence until the occurrence of some event. *E.g.* a grant to A. if he becomes a barrister. *Supra*, pp. 293–5.

[2] *Re Hollis' Hospital*, [1899] 2 Ch. 540.

[3] *Re Da Costa*, [1912] 1 Ch. 337.

[4] *Re Macleay* (1875), L. R. 20 Eq. 186.

[5] *Wynne* v. *Fletcher* (1857), 24 Beav. 430.

devise to A. for life on condition that he assumes the name and arms of the testator within 12 months.[1]

In all cases of this type there vests in the grantor, his heirs and assignees a right of re-entry, the exercise of which determines the estate of the grantee. On principle, therefore, a fee simple subject to a condition subsequent should be classified as an equitable interest, not as a legal estate, for since it may be defeated by a re-entry before its full course is run it can scarcely be described as "absolute." Nevertheless, for reasons already explained,[2] it has been given the status of a legal estate by the Law of Property (Amendment) Act 1926,[3] in words that are wide enough to include any right of re-entry. They state that

Right of entry for condition broken.

> a fee simple subject to a legal or equitable right of entry or re-entry is for the purposes of the Law of Property Act, 1925, a fee simple absolute.

Distinction between condition and limitation. There is a fundamental and somewhat subtle distinction[4] between limitations upon condition and determinable limitations. Some writers contend that the distinction is a mere matter of words. On this basis the effect of such expressions as *until, so long as, whilst, during*, is to create a determinable interest ; while such phrases as *on condition that, provided that, if, but if it happen that*,[5] will raise an interest upon condition.

Distinction between limitations on condition and determinable limitations.

But the distinction goes deeper than this. We must differentiate between a limitation properly so called, and a condition.

A limitation is a form of words which creates an estate and denotes its extent by designating the event upon which it is to commence and the time for which it is to endure.[6] It marks the utmost time for which the estate can continue. It appears in two forms. A direct limitation marks the time by denoting the size of the estate in familiar terms, *e.g.* by using such expressions as " for life " or " in fee simple " ; a determinable limitation gives an interest for one of the times possible in a direct limitation, but also denotes some event that may determine the estate during the continuance of that time. In the simple example of a grant to A. and his heirs, tenants of the Manor of Dale, the terminating event is incorporated in, and forms an essential part of, the whole

Meaning of "limitation."

---

[1] *Re Evans's Contract*, [1920] 2 Ch. 469.

[2] *Supra*, pp. 150–1.

[3] L.P.A. 1925 s. 7 (1) as amended by L.P.(A.)A. 1926 Sched. ; M. & B. p. 5, note 3.

[4] It has been referred to as " extremely artificial " by PENNYCUICK, V.-C. in *Re Sharp's Settlement Trusts*, [1973] Ch. 331, at p. 340 ; [1972] 3 All E. R. 151 ; and " as little short of disgraceful to our jurisprudence " by PORTER, M. R. in *Re King's Trusts* (1892), 29 L. R. Ir. 401, at p. 410.

[5] See *Sanders on Uses*, vol. i. p. 156 ; Shep. Touchstone, 122 ; Bac. Abr. Condition (A) ; Challis, *Law of Real Property* (3rd Edn.), p. 283.

[6] Sheppard's *Touchstone*, 117 ; Blackstone, vol. ii. p. 155. *Preston on Estates*, vol. i. pp. 40 *et seq.*

limitation, and if the estate expires because the tenancy of Dale is no longer in A.'s family, it is none the less considered to have lasted for the period originally fixed by the limitation. So in general the province of a limitation is to fix the period for the commencement and the duration of an estate, and to mark its determinable qualities.[1]

Meaning of "condition."

A condition, on the other hand, specifies some event which, if it takes place during the time for which an estate has already been limited to continue, will defeat that estate.

" And here is condition, because there is not a new estate limited over, but the estate to which it is annexed is destroyed." [2]

In short, if the terminating event is an integral and necessary part of the formula from which the size of the interest is to be ascertained, the result is the creation of a determinable interest ; but if the terminating event is external to the limitation, if it is a divided clause from the grant, the interest granted is an interest upon condition.[3]

Outwardly a condition resembles a determinable limitation, for the difference between a grant

to a woman for life, but if she remarries then her life interest shall cease,

and a grant

to a woman during widowhood

is not apparent at first sight. The natural inference is that the legal effect must be the same in each case. Nevertheless, certain practical distinctions between the two limitations existed at common law and to a diminished degree still exist.[4] The present position appears to be as follows.

Automatic termination of determinable interest.

(1) A determinable interest comes to an end automatically upon the occurrence of the terminating event, as for example upon the remarriage of a woman to whom an estate has been granted during her widowhood. This is inevitable, for according to the limitation itself, *i.e.* according to the words fixing the space of time for which the widow's right of enjoyment is to continue, her interest ceases with her remarriage and nothing remains to be done to defeat her right. There can, indeed, be no question of defeating what has already come to an end.[5]

---

[1] Fearne, *Contingent Remainders*, p. 11, Butler's note.

[2] *Serjeant Rudhall's Case*, (1596), Savile 76, cited *Re Hollis' Hospital*, [1899] 2 Ch. 540, 549.

[3] Fearne, *op. cit.*, p. 11, note (*h*) ; vol. ii. s. 36 (Smith, An Original View of Executory Interests) ; Challis, *Law of Real Property* (3rd Edn.), p. 260.

[4] "Although in some respects a condition and a limitation may have the same effect, yet in English law there is a great distinction between them"; *Re Moore* (1888), 39 Ch. 116, at p. 129, *per* COTTON, L.J.

[5] *Preston on Estates* vol. i. p. 47 ; Challis, *op. cit.*, p. 219 ; *Re Evans's Contract*, [1920] 2 Ch. 469, at p. 472.

The effect of a condition operating by way of re-entry, on the other hand, is to defeat an interest *before* it has reached the end of the period for which it has been limited. The interest becomes voidable upon the breach of the condition. It does not become void unless and until the grantor, his heir or assignee re-enters upon the land.[1]

No automatic termination of interest upon condition.

(2) The rule against perpetuities applies both to conditions subsequent and to a possibility of reverter arising on the grant of a determinable fee.

Applicability of the rule against perpetuities.

The position as regards common law conditions was established long before the rule came into existence, and the old authorities never doubted that a right of entry was enforceable at any distance of time by the grantor or his heirs.[2] But, after several dicta in favour of subjecting conditions to the rule,[3] the point was finally decided to that effect[4] and was later confirmed by the Law of Property Act 1925.[5]

Conditions subsequent.

As we have already seen, a possibility of reverter appertaining to a determinable fee simple has been subjected to the rule by the Perpetuities and Accumulations Act 1964.[6]

Possibilities of reverter.

(3) At common law, a right of entry affecting a fee simple was neither devisable nor alienable *inter vivos*, and availed only the grantor and his heirs.[7] This, however, is no longer the position. The Wills Act 1837 allows a testator to devise "all rights for condition broken and other rights of entry";[8] and the Law of Property Act 1925 deals with their assignment *inter vivos* by providing that:

Assignability

(a) Right of entry for condition broken.

> All rights and interests in land may be disposed of, including—
>> a right of entry into or upon land whether immediate or future, and whether vested or contingent.[9]

Whether a possibility of reverter is on the same footing in both these respects is not so clear. It has, indeed, been held that it may be disposed of by a testator since it is covered by the words of the Wills Act cited above.[10] But its assignment *inter vivos*

(b) Possibility of reverter.

---

[1] Co. Litt. 218*a*. At common law, the seisin transferred by livery cannot be divested without its actual resumption by re-entry, Co. Litt. 214*b*.

[2] Challis, *Law of Real Property* (3rd Edn.), pp. 187 *et seq.*

[3] *Re Macleay* (1875), L. R. 20 Eq. 186 ; *London and South Western Rail Co.* v. *Gomm* (1882), 20 Ch. D. 562, 582 ; *Dunn* v. *Flood* (1883), 25 Ch. D. 629.

[4] *Re Hollis' Hospital Trustees and Hagues' Contract*, [1899] 2 Ch. 540; *Re Da Costa*, [1912] 1 Ch. 337. A contrary view was expressed by PALLES, C.B., in *A.-G.* v. *Cummins*, [1906] 1 I. R. 406, and his view has prevailed in Northern Ireland, *Walsh* v. *Wightman*, [1927] N. I. 1.

[5] S. 4 (3).

[6] S. 12 (1) (*a*); *supra*, p. 355.

[7] Fearne, *Contingent Remainders*, Butler's note, p. 381.

[8] S. 3.

[9] L.P.A. 1925, s. 4 (2) (*b*).

[10] *Pemberton* v. *Barnes*, [1899] 1 Ch. 544; where it was held that the possibility of reverter arising upon the grant of a determinable fee in copyholds was within the Act.

presents some difficulty. In the view of the common law, what was left in the grantor of a determinable interest was not an estate but a possibility that he might acquire an estate at a future time. Such a *bare possibility*, as it was called, was not assignable at common law,[1] but it seems a reasonable assumption that it now falls within the wide language quoted above from the Law of Property Act 1925.

Void conditions.

(4) As will be seen in the next section, a condition attached to any limitation of property may prove to be void for a variety of reasons. A condition subsequent that is thus invalidated is totally cancelled, and the limitation takes effect as if it had not been imposed;[2] but a determinable interest fails altogether if the possibility of reverter is invalidated, for to treat it as absolute would be to alter its quantum as fixed by the limitation.[3]

Determinable interest, but not interest upon condition, might be followed by remainder.

(5) At common law, a remainder might be limited to take effect after a determinable life estate, but not after a life estate that was defeasible by a condition subsequent. If, for instance, there were a feoffment

to A. during widowhood and then to B. for life

the remainder to B. was valid, since by force of the limitation itself it took effect upon the natural determination of the particular estate. But had the limitation been

to A., a widow, for life on condition that if she remarried the land should remain to B. for life,

B.'s remainder would have come into conflict with three rules of ancient origin: a remainder was not allowed to cut short a particular estate;[4] none but the grantor and his heirs could exercise a right of re-entry; and in any event, the effect of re-entry was to defeat all the estates that depended upon the original livery of seisin.[5]

The matter has long been of only historical interest, for a settlor, minded to impose such a condition upon a widow's interest, could at an early date frame his limitation as a shifting use, and can now effect the same result by way of a future trust.

---

[1] As to the three different meanings of the word *possibility*, see Challis, *Law of Real Property* (3rd Edn.), p. 76, note.

[2] *Re Wilkinson*, [1926] Ch. 842, 846 ; *Re Croxon*, [1904] 1 Ch. 252. If the illegal condition is *precedent*, the gift fails entirely.

[3] *Re Moore* (1888), 39 Ch. D. 116. If, however, a possibility of reverter or a condition subsequent is void under the rule against perpetuities, the interest of the grantee becomes absolute ; Perpetuities and Accumulations Act 1964, s. 12.

[4] *Supra*, p. 299.

[5] Fearne, *Contingent Remainders*, pp. 261–2, p. 381, note ; *Preston on Estates*, vol. i. pp. 50 *et seq.*

SECTION II. VOID CONDITIONS

There are four types of conditions subsequent that are void when annexed to the grant of an estate or interest :—

(1) CONDITIONS REPUGNANT TO THE INTEREST GRANTED[1]

A condition that is repugnant to the interest to which it is annexed is absolutely void.[2] For instance, a condition attached to the grant of a fee simple that the grantee shall always let the land at a definite rent, or cultivate it in a certain manner or be deprived of all power of sale, is void on the ground of its incompatibility with that complete freedom of enjoyment, disposition and management that the law attributes to the ownership of such an estate.[3] It is not permissible to grant an interest and then to provide that the incidents attached to it by law shall be excluded. The most important examples of repugnant conditions that arise in practice are those designed to prohibit alienation or to exclude the operation of the bankruptcy laws.

Meaning of repugnancy.

Conditions against alienation. In accordance with the cardinal principle that the power of alienation is necessarily and inseparably incidental to ownership, it has been held in a long line of decisions that if an *absolute* interest is given to a donee—whether it be a fee simple, a fee tail, a life interest or any other interest, and whether it be in possession or *in futuro*—any restriction which *substantially* takes that power away is void as being repugnant to the very conception of ownership.[4] Therefore, a condition[5] that the donee

Total restraints void.

> shall not alienate at all,[6] or
>
> shall not alienate during a particular time, such as the life of a certain person[7], or during his own life,[8] or
>
> shall alienate only to one particular person[9], or to a small and diminishing class of persons, such as to one of his three brothers,[10] or

---

[1] For a trenchant criticism of this doctrine, see (1943), 59 *L. Q. R.* 343 (G. L. Williams).

[2] *Re Dugdale* (1888), 38 Ch. D. 176 ; *Bradley* v. *Peixoto* (1797), 3 Ves. 324.

[3] *Jarman on Wills* (8th Edn.), p. 1477.

[4] *Cf.* the position of a tenant for life under S.L.A. 1925 the exercise of whose powers cannot be prohibited or limited, s. 106 ; *supra*, p. 185.

[5] But a *covenant* against alienation is not repugnant. *Caldy Manor Estate, Ltd.* v. *Farrell,* [1974] 1 W. L. R. 1303 ; [1974] 3 All E. R. 753.

[6] Litt. s. 360 ; Co. Litt. 206*b*, 223*a* ; *Re Dugdale, supra.*

[7] *Re Rosher* (1884), 26 Ch. D. 801.

[8] *Corbett* v. *Corbett* (1888), 14 P. D. 7.

[9] *Muschamp* v. *Bluet* (1617), Bridg. J. 132 ; *Re Cockerill,* [1929] 2 Ch. 131.

[10] *Re Brown,* [1954] Ch. 39 ; [1953] 2 All E. R. 1342 ; M. & B. p. 7.

shall not adopt some particular mode of assurance such as a mortgage,[1] or

shall not bar an entail,[2]

is void.

Partial restraints valid.

A restraint that is partial, however, and which therefore does not substantially deprive the owner in fee of his power of alienation, is valid. Thus it has been held that a condition is valid which restrains the owner from alienating to a specified person,[3] or to anyone except a particular class of persons, provided, however, that the class is not too restricted.[4] But when does a restraint cease to be total ? In the case of *Re Macleay*,[5] where there was a devise

> " to my brother J. on the condition that he never sells out of the family,"

the condition was held by JESSEL, M.R., to be valid, though some doubt has been thrown on the correctness of this decision by a later case.[6]

The difficulty, indeed, is to ascertain the principle upon which such restraints have been permitted, for they would seem to be just as repugnant to ownership as a total restraint. Perhaps the truth is that the courts, losing sight of the fundamental doctrine of repugnancy, have, unintentionally and unwittingly, allowed the necessities of public policy to engraft certain exceptions on the main rule.[7]

Conditions excluding insolvency laws void.

Conditions excluding the operation of the bankruptcy laws.

Just as the donee of property cannot be deprived of the normal rights of ownership, so also is it impossible to render his interest immune from involuntary alienation for insolvency or bankruptcy.[8] It is not permissible, for instance, to annex to the grant of a life interest a condition that it shall not be liable to seizure for debt. Thus in *Graves* v. *Dolphin* [9] :

> a testator directed his trustees to pay £500 a year to his son for life, and declared that it should not on any account be subject or liable to the debts, engagements, charges or incumbrances of his son, but that it should always be payable to him and to no other person. The son became bankrupt, and it was held that the annuity became the property of his creditors.

---

[1] *Ware* v. *Cann* (1830), 10 B. & C. 433.
[2] *Sir Anthony Mildmay's Case* (1584), 6 Rep. 40a ; *Mary Portington's Case* (1613), 10 Rep. 35a ; *Dawkins* v. *Lord Penrhyn* (1878), 4 App. Cas. 51.
[3] Co. Litt. 223a.
[4] *Doe d. Gill* v. *Pearson* (1805), 6 East 173, (" except to four sisters or their children ").
[5] (1875), L. R. 20 Eq. 186.
[6] *Re Rosher* (1884), 26 Ch. D. 801. But the restriction was placed only on a sale, and it was to endure only for the life of J. See too *Re Brown*, [1954] Ch. 39 ; [1953] 2 All E. R. 1342 ; (1954), 70 *L. Q. R.* 15 (R. E. M.).
[7] *Ibid.*, at p. 813.
[8] *Re Machu* (1882), 21 Ch. D. 838 ; *Re Dugdale* (1888), 38 Ch. D. 176.
[9] (1826), 1 Sim. 66.

But, as we have seen in discussing the protective trust,[1] Contrast
there is no objection to the grant by one person to another of determinable
an interest which is to determine upon the bankruptcy of the limitation.
grantee. Lord ELDON, adverting to the distinction between
a determinable limitation and a limitation upon condition,
made this clear over a hundred years ago :—

" A disposition to a man until he shall become bankrupt, and
after his bankruptcy over, is quite different from an attempt to
give to him for his life, with a proviso that he shall not sell or alien
it. *If that condition is so expressed as to amount to a limitation,*
reducing the interest short of a life interest, neither the man nor
his assignees can have it beyond the period limited." [2]

The distinction at first sight seems fine and far from obvious,
but in fact it is fundamental. In one case the only interest passing
under the limitation is an interest *until* the donee becomes bankrupt ; in the other, an absolute interest is first limited for life, and
then an attempt is made to remove one of the incidents, namely
liability for debts, to which all absolute interests are subject.

Thus, if husband and wife both bring property into a marriage
settlement, the wife's property may be limited to the husband
until he becomes bankrupt and then over to the trustees. But the
husband cannot settle his own property upon himself in the same
manner, for this would be a fraud on the bankruptcy laws.[3] On
the other hand, it has long been recognized that a man may settle
his own property upon himself until he attempts to assign,
charge or encumber it, or until he does something that makes it
liable to be taken in execution by a particular creditor, and if so
over to another person. The limitation over, once it has taken
effect, is not avoided by the subsequent bankruptcy of the settlor.[4]

(2) CONDITIONS IN RESTRAINT OF MARRIAGE

The law as to the validity of conditions in restraint of marriage Personalty.
differs according as the gift is of real or of personal property.

The rules governing personalty have come to us from the
Roman Law through the ecclesiastical courts and the Court of
Chancery. It is marked by numerous and fine distinctions, and,
in the words of a learned judge, is " proverbially difficult " [5] ;
but it is sufficient for our purposes to say that a condition in
total restraint of marriage is void, while one in partial restraint
is good, provided that it is reasonable from the point of view of
public policy.[6]

---

[1] *Supra.* p. 364.
[2] *Brandon* v. *Robinson* (1811), 18 Ves. 429, at pp. 432, 433–4. See T.A.,
1925, s. 33, as to these protected life interests. *Supra*, pp. 364–5.
[3] *Mackintosh* v. *Pogose*, [1895] 1 Ch. 505, 511 ; *Re Brewer's Settlement*,
[1896] 2 Ch. 503.
[4] *Brooke* v. *Pearson* (1859), 27 Beav. 181. *Re Detmold* (1889), 40 Ch. D.
585.
[5] *Re Hewett*, [1918] 1 Ch. 458, 463, *per* YOUNGER, J.
[6] *Re Lanyon*, [1927] 2 Ch. 264.

For instance, a condition that a person shall not marry a named person,[1] a Papist,[2] a Scotchman,[3] or a domestic servant[4] is valid, but a condition that he shall not marry at all is void. But a partial restraint is not upheld unless there is a bequest over to another person in default of compliance with the condition. In the absence of such a bequest, the condition is treated as ineffectual on the ground that it has merely been imposed *in terrorem*, *i.e.* as an idle threat calculated to secure compliance by the donee.[5] A condition, however, is valid which restrains a *second* marriage, either of a man or of a woman.[6]

Realty.   The rules relating to real estate, on the other hand, are both few and simple. While a condition in general restraint of marriage if attached to a gift of personalty is void *per se*, in the case of realty it is not void *per se*, but only if there is an intention to promote celibacy. Thus in *Jones* v. *Jones* [7]

> a man after devising land to three women during their lifetime added :
>
> > " provided the said Mary . . . shall remain in her present state of single woman, otherwise . . . if she shall bind herself in wedlock, she is liable to lose her share of the said property immediately, and her share to be possessed and enjoyed by the other mentioned parties, share and share alike."

It was held that the condition was valid since its object was not to prevent her from marrying but to provide for her whilst unmarried.

The *in terrorem* doctrine does not apply to realty,[8] and it may be said that a condition in partial restraint of marriage attached to real estate is always good,[9] and that one in total restraint *may* be good. However, a general restraint cannot be imposed upon a tenant in tail, since it is incompatible with and repugnant to an interest that is expressly made descendible to the heirs born of the marriage of the donee.[10]

(3) CONDITIONS CONTRARY TO PUBLIC POLICY

Meaning of public policy.   Any condition that has a tendency to conflict with the general interest of the community, even though it will not necessarily do so, is void.[11] Thus in *Egerton* v. *Brownlow* :[12]

---

[1] *Re Bathe*, [1925] Ch. 377.
[2] *Duggan* v. *Kelly* (1848), 10 Ir. Eq. Rep. 473.
[3] *Perrin* v. *Lyon* (1807), 9 East 170.
[4] *Jenner* v. *Turner* (1880), 16 Ch. D. 188.   *Quaere*, however, whether this example and those given in the preceding two notes would not nowadays be treated as void for uncertainty ; see *infra*, pp. 375–6.
[5] *Re Whiting's Settlement*, [1905] 1 Ch. 96 ; *Re Hewett*, [1918] 1 Ch. 458 ; *Leong* v. *Chye*, [1955] A.C. 648 ; [1955] 2 All E. R. 903.
[6] *Allen* v. *Jackson* (1876), 1 Ch. D. 399.   [7] (1876), 1 Q. B. D. 279.
[8] *Jenner* v. *Turner* (1880), 16 Ch. D. 188, at p. 196, *per* BACON, V.-C.
[9] *Re Bathe*, [1925] Ch. 377.
[10] *Earl of Arundel's Case* (1575), 3 Dyer, 342*b*.
[11] *Egerton* v. *Brownlow*(1853), 4 H. L. Cas. 1 ; *Re Wallace*, [1920] 2 Ch. 274.
[12] (1853), 4 H L Cas. 1.

Lands were devised to Lord Alford for 99 years if he should so long live, and then to the heirs male of his body, with a proviso that if Lord Alford should not in his lifetime acquire the dignity of Duke or Marquis of Bridgewater, the estates should pass from his heirs male immediately on his decease.

After great conflict of opinion the condition was held invalid by the House of Lords as being contrary to public policy. But there were special considerations applicable to that case. For instance, since the rank to be obtained was among the highest in the peerage, and one that conferred legislative rights and imposed legislative duties upon the holder, there was a danger that efforts to obtain the qualifying position would be pushed so far as to come into conflict with the general interests of the community. These special considerations were recognized in a later case, where a limitation that property should go to a certain person provided that he acquired the title of baronet was held to be capable of taking effect upon the fulfilment of the condition.[1]

"A baronetcy is a barren title involving on the part of its holder the performance of no duties to the State, or the public, except those which are cast upon every good citizen. In this respect it differs most materially from a peerage, the subject of discussion in *Egerton* v. *Brownlow*. The public neither gains nor loses by the title being conferred. . . . In fact the possession of such a title by an individual is a matter of indifference, so far as the welfare of the State, or of the public at large, is concerned."[2]

Further, the House of Lords has held that a condition in a will under which a beneficiary would forfeit his interest if he should "be or become a Roman Catholic" was not void as being contrary to public policy. To invalidate it would go far beyond the mere avoidance of discrimination on religious grounds.

"To do so would bring about a substantial reduction of another freedom, firmly rooted in our law, namely that of testamentary disposition. Discrimination is not the same thing as choice: it operates over a larger and less personal area, and neither by express provision nor by implication has private selection yet become a matter of public policy."[3]

Finally, a condition whose object is to restrain a man from doing his duty,[4] or to cause the separation of a husband and wife who are at present unseparated, is contrary to public policy and

---

[1] *Re Wallace*, [1920] 2 Ch. 274. The condition here was precedent, but a condition, if contrary to public policy, is invalid whether precedent or subsequent. The *effect* of invalidity, however, is different ; *infra*, p. 378.

[2] At p. 289, *per* WARRINGTON, L.J.

[3] *Blathwayt* v. *Cawley (Baron)* [1975] 3 W.L.R. 684, at p. 697, per Lord WILBERFORCE ; see also Lord CROSS OF CHELSEA, at p. 700.

[4] *Re Sandbrook*, [1912] 2 Ch. 471 (condition held void which divested property if the donees "should live with or be or continue under the custody, guardianship or control of their father "). *Re Borwick*, [1933] Ch. 657 (condition held void which divested a gift if the infant donee during minority became a Roman Catholic, for this tended to influence the parent in the discharge of his duty of religious instruction).

void[1] ; but where in this latter case the parties are already separated, a limitation to a woman with a condition that the interest shall cease if she and her husband live together again, is valid as constituting a maintenance of the wife while she is unprovided for, unless there is evidence showing that the donor's object is to induce her not to return to her husband.[2]

(4) UNCERTAIN CONDITIONS.

Examples of uncertain conditions.
A condition subsequent, designed to defeat a vested estate, is void if it is uncertain either in expression or in operation. It must be possible, not only to affirm with precision exactly what the words imposing the condition mean, but also to ascertain with certainty the circumstances that will cause a forfeiture.[3] In a well-known passage Lord CRANWORTH stated the position as follows :

> " I consider that, from the earliest times, one of the cardinal rules on the subject has been this : that where a vested estate is to be defeated by a condition on a contingency that is to happen afterwards, that condition must be such that the court can see from the beginning, precisely and distinctly, upon the happening of what event it was that the preceding vested estate was to determine." [4]

Several cases have been concerned with conditions designed to secure the observance by a donee of a particular religion, as for example by requiring him " to be a member of " or " to conform to "[5] the Church of England, or not to marry any person " not of Jewish parentage and of the Jewish faith."[6] Such phrases are shrouded in uncertainty and are generally held to be ineffective. Of those, for instance, who profess membership of the Church of England, many are devout observers of its practice and doctrines, but the conduct of countless others affords little evidence of any religious conviction. Faith varies infinitely in degree, and, even if it were possible to do so, a donor does not normally specify the exact degree that will satisfy his anxiety.[7]

---

[1] *Re Moore* (1888), 39 Ch. D. 116 ; distinguished, *Re Thompson*, [1939] 1 All E. R. 681. *Re Caborne*, [1943] 1 Ch. 224 ; [1943] 2 All E. R. 7. *Re Johnson's Will Trusts*, [1967] Ch. 387 ; [1967] 1 All E. R. 152.

[2] See *Re Lovell*, [1920] 1 Ch. 122.

[3] *Re Sandbrook*, [1912] 2 Ch. 471, at p. 477, *per* PARKER, J. ; *Re Murray*, [1955] Ch. 69, at pp. 77–8 ; [1954] 3 All E. R. 129, at pp. 132–3, *per* Lord EVERSHED, M.R. Different considerations apply in the case of a condition precedent ; *Re Allen*, [1953] Ch. 810 ; [1953] 2 All E. R. 898 ; *Re Selby's Will Trusts*, [1966] 1 W. L. R. 43 ; [1965] 3 All E. R. 386 ; *Re Mills' Will Trusts*, [1967] 1 W. L. R. 837 ; [1967] 2 All E. R. 193.

[4] *Clavering* v. *Ellison* (1859), 7 H.L. Cas. 707, 725.

[5] *Re Tegg*, [1936] 2 All E. R. 878

[6] *Clayton* v. *Ramsden*, [1943] A.C. 320; [1943] 1 All E. R. 16; *Re Moss's Trusts*, [1945] 1 All E. R. 207. *Re Tarnpolsk*, [1958] 1 W. L. R. 1157, [1958] 3 All E. R. 479 ; *Re Krawitz's Will Trusts*, [1959] 1 W. L. R. 1192 ; [1959] 3 All E. R. 793. *Cf. Blathwayt* v. *Cawley (Baron)*, [1975] 3 W. L. R. 684 ; *Re Estate of Sir Adolph Tuck* (1975), 119 Sol. Jo. 868.

[7] *Re Donn*, [1944] Ch. 8.

Again, whether a person " conforms to " a particular religion defies any certain answer.[1] Does, for instance, conformity to the Church of England necessitate attendance at religious services ? If so, how regular must the attendance be ? On the other hand, a condition for the forfeiture of an interest if the donee should " become a convert to the Roman Catholic religion " has been upheld, for such a conversion requires the performance of certain definite acts.[2] The court can, therefore, say with certainty what has to be done and whether it has in fact been done.

Many other examples might be given of uncertain conditions. For instance, provisions that an interest should be forfeited if the donee " in any way associated, corresponded or visited with any of my present wife's nephews or nieces," [3] or " have social or other relationship with " a named person,[4] have been held void, since it is impossible to say with reasonable certainty which of the many connections included in the words " association " or " relationship " offend the prohibition.

Again, a condition that property shall be enjoyed by a beneficiary " only so long as she shall continue to reside in Canada " is too vague to be enforced, for there are many forms and degrees of residence and it is impossible to say precisely which of them fall under the ban.[5] But the law does not exact too high a standard of certainty. The condition need not be clear beyond a peradventure. So in one case a requirement of " taking up permanent residence in England " was held to be sufficiently certain, since the word " permanent " postulates an intention to live in a place for life as opposed to living there temporarily or for a fixed period.[6]

In several cases decided between 1945 and 1960, courts of first instance, in disregard of what had been conveyancing practice for at least a century, showed a surprising tendency to stigmatize as void for uncertainty clauses in a will or settlement providing for the forfeiture of an interest given to X. upon his failure to assume the surname and arms of Y. It has been held more than once, for instance, that to decree forfeiture if X. "disuses" the surname Y. does not show with sufficient precision what degree of disuser he must avoid.

Name and arms clauses.

---

[1] *Re Tegg, supra.*
[2] *Re Evans,* [1940] Ch. 629 ; *Blathwayt* v. *Cawley (Baron), supra.*
[3] *Jeffreys* v. *Jeffreys* (1901), 84 L.T. 417.
[4] *Re Jones,* [1953] Ch. 125 ; 1 All E. R. 357.
[5] *Sifton* v. *Sifton,* [1938] A.C. 656 ; [1938] 3 All E. R. 425. See also *Re Brace,* [1954] 1 W. L. R. 955, [1954] 2 All E. R. 354, when a condition requiring the donee " to provide a home for " X. was held to be so vague as to be unintelligible.
[6] *Re Gape's Will Trusts,* [1952] Ch. 743 ; [1952] 2 All E. R. 579. Compare *Bromley* v. *Tryon,* [1952] A.C. 265 ; [1951] 2 All E. R. 1058, when it was held that a condition for forfeiture if a beneficiary became entitled to specified settled land " or the bulk thereof " was not void for uncertainty, since " bulk " meant anything over half.

" What percentage short of 100 per cent. of the disuser of the name would amount to a disuser of it within the meaning of the clause ?"[1]

The Court of Appeal, however, has now overruled these decisions on the ground that they imposed an unreasonably rigorous test of certainty.[2]

"Each of us has a surname, and it seems to me altogether fanciful to suggest that there is any real ambiguity in a requirement that I should adopt and use a surname in place of that which I at present have : for the requirement does no more nor less than postulate that I should thereafter use the new surname, just as I at present use my existing name.   Equally, as it seems to me, there is no real ambiguity in a divesting provision expressed to take effect if I should at any time 'disuse' or 'discontinue to use' the surname which I have adopted."[3]

Effect of void conditions.   If realty is conveyed to a person on a condition which is void, then, in the case of a condition precedent, the conveyance is void, and the interest does not arise[4] ; but in the case of a condition subsequent the condition alone is void, and the donee takes an absolute interest in the property free from the restrictive clause.[5]

---

[1] *Re Bouverie*, [1952] Ch. 400, at p. 404, *per* VAISEY, J.

[2] *Re Neeld*, [1962] Ch. 643 ; [1962] 2 All E. R. 335.   The Court of Appeal also held that a name and arms clause is not contrary to public policy.   See too *Re Neeld (No. 3)*, [1969] 1 W. L. R. 988 ; [1969] 2 All E. R. 1025.

[3] *Re Neeld*, [1962] Ch. 643, at p. 667, *per* Lord EVERSHED.   See also p. 679, *per* UPJOHN, L.J., and p. 682, *per* DIPLOCK, L.J., as to disuser.

[4] A bequest of *personalty* subject to an illegal condition precedent is void if the condition is *malum in se*, *i.e.* wrong in itself, but if the condition is only *malum prohibitum*, *i.e.* indifferent in itself but contrary to a human law, the bequest takes effect unfettered by the condition ; *Re Elliott*, [1952] Ch. 217, [1952] 1 All E. R. 145.   See (1955), 19 *Conv.* (N.S.) 176 (V. T. H. Delany).

[5] Co. Litt. 206a ; *Re Croxon*, [1904] 1 Ch. 252 ; *Re Turton*, [1926] Ch. 96 (impossible condition).

BOOK II

ESTATES AND INTERESTS IN LAND

PART III

COMMERCIAL INTERESTS

SUMMARY

A. INTERESTS CONFERRING A RIGHT TO THE LAND ITSELF

CHAPTER I

LEASEHOLD INTERESTS[1]

SUMMARY

---

[1] See generally Foa, *Law of Landlord and Tenant* (8th Edn. 1957) ; Hill and Redman, *Law of Landlord and Tenant* (16th Edn. 1976) ; Woodfall, *Landlord and Tenant* (27th Edn. 1968) ; Evans, *Law of Landlord and Tenant* (1974) ; Partington, *Landlord and Tenant* (1975). In November 1970 work began on the preparation of a Landlord and Tenant Code. Three interim reports are to be published first.   See Report on Obligations of Landlords and Tenants (Law Com. No. 67, 1975) *infra*, p. 426 ; two others are due later on (a) termination of tenancies, and (b) covenants against assignment, alterations and change of use.   Law Commission Tenth Annual Report 1974–1975 (Law Com., No. 71) para. 18.

SECTION I. MEANING OF TERM OF YEARS ABSOLUTE

A leasehold is capable of subsisting as a legal estate,[1] but it must be created in the manner required by the law[2] and satisfy the definition of a "term of years absolute" contained in the Law of Property Act 1925.[3] Otherwise it is an equitable interest.[4] A term of years absolute means a term that is to last for a certain fixed period, even though it may be liable to come to an end before the expiration of that period by the service of a notice to quit ; the re-entry of the landlord [5] ; operation of law [6] ; or a provision for cesser on redemption, as in the case of a mortgage term.[7] It includes a term for less than a year[8], or for one year, or for a year or years and a fraction of a year, and also the tenancy from year to year that is common in the case of agricultural leases.

Meaning of terms of years.

The Act provides that[9]

Concurrent legal estates.

" A legal estate may subsist concurrently with or subject to any other legal estate in the same land in like manner as it could have done before the commencement of this Act,"

and it therefore follows, for instance, that the owner of a legal term may by sub-lease grant a legal sub-term to another person. In such a case two legal estates exist at once in the same land.

Reversion-ary leases.

A term of years absolute is a legal estate notwithstanding that it does not entitle the tenant to enter into immediate possession, but is limited to begin at a future date.[10]

Perpetually renewable leases.

There is no limit of time for which a lease may be made to endure ; periods of 99 or 999 years are common, and longer periods are possible, but leases cannot exist for unspecified or for indeterminate periods, such as leases in perpetuity or until war breaks out.[11] The nearest approach to a perpetual lease before 1926 was one which was perpetually renewable, that is one in which the lessor covenanted that he would from time to time grant a new lease on the determination of the one then existing, if the lessee should so desire and should pay a fine for the privilege.

Perpetually renewable leases were inconvenient[12] and were

---

[1] L.P.A. 1925 s. 1 (1).
[2] *Infra,* pp. 390 *et seq.*
[3] L.P.A. 1925, s. 205 (1) (xxvii).
[4] *Ibid.,* s. 1 (1) (*b*).
[5] *Infra,* pp. 435 ; 441.
[6] For example, where the purposes for which a portions term has been created are satisfied, the term merges in the reversion and ceases accordingly ; L.P.A. 1925, s. 5 (1) (2).
[7] *Infra,* p. 642.
[8] See *Re Land and Premises at Liss, Hants,* [1971] Ch. 986, at p. 991, *per* Goulding, J.
[9] L.P.A. 1925, s. 1 (5).
[10] *Infra,* p. 386.
[11] *Sevenoaks, Maidstone and Tonbridge Rail. Co.* v. *London, Chatham and Dover Rail. Co.* (1879), 11 Ch. D. 625, at p. 635.
[12] See remarks by Jessel, M.R., *Re Smith's Charity* (1882), 20 Ch. D. 516.

abolished as from January 1st, 1926. Those which existed on January 1st, 1926, were converted into leases for 2,000 years calculated from the date at which the existing term began ; and any perpetually renewable sub-lease granted by the tenant out of his interest was converted into a term of 2,000 years less one day.[1] Any fine that was due on renewal became payable as additional rent.[2]

Their abolition and conversion into leases for 2,000 years.

If a contract is made after 1925 which, when properly construed, provides for the grant of a lease with a covenant for perpetual renewal it operates as an agreement to grant a lease for 2,000 years, but the lessor is not entitled to convert into additional rent any fine that may have been reserved.[3] Thus a lessor may find to his discomfiture that a lease, though not expressly made renewable, is converted, by reason of the language used, into a term that will endure for 2,000 years unless the tenant chooses to determine it sooner. This will be the case, for instance, if a lease for three years certain contains a covenant that,

> the lessor will on the request of the tenant grant him a tenancy at the same rent containing the like provisions as are herein contained including the present covenant for renewal.[4]

Such a clause contains the seeds of its own reproduction[5] in the sense that a lease granted for a second period of three years would also contain a covenant for renewal, and so on *ad infinitum.*

The result, then, of the legislation is that there may be a valid contract for renewal, but not for perpetual renewal. In order to keep permissible renewals within reasonable bounds, however, it is enacted that an agreement to renew for a longer period than 60 years from the end of the lease in question shall be void.[6]

A term for 2,000 years that arises as a result of this legislation is in general subject to the covenants, conditions and provisions of the original lease, but the following special incidents have been attached to it by statute :—

Special incidents of the 2,000 years term.

(a) The lessee or his successor in title may terminate the lease by giving at least ten days' written notice before any date at which, but for its conversion, it would have expired if no renewal had taken place.[7]

(b) The lessee is bound to register with the lessor every

---

[1] L.P.A. 1922, s. 145, 15th Sched., para. 1.
[2] *Ibid.*, para. 12.
[3] *Ibid.*, para. 5.
[4] *Parkus* v. *Greenwood*, [1950] Ch. 644 ; [1950] 1 All E. R. 436 ; *Northchurch Estates, Ltd.* v. *Daniels*, [1947] Ch. 117 ; [1946] 2 All E. R. 524 ; *Caerphilly Concrete Products, Ltd.* v. *Owen*, [1972] 1 W. L. R. 372, at p. 376 ; [1972] 1 All E. R. 248 ; M. & B. p. 364, where SACHS L. J. refers to " an area of the law in which the courts have manoeuvred themselves into an unhappy position ". Cf. *Centaploy, Ltd.* v. *Matlodge, Ltd.*, [1974] Ch. 1 ; [1973] 2 All E. R. 720 ; M. & B. 378.
[5] An expression used by counsel in the court below, [1950] Ch. 33, at p. 34.
[6] L.P.A. 1922, 15th Sched., para. 7 (2).
[7] *Ibid.*, 15th Sched., para. 10 (1) (i).

assignment or devolution of the term within six months of its taking place.[1]

(c) A lessee who assigns the term to another, thereafter ceases to be liable on the covenants contained in the lease.[2] This applies even to the original lessee, and is therefore an exception to the general rule that despite an assignment he remains liable on his contractual obligations.[3]

Abolition of leases for lives, or until marriage.

There were certain other leases of a somewhat peculiar nature that have been modified by legislation.

A lease *at a rent, or in consideration of a fine,*[4] made

(i) for life or lives, *e.g.* to T. during the lives of A. and B. ; or

(ii) for a term of years determinable on a life or lives, *e.g.* to T. for 99 years if X. shall so long live ; or

(iii) for a term of years determinable on the marriage of the lessee, *e.g.* to T. for 20 years until T. marries,

now takes effect as a lease for 90 years.[5] This lease may be terminated upon the death or the marriage, as the case may be, of the original tenant, for after these events have occurred a month's notice in writing to terminate the tenancy upon one of the usual quarter days may be given by either side.[6]

SECTION II.   THE NATURE OF A TERM OF YEARS

For a term of years to arise and for the relation of landlord and tenant to be created, one person, called the landlord or lessor, must confer upon another, called the tenant or lessee, the right to the exclusive possession of certain land for a period that is definite or capable of definition.   The lessor retains an interest which is called a reversion.

Distinction between licence and lease.

Exclusive Possession.   A necessary feature of a lease is that the lessee shall acquire the right of possession to the exclusion of the lessor.[7]   This does not mean, however, that whenever a person is let into exclusive possession he necessarily becomes a lessee.   It may well be that he obtains only a personal privilege in

---

[1] *Ibid.*, para. 10 (1) (ii).

[2] *Ibid.*, 15th Sched., para. 11 (1).

[3] *Infra,* pp. 457 *et seq.*

[4] A fine is usually the single payment of a lump sum made by the tenant, and is additional to the rent. By statute the word includes " a premium or foregift and any payment, consideration or benefit in the nature of a fine, premium or foregift " ; L.P.A. 1925, s. 205 (1) (xxiii). The rent or fine excludes beneficial tenancies for life under a settlement. These are equitable interests and subject to S.L.A. 1925. *Binions* v. *Evans,* [1972] Ch. 359, at p. 366 ; [1972] 2 All E. R. 70 ; *Ivory* v. *Palmer,* [1975] I. C. R. 340.

[5] L.P.A. 1925, s. 149 (6).

[6] *Ibid.*

[7] *L. and N. W. Rail. Co.* v. *Buckmaster* (1874), 10 Q. B. 70, 76.

the shape of a licence which may be revoked according to the express or implied terms of the contract.[1]   Whether a transaction creates a lease or a licence, whatever label the parties may have used, is a question of intention to be inferred from the circumstances.[2]   Although a person who is given exclusive possession of land is *prima facie* to be regarded as a tenant, yet he will be nothing more than a licensee if the inference from the circumstances and the conduct of the parties is that he shall have a mere personal privilege of occupation but no definite interest in the land.[3]

" In all the cases where an occupier has been held to be a licensee there has been something in the circumstances, such as a family arrangement, an act of friendship or generosity, or such like, to negative any intention to create a tenancy." [4]

Thus licences rather than leases were created where an employer allowed his retiring servant to remain in his cottage rent free for the rest of his life [5] ; where a father, wishing to provide a home for his son and daughter-in-law, allowed them to occupy a house that he had bought in return for their promise to pay the instalments still due to a building society [6] ; where a landlord allowed the daughter of his deceased employee to remain in her father's cottage rather than evict her immediately [7] ; where a woman bought a house and allowed her brother to occupy it, rent free [8] ; and where a company allowed their former managing director to continue in occupation of a flat on the business premises.[9]

---

[1] *Infra*, pp. 577 *et seq.*

[2] *Heslop* v. *Burns*, [1974] 1 W. L. R. 1241 ; [1974] 3 All E. R. 406 ; M. & B. p. 371.   See Generally Megarry, *Rent Acts* (10th Edn.), pp. 53–64.

[3] *Booker* v. *Palmer*, [1942] 2 All E. R. 674, at p. 677 ; *Errington* v. *Errington and Woods*, [1952] 1 K. B. 290, and authorities cited *ibid.* at p. 297 ; [1952] 1 All E. R. 149 ; M. & B. p. 472 ; *Cobb* v. *Lane*, [1952] 1 All E. R. 1199 ; *Murray, Bull & Co., Ltd.* v. *Murray*, [1953] 1 Q. B. 211 ; [1952] 2 All E. R. 1079 ; *Isaac* v. *Hotel De Paris, Ltd.*, [1960] 1 W. L. R. 239 ; [1960] 1 All E. R. 348 ; *Finbow* v. *Air Ministry*, [1963] 1 W. L. R. 697 ; [1963] 2 All E. R. 647 ; *Appah* v. *Parncliffe Investments, Ltd.*, [1964] 1 W. L. R. 1064 ; [1964] 1 All E. R. 838 ; *Strand Securities, Ltd.* v. *Caswell*, [1965] Ch. 958, at p. 980 ; [1965] 1 All E. R. 820 ; *Abbeyfield (Harpenden) Society, Ltd.* v. *Woods*, [1968] 1 W. L. R. 374 ; [1968] 1 All E. R. 352 ; *Hughes* v. *Griffin*, [1969] 1 W. L. R. 23 ; [1969] 1 All E. R. 460 ; *Barnes* v. *Barratt*, [1970] 2 Q.B. 657 ; [1970] 2 All E.R. 483 ; *Shell Mex and B.P. Ltd.* v. *Manchester Garages Ltd.*, [1971] 1 W. L. R. 612 ; [1971] 1 All E. R. 841 ; *Binions* v. *Evans*, [1972] Ch. 359 ; [1972] 2 All E. R. 70 ; *Heslop* v. *Burns*, [1974] 1 W. L. R. 1241 ; [1974] 3 All E. R. 406 ; M. & B. p. 371 ; *Wang* v. *Wei* (1975), 119 Sol. Jo. 492.

[4] *Facchini* v. *Bryson*, [1952] 1 T. L. R. 1386, 1389, *per* DENNING, L.J.

[5] *Foster* v. *Robinson*, [1951] 1 K. B. 149.   Also where an evacuee was given the same privilege, *Webb Ltd.* v. *Webb*, Oct. 24, 1951, unreported, but referred to, [1952] 1 K. B. at 297.

[6] *Errington* v. *Errington and Woods, supra*; but see *infra*, pp. 583–5.

[7] *Marcroft Wagons Ltd.* v. *Smith*, [1951] 2 K. B. 496.

[8] *Cobb* v. *Lane, supra* ; *Heslop* v. *Burns, supra*.

[9] *Murray, Bull & Co.* v. *Murray*, [1953] 1 Q. B. 211 ; [1952] 2 All E. R. 1079. For the law relating to licences, see *infra*, pp. 577 *et seq.*

The distinction between a lease and a licence may arise in a variety of situations. It is of particular importance in connection with the Rent Acts, which, as we shall see, accord substantial security of tenure to lessees, but not to licencees.[1]

As Sachs, L. J. said of the test for the distinction in *Barnes* v. *Barratt*:[2]

> " In this way, the law has adapted itself so as to deal with the complexities of the Rent Acts without causing patently unintended injustice to landlords, whilst guarding against improper avoidance by the latter of the provisions of those Acts."

There must be certain beginning and ending.

The Period must be Definite. Though a lease may be limited to endure for any specified number of years, however many, it cannot be limited in perpetuity.[3] The term must be for a definite period in the sense that it must have a certain beginning[4] and a certain ending.

Date for commencement of term must be fixed.

This does not necessarily mean that the parties must immediately fix the exact date of commencement, for it is open to them to agree that the lease shall *begin* upon the occurrence of an uncertain event, as for example,

upon the declaration of war by Great Britain[5] ; or
upon possession of the premises becoming vacant.[6]

Such an agreement, though at first conditional, becomes absolute and enforceable as soon as the event occurs.[7]

Reversionary leases.

A term expressed to begin from a past date or, as is more usual, from the date of the lease is called a lease *in possession*. It is also possible to create a *reversionary* lease, by which the term is limited to commence at some future date. Formerly such a term might be granted so as to commence at any time in the future, as, for instance, where a lease was made in 1917 to commence in 1946,[8] but a restriction has now been imposed upon this right by the Law of Property Act 1925, which provides that

> " A term, at a rent or granted in consideration of a fine, limited after the commencement of this Act to take effect *more than 21 years* from the date of the instrument purporting to create it, shall be void,

---

[1] *Infra,* p. 470.

[2] [1970] 2 Q.B. 657, at p. 669.

[3] *Sevenoaks, Maidstone and Tunbridge Rail. Co.* v. *London, Chatham and Dover Ry. Co.* (1879), 11 Ch. D. 625, at pp. 635-6.   The effect of an instrument purporting to create a perpetual lease at a rent may perhaps be either to create a yearly tenancy or to pass the fee simple to the lessee subject to the payment of an annual rentcharge in perpetuity ; *Doe d. Roberton* v. *Gardiner* (1852), 12 C. B. 319, at p. 333.

[4] *Harvey* v. *Pratt,* [1965] 1 W. L. R. 1025 ; [1965] 2 All E. R. 786 (contract for lease void for failing to specify date of commencement).

[5] *Swift* v. *Macbean,* [1942] 1 K. B. 375 ; [1942] 1 All E. R. 126.

[6] *Brilliant* v. *Michaels,* [1945] 1 All E. R. 121.   In this case, however, it was held that no final agreement had been made.

[7] *Ibid.,* at p. 126, citing Fry, *Specific Performance* (6th Edn.), p. 458.

[8] *Mann, Crossman and Paulin, Ltd.* v. *Registrar of the Land Registry,* [1918] 1 Ch. 202.

and any contract made after such commencement to create such a term shall likewise be void."[1]

The first limb of this enactment nullifies the creation of a reversionary lease limited to take effect more than 21 years from the date of the lease, *e.g.* a lease executed in 1975 for a term of ten years to run from 2000. The second limb nullifies a contract to create *such a term, i.e.* a term that will commence more than 21 years from the date of the lease by which it will eventually be created. For example, a contract made in 1975 to grant a lease for ten years in 1977, the term to run from 2000 is void.[2]

Thus, the Act relates the period of 21 years to the date of the lease, not to the date of the contract. Therefore a contract in a lease for 35 years giving the tenant an option to renew it for a further period of 35 years by making a written request to this effect twelve months before the expiration of the current term, is not void, since the contractual option, if exercised, will result in a term to begin upon the execution of the second lease. It is immaterial that it will be more than 21 years before the contractual right is exercised.[3]

The date upon which a lease is to terminate is generally expressed specifically, but in accordance with the maxim—*id certum est quod certum reddi potest*—it is sufficient if made to depend upon some uncertain event, provided that the event occurs before the lease takes effect; as for example where lands are let to

> A. for so many years as B. shall fix.

On the other hand a lease is void if the date of its termination remains uncertain after it has taken effect. It was accordingly held in *Lace* v. *Chantler*,[4] for instance, that an agreement to let a house

> for the duration of the war

did not create a valid tenancy.[5]

Date for termination of lease.

---

[1] S. 149 (3). This restriction does not affect terms, such as portions terms, taking effect in equity under a settlement.

[2] *Re Strand and Savoy Properties, Ltd.* [1960] Ch. 582 ; [1960] 2 All E. R. 327 ; M. & B. p. 361 ; *Weg Motors, Ltd.* v. *Hales*, [1961] Ch. 176 ; affd. [1962] Ch. 49 ; [1960] 3 All E. R. 762 ; affd. [1961] 3 All E. R. 181 ; see (1960), 76 L. Q. R. pp. 352–4 (R.E.M.).

[3] *Re Strand and Savoy Properties, Ltd., supra.*

[4] [1944] K. B. 368 ; [1944] 1 All E. R. 305 ; M. & B. p. 358.

[5] A conveyancing device by which the difficulty may be surmounted is to grant a lease for a fixed period determinable upon the happening of the uncertain event, *e.g.* to A. for 99 years terminable on the cessation of hostilities. In *Great Northern Rail. Co.* v. *Arnold* (1916), 33 T. L. R. 114, ROWLATT, J., managed even to construe a lease similar to that in *Lace* v. *Chantler* as a lease for 999 years terminable on the cessation of the 1914 War. The effect of *Lace* v. *Chantler* was to defeat so many leases made before and during the war of 1939 that it was found necessary to save them by a temporary measure, the Validation of War-time Leases Act 1944. The rule in *Lace* v. *Chantler* does not apply to periodic tenancies. *Re Midland Railway Co.'s Agreement*, [1971] Ch. 725 ; [1971] 1 All E. R. 1007 ; M. & B. p. 360 ; *Centaploy, Ltd.* v. *Matlodge, Ltd.*, [1974] Ch. 1. ; [1973] 2 All E. R. 720 ; M. & B. p. 378 ; *infra*, p. 466.

Interesse termini abolished.

There was a troublesome doctrine of the common law which established, in the case of a lease not operating under the Statute of Uses, that the lessee acquired no estate in the land until he actually entered into possession. Until that time he was said to have a mere right to take possession, and this right was called an *interesse termini*. This requisite of entry to perfect a lease was, however, abolished by the Law of Property Act 1925, and all terms of years absolute, whether created before or after the commencement of the Act, take effect from the date fixed for the commencement of the term without actual entry.[1]

SECTION III. CREATION OF TERMS OF YEARS

SUMMARY

(1) INTRODUCTORY NOTE

A term of years may be brought into existence either at law by a lease or in equity by a contract for a lease.

Lease.

A lease is a conveyance, and if made in the form required by law, it passes a *legal* term of years to the tenant and creates the legal relationship of landlord and tenant—either at once in the case of an immediate letting or at the agreed future date in the case of a reversionary lease. The tenant thereby acquires a proprietary interest in the land, which, being legal, is enforceable against all the world.[2]

Contract for lease.

A contract for a lease, on the other hand, does not operate as a conveyance at law, but is a contract that binds the parties, the one to grant a lease and the other to accept it.[3]

Such a contract does not create the relationship of landlord and tenant *at law*. But, as we shall see, the position of the parties *in equity* is different. An *equitable* term of years may pass to the person who holds under a contract for a lease.[4] If that contract is capable of being enforced by specific performance, then he will

---

[1] L.P.A. 1925, s. 149 (1), (2).
[2] *Supra*, p. 61.
[3] *Borman* v. *Griffith*, [1930] 1 Ch. 493.
[4] *Infra*, pp. 392 *et seq.*

hold under the same terms in equity as if a lease had actually been granted to him. The relationship of landlord and tenant will thus be created *in equity*, and as between the parties the rights and duties of that relationship will be the same as if the lease had been granted.[1] But, in this case, the tenant has only an equitable interest in the land, which, according to general principle, is enforceable against all the world *except* a bona fide purchaser for value of the legal estate without notice.[2]

A lease which is framed in formal and technical language will state that

> " The landlord hereby demises unto the tenant all that messuage or dwelling house, etc."

but the mere fact that an instrument is drafted as a contract does not preclude it from taking effect as an actual demise. Whether the contract operates as a lease or as a contract depends upon the intention of the parties, which must be collected from all the circumstances.[3]

We will now deal separately with these two modes of creation, beginning with the contract for a lease.

(2) CONTRACT FOR A LEASE

We have already discussed the requirements for a valid and enforceable contract for the sale or other disposition of land.[4] For a contract for a lease to be valid, there must be a final agreement on the terms of the lease, that is to say, on the parties, the property, the consideration or rent, the duration of the lease and any other special terms. For the contract to be enforceable, there must be either a memorandum in writing signed by the defendant, as required by section 40 of the Law of Property Act 1925, or an act of part performance by the plaintiff.

As we have seen, it is usual for a contract for the sale of land to precede the conveyance of the legal estate to the purchaser.[5] However, this is the exception rather than the rule in the case of a lease.[6] Where there is a building lease, a contract is often made first, and then a lease is subsequently granted when building is complete. But in most cases, the transaction is effected either by a contract for a lease, or by a lease, but rarely by a combination of both.[7]

---

[1] *Walsh* v. *Lonsdale* (1882), 21 Ch. D. 9 ; M. & B. p. 74 ; *infra*, p. 394.
[2] For further detail, and for the effect of registration under L.C.A. 1972, see *infra*, pp. 392 *et seq*.
[3] See Woodfall, *Landlord and Tenant* (27th Edn.), 192–193.
[4] *Supra*, pp. 112 *et seq*.
[5] *Supra*, p. 112.
[6] See *Hollington Bros., Ltd.* v. *Rhodes*, [1951] 2 T.L.R. 691, at p. 694.
[7] *Emmet on Title* (16th Edn.), p. 802.

(3) LEASES

(A) FORMALITIES

Deed un-necessary for leases not exceeding three years.

At common law a parol lease was sufficient to create the relation of landlord and tenant in the case of corporeal hereditaments, and there was no necessity to employ either a deed or a writing. This is still the law with regard to leases *not exceeding three years*, for the Law of Property Act 1925,[1] re-enacting in effect the Statute of Frauds 1677, provides that

> " the creation by parol of leases taking effect in possession for a term not exceeding three years (whether or not the lessee is given power to extend the term) at the best rent which can be reasonably obtained without taking a fine "

shall be valid.

Meaning of " lease not exceeding three years."

Thus a mere oral lease suffices to create a *legal* term of years, provided that it is to take effect in possession, that it reserves the best rent obtainable, and that it is not to last for longer than three years. A lease exceeds three years within the meaning of the Act only if it is for a definite term longer than that period. It is immaterial in such a case that it contains a provision allowing its earlier determination by notice.[2] On the other hand, a periodic tenancy for an indefinite period, such as one from year to year or week to week, may be validly created by a parol lease, for, though it may endure for much longer than three years, it may equally well be determined at an earlier date.

Leases exceeding three years.

Necessity of Deed. A lease, however, which exceeds three years will not pass a legal estate immediately and directly to the tenant unless it is made by deed. The history of this requirement is as follows. Section 1 of the Statute of Frauds 1677 enacted that

> " All leases . . . or terms of years . . . made or created . . . by parol, and *not put in writing, and signed by the parties* so making or creating the same, or their agents thereunto lawfully authorized by writing, shall have the force and effect of leases or estates *at will* only."

The second section excepted leases not exceeding three years at a rent of two-thirds at least of the full improved value of the land.

The next enactment was the Real Property Act 1845,[3] which required a further formality by providing that

> " A lease, required by law to be in writing, of any tenements or hereditaments . . . . made after the first day of October, 1845, shall be *void at law* unless also made by *deed*."

---

[1] S. 54 (2).
[2] *Kushner* v. *Law Society*, [1952] 1 K. B. 264 ; [1952] 1 All E. R. 404.
[3] S. 3.

Thus it was only in the case of leases exceeding three years that a deed became necessary, since it was these alone that had previously been " required by law to be in writing." An unsealed lease exceeding three years had and still has a greater effect than is indicated by the language of the two statutes cited, but since 1845 it has never sufficed to pass to the tenant an immediate legal interest equivalent to that which the parties intended to create. The Statutes of 1677 and 1845 have been in effect re-enacted by the Law of Property Act 1925 in the two following sections :—

Law of Property Act 1925.

" 54.—(1) All interests in land created by parol and not put in writing and signed by the persons so creating the same, or by their agents thereunto lawfully authorized in writing, have, notwithstanding any consideration having been given for the same, the force and effect of interests at will only.

(2) Nothing in the foregoing provisions . . . shall affect the creation by parol of leases taking effect in possession for a term not exceeding three years . . . at the best rent which can be reasonably obtained without taking a fine.

52.—(1) All conveyances of land or of any interest therein are *void for the purpose of conveying or creating a legal estate* unless made by deed.

(2) This section does not apply to—

(*d*) leases or tenancies or other assurances not required by law to be made in writing

We must now attempt to define the exact effect of a lease exceeding three years which fails to satisfy the statutory requirements.

(B) Effect of Leases exceeding Three Years which are not made in accordance with the required Formalities

The scope of the following inquiry is to ascertain, first what was the legal effect between 1677 and 1845 of a lease not put into writing as required by the Statute of Frauds; secondly, what has been the effect since 1845 of a lease not made by deed as required by the Real Property Act of that year. Inasmuch as both these Statutes have been re-enacted by the Law of Property Act 1925, the result of this inquiry will be a statement of the present law on the subject.

Scope of inquiry.

(i) **Effect at Common Law.** The Statute of Frauds said that a lease which was not put in writing should create a mere tenancy at will, and this was the view taken by the common law when a tenant did nothing more than enter into possession of the premises under a parol lease. But common law went further and presumed that a tenant who had not merely gone into possession, but had also paid rent on a yearly basis, became tenant from year to year, and that he held this yearly tenancy subject to such of the terms

Lease not in writing might create a yearly tenancy.

and conditions of the unwritten lease as were consistent with a yearly tenancy.[1]

Unsealed lease might create yearly tenancy.

The provision of the Real Property Act 1845 that an unsealed lease should be *void at law* was construed in the same manner. The document was void as a lease in the sense that it did not create the agreed term of years, but if the intended tenant entered into possession and paid rent at a yearly rate, he was presumed to be a yearly tenant.[2]

Position to-day at common law.

Moreover the above represents the legal position at the present day *if we confine our attention to the common law.* A conveyance of land, and this includes a lease,[3] is void under the Law of Property Act 1925 for the purpose of creating a legal estate unless made by deed (except of course in the case of a lease not exceeding three years), but nevertheless, if the tenant enters into possession and pays a yearly rent, he will become a yearly tenant. Again, by the same Act a term exceeding three years which is not put in writing is to have the force and effect of an equitable interest at will only, but, given the same two facts of possession and payment of rent, it also will be converted into a legal yearly tenancy. It is expressly provided that the requirements of the Act with regard to formalities shall not " affect the right to acquire an interest in land by virtue of taking possession."[4]

Void lease equivalent to contract for lease.

(ii) **Effect in Equity.** Equity, however, took a very different view of the effect of a lease for more than three years which was not put in writing as required by the Statute of Frauds, or which, after 1845, was not made by deed. While admitting that the statutes rendered such a lease incapable of passing the term agreed upon by the parties, courts of equity held that the abortive lease must be regarded as a *contract for a lease*, provided, of course, that the constituents of an enforceable contract, as described above,[5] were present. In other words, an *oral* lease followed by an act of part performance, and a *written* lease signed by the party to be charged and constituting a sufficient memorandum of the terms of the bargain, were both allowed to have the same effect as a contract for a lease. It becomes necessary, therefore, to ascertain what the effect has always been in equity of such a contract.

Effect in equity of contract for lease.

A contract for a lease is a contract to which the equitable remedy of specific performance is peculiarly appropriate. If a

---

[1] *Doe d. Rigge* v. *Bell* (1793), 2 S. L. C. 119 ; *Mann* v. *Lovejoy* (1826), Ry. & M. 355 ; *Clayton* v. *Blakey* (1798), 8 Term Rep. 3 ; *Richardson* v. *Gifford* (1834), 1 Ad. & El. 52 ; *Hamerton* v. *Stead* (1824), 3 B. & C. 478, at p. 483, *per* LITTLEDALE, J. See *infra*, p. 403.

[2] *Martin* v. *Smith* (1874), L. R. 9 Exch. 50. *Rhyl U.D.C.* v. *Rhyl Amusements, Ltd.*, [1959] 1 W. L. R. 465 ; [1959] 1 All E. R. 257, where the lease was void for lack of compliance with the Public Health Act 1875, s. 177.

[3] S. 205 (1) (ii).　　　　　　　　　　　　　　　　[4] S. 55 (c).

[5] *Supra*, p. 389.

party can prove to the satisfaction of the court that such a contract has been entered into, he can bring a suit for specific performance requiring the other party to execute a deed in the manner required by statute so as to create that legal term which the parties intended to create. One effect, therefore, of such a specifically performable contract is that the prospective tenant immediately acquires an equitable interest in the land in the sense that he has an equitable right to a legal estate.[1]

As was said in a case prior to 1845,[2]

" The defendant was let into possession under an agreement, which gave the parties a right to go into equity to compel the execution of it by making out a formal lease."

The same view was upheld even when the Real Property Act 1845 had enacted that a lease exceeding three years made otherwise than by deed should be void at law. As Lord CHELMSFORD said in *Parker* v. *Taswell*,[3]

" The legislature appears to have been very cautious and guarded in language, for it uses the expression ' shall be void at law.' If the legislature had intended to deprive such a document of all efficacy, it would have said that the instrument should ' be void to all intents and purposes.' There are no such words in the Act. I think it would be too strong to say that because it is void at law as a lease, it cannot be used as an agreement enforceable in Equity, the intention of the parties having been that there should be a lease, and the aid of Equity being only invoked to carry that intention into effect."

The effect of this divergence between the views of common law and equity was that, prior to the passing of the Judicature Act 1873, an unsealed lease and a contract for a lease resulted in the creation of two entirely different interests, according as the common law or the equitable doctrine was invoked. At common law the tenant acquired the interest of a tenant from year to year if he paid rent and entered into possession : in equity he was entitled to call for the execution of a legal lease and to have inserted therein all the provisions of the void lease or of the contract. *Effect of divergence between common law and equity.*

The Judicature Act, however, materially affected the position. It provides in effect that, whenever an action is brought in any court, the plaintiff may set up equitable claims and the defendant may raise equitable defences, and that, *Effect of Judicature Act.*

" Where there is any conflict or variance between the rules of equity and the rules of the common law with reference to the same matter, the rules of equity shall prevail."[4]

---

[1] *Palmer* v. *Carey*, [1926] A. C. 703, 706 (P.C.).
[2] *Doe d. Thompson* v. *Amey* (1840), 12 Ad. & El. 476, at p. 479, *per* Lord DENMAN, C.J.
[3] (1858), 2 De G. & J. 559, at p. 570.
[4] Judication Act 1873, s. 25 (11) ; now Judicature Act 1925, s. 44.

Doctrine of *Walsh* v. *Lonsdale*. The particular point of variance which existed in the case of an unsealed lease fell to be considered in the leading case of *Walsh* v. *Lonsdale*,[1] decided in 1882. In that case

Walsh v. Lonsdale.

> the plaintiff agreed in writing to take a lease of a mill for seven years, and part of the agreement was that a deed should be executed containing *inter alia* a provision that *on any given day* the lessor might require the tenant to pay one year's rent in advance. No deed was executed, and the plaintiff, who was let into possession, paid rent quarterly, but not in advance, for a year and a half. The landlord then demanded a year's rent in advance and upon refusal distrained for the amount. The plaintiff brought an action to recover damages for illegal distress, for specific performance of the contract for a lease and for an interim injunction to restrain the distress.
>
> The main ground upon which he rested his claim was that, as he had been let into possession and had paid rent under a contract which did not operate as a lease, he was in the position of a tenant from year to year and held the mill upon such of the agreed terms as were consistent with a yearly tenancy. The condition making a year's rent always payable in advance was obviously inconsistent with a yearly tenancy which could be determined by half a year's notice, and for this reason it was argued that the distress was illegal.

Contract for lease may be as efficacious as a lease.

This argument did not prevail. It was decided that a tenant who holds under a contract for a lease of which specific performance will be decreed occupies the same position *vis à vis the landlord*, as regards both rights and liabilities, as he would occupy if a formal lease under seal had been executed.

If a lease by deed had been executed in this case on the lines of the contract, the defendant would have been entitled to distrain for rent not paid in advance, and the mere fact that the formal lease had not been actually made was not to prejudice his rights. Sir GEORGE JESSEL, M.R., put the matter thus :—

> " There is an agreement for a lease under which possession has been given. Now since the Judicature Act the possession is held under the agreement. There are not two estates as there were formerly —one estate at common law by reason of the payment of the rent from year to year, and an estate in equity under the agreement. There is only one court, and the equity rules prevail in it. The tenant holds under an agreement for a lease. He holds, therefore, under the same terms in equity as if a lease had been granted, it being a case in which both parties admit that relief is capable of being given by specific performance. That being so, he cannot complain of the exercise by the landlord of the same rights as the landlord would have had if a lease had been granted. On the other hand, he is protected in the same way as if a lease had been granted ; he cannot be turned out by six months' notice as a tenant from year to year. He has a right to say : ' I have a lease in equity and you can only re-enter if I have committed such a breach of covenant as would, if a lease had been granted, have entitled you to re-enter according to the terms of a proper proviso for re-entry.' That being so, it appears to me that being a lessee in equity he cannot complain of the exercise of the right

---

[1] (1882), 21 Ch. D. 9 ; M. & B. p. 74.

of distress merely because the actual parchment has not been signed and sealed."

Such, then, is the doctrine of *Walsh* v. *Lonsdale*. It is one example of the principle that equity regards as already done what the parties to a transaction have agreed to do—a principle that is by no means confined to a contract for a lease, for it applies to any contract to convey or create a legal estate of which equity will order specific performance, as for instance, a contract for the sale of land,[1] or for the grant of a mortgage,[2] an easement[3] or a profit.[4]

In the context of landlord and tenant, *Walsh* v. *Lonsdale* has been followed,[5] qualified[6] and explained[7] in later cases and is now the governing rule whenever it is necessary to ascertain the effect of a lease or contract for a lease which is not made by deed as required by the Law of Property Act 1925. Section 52 (1)[8] of the Act provides that all conveyances of land

> " are void for the purpose of conveying or creating a legal estate unless made by deed,"

Contract may not be equivalent to lease.

but, if a tenant has an enforceable right to call for a deed, he is, as far as his rights and liabilities in relation to the landlord are concerned, in practically the same position as if he actually had a deed.

It must not, however, be concluded that a contract for a lease is as effective in all respects and against all persons as a lease. This is not so.[9] What JESSEL, M.R., meant was that if, in litigation between the parties, the circumstances would justify a decree for the execution of a sealed lease, then both in the Queen's Bench Division and in the Chancery Division, the case must be treated as if such a lease had been granted. There are at least three facts which illustrate the limitations of the doctrine, and the advantages of a lease as compared with a mere contract for a lease.

> First, the doctrine stands excluded if the contract is one of which equity will not grant specific performance.

Specific performance is still a discretionary remedy and will not be granted in all cases, as for instance where a lessee who seeks the aid of the court will be unable to perform the covenants

[1] *Supra*, p. 125.   [2] *Infra*, p. 649.
[3] *Infra*, p. 528.   [4] *Infra*, p. 566.
[5] *Lowther* v. *Heaver* (1889), 41 Ch. D. 248 ; *Coatsworth* v. *Johnson* (1886) 55 L. J. Q. B. 220 ; M. & B. p. 78 ; *Tottenham Hotspur, Football and Athletic Co., Ltd.* v. *Princegrove Publishers Ltd.*, [1974] 1 W. L. R. 113 ; [1974] 1 All E. R. 17.
[6] *Cornish* v. *Brook Green Laundry, Ltd.*, [1959] 1 Q. B. 394 ; [1959] 1 All E. R. 373, where it was held that it cannot be invoked if the contract to grant a term of years is subject to a condition precedent performable by the proposed tenant and not yet performed.
[7] *Manchester Brewery Co.* v. *Coombs*, [1901] 2 Ch. 608 ; M. & B. p. 422 ; *Gray* v. *Spyer*, [1922] 2 Ch. 22.
[8] *Supra*, p. 391.
[9] *Manchester Brewery Co.* v. *Coombs*, [1901] 2 Ch. 608, at p. 617.

in the lease owing to his insolvent state or where he has already committed a breach of a covenant that would have formed part of the lease. Thus, in *Coatsworth* v. *Johnson* [1] :—

> The plaintiff entered into possession under an agreement that the defendant would grant him a lease for twenty-one years. Before any rent was due or had been paid, the defendant gave him notice to quit and evicted him on the ground that he had done that which amounted to a breach of a covenant contained in the agreement and intended to be inserted in the lease.

The plaintiff sued in trespass, but failed. At common law, having paid no rent, he was a mere tenant at will and as such could be evicted at the pleasure of the defendant; in equity he was precluded from obtaining a decree for specific performance, since he had broken a covenant into which he had entered.

Further, specific performance will not be granted if the court has no jurisdiction to grant it. Thus a County Court has such jurisdiction only where the value of the property claimed by the plaintiff is in excess of £5,000. [2]

> Secondly, the statutory definition of " conveyance " [3] includes a lease but not a contract for a lease.

Thus, a tenant under a contract cannot claim those privileges which are granted by section 62 of the Law of Property Act 1925 [4] to one who takes a " conveyance " of land. [5]

> Thirdly, the doctrine does not in all cases affect the rights of third parties. [6]

Contract for a lease not always enforceable against third parties.

For instance, privity of estate exists between a landlord and an assignee from a tenant holding *under a lease*, so as to make the covenants enforceable by and against the assignee, [7] but no such privity exists in the case of an assignee from a person "whose only title to call himself a lessee depends on his right to specific performance of the agreement." [8] But a more important fact is that, since a contract confers a mere equitable right upon the lessee, it will not on general principles be enforceable against a bona fide purchaser for value of a legal estate without notice

---

[1] (1886), 55 L. J. Q. B. 220 ; M. & B. p. 78 ; *Warmington* v. *Miller*, [1973] Q. B. 877 ; [1973] 2 All E. R. 372.
[2] County Courts Act 1959, s. 52 (1) (d), as amended by Administration of Justice Act 1969, s. 5. *Foster* v. *Reeves*, [1892] 2 Q. B. 255 ; *cf. Cornish* v. *Brook Green Laundry, Ltd.*, [1959] 1 Q. B. 394 ; [1959] 1 All E. R. 373 ; *Kingswood Estate Co. Ltd.* v. *Anderson*, [1963] 2 Q. B. 169 ; [1962] 3 All E. R. 593 ; *Rushton* v. *Smith*, [1975] 3. W. L. R. 30 ; [1975] 2 All E. R. 905.
[3] L.P.A. 1925, s. 205 (1) (ii).
[4] *Infra*, pp. 530–2.
[5] *Borman* v. *Griffith*, [1930] 1 Ch. 493 ; M. & B. p. 387.
[6] *Manchester Brewery Co.* v. *Coombs*, [1901] 2 Ch. 608 ; M. & B. p. 422 ; *Purchase* v. *Lichfield Brewery Co.*, [1915] 1 K. B. 184 ; M. & B. p. 426.
[7] *Infra*, pp. 449 *et seq.*
[8] *Purchase* v. *Lichfield Brewery Co.*, *supra*, at p. 188, *per* LUSH, J. ; M. & B. pp. 421–422.

in the land to which the contract relates. To quote the words of Maitland :

" An agreement for a lease is not equal to a lease. An equitable right is not equal to a legal right ; between the contracting parties an agreement for a lease may be as good as a lease ; just so between the contracting parties an agreement for the sale of land may serve as well as a completed sale and conveyance. But introduce the third party and then you will see the difference. I take a lease ; my lessor then sells the land to X. ; notice or no notice my lease is good against X. I take a mere agreement for a lease, and the person who has agreed to grant the lease then sells and conveys to Y., who has no notice of my merely equitable right. Y. is not bound to grant me a lease." [1]

It must be observed, however, that a contract for a lease is now an *estate contract* within the meaning of the Law of Property Act 1925,[2] and that therefore it will be enforceable against third parties who acquire the land from the lessor, if it has been registered as a *land charge* at the Land Registry.[3] Registration constitutes notice to the whole world, lack of registration renders the contract void against a later purchaser of the legal estate for money or money's worth, even though in actual fact he may have known of its existence.[4] Thus

Contract for a lease is registrable.

if A. takes such a contract from B. and then B. wrongfully sells and conveys the land to an unsuspecting purchaser, Y., the estate contract of A. *if registered* will prevail against Y. in any court, but *if not registered* will be defeated by the conveyance, even though Y., far from being unsuspecting, actually knew that it had been made.

If, however, in the case given A. goes into possession of the land before the sale to Y. and pays rent on a yearly basis, he acquires a yearly tenancy which will be binding upon Y.[5] The failure of A. to register does not affect the *legal* estate that arises in him at common law under the rules already discussed. If this is so, Y. can, of course, determine the tenancy by half a year's notice.[6]

Summary. We have now reviewed the methods whereby the relation of landlord and tenant may be constituted, and it may be helpful in conclusion to summarize the present state of the law.

Summary statement of how relationship of landlord and tenant arises.

1. A parol, written or sealed lease not exceeding three years confers a legal term of years upon the tenant.

---

[1] Maitland, *Equity*, p. 158. But if, when Y. buys, I am in possession of the land, Y. will have constructive notice of my equitable right. *Hunt* v. *Luck*, [1902] 1 Ch. 428, at pp. 432, 433. *Supra*, p. 67.

[2] S. 2 (3) (iv).

[3] L.C.A. 1972, ss. 2 (4), Class C (iv) ; 4 (6) ; *infra*, p. 742. For the position in registered land, see *infra*, pp. 509–12.

[4] L.P.A. 1925, s. 199 (1). *Sharp* v. *Coates*, [1948] 1 All E. R. 136 ; on appeal, [1949] 1 K. B. 285 ; [1948] 2 All E. R. 871. See *Hollington Bros. Ltd.* v. *Rhodes*, [1951] 2 All E. R. 578 ; M. & B. p. 45.

[5] See *e.g. Bell Street Investments, Ltd.* v. *Wood* (1970), 216 Estates Gazette 585.

[6] *Infra*, p. 465.

2. A sealed lease exceeding three years has the same effect.

3. A written lease exceeding three years confers an equitable term upon the tenant by virtue of the doctrine of *Walsh* v. *Lonsdale*, provided that there is a sufficient memorandum as required by section 40 of the Law of Property Act 1925. Where there is such a memorandum there will be no occasion, owing to the superior efficacy of the *Walsh* v. *Lonsdale* doctrine, to rely upon the common law rule that possession plus payment of a yearly rent may raise a yearly tenancy. The contract should, however, be registered as a land charge.[1]

4. A parol lease exceeding three years will confer an equitable term of years upon the tenant under the doctrine of *Walsh* v. *Lonsdale* if a sufficient act of part performance is proved ; but if there is no act of part performance and therefore no enforceable contract, the parol lease will create a yearly tenancy if followed by possession and the payment of a yearly rent.

Suppose, for instance, an oral contract between A. the landlord and B. the tenant, who already holds under a lease expiring on December 25th, that B. shall have a new lease on the same terms as the present one. B. is in possession, but, as we have already seen,[2] the mere fact of *remaining on* in possession does not constitute an act of part performance, and therefore, if A. repudiates the contract, the want of an enforceable contract will debar B. from relying on the equitable doctrine of *Walsh* v. *Lonsdale*. There will be nothing, however, to prevent him from relying on the common law doctrine and claiming a yearly tenancy.

SECTION IV. TENANCIES FROM YEAR TO YEAR, AT WILL, AT SUFFERANCE AND BY ESTOPPEL

A tenancy from year to year differs from a tenancy for a fixed number of years, in that, unless terminated by a proper notice to quit, it may last indefinitely[3]; and from a tenancy at will, in that the death of either party or the alienation of his interest by either party does not effect its determination. It is practically the universal form of letting in the case of agricultural lands.[4]

It may arise either by express agreement, or by operation of law.

---

[1] *Infra*, p. 742.   [2] *Supra*, p. 122.

[3] The rule that the maximum duration of a term must be certainly known in advance of its taking effect does not apply to periodic tenancies. *supra*, p. 387. See *Re Midland Railway Co.'s Agreement*, [1971] Ch. 725, at p. 733 ; [1971] 1 All E. R. 1007 ; M. & B. p. 360 ; *Centaploy Ltd.* v. *Matlodge, Ltd.*, [1974] Ch. 1 ; [1973] 2 All E. R. 720 ; M. & B. p. 378.

[4] It is greater than a tenancy for one year, *Bernays* v. *Prosser*, [1963] 2 Q. B. 592.

1. Where the tenancy is created by express agreement, the phrase best adapted for carrying out the intention of the parties is " from year to year," since this enables the tenancy to be determined at the end of the first or any subsequent year.[1] But it sometimes happens that the parties by inadvertence use expressions which have the effect of creating a tenancy for at least two years, as for example:

> " for one year and so on from year to year,"

in which case the tenancy can be determined only by notice in the second or any later year.[2]

Yearly tenancy by express creation.

2. A tenancy from year to year will arise by operation or presumption of law whenever a person is in occupation of land with the permission of the owner, not as a licensee nor for an agreed period, and rent measured by reference to a year is paid and accepted. The two important cases where this occurs are where either a tenant at will or a tenant at sufferance pays a yearly rent.

Implied yearly tenancy.

(a) **Where a Tenant at Will pays a Yearly Rent.** A tenancy at will exists when A. occupies the land of B. as tenant with B's consent, on the understanding that either A. or B. may terminate the tenancy when he likes. LITTLETON says :—

Tenancy at will.

> " Tenant at will is where lands or tenements are let by one man to another, to have and to hold to him at the will of the lessor, by force of which lease the lessee is in possession. In this case the lessee is called tenant at will, because he hath no certain or sure estate, for the lessor may put him out at what time it pleaseth him." [3]

But such a tenancy equally arises when possession is held at the will of the lessee, and indeed it is important to notice that, even though a lease is made determinable at the will of the lessor only, it is also by implication determinable at the will of the lessee. In other words, every tenancy at will must be at the will of both parties.[4] In the words of Lord SIMONDS :—

> " A tenancy at will, though called a tenancy, is unlike any other tenancy except a tenancy at sufferance, to which it is next-of-kin. It has been properly described as a personal relation between the landlord and his tenant: it is determined by the death of either of them or by one of a variety of acts, even by an involuntary alienation, which would not affect the subsistence of any other tenancy." [5]

---

[1] *Doe d. Clarke* v. *Smaridge* (1845), 7 Q. B. 957.
[2] *Re Searle*, [1912] 1 Ch. 610; *Cannon Brewery* v. *Nash* (1898), 77 L. T. 648.
[3] Litt., s. 68.
[4] Co. Litt. 55a ; *Fernie* v. *Scott* (1871), L. R. 7 C. P. 202.
[5] *Wheeler* v. *Mercer*, [1957] A. C. 416, at p. 427; [1956] 3 All E. R. 631, at p. 634.

Implied tenancies at will.

A tenancy at will may be created either expressly[1] or by implication, as, for example, where a tenant, with the consent of his landlord, holds over after the expiry of the lease ; or where he goes into possession under a contract for a lease or under a void lease ;[2] or where a purchaser goes into possession prior to completion, or a prospective tenant goes into possession during negotiations for a lease.[3] These situations apart, the courts have restricted the scope of implied tenancies at will. They are now less inclined to infer such a tenancy from an exclusive possession of premises for an indefinite period,[4] being partly moved perhaps by a desire to temper the severity of the statutory rule that the lessor loses his right to recover the land if the tenant remains in occupation for thirteen years from the commencement of the tenancy without a written acknowledgment of the lessor's title.[5] It was formerly held, for instance, that a person allowed to occupy a house rent free was a tenant at will, not a licensee, on the ground that his right to exclusive possession was incompatible with the position of a mere licensee.[6] But in the modern view, no incompatibility exists,[7] and therefore the presumption that such an occupier is a tenant at will may well be rebutted by the surrounding circumstances.[8]

Tenancies at will disfavoured.

Despite the termination of his tenancy, a tenant at will has always been allowed a right to emblements, *i.e.* a right to re-enter the land at harvest and recover the crops that he has sown. This situation, in which the land reverted to the lessor but the right to enjoyment remained in effect with the tenant, seemed unsatisfactory to the common law courts and if the circumstances warranted it they were disposed to treat a tenancy at will as having been converted into one from year to year.[9]

Tenant at will may become yearly tenant.

Thus, it has been the law from an early date that the payment and acceptance of rent is presumptive evidence of an intention by

---

[1] *E.g. Manfield & Sons, Ltd.* v. *Botchin*, [1970] 2 Q. B. 612; [1970] 3 All E. R. 143 ; *Hagee (London), Ltd.* v. *A. B. Erikson and Lawson*, [1975] 3 W. L. R. 272 ; [1975] 3 All E. R. 234.

[2] *Supra*, p. 392.

[3] *British Railways Board* v. *Bodywright, Ltd.*, (1971), 220 Estates Gazette 651.

[4] See *Heslop* v. *Burns*, [1974] 1 W. L. R. 1241, at p. 1253, *per* Scarman, L. J. ; M. & B. p. 371

[5] Limitation Act 1939, s. 9 (1) ; *infra*, p. 897.

[6] *Lynes* v. *Snaith*, [1899] 1 Q. B. 486.   [7] *Supra*, pp. 384–6.

[8] *Cobb* v. *Lane*, [1952] 1 All E. R. 1199; *Hughes* v. *Griffin*, [1969] 1 W. L. R. 23 ; [1969] 1 All E. R. 460 ; *Heslop* v. *Burns, supra*.

[9] Smith's *Leading Cases* (13th Edn.), notes to *Clayton* v. *Blakey* (1798), 8 Term Rep. 3., vol. ii. p. 120.

the parties to establish a yearly tenancy, provided that the rent is contractually assessed on a yearly basis.[1] CHAMBRE, J., said:—

> " If he accepts yearly rent, or rent measured by any aliquot part of a year, the courts have said that is evidence of a taking for a year." [2]

The assessment of rent on a yearly basis is evidence of an intention to create a yearly tenancy, even though payment may fall due at more frequent intervals such as every quarter or month. If the rent is fixed by reference to some period less than a year it creates a shorter tenancy.[3] Where, for example, a lease for one year reserves a rent of £3 weekly, the tenant holds under a weekly tenancy if he remains in possession after the end of the year.[4]

But, the presumption in favour of a yearly tenancy raised by the payment and acceptance of rent may be rebutted by contrary evidence, as for instance by proof that, unknown to the lessor, the payments have been made by a squatter who disseised the original occupier.[5]

(b) **Where a Tenant at Sufferance pays a Yearly Rent** Tenancy at
This is the second case in which a tenancy from year sufferance.
to year may arise by presumption of law. Lord COKE
said :—

> " Tenant at sufferance is he that at first comes in by lawful demise and after his estate ended continueth in possession and wrongfully holdeth over." [6]

A man, for example, becomes a tenant at sufferance if having an estate *pur autre vie*,[7] he continues to hold after the death of the *cestui que vie*; or if being tenant for a fixed term, he " holds over," *i.e.* remains in possession without the consent of the landlord, after the term has come to an end.

Such a person differs from a tenant at will because his holding over after the determination of the term is a wrongful act, and he differs from a disseisor in that his original entry upon the land was lawful.[8]

A tenant at sufferance unless he is a tenant of premises Liabilities of
within the Rent Acts is in a precarious position. He may tenant at
be ejected at any moment and has no right to emblements, sufferance.
while he becomes liable to statutory penalties if he remains

---

[1] *Clayton* v. *Blakey, supra.*
[2] *Richardson* v. *Langridge* (1811), 4 Taunt. 128.
[3] *Ladies' Hosiery and Underwear, Ltd.* v. *Parker*, [1930] 1 Ch. 304.
[4] *Ibid.*, at pp. 327–9 ; *Adler* v. *Blackman*, [1953] 1 Q. B. 146 ; [1952] 2 All E. R. 945 ; M. & B. p. 376.
[5] *Tickner* v. *Buzzacott*, [1965] Ch. 426; [1965] 1 All E. R. 131. In this case, the original occupier was not a tenant at will but was holding under a lease for an unexpired period of 75 years. See too *Manfield & Sons, Ltd.* v. *Botchin*, [1970] 2 Q. B. 612 ; [1970] 3 All E. R. 143.
[6] Co. Litt. 57*b*.
[7] *Supra*, p. 265.
[8] Co. Litt. 57*b*, and Butler's note to 270*b*.

in occupation after he should have departed. In the view of the common law tenants at sufferance came under no liability to pay rent, since it was the folly of the owners that suffered them to continue in possession after their estate had ended,[1] but the Landlord and Tenant Act 1730[2] enacts that any tenant (or any other person getting possession under or by collusion with him) who shall wilfully hold over after the determination of the term, and after demand made and written notice given for delivery up of possession, shall pay double the yearly value of the lands for the time the premises are detained. A tenant is not deemed to hold over " wilfully " unless he is well aware that he has no right to retain possession.[3]

Similarly, by the Distress for Rent Act 1737, a tenant holding under a periodic tenancy who gives notice to quit and who does not give up possession in accordance with his notice is liable to pay double the rent for the time he remains in possession after the notice expires.[4] Such a person is not a tenant at sufferance, but his tenancy is statutorily prolonged at double rent.

Rights of tenant at sufferance.

On the other hand, a tenant at sufferance, since he is in possession, may maintain trespass against a third party or recover in ejectment against a mere wrongdoer,[5] and if he remains in possession for twelve years without paying rent, he defeats the right of the landlord and of those claiming under the landlord to recover the land.[6]

How tenancy at sufferance becomes a yearly tenancy.

Our present task, however, is to see how a tenancy at sufferance may be converted by implication of law into a tenancy from year to year. In brief this conversion takes place if the landlord waives the tort of the tenant.[7]

A. L. SMITH, L.J., explained this in *Dougal* v. *McCarthy*[8] :

> " If the landlord consents to such holding over by the tenant, and the tenant consents to remain in possession as tenant, then the implication of law is, unless there is evidence to rebut it, that the tenant holds over as tenant from year to year on the terms of the old tenancy so far as they are not inconsistent with a tenancy from year to year."

The best evidence of this consent is the payment and acceptance of rent on a yearly basis. But other indications suffice. Thus in *Dougal* v. *McCarthy*

---

[1] Cruise, *Digest*, Tit. ix., c. ii. s. 5.
[2] S. 1. Distinguish the statutory tenant, *i.e.* one who holds over under the Rent Acts. *Infra*, p. 478.
[3] *French* v. *Elliott*, [1960] 1 W. L. R. 40, [1959] 3 All E. R. 866.
[4] S. 18.
[5] *Asher* v. *Whitlock* (1865), L. R. 1 Q. B. 1 ; M. & B. p. 161.
[6] *Re Jolly*, [1900] 2 Ch. 616.
[7] *Right d. Flower* v. *Darby and Bristow* (1786), 1 Term Rep. 159.
[8] [1893] 1 Q. B. 736, at p. 743 ; *Lowther* v. *Clifford*, [1926] 1 K. B. 185, affd., [1927] 1 K. B. 130.

premises were let at an annual rent of £140 for one year ending February 1st. The tenants remained in possession after February 1st and on February 25th they received a demand from the landlord for £35, being one quarter's rent due in advance. The tenants did not answer this demand, but wrote on March 26th intimating their intention to discontinue the tenancy.

It was held that under the circumstances the parties must be taken to have consented to a tenancy from year to year on the terms of the original lease.

A. L. SMITH, L.J., said :—

" In the present case there is a direct statement by the landlord to the tenants that he consents to their holding over, because on February 25th, three weeks after the expiration of the tenancy, he writes asking for a quarter's rent as on a fresh tenancy. For a whole month the tenants do nothing, but hold over with notice that the landlord is demanding rent from them as tenants on the terms of the agreement which expired on February 1st. Speaking for myself, I should say that the proper inference from that was that the tenants consented to hold over on the terms of the old agreement."

If, however, the contractural tenant who holds over occupies premises that are within the Rent Acts, the landlord has no alternative but to accept the rent, for the tenant becomes a " statutory tenant " and not a tenant holding under a new contractual agreement.[1]

It will have been observed that where a yearly tenancy arises by implication of law there is often some instrument of agreement under which the premises were formerly held, or under which it was intended that they should be held. For instance, there is the old lease when a tenant holds over with the consent of the landlord and, as in *Walsh* v. *Lonsdale*,[2] there is the void lease or the contract for a lease where the formalities for the creation of the strict relationship of landlord and tenant are wanting. The problem that arises in these cases is whether the covenants and the terms of the instruments in question continue to bind the parties after they have changed their former position and the tenant holds from year to year. The general principle is that the yearly tenant holds the land subject to all the terms of the old or the void lease or the contract, as the case may be, where they are not inconsistent with the general nature of a yearly tenancy.

Terms upon which implied tenancy held.

Examples of terms which in this way will be read into an implied yearly tenancy are agreements to pay rent,[3] to keep a house in repair,[4] to keep the premises open as a shop and to promote its trade as far as possible.[5]

---

[1] *Morrison* v. *Jacobs*, [1945] 1 K. B. 577; [1945] 2 All E. R. 430; *infra*, p. 478.

[2] *Supra*, p. 394.   [3] *Lee* v. *Smith* (1854), 9 Exch. 662.

[4] *Cole* v. *Kelly*, [1920] 2 K. B. 106.

[5] *Sanders* v. *Karnell* (1858), 1 F. & F. 356.

On the other hand, covenants by the tenants to build,[1] or to paint every three years,[2] and a covenant by the lessor giving the tenant an option to purchase the freehold at a certain price[3] are incompatible with a yearly tenancy and will not be enforced.

Tenancy by estoppel.

Tenancy by Estoppel.[4] The doctrine of estoppel may be applied to create a tenancy. If a person purports to grant a lease of land in which he has no estate, he is estopped from repudiating the tenancy and the tenant is estopped from denying its existence. There thus arises what is called a *tenancy by estoppel* which, as between the parties estopped, possesses the attributes of a true tenancy.

> " It is true that a title by estoppel is only good against the person estopped and imports from its very existence the idea of no real title at all, yet as against the person estopped it has all the elements of a real title."[5]

Thus, the covenants contained in the lease are enforceable by the lessor against the tenant, and the successors in title to either party are themselves equally estopped.[6] The estoppel operates from the time when the landlord puts the tenant into possession, and ceases after the tenant has given up possession.[7] It applies to all types of tenancy.

Feeding the estoppel.

A tenancy by estoppel, however, may be transformed into an effective tenancy. The rule is that if the lessor later acquires the legal estate in the land, the effect is to " feed the estoppel " and to clothe the tenant also with a legal estate. The lessee then acquires a legal tenancy and ceases to rely on the estoppel. The tenancy commenced by estoppel, but for all purposes it has now become an estate or interest,[8] and it prevails against a later mortgage of the same land however short the interval of time may be between the feeding of the estoppel and the creation of the mortgage. For instance :

> P. agrees to purchase a house from V. and is let into possession before completion. Though at present entitled only to an equitable

---

[1] *Bowes* v. *Croll* (1856), 6 E. & B. 255, 264.

[2] *Pinero* v. *Judson* (1829), 6 Bing. 206.

[3] *Bradbury* v. *Grimble*, [1920] 2 Ch 548.

[4] For a full discussion see Spencer Bower and Turner ; *Estoppel by Representation* (2nd Edn.), pp. 169–88 ; (1964) 80 *L. Q. R.* 370 (A. M. Prichard).

[5] *Bank of England* v. *Cutler*, [1908] 2 K. B. 208, at p. 234, *per* Farwell, L.J.

[6] *Cuthbertson* v. *Irving* (1859), 4 H. & N. 742. If the lessor has any legal estate in the land, though one less in extent than that which he purports to lease, there is no estoppel. The tenant acquires the interest, whatever it may be, that the lessor holds ; *Hill* v. *Saunders* (1825), 4 B. & C. 529. There may be an estoppel if the lessor has an equitable interest. *Universal Permanent Building Society* v. *Cooke*, [1952] Ch. 95, at p. 102.

[7] *Harrison* v. *Wells*, [1967] 1 Q. B. 263 ; [1966] 3 All E. R. 524; (1967), 83 *L. Q. R.* 19 (P. V. B.).

[8] *Webb* v. *Austin* (1844), 7 Man. & G. 701, at p. 724, *per* Tindal, C.J., citing Preston, *Treatise on Abstracts*.

interest, he purports to lease the premises to T., whereupon a tenancy by estoppel arises between these two parties. The conveyance of the legal estate to P. is completed some weeks later and this is followed immediately by a mortgage of the premises to M. who has agreed to advance the purchase money and who pays it direct to V.

In a sense, the conveyance to P. (which feeds the estoppel and gives T. a legal tenancy), and the mortgage to M. constitute one indivisible transaction, but such is not the effect in law of what has been done. There is a *scintilla temporis* between the conveyance and the mortgage, with the result that the legal tenancy acquired by T. precedes and takes priority over M's mortgage.[1] Normally, M. may no doubt determine the tenancy by serving a notice to quit, but he cannot do so if the premises are controlled by the Rent Acts.

SECTION V. RIGHTS AND LIABILITIES OF LANDLORD AND TENANT

SUMMARY

In the majority of cases the rights and the liabilities of a landlord and a tenant are fixed by the express covenants that, having been settled by the parties, are incorporated in the lease or the contract under which the premises are held. But a contract may be silent on several matters of importance, or there may be no agreement at all, and therefore it is necessary to consider, first, what the position of the parties is where there are no express covenants, and then to notice shortly the usual covenants common to all ordinary leases.

---

[1] *Church of England Building Society* v. *Piskor,* [1954] Ch. 553 ; [1954] 2 All E. R. 85 ; M. & B. p. 381, overruling in this respect *Coventry Permanent Economic Building Society* v. *Jones,* [1951] 1 All E. R. 901.

(1) POSITION WHERE THERE ARE NO EXPRESS COVENANTS OR CONDITIONS

(A) IMPLIED OBLIGATIONS OF THE LANDLORD

(i) Quiet Enjoyment

Implied covenant for quiet enjoyment.

A covenant that the lessee shall have quiet enjoyment of the premises is implied in every lease that does not expressly deal with the matter.[1] The meaning of this is that the lessee shall be put into possession and that he shall be entitled to recover damages[2] if his enjoyment is substantially disturbed by the acts, either of the lessor or of somebody claiming under the lessor.[3] " It is a covenant for freedom from disturbance by adverse claimants to the property. "[4]   Instances are, where the lessor, having reserved the right to work minerals under the land, so works them as to cause the land to subside ;[5] or where, in a lease of shooting rights, he erects buildings so as substantially to reduce the area over which the rights are exercisable ;[6] or where, with a view to getting rid of the tenant, he removes the doors and windows of the demised premises,[7] or subjects him to persistent and prolonged intimidation ;[8] or where he erects scaffolding which obstructs access to the premises.[9]   There is no liability under the covenant, however, if the act of disturbance is committed by a person claiming not under the lessor, but under a title paramount to his.[10]

(ii) Fit for Habitation

Implied warranty in the case of a furnished house.

In general, there is no implied undertaking by the landlord that the premises are or will be fit for habitation ; and no covenant is implied that he will do any repairs whatever.   There are, however, four exceptions to this rule.

(a) **Furnished Houses.**   Upon the letting of a furnished house, there is an implied waranty, in the nature of a condition, that the premises shall be reasonably fit for habitation at the date fixed for the commencement of the tenancy.[11]   Thus,

---

[1] *Markham* v. *Paget*, [1908] 1 Ch. 697.   In early days there was no such implication unless the word *demise* had been used in the lease ; *ibid.*

[2] For criminal offences in this connection, see *infra*, p. 483.

[3] *Jones* v. *Lavington*, [1903] 1 K. B. 253 ; *Sanderson* v. *Berwick-upon-Tweed Corpn.* (1884), 13 Q. B. D. 547, at p. 551 ; *Matania* v. *National Provincial Bank Ltd.*, [1936] 2 All E. R. 633.

[4] *Hudson* v. *Cripps*, [1896] 1 Ch. 265, at p. 268 *per* NORTH, J.

[5] *Markham* v. *Paget*, [1908] 1 Ch. 697.

[6] *Peech* v. *Best*, [1931] 1 K. B. 1 (a case, however, of an express covenant).

[7] *Lavender* v. *Betts*, [1942] 2 All E. R. 72.

[8] *Kenny* v. *Preen*, [1963] 1 Q. B. 499; [1962] 3 All E. R. 814.

[9] *Owen* v. *Gadd*, [1956] 2 Q. B. 99; [1956] 2 All E. R. 28, a case of an express covenant, but equally applicable to an implied covenant.

[10] *Jones* v. *Lavington, supra*.

[11] *Collins* v. *Hopkins*, [1923] 2 K. B. 617.

if the house is infested with bugs,[1] if its drainage is defective,[2] or if it has been lately occupied by a person suffering from tuberculosis,[3]

the tenant is entitled to repudiate the tenancy and to recover damages. But provided that the house is fit for habitation at the beginning of the tenancy, the fact that it later becomes uninhabitable imposes no liability upon the landlord.[4]

This implied condition does not extend to unfurnished premises.[5] Nor is a landlord who retains control of the means of access to demised premises in multi-storey blocks, such as lifts and staircases, under an implied duty to keep them in repair.[6]

(b) **Housing Act 1957.** The Housing Act 1957[7] provides for the protection of persons taking houses at a low rental. Where a contract is made on or after July 6th, 1957, for letting for human habitation a house or part of a house at a rent not exceeding £80 a year in Greater London and £52 elsewhere, there shall be implied a condition by the landlord, notwithstanding any stipulation to the contrary, that the house is fit for human habitation at the commencement of the tenancy, and that he will keep it so throughout the tenancy.[8] There is no such implication, however, if the letting is for at least three years upon the terms that the tenant will put the house into a condition reasonably fit for human habitation, and if the lease is not determinable by either party before the expiration of three years.[9]

Whether the statutory condition has been broken is a question of fact and one not always easy to determine, but the Act provides that a house shall be deemed to be unfit for human habitation if and only if it is unreasonably defective in respect of one or more of the following matters—repair, stability, freedom from damp, internal arrangement, natural lighting, ventilation, water supply, drainage and sanitary conveniences, facilities for preparation and cooking of food and for the disposal of waste water.[10]

In the event of a breach of the implied condition, the tenant may repudiate the tenancy and also recover damages,[11] provided

Housing Act 1957.

---

[1] *Smith* v. *Marrable* (1843), 11 M. & W. 5.
[2] *Wilson* v. *Finch-Hatton* (1877), 2 Ex. D. 336.
[3] *Collins* v. *Hopkins, supra.*   [4] *Sarson* v. *Roberts,* [1895] 2 Q. B. 395.
[5] *Hart* v. *Windsor* (1843), 12 M. & W. 68 ; *Robbins* v. *Jones* (1863), 15 C. B. N. S. 221 ; *Cruse* v. *Mount,* [1933] Ch. 278 ; *Bottomley* v *Bannister,* [1932] 1 K. B. 458. ; *Otto* v. *Bolton and Norris,* [1936] 2 K. B. 46 ; [1936] 1 All E. R. 960.
[6] *Liverpool City Council* v. *Irwin,* [1975] 3 W.L.R. 663 ; [1975] 3 All E. R. 658.
[7] See (1962) 26 Conv. (N.S.) 132 (W. A. West) ; (1974) 34 M:L.R. 377 (J. I. Reynolds).
[8] Housing Act 1957, s. 6 (1), (2). In the case of a contract made before July 6, 1957, and after July 31, 1923, the equivalent figures are £40 for London and £26 elsewhere ; *ibid.*   [9] Housing Act, 1957, s. 6 (2) proviso.
[10] S. 4, as amended by Housing Act 1969, s. 71. As to the test of unfitness in the case of disrepair, see *Summers* v. *Salford Corpn.,* [1943], A.C. 283, *per* LORD ATKIN at p. 289 ; [1943] 1 All E. R. 68, at p. 70.
[11] *Walker* v. *Hobbs & Co.* (1889) 23 Q. B. D. 458.

that the landlord had notice of the existence of the defect and failed to remedy it.[1] The landlord's obligation is restricted to cases where the house is capable of being made fit at reasonable expense for human habitation.[2]

(c) **Housing Act 1961.** The statutory obligations of the landlord have been further increased by the Housing Act 1961,[3] if he has let a dwelling-house after October 24, 1961, for a term of less than seven years.[4] In the case of such a lease, he is subjected to an implied covenant—

(*a*) to keep in repair the structure and exterior of the house[5] (including drains, gutters and external pipes) ; and

(*b*) to keep in repair and proper working order[6] the installations in the house—

(i) for the supply of water,[7] gas and electricity, and for sanitation (including basins, sinks, baths and sanitary conveniences), and

(ii) for space heating or heating water.

Moreover, it is enacted that any covenant to repair by the tenant shall be of no effect in so far as it relates to the above matters.[8]

These obligations do not require the landlord to reinstate the premises if they are damaged by fire or by tempest, flood or other inevitable accident; or to effect repairs necessitated by the tenant's failure to use the premises in a tenant-like manner.[9]

The parties cannot contract out of the Act,[10] but with their consent the County Court may exclude or modify the repairing obligations of the landlord if it is considered reasonable to do so.[11]

Local authorities have wide powers under the Housing Acts of requiring the person who has control of a house to make it fit for human habitation,[12] or to carry out repairs where, even though the house is not unfit,

---

[1] *Morgan* v. *Liverpool Corpn.*, [1927] 2 K. B. 131 ; *McCarrick* v. *Liverpool Corpn.*, [1947] A. C. 219 ; [1946] 2 All E. R. 646 ; *O'Brien* v. *Robinson*, [1973] A. C. 912 ; [1973] 1 All E. R. 583.

[2] *Buswell* v. *Goodwin*, [1971] 1 W. L. R. 92, at pp. 96–7 ; [1971] 1 All E. R. 418.

[3] See (1962), 26 *Conv.* (N.S.) 187 (W. A. West).

[4] *Parker* v. *O'Connor*, [1974] 1 W. L. R. 1160 ; [1974] 3 All E. R. 257.

[5] *Brown* v. *Liverpool Corpn.*, [1969] 3 All E. R. 1345 (outside steps and path held to be essential part of access and therefore included) : *cf. Hopwood* v. *Cannock Chase D.C.*, [1975] 1 W. L. R. 373 ; [1975] 1 All E. R. 796.

[6] But not to put in a new efficient system. *Liverpool City Council* v. *Irwin*, [1975] 3 W.L.R. 663, at p. 669 ; [1975] 3 All E. R. 658.

[7] *Sheldon* v. *West Bromwich Corporation* (1973), 25 P. & C. R. 360.

[8] Housing Act, 1961, s. 32 (1). A lease is treated as one for less than seven years if, though made for that period or longer, it is determinable at the lessor's option within seven years ; *ibid.*, s. 33 (2). See *Parker* v. *O'Connor*, [1974] 1 W. L. R. 1160 ; [1974] 3 All E. R. 257. As to what is a " house " within the meaning of the Act, see *Okereke* v. *Brent London Borough Council*, [1967] 1 Q. B. 42 ; [1966] 1 All E. R. 150.

[9] *Ibid.*, s. 32 (2).

[10] *Ibid.*, s. 33 (7).

[11] *Ibid.*, s. 33 (6).

[12] Housing Act 1957, ss. 9–15, 39.

" substantial repairs are required to bring it up to a reasonable standard, having regard to its age, character and locality. "[1]

**A tenant may prefer to invoke action of the local authority rather
than to enforce his rights directly under the covenant.**

(d) **Defective Premises Act 1972.** A landlord's duty
towards his tenant has been increased in two respects by the Defective Premises Act 1972. The Act applies as from January 1st,
1974 to all types of tenancy, and any agreement to contract out of
it is void.[2]

Defective
Premises Act
1972.

(i) Duty to build dwellings properly

Under section 1 any person who takes on work for or in
connection with the provision of a dwelling, whether by the
erection, conversion or enlargement of a building, is under a duty
to see that the work is done in a workmanlike or professional
manner, with proper materials and so that as regards that work the
dwelling will be fit for habitation when completed. Landlords
most likely to be affected by this wide provision are local authorities or housing associations, or, in the private sector, those who
themselves carry out any work in converting a house.[3] The
tenant may recover damages for any damage or injury that arises
within six years of the dwelling being completed.[4] The remedy
lies not only against the landlord, if he has the duty, but also
against third parties, including the builder and architect.[5]

(ii) Duty of care for safety

Under section 4 of the Act,[6] a landlord owes to all persons,
who might reasonably be expected to be affected by defects in the
state of the premises, a duty to take reasonable care to see that
they are reasonably safe from personal injury or from damage to
their property. Such a duty arises when the landlord is under an
obligation to the tenant for the maintenance or repair of the premises, or when he has an express or implied right to enter the
premises to maintain and repair them. This duty, however, is
owed only if the landlord knows or ought to have known of the
defect, and if the defect arises from his failure to carry out his
obligation or right to maintain or repair.

(iii) No Derogation from Grant[7]

The only other covenant to which a landlord becomes implicitly subject is one that he shall not derogate from his grant.

Implied
covenant
not to
derogate
from grant.

---

[1] Housing Act 1969, s. 72.   [2] S. 6.
[3] Evans, *Law of Landlord and Tenant*, p. 179.   [4] S. 1 (5).
[5] See also Health and Safety at Work etc. Act 1974, s. 71.
[6] Replacing Occupiers' Liability Act 1957, s. 4.
[7] For a comprehensive discussion, see (1964), 80 *L. Q. R.* 244 (D. W.
Elliott) ; criticized in part, 81 *L. Q. R.* 28 (M. A. Peel) ; *Molton Builders, Ltd.*
v. *Westminster City Council* (1974), 234 Estates Gazette 115 ; *affd.* (1975) 30
P. & C. R. 182.

He must not frustrate the use of the land for the purposes for which it was let ;[1]   or, as BOWEN, L.J., put it, " a grantor having given a thing with one hand is not to take away the means of enjoying it with the other. "[2]   WOOD, V.-C., in one case said:—

> " If a landowner conveys one of two closes to another, he cannot afterwards do anything to derogate from his grant ; and if the conveyance is made for the express purpose of having buildings erected upon the land so granted, a contract is implied on the part of the grantor to do nothing to prevent the land from being used for the purpose for which to the knowledge of the grantor the conveyance is made.[3]

This general principle of law becomes particularly applicable when the lessor makes an inconsiderate use of land adjacent to the tenant's holding. Thus where lands were leased to a tenant for the purpose of carrying on the business of a timber merchant, and the landlord proceeded to erect buildings on adjoining land in such a way as to interrupt the free flow of air to the tenant's drying sheds, it was held that damages were recoverable against the landlord's assigns for breach of the implied covenant.[4] Again, where a flat is leased in a building, the whole of which is clearly intended to be used solely by residential tenants, the landlord commits a breach of the covenant if he subsequently lets the greater part of the premises for business purposes.[5]

(B) IMPLIED OBLIGATIONS AND RIGHTS OF THE TENANT

(i) Obligations

Obligation not to commit waste. A tenant, including one from year to year,[6] is subject to an implied obligation to keep and to deliver up the premises in a tenant-like manner and to keep the fences in a state of repair.[7]

Liability
for waste.

Further, tenants are subject to the doctrine of waste,[8] though in varying degrees.

---

[1] *Browne* v. *Flower*, [1911] 1 Ch. 219, at pp. 225–7, where illustrations are given by PARKER, J.
[2] *Birmingham, Dudley and District Banking Co.* v. *Ross* (1888), 38 Ch. D. 295, 313.
[3] *North Eastern Rly. Co.* v. *Elliot* (1860), 1 J. & H. 145, 153.
[4] *Aldin* v. *Latimer Clark Muirhead & Co.*, [1894] 2 Ch. 437 ; *Harmer* v. *Jumbil (Nigeria) Tin Areas Ltd.*, [1921] 1 Ch. 200. The principle is also applicable if the tenant is prevented from entering the lessor's land in order to execute essential repairs to the demised premises ; *Ward* v. *Kirkland*, [1967] Ch. 194, at pp. 226–227 ; [1966] 1 All E. R. 609, at p. 617.
[5] *Newman* v. *Real Estate Debenture Corpn. Ltd.* [1940] 1 All E. R. 131 ; distinguished in *Kelly* v. *Battershell*, [1949] 2 All E. R. 830.
[6] *Marsden* v. *Edward Heyes, Ltd.*, [1927] 1 K. B. 1.
[7] *Cheetham* v. *Hampson* (1791), 4 Term Rep. 318 ; *Goodman* v. *Rollinson* (1951), 95 Sol. Jo. 188. For the tenant of an agricultural holding, see *Wedd* v. *Porter*, [1916] 2 K. B. 91.
[8] *Supra*, pp. 267–71.

A tenant for a fixed number of years is liable for voluntary and also for permissive waste,[1] though perhaps a doubt still lingers with regard to the latter question.[2]

A tenant from *year to year* is liable for voluntary waste, but otherwise his only obligation, it would seem, is to use the premises in a "tenant-like" manner.[3] This expression is obscure if not unintelligible, and all that it means apparently is that the tenant must do such work as is necessary for his own reasonable enjoyment of the premises.[4] There is some authority for the view that he must keep the premises wind and water tight in the sense that, although he is not bound to do anything of a substantial nature, he must carry out such repairs as are necessary to prevent the property from lapsing into a state of decay.[5] The existence of this obligation, however, has been doubted by the Court of Appeal.[6]

A tenant *at will* is not liable for either kind of waste, though the effect of the commission by him of any act of voluntary waste is to terminate his tenancy and to render him liable to an action of trespass.[7] A tenant *at sufferance* is liable for voluntary waste, but probably not for permissive waste.[8]

(ii) Rights

(a) **Estovers.** A tenant for years, notwithstanding the doctrine of waste, is entitled to take estovers from the land, that is to say, wood, even though it be timber,[9] for the purpose of carrying out certain repairs. Estovers fall into three classes, namely : 1. house-bote (wood to be used either as fuel or for building purposes) ; 2. plough-bote (wood for making and repairing agricultural implements) ; and 3. hay-bote (wood for repairing hedges).[10]

This right is limited by immediate necessity : a tenant cannot cut and store wood with a view to future requirements.

(b) **Emblements.** A tenant for years is entitled at common law to emblements.[11] It is obvious that a tenant for a fixed term of

---

[1] *Yellowly* v. *Gower* (1855), 11 Exch. 274.

[2] See cases collected in Hill and Redman, *Law of Landlord and Tenant* (16th Edn.), p. 212.

[3] *Warren* v. *Keen*, [1954] 1 Q. B. 15 ; [1953] 2 All E. R. 1118.

[4] See the illustrations given by DENNING, L. J., in *Warren* v. *Keen, supra,* at p. 20. The expression is an extension to tenants generally of the rule that the agricultural tenant must farm the land in a " husbandlike " manner. In this context, " husbandlike " has a definite meaning. The tenant must observe the custom of the country, *i.e.* the local usages of husbandry.

[5] *Ferguson* v. ———— (1797), 2 Esp. 590 ; *Wedd* v. *Porter, supra,* at p. 100.

[6] *Warren* v. *Keen, supra.*

[7] *Countess of Shrewsbury's Case* (1600), 5 Co. Rep. 13*b*.

[8] *Burchell* v. *Hornsby* (1808), 1 Comp. 360.

[9] For the definition of " timber ", see *supra*, pp. 269–70.

[10] Co. Litt. 41*b*.; *cf. infra*, p. 564.   [11] See *supra*, pp. 266–7.

years cannot be entitled to this right, because he knows when his tenancy will end, and it is his own fault if he sows crops which will not come to maturity until after that date. But there may be cases where a tenancy comes to an end unexpectedly, as for instance upon the sudden determination of a tenancy at will or upon the determination of the estate out of which the term has been created, in which the common law right to emblements exists. The right is obviously inconvenient to both parties, and in one type of case, *i.e.* where the lessor's estate ended prematurely, it was modified by the Landlord and Tenant Act 1851. This provided that a tenant for years at a rack rent (*i.e.* a rent which represents the full annual value of the land),[1] whose lease expired owing to the failure of his lessor's estate, should in lieu of emblements be entitled to remain in occupation until the end of the current year of tenancy.

Agricultural Holdings Act 1948.
This Act has, however, in the case of agricultural tenancies been replaced by the Agricultural Holdings Act 1948,[2] which provides that a tenant at a rack rent, whose term ceases by the death, or the cesser of the estate, of a landlord entitled only for life or for any other uncertain interest, shall continue to hold and occupy the holding until the occupation is determined by a twelvemonth's notice to quit, expiring at the end of a year of the tenancy.

(c) **Right to remove Certain Fixtures.** The extent of this right of removal has already been discussed.[3]

(2) POSITION WHERE THERE ARE EXPRESS COVENANTS AND CONDITIONS

Nature of covenants generally entered into.
In the majority of cases the rights and the liabilities of a lessor and a lessee are regulated by express covenants inserted in the lease, but, as the number of matters that may be the subject of agreement is infinite, and as the agreed terms will naturally vary widely in different cases, it is obvious that in a treatise of this limited scope we cannot do more than notice shortly the more important covenants that find a place in a normal lease.

Generally speaking, and where no exceptional circumstances exist, a lessee will enter into covenants with regard to the payment of rent, rates and taxes, and the maintenance, repair and insurance of the premises; while the lessor will undertake to keep the lessee in quiet enjoyment, and may perhaps take upon himself part of the burden of repairs. The following covenants require special mention :—

---

[1] *Re Sawyer and Withall*, [1919] 2 Ch. 333.
[2] S. 4 (1).
[3] *Supra*, pp. 138–43.

(A) COVENANT BY TENANT TO PAY RENT

The rent payable by a tenant for years is properly called a rent-service,[1] and though it generally consists of the payment of money, it may equally well take the form of the delivery of personal chattels,[2] as corn, or the performance of personal services.[3] The rent must be certain, but this does not mean that it must be certain at the date of the lease. Rent is sufficiently certain if it can be calculated with certainty at the time when payment comes to be made. Thus a condition in a council tenant's rent book, providing that the rent was " liable to be increased or decreased on notice being given " was held to be valid.[4] The covenant should state precisely the dates at which rent is payable, but if no mention is made of the matter, payment is due at the end of each period by reference to which the rent has been assessed. Thus in the case of a yearly rent nothing need be paid until the end of each year of the term.[5] If a day for payment is fixed, it becomes due on the first moment of that day and is held to be in arrear if it is not paid by midnight.[6]

The liability to pay rent is unaffected by the subsequent occurrence of some unforeseen event which operates to the detriment of the tenant. This is consonant to the general principle that if a man deliberately assumes an absolute obligation, he cannot escape liability by proof that subsequent events have made performance a matter of hardship, for he might have expressly guarded against what has happened.[7] Thus a tenant must continue to pay his rent notwithstanding that the premises are utterly destroyed by fire,[8] or by a hostile bomb,[9] or are requisitioned by the Crown acting under statutory powers or under the prerogative,[10] even though the Crown itself is the lessor.[11]

Rent-service.

Payment of rent not excused by subsequent events.

---

[1] *Infra*, p. 418.   [2] Co. Litt. 142a.
[3] *Duke of Marlborough* v. *Osborn* (1864), 5 B. & S. 67.
[4] *Greater London Council* v. *Connolly*, [1970] 2 Q. B. 100 ; [1970] 1 All E. R. 870. Hill and Redman, *Law of Landlord and Tenant* (16th Edn.), p. 311 ; Woodfall, *Landlord and Tenant* (27th Edn.), vol. 1. p. 302. See also in connexion with options to renew and rent revision at the time of renewal *Smith* v. *Morgan*, [1971] 1 W. L. R. 803 ; [1971] 2 All E. R. 1500 ; *Brown* v. *Gould*, [1972] Ch. 53 ; [1971] 2 All E. R. 1505 ; M. & B. p. 366 ; *Bushwall Properties Ltd.* v. *Vortex Properties Ltd.*, [1975] 1 W.L.R. 1649 ; *cf. King's Motors (Oxford) Ltd.*, v. *Lax* [1970] 1 W. L. R. 426 ; [1969] 3 All E. R. 665. See also *Talbot* v. *Talbot*, [1968] Ch. 1 ; [1967] 2 All E. R. 920.
[5] *Coomber* v. *Howard* (1845), 1 C. B. 440; *Collett* v. *Curling* (1847), 10 Q. B. 785.
[6] *Dibble* v. *Bowater* (1853), 2 E. & B. 564.
[7] *Jacobs, Marais & Co.* v. *Crédit Lyonnais* (1884), 12 Q. B. D. 589, at p. 603 ; *Atkinson* v. *Ritchie* (1809), 10 East 530, at p. 533.
[8] *Matthey* v. *Curling*, [1922] 2 A. C. 180.
[9] See *Redmond* v. *Dainton*, [1920] 2 K. B. 256 ; *Denman* v. *Brise*, [1949] 1 K. B. 22 ; [1948] 2 All E. R. 141.
[10] *Whitehall Court* v. *Ettlinger*, [1920] 1 K. B. 680. But see the Landlord and Tenant (Requisitioned Land) Act 1942, which allows a tenant to disclaim a lease if the land is requisitioned by the Crown.
[11] *Crown Land Commissioners* v. *Page*, [1960] 3 Q. B. 274 ; [1960] 2 All E. R. 726.

Doctrine of
frustration
inapplicable.

The present rule, though doubts have been cast upon its soundness by high authority,[1] is that in such cases a tenant cannot rely upon the contractual doctrine of frustration, under which a contract is discharged if the common venture of the parties is frustrated by the occurrence of some unexpected event that strikes at the root of the agreement.[2]   When the doctrine applies, the contractual rights and obligations cease automatically upon the occurrence of the frustrating event.   But a lease creates more than a contract.   It creates an estate.   Indeed, it is the transfer of this estate to the tenant that represents the common venture of the parties.   Whatever may be the effect of extraneous circumstances upon the contractual side of the lease, the estate remains vested in the tenant and the land remains available to him. Therefore, the rule is that the estate does not cease merely because it has become burdensome or even because the performance of one or more of the contractual obligations has become impossible.

> If, for example, the tenant is entitled and bound to erect houses on the demised land, which it is his design to sub-let at profitable rents, and then before he begins the work all building operations are forbidden by the Secretary of State for the Environment, the rule is that the impossibility of performing this particular term of the contract does not cause the cessation of the estate to which it is incident.[3]

The landlord's remedies for the recovery of rent will be considered later[4].

(B) COVENANT TO REPAIR[5]

Various expressions are used by practitioners to describe the extent of the obligation imposed by a covenant to repair the premises.   The following are typical examples :—

" good tenantable repair " ;

" good and tenantable order and repair " ;

---

[1] Viscount SIMON and Lord WRIGHT in *Cricklewood Property and Investment Trust, Ltd.* v. *Leighton's Investment Trust, Ltd.*, [1945] A. C. 221 ; [1945] 1 All E. R. 252.

[2] *London and Northern Estates Co.* v. *Schlesinger*, [1916] 1 K. B. 20 ; *Whitehall Court, Ltd.* v. *Ettlinger*, [1920] 1 K. B. 680 ; *Matthey* v. *Curling*, [1922] 2 A. C. 180 ; *Swift* v. *Macbean*, [1942] 1 K. B. 375; [1942] 1 All E. R. 126; *Denman* v. *Brise*, [1949] 1 K. B. 22; [1948] 1 All E. R. 141 ; *Cricklewood Property and Investment Trust, Ltd.* v. *Leighton's Investment Trust, Ltd.*, *supra*, *per* Lord RUSSELL of KILLOWEN and Lord GODDARD.

[3] See the opinions of Lord RUSSELL of KILLOWEN and Lord GODDARD in the *Cricklewood Case, supra ;* and the decision of the Court of Appeal in *Denman* v. *Brise*, [1949] 1 K. B. 22.   See Cheshire and Fifoot, *The Law of Contract* (8th Edn.), pp. 550–551.

[4] *Infra*, pp. 428 *et seq.*

[5] Whether the matter has been dealt with by covenant or not, the lessor is under a statutory obligation to repair a dwelling-house that has been let for less than seven years ; *supra*, p. 408.

" well and substantially repair " ;
" perfect repair."

By the use of appropriate language, the parties can, of course, settle the standard of repair as high or as low as they choose, but it is generally admitted that such epithets as " good," " perfect " or " substantial " do not increase the burden connoted by the simple word " repair."[1] By way of caution, it should be noticed that, if the premises are in a state of disrepair at the beginning of the lease, a covenant by the tenant to " keep " them in repair obliges him to put them in the required state at his own expense.[2]

Covenant to repair.

The extent of the obligation assumed by a covenantor who has agreed to repair the premises is this :—

Extent of obligation.

> After making due allowance for the locality, character and age of the premises at the time of the lease, he must keep them in the condition in which they would be kept by a reasonably minded owner.[3]

The locality is a material consideration, for the state of repair suitable for a house, say, in Grosvenor Square, differs from that which is appropriate to a house in Spitalfields.

Locality is material.

The character of the premises is also material. Thus the standard of repairs will vary according as the premises are the mansion house or a labourer's cottage on the estate. The essential fact to notice, however, is that it is the character of the premises at the beginning, not at the end, of the lease that is material in this context.

Character of premises is material.

> Thus in one case a new house, situated in what was then a fashionable part of London was let in 1825 to a good class of tenant on a 95 year lease. In course of time the character of the neighbourhood deteriorated to such an extent that the only persons willing to occupy the house expected nothing more than that the rain should be kept out.

The covenantor, therefore, argued that the standard of repair required of him was to be measured by the needs and expectations of prospective tenants in 1920. The argument failed. The obligation of a covenantor is neither increased nor diminished in extent by a change in the character of the neighbourhood.[4]

The age of a house is also material, though only in the sense that the covenantor's obligation is not to bring it up to date, but to keep it in a reasonably good condition for a building of that age.

Age of premises is material.

---

[1] *Anstruther-Gough-Calthorpe* v. *McOscar*, [1924] 1 K. B. 716 ; at pp. 722–723, 729 ; but see pp. 731–2.

[2] *Payne* v. *Haine* (1847), 16 M. & W. 541.

[3] *Proudfoot* v. *Hart* (1890), 25 Q. B. D. 42 ; *Lurcott* v. *Wakely and Wheeler* [1911] 1 K. B. 905 ; *Anstruther-Gough-Calthorpe* v. *McOscar*, [1924] 1 K. B. 716 ; *Lloyd's Bank Ltd.* v. *Lake*, [1961] 1 W. L. R. 884 ; [1961] 2 All E. R. 30.

[4] *Anstruther-Gough-Calthorpe* v. *McOscar*, *supra.*

He cannot escape liability by the allegation that to keep so old a building in the covenanted condition requires renewal, not mere repairs. Repair always involves renewal. The covenant must be fulfilled, even though this necessitates the replacement of part after part until the whole is renewed.[1] The correct antithesis is between renewal and reconstruction. The former is required, the latter not. Whether the work necessary for the maintenance of a building is renewal or reconstruction is a question of degree, the test being whether the replacement affects a subordinate part or substantially the whole of the building.[2]

> Thus the tenant of a house is not bound to replace defective foundations by foundations of an entirely different character;[3] but he must demolish and replace a dangerous wall if it is but a subsidiary part of the whole building.[4]

Exception of fair wear and tear. It is usual to qualify the covenant to repair by a clause to the effect that the covenantor shall not be liable for " fair wear and tear," or, what signifies the same thing, for " reasonable wear and tear." The effect of these words is to exempt the covenantor from liability for damage that is due to the ordinary operation of natural causes, always presuming that he has used the premises in a reasonable manner.[5] As TINDAL, C.J., put it in a case where a tenant had invoked such a clause :

> " What the natural operation of time flowing on effects, and all that the elements bring about in diminishing value, constitute a loss which, so far as it results from time and nature, falls upon the landlord."[6]

But where the defect, though initially due to natural causes, will obviously cause further and lasting damage unless rectified, the clause will not continue to avail a covenantor who stands idly by and allows the ravages of time and nature to take their course. TALBOT, J., made this clear in a passage later adopted by the House of Lords.

> " The tenant," he said, " is bound to do such repairs as may be required to prevent the consequences flowing originally from wear and tear from producing others which wear and tear would not directly produce. For example, if a tile falls off the roof, the tenant is not liable for the immediate consequences ; but, if he does

---

[1] *Lurcott* v. *Wakely and Wheeler*, [1911] 1 K. B. 905, at pp. 916-17, *per* FLETCHER-MOULTON, L.J.

[2] *Ibid. Sotheby* v. *Grundy*, [1947] 2 All E. R. 761.

[3] *Lister* v. *Lane and Nesham*, [1893] 2 Q. B. 212 ; *Sotheby* v. *Grundy*, *supra* ; *Pembery* v. *Lamdin*, [1940] 2 All E. R. 434 (landlord's covenant) ; *Brew Brothers* v. *Snax (Ross), Ltd.*, [1970] 1 Q. B. 612 ; [1970] 1 All E. R. 587, (tenant's covenant).

[4] *Lurcott* v. *Wakely and Wheeler*, [1911] 1 K. B. 905.

[5] *Haskell* v. *Marlow*, [1928] 2 K. B. 45, 59.

[6] *Gutteridge* v. *Munyard* (1834), 1 Mood. & R. 334, at p. 336. The words quoted do not appear in the report 7 C. & P. 129.

nothing and in the result more and more water gets in, the roof and walls decay and ultimately the top floor, or the whole house, becomes uninhabitable, he cannot say that it is due to reasonable wear and tear. . . . On the other hand, take the gradual wearing away of a stone floor or staircase by ordinary use. This may in time produce a considerable defect in condition, but the whole defect is caused by reasonable wear and tear, and the tenant is not liable in respect of it." [1]

A covenant against the making of improvements without consent is statutorily subject to a proviso that consent shall not unreasonably be withheld, though the landlord is entitled to demand the payment of a reasonable sum for any damage or loss of value that may be caused to the premises or to neighbouring premises belonging to him. [2] The word " improvements " refers to improvements from the point of view of the tenant, and the statute applies even though what he proposes to do, *e.g.* the demolition of part of the main structure of a building, will temporarily diminish the value of the premises. [3] In such a case no injury is, in theory, suffered by the landlord, since he is permitted by the statute to demand an undertaking from the tenant that the premises will be reinstated.

Covenant not to make improvements without consent.

As in the case of a covenant to pay rent, [4] a covenant to repair imposes an absolute obligation for the non-performance of which the covenantor remains liable, notwithstanding that owing to some extraneous cause beyond his control, such as the refusal of the authorities to grant him a building licence [5] or the requisitioning of the premises, [6] he is unable to execute the necessary work.

Covenant to repair imposes absolute obligation.

Apart from forfeiture, [7] the usual remedy for breach of a covenant to repair is damages. Injunction and specific performance are inappropriate where the covenant is broken by the tenant, [8] because damages are an adequate remedy for the landlord. On the other hand, where it is the landlord who breaks the covenant, damages may be inadequate for the tenant; and, in the case of dwellings, the Housing Act 1974 gives the court discretion to

Remedies for breach of covenant to repair.

---

[1] *Haskell* v. *Marlow, supra*, at p. 59. This decision was overruled by the Court of Appeal in *Taylor* v. *Webb*, [1937] 2 K. B. 283 ; [1937] 1 All E. R. 590, but the principles laid down in this second case, after being stigmatized by a later Court of Appeal as inconsistent with earlier authorities, *Brown* v. *Davies*, [1958] 1 Q. B. 117 ; [1957] 3 All E. R. 401, were finally overruled by the House of Lords in *Regis Property Co. Ltd.* v. *Dudley*, [1959] A. C. 370 ; [1958] 3 All E. R. 491, and the authority of *Haskell* v. *Marlow* restored.

[2] Landlord and Tenant Act 1927, s. 19 (2). The tenant may apply to the High Court or the County Court for a declaration that the landlord has unreasonably withheld his consent ; Landlord and Tenant Act 1954, s. 53 (1) (*b*).

[3] *Lambert* v. *Woolworth & Co.*, [1938] Ch. 883 ; [1938] 2 All E. R 664.

[4] *Supra*, pp. 413–4.

[5] *Eyre* v. *Johnson*, [1946] K. B. 481 ; [1946] 1 All E. R. 719.

[6] *Smiley* v. *Townshend* [1950] 2 K. B. 311 ; [1950] 1 All E. R. 530. But the Landlord and Tenant (Requisitioned Land) Act 1944 relieves the tenant of liability for damages to the land during the period of requisition.

[7] *Infra*, pp. 435, 441.

[8] *Hill* v. *Barclay* (1810), 16 Ves. 402.

order specific performance of the covenant whether or not the breach relates to part of the premises let to the tenant.[1]

The measure of damages *at common law* for breach of a contract to repair varies according as the breach occurs during the tenancy or at the end of the tenancy. In the first case the measure is the amount by which the value of the reversion has diminished; but in the second case, where the premises are delivered up in disrepair, it is the amount that it will cost to carry out the repairs required by the covenant.[2] If, for instance, a tenant converts into flats a house which he has covenanted to keep suitable for single occupation, the first rule applies and the measure of damages is not necessarily the full cost of reinstatement, but the sum that represents the loss which the lessor has sustained.[3] It was found that the second rule might inflict unnecessary hardship upon an outgoing tenant, since it enabled a landlord to recover substantial damages even though the performance of the covenant would have been entirely useless, as, for instance, where the premises were to be demolished, or where the want of repair would not diminish by one penny the rent obtainable on a re-letting. It is, therefore, provided by the Landlord and Tenant Act 1927[4] that **whether the breach is of a covenant to repair during the currency of a lease or to leave premises in repair at the termination of a lease,**

> the damages shall in no case exceed the amount (if any) by which the value of the reversion (whether immediate or not) in the premises is diminished.

The diminution in the value of the reversion is the amount that it will cost within the terms of the covenant to make the house reasonably fit for the class of tenant likely to take it. The fact that the landlord has been able to relet it, though spending less than that amount on repairs, is an irrelevant consideration.[5] In other words the primary test of the measure of damages still seems to be the cost of doing the covenanted repairs. There are many cases where the sale of the property unrepaired will fetch as high a price as its sale in a state of good repair, so that in one sense the value of the reversion as a whole is undiminished, as, for example, where the tenancy relates only to a few rooms in a large building and they cannot be made fit for occupation unless the covenanted repairs are done. In such a case it is now

---

[1] Ss. 125, 129 (1). *Jeune* v. *Queens Cross Properties, Ltd.,* [1974] Ch. 97 ; [1973] 3 All E. R. 97 (specific performance granted before the Act). See (1975) 119 Sol. Jo. 362 (H. E. Markson).
[2] *Joyner* v. *Weeks,* [1891] 2 Q. B. 31.
[3] *Westminster (Duke)* v. *Swinton,* [1948] 1 K. B. 524 ; [1948] 1 All E. R. 428. See also *James* v. *Hutton and J. Cook & Sons, Ltd.,* [1950] 1 K. B. 9 ; [1949] 2 All E. R. 243.
[4] S. 18 (1) ; *Haviland* v. *Long,* [1952] 2 Q. B. 80 ; [1952] 1 All E. R. 463.
[5] *Jaquin* v. *Holland,* [1960] 1 W. L. R. 258 ; [1960] 1 All E. R. 402 ; *Hanson* v. *Newman,* [1934] 1 Ch. 298.

recognized that the cost of the necessary repairs *prima facie* represents the diminution in value of the reversion.[1]

In one particular case the landlord is denied any right to damages. The Act provides that no damages shall be recoverable for breach of the covenant

No damages recoverable if premises to be demolished.

> " if it is shown that the premises, in whatever state of repair they might be, would at or shortly after the termination of the tenancy have been or be pulled down, or such structural alterations made therein as would render valueless the repairs covered by the covenant or agreement."[2]

Thus the Act requires the tenant to prove that the landlord had decided to demolish the premises and that this decision still held at the end of the lease. If this be shown, it is immaterial that the decision is later changed and the premises not demolished.[3] Damages are irrecoverable.[4] The onus, therefore, that lies upon the tenant is to show that the demolition or structural alteration of the premises was firmly intended, not merely contemplated, by the landlord and also that the achievement of the plan was reasonably possible.[5] Damages will, however, be recoverable, if the premises are demolished as a result of the tenant's breach of his covenant to repair.[6]

(C) COVENANT BY TENANT TO INSURE AGAINST FIRE

By the Fires Prevention (Metropolis) Act 1774[7] no action may be brought against any person in whose house a fire shall *accidentally* begin, though it is expressly enacted that this provision shall not defeat an agreement made between landlord and tenant. The result is that, when the property has been burnt, a landlord can maintain an action against his tenant in two cases :—

Covenant to insure.

> first, where the tenant has covenanted to repair, for his contractual liability is not excluded by the happening of an inevitable accident against which he might have expressly protected himself[8] ; and
>
> secondly, where the fire has begun or been allowed to spread by reason of the negligence of the tenant or of those for whom he is responsible.[9]

---

[1] *Jones* v. *Herxheimer*, [1950] 2 K. B. 106 ; [1950] 1 All E. R. 323 ; *Smiley* v. *Townshend*, [1950] 2 K. B. 311, at pp. 322–3 ; [1950] 1 All E. R. 530, at p. 534.

[2] Landlord and Tenant Act 1927, s. 18 (1).

[3] *Keats* v. *Graham*, [1960] 1 W. L. R. 30 ; [1959] 3 All E. R. 919.

[4] *Salisbury* v. *Gilmore*, [1942] 2 K. B. 38 ; [1942] 1 All E. R. 457.

[5] *Cunliffe* v. *Goodman*, [1950] 2 K. B. 237 ; [1950] 1 All E. R. 720.

[6] *Hibernian Property Co. Ltd.* v. *Liverpool Corpn.*, [1973] 1 W. L. R. 751 ; [1973] 2 All E. R. 1117.

[7] S. 86. The Act applies to the whole of England. As to its interpretation, see *Goldman* v. *Hargrave*, [1967] 1 A.C. 645 ; [1966] 2 All E. R. 989 ; *Mason* v. *Levy Auto Parts of England, Ltd.*, [1967] 2 Q. B. 530 ; [1967] 2 All E. R. 62.

[8] *Redmond* v. *Dainton*, [1920] 2 K. B. 256.

[9] *Musgrove* v. *Pandelis*, [1919] 2 K. B. 43.

But, in addition, it is usual for a tenant to covenant that he will insure the demised buildings to their full value and will keep them insured during the term. It has been held in such a case that the omission to keep the premises insured for any period, no matter how short, and even though no fire breaks out during the period, constitutes a breach of the covenant.[1]

If the landlord himself takes out a policy without having agreed to do so, he is not liable to expend the insurance money on the reinstatement of the premises in the event of their destruction, unless the cost of the premiums is reflected in the rent.[2]

(D) COVENANT BY TENANT NOT TO ASSIGN OR UNDERLET

Covenant not to assign.

Unless there is a special agreement to the contrary, a tenant is free to grant his interest to a third party either by assignment or by underlease,[3] but as it is undesirable from the landlord's point of view that the premises should fall into the hands of an irresponsible person, it is usual to provide for the matter by express covenant.

What is a breach of the covenant?

The courts, however, have always construed this covenant with great strictness and have insisted that the restraint imposed upon the tenant shall not go beyond the letter of the express agreement.[4] Thus, a covenant *not to assign or underlet* is not broken by an equitable mortgage accompanied by deposit of the deeds,[5] nor by a deed of arrangement whereby the tenant constitutes himself trustee for his creditors,[6] nor by permitting another person to have the use of the premises without giving him legal possession,[7] nor in general by any transfer which is involuntary, as, for instance, one which results from the bankruptcy of the tenant.[8] A provision that "this lease shall be non-assignable" does not embrace a sub-lease of the premises.[9] An agreement *not to sublet* is not broken by a sub-lease of part of the premises.[10] A covenant *not to part with the possession of the premises or any part thereof* is not broken by the grant of a licence to place an advertisement hoarding on the wall of the demised premises, since

---

[1] *Penniall* v. *Harborne* (1848), 11 Q. B. 368.
[2] *Mumford Hotels, Ltd.* v. *Wheler*, [1964] Ch. 117; [1963] 3 All E. R. 250. Cf. *Re King*, [1963] Ch. 459 ; [1963] 1 All E. R. 781.
[3] *Keeves* v. *Dean*, [1924] 1 K. B. 685, 691.
[4] *Church* v. *Brown* (1808), 15 Ves. 258, at p. 265, *per* Lord ELDON ; *Grove* v. *Portal*, [1902] 1 Ch. 727, 731.
[5] *Doe d. Pitt* v. *Hogg* (1824), 4 Dow. & Ry. 226.
[6] *Gentle* v. *Faulkner*, [1900] 2 Q. B. 267.
[7] *Chaplin* v. *Smith*, [1926] 2 K. B. 198.
[8] *Re Riggs, Ex p. Lovell*, [1901] 2 K. B. 16. As to whether a bequest of a leasehold interest breaks a covenant not to assign, see (1963), 27 *Conv.* (N. S.), 159 (D. G. Barnsley).
[9] *Sweet and Maxwell, Ltd.* v. *Universal News Services, Ltd.*, [1964] 2 Q. B. 699; [1964] 3 All E. R. 30.
[10] *Cook* v. *Shoesmith*, [1951] 1 K. B. 752.

the tenant is not thereby deprived of legal possession.[1] It would seem that the letting of lodgings is no breach of a covenant *not to underlease the premises.*[2]

The result of a tenant's breach depends upon the nature of the covenant by which he has bound himself. A covenant is either absolute or qualified. *[margin: Two classes of covenant.]*

An absolute covenant is one which imposes an unconditional prohibition upon the tenant, there being no provision for its relaxation at the will of the lessor. In this case any assignment contrary to the terms of the covenant renders the tenant liable, notwithstanding that it is in no way prejudicial to the lessor's interest. *[margin: Absolute covenant.]*

A qualified covenant, which is far more common in practice, is one which merely prohibits an assignment *without the consent of the lessor.* It has long been usual to qualify this type of covenant even further by a provision that the lessor's *consent shall not be unreasonably withheld,* and the Landlord and Tenant Act 1927 makes this qualification inevitable by providing that :— *[margin: Qualified covenant.]*

> A covenant against " assigning, underletting, charging or parting with the possession of demised premises without licence or consent," shall, despite any contrary agreement, be subject to a proviso that " such licence or consent is not to be unreasonably withheld." [3]

Thus, the Act requires that the grounds for the refusal of consent shall in fact be reasonable, and therefore its operation cannot be curtailed by a provision in the lease that certain specified grounds shall not be deemed unreasonable.[4] But, if the lease contains a covenant that, before the tenant assigns or underlets, he must first offer to surrender his lease to the landlord, the landlord may demand surrender and so obtain the value of a premium obtainable on an assignment.[5]

It is enacted by the Law of Property Act 1925 that the lessor may

---

[1] *Stening v. Abrahams,* [1931] 1 Ch. 470 ; *Lam Kee Ying Sdn. Bhd. v. Lam Shes Tong* [1975] A. C. 247 ; [1974] 3 All E. R. 137.

[2] *Doe d. Pitt v. Laming* (1814), 4 Camp. 73, at p. 77 ; *Greenslade v. Tapscott* (1834), 1 Cr. M. & R. 55, doubting the last case; *Victoria Dwellings Association, Ltd. v. Roberts,* [1947], L. J. N. C. C. C. R. 177 ; *Phillips v. Woolf,* [1953] C. L. Y. 1966 ; *Re Smith's Lease,* [1951] 1 All E. R. 346.

[3] S. 19 (1) (*a*) ; this section does not apply to an absolute covenant ; *per* ROMER, L.J., in *F. W. Woolworth & Co. Ltd., v. Lambert,* [1937] Ch. 37, at pp. 58, 59 ; but see DANCKWERTS, L.J., in *Property and Bloodstock, Ltd. v. Emerton,* [1968] Ch. 94, at p. 120. Nor does it apply to the lease of an agricultural holding s. 19 (4).

[4] *Re Smith's Lease,* [1951] 1 All E. R. 346.

[5] *Adler v. Upper Grosvenor Street Investment, Ltd.,* [1957] 1 W. L. R. 227 ; [1957] 1 All E. R. 229 ; (1957) 73 L.Q.R. 157 (R.E.M.) ; followed in *Creer v. P. & O. Lines of Australia Pty., Ltd.* [1971], 45 A.L.J.R. 697 ; (1972) 88 L.Q.R. 317 ; but doubted by C. A. in *Greene v. Church Comrs. for England,* [1974] 3 W. L. R. 349 ; [1974] 3 All E. R. 609. This surrender proviso is registrable as an estate contract, L.C.A. 1972, s. 2 (4) ; *Greene v. Church Comrs. for England, supra.*

not require the payment of a fine in return for his consent, unless express provision for such a payment is contained in the lease.[1]

Effect of breach of qualified covenant. If the tenant disregards a qualified covenant of this nature and assigns the premises without the consent of the lessor, the result is as follows :—

> If he omits to apply for consent, he is liable in any event to the payment of damages, and also at common law to the forfeiture of his interest if a right of re-entry[2] is contained in the lease.[3]   He may, however, apply to the court for relief against such forfeiture.[4]
>
> If on the other hand he makes a formal request for consent and meets with a refusal, then, provided that the refusal is in fact unreasonable, he incurs no liability whatsoever for his breach of covenant.[5]   But he has no right to recover damages.[6]

The distinction was well put by Neville, J., in a case where the lessor had agreed not to withhold his consent to an assignment to *a respectable and responsible person*.

> " It is obviously a formality to apply for the consent of the landlord in a case where under the terms of the covenant he has no power to prevent the assignment by withholding his consent.   It matters not, where the proposed assignee is a respectable and responsible person, whether the landlord gives or does not give his consent.   The cases show that if, on the one hand, . . . the landlord has been asked and has withheld his consent, the lessee retains his interest under the lease, whereas if he has not been asked and so is unable to give the consent that he should give, the withholding of which is inoperative if the request be made, then the whole of the property of the lessee becomes the property of the lessor.[7]   It certainly seems strange that so small and perfectly indifferent a matter should make such a difference, but so stands the law."[8]

The onus of proving that consent has been unreasonably refused lies on the tenant,[9] but the crucial question is—What

---

[1] S. 144 ; *Gardner & Co., Ltd.* v. *Cone*, [1928] Ch. 955 ; *Comber* v. *Fleet Electrics, Ltd.*, [1955] 2 All E. R. 161.   An increase in rent as a condition to giving consent is in the nature of a fine *Jenkins* v. *Price*, [1907] 2 Ch. 229.

[2] *Infra*, p. 441.

[3] *Barrow* v. *Isaacs & Son*, [1891] 1 Q. B. 417 ; *Creery* v. *Summersell and Flowerdew & Co., Ltd.*, [1949] Ch. 751.

[4] *House Property and Investment Co., Ltd.* v. *Walker (James), Goldsmith and Silversmith, Ltd.*, [1948] K. B. 257 ; [1947] 1 All E. R. 789 ; *i.e.* relief under L.P.A. 1925, s. 146 (2), *infra*, p. 446.

[5] The tenant may apply to the High Court or to the County Court for a declaration that the landlord has unreasonably withheld his consent.   Landlord and Tenant Act 1954, s. 53 (1) (a).

[6] *Treloar* v. *Bigge* (1874), L. R. 9 Exch. 151 ; *Fuller's Theatre and Vaudeville Co., Ltd.* v. *Rofe*, [1923] A. C. 435 ; *Wilson* v. *Fynn*, [1948] 2 All E. R. 40. As to joinder of parties if the assignee sues the landlord for a declaration that the assignment is effective, see *Theodorou* v. *Bloom*, [1964] 1 W. L. R. 1152; [1964] 3 All E. R. 399.

[7] *I.e.* at common law and if the lease contains a right of re-entry.   But see *supra*, note 4.

[8] *Lewis and Allenby (1909), Ltd.* v. *Pegge*, [1914] 1 Ch. 782, at p. 785.

[9] *Shanly* v. *Ward* (1913), 29 T. L. R. 714.

does the law regard as a reasonable refusal? It was suggested by TOMLIN, J., that the question is capable of submission to a precise test, namely, the reason for which consent is withheld must be connected either with the personality of the assignee or with the manner in which he proposes to use the premises.[1]

Grounds on which lessor is justified in with-holding consent.

> In conformity with this opinion, TOMLIN, J., held that it was unreasonable for a landlord, who had let Blackacre to X. and White-acre to Y., to forbid an assignment of Blackacre by X. to Y., on the ground that Y. might terminate his tenancy of Whiteacre.[2]

This proposed test, after being doubted by Lord DUNEDIN and Lord PHILLIMORE,[3] and never consistently followed,[4] has been disapproved by the Court of Appeal.[5] In forming his opinion the landlord need not confine his attention to matters arising during the currency of the lease. Whether an act is reasonable must be determined not on abstract considerations, but in the light of the particular circumstances.[6] It is safer, therefore, to be content with the somewhat elusive statement that the lessor must have some fair, solid and substantial cause for disallowing an assign-ment.[7] To give a few instances, it has been held that a landlord has a valid reason for withholding his consent,

> if he considers that other property belonging to him will be injured by the use that the assignee intends to make of the demised premises [8] ; or
> if, where the lease is of a tied public-house, he fears that the value of the trade will depreciate because the assignee is a foreigner who does not intend to reside on the premises[9] ; or
> if the effect of the assignment will be to nullify a collateral agreement made at the time of the lease[10]; or
> if the sole or substantial object of the parties is that the

---

[1] *Houlder Bros. & Co., Ltd.* v. *Gibbs*, [1925] Ch. 198, at p. 209. The suggestion was approved by EVERSHED, J., in *Re Swanson's Agreement*, [1946] 2 All E. R. 628, but all that he said on the matter was *obiter* ; see the remarks of TUCKER, L.J., in *Lee* v. *Carter* (*K.*), *Ltd.*, [1949] 1 K. B. 85, at p. 96 ; [1948] 2 All E. R. 690, at p. 695.

[2] *Houlder Bros. & Co., Ltd.* v. *Gibbs, supra.* The decision was affirmed at p. 575.

[3] *Viscount Tredegar* v. *Harwood*, [1929] A. C. 72, at pp. 78, 81.

[4] *Premier Confectionery (London) Co., Ltd.* v. *London Commercial Sale Rooms, Ltd.*, [1933] Ch. 904 ; *Wilson* v. *Fynn*, [1948] 2 All E. R. 40 ; *Lee* v. *Carter* (*K.*), *Ltd., supra* ; *Re Town Investments Ltd. Underlease*, [1954] Ch. 301 ; [1954] 1 All E. R. 585.

[5] *Swanson* v. *Forton*, [1949] Ch. 143 ; [1949] 1 All E. R. 135.

[6] *Houlder Bros. & Co., Ltd.* v. *Gibbs*, [1925] Ch. 575, at p. 584, *per* WARRING-TON, L.J.; *Re Greater London Properties Ltd.'s Lease*, [1959] 1 W. L. R. 503 ; [1959] 1 All E. R. 728.

[7] *Treloar* v. *Bigge* (1874), L. R. 9 Exch. 151, 155; *Barrow* v. *Isaacs & Son*, [1891] 1 Q. B. 417, 419 ; *Mills* v. *Cannon Brewery Co., Ltd.*, [1920] 2 Ch. 38, at p. 45 ; *Whiteminster Estates Ltd.* v. *Hodges Menswear Ltd.* (1974), 232 Estates Gazette 715.

[8] *Bridewell Hospital (Governors)* v. *Fawkner and Rogers* (1892), 8 T. L. R. 637.

[9] *Mills* v. *Cannon Brewery Co., Ltd. supra.* Distinguish *Parker* v. *Boggon*, [1947] K. B. 346 ; [1947] 1 All E. R. 46.

[10] *Wilson* v. *Fynn*, [1948] 2 All E. R. 40.

assignee shall acquire a statutory tenancy protected by the Rent Acts[1] ; or

if the rent reserved in a proposed sub-lease is well below that obtainable in the open market, but the sub-lessee agrees to pay a large sum by way of premium;[2] or

if the assignment will embarrass the future development of the property of which the demised premises form part.[3]

Is the test of reasonableness objective or subjective? No decisive answer has yet been given to the fundamental question whether the test of reasonableness is objective, not subjective, as some affirm[4] but others deny.[5] Must the court merely enquire whether the landlord's refusal of consent is in fact unreasonable? Or, must it also consider what influenced his mind in reaching his decision? This difference of opinion is not purely academic, for if the state of his mind is relevant, certain difficult problems will inevitably arise.

For instance, if the landlord has justified his refusal on some unsupportable ground he will presumably be unable at the date of the trial to rely upon an alternative and better ground.[6] Again, a refusal will apparently be ineffectual if, though justifiable in the circumstances, it is justified on inadmissible grounds, as for instance where the proposed assignee is in fact an undischarged bankrupt, but the landlord's only declared objection is to his religion.

It is submitted that the question must be approached objectively, and that, as it has been aptly put, the landlord's "mental processes or uttered words" are irrelevant.

> "In short, what must be tested for unreasonableness is the withholding and not the landlord, the act and not the man."[7]

Racial objections. The Race Relations Act 1965[8] provides that it is unreasonable to withhold consent " on the ground of colour, race or ethnic or national origins," but where the tenancy is of part of a dwellinghouse this does not apply if the landlord occupies the remainder as his own residence and the tenant is entitled in common with

---

[1] *Lee* v. *Carter (K.), Ltd., supra ; Swanson* v. *Forton, supra ; Dollar* v. *Winston,* [1950] Ch. 236 ; [1949] 2 All E. R. 1088, n. ; dist. *Bookman (Thomas) Ltd.* v. *Nathan,* [1955] 1 W. L. R. 815, [1955] 2 All E. R. 821 ; *Re Cooper's Lease* (1968), 19 P. & C.R. 541 ; *Welch* v. *Birrane* (1974), 29 P. & C.R. 102.

[2] *Re Town Investments Ltd. Underlease,* [1954] Ch. 301 ; [1954] 1 All E. R. 585.

[3] *Pimms, Ltd.* v. *Tallow Chandlers Co.,* [1964] 2 Q. B. 547; [1964] 2 All E. R. 145.

[4] *Re Smith's Lease,* [1951] 1 All E. R. 346, at p. 349, *per* ROXBURGH, J.

[5] *Lovelock* v. *Margo,* [1963] 2 Q. B. 786, at p. 789; [1963] 2 All E. R. 13 at p. 15, *per* Lord DENNING, M. R.

[6] *Parker* v. *Boggon,* [1947] K. B. 346; [1947] 1 All E. R. 46 where MACNAGHTEN, J. was prepared to allow a better ground to be put forward. See also *Sonnenthal* v. *Newton* (1965), 109 Sol. Jo. 333.

[7] (1963), 79 L. Q. R. 479, 482 (R. E. M.).

[8] S. 5. See also Race Relations Act 1968, ss. 1, 5, 7 ; and Sex Discrimination Act 1975, s. 31.

him to the use of any accommodation other than that required for the purposes of access.

It is also provided by the Landlord and Tenant Act 1927 that in the case of a lease for more than 40 years made in consideration of the erection or the substantial improvement, alteration or addition of buildings, the tenant may, notwithstanding a prohibition of assignment without the lessor's consent, assign the premises without such consent, provided that the assignment is made more than seven years before the end of the term, and provided that within six months after its completion it is notified in writing to the lessor.[1]

Special case of building leases.

The rule at common law as laid down in *Dumpor's Case*[2] is that a condition is an entire and indivisible thing and therefore incapable of enforcement if once the person entitled to enforce it has allowed it to be disregarded. The effect of this doctrine was that, if a lease from A. to B. contained a covenant or condition against assigning without licence, and A. permitted B. to assign to C., A.'s right to stop further assignments was utterly gone. When once consent had been given to an assignment, the term became freely assignable. Again, and as a result of the same doctrine, if a lease was made to several lessees, upon condition that neither they nor any one of them should assign without a licence, a licence given to one of the lessees destroyed the condition with regard to the others. Again, if a tenant was allowed to assign part of the land leased, the condition ceased to apply to the whole of the land.

Doctrine of Dumpor's Case.

This absurd doctrine was, however, abrogated by statute[3] in 1859 so far as conditions contained in leases were concerned, and the present position is regulated by the Law of Property Act 1925.[4] This provides that,

Present position.

" where a licence is granted to a lessee to do any act, the licence, unless otherwise expressed, extends only—

    (*a*) to the permission actually given ; or

    (*b*) to the specific breach of any provision or covenant referred to ; or

    (*c*) to any other matter thereby specifically authorised to be done ;

and the licence does not prevent any proceeding for any subsequent breach unless otherwise specified in the licence."

Moreover, it is enacted that where a lease contains a covenant or condition against assigning or doing any other act without licence, and a licence is granted to one or more of several lessees, or is granted in respect only of part of the property, it shall not operate to extinguish the lessor's remedy in case the covenant is

---

[1] S. 19 (1) (*b*). This section does not apply if the lessor is a Government department, a local or public authority, or a statutory or public utility company.

[2] (1603), 4 Co. Rep. 119 b. Smith's *Leading Cases* (13th Edn.), vol. i. p. 35. Holdsworth, *History of English Law*, vol. vii. p. 282.

[3] L.P.(A.)A. 1859, s. 1.   [4] S. 143 (1).

broken either by the other lessees or with regard to the rest of
the property.[1]

The result is that the rule in *Dumpor's Case* no longer applies
to leases.

"Usual
covenants."

Although there are many other covenants which may figure
in a lease, those that are normally found have been mentioned.
It should be noticed that, where the lease is preceded by a contract
for a lease,[2] there is an implied term of the contract that it shall
include the *usual covenants*. It was generally considered, on the
authority of *Hampshire* v. *Wickens*,[3] that the only covenants by a
tenant which could be described as " usual " were :—

> to pay rent ;
> to pay tenant's rates and taxes ;
> to keep and deliver up the premises in repair ;
> to allow the lessor to enter and view the state of repair ;

and that the covenant for quiet enjoyment was the only usual
covenant binding the lessor.

It has now been decided, however, that the list is neither fixed
nor closed. The question whether particular covenants are
usual is a question of fact dependent upon the circumstances
of each case, which can be resolved only after considering the
evidence of conveyancers, the practice in the particular district
and the character of the property.[4]

(3) LAW COMMISSION REPORT ON OBLIGATIONS OF LANDLORDS AND TENANTS, 1975

In 1975 the Law Commission recommended[5] that standard
covenants should be implied into leases and contracts of tenancy.
These are to be either overriding covenants, which are mandatory,
or variable covenants, which can be varied or excluded by agreement.[6] The legislation introducing them would not be retrospective.[7]

The proposed covenants restate the existing law and in part
reform it. The main proposals in outline are as follows.

(A) POSSESSION AND QUIET ENJOYMENT[8]

There should be an overriding covenant in every tenancy that
the tenant should peacefully hold and enjoy the premises for the

---

[1] L.P.A. 1925, s. 143 (3).   [2] *Supra.*, p. 389.
[3] (1878), 7 Ch. D. 555, at p. 561, *per* JESSEL, M.R. ; *Charalambous* v. *Ktori*,
[1972] 1 W. L. R. 951 ; [1972] 3 All E. R. 701.
[4] *Flexman* v. *Corbett*, [1930] 1 Ch. 672.
[5] Law Com. No. 67 (1975). It contains a draft Landlord and Tenant
(Implied Covenants) Bill. See (1975) 236 Estates Gazette, pp. 29, 115, 189,
269 (W. A. West and D. Lloyd Evans).
[6] Paras. 11–13, 28–29.   [8] Paras. 26–27.
[7] Paras. 31–62.

purpose of the tenancy without interruption or disturbance by the landlord or by any person lawfully asserting or enforcing a title or right, whether derived from or superior to the title of the landlord. Subject to qualifications, a landlord would become responsible for the acts of all persons with lawful rights and not only of those deriving title under him. Actionable interruption would be extended to cover enforcement of any restriction affecting the use of the premises for " the purpose of the tenancy ".

(B) Derogation from Grant[1]

No change is recommended.

(C) Repairing Obligations[2]

These are to be determined in relation to the length of the letting and the nature of the premises. There are to be four different classes :[3]

    (a) all residential lettings for less than seven years ;
    (b) furnished residential lettings up to 20 years ;
    (c) all other lettings up to 20 years (including unfurnished residential lettings for seven years or more) ;
    (d) all lettings whether residential or not for over 20 years.

It is only in class (a) that there is to be an overriding covenant. This would cover all tenancies and be by the landlord to repair the structure and exterior of a dwelling let for a term of less than seven years. This would be, in effect, a re-enactment with minor variations of sections 32 and 33 of the Housing Act 1961.[4]

In classes (b) to (d) variable covenants are recommended, *i.e.* in (b) by the landlord to keep the entirety of the premises in repair ; in (c), subject to the covenants in (a) and (b), by the landlord to repair the structure and exterior of the premises, and by the tenant to repair all other parts ; and, finally, in (d) by the tenant to keep the entirety of the premises in repair, even if they are furnished dwellings.

The present implied obligation of tenants is to be replaced by a variable covenant to take proper care of the premises as a good tenant, to make good wilful damage and not to make alterations to the detriment of the interest of the landlord. This would be wide enough to include what would now be grounds for an action in tort for waste.[5]

---

[1] Paras. 63–67.
[2] Paras. 108–157.
[3] Agricultural tenancies are excluded, being covered by the detailed code in Agriculture (Maintenance, Repair and Insurance of Fixed Equipment) Regulations 1973 (S.I. 1973 No. 1473). Paras. 118–119.
[4] *Supra*, p. 408.
[5] Para. 139.

(D) Payment of Rent[1]

There should be an overriding tenant's covenant to pay any rent due, and, unless otherwise provided by the contract, rent should be payable in advance for quarterly tenancies or tenancies for shorter periods and in arrear for other cases.

(E) Protection of Premises[2]

As a corollorary to the landlord's covenant of quiet enjoyment, there should be implied an overriding covenant by the tenant to protect the landlord's premises *e.g.* to take steps to prevent, and to notify the landlord of, encroachment, to prevent any nuisance on the premises, and not to allow them to be used for any illegal purpose.

(F) Disclosure of Identity[3]

There should be overriding covenants that the tenant should be informed of the landlord's name and address, and vice versa.

SECTION VI. REMEDIES OF THE LANDLORD FOR THE ENFORCEMENT OF THE COVENANTS

SUMMARY

From the point of view of remedies, the covenant to pay rent must be distinguished from all other covenants entered into by the tenant. These two classes will now be treated separately.

(1) COVENANT TO PAY RENT

A rent is either a rentservice or a rentcharge.

Rent due from tenant is a rent service.

1. **Rentservice** consists of an annual return, made by the tenant in labour, money or provisions, in retribution for the

---

[1] Paras. 68–70.
[2] Paras. 78–89.
[3] Paras. 90–107. Under Housing Act 1974, s. 121, any person who demands or receives rent or acts as the landlord's agent must supply his landlord's name and address in writing, on receipt of a written request by the tenant of a dwelling. The maximum penalty for failure to comply without reasonable excuse is a fine of £200.

land that passes,[1] and this is the rent which is due whenever a tenant holds his lands of a reversioner.[2] A reversion is an estate that arises by operation of law whenever the owner of an estate carves a smaller estate, called a *particular estate*, out of it in favour of another. The residue of the estate continues in him that made the particular estate.[3]

Thus, where lands are leased at a rent for a term of years, the lessor is the *reversioner* and the rent payable by the tenant is called a *rentservice*.

Since rentservice is that rent which is due from a tenant who holds of a reversioner, it follows that rent which is reserved on the grant of an estate in fee simple cannot be a rentservice, for since *Quia Emptores* such a grantee no longer holds of the grantor, but is substituted for him. There is no reversion, no residue left in the grantor.

The origin of the term rentservice lies far back in legal history. Originally the services due from a tenant took many forms, but in course of time they were commuted into fixed money payments called rents service, since they represented the services that formerly issued out of the land. If the tenant failed to perform the services or to pay the rent into which they had been commuted, the lord enjoyed of common right, *i.e.* independently of statute or agreement, the remedy of distress, a feudal institution of very ancient origin, which entitled him to seize cattle and other chattels found upon the land. This remedy existed of common right only where the distrainor had an interest in the shape of a reversion in the land upon which the chattels lay, for otherwise it could scarcely be said with justice that there was anything he was entitled to seize.[4]

Why called rentservice.

The Court of Appeal has recently emphasized that rent is a contractual sum to which a landlord becomes entitled for the use of his land, and, therefore, " the time and manner of the payment is to be ascertained according to the true construction of the contract, and not by reference to out-dated relics of mediaeval law."[5]

2. **Rentcharge.** From a rentservice must be distinguished a rentcharge. This differs from rentservice in that its owner has no tenurial interest in the land out of which it is payable, and having no such interest, is not entitled as of common right to the remedy of distress. It is, then, any rent *expressly* made payable out of land, other than rent payable by a

Distinction between rentservice and rentcharge.

---

[1] Gilbert on *Rents*, p. 9. For the history of the subject, see Holdsworth, *History of English Law*, vol. vii. pp. 262 *et seq.*

[2] Litt., s. 213.

[3] Co. Litt. 22b.

[4] Litt., s. 213; Gilbert, p. 9; Co. Litt. 78b, 142b; Bac. Abr. tit., Rent (A) 1.

[5] *C. H. Bailey, Ltd.* v. *Memorial Enterprises, Ltd.* [1974] 1 W. L. R. 728, at p. 732, *per* Lord DENNING M.R. ; see also *Property Holding Co., Ltd.* v. *Clark*, [1948] 1 K. B. 630, at p. 648 *per* EVERSHED, L.J.

tenant to a reversioner. For instance, if A. sells land to B. in fee simple, he may agree to accept an annual sum of money from B. in perpetuity instead of a lump sum down, and if it is expressly agreed that the fee simple estate shall be charged in favour of A. with a power of distress should the rent fall into arrears, the rent (whatever name may be given to it by local usage, such as quit rent, ground rent, chief rent, etc.) is a rentcharge.

> " It is called a rentcharge because the land for payment thereof is charged with a distresse."[1]

Rentseck.

Formerly, if a rent was made payable out of a fee simple and for some reason an express power of distress was not reserved, the rent was called a *rentseck* or dry rent—*dry* because it did not confer the power to distrain.[2]

Thus, at common law the three kinds of rent are rentservice, rentcharge and rentseck.   But rentsseck have long ceased to exist, for the inability of their owners to distrain was removed by the Landlord and Tenant Act 1730,[3] which enacted that the owners of rentsseck, rents of assize and chief rents should have the same remedy by distress as was available to the owner of a rentservice.

LINDLEY, L.J., said :—

> " Bearing in mind what was done by the Act of Geo. II, which by section 5 gave a power of distress for all rents, there is now no magic in the word rentcharge.   Whether you speak of a rentcharge or only of a rent, if it is a rent and not merely a sum covenanted to be paid, seems to me to be utterly immaterial, because under the Act of Geo. II you have a power of distress in respect of it."[4]

The same remedy is given by the Law of Property Act 1925.[5] For the purpose of this Act, " rent "

> " includes a rentservice or a rentcharge, or other rent, toll, duty, royalty, or annual or periodical payment, in money or money's worth, reserved or issuing out of or charged upon land, but does not include mortgage interest."[6]

This is not the place to elaborate the subject of rentcharges.[7] The historical difference between them and rentservice has been demonstrated, and we may now proceed to set out the remedies that are available to a landlord for the recovery of the rent service due to him.

(A) DISTRESS

Nature of distress.

The right of distress which has existed in England since the Conquest was originally allowed for the enforcement of a great

---

[1] Co. Litt. 144a.   See also *Jenkin R. Lewis, Ltd.* v. *Kerman* [1971] Ch. 477, at p. 484.
[2] Litt. s. 218.   [3] S. 5.
[4] *Re Gerard (Lord) and Beecham's Contract*, [1894] 3 Ch. 295, at p. 313.
[5] S. 121.   [6] S. 205 (1) (xxiii).
[7] *Infra*, p. 624.

number of services that in feudal days might be incident to tenure, such as rent-service, suit-service, heriot-service, aids, reliefs and so on, but most of these are now obsolete, and practically the only purposes for which common law distress is exercisable is the recovery of rent in arrear.[1]

The value of the remedy to a landlord is that he can seize and sell the chattels found on the land and thus procure the rent without the necessity of taking legal proceedings.

Value of distress.

This is a self-help remedy[2] which operates outside the machinery of the courts except in the case of tenancies subject to the Rent Acts. In 1969 the Payne Committee recommended the abolition of "the highly complex technical and archaic law " of distress for rent.[3]

It is essential that the reversion should be vested in the distrainor at the time when the rent falls due and also when the distress is levied.

Reversion must be in distrainor.

> Thus if L. has assigned the reversion to X. at a time when rent is due, L. cannot distrain, since he no longer holds the reversion; and X. is under the same disability, since he was not the reversioner at the critical moment.

Distress cannot be made until the rent is in arrears, which does not occur until the day after it is due,[4] nor can it be levied between sunset and sunrise.[5]

When it may be made.

As a general rule the right of seizure is confined to chattels upon the actual land out of which the rent issues, but it may be extended by agreement to other premises, and by the Distress for Rent Act 1737 goods which have been fraudulently and secretly removed by a tenant after the rent became due, in order to avoid distress, may be seized by the landlord within 30 days wherever found.

Where it may be made.

A distrainor may enter the demised premises and may commit in so doing what in any one else would be a trespass,[6] as for example by entry through an unlocked door;[7] but he may neither break open a door whether of the living house or of an outhouse,[8] nor effect an entrance through a closed but unfastened window.[9]

Involves a right of entry.

The general rule of the common law is that all personal chattels

What may be seized.

---

[1] The common law right to recover compensation by way of distress for damage caused by trespassing livestock has been replaced by a statutory provision for detention and sale. Animals Act 1971, s. 7.

[2] At common law he could only retain the goods: a power of sale was given by the Distress for Rent Act 1689, s. 1.

[3] Report of the committee on the Enforcement of Judgment Debts (1969), Cmnd. 3909, paras. 912–932 ; see also Law Com. Interim Report on Distress for Rent (1966) ; Law Com. Report on Rentcharges 1975 (Law Com. No. 68), para. 94.

[4] *Duppa* v. *Mayo* (1670), 1 Wms. Saund. 287 ; *Re Aspinall*, [1961] Ch. 526 ; [1961] 2 All E. R. 751.

[5] *Tutton* v. *Darke* (1860), 29 L. J. Ex. 271.

[6] *Long* v. *Clarke*, [1894] 1 Q. B. 119, 122.

[7] *Southam* v. *Smout*, [1964] 1 Q. B. 308; [1963] 3 All E. R. 104.

[8] *American Concentrated Must Corpn.* v. *Hendry* (1893), 62 L. J. Q. B. 388.

[9] *Nash* v. *Lucas* (1867), L. R. 2 Q. B. 590.

found upon the premises out of which the rent issues, whether they belong to the tenant or to a stranger, can be distrained, but this extensive power is cut down in two ways :—

Privileged things.

1. SOME THINGS ARE PRIVILEGED FROM DISTRESS.

It is outside the scope of this work to deal with this question in detail, and the reader is referred to the notes given in Smith's *Leading Cases* to *Simpson* v. *Hartopp*.[1] It will suffice here to say that the following articles are absolutely privileged in the sense that they can never be seized :—

Absolutely privileged.

machinery belonging to a third person which is on an agricultural holding under a contract of hire [2];

livestock belonging to a third person which is on an agricultural holding solely for breeding purposes [3];

animals *ferae naturae*;

things delivered to a person in the way of his trade, such as cloth given to a tailor to be made into a suit ;

things in actual use, such as a horse drawing a cart ;

things in the custody of the law, such as property already taken in execution ;

clothes, bedding and tools up to the value of £50.

Conditionally privileged.

The following things are conditionally privileged, that is to say, they can be seized only if there is not a sufficiency of other distrainable goods to be found upon the premises :

beasts of the plough ;

sheep and instruments of husbandry ;

the instruments of a man's trade or profession, such as the text-books of a solicitor ;

the live-stock of a third person found on the land of an agricultural tenant as a result of a contract of agistment.[4]

Lodger's goods.

2. GOODS BELONGING TO AN UNDER-TENANT OR A LODGER ARE PROTECTED. BLACKBURN, J., said :—

" The general rule at common law was that whatever was found upon the demised premises, whether belonging to a stranger or not, might be seized by the landlord and held as a distress till the rent was paid or the service performed. This state of things produced no harm, because at common law the landlord not being able to sell the distress he generally gave up the goods as soon as he found they were not the tenant's, as his continuing to hold them would not induce the tenant to pay. But in the reign of William and Mary a very harsh and unjust law was passed by which the right was given to the landlord to sell any goods seized, and to apply the proceeds to the payment of the rent unless the tenant or the owner of the goods first paid it ; and this held out a great temptation to a landlord to seize the goods of a stranger although he knew they were not the tenant's." [5]

---

[1] (1744), Willes 512 ; *Smith's Leading Cases* (13th Edn.), vol. i. p. 137.
[2] Agricultural Holdings Act 1948, s. 20.   [3] *Ibid.*
[4] *Ibid.*, s. 19 (1). If distrained because of an insufficiency of other goods the landlord cannot thereby recover more than the amount due and unpaid under the contract of agistment.
[5] *Lyons* v. *Elliott* (1876), 1 Q. B. D. 210, at p. 213.

This has gradually been put on a more equitable footing, and at the present day the Law of Distress Amendment Act 1908,[1] except in the case of certain specified goods,[2] provides a means by which a lodger or under-tenant or indeed any person not being a tenant of the premises and not having any beneficial interest in the tenancy, may avoid the seizure of his belongings. Suppose for instance that

L. has leased premises to T., and that X. is the lodger or the under-tenant of T. If in such a case L. levies a distress on any goods belonging to X. for arrears of rent due from T., X. may serve L. with a notice declaring that

T. has no right of property in the goods ;
the goods are not goods excepted from the Act ;
so much rent is due from X. to T. ;
future instalments will become due on stated days ;
he will pay such rent to L.

With this notice, which is of no effect unless it contains the requisite statements,[3] X. must also send an inventory of his goods. If L. distrains on the goods of X. after receipt of this notice and inventory, he is guilty of an illegal distress, and X. may apply to a justice of the peace or to a magistrate for the restoration of his goods. The protection afforded by the Act applies only to a tenant whose rent equals the full annual value of the premises.

How Distress is Levied. No person can distrain for rent unless he is a certificated bailiff, that is, unless he has been authorized to levy distress (either in the one particular case or in general cases) by a certificate in writing under the hand of a county court judge.[4]

Such a bailiff should be provided by the landlord with a distress warrant authorizing him to make the levy. The first step is to seize and impound the goods. At common law the impounding had to take place off the premises, but now it is lawful to secure the goods in some part of the premises themselves.[5]

The usual practice is to leave a man in possession, but this is not essential, for goods are deemed to be impounded if what is called " walking possession " is taken of them, *i.e.* if they are left on the premises but periodically inspected by the bailiff.[6] Anyone who interferes with goods after they have been impounded is liable in treble damages for pound breach.[7] As soon as the seizure is complete, the landlord is bound to give the tenant[8] notice of the

Procedure.

Impounding.

---

[1] S. 1.
[2] *I.e.*, goods belonging to the husband or wife of the tenant ; goods comprised in a bill of sale, hire purchase agreement or settlement made by the tenant.
[3] *Druce & Co., Ltd.* v. *Beaumont Property Trust, Ltd.*, [1935] 2 K. B. 257.
[4] Law of Distress Amendment Act 1888, s. 7.
[5] Distress for Rent Act 1737, s. 10.
[6] *Lavell* v. *O'Leary*, [1933] 2 K. B. 200.
[7] Distress for Rent Act 1689, s. 3 (1).   [8] *Ibid.*, s. 1.

distress and of the place, if any, to which the goods have been removed,[1] and he is not at liberty to sell them until five days have elapsed since the service of the notice.   Thus a tenant is allowed five days within which to pay what is due, but he is entitled to an extension of this period to 15 days if he makes a request in writing to this effect to the landlord and gives security for any additional expense that the delay may involve.[2]   The sale is generally though not necessarily by auction, and it usually takes place on the premises unless the tenant has requested in writing that the goods shall be removed to a public auction-room.   If it does not produce sufficient proceeds, no second sale is as a general rule permissible.[3]

Only six years' arrears of rent may be recovered by the remedy of distress, whether or not the lease is under seal.[4]   When the demised premises consist of an agricultural holding only one year's arrears are recoverable by this method.[5]

(B) ACTION FOR ARREARS OF RENT

Whether a lease is made by deed or not, only six years' arrears of rent are recoverable by action.[6]   Thus a landlord must bring his action within six years after the rent has become due or has been acknowledged in writing to be due, or after some payment has been made by the tenant.[7]   A payment of part of the rent does not entitle the landlord to sue for the remainder more than six years after it became due.[8]

But while the relation of landlord and tenant continues under a lease for a fixed term of years, the right of the landlord to recover rent is not *totally* barred by non-payment no matter how long the rent is in arrear.[9]   Suppose, for instance, that

A. holds lands of B. for 99 years at £100 a year, and that A. has not paid rent for 25 years.   B.'s right to recover rent is not extinguished, but is limited to the recovery of the last six years' arrears.

The only case in which the right of a landlord is extinguished altogether occurs where for a period of 12 years the rent has been paid to a third person who wrongfully claims to be entitled to the reversion.[10]

---

[1] Distress for Rent Act 1737, s. 9.
[2] Law of Distress Amendment Act 1888, s. 6.
[3] *Rawlence and Squarey* v. *Spicer*, [1935] 1 K. B. 412.
[4] Limitation Act 1939, s. 17.
[5] Agricultural Holdings Act 1948, s. 18.
[6] Limitation Act 1939, s. 17.
[7] *Ibid.*, s. 23 (4).
[8] *Ibid.*, proviso.
[9] *Grant* v. *Ellis* (1841), 9 M. & W. 113 ; *Archbold* v. *Scully* (1861), 9 H. L. C. 360.
[10] *Lehain* v. *Philpott* (1875), L. R. 10 Ex. 242 ; *infra*, pp. 896–7.

The rule is that a landlord cannot pursue the two remedies of action and distress at one and the same time. If he has levied a distress, he cannot bring an action for recovery until he has sold the distrained articles and found the purchase money insufficient to satisfy his demand.[1] If he has sued to judgment first, then, even though the judgment remains unsatisfied, he loses his remedy of distress altogether for that particular rent.[2]

Inter-relation of remedies.

(C) Express Proviso for Re-entry

The breach of a covenant by a tenant does not entitle the lessor to resume possession by a re-entry upon the premises, unless the right to do so is expressly reserved in the lease. On the other hand, an undertaking by the tenant which is framed not as a mere covenant, but as a condition, carries with it at common law a right of re-entry if the condition is broken. Whether a stipulation amounts to a covenant or a condition is sometimes a question of considerable nicety, but it depends entirely upon the intention of the parties. A condition is a clause which shows a clear intention on the part of the landlord, not merely that the tenant shall be personally liable if he fails in his contractual duties, but that the lease shall determine in the event of such a failure. The tenancy is to remain conditional upon the fulfilment by the tenant of his obligations. In an early case, Bayley, J., said :

Distinction between covenant and condition.

" In a lease for years no precise form of words is necessary to make a condition. It is sufficient if it appear that the words used were intended to have the effect of creating a condition. They must be the words of the landlord, because he is to impose the condition." [3]

In this case it was " stipulated and conditioned " in the lease that the tenant should not assign or underlet the premises, otherwise than to his wife or children, and it was held that these words were sufficient to create a condition. Mere words of agreement, however, as for example when the tenant " agrees that he will not assign the premises without the consent of the landlord," create nothing more than a covenant.[4]

It is, however, the usual practice for a lease to contain, in clear and unmistakable language, an express clause which reserves to the lessor the right of re-entry if one or more of the covenants are broken, and which provides that upon re-entry the lease shall be forfeited. The virtue of this is that the lessor, if he finds himself saddled with an impecunious tenant who is a persistent defaulter in the payment of rent, may regain possession instead of being driven to constant litigation.

Express proviso for re-entry and forfeiture of lease.

---

[1] *Archbold* v. *Scully, supra.*
[2] *Chancellor* v. *Webster* (1893), 9 T. L. R. 568.
[3] *Doe d. Henniker* v. *Watt* (1828), 8 B. & C. 308, at p. 315.
[4] *Crawley* v. *Price* (1875), L. R. 10 Q. B. 302.

The following is a precedent of a proviso for forfeiture :—

"Provided always that if any part of the said rent shall be in arrears for 21 days, whether lawfully demanded or not, the lessor or his assigns may re-enter upon the said premises, and immediately thereupon the said term shall absolutely determine."

Breach of condition renders lease voidable.

In such a case the effect of allowing the rent to fall into arrears for more than 21 days is to render the tenant's interest liable to forfeiture, and not *ipso facto* to cause a forfeiture. However clearly the proviso may state that the lease shall be void on breach of condition, it has been held in a long series of decisions that its only effect is to render the lease voidable.[1] It is at the option of the landlord whether the tenancy shall be determined or not, and it is only if he does some act which shows his intention to end it that the lease will be avoided.[2] Thus an actual entry by the landlord or the grant of a lease to a new tenant works a forfeiture, but the usual practice at the present day is to sue for the recovery of possession instead of making a re-entry,[3] for, as Willes, J., said,

"The bringing of an action of ejectment is equivalent to the ancient entry. It is an act unequivocal in the sense that it asserts the right of possession upon every ground that may turn out to be available to the party claiming to re-enter."[4]

It is the service of the writ for possession, and not its issue which is equivalent to re-entry.[5]

Condition of forfeiture may be waived.

Waiver. The question whether the landlord has by some unequivocal act elected to treat the lease as forfeited is an important one from the point of view of waiver. Common law dislikes conditions of forfeiture, and it will always treat such a condition as waived and therefore unenforceable if, after the act of forfeiture has been committed, the landlord clearly shows that he regards the tenancy as still existing. The two essentials for waiver are that,

1. the landlord must be aware of the commission of an act of forfeiture by the tenant, and
2. he must do "some unequivocal act recognizing the continued existence of the lease."[6]

Thus a merely passive attitude on his part has no effect,[7] but on the other hand (and this applies to all conditions of forfeiture, whether in respect of the non-payment of rent or of the non-performance of other covenants),

---

[1] *Davenport* v. *R.* (1877), L. R. 3 App. Cas. 115, at p. 128.
[2] *Toleman* v. *Portbury* (1871), L. R. 6 Q. B. 245, at p. 250.
[3] In the case of tenancies of residential premises a re-entry other than pursuant to a court order for possession is prohibited. See *infra*, p. 483.
[4] *Grimwood* v. *Moss* (1872), L. R. 7 C. P. 360, at p. 364.
[5] *Canas Property Co., Ltd.* v. *K. L. Television Services, Ltd.*, [1970] 2 Q. B. 433 ; [1970] 2 All E. R. 795 ; *Richards* v. *De Freitas* (1974) 29 P. & C. R. 1.
[6] *Matthews* v. *Smallwood*, [1910] 1 Ch. 777, at p. 786, *per* Parker, J. ; *Dendy* v. *Nicholl* (1858), 4 C. B. N. S. 376.
[7] *Perry* v. *Davis* (1858), 3 C. B. (N. S.) 769.

1. if, after the act of forfeiture has been committed, he demands or sues for rent,[1] or accepts payment of it notwithstanding that his acceptance is stated to be " without prejudice ",[2] or a clerk of his agents accepts it by mistake,[3] or
2. if he distrains for rent whether due before or after the breach;[4] or
3. if he grants a new lease to the defaulting tenant;[5] or
4. if he or some person authorized by him unequivocally demands the rent that is due,[6]

each of these acts is strong evidence that he has elected not to avoid the lease.[7] At bottom, however, the question always is *quo animo* was the act done.[8]

The waiver of a covenant or of a condition does not operate as a general waiver, but extends only to the particular breach in question.[9] An important distinction should be noticed between continuing and non-continuing breaches of covenant, for acceptance of rent or the levy of distress after the breach of a continuing covenant, *e.g.* to insure the premises or to keep them in repair, waives the forfeiture only up to the date of distress or payment of rent. The proviso for re-entry may be enforced if the breach subsequently continues.[10]

But when once a landlord unequivocally and finally elects to treat a lease as void, as, for instance, where he serves a writ for recovery of the land, no subsequent receipt of rent or other act will amount to waiver so as to deprive him of his right to enforce the clause of re-entry.[11]

What Constitutes a Demand of Rent. In the precedent which is set out above it will be noticed that the landlord reserves

Demand of rent.

---

[1] *Dendy* v. *Nicholl, supra.* Dist. *Clarke* v. *Grant,* [1950] 1 K. B. 104; [1949] 1 All E. R. 768.
[2] *Segal Securities, Ltd.* v. *Thoseby,* [1963] 1 Q. B. 887; [1963] 1 All E. R. 500. It is a question of fact whether money has been tendered and accepted as rent; if answered affirmatively, the consequences as regards waiver raise a question of law; *Windmill Investments (London), Ltd.* v. *Milano Restaurant, Ltd.,* [1962] 2 Q. B. 373 ; [1962] 2 All E. R. 680 ; See also *Bader Properties, Ltd.* v. *Linley Property Investments, Ltd.,* (1967), 19 P. & C. R., 620, pp. 638–41 ; *David Blackstone, Ltd.* v. *Burnetts (West End), Ltd.,* [1973] 1 W. L. R. 1487 ; [1973] 3 All E. R. 782.
[3] *Central Estates (Belgravia), Ltd.* v. *Woolgar (No. 2),* [1972] 1 W. L. R. 1048 ; [1972] 3 All E. R. 610.
[4] *Doe d. David* v. *Williams* (1835), 7 C. & P. 322.
[5] *Ward* v. *Day* (1864), 5 B. & S. 359.
[6] *Creery* v. *Summersell and Flowerdew & Co., Ltd.,* [1949] Ch. 751 ; *David Blackstone, Ltd.* v. *Burnetts (West End), Ltd. supra* (demand for future rent) ; *Welch* v. *Birrane* (1974) 29 P. & C. R. 102.
[7] *Ibid.,* at p. 761.   [8] *Ibid.*
[9] L.P.A. 1925, s. 148.
[10] *Doe d. Hemmings* v. *Durnford* (1832), 2 Cr. & J. 667 ; *Doe d. Baker* v. *Jones* (1850), 5 Exch. 498.
[11] *Civil Service Co-operative Society, Ltd.* v. *McGrigor's Trustee,* [1923] 2 Ch. 347 ; *Evans* v. *Enever,* [1920] 2 K. B. 315.

Common Law rule.

a power of re-entry for non-payment of rent *whether lawfully demanded or not*. The object of inserting these words is to avoid the strictness of the common law which requires the landlord, failing a contrary agreement, to make a formal demand upon the premises themselves for the exact amount of rent due, and to make it between the hours of sunrise and sunset so as to afford the tenant an opportunity of counting out the money while light remains.[1] This common law rule has, however, been partly abrogated by a statute which enacts that, even though the formal demand has not been dispensed with in the lease, yet, if one-half year's rent is in arrear and there are not sufficient distrainable goods upon the premises and a power of re-entry has been reserved, the landlord can recover the premises by action at the end of the period fixed in the proviso for re-entry without making any formal demand of rent.[2] The restricted nature of this statutory modification makes it desirable, in the interests of a sure and speedy remedy, to obviate by express words the necessity for a formal demand.

Relief granted against forfeiture for non-payment of rent.

Relief against Forfeiture. One of the aims of the old Court of Chancery was to prevent the enforcement of a legal right from producing hardship, and therefore, since the sole object of a right of re-entry was to give a landlord security for the rent, it was always prepared to relieve the tenant against the forfeiture, provided that he paid all that was due by way of arrears of rent, together with costs and interest. In this way, the landlord obtained all that the right of re-entry was intended to secure to him, and it would be inequitable for him to take advantage of the forfeiture.[3]

Time within which relief must be sought.

Originally a tenant might petition for and obtain this relief at any time after he had been ejected under the power of re-entry, but his right has been restricted by statute. The present position depends upon the Common Law Procedure Act 1852[4] (which re-enacted in this particular the Landlord and Tenant Act of 1730), and upon the Judicature Act 1925. The result of these Acts is as follows:—

> If the lessor sues for possession and the tenant at any time before the trial pays or tenders to the lessor or pays into court the rent and arrears and costs, all further proceedings are stayed and he regains possession under the old lease.[5]

---

[1] Notes to *Duppa* v. *Mayo* (1668), 1 Wms. Saund. 282, at p. 287.
[2] Common Law Procedure Act 1852, s. 210.
[3] *Howard* v. *Fanshawe*, [1895] 2 Ch. 581 ; and authorities there cited.
[4] Ss. 210–12.
[5] Common Law Procedure Act 1852, s. 212. For a " trial " to come within the meaning of this section, it must be an effective trial binding on all the necessary parties ; *Gill* v. *Lewis*, [1956] 2 Q. B. 1 ; [1956] 1 All E. R. 884, where judgment was signed against only one of two joint tenants.

It has now been held, however, that there is no case for such a stay of proceedings unless six months' rent is in arrear.[1]

If the tenant does not, or cannot, take this opportunity and judgment is given against him, he may, nevertheless, apply for relief within six months after execution of the judgment.[2] If he applies within this period, the court is empowered by the Act of 1925 to relieve him from the forfeiture subject to such terms and conditions as to payment of rent, costs and otherwise, as could formerly have been imposed by the old Court of Chancery. The effect of a grant of relief is that he holds the land according to the terms of the original lease without the necessity of a new lease.[3]

The grant of relief within this extended time of six months, however, is a matter of discretion, the general principle being that, so far as rent is concerned, the landlord can claim nothing more than to be restored to the position that he would have occupied had the forfeiture not been incurred. The position has been stated in the following authoritative passage:

" The function of the court in exercising this equitable jurisdiction is to grant relief when all that is due for rent and costs has been paid up, and (in general) to disregard any other causes of complaint that the landlord may have against the tenant. The question is whether, provided all is paid up, the landlord will not have been fully compensated ; and the view taken by the court is that if he gets the whole of his rent and costs, then he has got all that he is entitled to so far as rent is concerned, and extraneous matters of breach of covenant, and so forth, are, generally speaking, irrelevant."[4]

Even so, however, exceptional circumstances may justify the refusal of relief, such as the inordinate conduct of the tenant himself or the fact that the landlord has altered his position in the belief that the forfeiture is effective. Thus, for instance, relief was refused to a tenant who did not apply until just before the six months had elapsed, by which time the landlord, after incurring expenditure upon the maintenance of the property, had "made an arrangement" to let another party into possession.[5]

If relief is granted upon conditions to be performed within a limited time, the court has jurisdiction to extend the time if it is just and equitable to do so.[6]

Relief may be granted to the tenant where the landlord, instead of bringing an action for recovery of the land, enters into

---

[1] *Standard Pattern Co., Ltd.* v. *Ivey*, [1962] Ch. 432; [1962] 1 All E. R. 452 criticized (1962), 78 *L. Q. R.* pp. 168–71 (R. E. M.).

[2] Common Law Procedure Act 1852, s. 210–212.

[3] Supreme Court of Judicature (Consolidation) Act 1925, s. 46.

[4] *Gill* v. *Lewis*, [1956] 2 Q. B. 1, at p. 13, [1956] 1 All E. R. 844, at p. 853, *per* JENKINS, L. J. See also *Belgravia Insurance Co., Ltd.* v. *Meah*, [1964] 1 Q. B. 436; [1963] 3 All E. R. 828 ; M. & B. p. 394.

[5] *Stanhope* v. *Haworth* (1886), 3 T. L. R. 34.

[6] *Chandless-Chandless* v. *Nicholson*, [1942] 2 K. B. 321 ; [1942] 2 All E. R.

peaceable possession. In such a case the tenant cannot claim relief under the Act which only applies where the landlord sues for possession. He may however, rely on the ancient equitable jurisdiction of the court, and, provided that he acts with reasonable promptitude, may obtain relief even if he brings his action more than six months after the landlord resumes possession.[1]

Relief to under-lessees.

Relief to Under-lessees. The old rule was that, if the lease contained a proviso for re-entry, an under-lessee from the original tenant could be evicted if the original tenant committed an act of forfeiture, but the Law of Property Act 1925,[2] re-enacting the Conveyancing Act 1892, provides that where a head lessor proceeds by action or otherwise to enforce a forfeiture, the court may, on the application of an under-lessee, vest the property in the under-lessee for part or the whole of the remainder of the term and upon such conditions as are thought fit. The general principle here is that the landlord is entitled to be restored to his former position, but only in respect of the part of the premises occupied by the under-lessee. It would not be equitable, for instance, that the latter should be required to pay the rent due to the landlord in respect of the whole of the premises.[3] The proper way of giving effect to the statute is to create a new lease in favour of the sub-tenant, but one that is implicitly subject to the terms and conditions contained in the original lease.[4] In no case, however, may he be granted a lease for any longer term than he is entitled to under the sub-lease.[5]

Mortgagees and squatters.

Relief is available to the mortgagee of a leasehold interest holding under a sub-demise or under a charge by way of legal mortgage.[6] It is not available to a squatter who has dispossessed a lessee.[7]

(2) COVENANTS OTHER THAN THE COVENANT TO PAY RENT

(A) DAMAGES OR INJUNCTION

Damages or injunction.

If the tenant fails to observe any of the covenants contained in the lease, it is open to the lessor either to sue for damages for

---

[1] *Howard* v. *Fanshawe*, [1895] 2 Ch. 581 ; *Lovelock* v. *Margo*, [1963] 2 Q. B. 786 ; [1963] 2 All E. R. 13. *Thatcher* v. *C. H. Pearce & Sons (Contractors) Ltd.*, [1968] 1 W. L. R. 748 (four days over six months). See (1969), J. P. L., pp. 251–252. For the special rules that govern the jurisdiction of the County Court to grant relief, see the County Courts Act 1959, s. 191, as amended by the County Courts (Jurisdiction) Act 1963, s. 1 (1) (*a*).
[2] S. 146 (4).
[3] *Chatham Empire Theatre* (1955) *Ltd.* v. *Ultrans Ltd.*, [1961] 1 W. L. R 817 ; [1961] 2 All E. R. 381.
[4] *Chelsea Estates Investment Trust Co., Ltd.* v. *Marche*, [1955] Ch. 328; [1955] 1 All E. R. 195.
[5] *Factors (Sundries), Ltd.* v. *Miller*, [1952] 2 All E. R. 630.
[6] *Belgravia Insurance Co., Ltd.* v. *Meah*, [1964] 1 Q. B. 436; [1963] 3 All E. R. 828 ; M. & B. p. 394. As to these forms of mortgage, see *infra*, p. 642.
[7] *Tickner* v. *Buzzacott*, [1965] Ch. 426; [1965] 1 All E. R. 131.

breach or to obtain an injunction to restrain the breach.[1] This
remedy is available, for instance, notwithstanding the Agricultural
Holdings Act 1948, where a tenant farmer fails to observe the
rules of good husbandry.[2]

(B) ENFORCEMENT OF FORFEITURE

As a further safeguard to the landlord it is the common
practice, just as in the case of the covenant to pay rent, to ensure
the observance of all other covenants by inserting an express
proviso for re-entry and forfeiture in the event of their breach.
The following is a typical clause in a lease :—

Condition of forfeiture.

> " If there shall be any breach or non-observance of any of the cove-
> nants by the tenant hereinbefore contained, then and in any such
> case the lessor may, at any time thereafter, into and upon the demised
> premises, or any part thereof, in the name of the whole, re-enter,
> and the same have again, repossess and enjoy as in his former estate. "[3]

In two respects, what has already been said above about
forfeiture for non-payment of rent applies equally to these other
covenants, namely, the effect of a breach is to render the lease
voidable, not void ; and the right of avoidance is lost by any act
on the part of the lessor which amounts to a waiver of the condition.[4] But until the legislature intervened, the jurisdiction of
the court to relieve the tenant varied according as the forfeiture
was due to non-payment of rent or to the breach of a covenant
relating to some other matter. The question soon arose whether
equity would protect a tenant against the loss of his interest under
such a clause if, having incurred a forfeiture by breaking one of
the covenants, he was prepared to put the matter right by paying
all costs and compensation. To cite the words of KAY, L.J. :—

No relief against forfeiture.

> " At first there seems to have been some hesitation whether this
> relief " [grantable in the case of non-payment of rent] " might not be
> extended to other cases of forfeiture for breach of covenants such
> as to repair, to insure, and the like, where compensation could be made ;
> but it was soon recognized that there would be great difficulty in
> estimating the proper amount of compensation; and since the decision
> of Lord ELDON in *Hill* v. *Barclay*[5] it has always been held that equity

---

[1] *Coward* v. *Gregory* (1866), L. R. 2 C. P. 153.

[2] *Kent* v. *Conniff*, [1953] 1 Q. B. 361 ; [1953] 1 All E. R. 155.

[3] In this case forfeiture is provided for by the act of the parties, but it
also occurs by operation of law if the tenant asserts a title in himself adverse
to the landlord (*e.g.* by a written declaration that he, not the landlord, is
entitled to the freehold), or if he lets a stranger into possession with the
intention of enabling him to set up such an adverse title. But in all cases,
it is a question of fact whether the tenant's act shows an intention to deny the
landlord's title ; *Wisbech St. Mary Parish Council* v. *Lilley*, [1956] 1 W. L. R.
121 ; [1956] 1 All E. R. 301 ; *Warner* v. *Sampson*, [1959] 1 Q. B. 297 ;
[1959] 1 All E. R. 120. See generally, Hill and Redman, *Law of Landlord
and Tenant* (16th Edn.), p. 461.

[4] *Supra.*, pp. 436–7.

[5] (1810), 16 Ves. 402.

would not relieve, merely on the ground that it could give compensation, upon breach of any covenant in a lease except the covenant for payment of rent.   But of course this left unaffected the undoubted jurisdiction to relieve in case of breach occasioned by fraud, accident, surprise, or mistake." [1]

This denial of relief was maintained even though the breach, instead of causing loss to the landlord, operated to his advantage by restoring to him, at a much earlier date than he had a right to expect, premises upon which the tenant in the expectation of continued tenure might have already expended large sums of money. The strongest example of this was where a tenant failed to reinsure for a short time after the previous year's policy had run out. If in such a case no fire had occurred in the uninsured period the landlord had obviously lost nothing, and yet it was held in several cases that such a breach was sufficient to produce a forfeiture against which no relief could be given.[2]   This particular case of forfeiture (by failure to insure) received legislative attention in 1859,[3] when relief was made possible on certain conditions, but it still remained true that the merely technical and innocuous breach of any other covenant inevitably led to the loss of his interest by the tenant if the landlord chose to take advantage of a proviso for re-entry.

Changes by Conveyancing Act 1881.   The law, however, was fundamentally changed in two respects by the Conveyancing Act of 1881,[4] which first required certain conditions to be satisfied before forfeiture could be enforced, and then gave the tenant the right to petition for relief.

These provisions were re-enacted by section 146 of the Law of Property Act 1925 and amended by three further Acts in 1927, 1938 and 1954.[5]   The law now stands as follows :—

Notice to tenant required.   1. **The Statutory Restriction on the Landlord's Right to Enforce a Forfeiture.** Section 146 of the Law of Property Act 1925 provides as follows :—

" A right of re-entry or forfeiture under any proviso or stipulation in a lease for a breach of any covenant or condition in the lease shall not be enforceable, by action or otherwise, unless and until the lessor serves on the lessee a notice—

    (a) specifying the particular breach complained of ; and

    (b) if the breach is capable of remedy, requiring the lessee to remedy the breach ; and

    (c) in any case, requiring the lessee to make compensation in money for the breach ;

---

[1] *Barrow* v. *Isaacs & Son*, [1891] 1 Q. B. 417, 425 ; *Shiloh Spinners, Ltd.* v. *Harding*, [1973] A. C. 691, at pp. 722 *et seq. per* Lord Wilberforce ; M. & B. p. 407.

[2] See, *e.g.*, *Doe d. Muston* v. *Gladwin* (1845), 6 Q. B. 953.

[3] Law of Property Amendment Act 1859, ss. 4–9 ; later repealed by the Conveyancing Act 1881.   [4] S. 14.

[5] Landlord and Tenant Act 1927 ; Leasehold Property (Repairs) Act 1938 ; Landlord and Tenant Act 1954.

and the lessee fails, within a reasonable time thereafter, to remedy the breach, if it is capable of remedy, and to make reasonable compensation in money, to the satisfaction of the lessor, for the breach."

The section has effect notwithstanding any stipulation to the contrary.[1] A period of three months is normally regarded as a " reasonable time," but in special circumstances it may be much less.[2] This statutory rule is designed to afford the tenant an opportunity of considering the matter before an action is brought against him and of making up his mind whether he can admit the breach and whether he ought to offer compensation.[3]

To eliminate the risk of the notice not reaching the occupying tenant, it is enacted by the Landlord and Tenant Act 1927,[4] that *in the case of a covenant to repair* a right of re-entry shall not be enforceable unless the lessor proves that service of the notice was known either—

(a) to the lessee ; or
(b) to an under-lessee holding under an under-lease which reserved a nominal reversion only to the lessee ; or
(c) to the person who last paid the rent,

and that a reasonable interval had elapsed since the time when the fact of service was *known to* such person. The sending of a registered letter to a person is, however, to be regarded *prima facie* as good service.[5]

It is now established that the statutory notice need not contain a demand for compensation if the lessor does not desire to be indemnified.[6] We must now see whether the statutory notice will be ineffective if it omits to require a breach to be remedied. If a positive covenant has been broken, *e.g.* a covenant to repair, that is capable of remedy and accordingly the notice must require it to be remedied. Where, however, the covenant which has been broken is a

Position where negative covenant not remediable.

---

[1] L.P.A. 1925, s. 146 (12). A forfeiture in the guise of a surrender remains a forfeiture for the purposes of s. 146. *Plymouth Corpn.* v. *Harvey*, [1971] 1 W. L. R. 549 ; [1971] 1 All E. R. 623.

[2] *Civil Service Co-operative Society, Ltd.* v. *McGrigor's Trustee*, [1923] 2 Ch. 347 ; *Scala House and District Property Co., Ltd.* v. *Forbes*, [1974] Q. B. 575 ; [1973] 3 All E. R. 308 ; M. & B. p. 400 (fourteen days held to be sufficient where breach of covenant incapable of remedy).

[3] *Horsey Estate, Ltd.* v. *Steiger*, [1899] 2 Q. B. 79, at p. 91.

[4] S. 18 (2).

[5] If a tenant is making a claim under the Leasehold Reform Act 1967 (*infra*, p. 491), no proceedings to enforce any right of re-entry or forfeiture may be brought during the currency of the claim without the leave of the court, which shall not be granted unless it is satisfied that the claim was not made in good faith, *i.e.* to avoid forfeiture. Ss. 22, 34, Sched. 3, para. 4 (1). *Central Estates (Belgravia) Ltd.* v. *Woolgar*, [1972] 1 Q. B. 48 ; [1971] 3 All E. R. 651.

[6] *Lock* v. *Pearce*, [1893] 2 Ch. 271. *Rugby School (Governors)* v. *Tannahill*, [1935] 1 K. B. 87.

negative one, there is some difficulty. If, for instance, the tenant has agreed not to permit the premises to be used for illegal or immoral purposes and he is convicted of using them for habitual prostitution, it may be that the landlord is already branded locally as the owner of a brothel. If so, the tenant may no doubt discontinue his immoral use of the premises, his only mode of re-demption, but mere cesser will not wipe out the past and **remove the stigma on the landlord's reputation. In this sense the breach is not capable of remedy. If, therefore, the landlord can show that he has suffered lasting damage of this nature, his statutory notice need not require the breach to be remedied.**[1] But the position is different where the action for forfeiture is brought against the original tenant in respect of immoral user permitted not by him, but by his sub-tenant or assignee. In these circumstances, it is the duty of the original tenant to take immediate steps to stop the wrongful user and also to enforce the forfeiture against the wrongdoer. It is only if he fails to do so within a reasonable time after learning the facts that the breach will be regarded as incapable of remedy.[2]

The Court of Appeal has held that a covenant not to sub-let is a once-for-all breach which cannot be remedied, even by obtaining a surrender from the tenant of the sub-lease.[3] In reaching that decision, Russell, L.J. reviewed the cases of *user* of premises in breach of covenant and said :[4]

" We have a number of cases . . . in which the decision that the breach is not capable of remedy has gone upon the ' stigma ' point, without considering whether a short answer might be—if the user had ceased before the section 146 notice—that it was *ex hypothesi* incapable of remedy, leaving the lessee only with the ability to seek relief from forfeiture and the writ unchallengeable as such. "

Hitherto, as we have seen, the test applicable to such breaches has been whether or not the stigma attaching to the premises can be removed by cesser of the immoral or illegal user. It might be preferable to adopt the approach of Russell, L.J. and to

---

[1] *Rugby School (Governors)* v. *Tannahill*, [1935] 1 K. B. 87 ; *Egerton* v. *Esplanade Hotels London, Ltd.*, [1947] 2 All E. R. 88 ; *Hoffman* v. *Fineberg*, [1949] Ch. 245 ; [1948] 1 All E. R. 592. *D. R. Evans & Co., Ltd.* v. *Chandler* (1969), 211 Estates Gazette 1381.
[2] *Glass* v. *Kencakes, Ltd.*, [1966] 1 Q. B. 611; [1964] 3 All E. R. 807; These difficulties will be avoided if the statutory notice requires the tenant to remedy the breach *if it is capable of remedy*. The landlord can then claim in his action (1) that the breach is incapable of remedy, or (2) if it is capable of remedy that it has not been remedied ; *ibid.*, pp. 629–30.
[3] *Scala House and District Property Co., Ltd.* v. *Forbes* [1974] Q. B. 575 ; [1973] 3 All E. R. 308 ; M. & B. p. 400 ; (1973) 89 L. Q. R. 460 (P.V.B.) ; (1973) 37 Conv. (N.S.) 455 (D. Macintyre).
[4] *Ibid.*, at p. 588.

revert to the " attractive and easy " view[1] that *all* negative covenants are incapable of remedy. Recovery of possession by the landlord would then depend solely on whether the court would grant to the tenant relief from forfeiture under section 146 (2).

As regards the details which must be brought to the knowledge of the tenant, the rule has been laid down that the notice must be sufficiently precise to direct his attention to the particular things of which the landlord complains, so that he may understand with reasonable certainty what he is required to do and may be in a position to put matters right before the action is brought.[2]

Notice to be distinct.

If, for instance,

> the tenant holds half a dozen houses from the landlord and he is merely notified that he has broken his covenant to repair, the notice will be bad as not indicating which of the houses are involved.

Where a landlord sues for damages or to enforce a forfeiture in respect of a covenant to keep or put the premises in repair, he is subject to a further statutory restriction under the Leasehold Property (Repairs) Act 1938.[3] This Act applies to premises, other than an agricultural holding, which have been let for a period of not less than seven years, of which at least three years remain unexpired. The landlord must serve on the tenant a notice under section 146 of the Law of Property Act 1925 not less than one month before the commencement of the action, and inform him in that notice of his right to serve a counter-notice.[4] The tenant may within 28 days of receiving the notice serve a counter-notice on the landlord claiming the benefit of the Act.

Exceptional case of the covenant to repair.

The effect of a counter-notice is that no proceedings whatsoever may be taken by the landlord for the enforcement of any right of re-entry or forfeiture, or for the recovery of damages, in respect of a breach of the repairing covenant, unless he first obtains the leave of the County Court.[5] But as soon as the lease has less than three years to run, there is no longer any need to apply for this leave.[6] The circumstances in which leave is to be

Effect of counter-notice.

---

[1] *Hoffmann* v. *Fineberg*, [1949] Ch. 245, at p. 254 *per* HARMAN, J., referring to the ratio of MACKINNON, J. in *Rugby School (Governors)* v. *Tannahill* at first instance [1934] 1 K. B. 695, at pp. 700–1. While affirming his decision, C.A. rejected his view that all breaches of negative covenant are irremediable [1935] 1 K. B. 87, at pp. 90, 92.

[2] *Fletcher* v. *Nokes*, [1897] 1 Ch. 271, 274 ; approved *Fox* v. *Jolly*, [1916] A. C. 1.

[3] Leasehold Property (Repairs) Act 1938, s. 1 (1) ; as amended by the Landlord and Tenant Act 1954, s. 51 (1).

[4] *Ibid.*, s. 1 (4) *Middlegate Properties, Ltd.* v. *Messimeris*, [1973] 1 W. L. R. 168 ; [1973] 1 All E. R. 645.

[5] *Ibid.*

[6] *Baker* v. *Sims*, [1959] 1 Q. B. 114 ; [1958] 3 All E. R. 326.

given are specifically enumerated by the statute.[1] At this stage of the proceedings the landlord need only show a *prima facie* case of a breach by the tenant.[2]

The Act applies to leases created and to breaches occurring before or after June 23, 1938, when it came into operation.[3]

Power of court to grant or refuse relief.

2. The Right of the Tenant to Claim Relief. After requiring the above preliminaries from a lessor before he can enforce a forfeiture the Act of 1925 then provides that, when the lessor is proceeding by action or entry to recover the premises, the lessee may apply to the court for relief, and the court may, after reviewing the circumstances of the case and the conduct of the parties, refuse such relief, or grant it upon such terms as to costs, expenses, damages, compensation, penalty, etc., as seem fit.[4] This application must be made by all the tenants if the premises are held by joint lessees.[5] Where relief is granted on terms to be performed within a specified time, the court has jurisdiction to extend that time.[6]

Attempts have been made to specify the principles upon which this relief should be granted or withheld,[7] but the House of Lords has held that though such statements are useful and may reflect the judicial view for normal cases, yet the discretion given by the statute is so wide that it is better not to lay down rigid rules for its exercise.[8] Although the court will rarely exercise its discretion in favour of a lessee who knowingly suffers premises to be used for immoral

---

[1] Leasehold Property (Repairs) Act 1938, s. 1 (5) ; (a) where substantial damage has been caused, or will be caused if breach not remedied ; (b) where an immediate remedy is required for giving effect to any enactment, by-law or order of a local authority respecting the safety, repair, maintenance or sanitary condition of the house; (c) where the tenant does not occupy the whole of the house and the breach is injurious to the other occupant; (d) where the cost of repair is relatively small as compared with the much greater expense that a postponement will involve; (e) or where it is " just and equitable " that leave should be given. It is sufficient to give the court jurisdiction if the landlord proves any one of these five facts, *Phillips* v. *Price*, [1959] Ch. 181 ; [1958] 3 All E. R. 386.

[2] *Sidnell* v. *Wilson*, [1966] 2 Q. B. 67 ; [1966] 1 All E. R. 681 ; *Charles A. Pilgrim, Ltd.* v. *Jackson* (1975), 29 P. & C. R. 328.

[3] Leasehold Property (Repairs) Act 1938, s. 5.

[4] L.P.A. 1925, s. 146 (2).

[5] *T. M. Fairclough & Sons, Ltd.* v. *Berliner*, [1931] 1 Ch. 60.

[6] *Starside Properties, Ltd.* v. *Mustapha* [1974] 1 W. L. R. 816 ; [1974] 2 All E. R. 567. If the conditions are not performed, the order for relief falls to the ground. *City of Westminster Assurance Co., Ltd.* v. *Ainis* (1975), 29 P. & C. R. 469.

[7] *E.g. Rose* v. *Hyman*, [1911] 2 K. B. 234.

[8] *Hyman* v. *Rose*, [1912] A. C. 623.

purposes, it may nevertheless do so where there are special mitigating circumstances.[1]

The result is that, even after the statutory notice under section 146 has been served, and even though there has been no compliance with its requirements after a reasonable interval, the tenant may still apply for relief. As regards the time within which he must apply, however, he is in a worse position than in the case of a covenant to pay rent.[2] The particular section of the Act which deals with forfeiture opens with the words : Limitation of time.

"Where a lessor is proceeding . . . to enforce such a right of re-entry or forfeiture."

and it has been held that the lessor cannot be said to be *proceeding* where he has sued to judgment and has obtained possession of the premises by way of execution.[3] In other words, a tenant will irretrievably lose his right to relief unless he makes application before the landlord has actually re-entered.

3. **Exceptional Cases.** The particular sub-sections of the Act already considered are general in nature and would, without more, apply to every covenant contained in a lease, but there are three covenants for the breach of which a lessor need not serve the statutory notice as a preliminary to enforcing the forfeiture, and in respect of which relief is not grantable. The covenants so excepted are the following :— Exceptions to the statutory requirements.

1. THE COVENANT TO PAY RENT.[4]

2. THE COVENANT FOR INSPECTION IN A MINING LEASE. If a mining tenant, under obligation to pay royalties according to the quantity of minerals gotten, breaks the covenant by which he has agreed to give access to his books and accounts, forfeiture may be enforced without service of the statutory notice and no relief is grantable.[5]

3. THE CONDITION OF FORFEITURE ON THE BANK-RUPTCY OF THE TENANT *IN CERTAIN CASES.* It is common to provide in a lease that the premises shall be for-feited to the lessor if the tenant becomes bankrupt or if his interest is taken in execution. There are certain classes of

---

[1] *Borthwick-Norton* v. *Romney Warwick Estates, Ltd.,* [1950] 1 All E. R. 798 ; *Borthwick-Norton* v. *Dougherty,* [1950] W. N. 481 ; *Central Estates (Belgravia), Ltd.* v. *Woolgar (No. 2)* [1972] 1 W. L. R. 1048 ; [1972] 3 All E. R. 610. See also *Earl Bathurst* v. *Fine,* [1974] 1 W. L. R. 905 ; [1974] 2 All E. R. 1160 (relief refused to unsatisfactory tenant, where his personal qualifications were important).
[2] *Supra,* pp. 438–40.
[3] *Rogers* v. *Rice,* [1892] 2 Ch. 170.
[4] L.P.A. 1925, s. 146 (11) ; *supra,* pp. 428 *et seq.*
[5] L.P.A. 1925, s. 146 (8) (ii).

property in which it is vital to the landlord that he should recover his property in either of these events, and where the lease relates to such property the Act provides that the statutory provisions shall be excluded. The following are the leases concerned [1] :—

Leases of

(a) agricultural or pastoral land,

(b) mines or minerals,

(c) a public house or beer shop,

(d) a furnished house,

(e) any property with respect to which the personal qualifications of the tenant are of importance for the preservation of the value or character of the property,[2] or on the ground of neighbourhood to the lessor, or to any person holding under him.

In such a lease, then, the lessor can proceed to enforce a forfeiture as soon as the bankruptcy occurs, and the tenant has no claim to relief.

If the demised land is not within one of the classes enumerated above, the extent to which the statutory provisions concerning notice and relief apply depends upon whether the lessee's interest is sold, or is not sold, for the benefit of his creditors within one year from the bankruptcy or taking in execution. The two rules on the matter, which are designed to enable the trustee in bankruptcy to decide whether he will disclaim the lease or use it for the benefit of the creditors, are as follows [3] :—

(a) If the interest is sold within the year, the statutory provisions apply without any limit of time. This means, in the case of bankruptcy, that if the trustee in bankruptcy is able to sell the tenant's interest under the lease within the year for the benefit of the creditors, then, despite proceedings for forfeiture, he can apply for relief even after the year has elapsed, and the court may grant the application and confirm the title of the purchaser.[4]

(b) If the interest is not sold within the year, the statutory provisions apply only during that year, *i.e.*, although the landlord cannot take steps to regain possession during that period without serving the statutory notice and without the risk of defeat by a successful application for relief, yet, after the year has elapsed, his right to recover the premises is absolute. No notice need be served, no relief can be granted.[4]

In practice, however, leases do not usually contain a proviso for forfeiture on the bankruptcy of the tenant, except in the five cases enumerated above, since it is troublesome for the landlord to be deprived of his rent until a decision has been

---

[1] *Ibid.*, s. 146 (9).

[2] *Earl Bathurst v. Fine*, [1974] 1 W. L. R. 905 ; [1974] 2 All E. R. 1160.

[3] *Ibid.*, s. 146 (10).

[4] *Civil Service Co-operative Society* v. *McGrigor's Trustee*, [1923] 2 Ch. 347, 355 ; *Horsey Estate, Ltd.* v. *Steiger*, [1899] 2 Q. B. 79 ; *Gee v. Harwood*, [1933] 1 Ch. 712 ; affd., [1934] A. C. 272.

reached by the trustee, and if he accepts rent falling due after the date of bankruptcy the forfeiture is thereby waived.[1]

Relief in case of decoration covenants. A special rule has been introduced by the Act for covenants relating to the internal decorative repair of a house. It is provided that where a statutory notice has been served by the landlord indicating a breach of such a covenant, the court, after reviewing all the circumstances and in particular the length of the term, may wholly or partially relieve the tenant from liabilities for such repairs. But this power to set a covenant aside is not exercisable when a tenant, having expressly agreed to put the property in a decorative state of repair, has never performed the covenant, nor is it to apply to anything which is necessary for keeping the property in a sanitary condition or in a state which makes it fit for human habitation.[2]

Relief to Under-lessees. The jurisdiction of the court to relieve an under-lessee, or a person deriving title under him,[3] against a forfeiture due to the under-lessor's failure to pay rent[4] is equally exercisable where the failure relates to some other covenant.[5] This is so, even though the nature of the breach, *e.g.* the bankruptcy of a publican, preludes the under-lessor from applying for relief.[6] It is a jurisdiction that should be sparingly exercised.[7]

Relief to under-lessees.

SECTION VII. COVENANTS WHICH RUN WITH THE LAND AND WITH THE REVERSION[8]

Introductory Note. A covenant in a lease is *prima facie* a contract binding only on the lessor and the lessee—the actual contracting parties. But it was early seen that to enforce this doctrine of privity of contract was highly undesirable in the case of leases, since both parties had transmissible interests the value of which depended largely upon the obligations that each had assumed. Thus the mediæval land law, although it never lost sight of the general principle that a stranger to a contract cannot sue or be sued upon it, did recognize that covenants contained in a lease might have a wider operation than ordinary contracts. As HOLDSWORTH remarked,

Scope of inquiry.

" they were regarded in a sense as being annexed to an estate in the land, so that they could be enforced by anyone who took that estate in the land."[9]

---

[1] *Doe d. Gatehouse* v. *Rees* (1838), 4 Bing N.C. 384.
[2] L.P.A. 1925, s. 147.
[3] *Re Good's Lease*, [1954] 1 W. L. R. 309 ; [1954] 1 All E. R. 275 ; as, for example, a mortgagee by way of sub-demise ; *Grand Junction Co., Ltd.* v. *Bates*, [1954] 2 Q. B. 160 [1954] 2 All E. R. 385.
[4] *Supra*, pp. 438–40.   [5] L.P.A. 1925, s. 146 (4).   [6] L.P.(A.)A. 1929, s. 1.
[7] *Creery* v. *Summersell and Flowerdew & Co., Ltd.*, [1949] Ch. 751.
[8] Holdsworth, *History of English Law*, vol. vii. pp. 287–92.
[9] *Ibid.*, vol. iii. p. 158.

The scope, then, of our present inquiry is to ascertain in what circumstances persons other than the original lessor and lessee can sue or be sued upon the covenants. Two events may occur— an assignment of the term by the tenant or an assignment of the reversion by the lessor.[1] In each case the two questions that arise are whether the benefit and burden of the covenants pass to the assignee. In short, do the covenants run with the land and with the reversion. Four cases, therefore, fall to be considered :—

Four cases to be considered.

1. The lessee assigns his interest to A. Can A. enforce the covenants inserted in the lease in favour of the lessee ? Does the benefit of these covenants run with the land?

2. The lessee assigns his interest to A. Can A. be sued on the covenants inserted in the lease in favour of the lessor ? Does the burden of the covenants entered into by the lessee run with the land ?

3. The lessor assigns his interest, *i.e.* the reversion, to Z. Can Z. enforce the covenants inserted in the lease in favour of the lessor ? Does the benefit of the covenants run with the reversion ?

4. The lessor assigns his reversion to Z. Can Z. be sued upon the covenants inserted in the lease in favour of the lessee ? Does the burden of the lessor's covenants run with the reversion ?

Limits of present discusion.

In this section we are concerned only with the rules laid down by common law and by statute. It must be realized, however, that these rules may in certain limited circumstances be modified by the doctrine of *Tulk* v. *Moxhay*, under which a covenant between landlord and tenant is sometimes enforceable by and against third parties in cases where this would be impossible either at common law or under the statutes that we shall presently consider.[2]

Covenants touching and concerning the land.

It will simplify our task if, before dealing separately with the four divisions of the subject given above, we describe what is meant by covenants that *touch and concern the land demised*, for it is only these, as distinct from those merely affecting the person, that are capable of running either with the reversion or with the land.

From the present point of view all covenants fall into one or other of two classes, being either personal to the contracting parties, or such as touch and concern the land.

The time-honoured expression " touching and concerning the land " has been replaced in the Law of Property Act 1925 by the phrase *having reference to the subject-matter of the lease*.[3] This affords a clue to the meaning of what is at first sight a little vague. If the covenant has direct reference to the land, if it lays down something which is to be done or is not to be done upon the

---

[1] For the meaning of assignment, see *infra*, pp. 459–61.
[2] *Infra*, pp. 597 *et seq.*   [3] Ss. 141, 142.

land, or, and perhaps this is the clearest way of describing the test, *if it affects the landlord in his normal capacity as landlord or the tenant in his normal capacity as tenant*, it may be said to touch and concern the land.

Lord RUSSELL, C.J., said :—

" The true principle is that no covenant or condition which affects merely the person, and which does not affect the nature, quality, or value of the thing demised or the mode of using or enjoying the thing demised, runs with the land " ;[1]

and BAYLEY, J., at an earlier date asserted the same principle :

" In order to bind the assignee, the covenant must either affect the land itself during the term, such as those which regard the mode of occupation, or it must be such as *per se*, and not merely from collateral circumstances, affects the value of the land at the end of the term."[2]

If a simple test is desired for ascertaining into which category a covenant falls, it is suggested that the proper inquiry should be whether the covenant affects either the landlord *qua* landlord or the tenant *qua* tenant. A covenant may very well have reference to the land, but, unless it is reasonably incidental to the relation of landlord and tenant, it cannot be said to touch and concern the land so as to be capable of running therewith or with the reversion.[3] Tested by this principle the following covenants have been held to touch and concern the land :—

> Covenants by the tenant—
>> to pay rent or taxes ;[4]
>> to repair or leave in repair ;[5]
>> to spend a stated yearly sum on repairs, or in default to pay to the landlord the difference between this sum and the amount actually expended ;[6]
>> to lay dung on the land annually ;[7]
>> to renew tenant's fixtures ;[8]
>> to reside on a farm during the term ;[9]
>> by a publican tenant to buy all beer from the lessor ;[10]
>> not to assign or under-let ;[11]
>> not to allow a third party, X., to be concerned in the conduct of the business carried on at the demised premises.[12]

Examples of covenants touching and concerning the land.

---

[1] *Horsey Estate, Ltd.* v. *Steiger*, [1899] 2 Q. B. 79, 89.
[2] *Mayor of Congleton* v. *Pattison* (1808), 10 East, 130, at p. 138 ; cited Behan, *Covenants affecting Land*, p. 52, *q.v.*
[3] Approved in *Breams Property Investment Co., Ltd.* v. *Stroulger*, [1948] 2 K. B. 1, at p. 7 ; [1948] 1 All E. R. 758, at p. 759.
[4] *Parker* v. *Webb* (1700), 3 Salk. 5.
[5] *Martyn* v. *Clue* (1852), 18 Q. B. 661.
[6] *Moss' Empires, Ltd.* v. *Olympia (Liverpool), Ltd.*, [1939] A. C. 544.
[7] *Sale* v. *Kitchingham* (1713), 10 Mod. 158.
[8] *Williams* v. *Earle* (1868), L. R. 3 Q. B. 739.
[9] *Tatem* v. *Chaplin* (1793), 2 H. Bl. 133.
[10] *Clegg* v. *Hands* (1890), 44 Ch. D. 503.
[11] *Goldstein* v. *Sanders*, [1915] 1 Ch. 549.
[12] *Lewin* v. *American and Colonial Distributors, Ltd.*, [1945] Ch. 225, at p. 236 ; [1945] 2 All E. R. 271, n.

Covenants by the landlord—
> to renew the lease ; [1]
> to supply the demised house with good water ; [2]
> not to build on adjoining land so as to depreciate the amenity of the demised land ; [3]
> to erect a new building in place of an old one ; [4]
> to keep a housekeeper to act as servant of the lessee ; [5]
> not to serve a notice to quit for three years, unless he requires the premises for his own occupation. [6]

Personal covenants.

On the other hand personal, or collateral, covenants do not touch and concern the land, since they have no direct reference to the subject-matter of the lease. The word *collateral*, admittedly ambiguous, in this context indicates a covenant relating to a matter not normally relevant to the relationship of landlord and tenant. For instance, a covenant by either party to pay a sum of money to the other is merely collateral, [7] unless it is inextricably bound up with other covenants that touch and concern the land. [8]

> Thus a covenant by a lessee, in furtherance of his express undertaking to repair, to expend £500 yearly upon repairs, or to pay the lessor the difference between this amount and what is actually expended, is not a bare obligation personal to the contracting parties. It touches and concerns the land, since it is part and parcel of the repairing covenant. [9]

In *Thomas* v. *Hayward* [10] :—

> Where the lessor of a public house had covenanted that he would not open another beer or spirit house within half a mile of the demised premises, the question arose whether this covenant could be enforced by an assignee of the lessee.

It was held that it could not, because it was collateral in the sense that it did not oblige the lessor to do or to refrain from doing anything on the demised premises. On the other hand a covenant by the tenant of a public house to conduct the business in such a manner as to afford no ground for the suspension of the licence, was held to touch the land, since it concerned the manner in which the covenantor was to use the premises as tenant. [11]

---

[1] *Muller* v. *Trafford*, [1901] 1 Ch. 54; *Weg Motors, Ltd.* v. *Hales*, [1961] Ch. 176 ; [1960] 3 All E. R. 762 ; affd. [1962] Ch. 49 ; [1961] 3 All E. R. 181.
[2] *Jourdain* v. *Wilson* (1821), 4 B. & Ald. 266.
[3] *Ricketts* v. *Enfield Churchwardens*, [1909] 1 Ch. 544.
[4] *Easterby* v. *Sampson* (1830), 6 Bing. 644.
[5] *Barnes* v. *City of London Real Property Co.*, [1918] 2 Ch. 18.
[6] *Breams Property Investment Co., Ltd.* v. *Stroulger*, [1948] 2 K. B. 1 ; [1948] 1 All E. R. 758.
[7] *Re Hunter's Lease*, [1942] Ch. 124; [1942] 1 All E. R. 27.
[8] *Moss' Empires, Ltd.* v. *Olympia (Liverpool), Ltd.*, [1939] A. C. 544 ; [1939] 3 All E. R. 460 ; *Boyer* v. *Warbey*, [1953] 1 Q. B. 234 ; [1952] 2 All E. R. 976.
[9] *Moss' Empires, Ltd.* v. *Olympia (Liverpool), Ltd.*, *supra.*
[10] (1869), L. R. 4 Ex. 311.
[11] *Fleetwood* v. *Hull* (1889), 23 Q. B. D. 35.

A covenant that entitles the tenant to purchase the fee simple at a given price at any time during the term, affects the parties *qua* vendor and purchaser, not *qua* landlord and tenant. It is collateral to the lease and as such it cannot run as a matter of course with the land or with the reversion as being one that touches and concerns the land.[1] Nevertheless, if it does not infringe the rule against perpetuities,[2] its effect is to confer upon the tenant an equitable interest in the land[3] which, like any other piece of property, is freely assignable unless the terms of its grant show that it is personal to him. Therefore, the option, will pass on an assignment of the demised land and will be enforceable against the landlord; and if registered as an estate contract[4] it will be enforceable against an assignee of the reversion.[5]

Option to purchase the fee simple.

We can now take up the four cases that have been indicated above and determine in what circumstances the covenants will run in each case. The rules depend partly upon the common law as finally enunciated in *Spencer's Case*, 1583,[6] and partly upon statutes. The statutes that formerly regulated the matter were the Grantees of Reversions Act,[7] passed in 1540 after the dissolution of the monasteries, and the Conveyancing Act 1881,[8] but both these were repealed and replaced by the Law of Property Act 1925.[9]

Running of covenants at common law and by statute.

1. *The lessee assigns his interest to A. Can A. enforce the covenants which were inserted in the lease in favour of the lessee?* The rule even at common law is that the benefit of the covenants runs with the land, enabling an assignee (A.) from the lessee to sue the lessor on any covenants which touch and concern the land demised and which enure for the benefit of the lessee, such as a covenant by the lessor to supply the demised premises with pure water. The authority for this rule is *Spencer's Case*, in the fourth resolution of which the court, dealing with a covenant for quiet enjoyment, said :—

Benefit of covenant runs with land.

" for the lessee and his assignee hath the yearly profits of the land, which shall grow by his labour and industry for an annual rent ; and therefore it is reasonable when he hath applied his labour and employed his cost upon the land, and be evicted, (whereby he loses all) that he shall take such benefit of the demise and grant, as the first lessee might. . . ."

2. *The lessee assigns his interest to A. Can A. be sued upon*

---

[1] A right of pre-emption is also collateral. *Collison* v. *Lettson* (1815), 6 Taunt. 224. *Charles Frodsham & Co., Ltd.* v. *Morris* (1972), 229 Estates Gazette 961.

[2] *Supra*, p. 347.

[3] *London and South Western Rail Co.* v. *Gomm* (1882), 20 Ch.D. 562; *supra*, pp. 128, 338–9.

[4] *Infra*, p. 742.

[5] *Griffith* v. *Pelton*, [1958] Ch. 205; [1957] 3 All E. R. 75, explaining *Woodall* v. *Clifton*, [1905] 2 Ch. 257; *Re Button's Lease*, [1964] Ch. 263 ; [1963] 3 All E. R. 708. See generally (1958), 74 *L. Q. R.* 242 (W. J. Mowbray).

[6] (1583), 5 Co. Rep. 16 ; M. & B. p. 414.   [7] 32 Hen. 8, c. 34, s. 1.

[8] Ss. 10, 11.   [9] Ss. 141, 142.

Burden of
covenant
runs with
land.

the covenants which were inserted in the lease in favour of the lessor ? The common law answers this also in the affirmative, provided that the covenant touches and concerns the land, for it is said in *Spencer's Case* that :—

> " When the covenant extends to a thing *in esse*, parcel of the demise, the thing to be done by force of the covenant is *quodammodo* annexed and appurtenant to the thing demised, and shall go with the land and shall bind the assignee, although he be not bound by express words."

Distinction
between
thing *in esse*
and *in posse.*

It is true that the judgment then proceeded to draw a distinction between a covenant which referred to something already in existence (such as to repair an existing wall), and one which related to a thing not in existence at the time of the lease (such as a covenant to build a new wall), and laid down that though the former would bind assignees in all cases, yet the latter would not do so unless the original lessee had covenanted for himself *and his assigns*. This distinction rested upon no solid basis, but, though adversely criticized,[1] it remained law until 1926. It has been abolished by the Law of Property Act 1925, which provides that [2] :—

> " A covenant relating to any land of a covenantor or capable of being bound by him, shall, unless a contrary intention is expressed,[3] be deemed to be made by the covenantor on behalf of himself his successors in title and the persons deriving title under him or them, and, subject as aforesaid, shall have effect as if such successors and other persons were expressed.
>
> This subsection extends to a covenant to do some act relating to the land, notwithstanding that the subject-matter may not be in existence when the covenant is made."

This section, however, applies only to covenants made on or after January 1st, 1926. In the case of a lease executed before 1926, the burden of a covenant relating to something not in existence will not run with the land unless it was expressly imposed upon the lessee *and his assigns*.

Benefit of
covenant
runs with
reversion.

3. *The lessor assigns his interest, i.e. the reversion, to Z. Can Z. enforce the covenants which were inserted in the lease in favour of the lessor ?* The rule at common law is that the grantee of a reversion can sue upon an implied covenant, that is, one which automatically results from the relationship of landlord and tenant (such as a covenant to pay rent), but he cannot sue upon express covenants contained in the lease.[4] The difficulty is said to be that in the case of a reversion there is no corporeal thing to which the covenant can be regarded as annexed, such as there is where the land is assigned.[5]

---

[1] *Minshull* v. *Oakes* (1858), 2 H. & N. 793. See Behan, *Covenants affecting Land*, pp. 75 *et seq.*   [2] S. 79 (1).

[3] *Re Royal Victoria Pavilion, Ramsgate*, [1961] Ch. 581 ; [1961] 3 All E. R. 83 ; M. & B. p. 702.

[4] Platt on Covenants, p. 531 ; *Wedd* v. *Porter*, [1916] 3 K. B. 91, at pp. 100–101.

[5] *E.g.* Smith's *Leading Cases* (13th Edn.), vol. i. pp. 61–2.

A mitigation of this strict rule of the common law became urgent when the monasteries were dissolved by Henry VIII in 1539, because, if the law had not been altered, it would have precluded the grantees of the monastic lands from enforcing against existing lessees the express covenants in leases granted by the monasteries before their dissolution. Hence the Grantees of Reversions (1540), which, though designed merely to accommodate grantees of monastic lands, soon came to be regarded as having universal application and as laying down the law for assignees of reversions in general. This statute, which remained the only law on the subject until the Conveyancing Act of 1881, enacted that assignees of reversions should have the same right of enforcing forfeitures, and the same right of suing for a breach of any covenant, as the original lessors.[1]

Both these statutes have been repealed, and the right of an assignee of a reversion to enforce the covenants now rests upon the Law of Property Act 1925,[2] which, in a section that applies to all leases whether made before 1926 or after 1925, provides that :

Provisions o the Law of Property Act 1925.

" (1) Rent reserved by a lease, and the benefit of every covenant or provision therein contained, having reference to the subject-matter thereof,[3] and on the lessee's part to be observed or performed, and every condition of re-entry and other condition therein contained, shall be annexed and incident to and shall go with the reversionary estate in the land, or in any part thereof, immediately expectant on the term granted by the lease, notwithstanding severance of that reversionary estate, and without prejudice to any liability affecting a covenantor or his estate.

(2) Any such rent, covenant or provision shall be capable of being recovered, received, enforced and taken advantage of, by the person from time to time entitled, subject to the term, to the income of the whole or any part, as the case may require, of the land leased.

(3) Where that person becomes entitled by conveyance or otherwise, such rent, covenant or provision may be recovered, received, enforced or taken advantage of by him notwithstanding that he becomes so entitled after the condition of re-entry or forfeiture has become enforceable, but this subsection does not render enforceable any condition of re-entry or other condition waived[4] or released before such person becomes entitled as aforesaid."

One result of this enactment, which provides, in repetition of the Conveyancing Act 1881, that " rent reserved by a lease,[5] and the benefit of every covenant or provision therein contained " shall pass with the reversion, is to abolish the old construction put upon the Grantees of Reversions (1540), viz. that the assignee of a reversion could not sue upon the covenants unless the original lease was under seal. The rule now is that the assignee can sue if the lease is in writing or if the tenancy is the result of a written

Lease must be in writing.

---

[1] S. 10.   [2] S. 141.
[3] *I.e.*, touching and concerning the land demised.
[4] *London and County (A. and D.) Ltd.* v. *Wilfred Sportsman, Ltd.*, [1971] Ch. 764 ; [1970] 2 All E. R. 600 ; M. & B. p. 420.
[5] " Lease " includes " an under-lease or other tenancy " ; s. 154.

agreement for a lease,[1] even though in the latter case the agreement is signed by the landlord only.[2] The same is the case if a parol lease is made for a period not exceeding three years, or if a parol agreement for a lease of any length is followed by a sufficient act of part performance.[3]

Breach of covenant committed before assignment.

The Court of Appeal has held that, under this section of the Act, the assignee of the reversion is the only person entitled to sue the tenant for any breach of covenant, whether of a continuous nature or not and even though committed before the date of the assignment.[4]

> " The expression ' go with ' must be intended to add something to the concept involved in the expression ' annexed and incident to ' and in my view connotes the transfer of the right to enforce the covenant from the assignor to the assignee with the consequent cessation of the right of the assignor to enforce the covenant against the tenant."[5]

Burden of covenant runs with reversion.

4. *The lessor assigns his reversion to Z. Can Z. be sued upon the covenants which were inserted in the lease in favour of the lessee?* There was no right of action against Z. at common law, but a right was given by the Grantees of Reversions (1540) which enacted that a lessee and his assigns should have the same remedy against the assignees of the lessor as the original lessee would have had against the lessor. This enactment was attended by certain difficulties, which are no longer of interest, since they were removed by the Conveyancing Act 1881,[6] in a section now replaced by the Law of Property Act 1925, and applicable to all leases whenever made.[7] This section runs as follows :—

> " The obligation under a condition or of a covenant entered into by a lessor with reference to the subject-matter of the lease shall, if and as far as the lessor has power to bind the reversionary estate immediately expectant on the term granted by the lease, be annexed and incident to and shall go with that reversionary estate, or the several parts thereof, notwithstanding severance of that reversionary estate, and may be taken advantage of and enforced by the person in whom the term is from time to time vested by conveyance, devolution in law, or otherwise ; and, if and as far as the lessor has power to bind the person from time to time entitled to that reversionary estate, the obligation aforesaid may be taken advantage of and enforced against any person so entitled."

The word " covenant " as used in this section is not confined to its strict meaning of a contract under seal, but includes any promise

---

[1] *Rickett* v. *Green*, [1910] 1 K. B. 253 ; M. & B. p. 425 ; *Boyer* v. *Warbey*, [1953] 1 Q. B. 234 ; [1953] 1 All E. R. 269 ; M. & B. p. 427.
[2] *Rye* v. *Purcell*, [1926] 1 K. B. 446.
[3] *Boyer* v. *Warbey, supra.*
[4] *Re King*, [1963] Ch. 459 ; [1963] 1 All E. R. 781 ; M. & B. p. 418 (covenant to repair and reinstate) ; *London and County (A. and D.), Ltd.* v. *Wilfred Sportsman, Ltd.*, [1971] Ch. 764; [1970] 2 All E. R. 600 (covenant to pay rent) ; M. & B. p. 420 ; *Arlesford Trading Co., Ltd.* v. *Servansingh*, [1971] 1 W. L. R. 1080 ; [1971] 3 All E. R. 1130.
[5] *Ibid.*, at p. 497, *per* DIPLOCK, L. J.
[6] S. 11.   [7] S. 142 (1).

touching and concerning the land[1] that is contained in a tenancy agreement made otherwise than by deed.[2]

One particular difficulty which arose under the Grantees of Reversions (1540) was that, owing to its indivisible nature,[3] a condition could not be enforced by an assignee of *part* of the reversion. If the reversion was severed, the condition could not be apportioned. The statutory rule, however, now is that, where such a severance has taken place, every condition contained in the lease is apportioned and remains annexed to the severed parts of the reversion.[4] If the owner of a severed part of the reversion determines the tenancy by a notice to quit,[5] the lessee is permitted within one month to determine the whole tenancy by serving notice on the owner in whom the rest of the reversion is vested.[6]

Before we conclude the subject of covenants that run with the land or the reversion, there are two general observations of considerable importance to be made :—

1. First, there can be no question of the enforcement of covenants between two parties unless there exists between them either privity of estate or privity of contract. *Privity of contract* denotes that relationship which exists between the lessor and the lessee—and between them only—by virtue of the covenants contained in the lease. This relationship is created by the contract itself and continues to subsist between the lessor and lessee despite an assignment of their respective interests. *Privity of estate* describes the relationship between two parties who respectively hold the same estates as those created by the lease. This is the position where one holds the original reversion and the other the original term, or rather, the whole of what is now left of the original term. Thus there is privity of estate between the lessor and an assignee from the lessee of the residue of the term ; also between the lessee and an assignee of the reversion ; also between an assignee of the reversion and an assignee of the residue of the term. In the absence of assignment, therefore, there is privity both of contract and of estate between the lessor and lessee.[7]

---

[1] *Davis* v. *Town Properties, etc.*, [1903] 1 Ch. 797.

[2] *Weg Motors, Ltd.* v. *Hales*, [1962] Ch. 49 ; [1961] 3 All E. R. 181.

[3] *Supra*, pp. 425–6.

[4] L.P.A. 1925, s. 140 (1) ; replacing L.P.(A.)A. 1859, s. 3, and Conveyancing Act 1881, s. 12.

[5] See, *e.g.*, *Smith* v. *Kinsey*, [1936] 3 All E. R. 73.

[6] L.P.A. 1925, s. 140 (2). See *Jelley* v. *Buckman*, [1974] Q. B. 488 ; [1973] 3 All E. R. 853 (after severance of reversion tenant continues to hold under single tenancy).

[7] *Bickford* v. *Parson* (1848), 5 C. B. 920, at p. 929. See also *Platt on Leases*, vol. ii. p. 351 : " Privity of estate is the result of tenure ; it subsists by virtue of the relation of landlord and tenant, and follows alike the devolution of the reversion, and of the term."

Original
lessee always
liable to
original
lessor.

There are certain important rules that flow from this general principle. Thus :

" It is perfectly settled by a multitude of decisions that, notwithstanding an assignment of his lease, the lessee continues liable on the personal privity of the contract to the payment of the rent and the performance of the covenants during the whole term ; although the lessor concur in the assignment, or, by acceptance of rent or otherwise, recognize the assignee as his tenant. " [1]

Assignee
liable and
entitled only
in respect
of matters
occurring
while he
holds the
land.

Again, as the liability of an assignee of the tenant is based upon the privity of estate between him and the lessor or the latter's assignee,[2] it follows that the tenant's assignee cannot be liable for a breach of covenant committed before he took the estate under the assignment,[3] and cannot sue the lessor for breaches committed prior to that time. Lastly, and consistently with the same principle, an assignee ceases to be liable for breaches occurring after he has assigned his interest to a third party, for such a re-assignment obviously destroys the privity of estate which previously existed.[4] He is liable, however, even for these subsequent breaches, if he expressly covenants with the landlord at the time of taking the assignment that he will perform the terms of the lease.[5] Moreover, in any event, he remains liable after re-assignment for any breaches which occurred while the tenancy was vested in him.[6]

Implied
indemnity
by assignee.

It will thus be seen that, where one of the lessee's covenants has been broken after an assignment of the term, the lessor has the option of suing either the original lessee on the privity of contract or the particular assignee who had the estate when the breach occurred, but although this joint liability undoubtedly exists, the rule is that the assignee in possession is the principal debtor, while the lessee occupies the position of a surety.[7] Nevertheless the continuing liability of the original lessee is an obvious menace to him, and it became the invariable practice for every assignee expressly to covenant to indemnify his assignor against future breaches of the provisions contained in the lease. This is no longer necessary, for it is now enacted that every assignment for valuable consideration shall be deemed to include a covenant by the assignee that he will pay all rent falling due in the future and will perform all the covenants, agreements and

---

[1] *Platt on Leases*, vol. ii. pp. 352–3. Distinguish, however, the liability of a lessee who acquires a statutory term of 2000 years under the provisions for converting perpetually renewable leases ; *supra*, pp. 382–3.

[2] *Purchase* v. *Lichfield Brewery Ltd.*, [1915] 1 K. B. 184 ; M. & B. p. 426.

[3] *Grescot* v. *Green* (1699), 1 Salk. 199.

[4] *Paul* v. *Nurse* (1828), 8 B. & C. 486.

[5] *(J.) Lyons & Co., Ltd.* v. *Knowles*, [1943] 1 K. B. 366 ; [1943] 1 All E. R. 477.

[6] *Harley* v. *King* (1835), 2 C. M. & R. 18 ; cf. *Richmond* v. *Savill*, [1926] 2 K. B. 530.

[7] *Humble* v. *Langston* (1841), 7 M. & W. 517, at p. 530, *per* PARKE, B.

conditions binding upon the original lessee. This implied covenant of indemnity binds all persons, such as later assignees, deriving title under the assignee.[1] To take an example:

> L. leases land to T. Later successive assignments of the land are made first to U., then to V., and finally to W. If L. sues T. for the breach committed by W. of some condition contained in the lease, the implied covenant of indemnity entitles T. to make U. a party to the action. Similarly U. can join V., and V. can join W. as a party. In this way judgment can be given against the person who has actually committed the breach.[2]

2. The second observation is that the rules laid down above with regard to the running of covenants apply only where there has been an assignment in the true and proper sense of that term, for it is only then that privity of estate exists between the reversioner and the person who is in occupation of the land. The term " assignee " is very comprehensive: it applies to all persons who take the estate either by act of party or by act of law, such as the executors of a lessee or assignee, and persons taking the premises by way of execution for debt, but in the eyes of the law no person occupies the position of assignee of the land unless he takes the *identical term* which the lessee had, and also takes the *whole of that term*.[3]

There must be an "assignment."

Thus if the lessee, on making what purports to be an assignment of his term, reserves to himself a reversion, no matter how trifling it may be—as where he assigns the remainder of his lease less one day—the transaction amounts to an under-lease and not to an assignment. In such a case it is obvious that there is neither privity of contract nor privity of estate between the superior landlord and the under-lessee, and therefore neither of them can sue or be sued *at law* upon the covenants of the lease,[4] though as we shall see later the under-lessee may be liable under the equitable doctrine of *Tulk* v. *Moxhay* on purely negative covenants.[5] But there is no magic in words. If a man has acquired an interest in the tenancy and a question arises with regard to his position, the first point that falls to be considered is whether he has taken the whole of the tenant's interest. Thus where the tenant executes a deed couched in the form of an under-lease, which purports to sub-let the property for the whole of the remainder of his term

Whole interest must be transferred.

---

[1] L.P.A. 1925, s. 77 (1) (c) ; 2nd Sched., Part IX.
[2] As to the nature of this covenant see *Butler Estates Co.* v. *Bean*, [1942] 1 K. B. 1 ; [1941] 2 All E. R. 793.
[3] *Platt on Leases*, vol. ii. pp. 419–20.
[4] *South of England Dairies Co.* v. *Baker*, [1906] 2 Ch. 631 ; M. & B. p. 420.
[5] *Infra*, p. 602, note 5.

or for a longer period, the transaction amounts to an assignment.[1]

Identical interest must be transferred.

The other point, as we have observed, is that if there is to be an assignment, the alienee must take the identical interest which the alienor possessed. If, for instance, a tenant deposits his lease with X. by way of mortgage, X. obtains a mere equitable right to the land and not the legal term to which the tenant was entitled. Therefore, whether he goes into possession or not, he can neither sue nor be sued on the covenants.[2] A similar result again ensues where a person obtains a title under the Limitation Act against the lessee, as was decided in *Tichborne* v. *Weir*.[3] The facts of this case were as follows :—

Tichborne v. *Weir*.

In 1802 D. leased land to B. for 89 years.

In 1836 G. seized the land and remained in possession of it until 1876, paying D. the rent which had been fixed by the lease of 1802.

In 1876 G. by deed assigned all his interest to the defendant, who remained in possession until 1891, paying the same rent to the plaintiff, who had succeeded to D.

The original lease between D. and B. contained a covenant by B. to keep the premises in repair, and the plaintiff now sued the defendant for breach of that covenant. The right of the original covenantor B. to his tenancy of the land had been extinguished by lapse of time when the defendant came to the land in 1876, but the question that arose was whether the defendant was an assignee of B. through G. It was clear, if the identical lease which was vested in B. had passed to G. and from him to the defendant, that the latter would be liable as assignee on the repairing covenant, and it was strenuously argued that the effect of the Real Property Limitation Act, which was the statute then in force, was to transfer the term from B. to G.

But it was held that the only effect of the statute was to extinguish B.'s right of recovering the land and not to convey what he had to G. It therefore followed that the defendant was not liable on the repairing covenant, because, not possessing the very estate to which it was attached, he was not an assignee.

O'Connor v. *Foley*.

But the limits of the decision must be noted. It was said by a learned Irish judge [4] :—

" It appears to me to decide only this, that the Statute of Limitations operates by way of extinguishment, and not by way of assignment of the estate, which is barred ; and that a person who becomes entitled to a leasehold interest by adverse

---

[1] *Beardman* v. *Wilson* (1868), L. R. 4 C. P. 57 ; *Hallen* v. *Spaeth*, [1923] A. C. 684 ; *Milmo* v. *Carreras*, [1946] K. B. 306 ; [1946] 1 All E. R. 288 ; M. & B. p. 420.

[2] *Cox* v. *Bishop* (1857), 8 De G. M. & G. 815 ; M. & B. p. 425. He may, however, be liable under the doctrine of *Tulk* v. *Moxhay*, *infra*, pp. 597 *et seq.*

[3] (1892) 67 L. T. 735 ; M. & B. pp. 167, 700 ; followed in *Taylor* v. *Twinberrow*, [1930] 2 K. B. 16.

[4] FitzGibbon, L.J., in *O'Connor* v. *Foley*, [1906] 1 I. R. 20, at p. 26.

possession for the prescribed period is not liable to be sued *in covenant as assignee* of the lease, unless he has estopped himself from denying that he is assignee."

So, in the first place, the decision will not apply where the occupier of the lands has estopped himself from denying that he holds on all the terms of the original lease,[1] but although this point was pressed in *Tichborne* v. *Weir*, it was held that the terms under which the defendant paid rent did not warrant the conclusion that he stood for all purposes in the shoes of the original tenant B.[2] But where a lease contains a proviso that the rent shall be reduced by a half if all the covenants are duly observed, and an adverse possessor avails himself of the privilege, he is estopped from denying that he is subject to the burden of the lease.[3]

Secondly, the case only goes to show that an adverse possessor cannot be sued in covenant as assignee, and when we come to deal with equitable doctrines, we shall see that he is liable on such negative covenants as create an equitable burden on the estate he takes.[4]

SECTION VIII. DETERMINATION OF TENANCIES

SUMMARY

1. TENANCIES FOR A FIXED PERIOD

A tenancy for a fixed period may be terminated by forfeiture, surrender, merger, enlargement, effluxion of time, or, where an agreement to that effect has been made, by a notice to quit given by either party. There is no need to add to the account already given of forfeiture.[5]

Modes of determination.

Surrender. Surrender occurs where the tenant yields up his estate to the lessor. In the case of a joint tenancy, a surrender is not effective unless made by all the tenants.[6]

The express surrender of a lease not exceeding three years may be effected by a written instrument,[7] but in terms for longer periods it must be made by deed.[8]

Express surrender.

---

[1] As for instance in *Rodenhurst Estates, Ltd.* v. *Barnes, Ltd.*, [1936] 2 All E. R. 3.

[2] For another instance, see *Official Trustee of Charity Lands* v. *Ferriman Trust, Ltd.*, [1937] 3 All E. R. 85.

[3] *Ashe* v. *Hogan*, [1920] 2 I. R. 159.

[4] *Re Nisbet and Potts' Contract*, [1905] 1 Ch. 391 ; M. & B. pp. 168, 700, *infra*, pp. 435–40 ; 441–9.

[5] *Supra*, pp. 435–40 ; 441–9.

[6] *Leek and Moorlands Building Society* v. *Clark*, [1952] 2 Q. B. 788 ; [1952] 2 All E. R. 492.

[7] L.P.A. 1925, ss. 53 (1) ; 54 (2).   [8] *Ibid.*, s. 52.

Surrender by operation of law.

If, however, the intention of the parties as inferred from their conduct is that the lease should be yielded up, surrender results by operation of law without the necessity either of a writing or a deed.[1] This doctrine rests upon the principle of estoppel.[2] It operates where the owner of a particular estate, such as a tenant for years, is a party to some transaction that would not be valid if his estate continued to exist. If, for example, the lessor grants to him a new lease which is to begin during the currency of the existing lease, the latter is implicitly surrendered and the tenant is estopped from disputing the validity of the new lease.[3] Before there can be such an implied surrender, there must be something in the nature of an agreement, and that agreement must amount to more than a mere variation of the terms of an existing tenancy.[4]

Other examples of implied surrender occur, if

possession is delivered by the tenant to the lessor and accepted by the latter [5] ;

the tenant is permitted to remain in occupation of the premises as a licensee paying no rent [6] ;

the lessor grants a new lease to a third party, or accepts a third party as the new tenant, with the assent of the existing tenant.[7]

Union of term and reversion in one person.

Merger. The term of years and the reversion are concurrent interests that cannot be held by one and the same person at the same time. If, therefore, they become united in one person in the same right, as for example where the lessor conveys the fee simple to the tenant, the term is at common law immediately destroyed. It is said to be "merged," *i.e.* sunk or drowned in the greater estate.[8] It will be explained later, however, that in equity the union of a smaller and a greater estate in one person does not always result in merger.[9]

Enlargement. A tenant may by deed enlarge his lease into a fee simple under the Law of Property Act 1925.[10]

Before the enlargement can be effected, however, the following conditions must exist :

(i) The term must originally have been created for not

---

[1] L.P.A. 1925, s. 52 (2) (c).

[2] For its operation in the creation of a tenancy, see *supra*, p. 404.

[3] *Lyon* v. *Reed* (1844), 13 M. & W. 285 ; *Fenner* v. *Blake*, [1900] 1 Q. B. 426 ; *Knight* v. *Williams*, [1901] 1 Ch. 256. To produce a surrender, the new lease must be effective, not, for example, one which is beyond the powers of the lessor, *Barclays Bank, Ltd.* v. *Stasek*, [1957] Ch. 28 ; [1956] 3 All E. R. 439.

[4] *Smirk* v. *Lyndale Developments, Ltd.*, [1975] Ch. 317, at p. 339 *per* Lawton, L.J. An agreed increase in rent does not necessarily amount to an implied surrender, *Jenkin R. Lewis & Son, Ltd.* v. *Kerman*, [1971] Ch. 477 ; [1970] 1 All E. R. 833 ; affd. ; [1970] 3 All E. R. 414.

[5] *Dodd* v. *Acklom* (1843), 6 Man. & G. 672.

[6] *Foster* v. *Robinson*, [1951] 1 K. B. 149 ; [1950] 2 All E. R. 342.

[7] *Wallis* v. *Hands*. [1893] 2 Ch. 75 ; *Metcalfe* v. *Boyce*, [1927] 1 K. B. 758.

[8] Blackstone, vol. ii. p. 177.   [9] *Infra*, p. 910.

[10] S. 153. See (1958) 22 *Conv.* (N.S.) 101 (T. P. D. Taylor).

less than 300 years, and at the time of the proposed enlargement there must be at least 200 more years to run.

(ii) There must be no trust or right of redemption[1] still existing in favour of the reversioner.

(iii) The term must not be one which is liable to be determined by re-entry for condition broken.

(iv) There must be no rent of any money value.[2]

A fee simple, so acquired by enlargement, is subject to all the same covenants, provisions and obligations as the lease would have been subject to if it had not been so enlarged.[3]

Effluxion of time. In principle there is no need for a notice to quit in the case of a lease for a definite term, since the tenancy terminates automatically upon the expiration of the agreed period. The scope of this rule, however, has been drastically restricted by legislation, for there are several cases in which there is no automatic cessation of a tenancy upon the expiration of the period for which it was granted. These cases are the following :— *Special cases.*

Ordinary Residential Lettings.[4]
Lettings by Resident Landlords.[5]
Long Tenancies.[6]
Business Tenancies.[7]
Agricultural Holdings.[8]

In the result there are comparatively few cases in which effluxion of time has its normal effect.

Notice to quit. A notice to quit is necessary in the case of yearly and other periodic tenancies, and also in the case of a lease for a fixed period if a stipulation to that effect is made. There is special protection in the case of a dwelling house. The Rent Act 1957[9] provides that no notice shall be valid unless it is given not less than four weeks before the date on which it is to expire ; the notice must be in writing and contain such information as may be prescribed by the Secretary of State.[10] The common law rule applies in this context and the provision is satisfied by a notice given on one day to expire that day four weeks hence.[11] *When necessary.*

---

[1] *I.e.* under a mortgage. See *infra*, p. 653.

[2] *Re Chapman and Hobbs*, (1885), 29 Ch. D. 1007 ; *Re Smith and Stott* (1883), 29 Ch. D. 1009.

[3] L.P.A. 1925, s. 153 (8) ; see p. 596, *infra*.

[4] *Infra*, p. 469.

[5] *Infra*, p. 484.

[6] *Infra*, p. 490.

[7] *Infra*, p. 499.

[8] *Infra* p. 507.

[9] S. 16. This section only applies where the true relation between the parties is that of landlord and tenant ; *Alliance Building Society* v. *Pinwill*, [1958] Ch. 788 ; [1958] 2 All E. R. 408. *Crane* v. *Morris*, [1965] 1 W. L. R. 1104 ; [1965] 3 All E. R. 77. Four weeks is also the minimum notice for a residential contract in respect of a caravan. Caravan Sites Act 1968, s. 2.

[10] Housing Act 1974, s. 123. See Notices to Quit (Prescribed Information) (Protected Tenancies and Part VI Contracts) Regulations 1975 (S.I. No. 2196).

[11] *Schnabel* v. *Allard*, [1966] 3 All E. R. 816;

Essentials of validity.

Since the notice is a unilateral act performed in the exercise of a contractual right, it must conform strictly to the terms of the contract.[1] The onus of proving its validity lies upon the person by whom it is given.[2] Two matters in particular upon which its validity depends may be observed.

Must indicate the correct day.

(i) First, it is void unless it either names the correct date for the termination of the tenancy[3] or uses a formula from which the correct date is ascertainable with certainty. A familiar example of the latter is when the notice requires the yearly tenant to quit the premises

" at the expiration of the year of your tenancy, which shall expire next after the end of one half-year from the service of this notice."[4]

Must be unconditional.

(ii) Secondly, a notice to quit must be unconditional. It must be expressed in such decisive and unequivocal terms, that the person to whom it is directed can entertain no reasonable doubt as to its intended effect. In particular, although no precise form is required, " there must be plain unambiguous words claiming to determine the existing tenancy at a certain time." [5] Thus a notice given by a tenant would be ineffective if it expressed his intention to quit the premises on March 25, unless he was unable to obtain alternative accommodation.

Where, however, the naming of a certain day for the termination of the tenancy is followed by an intimation that the lease shall continue if the other party assents to certain terms, as for example to an increase [6] or diminution [7] of rent, the courts are inclined to treat the document as a valid notice accompanied by an offer of a new tenancy capable of acceptance or refusal by the other party. In *Dagger* v. *Shepherd*, [8] for instance, the question arose whether a notice, given on December 21, directing the tenant to quit the premises

" on or before the 25th March next "

was valid and effective. It was objected by the tenant that the notice was void for uncertainty, since he was left in doubt as to its intended effect. In his submission the document contained nothing more than a statement that the tenancy was to end on some unspecified date between December 21 and March 25. The court, however, rejected this submission. It construed the document as an irrevocable notice to quit on March 25 in any event,

---

[1] *Dagger* v. *Shepherd*, [1946] K. B. 215, at p. 220 ; [1946] 1 All E. R. 133, at p. 135 ; *Hankey* v. *Clavering*, [1942] 2 K. B. 326, at p. 330 ; [1942] 2 All E. R. 311, at p. 314.
[2] *Lemon* v. *Lardeur*, [1946] K. B. 613 ; [1946] 2 All E. R. 329.
[3] *Hankey* v. *Clavering*, *supra*.
[4] *Addis* v. *Burrows*, [1948] 1 K. B. 444 ; [1948] 1 All E. R. 177.
[5] *Gardner* v. *Ingram* (1889), 61 L. T. 729, at p. 730, *per* Lord Coleridge.
[6] *Ahearn* v. *Bellman* (1879), 4 Exch. D. 201 ; but Lord Esher vigorously dissented.
[7] *Bury* v. *Thompson*, [1895] 1 Q. B. 696.
[8] [1946] K. B. 215 ; [1946] 1 All E. R. 133.

but followed by an offer to accept the termination of the tenancy at any earlier date at which the tenant might elect to give up possession.

Must relate to the whole of the premises.

(iii) A notice to quit given by a lessor must relate to the whole of the premises. It is void if it directs the tenant to surrender possession of part only of what he holds, unless this is permitted by the lease itself or by statute.[1] Such a statutory power is vested in the lessor of an agricultural holding if he requires part of the land for certain purposes, such as the erection of cottages or the provision of allotments, specified by the Agricultural Holdings Act 1948.[2] If, however, he takes advantage of this power, the tenant may treat the notice as a notice to quit the entire holding.[3]

2. YEARLY AND OTHER PERIODIC TENANCIES

Half a year's notice necessary.

A tenancy from year to year does not expire at the end of the first or any subsequent year, but continues until it is determined by a notice served either by the landlord or tenant.[4] It has been the rule since the reign of Henry VIII that not less than half a year's notice is necessary, unless a different agreement has been made by the parties.

Meaning of " half a year."

It is well established what is meant by " half a year." If the tenancy began on one of the usual quarter days[5], it means the interval between a quarter day and the next quarter day but one, notwithstanding that, measured by days, such a period may not amount to half a year.[6] Thus in a Lady Day tenancy notice to quit will be good if given on or before Michaelmas Day, though the actual period is five days short of 182. If the tenancy began at some day falling between two quarter days, then the length of notice must be 182 days at least.[7]

Exceptions to the rule.

There are two exceptions to the rule requiring half a year's notice.

Contrary agreement.

(i) First, where the parties have made a different arrangement.

" I know of nothing which prevents parties, in entering into an agreement for a tenancy from year to year, from stipulating that it should be determinable by a notice to quit shorter than the usual six months' notice ; or that the notices to quit to be given by the landlord and the tenant respectively should be of unequal length ; or that the tenancy should be determinable by the one party only by notice to

---

[1] *Re Bebington's Tenancy*, [1921] 1 Ch. 559. The actual decision is now out of date owing to L.P.A. 1925, s. 140 (1), (2) ; *supra*, p. 457.

[2] S. 31.   [3] S. 32.

[4] See *Youngmin* v. *Heath*, [1974] 1 W. L. R. 135 ; [1974] 1 All E. R. 461 (personal representative of deceased weekly tenant liable for rent until notice to quit given).

[5] Lady Day (March 25) ; Midsummer Day (June 24) ; Michaelmas (September 29) ; Christmas (December 25).

[6] *Right d. Flower* v. *Darby* (1786), 1 Term Rep. 159.

[7] 1 Wms. Saunders 276 C ; *Sidebotham* v. *Holland*, [1895] 1 Q. B. 378, at p. 384.

quit and by the other party either by notice to quit or in some other way."[1]

Any such agreement must not be repugnant to the nature of a yearly tenancy. Thus, a term which prevents the landlord from ever determining the tenancy has been held void.[2] On the other hand, a proviso that the landlord cannot determine the tenancy until he requires the premises for some purpose, such as his own use or occupation, has been held valid.[3]

Agricultural holding.

(ii) Secondly, it is provided by statute in the case of an agricultural holding, that, notwithstanding any express stipulation to the contrary, a notice to quit shall be invalid if it purports to terminate the tenancy before the expiration of twelve months from the end of the current year of tenancy.[4]

Notice must be so given as to expire at end of current year.

A yearly tenancy is terminable only at the end of the current year, and therefore a notice, given for example by the landlord, must require the tenant to quit the holding on that date—no earlier, no later. Literally interpreted, the end of the current year is midnight of the day prior to the anniversary of the day on which the tenancy began.

For instance, if a yearly tenancy began on September 29,[5] its current period ends each year on September 28. In strictness, therefore, a notice given, say, by the landlord, must direct the tenant to quit on September 28 and it must reach the tenant at least half a year before that day. A notice, for instance, that is not served upon him till after March 25, and which directs him to quit on the next ensuing September 28 is bad, and he will be entitled to remain until September 28 in the following year.

The courts, however, after some hesitation, have extended the strict meaning of the expression " end of the current year " to include the anniversary of the day on which the tenancy began. " A notice to quit at the first moment of the anniversary," said LINDLEY, L.J., " ought to be just as good as a notice to quit on the last moment of the day before." [6] A notice, therefore, given not later than Lady Day, will be good if it purports to terminate a Michaelmas tenancy on September 29.[7]

---

[1] *Allison* v. *Scargall,* [1920] 3 K. B. 443, at p. 449, *per* SALTER, J.

[2] *Centaploy, Ltd.* v. *Matlodge, Ltd.,* [1974] Ch. 1 ; [1973] 2 All E. R. 720 ; M. & B. p. 378.

[3] *Re Midland Railway Co.'s Agreement,* [1971] Ch. 725 ; [1971] 1 All E. R. 1007 ; M. & B. p. 360 ; *Breams Property Investment Co., Ltd.* v. *Stroulger,* [1948] 2 K. B. 1 ; [1948] 1 All E. R. 758.

[4] Agricultural Holdings Act 1948, s. 23, *infra,* p. 508.

[5] There is a presumption that a tenancy " from a named date commences on the first moment of the day following. *Ladyman* v. *Wirral Estates, Ltd.,* [1968] 2 All E. R. 197.

[6] *Sidebotham* v. *Holland,* [1895] 1 Q. B. 378, at p. 383.

[7] *Sidebotham* v. *Holland, supra* ; *Crate* v. *Miller,* [1947] K. B. 946 ; [1947] 2 All E. R. 45 ; dealing with the analogous case of a weekly tenancy.

Similar rules apply in the case of other periodic tenancies. Other
periodic
tenancies. Subject to the statutory rule in the case of a dwelling house,[1] the length of the notice must be not less than the length of the tenancy, *e.g.* at least seven days' notice is necessary to terminate a weekly tenancy, and the notice must purport to terminate the tenancy at the end of the current period,[2] *i.e.* either on the anniversary of the date of its commencement[3] or on the preceding day. In computing the period of seven days or other the appropriate period, the day of expiry but not the day of service is included. Thus, a tenancy that began on a Saturday may be terminated by a notice to quit given on a Saturday, notwithstanding that this does not give the tenant seven clear days' notice.

> In *Lemon* v. *Lardeur*,[4] a tenant who held on a four-weekly tenancy was given " a month's notice as from August 1, 1945, to vacatè " the premises. No evidence was given of the date on which the tenancy began.

The notice was invalid, for, since it had not been shown that August 1 was the first day of one of the four-weekly periods, it was impossible to ascertain whether the month's notice would expire at the end of the current period.

These rules may be varied by the parties. Subject to the statutory rule that four weeks notice is necessary to terminate a lease of a dwelling-house, the length of the notice and the date at which it may be given are matters upon which they may make what arrangement they like.[5]

3. TENANCIES AT WILL

A tenancy at will may be expressly terminated at any time by Express
determina-
tion. either party. The strict rules that govern a notice to quit do not, however, apply in this case, for it has been said by high authority that :

> " Anything which amounts to a demand of possession, although not expressed in precise and formal language, is sufficient to indicate the determination of the landlord's will."[6]

Thus a declaration, that the landlord will take steps to recover Implicit
determina-
tion :
(i) by lessor possession unless the tenant complies with certain conditions, determines the tenancy if the conditions are not accepted.[7]

---

[1] Rent Act 1957 s. 16 ; Housing Act 1974, s. 123 ; *supra*, p. 463, *infra*, p. 483.

[2] *Lemon* v. *Lardeur*, [1946] K. B. 613 ; [1946] 2 All E. R. 329 ; *Queen's Club Garden Estates, Ltd.* v. *Bignell*, [1924] 1 K. B. 117 ; *Bathavon R.D.C.* v. *Carlisle*, [1958] 1 Q. B. 461 ; [1958] 1 All E. R. 801.

[3] *Crate* v. *Miller*, *supra*.

[4] [1946] K. B. 613.

[5] *Land Settlement Association, Ltd.* v. *Carr*, [1944] K. B. 657 ; [1944] 2 All E. R. 126. As regards the actual decision in this case, see Agricultural Holdings Act 1948, s. 2 (1).

[6] *Doe d. Price* v. *Price* (1832), 9 Bing. 358, at p. 358, *per* TINDAL, C.J.

[7] *Doe d. Price* v. *Price*, *supra* ; *Fox* v. *Hunter-Paterson*, [1948] 2 All E. R. 813.

The tenancy is also implicitly determined if the lessor does acts inconsistent with its continuance, as for instance if he alienates the reversion or removes material, such as stones from the land.[1]

(ii) by tenant.   Implicit determination also occurs if the tenant does acts incompatible with his limited rights, as for instance if he commits waste or assigns the land to a stranger.[2]

The death of either party also determines the tenancy.

A premature determination is not allowed to prejudice the rights of either party. If the tenant quits before the day on which his rent is due, he does not escape liability;[3] while if he has sown crops he has a right at common law to re-enter and reap them if the lessor determines the tenancy before they are ripe.[4]

SECTION IX. SECURITY OF TENURE AND CONTROL OF RENT

SUMMARY

Introduction.   Land in overcrowded England is a scarce commodity which all need but many cannot afford to own. The forces of supply and demand, if left unchecked, would give landlords a bargaining superiority over their tenants which twentieth-century ideas of social justice have been unwilling to accept. In consequence, ever since the First War, legislation has been used to redress the balance in favour of the tenant. Restrictions have been imposed upon the amount of rent recoverable and the landlord's common law right to recover possession. Different governments have taken different views about the degree to which tenants ought to be protected, but the need for protection of some kind is today generally accepted and it is highly unlikely that landlord and tenant will ever be restored to their nineteenth-century freedom of contract.

Separate statutory codes of protection.   Statutory protection was at first afforded only to tenants who held periodic tenancies or short leases of unfurnished residential premises,[5] but an improved version of this original scheme now applies to most ordinary residential lettings,[6] while different

---

[1] *Doe d. Bennett* v. *Turner* (1840). 7 M. & W. 226.
[2] *Pinhorn* v. *Souster* (1853), 8 Exch. 763, 772.
[3] Cruise, *Digest*, Tit. ix., c. 1, s. 13.
[4] Co. Litt. 55b ; see *supra*, p. 411.
[5] Increase of Rent and Mortgage Interest (War Restrictions) Act 1915.
[6] The Rent Acts 1968 and 1974.

systems of control have been devised for lettings by resident landlords,[1] long leaseholders,[2] business tenants[3] and agricultural holdings.[4] The result of somewhat haphazard historical development is that there are today six distinct statutory codes of protection, in many respects radically different from each other. The detailed provisions of this legislation are extremely complex[5] and the subject-matter of a number of specialized works. What follows is no more than a brief outline of how the various codes operate.

(1) ORDINARY RESIDENTIAL LETTINGS[6]

Statutory control of residential lettings dates back to 1915, but almost all the provisions now in force will be found consolidated in the Rent Acts 1968 and 1974. The key concept in the Acts is the " protected tenancy," defined as a tenancy :—

Ordinary residential lettings.

   (i) " under which a dwelling-house (which may be a house or part of a house) is let as a separate dwelling,"[7] and

   (ii) which does not fall within any of the exceptions listed in the Act.[8]

Any tenancy which qualifies as a " protected tenancy " is entitled to the benefit of the Acts' provisions about security of tenure. But for the purposes of determining the maximum recoverable rent, protected tenancies are a genus divided into two species : the " controlled tenancy " and the " regulated tenancy " . This distinction exists for historical reasons. Controlled tenancies are those tenancies of premises of low rateable value which survived the massive decontrol introduced by the Rent Act of 1957 and which are still subject to the rent provisions of that Act.[9] Regulated tenancies are the residuary category ; all those protected tenancies which are not controlled. Generally speaking, this means the tenancies which were brought into protection by the Rent Acts of 1965 and 1974.[10] The following discussion of the Rent Acts 1968 and 1974 is therefore divided into three main parts : the definition of the protected tenancy and its exceptions ;

Controlled and regulated tenancies.

---

   [1] Part VI of the Rent Act 1968 as applied by the Rent Act 1974. See *infra*, p. 484.

   [2] Part I of the Landlord and Tenant Act 1954 and Part I of the Leasehold Reform Act 1967. See *infra*, p. 490.

   [3] Part II of the Landlord and Tenant Act 1954. See *infra*, p. 499.

   [4] The Agricultural Holdings Act 1948. See *infra*, p. 507.

   [5] There is to be further consolidation of the Rent Acts " even though the last Rent Act consolidation was as recent as 1968 ". Law Com. Ninth Annual Report 1973–1974 (Law Com. No. 64), para. 51.

   [6] For detailed discussion, see Megarry on *The Rent Acts* (10th Edn.) ; Farrand, *The Rent Act 1974.*

   [7] Rent Act 1968, s. 1 (1).

   [8] The exceptions are contained in ss. 1 (1) (*a*), 2, 4 and 5.

   [9] The relevant provisions of the Rent Act 1957 are now consolidated in the Rent Act 1968. See *infra*, p. 475.

   [10] See Rent Act 1968, s. 7 (2) and Rent Act 1974, s. 1 (3). The relevant provisions of the Rent Act 1965 are also consolidated in the Rent Act 1968.

the rent provisions applicable to controlled and regulated tenancies respectively, and the provisions for security of tenure applicable to all protected tenancies.

(A) THE PROTECTED TENANCY

Definition of protected tenancies.

(i) House or part of a house . . . let as a separate dwelling

Every word of this definition has been the subject of judicial interpretation and the last five words are among the most litigated on the statute book.

(a) **House or part of a house.** A " house " includes a flat and even a hotel,[1] but the premises must be structurally suitable for occupation as a residence and must have some degree of permanence. Caravans are therefore not within the definition and their occupants are protected, if at all, by different legislation.[2]

(b) **Let.** The use of the word " let " connotes the relationship of landlord and tenant.[3] Contractual licensees, such as lodgers and other persons not having exclusive possession, are therefore not within the Act. Even exclusive possession may not be enough to create a tenancy.[4] The question depends upon the intention of the parties, *i.e.* whether they intended to create those mutual rights and obligations which the law would classify as a tenancy.[5] If, however, the court is satisfied that such was their intention, it will pay no regard to the fact that they have chosen to label their relationship a licence.[6] The most common example of the residential licensee is the " service occupant," *i.e.* the employee who is required by his contract of employment to occupy a particular dwelling for the better performance of his duties. Caretakers occupying flats in blocks or office buildings and agricultural workers in tied cottages[7] usually come within this category. But a service occupant must be distinguished from a " service tenant," *i.e.* a person to whom a dwelling-house is let in consequence of his employment, but who is not required to live there for the better performance of his duties.[8] Service tenants are within the Rent Acts, although the Acts contain a special provision to enable the employer to recover possession from a tenant who has left his service.[9]

---

[1] *Luganda* v. *Service Hotels, Ltd.*, [1969] 2 Ch. 209 ; [1969] 2 All E. R. 692.
[2] The Caravan Sites Act 1968 and the Mobile Homes Act 1975.
[3] Compare the definition of a " Part VI contract " in Rent Act 1968, s. 70 (1). See *infra*, p. 484.
[4] *Marcroft Wagons, Ltd.* v. *Smith*, [1951] 2 K. B. 496 ; [1951] 2 All E. R. 271.
[5] *Cobb* v. *Lane*, [1952] 1 All E. R. 1199. See *supra*, pp. 384–6.
[6] *Facchini* v. *Bryson*, [1952] 1 T. L. R. 1386.
[7] But see s. 33 of the Rent Act 1965, as amended by s. 99 of the Agriculture Act 1970.
[8] *Torbett* v. *Faulkner*, [1952] 2 T. L. R. 659.
[9] Rent Act 1968, Sched. 3, Part I, Case 7. See *infra*, p. 482.

(c) **As.** The requirement that the house must be let *as* a separate dwelling means that one has regard to the purpose for which it was let, which will not necessarily be the same as the purpose for which it is actually being used. If a lease contains a covenant confining the use of the premises to business purposes, the tenancy will not be protected merely because the tenant in fact uses them as a dwelling.[1] If there is no specific user covenant in the lease, the question will turn upon the use contemplated by the parties at the time of the letting,[2] and if they had no particular use in mind, it will depend upon the *de facto* use of the premises at the time when the question arises for decision.

(d) **A.** The house (or part of a house) must be let as a single dwelling. A house let to one person as a number of separate dwellings in multiple occupations is not protected.[3]

(e) **Separate.** The requirement that the premises must be let as a separate dwelling would, if unqualified, exclude all cases where the tenant shares some living accommodation, either with another tenant or with his landlord.[4] This was in fact the position before 1949, by which time the courts had evolved a great deal of learning on what constituted sharing and what amounted to " living accommodation". Now, however, the tenant who shares with another tenant nevertheless has a protected tenancy,[5] while a tenant who shares with his landlord is given the same protection as any other tenant who has a resident landlord.[6]

(f) **Dwelling.** The word " dwelling " has its ordinary meaning of premises used for normal domestic purposes such as cooking, feeding and sleeping, of which " sleeping seems to be the most important".[7] If premises are let partly as a dwelling and partly for business purposes (as in the common case of a shop with living accommodation above) the tenancy will be protected only if it is " controlled,"[8] *i.e.* one of the tenancies which survived decontrol after 1957.[9] If it does not qualify as a controlled tenancy, it will be subject only to the code governing business tenancies[10] and not come within the Rent Acts at all.[11]

(ii) The exceptions

The Act contains a fairly long list of exceptions.[12] Only the more important ones will be considered here. Exceptions.

---

[1] *Wolfe* v. *Hogan*, [1949] 2 K. B. 194 ; [1949] 1 All E. R. 570.
[2] *Ibid.*
[3] *Horford Investments, Ltd.* v. *Lambert*, [1973] 3 W. L. R. 872 ; [1974] 1 All E. R. 131.
[4] *Neale* v. *Del Soto*, [1945] K. B. 144 ; [1945] 1 All E. R. 191 ; *Goodrich* v. *Paisner*, [1957] A. C. 65 ; [1956] 2 All E. R. 176.
[5] Rent Act 1968, s. 102.   [6] *Ibid.*, s. 101. See p. 484, *infra.*
[7] Megarry, *op cit.*, p. 85.   [8] Rent Act 1968, s. 9 (1).
[9] See *infra*, p. 475.   [10] See *infra*, p. 499.
[11] Rent Act 1968, s. 9 (5).
[12] See Rent Act 1968, ss. 1 (1) (*a*), 2, 4 and 5.

(a) **Houses let by an exempted body.** Houses let by
certain specified bodies, which include local authorities, new town
corporations, housing trusts and housing associations are not
protected by the Rent Acts.[1] This is numerically by far the
most important exception. In 1974 there were about 9.5 million
dwellings in the United Kingdom let to tenants. Of these, more
than two-thirds were let by local authorities and new town corporations, and therefore not protected.[2] Similar exemption has
been conferred upon educational institutions and similar bodies
who let premises to students.[3]

(b) **Lettings by resident landlords.** A tenancy is not
protected if the dwelling forms part of a building (other than a
purpose-built block of flats) in which the landlord was also residing when the tenancy began and in which he has since continued
to reside.[4] Such tenancies are subject to a different system of
control, to be discussed later in this section,[5] under which there is
far less security of tenure.

This exception was introduced by the Rent Act 1974 and is
hedged about with qualifications of great complexity which can
only be explained (though not excused) by its legislative history.
Until 1974 the law took no account of whether or not the landlord
resided on the premises. Instead, there was a general exception
for furnished lettings, *i.e.* cases in which the dwelling was " bona
fide let at a rent which [included] payments in respect of . . . use
of furniture "[6] and " the amount of rent . . . fairly attributable
to . . . use of furniture . . . [formed] a substantial part of the whole
rent ".[7] Such tenancies were subject to the alternative code,
giving a lesser degree of security of tenure, which has now been
applied to lettings by resident landlords. The furnished tenancy
exception was socially controversial because despite the requirement of " substantiality ", it was comparatively easy and inex-
pensive for a landlord to provide enough furniture to prevent the
tenant from acquiring security of tenure.[8] This was hard on
the many persons (including a substantial proportion of recent
immigrants and " single-parent families ") who had to take furnished accommodation because they could not find or afford any
other. On the other hand, there is a need for a pool of short-
term accommodation which would dry up if all tenants were given
full protection. This latter consideration persuaded the majority

---

[1] Rent Act 1968, s. 5.
[2] See *Housing in Britain* (H.M.S.O. 1975) p. 24
[3] Rent Act 1968, s. 2 (1) (*bb*) (inserted by Rent Act 1974, s. 2 (1)).
[4] *Ibid.*, s. 5A (inserted by Rent Act 1974, s. 2 (3) and Sched. 2, para. 1).
[5] See p. 484, *infra.*
[6] Rent Act 1968, s. 2 (1) (*b*).
[7] *Ibid.*, s. 2 (3).
[8] See *Woodward* v. *Docherty*, [1974] 1 W. L. R. 966 ; [1974] 2 All E. R.
844.

of the Francis Committee on the Rent Acts[1] and the government of the day[2] to preserve the furnished lettings exception. The Labour government of 1974 took a different view, but tried to preserve the pool of short-term accommodation by introducing the new exception for resident landlords.

The 1974 Act deals in two ways with the amount of residence which a landlord must put in to keep his tenant within the exception. In the first place, it provides obscurely and referentially that his residence must be " substantial " to the same extent as that of an ordinary residential tenant who wishes to retain protection.[3] As we shall see,[4] this allows for a good deal of constructive residence while the landlord is physically absent on holiday or business, occupying another house or for some other reason. Secondly, the Act specifies periods of non-residence which may be overlooked, such as up to six months for a successor landlord to move in and up to a year after a landlord has died and while the premises are vested in his estate.[5]

Finally it is important to notice two cases in which the exception for resident landlords does not apply. First, the 1974 Act preserves the protection which their unfurnished tenants had previously enjoyed.[6] In the case of tenancies which commenced before August 14th, 1974 it is therefore still necessary to ask whether, according to the law as it then stood, they were furnished or unfurnished.[7] In the latter case they will continue to be protected. Secondly, a resident landlord who, after the passing of the Act, grants to an existing tenant a new tenancy for a " term of years certain " thereby loses the benefit of the exception.[8] The reason for this outwardly irrational rule is that, as we shall see, the limited security of tenure enjoyed under their separate code by the tenants of resident landlords can operate only on periodic tenancies.[9] For this reason it was common, in the days when the code applied principally to furnished tenancies, to exclude any security of tenure by the easy device of granting a series of tenancies for fixed periods. It is this loophole which the 1974 Act seeks to stop up. It might have been thought sufficient to provide for the statutory conversion of fixed term tenancies into periodic tenancies,[10] which would then have fitted into the statutory machinery. Instead, a landlord who is so misguided as to

---

[1] *Report of the Committee on the Rent Acts* (1971) Cmnd. 4609, pp. 202–6, 233–7.
[2] See the White Paper, *Fair Deal for Housing* (1971) Cmnd. 4728, para. 28 (i).
[3] Rent Act 1968, s. 5A (7).   [4] See pp. 478–9, *infra.*
[5] Rent Act 1968, s. 5A (2).
[6] This is the effect of Rent Act 1968, s. 5A (1) and Rent Act 1974, Sched. 3, para. 1.
[7] See *Woodward* v. *Docherty* [1974] 1 W. L. R. 966 ; [1974] 2 All E. R. 844.
[8] Rent Act 1968, s. 5A (5) (*b*).   [9] See p. 490, *infra.*
[10] Compare the Agricultural Holdings Act 1948, ss. 2 (1) and 3 (1), discussed at p. 507, *infra.*

think that he can use the old device to avoid giving his tenant limited security is punished by giving the tenant the full security of the Rent Acts.

(c) **Lettings with board or attendance.**   A tenancy is not protected if the dwelling is " bona fide let at a rent which includes payments in respect of board or attendance."[1]   Such tenancies are for the most part subject to the same code as lettings by resident landlords.[2]   This is all that remains of the exception which originally included furnished lettings.   " Attendance " means " service personal to the tenant provided by the landlord in accordance with his covenant for the benefit or convenience of the individual tenant in his use or enjoyment of the demised premises ".[3]   In order to bring a tenancy within the exception on the ground that attendance is provided, the amount of rent " fairly attributable to the attendance " must form a " substantial part of the whole rent ".[4]   In the case of board, however, the provision of any board which is not *de minimis* will be sufficient to exclude the Acts.

(d) **Holiday lettings.**   These are outside the Rent Acts[5] or any other system of control.[6]

(e) **Tenancies at a low rent.**   Tenancies at a rent amounting to less than two-thirds of the rateable value of the premises are excluded.[7]   The effect of this provision is to exclude tenants under leases, usually for long terms such as 99 years, which have been granted at a low or " ground " rent in return for payment of a substantial premium.   Such tenants are, from an economic point of view, owner-occupiers, and the machinery of rent restriction and security of tenure provided by the Rent Acts is not appropriate for them. As we shall see, they have substantial protection under other statutory codes.[8]

(f) **Houses of high rateable value.**   Houses with a rateable value exceeding £1,500 in Greater London or £750 outside London are not subject to protection.[9]   At this level there is no hardship in allowing a free market.   The exception is not quantitatively important because almost all such houses are owner-occupied.

---

[1] Rent Act 1968, s. 2 (1) (b) or amended by Rent Act 1974, s. 1 (4).
[2] See p. 484, *infra.*
[3] Viscount SIMON in *Palser* v. *Grinling*, [1948] A. C. 291, at p. 310 ; [1948] 1 All E. R. 1, at p. 8.
[4] Rent Act 1968, s. 2 (3).
[5] *Ibid.*, s. 2 (1) (*bbb*) (inserted by Rent Act 1974, s. 2 (1)).
[6] *Ibid.*, s. 70 (5).
[7] *Ibid.*, s. 2 (1) (*a*).
[8] See *infra*, p. 490.
[9] Rent Act 1968, s. 1 (1) (*a*), as substituted by Counter-Inflation Act 1973, s. 14.   There are also provisions to deal with houses excluded by earlier limits under pre-1973 valuation lists.

(B) Control of Rents

The Rent Act 1968 contains elaborate provisions for determining, or providing machinery to determine the maximum rent recoverable from a tenant who has a protected tenancy. These provisions differ according to whether the protected tenancy is " controlled " or " regulated ".

(i) Controlled tenancies

(a) **Definition.** A controlled tenancy is one which remains in existence after having survived the decontrol of the Rent Act 1957 and other legislation. The 1957 Act excluded from control all tenancies created on or after July 6th, 1957 and all tenancies then existing of premises having a rateable value in 1956 of more than £40 in Greater London or £30 elsewhere. A controlled tenancy must therefore have been in existence before July 6th, 1957 and the premises must have had a 1956 rateable value below the limits laid down by the 1957 Act.[1] Premises erected or converted after August 29th, 1954 had been decontrolled by earlier legislation and a controlled tenancy must therefore be of premises which were in existence before that date.[2] Another general decontrol of premises exceeding £70 in rateable value took place by virtue of provisions in the Housing Act 1972.[3] Furthermore, since 1969 there has been in existence machinery to enable landlords of premises in good repair and provided with standard amenities to convert controlled into regulated tenancies.[4] Notwithstanding these apparently formidable obstacles to their continued existence, there were in 1975 still half a million controlled tenancies.[5]

(b) **Maximum rents.** The maximum rent recoverable under a controlled tenancy is related to the gross value[6] of the premises on November 7th, 1956.[7] In the normal case where the tenant is responsible for internal decoration and the landlord for all other repairs, the rent is twice the gross value.[8] If the landlord is responsible for decoration as well, the rent will be seven-thirds

Controlled tenancies.

---

[1] Rent Act 1968, Sched. 2, Part I, paras. 1 (*a*) and (*d*).

[2] *Ibid.*, Sched. 2, Part I, para. 1 (*b*).

[3] Housing Act 1972, s. 35. This provided for a general decontrol in stages, starting with premises of higher rateable value. The process was arrested when s. 35 was repealed by s. 9 of the Housing Rents and Subsidies Act 1975.

[4] Part III of the Housing Finance Act 1972, replacing (with improvements) similar provisions in the Housing Act 1969.

[5] *Housing in Britain*, p. 29.

[6] " Gross value " means the letting value of premises by the year on the assumption that the landlord bears the cost of all repairs and insurance. See s. 19 of the General Rate Act 1967.

[7] Rent Act 1968, s. 52 and Sched. 8.

[8] *Ibid.*, s. 52 (2) (*b*).

times the gross value ;[1] if the tenant is responsible for all repairs, the multiplier will be four-thirds,[2] and intermediate variations on the distribution of liability for repairs will produce rents between these two extremes.[3]　If a landlord fails to do necessary repairs for which the tenant is not responsible under the terms of the tenancy, the tenant can apply to the local authority for a " certificate of disrepair".　While this certificate is in force the tenant may reduce the rent to four-thirds of the gross value.[4]

There are provisions for some increase in the maximum rent to allow the landlord a modest return on money spent on improvements made with the tenant's consent[5] and on repairs[6] but otherwise the rent is rigidly tied to some multiple of the 1956 gross value.　The result is that controlled tenants pay on average substantially less than the rents which regulated tenants pay for equivalent accommodation.

(ii) Regulated tenancies

Regulated
tenancies.

(a) Definition. Regulated tenancies are all protected tenancies which are not controlled.[7]

(b) Maximum rents. The maximum recoverable rent under a regulated tenancy is ordinarily the amount which an independent official called the Rent Officer has determined and registered as the " fair rent " for the premises.[8]　An application for registration can be made by the parties jointly or by either of them.[9]　A party who is dissatisfied with the determination of the Rent Officer can appeal to a body called the Rent Assessment Committee, whose decision is final.[10]　Application can be made to the Rent Officer to vary the amount which has been registered as a fair rent, but except in special circumstances, not within three years from the date of registration.[11]

The statutory formula for determining the fair rent is that " regard shall be had . . . to all the circumstances (other than personal circumstances) and in particular to the age, character, locality and state of repair of the dwelling-house, and, if any furniture is provided for use under the tenancy, to the quantity, quality, and condition of the furniture,"[12] but subject to the assumption that the demand for similar dwelling houses in the

---

[1] Rent Act 1968, Sched. 8, para. 2 (1) (*a*).
[2] *Ibid.*, para. 1 (2).　　　　　　　　[3] *Ibid.*, para. 1 (3).
[4] *Ibid.*, Sched. 9, Part II.　　　　　[5] *Ibid.*, s. 56.
[6] Housing Rents and Subsidies Act 1975, s. 10.
[7] Rent Act 1968, s. 7 (2).　　　　　[8] *Ibid.*, ss. 20 (2), 22 (2).
[9] *Ibid.*, s. 44 (1).　　　　　　　　　[10] *Ibid.*, Sched. 6, para. 6.
[11] *Ibid.*, s. 44 (3).　A landlord may apply up to 3 months in advance of the expiry of the 3 year period : see Rent Act 1974, s. 4.
[12] *Ibid.*, s. 46 (1) as amended by the Rent Act 1974.

locality[1] is not substantially greater than the supply.[2]   Econo-
mists may object on the ground that it is meaningless to speak of
supply or demand except in relation to a given rent, but in practice
the Rent Officers and Rent Assessment Committees make a more
or less arbitrary allowance for " scarcity " in areas of overcrowding
or housing shortage.[3]   Furthermore, any changes in fair rents are
subject to the Government's statutory powers to restrict or prevent increases which would otherwise take place.[4]

(iii) Enforcement

It is not an offence to let premises at a rent in excess of the
statutory maximum,[5] but the excess cannot be recovered from the
tenant and it if has already been paid, the landlord is liable to have to
refund it.[6]   There is however a special two year limitation period
for the recovery by a tenant of excess rent.[7]   It is an offence to try
to evade the Acts by charging a premium for the grant or assignment of a protected tenancy[8] and the amount of any such premium
can also be recovered by the tenant.[9]   " Premium " is widely defined[10] and includes payments to third parties[11] or excessive payments for furniture and fittings.[12]

*Enforce-
ment of
rent control.*

(iv) Reform

The existence of controlled tenants paying a rent far lower than
the rent which a regulated tenant would pay for identical
premises has caused a good deal of unfairness.   Many landlords
of such premises are poorer than their tenants, but receive a rent
which makes it uneconomic for them to do any repairs.   This may
lead to the issue of a certificate of disrepair and a further reduction
of the rent, without any corresponding incentive to do the repairs.
The result is that many houses with controlled tenants have been
falling into decay.[13]   It remains to be seen whether recent legislation allowing a landlord to charge for his expenditure on repairs[14] will do anything to arrest this process.

Reform.

---

[1] On the meaning of " the locality " see *Palmer* v. *Peabody Trust* [1975]
Q. B. 604 ; [1974] 3 All E. R. 355 ; and *Metropolitan Property Holdings,
Ltd.* v. *Finegold* [1975] 1 W. L. R. 349 ; [1975] 1 All E. R. 389.   A popular
local amenity does not create a disregardable " scarcity " but s. 8 of the Housing
Rents and Subsidies Act 1975 prevents tenants from having their rents raised
on account of the introduction of new amenities.
[2] Rent Act 1968, s. 46 (2).   [3] The *Francis Report*, pp 57–62.
[4] See the Housing Rents and Subsidies Act 1975, s. 11, replacing orders
made under the Counter-Inflation Act 1973, s. 11.
[5] But the creation of such an offence is recommended in the *Francis Report*,
pp. 117–8.
[6] Rent Act 1968, s. 62 (1).   [7] *Ibid.*, s. 62 (3).
[8] *Ibid.*, ss. 85, 86.   [9] *Ibid.*, ss. 85 (4), 86 (7), 90.
[10] *Ibid.*, s. 92 (1).
[11] *Elmdene Estates, Ltd.* v. *White,* [1960] A. C. 528 ; [1960] 1 All E. R. 306.
[12] Rent Act 1968, ss. 88, 89, 92 (1).
[13] See the *Francis Report*, pp. 96–9.
[14] Housing Rents and Subsidies Act 1975, s. 10.

(C) Security of Tenure

(i) The Statutory Tenancy

Meaning of statutory tenancy.

At common law, as we have seen, a tenancy can come to an end in a number of different ways.[1] Effluxion of time, the expiration of a notice to quit, surrender and forfeiture are the most common. At the end of his tenancy the tenant is obliged to yield up possession of the demised premises to his landlord. But in the case of a protected tenancy, the termination of the contractual term, for whatever reason, is automatically followed by what the Acts call a " statutory tenancy."[2] This phrase, which Parliament has borrowed from the judges,[3] is to some extent a convenient misnomer. The statutory tenant has no tenancy in the sense of an estate in the land. He has a " status of irremovability ; "[4] a statutory right to remain in possession, subject to and with the benefit of " all the terms and conditions of the original contract of tenancy, so far as they are consistent with the provisions of this Act."[5]

(a) **Creation.** In order to bring into existence a statutory tenancy it is necessary, first, that there should have been a contractual protected tenancy, secondly, that it should have come to an end, and thirdly, that the tenant should be occupying all or part of the premises as his residence. The method by which the contractual tenancy is terminated is immaterial ; even if the contractual tenancy has been forfeited by an order of the court, it will nevertheless be replaced by a statutory tenancy and the court may have to give separate consideration to the question of whether grounds exist for making an order for possession and whether such an order should be made.[6] The third requirement has been evolved by the courts with little statutory assistance.[7] It reflects the view that the object of the Rent Acts is " to protect a resident in a dwelling house "[8] and not to protect a person who is merely allowing someone else to live there, whether as sub-tenant[9] or otherwise. The tenant's own residential use must be " substantial." He can sub-let parts as long as he continues himself to reside in the premises as well.[10] He need not be there all the time,

---

[1] See *supra*, p. 463.
[2] Rent Act 1968, s. 3 (1).
[3] See Megarry, *op. cit.*, p. 196, attributing paternity to Lord Coleridge, J. in preference to the claims of Scrutton, L.J.
[4] *Keeves* v. *Dean*, [1924] 1 K. B. 685, at p. 686, *per* Lush, J.
[5] Rent Act 1968, s. 12 (1).
[6] *Wolmer Securities, Ltd.* v. *Corne*, [1966] 2 Q. B. 243 ; [1966] 2 All E. R. 691.
[7] *Skinner* v. *Geary*, [1931] 2 K. B. 546 is the leading case.
[8] *Haskins* v. *Lewis*, [1931] 2 K. B. 1, at p. 14.
[9] A sub-tenant may have separate protection against the landlord. See Megarry, *op. cit.*, pp. 454–69.
[10] *Berkeley* v. *Papadoyannis*, [1954] 2 Q. B. 149 ; [1954] 2 All E. R. 409.

as long as he preserves sufficient intention to return and leaves some visible indication of continued occupation.[1] The presence of the tenant's furniture, wife or other member of his family[2] are the usual ways in which the latter requirement is satisfied while the tenant is away on business, at sea, on military service[3] or in gaol.[4] Whether in any given case the tenant can show the necessary *animus* and *corpus* of continued residence is a question of fact and degree.[5]

(b) **Transmission.** A statutory tenancy is a personal status and therefore not an assignable item of property, but there are special statutory provisions for the substitution of a new statutory tenant or " transmission " of the statutory tenancy on death.[6] If a statutory tenant dies leaving a widow who was residing with him at his death, the widow is entitled to retain possession as a " statutory tenant by succession."[7] If he leaves no such widow, the statutory tenancy can be transmitted to any member of his family who was residing with him at his death. If there was more than one member of the family so residing, they can agree among themselves who shall become the new statutory tenant, or if they cannot agree, they can ask the county court to decide.[8] A protected tenancy can undergo two transmissions on death,[9] but a controlled tenancy can survive only one transmission as such ; after the second transmission it becomes a regulated tenancy.[10]

(c) **Determination.** As long as the premises remain within the Rent Acts, a statutory tenancy can ordinarily be determined only by the tenant actually yielding up possession or by an order for possession made by the court.[11] Such an order, as we shall see, can be made only on certain specified grounds. There must be an actual yielding up of possession ; a mere notice of intention to do so, or an agreement to surrender is insufficient.[12] It is not unlawful for a landlord to offer a protected tenant money or some other consideration for giving up his tenancy,[13] and landlords frequently do so, but the agreement is not enforceable by the landlord if the tenant changes his mind and refuses to go. The court cannot even make an order for possession by consent unless one

---

[1] *Brown* v. *Brash*, [1948] 2 K. B. 247 ; [1948] 1 All E. R. 922.
[2] *Brown* v. *Draper*, [1944] K. B. 309 ; [1944] 1 All E. R. 246.
[3] *Ibid.*, p. 314.
[4] *Brown* v. *Brash, supra.*
[5] *Hallwood Estates, Ltd.* v. *Flack* (1950), 66 (pt. 2) T. L. R. 368, at pp. 374, 376.
[6] See Rent Act 1968, Sched. 1.
[7] *Ibid.*, s. 3 (3) ; Sched. 1. paras. 2, 6.
[8] *Ibid.*, Sched. 1, paras. 3, 7.
[9] *Ibid.*, paras. 6, 7, and Housing Finance Act 1972, s. 47.
[10] *Ibid.*, Sched. 2, para. 5.
[11] *Brown* v. *Draper*, [1944] K. B. 309 ; [1944] 1 All E. R. 246.
[12] Megarry, *op. cit.*, p. 226.
[13] But it is unlawful for a statutory tenant to ask for payment or other consideration from a third party, such as the incoming tenant. See Rent Act 1968, s. 13 (1).

of the specified grounds exist. In their absence it lacks jurisdiction to make such an order. Thus a husband may remain a
statutory tenant *malgré lui* if his deserted wife is left in possession
of the premises and refuses to move.[1] Unless the wife has been
guilty of some matrimonial misconduct, the husband will probably
be unable to evict her, while the landlord will be unable to obtain
an order for possession, even with the husband's consent, unless
one of the specified grounds exists.[2]

(ii) The Grounds for Possession

Grounds for
possession
of statutory
tenancy.

The court may make an order for possession, which determines
the statutory tenancy only if the judge is satisfied of the existence
of one of the grounds for possession specified in the Acts. In
some cases, the establishment of a statutory ground for possession
concludes the matter. An order for possession is then mandatory.[3]
Ordinarily, however, the judge may not make such an order unless
he considers it reasonable to do so.[4] The latter requirement
gives the judge a wide discretion, enabling him to consider all
relevant circumstances at the date of the hearing.[5] For example,
the existence of any arrears of rent is one of the specified grounds for
possession, but judges seldom make an order for possession without first having given the tenant a generous opportunity to bring
his payments up to date. There are eighteen specified grounds
for possession, seventeen being set out in a Schedule to the Act
of 1968 as amended[6] and one, rather curiously, in the body of the
Act itself.[7] Some of the more important ones will be noticed
below.

(a) **Alternative accommodation.** The court can make an
order for possession if it is satisfied that " suitable alternative
accommodation " is available for the tenant or will be available for
him when the order takes effect.[8] Alternative accommodation
is suitable if (as will normally be the case) the tenant will have a
protected tenancy or equivalent security of tenure,[9] and if the
premises are reasonably suitable to the means of the tenant and the
needs of his family as regards proximity to place of work, extent and
character.[10] Although the alternative accommodation must be
suitable for the tenant and his family, it need not be as pleasant and

---

[1] Not so in the case of a deserted mistress : *Colin Smith Music, Ltd.* v.
Ridge, [1975] 1 W. L. R. 463 ; [1975] 1 All E. R. 290.
[2] *Old Gate Estates Ltd.* v. *Alexander*, [1950] 1 K. B. 311 ; [1949] 2 All E. R.
822 ; *Middleton* v. *Baldock*, [1950] 1 K. B. 657 ; [1950] 1 All E. R. 708.
[3] Rent Act 1968, s. 10 (2) and Sched. 3, Part II.
[4] *Ibid.*, s. 10 (1) and Sched. 3, Part I.
[5] *Rhodes* v. *Cornford*, [1947] 2 All E. R. 601.
[6] Rent Act 1968, Sched. 3, as amended by Rent Act 1974.
[7] The " alternative accommodation " ground.
[8] Rent Act 1968, s. 10 (1) (a).
[9] *Ibid.*, Sched. 3, Part IV, para. 2.
[10] *Ibid.*, Sched. 3, Part IV, para. 3.

commodious as the existing premises. The test is suitability to the means and needs of the tenant and not comparison with what the tenant has got.[1] Indeed, landlords would seldom in practice offer alternative accommodation if it had to be in all respects equivalent to the existing premises. Furthermore, the tenant can be required to give up a controlled tenancy even though the alternative accommodation will be regulated and therefore at a much higher rent. If the tenant has the means to pay, the accommodation will nevertheless be suitable.[2] An offer of alternative accommodation is therefore the most practical way of increasing the return on premises let to controlled tenants ; once possession is recovered, they can either be re-let on regulated tenancies, or the house sold with vacant possession for a much higher figure than it would have fetched subject to a controlled tenancy. It should however be observed that although comparisons with the existing premises and rent are not admissible on the question of suitability, they are nevertheless matters which the judge may take into account in deciding whether or not it is reasonable to make an order for possession.[3]

An ingenious piece of judicial interpretation has made the " alternative accommodation " provisions a means of regaining possession of parts of the premises which the protected tenant has sub-let. We have seen that as long as the tenant himself resides somewhere on the premises, he may sub-let the rest and retain his statutory tenancy of the whole. A controlled tenant may thus be able to make more out of sub-lettings of parts than he pays his landlord for the whole premises. But the landlord may be able to put an end to this situation by offering the tenant as " alternative accommodation " a tenancy of the part of the premises which he is actually occupying, and on this ground seeking an order for possession of the whole.[4] As the tenant is voluntarily confining himself to the part in question, it is difficult for him to say that it is not suitable to his needs. The end result is that the tenant obtains a new tenancy of his part,[5] while the landlord takes over his sub-tenants.

(b) **Non-payment of rent or breach of tenancy obligation.**[6] This is, of course, the most common ground upon which orders for possession are made. Again, the judge must also decide whether it would be reasonable to make an order and he may (and frequently does) suspend the operation of the order on condition

---

[1] *Warren* v. *Austen*, [1947] 2 All E. R. 185.
[2] *Cresswell* v. *Hodgson*, [1951] 2 K. B. 92 ; [1951] 1 All E. R. 710.
[3] *Warren* v. *Austen*, [1947] 2 All E. R. 185 ; *Redspring, Ltd.* v. *Francis*, [1973] 1 W. L. R. 134 ; [1973] 1 All E. R. 640.
[4] *Mykolyshyn* v. *Noah*, [1970] 1 W. L. R. 1271 ; [1971] 1 All E. R. 49.
[5] Rent Act 1968, Sched. 2, para. 4 spares the tenant the ultimate indignity of having his own tenancy converted from controlled to regulated.
[6] *Ibid.*, Sched. 3, Part 1, Case 1. Ill-treatment of the furniture is a separate ground under Case 3A, inserted by Rent Act 1974.

that the tenant pays the arrears, remedies the breach or refrains from committing it again in future.

(c) **Nuisance or annoyance or illegal or immoral user.** It is a ground for possession if the tenant, his sub-tenant or lodger or any person residing with the tenant has been guilty of conduct falling within this description,[1] though the degree of control which the tenant could have exercised over the person in question would no doubt be taken into account in deciding whether it was reasonable to make an order.[2]

(d) **Premises reasonably required for employee.** This ground for possession lies only against a "service tenant," *i.e.* a person to whom the premises were let in consequence of his employment.[3] The court may make an order for possession if the tenant has ceased to be in the landlord's employment and the premises are reasonably required for some person already in his whole-time employment or with whom he has entered into a contract of employment conditional upon housing being provided.[4] This produces the rather awkward result that the landlord cannot safely launch proceedings for possession until he has secured an employee, at least under a conditional contract, but an employee cannot be installed in the premises until the action to evict his predecessor has run its course, usually over a period of months.

(e) **Premises required by landlord or member of his family.** It is a ground for possession that the landlord reasonably requires the premises for occupation as a residence by himself, his mother, father or son or daughter over 18, or in the case of a regulated tenancy, his mother-in-law or father-in-law.[5] But there are two important exceptions to this ground for possession. The first is that it cannot be invoked by someone who has become a " landlord by purchase," that is to say, has bought the landlord's interest during the currency of the tenancy.[6] One cannot therefore obtain a residence by buying a house subject to a protected tenancy and then seeking possession on the ground that it is reasonably required for occupation by the new landlord. Secondly the court cannot make an order if the tenant can show that " greater hardship would be caused by granting the order or judgment than by refusing it ".[7] There is hardly any limit to the circumstances which the court may consider in deciding this question : the need

---

[1] Rent Act 1968, Sched. 3, Part 1, Case 2.
[2] *Abrahams* v. *Wilson*, [1971] 2 Q. B. 88 ; [1971] 2 All E. R. 1114.
[3] See *supra*, p. 470.
[4] Case 7.
[5] Case 8.
[6] But not if he bought it before November 7, 1956 (in the case of a controlled tenancy), March 23, 1965 (in the case of a regulated tenancy) or May 24th 1974 (in the case of a regulated furnished tenancy). See Case 8, as amended by Rent Act 1974, Sched. 1, para. 3.
[7] Rent Act 1968, Sched. 3, Part III, para. 1.

for young couples to have space in which to bring up families and the hardship involved in making old people leave familiar friends and surroundings are among the more obvious examples. Nor is the court confined to considering the consequences upon the landlord and tenant alone ; their families, dependants and other persons affected must also be taken into account.[1]

(f) Recovery of possession by owner-occupier. Since 1965 a person who wishes to let a house which he has been occupying as his own residence (for example, because he has been posted abroad) may, if he gives an appropriate notice before granting the tenancy, be able to recover possession at any later date on the ground that he requires it as a residence for himself or any member of his family who lived with him when he last occupied it as his residence.[2] This ground differs from the last one in several respects ; it is confined to owner-occupiers who have given the necessary notice, there is no need for them to show that their wish to resume residence is " reasonable," the " greater hardship " defence is excluded and the class of persons for whom possession can be obtained is extended to any member of the landlord's family, but confined to those who were residing with him in the premises. Furthermore, once this ground is established an order for possession is mandatory.

(g) Dwelling bought for retirement. An employee who buys his rose-covered country cottage or seaside villa with a view to retirement can let it with comparative safety if he gives the tenant notice in writing that he will require possession when he retires.[3] In such a case an order for possession is mandatory and even if he has forgotten to serve the necessary notice, the court may still make an order if it is of opinion that it would be just and equitable to do so. This ground does not appear to be available to the self-employed.

(iii) Unlawful Eviction and Harassment

Residential tenants and other residential occupiers (which includes licensees and persons whose tenancies have come to an end) may not lawfully be evicted without an order of the court.[4] In such cases, therefore, the landlord's right to make a " peaceful re-entry "[5] is abolished. It is a criminal offence for any person unlawfully to deprive the residential occupier of his occupation of the premises or any part thereof.[6] The separate offence of harassment consists in doing certain specified acts with the intention of causing a residential occupier to give up the occupation

(margin note: Unlawful eviction and harassment.)

---

[1] *Harte* v. *Frampton*, [1948] 1 K. B. 73 ; [1947] 2 All E. R. 604.
[2] Case 10.
[3] Case 10A, inserted by Rent Act 1974.
[4] Rent Act 1965, s. 31.   [5] See *supra*, p. 436.
[6] Rent Act 1965, s. 30 (1).

of all or part of the premises or to refrain from exercising any of his rights, such as a right to the use of shared accommodation.[1] The specified acts are acts calculated to interfere with the peace or comfort of the occupier or members of his household or the persistent withdrawing or withholding of services reasonably required for the occupation of the premises as a residence. Prosecutions for these offences can be brought by the victim, the police or the local authority, although in practice the police refer complaints to the local authority.[2]

(2) LETTINGS BY RESIDENT LANDLORDS

Lettings by resident landlord.

The present system of control for lettings by resident landlords derives from that set up just after the Second War to deal with furnished lettings.[3] Its provisions are now consolidated in Part VI of the Rent Act 1968, which is still headed " Furnished Lettings ". Since 1974, however, the fact that a letting is furnished does not prevent it from being an ordinary protected tenancy.[4] On the other hand, lettings by resident landlords (whether furnished or unfurnished) have now been excluded from the definition of protected tenancies and brought within Part VI. But the substitution has been untidy and left some loose ends within the Part VI code. These include contractual licences to occupy furnished dwellings, lettings in which the rent includes a payment for attendance sufficiently substantial to prevent the creation of a protected tenancy[5] and lettings which include payments for board which do not form a substantial part of the rent.[6]

As in the previous section, the following discussion of Part VI is divided into three parts. First, the definition of a " Part VI contract "—the code's equivalent of a protected tenancy. Secondly, the provisions for control of rents and thirdly, security of tenure.

(A) The Part VI Contract

Definition of " Part VI contract "

Originally, the key concept of the code was the " Part VI contract ", which the Act still defines as :—

> " a contract whereby one person grants to another person, in consideration of a rent which includes payment for the use of furniture or for services, the right to occupy as a residence a dwelling to which [Part VI] applies . . . "[7]

---

[1] Rent Act 1965, s. 30 (2). The section does not give rise to a civil action for damages. *McCall* v. *Abelesz*, (1975) *Times*, Dec. 24.

[2] The *Francis Report, supra*, pp. 105–6.

[3] The Furnished Houses (Rent Control) Act 1946.

[4] See p. 472, *supra*.

[5] See p. 474, *supra*.

[6] *Ibid*. and Rent Act 1968, s. 70 (3) (*b*).

[7] Rent Act 1968, s. 70 (1).

Since 1974, however, this definition looks like Hamlet without the Prince of Denmark. Most furnished tenancies have become regulated and thereby excluded from Part VI.[1] Instead, the main business of the code is supplied by section 102A of the Rent Act 1968,[2] which provides that a tenancy within the resident landlord exception[3] :—

> " shall be treated for the purposes of Part VI of this Act as a contract to which that Part applies, notwithstanding that the rent may not include payment for the use of furniture or for services. "

Despite this diminished importance of the original definition of a Part VI contract, it contains certain words and phrases which require closer examination.

(i) " A contract ... "

Part VI applies to contracts, which may be tenancies but can also be mere contractual licences. Although the parties to the contract are designated " lessor " and " lessee," the Act contains an elaborate definition of these words which makes it clear that for the purposes of Part VI they are terms of art which include licensor and licensee.[4] It is necessary that the lessee should be entitled to exclusive occupation of some part of the premises,[5] but the term " exclusive occupation " must not be confused with the exclusive possession which may distinguish a tenant from a licensee. The lodger in his furnished bed-sitting room does not have exclusive possession of any part of the house and is therefore a licensee, but he has exclusive occupation of his room and the protection of Part VI if no other person is entitled to occupy it.[6]

Until 1974 it did not matter whether the occupier of furnished premises was a tenant or a licensee. In both cases he held under a Part VI contract. But since the 1974 Act the tenant (unless he has a resident landlord) will have a protected tenancy while the licensee is still within Part VI.

(ii) " right to occupy as a residence "

The contract need not make express reference to the lessee's right to occupy the premises as his residence, but he must in fact be residing there and must be within his contractual rights in doing so. Some degree of permanence is therefore necessary. An ordinary stay at an hotel will not create a Part VI contract and

---

[1] See pp. 472–3, *supra*.
[2] Inserted by Rent Act 1974, Sched. 2, para. 4.
[3] See p. 472, *supra*.
[4] Rent Act 1968, s. 84 (1).
[5] *Ibid.*, s. 70 (2).
[6] *R.* v. *Battersea, etc. Rent Tribunal, Ex parte Parikh*, [1957] 1 W. L. R. 410 ; [1957] 1 All E. R. 352 ; *Luganda* v. *Service Hotels, Ltd.* [1969] 2 Ch. 209 ; [1969] 2 All E. R. 692.

there is a specific provision which excludes holiday lettings of any kind.[1] On the other hand, the occupant of a room in a residential hotel is likely to be protected by Part VI[2] unless he makes payments in respect of board which form a substantial part of his rent.[3]

(iii) " a dwelling to which [Part VI] applies "

A dwelling means a house or part of a house[4] and these terms have the same meanings as they do in the case of protected tenancies.[5] Houses of high rateable value are similarly excluded.[6]

(B) Control of Rents

Control of rents.

Jurisdiction to determine the maximum rent recoverable under a Part VI contract is vested in a statutory body called a Rent Tribunal, which consists of a Chairman and other members (usually two) appointed by the Secretary of State for the Environment.[7] There are about forty Rent Tribunals in England and Wales, each operating within a prescribed area.

(i) Reference procedure

Reference procedure.

A Part VI contract can be referred to the Rent Tribunal by either of the parties or by the local authority.[8] A reference ordinarily involves filling in a prescribed form giving particulars of the contract, the parties and the premises, and sending it to the appropriate Rent Tribunal. If the reference has been made by the lessee, the Tribunal may require the lessor to give certain further information for its assistance in fixing the rent, such as the value of any furniture and the cost of any services he is providing.[9] A hearing before the Tribunal will follow, usually preceded earlier on the same day by an inspection of the premises. Procedure before a Rent Tribunal is extremely informal and the parties are seldom represented by lawyers.

(ii) Determining the rent

Determining the rent.

Part VI is even less explicit than the unfurnished code in providing the Tribunal with criteria for determining an appropriate rent. The Act merely says that the Tribunal shall do one of three things : approve the rent payable under the contract ; reduce the

---

1 Rent Act 1968, s. 70 (5).
2 *Luganda* v. *Service Hotels, Ltd.,* [1969] 2 Ch. 209 ; [1969] 2 All E. R. 692.
3 Rent Act 1968, s. 70 (3) (*b*).
4 *Ibid.,* s. 84 (1).
5 See *supra,* p. 470.
6 Rent Act 1968, s. 71 (1), as amended by Rent Act 1974, s. 6.
7 *Ibid.,* s. 69 (1) and Sched. 10.
8 *Ibid.,* s. 72 (1).
9 *Ibid.,* s. 72 (2).

rent to " such sum as they may, in all the circumstances, think reasonable " ; or dismiss the reference altogether.[1]

In fixing the rents of unfurnished premises falling within the resident landlord exception, the Tribunal will no doubt operate along much the same lines as a Rent Officer dealing with a protected tenancy. In the case of furnished premises, the normal practice is for the Tribunal to start by considering what would be a fair rent for the accommodation if it were unfurnished. In deciding what for this purpose would be a reasonable rent, the Tribunal is entitled to disregard a " scarcity element " in the market rent and start from a lower figure than the premises are likely to fetch if let unfurnished upon the open market.[2] The Tribunal may thus perform the same calculation which Rent Officers and Rent Assessment Committees are required to perform by section 46 (2) of the Rent Act 1968[3] but they are not obliged to do so. In practice it is usual for Tribunals to have regard to the fair rents determined by Rent Officers or Rent Assessment Committees for regulated tenancies of comparable accommodation in the area.[4]

The Tribunal will then add to the unfurnished rent an amount which it considers sufficient to cover the landlord's costs and reasonable profit for providing furniture and services.[5] In valuing services, the Tribunal is not confined to those which the landlord is contractually obliged to provide. It will take into account all services in fact provided and which appear reasonably likely to continue.[6] The Francis Committee emphasised the importance of allowing landlords sufficient profit to encourage them to maintain the supply of furnished accommodation,[7] but Parliament has been less impressed by this argument. Rents under Part VI contracts are subject to restrictions on increase imposed by Government orders.[8]

(iii) Registration of rents

Local authorities are required to keep a register of the Part VI contracts for premises within their areas which have been referred to the Rent Tribunal, stating the rent determined by the Tribunal and certain prescribed particulars of the contract and the premises.

Registration of rents.

---

[1] Rent Act 1968, s. 73 (1).
[2] *John Kay, Ltd.* v. *Kay*, [1952] 2 Q. B. 258 , [1952] 1 All E. R. 813.
[3] See *supra*, p. 476.
[4] The *Francis Report, supra*, p. 148.
[5] *Ibid.*, pp. 148–50.
[6] *R.* v. *Paddington and St. Marylebone Rent Tribunal, Ex parte Bell, London and Provincial Properties, Ltd.*, [1949] 1 K. B. 666 ; [1949] 1 All E. R. 720.
[7] At p. 150 : " the letting of furnished dwellings is a business which normally entails the landlord in a good deal of work and it is idle to suppose that landlords will embark on or continue in such a business if it is not worth their while to do so. "
[8] Under the Housing Rents and Subsidies Act 1975, s. 11, replacing the Counter-Inflation Act 1973, s. 11.

Once a rent has been registered, it operates *in rem* and becomes the maximum recoverable rent for any letting of the premises under a Part VI contract.   Even if the premises are completely redecorated or refurnished, the registered rent will continue to apply until a new rent has been determined upon a fresh reference to the Tribunal.

(iv) Reconsideration

Reconsideration of registered rent.

Either or both of the parties to a Part VI contract or the local authority may apply to the Rent Tribunal for reconsideration of the registered rent.[1]   An application on the grounds of some change in circumstances (*e.g.* improvement or deterioration in services or furniture supplied by the landlord) may be made at any time, but otherwise (except in the case of a joint application) the Tribunal need not entertain a reference made within three years of the date on which a rent was last registered.[2]

(v) Enforcement

Enforcement.

It is an offence to require or receive a payment on account of rent under a Part VI contract which is in excess of the rent registered for the premises.[3]   The exaction of premiums for the grant, renewal, continuance or assignment of rights under a Part VI contract is similarly forbidden[4] and excess payments are recoverable by the lessee.[5]

(vi) Reform

Reform.

The processes of determining fair rents for regulated tenancies and Part VI contracts cover so much common ground that there is little justification for maintaining two separate organisations to operate the two codes.   In practice there is a certain amount of integration because the same people tend to be members of both Rent Tribunals and Rent Assessment Committees, but the Francis Committee has recommended further steps towards the assimilation of the administration of the two codes.   It is suggested that the rent under a Part VI contract should be determined in the first instance by the Rent Officer in the same way as the rent under a regulated tenancy, with a single " second-tier tribunal " to hear appeals from the decisions of Rent Officers under both codes.[6]

---

[1] Rent Act 1968, s. 75 (1) as amended by Rent Act 1974, s. 7 (4).
[2] *Ibid.*, s. 73 (5) as substituted by Rent Act 1974, s. 7 (2).
[3] *Ibid.*, s. 76 (1).
[4] *Ibid.*, s. 87 (2).
[5] *Ibid.*, ss. 76 (2), 87 (5) and 90 (1).
[6] The *Francis Report*, pp. 209–10.

(C) SECURITY OF TENURE

Lessees under Part VI contracts are able to obtain some degree of security of tenure. But the machinery is entirely different from that applicable to protected tenancies. Instead of a statutory tenancy determinable only by the voluntary act of the tenant or an order of court, capable of enduring for three lifetimes,[1] Part VI provides only that in certain circumstances and for a limited period the operation of a notice to quit may be deferred. This deferment may happen in two ways. First, a reference to the Tribunal at a time when no notice to quit has been served will automatically confer a period of security during which such notice cannot take effect. Secondly, a lessee who is already under notice can apply to the Tribunal for the express grant of a period of security during which the operation of the notice will be deferred.

Security of tenure.

(i) Automatic security

A reference to the Rent Tribunal ordinarily confers upon the lessee security of tenure for six months after the Tribunal has given its decision.[2] A notice to quit served at any time after the reference cannot take effect until this period has expired. But the Tribunal has a discretion to substitute a shorter period in suitably undeserving cases[3] and if it should decide to dismiss the reference altogether, the notice can take effect seven days after the decision.[4]

Automatic security.

(ii) Express grant of security

A lessee under a Part VI contract who has been served with a notice to quit may apply to the Rent Tribunal for security of tenure and the Tribunal may defer the operation of the notice for up to six months.[5] The application must be made before the notice to quit has expired. A Part VI tenant whose notice to quit has expired is past help and there is nothing which either the Rent Tribunal or the County Court can do for him. But it does not matter whether the non-expiry of the notice is because the date which it specifies has not yet arrived or because it has been artificially extended by automatic security after an earlier reference or by a previous grant of security.[6] It is therefore theoretically possible for a lessee to obtain successive grants of security *ad infinitum*, always applying again just before the current period expires. In practice, however, Rent Tribunals are reluctant to grant extended periods of security.[7]

Express grant of security.

---

[1] See *supra*, p. 479.
[2] Rent Act 1968, s. 77 (1).
[3] *Ibid.*, s. 77 (2) (*a*).
[4] *Ibid.*, s. 77 (2) (*b*).
[5] *Ibid.*, s. 78.
[6] *Ibid.*, s. 78 (1) (*d*).
[7] The *Francis Report*, p. 151.

(iii) **Reduction of security**

Reduction
of
security.

We have seen that a Tribunal may substitute a shorter period for the normal six months automatic security following a reference. In addition, if the lessee has been guilty of a breach of contract, nuisance or other misbehaviour, the landlord may apply to the Tribunal for the reduction of a period of security already in operation.[1] A direction that the period of security be reduced is a black mark against the lessee which bars him from making any further applications.[2]

(iv) **Part VI contracts for fixed terms**

Part VI
contracts
for fixed
terms.

As we have seen, the machinery by which Part VI confers security of tenure is by deferring the operation of a notice to quit. But contracts for a fixed term expire by effluxion of time without the need for a notice to quit. There is consequently nothing upon which the security of tenure machinery can bite. It is therefore possible to prevent lessees from obtaining security under Part VI by avoiding the creation of a periodic tenancy and granting instead a series of short terms for fixed periods. For resident landlords, however, this remedy has consequences much worse than the disease ; the tenancy becomes protected under the Rent Acts.[3]

(3) LONG TENANCIES

A long tenancy for the purposes of the landlord and tenant codes means primarily a tenancy granted for a term exceeding twenty-one years.[4] In 1967 it was estimated that about a million and a quarter houses in England and Wales were let on long tenancies. Most of them originate in the Victorian and Edwardian practice of developing land for residential purposes by means of " building leases ". This usually involved an agreement between a landowner and a speculative builder. The builder would enter upon the land and put up houses. When the houses were completed, the landowner would let them to the builder on long leases. Ninety-nine years was a common period.[5] The leases would reserve a rent representing the value of the site as building land but ignoring the value of the houses, which the builder had erected at his own expense. It was therefore called a " ground rent ". The landowner would thus obtain an immediate enhanced return on his land and the somewhat distant prospect of the reversion in the houses when the leases came to an end. The builder would make

Building
leases.

---

[1] Rent Act 1968, s. 80.   [2] *Ibid.*, s. 80 (3).
[3] *Ibid.*, s. 5A (5) (*b*). See p. 473, *supra*.
[4] Landlord and Tenant Act 1954, s. 2 (4) ; Leasehold Reform Act 1967, s. 3 (1).
[5] Because leases for 100 years and over attracted a higher rate of stamp duty.

his profit by selling the leases to individual purchasers for capital sums. Or sometimes the landowner would grant the leases directly to individual purchasers nominated by the builder, in return for payment of a capital sum to the builder and the reservation of a ground rent for himself. In all these cases the main object of the builder was to take his profit and disappear from the scene, but more recently some developers of residential estates have chosen to grant long leases rather than sell freeholds in order to retain control over the management of the estate. Positive covenants are easier to enforce against tenants than against freeholders and the expiry of all leases simultaneously would allow the landlords to undertake a comprehensive redevelopment.

Long tenancies seldom fall within the Rent Acts. This is not because the Acts exclude long tenancies as such[1] but because they are usually within the exception for tenancies granted at a low rent.[2] Such tenancies are, however, by no means lacking in statutory protection. In fact they enjoy the exclusive benefit of two separate codes. The first and most important is that contained in Part I of the Leasehold Reform Act 1967. This allows a duly qualified long leaseholder of a dwelling house to acquire the freehold or an extended long tenancy upon terms which the Act describes as " fair "[3] but which can be highly advantageous to the tenant. The existence of these rights has reduced the importance of the second code, contained in Part I of the Landlord and Tenant Act 1954, which merely allows the tenant to remain in possession at a regulated rent after the expiration of his lease. The following is a brief account of both statutes.

Long tenancies protected by two separate codes.

(A) THE LEASEHOLD REFORM ACT 1967[4]

The Act confers upon a duly qualified tenant the right to acquire the freehold (commonly called "enfranchisement" of the tenancy) or an extended long lease of his house and premises. The discussion of the Act can conveniently be divided into four parts. First, the conditions which must be satisfied by the tenant ; secondly, the procedure by which he must exercise his rights ; thirdly, the nature of the interests he may acquire and finally the terms upon which he may do so.

Leasehold Reform Act 1967.

(i) The Qualifying Conditions

The qualifying conditions concern the terms of the tenancy, the character and value of the premises and the way in which they have been occupied.

Qualifying conditions.

---

[1] They were excluded by the Rent Act 1957, s. 21 (1), but reinstated as regulated tenancies by Leasehold Reform Act 1967, s. 39.

[2] Rent Act 1968, s. 2 (1) (*a*).

[3] Leasehold Reform Act 1967, s. 1 (1).

[4] See Hague, *Leasehold Enfranchisement.*

(a) **Long tenancy at a low rent.** A tenant must hold under a tenancy granted originally for a term of years certain exceeding twenty-one years[1] and at a rent which is less than two-thirds of the rateable value of the premises.[2] He need not of course be the original tenant. It is possible to buy a long lease which has only a short time left to run and then (subject only to the residence requirements discussed below) claim the benefits of the Act. A tenant who had bought the short residue of a long lease in the years immediately before the passing of the Act found that Parliament had given him a substantial windfall gain.

(b) **House, not flat.** The Act applies to houses in the ordinary sense of that word (" any building designed or adapted for living in and reasonably so called "[3]) but not to flats or maisonettes. These are excluded by a quaint proviso declaring that the Act does not apply to a house " of which a material part lies above or below a part of the structure not comprised in the house ".[4] Flats and maisonettes were excluded because until effect is given to the Wilberforce Report on Positive Covenants[5] their conversion into freeholds can present some awkward conveyancing problems. The Government's White Paper which preceded the Act also said rather mysteriously that " different considerations of equity " applied to flats,[6] although it is not easy to guess what these could be. The sale of flats on long leases has become a widespread practice in recent years, being considered a more profitable proposition than letting them on short regulated tenancies.[7] Long leases of flats may therefore be brought within the Act by future legislation when the conveyancing problems have been solved.

(c) **Rateable value.** The Act does not apply to houses having a rateable value exceeding £1,500 in Greater London or £750 elsewhere.[8]

(d) **Occupation as a residence.** The tenant may exercise his rights only when he has been occupying the house or some part of it in right of his tenancy as his only or main residence for the last five years or for five out of the last ten years.[9] A tenant who has

---

[1] Leasehold Reform Act 1967, s. 3 (1).
[2] *Ibid.*, s. 4. [3] *Ibid.*, s. 2 (1).
[4] *Ibid.*, s. 2 (2) ; see *Parsons* v. *Trustees of Henry Smith's Charity*, [1974] 1 W. L. R. 435 ; [1974] 1 All E. R. 1162.
[5] See *infra*, p. 596.
[6] *Leasehold Reform in England and Wales* (1966) Cmnd. 2916, para. 8.   For the Government's view on the considerations of equity applicable to houses, see *infra*, p. 496.
[7] Besides not having to concern himself with the Rent Officer, the landlord can indirectly profit from the fact that the tenant will finance the purchase by a mortgage on which interest payments and sometimes part of the capital repayments are deductible for tax, while rent payments are not.
[8] Leasehold Reform Act 1967, s. 1 (1) (a) ; as amended by Housing Act 1974, s. 118 (1). In the case of long tenancies created after February 18th, 1966 the limits are £1,000 and £500 respectively.
[9] *Ibid.*, s. 1 (1) (b).

more than one residence may claim only in respect of his " main " residence.[1] Thus a man with a freehold principal residence in London and a long lease of a country cottage, or a principal residence abroad and a long leasehold pied-à-terre in London, cannot claim the benefits of the Act at all. Sometimes the question of deciding which of two houses is a tenant's " main " residence will involve difficult questions of fact and degree.

It is sufficient if the tenant resides in only part of the house comprised in his tenancy.[2] Thus, although the tenant of a flat cannot qualify under the Act,[3] a tenant of the whole house who has converted it into flats and resides in one, underletting the rest, can claim the freehold of the house. It is also no objection that part of the house is used for business premises, either by the tenant or his sub-tenant or licensee.[4] A tenant of a shop with living accommodation above can therefore qualify if he lives on the premises, whether he uses the shop himself or underlets it to someone else.[5]

It is ordinarily necessary that the statutory period of residence should coincide with the existence of a long tenancy at a low rent.[6] Thus a tenant who has been occupying a house for seven years under a short tenancy at a full rent and then buys a long lease at a low rent cannot claim the freehold at once on the ground that he has already been in residence for more than five years. But there is an exception in favour of a tenant who has succeeded to a qualifying tenancy by reason of the death of a member of his family.[7] Such a tenant may include any period during which he was residing with his predecessor in the house.

The object of the residence provisions was to confine the benefits of the Act to persons who were genuinely occupying the property as their homes and to exclude speculators who might buy up leases simply to make a profit by acquiring the freeholds. But the benefit of a tenant's notice claiming the freehold or an extended lease is assignable together with the tenancy[8] and there is nothing to stop a speculator from buying the lease and the benefit of the notice from an outgoing tenant who was residentially qualified and served his notice before completion.

(ii) Enfranchisement procedure

A tenant exercises his rights under the Act by serving upon his landlord a notice in the prescribed statutory form, stating that he

Enfranchisement procedure.

---

[1] Compare the capital gains tax exemption provisions in s. 29 of the Finance Act 1965.
[2] Leasehold Reform Act 1967, s. 1 (2). See *Harris* v. *Swick Securities, Ltd.*, [1969] 1 W. L. R. 1604 ; [1969] 3 All E. R. 1131.
[3] *Ibid.*, s. 2 (2). See *supra.*
[4] *Ibid.*, s. 1 (2).
[5] *Lake* v. *Bennett*, [1970] 1 Q. B. 663 ; [1970] 1 All E. R. 457.
[6] Leasehold Reform Act 1967, s. 1 (1) (b).
[7] *Ibid.*, s. 7. " Family " is narrowly defined.
[8] *Ibid.*, s. 5 (2).

desires to acquire the freehold or an extended lease. In particular the notice must make it clear whether he wants the one or the other. A notice claiming the freehold or an extended lease in the alternative is invalid.[1] The effect of service of the notice is to create a contract between landlord and tenant, registrable as an estate contract[2] under which the one is bound to grant and the other to take the freehold or an extended lease, as the case may be, on the terms laid down by the Act.[3]

(iii) Freehold or extended lease

Freehold
or extended
lease.

(a) **Freehold.** A tenant who claims the freehold is entitled to have it conveyed to him free of encumbrances.[4] Any intermediate leasehold interests will be merged in the freehold and there are provisions for dividing up the purchase money between the freeholder and intermediate leaseholders according to the value of their respective interests.[5]

The effect of enfranchisement is of course ordinarily to extinguish the covenants between landlord and tenant in the lease and thereby to deprive the landlord of all rights which he may have had under the lease to control the use, appearance or state of repair of the house. The Act did however provide for exceptional cases in which the former landlord was allowed to retain " powers of management ".[6] This exception was intended to apply to substantial residential estates which were held from one landlord where the Secretary of State for the Environment certified that it was in the general interest " in order to maintain adequate standards of appearance and amenity and regulate development in the area " that the landlord should retain some control. Applications for the Minister's certificate had to be made before January 1st, 1970.[7] If the certificate was granted, the landlord could apply to the High Court for approval of a scheme giving him the appropriate powers.

The powers of management which a landlord may retain by virtue of a successful application for a certificate and scheme are very limited. They concern principally the regulation of the use or appearance of the houses and the enforcement of obligations concerning repair and the upkeep of common parts and facilities. But the landlord cannot prevent the tenants from acquiring their freeholds or reserve any right to re-acquire them, even for the purposes of redevelopment. He therefore loses all direct financial

---

[1] *Byrnlea Property Investments, Ltd.* v. *Ramsay,* [1969] 2 Q. B. 253 ; [1969] 2 All E. R. 311.

[2] Leasehold Reform Act 1967, s. 5 (5).

[3] *Ibid.,* ss. 8 (1) and 14 (1).

[4] *Ibid.,* s. 8 (1).

[5] *Ibid.,* Sched. 1.

[6] *Ibid.,* s. 19.

[7] For houses which became enfranchisable only by virtue of the increases in rateable value limits effected by Housing Act 1974, s. 118, the date is July 31st, 1976.

interest in the houses which have been enfranchised. As the application for a certificate and scheme is lengthy and expensive, a landlord would have to be very public spirited to seek a scheme for an estate on which most of the houses qualified for enfranchisement. In such cases, however, applications could be made by a representative body of tenants.[1] Applications for schemes by landlords have tended to be confined to estates which include a substantial number of houses which, by reason of their high rateable value, do not qualify for enfranchisement. Here it is worthwhile for the landlord to retain control of the enfranchised houses in order to maintain the amenities and value of the others.

(b) Extended lease. A tenant who claims an extended lease is entitled to the grant of a new tenancy, in substitution for the existing tenancy, for a term expiring fifty years after the term date of the existing tenancy[2] and on terms as to rent which will be considered in the next section.

Compared with the freehold, the extended tenancy is a weak and unattractive thing and it is seldom in practice requested. After the expiry of the original term it carries no further rights, either to claim the freehold or even another extension.[3] A tenant under an extended tenancy does not even have the ordinary long leaseholder's right to remain in possession at a regulated rent after the expiry of his term.[4] Furthermore, the landlord may at any time from twelve months before the commencement of the last fifty years of the term apply to the court for an order terminating the tenancy (on payment of compensation) if he can show that he intends to demolish or reconstruct the whole or a substantial part of the house and premises.[5]

(iv) Terms of acquisition

(a) Extended tenancy. The rent for the new substituted tenancy is the old rent for the remainder of the old term and then, for the fifty year extension, a " modern ground rent " representing the letting value of the site without including anything for the value of the buildings on the site, calculated at the date when the extension commences, with a review after twenty-five years.[6]

Terms of acquisition.

(b) Freehold. The Act now contains two different methods of calculating the price which the tenant must pay for the freehold. The first, contained in the original Act, now applies to houses of

---

[1] Leasehold Reform Act 1969, s. 19 (13). Most applications were in fact made by tenant's associations.

[2] *Ibid.*, s. 14 (1).

[3] *Ibid.*, s. 16 (1) (*a*) and (*b*).

[4] Parts I and II of the Landlord and Tenant Act 1954 are excluded by s. 16 (1) (*c*).

[5] Leasehold Reform Act 1967, s. 17.

[6] *Ibid.*, s. 15 (2).

a rateable value of less than £500 (£1,000 in Greater London). The second, introduced by the Housing Act 1974, applies to houses of greater rateable value.[1] Under the original scheme, the price of the freehold is the price which it would fetch if sold in the open market by a willing seller subject to the lease, on the assumption that the lease had already been extended by fifty years in accordance with the Act,[2] but without regard to any enhanced bid which might be expected from the tenant himself or a member of his family.[3] In practice, therefore, the price will be the capitalised value of the rent payable under the lease together with the value (if any) of the reversion to the site upon which the house stands. In the case of a lease which still has a very long time to run, the calculation is comparatively easy because the reversion has no value. No one will give anything simply for the right to possession of a building plot in 90 years' time. The value is therefore simply a capitalisation of the rent. Thus the freehold reversion upon a lease of a house at a ground rent of £20 a year with 70 years unexpired is likely to be worth today about twelve years' purchase or £240. On the other hand, as the term date approaches, the reversion begins to acquire some value. If the lease has, say, 20 years left to run, one can value the site and estimate what someone would give for the right to possession in twenty years' time. This value must then be added to the value of the right to receive the rent for the rest of the term. If the parties cannot agree on the value, it must be determined by the Lands Tribunal.[4]

The terms upon which the freehold can be acquired are perhaps the most controversial feature of the Leasehold Reform Act 1967. The exclusion of the value of the reversion to the building means that the terms can be highly advantageous to the tenant whose lease has a short period left unexpired. This method of calculation was intended to give effect to the Government's declaration in the White Paper that " the price of enfranchisement must be calculated in accordance with the principle that in equity the bricks and mortar belong to the qualified leaseholder and the land to the landlord ".[5] The word " equity " is clearly used in the sense of social justice and not in any sense which would have been recognised by Lord ELDON. Even so, it is not easy to understand. It is presumably intended to reflect the situation on the grant of a building lease, when the landlord reserves a rent which reflects the value of the land alone and the builder is able to dispose at a profit of the building he has erected.[6] At this stage, however, the reversion is so remote

---

[1] See p. 497, *infra*.
[2] Leasehold Reform Act 1967, s. 9 (1).
[3] Housing Act 1969, s. 82.
[4] Leasehold Reform Act 1967, s. 21 (1).
[5] *Leasehold Reform in England and Wales, supra,* para. 4.
[6] See *supra*, pp. 490–1.

that the question of whether it should in equity be a reversion in the land alone or the land and building is entirely academic ; in either case it will have no value.   But the position is very different when the lease is approaching its end, as was the case with many Victorian building leases at the time when the Act was passed.   At this point the reversion has a value which is enhanced by the fact that it includes the house as well as the land and a person who bought the reversion would have paid a price which reflected this enhanced value.   A purchaser of the residue of the term will have paid a price which was correspondingly lower in order to allow for the fact that he was buying a wasting asset.   The " equity " of the Act deprives the landlord of part of the value of his reversion and gives the tenant a windfall gain.   It can be justified only on the general ground that it is desirable to enrich tenants at the expense of their landlords.

It was no doubt for these reasons that a different method of calculating the price was applied to the more expensive houses which were brought within the scope of the Act by the Housing Act 1974.   In the case of houses having a rateable value of more than £500 (£1,000 in Greater London) the price is calculated upon a set of assumptions which result in the tenant paying more or less the market value of the reversion, including the reversion to the building as well as the site.[1]

(B) PART I OF THE LANDLORD AND TENANT ACT 1954[2]

Part I of the Landlord and Tenant Act 1954 gives security of tenure to long leaseholders who, at common law, would be obliged to give up possession on the ground that their leases had terminated by effluxion of time.   In effect, it allows them to remain in possession as regulated tenants.   Nowadays, however, such tenants will usually also be entitled to the more attractive privileges of the Leasehold Reform Act 1967.   The importance of the earlier code is therefore very much diminished.

Landlord and Tenant Part I.

(i) The Qualifying Tenancy

The Act protects the tenant if he holds under a long tenancy at a low rent[3] and if he satisfies what the Act calls the " qualifying condition".[4]   This requires him to show that if his tenancy had not been at a low rent, he would have been entitled to retain possession of all or part of the premises under the Rent Act 1968.   Thus

Qualifying tenancy.

---

[1] See Housing Act 1974, s. 118 (4).
[2] See Woodfall *Landlord and Tenant* (27th Edn:), pp. 1574–1605.
[3] For the meaning of this phrase, see *supra*, p. 492.
[4] Landlord and Tenant Act 1954, s. 2 (1).

the premises must have been let as a separate dwelling,[1] they must fall within the appropriate limits of rateable value,[2] the tenant must have been occupying them wholly or in part as his residence,[3] and so forth.   The crucial moment when the qualifying condition must be satisfied is on what the Act calls " the term date,"[4] *i.e.* the date on which the tenancy would expire at common law.   Thus in *Herbert* v. *Byrne*[5] the tenant bought the last five months' residue of the 99 year lease which was due to expire at Christmas 1962. In November 1962 he moved in a few pieces of his furniture and when Christmas came he was " pigging it " in a part of the house while his family lived elsewhere.   The whole exercise was admittedly performed solely in order to obtain the protection of the Act, but the Court of Appeal held that he satisfied the qualifying condition on the relevant date and had therefore succeeded.

(ii) Security of Tenure

Security of tenure.

At common law the landlord would be entitled to possession on the term date.   But the Act provides that he shall be entitled to possession only if he can show the existence of certain specified grounds.[6]   These grounds are similar to those upon which a court may make an order for possession under the Rent Act[7] but with one important addition, namely, that for the purposes of redevelopment after the termination of the tenancy the landlord proposes to demolish or reconstruct the whole or a substantial part of the relevant premises.[8]   If the landlord is unable to prove the existence of any of the statutory grounds, the tenant is entitled to retain possession as a regulated tenant,[9] paying a fair rent determined by the Rent Officer in the normal way.[10]

The machinery by which the Act provides security of tenure is rather different from that applicable to ordinary short protected tenancies.   Instead of a statutory tenancy which springs into existence immediately upon the expiry of the contractual term,[11] the Act artificially prolongs the existence of the long tenancy until it has been determined in accordance with a complicated procedure of notices, counter-notices and (if necessary) applications to the County Court.   If the landlord wishes to retake possession, he must serve the appropriate notice on the tenant at least six months but

---

[1] See *supra*, p. 470.
[2] See *supra*, p. 474.
[3] See *supra*, p. 478.
[4] Landlord and Tenant Act 1954, s. 2 (6).
[5] [1964] 1 W. L. R. 519 ; [1964] 1 All E. R. 882.
[6] Landlord and Tenant Act 1954, s. 12.
[7] See *supra*, p. 480.
[8] Landlord and Tenant Act 1954, s. 12 (1) (a).
[9] *Ibid.*, ss. 6 (1) (a) and 22 (1).
[10] Leasehold Reform Act 1967, Sched. 5. para. 4.
[11] See *supra*, p. 478.

less than twelve months in advance, stating the ground upon which he claims that he is entitled to possession.[1]   If the tenant replies with a counter-notice electing to remain in possession, or simply stays there and continues to fulfil the " qualifying condition "[2] the landlord must apply to the court for an order for possession.[3]   If he is successful, the tenancy will of course come to an end.   If he is unsuccessful, or if he did not want to retake possession in the first place, he may terminate the long tenancy by a notice proposing a statutory tenancy.[4]   Such a notice must specify the date upon which the long tenancy is to come to an end.   Except in the case of a notice served after an unsuccessful application for possession (when the minimum period is three months)[5] the notice must also be given at least six months but less than one year in advance.[6]   The notice must also propose the terms of the new statutory tenancy (apart from the rent) and in particular the obligations of the parties concerning repairs.[7]   If these are not agreed, they must be settled by an application to the court.[8]   The rent will continue (in the absence of agreement between the parties) at the old rate[9] until a fair rent for the statutory tenancy has been determined by the Rent Officer.[10]

(4) BUSINESS TENANCIES[11]

Protection is necessary for business tenants principally because a tenant with an established business is in a vulnerable position. If he has built up a goodwill attaching to the premises, such as that of a successful shopkeeper, he may suffer a severe loss of custom if he is required to remove elsewhere at the end of his tenancy. Furthermore, he will often have adapted the premises at his own cost to the needs of his particular business, so that removal would involve him in considerable further outlay.   A landlord may therefore be able to extract a higher rent from his sitting tenant than he would obtain by letting the premises to a new tenant in the open market.   Parliament has thought it unfair that the landlord should be able to force the tenant to pay this additional rent merely to preserve goodwill and improvements created by his own effort and expense.   It has therefore made provision for a system of security

---

[1] Landlord and Tenant Act 1954, s. 4 (2), (3) (*b*).
[2] *Ibid.*, s. 13 (1).   For the meaning of " qualifying condition," see *supra*, p. 497.
[3] *Ibid.*, s. 13 (1).
[4] *Ibid.*, s. 4 (3) (*a*).
[5] *Ibid.*, s. 14 (3).
[6] *Ibid.*, s. 4 (2).
[7] *Ibid.*, s. 7 (3).
[8] *Ibid.*, s. 7 (1).
[9] Leasehold Reform Act 1967, Sched. 5, para. 3 (1).
[10] *Ibid.*, para. 4.
[11] See Woodfall on *Landlord and Tenant* (27th Edn., 1968), Chapter 22.

of tenure and rent control which is now contained in Part II of the
Landlord and Tenant Act 1954, as amended by Part I of the Law
of Property Act 1969.

(A) The Qualifying Tenancy

Qualifying
tenancy.

A tenancy qualifies for the protection of Part II of the Landlord
and Tenant Act 1954 if the property comprised in the tenancy " is
or includes " premises which are occupied by the tenant " and are
so occupied for the purposes of a business carried on by him or for
those and other purposes ".[1] There are some features of this
definition which require closer examination.

(i) " is or includes premises . . . occupied by the tenant . . ."

A tenant will enjoy the protection of the Act if he occupies
any part of the property comprised in his lease for the purposes
of his business, although his protection will ordinarily extend only
to what the Act defines as his " holding ". This means the part
of the property occupied by the tenant himself (whether for business
or other purposes) or by a person employed in his business.[2] Thus
the tenant of a shop with a flat above who carries on business in
the shop and lives in the flat, or sub-lets it to an assistant or manager
working in the shop will enjoy protection in respect of the whole
premises. If he has sub-let the flat to someone who does not work
in the shop, the tenancy will be within the Act but his " holding "
will be the shop alone.[3] If he has sub-let the whole premises, his
tenancy will not be protected at all, although that of the sub-tenant
probably will be.

(ii) " occupied for the purposes of a business "

" Business " is very widely defined, to include a " trade, profession or employment " and, rather curiously, " *any* activity carried
on by a body of persons, whether corporate or unincorporate ".
Thus the tenancy of a members' tennis club has been held within
the Act, because playing tennis is undoubtedly an activity and it
was carried on by a body of persons.[4] For an individual, on the
other hand, activity is not enough. It must be a " trade, profession or employment ". Accordingly a tenant who ran a free
Sunday school in a disused shop was held to be outside the
definition.[5]

---

[1] Landlord and Tenant Act 1954, s. 23 (1).
[2] *Ibid.*, s. 23 (3).
[3] *Narcissi* v. *Wolfe*, [1960] Ch. 10 ; [1959] 3 All E. R. 71.
[4] *Addiscombe Garden Estates, Ltd.* v. *Crabbe*, [1958] 1 Q. B. 513 ; [1957]
3 All E. R. 563.
[5] *Abernethie* v. *A.M. & J. Kleiman*, [1970] 1 Q. B. 10 ; [1969] 2 All E. R.
790.

Under the Rent Act, where the key phrase is " let as a separate dwelling," attention is concentrated on the purpose for which the premises were let rather than the purpose for which they are actually being used.[1] The business code, on the other hand, is more concerned with actual user at the time when the question has to be decided. *Prima facie*, the fact that the tenant is carrying on business upon the premises is enough. But in some cases the fact that the business user is in breach of covenant will exclude the application of the Act.[2] And there is nothing in the Act to restrict the landlord's common law rights to forfeit the tenancy for breach of covenant.[3]

(iii) " or for those and other purposes "

The tenant need use only a part of the premises for the purposes of his business, or he may use the same part for business purposes some of the time and other purposes at other times. An exception to this rule is where, by reason of a partial residential use, the letting qualifies under the Rent Acts as a controlled tenancy. In that case, the Rent Acts take priority and the business code is excluded.[4] On the other hand, the Landlord and Tenant Act 1954 takes precedence over a regulated tenancy and consequently all lettings since 1956 which have included an element of business use have been excluded from the Rent Acts.[5]

(B) Security of Tenure and Rent

The Act gives a business tenant security of tenure by providing, first, that his tenancy (whether periodic or for a term certain) cannot be terminated except by the notice procedure laid down by the Act, and secondly, that upon the termination of his tenancy the tenant shall be entitled as of right to the grant of a new tenancy unless the landlord can establish one of a list of specified grounds of opposition.

Security of tenure and rent.

(i) Termination procedure

A business tenancy can be terminated only in accordance with the system of notices, counter-notices and applications to court provided by the Act.[6] Until this procedure has run its course, the tenancy continues, whatever its term might be. At common law, if a tenant for a term certain at an annual rent holds over after the end of the term and rent continues to be paid at the old rate,

Termination procedure.

---

[1] See *supra*, p. 471.
[2] Landlord and Tenant Act 1954, s. 23 (4).
[3] *Ibid.*, s. 24 (2).
[4] Rent Act 1968, s. 9 (1), (3). See *supra*, p. 471.
[5] *Ibid.*, s. 9 (5). See *supra*, p. 471.
[6] Landlord and Tenant Act 1954, s. 24 (1).

the normal inference is that he is holding over as a tenant from year to year.[1]　But a business tenant who stays after the term date is not holding over.　There can be no inference of a tenancy from year to year because the old tenancy has not yet come to an end.

(a) **Termination by landlord**. The landlord may terminate the tenancy by a notice in a prescribed form, specifying the date of termination.[2]　This must be at least six months but not more than twelve months after service of the notice and not earlier than the date on which the tenancy would have terminated, or could have been terminated, at common law.[3]　A landlord's notice to terminate is commonly known as a " section 25 notice ".

The notice must state whether or not the landlord would oppose the grant of a new tenancy, and if he intends to do so, the statutory grounds upon which he will rely.[4]

A tenant who has been served with a section 25 notice must within two months serve a counternotice stating whether or not he is willing to give up possession of the premises.[5]　If he does not serve such a notice (or states that he is willing to give up possession) the tenancy will end upon the date specified in the notice.　Having served the necessary counter-notice, a tenant who wishes to preserve his right to a new tenancy must apply to the court more than two months but within four months after the date of service of the section 25 notice.[6]　If he does not, the tenancy will again expire on the date specified in the notice.　The negotiation of the terms of a new tenancy usually takes some time, but a tenant who has been served with a section 25 notice and allows the four months to pass in negotiation without protecting himself by an application to court will find that he has lost all his rights.　Once an application for a new tenancy has been made, the old tenancy continues until three months after the proceedings have been " finally disposed of ".[7]

(b) **Termination by tenant**.　A tenant who simply wants to go out of possession can terminate his tenancy in any way open to him at common law.[8]　Furthermore, a tenant who holds under a tenancy for a term of years certain exceeding one year, or a term of years certain and thereafter from year to year, can serve a notice requesting the grant of a new tenancy.[9]　This notice is the counterpart of the landlord's section 25 notice.　Like the section 25 notice,

---

[1] See *supra*, p. 400.
[2] Landlord and Tenant Act 1954, s. 25 (1).
[3] *Ibid.*, s. 25 (2).
[4] *Ibid.*, s. 25 (6).
[5] *Ibid.*, s. 29 (2).
[6] *Ibid.*, s. 29 (3).　*Cf. Kammins Ballrooms Co., Ltd.* v. *Zenith Investments (Torquay) Ltd.*, [1971] A.C. 850 ; [1970] 2 All E. R. 871.
[7] *Ibid.*, s. 64.
[8] *Ibid.*, s. 24 (2).
[9] *Ibid.*, s. 26 (1).

it must specify the date on which the current tenancy is to terminate, and it is subject to the same time limits.[1] A landlord who wishes to oppose the grant of a new tenancy must serve a counter-notice stating his grounds of opposition within two months of the tenant's notice,[2] but whether he does so or not, the tenant will lose his right to a new tenancy unless he follows up his notice by an application to the court more than two months but not more than four months after the date of his notice.[3]

(c) **Who is the " landlord " ?** The scheme of the Act contemplates an exchange of notices followed by negotiations for a new tenancy and, if necessary, the adjudication of the court, between landlord and tenant. " Tenant," however, includes a sub-tenant[4]; the immediate landlord of the tenant carrying on the business may himself hold only a leasehold interest. But there is little point in the grant of a new tenancy by a " landlord " whose own interest in the premises is shortly about to expire. The Act deals with this problem by disregarding altogether a landlord who has himself only a short remaining leasehold interest. For the purposes of the Act, the " landlord " must be the owner of the fee simple or a leasehold interest which will not come to an end within fourteen months by effluxion of time or in respect of which a notice to terminate has been served under the Act.[5] If the immediate landlord does not fulfil these conditions, the competent landlord for the purposes of the Act will be the next superior landlord who does.

(ii) The grounds of opposition

The Act specifies seven grounds upon which a landlord may oppose the grant of a new tenancy.[6] These may be briefly summarised as follows : (a) the tenant's failure to repair (b) persistent delay in paying rent (c) other misbehaviour by the tenant (d) alternative accommodation available (e) that the tenant is, in relation to the landlord, a subtenant of part of the property originally let and that the landlord could realise a better rent by reletting the property as a whole (f) the landlord's intention to demolish or reconstruct the premises and (g) the landlord's intention to occupy the premises himself, either for the purposes of his business or as a residence. The last two grounds are in practice the most frequently relied upon and the only ones upon which any further comment will be made.

Grounds of opposition by landlord.

(a) **Intention to demolish or reconstruct.** The burden is upon the landlord to establish the necessary intention at the time of the hearing.[7] " Intention " involves more than thinking

---

[1] Landlord and Tenant Act 1954, s. 26 (2).
[2] *Ibid.*, s. 26 (6).
[3] *Ibid.*, s. 29 (3).
[4] *Ibid.*, s. 69 (1).
[5] *Ibid.*, s. 44 (1).
[6] *Ibid.*, s. 30 (1) (a) to (g).
[7] *Betty's Cafés, Ltd.* v. *Phillips Furnishing Stores, Ltd.*, [1959] A.C. 20 ; [1958] 1 All E. R. 607.

that demolition or reconstruction would be desirable. The land-lord must be able to show that he means business. As Lord ASQUITH said in a famous passage[1] :—

> " An ' intention ' . . . connotes a state of affairs which the party
> ' intending ' . . . does more than merely contemplate : it connotes a
> state of affairs which, on the contrary, he decides, so far as in him lies,
> to bring about, and which, in point of possibility, he has a reasonable
> prospect of being able to bring about, by his own act of volition . . .
> The term ' intention ' [is] unsatisfied if the person professing it has
> too many hurdles to overcome, or too little control of events . . .
> [The scheme must have] moved out of the zone of contemplation—
> out of the sphere of the tentative, the provisional and the explor-
> atory—into the valley of decision."

The landlord may therefore have to satisfy the court that his scheme of redevelopment is commercially viable, that he has the means to carry it through and the necessary planning permissions and other consents, or a reasonable prospect of obtaining them.

The landlord must also show that he could not reasonably carry out his work of demolition or reconstruction without ob-taining possession of the holding.[2] " Possession " in this con-text means legal possession, not merely physical occupation of the premises. Thus a landlord who has reserved a wide right to enter and do works upon the premises may be entitled to go into occupation for a lengthy period without ousting his tenant from legal possession.[3] Such a right will prevent him from opposing the grant of a new tenancy in similar terms. Even if the lease does not include such rights of entry, the tenant may be able to preserve his right to a new lease by offering to include them. The Act provides that the landlord cannot oppose the grant of a new tenancy on this ground if the tenant agrees to the inclusion of terms giving the landlord reasonable access and other facilities and the work could then be carried out without obtaining possession and without interfering " to a substantial extent or for a substantial time " with the use of the holding for the purposes of the tenant's business.[4] Similarly, the tenant may be entitled to claim a new tenancy of " an economically separable part "[5] of the holding if possession of the rest and (if necessary) access and facilities over the part retained would be reasonably sufficient to enable the landlord to carry out his work.[6]

---

[1] *Cunliffe* v. *Goodman*, [1950] 2 K. B. 237, at pp. 253–254 ; [1950] 1 All E. R. 720.

[2] Landlord and Tenant Act 1954, s. 30 (1) (*f*).

[3] *Heath* v. *Drown*, [1973] A. C. 498 ; [1972] 2 All E. R. 561.

[4] Landlord and Tenant Act 1954, s. 31A (1) (*a*).

[5] Defined in Landlord and Tenant Act 1954, s. 31A (2).

[6] *Ibid.*, s. 31A (1) (*b*). On the other hand, if the landlord wants to use the whole holding for the purposes of the works, the tenant cannot argue that the landlord could do as well or better by using only a part. See *Decca Navigator Co., Ltd.* v. *Greater London Council*, [1974] 1 W. L. R. 748 ; [1974] 1 All E. R. 1178.

(b) Intention to use for own business or residence.
Again the burden is upon the landlord to establish the necessary
intention at the time of the hearing. The Act provides, however,
that the landlord cannot rely upon this ground if his own interest
was purchased or created less than five years before " the termination of the current tenancy."[1] The purpose of this provision, as
in the case of the parallel provision in the Rent Act,[2] is to prevent
persons wanting premises with vacant possession from buying
them over the heads of sitting tenants and then opposing their
normal security of tenure on the ground that they are required for
the landlord's own use.

(iii) Compensation

A tenant who is unable to obtain a new tenancy because the
landlord can establish one of the grounds of opposition listed above
as (e), (f) or (g) is entitled to be paid compensation for disturbance.[3]
If his business has been carried on at the premises (whether by
himself or a predecessor) for more than fourteen years, the compensation will be twice the rateable value of the premises.[4] Otherwise it will be once the rateable value.[5] A tenant need not go to
court and lose merely in order to claim his compensation. If the
landlord states in his section 25 notice, or his counter-notice
opposing the tenant's request for a new tenancy, that he intends to
rely on grounds (e), (f) or (g), the tenant will be entitled to his compensation if he makes no application to court, or makes one and
later withdraws it.[6]

Tenant's compensation for disturbance.

(iv) Terms of the new tenancy

If the parties cannot agree on the terms of the new tenancy,
they must be fixed by the court. The court has a discretion in
fixing the length of the term but must not exceed fourteen years.[7]
Other terms (apart from rent) must be fixed by having regard to
the terms of the current tenancy and to "all relevant circumstances."[8]

Terms of new tenancy.

(v) Rent

The rent under the new tenancy is that which the premises
could command if let in the open market, but disregarding any
effect on the rent of the fact that the tenant or his predecessors in
title have been in occupation, or any goodwill attaching to the
holding on account of the tenant's business, or any improvements
made during the current tenancy or in certain cases in previous

Rent.

---

[1] Landlord and Tenant Act 1954, s. 30 (2).
[2] Rent Act 1968, Sched. 3, Part 1, case 8 ; *supra*, p. 483.
[3] Landlord and Tenant Act 1954, s. 37 (1).
[4] *Ibid.*, 37 (2) (*a*) and (3).   [5] *Ibid.*, s. 37 (2) (*b*).
[6] Until the Act was amended by L.P.A. 1969 the tenant had to go to court.
[7] Landlord and Tenant Act 1954, s. 33.
[8] *Ibid.*, s. 35.

tenancies within the past twenty-one years.[1]   When the court has to determine the rent, it will usually do so after hearing the evidence of expert surveyors, giving their opinions of the letting value of the premises supported by evidence of lettings of comparable properties in the same area.   It may be questioned whether the court's function could not be better performed by a body which was itself expert in these matters, such as the Lands Tribunal.

Until 1970, the tenant continued to be liable only for the rent under the old tenancy until it was duly terminated in accordance with the Act and the new tenancy had begun.   In the absence of contrary agreement, as we have seen, the old tenancy could not terminate until three months after the proceedings for the grant of the new tenancy had been finally disposed of.[2]   In times of inflation, when the difference between the old rent and the new might be very considerable, it was therefore greatly in the tenant's interest to prolong the proceedings (and his tenancy) as much as possible.   Time might be gained by taking fine points on the validity of the section 25 notice and similar procedural matters, while even an unsuccessful appeal to the House of Lords might be financed out of the difference in rents.   This situation led to an amendment which allowed the landlord or tenant to apply to the court to fix an interim rent, payable from the date of termination specified in the section 25 notice or the tenant's request for a new tenancy or the date of the application to fix the interim rent, whichever is the later.[3]   The interim rent is also a market rent, based upon the assumption that the tenancy is to be from year to year.[4]

(vi) Contracting out

Contracting out.

Until 1970 the parties could not by agreement exclude the provisions of the Act.[5]   But it was found that this prohibition discouraged landlords from granting temporary lettings of premises which they intended eventually to use themselves or redevelop. Whatever the terms of the letting, the protected tenant will be entitled to at least six months' notice to terminate[6] and can usually prolong his tenancy for several months more by an unsuccessful application for a new tenancy.[7]   When it finally expires, he may delay the landlord still further by compelling him to commence

---

[1] Landlord and Tenant Act 1954, s. 34.
[2] *Ibid.*, s. 64.   See *supra*, p. 502.
[3] *Ibid.*, s. 24A.   See *Stream Properties, Ltd.* v. *Davis*, [1972] 1 W. L. R. 645 ; [1972] 2 All E. R. 746.
[4] In times of inflation the rent for a tenancy from year to year will be less than that of a tenancy at a fixed rent for a term of years.   See *Regis Property Co., Ltd.* v. *Lewis and Peat, Ltd.*, [1970] Ch. 695 ; [1970] 3 All E. R. 227 ; *English Exporters (London), Ltd.* v. *Eldonwall, Ltd.*, [1973] Ch. 415 ; [1973] 1 All E. R. 726.
[5] Landlord and Tenant Act 1954, s. 38 (1).
[6] See *supra*, p. 502.
[7] See *supra*, p. 502.

proceedings for possession. Many landlords therefore preferred to leave their buildings temporarily empty. The Act now allows the parties to agree to exclude the Act if their agreement is approved by the court, which will have to be satisfied that the tenant understands his position and has not been oppressed or overborne.[1]

(5) AGRICULTURAL HOLDINGS[2]

Tenant farmers need security of tenure to encourage them to spend money on improving the land and buying stock and other capital equipment. Some statutory protection was introduced soon after the First War,[3] but this was greatly strengthened and improved during and after the Second War as part of the general effort made to increase home food production at the time. The code now in force is still largely contained in the Agricultural Holdings Act 1948, although there have been some later amendments.[4]

(A) The Agricultural Holding

The key concept in the Agricultural Holdings Act 1948 is the " agricultural holding." This is defined as " the aggregate of the agricultural land comprised in a contract of tenancy "[5] but excluding service tenancies granted during the continuance of some office or employment. " Agriculture " is very widely defined[6] and there is no minimum size for an agricultural holding but " agricultural land " means land which is not merely used for agriculture but is " so used for the purposes of a trade or business."[7] This provision excludes a tenancy of a plot of land used as a private garden. The Agricultural holding.

(B) Security of Tenure

(i) The deemed yearly tenancy

The Act confers security of tenure by limiting the circumstances in which a landlord can validly serve a notice to quit. *Prima facie* this machinery can operate only on periodic tenancies, because only in such cases is a notice to quit necessary to terminate the tenancy. But the Act deals with this problem in sweeping fashion by providing that tenancies for an interest less than a tenancy from year to year shall take effect as if they were yearly tenancies,[8] while a tenancy for a term certain of two years or upwards shall (unless a notice to quit has been served) thereafter Security of tenure.

---

[1] Landlord and Tenant Act 1954, s. 37 (4).
[2] See Muir Watt, *Agricultural Holdings* (12th Edn. 1967).
[3] The Agricultural Holdings Act 1923.
[4] Principally in the Agriculture Act 1958.
[5] Agricultural Holdings Act 1948, s. 1 (1).
[6] *Ibid.*, s. 94 (1).   [7] *Ibid.*, s. 1 (2).   [8] *Ibid.*, s. 2 (1).

continue as a yearly tenancy.[1] Licences to occupy the land for
any period also take effect as tenancies from year to year.[2] Thus
most agricultural tenancies, whatever their express terms, are
deemed to be or become yearly tenancies.

It will be noticed, however, there is a curious gap in these
provisions. A tenancy for a term certain which is more than a year
but less than two years does not appear to be converted into a
yearly tenancy. It will therefore expire by effluxion of time and
the security of tenure machinery cannot apply to it.[3] Furthermore,
the Act contains an express exception in the case of a letting or
licence " in contemplation of the use of the land only for grazing
or mowing during some specified period of the year."[4] The owner
of a country house who has some surplus fields can therefore let
them to a neighbouring farmer for grazing for up to 364 days at
a time[5] without committing himself to the security of tenure provisions of the Act.

(ii) The notice to quit

At common law a yearly tenancy may be terminated by at
least six months' notice expiring on the anniversary of the tenancy.[6]
For an agricultural holding the notice period is extended to one
year.[7] The common law requirement that the notice must terminate on the anniversary is retained. It may therefore be up to
two years before a notice to quit can expire.

(iii) Validity of notice to quit

A notice to quit an agricultural holding can operate effectively
in only two kinds of circumstances. The first is when the landlord
at the time of service can rely upon one of seven specified grounds[8]
(commonly known to land agents as " the seven deadly sins ").
The second is when the local Agricultural Land Tribunal consent
to the operation of the notice after it has been served.[9] This
consent also may be given only upon certain specified grounds.

The grounds upon which a notice may be served and operate
without further consent may be summarised briefly as follows :
(a) consent of the Agricultural Land Tribunal given before service
(b) land required for non-agricultural use (c) bad husbandry by the
tenant (d) failure to pay rent after statutory demand (e) breach of

---

[1] Agricultural Holdings Act 1948, s. 3 (1).
[2] *Ibid.*, s. 2 (1). But see *Bahamas International Trust Co., Ltd.* v. *Thread-
gold*, [1974] 1 W. L. R. 1514 ; [1974] 3 All E. R. 881.
[3] *Gladstone* v. *Bower*, [1960] 2 Q. B. 284 ; [1960] 3 All E. R. 353.
[4] Proviso to Agricultural Holdings Act 1948, s. 2 (1).
[5] *Reid* v. *Dawson*, [1955] 1 Q. B. 214 ; [1954] 3 All E. R. 498 ; *Scene Estate,
Ltd.* v. *Amos*, [1957] 2 Q. B. 205 ; [1957] 2 All E. R. 325.
[6] See *supra*, p. 465.
[7] Agricultural Holdings Act 1948, s. 23 (1).
[8] *Ibid.*, s. 24 (2) (*a*) to (*g*).   [9] *Ibid.*, ss. 24 (1), 25 (1).

covenant by the tenant (f) bankruptcy (g) death of " the tenant with whom the contract of tenancy was made."

The last ground is in practice the most important because it is the only one which (unless the tenant is a limited company) must become available to the landlord sooner or later. A tenant farmer can therefore usually expect to retain possession during his lifetime. But the provision that the death must be that of the tenant " with whom the contract of tenancy was made " produces a curious result when the tenancy has been assigned. The assignee acquires in effect a statutory estate *pur autre vie* which is liable to termination on the death of a person who no longer has any connection with the land.[1]

(iv) Notice procedure

A tenant who has been served with a notice to quit and wishes to invoke the security of tenure provisions of the Act must serve a counter-notice. If the notice does not purport to have been given on one of the seven permitted grounds, he must simply claim the protection of the relevant section.[2] If the notice relies on certain of the permitted grounds, the tenant's notice must claim an arbitration on whether the appropriate ground existed.[3] There are stringent time limits for these notices and the tenant may lose all protection if they are not correctly served.[4] It is perhaps questionable whether such a complicated procedure is suitable for farmers.

(C) RENT

The rent for an agricultural holding is, in the absence of agreement, fixed by an arbitrator appointed under the Act.[5] The landlord is entitled to the rent which the holding could command if let on the open market, but disregarding the fact that the tenant is in occupation, the improvements he has made and certain other matters.[6] The rent may be reviewed (by agreement or arbitration) at intervals of not less than three years.[7]

SECTION X. REGISTERED LAND[8]

As we have seen, a term of years absolute is one of the two legal estates which can be registered as a separate title on the property

---

[1] *Clarke* v. *Hall*, [1961] 2 Q. B. 331 ; [1961] 2 All E. R. 365.

[2] Agricultural Holdings Act 1948, s. 24 (1).

[3] See The Agriculture (Notices to Remedy and Notices to Quit) Order 1964, Article 9.

[4] As in *Magdalen College, Oxford* v. *Heritage*, [1974] 1 W. L. R. 441 ; [1974] 1 All E. R. 1065.

[5] Agricultural Holdings Act 1948, s. 8.

[6] *Ibid.*, s. 8 (2).   [7] *Ibid.*, s. 8 (3).

[8] See generally Ruoff and Roper, chap. 23. Barnsley, *Conveyancing Law and Practice*, pp. 410–18. *Registered Land Practice Notes* (1972), pp. 14–15 ; M. & B. pp. 434–5. Law Commission Working Paper No. 32 (Law Com. 1971).

register.[1]   Not every lease is so registrable, but if it is, then the legal estate will not finally pass to the lessee until registration is completed in accordance with the provisions of the Land Registration Act 1925.

The provisions on the registrability of a leasehold title[2] are complex, but may be set out briefly as follows.

(a) Where the title to the reversion is registered, then, if the lease is granted for a term exceeding 21 years, the title to the lease *must* be registered.[3]   This is the rule whether or not the land is in an area of compulsory registration.

(b) Where the title to the reversion is not registered, there is a difference between those areas where registration is compulsory and those where it is voluntary.

If the land is in a compulsory area, then

(i) where a lease is granted for a term of 40 years or more (or is assigned on sale when it has 40 or more years to run) it *must* be registered.[4]

(ii) where a lease is granted for a term exceeding 21 years but less than 40 years (or is assigned on sale when it has less than 40 years but more than 21 years to run) it *may* be registered.[5]

But if the land is in a voluntary area, registration may only be effected in the special cases specified by the Registrar under the Land Registration Act 1966.[6]

(c) There are exceptions to the above rules in that certain types of lease, no matter what the length of their term, cannot be registered substantively.   Such leases are

(i) Leases " containing an absolute prohibition against all dealings therewith *inter vivos*,"[7] and

(ii) Mortgage terms " where there is a subsisting right of redemption."[8]

It is important to notice the effect of the substantive registration of a compulsorily registrable lease. It is only on registration that the lessee finally acquires a legal estate : furthermore, as part of the machinery of registration, notice of the lease is automatically entered by the Registrar against the lessor's registered title, if the land certificate is lodged in the registry.[9]   We must now consider

---

[1] *Supra*, p. 108.

[2] For the kinds of leasehold title which may be registered, see *supra*, pp. 108–9 ; *infra*, pp. 768–9.

[3] L.R.A. 1925, ss. 19 (2), 22 (2).

[4] *Ibid.*, s. 123.   [5] *Ibid.*, s. 8 (1) (a).

[6] L.R.A. 1966, s. 1 (2), *supra*, p. 104, note 7.   [7] L.R.A. 1925, s. 8 (2).

[8] *Ibid.*, ss. 8 (1) (a), 19 (2) (b), 22 (2) (b).

[9] L.R.R. 1925, r. 46.   For an account of the procedure see *Strand Securities, Ltd.* v. *Caswell*, [1965] Ch. 958, at pp. 976–979 ; [1965] 1 All E. R. 820, *per* Lord DENNING M.R.   M. & B. p. 431.

the effect of the failure on the part of the lessee to register his lease. There are two different situations. If, on the one hand, he must register it because his lessor's title is itself registered (*e.g.* a lease for more than 21 years), then until registration is completed " the transferor shall be deemed to remain proprietor of the registered estate."[1] If, on the other hand, he must register it because the land is in a compulsory area (*e.g.* a lease for 40 years or more) then, if he does not apply for registration within two months, the transaction is " void so far as regards the grant . . . of the legal estate."[2] In the latter case the lessee acquires the legal estate at the time of the grant, but if he fails to register it within the time limit, it reverts to the lessor. " The effect of not registering the title to a lease when granted would at best seem to be that the lessee holds the demised premises, not as legal owner of the term, but as a person who has entered into a binding agreement for a lease."[3]

From these complexities of what must and what may be registered, it is clear that a lease granted for a term of 21 years or less (and a lease which has 21 years or less unexpired[4]) cannot be substantively registered.[5] Nor can a contract for a lease : this is, as we have seen, an equitable interest and is therefore incapable of registration as a legal estate.[6] But this does not mean that such transactions afford no protection to a lessee or to a holder under an agreement for a lease.

Under section 70 (1) (*k*) of the Land Registration Act 1925 :—

> "leases for any term or interest not exceeding twenty-one years, granted at a rent without taking a fine "

are overriding interests, and here the lessee is protected against a transferee from the lessor without the need for any entry on the register. If the lease is not an overriding interest under this paragraph, *i.e.* a fine has been taken or no rent has been reserved, then the right is a minor interest and the lessee should protect it by the entry of a notice or, if a notice cannot be entered, of a caution on his lessor's registered title. A contract for a lease may be protected by similar entries.[7] The question now arises as to how far such a lessee or a holder under a contract for a lease is protected if he fails to enter a notice or a caution on the register. It

---

[1] L.R.A. 1925, ss. 18 (5), 19 (1), 19 (2), 21 (5), 22 (1), 22 (2).
[2] *Ibid.*, s. 123 (1). [3] Ruoff and Roper, p. 199.
[4] L.R.A. 1925, ss. 8 (1) (*a*), 19 (2) (*a*), 22 (2) (*a*). If originally granted for more than 21 years, the Registrar may in certain circumstances allow registration, Ruoff and Roper, pp. 479–81.
[5] Nor can (*a*) a lease which contains " an absolute prohibition against all dealings therewith inter vivos " (*b*) a mortgage term where there is a subsisting right of redemption. *Supra*, p. 510. Leases under (*a*) should be protected in all cases where they are not overriding interests by virtue of s. 70 (1) (*k*) by entry of a notice on the lessor's title. Mortgage terms are best protected by registration of a charge under s. 26.
[6] *Supra*, p. 106.
[7] It cannot be protected as an overriding interest under L.R.A. 1925, s. 70 (1) (*g*). *City Permanent Building Society* v. *Miller*, [1952] Ch. 840 ; [1952] 2 All E. R. 621 ; *infra*, p. 773.

is here that there is a striking difference between the two systems
of conveyancing. In the unregistered system, failure to register
a contract for a lease as a land charge under the Land Charges Act
1972 renders it void as against a purchaser of the legal estate for
money or money's worth, even if the purchaser has actual notice
of the agreement.[1] But in registered land the position is both
similar and different. On the one hand the failure to protect a
contract as a minor interest by an entry on the lessor's registered
title has similar consequences ; it will be overridden if the lessor
makes a registered disposition for valuable consideration.[2] On the
other hand the contract may be saved by section 70 (1) (g) of
the Land Registration Act 1925, under which

> "the rights of every person in actual occupation of the land or in
> receipt of the rents and profits thereof, save where inquiry is made
> of such person and the rights are not disclosed"

are overriding interests.[3] Accordingly if the lessee is let into
occupation before formal transfer and there is no entry on the
register of his interest, the mere fact of the occupation turns his
minor interest into an overriding one.[4] It would seem that a
lessee in occupation (irrespective of the length of his lease) can
always rely on just his occupation for protection. A lessor in
receipt of rent, or in occupation through a servant or agent is also
protected in this way, but a tenant who allows another to occupy his
property rent free is not.[5]

The Registrar is required to notify on the register the determination, whether whole or partial, of a lease. It must be proved
to his satisfaction that it has so determined. The general principles which govern the determination of leases apply equally to
registered as to unregistered land. A lease which is determined
by effluxion of time will only be cancelled on the register, if the
Registrar is satisfied that it has not been statutorily extended,
e.g. under the Landlord and Tenant Act 1954.[6]

---

[1] *Supra*, p. 397.
[2] *Infra*, p. 779.
[3] *Supra*, p. 109 ; *infra*, p. 773.
[4] *Woolwich Equitable Building Society* v. *Marshall*, [1952] Ch. 1 ; [1951]
2 All E. R. 769 ; *Mornington Permanent Building Society* v. *Kenway*, [1953]
Ch. 382 ; [1953] 1 All E. R. 951.
[5] *Strand Securities Ltd.* v. *Caswell*, [1965] Ch. 958 ; [1965] 1 All E. R. 820.
M. & B. p. 114.
[6] See ss. 1–3, 23, 24 ; Rent Act 1968, s. 117 (2), Sched. 15.

B. INTERESTS CONFERRING A RIGHT ENFORCEABLE AGAINST THE LAND OF ANOTHER

CHAPTER II

EASEMENTS AND PROFITS

SUMMARY

SECTION I.   RIGHTS *IN ALIENO SOLO* GENERALLY

Incorporeal interests.

Introductory Note. In this chapter our concern is with rights *in alieno solo*, *i.e.* with the case where X. possesses some right that is enforceable against the land of another. If the owner of Blackacre is entitled to an easement, such as a right of way, over Whiteacre, he is said, in the curious language of English law, to have an incorporeal interest. Perhaps it is more intelligible to describe him as holding an interest in an incorporeity.[1]

Like corporeal estates and interests, incorporeal interests may exist at law and in equity. A legal interest must be created by deed,[2] and can exist only for the same periods as those for which a legal estate can exist. Thus a legal easement may exist in fee simple or for a term of years absolute. An easement for any other period, or an easement created otherwise than by deed, must be equitable only.[3]

Servitudes.

Servitudes. As we have seen, the *jura in re aliena* which are known to English Law cover a very wide field and include such diverse subjects as rentcharges,[4] advowsons, tithes and so on,[5] but our present concern is solely with what Roman lawyers called "praedial servitudes". Though servitude is a word that is occasionally adopted by the judges,[6] it is not admitted as a term of art in English Law, and yet it is a suitable expression to denote the particular legal interests which form the subject of this chapter.

Definition.

A praedial servitude in Roman Law meant a right *in rem*, annexed to a definite piece of land, the *praedium dominans*, which entitled the owner of that land to do something or to prevent the doing of something on another piece of land, the *praedium serviens*.[7] This is a sufficiently accurate description of easements and profits which represent the praedial servitudes of English Law.

---

[1] *Supra*, pp. 136–8.
[2] *Infra*, pp. 526, 528.
[3] *Infra*, pp. 526–7.
[4] *Infra*, pp. 624 *et seq.*
[5] *Supra*, p. 138, note 1.
[6] *E.g. Dalton* v. *Angus* (1881), L. R. 6 App. Cas. 740, at p. 796 ; *per* Lord Selborne.
[7] Moyle, *Institutes of Justinian* (5th Edn.), p. 214.

An easement is a privilege without a profit,[1] that is to say, it is   Easements
described.
a right attached to one particular piece of land which allows the
owner of that land (the dominant owner) either to use the land of
another person (the servient owner) in a particular manner, as by
walking over or depositing rubbish on it or to restrict its user by
that other person to a particular extent, but which does not allow
him to take any part of its natural produce or its soil.[2]

Thus an easement may be either positive or negative.[3] It is   Positive and
negative
easements.
positive if it consists of a right to do something upon the land of
another, as, for example, to walk or to place erections such as
signboards thereon.

A negative easement, on the other hand, does not permit the
execution of an act, but imposes a restriction upon the use which
another person may make of his land.   For instance, the easement
of light signifies that the servient owner may not build so as
unreasonably to obstruct the flow of light, and again an easement of
support implies that the servient owner must not interfere with
his own land or building so as to disturb his neighbour's.

An easement confers upon its owner no proprietary or possessory right in the land affected.   It merely imposes a particular
restriction upon the proprietary rights of the owner of the servient
land.   A right which entitles one person to the unrestricted use of
the land of another may be an effective right to ownership or
possession, but it cannot be an easement.[4]

A *profit à prendre* is a right to enter another's land and to   Definition
of a profit.
take something off that land,[5] and it is this participation in the
produce of the soil or in the soil itself that principally distinguishes a profit from an easement.   A right is a profit only if the
thing to be taken is something that is capable of ownership.
Thus the rights to pasture cattle on another's land, or to take sand
or fish from another's river, or to take turf, stones or pheasants
from another's estate are all examples of profits, for such things are
capable of ownership; but a right to collect and carry away water
from a spring on another person's land, or to water cattle in
another's stream is an easement, since water is no part of the soil
like sand, nor the produce of soil like grass, and unless stored in a
tank or other receptacle is not capable of private ownership.[6]

---

[1] *Hewlins* v. *Shippam* (1826), 5 B. & C. 221 ; Termes de la Ley, *sub voce*
" Easement."
[2] *Manning* v. *Wasdale* (1836), 5 A. & E. 758.
[3] *Dalton* v. *Angus* (1881), 6 App. Cas. 740, 821.
[4] *Copeland* v. *Greenhalf*, [1952] Ch. 488 ; [1952] 1 All E. R. 809 ; dist.
Ward v. *Kirkland*, [1967] Ch. 194 ; [1966] 1 All E. R. 609 ; *Wright* v. *Macadam*
[1949] 2 K. B. 744 ; [1949] 2 All E. R. 565.   See also *Grigsby* v. *Melville*,
[1972] 1 W. L. R. 1355 ; [1973] 1 All E. R. 385 ; affirmed [1974] 1 W. L. R.
80 ; [1973] 3 All E. R. 455 ; *infra*, p. 525.
[5] *Duke of Sutherland* v. *Heathcote*, [1892] 1 Ch. 475, 484.
[6] Co. Litt. 4*a* ; Blackstone, vol. ii. 18 ; *Mason* v. *Hill* (1833), 5 B. & Ad. 1 ;
Race v. *Ward* (1855), 4 E. & B. 702 ; *Lowe* v. *J. W. Ashmore, Ltd.*, [1971] Ch.
545, 557.

SECTION II. EASEMENTS[1]

SUMMARY

(A) CHARACTERISTICS OF EASEMENTS

Introductory Note. A question that not infrequently arises is whether some right exercisable over the land of another is an easement or a right of an inferior nature, and it is a question of crucial importance. An owner may grant a multitude of different rights over his land to X., but it will make a world of difference to the position of X. whether they are easements or not. A legal easement is a *jus in rem*, not a mere *jus in personam*; it permanently binds the land over which it is exercisable and permanently avails the land for the advantage of which it exists.[2] If X. acquires an easement either in fee simple or for a term of years absolute, he becomes the owner of an actual legal interest in the land[3] and can enforce it against anybody who comes to the land whether by way of purchase, lease, gift or as a squatter, and whether with or without notice of the easement.

Thus at common law the benefit of an easement passes with a transfer of the land to which it is annexed without being specially mentioned,[4] and it is now expressly provided that a conveyance of land shall be deemed to include and shall operate to convey all easements which are attached to the land conveyed.[5]

On the other hand, if X. is given some right over the land of Y which may bear some similarity to an easement but which nevertheless the law does not regard as an easement, X. acquires a

Importance of distinguishing between easements and other rights.

Personal rights distinguished from easements.

---

[1] See generally Gale, *Law of Easements* (14th Edn.)
[2] *Leech* v. *Schweder* (1874), L. R. 9 Ch. App. 463, at p. 474; L.P.A. 1925, s. 187 (1).
[3] *Infra*, p. 526.　　　　　　　　[4] Co. Litt. 121b.
[5] L.P.A. 1925, s. 62 (1), re-enacting Conveyancing Act 1881, s. 6 (1) ; *infra*, pp. 530-2.

mere personal right. Its infringement may give him a remedy in damages against Y, and if negative in nature it may be enforceable in equity against a person who acquires Y's land with notice of its existence,[1] but it is not a real right enforceable irrespective of notice against all subsequent owners of that land. Neither can a right be given the status of an easement at the free will of the parties who create it, for the rule is that no right over land will be regarded as an easement unless it possesses certain attributes which the law has determined.

This being so, the first task must be to discover what those attributes and characteristics are.

Characteristics. If an interest is to be an easement it must possess the four following characteristics [2] :—

(1) **There must be a dominant and a servient tenement.**[3] The very nature of an easement, as being a right *in alieno solo*, requires that there shall be a tenement over which it is exercisable, the *servient tenement*, but in addition to this the law requires that there shall be another tenement, the *dominant tenement*, for the benefit of which the easement exists. To adopt legal phraseology an easement must be appurtenant or attached to land.

Easement must be appurtenant to land.

> If X., the owner of Blackacre, has acquired a right of way over the adjoining tenement Whiteacre, he is entitled to an easement of way not because he is X., but because he is the fee simple owner of Blackacre. The easement exists because Blackacre exists.[4]

> It follows from this that there cannot be an easement *in gross*,[5] *i.e.* an easement that is independent of the ownership of land by the person who claims the right. Of course a person who does not own a yard of property may be granted a privilege to pass over Whiteacre, but though this may give him a personal right it certainly does not entitle him to an easement. It amounts to a licence confined in its effect to the actual parties.[6]

(2) **An easement must accommodate the dominant tenement.** It is a fundamental principle that an easement must not only be appurtenant to a dominant tenement, but must also be connected with the normal enjoyment of that

Easement must accommodate dominant tenement.

---

[1] See the doctrine of *Tulk* v. *Moxhay*, *infra*, p. 597, *et seq.*

[2] *Re Ellenborough Park*, [1956] Ch. 131 ; [1955] 2 All E. R. 38 ; M. & B. p. 490 ; (1964), 28 *Conv.* (N.S.) 450 (M. A. Peel).

[3] Holdsworth, *History of English Law*, vol. vii. pp. 324 *et seq.*

[4] *Rangeley* v. *Midland Rail Co.* (1868), 3 Ch. App. 306, 311 ; *Ackroyd* v. *Smith* (1850), 10 C. B. 164, 188 ; *Hawkins* v. *Rutter*, [1892] 1 Q. B. 668.

[5] *Ackroyd* v. *Smith, supra* : *Weekly* v. *Wildman* (1698), Ld. Raym. 406, *per* TREBY, C.J. In the U.S.A. both easements and profits may be *in gross*. See American Law Institute *Restatement of the Law of Property* (1944), vol. 5. paras. 454, 489–96. [6] *Infra*, pp. 577 *et seq.*

tenement.[1] There must be a direct *nexus* between the enjoyment of the right and the user of the dominant tenement.[2] This requirement has been stated in various ways:—

"An easement must be connected with the enjoyment of the dominant tenement and must be for its benefit."[3]

"It must have some natural connection with the estate, as being for its benefit."[4]

"The incident sought to be annexed, so that the assignee of the land may take advantage of it, must be beneficial to the land in respect of the ownership." [5]

To take a simple example, a right of way in order to rank as an easement need not lead right up to the dominant tenement, but it must at least have some natural connection with it.[6] You cannot, remarked BYLES, J., have a right of way over land in Kent appurtenant to an estate in Northumberland,[7] for a right of way in Kent cannot possibly be advantageous to Northumberland land.[8] We may expand the statement of the principle thus : a right enjoyed by one over the land of another does not possess the status of an easement unless it accommodates and serves the dominant tenement, and is reasonably necessary for the better enjoyment of that tenement, for if it has no necessary connexion therewith, although it confers an advantage upon the owner and renders his ownership of the land more valuable, it is not an easement at all, but a mere contractual right personal to and only enforceable between the two contracting parties.[9]

Whether the necessary *nexus* exists depends greatly upon the nature of the dominant tenement and the nature of the right alleged. If, for example, the dominant tenement is a residential house and if there is annexed to it by express grant a right to use an adjoining garden for purposes of relaxation and pleasure, this is a clear case where the right is sufficiently connected with the normal enjoyment of the house to rank as an easement.[10] The fact that the right enhances the value of the dominant tenement is a relevant, but not a decisive, consideration.[11] The principle is perhaps best illustrated by *Hill* v. *Tupper*,[12] where the facts were as follows :—

---

[1] *Ackroyd* v. *Smith* (1850), 11 C. B. 10.

[2] *Re Ellenborough Park*, [1956] Ch. 131, at p. 174 ; [1955] 2 All E. R. 38, at p. 42.

[3] Gale on Easements (12th Edn.), p. 20. *Clapman* v. *Edwards*, [1938] 2 All E. R. 507.

[4] *Bailey* v. *Stephens* (1862), 12 C. B. (N.S.) 91, at p. 115, *per* BYLES, J.

[5] *Ibid.*

[6] *Todrick* v. *Western National Omnibus Co.*, [1934] Ch. 561 ; *Birmingham, Dudley and District Banking Co.* v. *Ross* (1888), 38 Ch. D. 295, at p. 314 ; *Pugh* v. *Savage*, [1970] 2 Q. B. 373 ; [1970] 2 All E. R. 353 (intervening land between dominant and servient tenements).

[7] *Bailey* v. *Stephens* (1862), 12 C. B. (N.S.) 99.

[8] *Todrick* v. *Western National Omnibus Co.*, [1934] Ch. 561, at p. 580, ROMER, L.J.

[9] Cited with approval in *Re Ellenborough Park*, *supra.*, at p. 170.

[10] *Re Ellenborough Park*, [1956] Ch. 131 ; [1955] 2 All E. R. 38 ; M. & B. p. 490.   [11] *Ibid.*, at pp. 173, 43 respectively.

[12] (1863) 2 H. & C. 121 ; M. & B. p. 488.

A canal company leased land adjoining the canal to Hill and gave him the " sole and exclusive right " to let out pleasure boats on the canal. Tupper, an innkeeper, disregarded this privilege by himself letting out boats for fishing purposes. Hill thereupon brought an action in his own name against Tupper, his alleged cause of action being a disturbance of his easement to put boats on the canal.

It was held that the right conferred upon Hill by the contract with the company was not an easement but a mere licence personal to himself, since it was acquired in order to exploit an independent business enterprise, not to accommodate the riparian land as such.[1] The right was not beneficial to the land as land ; rather, the land was required for the exploitation of the right.

The principle applies equally to profits appurtenant, and may be illustrated by the remark of Coke that the right of cutting turfs for fuel cannot be claimed as appurtenant to land, but only to a house, because the use of fuel has no connection with land as such. In the leading case of *Bailey* v. *Stephens*,[2]

A., who was seised in fee of a piece of land called Bloody Field, claimed the right to enter an adjoining close for the purpose of cutting down, carrying away and converting to his own use the trees and wood growing thereon. It was held that, as the wood was not employed for the beneficial enjoyment of Bloody Field, it was not connected therewith and so was not a valid profit.

(3) Dominant and servient owners must be different persons. If one person owns two adjoining properties which, physically speaking, are separate properties, any rights that he may have been in the habit of exercising over one or other of them, as, for example, by passing over one to reach the highway, are not easements (though they are often called " quasi-easements "), because they derive from his ownership not of the quasi-dominant land, but of the quasi-servient land itself.[3] FRY, L.J., in one case said :—

Owner cannot have easements over his own land.

" Of course, strictly speaking, the owner of two tenements can have no easement over one of them in respect of the other. When the owner of Whiteacre and Blackacre passes over the former to Blackacre, he is not exercising a right of way in respect of Blackacre ; he is merely making use of his own land to get from one part to another ".[4]

---

[1] *Re Ellenborough Park, supra*, at pp. 175, 45 respectively. Contrast the Pennsylvanian case of *Miller* v. *Lutheran Conference and Camp Association*, [1938] 331 Pa. 241 ; Aigler, Smith and Tefft, *Cases on Property* (1960), vol. ii. p. 212, where a somewhat similar right was treated as an easement *in gross* capable of assignment.

[2] (1862), 12 C. B. (N.S.) 91.

[3] *Bolton* v. *Bolton* (1879), 11 Ch. D. 968.

[4] *Roe* v. *Siddons* (1888), 22 Q. B. D. 224, at p. 236 ; and see *Metropolitan Rail Co.* v. *Fowler*, [1892] 1 Q. B. 165 ; *Derry* v. *Sanders*, [1919] 1 K. B. 223.

Thus, if X. is the owner of two separate tenements and he lets one of them to a tenant, the latter cannot acquire by prescription an easement over the other, for his occupation is in the eyes of the law the occupation of his landlord, a person who cannot acquire an easement against himself.[1] As will be seen later, however, the right to light is exceptional in this respect.[2]

If the principle were otherwise and if rights exercised by a man over one of two properties both owned by him were to be treated as easements, they would necessarily remain vested in him after a sale of the quasi-servient tenement. They would also pass without express mention to a purchaser of the quasi-dominant tenement. But these consequences do not ensue. To quote an ancient instance :—

> " J. S. had a close, and a wood adjoining to it, and time out of mind a way had been used over the close to the wood to carry and re-carry. He granted the close to one, and the wood to another. The question was, if the grantee of the wood shall have the way ? And it was adjudged he should not, for the grantor by the grant of the close had excluded himself of the way, because it was not saved to him ; and he himself could not use it, no more can his grantee."[3]

The moral to be drawn from this rule is that, when a large estate is split up and sold to different purchasers, any quasi-easements which were enjoyed by the former owner should be expressly reserved to the purchaser of the quasi-dominant tenement.[4]

Right to easements depends upon grant, actual or presumed.

(4) **A right over land cannot amount to an easement unless it is capable of forming the subject-matter of a grant.** As we shall see, apart from statute, every easement must originate in a grant, either express, implied or presumed. It follows from this that no right can have the status of an easement unless it is the possible subject-matter of a grant.[5] This in turn requires that its nature and extent should be capable of exact description. Its sphere of operation must be precise and certain. If it is so vague or so indeterminate as to defy precise definition, it cannot rank as an easement.[6] This requirement, which is common to all forms of grant, is especially important in the present context, for a

---

[1] *Warburton* v. *Parke* (1857), 2 H. & N. 64; *Gayford* v. *Moffatt* (1868), L. R. 4 Ch. App. 133. A tenant may, however, grant an easement, for a period not exceeding that of his lease, in favour of another tenant of the same landlord ; *infra*, p. 541.

[2] *Infra*, pp. 553 ; 558.

[3] *Dell* v. *Babthorpe* (1593), Cro. Eliz. 300.

[4] *Wheeldon* v. *Burrows* (1879), 12 Ch. D. 31, 49 ; *infra*, pp. 534–7.

[5] *Potter* v. *North* (1669), 1 Wms. Saund. 347, *arguendo* ; *Goodman* v. *Mayor of Saltash* (1882), 7 App. Cas. 633, at p. 654 ; *Dalton* v. *Angus* (1881), 6 App. Cas. 740, at p. 795 ; *Chastey* v. *Ackland* (1895), 11 T. L. R. 460 ; *Harris* v. *De Pinna* (1886), 33 Ch. D. 238, at p. 262 ; *Bryant* v. *Lefever* (1879), 4 C. P. D. 172, at p. 178, BRAMWELL, L.J.

[6] For a criticism of the statement in the text, see (1942), 30 *California Law Review*, pp. 133 *et seq.* (A. F. Conard).

right over the land of another is allowed to ripen into an easement if it has been enjoyed for a long time without any interruption by the servient owner, but this necessarily implies that there should be something definite capable of interruption.[1]

A right to the flow of light to a particular window satisfies the test of certainty, for not only does the light pass over the servient tenement along a defined channel, but it can be interrupted by an obstruction placed across its line of approach.[2] Again, it has been held that a *jus spatiandi*, *i.e.* a right to wander at large over the servient tenement, is sufficiently determinate to constitute an easement if it is limited by express grant to a particular house or group of houses and is exercisable over an adjoining garden.[3] So also the right to a flow of air can subsist as an easement if it is claimed in respect of some definite channel, such as a ventilator in a building,[4] but not if what is claimed is that the current of air flowing indiscriminately over the entire servient tenement shall not be interrupted.[5]

In *Harris* v. *De Pinna*,[6] where such a claim to the general flow of air was made, BOWEN, L.J., said :—

> " It would be just like amenity of prospect, a subject-matter which is incapable of definition. So the passage of undefined air gives rise to no rights and can give rise to no rights for the best of all reasons, the reason of common sense, because you cannot acquire any rights against others by a user which they cannot interrupt."

Other practical consequences result from the general principle that an easement must originate in a grant. For instance, a claimant to an easement must be a person capable of receiving a grant, that is, he must be a definite person or a definite body such as a corporation. Thus a claim put forward by a vague fluctuating body of persons, such as the inhabitants of a village, will not be sustainable as an easement.[7] *Must be a capable grantee.*

Again, the same principle demands that the servient owner should have been lawfully entitled to grant the right claimed to be an easement. Thus a claim[8] against a company incorporated by statute will fail upon proof that the grant was *ultra vires*.[9] *Must be a capable grantor.*

---

[1] *Webb* v. *Bird* (1862), 13 C. B. (N.S.) 841, 843.
[2] *Harris* v. *De Pinna* (1886), 33 Ch. D. 238, at p. 259.
[3] *Re Ellenborough Park*, [1956] Ch. 131 ; [1955] 2 All E. R. 38 ; M. & B. p. 490.
[4] *Cable* v. *Bryant*, [1908] 1 Ch. 259 ; M. & B. p. 490.
[5] *Webb* v. *Bird, supra* ; *Bryant* v. *Lefever* (1879), 4 C.P.D. 172 ; M. & B. p. 488.
[6] (1886), 33 Ch. D. 238, at p. 262. This may, however, be enforceable under the doctrine of non-derogation from grant. See *Aldin* v. *Latimer Clark, Muirhead & Co.*, [1894] 2 Ch. 437 ; *supra*, p. 410.
[7] But a local customary right may be established. *Infra*, pp. 526 ; 571 *et seq.*
[8] *Paine & Co., Ltd* v. *St. Neots Gas and Coke Co.*. [1939] 3 All E. R. 812.
[9] *Mulliner* v. *Midland Rail Co.* (1879), L. R. 11 Ch. D. 611.

Such, then, are the essential characteristics of easements, and it is important that they should be borne in mind, for otherwise certain judicial statements that new kinds of rights *in rem* cannot be created at will may be misunderstood.   Thus Lord BROUGHAM said[1] :—

> " There are certain known incidents to property and its enjoyment, among others, certain burdens wherewith it may be affected, or rights which may be created and enjoyed over it by parties other than the owner. . . . But it must not therefore be supposed that incidents of a novel kind can be devised and attached to property at the fancy or caprice of any owner ;   . . . great detriment would arise and much confusion of rights, if parties were allowed to invent new modes of holding and enjoying real property, and to impress upon their land and tenements a peculiar character, which should follow them into all hands, however remote."

List of easements not closed. This means not that an easement of a kind never heard of before cannot be created, but that a new species of incorporeal hereditament or a new species of burden cannot be brought into being and given the status and legal effect of an easement.   In other words, if a right exhibits the four characteristics described above, it is an easement that will run with the dominant and against the servient tenement, even though its object may be to fulfil a purpose for which it has not hitherto been used; but if it lacks one or more of those characteristics, it may, indeed, be enforceable between the parties who create it, but it cannot, like an easement, be enforceable by or against third parties.[2]   One of the main purposes of law is to keep pace with the requirements of society and to adapt itself to new modes of life and new business methods, a fact that was present to the mind of Lord ST. LEONARDS when he said :—

> " The category of servitudes and easements must alter and expand with the changes that take place in the circumstances of mankind."[3]

Thus in a case where an easement was claimed to place stores and casks upon land reclaimed from the sea, the Privy Council said:—

> " The law must adapt itself to the conditions of modern society and trade, and there is nothing in the purposes for which the easement is claimed inconsistent in principle with a right of easement as such."[4]

Examples of easements. **Examples of Easements.** The following list of easements, which begins with the most important kinds and which,

---

[1] *Keppell* v. *Bailey* (1834), 2 My. & K. 517, at p. 535.   See also *Hill* v. *Tupper*, (1863), 2 H. &. C. 121, at pp. 127–8, *per* POLLOCK, C.B.
[2] *Re Ellenborough Park*, [1956] Ch. 131, at pp. 140–1 ; [1955] 2 All E. R. 38, at pp. 42–3.
[3] *Dyce* v. *Hay* (1852), 1 Macq. 305.
[4] *A.-G. of Southern Nigeria* v. *John Holt & Co.*, [1915] A. C. 599, at 617 ; *Simpson* v. *Godmanchester Corpn.*, [1896], Ch. 214, 219 ; *Dowty Boulton Paul, Ltd.* v. *Wolverhampton Corpn. (No. 2)*, [1973] 2 W. L. R. 618, at p. 624 ; [1973] 2 All E. R. 491 (" A tendency in the past to freeze the categories of easements has been overtaken by the defrosting operation in *Re Ellenborough Park* ", *per* RUSSELL, L.J.).

of course, is not exhaustive, will afford some idea of how great
their variety is :—

(a) Rights of *way*, whether for general or special purposes, and
whether exercisable in all modes or limited to a carriage way,   **Way.**
bridle way, foot way or a way for cattle.

(b) A right that the *light* flowing over adjoining land to a window
shall not be unreasonably obstructed.[1]   **Light.**

(c) Rights in connection with *water*, such as a right to enter upon
adjoining land to divert the course of a stream for irrigation   **Water.**
purposes, or a right to pollute a river or to discharge water on
to the land of another.[2]

(d) A right to the *support* of buildings by adjoining land or buildings.
Though a landowner has a natural right to have his *land*   **Support.**
supported by adjoining land, yet a right to have *buildings*
supported can be claimed only if it has actually been
acquired as an easement.[3]

(e) Right to have a *fence* maintained by an adjoining owner.   **Fencing.**

This has been recognised by the Court of Appeal as " a right
in the nature of an easement". As Lord DENNING said in *Crow* v.
Wood [4] :—

" It is not an easement strictly so called because it involves the
servient owner in the expenditure of money. It was described by Gale
as a ' spurious kind of easement '.[5] But it has been treated in practice
by the courts as being an easement . . . [6]

It seems to me that it is now sufficiently established—or at any
rate, if not established hitherto, we should now declare—that a right
to have your neighbour keep up the fences is a right in the nature of an
easement which is capable of being granted by law so as to run with the
land and to be binding on successors. It is a right which lies in grant
and is of such a nature that it can pass under section 62 of the Law of
Property Act 1925." [7]

Such are the only easements commonly found in practice,   Miscel-
but we may add examples of some variations and extensions of   laneous
these interests :[8]—   easements.

(i) Right to hang clothes on a line passing over neighbouring soil.[9]
(ii) Right to run telephone lines over neighbouring land.[10]

---

[1] See generally *Colls* v. *Home and Colonial Stores, Ltd.* [1904] A. C. 179 ;
M. & B. p. 568 ; *infra*, pp. 551–3.
[2] A landowner may have certain natural rights in respect of water, *supra*,
p. 156, *infra*, p. 526.
[3] The leading case is *Dalton* v. *Angus & Co.* (1881), 6 App. Cas. 740. See
also London Buildings Acts (Amendment) Act 1939, s. 50.
[4] [1971] 1 Q. B. 77, at p. 84. See (1971), 87 *L.Q.R.* 13 (P. V. Baker).
[5] *Easements* (11th Edn.), p. 432 ; see too *Lawrence* v. *Jenkins* (1873),
L. R. 8 Q. B. 274, at p. 279, *per* ARCHIBALD, J. *Cf. Hilton* v. *Ankesson* (1872),
27 L. T. 519.
[6] See *Jones* v. *Price*, [1965] 2 Q. B. 618, at p. 633, *per* WILMER, L.J., and
at p. 639, *per* DIPLOCK, L.J. ; *Egerton* v. *Harding*, [1975] Q. B. 62 ; [1974] 3
All E. R. 689.
[7] *Infra*, p. 530. It may also be acquired (1) as an easement by prescription,
Lawrence v. *Jenkins* (1873), L.R. 8 Q. B. 274 ; *Jones* v. *Price*, [1965] 2 Q. B.
618 ; [1965] 2 All E. R. 625 ; (2) by custom, *Egerton* v. *Harding*, [1975]
Q. B. 62 ; [1974] 3 All E. R. 689.
[8] For further examples see Gale on *Easements* (14th Edn.), pp. 35–37.
[9] *Drewell* v. *Towler* (1832), 3 B. & Ad. 735.
[10] *Lancashire Telephone Co.* v. *Manchester Overseers* (1884), 14 Q. B. D. 267.

   (iii) Right to use a close for the purpose of mixing muck and preparing manure thereon for the use of an adjoining farm.[1]
   (iv) Right to fix a signboard to the walls of another's house.[2]
   (v) Right of a landowner to use a particular seat in a parish church.[3]
   (vi) Right to nail trees to a wall.[4]
   (vii) Right to lay stones upon adjoining land to prevent sand from being washed away by the sea.[5]
  (viii) Right to use a lavatory situated on the servient tenement.[6]
   (ix) Right to use a letter-box.[7]
   (x) Right to use an airfield.[8]

Summary. New easements may arise, but no right which fails to exhibit the four characteristics described above can exist as an easement. Whether or not a new right, complying with the accepted requirements of an easement, will be judicially recognised or not is very difficult to forecast.

There are, however, two situations in which such recognition is unlikely to be granted. Firstly, where the owner of the servient tenement would be under a duty to spend money.[9] There is only one right in this category, that of fencing, and its exceptional nature is recognised by the Court of Appeal.[10] Secondly, where the easement is negative, in the sense that it gives the owner of the dominant tenement a right to stop his neighbour doing something on his (the neighbour's) own land. This has long been recognised in the cases of the easement of light and support. But in *Phipps* v. *Pears*,[11] where the premises had been exposed to damp and frost owing to the demolition of an adjacent house, the Court of Appeal held that there was no easement of protection against the weather. Lord DENNING said[12]:

> " A right to protection from the weather . . . is entirely negative. Seeing that it is a negative easement, it must be looked at with caution. Because the law has been very chary of creating any new negative easements. . . . If such an easement were to be permitted, it would unduly restrict your neighbour in his own enjoyment of his own land."

---

  [1] *Pye* v. *Mumford* (1848), 11 Q. B. 666.
  [2] *Moody* v. *Steggles* (1879), L. R. 12 Ch. D. 261.
  [3] *Mainwaring* v. *Giles* (1822), 5 B. & Ald. 356 ; *Brumfitt* v. *Roberts* (1870), L. R. 5 C. P. 224.
  [4] *Hawkins* v. *Wallis* (1763), 2 Wils. 173.
  [5] *Philpot* v. *Bath* (1905), 21 T. L. R. 634.
  [6] *Miller* v. *Emcer Products, Ltd.*, [1956] Ch. 304 ; [1956] 1 All E. R. 23 7 ; M. & B. p. 500.
  [7] *Goldberg* v. *Edwards*, [1950] Ch. 247 ; M. & B. p. 520.
  [8] *Dowty Boulton Paul, Ltd.* v. *Wolverhampton Corpn.* (No. 2), [1973] 2 W. L. R. 618 ; [1973] 2 All E. R. 491.
  [9] *Regis Property Co. Ltd.* v. *Redman* [1956] 2 Q. B. 612 ; [1956] 2 All E. R. 335 (covenant to supply hot water and central heating, involving the performance of services, not an easement).
  [10] *Jones* v. *Price*, [1965] 2 Q. B. 618 ; *Crow* v. *Wood*, [1971] 1 Q. B. 77 ; [1970] 3 All E. R. 425 ; M. & B. p. 502.
  [11] [1965] 1 Q. B. 76 ; [1964] 2 All E. R. 35 ; M. & B. p. 500 ; (1964), 80 L.Q.R. 318 (R.E.M.) ; (1964), 27 M.L.R. 614 (H. W. Wilkinson).
  [12] At p. 83.

It is, however, possible for such rights to be framed as covenants which may be enforceable under the doctrine of *Tulk* v. *Moxhay*.[1]

Finally, it must be remembered that no right will be recognized as an easement which is in effect a claim to joint possession of the servient tenement. Thus in *Copeland* v. *Greenhalf*,[2] it was held that a wheelwright had no easement to store and repair an unlimited number of vehicles on a strip of his neighbour's land. The question is really one of degree. As ROMER, L.J. said in *Miller* v. *Emcer Products, Ltd.*,[3] where a right to use a lavatory situated on the servient tenement was held to be an easement :

> " It is true that during the times when the dominant owner exercised the right the owner of the servient tenement would be excluded, but this in greater or less degree is a common feature of many easements (for example, rights of way) and does not amount to such an ouster of the servient owner's rights as was held by UPJOHN, J. to be incompatible with a legal easement in *Copeland* v. *Greenhalf*."

There may, however, be a successful claim by reason of adverse possession under the Limitation Act 1939.[4]

(B) EASEMENTS DISTINGUISHED FROM OTHER RIGHTS

Having seen something of the nature of easements, we will conclude this part of the subject by adverting to other rights of a somewhat similar nature from which they must be distinguished.[5]

1. **Licences.** A licence is created in favour of B. if, without being given any legal estate or interest, he is permitted by A. to enter A.'s land for an agreed purpose. It is an authority that justifies what would otherwise be a trespass. Licences.

We shall discuss later the categories of licence and the different rules which are applicable to each of them.[6] Here it is sufficient to mention that an easement is narrower than a licence.

Thus an easement must be created by a deed of grant, whether actual, implied or presumed ; whereas a licence may be created informally ; further an easement is not a personal right, but is of necessity annexed to a dominant tenement ; and, once established, there can never be any question of its unilateral revocation by the servient owner.

---

[1] *Infra*, p. 597.
[2] [1952] Ch. 488 ; [1952] 1 All E. R. 809 ; M. & B. p. 496. Dist. *Wright* v. *Macadam*, [1949] 2 K. B. 744 ; [1949] 2 All E. R. 565 ; M. & B. p. 516 ; (right to store domestic coal in shed held to be an easement). This case was not cited in *Copeland* v. *Greenhalf*. *Ward* v. *Kirkland*, [1967] Ch. 194 ; [1966] 1 All E. R. 609. See too *Grigsby* v. *Melville*, [1972] 1 W. L. R. 1355 ; [1973] 1 All E. R. 385 ; affd. [1974] 1 W. L. R. 80 ; [1973] 3 All E. R. 455 ; M. & B. p. 498 (claim to exclusive right of storage in cellar under drawing-room floor).
[3] [1956] Ch. 304, at p. 316 ; [1956] 1 All E. R. 237 ; M. & B. p. 500 ; (1956) 72 L.Q.R. 172 (R.E.M.).
[4] *Infra*, pp. 883 *et seq.* See (1968) Conv. (N.S.) 270 (M. J. Goodman).
[5] For the difference between an easement and a profit, see *infra*, pp. 558–60.
[6] *Infra*, pp. 577 *et seq.* For the difference between a licence and a lease see *supra*, pp. 384–6.

2. **Local customary rights.** Indefinite and fluctuating classes of persons, such as the inhabitants of a village, may be entitled to exercise over another's land rights which, if the matter rested between the servient owner and a definite dominant owner, would properly be termed easements. Illustrations from the cases are

(i) where the inhabitants of a village pass across another's land on their way to church,[1] or

(ii) where the fishing inhabitants dry their nets on certain property.[2]

Such rights are not easements, for an easement lies in grant, and a vague and fluctuating body of persons such as fishing inhabitants is incapable of taking under a grant. If, therefore, they are to be established, some other title than grant must be shown, and this, as we shall see later, is what the law calls *custom*.[3]

3. **Natural rights of property.** This is an expression often used to describe a right that is one of the ordinary and inseparable incidents of ownership, though its exercise requires an adjacent owner to forbear from doing something on his own land that otherwise he would be free to do. The epithet " natural " serves to distinguish such rights from easements, which do not automatically accompany ownership but must be acquired by grant, either actual, implied or presumed.[4] Thus *ex jure naturae*,

an owner has a right to so much support from his neighbour's land as will support his own land, unincumbered by buildings, at its natural level;[5] and a riparian owner is entitled to demand that other riparian owners shall not divert the natural course of the stream.[6] Such natural rights differ from easements in at least two respects—their existence does not depend upon some form of grant, and they cannot be extinguished by unity of seisin.[7]

(C) LEGAL AND EQUITABLE EASEMENTS

An easement is capable of subsisting as a legal interest. It will be legal if (a) it complies with the Law of Property Act 1925 and is held for " an interest equivalent to an estate in fee simple absolute in possession or a term of years absolute "[8] and (b) is created either by statute, deed or prescription.[9] If it does not satisfy both re-

---

[1] *Brocklebank* v. *Thompson*, [1903] 2 Ch. 344.
[2] *Mercer* v. *Denne*, [1905] 2 Ch. 538.
[3] *Infra*, pp. 571–7.
[4] *Bonomi* v. *Backhouse* (1859), E. B. & E. 654.
[5] *Bonomi* v. *Backhouse*, *supra*.   [6] *Supra*, pp. 130 *et seq.*
[7] Jenks, *Modern Land Law*, p. 166. For extinguishment of easements, see *infra*, p. 555.
[8] S. 1 (2) (a).   [9] *Infra*, pp. 528 *et seq.*

quirements, then it may be an equitable easement : *e.g.* if it is for the life of the grantee (even if it is created by deed), or if it is created for value informally,[1] as for instance by a contract to grant an easement.

This distinction is important in relation to the enforceability of the easement against third parties. In accordance with general principle, a legal easement is enforceable against all the world, an equitable easement against all the world except the bona fide purchaser for value of the legal estate without notice. An equitable easement is registrable as a Class D (iii) Land Charge under the Land Charges Act 1972,[2] and if it is not so registered, is void against a purchaser of the legal estate for money or money's worth. Importance of distinction.

It is therefore important to define an equitable easement. The Law of Property Act 1925 refers to : Scope of equitable easement.

> Any easement, liberty, or privilege over or affecting land and being merely an equitable interest (in this Act referred to as an " equitable easement ").[3]

In spite of some earlier views to the contrary,[4] it is now settled that this definition is to be construed narrowly.[5] It may be limited to such proprietary interests in land as would before 1926 have been recognized as capable of being conveyed or created at law, but which since 1925 only take effect as equitable interests, as for instance, an easement granted for the life of the grantee.[6] It thus excludes such informal equitable rights as an equitable right of re-entry,[7] or any rights arising in equity by reason of an estoppel licence or the doctrine of mutual benefit and burden.[8] The effect of this in unregistered conveyancing is that there are certain informal third party rights which do not require registration ; they cannot therefore be void for want of registration as land charges, and their enforceability against third parties depends solely on the doctrine of notice.[9]

---

[1] *Infra*, p. 528.

[2] Ss. 2 (5), 4 (6).

[3] S. 2 (3) (iii) ; the definition in L.C.A. 1972, s. 2 (5) substitutes the word " right " for " liberty ".

[4] See (1935), 15 Bell Yard 18 (G. Cross).

[5] *Shiloh Spinners, Ltd.* v. *Harding*, [1973] A. C. 691 ; [1973] 1 All E. R. 90, *supra*, p. 103.

[6] *E. R. Ives Investment Ltd.* v. *High,* [1967] 2 Q.B. 379 at p. 395 *per* Lord DENNING ; [1967] 1 All E. R. 504 ; M. & B. p. 478 ; (1937) 53 L.Q.R. 259 (C. V. Davidge) ; (1948), 12 *Conv.* (N.S.) 202 (J. F. Garner).

[7] *Shiloh Spinners, Ltd.* v. *Harding, supra.*

[8] *E. R. Ives Investment Ltd.* v. *High, supra* followed in *Poster* v. *Slough Estates Ltd.,* [1969] 1 Ch. 495 ; [1968] 3 All E. R. 257 ; M. & B. p. 504 (right of entry to remove fixtures at end of lease). See also *Lewisham Borough Council* v. *Maloney* [1948] 1 K. B. 50 ; [1947] 2 All E. R. 36 (requisitioning authority's right to possession) ; (1969) 33 *Conv.* (N.S.) 135 (P. Jackson).

[9] See *supra*, p. 103.

(D) THE METHODS BY WHICH EASEMENTS MAY BE CREATED

The basic principle is that every easement must have had its origin in grant.[1]

All the methods of acquisition except one are traceable to a grant which has been or which might have been made, and the one exception, namely statute, is not of frequent occurrence. It may facilitate exposition to set the subject out in the form of a genealogical table.

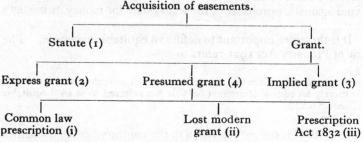

Acquisition of easements.

Statute (1)   Grant.

Express grant (2)   Presumed grant (4)   Implied grant (3)

Common law   Lost modern   Prescription
prescription (i)   grant (ii)   Act 1832 (iii)

The figures in parentheses denote the order of treatment in the following pages.

(1) **Acquisition by Statute.** An example of statutory creation is an Inclosure Act. This is a statute that discharges land from rights of common to which it has hitherto been subject and distributes it in plots among a number of absolute owners.[2] As part of the scheme of distribution easements of way over adjoining plots are frequently reserved to the respective owners.[3] Modern examples of easements created by statute are to be found in local Acts of Parliament.

Deed necessary at common law.
(2) **Acquisition by express grant.** An easement is an incorporeal hereditament and therefore, in accordance with the historic rule of the common law, it must be granted by deed, for

> " the deed of incorporeate inheritances doth equal the livery of corporeate."[4]

Effect of mere parol or written grant in equity.
At common law, a grant of an easement made orally or by an unsealed writing creates only a licence.[5] But this may create an equitable easement where equity acts on the principle that what ought to be done must be regarded as actually done—a view which has given us the doctrine of *Walsh* v. *Lonsdale*.[6] If the grant is

---

[1] *Angus* v. *Dalton* (1877), 3 Q. B. D. 102, *per* COCKBURN, C.J.
[2] *Infra*, p. 569.
[3] For example, *Adeane* v. *Mortlock* (1839), 5 Bing. N. C. 236.
[4] Co. Litt. 9a, b ; L.P.A., 1925, s. 52 (1).
[5] *Wood* v. *Leadbitter* (1845), 13 M. & W. 838 ; M. & B. p. 438 ; *Fentiman* v. *Smith* (1803), 4 East 107, *infra*, pp. 578–9.
[6] *Supra*, pp. 394 *et seq.*

made by an unsealed writing and is for value, equity will treat this as a contract to grant a legal interest in land, and if the agreement is specifically enforceable, it will then treat the situation as if the grant by deed had already been made.[1] If, however, the grant is only made orally, then the doctrine of part performance must be invoked[2] and equity may rectify the want of a deed when the altered position of one of the parties gives him an equitable right against the other party.[3]

The leading case on the subject is *McManus v. Cooke*,[4] the facts of which may be thus summarized :—

> Between adjoining properties belonging the one to X. and the other to Y. there was a high party wall of unnecessary width. It was orally agreed between X. and Y. that in order to give more space to each owner the wall should be pulled down by X. and replaced by one which was lower and thinner, the work to be at their joint expense. It was also agreed orally that each of the parties should erect a lean-to skylight, and that both of these should rest on the new wall and incline upwards and outwards to the respective houses. X. duly carried out his part of the work, but Y., instead of building a lean-to skylight on his side, built one so shaped that part of it showed above the wall and in consequence obstructed the access of light to X.'s skylight. X. sued for an injunction to restrain Y. from maintaining an erection which infringed the agreement.

KAY, J., decided in favour of the plaintiff X. on the ground that the effect of the oral agreement was to give each party an easement of light over the other's land, and that despite the want of a deed this easement was enforceable by the party who had gone to expense in carrying out his side of the agreement, thereby giving to Y. all the advantages to which he was entitled under the contract.

If the dominant tenement has not been clearly described by the parties, the court will identify it by construing the instrument that created the easement, and for this purpose extrinsic evidence of the circumstances in which the instrument was executed is admissible.[5]

Dominant tenement must be identified.

If the owner of two adjoining properties desired, upon the sale of one of them, to retain an easement over that one, he could not do so at common law either by way of *exception* from the grant or by way of *reservation*.[6] The only things that could be excepted were specific parts of the land, such as timber and minerals ; and the word " reservation " was only appropriate where services, such as the payment of rent, were to be rendered for the tenure of land.[7]

Easement could not formerly be excepted or reserved.

---

[1] *May v. Belleville*, [1905] 2 Ch. 605.
[2] *McManus v. Cooke* (1887), 35 Ch. D. 681 ; M. & B. p. 75. *Supra*, pp. 121 *et seq.*
[3] *Dunn v. Spurrier* (1803), 7 Ves. 231, at p. 235 ;. *Duke of Devonshire v Eglin* (1851), 14 Bear. 530.   [4] (1887), 35 Ch. D. 681 ; M. & B. p. 75.
[5] *Johnstone v. Holdway*, [1963] 1 Q. B. 601 ; [1963] 1 All E. R. 432 ; M. & B. p. 559; *The Shannon, Ltd. v. Venner, Ltd.*, [1965] Ch. 682 ; [1965] 1 All E. R. 590.
[6] *Durham and Sunderland Rail Co. v. Walker*, [1842] 2 Q. B. 940.
[7] Leake, *Uses and Profits of Land*, p. 265.

It was formerly necessary, therefore, either that the conveyance of the land should be executed by the *grantee* (whereupon the easement would arise by way of re-grant from him),[1] or that the conveyance should be made to him *to the use* that the vendor should enjoy the easement and subject thereto *to the use* of the purchaser in fee simple.[2]

With the repeal of the Statute of Uses the latter method is now impossible, and the former is unnecessary, for the Law of Property Act 1925 provides[3] that

" a reservation of a legal estate shall operate at law without any execution of the conveyance by the grantee of the legal estate out of which the reservation is made, or any regrant by him. "

Such a reservation, however, still operates by way of re-grant. Thus, where an easement is reserved by a vendor of land, the terms of the reservation in cases of doubt are to be construed against the purchaser and not against the vendor.[4]

Statutory effect of a conveyance of a dominant tenement. Finally, it is of the greatest practical importance to observe that, owing to section 62 of the Law of Property Act 1925, a grant of land may have a far-reaching, and sometimes an unexpected, effect upon the creation of easements. This section provides that unless a contrary intention is expressed in the conveyance :

" A conveyance of land shall be deemed to include and shall by virtue of this Act operate to convey, with the land, all buildings, erections, fixtures, commons, hedges, ditches, fences, ways, waters, watercourses, liberties, privileges, easements, rights, and advantages whatsoever, appertaining or reputed to appertain to the land or any part thereof, or, at the time of conveyance, demised, occupied, or enjoyed with, or reputed or known as part or parcel of or appurtenant to the land or any part thereof." [5]

The object of this section is to ensure that a purchaser, without inserting numerous descriptive terms, usually called *general words*, in the conveyance, shall automatically acquire the benefit not only of easements and other rights appurtenant to the land in the strict sense, but also of quasi-easements and other privileges which have hitherto been enjoyed in respect of the land. It is obvious that easements already appurtenant to the land conveyed continue in favour of the purchaser, but the statutory words are so sweeping and comprehensive that the conveyance, unless expressly limited in its operation, may have an effect far wider

---

[1] *Wickham* v. *Hawker* (1840), 7 M. & W. 63.
[2] Conveyancing Act 1881, s. 62 (1).   [3] S. 65 (1).
[4] *Johnstone* v. *Holdway*, [1963] 1 Q. B. 601 ; [1963] 1 All E. R. 432 ; *St. Edmundsbury and Ipswich Diocesan Board of Finance* v. *Clarke (No. 2)*, [1975] 1 W. L. R. 468 ; [1975] 1 All E. R. 772 ; M. & B. p. 506.
[5] S. 62 (1) ; re-enacting Conveyancing Act 1881, s. 6 (1).

than the vendor intends. The effect indeed may be catastrophic in the sense that privileges which have hitherto been enjoyed by the permission of the vendor in respect of the land conveyed, a permission which could at any moment have been withdrawn, may acquire the status of permanent easements as a result of the conveyance.

> Suppose, for example, that A., the owner of two adjoining closes, Blackacre and Whiteacre, leases Blackacre to X., and as a friendly act allows X. to use a path over Whiteacre as a short cut to the main road and also to store his coal in a shed on Whiteacre. Later A. sells and conveys the fee simple of Blackacre to X.

In this case at the time of the conveyance there is a " privilege . . . enjoyed with the land " conveyed. The statute therefore comes into operation, and the effect of the conveyance, unless it expresses a contrary intention,[1] is that a right of way over Whiteacre and a right to use the shed become appurtenant to Blackacre.[2]

> Again, if B., the owner of a mansion and park, allows Y., the tenant of the lodge at one of the gates, to use the main drive as a means of access to the neighbouring village, and later sells and conveys the fee simple of the lodge to him, a similar result follows. Y. acquires an easement of way over the drive.[3]

The permissive nature of the privilege enjoyed prior to the conveyance is quite irrelevant in these cases. The question is not whether the purchaser had an enforceable right to enjoy the privilege, but whether it was in fact enjoyed by him *qua* occupant of the land prior to the conveyance.[4]

No right will be conveyed by virtue of the Act, however, unless it is one capable of being granted at law, or in other words unless it is a right known to the law.[5]

The right must be one known to the law.

Neither will the Act operate unless, as in the examples given

---

[1] This may be expressed by a condition of sale. See Law Society Contract and Conditions of Sale 1973 Condition 4 (2) (c) ; National Conditions of Sale (18th Edn.) Condition 14 (1).

[2] *International Tea Stores Co.* v. *Hobbs*, [1903] 2 Ch. 165 ; *Wright* v. *Macadam*, [1949] 2 K. B. 744 ; [1949] 2 All E. R. 565 ; M. & B. p. 516.

[3] *International Tea Stores Co.* v. *Hobbs*, *supra*, at p. 172 ; *Goldberg* v. *Edwards*, [1950] Ch. 247 ; M. & B. p. 520.

[4] *Wright* v. *Macadam*, [1949] 2 K. B. 744, at pp. 750–1; [1949] 2 All E. R. 565, at pp. 570–1. *Phipps* v. *Pears*, [1965] 1 Q. B. 76; [1964] 2 All E. R. 35; M. & B. p. 522. For a critical attitude to this effect of s. 62 (1), see *Wright* v. *Macadam*, *supra*, at p. 755, *per* TUCKER, L.J. ; *Green* v. *Ashco Horticulturist, Ltd.* ; [1966] 1 W. L. R. 889 at p. 896, *per* CROSS, J.

[5] *International Tea Stores Co.* v. *Hobbs*, [1903] 2 Ch. 165, at p. 172 ; *Goldberg* v. *Edwards*, [1950] Ch. 247. *Ward* v. *Kirkland*, [1967] Ch. 194 ; [1966] 1 All E. R. 609 ; *Green* v. *Ashco Horticulturist, Ltd.* [1966] 1 W. L. R. 889 ; [1966] 2 All E. R. 232 ; *Phipps* v. *Pears*, *supra* ; *Crow* v. *Wood*, [1971] 1 Q. B. 77 ; [1970] 3 All E. R. 425 ; M. & B. p. 502.

Diversity
of occupa-
tion before
conveyance
essential.

above, there has been some diversity of ownership or occupation of
the two closes prior to the conveyance.[1] If, for instance, the vendor, the common owner and occupier of Blackacre and Whiteacre,
has been in the habit of passing over Blackacre in order to reach
the highway, his conveyance of Whiteacre does not entitle the
purchaser to invoke the statute and to establish a right of way over
Blackacre. What the vendor was accustomed to do was attributable to his general rights as the occupying owner of both closes, not
to a privilege deriving from his occupation of Whiteacre, as distinct
from his occupation of Blackacre.[2] In order to substantiate
his claim, the purchaser would have to bring himself within the
doctrine of an implied grant under the rule in *Wheeldon* v.
Burrows.[3]

Meaning of
"convey-
ance."

Neither does the statute operate unless there has been a
" conveyance " of land, a word which statutorily includes

> " a mortgage, charge, lease, assent, vesting declaration, vesting
> instrument, disclaimer, release and every other assurance of property
> or of an interest therein by any instrument, except a will." [4]

This definition does not comprise an oral lease.[5] Nor does it
comprise a contract for a lease or for the sale of land, since an
assurance is " something which operates as a transfer of property" [6]
and a mere contract has no such operation, notwithstanding
that under the doctrine of *Walsh* v. *Lonsdale* [7] it is for many
purposes as effective as a lease.[8]

Enough has now been said to show that a vendor, who retains
property adjoining that sold, should be extremely vigilant to
ensure that any advantages or privileges hitherto enjoyed in
respect of the land sold are expressly excepted from the
conveyance, unless he wishes them to continue.

If an intention is shown in the preliminary contract of sale
that a certain privilege shall not pass to the purchaser, the vendor
is entitled to insert a clause in the deed of conveyance restrictive
of the operation of the statute.[9] Moreover, in such a case he is
entitled to have the conveyance rectified if, owing to the common
mistake of the parties, it does not include a restrictive clause of
this nature.[10]

Depends
upon pre-
sumed in-
tention of
parties to
grant.

(3) Acquisition by implied grant.[11] An owner, as we

have seen, cannot have an easement over his own land.[12] Where,

---

[1] *Long* v. *Gowlett*, [1923] 2 Ch. 177 ; M. & B. p. 523 ; (1966) 30 Conv.
(N.S.) 346–8 (P. Jackson) ; *Ward* v. *Kirkland, supra*, at pp. 227–31. See,
however, *Wright* v. *Macadam, supra*, at p. 748, *per* Jenkins, L.J.)

[2] *Ibid.*, at pp. 200–1. The right to light, however, stands on a different
footing ; *ibid.*, at pp. 202–3, citing *Broomfield* v. *Williams*, [1897] 1 Ch. 602.

[3] *Infra*, p. 534.   [4] L.P.A. 1925, s. 205 (1) (ii).

[5] *Rye* v. *Rye*, [1962] A. C. 496 ; [1962] 1 All E. R. 146 ; M. & B. p. 384.

[6] *Re Ray*, [1896] 1 Ch. 468, at p. 476.   [7] *Supra*, p. 394.

[8] *Borman* v. *Griffith*, [1930] 1 Ch. 493 ; M. & B. p. 387 ; *infra*, p. 536.

[9] *Supra*, p. 531.   [10] *Clark* v. *Barnes*, [1952] 2 Ch. 368.

[11] See generally Farrand, *Contract and Conveyance* (2nd Edn.) pp. 377–92.

[12] *Supra*, p. 519.

however, he has been accustomed to use one part in a particular manner, as for example by crossing a field to reach the highway, his practice is conveniently described as the exercise of a *quasi-easement*. If he later severs his ownership by granting part only of the land to another, such a quasi-easement is capable of ripening by implication into an easement properly so called in favour either of the land granted or the land retained.

The principle of this mode of creation is that although there has been no express mention of an easement in the grant of the land, yet it may very well be that the common intention of the parties cannot be carried out unless some particular easement is deemed to arise by implication. For the purposes of the doctrine, however, a lease and a devise are on the same footing as a grant.

The premises for the application of the doctrine are, first, that A., the owner of two separate tenements, has been in the habit of enjoying certain quasi-easements over one of them; and secondly, that the common ownership of A. has been severed. That is, if A. sells the quasi-servient tenement, certain easements may be implied in his favour (implied reservation); if he sells the quasi-dominant tenement, certain easements may be implied against him (implied grant); while the question of implication may also arise when he disposes of both the tenements to different persons. We will now consider these three cases separately.

(*a*) The common owner sells the quasi-servient tenement. What quasi-easements over that tenement will be implied in favour of the quasi-dominant tenement retained by the vendor?

The law is disinclined to imply easements in favour of a grantor. The reason is not far to seek. In the case of a grant of land the law is guided by two principles: the words of a deed must be construed as far as possible in favour of the grantee,[1] and the grantor cannot derogate from his own absolute grant by claiming rights over the thing granted.[2]

Easements not implied in favour of grantor.

If the grantor intends to retain a right over the land, it is his duty to reserve it expressly in the grant.[3] As a general rule there will be no implication in his favour.[4] There are, no doubt, exceptions to this rule, the most obvious of which are the way of necessity and the mutual easements of support between two adja-

Except in case of a way of necessity.

---

[1] *Neill* v. *Devonshire* (1882), 8 App. Cas. 135, *per* Lord Selborne, at p. 149.

[2] *Suffield* v. *Brown* (1864), 4 De G. J. & S. 194, *per* Lord Westbury. See generally (1964), 80 L. Q. R. 244 (D. W. Elliott). The rule may be varied by contract, see, *e.g.*, the draft forms of standard contracts of sales of land published by the Lord Chancellor under the Law of Property Act 1925, s. 46, which provide that a vendor who sells a house reserving adjoining land shall retain the right to build on such land. This right may, of course, operate to the prejudice of the house sold.

[3] *Wheeldon* v. *Burrows* (1879), 12 Ch. D. 31, at p. 49, *per* Thesiger, L.J.

[4] *Wheeldon* v. *Burrows*, *supra*.; *Aldridge* v. *Wright*, [1929] 2 K. B. 117; *Liddiard* v. *Waldron*, [1934] 1 K. B. 435; *Re Webb's Lease*, [1951] Ch. 808; [1951] 2 All E. R. 131; M. & B. p. 527.

cent buildings.[1]   A way of necessity arises where land which is entirely surrounded by other land is segregated by the common owner, and either retained by him or conveyed to another person. In such a case a way is implied both in favour of the grantor and against him.[2]

> " Where a man, having a close surrounded with his own land, grants the close to another in fee, for life or for years, the grantee shall give a way to the close over the grantor's land as incident to the grant ; for without it he cannot derive any benefit from the grant. "[3]

This rule applies where the landlocked close is devised,[4] and also where part of the surrounding land is owned by third persons.[5]

The same doctrine also applies where the grantor disposes of the surrounding land and keeps that which is enclosed.[6]

Extent of way of necessity.
The extent of the implied right is strictly limited and depends upon the mode of enjoyment of the surrounded land prevailing at the time of the grant.   The way may be used for any purpose which is essential to maintain that mode of enjoyment : it may not be used for other purposes.   Thus :

> Where at the time of the grant the surrounded close was used only for agricultural purposes, it was held that the grantor was not entitled to carry over it timber and other materials.[7]

There are, perhaps, other cases in which easements will be implied in favour of a grantor without express reservation,[8] but they defy exhaustive enumeration and all that can be said is that the scales are heavily weighted against him.   The necessary inference from the circumstances must be that he was intended to retain the precise easement that he claims.[9]

(b) The common owner sells the quasi-dominant tenement. What quasi-easements over the part retained by him will be implied in favour of the grantee ?

Continuous and apparent easements implied in favour of grantee.
The law is much more inclined to imply easements in favour of the grantee than in favour of the grantor, and the extent to which the implication goes is clearly indicated in the leading case of *Wheeldon* v. *Burrows*,[10] where Thesiger, L.J., said :—

---

[1] *Richards* v. *Rose* (1853), 9 Exch. 218 ; *Shubrook* v. *Tufnell* (1882), 46 T. L. R. 886.   [2] See (1973) 89 L. Q. R. 87 (E. H. Bodkin).
[3] *Pomfret* v. *Ricroft*, 1 Wms. Saund. 321 n (6) ; *Union Lighterage Co.* v. *London Graving Dock Co.*, [1902] 2 Ch. 557, 573 ; *Pinnington* v. *Galland* (1853), 9 Ex. 1.
[4] *Pearson* v. *Spencer* (1861), 1 B. & S. 571.
[5] *Barry* v. *Hasseldine*, [1952] Ch. 835 ; [1952] 2 All E. R. 317.
[6] *Pomfret* v. *Ricroft* (1669) 1 Wms. Saund., 321 n. (6) ; *London Corpn.* v. *Riggs* (1880), 13 Ch. D. 798 ; M. & B. p. 524.
[7] *London Corpn* v. *Riggs, supra* ; *Serff* v. *Acton Local Board* (1886), 31 Ch. D. 679.
[8] *Re Webb's Lease*, [1951] Ch. 808, 816–7, 823 ; [1951] 2 All E. R. 131, 136–7, 141 ; M. & B. p. 527.   [9] *Ibid.*, at p. 828.
[10] *Wheeldon* v. *Burrows* (1878), 12 Ch. D. 31, 49.   *Cf.* the formulation in the same case at pp. 58–59 and on the difference, see *Ward* v. *Kirkland*, [1967] Ch. 194 at p. 224 *per* Ungoed-Thomas, J. ; [1966] 1 All E. R. 609 ; M. & B. p. 512 ; (1967), 83 *L. Q. R.* 240 (A. W. B. Simpson).

"... on the grant by the owner of a tenement of part of that tenement as it is then used and enjoyed, there will pass to the grantee all
those continuous and apparent easements (by which, of course, I
mean quasi-easements), or, in other words, all those easements
which are necessary to the reasonable enjoyment of the property
granted, and which have been and are at the time of the grant used
by the owner of the entirety for the benefit of the part granted. "

Thus, for instance, it has been law since 1663[1] that if a man
grants a house in which there are windows, he cannot build on his
own adjoining land so as to obstruct the light.   The principle of
such a case is that the grantor is assumed to have intended that his
grant shall be effectual, and when two properties are severed, the
parties to the severance, both the man who gives and the man who
takes, must be presumed to intend that such reasonable incidents
shall go with the thing granted as will enable the person who takes
it to enjoy it in a proper and substantial way.[2]

It will be noticed that, unlike section 62 of the Law of Property
Act 1925,[3] the rule in *Wheeldon* v. *Burrows* is limited to continuous
and apparent easements.   Strictly speaking a continuous easement is one, such as the right to light, the constant enjoyment of
which does not, as in the case of a right of way, require the active
intervention of the dominant owner.   The word " continuous, "
however, is not in this context to be taken in its strict sense but
rather in the sense of permanence.   The two words " continuous " and " apparent " must be read together and understood
as pointing to an easement which is accompanied by some obvious
and permanent mark on the land itself, or at least by some mark
which will be disclosed by a careful inspection of the premises.[4]
Instances are :

    (i) watercourses consisting of some actual construction such
            as pipes[5] ;

    (ii) a made road[6] ;

    (iii) light flowing through windows[7] ;

    (iv) drains which can be discovered with ordinary care,[8]
            and so on.

A right of way is not necessarily such a quasi-easement as
will pass under the rule in *Wheeldon* v. *Burrows*.   To do so it
must be apparent.   There is no difficulty where there is a definite
made road over the quasi-servient tenement to and for the

When a way is implied.

---

    [1] *Palmer* v. *Fletcher* (1663), 1 Lev. 122; *Phillips* v. *Low*, [1892] 1 Ch. 47.
    [2] *Bayley* v. *G. W. R.* (1884), 26 Ch. D. 434, *per* BOWEN, L.J., at p. 452;
Aldridge v. *Wright*, [1929] 2 K. B. 117.
    [3] *Supra*, p. 530.
    [4] *Pyer* v. *Carter* (1857), 1 H. & N. 916, 922, adopting *Gale on Easements*.
Ward v. *Kirkland*, [1967] Ch. 194 ; [1966] 1 All E. R. 609 (right to enter neighbour's land to repair and maintain a wall held to be not continuous and apparent).
    [5] *Watts* v. *Kellson* (1871), 6 Ch. App. 166 ; *Schwann* v. *Cotton*, [1916] 2 Ch.
120 ; affd., [1916] 2 Ch. 459.
    [6] *Brown* v. *Alabaster* (1887), 37 Ch. D. 490.
    [7] *Allen* v. *Taylor* (1880), 16 Ch. D. 355.
    [8] *Pyer* v. *Carter* (1857), 1 H. & N. 916.

apparent use of the quasi-dominant tenement. Such will clearly pass upon a severance of the common tenement.[1] But the existence of a formed road is not essential, and if there are other indicia which show that the road was being used at the time of the grant for the benefit of the quasi-dominant tenement and that it is necessary for the reasonable enjoyment of that tenement,[2] it will pass to a purchaser of the latter.[3] Thus :

> A man built four cottages on his own land and left a strip between the rear of the cottages and the boundary of his land in order to afford a back means of access to the main highway. It was held that the quasi-easement of way was sufficiently continuous and apparent to pass under the present doctrine, for at the time of the grant the strip, though not formed into a made road, was worn and marked with rough tracks, so that no one seeing it could doubt that it was used as a way to the cottages.[4]

Doctrine of Wheeldon v. Burrows of less importance now.

This doctrine of *Wheeldon* v. *Burrows* is of particular importance in those cases where section 62 of the Law of Property Act 1925[5] is inapplicable because there has been no diversity of occupation prior to a conveyance,[6] or because there has been no "conveyance" as defined by the Act.[7] Thus in *Borman* v. *Griffith*[8] :—

> X., who owned a large park containing two houses, The Gardens and The Hall, agreed in writing to lease the former to the plaintiff for seven years. A drive ran from the public road to The Hall, passing *en route* close to The Gardens. There was no separate drive for The Gardens, but at the time of the agreement X. was constructing, and he later completed, an unmetalled way which ran from the back door of the house to the public road. The agreement reserved no right of way to the plaintiff, but he constantly used The Hall drive in preference to the unmetalled way. Later, the defendant took a lease from X. of The Hall and the rest of the park, and began to obstruct the plaintiff in his use of the drive. In the ensuing action the plaintiff claimed to be entitled to a right of way over the drive.

The question, therefore, was whether the plaintiff had acquired the quasi-easement which the common owner of the whole land had exercised over the drive when passing from The Gardens to the public road. There was clearly no easement of necessity, since the unmetalled way provided a means of approach to the

---

[1] *Brown* v. *Alabaster* (1887), 37 Ch. D. 490 ; *Davies* v. *Sear* (1869), L. R. 7 Eq. 427.

[2] " Necessary " must not be confused with " necessity " (see " way of necessity," *supra*, p. 534. A way of necessity is one without which the property cannot be used at all, but " necessary " in the present connection indicates that the way conduces to the reasonable enjoyment of the property.

[3] *Hansford* v. *Jago*, [1921] 1 Ch. 322 ; *Borman* v. *Griffith*, [1930] 1 Ch. 493, 499. This paragraph was cited with approval in *Ward* v. *Kirkland* [1965] Ch. 194 at p. 225.

[4] *Hansford* v. *Jago, supra.*   [5] *Supra*, pp. 530–2.   [6] *Supra*, p. 532.

[7] *Supra*, p. 532. S. 62, however, is wider, in that the right need not be " continuous and apparent ", nor " necessary to the reasonable enjoyment of the property granted ".

[8] [1930] 1 Ch. 493 ; M. & B. p. 387 ; *Horn* v. *Hiscock* (1972), 223 Estates Gazette 1437 ; *Sovmots Investments, Ltd.* v. *Secretary of State for the Environment*, [1976] 2 W. L. R. 73.

outside world. It was equally clear that section 62 was inapplicable to a contract for a lease. Nevertheless it was held that an easement of way had arisen by implication in favour of the plaintiff according to the doctrine of *Wheeldon* v. *Burrows*. Thus, under that doctrine a grantee acquires only those easements to which he has an implied contractual right ; but under section 62 of the Law of Property Act 1925, the conveyance may vest in him an easement to which he has no contractual right whatsoever.[1]

In the normal case, the quasi-easement that passes by implication to the purchaser or lessee of the quasi-dominant tenement is already in existence at the time of the contract. But the law recognizes that one, not hitherto enjoyed, shall also be implied in his favour if this is necessary to effectuate the common intention of the parties.[2] In one case, for instance :— *Fresh easement may be implied.*

> Three cellars were let for the purpose of being used as a restaurant. By certain statutory regulations no premises could be used for this purpose unless they were provided with a ventilation system. In the circumstances, it was impossible to do this without affixing a duct to the outside walls of the landlord's building.

The Court of Appeal granted a declaration that the tenant was entitled to construct and maintain the duct.[3]

(c) The common owner severs his property and sells one part to X. and the other part to Y. What quasi-easements hitherto enjoyed by the common owner over the quasi-servient tenement will pass to the purchaser of the quasi-dominant tenement?

Where, instead of a sale of part of the land and a retention by the common owner of the other part, there have been simultaneous sales effected by separate but *contemporaneous* conveyances to different persons, all those continuous and apparent quasi-easements which were in use at the time of the sales pass by implication with the respective parts.[4] In other words, when the sales are by the same vendor and take place at one and the same time, the rights of the parties are exactly the same as if the common owner had sold the dominant part and kept the rest of the land. *Contemporaneous sales.*

Thus in *Schwann* v. *Cotton*,[5]

> where a testator devised Blackacre to X. and Whiteacre to Y., it was held that a right to the free passage of water which flowed

---

[1] (1952), 15 *M. L. R.* pp. 265–6 (A. D. Hargreaves).

[2] *Pwllbach Colliery Co., Ltd.* v. *Woodman*, [1915] A. C. 634, at p. 646.

[3] *Wong* v. *Beaumont Property Trust, Ltd.*, [1965] 1 Q. B. 173; [1964] 2 All E. R. 119 ; M. & B. p. 512. The court classified this as an easement of necessity, but this must have been *per incuriam*. " An easement is surely not an ' easement of necessity ' merely because it is necessary to give effect to the intention " (1964), 80 *L. Q. R.*, 322 (R. E. M.). An easement of necessity is based on public policy, not on presumed intention ; (1964), 27 M. L. R., 721 (H. W. Wilkinson).

[4] *Allen* v. *Taylor* (1880), L. R. 16 Ch. D. 355 ; *Swansborough* v. *Coventry* (1832), 9 Bing. 305 ; *Barnes* v. *Loach* (1879), 4 Q. B. D. 494 ; *Schwann* v. *Cotton*, [1916] 2 Ch. 120; 459 (C. A.); *Hansford* v. *Jago*, [1921] 1 Ch. 322.

[5] *Supra.*

through an underground pipe running across Blackacre to White-acre passed by implication to the devisee of Whiteacre.

Separate
sales.

If the sales are not simultaneous, the later purchaser is in the same position as his vendor. So if the vendor first sells the quasi-servient tenement, he will not, in the absence of an express reserva-tion, be entitled to easements over the part sold, except a way of necessity where one exists, nor will a subsequent purchaser from him be in any better position ;[1] but if the vendor first sells the quasi-dominant tenement, the purchaser thereof can enforce quasi-easements against a subsequent purchaser of the quasi-servient tenement to the same extent as he could have done against the vendor.

(4) Acquisition by presumed grant. Proof of the exist-ence of an easement may be, and usually is, based upon a mere presumption that at some time in the past it has been granted by deed. There are three possible methods by which a claimant may avail himself of this presumption, for he may plead prescription

  (i) at common law ; or
  (ii) under the doctrine of lost modern grant ; or
  (iii) under the Prescription Act 1832

Why grant is
presumed.

Each method is based upon identical reasoning. The estab-lished principle no doubt is that an easement must be created by deed of grant, since incorporeal hereditaments lie in grant.[2] On the other hand, it is obviously undesirable that a man should be deprived of an easement long and continuously enjoyed merely because its formal creation by deed is incapable of proof. There-fore, in accordance with the maxim—*omnia praesumuntur rite et sollemniter esse acta*—the law is prepared to infer from this long enjoyment that all those acts were done that were necessary to create a valid title.[3] In this way, a claim, founded upon factual enjoyment without interruption by the servient owner, is referred to a lawful origin.

Long enjoyment, however, is not in itself sufficient to raise the presumption of a grant. It must be of a particular nature, and this is so whether an easement is claimed either by prescription at common law, or under the doctrine of lost modern grant or under the Prescription Act 1832. As we shall see, the user must be as of right and continuous, and only a grant in fee simple will be presumed.

All forms of prescription ultimately depend on the acquies-cence of the servient owner. Why should long user confer a right protected by the courts ? The answer is, that if the

---

[1] *Murchie* v. *Black* (1865), 19 C. B. (N. S.) 190.
[2] *Supra,* p. 520.
[3] *Philipps* v. *Halliday,* [1891] A. C. 228, 231 ; *Foster* v. *Warblington Urban Council,* [1906] 1 K. B. 648, 679.

servient owner has allowed somebody to exercise an easement over his land for a considerable period and if he has omitted to prevent such exercise when he might very well have done so, it is only reasonable to conclude that the privilege has been rightfully enjoyed, for otherwise some attempt to interfere with it would long ago have been made by any owner who possessed even a modicum of common sense.   FRY, J., in one case said [1] :—

> " In my opinion, the whole law of prescription and the whole law which governs the presumption or inference of a grant or covenant rest upon acquiescence. The courts and the judges have had recourse to various expedients for quieting the possession of persons in the exercise of rights which have not been resisted by the persons against whom they are exercised ; but in all cases it appears to me that acquiescence and nothing else is the principle upon which these expedients rest. It becomes then of the highest importance to consider of what ingredients acquiescence consists. . . . I cannot imagine any case of acquiescence in which there is not shewn to be in the servient owner :
>
> > (1) a knowledge of the acts done ;
> > (2) a power in him to stop the acts or to sue in respect of them ; and
> > (3) an abstinence on his part from the exercise of such power."

User as of right.   This stress upon the element of acquiescence gives the clue to the kind of user required for a prescriptive title. In technical language, it must be *user as of right*,[2] or, to use the expression taken by Coke from Bracton,[3] *longus usus nec per vim, nec clam, nec precario*. The servient owner cannot be said to have acquiesced in an easement that has been enjoyed *vi, clam* or *precario*.

Thus, if the dominant owner has used coercion, or if his user is contentious in the sense that the servient owner continually and unmistakably protests against it, there is clearly no acquiescence, and the user, being *vi*, will not avail the claimant.[4] Again, there is no acquiescence if the user has been *clam, i.e.* by stealth, for a man cannot assent to something of which he is ignorant, and the law allows no prescriptive right to be acquired where there has been any concealment or where the enjoyment has not been

User must not be violent;

nor secret;

---

[1] *Dalton* v. *Angus* (1881), 6 App. Cas. 740, at p. 773. Lord PENZANCE was " in entire accord with " FRY, J. (p. 803), and Lord BLACKBURN (at p. 823) described it as " a very able opinion." THESIGER, L.J., has used very similar language to that of FRY, J., in *Sturges* v. *Bridgman* (1879), 11 Ch. D. 852, at p. 863.

[2] *Gardner* v. *Hodgson's Kingston Brewery Co. Ltd.*, [1903] A. C. 229 ; M. & B. p. 536 ; *Tickle* v. *Brown* (1836), 4 A. & E. 369 ; *Healey* v. *Hawkins*, [1968] 1 W. L. R. 1967 ; [1968] 3 All E. R. 836 ; M. & B. p. 537.

[3] Co. Litt., 113*b*.

[4] *Eaton* v. *Swansea Waterworks Co.* (1851), 17 Q. B. 267 ; *Dalton* v. *Angus* (1881), 6 App. Cas. 740, at p. 786 ; *Hollins* v. *Verney* (1884), 13 Q. B. D. 304, at p. 307.

nor precarious.

open.[1] It must always be found that the servient owner had actual or constructive knowledge of the enjoyment upon which the claimant relies.[2] Lastly, where the user has been *precario*, that is, where it is enjoyed by the permission of the servient owner and the permission is one which he may withdraw at any moment, it cannot be said that he has acquiesced in the existence of the easement as a matter of right. To ask permission is to acknowledge that no right exists. In this case an explanation of the user is forthcoming, and an irrevocable right to the perpetual enjoyment of the easement is not consistent with the explanation. What a plaintiff must show is that he claims the privilege not as a thing permitted to him from time to time by the servient owner, but as a thing that he has a right to do.

For instance :

A woman relied upon sixty years' user of a cartway from her stables through the yard of an adjoining inn, but on it appearing that she had paid 15s. each year for this privilege, it was held by the House of Lords that the user, being *precario*, was not *as of right*.[3]

Thus a common method of preventing user from developing into a right is to exact a small periodical payment, and although in such a case there is in one sense a right to enjoy what has been paid for, yet it does not amount to a right to a permanent easement, but at the most to a right to damages for breach of contract.[4]

Continuous user.

User must be continuous. In addition to being *as of right*, user must also be continuous, though the continuity varies according to the nature of the right in question. For instance, a right of way from the nature of the case admits only of occasional enjoyment, and therefore if it is used as and when occasion demands, the requirement of continuity is satisfied.[5] But so far as a discontinuous easement, such as a right of way, is concerned, it is impossible to define what in every case constitutes sufficient continuity of user. Every case must depend upon the exact nature of the right claimed, and all that can be said is that the user must be such as to disclose to the servient owner the fact that a continuous right to enjoyment is being asserted and that therefore

---

[1] *Union Lighterage Co.* v. *London Graving Dock Co.*, [1902] 2 Ch. 557 ; M. & B. p. 548, in which a dock-owner's claim to an easement of support by means of invisible rods sunk under the adjoining land was disallowed ; *Dalton* v. *Angus, supra*, at p. 827. *Liverpool Corporation* v. *Coghill*, [1918] 1 Ch. 307 (injurious substances discharged into the public sewer at night for more than 20 years).

[2] *Lloyds Bank* v. *Dalton Ltd.*, [1942] Ch. 466 ; [1942] 2 All E. R. 352 ; *Davies* v. *Du Paver*, [1953] 1 Q. B. 184 ; [1952] 2 All E. R. 991 ; M. & B. p. 546

[3] *Gardner* v. *Hodgson's Kingston Brewery Co., Ltd.*, [1903] A. C. 229 ; M. & B. p. 536 ; *Diment* v. *N. H. Foot, Ltd.*, [1974] 1 W. L. R. 1427 ; [1974] 2 All E. R. 785 ; M. & B. p. 533 (agent's knowledge).

[4] *Ibid.*, at p. 231.

[5] *Dare* v. *Heathcote* (1856), 25 L. J. Ex. 245.

it ought to be resisted if it is not to ripen into a permanent right.[1]

The right which is claimed on the ground of its continuous and uninterrupted exercise for a period of time need not have been exercised by the same person throughout the whole period : it is sufficient that it has been exercised by the successive owners of the estate in the dominant tenement to which the easement is appurtenant. Nor need it continue to be exercised in precisely the same manner ; thus, where the dominant and servient owners agreed upon a variation of the route of a right of way for their own convenience, it was held that the user of the substituted route was substantially an exercise of the old right.[2]

Continuous user by successive owners.

User in fee simple. Since the basis of a prescriptive claim is immemorial user, an easement can be prescribed for only in respect of a fee simple estate. The rule is absolute that an easement claimed either by prescription at common law, or under the doctrine of a lost grant or under the Prescription Act 1832 must be claimed in favour of the fee simple estate in the servient tenement.[3] An easement may be granted expressly for a lesser interest than a fee simple, but it cannot arise by virtue of a presumed grant. A tenant for years, no matter what the length of his lease may be, cannot for instance acquire a right of way over the adjoining land of his lessor.[4] He may, however, acquire by prescription an easement against the land of a stranger, though if he does so it enures for the benefit of the fee simple and does not cease with the cessation of his leasehold interest.[5] Furthermore, if the servient tenement is occupied by a tenant for years[6] or a tenant for life[7] at the beginning of the period of user, there can be no claim for an easement by prescription. But if the user begins against a fee simple owner, then the fact that the servient tenement is subsequently let or settled will not prevent this claim.[8]

No presumed grant except in respect of the fee simple in both tenements.

Owing, however, to the wording of the Prescription Act 1832, the right to light is an exception to these rules.[9]

Exceptional case of light.

---

[1] *Hollins* v. *Verney* (1884), 13 Q. B. D. 304, at p. 315. In that case a right of way was claimed for the purpose of removing wood cut upon adjoining land, but the evidence showed that the right had been exercised only on three occasions at intervals of twelve years. The Court of Appeal held that there had not been sufficient continuity of enjoyment.

[2] *Davis* v. *Whitby*, [1974] Ch. 186 ; [1974] 1 All E. R. 806 ; M. & B. p. 551 ; *Payne* v. *Shedden* (1834) 1 Mood. & R. 382.

[3] *Bright* v. *Walker* (1834), 1 Cr. M. & R. 211, 221 ; *Wheaton* v. *Maple & Co.*, [1893] 3 Ch. 48 ; *Kilgour* v. *Gaddes*, [1904] 1 K.B. 457, 466 ; M. & B. p. 538. So far as the doctrine of the lost modern grant is concerned, this rule would appear to be contrary to principle ; see (1958), 74 *L. Q. R.* pp. 82–96 (V. T. H. Delany).

[4] *Gayford* v. *Moffatt* (1868), 4 Ch. App. 133 ; *Kilgour* v. *Gaddes, supra.*

[5] *Wheaton* v. *Maple & Co., supra*, at p. 63. *Pugh* v. *Savage*, [1970] 2 Q. B. 373 ; [1970] 2 All E. R. 353.

[6] *Daniel* v. *North* (1809), 11 East. 372.

[7] *Roberts* v. *James* (1903), 89 L. T. 282.

[8] *Palk* v. *Shinner* (1852), 18 Q. B. 215 ; *Pugh* v. *Savage, supra.*

[9] *Infra*, p. 553.

Methods of prescription. We must now discuss the three methods of prescription.

Enjoyment
during time
immemorial.

(i) **Prescription at Common Law.**[1] At common law a man may assert a prescriptive title to an easement founded upon long enjoyment. This, however, immediately raises the question —how long must his enjoyment have lasted before a grant in his favour will be presumed ? The conclusion reached by the courts was that he must have enjoyed his right for *time immemorial*, that is to say, " from time whereof the memory of men runneth not to the contrary. "[2]

Meaning of
time im-
memorial.

It is obvious that this designation of what is generally termed *legal memory* is vague and unsatisfactory, and so the courts soon solved the difficulty in a rough and ready fashion by fixing some date at which the memory of man was supposed to begin. They did not choose a date at random, but took as their guide the statutes that from time to time restricted the period within which actions for the recovery of land had to be brought. At first those statutes, instead of fixing a given number of years, adopted the singular expedient of making the period of limitation run from particular dates or events as, for example, from the last return of King John into England. The last statute which adopted this plan was the Statute of Westminster in 1275, which fixed the first year of the reign of Richard I, *i.e.* 1189, as the period of limitation for the recovery of land by a writ of right. These statutes were, of course, not concerned with prescription, but the courts, from time to time, adopted the various statutory dates as the time at which *legal memory* was to be taken as beginning. Thus after the Statute of Westminster, a prescriptive claim to an easement had to be based on an enjoyment carried back to 1189. Unfortunately, this policy of keeping in line with successive statutes of limitation was not maintained, for when the legislature set up a different principle in 1623[3] by enacting that actions for the recovery of land must be brought within a fixed number of years (20 years for the action of ejectment), the courts omitted to restrict *legal memory* to the same period.[4] So, absurd though it is, 1189 is at the present day still considered to be the time from which a claimant who is prescribing at common law must prove enjoyment of the easement. The result has been the adoption of what COCKBURN, C.J., described as a " somewhat startling rule," [5] for, in order to lighten the burden of a claimant, the courts are willing to presume that enjoyment has lasted from

---

[1] For the history of prescription, see Holdsworth, *History of English Law*, vol. vii. pp. 343 *et seq*.
[2] Co. Litt. 170.
[3] Following 32 Henry VIII, c. 2.
[4] For the above see the judgment of COCKBURN, C.J.; *Bryant* v. *Foot* (1867), L. R. 2 Q. B. 161, at pp. 180-1 ; M. & B. p. 530.
[5] *Bryant* v. *Foot, supra*, at p. 181.

1189 if proof is given of an actual enjoyment from as far back as living witnesses can speak.[1] A lifetime's enjoyment or even a shorter period raises the presumption that the enjoyment has stretched back to the reign of Richard I.[2]

This principle that the court will be satisfied with something like a lifetime's enjoyment affords some alleviation to claimants who, in strict theory of law, should stretch their enjoyment back to 1189, but in the majority of cases it is ineffectual because of another difficulty that confronts a claim based on prescription. If it can be shown that there was a time subsequent to 1189 when for some reason or other the easement could not possibly have existed, it is obvious that user enjoyed even for several centuries will be of no avail, since despite its length it must have started after the removal of the impossibility, and that was after 1189.[3] This almost precludes prescription at common law in the case of easements appurtenant to buildings, such as a right to light, for proof that the building did not exist in the time of Richard I must inevitably defeat the claim.[4]

(ii) **Prescription under Lost Modern Grant.** The " lost modern grant, " represents the second stage in the history of acquisition by presumed grant. If easements which were fortified by long enjoyment, but for the grant of which no deed could be produced, were to receive the protection they deserved, it was soon seen that something must be done to turn the flank of the rule that a prescriptive claim at common law failed if it was shown that the easement must have come into existence at some time later than 1189. Stimulated by a determination to support ancient user at all costs, judicial astuteness in course of time evolved the very questionable theory[5] of the lost modern grant. After actual enjoyment of an easement has been shown for a reasonable length of time, the court presumes that an actual grant was made at the time when enjoyment began, but that the deed has been lost. The justification for this attitude is that if a claimant, despite his inability to prove enjoyment back to 1189 or to produce a deed of grant, has clearly exercised the easement for (say) the last 60 years, it is possible that at some time an actual grant was made to him or his predecessor, and that it was subsequently lost. Therefore, since long enjoyment must be upheld, the only course open to the

Fiction of lost modern grant.

Its justification.

---

[1] First Report of Real Property Commissioners, p. 51.

[2] *Bailey* v. *Appleyard* (1838), 8 A. & E. 161, at p. 166. See *Darling* v. *Clue* (1864), 4 F. & F. 329, at p. 334, *per* WILLES, J. " At common law twenty years uninterrupted user as of right will be prima facie evidence of the right liable to be rebutted." ; see also *Bealey* v. *Shaw* (1805), 6 East 208, at p. 215, *per* Lord ELLENBOROUGH.

[3] *Hulbert* v. *Dale*, [1909] 2 Ch. 570, at p. 577.

[4] *Bury* v. *Pope* (1587), Cro. Eliz. 118 ; *Norfolk* v. *Arbuthnot* (1880), 5 C. P. D. 390 ; Real Property Commission, First Report, 1829, p. 51.

[5] *Bryant* v. *Foot* (1867), L. R. 2 Q. B. 161, at p. 181, *per* COCKBURN, C. J.

court is to leave it to the jury to presume that the grant was in
fact made.

The virtue of this theory is that it avoids the disaster which
overtakes common law prescription when it is shown that the
easement could not have existed (say) in 1750, for it does not
matter what the state of affairs was then if you rely on a grant
made some years later.

COCKBURN, C.J., said[1] :—

> " Juries were first told that from user, during living memory or
> even during twenty years, they might presume a lost grant or deed,
> [and here the courts did act by analogy to the Limitation Act 1623][2] ;
> next they were recommended to make such presumption ; and lastly,
> as the final consummation of judicial legislation, it was held that a jury
> should be told, not only that they might, but also that they were bound
> to presume the existence of such a lost grant, although neither judge
> nor jury, nor anyone else, had the shadow of a belief that any such
> instrument had ever really existed."

So the lost grant fiction rested and still rests upon the basis of
long user, and though in theory the user is merely presumptive
evidence, in practice and effect it is decisive.   At the present day
it is the last expedient of a claimant who finds himself unable to
rely upon prescription at common law or upon the provisions of the
Prescription Act.[3]

**Period of
enjoyment.**   The general rule is that twenty years' enjoyment is enough to
raise the presumption,[4] and a period of twenty-one years, eight and
a half months has been held to suffice.[5]

**User as of
right
necessary.**   The same kind of user must be shown as in the case of prescription at common law, so that if it is *vi*, *clam* or *precario* the
doctrine will not be invoked by the court.[6]   Again, in accordance
with general principles, it must be clear that there was some
person or body of persons to whom the grant might have been
made[7] ; that there was a fee simple owner capable of executing
the grant[8] ; and that the right claimed was one which might have
been the subject-matter of a grant.[9]

**How claim
may be
defeated.**   In *Tehidy Minerals, Ltd.* v. *Norman*,[10] the Court of Appeal,
after reviewing the difference of judicial opinion in *Dalton* v. *Angus*

---

[1] *Bryant* v. *Foot* (1867), L. R. 2 Q. B. 161, at p. 181.
[2] *Bright* v. *Walker* (1843), 1 Cr. M. & R. 211, 217, PARKE, B.
[3] *Hulley* v. *Silversprings Bleaching and Dyeing Co., Ltd.*, [1922] 2 Ch. 268 ;
see *e.g. Hulbert* v. *Dale*, [1909] 2 Ch. 570 ; M. & B. p. 415 (easement) ; *Tehidy
Minerals Ltd.* v. *Norman*, [1971] 2 Q. B. 528 ; [1971] 2 All E. R. 475 ; M. & B.
p. 542 (profit à prendre).
[4] *Bryant* v. *Foot* (1867), L. R. 2 Q. B. 161 ; *per* COCKBURN, C.J., at 181.
[5] *Tehidy Minerals, Ltd.* v. *Norman*, *supra.*
[6] *Hanna* v. *Pollock*, [1900] 2 Irish Reports, 664, at p. 671 ; *Partridge* v.
Scott (1838), 3 M. & W. 220 ; *Oakley* v. *Boston*, [1975] 3 W. L. R. 478 ; [1975]
3 All E. R. 405.
[7] *Tilbury* v. *Silva* (1890), 45 Ch. D. 98, at p. 122.
[8] *Daniel* v. *North* (1809), 11 East, 372; *Oakley* v. *Boston*, *supra.*
[9] *Bryant* v. *Lefever* (1879), 4 C. P. D. 172.
[10] [1971] 2 Q. B. 528 ; [1971] 2 All E. R. 475.

and Co.[1] decided that the presumption of a lost modern grant cannot be rebutted by evidence that no such grant was in fact made. If for instance a claim to an easement of support in respect of a house were made, it might be a simple matter to prove that no grant had ever been executed, but it would not be a good reason for refusing to apply the doctrine. The doctrine is plainly a fiction ; it is a means to an end, and the end is that some technical ground may be found for upholding a right that has been openly enjoyed.

A lost grant, however, will not be presumed if, during the period of user, there was no person capable of making the grant, or if such a grant would have been in contravention of a statute.[2]

As Buckley, L.J. said[3] :

> " In our judgment *Angus* v. *Dalton* decides that, where there has been upwards of 20 years' uninterrupted enjoyment of an easement, such enjoyment having the necessary qualities to fulfil the requirements of prescription, then unless, for some reason such as incapacity on the part of the person or persons who might at some time before the commencement of the 20-year period have made a grant, the existence of such a grant is impossible, the law will adopt a legal fiction that such a grant was made, in spite of any direct evidence that no such grant was in fact made.
>
> If this legal fiction is not to be displaced by direct evidence that no grant was made, it would be strange if it could be displaced by circumstantial evidence leading to the same conclusion, and in our judgment it must follow that circumstantial evidence tending to negative the existence of a grant (other than evidence establishing impossibility) should not be permitted to displace the fiction."

(iii) **Prescription under the Prescription Act 1832.** The two chief objects of the Prescription Act were to shorten the time of legal memory, and to make it impossible in actions brought under the Act for a claim to be defeated by proof that at some point of time later than 1189 the easement could not have existed. For these purposes the act separates the right to light from all other easements, and deals with each class in a different manner. *Object of the Act.*

(a) **Easements other than the easement of light.**
Section 2 enacts in effect that

> where an easement has been actually enjoyed without interruption for twenty years, it shall not be defeated by proof that it commenced later than 1189, but it may be defeated in any other way possible at common law. *Effect of enjoyment for 20 years.*

Thus a claimant who relies on the Act is untroubled by the doctrine of legal memory, but he may still be met by the

---

[1] (1877), 3 Q. B. D. 85 ; on appeal, (1878), 4 Q. B. D. 162 ; affd., *sub nom. Dalton* v. *Angus* (1881), 6 App. Cas. 740. The views are summarized in *Tehidy Minerals, Ltd.* v. *Norman* [1971] 2 Q. B. 528 at pp. 547, *et seq.*
[2] *Neaverson* v. *Peterborough Rural Council*, [1902] 1 Ch. 557.
[3] *Tehidy Minerals, Ltd.* v. *Norman, supra,* at p. 552.

defences admissible in a case where common law prescription is pleaded, as for instance that the right is not the possible subject-matter of a grant[1]; or that the enjoyment has been contentious, secret or precarious.

Effect of enjoyment for 40 years.

The same section goes on to enact that an easement which has been enjoyed without interruption for forty years shall be deemed absolute and indefeasible unless it appears that it was enjoyed by some consent or agreement expressly given by deed or writing.

The advantage derived from enjoyment for the longer of these periods will be explained below.[2]

Enjoyment must immediately precede action.

The two periods specified do not mean *any* period of twenty or forty years, but the period *next before some suit or action* wherein the claim is brought into question.[3]   Thus, the plaintiff must prove uninterrupted enjoyment for the period which immediately precedes and which terminates in an action.[4]   For instance,

suppose that a claimant proves that he and his predecessors in title have enjoyed a right of way over adjoining lands for more than a hundred years, except for a short period of eighteen months twelve years ago, when he happened to be seised in fee of both tenements. Although this is a case where the court will still presume a lost modern grant,[5] a claim under the Act will fail, because during part of the *last* twenty years he has enjoyed the privilege not as the owner of an easement over the land of another, but as the owner of the servient tenement.[6]

Meaning of interruption.

It is essential that the enjoyment for the period of twenty or forty years should be uninterrupted, but the Act provides that nothing is to be deemed a statutory interruption unless it has been submitted to or acquiesced in by the dominant owner for one year after he had notice of the interruption and of the person responsible therefor.[7]

" Interruption " means some overt act, such as the obstruction of a right of way, which shows that the easement is disputed.[8]   Thus,

---

[1] *Staffordshire Canal Co.* v. *Birmingham Canal Co.* (1866), L. R. 1 H. L. 254, at p. 278.

[2] *Infra*, pp. 548–50.   [3] Prescription Act 1832, s. 4.

[4] *Jones* v. *Price* (1836), 3 Bing. N. C. 52 ; *Parker* v. *Mitchell* (1840), 11 A. & E. 788 ; *Hyman* v. *Van den Bergh*, [1907] 2 Ch. 516 ; affd., [1908] 1 Ch. 167 ; M. & B. p. 548 ; *Oakley* v. *Boston* [1975] 3 W. L. R. 478 ; [1975] 3 All E. R. 405.

[5] *Cf. Hulbert* v. *Dale*, [1909] 2 Ch. 570 ; M. & B. p. 540.

[6] *Bright* v. *Walker* (1834), 1 Cr. M. & R. 211, 219.

[7] S. 4.

[8] *Carr* v. *Foster* (1842), 3 Q. B. 581, *per* Parke, B.

if A. has regularly passed over a track on B.'s land for twenty-five years and is then sued in trespass by B., his user of the way for the twenty years next preceding the action will entitle him to judgment. If, however, before his right has been contested, he submits to or acquiesces in an interruption that continues for one year, his previous enjoyment for twenty-five years becomes unavailing to him and he must start it afresh in order to satisfy the statute.

The crucial question, therefore, is—what amounts to submission or acquiescence ? This is a question of fact dependent upon the circumstances, but the test that should be applied seems a little obscure.

Suppose, in the case above, that B. erects a wall across the track over which A. has been passing for twenty-five years and that A., though he protests violently and threatens legal proceedings, lets thirteen months elapse without forcing the issue by a positive act of resistance.[1]

Does his protest suffice to negative his submission to or acquiescence in the interruption ? It has been held that he need not go so far as to remove the obstruction or to take legal proceedings. It is said to be enough that he communicate to the servient owner, with sufficient force and clarity, his opposition to the interruption.[2] This vague test is scarcely satisfactory. Strictly speaking, no doubt, submission or acquiescence is a state of mind, but if a dissident state of mind, unfortified by some positive act of resistance, is to nullify an aggressive act of interruption, what certainty will remain in the title to the servient tenement ? A single protest will remain effective after the year has elapsed and the statutory rule that interruption for a year shall defeat a claimant will be deprived of its intended force. The weight of judicial opinion, however, is disinclined to regard inactivity by the dominant owner for longer than a year after the interruption and after his protest as necessarily fatal to his claim.[3]

An interruption that occurs after the enjoyment of an easement has persisted for nineteen years and a fraction of a year will not avail the servient owner, provided that the dominant owner sues to vindicate his right within a year afterwards.[4] The interruption is not yet an interruption within the meaning of the statute. Nevertheless, the acquisition of an easement requires enjoyment for the full period of twenty years immediately preceding an

Effect of enjoyment for 19 years and a fraction.

---

[1] *Cf. Davies* v. *Du Paver,* [1953] 1 Q. B. 184 ; [1952] 2 All E. R. 991 ; M. & B. p. 546.
[2] *Bennison* v. *Cartwright* (1864), 5 B. & S. 1 ; *Glover* v. *Coleman* (1874), 10 C. P. 108.
[3] *Davies* v. *Du Paver, supra,* (where, however, that view was not shared by SINGLETON, L.J.) ; *Ward* v. *Kirkland,* [1967] Ch. 194 ; [1966] 1 All E. R. 609.
[4] *Flight* v. *Thomas* (1840), 8 Cl. & Fin. 231.

action, and therefore if the servient owner brings an action before the period has elapsed he will be entitled to a declaration that no easement exists, notwithstanding the deficiency of the interruption.[1]

User must be as of right.

The nature of the enjoyment necessary for the statutory periods, must be similar to that required at common law, that is to say, it must be *as of right*.[2] This is so even where user has been shown for the full period of forty years. The Act does not mean that easements enjoyed for forty years otherwise than by written permission are in all circumstances indefeasible, but only if their enjoyment has been open and notorious. Lord MACNAGHTEN gave a warning against reading too much into the Act :—

Difference between the two periods of 20 and 40 years.

> " The Act was passed, as its preamble declares, for the purpose of getting rid of the inconvenience and injustice arising from the meaning which the law of England attached to the expressions ' time immemorial ' and ' time whereof the memory of man runneth not to the contrary.' The law as it stood put an intolerable strain on the consciences of judges and jurymen. The Act was an Act ' for shortening the time of prescription in certain cases.' And really it did nothing more." [3]

This enables us to appreciate the significance of enjoyment for the longer period of forty years. A hasty reading of section 2 might induce the belief that a right enjoyed for forty years is indefeasible unless it can be proved that it was enjoyed by virtue of a written grant. But this is not so. In the case of enjoyment for the *shorter* period the claim cannot be met by the objection that enjoyment originated subsequently to 1189, but it can be met and defeated by any one of the common law defences, namely :—

(a) that the right claimed lacks one or more of the characteristics essential to an easement [4] ; or,

(b) that the right in question, though enjoyed for twenty years, is prohibited by law, as, for example, because a grant would have been *ultra vires* the grantor [5] or the grantee [6] ; or,

(c) that the user was not *as of right*,[7] *i.e.* that it was forcible, or secret, or enjoyed by permission *whether written or oral*.[8]

---

[1] *Reilly* v. *Orange*, [1955] 2 Q. B. 112 ; [1955] 2 All E. R. 369 ; M. & B. p. 550.
[2] *Tickle* v. *Brown* (1836), 4 A. & E. 369, at p. 382 ; *Bright* v. *Walker* (1834), 1 Cr. M. & R. 211 ; *Lyell* v. *Hothfield*, [1914] 3 K. B. 911.
[3] *Gardner* v. *Hodgson's Kingston Brewery Co. Ltd.*, [1903] A. C. 229, at p. 236.
[4] *Mouncey* v. *Ismay* (1865), 3 H. & C. 486.
[5] *Rochdale Canal Co.* v. *Radcliffe* (1852), 18 Q. B. 287, at p. 315 ; *Staffordshire Canal Co.* v. *Birmingham Canal Co.* (1866), L. R. 1 H. L. 254, at p. 278.
[6] *National Manure Co.* v. *Donald* (1859), 4 H. & N. 8.
[7] *Supra*, pp. 539–40.
[8] *Burrows* v. *Lang*, [1901] 2 Ch. 502.

Next, a claim to an easement based upon forty years' enjoyment can likewise be defeated upon the first two grounds, and also by proof that the user was forcible or secret or enjoyed by *written* permission. What is not sufficient to nullify a user lasting for this longer period is the oral permission of the servient owner. On general principles user that is precarious in any sense cannot originate an easement, but the statute, by enacting that user for forty years is not to be considered precarious unless enjoyed by written permission, has, in the case of this longer period, given a special and restricted meaning to " precarious " if the claim is based on statutory prescription.[1] The difference, then, between the two periods is that an oral consent may defeat enjoyment for twenty years, but not enjoyment for forty years.

The circumstances when this may do so have been elucidated by the courts. It is clear that permission of any sort, whether written or oral is fatal to a claim based upon prescription at common law, however long the enjoyment may have lasted. The case of a claim based on the statutory periods, however, depends upon whether the permission is given during or at the beginning of the period of user. If permission is given from time to time *during* the twenty or forty years, the user becomes *precario* and this is fatal to the claim.[2] On the other hand, if the permission is given at the *beginning* of the period of user and extends over the whole period[3] (*i.e.* a permission given more than twenty or forty years ago and not since renewed), then, if it is written, it is fatal to a claim based upon either of the statutory periods, and, if oral, it is only fatal to a claim based upon the twenty year period.

What constitutes permission.

As GOFF, J., said in *Healy* v. *Hawkins* : [4]

" In principle it seems to me that once permission has been given, the user must remain permissive and not be capable of ripening into a right save where the permission is oral and the user has continued for 40 . . . years, unless and until, having been given for a limited period only, it expires or, being general, it is revoked, or there is a change in circumstances from which revocation may fairly be implied. . . .

Of course, when the user has continued for 40 . . . years a prior parol consent affords no answer, because it is excluded by the express terms of section 2 of the Prescription Act, but, even so, permission given during the period will defeat the claimant because it negatives user as of right. That is, in my

---

[1] *Gardner* v. *Hodgson's Kingston Brewery Co., Ltd.*, [1901] 2 Ch. 198, 214 ; for the facts see *supra*, p. 540. The annual payment of 15/– had been orally fixed some 60 years before the action. That was held, however, to be no evidence that an oral agreement granting the easement had in fact been made.

[2] *Gardner* v. *Hodgson's Kingston Brewery Co., Ltd.*, [1903] A. C. 229 ; M. & B. p. 536, 545.

[3] Whether it does so depends on the circumstances, *Gaved* v. *Martyn* (1865), 19 C. B. N. S. 732 ; *Healey* v. *Hawkins*, [1968] 1 W. L. R. 1967 ; [1968] 3 All E. R. 836 ; M. & B. p. 537. See (1968) 32 Conv. (N.S.) 40 (P. S. Langan).

[4] At p. 1973.

judgment, the explanation of the distinction drawn by the House of Lords in *Gardner* v. *Hodgson's Kingston Brewery* between antecedent and current parol consents."

Another difference is that certain disabilities of the servient owner, which obstruct a claim based on twenty years user, do not affect a claimant who has enjoyed an easement for forty years.

Savings for disabilities.

Disabilities. The Act provides that a right, even though enjoyed for the statutory periods, shall not ripen into a legal easement if the servient owner has been under certain disabilities. The time during which such person may have been an infant, idiot, *non compos mentis* or tenant for life, or during which an action has been pending and diligently prosecuted, is excluded by section 7 from the period of twenty years, though it begins to run again *at the point where it was interrupted* as soon as the disability is removed. Suppose, for instance, that

the claimant began to exercise the right in 1941, when the servient owner was the fee simple owner. In 1946 the latter became tenant for life under a settlement, but on his death in 1958 his successor came to the estate as tenant in fee simple. The claimant has exercised the right continuously from 1941 until 1975, when the action is brought. Five of these thirty-four years preceded the disability of a tenancy for life and seventeen came afterwards. The twelve years during which the disability lasted must of course be excluded, but the question is whether the claimant may add the periods of five and seventeen years together and allege enjoyment for the statutory period ; or whether he will be defeated by his inability to show enjoyment for the last twenty years.

He will not be defeated, for the rule is that a claimant must show twenty years' enjoyment either

(i) wholly before the disability if it still exists at the time of the action, or

(ii) partly before or partly after, if the disability be ended.[1]

Except for that of a tenancy for life, these disabilities do not affect a claim based on a forty years' enjoyment [2] ; that is to say, an uninterrupted user as of right for so long will confer an absolute title, no matter what the position of the servient owner may have been. Section 8, however, provides that where the servient tenement has been held during the whole or any part of the forty years for a term of life or for a term of years exceeding three years, the period during which such

---

[1] *Cf. Clayton* v. *Corby* (1843), 2 Q. B. 813.   [2] S. 7.

term lasted shall be excluded in the computation, provided that the claim is resisted by the reversioner within three years of the determination of the term.[1]

A curious feature of these rules is that the deduction of the time during which the servient tenement has been held by a tenant for a term exceeding three years only affects the computation of the longer period of forty years. Thus an easement of way may be acquired by twenty years user, though for the greater part of that time the servient tenement has been in the hands of a tenant.[2]

None of the disabilities applies to the easement of light.

(*b*) **The easement of light.** As the Act treats this particular easement quite differently from all others, it is necessary to cite the section dealing with it in full [3] :— **Light.**

> " When the access and use of light to and for any dwelling house, workshop or other building shall have been actually enjoyed therewith for the full period of twenty years without interruption, the right thereto shall be deemed absolute and indefeasible, any local usage or custom to the contrary notwithstanding, unless it shall appear that the same was enjoyed by some consent or agreement expressly made or given for that purpose by deed or writing."

We have seen that where a claim to an easement is made under the Act, it must clearly appear that the enjoyment has been *as of right*, and the reason is that the statutory words *claiming right thereto* have been construed as equivalent to the common law expression *as of right*. Since these words, however, are omitted from the section dealing with light, it follows that in the case of this particular easement a fresh mode of creation has been statutorily introduced.[4] All that the claimant need show, if he claims not at common law but under the Act, is actual user and absence of written agreement,[5] but the user must have continued for the period of twenty years next before the action in which the claim is brought into question. In other words, the right is not absolute and indefeasible after twenty years' user, but remains merely inchoate until it has been established in legal proceedings.[6] To defeat a claim to light, based upon

Its enjoyment need not be " as of right."

---

[1] The section is in words restricted to ways and watercourses, but there is reason to believe that the word " convenient " has slipped into the section instead of " easement," see *Wright* v. *Williams* (1836), 1 M. & W. 77.

[2] *Palk* v. *Shinner* (1852), 18 Q. B. 568.

[3] S. 3.

[4] *Per* BOWEN, L.J. ; *Scott* v. *Pape* (1886), 31 Ch. D. 554, at p. 571.

[5] *Truscott* v. *Merchant Taylors' Co.* (1856), 11 Exch. 855 ; *Frewen* v. *Phillips* (1861), 11 C. B. N. S. 149 ; *Colls* v. *Home and Colonial Stores Ltd.*, [1904] A. C. 179, at p. 205 ; *Kilgour* v. *Gaddes*, [1904] 1 K. B. 457.

[6] *Hyman* v. *Van Den Bergh*, [1907] 2 Ch. 516 ; affd., [1908] 1 Ch. 167 ; M. & B. p. 548. The reason is that the third section, cited above, must be read in connexion with the fourth section which requires the period to be *next before* some action.

user for the statutory period, the servient owner must produce an express agreement by deed or writing which shows that the user has been permissive during the last twenty years.[1] Thus, for instance, user of light for twenty years is not dismissed as precarious, merely because it has been enjoyed under an oral permission extending over the whole period.[2] Even the payment of rent by the dominant owner under an oral agreement will not prevent the acquisition of the easement,[3] unless some receipt or acknowledgment has been given which can be construed as a written agreement.

Interruption of enjoyment.

A right to light cannot, of course, be acquired if its enjoyment has been effectively interrupted within the meaning of the Prescription Act, *i.e.* if there has been some adverse act by the servient owner which has lasted for at least one year.[4] In this type of easement, the adverse act must in the nature of things take the form of some physical structure, such as a hoarding, so sited as to obstruct the flow of light to the dominant tenement. An alternative to this cumbrous and unsightly method, however, has been introduced by the Rights of Light Act 1959,[5] which enables the access of light to be notionally obstructed by the registration of a notice as a local land charge.

Notional interruption by registered notice.

A notice in the prescribed form must be submitted to the local authority by the servient owner,[6] and it must state that its registration is intended to represent the obstruction to the access of light that would be caused by an opaque structure of certain specified dimensions, whether of unlimited height or not, erected upon the servient tenement.[7] The notice must also be accompanied by a certificate from the Lands Tribunal certifying either that adequate notice of the proposed registration has been given to all persons likely to be affected, or that the case is one of exceptional urgency and that therefore registration for a limited time is essential.[8] The notice, if not cancelled, expires one year after registration or, where accompanied by a certificate of exceptional urgency, at the end of the period specified in the certificate.[9]

---

[1] *Foster* v. *Lyons*, [1927] 1 Ch. 219; *Willoughby* v. *Eckstein*, [1937] Ch. 167, [1937] 1 All E. R. 257.   [2] *Mallam* v. *Rose*, [1915] 2 Ch. 222.
[3] *Plasterers' Co.* v. *Parish Clerks' Co.* (1851), 6 Exch. 630.
[4] *Supra*, p. 546.
[5] As amended by Local Land Charges Act 1975, s. 17, Sched. 1.   The Act embodies the recommendations of the Harman Committee on Rights of Light, 1958 (Cmnd. 473). See *Hawker* v. *Tomalin* (1969), 20 P. & C. R. 550, 551, *per* HARMAN, J.
[6] *I.e.* the owner of a legal fee simple or of a term of years absolute of which at least seven years remain unexpired, or the mortgagee in possession of such a fee or term; Rights of Light Act 1959, s. 7 (1).
[7] Rights of Light Act 1959, s. 2 (1), (2). Lands Tribunal Rules 1975 (S.I. 1975 No. 299); Local Land Charges Rules 1966 (S.I. 1966 No. 579) as amended. See *infra*, p. 748.
[8] *Ibid.*, s. 2 (3). 402 definite and 39 temporary certificates were issued between 1965 and 1975. See (1976) 126 N. L. J. 143 (W. A. Greene).
[9] *Ibid.*, s. 3 (2).

For the purpose of determining whether a right to light has been acquired either at common law or under the Prescription Act, the access of light to the dominant tenement is to be treated as obstructed by a registered notice to the same extent and with the like consequences as if the structure specified in the application for registration had in fact been erected[1]; and any right of action that the dominant owner would have had in that event is available by reason of the notice.[2]   In order to obviate the difficulties that may arise where the right is interrupted after it has been enjoyed for nineteen years and a fraction,[3] the Act provides in effect that the enjoyment by the dominant owner of the flow of light shall be notionally prolonged for one year if he sues for cancellation of the notice.[4]

Owing to the wording of the Prescription Act 1832 the right to light is an exception to the rule that an easement can be prescribed for only in respect of a fee simple.[5]   It is peculiar in two respects :—

> First, the fee simple estate of a landlord is bound by an easement of light acquired over the land while in the occupation of a tenant.[6]
>
> A., the fee simple owner of Blackacre, leases it to a tenant for 25 years.   During the tenancy, X., the owner of an adjoining house, builds a window overlooking Blackacre and enjoys access of light to it for twenty years.   A right to light is thereby acquired that is enforceable against A., his tenant and all successors in title of Blackacre.
>
> Secondly, if two tenements are held by different lessees under a common landlord, and one lessee enjoys the use of light over the other tenement for the necessary period, he and his successors acquire an indefeasible right to the light not only against the other tenant, but also against the common landlord and all succeeding owners of the servient tenement.[7]

Common law not displaced by the Prescription Act 1832.   The Act is only supplementary to the common law—it provides an additional method of claiming easements, but leaves the other two methods untouched.   If, for instance, the claimant is unable to show enjoyment for the statutory period of the last twenty years, as will happen if there has been unity of possession for part of that period, he may either prescribe at common law or invoke the doctrine of a lost grant.[8]   Normally, he will rely on the Act.   Failing this, he will base his case on prescription at

Effect of registration

Light not limited to prescription in respect of fee simple.

Prescription Act 1832 only supplements the common law.

---

[1] Rights of Light Act 1959, s. 2 (1).   [2] *Ibid.*, s. 3 (3).
[3] *Supra*, pp. 547–8.
[4] Rights of Light Act 1959, s. 1 (1) (2).   [5] *Supra*, p. 541.
[6] *Simper* v. *Foley* (1862), 2 John. & H. 555.
[7] *Morgan* v. *Fear*, [1907] A. C. 425 ; M. & B. p 571 ; *Willoughby* v. *Eckstein*, [1937] Ch. 67, at p. 170.
[8] See *Hulbert* v. *Dale*, [1909] 2 Ch. 570, argument of counsel at p. 573.

common law ; and failing that, he will plead a lost modern grant, but only if driven to it, for, as Lord LINDLEY said,

" that doctrine only applies where the enjoyment cannot be otherwise reasonably accounted for."[1]

Although a plaintiff can succeed only on one ground, it may be advisable to plead alternative claims by statute, common law prescription and lost modern grant.[2]

(E) EXTENT OF EASEMENTS

In ascertaining the nature and extent of an easement, the principles to be applied vary with the method of its creation. As WILLES, J., said in *Williams* v. *James* [3]

" The distinction between a grant and prescription is obvious. In the case of proving a right by prescription the user of the right is the only evidence. In the case of a grant the language of the instrument can be referred to, and it is of course for the court to construe that language ; and in the absence of any clear indication of the intention of the parties, the maxim that a grant must be construed most strongly against the grantor must be applied. "

Extent of
easement
created by
(i) Express
grant.

It follows that, if the easement is created by express grant, the question is one of construing the terms of the grant, and, in cases of difficulty, the physical circumstances of the *locus in quo* must be considered. Thus, in determining whether the grant or reservation of " a right of way " is a right exercisable on foot only or with vehicles and, if so, what kind of vehicles, the condition of the way itself and the nature of the dominant tenement may be taken into account.[4] Furthermore, an unrestricted right of way is not confined to the use of the dominant tenement contemplated by the parties at the time of the grant. Thus, where an unrestricted right of way was granted as appurtenant to a house, and the house was subsequently converted into an hotel, its owner became entitled to a right of way for the general purposes of the hotel.[5]

---

[1] *Gardner* v. *Hodgson's Kingston Brewery Co., Ltd.*, [1903] A. C. 229, 240.
[2] See Bullen and Leake and Jacob, *Precedents of Pleadings* (12th Edn.), p. 1049.   The three alternative claims were pleaded together in *Bailey* v. *Stephens* (1862), 12 C. B. N. S., 91 ; *Norfolk* v. *Arbuthnot* (1880), 5 C. P. D. 590 ; *Wheaton* v. *Maple*, [1893] 3 Ch. 48 ; *Roberts* v. *James* (1903), 89 L. T. 282.   See too *Pugh* v. *Savage*, [1970] 2 Q. B. 373 ; [1970] 2 All E. R. 353.
[3] (1867), L. R. 2 C. P. 577, at p. 581.
[4] *Cannon* v. *Villars* (1878), 8 Ch. D. 415, at p. 420 ; *St. Edmundsbury and Ipswich Diocesan Board of Finance* v. *Clark* (*No. 2*), [1975] 1 W. L. R. 468 ; [1975] 1 All E. R. 772 ; M. & B. p. 558.
[5] *White* v. *Grand Hotel Eastbourne, Ltd.*, [1913] 1 Ch. 113 ; *Kain* v. *Norfolk*, [1949] Ch. 163 ; [1949] 1 All E. R. 176 ; *Bulstrode* v. *Lambert*, [1953] 1 W. L. R. 1064 ; [1953] 2 All E. R. 728 ; *Keefe* v. *Amor*, [1965] 1 Q. B. 334 ; [1964] 2 All E. R. 517 ; M. & B. p. 554 ; *McIlwraith* v. *Grady*, [1968] 1 Q. B. 468 ; [1967] 3 All E. R. 625 ; *Jelbert* v. *Davis* [1968] 1 W. L. R. 589 ; [1968] 1 All E. R. 1182 ; M. & B. p. 557 ; (1968) 112 Sol. Jo. 172 (S. M. Cretney) ; *Bracewell* v. *Appleby*, [1975] Ch. 408 ; [1975] 1 All E. R. 993.

If the easement is created by implied grant, we have already seen that where it is implied in favour of the grantor, an easement of necessity is strictly limited to the circumstances of the necessity prevailing at the time of the grant.[1]   In the case of an easement implied in favour of the grantee, there seems to be little authority on the question of its extent.[2]

(ii) Implied grant.

The extent of a prescriptive easement is commensurate with its user.   Once the purposes for which it has been used during the period of its acquisition have been determined by evidence, its use for purposes radically different in character is not permissible. In other words, the burden upon the servient tenement must not be increased by reason of a radical change in the character of the dominant tenement.[3]   For example, a right of way that has been used to carry agricultural produce to a farm cannot lawfully be used to meet the requirements of a factory into which the farm is later converted.[4]   But if the character or nature of the user remains constant, there is no objection to an increase in its intensity.[5]   A right of way appurtenant to a golf club, for instance, is not misused merely because the membership of the club has greatly increased.[6]

(iii) Prescription.

(F) EXTINGUISHMENT OF EASEMENTS

An easement may be extinguished by release or as the result of unity of seisin.

(1) **Release**.   An extinguishment may be effected by a release, either express or implied.

Express release.

The dominant owner is free to execute a deed of release relieving the servient tenement from the burden of any easement to which it is subject.   At common law a deed is necessary,[7] but if the servient owner, in reliance on an agreement to release, has prejudiced his position to such an extent that it would be inequitable and oppressive to treat the easement as still in being, equity will disregard the absence of formalities and will hold the dominant

---

[1] *Supra*, p. 534.

[2] *Milner's Safe Co., Ltd.* v. *Great Northern and City Rail Co.*, [1907] 1 Ch. 208.

[3] *Wimbledon and Putney Common Conservators* v. *Dixon* (1875), 1 Ch. D. 362.

[4] *Williams* v. *James* (1867), L. R. 2 C. P. 577, at p. 582, *per* WILLES, J.

[5] *British Railways Board* v. *Glass*, [1965] Ch. 538 ; [1964] 3 All E. R. 418 ; M. & B. p. 560 (LORD DENNING, M.R., dissenting).   (1965), 87 *L. Q. R.* 17 (R. E. M.) ; *Woodhouse & Co., Ltd.* v. *Kirkland, Ltd.*, [1970] 1 W. L. R. 1185 ; [1970] 2 All E. R. 560 (considerable increase in number of customers using right of way held to be " mere increase in user and not a user of a different kind or for a different purpose ") ; *Giles* v. *County Building Constructors (Hertford) Ltd.* (1971), 22 P. & C. R. 978 (erection of seven modern dwelling units in place of two houses held to be " evolution rather than mutation ").

[6] *Ibid.*, at p. 568, *per* DAVIES, L.J.

[7] Co. Litt., 264b.

owner to his bargain.[1]   If, for instance, a person who is entitled to an easement of light orally agrees to an alteration in the servient tenement which must necessarily obstruct the flow of light to the window, he cannot, after expense has been incurred in making the alteration, bring an action in respect of the resulting obstruction.

Implied release.

But a more important and at the same time more difficult point is whether in any given case there has been an implied release or abandonment of the easement by the dominant owner.

The general principle is that whether he intended to abandon his right depends upon the proper inference to be drawn from the circumstances.[2]

Non-user.

No one circumstance necessarily implies an abandonment, and thus, it has been laid down again and again that mere non-user is not decisive of the question.[3]   If the non-user is explicable only on the assumption that the dominant owner intended to give up his right, it will amount to an abandonment, but not if there are other circumstances which go to show that he regarded the right as still alive.   In other words, a cessation may show either an abandonment or a mere abeyance of an easement according to the particular circumstances of each case.

The principle was re-stated by POLLOCK, M.R. in *Swan* v. *Sinclair* :

" Non-user is not by itself conclusive evidence that a private right of easement is abandoned.   The non-user must be considered with, and may be explained by, the surrounding circumstances.   If those circumstances clearly indicate an intention of not resuming the user then a presumption of a release of the easement will, in general, be implied and the easement will be lost." [4]

Thus in the leading case of *Moore* v. *Rawson,*[5]

a plaintiff, who had some ancient windows, pulled down the wall in which they were situated and rebuilt it as a stable with no windows. Some fourteen years later the defendant erected on his adjoining land a building which would have obstructed the flow of light to the windows had they still been there.   After another three years the plaintiff made a window in the stable in the exact spot where one of the old windows had been, and then proceeded to bring an action against the defendant for obstruction of light.

It was held that he could not succeed, because, in erecting a building entirely different from the old one, he had shown an intention to abandon the enjoyment of his former right.

---

[1] *Davies* v. *Marshall* (1861), 10 C. B. (N. S.) 697 ; *Waterlow* v. *Bacon* (1866), L. R. 2 Ch. 514.

[2] *Cook* v. *Bath Corpn.* (1868), L. R. 6 Eq. 177.

[3] *R.* v. *Chorley* (1848), 12 Q. B. 515 ; *Ward* v. *Ward* (1852), 7 Exch. 838; *Crossley & Sons, Ltd.* v. *Lightowler* (1867), 2 Ch. App. 478.

[4] *Swan* v. *Sinclair*, [1924] 1 Ch. 254, 266 ; affd., [1925] A. C. 227 ; see also *Tehidy Minerals, Ltd.* v. *Norman* [1971] 2 Q. B. 528, at p. 553 ; [1971] 2 All E. R. 475 ; M. & B. p. 573.

[5] *Moore* v. *Rawson* (1824), 3 B. & C. 332 ; M. & B. p. 573.

However, as was stated by HOLROYD, J.,

> " If he had done some act to shew that he intended to build another in its place, then the new house, when built, would in effect have been a continuation of the old house, and the rights attached to the old house would have continued. If a man has a right of common attached to his mill, or a right of turbary attached to his house, if he pulls down the mill or the house, the right of common or of turbary will *prima facie* cease. If he shows an intention to build another mill or another house, his right continues."

Furthermore, the easement may be extinguished where the dominant tenement is so altered as to throw a substantially increased burden on the servient tenement to the prejudice of its owner.[1]

The same principle can be seen at work in the case of rights of way. So : **Non-user of way.**

> where the exercise of a right of way had been discontinued for many years because the dominant owner had a more convenient route over his own land, it was held that the non-user was adequately explained and did not constitute an abandonment.[2]

But any non-user of a right of way caused by something which is adverse to the enjoyment of the right will be regarded as an abandonment.[2] Thus in *Swan* v. *Sinclair*[3] :—

> Certain houses were put up for sale in lots in 1871, one of the conditions being that a strip of land running at the back of the houses should be formed into a roadway, and that the purchaser of each lot should have a right of way along the road when made. At the time when the action was brought in 1923 the road had not been constructed, fences lay across its proposed site between each pair of lots, and in 1883 the then owner of lot 1 nearest the exit of the proposed road had levelled up the site, and by so doing had caused a sheer drop of 6 feet to occur between that lot and lot 2. The plaintiff was now desirous of building a garage on lot 2, and the question arose whether he was still entitled to a right of way over the strip of land at the back of lot 1.
>
> The majority of the court dismissed his claim on the ground that, though as a rule mere non-user is insufficient to extinguish a right of way, yet in this case the continued existence of the dividing fences and the raising the level of lot 1 were circumstances adverse to a right of enjoyment, sufficient to show an intention on the part of the various owners to abandon the project.

(2) **Unity of seisin.** Easements are also extinguished by unity of seisin, that is to say, if the fee simple of both the dominant and the servient tenements become united in the same owner, all easements properly so called come to an end, for the owner can do **Unity of seisin.**

---

[1] *Ankerson* v. *Connelly*, [1906] 2 Ch. 544 ; affd., [1907] 1 Ch. 678 (easement of light) ; *Ray* v. *Fairway Motors (Barnstaple) Ltd.* (1969), 20 P. & C. R. 261 (easement of support) ; *Lloyds Bank Ltd.* v. *Dalton*, [1942] Ch. 466, at pp. 471–2, *per* BENNETT, J. ; [1942] 2 All E. R. 352 ; *Gale on Easements* (14th Edn.), pp. 320 *et seq.*

[2] *Ward* v. *Ward* (1852), 7 Exch. 838.

[3] [1924] 1 Ch. 254 ; affd., [1925] A. C. 227.

what he likes with his own land, and any right that formerly ranked as an easement because it was exercisable over another's land is now merely one of the ordinary incidents of his ownership.[1] An easement which has been destroyed by this union of title in one hand may, however, revive under the doctrine of implied grant if the property is again severed into its original parts.[2] A complete extinguishment occurs when both the tenements become united in one person for an estate in fee simple, but if he acquires only a particular estate in one of them, as for instance a life interest or a term of years, the easement is merely suspended and will revive again if upon the determination of his particular estate the tenements are once more in different hands.[3]

Unity of seisin without unity of possession does not extinguish an easement of light, as, for example, where the owner of the servient tenement acquires the fee simple in the dominant tenement while the latter is in the possession of a tenant for years.[4] It is doubtful, however, whether this is true in the case of easements other than light.[5]

SECTION III.   PROFITS À PRENDRE

SUMMARY

(A) GENERAL NATURE OF *PROFITS À PRENDRE*

Profits distinguished from easements.

Introductory Note. *Profits à prendre* differ from easements in the fact that they import the taking of some thing which is capable of ownership from the servient tenement. Such things are numerous and diverse, as for instance, the soil itself, the grass growing on or the minerals lying below the soil, animals such as fish and fowl,[6] sand from the seashore, ice from a canal, heather, turf, acorns and so on.

---

[1] Co. Litt., 313a.   *Lord Dynevor* v. *Tennant* (1888), 13 App. Cas 279.
[2] *Gale on Easements* (14th Edn.), p. 311 ; *supra*, p. 532.
[3] *Thomas* v. *Thomas* (1835), 2 Cr. M. & R. 34.
[4] *Richardson* v. *Graham*, [1908] 1 K. B. 39 ; M. & B. p. 575.
[5] In *Buchby* v. *Coles* (1814), 5 Taunt. 311, MACDONALD, C. B., was of opinion that a right of way was not extinguished by mere unity of seisin (at p. 315), but the Court of Common Pleas expressed a " decided opinion " to the opposite effect (pp. 315–6) and counsel abandoned the argument.
[6] *Peech* v. *Best*, [1931] 1 K. B. 1, at p. 9.

But in addition to this fundamental distinction there are the following important differences between easements and profits :

(*a*) Unlike an easement,[1] a profit may be granted in gross to be held independently of the ownership of land.[2] From early times it was held that an express grant by deed to a man, his heirs and assigns of a perpetual right to a profit was a valid grant,[3] and as the possibility of a grant is the basis of all the methods whereby profits as well as easements may be acquired, it was later held that a profit in gross might be prescribed for at common law.[4] Such profits in gross are not common, but once established they may be sold or leased to a third party,[5] and they will pass under a will or intestacy.

(*b*) Profits as well as easements may be prescribed for under the Prescription Act 1832, but the statutory periods of enjoyment are fixed at 30 and 60 years respectively instead of 20 and 40.[6]

(*c*) Inasmuch as a profit imports the privilege of carrying away something from the servient tenement, the dominant owner enjoys such possessory rights as will enable him to maintain trespass or nuisance at common law for an infringement of his right, but the owner of an easement is restricted to the remedies of abatement or an action of nuisance.[7]

(*d*) A right in the nature of an easement can be acquired by an indefinite and fluctuating class of persons such as the inhabitants of a village, while a *profit à prendre* cannot be directly claimed by such persons, for otherwise the result would be to exhaust the servient tenement,[8] though in exceptional cases it can be indirectly acquired, as we shall see later.[9]

(*e*) A profit may be *appendant* to land, that is annexed to the land by operation of law, but an easement may not. If before the passing of the Statute *Quia Emptores* in 1289 the lord of a manor granted *arable* land to be held of him by a freehold tenant, the common law automatically appended to the grant a right in the tenant to pasture upon the waste lands of the

---

[1] *Supra*, p. 517.

[2] *Chesterfield* v. *Harris*, [1908] 2 Ch. 397, *per* BUCKLEY, L.J., at p. 421.

[3] 1495, Y. B. 11 Hen., fol. 8*a*, cited by PARKE, B., *Wickham* v. *Hawker* (1840), 7 M. & W. 63, at p. 79.

[4] *Welcome* v. *Upton* (1840), 6 M. & W. 536; *Johnson* v. *Barnes* (1872), L. R. 7 C. P. 592; 8 C. P. 527; *Shuttleworth* v. *Le Fleming* (1865), 19 C. B. N S.. 687; *Goodman* v. *Saltash Corpn.* (1882), L. R. 7 App. Cas. 633, at p. 658.

[5] *Goodman* v. *Saltash Corpn.*, *supra*.

[6] Prescription Act 1832, s. 1. The period of 20 years enjoyment is sufficient for prescription under lost modern grant. *Tehidy Minerals, Ltd.* v. *Norman*, [1971] 2 Q. B. 528, 545.

[7] *Fitzgerald* v. *Firbank*, [1897] 2 Ch. 96; *Peech* v. *Best*, *supra*; *Nicholls* v. *Ely Beet Sugar Factory, Ltd*, [1936] 1 Ch. 343.

[8] *Infra*, pp. 574.   [9] *Infra*, pp. 575–7.

manor such cattle as were necessary to plough and manure the arable land.[1]

This right of pasture was held to be appendant, and necessarily appendant, to a grant of arable land within a manor, for the grantee obviously could not till the arable land without beasts of plough, and he would have no means of sustaining the animals unless he could pasture them on the manorial waste.[2] This right, therefore, arose of common right upon the grant of arable land within a manor and it must be distinguished from profits or easements appurtenant to land, which are opposed to common right and must be deliberately acquired by an actual or presumed grant.[3] Profits appendant are still possible, but they must have come into existence before 1289,[4] for the effect of *Quia Emptores* is that all sales by the lord of a manor since that date take the land out of the manor altogether, so that the grantee does not hold of the manor in the waste of which he claims a right.

Similarities between easements and profits.

Apart from the differences indicated, the nature of a profit is in general similar to that of an easement. Thus, for instance, it is necessary that a profit which is *appurtenant* to land should be connected with the dominant tenement in the sense of increasing its beneficial enjoyment.[5] The law does not recognize an unlimited profit appurtenant, as for instance a right to cut turf[6] or to catch salmon[7] for sale, or to dig clay wherever it is required for making bricks.[8] A profit appurtenant must be limited, and the limit is arrived at by estimating the needs of the dominant tenement.[9]

Further, a profit, like an easement is capable of subsisting as a legal interest; it may also be equitable[10] and, if so, is registrable as a Class D (iii) land charge under the Land Charges Act 1972.[11]

(B) CLASSES OF *PROFITS À PRENDRE*

Two classes of profits.

Profits fall into two classes, namely those enjoyed by their owner to the exclusion of everybody else, and those enjoyed by

---

[1] Co. Litt. 122*a*; Blackstone, vol. ii. p. 33. *Dunraven* v. *Llewellyn* (1850), 15 Q. B. 791, 810; Holdsworth, *History of English Law*, vol. iii. pp. 147 *et seq.*; Hall, *Law of Profits à Prendre and Rights of Common*, p. 224.

[2] Blackstone, vol. ii. p. 33.

[3] *Tyrringham's Case* (1584), 4 Co. Rep. 36*b*; *Warrick* v. *Queen's College, Oxford* (1871), L. R. 6 Ch. App. 716.

[4] See *Davies* v. *Davies*, [1975] Q. B. 172; [1974] 3 All E. R. 817.

[5] *Clayton* v. *Corby* (1843), 5 Q. B. 415, 419; *Bailey* v. *Stephens* (1862), 12 C. B. (N. S.) 91; *cf. supra*, pp. 517–9.

[6] *Valentine* v. *Penny* (1604), Noy. 145.

[7] *Chesterfield* v. *Harris*, [1908] 2 Ch. 397; [1911] A. C. 623.

[8] *Clayton* v. *Corby, supra*.

[9] See *infra*, pp. 561–3, in reference to common of pasture.

[10] *Mason* v. *Clarke*, [1955] A. C. 778; [1955] 1 All E. R. 914; M. & B. p. 56; *infra*, p. 566; see *Lowe* v. *J. W. Ashmore, Ltd.*, [1971] Ch. 545, esp. at pp. 557–8.

[11] S. 2 (5). *Supra* pp. 526–7, which apply *mutatis mutandis* to profits.

him in common with other persons including the owner of the servient tenement.

The first are called " several " *profits à prendre*, and the latter *profits à prendre* in "common," or rights of common, or more often simply *commons*.

> "Common may be said to exist where two or more take, in common with each other, from the soil of a third person a part of the natural produce."[1]

Distinction between profits and commons.

Thus, while every common is a *profit à prendre*, it does not follow that all *profits à prendre* are commons.

Profits à prendre are rights which have existed from a very early date in the history of this country, and which in their origin[2] were exercised by numbers of persons in common with each other. Moreover, that is the form in which they are most frequently found nowadays. It may of course happen that a man possesses the right to take something off the land of another without affecting the right of the owner to take similar things for his own use ; or he may be entitled to the exclusive right of taking something, as often occurs in the case of pasturage rights over the Sussex Downs ; but the type of profit that a practising lawyer will most likely have to consider is a right of common properly so called.

Classification of rights of common. Rights of common are classified into

  (i) rights appendant,
  (ii) rights appurtenant,
  (iii) rights in gross, and
  (iv) rights *pur cause de vicinage*. A common *pur cause de vicinage*, which is the only one we have not explained, is restricted to the right of pasturage, and arises where adjacent commons are open and unfenced and there is a custom for the cattle to inter-common, that is, for the cattle rightfully put upon the common of one manor to stray and feed upon the common of the adjoining manor without being treated as trespassers.[3]

Rights of common may also be classified according to their subject-matter into four kinds, namely, common of pasture, of piscary, of turbary and of estovers.[4]

(1) Common of pasture. This, the most usual common, arises when the owner of cattle is, in common with others, entitled to put his cattle to feed on the land of another.[5]

Common of pasture.

---

[1] *Woolrych on Commons*, p. 13.
[2] For the history of profits, see the 11th Edn. of this book, pp. 547–8.
[3] Co. Litt. 122*a* ; *Tyrringham's Case* (1584), 4 Co. Rep. 37.
[4] Blackstone, vol. ii. p. 32 ; Co. Litt. 122*a*.
[5] *Tyrringham's Case* (1584), 4 Co. Rep. 36*b*, 37.

Limited as
to kind of
animals.

In the case of a common *appendant* the right is limited to " commonable cattle," that is, horses and oxen to plough the land and cows and sheep to manure it.[1] A common *appurtenant* is not limited in this way, but depends upon the extent of the enjoyment proved or upon the terms of the grant if there is one, and so a right may well be established to pasture such animals as hogs, goats and geese.[2] Common in gross may also be enjoyed in respect of any animal. Commons of pasture appendant and appurtenant are also restricted in another manner, as we have already had occasion to notice, for there is no right to pasture an unlimited number of commonable cattle. The rule at common law is that the right is exercisable only in respect of cattle *levant et couchant* on the land, *i.e.* the number that the dominant tenement is capable of supporting through the winter.[3] Again a right of pasturage in gross cannot be prescribed for unless it is restricted in the same manner.[4]

Limited as
to number.

This doctrine of *levancy et couchancy* has, however, now been abolished by the Commons Registration Act 1965,[5] which requires all rights of grazing to be registered, but limits registration to a defined number of animals.[6] In the case of a common in gross there is no objection in principle to the existence of pasture without stint, or, in other words, to a right to put an unlimited number of cattle on the servient tenement, because, as it is not appurtenant to anything, there is no dominant tenement with reference to the needs of which the content of the right must be proportioned. Thus, as was said by Buckley, L.J.,[7]

Common
without
stint.

> " it may well be that there can exist in law a right in gross to enter and take without limitation—without stint—the profits or proceeds of another's land commercially for the purposes of sale."

Such an unstinted right might no doubt be granted expressly by deed, but though there is no objection to it in principle, the case of *Mellor* v. *Spateman*[8] clearly decided that it could not be prescribed for.

> " And the court did not dislike any part of the plea, but only it was not said in the plea '*levant et couchant* within the town.'

---

[1] *Tyrringham's Case* (1584), 4 Co. Rep. 37. This pasture may be claimed for certain animals only, *e.g.* sheep (when it is called " sheep walk "), *Robinson* v. *Duleep Singh* (1879), L. R. 11 Ch. D. 798 ; or swine (called common of " pannage ") *Chilton* v. *Corpn. of London* (1878), L. R. 7 Ch. D. 562.
[2] *Bennett* v. *Reeve* (1740), Willes 246 ; *Tyrringham's Case, supra.*
[3] *Robertson* v. *Hartopp* (1889), 43 Ch. D. 484, 517. Holdsworth, *History of English Law*, vol. vii. p. 320 and authorities there cited.
[4] *Mellor* v. *Spateman* (1669), 1 Saund 339.
[5] *Infra*, p. 564.   [6] S. 15.
[7] *Lord Chesterfield* v. *Harris*, [1908] 2 Ch. 397, at p. 421.
[8] (1669), 1 Wms Saund. 339

And KELYNGE, C.J., said positively that there cannot be any common in gross without number."[1]

The old expression *common sans nombre* which is met with in earlier cases is not inconsistent with this principle, for it merely meant that the right was for beasts *levant et couchant*, the point being in such a case that the number was not positively fixed at a definite figure.

(2) **Common of piscary.** A stranger may acquire a right to catch fish in inland waters, such as lakes, ponds and non-navigable rivers, belonging to private owners. This right takes two forms :

Common of piscary.

    (i) A " several fishery " or a " free fishery," which is not a right of common, is a right to take fish *in alieno solo* and to exclude the owner of the water from the right to take fish himself [2] ; while

Several fishery.

    (ii) A " common of fishery " is a liberty of fishing in another man's water in common with other persons.[3]

Common of fishery.

" Common of piscary being given for the sustenance of the tenant's family " [4] must, if appurtenant to a house, be limited to the needs of that house, and the fish cannot be caught for sale.[5] It should be noted that though the fishery in arms of the sea and in tidal rivers is open to all subjects of the realm,[6] yet a prescriptive right to a several fishery or a common of fishery therein may be established.[7] The presumption, however, is in favour of the public.

(3) **Common of turbary.** Common of turbary is the right of cutting turf or peat in another man's land to be expended as fuel in the house of the commoner.[8] For the last 400 years this right has always been treated as a common appurtenant, with the qualification that it must be appurtenant to an ancient house or to a new house erected in continuance of the ancient one.[9] It cannot be appurtenant to land,[10] for, as we have seen, a thing which is appurtenant must agree in nature and quality with the thing to which it is attached, and the idea of using fuel on land apart from a house is absurd.

Turbary.

---

[1] At p. 346.
[2] *Foster* v. *Wright* (1878), L. R. 4 C. P. D. 438, at p. 449.
[3] Blackstone, vol. ii. p. 34 ; *Seymour* v. *Courtenay* (1771), 5 Burr. 2817 ; MANSFIELD, C.J.
[4] Blackstone, vol. ii. p. 35.
[5] *Chesterfield* v. *Harris*, [1908] 2 Ch. 397.
[6] *Fitzwalter's Case* (1674), 1 Mod. 105 ; *Carter* v. *Murcot* (1768), 4 Burr. 2162, at p. 2164.
[7] *Carter* v. *Murcot, supra.*
[8] Blackstone, vol. ii. p. 34.
[9] *A.-G.* v. *Reynolds*, [1911] 2 K. B. 888 ; *Warrick* v. *Queen's College, Oxford* (1871), L. R. 6 Ch. App. 716, 730.
[10] *Tyrringham's Case* (1584), 5 Co. Rep. 37.

Estovers.

(4) Common of estovers. BLACKSTONE has said :—

" Common of estovers or *estouviers*; that is, necessaries (from *estoffer*, to furnish), is a liberty of taking necessary wood, for the use or furniture of a house or farm, from off another's estate. The Saxon word, *bote*, is used by us as synonymous to the French *estovers*; and therefore house-bote is a sufficient allowance of wood to repair or to burn in the house (which latter is sometimes called fire-bote); plough-bote and cart-bote are wood to be employed in making and repairing instruments of husbandry; and hay-bote, or hedge-bote, is wood for repairing hays, hedges or fences."[1]

This right, which very closely resembles common of turbary, is generally appurtenant to a house,[2] though of course it may be attached to land for the purpose of repairing fences. When it is appurtenant to a house, the wood taken must be expended on that house, and cannot be used for the reparation of new buildings which may have been erected, or as fuel in new fireplaces which may have been built in the original house.[3] But when the old dominant house is demolished and replaced by another one, the right continues to exist according to its original extent :—

" If an ancient cottage which had common be fallen down, and another cottage be erected in the place where the old cottage stood; this is no new cottage, but it may claim common as an ancient cottage by prescription."[4]

A right similar to the common of estovers and also called estovers is given at common law to a tenant for life or years enabling him to cut timber which would otherwise be waste.[5] The only difference between the common law right and that which we have just considered is that the former arises in the tenant by virtue of the possession of the land rented and is exercisable over that land, while the latter is a profit to be taken out of somebody else's land.

Commons Registration Act 1965.

Registration of Commons. The Commons Registration Act 1965[6] required the registration with county and county borough councils of common land,[7] in England and Wales of

---

[1] Blackstone, vol. ii. p. 35.
[2] *A.-G.* v. *Reynolds*, [1911] 2 K. B. 888.
[3] *Luttrel's Case* (1602), 4 Co. Rep. 86a.
[4] *Bryers* v. *Lake*, cited Hall, *Law of Profits à Prendre and Rights of Common*, p. 322.
[5] *Supra*, p. 411.
[6] See generally Harris and Ryan, *Common Land*; Campbell, *Law of Commons* (2nd Edn. 1973); Report of Royal Commission on Common Land, 1955–1958 (Cmnd. 462); (1972) 122 N. L. J. 1127 (V. Chapman). Decisions of the Commons Commissioners are reported in Current Law. See (1973) 117 Sol. Jo. 537; (1974) 118 Sol. Jo. 434 (I. Campbell). There will be further legislation about the management and improvement of registered common land as well as about its user by the public.
[7] The Act also applies to town and village greens. Ss. 1 (1), 22 (1). *New Windsor Corporation* v. *Mellor* [1975] Ch. 380; [1975] 3 All E. R. 44.

persons claiming to be or found to be its owners, and of claims to rights of common over such land before August 1970.[1]

The expression '' rights of common '' includes :—[2]

cattlegates or beastgates[3] and rights of sole or several vesture or herbage[4] or of sole or several pasture, but does not include rights held for a term of years or from year to year.[5]

Registration under the Act is provisional only ;[6] objections may be made to a Commons Commissioner,[7] with an appeal to the High Court on a point of law.[8] Registration then becomes final, if no objection has been lodged, or, if there is an objection, after the Commissioner or the Court have confirmed the registration.[9] Final registration is conclusive evidence of the matters registered as at the date of registration.[10]

After July 1970, no land capable of being registered under the Act is to be deemed to be common land unless it is so registered, and no rights of common shall be exercisable over any such land unless they are either registered under the Act or have been previously registered under the Land Registration Act 1925.[11] Thus not only are unregistered rights existing before that date extinguished, but there can be no future acquisition of rights over registered commons.[12] New commons may, however, arise, for example, by grant or by prescription, and be registered.[13] In this case there is no time limit as regards application for registration, nor does the land cease to be common land nor do the rights cease to be exercisable, if not registered.

(C) ACQUISITION OF *PROFITS À PRENDRE*.

It will not be necessary to consider this topic at any length for the methods by which easements may be acquired are applicable, with very few exceptions, to the acquisition of *profits à*

---

[1] Commons Registration Act 1965, ss. 1–4. S. I. 1970, No. 383. The Act does not apply to the New Forest, Epping Forest or to any land exempted by an order of the Secretary of State. S. 11.

[2] *Ibid.*, s. 22 (1).

[3] Cattlegate or beastgate, sometimes called *stinted pasture*, is a right to pasture a fixed number of beasts on the land of another, generally for a part of the year only. See, *e.g. Rigg* v. *Earl Lonsdale* (1857), 1 H. & N. 923.

[4] The right of sole vesture, *vestura terras*, is not merely to graze cattle, but to take away the product of the land, such as grass, corn, underwood, turf, peat, and so forth.

[5] Commons Registration Act 1965, s. 22 (1).

[6] *Ibid.*, s. 4 (5).

[7] Objections had to be lodged before August 1972, S. I. 1968, No. 989 ; S. I. 1970, No. 384.

[8] Commons Registration Act 1965, s. 18. See *Wilkes* v. *Gee* [1973] 1 W. L. R. 742 ; [1973] 2 All E. R. 1214.

[9] *Ibid.*, ss. 6, 7.

[10] *Ibid.*, s. 10.

[11] *Ibid.*, s. 1 (2). S. I. 1970, No. 383. *Central Electricity Generating Board* v. *Clwyd C.C.* ; [1976] All E. R.

[12] *Ibid.*, s. 13 (b). S. I. 1969, No. 1843, r. 3 (2).

[13] S. I. 1969, No. 1843, r. 3 (1), and note 5 on p. 11.

prendre, whether rights of common or not.   At the outset we can
dismiss profits appendant because they have been impossible of
acquisition since *Quia Emptores* in 1289, and a claimant will be
required to prove that he holds arable land which was granted by
the lord of a manor to a freehold tenant before that date.[1]

The six possible methods of acquiring easements are set out
on page 528.   We will take each one of these and show to what
extent it applies to profits :—

Statute.
(1) Statute. Profits may be acquired by statute, as when
Inclosure Acts confer new rights upon manorial lords by
way of compensation for the interest lost by them in the soil
itself.

Deed of
grant.
(2) Express grant. Profits, whether appurtenant or in gross,
may be created by an express grant, which at common law
must be made by deed.[2]   The want of a deed, however, is
not necessarily fatal to the grantee, for if he can prove a
specifically enforceable contract for the grant of the profit,
i.e. an agreement for value that is either evidenced by a written
memorandum or fortified by an act of part performance, he
may invoke the familiar doctrine of equity that the grantor
must be regarded as having already done what he ought to
have done.

Thus in an early case[3] :

Position in
Equity
where no
deed.
The defendant signed a written memorandum by which he agreed in
return for valuable consideration that the plaintiff should have the
exclusive right of sporting over and killing the game on the defendant's lands, but some years later he revoked the agreement.

At the instance of the plaintiff, WOOD, V.-C., decreed
specific performance by ordering the execution of a formal
deed and meanwhile granting an injunction forbidding the
defendant to interfere with the enjoyment of the right.

Profits
appurtenant
pass under
the general
words.
Section 62 of the Law of Property Act 1925, which, as
we have already seen, provides that a conveyance of land shall
operate to pass rights and advantages appertaining to the
land at the time of the conveyance,[4] applies not only to easements but also to profits, such as a right of depasturing sheep
on an adjoining mountain.[5]

Profits do
not arise by
implied
grant.
(3) Implied grant. The next method whereby *easements*
may be acquired is that of an implied grant under the
doctrine of *Wheeldon* v. *Burrows*, but since this is confined

---

[1] Viner's Abridgement—Common C. p. 1 ; Comyns' Digest, Tit. Covenant B.
[2] Co. Litt. 9 *a, b* ; *Wood* v. *Leadbitter* (1845), 13 M. & W. 838, at pp. 842–3 ;
Mason v. *Clarke*, [1954] 1 Q. B. 460 ; [1954] 1 All E. R. 189.
[3] *Frogley* v. *Lovelace* (1859), John. 333 ; *Mason* v. *Clarke*, [1955] A. C.
778 ; [1955] 1 All E. R. 914 (part performance); M. & B. p. 77.
[4] *Supra*, p. 530.
[5] *White* v. *Williams*, [1922] 1 K. B. 727 ; *White* v. *Taylor* (*No.* 2), [1969]
1 Ch. 160 ; [1968] 1 All E. R. 1015.

to interests of a continuous and apparent nature, it can have no application to profits, which can scarcely possess either of these characteristics.

(4) **Prescription at common law.** Profits can be acquired by prescription at common law, and when this method of claim is adopted it must conform to all those general principles which obtain in the case of easements, so that

(i) the possibility of a grant must be shown ;

(ii) user is required to be *as of right* ; and

(iii) the claim is liable to be defeated by proof of its origin since 1189.

Prescription.

There is this difference, however, between easements and profits, that although a man can only prescribe in a *que estate* for an easement, he may prescribe in himself and his ancestors for a profit.[1] Examples of this personal prescription are rare,[2] since profits in gross themselves are rare, and such cases as are to be found in the Law Reports refer to *several* profits and not to rights of common.[3] Where a man does prescribe in the person, he must adduce evidence to show that either he and his ancestors, or some other person and *his* ancestors from whom the plaintiff acquired the title to the profit, have enjoyed the right from time immemorial.[4]

(5) **Lost modern grant.** *Profits à prendre* may be claimed by virtue of a lost modern grant, but instances are rarely found. If a claim is so made, it must conform to the rules and surmount the objections that apply where an easement is founded on a lost grant.[5]

Lost modern grant.

(6) **Prescription Act 1832.** The Prescription Act 1832 treats profits differently from easements in that it requires longer periods of enjoyment. The periods fixed for profits are 30 years and 60 years instead of 20 and 40. But, for the purposes of the Commons Registration Act 1965,[6] the time during which the servient tenement has been requisitioned, or a right of grazing has been prevented by reason of animal health, must be ignored in computing the period of 30 or 60 years or in determining whether there has been an interruption within the meaning of the Prescription Act.[7] Further, any

Prescription Act 1832.

---

[1] Co. Litt. 122*a*.

[2] *Shuttleworth* v. *Le Fleming* (1865), 19 C. B. (N. S.) 687, *per* Montague Smith, J.

[3] Cases are :—*Welcome* v. *Upton* (1840), 6 M. & W. 536; *Shuttleworth* v. *Le Fleming, supra* ; *Johnson* v. *Barnes* (1873), L. R. 8 C. P. 527.

[4] *Welcome* v. *Upton* (1839), 5 M. & W. 398.

[5] *Neaverson* v. *Peterborough R.D.C.*, [1902] 1 Ch. 557 ; *Mills* v. *New Forest Commission* (1856), 18 C. B. 60.

[6] *Supra*, p. 564.

[7] Commons Registration Act 1965, s. 16.

objection to the registration of a right of common under the Commons Registration Act is deemed to be a suit or action within section 4 of the Prescription Act.[1] Otherwise the provisions of the Act of 1832 are exactly the same for both interests.

Applies only to profits appurtenant. The Act applies only to profits appurtenant, not to those in gross, for it requires the claimant to allege in his pleading that the right has been enjoyed " by the occupiers of the tenement in respect whereof the same is claimed. . . ."[2] As MONTAGUE SMITH, J., said in the leading case :—

> " The whole principle of this pleading assumes a dominant tenement and an enjoyment of the right by the occupiers of it. The proof must of course follow and support the pleading. It is obvious that rights claimed in gross cannot be so pleaded or proved."[3]

(D) EXTINGUISHMENT OF *PROFITS À PRENDRE*.

Several profits and profits in common may be extinguished by any of the following methods :—

(1) **Unity of Seisin.** If the owner of the profit or common also becomes owner of the land over which the right is exercisable, the right is extinguished, provided that his estates in the right and in the land are similar both in quantum and in quality.[4] Thus a profit appurtenant is extinguished if one person becomes seised in fee both of the dominant and of the servient tenement, but if the owner of the profit takes a lease of the servient tenement, the result of this unity of possession, as distinguished from unity of seisin in the former case, is that the profit is only suspended and will revive again upon the expiration of the lease.[5]

(2) **Release.** A release of a profit in favour of the servient owner extinguishes the right in the sense that it ceases to exist as a right *in alieno solo*, since a man cannot have a profit or common in his own land.

(3) **Alteration of dominant tenement.** Although it has been said that

> " Common is obtained by long sufferance and also it may be lost by long negligence."[6]

it is not true that mere non-user of a profit will by itself produce an extinguishment of the right,[7] but if the character

---

[1] Commons Registration Act 1965, s. 16 (2).
[2] Prescription Act 1832, s. 5.
[3] *Shuttleworth* v. *Le Fleming* (1865), 19 C. B. (N. S.) 687, at p. 711.
[4] *Tyrringham's Case* (1584), 4 Co. Rep. 36b ; *White* v. *Taylor* [1969] 1 Ch. 150 ; [1967] 3 All E. R. 349 ; Hall, *Law of Profits à Prendre and Rights of Common*, p. 335.
[5] Co. Litt. 313a, 114b.
[6] *Gateward's Case* (1607), 3 Leonard 202.
[7] *Seaman* v. *Vawdrey* (1810), 16 Ves. 390.

of the dominant tenement is so altered as to make any further appurtenancy impossible, a presumption is raised in favour of extinguishment. If, for instance, land to which a common of pasture was appurtenant entirely loses its agricultural character by conversion into a building estate, the common is destroyed, but if the conversion is not irrevocable, as where arable land is turned into an orchard, the profit is merely suspended and is capable of being resumed on the restoration of the land to its original state.[1]

(4) Approvement and inclosure of commons. Rights of common may be partially extinguished by the process known as approvement or wholly extinguished by inclosure.

Approvement.

Approvement. Even at common law it appears that the lord of a manor was entitled to *approve* the manorial waste upon which the freehold tenants had the right of pasturing their cattle, by appropriating part thereof to himself and holding it in separate ownership.[2] This practice was justified by the lords on the ground that the multiplicity of commoners rendered the manor unprofitable, but as it not unnaturally caused dissension it was ultimately regulated by two statutes—the Statute of Merton 1235, Chapter 4, and the Statute of Westminster the Second 1285, Chapter 46.[3] These expressly permitted the lord of a manor to appropriate or approve the manorial waste, subject to the condition that he left sufficient pasturage for the commoners, determined according to the aggregate number of animals which they were entitled to turn out, and not according to the number which they had for a fixed number of years been in the habit of turning out.[4]

Approvement.

The Commons Act 1876 requires a person seeking to approve a common to publish his intention in the local press on three successive occasions,[5] and the Law of Commons (Amendment) Act 1893 further provides that an approvement of any part of a common purporting to be made under the Commons Acts of 1236 and 1285 shall not be valid unless it is made with the consent of the Board of Agriculture and Fisheries (now the Secretary of State for the Environment).

Inclosure. The other method of deliberate extinguishment is inclosure under the various Inclosure Acts. Inclosure differs in three respects from approvement :—

Inclosure.

---

[1] *Carr* v. *Lambert* (1866), L. R. 1 Exch. 168 ; *Tyrringham's Case* (1584), 4 Co. Rep. 36b.

[2] See authorities collected—Hall, *Law of Profits à Prendre and Rights of Common*, pp. 345 *et seq*.

[3] The Statute Law Revision Act 1948 renamed these two chapters as the Commons Act 1236, and the Commons Act 1285. The former was repealed *in toto* by the Statute Law Revision Act 1953.

[4] *Robertson* v. *Hartopp* (1888), 43 Ch. D. 484.

[5] S. 31.

(i) it applies to all kinds of commonable rights, such as common of turbary and estovers, and is not restricted to pasture ;

(ii) it involves the discharge of the whole of the lands from the rights of common ; and finally

(iii) it does not depend upon the discretion of any one man, but requires for its validity the sanction of an Act of Parliament.

Inclosure is the process whereby a commoner, in place of the rights over the manorial waste which he formerly enjoyed, is granted a definite piece of land to be held in fee simple. It is now virtually a dead letter, but in the comparatively short period of a hundred years, from about 1760 to 1860, it led to the almost entire disappearance of those rights of common which from the earliest days had been such a striking feature of English landholding. To understand this sudden and rapid extinction of ancient rights, it is necessary to realize that even as late as the eighteenth century the greater part of the cultivated land of England was still farmed under the medieval village community system. That system[1] had outlived its *raison d'être* and had become by the eighteenth century nothing but a hindrance to proper cultivation.

Private Inclosure Acts.

At first inclosures were carried out by private Acts of Parliament by which allotments of land to be held in separate ownership and discharged from commonage were awarded to the lord and the commoners. The expense of these private Acts was very great, and in 1801 the procedure was simplified by the passing of the Inclosure (Consolidation) Act, which set out a number of general provisions capable of being incorporated into private Acts.

The Inclosure Act 1845 established a central body in the shape of the Inclosures Commissioners for England and Wales, whose duties are now carried out by the Secretary of State for the Environment, and required the consent of Parliament for inclosures.[2]

Central body set up to superintend inclosures.

The result of this Act, was that between 1845 and 1875, 590,000 acres were inclosed and divided among 25,930 persons. But during the last decade of this period it became practically impossible to obtain parliamentary sanction for inclosure awards, since, under the influence of the Commons Preservation Society, the nation became convinced that one of the most urgent national needs was the provision of open spaces. The new policy was not to parcel out common lands among private owners, but to throw them open to the public and provide for their management and regulation by public bodies. Effect was given to this by the Commons Act 1876, which, after reciting that

Movement against inclosures.

---

[1] See Holdsworth, *History of English Law*, Vol. ii. pp. 56 *et seq.* and the 11th Edn. of this book, pp. 547–8.

[2] Or the Secretary of State for Wales, S. I. 1967 No. 156; S. I. 1970 No. 1681.

" inclosure in severalty as opposed to regulation of commons should not be herein-after made unless it can be proved to the satisfaction of the said Commissioners and of Parliament that such inclosure will be of benefit to the neighbourhood as well as to private interests,"

contained provisions designed to protect the public and to give local authorities an opportunity of acquiring land for the public. Thus the Secretary of State for the Environment when making a provisional award for submission to Parliament must now insert provisions, where applicable, for securing free access to any particular prospect, the preservation of objects of historical interest, the reservation of the right of playing games where a recreation ground has not been set out, and so on.[1]

Interests of public favoured.

The procedure for an inclosure is governed by the Act of 1876, and the stages are as follows :

How inclosure is effected.

(i) An application supported by persons representing at least one-third of the value of the lands must first be made to the Secretary of State for the Environment.

(ii) The application must explain why inclosure is preferable to the regulation of the land as a public common.

(iii) If the Secretary of State is of opinion that a *prima facie* case has been made out he orders a local inquiry to be made by one of his officers.

(iv) The Officer inspects the locality, holds a public meeting at which he hears the views of all persons who wish to be heard and makes a report to the Secretary of State.

(v) The Secretary of State, if he is satisfied that the matter ought to go further, prepares a draft provisional order which is ultimately submitted to Parliament.

So then at the present day inclosures are still possible, but owing to the very strong case which must be made out by the petitioners, and also to the important part played by local authorities, who are afforded facilities for making a portion of the land common to the public, it is unlikely that they will be continued.

Inclosure now rare.

SECTION IV. RIGHTS IN THE NATURE OF EASEMENTS AND PROFITS ACQUIRED BY FLUCTUATING AND UNDEFINED CLASSES OF PERSONS

There is no doubt that indefinite and fluctuating classes of persons, such as the inhabitants of a village, may acquire rights, analogous in nature to easements, over the land of another.[2] For example, they have succeeded in establishing rights to enter another's close and take water from a spring,[3] to dry their fishing

Fluctuating classes may acquire rights in the nature of easements.

---

[1] S. 7. See also L.P.A. 1925, ss. 193, 194 (rights of the public over commons and waste lands).

[2] *Gateward's Case* (1607), 6 Co. Rep. 59*b*; *Race* v. *Ward* (1855), 4 E. & B. 702.

[3] *Weekly* v. *Wildman* (1698), 1 Ld. Raym. 405; *Race* v. *Ward, supra.*

nets on the land of a private person, [1] to hold horse races [2] or a fair [3] on such land, and to pass to church [4] or market over a man's private property.

Method of acquisition is custom.

Such rights are not easements capable of acquisition by prescription, for all forms of prescription pre-suppose the possibility of a grant, and no grant can be made to an indefinite body of persons. Nevertheless, the law, in its anxiety to protect the long sustained enjoyment of a privilege, has surmounted the technical difficulty incident to prescription by allowing rights of this nature to be established by *custom*. Hence the name *customary* rights. Custom is an unwritten rule of law which has applied from time immemorial in a particular locality and which displaces the common law in so far as that particular locality is concerned. [5] To quote the words of TINDAL, C.J. [6] :

> " A custom which has existed from time immemorial without interruption within a certain place, and which is certain and reasonable in itself, obtains the force of a law, and is, in effect, the common law within that place to which it extends, though contrary to the general law of the realm."

Requisites for valid custom.

It has been said [7] that a custom must be

(1) certain, [8]

(2) not unreasonable, [9]

(3) commencing from time immemorial,

(4) continued without interruption, and

(5) applicable to a particular district.

The two outstanding requirements are existence from time immemorial[10] and restriction to a definite locality.[11]

Length of enjoyment.

Strictly speaking the first of these requirements means that the custom must have existed since 1189, but although the nature of the right precludes the court from presuming a lost modern grant if enjoyment cannot be proved for so long, yet the practice is to presume that the right originated at the proper time

---

[1] *Mercer* v. *Denne*, [1905] 2 Ch. 538.
[2] *Mouncey* v. *Ismay* (1865), 3 H. & C. 486.
[3] *Tyson* v. *Smith* (1838), 9 Ad. & El. 406.
[4] *Brocklebank* v. *Thompson*, [1903] 2 Ch. 344.
[5] See *Termes de la Ley, sub voce* " Custom " ; *Tanistry Case* (1608), Dav. Ir. 29, Litt. s. 169 ; *Hammerton* v. *Honey* (1876), 24 W. R. 603.
[6] *Lockwood* v. *Wood* (1844), 6 Q. B. 50, at p. 64.
[7] *Mercer* v. *Denne*, [1905] 2 Ch. 538 ; *New Windsor Corporation* v. *Mellor*, [1975] Ch. 380 ; [1975] 3 All E. R. 44 (right to indulge in lawful sports and pastimes).
[8] *I.e.* the persons entitled to the right must be certain and not, *e.g.*, " poor householders " ; *Selby* v. *Robinson* (1788), 2 Term Rep. 758.
[9] *E.g.* a custom to do something which would exhaust the subject-matter, is void, as for inhabitants of a parish to fish in a river—*Bland* v. *Lipscombe* (1854), 4 E. & B. 713 *n*.
[10] Blackstone, vol. i. p. 76 ; *Chapman* v. *Smith* (1754), 2 Ves. Sen. 505.
[11] *R.* v. *Rollett* (1875), L. R. 10 Q. B. 469, at p. 480.

if it is obviously of respectable antiquity.[1]   It is generally enough to show continuous enjoyment going as far back as living testimony can go.

To quote Tindal, C.J., again :

> " As to the proof of the custom, you cannot, indeed, reasonably expect to have it proved before you that such a custom did in fact exist before time of legal memory, that is, before the first year of the reign of Richard I ; for if you did, it would in effect destroy the validity of almost all customs ; but you are to require proof, as far back as living memory goes, of a continuous, peaceable, and uninterrupted user of the custom." [2]

Although the presumption in favour of enjoyment from time immemorial will readily be raised, it can undoubtedly be rebutted by positive evidence showing that it actually began at some later date.[3]   The courts, however, are slow to rebut the presumption. In *Mercer* v. *Denne*

> it was proved by witnesses that for as long as they could remember— a matter of 70 years—the fishing inhabitants of Walmer had used part of the defendant's beach for the purpose of drying their nets. The defendant, having proved that in 1844 a considerable portion of this part of the beach was under water, argued that the custom of using that particular portion must be disallowed as obviously having arisen since 1189.

In rejecting this plea Farwell, J., said [4] :—

> " A defendant may no doubt defeat a custom by shewing that it could not have existed in the time of Richard I, but he must demonstrate its impossibility, and the onus is on him to do so if the existence of the custom has been proved for a long period ; this was done, for instance, in *Simpson* v. *Wells*,[5] where the claim of a custom to set up stalls at the Statute Sessions for the hiring of servants was defeated by shewing that such sessions were introduced by the Statutes of Labourers, the first of which was in the reign of Edward III.   But no such impossibility is shewn in the present case.   If the beach was of its present extent in 1795, why am I bound to infer that it cannot have been the same in 1189 from the mere fact that between 1795 and 1844 the extent diminished and has since again increased ?   The mere non-user during the period that the sea flowed over the spot is immaterial, for it was no interruption of the right but only of the possession, and an ' interruption of the possession only for ten or twenty years will not destroy the custom.'[6] "

A customary right, once acquired, cannot be lost by mere non-user or by waiver.[7]

---

[1] *Mercer* v. *Denne, supra*, at p. 556 ; *Wolstanton, Ltd. and A.-G. of Duchy of Lancaster* v. *Newcastle-under-Lyme Borough Council*, [1940] A. C. 860, at p. 876 ; [1940] 3 All E. R. 101, at p. 109.

[2] *Bastard* v. *Smith* (1837), 2 Mood. & R. 129, at p. 136.

[3] *Hammerton* v. *Honey* (1876), 24 W. R. 603, *per* Jessel, M.R., at p. 604.

[4] [1904] 2 Ch. 534, at p. 555.   [5] (1872), 7 Q. B. 214.

[6] Blackstone, vol. 1. p. 77 ; Co. Litt. 114b.

[7] *Wyld* v. *Silver*, [1963] Ch. 243 ; [1962] 3 All E. R. 309 ; *New Windsor Corporation* v. *Mellor*, [1975] Ch. 380 ; [1975] 3 All E. R. 44.

Custom and prescription. Enough has been said to show that custom bears a close and striking resemblance to prescription. Both methods depend on continuous and uninterrupted enjoyment which has lasted for the time whereof the memory of man runneth not to the contrary, and both are liable to be defeated in the same manner. Coke, C.J., emphasized the resemblance in quaint language :—

> " Prescription and custom are brothers, and ought to have the same age, and reason ought to be the father, and congruence the mother, and use the nurse, and time out of memory to fortify them both." [1]

But for all that there is an important difference between the two methods, for while prescription always connects the right with a definite person, custom connects it with some particular locality. Prescription is personal, custom is local. A right is always prescribed for in the name of a certain person and his ancestors, or of those whose estate he owns, or in the name of corporations and their predecessors.[2] But a right claimed by custom is not alleged to be vested in any definite person or body of persons, but is claimed on the ground that it is vested in the shifting class of persons connected from time to time with the definite locality to which the right is attached.[3] In custom you first prove the attachment of the right to a locality and then prove your connection with that locality; while in prescription you show the existence of the right in some person from whom your title is derived, or else you prove yourself to be the owner of a tenement to which the right is attached.

The importance of the distinction lies in the fact that persons who are quite unable to establish their claim to an easement by means of prescription, because prescription pre-supposes a grant to some definite person, may very well succeed under the cover of custom. A customary right is part of the general law applicable to a particular locality; and persons resident there, whether capable grantees or not, are entitled to enjoy the benefit of the law which runs throughout the locality.

Profits à prendre. So far our account has been restricted to the capacity of a fluctuating and ever-changing class of persons to establish a claim to quasi-easements, and it remains to be considered whether such persons can sustain a claim to *profits à prendre.* It has been the law at least since 1607 [4] that indefinite persons cannot acquire a profit by custom.[5] James, L.J., in one case, said :—

---

[1] *Rowles* v. *Mason* (1612), 2 Brownl. 192, at p. 198.
[2] *Per* Sir Edward Coke, 4 Co. Rep. 32a.
[3] Co. Litt. 113b ; Blackstone, vol. ii. p. 263 ; *Foiston* v. *Crachroode* (1587), 4 Co. Rep. 32a ; *Gateward's Case* (1607), 6 Co. Rep. 59b.
[4] *Gateward's Case, supra.*
[5] *Ibid. Race* v. *Ward* (1855), 4 E. & B. 702 ; *Chilton* v. *London Corpn.* (1878), 7 Ch. D. 735 ; *Constable* v. *Nicholson* (1863), 14 C. B. (N. S.) 230.

" Of course it is settled and clear law that you cannot have any right to a *profit à prendre in alieno solo* in a shifting body like the inhabitants of a town or residents of a particular district."[1]

Were the rule otherwise the result would be to exhaust and destroy the subject-matter of the custom. Thus claims by inhabitants or classes of persons equally indefinite have been disallowed where the customs alleged were to enjoy common of pasture,[2] to collect dead wood for fuel,[3] to carry away sand that has drifted from the sea shore,[4] or to take minerals from the soil.[5]

But in all cases where ancient claims are in question we have to reckon with the tendency of the courts to presume everything reasonably possible in order to uphold a right of which there has been long enjoyment, and it is in furtherance of this general principle that two methods have been evolved whereby fluctuating classes can in certain circumstances maintain a claim even to profits *in alieno solo.* These may be termed (1) the " presumed Crown grant " method and (2) the " presumed charitable trust " method.

1. To take the Crown grant first, we start with this, that although a private person cannot make a grant to indefinite classes of persons, yet the Crown may do so. Lord ROMILLY said [6] :

> " The distinction between a grant by a private individual and a grant by the Crown is this, that as the Crown has the power to create corporations, so, if it is necessary for the purpose of establishing the validity of the grant, the grantees will be treated as a corporation *quoad* the grant, which is not the case with a grant by a private individual, because a private individual has no power of creating a corporation."

Can be claimed under presumed Crown grant

The Crown by virtue of this power may make a grant to the inhabitants of a town, with the result that they become by implication a corporation for the purposes of the grant and, as such, capable of enjoying a profit in the land of another. So in *Willingale* v. *Maitland,*

> where an actual Crown grant had been made in the time of Elizabeth to the inhabitants of a parish allowing a certain section of the parishioners to lop the branches of trees growing in the waste of a manor, it was held on demurrer that the grant was legal.[7]

Cases where an actual grant can be found must be rare, and the real question is whether the court will presume a grant so as to incorporate the inhabitants and thus render them eligible to take profits. All that can be said is that such

---

[1] *Commissioners of Sewers of the City of London* v. *Glasse* (1872). 7 Ch. App. 456, 465.
[2] *Grinstead* v. *Marlowe* (1792), 4 Term Rep. 717.
[3] *Selby* v. *Robinson* (1788), 2 T. R. 758.
[4] *Blewett* v. *Tregonning* (1835), 3 Ad. & El. 554.
[5] *A.-G.* v. *Mathias* (1858), 4 K. & J. 579.
[6] *Willingale* v. *Maitland* (1866), L. R. 3 Eq. 103, at p. 109.
[7] *Ibid.*

a presumption will be raised only where the circumstances that have accompanied the enjoyment go to show that the claimants have always regarded themselves as a corporation and have acted as such.

Such a grant was presumed in the *Faversham Fishery Case*[1]; but in *Lord Rivers* v. *Adams*,[2] where it appeared that the enjoyment of an alleged right of inhabitants to carry away wood from a manorial waste was inconsistent with the fact that the tenants of the manor had openly asserted and exercised control over the wood, the court refused to raise the presumption.

Kelly, C.B., in this case said :—

> " If the inhabitants had held meetings in reference to this right, or appointed any officer to look to the right, or done any act collectively of that description, the case would be different. We should then have the inhabitants acting in a corporate capacity in reference to this right, and from their doing so, and from their existence *de facto* as a corporation, we might according to the ordinary rule find a legal origin by a grant from the Crown." [3]

Can be claimed under presumed charitable trust.

2. The second method, whereby uncertain bodies may establish a claim to profits, namely, that of a presumed charitable trust, is very similar to the one just described. It depends upon the decision of the House of Lords in *Goodman* v. *Mayor of Saltash*,[4] where the following principle was in effect established.

Where it appears that a definite body capable of taking by grant, such as the corporation of a borough, has enjoyed a profit *in alieno solo* for a great number of years, and where it also appears that an indefinite body has shared in this enjoyment, then the court presumes a lost grant in favour of the corporation, but declares that the corporation must hold the profit in trust for the indefinite body

In *Goodman* v. *Mayor of Saltash* :—

Two facts were clearly proved : first, that the Corporation of Saltash had from time immemorial exercised the right of dredging for oysters in the river Tamar ; secondly, that the free inhabitants of ancient tenements in the borough had each year from Candlemas (22nd February) to Easter Eve exercised a similar right for the previous 200 years. An action was brought by the corporation against two free inhabitants of ancient tenements for trespass committed in the Tamar and for converting to their own use quantities of oysters.

---

[1] *Re Free Fishermen of Faversham* (1887), 36 Ch. D. 329 ; see especially *per* Bowen, L.J., at p. 343.

[2] (1878), L. R. 3 Ex. D. 361.

[3] *Lord Rivers* v. *Adams* (1878), L. R. 3 Ex. D. 361, at pp. 366-7.   This is a most instructive case on the whole subject of claims to profits by fluctuating bodies.   [4] (1882), 7 App. Cas. 633.

After holding that the free inhabitants could not be presumed to be separately incorporated, the House addressed itself to the task of discovering a legal origin for the right which undoubtedly had been enjoyed for a very considerable time. The majority of the House (Lord BLACKBURN dissenting) held that the fishery must have originally been granted to the corporation subject to a condition that the free inhabitants were to be allowed to fish for a certain period each year. Lord CAIRNS said :—

> " It appears to me that there is no difficulty at all in supposing such a grant, a grant to the corporation before the time of legal memory of a several fishery, a grant by the Crown, with a condition in that grant in some terms which are not before us, but which we can easily imagine—a condition that the free inhabitants of ancient tenements in the borough should enjoy this right, which as a matter of fact the case tells us they have enjoyed from time immemorial.... Such a condition would create that which in the very wide language of our courts is called a charitable, that is to say a public, trust or interest, for the benefit of the free inhabitants of ancient tenements." [1]

But for this principle to apply, it must be established that the enjoyment of the profit was regarded by the indefinite body of persons as a right to which they were entitled without anybody's permission, not as a privilege of little significance that was tolerated by the indulgence or good nature of the servient owner. [2]

Claim must be as of right.

In conclusion, then, we may say that before a fluctuating class can sustain a claim to a profit, they must show either that a grant was probably made in such a way as to incorporate them, or that there is some definite corporation which is capable of taking a grant and of holding the right granted in trust for them.

SECTION V. LICENCES [3]

As we have already seen, a licence is a permission to enter upon the land of another for an agreed purpose. [4]   It is an authority that justifies what would otherwise be a trespass.   We must now consider two separate aspects of the law of licences.   First, the extent to which the licensee has the right to enjoy his licence, or, looked at the other way round, the extent to which the licensor may revoke it and eject him.   And then, secondly, when it has been decided that a licence is enforceable against the licensor, the extent to which it is also enforceable against a successor in title to his land.

---

[1] At p. 650.
[2] *Alfred F. Beckett Ltd.* v. *Lyons*, [1967] Ch. 449 ; [1967] 1 All E. R. 833.
[3] See generally Hanbury's *Modern Equity* (9th Edn.), pp. 674 *et seq.* ; M. & B. pp. 436 *et seq.*
[4] *Supra*, p. 525.

(A) EFFECT OF LICENCE AS BETWEEN LICENSOR AND LICENSEE

Licences may be divided into four categories :

Bare or gratuitous licence.

(1) **A bare or gratuitous licence**, which is a mere permission to the licensee to enter upon the licensor's land, as for instance when permission is given to play cricket on a field. As we shall see, this permission may be withdrawn at any time by the licensor.

Licence coupled with a grant or interest.

(2) **A licence coupled with a grant or interest**, on the other hand, may be irrevocable. It is said to be *coupled with a grant or interest* when the licensee, having been granted a definite proprietary interest in the land or in chattels lying on the land, is given permission to enter in order that he may enjoy or exploit the interest. Such a licence, as distinct from a *bare* licence, is of this nature if given to a man who is entitled to chattels,[1] or to growing timber[2] or to game on the land.[3] There are here two separate matters—the grant and the licence.

> " But a licence to hunt in a man's park and to carry away the deer killed to his own use ; to cut down a tree in a man's ground and to carry it away the next day after to his own use, are licences as to the acts of hunting and cutting down the tree ; but as to the carrying away of the deer killed and the tree cut they are grants."[4]

Such a licence is not effective at common law unless the grant is formally valid. Thus a grant by an unsealed writing of a right to shoot and carry away game, coupled with a licence to enter the land, is ineffective, since a deed is necessary at common law for the grant of a *profit à prendre*.[5] But the rule in equity, which now prevails and which is illustrated in another context by *Walsh* v. *Lonsdale*,[6] is that a contract to grant an interest is treated as if the formalities required by law had been observed. Thus a properly evidenced contract to grant a right of shooting over land is specifically enforceable and is as effective as an actual grant under seal.[7] Equity may grant an injunction to the licensee to prevent the licensor from revoking the licence contrary to the terms of the grant.

Contractual licence.

(3) **A contractual licence** is a licence supported by consideration, as for instance where the licensee buys a ticket for a theatre or a race meeting,[8] or where he is contractually entitled to the exclusive privilege of supplying refreshments in a theatre.[9]

In considering the effect of these licences as between licensor and

---

[1] *Wood* v. *Manley* (1839), 11 Ad. & El. 34.
[2] *James Jones & Sons, Ltd.* v. *Earl of Tankerville*, [1909] 2 Ch. 440 ; M. & B. p. 440.
[3] *Frogley* v. *Earl of Lovelace* (1859), John. 333.
[4] *Thomas* v. *Sorrell* (1673), Vaugh. 330, at p. 351, *per* VAUGHAN, C.J.
[5] *Wood* v. *Leadbitter* (1845), 13 M. & W. 838. M. & B. p. 438.
[6] *Supra*, pp. 394-8.
[7] *Hurst* v. *Picture Theatres, Ltd.* [1915] 1 K. B. 1 ; M. & B. p. 439 ; *Frogley* v. *Earl of Lovelace*, *supra*.
[8] *Wood* v. *Leadbitter*, *supra* ; *Hurst* v. *Picture Theatres, Ltd.*, *supra*.
[9] *Frank Warr & Co., Ltd.* v. *London County Council*, [1904] 1 K. B. 713.

licensee, common law drew a distinction between a mere licence, Effect of
licence at
common law. whether gratuitous or contractual, and a licence coupled with a grant. We have seen that a licence coupled with a grant may be irrevocable. On the other hand a mere licence may, at common law, be revoked at any moment, whether it is part of a contract or a mere indulgent permission unsupported by consideration, as for example, a permission to practise golf in a park. Its only legal effect is that until revoked it precludes the licensor from maintaining an action of trespass.[1] If, however, a licensee remains on the land after his permission to be there has been withdrawn, he is treated by the common law as a trespasser, even though the withdrawal is in complete disregard of the contract.[2] He cannot enforce a contractual right to occupation, although it is conceded that he may recover damages.[3] At common law it is immaterial that he has entered the land and has acted to his financial detriment in the belief that his right to occupation is legally secure.

In 1845 the Court of Exchequer decided the case of *Wood* v. *Leadbitter*. The plaintiff bought a ticket for admission to the grandstand at Doncaster racecourse. The plaintiff was ordered to leave by the defendant, who was the servant of the steward of the course, and, on his refusal to go, he was physically removed, no more force being used than was reasonably necessary. In refusing his action for damages for assault and false imprisonment, Baron ALDERSON stated the distinction between a mere licence and a licence coupled with a grant as follows [4] :

> " A mere licence is revocable ; but that which is called a licence is often something more than a licence ; it often comprises or is connected with a grant, and then the party who has given it cannot in general revoke it, so as to defeat his grant, to which it is incident. It may further be observed that a licence under seal (provided it be a mere licence) is as revocable as a licence by parol; and on the other hand a licence by parol, coupled with a grant is as irrevocable as a licence by deed, provided only that the grant is of a nature capable of being made by parol."

The judgment, indeed, contained dicta suggesting that the particular licence in issue, which was to enter a racecourse for the purpose of viewing the races, would have been irrevocable had it been made by deed. These dicta, however, must now be disregarded, since they reflected the view current in 1845 that an easement might be created in gross, a view that was not finally rejected until twenty-three years later.[5]

---

[1] *Thomas* v. *Sorrell* (1673), Vaugh. 330, 351. Any revocation must be clear and reasonable; *Minister of Health* v. *Bellotti*, [1944] K. B. 298 ; [1944] 1 All E. R. 238 ; *Mellor* v. *Watkins* (1874), 9 Q. B. 400.

[2] *Wood* v. *Leadbitter* (1845), 13 M. & W. 838 ; M. & B. p. 438; *Thompson* v. *Park*, [1944] K. B. 408 ; [1944] 2 All E. R. 477 ; M. & B. p. 444.

[3] *Kerrison* v. *Smith*, [1897] 2 Q. B. 445.

[4] (1845), 13 M. & W. 838, at pp. 844–5.

[5] *Rangeley* v. *Midland Ry. Co.* (1868), L. R. 3 Ch. App. 306. For a doctrine of long standing, but little relied on, that a licence is irrevocable if it has been acted on, see *Webb* v. *Paternoster* (1619), Palm. 71 ; *Hounslow London*

Effect of
licence
in equity.

In 1915, the influence of the Judicature Act 1873 upon a licence was considered for the first time by the Court of Appeal in *Hurst* v. *Picture Theatres Ltd.*,[1] but even as late as this the confusion evident in *Wood* v. *Leadbitter* concerning the effect of a deed still pervaded the reasoning of the majority of the Court.

> The plaintiff, who had been wrongfully ejected from a cinema theatre for which he had bought a ticket, elected to sue the owners for assault and false imprisonment rather than for breach of contract, since, if he could establish this cause of action, he would recover substantial, not merely nominal, damages.   He succeeded.

This required proof that the licence was irrevocable during the continuance of the performance, but the Court of Appeal overcame the difficulty by holding that it was coupled with an interest and that despite the absence of a deed the plaintiff was entitled in equity to a decree for the specific performance of his contractual right to view the complete entertainment.   The fatal defect in this reasoning, of course, was that there was no proprietary interest capable of being contained in a grant.

> " The right to see a spectacle cannot, in the ordinary sense of legal language, be regarded as a proprietary interest. Fifty thousand people who pay to see a football match do not obtain fifty thousand interests in the football ground." [2]

A more successful way of softening the rigidity of the common law was indicated in the dicta of the House of Lords in *Winter Garden Theatre (London), Ltd.* v. *Millennium Productions, Ltd.*,[3] This case finally established that the rights of the parties to a contractual licence must be determined upon the proper construction of the contract.   Their Lordships favoured the argument that, if on its construction a contractual licence is irrevocable, then, even though it is not coupled with a grant, its revocation in breach of the contract should be prevented where possible[4] by the grant of an injunction.[5]   In other words, equity does what it

---

Borough Council v. *Twickenham Garden Development, Ltd.*, [1971] Ch. 223, at p. 255 ; [1970] 3 All E. R. 326 ; M. & B. p. 451 ; (1965) 29 Conv. (N.S.) 19 (M. C. Cullity) ; M. & B. pp. 437–8.

[1] *Hurst* v. *Picture Theatres, Ltd.*, [1915] 1 K. B. 1 ; M. & B. p. 439.   See also *Cowell* v. *Rosehill Racecourse* (1937), 56 C. L. R. 605 (Australia).

[2] *Cowell* v. *Rosehill Racecourse Co., Ltd.* (1937), *supra*, at p. 616, *per* LATHAM, C.J., whose judgment is conveniently summarized by Lord EVERSHED in (1954), 70 *L. Q. R.*, p. 333 : see the dissenting judgment of PHILLIMORE, L.J., in *Hurst* v. *Picture Theatres, Ltd.*, [1915] 1 K. B. 1.   See also *Vaughan* v. *Hampson* (1875), 33 L. T. 15 (right to attend a creditors' meeting) described as " a curiosity " in *Hounslow Borough Council* v. *Twickenham Garden Development, Ltd.*, *supra*, at p. 254.

[3] [1948] A. C. 173 ; [1947] 2 All E. R. 331 ; M. & B. p. 445 ; for a critique of this case see *Hounslow London Borough Council* v. *Twickenham Garden Developments, Ltd.*, *supra*, at pp. 245 *et seq.* ; (1971) 87 L. Q. R. 309 ; *Mayfield Holdings, Ltd.* v. *Moana Reef, Ltd.*, [1973] 1 N.Z.L.R. 309.

[4] *Thompson* v. *Park*, [1944] K. B. 408 ; [1944] 2 All E. R. 477 ; M. & B. p. 444.

[5] The House of Lords construed the licence as being revocable by the licensor, and so their views were obiter.   The Court of Appeal, however, had construed it as irrevocable and had protected the licensee by granting an injunction against the licensor.   [1946] 1 All E. R. 678, at p. 684, *per* Lord GREENE, M.R.; M. & B. p. 448.   For a full discussion of contractual licences see MEGARRY, J. in *Hounslow London Borough Council* v. *Twickenham Garden Developments Ltd.*, *supra*, where this approach was followed.

can by means of a decree of injunction to preserve the sanctity of a
bargain[1] and by that remedy it is prepared to restrain a revocation
that would derogate from the right of occupation conferred by the
contract. If the contract does not expressly state the time for
which the licence is to last, a promise by the licensor must be
implied that he will not revoke the permission in a manner contrary to the intention of the parties.[2] The exact scope of the
implied promise, if any, must be ascertained in each case, for it
will, of course, vary with the circumstances. For instance a
spectator who buys a ticket for a theatre is a licensee with a right
to occupy his seat until the spectacle is over;[3] a licence of the
" front of the house rights " at a theatre cannot be revoked until a
reasonable time has been afforded to the licensee for his withdrawal.[4] In those cases such as *Hurst* v. *Picture Theatres, Ltd.*,
where there is no time or opportunity to obtain an injunction, the
court will presumably give judgment on the basis of what the
rights of the parties would have been, had the grant of this remedy
been practicable.

(4) **A licence by estoppel.** A further intervention has been
made by equity where the doctrine of estoppel operates. A long
line of cases[5] has established that where a licensee has been
permitted or encouraged by the licensor to act in such a way that
an estoppel arises in his favour, the licensor will be bound by it
and will be unable to eject the licensee inconsistently with the
representation which forms the basis of estoppel. As Lord
Kingsdown said :

> " If a man, under a verbal agreement with a landlord for a certain
> interest in land, or, what amounts to the same thing under an ex-
> pectation, created or encouraged by the landlord, that he shall have

Licence by
estoppel.

---

[1] *Winter Garden Theatre (London), Ltd.* v. *Millennium Productions, Ltd.*,
[1948] A. C. 173, 202, *per* Lord Uthwatt ; [1947] 2 All E. R. 331, 343.

[2] *Errington* v. *Errington and Woods*, [1952] 1 K. B. 290; [1952] 1 All E.R. 149.

[3] *Hurst* v. *Picture Theatres, Ltd.*, [1915] 1 K. B. 1.

[4] *Winter Garden Theatre (London), Ltd.* v. *Millennium Productions, Ltd.*,
[1948] A. C. 173 ; [1947] 2 All E. R. 331.

[5] *East India Co.* v. *Vincent* (1740), 2 Atk. 83 ; *Dann* v. *Spurrier* (1802),
7 Ves.Jr. 231 ; *Duke of Devonshire* v. *Eglin* (1851), 14 Beav. 530 ; *Duke of
Beaufort* v. *Patrick* (1853), 17 Beav. 60 ; *Unity Joint Stock Mutual Banking
Association* v. *King* (1858), 25 Beav. 72 ; *Ramsden* v. *Dyson* (1866), L. R. 1
H. L. 129 ; *Willmott* v. *Barber* (1880), 15 Ch. D. 96 ; *Plimmer* v. *Wellington
Corpn.* (1884), 9 App. Cas. 699 ; M. & B. p. 453 ; *Foster* v. *Robinson*, [1951]
1 K. B. 149 ; [1950] 2 All E. R. 342 ; *Errington* v. *Errington and Woods*, [1952]
1 K. B. 290 ; [1952] 1 All E. R. 149 ; M. & B. p. 472 ; *Vaughan* v. *Vaughan*,
[1953] 1 Q. B. 762 ; [1953] 1 All E. R. 209 ; *Hopgood* v. *Brown*, [1955] 1 W. L. R.
213 ; [1955] 1 All E. R. 550 ; M. & B. p. 481 ; *Armstrong* v. *Sheppard and
Short*, [1959] 2 Q. B. 384 ; [1959] 2 All E. R. 651 ; *Inwards* v. *Baker*, [1965] 2
Q. B. 29 [1965] ; 1 All E. R. 446 ; M. & B. p. 475 ; *Ward* v. *Kirkland*, [1967]
Ch. 194 ; [1966] 1 All E. R. 609 ; *E. R. Ives Investment Ltd.* v. *High*, [1967]
2 Q. B. 279 ; [1967] 1 All E. R. 504 ; M. & B. p. 478 ; *Binions* v. *Evans*,
[1972] Ch. 359 ; [1972] 2 All E. R. 70 ; M. & B. p. 467 ; *Hussey* v. *Palmer*,
[1972] 1 W. L. R. 1286 ; [1972] 3 All E. R. 744 ; *Siew Soon Wah* v. *Yong
Tong Hong*, [1973] A. C. 836 ; *Dodsworth* v. *Dodsworth* (1973), 228 Estates
Gazette 1115 ; M. & B. p. 458 ; *Holiday Inns Inc.* v. *Broadhead* (1974), 232
Estates Gazette 1087 ; *Crabb* v. *Arun District Council*, [1975] 3 W. L. R. 847 ;
[1975] 3 All E. R. 865. See Snell, *Equity* (27th Edn.) pp. 565–8.

a certain interest, takes possession of such land, with the consent of
the landlord and upon the faith of such promise or expectation,
with the knowledge of the landlord, and without objection by him,
lays out money upon the land, a Court of equity will compel the
landlord to give effect to such promise or expectation. "[1]

If, for example, A encourages B to build a house on A's land
under the express or implied undertaking that B will be allowed to
reside in the house for a period of time, A cannot eject B as soon as
the house is built.[2]

The permission given by A to B may be gratuitous or for value.
If it is for value, then B may rely either on the contract or on the
estoppel. If the remedy which B is seeking is damages, then he
must of course prove the contract : if however the permission is
gratuitous, the estoppel may be the only basis of his protection.
And, as we shall see, if it is correct to say that " licences by estoppel
are protected against third parties taking with notice, but contractual licensees are not, the protection based on estoppel will be
essential if the licensor has transferred the property to a third
party ".[3]

The extent of the protection accorded to a licensee by estoppel
varies with the circumstances. They may be such as to entitle
him to call for the conveyance of the legal estate, as in *Dillwyn* v.
Llewelyn,[4] or to enjoy the licence indefinitely,[5] or to remain on the
land as long as he wishes or for his life,[6] or subject to payment of its
value,[7] or until the licensor has reimbursed him for any expenditure on improvements.[8] In *E. R. Ives Investment, Ltd.* v.
High, Lord DENNING in considering the extent of the " equity
arising out of acquiescence " in that case said[9] :

> " The Court will not allow that expectation to be defeated when
> it would be inequitable so to do. It is for the court in each case to
> decide in what way the equity can be satisfied."

These examples show how broad is the discretion which the
court may exercise.[10] The granting of positive remedies, however,
causes conveyancing difficulties. If, as in *Dillwyn* v. *Llewelyn*,

---

[1] *Ramsden* v. *Dyson* (1866), L. R. 1 H. L. 129, at p. 170, *per* Lord KINGS-
DOWN ; *Willmott* v. *Barber*, (1880) 15 Ch. D. 96, at pp. 105–6, *per* FRY, J. ;
Crabb v. *Arun District Council*, [1975] 3 W. L. R. 847 ; [1975] 3 All E. R. 865.
[2] *Dillwyn* v. *Llewelyn* (1862), 4 De G.F. & J. 517 ; *Inwards* v. *Baker*,
supra.
[3] Hanbury, *op. cit.*, p. 680.
[4] (1862), 4 De G.F. & J. 517 ; M. & B. p. 456.
[5] *Plimmer* v. *Wellington Corpn.* (1884), 9 App. Co. 699 ; *Ward* v. *Kirkland*,
[1967] Ch. 194 ; [1966] 1 All E. R. 609.
[6] *Inwards* v. *Baker*, [1965] 2 Q. B. 29 ; [1965] 1 All E. R. 446 ; M. & B.
p. 475 (son builds bungalow on father's land).
[7] *Duke of Beaufort* v. *Patrick* (1853), 17 Beav. 60.
[8] *Dodsworth* v. *Dodsworth* (1973), 228 Estates Gazette 1115 ; M. & B. p. 458.
[9] [1967] 2 Q. B. 379, at p. 395 ; [1967] 1 All E. R. 504.
[10] For a solution on the basis of a constructive trust, see *Bannister* v. *Bannister*,
[1948] 2 All E. R. 133 ; *cf. Binions* v. *Evans*, [1972] Ch. 359 ; [1972] 2 All E. R.
70 ; M. & B. p. 467 ; *Hussey* v. *Palmer*, [1972] 1 W. L. R. 1286 ; [1972]
3 All E. R. 744. *Infra*, p. 585.

the licensee is entitled to call for the conveyance of the legal fee simple, the beneficial interest in the land is separated from the legal estate and is not apparent from the title deeds. Where the licensee is entitled to a limited interest, this may make him a tenant for life under the Settled Land Act 1925, under which the legal estate must be vested in him and he and he alone has the power to make title.[1] Furthermore, the automatic ordering of a conveyance does not necessarily result in automatic justice. In *Dillwyn* v. *Llewelyn* the son received a free gift of the land in return for his expenditure on a house, which he had built on it with his father's encouragement. Such a clear cut solution may cause injustice to those who would otherwise be entitled to the land, especially if the value of the site is greater than the value of the house.

(B) THE LICENSEE AND THIRD PARTIES

As between the parties themselves, then, the effect of a licence is reasonably clear. Difficulties have arisen, however, when we ask whether the licensee acquires a personal right enforceable only against the licensor or a proprietary interest binding upon the licensor's successors in title. The answer depends on the category of licence. If it is bare, then, as it is revocable by the licensor, it clearly does not bind his successors in title. If, however, the licence is coupled with a grant or interest, it is irrevocable by the licensor. If the interest granted is legal, it binds any successor in title; if it is equitable, as for instance, where there is a contract to grant by an unsealed writing, the interest, and with it the licence, binds all successors in title except a bona fide purchaser of the legal estate from the licensor. Such a contract, however, is registrable under section 2 (4) of the Land Charges Act 1972, and, if not registered, will be void against a purchaser of a legal estate in the land for money or money's worth.[2] *{Effect of licence on successor in title of licensor.}* *{Licence coupled with grant or interest.}*

As to whether a contractual licence is binding on third parties may be considered by reference to the case of *Errington* v. *Errington and Woods*[3] where the facts were as follows :— *{Contractual licence.}*

> A father bought a house for £750. He paid £250 in cash and borrowed £500 from a building society, the loan being secured by a mortgage of the house and repayable by instalments of fifteen shillings a week. He allowed his son and daughter-in-law to go into possession and told them that if they paid all the instalments he would

---

[1] *Supra*, pp. 168, 176. *Binions* v. *Evans*, [1972] Ch. 359 ; [1972] 2 All E. R. 70, *infra*, p. 585. But see *Dodsworth* v. *Dodsworth*, (1973) 228 Estates Gazette 1115 *per* RUSSELL, L.J.; M. & B. p. 458 ; *Ivory* v. *Palmer*, [1975] I. C. R. 340, where C. A. held that a right of occupation " expressed to be granted for the period of a job, which in its turn is described as a job for life " did not create a Settled Land Act tenancy. " *Binions* v. *Evans* stretched to the very limit the application of the Settled Land Act 1925 ", *per* CAIRNS, L. J. at p. 347.

[2] S 4 (6). *Infra*, p. 742.

[3] [1952] 1 K. B. 290; [1952] 1 All E. R. 149 ; M. & B. p. 472.

convey the legal estate to them. They paid the instalments as they became due, but the payments were not all completed when the father died nine years later having devised the house to his widow. The son then left his wife, but the latter remained in occupation of the house and continued to pay the instalments.

An action brought by the widow for possession against the daughter-in-law was dismissed. The Court of Appeal held that the son and daughter-in-law were neither tenants at will nor weekly tenants, but licensees entitled to occupy the house as long as they paid the instalments. This licence was binding upon the licensor's devisee.

Substantially, the reasoning adopted by the court was that, since the son and daughter-in-law were entitled in equity to restrain the revocation of the licence contrary to the terms of the implied contract, they acquired in effect an equitable interest, or at least an equity,[1] in the land that was capable of binding third parties, as in the case of a restrictive covenant.[2]

This reasoning must be considered afresh in the light of *National Provincial Bank, Ltd.* v. *Ainsworth*,[3] in which the House of Lords finally rejected the so-called 'deserted wife's equity'. It overruled the cases in which it had been held that a wife deserted by her husband had an equity, *qua* licensee, to continue in occupation of the matrimonial home subject to any order to the contrary that might be made by the court under section 17 of the Married Women's Property Act 1882.[4] But, though the decision is an authority only on this particular matter, the position of contractual licenses inevitably came under review, and it is a reasonable inference from the observations of their Lordships that if the occasion arises they will not accept the ground upon which *Errington* v. *Errington and Woods* was decided.

Lord UPJOHN, Lord WILBERFORCE and in the Court of Appeal, RUSSELL, L.J. associated themselves with the strictures on the decision made by Professor Wade[5] and, although they refrained from expressing a final opinion upon the position of a contractual licensee let into occupation of land, their disinclination to regard him as possessing more than a personal right is reasonably evident. RUSSELL, L.J., in particular, resisted the view that this personal right is converted into some form of equitable interest binding on third parties merely because the licensor may be restrained from revoking his permission.[6] Moreover, there was an equal disinclination to temper the authority of *King* v. *David Allen & Sons*,

---

[1] *Supra*, p. 70.

[2] This reasoning was defended by the author in (1953) 16 M.L.R. 1; but rejected by Professor H. W. R. Wade in (1952), 68 *L. Q. R.* 337. For an attack on the decision from a different angle, see (1953), 69 *L. Q. R.* 466 (A. D. Hargreaves). See also *Re Solomon*, [1967] Ch. 573 at pp. 582–6, *per* GOFF, J.

[3] [1965] A. C. 1175; [1965] 2 All E. R. 472.

[4] This decision gave rise to the Matrimonial Homes Act 1967, *supra*, p. 233.

[5] See note 2, *supra*.

[6] [1964] Ch. 665, at p. 698.

Billposting, Ltd.[1] and *Clore* v. *Theatrical Properties, Ltd.*,[2] which held that the rights of a contractual licensee cannot be enforced against third parties.

A contractual licence has, however, been enforced against a purchaser who took a conveyance of land expressly subject to a licence, having in consequence paid a reduced price. In *Binions* v. *Evans*,[3]

> Mrs. Evans was the widow of an employee of the Tredegar Estate. In 1968 the Estate entered into a written agreement with her under which she was permitted to reside in a cottage on the Estate for the remainder of her life free of rent and rates. She agreed to keep the cottage in a proper manner. In 1970 the Estate sold and coveted it to the plaintiffs expressly subject to the agreement. The plaintiffs paid a reduced price because of this. Six months later they claimed possession of the cottage.

The Court of Appeal unanimously held that Mrs. Evans was protected, but differed in their reasons. MEGAW and STEPHENSON, L.JJ. held that the agreement conferred a life interest and that Mrs. Evans was a tenant for life under the Settled Land Act 1925.[4] Lord DENNING, however, held that the plaintiffs were bound by Mrs. Evans's contractual licence, saying, firstly, that the plaintiffs, having purchased *expressly subject* to the rights of Mrs. Evans, could not ignore them ; and, secondly, on the wider ground that the contractual licence created a constructive trust[5] which bound the plaintiffs to permit her to reside in the cottage during her life or as long as she wished. It is submitted that the former view is preferable. It is difficult to see how the wider view is consistent with earlier authority on contractual licences, and the expressions of opinion in the House of Lords in *National Provincial Bank, Ltd.* v. *Ainsworth.*

Finally we must consider how far an estoppel licence is enforceable against a successor in title of the licensor. It does not follow from what we have so far said that the actual decision in *Errington* v. *Errington and Woods* was wrong. In fact, the prevalent view seems to be that it is sustainable on the principle of estoppel by acquiescence. As we have seen,[6] a supervening equity to be protected vests in the licensee by estoppel and this has been protected against a purchaser from the licensor of the legal estate for value with actual or constructive notice.[7]

Licence by estoppel.

---

[1] [1916] 2 A. C. 54 ; M. & B. p. 465.

[2] [1936] 3 All E. R. 483 ; M. & B. p. 466.

[3] [1972] Ch. 359 ; [1972] 2 All E. R. 70 ; M. & B. p. 467 ; (1972) 88 L. Q. R. 336 (P. V. B.) ; (1972) 36 Conv. (N.S.) 277 (D. J. Hayton) ; (1973) C.L.J. 123 (R. J. Smith) ; (1973) 117 Sol. Jo. 23 (B. W. Harvey).

[4] Following *Bannister* v. *Bannister*, (1948) 2 All E. R. 133. This is not without difficulty, *supra*, p. 583, n. 1. MEGAW, L.J. also suggested at p. 371 that the plaintiffs would be guilty of the tort of interference with existing contractual rights if they were to evict the defendant.

[5] On constructive trusts, see Snell, Ch. 5 ; Hanbury, Ch. 13.

[6] *Supra*, p. 581.

[7] *Hopgood* v. *Brown*, [1955] 1 W. L. R. 213 ; [1955] 1 All E. R. 550 ; M. & B. p. 481.

Thus in *E.R. Ives Investment Ltd.* v. *High*[1] the defendant, High, built a house on his own land. His neighbour then erected a block of flats whose foundations encroached on High's land. They agreed orally that the foundations should remain and that High should have a right of way across the neighbour's yard. High, relying on this agreement, built a garage on his own land so sited that it could only be approached across the yard. The neighbour sold the block of flats to a purchaser, who resold it to the plaintiffs, expressly subject to High's right of way. The right of way was not a legal interest since it had not been formally created ; nor had it been registered as an equitable easement under the Land Charges Act 1925. The Court of Appeal held that High had a right by estoppel, which, not being registrable as a land charge,[2] was binding on the plaintiffs who had purchased the legal estate of the licensor with actual notice.[3]

The law on this point is still in the process of development,[4] but it seems that a new right *in alieno solo* is emerging in the twentieth century as did one in the previous century under the doctrine of *Tulk* v. *Moxhay*.[5]

SECTION VI.   REGISTERED LAND[6]

An easement, right or privilege may be created over registered land in the same way as it can over unregistered land.

Express grant.

When it is created by express grant, it may appear on either the property register of the title to the dominant tenement, or on the charges register of that to the servient tenement, or on both. Provision is made for the entry of a right on the property register, if it is appurtenant to land and is capable of subsisting as a legal estate.[7] The noting of a profit in gross, as opposed to a profit appurtenant, is thus excluded. As far as the charges register is concerned, the Registrar has a mandatory duty to enter a note thereon of any easement, right or privilege which has been created by an instrument[8] and which adversely affects the servient land at the time of first registration.[9] Thereafter, he has a discretion to

---

[1] [1967] 2 Q. B. 379 ; [1967] 1 All E. R. 504 ; M. & B. p. 478.

[2] *Supra*, p. 527.

[3] *Supra*, p. 103.   The C.A. also relied on the doctrine of *Halsall* v. *Brizell* [1957] Ch. 169 ; [1957] 1 All E. R. 371, that he who takes the benefit must accept the burden.   *Infra*, p. 596.

[4] For an appraisal of the difficulties see (1967), 31 Conv. (N.S.) 341 (F. R. Crane) ; (1969) A.S.C.L. 354 (E. H. Burn) ; Hanbury's *Modern Equity* (9th Edn.), pp. 688–9.

[5] *Infra*, pp. 597 *et seq*.

[6] Barnsley, *Conveyancing Law and Practice*, pp. 427–30.

[7] L.R.R. 1925, rr. 3 (2) (c), 252–257.   See *Re Evans' Contract*, [1970] 1 W.L.R. 583 ; [1970] 1 All E. R. 1236.

[8] This does not include a statute, unless the statute creates a settlement. L.R.A. 1925, s. 3 (vii).

[9] L.R.A. 1925, s. 70 (2).   *Re Dances Way, West Town, Hayling Island*, [1962] Ch. 490, at p. 508 ; [1962] 2 All E. R. 42 ; M. & B. p. 578.

enter a notice of an adverse easement etc. upon proof of its existence.[1]

Furthermore, even if the easement etc. is not referred to on the property register, it will nevertheless be enjoyed by each registered proprietor of the dominant tenement. This stems from the rule that section 62 of the Law of Property Act 1925, under which general words may be implied in a conveyance, applies equally to a transfer of registered land.[2]

In this context it is important to reiterate the rule that in order to perfect the title of any easement or profit at law, the disposition creating it must itself be completed by registration.[3] Until this has been done, the grantor remains the proprietor. The consequence is that the transaction takes effect in equity, and a type of equitable easement, peculiar to registered conveyancing, is thereby created.

In the case of an easement created by implied grant,[4] it would appear that the rule in *Wheeldon* v. *Burrows* applies also to registered land, although there is no specific reference to it in the Land Registration Act or the Rules. It is clear, however, that an easement or profit may be created by implied grant under section 62 of the Law of Property Act 1925. Here too no legal right can be created until the grantee is registered as proprietor. *Implied grant.*

Rule 250 (1) of the Land Registration Rules 1925 provides[5] :— *Prescription.*

> " easements, rights and privileges adversely affecting registered land may be acquired in equity by prescription in the same manner and to the same extent as if the land were not registered."

An easement or profit acquired by prescription will take effect at law if it is capable of subsisting as a legal interest, and in equity, in any other case.[6] If it takes effect at law, it becomes an overriding interest,[7] and, if the Registrar thinks fit, he may enter a notice of it on the charges register of the servient tenement, and on the property register of the dominant tenement.[8]

As far as the running of the burden of an easement or profit is concerned, a purchaser of the servient tenement, in accordance

---

[1] L. R. A. 1925, s. 70 (3). L.R.R. 1925, r. 41 (1). The difficulties in determining from available evidence the nature and extent of easements is considerable. See generally *Re Dances Way, supra.*

[2] L.R.R. 1925, r. 251. See also L.R.A. 1925, ss. 5–7, 9–12, 19 (3), 20 (1), 22 (3), 23 (1), 72.

[3] L.R.A. 1925, ss. 19 (2), 22 (2).

[4] See Ruoff and Roper, pp. 103–4. Farrand *Contract and Conveyance,* (2nd Edn.), pp. 390–2.

[5] See also L.R.A. 1925, s. 75 (5).

[6] The possibility of an easement being acquired in equity by prescription is " perplexing. " Ruoff and Roper, p. 694

[7] L.R.A. 1925, s. 70 (1) (a) *infra.*

[8] *Ibid.,* s. 75 (3) ; L.R.R. 1925, r. 250 (2). Ruoff and Roper, pp. 104, 693–695. In most cases, as easements in course of prescription are inchoate until court action, the note in the property register will merely state that the easement is claimed and not that it actually subsists.

with the general principles of registered conveyancing, takes subject to any rights which appear on the register.   He also takes subject to any overriding interests, and, in this context, section 70 (1) (a) of the Land Registration Act 1925 provides that the following are such :

> " Rights of common,[1] drainage rights, customary rights (until extinguished), public rights, profits à prendre, rights of sheepwalk, rights of way, watercourses, rights of water, and other easements not being equitable easements required to be protected by notice on the register."[2]

From this it would seem that an equitable easement (but not an equitable profit à prendre) is not an overriding interest.[3]   It can, therefore, only be protected if an entry has been made on the register of the title to the servient tenement.   So far this is similar in effect to the position under unregistered conveyancing.   The difference lies in respect of those equitable rights which do not qualify as equitable easements under Class D (iii) of the Land Charges Act 1972.[4]   As we have seen, in unregistered land these rights are not registrable and the court can apply the doctrine of notice to them.   " This may enable the judge to arrive at a fairer result in the particular case than he could have reached had the equity been registrable but unregistered ".[5]   In registered land, however, they must be protected by the entry of a notice or caution on the register, otherwise[6] they will be void against a purchaser for valuable consideration from the registered proprietor, unless they are overriding interests.   In *Inwards* v. *Baker*,[7] for example, where a son expended money in building a bungalow on his father's unregistered land, under the expectation created by his father that he could remain there, the Court of Appeal held that the son's right to remain in the bungalow for life or as long as he wished was enforceable against a purchaser with notice.   It would seem that, if the title to the land were registered, the son's right would be protected by virtue of his actual occupation as an overriding interest under section 70 (1) (g) of the Land Registration Act 1925.[8]   On the other hand, such protection would not be accorded to the estoppel licensee in *E.R. Ives Investment Ltd.* v.

---

[1] No rights of common can be registered under L.R.A. 1925 over land which is capable of registration under the Commons Registration Act 1965, s. 1 (1).   See also s. 12.   *Supra*, p. 564.

[2] See also L.R.R. 1925, r. 258 ; *infra*, p. 776.

[3] Ruoff and Roper, pp. 102–3 ; *Payne* v. *Adnams* (1971), C. L. Y. 6486 ; Barnsley, pp. 43–44, Farrand, pp. 189–90, Hayton, *Registered Land*, pp. 59–60 ; (1969), 33 Conv. (N.S.) p. 138 (P. Jackson).

[4] *Supra*, pp. 526–7.

[5] *Poster* v. *Slough Estates, Ltd.*, [1969] 1 Ch. 495, at p. 507 ; [1968] 3 All E. R. 257, *per* CROSS, J.

[6] L.R.A. 1925, ss. 49 (1) (f), 54 (1).   Ruoff and Roper, pp. 763–4, 768.

[7] [1965] 2 Q. B. 29 ; [1965] 1 All E. R. 446 ; M. & B. p. 475.

[8] *Infra*, p. 773.

High,[1] where the garage was sited on his own land.　Nor would the intermittent user of his right over the licensor's land amount to actual occupation.[2]

SECTION VII.　LAW REFORM COMMITTEE REPORT ON ACQUISITION OF EASEMENTS AND PROFITS BY PRESCRIPTION[3]

In *Tehidy Minerals Ltd.* v. *Norman*, BUCKLEY, L.J. said[4] :—

" The co-existence of three separate methods of prescribing is, in our view, anomalous and undesirable, for it results in much unnecessary complication and confusion.　We hope that it may be possible for the Legislature to effect a long-overdue simplification in this branch of the law."

In 1966 the Law Reform Committee recommended the abolition of the prescriptive acquisition of easements and of profits à prendre ;[5] in the former case by a majority of eight to six, in the latter unanimously.　The Committee, however, also considered the ways in which prescriptive acquisition—if it should be retained for easements—should operate, and was unanimous on the new system to be adopted.

The main recommendations, in brief outline, are :—

(1) All existing methods of acquisition of easements and profits by prescription should be abolished.　This recommendation includes the abolition of prescription at common law and under the doctrine of a lost modern grant, and the repeal of the Prescription Act 1832.[6]

---

[1] [1967] 2 Q. B. 379 ; [1967] 1 All E. R. 504 ; M. & B. p. 478 ; *supra*, p. 586.

[2] *Epps* v. *Esso Petroleum Co., Ltd.*, [1973] 1 W. L. R. 1071 ; [1973] 2 All E. R. 465 ; M. & B. p. 141.　See also *Lee-Parker* v. *Izzet (No. 2)*, [1972] 1 W. L. R. 775 ; [1972] 2 All E. R. 800.

[3] Fourteenth Report (1966), Cmnd. 3100.　See (1967), 30 *M. L. R.* 189 (H. W. Wilkinson).　M. & B. pp. 579–80

The Law Commission will next prepare a report recommending changes in the law relating to easements, covenants (both negative and positive) and prescription.　It does not expect to submit it for some time (Law Com. No. 58. Eighth Annual Report 1972–1973, para. 21).　A Working Paper (1971 No. 36) suggests that " easements and covenants should be assimilated along lines hitherto regarded as appropriate to easements " (para. 9) and, in relation to prescription, " as at present advised we are inclined to agree in principle with the majority, but only on the basis that some alternative to prescription can be found.　In the meantime it will be assumed that prescription will continue. " (para. 99).　It should be reformed along the lines recommended by the Law Reform Committee (Proposition 10).　For further criticism of the Prescription Act 1832, see Holdsworth, *Historical Introduction to the Land Law*, pp. 284–6 ; *History of English Law*, vol. vii pp. 350–62 ; Simpson, *Introduction to the History of Land Law*, pp. 250–51, Underhill, *Century of Law Reform*, p. 308.

[4] [1971] Q. B. 528, at p. 543.

[5] Paras. 32, 98.

[6] Paras. 40, 98, 99 (1)–(3).

(2) The following method should be adopted, if it were decided to substitute a new system for easements only : [1]

(a) The prescriptive period should be a period in gross of 12 years (*i.e.*, it need not be " next before action brought ").[2]

(b) There should be no " disabilities." [3]

(c) An easement should be capable of being acquired against the owner of a limited interest in the servient land so as to subsist as long as that servient owner's interest subsists.[4] Prescription by the owner of a limited interest in the dominant land should continue, as at present, in favour of the freeholder.[5] A tenant should be able to prescribe against his landlord and vice-versa.[6]

(d) Enjoyment :

(i) by force should not count in favour of the dominant owner ;[7]

(ii) must have been actually known to the servient owner or ought reasonably to have been known to him ;[8]

(iii) must be of such a kind and frequency as would only be justified by the existence of an easement ;[9]

(iv) by consent or agreement, whether written or oral, should not count. If so enjoyed for one year or more, the consent, like an interruption, would prevent earlier enjoyment being added to later enjoyment for the purpose of making up the required total of 12 years. A consent which is indefinite in duration should operate for one year.[10]

(e) Notional interruption, on the lines of the Rights of Light Act 1959, should be extended to easements generally ; this should be by registration against the dominant land in the local land charges register after notice given. Interruption, notional or actual, should endure for 12 months in order to be effective.[11]

(f) An easement, acquired by prescription, should be lost by 12 years continuous non-user.[12]

(3) The Committee is unanimous about provisions to facilitate, subject to compensation where appropriate, the acquisition of

---

[1] Para. 99 (6).

[2] Paras. 41–43. Prescription Act 1832, s. 4.

[3] Para. 44. *Ibid.*, ss. 7, 8.

[4] Paras. 47–49.   [5] Para. 50.

[6] Para. 51.   [7] Para. 57.

[8] Para. 58.   [9] Para. 59.

[10] Paras. 61–63.

[11] As at present. Prescription Act 1832, s. 4. Paras. 64–69, 75.

[12] Para. 81.

easements of support for buildings by land or for buildings by buildings.[1]

(4) Shelter of a building by an adjoining building should be treated in the same way as support.[2]

(5) The Lands Tribunal should be empowered to discharge easements or substitute more convenient ones, subject to payment of compensation where appropriate.[3]

---

[1] Paras. 89–95, 99 (8)–(11).
[2] Paras. 96, 99 (12) ; *Phipps* v. *Pears*, [1965] 1 Q. B. 76 ; [1964] 2 All E. R. 35 ; *supra*, p. 524.
[3] Paras. 97, 99 (13).

CHAPTER III

RESTRICTIVE COVENANTS

SUMMARY

Does a covenant relating to land affect only the contracting parties?

It sometimes happens that a landowner desires to impose a positive or a negative duty upon the owner of neighbouring land with the object of preserving the saleable value or the residential amenities of his own property. X., the owner of Whiteacre, for instance, who sells part of his garden (Blackacre) to Y., may wish to control the manner in which Y. uses the land. Accordingly X. may require Y. to covenant that he will not build shops on Blackacre or that he will construct and maintain a road across it for the benefit of X. and his successors in title. Such a covenant remains binding *qua* contract between X. and Y. personally, but does its benefit run with Whiteacre and its burden with Blackacre in the sense that it is enforceable by the successors in title of the former against the successors in title of the latter?

If the privilege granted by the covenant constitutes a legal easement, there is no difficulty. It permanently binds the servient Blackacre and permanently enures for the benefit of the dominant Whiteacre. If the covenant is contained in a lease, again there is no difficulty, for it will normally run both with the land and with the reversion.[1] Otherwise there is the fundamental objection that a stranger to a contract can neither enforce nor be found by its terms.[2]

We must now consider the extent to which in this context the doctrine of privity of contract has been relaxed, first by the common law, secondly by equity.[3]

SECTION I. THE EXTENT TO WHICH COVENANTS MADE ON THE OCCASION OF A SALE IN FEE SIMPLE RUN AT COMMON LAW[4]

Benefit may run at Common Law. The rule at law for several centuries has been that the *benefit* of covenants, whether positive or negative, which are made with a covenantee, having an interest in the land to which they relate, passes to his successors in title.[5] Thus in *Sharp* v. *Waterhouse*[6] it was admitted that— *(margin: Common Law rule; benefit may run.)*

A covenant by the owner of a mill that he " his heirs executors and administrators " would supply pure water to the adjacent land of X., ran with that land and could be put in suit by X.'s devisee.

The covenantor is liable to the successors in title of the covenantee merely because of the covenant that he has made, not because of his relationship to any servient tenement.[7] He is liable even though he himself owns no land.[8]

Four things, however, are essential to bring this rule into operation at common law:—

(i) The covenant must touch and concern the land of the covenantee.[9]

---

[1] *Supra*, p. 449 *et seq.*

[2] See Cheshire and Fifoot, *Law of Contract* (8th Edn.), pp. 428 *et seq.*

[3] See generally Preston and Newsom, *Restrictive Covenants Affecting Freehold Land* (5th Edn. 1971) ; Farrand, *Contract and Conveyance* (2nd Edn. 1973) pp. 404 *et seq.* ; (1971) 87 *L. Q. R.* 539 (D. J. Hayton).

[4] See (1954), 18 *Conv.* (N.S.) 546 (E. H. Scammell).

[5] *The Prior's Case* (1369), Y. B. 42 Ed. III., pl. 14, fol. 3 A. ; Co. Litt. 384a ; *Shayler* v. *Woolf*, [1946] Ch. 320 ; [1946] 2 All E. R. 54 (express assignment by covenantee of the benefit of the covenant) ; *Smith and Snipes Hall Farm, Ltd.* v. *River Douglas Catchment Board*, [1949] 2 K. B. 500 ; [1949] 2 All E. R. 179 ; 1 Smith's *Leading Cases* (13th Edn.), pp. 51, 65, 73. M. & B. p. 704.

[6] (1857), 7 E. & B. 816.

[7] *Smith and Snipes Hall Farm, Ltd.* v. *River Douglas Catchment Board, supra.*

[8] *Ibid.*   [9] *Rogers* v. *Hosegood*, [1900] 2 Ch. 388, at p. 395.

(ii) There must be an intention that the benefit should run with the land owned by the covenantee at the date of the covenant.[1]

At common law the benefit of a covenant prima facie enures only in favour of the covenantee and his heirs, and, if a wider operation is intended, it is essential that the intention be stated in the covenant.

(iii) The covenantee, at the time of making the covenant, must have the legal estate in the land which is to be benefited.[2]

(iv) An assignee who seeks to enforce the covenant must have the same estate in the land as the original covenantee, for the covenant is incident to that estate.[3]

Thus, at common law a covenant taken by an owner in fee simple does not avail his lessee. This rule, however, has been abrogated for covenants made after 1925 by the statutory provision that:—

" A covenant relating to any land of the covenantee shall be deemed to be made with the covenantee and his successors in title and the persons deriving title under him or them, and shall have effect as if such successors and other persons were expressed."[4]

In the present context, of course, this provision will avail a successor in title, such as a lessee, only where the covenant is one that touches and concerns the land that he holds.

The benefit of a covenant may also be transferred by assignment as a chose in action under section 136 of the Law of Property Act 1925. To be effective at law, the assignment must be in writing, and express notice in writing given to the covenantor.[5]

Burden does not run.

Burden does not run at Common Law.—In *Austerberry* v. *The Corporation of Oldham*[6] the view was expressed by two Lords Justices that the burden of a positive covenant made between a vendor and a purchaser does not run with the fee simple at common law.

---

[1] *Rogers* v. *Hosegood,* [1900] 2 Ch. 388, at p. 396 ; *Shayler* v. *Woolf,* [1946] Ch. 320 ; [1940] 2 All E. R. 54 ; *Smith and Snipes Hall Farm Ltd.* v. *River Douglas Catchment Board, supra,* at p. 506.
[2] *Webb* v. *Russell* (1789), 3 Term Rep. 393.
[3] *Smith and Snipes Hall Farm, Ltd.* v. *River Douglas Catchment Board,* [1949] 2 K. B. 500, at p. 516.
[4] L.P.A. 1925, s. 78 (1) ; *Smith and Snipes Hall Farm, Ltd.* v. *River Douglas Catchment Board, supra.* For a criticism of this decision of the Court of Appeal see 18 Conv. (N.S.), at pp. 553–6. It would seem that the section was intended to abrogate (ii) and not (iv) and thus to be a " word-saving " section only. *Smith and Snipes Hall Farm Ltd.* v. *River Douglas Catchment Board* (where one of the plaintiffs was a yearly tenant) was followed in *Williams* v. *Unit Construction Co. Ltd.* (1955), 19 *Conv.* (N.S.) 262 (where the plaintiff was a weekly tenant). See also Wolstenholme and Cherry, Vol. 1, pp. 162–3 ; (1972B) 31 C. L. J. 157, pp. 171–5, (H. W. R. Wade).
[5] See Cheshire and Fifoot, *op cit.,* pp. 489 *et seq.*
[6] (1885), 29 Ch. D. 750; M. & B. p. 685.

In that case

> A. conveyed part of his land to trustees with a view to their forming it into a road, which was to pass across the land of A. and other adjacent owners. The trustees for themselves, their heirs and assigns covenanted with A., his heirs and assigns that they would form this strip of land into a road and would ever afterwards keep it in repair. The road was duly made, and later A. sold to the plaintiff the part of his land which ran along both sides of the road. The Corporation of Oldham then took the road over from the trustees and sought to make the plaintiff bear a share of the cost of its maintenance, but he resisted this claim on the ground that the benefit of the original covenant had passed from A. to himself, and the burden of it from the trustees to the Corporation.

It will be noticed that the plaintiff was obliged to prove two things, namely, that the benefit of the covenant had passed to him and that the burden had passed to the Corporation. In neither case did he succeed. As regards his right to take the benefit, it was held that no such right was acquired by him, because the covenant, since it did not pointedly refer to the covenantee's land, but was meant to confer the boon of a road on the public, lacked the primary essential of being one which touched and concerned the land. Then LINDLEY and FRY, L.JJ., expressed their strong opinion that, apart from the case of landlord and tenant, the burden of a covenant can never run with the land of the covenantor at law.

A decision in accordance with these opinions was ultimately given in the case of *E. and G. C., Ltd.* v. *Bate*[1] where the point arose in a neat form.

> In 1909 A. conveyed a strip of land to X. and covenanted to construct a road upon part of it when required to do so. Both parties owned land abutting on the proposed road.

It was held in 1935 that an assignee of the covenantee, X., was not entitled to recover damages for breach of covenant from the defendant, who was the devisee of A.'s land.

There are however, " a number of current techniques and devices by which lawyers attempt to surmount or circumvent the difficulties of enforcing positive covenants." [2] Among these the best known are :— *Devices to enable burden to run.*

(i) Instead of selling land, to lease it and to enforce the positive covenant under the doctrine of privity of estate.[3]

(ii) Chains of Indemnity Covenants.

As we have seen, an original covenantor remains liable even after he has parted with the land, and so he may protect himself by taking a covenant of indemnity from his purchaser. Each succes-

---

[1] (1935), 79 L. J. News. 203.
[2] Report of the Committee on Positive Covenants Affecting Land (1965), Cmnd. 2719, para. 8, whence the quotations in this paragraph are taken. For other methods of circumvention, see also M. & B. pp. 687–9 ; George, *The Sale of Flats* (3rd Edn. 1970), pp. 14–16, 70–6 ; (1973) 37 Conv. (N.S.) 194 (A. M. Prichard). [3] *Supra*, pp. 449 *et seq.*

sive purchaser may give a similar covenant to his vendor with the result that a chain of indemnity covenants is created. In theory the original covenantee should be able to secure the indirect enforcement of the positive covenant by the current owner of the land by suing the original covenantor. " But in practice this device sooner or later becomes ineffective, either in consequence of the death or disappearance of the original covenantor, or because a break occurs in the chain of indemnities."

(iii) The doctrine of *Halsall* v. *Brizell*.[1]

" In some cases a positive covenant can be enforced in practice by the operation of the maxim ' *qui sentit commodum sentire debet et onus* ' ". This obliges a person who wishes to take advantage of a service or facility (*e.g.* a road or drains) to comply with any corresponding obligation to contribute to the cost of providing or maintaining it. The maxim cannot, however, be invoked where the burdened owner does not enjoy any service or facility to which his obligations attach or has no sufficient interest in the continuance of these benefits."

(iv) Enlargement of long leases into freeholds.

This is an " untried and artificial " device, whereby a long lease is enlarged under section 153 of the Law of Property Act 1925, and the freehold is then subject " to all the same covenants . . . as the term would have been subject to if it had not been so enlarged."[2]

Proposed
amendment
of the law.

Thus, in spite of these methods of circumvention, the burden of a covenant, whether positive or negative, does not run at common law with the servient land upon which it is imposed. As we are about to see, this rule has been radically relaxed by equity in the case of a negative covenant which merely restricts an owner from making certain defined uses of his land, but it still governs a positive covenant, such as one to maintain a fence for the benefit of a neighbouring owner or to contribute towards the cost of constructing and maintaining a private road. That such a covenant should be unenforceable against the successors in title of the covenantor is in many cases unreasonable, as, for instance, where the purchaser of a flat has entered into positive covenants that are essential to the comfort of his neighbours in the same building. However, in 1965 the Wilberforce Committee recommended that :—

"the assignability and enforcement of positive covenants should, as far as possible, be assimilated to that of negative covenants."[3]

---

[1] [1957] Ch. 169 ; [1957] 1 All E. R. 371 ; *E. R. Ives Investment, Ltd.* v. *High,* [1967] 2 Q. B. 379 ; [1967] 1 All E. R. 504 ; *Montague* v. *Long* (1972), 24 P. & C. R. 240. See too (1957), 73 *L. Q. R.* 154 (R. E. Megarry).

[2] *Supra,* p. 462.

[3] Report of the Committee on Positive Covenants affecting Land 1965, (Cmnd. 2719), para. 10 ; Law Commission Report on Restrictive Covenants 1967 (Law Com. No. 11), para. 30 ; Law Commission Working Paper on

SECTION II. THE EXTENT TO WHICH RESTRICTIVE COVENANTS, WHETHER MADE BETWEEN LESSOR AND LESSEE, OR BETWEEN THE VENDOR AND THE PURCHASER OF A FEE SIMPLE, RUN WITH THE LAND IN EQUITY

(A) GENERAL NATURE OF THE EQUITABLE DOCTRINE.

In the historic case of *Tulk* v. *Moxhay*,[1] the common law rule, that the burden of a covenant does not run with the land of the covenantor except in the case of a lease, was radically modified by equity so far as negative covenants are concerned. The general effect of the doctrine established by this case is that, subject to certain conditions to be discussed at length later, a covenant *negative in substance* entered into by the owner of Blackacre with the neighbouring owner of Whiteacre, imposes an equitable burden upon Blackacre that is enforceable to the same extent as any other equitable interest, such as a contract for a lease. The right to obtain an injunction against a breach of the negative undertaking will pass to the subsequent owners of Whiteacre, and the duty to observe it will pass to all persons who take the burdened Blackacre, except a purchaser for value of the legal estate therein without notice, actual or constructive, of the covenant. The facts of *Tulk* v. *Moxhay* were as follows :— *The doctrine of Tulk v. Moxhay.*

In 1808 the plaintiff, being then the owner in fee of the vacant piece of ground in the middle of Leicester Square, London, sold the ground to one Elms in fee, Elms covenanting for himself, his heirs and assigns that he and they would

"keep and maintain the said piece of ground and Square Garden, and the iron railing round the same in its then form, and in sufficient and proper repair as a Square Garden and Pleasure Ground, in an open state, uncovered with any buildings in neat and ornamental order."

The piece of ground passed by divers conveyances into the hands of the defendant Moxhay, who, although he had made no similar covenant with his immediate vendor, admitted that he took the land with notice of the original covenant. The defendant then openly proposed to erect buildings upon the square, but the plaintiff, who still remained the owner of several adjacent houses, succeeded in obtaining an injunction to stop the breach of covenant.

Appurtenant Rights (No. 36, 1971) recommends that positive covenants to carry out or pay for work on land be enforceable as Land Obligations (paras. 41–4 ; Propositions 5 and 6). The Law Commission will next prepare a report recommending changes in the law relating to easements, covenants (both negative and positive) and prescription. It does not expect to submit this for some time. Eighth Annual Report 1972–1973 (Law Com. No. 58), para. 21. See also (1972B) 31 C. L. J. 157 (H. W. R. Wade).

[1] (1848), 2 Ph. 774; M. & B. p. 693.

This doctrine has been the subject of development, in the course of which the nature of the right and obligation arising from a restrictive covenant has undergone a radical change.[1] The earlier decisions, culminating in *Luker* v. *Dennis*,[2] in 1877, proceeded solely upon the fact of notice,[3] since this was the element that Lord Cottenham stressed in *Tulk* v. *Moxhay* in the following words :—

> " It is said that, the covenant being one which does not run with the land, this court cannot enforce it ; but the question is, not whether the covenant runs with the land, but whether a party shall be permitted to use the land in a manner inconsistent with the contract entered into by his vendor, and with notice of which he purchased."[4]

To rest the enforcement of a contract against a third party on this basis is not without its dangers.

First, if the emphasis is laid upon whether the conscience of the third party acquiring the land of the covenantor is affected, instead of upon whether the land itself is affected, there will be certain persons, such as a squatter obtaining a title by twelve years' adverse possession,[5] who will enjoy an immunity that they do not deserve.

Secondly, if notice alone justifies the issue of an injunction, the remedy can scarcely be withheld in principle even though the contract is collateral in the sense that its purpose is not to protect the covenantee's land against an undesirable use of the covenantor's land, but to confer some personal privilege upon the covenantee. The doctrine of *Tulk* v. *Moxhay* was indeed carried to these lengths in *Luker* v. *Dennis*.[6]

> A publican, who already held a lease from X. of a public house called the " Milton Arms," took a lease of a second house, the " Sutton Arms," from a different landlord who was a brewer.
>
> In this second lease he covenanted for himself and his assigns that he would buy from the brewer all the beer which he sold not only at the " Sutton Arms," but also at the " Milton Arms." Later the publican assigned the " Milton Arms " lease to the defendant, who took with notice that the public house was " tied " by the covenant to the brewer—that is to say, to a person who, apart from the covenant, was an absolute stranger to the property.
>
> It was held that the defendant was bound by the covenant, since he had notice of it at the time when he took the assignment. It was regarded as immaterial that no proprietary relation in respect of the " Milton Arms " such as that of vendor and purchaser, or lessor and lessee, existed between the original covenanting parties.

This was an indefensible extension of a contractual liability to a non-contracting party, but it was the last case in which *Tulk* v. *Moxhay* was based on the doctrine of notice pure and simple. Since the end of the nineteenth century the judicial approach to

---

[1] See especially Behan, *Covenants affecting Land*, pp. 27 *et seq.*
[2] (1877), 7 Ch. D. 227.
[3] *London County Council* v. *Allen*, [1914] 3 K. B. 642, at pp. 658–9, 664–6.
[4] *Tulk* v. *Moxhay*, (1848), 2 Ph. 774, at p. 777.
[5] *Infra*, pp. 603–4.   [6] (1877), 7 Ch. D. 227.

the matter has altered. The courts, choosing as the appropriate analogy either the negative easement, such as the right to light, or the tenant's covenant that is annexed to the land by virtue of *Spencer's* case,[1] have required a restrictive covenant to possess what may be called a real, as distinct from a personal, flavour, before it becomes available to and enforceable against third parties. It must, as VAUGHAN WILLIAMS, L.J., said, " arise from the relation of two estates one to the other,"[2] or, to use more familiar language, it must touch and concern the dominant tenement of the covenantee and must be intended to protect that land against certain users of the servient tenement. But once it satisfies this requirement it creates an equitable right that will run with the dominant tenement and a corresponding equitable obligation binding on the servient tenement. Being an equitable burden, it affects every person in the world who comes to the servient tenement, except one who acquires the legal estate for value therein without notice, actual or constructive, of the covenant. The position cannot be better described than in the words of COLLINS, L.J. :—

> " When the benefit has been once clearly annexed to one piece of land, it passes by assignment of that land, and may be said to run with it ... without proof of special bargain or representation on the assignment. In such a case it runs, not because the conscience of either party is affected, but because the purchaser has bought something which inhered in or was annexed to the land bought. That is the reason why, in dealing with the burden, the purchaser's conscience is not affected by notice of covenants which were part of the original bargain on the first sale, but were merely personal and collateral, while it is affected by notice of those which touch and concern the land. The covenant must be one that is capable of running with the land before the question of the purchaser's conscience and the equity affecting it can come into discussion." [3]

Notice alone insufficient to impose liability.

As the law now stands, certain essentials must be satisfied before the burden of a covenant can be laid upon an assignee of the servient tenement or before its benefit can be exploited by an assignee of the dominant tenement. These will now be stated.

(B) CONDITIONS PRECEDENT TO THE ENFORCEMENT OF A RESTRICTIVE COVENANT IN EQUITY

(1) THE RUNNING OF THE BURDEN WITH THE LAND OF THE COVENANTOR

The burden of a restrictive covenant will bind an assignee of the servient tenement if the following essentials are satisfied.

---

[1] *L. and S. W. Rail Co.* v. *Gomm* (1882), 20 Ch. D. 562, at p. 583 ; M. & B. p. 699.
[2] *Formby* v. *Barker*, [1903] 2 Ch. 539, at p. 553. No such relation existed, for instance, in *Tophams, Ltd.*, v. *Earl of Sefton*, [1967] 1 A. C. 50 ; [1966] 1 All E. R. 1039.   [3] *Rogers* v. *Hosegood*, [1900] 2 Ch. 388, at p. 407.

Doctrine does not apply to positive covenants.

(a) The Covenant must be Negative in Nature. It is essential that the covenant should be negative in substance, not a positive one requiring the expenditure of money for its performance.[1] This condition is satisfied if the owner of the land undertakes to use the premises for private residence only, or to keep certain windows obscured, or not to build, not to open a public house, not to carry on a business, and so on. But in every case it is the substance and not the form of the contract that must be regarded, for if an undertaking, though couched in affirmative terms, clearly implies a negative, it will be caught by the doctrine of *Tulk* v. *Moxhay*. Indeed, in that case itself, the covenant was not in terms restrictive, but its provision that the piece of ground was to be used only as an ornamental garden implied a prohibition against building.[2] Again, a covenant to give the first refusal of land is regarded as negative in substance, since in effect it is a promise not to sell without giving the covenantee an option to buy.[3]

Necessity for protection of dominant land.

(b) The covenantee must at the time of the creation of the covenant and afterwards own land for the protection of which the covenant is made. A restrictive covenant taken from the purchaser of a freehold estate is a mere covenant in gross personal to the contracting parties, unless it imposes an equitable burden upon the covenantor's land for the protection of land owned by the covenantee. Equity, acting on the analogy of a negative easement, will not regard a restrictive covenant as other than personal, unless there is the relation of dominancy and serviency between the respective properties.

Effect of covenant if there is no dominant land.

It follows, therefore, that, if the covenantee retains no adjacent land or owns no land capable of being protected by the covenant, the covenant cannot be enforced against a person other than the covenantor, even if he has notice of it.[4]

Thus in *London County Council* v. *Allen*,[5]

---

[1] *Haywood* v. *Brunswick Permanent Benefit Building Society* (1881), 8 Q. D. B. 403. Positive and negative obligations may be set out in a single covenant. "There cannot be any doctrine of contagious proximity whereby the presence of the positive inhibits the enforcement of the neighbouring negative." *Shepherd Homes, Ltd.* v. *Sandham (No. 2)*, [1971] 1 W. L. R. 1063; [1971] 2 All E. R. 1267, *per* Megarry, J.

[2] *Clegg* v. *Hands* (1890), 44 Ch. D. 503, 519.

[3] *Manchester Ship Canal Co.* v. *Manchester Racecourse Co.*, [1902] 2 Ch. 37.

[4] But a lessor's interest in the reversion suffices to make a covenant touching and concerning the land enforceable against a sub-lessee; *Hall* v. *Ewin* (1887), 37 Ch. D. 74; *Regent Oil Co.* v. *J. A. Gregory (Hatch End), Ltd.*, [1966] Ch. 402, 432-3; [1965] 3 All E. R. 673. For statutory exceptions to the rule see (a) covenants arising by use of special statutes, such as National Trust Act 1937, s. 8; *Gee* v. *The National Trust*, [1966] 1 W. L. R. 170; [1966] 1 All E. R. 954; Green Belt (London and Counties) Act 1938, s. 22; Water Act 1945, s. 15; Forestry Act 1947, s. 1; National Parks and Access to the Countryside Act 1949, s. 16; (b) covenants entered into with local authorities under Local or Private Acts; Housing Act 1957, s. 151; T.C.P.A. 1971, s. 52.

[5] [1914] 3 K. B. 642; M. & B. p. 694; *Formby* v. *Barker*, [1903] 2 Ch. 539; M. & B. p. 697.

A, a builder, in return for permission to lay out a new street on his land, entered into a covenant with L.C.C. not to build upon a plot of land which lay across the end of the proposed street. The plot was eventually conveyed to Mrs. A, who built on it and mortgaged it to B. The Court of Appeal held that the restrictive covenant was not binding on Mrs. A and B, even if they had had notice of it.

BUCKLEY, L.J. in the course of his judgment said :[1]

"In the present case we are asked to extend the doctrine of *Tulk* v. *Moxhay* so as to affirm that a restrictive covenant can be enforced against a derivative owner taking with notice by a person who never has had or who does not retain any land to be protected by the restrictive covenant in question. In my opinion the doctrine does not extend to that case. The doctrine is that a covenant not running with the land, but being a negative covenant entered into by an owner of land with an adjoining owner, binds the land in equity and is enforceable against a derivative owner taking with notice. The doctrine ceases to be applicable when the person seeking to enforce the covenant against the derivative owner has no land to be protected by the negative covenant. The fact of notice is in that case irrelevant."[2]

Again, once a covenantee has assigned the whole of the dominant land, he cannot enforce the covenant against the servient owner. His one remedy is to sue the covenantor personally on the contract, but even so he is entitled only to nominal damages, not to an injunction. The principle of *London County Council* v. *Allen*[3] is that the equitable doctrine ought to be applied with the sole object of protecting the enjoyment of the land which the covenant was intended to protect. If it were possible for a covenantee to enforce a covenant, despite the fact that he never retained any land at all or that he later disposed of the land which he had retained, the result would be to place an unwarranted and useless burden upon subsequent purchasers from the covenantor.[4]

(c) The covenant must touch and concern the dominant land. The covenant must be capable of benefiting the dominant land in the sense that it must be one which touches and concerns that land.[5] To satisfy this condition in the case where a freehold estate is conveyed,

> "the covenant must either affect the land as regards mode of occupation, or it must be such as *per se*, and not merely from collateral circumstances, affects the value of the land."[6]

The covenant must touch and concern the dominant land.

---

[1] At p. 654.

[2] See, however, p. 600, note 4, *supra*, as to the modern statutory power of local authorities to enforce restrictive covenants otherwise than for the protection of land.

[3] [1914] 3 K. B. 642; *Formby* v. *Barker*, [1903] 2 Ch. 539; *Kelly* v. *Barrett*, [1924] 2 Ch. 379.

[4] *Chambers* v. *Randall*, [1923] 1 Ch. 149, at p. 157; *Re Union of London and Smith's Bank, Ltd.'s Conveyance, Miles* v. *Easter*, [1933] Ch. 611, at p. 632.

[5] *Rogers* v. *Hosegood*, [1900] 2 Ch. 388, at p. 395; *Kelly* v. *Barrett*, [1924] 2 Ch. 379, at p. 395; *Marquess of Zetland* v. *Driver*, [1939] Ch. 1, at p. 8; [1938] 2 All E. R. 158, at p. 161.

[6] *Rogers* v. *Hosegood*, *supra*, at p. 395, *per* FARWELL, J., adopting BAYLEY, J., in *Congleton Corpn.* v. *Pattison* (1808), 10 East. 130.

Whether the covenant benefits the dominant land is a question of fact to be determined on expert evidence presented to the court.[1] The onus is on the defendant to show that it does not do so, either originally or at the date of the action.[2] This means that, if there were possible opinions either way, the defendant will still fail unless he can show that the opinion that the covenant benefits the land could not reasonably be held.[3]

Intention that burden of covenant shall run.

(d) It must be the common intention of the parties that the burden of the covenant shall run with the land of the covenantor. This intention may appear from the wording of the covenant itself, as, for instance, where the covenant is made by the covenantor for himself, his heirs and assigns. Covenants which are made after 1925 and relate to any land of the covenantor are deemed by section 79 of the Law of Property Act 1925 to be made by the covenantor on behalf of himself his successors in title and the persons deriving title under him or them, unless a contrary intention is expressed.[4]

Persons against whom restrictive convenant is enforceable.

We must now examine more closely the effect of a covenant which satisfies the four conditions set out above, and in particular consider those persons against whom the covenant is enforceable.

Restrictive covenants as equitable interests.

The doctrine of *Tulk* v. *Moxhay* stands on quite a different footing from the rules which regulate the running of covenants at law, and being of a far more elastic nature it affects a more extensive class of persons and embraces a more extensive class of covenants. The essence of the matter is that when once the above conditions are satisfied a restrictive covenant becomes an equitable interest, and as such is enforceable on general principles against all persons who acquire the burdened land, with the one exception of the purchaser for valuable consideration of the legal estate therein without notice of the covenant. Moreover, the occupier of the burdened land is liable irrespectively of the character of his occupation. This is in sharp contrast with the common law and statutory rules that govern covenants contained in a lease. Under these rules, as we have seen,[5] the burden of a covenant, whether positive or negative, that touches and concerns the land passes to an assignee of the tenant, and it is immaterial that the landlord retains no dominant land.[6] But no one is an

---

[1] *Marten* v. *Flight Refuelling Ltd.*, [1962] Ch. 115, at p. 137 ; *Earl of Leicester* v. *Wells-next-the-Sea U.D.C.*, [1973] Ch. 110 ; [1972] 3 All E. R. 77 ; *Wrotham Park Estate Co., Ltd.* v. *Parkside Homes, Ltd.*, [1974] 1 W. L. R. 799 ; [1974] 2 All E. R. 321.

[2] *Wrotham Park Estate Co., Ltd.* v. *Parkside Homes, Ltd.*, *supra*.

[3] (1974) J. P. L. at p. 133 (G. H. Newsom).

[4] *Re Royal Victoria Pavilion (Ramsgate)*, [1961] Ch. 581 ; [1961] 3 All E. R. 83 ; *Tophams, Ltd.* v. *Earl of Sefton*, [1967] 1 A. C. 50, at p. 81 ; [1966] 1 All E. R. 1039 ; *supra*, p. 454.

[5] *Supra*, p. 459, note 5.

[6] *Regent Oil Co., Ltd.* v. *J. A. Gregory (Hatch End), Ltd.*, [1966] Ch. 402; [1965] 3 All E. R. 673.

assignee for this purpose unless there is privity of estate between him and the reversioner. Thus, though the burden is traditionally said to run with the land, what in fact it runs with is the estate created by the lease. Under the developed doctrine of *Tulk* v. *Moxhay*, on the other hand, it runs with the servient land as such, and there is no question of privity of estate. A restrictive covenant is enforceable against the successors in title of the original covenantor, including a mere occupier of the land.[1]

The effect of this distinction between running with the land and running with the estate may be illustrated by a reference to three classes of persons who are all caught by the doctrine of *Tulk* v. *Moxhay*, but none of whom is liable at common law under the rules derived from *Spencer's* case.

A restrictive covenant imposed upon a lessee binds an under-lessee, despite the absence of privity of estate between him and the lessor.[2]   **Under-lessees.**

A person who is merely occupying land without having any definite estate or interest therein is bound by restrictive covenants. Thus in *Mander* v. *Falcke*,[3]   **Mere occupiers.**

> a lessee who had covenanted not to use the demised premises for purposes which would cause annoyance or inconvenience to adjoining property owned by the lessor granted an under-lease of the premises. The reversion was ultimately assigned to the plaintiff and the under-lease became vested in X. Apparently X. did not occupy the premises himself, but allowed his father to have possession, and the evidence clearly showed that the latter, while purporting to keep an oyster bar, was in fact using the place as a brothel to the great scandal of the neighbourhood.

In an injunction to restrain a breach of the covenant it was argued that such relief could not be granted against the father, as he had no interest whatever, either legal or equitable, in the land. This argument failed, and an injunction was granted against the father, LINDLEY, L.J., saying :

> " I treat him simply as an occupier managing the business. He may be neither an assignee nor purchaser, but he is in occupation, and that is enough to affect him, he having notice of the covenants in the lease." [4]

A person who acquires a title to land by lapse of time under the Limitation Act is bound by any restrictive covenants which are annexed to the land. We have seen that a covenant entered into between landlord and tenant does not at law bind a person who by long-continued possession of the premises acquires a superior right to the tenant, because the effect of the Limitation Act is merely to extinguish the right of the tenant and not to transfer his identical interest to the adverse possessor.[5]   There   **Disseisors.**

---

[1] L.P.A., 1925, s. 79 (2).
[2] *Clements* v. *Welles* (1863), L. R. 1 Eq. 200 ; *Hall* v. *Ewin* (1887), 37 Ch. D. 74 ; *John* v. *Holmes*, [1900] 1 Ch. 188.
[3] [1891] 2 Ch. 554.   [4] At p. 557.
[5] *Tichborne* v. *Weir* (1892), 67 L. T. 735 ; M. & B. p. 700. *Supra*, pp. 460-1.

is no privity of estate between the disseisor and the lessor. This lack of privity, however, will not free a disseisor of the servient land from a restrictive covenant unless he can prove that he is a purchaser for value of the legal estate without notice. The case of *Re Nisbet and Potts' Contract*[1] affords an illustration.

> Lands were sold in 1867 by A. to W., a covenant being entered into by the latter that he would not build on the purchased property within 30 feet of a certain road. This covenant was for the benefit of other property owned by A. In 1872 W. re-sold the land to X. with a similar covenant. Somewhere about 1878 Y. wrongfully seized the land and remained in occupation for over 12 years, after which he automatically acquired what is called a possessory title, and became entitled to keep the land as against X. In 1890 Y.'s son, who had succeeded his father, sold the land to Z., who agreed that instead of requiring the title to be proved for the last 40 years[2] he would be content with proof that Y. had been in possession since before 1878. Later still the land was sold to Nisbet, and he agreed in 1903 to sell it to Potts. The question was whether Potts, if he took a conveyance of the land, would be subject to the restrictive covenant imposed by the original deed of 1867.

It was argued that the covenant no longer bound assignees of the servient land, for Y., who had seized the land in 1878, acquired a title quite independent of any prior holder's title, and that, even if it made any difference, which was denied, neither Z. nor Nisbet had notice of the covenant and therefore could not be bound thereby. But it was held that the equitable interest created by the covenant remained enforceable against Z. and Nisbet, unless they could satisfy the Court that they had acquired the legal estate for valuable consideration without notice.

They certainly had acquired the legal estate for value without actual notice, but nevertheless they were affected by constructive notice, for if they had insisted, as they might have done, upon proof of a good root of title at least 40 years old, they would have been led back through the squatter Y. to the original covenantor W. If they chose to accept less than they might have done, they were bound to take the consequences.

Further, it was clear that the lapse of time and the changes of title that had occurred since 1867 did not bar the remedy of the person in whom the benefit of the covenant was now vested. Time under the Limitation Act does not begin to run against a person until his right of action accrues. In the instant case no right of action would accrue until the covenant was broken, and there had been no question of this until 1903.

Binding effect of restrictive covenants. A final word is now required as to the binding effect of restrictive covenants.

---

[1] [1905] 1 Ch. 391 ; [1906] 1 Ch. 386; M. & B. p. 700.
[2] *Supra*, p. 65.

Since 1925 restrictive covenants have been divided into two classes :—

1. those created before January 1st, 1926, when the Law of Property Act 1925 came into force ;

2. those created after 1925.

1. The rule which governs covenants created before January 1st, 1926, is that laid down above, viz. that they bind all persons who acquire the burdened land, with the exception of a purchaser for value of the legal estate therein without notice, actual or constructive, of the covenants. Such a purchaser can, however, pass a title free from the restriction to a purchaser from him, even though the latter has actual notice of the covenant.[1]

2. Covenants created after 1925, except those made between lessor and lessee,[2] are void against a purchaser (including a mortgagee and lessee) of the *legal estate* in the burdened land *for money or money's worth*, unless they are registered as land charges in the appropriate register.[3] If not registered they are void against the purchaser for value of the legal estate even though he had express notice of them. Thus non-registration does not avail an assignee of a mere equitable interest in the burdened land, or an assignee of the legal estate who does not give money or money's worth. The reason why a restrictive covenant between a lessor and lessee cannot be registered, is that it is a simple and normal step for an assignee to inspect the lease which contains the terms of the tenancy.

(2) THE RUNNING OF THE BENEFIT WITH THE LAND OF THE COVENANTEE

Suppose that on the sale of Whiteacre to X. a restrictive covenant has been taken from him for the protection of Blackacre still retained by the vendor, A. ; and suppose further that A. has subsequently sold Blackacre, the dominant land, to B. Can B. enforce the covenant against X. or against Y. who is an assignee of X.'s land ? The answer is that enforcement is not automatic merely because the dominant land has come into the hands of B. B. must go further. He must prove, not only that he has acquired the land, but also that he has acquired the benefit of the covenant itself.

---

[1] *Wilkes* v. *Spooner,* [1911] 2 K. B. 473; M. & B. p. 29.
[2] *Dartstone, Ltd.* v. *Cleveland Petroleum Co., Ltd.,* [1969] 1 W. L. R. 1807; [1969] 3 All E. R. 668 ; (1956) 20 Conv. (N.S.) 370 (R. G. Rowley).
[3] L.C.A. 1972, ss. 2 (5) Class D (ii), 4 (6) ; s. 17 (1), *infra*, pp. 743-4.

When it is
necessary to
rely on
equitable
rules.

We have already seen that the benefit of a covenant runs at common law subject to certain conditions.[1] If B. can satisfy these, there is no need for him to rely on the rules evolved by equity for the running of the benefit.   There are however circumstances in which the common law rules are inapplicable, and it is then that B. must prove that he has satisfied the conditions which equity imposes.

The situations in which B. must do this are

(*a*) where B. is, or A. the original covenantee, was, a mere equitable owner of Blackacre.[2]

(*b*) where B. does not have the same legal estate in Blackacre as A. had.   This would only apply to covenants made before 1926.[3]

(*c*) where Whiteacre has been conveyed to Y. and enforcement against Y. depends upon the equitable doctrine of *Tulk* v. *Moxhay*.[4]

(*d*) where B. relies upon an express assignment of the benefit of the covenant from A., and the assignment does not comply with section 136 of the Law of Property Act 1925.[5]

(*e*) Where part only of Whiteacre has been conveyed to B, for " at law, the benefit could not be assigned in pieces. It would have to be assigned as a whole or not at all."[6]

(*f*) where B. relies upon his land being part of a scheme of development.[7]

In these situations there are only three ways[8] in which B. can show that he has acquired the benefit of the covenant itself, namely by proving :

Ways in
which bene-
fit passes.

(*a*) that the benefit of the covenant has been effectively annexed to the dominant land, and that he has acquired the whole of that land, or the part of it to which the covenant was annexed; or,

(*b*) that the benefit of the covenant was separately and expressly assigned to him at the time of the sale ; or,

(*c*) that both the dominant and servient lands are subject to a scheme of development.

---

[1] *Supra*, p. 593.
[2] *Fairclough* v. *Marshall* (1878), 4 Ex. D. 37 ; *Rogers* v. *Hosegood*, [1900] 2 Ch. 388 (a mortgagor before 1926) ; M. & B. p. 710.
[3] L.P.A. 1925, s. 78 (1) ; *supra*, p. 594.
[4] *Renals* v. *Cowlishaw* (1878), 9 Ch. D. 125, ; M. & B. p. 713 ; *Re Union of London and Smith's Bank, Ltd.'s Conveyance, Miles* v. *Easter*, [1933] Ch. 611, *per* ROMER, L.J. at p. 630 ; M. & B. p. 723 ; *Marten* v. *Flight Refuelling, Ltd.*, [1962] Ch. 115 ; [1961] 2 All E. R. 696.
[5] *Infra*, pp. 610 et seq.
[6] *Re Union of London and Smith's Bank, Ltd's Conveyance*, *supra*, at p. 630, *per* ROMER, L.J.   [7] *Infra*, pp. 612 et seq.
[8] *Re Pinewood Estate, Farnborough*, [1958] Ch. 280 ; [1957] 2 All E. R. 517 ; M. & B. p. 709.

Let us take these methods separately.

(a) Annexation of Covenant to Dominant Land

Whether or not the benefit of a restrictive covenant runs with the dominant land by virtue of its express annexation to that land depends on the intention of the parties to be inferred from the language which they used in the deed creating the covenant. This intention to annex is commonly inferred when the covenant is made " with so and so, owners or owner for the time being of whatever the land may be. Another method is to state by means of an appropriate declaration that the covenant is taken ' for the benefit of ' whatever the lands may be." [1]

Annexation inferred from language of covenant.

Thus in *Rogers* v. *Hosegood* [2] the following covenant was held to be annexed to the land.

> " with intent that the covenants might so far as possible bind the premises thereby conveyed and every part thereof and might enure to the benefit of the vendors ... their heirs and assigns and others claiming under them to all or any of their lands adjoining or near to the said premises."

Furthermore, the exact land to which the parties intend to annex the benefit of the covenant must be ascertainable. Whether this is so depends primarily upon the construction of the deed of conveyance. A competent draftsman will describe the land in precise terms, as for instance by declaring that the covenant is taken for the benefit of " the property known as Blackacre " ; or for the " land marked red on the plan drawn on these presents." If the description is more vague, as for instance " the land adjoining " the servient land, extrinsic evidence is admissible to identify the particular land that the parties had in mind. [3]

Dominant land must be ascertainable.

In summary, the land must be clearly, [4] or easily, [5] identified in the conveyance creating the covenant. As we shall see, this is a stricter rule of identification than that which applies in the case of express assignment. [6]

Even if the language of the covenant indicates an intention to annex the benefit of the covenant to the whole of the land of the covenantee, such annexation will not be effected, unless substantially the whole of the land is capable of benefiting. Thus in *Re Ballard's Conveyance* [7]

> the benefit of a covenant which imposed a restriction on 18 acres was annexed by the conveyance to " the Childwickbury Estate."

---

[1] *Drake* v. *Gray*, [1936] Ch. 451 at p. 456 ; [1936] 1 All E. R. 363, *per* GREENE, L. J.

[2] [1900] 2 Ch. 388 ; M. & B. p. 710. *Cf. Renals* v. *Cowlishaw* (1878), 9 Ch. D. 125 ; M. & B. p. 713 (covenant with the vendors " their heirs, executors, administrators and assigns " held insufficient to annex, since no dominant land was specified).

[3] See Preston and Newsom, *Restrictive Covenants* (5th Edn.), p. 16.

[4] *Newton Abbot Co-operative Society, Ltd.* v. *Williamson and Treadgold, Ltd.*, [1952] Ch. 286, at p. 289 ; [1952] 1 All E. R. 679, *per* UPJOHN, J.

[5] *Marquess of Zetland* v. *Driver*, [1939] Ch. 1 at p. 8 ; [1938] 2 All E. R. 158, *per* FARWELL, J.

[6] *Infra*, pp. 610–1.   [7] [1937] Ch. 473 ; [1937] 2 All E. R. 691.

The area of this estate was about 1700 acres, far the largest part of which could not possibly be directly affected by a breach of the covenant.

Although it would seem that an injury to a part of any unity is inevitably an injury to the whole, CLAUSON, J. held that the covenant was not enforceable by assignees of the whole of the dominant land. Moreover, he refused to sever the covenant and thus to regard it as annexed to the part of the land that was in fact touched and concerned. The decision seems to amount to this : that if a convenantee over-estimates to a moderate degree the area of the dominant land capable of deriving advantage from a restrictive covenant, his attempt to preserve the amenities of the neighbourhood and to maintain the selling value of what he retains will fail.[1] Why the well-known doctrine of severance should be excluded from this type of contract is difficult to appreciate.[2]

On the other hand, a covenant which is annexed to the whole *or any part or parts* of the dominant land is enforceable by a successor in title to any part of that land which is in fact benefited by the covenant. In *Marquess of Zetland* v. *Driver*,[3] for instance :

> The covenant was expressed to be for the benefit and protection of " such part or parts of the [dominant land] (a) as shall for the time being remain unsold or (b) as shall be sold by the vendor or his successors in title with the express benefit of this covenant." Certain parts of the unsold land were contiguous to the land of the covenantor, but other parts were more than a mile distant. The covenant, therefore, did not benefit the whole of the dominant land.

It was held that the person who succeeded to the dominant land could enforce the covenant against a purchaser of the servient land. The Court of Appeal, without expressing approbation of *Re Ballard's Conveyance*, distinguished it on the ground that :—

> " in that case the covenant was expressed to run with the whole estate, whereas in the present case . . . the covenant is expressed to be for the benefit of the whole or any part or parts of the unsold settled property."[4]

Extrinsic evidence is admissible to show whether a covenant is capable of operating to the advantage of the dominant land.[5]

Effect of annexation.

The benefit of a restrictive covenant, once it has been annexed to the dominant land, runs automatically with that land and is enforceable by the successors in title of the covenantee, even though they do not learn of its existence until after execution of

---

[1] (1941), 57 *L. Q. R.* pp. 210–1 (G. R. Y. Radcliffe).
[2] See Elphinstone, *Covenants affecting Land*, p. 60, note 10.
[3] [1939] Ch. 1 ; [1938] 2 All E. R. 158.   [4] *Ibid.*, at p. 10.
[5] *Marten* v. *Flight Refuelling, Ltd.*, [1962] Ch. 115 ; [1961] 2 All E. R. 696 ; M. & B. p. 729 ; *Earl of Leicester* v. *Wells-next-the-Sea U.D.C.*, [1973] Ch. 110 ; [1972] 3 All E. R. 77 (expert evidence admitted to show that a covenant restricting 19 acres afforded " great benefit and much needed protection to the Holkham Estate as a whole " *i.e.* to 32,000 acres). In *Re Ballard's Conveyance supra*, no evidence was offered to show benefit to the dominant land as a whole.

the conveyance.[1] If a successor in title acquires the whole of the land, the benefit passes to him without question ; but if he acquires only part he must show that the benefit was annexed to that particular part alone or to each portion of the whole.

For instance, A., the owner of a large property, sells part of it to Y. and takes a covenant that no public house shall be opened on it. This covenant is annexed to A's land. Later A. sells part of the dominant land to B. If B. seeks to enforce the covenant by virtue of its annexation to A's land, he must prove that its benefit was annexed to each and every part of those lands or to the very part bought by him.

Whether or not there has been effective annexation to each and every part of the land is once again a question of construction of the language of the covenant. Thus in *Re Selwyn's Conveyance*[2] it was held that

> a covenant " to enure for the protection of the adjoining or neighbouring land part of, or lately part of, the Selwyn Estate "

was annexed to each part of the dominant land.

Furthermore, even if the covenant has been annexed only to the whole of the dominant land, a purchaser of part of it will be able to enforce the covenant if the benefit of the covenant has been expressly assigned to him.[3]

Finally we must consider what effect section 78 (1) of the Law of Property Act 1925 has on these rules of annexation.

Effect of s. 78(1) Law of Property Act 1925.

> " A covenant relating to any land of the covenantee shall be deemed to be made with the covenantee and his successors in title and the persons deriving title under him or them, and shall have effect as if such successors and other persons were expressed.
>
> For the purposes of this subsection in connexion with covenants restrictive of the user of land " successors in title " shall be deemed to include the owners and occupiers for the time being of the land of the covenantee intended to be benefited."

A possible construction of the section in this context is that where a covenant relates to the land of the covenantee (i.e., touches and concerns it) the benefit is annexed to the land without the need to use appropriate language from which an intention to annex

---

[1] *Rogers* v. *Hosegood,* [1900] 2 Ch. 388 ; M. & B. p. 710.

[2] [1967] Ch. 674 ; [1967] 1 All E. R. 339. *Cf. Russell* v. *Archdale,* [1964] Ch. 38 ; [1962] 2 All E. R. 305 ; M. & B. p. 719 ; *Re Jeff's Transfer (No. 2),* [1966] 1 W. L. R. 841 ; [1966] 1 All E. R. 937 ; *Stilwell* v. *Blackman,* [1968] Ch. 508 ; [1967] 3 All E. R. 514 ; M. & B. p. 721 ; *Griffiths* v. *Band* (1974), 29 P. & C. R. 243 (" this somewhat muddy corner of legal history ", *per* GOULDING, J., at p. 246) ; See Law Commission : Report on Restrictive Covenants 1967 (Law Com. No. 11), p. 15 which recommends that the benefit of a land obligation (*infra,* p. 621) should be annexed to each and every part unless a contrary intention is expressed. See too a valuable article in (1968), 84 *L. Q. R.* 22 (P. V. Baker).

[3] *Russell* v. *Archdale, supra.* (against the original convenantor who was still owner of the servient land) ; *Stilwell* v. *Blackman, supra* (against a successor in title of the original covenantor).

may be inferred. The alternative and better view is that it is a mere " word-saving " section and makes it unnecessary to include in the covenant an express reference to the covenantee's successors in title.[1]

(b) Express Assignment of Covenant

Limits within which assignment of covenant allowed.

Failure to establish the annexation described above is not necessarily fatal to an assignee of the covenantee's land, for he will succeed in an action for an infringement of the restriction if he shows that he is not only an assignee of the land, but also the express assignee of the *covenant* itself.[2]

As we have already seen, the benefit of a covenant may be transferred at law by assignment as a chose in action under section 136 of the Law of Property Act 1925.[3] " Where the defendant is liable at law (as the original convenantor or his personal representative) there is no difficulty peculiar to the case of covenants affecting land : such an action is governed by the ordinary rules as to the assignment of a chose in action. But where the defendant is sued as an assign of the land burdened by the covenant, the plaintiff can only establish the defendant's liability in equity under the rule in *Tulk* v. *Moxhay*."[4]

The equitable rules under which an express assignment is permissible were crystallised by ROMER, L.J. in *Re Union of London and Smith's Bank Ltd.'s Conveyance, Miles* v. *Easter.*[5]

(i) The covenant must have been taken for the benefit of the land of the covenantee and (ii) that land must be indicated with reasonable certainty. This indication need not appear in the conveyance creating the covenant. It is sufficient if in the light of the attendant circumstances the identity of the dominant land is in some other way ascertainable with reasonable certainty. (iii) It must also be retained in whole or part by the plaintiff and (iv) be capable of benefiting from the covenant. (v) The assignment of the covenant and the conveyance of the land to which it relates must be contemporaneous.

Whether the first two requirements were satisfied was neatly raised in *Newton Abbot Co-operative Society Ltd.* v. *Williamson and Treadgold, Ltd.*[6] on the following facts:

The owner of Devonia, in which she carried on the business of an ironmonger, sold a shop on the opposite side of the street to a pur-

---

[1] Preston and Newsom, *Restrictive Covenants* (5th Edn.), pp. 52–3 ; for a contrary view, see (1972B) C. L. J. 157, at p. 171 (H. W. R. Wade). See too Farrand, *Contract and Conveyance*, (2nd Edn.), p. 413. *Cf.* the effect at common law, *supra*, p. 594. For the view that the benefit passes under L.P.A. 1925, s. 62 on any conveyance of the benefited land, see (1971) 87 L. Q. R. 539, at p. 570 (D. J. Hayton).
[2] *Reid* v. *Bickerstaff*, [1909] 2 Ch. 305, at p. 320 ; *Re Union of London and Smith's Bank, Ltd.'s Conveyance, Miles* v. *Easter*, [1933] Ch. 611.
[3] *Supra*, p. 594.
[4] Preston and Newsom, *Restrictive Covenants* (4th Edn.), p. 30.
[5] [1933] Ch. 611, at pp. 631–2 ; M. & B. p. 723.
[6] [1952] Ch. 286 ; [1952] 1 All E. R. 279 ; M. & B. p. 724, approved by WILBERFORCE, J. in *Marten* v. *Flight Refuelling, Ltd.*, [1962] Ch. 115, at p. 133 ; [1961] 2 All E. R. 696. But see (1952), 68 L. Q. R. 353 (Sir Lancelot Elphinstone).

chaser who traded there as a grocer. The purchaser covenanted not to trade as an ironmonger at the premises. The conveyance did not define any dominant land for the benefit of which the covenant was taken, but simply described the vendor as 'of Devonia'.

UPJOHN, J. held in the first place that the covenant was not a mere covenant in gross. Its objects were not only to protect the vendor personally against competition, but also to enhance the selling value of Devonia if sold to someone intending to trade there as an ironmonger. The learned judge further held that the identity of the dominant land was sufficiently clear. The only reasonable inference to draw from the surrounding circumstances, especially from the propinquity of the two shops, was that the covenant was taken for the benefit not only of the vendor's business, but also of the land that she retained.

Nevertheless, in order to appreciate the limits within which assignment is permissible it is essential to stress that the reason why equity allows a restrictive covenant to be enforced against third parties is that the land of the covenantee may be protected, and in particular, that its sale value shall not be diminished.[1] Such a covenant is not an independent entity having its own intrinsic value. It has no *raison d'être* apart from the land for whose protection it was taken. Therefore, as we have already seen, even the covenantee himself cannot enforce the covenant against an assignee of the covenantor after he has disposed of the whole of his dominant land, for it is obvious that he no longer requires protection.[2] This theory, that the maintenance of the value of the covenantee's land is the sole justification for allowing restrictive covenants to run in favour of his successors in title, leads to this result, that the express assignment of the benefit of a covenant is ineffective unless it is contemporaneous with the assignment of the land affected. The covenant has spent its force if the covenantee has not required its aid in disposing of the dominant land.[3]

Assignment and conveyance must be contemporaneous.

" But if he has been able to sell any particular part of his property without assigning to the purchaser the benefit of the covenant, there seems no reason why he should at a later date and as an independent transaction be at liberty to confer upon the purchaser such benefit. To hold that he could do so would be to treat the covenant as having been obtained, not only for the purpose of enabling the covenantee to dispose of his land to the best advantage, but also for the purpose of enabling him to dispose of the benefit of the covenant to the best advantage." [4]

---

[1] *Chambers* v. *Randall*, [1923] 1 Ch. 149 ; *Re Union of London and Smith's Bank, Ltd.'s Conveyance, Miles* v. *Easter,* [1933] Ch. 611, at p. 632.
[2] See last note.
[3] *Chambers* v. *Randall, supra* ; *Re Union of London and Smith's Bank, Ltd.'s Conveyance, Miles* v. *Easter, supra* ; *Re Rutherford's Conveyance,* [1938] 1 Ch. 396 ; [1938] 1 All E. R. 495.
[4] *Re Union of London and Smith's Bank, Ltd.'s Conveyance, Miles* v. *Easter, supra,* at p. 632, *per* ROMER, L.J.

Subject to these limitations, however, an express assignment of a covenant to a purchaser of the whole or part of the dominant land made at the time of the purchase is effective.

The benefit of a restrictive covenant is also capable of assignment by operation of law. Thus on the death of the covenantee it passes to his executors and is held by them as bare trustees for the devisee of the dominant land and becomes assignable by him.[1]

There remains to be noticed the question whether the express assignment of the benefit of a restrictive covenant annexes it to the dominant land, so that it will thereafter run automatically with that land without the necessity for any further express assignment. There are judicial dicta which support the view that an express assignment has this effect of annexation,[2] but recent cases are against it. The decision in *Re Pinewood Estate, Farnborough*[3] assumes without argument that a chain of assignments is necessary, and that in *Stilwell* v. *Blackman*[4] is inconsistent with the dicta.

(c) *Scheme of Development (or Building Scheme)*[5]

Meaning of scheme of development. The third case in which a restrictive covenant is enforceable by and against persons other than the original covenanting parties is when lands are held by their respective owners under a scheme of development.

A scheme of development comes into existence where land is laid out in plots and sold to different purchasers or leased to different lessees, each of whom enters into a restrictive covenant with the common vendor or lessor agreeing that his particular plot shall not be used for certain purposes. In such a case these restrictive covenants are taken because the whole estate is being developed on a definite plan, and it is vital, if the value of each plot is not to be depreciated, that the purchasers or lessees should be prevented from dealing with their land so as to lower the tone of the neighbourhood. When the existence of a scheme of

---

[1] *Newton Abbot Co-operative Society, Ltd.* v. *Williamson and Treadgold, Ltd.*, [1952] Ch. 286 ; [1952] 1 All E. R. 279 ; M. & B. p. 724 ; *Earl of Leicester* v. *Wells-next-the-Sea U.D C.* [1973] Ch. 110 ; [1972] 3 All E. R. 77 (special executors of settled land held to be bare trustees of benefit of restrictive covenant for beneficiary under S.L.A. 1925, s. 7 (1)).

[2] *Renals* v. *Cowlishaw* (1878), 9 Ch. D. 125, at pp. 130–31 ; *Rogers* v. *Hosegood*, [1900] 2 Ch. 388, at p. 408 ; *Reid* v. *Bickerstaff*, [1909] 2 Ch. 305, at p. 320.

[3] [1958] Ch. 280 ; [1957] 2 All E. R. 517. See the criticism in (1957), *C. L. J.* 146 (H. W. R. Wade).

[4] [1968] Ch. 508 ; [1967] 3 All E. R. 514 ; (1968), 84 *L. Q. R.* at pp. 29–32 (P. V. Baker).

[5] " Scheme of development is the genus : building scheme a species." *Brunner* v. *Greenslade*, [1971] Ch. 993, at p. 999 ; [1970] 3 All E. R. 833, *per* MEGARRY, J. For recent successful schemes, see *Re Dolphin's Conveyance*, [1970] Ch. 654 ; [1970] 2 All E. R. 664 ; M. & B. p. 738 ; *Eagling* v. *Gardner*, [1970] 2 All E. R. 838 ; *Brunner* v. *Greenslade, supra* ; *Texaco Antilles, Ltd.* v. *Kernochan*, [1973] A.C. 609 ; [1973] 2 All E. R. 118. This is in marked contrast to the usual fate of schemes during the previous four decades. Perston and Newsom, pp. 47–8.

development has been established, the rule is that each purchaser and his assignees can sue or be sued by every other purchaser and his assignees for a breach of the restrictive covenants.[1] In such an action for breach it is immaterial whether the defendant acquired his title before or after the date on which the plaintiff purchased his plot. In other words, the restrictive covenants constitute a special local law for the area over which the scheme extends, and not only the plot-owners, but even the vendor himself, become subject to that law,[2] provided that the area and the obligations to be imposed therein are defined. " They all have a common interest in maintaining the restriction. This community of interest necessarily requires and imports reciprocity of obligation. "[3]

Pre-eminent among the essentials for the enforcement of a scheme of development is proof of a common intention that the restrictive covenants have been taken for the mutual benefit of the respective purchasers.[4] This community of interest and intention may be evidenced by the existence of a deed of mutual covenant to which all the several purchasers are parties,[5] or it may be inferred on the construction of the conveyances of the several parts of the estate.[6] If, however, the necessary intention cannot be derived solely from the formal documents, but extrinsic evidence is also required, a scheme of development may nevertheless come into existence. In these circumstances the conditions formulated by PARKER, J., in *Elliston* v. *Reacher*[7] must exist before the benefit and the burden of the restrictive covenants can pass to the various purchasers and their assignees :

    (*a*) **Both the plaintiff and the defendant to the action for breach of the restrictive covenant must have derived their titles to the land from a common vendor.**

    (*b*) Before the sale of the plots to the plaintiff and the defendant, the common vendor must have laid out his estate for sale in lots[8] subject to restrictions which it was intended to impose on all the

---

[1] *Spicer* v. *Martin* (1888), 14 App. Cas. 12 ; *Renals* v. *Cowlishaw* (1878), 9 Ch. D. 125 ; affirmed (1879), 11 Ch. D. 866 ; *Hudson* v. *Cripps*, [1896] 1 Ch. 265 (lease).
[2] *Reid* v. *Bickerstaff*, [1909] 2 Ch. 305 at p. 319 ; *Brunner* v. *Greenslade*, [1971] Ch. 993, at p. 1004. The scheme may expressly entitle the vendor to dispose of plots free from its restrictions ; *Mayner* v. *Payne*, [1914] 2 Ch. 555.
[3] *Spicer* v. *Martin* (1888), 14 App. Cas. 12, at p. 25, *per* Lord MACNAGHTEN.
[4] *Nottingham Patent Brick and Tile Co.* v. *Butler* (1886), 15 Q. B. D. 261, at p. 268, *per* WILLS, J. ; approved in *White* v. *Bijou Mansions, Ltd.*, [1938] Ch. 351, at p. 361 ; [1938] 1 All E. R. 546, at p. 552. See Preston and Newsom, *Restrictive Covenants* (5th Edn.), pp. 40 *st seq.*
[5] *Baxter* v. *Four Oaks Properties, Ltd.*, [1965] Ch. 876 ; [1965] 1 All E. R. 906 ; M. & B. p. 738 (where the common vendor had not laid out the estate in lots before the sale).
[6] *Re Dolphin's Conveyance*, [1970] Ch. 654 ; [1970] 2 All E. R. 664 ; M. & B. p. 738 (where there was no common vendor and no lotted estate). See (1970), 114 Sol. Jo. 798 (G. H. Newsom) : 86 *L. Q. R.* 445 (P. V. Baker).
[7] [1908] 2 Ch. 374, at p. 385 ; M. & B. p. 736 ; for a recent case in which all the conditions are considered see *Eagling* v. *Gardner*, [1970] 2 All E. R. 838.
[8] *Lawrence* v. *South County Freeholds, Ltd.*, [1939] Ch. 656, at p. 674.

lots, and which were consistent only with some general scheme of development.[1]

(c) The restrictions were intended by the common vendor to be and were for the benefit of all the lots sold. This intention is gathered from all the circumstances of the case, but if the restrictions are obviously calculated to enhance the value of each lot, the intention is readily inferred.

To a certain extent these three conditions overlap, but the basic requirement is the existence of common regulations obviously intended to govern the area that is to be developed.

" The material thing I think is that every purchaser . . . must know when he buys what are the regulations to which he is subjecting himself, and what are the regulations to which other purchasers on the estate will be called upon to subject themselves. Unless you know that, it is quite impossible in my judgment to draw the necessary inference, whether you refer to it as an agreement or as a community of interest importing reciprocity of obligation."[2]

(d) The original purchasers must have bought their lots on the understanding that the restrictions were to enure for the benefit of the other lots.

(e) The geographical area to which the scheme extends must be ascertained with reasonably clear definitiveness.[3]

These conditions are " a valuable, and perhaps complete guide to what has to be sought in the extrinsic evidence when such evidence is the foundation of the case."[4] This may include parol evidence from the common vendor[5] and evidence of what was said and done before the contract which preceded the conveyances.

The common vendor may reserve the power to waive or vary the restrictive covenants, especially in the case of land of which he has not yet disposed.[6] Furthermore the restrictions which he imposes need not be uniform.[7]

The subject-matter of a scheme generally consists of freehold land which is to be sold in plots to persons who desire to erect houses, but it may equally well comprise houses or a block of flats that have been already built,[8] and leaseholds as well as freeholds.[9]

---

[1] *Willé* v. *St. John*, [1910] 1 Ch. 84 ; affd., [1910] 1 Ch. 325.

[2] *White* v. *Bijou Mansions*, [1938] Ch. 351, at p. 362 ; [1938] 1 All E. R. 546, at p. 552, *per* GREENE, M.R.

[3] *Osborne* v. *Bradley*, [1903] 2 Ch. 446 ; *Torbay Hotel, Ltd.* v. *Jenkins*, [1927] 2 Ch. 225.

[4] (1970), 114 Sol. Jo. at p. 800.

[5] *Kelly* v. *Battershell*, [1949] 2 All E. R. 830, at p. 843.

[6] *Elliston* v. *Reacher*, [1908] 2 Ch. 665, at p. 672. *Pearce* v. *Maryon-Wilson*, [1935] Ch. 188 ; *Re Wembley Park Estate Co., Ltd's Transfer*, [1968] Ch. 491, at p. 497 ; [1968] 1 All E. R. 457.

[7] *Collins* v. *Castle* (1887), 36 Ch. D. 243, at p. 253 ; *Elliston* v. *Reacher*, [1908] 2 Ch. 374, at p. 384.

[8] See *Torbay Hotel Ltd.* v. *Jenkins*, [1927] 2 Ch. 225, at p. 241.

[9] See *Spicer* v. *Martin* (1888), 14 App. Cas. 12 ; *Hudson* v. *Cripps*, [1896] 1 Ch. 265.

There may also be a sub-scheme within an area which is itself subject to a scheme of development.[1]

(C) SECTION 56, LAW OF PROPERTY ACT 1925

We have seen how a person may show that he has acquired the benefit of a covenant at law and in equity. We must now consider how far someone may enforce a covenant by reliance on section 56 of the Law of Property Act 1925.[2]

" A person may take an immediate or other interest in land or other property, or the benefit of any condition, right of entry, covenant or agreement over or respecting land or other property, although he may not be named as a party to the conveyance or other instrument. "

This section reproduces and extends section 5 of the Real Property Act 1845, which abrogated the technical rule of common law that

" a grantee or covenantee, though named as such in an indenture under seal expressed to be made inter partes, could not take an immediate interest as grantee nor the benefit of a covenant as covenantee unless named as a party to the indenture."

It is important to notice that this section is not concerned with the *passing* of the benefit of a covenant. It is concerned with the *giving* of the benefit of a covenant, at the time when the covenant is created, to a person other than the covenantee. The section in effect makes the person claiming the benefit of the covenant into an original covenantee, even though he was not named as a party to the deed in which the covenant was created.

The application of section 56 is not confined to covenants that touch and concern the land,[3] nor is it confined to restrictive covenants in equity. Its application in the latter context may, however, enable an earlier purchaser of a plot of land on an estate, which is not subject to a scheme of development, to enforce a restrictive covenant against a later purchaser of a plot from the common vendor.

Thus, in *Re Ecclesiastical Commissioners for England's Conveyance*,[4]

In 1887, the purchaser of Blackacre entered into restrictive covenants in favour of the Ecclesiastical Commissioners, the vendors.

---

[1] See *Knight* v. *Simmonds*, [1896] 1 Ch. 663 ; *King* v. *Dickeson* (1889), 40 Ch. D. 596 ; *Lawrence* v. *South County Freeholds, Ltd.*, [1939] Ch. 656 ; [1939] 2 All E. R. 503 ; *Brunner* v. *Greenslade*, [1971] Ch. 993 ; [1970] 3 All E. R. 833.

[2] On the section generally, see Cheshire and Fifoot, *Law of Contract* (8th Edn.) pp. 439–42 ; *Beswick* v. *Beswick*, [1968] A.C. 58 ; [1967] 2 All E. R. 1197, especially Lord PEARCE, at pp. 93–4, and Lord UPJOHN, at pp. 102–7 ; (1967) 30 M. L. R. 687 (G. H. Treitel).

[3] *Re Ecclesiastical Commissioners for England's Conveyance*, [1936] Ch. 430 ; at p. 438 ; but see *Grant* v. *Edmondson*, [1931] 1 Ch. 1

[4] [1936] Ch. 430 ; M. & B. p. 747. See also *Forster* v. *Elvet Colliery Co., Ltd.*, [1908] 1 K. B. 629 ; *affirmed sub. nom. Dyson* v. *Forster*, [1909] A. C. 98.

A separate covenant was also included in the conveyance, providing that the benefit of the covenants should avail the vendors' " assigns, owners for the time being of the land adjoining or adjacent to " Blackacre.   Prior to 1887, the commissioners had sold various freehold plots, situated near Blackacre, to different purchasers and these had passed into other hands by the time of the action.

It was held that the successors in title of the adjacent owners were entitled to enforce the covenants although their respective predecessors in title had not joined in the conveyance of 1887.

The section will not avail a person unless he might have been a party to the deed in question.   If he is an ascertainable person at the time of the execution of the deed which purports to grant him an interest in property[1] or to make a covenant available to him, he and his successors in title are in as good a position as if he had been one of the original parties.   On the other hand, a deed is inoperative in so far as it purports to extend the advantage of a covenant to an unascertainable person, such as the future owner of specified land.[2]   It will, therefore, not enable a later purchaser to enforce a restrictive covenant against an earlier purchaser from a common vendor.   In order to succeed, he must prove that the benefit of the covenant has passed to him by annexation, express assignment or under a scheme of development.

(D) DISCHARGE AND MODIFICATION OF RESTRICTIVE COVENANTS[3]

(1) Section 84 of the Law of Property Act 1925

Mode of discharging obsolete covenants.

The Law of Property Act 1925 provides for the total extinction of restrictive covenants.   Under the law apart from the Act a covenantee (including his assignees) is deprived of his right to enforce the covenant if he has submitted to a long course of usage wholly inconsistent with its continuance, as where he remains inactive for a considerable time while open breaches of the covenant are taking place ;[4] if he disregards breaches in such a way as to justify a reasonable person in believing that future breaches will be disregarded ;[5] or if the character of the neighbourhood in which the protected property lies is so entirely altered that it would be

---

[1] *Stromdale and Ball, Ltd.* v. *Burden*, [1952] 2 Ch. 223 ; [1952] 1 All E. R. 59 ; M. & B. p. 753 ; *Drive Yourself Hire Co. (London), Ltd.* v. *Strutt*, [1954] 1 Q. B. 250 ; [1953] 2 All E. R. 1475.

[2] *Kelsey* v. *Dodd*, (1881) 52 L. J. Ch. 24, at p. 39 ; *White* v. *Bijou Mansions, Ltd.*, [1937] Ch. 610, at p. 625 ; [1937] 3 All E. R. 269, 277 ; affirmed [1938] Ch. 351, at p. 365 ; 1 All E. R. 546, at p. 554; M. & B. p. 749.

[3] See generally Preston and Newsom, *Restrictive Covenants* (5th Edn.), pp. 172 *et seq.*

[4] *Gibson* v. *Doeg* (1857), 2 H. & N. 615 ; *Hepworth* v. *Pickles*, [1900] 1 Ch. 108 ; *Re Summerson*, [1900] 1 Ch. 112 n. ; discussed in *Lloyds Bank, Ltd.* v. *Jones*, [1955] 2 Q. B. 298, 320-2 ; [1955] 2 All E. R. 409.

[5] *Chatsworth Estates Co.* v. *Fewell*, [1931] 1 Ch. 224; M. & B. p. 756.

inequitable and senseless to insist upon the rigorous observance of a covenant that is no longer of any value.[1]

Section 84 of the Law of Property Act 1925[2] develops this last ground of extinction, and sets up a new method whereby restrictions may be discharged or modified.[3]

The first point to notice is that the Act mainly applies to restrictions imposed on freehold estates. It has no application to leaseholds which are subject to restrictive covenants, except where the lease was originally made for more than 40 years, and 25 years of this term have expired when the question of extinction arises.[4]

It is then provided that any person interested in any such freehold or leasehold land[5] affected by the restrictive covenant,[6] may apply to the Lands Tribunal to have the restriction either wholly or partially discharged, or modified.[7]

In making an order discharging or modifying a restriction the Tribunal may direct the applicant to pay to any person entitled to the benefit of the restriction such sum by way of consideration as it may think it just to award.[8] This must fall under one of the following heads :

either (i) a sum to make up for any loss or disadvantage suffered by that person in consequence of the discharge or modification ;[9] or (ii) a sum to make up for any effect which the restriction had, at the time when it was imposed, in reducing the consideration then received for the land affected by it.

Before making any order the tribunal must be satisfied :

" (a) that by reason of changes in the character of the property or the neighbourhood or other circumstances of the case which the

---

[1] *Chatsworth Estates Co.* v. *Fewell, supra* ; see generally, Behan, *Covenants affecting Land*, pp. 148 *et seq.* ; Elphinstone, *Covenants affecting Land*, pp. 110 *et seq.* ; *Westripp* v. *Baldock*, [1938] 2 All E. R. 779 ; affd. [1939] 1 All E. R. 279. (1966), 5 *Melbourne University Law Review*, pp. 209–14 (D. Mendes da Costa).

[2] As amended by L.P.A. 1969, s. 28. See Law Commission Report on Restrictive Covenants, 1967 (Law Com. No. 11), pp. 21–6 ; (1974) J. P. L. 72, 130 ; (1975) J. P. L. 644 (G. H. Newsom).

[3] S. 84 (1) ; see *Richardson* v. *Jackson*, [1954] 1 W. L. R. 447 ; [1954] 1 All E. R. 437. A list of the applications made under the section and of their results is given in *Current Law* under the heading " Real Property and Conveyancing ". Some are reported in P. & C. R., Estates Gazette and J. P. L.

[4] S. 84 (12), as amended by Landlord and Tenant Act 1954, s. 52. The 25 years is reckoned from the date of the lease, and not from any earlier date at which the term is expressed in the lease to begin ; *Earl of Cadogan* v. *Guinness*, [1936] Ch. 515 ; [1936] 2 All E. R. 29.

[5] The tribunal should be more reluctant to interfere with leasehold than freehold covenants ; *Ridley* v. *Taylor*, [1965] 1 W. L. R. 611 ; [1965] 2 All E. R. 51 ; M. & B. p. 762.

[6] It may be personal only. *Shepherd Homes, Ltd.* v. *Sandham (No. 2)*, [1971] 1 W. L. R. 1062 ; [1971] 2 All E. R. 1267.

[7] Lands Tribunal Rules 1975 (S. I. 1975 No. 299).

[8] L.P.A. 1925, s. 84 (1), as amended by L.P.A. 1969, s. 28 (3). See generally (1976) J. P. L. 18 (W. A. Leach).

[8] L.P.A. 1925, s. 84 (1), as amended by L.P.A. 1969, s. 28 (3).

[9] *S.J.C. Construction Co., Ltd.* v. *Sutton London Borough Council* (1975), 29 P. & C. R. 322 (" there is no method prescribed by the Act by which it is to be assessed ; it is essentially a question of quantum ", *per* Lord DENNING, M.R., at p. 326.

Lands Tribunal may deem material, the restriction ought to be deemed obsolete ; or

(*aa*) that the continued existence thereof would impede some reasonable user of the land for public or private purposes or, as the case may be, would unless modified so impede such user ; or

Under this paragraph the Lands Tribunal must be satisfied that the restriction, in impeding the user, either

(i) does not secure to persons entitled to the benefit of it any practical benefits of substantial value or advantage to them ; or

(ii) is contrary to the public interest ;

and that money will be an adequate compensation for the loss or disadvantage (if any) which any such person will suffer from the discharge or modification.[1]

" (*b*) that the persons of full age and capacity for the time being or from time to time entitled to the benefit of the restriction, whether in respect of estates in fee simple or any lesser estates or interests in the property to which the benefit of the restriction is annexed, have agreed, either expressly or by implication,[2] by their acts or omissions, to the same being discharged or modified ; or

(*c*) that the proposed discharge or modification will not injure the persons entitled to the benefit of the restriction."

The Lands Tribunal may, however, add further restrictive provisions if it appears to it to be reasonable to do so. This cannot be done unless the applicant accepts them, but, if he does not, the application may be refused.

Scope of changes made by L.P.A. 1969.

The substantive change made by the Law of Property Act 1969 was to widen the scope of section 84 of the Law of Property Act 1925, and, in particular, to redraft paragraph (*aa*), so as to enable the Lands Tribunal " to take a broader view of whether the use of land is being unreasonably impeded ; and to make clear provision for an award of monetary compensation where the Tribunal thinks that the injury which an objector would suffer by a modification or discharge can be properly compensated in that way."[3] To enable it to take this broader view the Tribunal must take into account the development plan and any declared or ascertainable pattern for the grant or refusal of planning permissions in the relevant areas, as well as the period at which and context in which the restriction was created or imposed and any other material circumstances.[4]

---

[1] L.P.A. 1925, s. 84 (1A). For the formulation of the questions to be answered by the Lands Tribunal, see *Re Bass Ltd's Application* (1973), 26 P. & C. R. 156 ; M. & B. p. 763.

[2] See *Re Memvale's Securities Ltd's Application* (1975), 233 Estates Gazette 689.

[3] Law Commission Report on Restrictive Covenants, 1967 (Law Com. No. 11), p. 23.

[4] L.P.A. 1925, s. 84 (1B). See *Re Collins' Application* (1975), 30 P. & C. R. 527 ; M. & B. p. 771.

Since 1969 the new paragraph (*aa*) and the power to award compensation have resulted in an increased number of cases before the Lands Tribunal.[1] A number of important criteria have been established for deciding whether a covenant should be modified or discharged. In particular, where the applicant has obtained planning permission for the proposed user, the effect is very persuasive in considering whether that user is reasonable. The proposition that impeding that user is contrary to the public interest may also be aided by a planning permission, but in rather a different way. The question is not whether the proposed user is in the public interest, but whether impeding the proposed user is contrary to it.

Whether impeding user is contrary to public interest.

> " There is here more that a narrow nuance of difference : a planning permission only says, in effect, that a proposal will be allowed ; it implies that such a proposal will not be a bad thing, but it does not necessarily imply that it will be positively a good thing. "[2]

Consistently with this restrictive approach, the President of the Lands Tribunal said in 1975 :[3]

> " For an application to succeed on the ground of public interest it must be shown that that interest is so important and immediate as to justify the serious interference with private rights and the sanctity of contract. "

An acute shortage of building land in a particular locality does not establish that any restriction which prevents development of land is *ipso facto* contrary to the public interest. The question of public interest must be considered in a broad context.[4] And the argument of public interest succeeded in a case where there was a scarcity of land available for building development, and, if the restriction were not modified, building work costing £47,000 would have to be demolished. That was to be avoided in " the present economic circumstances of the country ".[5]

Further, in considering whether the proposed user secures to the applicant practical benefits of substantial value or advantage,[6] the Lands Tribunal has observed that the words " value or

---

[1] See generally (1974) J. P. L. 72, 130 ; (1975) J. P. L. 644 (G. H. Newsom) ; M. & B. pp. 759–72.

[2] *Re Bass Ltd.'s Application* (1973), 26 P. & C. R. 156 ; M. & B. p. 763.

[3] *Re Collins' Applications* (1975), 30 P. & C. R. 527 *per* Douglas Frank, Esq. Q.C. ; M. & B. p. 771.

[4] *Re Beardsley's Application* (1972), 25 P. & C. R. 233 ; M. & B. p. 769 ; *Re Gardner's Application* (1974) J. P. L. 728.

[5] *Re S.J.C. Construction Co., Ltd.'s Application* (1974), 28 P. & C. R. 200 ; M. & B. p. 769 ; affirmed by C.A. on method of assessing compensation *sub. nom. S.J.C. Construction Co., Ltd.* v. *Sutton London Borough Council* (1975), 29 P. & C. R. 322, *supra*, p. 617, n. 9.

[6] *Re John Twiname, Ltd.'s Application* (1972), 23 P. & C. R. 413, at pp. 417–18 ; *Re Wards Construction (Medway), Ltd.'s Application* (1973), 25 P. & C. R. 223, at p. 231 (" even ordinary people not infrequently value space and quiet and light ") ; *Re Gossip's Application* (1973), 25 P. & C. R. 215, at p. 220 (" houses built on the application land would overlook the garden and the principal rooms, albeit somewhat screened by a hawthorn, a poor substitute for a covenant ").

advantage " are not intended to be assessed in terms of pecuniary value only.[1]

The statutory provisions apply to restrictive covenants entered into either before or after the commencement of the Act, but do not apply where the restriction was imposed on the occasion of a disposition made gratuitously, or for a nominal consideration, for public purposes.[2] Any person aggrieved by the decision of the tribunal on the ground that it is erroneous in point of law may require that a case be stated for the decision of the Court of Appeal.[3]

Statutory power to declare whether restriction binding.

In order to meet the case where it may be doubtful whether an effectual restrictive covenant has been imposed on land and if so what persons it now affects, the Act confers jurisdiction upon the court,

(*a*) to declare whether or not in any particular case any free-hold land is, or would in any given event be, affected by a restriction imposed by any instrument ; or

(*b*) to declare what is the nature and extent of the restriction thereby imposed and whether the same is, or would in any given event be, enforceable and if so by whom.[4]

Housing Act 1957.

If it is proved that a house cannot readily be let as a single tenement but can readily be let if converted into two or more tenements, the Housing Act 1957 empowers the County Court to vary any provisions in a lease or any restrictive covenant affecting the lease if these impede the proposed conversion.[5] Such a variation is not permissible unless the converted tenements will be wholly contained within one house.[6]

Town and Country Planning Act 1971.

The Town and Country Planning Act 1971,[7] authorizes a local planning authority, subject to the payment of compensation, to carry out a scheme of development, notwithstanding that it interferes with an easement or infringes a restrictive covenant.

(2) UNITY OF SEISIN

A restrictive covenant will be discharged when a person becomes entitled to both the dominant and servient lands to which it relates.[8] This is similiar to the extinguishment of an easement by the unity of ownership and possession.[9] In *Texaco Antilles*,

---

[1] *Re Bass, Ltd.'s Application, supra.*
[2] L.P.A. 1925, s. 84 (7).
[3] Lands Tribunal Act 1949, s. 3 (4) proviso.
[4] L.P.A. 1925, s. 84 (2), as amended by L.P.A. 1969, s. 28 (4). *Re Sunny-field*, [1932] 1 Ch. 79 ; *Re Freeman-Thomas Indenture*, [1957] 1 All E. R. 532.
[5] S. 165. See Preston and Newsom, *Restrictive Covenants* (5th Edn.), Appendix II.
[6] *Josephine Trust, Ltd.* v. *Champagne*, [1962] 2 Q. B. 160; [1962] 3 All E. R. 136.
[7] S. 127. See Local Government Act 1972, ss. 120 (3), 124 (2).
[8] *Texaco Antilles, Ltd.* v. *Kernochan*, [1973] A.C. 609 ; [1973] 2 All E. R. 118 ; M. & B. p. 758.
[9] *Supra*, p. 557.

Ltd. v. *Kernochan,*[1] however, the Privy Council held that, if there is a scheme of development, unity of seisin does not automatically discharge a covenant within the area of unity, and that on severance it revives, unless there is evidence from the circumstances surrounding the severance that the parties intended that it should not do so.

(E) LAW COMMISSION REPORT ON RESTRICTIVE COVENANTS 1967[2]

This report recommends fundamental changes in the law relating to restrictive covenants. These are set out in twelve Propositions, the general effect of which is summarised in paragraph 27 of the Report itself :

" Briefly stated, these Propositions recommend the creation of a new interest in land called a Land Obligation, which will be available to regulate matters now dealt with by covenants as to user. Land Obligations will be capable of creation in respect of freehold or leasehold interests in land, but will not apply to rights between lessor and lessee in respect of the demised land. They will be imposed on specified land for the benefit of other specified land so that the burden and benefit will run automatically with the land until released, modified, discharged, or, for example, in the case of an obligation affecting a leasehold interest, brought to an end by effluxion of time : and they will be enforceable only by and against the persons currently concerned with the land as owners of interests in it or occupiers of it. They will thus in nature and attributes be more akin to easements than to covenants."

The Propositions " are intended to apply only to obligations entered into after a day to be appointed for the purposes of the new legislation[3] and ' pre-appointed day ' restrictive covenants should be left to take effect in accordance with the existing law."[4]

Although the Propositions are specifically confined to restrictive covenants, paragraph 30 states :

" The substance of our proposals is applicable in principle ... to positive as well as to restrictive obligations, subject to any necessary modifications, and we consider that a common code could and should be devised from the Wilberforce recommendations[5] and these Propositions."

SECTION III. REGISTERED LAND

Under section 40 (1) of the Land Registration Act 1925, a proprietor of registered land may " by covenant ... impose or make binding, *so far as the law permits*, any obligation or reservation with respect to the building on or other user of the registered

---

[1] [1973] A.C. 609 ; [1973] 2 All E. R. 118 ; *Brunner* v. *Greenslade,* [1971] Ch. 993 ; [1970] 3 All E. R. 833.
[2] Law Com. No. 11.
[3] Para. 34. [4] Para. 35.
[5] Report of the Committee on Positive Covenants affecting Land 1965 (Cmnd. 2719), *supra*, p. 596.

land ".[1] This power is made " subject to any entry to the contrary on the register, and without prejudice to the rights of persons entitled to overriding interests (if any) and to any incumbrances entered on the register, who may not concur therein."   Subject to this limitation, however, the power to create restrictive covenants and the substantive law relating to the running of the burden and the benefit are similar to those relating to unregistered land.

Burden of restrictive covenants.

Section 50 (1) provides[2] for the entry of a notice of " a restrictive covenant or agreement (not being a covenant or agreement made between a lessor and lessee)."[3] If the burden of such a covenant is to run with the land of the covenantor, it should be protected by a notice on the charges register of the title to the servient land, otherwise it will be defeated by a registered disposition of that land for valuable consideration.[4] Thus the position of a purchaser of registered land who is affected by notice of a restrictive covenant entered on the register, is similar to that of a purchaser of unregistered land where the restrictive covenant is registered as a land charge under the Land Charges Act 1972. Further, it should be observed that the entry of a notice of the burden of a restrictive covenant merely gives notice[5] and does not mean that the covenant is necessarily enforceable against the servient land.[6]

Benefit of restrictive covenants.

The benefit of a covenant is not in practice entered on the register of the title to the dominant land.   " There are scarcely any instances (unless there is a properly constituted building scheme) in which any applicant is in a position to prove to the Registrar that he has the benefit of restrictive covenants. . . . There is no provision in the Acts or Rules authorising the Registrar to enter the benefit of covenants on the register of title. It is possible, however, that in a quite exceptional and clear case he might enter notice that such a benefit was claimed."[7]

Positive covenants.

The Acts and Rules contain no provision for making entries relating to positive covenants since in this case the burden does not run with the land. In practice, they are often intermixed with restrictive covenants, and where this occurs they are not

---

[1] See generally Ruoff and Roper, pp. 374–5, 753–9 ; Registered Land Practice Notes 1972, pp. 25–9, as amended by (1974) L. S. G. p. 395. Farrand, *Contract and Conveyance* (2nd Edn.), pp. 427–9 ; Barnsley, *Conveyancing Law and Practice*, pp. 430–3.

[2] See also L.R.R. 1925, rr. 7 (c), 212 ; L.R.A. 1925, s. 40 (3).

[3] See Ruoff and Roper, p. 490 ; *Newman* v. *Real Estate Debenture Corpn., Ltd. and Flower Decorations, Ltd.*, [1940] 1 All E. R. 131.

[4] L.R.A. 1925, ss. 20 (1) (a), (4) ; 23 (1) (a), (5). See *Hodges* v. *Jones*, [1935] Ch. 657, at p. 671, where LUXMOORE, J., states that a restrictive covenant is not an overriding interest.

[5] L.R.A. 1925, s. 50 (2).

[6] *Ibid.*, s. 52. *Cator* v. *Newton and Bates*, [1940] 1 K. B. 415 ; [1939] 4 All E. R. 457.

[7] Ruoff and Roper, p. 757. L.R.R. 1925, r. 3 (2) (c), is unfortunately worded as the Acts and Rules contain no provision for noting the benefit of covenants.

edited out of the restrictive covenant entry. Furthermore, in order to preserve a record of positive covenants (including indemnity covenants) where they are not referred to on the register by reason of such intermixing, the Land Registry, in most cases where they have been imposed on land after it has been registered, will by way of concession refer to them on the register and sew up a copy in the Land or Charge Certificate.[1]

Any release, discharge or modification of a restrictive covenant should be noted on the register.[2] Where the covenant is discharged, modified or dealt with by an order under section 84 of the Law of Property Act, or the court refuses to grant an injunction to enforce it, the entry is either cancelled or reference is made to the order, and a copy is filed at the registry.[3]

Discharge and modification.

SECTION IV. COVENANTS AND PLANNING

Tulk v. *Moxhay*[4] was decided in 1848 and the doctrine to which it gave rise was one of the bases for control of land use by private landowners during the suburban expansion of the 19th century. Together with leasehold and reciprocal positive freehold covenants, it is fundamental to all private planning. Private planning, however, co-exists side by side with the public control of the use and development of land in the hands of local planning authorities under the principal planning statute, the Town and Country Planning Act of 1971.[5]

It is important to notice that these two methods of control, private and public, are cumulative.[6] A purchaser of land must not only satisfy himself about the existence of private covenants that may bind the land which he is buying, but he must also investigate its planning aspect.

An outline of the public planning law is given in Book IV below.[7]

---

[1] This concession is not applied where the document imposing such covenants is for some reason itself sewn up in the Land or Charge Certificate, nor in the case of positive covenants imposed prior to first registration. In the first case the sewn up document can be perused, and in the second the record is preserved in the pre-registration deeds which are returned to the applicant. The concession does not in general extend to the benefit of positive covenants being entered on the title because of practical difficulties and doubts about enforcement.

[2] L.R.R. 1925, r. 212.

[3] L.R.A. 1925, s. 50 (3).

[4] (1848), 2 Ch. 774; M. & B. p. 693.

[5] See Law Commission Report on Restrictive Covenants (1967 Law Com. No. 11), paras. 16–19.

[6] See (1964), 28 *Conv.* (N. S.), 190 (A. R. Mellows).

[7] Pp. 935 *et seq.*

CHAPTER IV

RENTCHARGES[1]

SUMMARY

SECTION I.   NATURE OF A RENTCHARGE

Distinction
between
rentcharge
and rent-
service.

Origin and History. We have already seen that a rent payable by a tenant to a landlord is called rent-service because of the tenure which exists between the parties, but that it is called a rentcharge if there is no tenure between the creditor and the debtor from whose land it issues.[2]   In former days this lack of

---

[1] See generally Barnsley, *Conveyancing Law and Practice*, pp. 298–301, 507–9 ; Easton, *Law of Rentcharges* (2nd Edn. 1931).
[2] *Supra*, pp. 428–30.

624

tenurial interest between the parties meant that the rent owner had no automatic right at law to distrain upon the land of the debtor for the recovery of arrears, and generally speaking, rentcharges, though of considerable antiquity, were regarded as contrary to the policy of the common law, since the debtor was rendered less able to perform the military service due to his overlord, while the rent owner himself was free from all feudal obligations in respect of the land.[1] It became usual, therefore, for the parties to enter into an express agreement that the creditor should have a power of distress over the debtor's land. A rent supported in this way by a specially reserved power of distress, as distinct from a rent-service where such power existed of common right, was called a rentcharge, since the land liable for payment was charged with a distress.[2] We have seen that there is no longer any necessity to charge the land expressly, for the Law of Property Act 1925, re-enacting the Landlord and Tenant Act 1730, and the Conveyancing Act 1881 confers the right of distress upon all rentcharge owners.[3]

A rentcharge may therefore be defined as an annual sum of money issuing and payable out of land, the due payment of which is secured by a right of distress that is not the result of tenure between the parties but is either expressly reserved or allowed by statute.[4]

Definition of rent-charge.

Creation. There are three distinct transactions that may lead to the creation of such a rent :—

first, the owner of an estate may grant the whole of his estate to A., leaving no reversion in himself, but reserving a rent to be paid to him out of the land ;

secondly, he may retain the whole of his estate, but grant a rent to another payable out of the land ; and

thirdly, the owner of a reversion to which a rent-service is attached may sever the rent from the reversion, either by granting the reversion to a stranger and keeping the rent, or by granting the rent to a stranger and keeping the reversion.[5]

In each of these cases it will be seen that, since no tenure exists between the debtor and creditor, the rent lacks the characteristic of a rent-service.

---

[1] Cruise *Digest*, Tit. xxviii. c. i. ss. 1, 7.
[2] Co. Litt., 144*a*.
[3] L.P.A. 1925, s. 121.; *supra*, p. 429.
[4] See Co. Litt., 143*b*, 147*b*.
[5] Leake, *Uses and Profits of Land*, 373, 385.

Rentcharge
is real
property.

Incidents. A rentcharge is an incorporeal interest that may be limited for all the estates recognized at common law.[1]

Thus it may be limited to a person for an estate in fee simple, in tail, for life, for years or in remainder, but under the Law of Property Act 1925 the interest conferred on the rent owner is a legal interest only where it is in possession and either perpetual or for a term of years absolute.[2] Thus, an annual sum of money granted to a widow for life and charged upon the settled lands by a marriage settlement confers a mere equitable interest. Furthermore, a rentcharge can only be legal if the proper formalities for its creation have been observed.

No rent-
charge on a
rentcharge at
common law.

As the essence of a rentcharge lies in the power of the owner to distrain upon lands, it follows that, strictly speaking, it can issue only out of corporeal hereditaments. A dominant owner, for instance, cannot charge a right of way to which he is entitled, since there is nothing on which the rent owner can distrain, though of course the debtor will be liable for the amount he has agreed to pay.[3] For the same reason at common law a rent cannot be reserved out of a rent,[4] and therefore if A., who is entitled to a rentcharge of £50, grants it to B., but reserves to himself thereout a rentcharge of £25, the reservation is void in the sense that the £25 does not constitute a rentcharge properly so called.

Rule altered
by statute.

But this rule of the common law has in part been abrogated by the Law of Property Act 1925, which enacts that a rentcharge or annual sum of money (not being a rent-service) may be reserved out of or charged on another rentcharge in the same manner as it could have been charged on land.[5] In such a case the ordinary remedies of distress and entry upon the lands are impossible, and therefore it is provided that where the rent is in arrears for twenty-one days, the owner of the second rent (£25) shall have power to appoint a receiver of the rent (£50) on which it is charged. The receiver is then entitled to acquire the £50 by action, distress or otherwise, and out of this to pay arrears, expenses and his own remuneration.

SECTION II.   CREATION OF A RENTCHARGE

A rentcharge may be created by instrument *inter vivos*, by will, or by statute.

Creation by
deed of
grant.

(1) **By Instrument** *inter vivos*.   At common law a rentcharge, if created *inter vivos*, must be granted by deed.[6] But the

---

[1] Cruise *Digest*, Tit. **xxviii**. c. ii. ss. 1–3.

[2] S. 1 (1) (b). A rentcharge, provided that it is not limited to take effect upon the determination of some other interest, is " in possession " notwithstanding that its payment is to commence at some time subsequently to its creation. Law of Property (Entailed Interests) Act 1932, s. 2.

[3] Co. Litt., 47a.

[4] *Stafford* v. *Buckley* (1750), 2 Ves. Sen. 170, 177.

[5] L.P.A. 1925, s. 122.   This occurs very rarely in practice.

[6] Co. Litt., 169a ; *Hewlins* v. *Shippam* (1826), 5 B. & C. 221, at p. 229.

equitable principle underlying the doctrine of *Walsh* v. *Lonsdale* applies here just as it does in the case of an agreement to grant a term of years[1] or an easement, so that, where one person has agreed in a signed memorandum to grant a rentcharge to another, an equitable rentcharge may be created.[2]

The quantum of the interest in a rentcharge depends upon the words of limitation which are inserted in the deed of grant, and the rule is that such words are construed in exactly the same way as in a grant of corporeal hereditaments. Thus before 1926, in order to pass a perpetual rentcharge it was necessary to convey the rent to the grantee *and his heirs*, or to the grantee *in fee simple*, but the changes which have been effected by the Law of Property Act 1925 in regard to words of limitation sufficient to pass a fee simple estate in land[3] apply to rentcharges, and at the present day the effect of a grant which contains no technical words of limitation is to give the grantee a perpetual rentcharge, or if that is impossible owing to the grantor only having a smaller estate, then to give him a rent for the whole interest—whatever that may be—possessed by the grantor. This rule is, however, displaced if a contrary intention is shown in the conveyance, and in such a case the size of the grantee's interest will depend upon the intention of the parties.[4]

Words of limitation.

Perhaps the most usual example of the grant of a perpetual rentcharge occurs where a vendor on the sale of a fee simple instead of receiving the purchase money in the form of a lump sum, reserves to himself a rent—generally known as a *fee farm rent* or a *chief rent*—which is payable to him and his heirs in perpetuity.[5] Several statutes have sanctioned this practice.[6] One drawback is that a positive covenant by the purchaser, such as to build and repair buildings, does not run with the land and bind his successors in title, though they remain liable for the rent.[7] Moreover, the benefit of a covenant to pay a rentcharge does not run with the rentcharge so as to entitle an assignee thereof to maintain an action *on the covenant* against the covenantor or his assignee.[8] Thus,

Fee farm rents.

A covenant to pay a rentcharge is only in gross.

> where A. granted a fee simple to B. on the terms that A. his heirs and assigns should be entitled to a rent issuing out of the land, and the conveyance contained a covenant by B. to pay the rent to A. his heirs and assigns, it was held that X.,

---

[1] *Supra*, pp. 394 *et seq*.

[2] *Jackson* v. *Lever* (1792), 3 Bro. C.C. 605.

[3] *Supra*, p. 153. L.P.A. 1925, s. 60.

[4] S. 60 (1). See Megarry and Wade, *Law of Real Property* (4th Edn.), p. 795, for an argument that s. 60 may not apply to the creation of rentcharges by deed.

[5] *Supra*, pp. 150-1.

[6] *E.g.* Lands Clauses Consolidation Act 1845, s. 10.

[7] *Haywood* v. *Brunswick Building Soc.* (1881), 8 Q. B. D. 403.

[8] *Grant* v. *Edmondson*, [1931] 1 Ch. 1. But see *infra*, p. 631, as to liability of the *terre tenant* in debt.

to whom A. had demised the rent for 1000 years, could not sue B. on the covenant.[1]

The technical nature of this rule was demonstrated by P. O. LAWRENCE, L.J. :—

" Whatever may be the foundation of the rule, and whether it rests on the broader principle that (except as between lessor and lessee) no covenant can run with an incorporeal hereditament, or whether it rests on the narrower principle that a covenant to pay a rent-charge is a collateral covenant or a covenant in gross which does not touch or concern the rentcharge, or whether it rests on no principle and is merely arbitrary, I am of opinion that it is too firmly established to be disturbed by this court." [2]

Creation by will.

(2) **By Will.** A rentcharge may be validly created by will, and whether it is so or not depends upon the intention of the testator. If he directs that an annual sum shall be paid to a donee and uses words which show that the money is to be a charge upon the land and not upon his personal property, it is a rentcharge as distinct from an annuity, as for instance where he devises land to A.

" subject to and charged and chargeable with the payment of £100 a year to B. for 25 years." [3]

Section 28 of the Wills Act 1837[4] only applies to the transfer of an existing rentcharge ; it does not apply to the creation of a new one. Thus, if a rentcharge is created by will without any words of limitation, the devisee can take it only for life.[5]

Creation by statute.

(3) **By Statute.** There are two distinct series of enactments under which an owner of land may carry out certain improvements and arrange that the cost shall be charged upon the land and reimbursed in full, together with interest, by a definite number of annual payments. The chief statute of the first class is the Improvement of Land Act 1864, which allows " landowners " (*i.e.* anyone except a lessee at a rack rent[6] who is in actual possession of the rents and profits) to borrow money for improvements from certain private land improvement companies.

Improvement of Land Act 1864.

Money may not be borrowed in this way for every improvement, but only for those specified in the Settled Land Act 1925.[7] No rentcharge can be imposed upon the land until the Secretary of State for the Environment[8] has, on the application of the land owner, satisfied itself that the suggested improvement will permanently increase the yearly value of the

---

[1] *Milnes* v. *Branch* (1816), 5 M. & S. 411.

[2] *Grant* v. *Edmondson*, [1931] 1 Ch. 1, at p. 26. See (1931), 47 *L. Q. R.* 380 (W. Strachan).

[3] *Ramsay* v. *Thorngate* (1849), 16 Sim. 575.

[4] *Supra*, p. 152.

[5] *Nichols* v. *Hawkes* (1853), 10 Hare 342.

[6] *I.e.* the full yearly value of the land.

[7] *Supra*, p. 181. The improvements specified in the 1864 Act are all covered by those set out in the Settled Land Act 1925, and the latter are expressly brought within the operation of the earlier Act

[8] Or the Secretary of State for Wales. S. I. 1967 No. 156 ; S. I. 1970 No. 1681.

land to an extent greater than the annual rentcharge which is contemplated.[1]

If satisfied on this point the Secretary of State issues a provisional Order which specifies the sum to be charged upon the land, the rate of interest and the number of years within which it must be paid off. The rate of interest is now left to the discretion of the Secretary of State,[2] but the period for payments must not exceed forty years.[3] After the improvements are completed the Secretary of State issues an absolute Order imposing the annual sum as a rentcharge upon the fee simple, and this has priority over all existing and future incumbrances affecting the land with certain specified exceptions.[4] The remedies for its recovery are the same as in the case of other rentcharges,[5] except that the landowner is not personally liable.

The second class of statute is represented by the Settled Land Act 1925, which allows a limited owner to raise money for the purpose of carrying out permanent improvements on the settled land. Prior to January 1st, 1926, there was an important difference between the operation of the Improvement of Land Acts and that of the Settled Land Acts in this matter, for, while under the former a tenant for life could raise new money for the purpose, all that the Settled Land Acts did was to authorize the expenditure upon improvements of capital money which happened to be in the hands of the trustees. A tenant for life could not raise new money by mortgage under the Settled Land Acts for carrying out improvements, but this power, as we have seen, has now been expressly conferred upon him by the Settled Land Act 1925.[6]

Settled Land Act 1925.

SECTION III. REMEDIES FOR THE RECOVERY OF A RENTCHARGE

The following remedies are available to a rentcharge owner :

(1) **Distress.** A power to distrain upon the land out of which the rent issues is, as we have seen, an implicit incident of a rentcharge, though formerly it had to be specially reserved. Even when the Landlord and Tenant Act 1730 had conferred the power of distress on rent owners, it was the usual practice to insert an express provision to the same effect in all instruments creating rentcharges, but this has ceased to be the practice in the case of instruments coming

Distress when 21 days' rent due.

---

[1] There are certain improvements which may be allowed although they will not permanently increase the yearly value of the land, *i.e.* construction of waterworks for the use of residents on the estate (40 & 41 Vict. c. 31, s. 5); erection of mansion house under Limited Owners Residence Acts 1870, 1871 ; planting, Improvement of Land Act 1864, s. 15 ; erection or improvement of farmhouse or cottage for use of workers on the land, Agricultural Credits Act 1923, s. 3 (3).
[2] Agricultural Credits Act 1923, s. 3 (1).
[3] Improvement of Land Act 1899, s. 1 (1).   [4] *Ibid.*, s. 59.
[5] *Infra.*   [6] S.L.A. 1925, s. 71 (1) (ii) ; *supra*, p. 181.

into effect after December 31st, 1881. The Conveyancing Act of that year provides that where any rent (not incident to the relationship of làndlord and tenant) is in arrears for 21 days, the person entitled to receive it may enter into and distrain upon the land charged or any part thereof, and dispose of any distrainable objects according to the general law.[1] This remedy is now re-enacted by the Law of Property Act 1925.[2]

Entry when 40 days' rent due.

(2) Entry upon the land charged. The Law of Property Act 1925 provides that, when a rentcharge is in arrears for 40 days, even though no legal demand has been made for payment, the owner may enter into possession of and hold the land charged or any part thereof and take the income thereof until all arrears and costs and expenses occasioned by the non-payment of the rent are satisfied.[3] The Act, it will be noticed, does not give the owner of the rent a power of entry that will cause a forfeiture of the debtor's interest in the land, as is usual between landlord and tenant, but such a power may be, and generally is, reserved in the instrument of creation.

As we have seen, neither type of power, whether to hold the land until payment or to determine the debtor's interest, is subject to the rule against perpetuities.[4]

Appointment of trustees when 40 days' rent due.

(3) Lease to trustees. When a rentcharge is in arrears for 40 days, the person entitled to payment, whether taking possession or not, may by deed lease the whole or part of the land to a trustee for a term of years, with or without impeachment of waste, on trust to raise and pay the rent together with all arrears, costs and expenses.[5] The trustee may adopt any *reasonable means*[6] to raise the money, as for instance by the mortgage, assignment or sublease of the term vested in him, or by appropriating the income of the land, but he cannot create a *legal* mortgage unless the rentcharge itself is held for a legal estate.

The above three remedies are not enforceable if a contrary intention is expressed in the instrument under which the annual sum arises,[7] and they are subject to the provisions of such instrument. Moreover, when a rentcharge is charged on another rentcharge, the above remedies are excluded and replaced by a right in the rent owner to appoint a receiver of the annual sum charged whenever payment is in arrears for 21 days.[8]

---

[1] *Supra*, p. 429.
[2] Section 121 (3).
[3] Section 121 (2).
[4] L.P.A. 1925, s. 121 (6), *supra*, p. 340 (right to enter for purpose of distraint or leasing) ; Perpetuities and Accumulations Act 1964, s. 11 (1), *supra*, p. 357 (right to effect forfeiture).
[5] L.P.A. 1925, s. 121 (4).
[6] *Ibid.*
[7] *Ibid.*, s. 121 (5).
[8] *Ibid.*, s. 122, *supra*, p. 626.

(4) **Action of debt.** It is well settled that an action of debt for the recovery of arrears lies against the *terre tenant* for the time being of the whole or part only of the land charged,[1] provided that he holds a freehold as distinct from a leasehold interest.[2] It is no defence that the profits of the land do not equal in amount the value of the rentcharge. Thus in *Pertwee* v. *Townsend* :[3]

> Lands were charged with the payment of a rentcharge of £80 a year. A certain portion of these lands was acquired by the defendant's predecessor in title, who released the rest of the land from the burden of the charge and imposed it upon the portion so acquired. At the time of the action for the recovery of £80, being one year's arrears, the defendant was able to show that the annual profits of the portion charged, of which he was tenant for life, amounted only to £7 5s., but nevertheless he was held personally liable for the whole £80.

COLLINS, J., said [4]:—

> " The defendant holds the land subject to a charge, and he cannot keep the land and refuse to pay the charge. If he does refuse, the remedy against him is personal for the amount of the charge itself."

Where land which is subject to a rentcharge is split up as the result of some conveyance, and the charge is either made payable out of one of the portions or apportioned between them, the parties possess certain statutory rights whose object it is to give effect to any such arrangement that may have been made. This kind of apportionment is equitable as distinct from legal apportionment, since it is made without the consent of the owner of the rentcharge. The Law of Property Act 1925 [5] provides that where in such a case the rentcharge, without the consent of the owner, is

(a) charged exclusively on the land conveyed in exoneration of the land retained, or

(b) charged exclusively on the land retained in exoneration of the land conveyed, or

(c) apportioned between the land conveyed and the land retained,

then the agreement, without prejudice to the rights of the rent owner, shall be binding between the grantor and the grantee under the conveyance and their respective successors in title. If the owner of part of the land fails to pay the rentcharge in accordance with the agreement or fails to perform some covenant, and the owner of the other part is in consequence obliged to pay the

---

[1] *Thomas* v. *Sylvester* (1873), L. R. 8 Q. B. 368. A *terre tenant* is the person who has the actual possession or occupation of land.

[2] *Re Herbage Rents*, [1896] 2 Ch. 811. Distress, however, may be levied on the premises.

[3] [1896] 2 Q. B. 129.   [4] At p. 134.   [5] S. 190.

charge or damages, the latter may distrain upon the land of the former and may also take the income thereof until he has been satisfied.[1]

SECTION IV.   EXTINCTION OF A RENTCHARGE

There are several ways in which a rentcharge may be extinguished and the land freed from liability.

Release of whole land.

(1) **Release.** If the rent owner releases the whole of the land charged from any further liability to pay, the rent is extinguished. Indeed, on the somewhat questionable ground that a rent, being entire and issuing out of every part of the land, cannot be thrown upon one particular part nor apportioned between several parts, the old rule was that a release of *part* of the land discharged the whole land and produced a total extinguishment of the rent.[2] But the Law of Property Act 1925,[3] re-enacting the Law of Property Amendment Act 1859, provides that the release from a rentcharge of part of the lands charged shall not extinguish the whole rentcharge, but shall only render it unenforceable against the part released. This provision, however, is not to prejudice the rights of the persons who are interested in the unreleased part of the lands unless they concur in or confirm the release. The effect of this enactment is that where the owner of land which is subject to a rentcharge sells the land in separate portions to different persons, and only one portion is released from the charge by the rent owner, the purchasers of the unreleased portions will be liable for the whole rent if they concur in the release, but will be liable only for an apportioned part if they do not concur.[4]

Release of part of land.

Merger at common law.

(2) **Merger.** A rentcharge may also be extinguished by merger.[5] The rigid rule of common law is that, whenever a lesser and a greater estate in the same lands become united in one person in his own right, the lesser estate is merged in the greater and extinguished without regard to the intention of the parties. As we shall see later, however, the equitable view that no merger occurs if it is contrary to the intention of the party in whom the two estates vest now obtains in all courts,[6] and it will suffice to say here that this principle applies to the merger of a rentcharge. Thus :

---

[1] S. 190 (2) ; *Whitham* v. *Bullock*, [1939] 2 K. B. 81 ; [1939] 2 All E. R. 310.
[2] Co. Litt., 147*b*.   [3] S. 70.
[4] *Booth* v. *Smith* (1884), 14 Q. B. D. 318.
[5] As to merger generally, see *Forbes* v. *Moffatt* (1811), 18 Ves. 384, Tudor, *Leading Cases on Real Property* (4th Edn.), p. 244. *Infra*, pp. 910 *et seq.*
[6] *Infra*, pp. 899–900.

if the absolute owner of a rentcharge also becomes absolute owner in his own right of the land charged, either by grant or by devise, there is *prima facie* a merger of the rent in the estate because there is no obvious advantage in keeping both the interests alive.[1]

But on the other hand :

if the person who is responsible for the rent mortgages the land charged to the rent owner, there is no merger, since the two interests do not unite in one person in the same right.

(3) **Statute.** Lastly, means have been devised by statute[2] whereby the owner of the land charged, or any person interested therein, may redeem a rentcharge by payment to the rent owner of a capital sum of money certified by the Secretary of State for the Environment[3] as being a fair equivalent for the rent. An estate owner who desires to free his land by this method must request the Secretary of State to certify the amount payable, and when this has been done he is entitled, after serving a month's notice, to pay the amount to the rent owner provided that the latter is entitled to give a good discharge for the capital value of the rent.[4] But if the rent owner cannot be found or ascertained, or if he is unable or unwilling to prove his right to give a discharge, or if the redemption is held up owing to complications of title, the Secretary of State may authorize the owner of the land charged to pay the redemption money into court. When the certified capital sum has been paid to the rent owner or into court, the Secretary of State issues a certificate to the effect that the land is discharged from the rent.[5]

Redemption of rent-charge.

This statutory mode of redemption does not apply to a rent reserved on a lease or tenancy, but it does include a rent reserved on a sale of land, or made payable under a grant for building purposes, and a rent may be redeemed even though it is not perpetual.[6] If an estate owner desires to discharge part of his land from a rentcharge, the Secretary of State may apportion the rent between the parts of the land indicated by the owner, and then any such apportioned part may be redeemed.[7]

---

[1] *Freeman* v. *Edwards* (1848), 2 Ex. 732.
[2] L.P.A. 1925, s. 191, as amended by Finance Act 1962, Sched. XI, Pt. VI.
[3] Or the Secretary of State for Wales S. I. 1967, No. 156 ; S. I. 1970, No. 1681.
[4] *Ibid.*
[5] *Ibid.*   [6] *Ibid.*, s. 191 (1).
[7] *Ibid.*, s. 191 (7). Application for apportionment may also be made under Landlord and Tenant Act 1927, s. 20.

SECTION V. REGISTERED LAND

A rentcharge may be created over registered land[1] in the same
way as it can over unregistered land. Thus, unless there is some
entry on the register to the contrary, the proprietor of registered
freehold land may grant a rentcharge in possession, either perpetual or for a term of years absolute in any form which sufficiently
refers to the registered land.[2] He may also transfer the fee simple
in possession of his registered land or any part of it subject to the
reservation thereout of a rentcharge in possession.[3]

Unlike legal easements and profits à prendre, a legal rentcharge
is capable of being substantively registered with a separate title.[4]
Further, unlike leases, a rentcharge granted for any term of years,
no matter how short, may be so registered. As to compulsory
registration, the mere fact that the land affected by a rentcharge
lies in a compulsory area never makes registration of the rentcharge
itself compulsory, since section 120 (1) of the Land Registration
Act 1925 in effect exempts from compulsory registration the title
to an incorporeal hereditament.[5] However substantive registration of any rentcharge capable of such registration is always compulsory where the rentcharge issues out of land which is already
registered.

On the other hand a rentcharge for life is not capable of substantive registration, although it may and should be noted as a
general equitable charge against the registered title of the land
charged ;[6] nor too can a perpetual or other rentcharge which takes
effect under a settlement be registered.

In order to be effective at law, any disposition under which a
rentcharge is created, whether by a deed of grant or by a transfer,
must, like all other kinds of disposition, be completed by registration.[7] In the case of a rentcharge, there are thus " two processes,
namely, the substantive registration of the title to the rentcharge
... and the entry of notice of the rentcharge as an incumbrance
against the title of the landowner ... When land is transferred
in consideration of a rentcharge ... the transferor will be registered
as the proprietor of the rentcharge under a separate title, and be
given a rentcharge certificate.[8] Simultaneously, the transferee is

---

[1] See generally Ruoff, *Rentcharges in Registered Conveyancing* (1961) and
Ruoff and Roper, chap. 28, where, at p. 590 it is said that " there is probably
no subject which receives a more meagre and fragmentary treatment in the
Land Registration Acts and Rules than that of rentcharges."

[2] L.R.A. 1925, s. 18 (1) (*b*) ; L.R.R. 1925, rr. 79, 113.

[3] *Ibid.*, s. 18 (1) (*d*). For rentcharges created by the proprietor of a
registered leasehold estate see L.R.A. 1925, s. 21 (1) (b) (c).

[4] *Ibid.*, s. 3 (xxv). L.R.R. 1925, rr. 50–52.

[5] *Supra*, p. 107, note 5.

[6] L.R.A. 1925, s. 49 (1) (*c*). Ruoff and Roper, p. 592.

[7] *Ibid.*, ss. 19 (2), 22 (2). L.R.R. 1925, rr. 107, 108.

[8] L.R.R. 1925, r. 108.

registered as the proprietor of the land, and the rentcharge is noted in the charges register of his title as an incumbrance.[1]   In the remarks column of the entry there will be a cross reference to the rentcharge title."[2]

SECTION VI.   LAW COMMISSION REPORT ON RENTCHARGES, 1975

In 1975 the Law Commission recommended[3] that, subject to certain exceptions, no further rentcharges should be created,[4] and that all existing rentcharges should be extinguished without compensation after, say, 60 years.[5]

The main exceptions are :[6]

(a) Rentcharges, such as those connected with family annuities, which cause the land charged therewith to be settled land for the purposes of the Settled Land Act 1925[7] or which affect settled land or land held on trust for sale ;

(b) Rentcharges created (typically in connection with freehold flat developments) for the purpose either of making positive covenants enforceable against successors in title or of financing the provision of common services ;

(c) Rentcharges created by or in accordance with court orders ;

(d) Certain terminable rentcharges created by or under statutory provisions, *e.g.*, where the charges are designed to enable the rent owners to recover over a period money spent or advanced for improvement works carried out on the land charged.[8]

New apportionment and redemption procedures are also recommended,[9] and, in particular, the administrative functions are to be transferred from the Secretary of State to District Councils, through which all steps are to be conducted.

---

[1] L.R.A. 1925, s. 49 (1) (*a*) : L.R.R. 1925, r. 107 (2).
[2] L.R.R. 1925, r. 108 ; Ruoff and Roper, p. 606.
[3] (1975) Law Com. No. 68.
[4] Paras. 38–42.
[5] Paras. 54–62.
[6] Paras. 46–53.
[7] S. 1 (1) (v).   *Supra*, p. 169.
[8] *E.g.*, S. L. A. 1925, s. 85.   *Supra*, p. 185.
[9] (1975) Law Com. No. 68, paras. 67–89.

CHAPTER V

MORTGAGES[1]

SUMMARY

---

[1] See generally Coote *Law of Mortgages* (9th Edn.) ; Fisher and Lightwood, *Law of Mortgage* (8th Edn.) ; Waldock, *Law of Mortgages* (2nd Edn.).

SECTION I. HISTORY OF THE METHODS
WHEREBY MORTGAGES HAVE BEEN EFFECTED

Definition and Terminology. A mortgage is a conveyance or other disposition of land designed to secure the payment of money or the discharge of some other obligation.[1] The party who conveys the property by way of security is called the mortgagor, the lender or obligee who obtains an interest in the property is called the mortgagee, and the debt for which the security is created is termed the mortgage debt. The mortgagee, since he is the grantee of a proprietary interest acquires a real, not merely a personal, security that prevails against the general body of creditors in the event of the mortgagor's bankruptcy.

Terminology.

History of Mortgages.[2] If we are to understand the radical alterations that were made by the legislation of 1925 in the methods of creating mortgages, it is necessary to appreciate the principles of the earlier law.

History.

The developed law of mortgages is the joint product of common law, equity and statute. In the earliest days of the common law a mortgage was a mere pledge, which took one of two forms. It might be agreed that the lender should enter into possession of the land, and should take the rents and profits in discharge of both the principal and the interest of the loan. This was called a *vivum vadium*, or living pledge, since it automatically and by its own force discharged the entire debt. But, on the other hand, the arrangement might be that the lender should take the rents and profits of the land in discharge of the interest only, in which case the transaction was called a *mortuum vadium*, a dead pledge, since it did not effect the gradual extinction of the debt.

Earliest position.

By the time of Littleton (1402-1481), however, a mortgage had become a species of estate upon condition created by a feoffment defeasible upon condition subsequent.

Position in time of Littleton.

The land was conveyed in fee simple to the mortgagee on condition that if the loan was repaid upon the day which had been fixed by agreement, the conveyance should be defeated, and the mortgagor be free to re-enter. If repayment was not made on the exact date fixed, then the estate of the mortgagee became absolute, and the mortgagor's interest in the land was extinguished. In the words of Littleton:

> " If a feoffment be made upon such condition, that if the feoffor pay to the feoffee at a certain day etc. 40 pounds of money, that then the feoffor may re-enter, etc., in this case the feoffee is called tenant in morgage, which is as much to say in French as mortgage, and in Latin *mortuum vadium*. And it seemeth that the cause why it is called mortgage is, for that it is doubtful whether the feoffor will

---

[1] See *Santley* v. *Wilde*, [1899] 2 Ch. 474, *per* LINDLEY, M.R. ; Lawson, *Introduction to the Law of Property*, p. 184.

[2] Holdsworth, *History of English Law*, vol. iii. p. 128 ; Plucknett, *Concise History of the Common Law* (5th Edn.), pp. 603-9.

pay at the day limited such sum or not, and if he doth not pay, then the land which is put in pledge upon condition for the payment of the money is taken from him for ever, and so dead to him upon condition etc. And if he doth pay the money, then the pledge is dead as to the tenant." [1]

That a feoffor should be bound to repay the loan on the exact day fixed or be precluded for ever from redeeming his property was a hard rule, and

> " what made the hardship on the debtor a glaring one was that the debt still remained unpaid and could be recovered from the feoffor notwithstanding that he had actually forfeited the land to his mortgagee." [2]

Alteration by equity. But by the time of Charles I, equity had so fundamentally altered this strict legal view that the law of mortgages was transformed.[3] The form as indicated by Littleton remained, but equity interfered on the general principle that relief should be granted against forfeiture for breach of a penal condition.[3] No longer was redemption to depend upon a strict compliance with the contract. In the view of equity the essential object of a mortgage is to afford security to the lender, and as long as the security remains intact there is no justification for expropriating the property of the mortgagor merely because of his failure to make prompt payment. In the words of Lord Nottingham :—

> " In natural justice and equity the principal right of the mortgagee is to the money, and his right to the land is only as a security for the money." [4]

Hence the rule ultimately established by courts of equity was that a mortgagor must be allowed to redeem his fee simple despite his failure to make repayment on the appointed day. Time was not to be of the essence of the transaction. This is still the rule, although a mortgage is no longer created by the conveyance of a fee simple estate. The position, then, is this :—

Equity of redemption. Upon the date fixed for repayment (which is usually six months after the creation of the mortgage, although in most cases neither mortgagor nor mortgagee intends that the loan shall be repaid on that date) the mortgagor has at common law a contractual right to redeem.

If this date passes without repayment, he obtains a right to redeem in equity.

> " The equity to redeem, which arises on failure to exercise the contractual right of redemption, must be carefully distinguished from the equitable estate, which, from the first, remains in the mortgagor, and is sometimes referred to as an equity of redemption." [5]

---

[1] Litt. s. 332.

[2] *Kreglinger* v. *New Patagonia Meat and Cold Storage Co., Ltd.*, [1914] A. C. 25, at p. 35, *per* Lord Haldane.

[3] Holdsworth, *History of English Law*, vol. v. p. 330.

[4] *Thornborough* v. *Baker* (1675), 3 Swans. 628, at p. 630.

[5] *Kreglinger* v. *New Patagonia Meat and Cold Storage Co., Ltd.*, [1914] A. C. 25, at p. 48, *per* Lord Parker.

This equity of redemption arises as soon as the mortgage is created, and is an equitable interest owned by the mortgagor. It is an interest in land which may be conveyed, devised or entailed, and it may descend on intestacy or pass as *bona vacantia* to the Crown.[1] It is destructible only by four events, namely, its release by the mortgagor, the lapse of time under the Limitation Act,[2] the exercise by the mortgagee of his statutory power of sale,[3] and a foreclosure decree, *i.e.* a judicial decree that the subject-matter of the mortgage shall be vested absolutely in the mortgagee free from any right of redemption.[4]

Position prior to 1926. Up to January 1st, 1926, the normal method by which a mortgage of the fee simple was created was for the mortgagor to convey the legal fee simple to the mortgagee together with a covenant to repay the loan in, say, six months' time, with a proviso, however, that if the loan were repaid at such date, the mortgagee would reconvey the legal estate. Outwardly it still seemed as if the mortgagee became absolute owner failing repayment within six months, but essentially, owing to the doctrine of the equity of redemption, the mortgagor was the true owner. Technically he was a mere equitable owner, but in the eyes of equity he was the real owner and, on his repaying the principal and interest with costs to the mortgagee, equity was prepared to grant specific performance of the proviso for reconveyance of the legal estate to him. *Summary of pre-1926 law.*

A still older method of creating a mortgage, used between the thirteenth and fifteenth centuries and worthy of notice because of its revival by the 1925 legislation, was for the mortgagor to lease his land to the mortgagee for a short term of years. If the debt was not repaid at the end of the lease, the right of the mortgagor was extinguished, and the term was automatically enlarged into a fee simple which vested absolutely in the mortgagee.[5] This method, however, fell into desuetude, mainly because the law in its growing strictness could not countenance this facile mode of enlarging a term of years into a fee. An attempt to resuscitate it was made about the beginning of the nineteenth century, but owing to certain disadvantages, such as the doubt whether the mortgagee was entitled to possession of the title deeds, it failed, and the term of years was used only in family settlements where it was desired to secure money lent for the payment of portions.[6] *Alternative form of mortgage under pre-1926 law.*

Mortgage of a term of years. If the security offered by the borrower was a leasehold interest, not the fee simple, there were *Mode of mortgaging leaseholds.*

---

[1] *Casborne* v. *Scarfe* (1738), 1 Atk. 603 ; *Re Sir Thomas Spencer Wells,* [1933] 1 Ch. 29 ; Waldock, *Law of Mortgages* (2nd Edn.), pp. 202 *et seq.*
[2] *Infra,* p. 662.   [3] *Infra,* p. 669.
[4] *Infra,* p. 673.
[5] Holdsworth, *History of English Law,* vol. iii. p. 129.
[6] (1925), 60 *L. J. News,* 46 (J. M. Lightwood).

two methods before 1926 by which the mortgage might be created. Usually the mortgagor subleased his term of years to the mortgagee for a period slightly shorter than the remainder of the term. This was the most desirable method, since the sublease did not involve privity of estate between the mortgagee and the superior landlord, and therefore the mortgagee was immune from liability on the covenants contained in the original lease, unless indeed there were negative covenants enforceable under the doctrine of *Tulk* v. *Moxhay*.[1] The alternative method was for the mortgagee to take an assignment of the whole remainder of the term, but in this case he became liable to covenants and conditions under the doctrine of *Spencer's Case*.[2]

Equitable mortgages.

Equitable Mortgages. In addition to the conveyance of a legal estate, whether a fee simple or a term of years, by way of security, it has long been possible, of course, to create an equitable mortgage by the grant of an equitable interest. This is necessarily the method where the borrower himself is a mere equitable owner, as, for instance, where before 1926 a mortgagor created a second mortgage in the same land : the legal estate had been conveyed to the first mortgagee and what the mortgagor conveyed to the second mortgagee was his equity of redemption. A further example of an equitable mortgage, made by a borrower who is an equitable owner, is where a tenant for life under a strict settlement mortgages his equitable life interest.

On the other hand it is also possible for an equitable mortgage to be created by the owner of a legal estate, as for instance where he agrees to create a legal mortgage ; this entitles the lender in equity to enforce specific performance of the promise. Indeed, without the grant even of an equitable interest, an owner may charge his land with the repayment of a loan and so entitle the lender in equity to enforce a judicial sale of the property. These equitable mortgages are considered in more detail later.[3]

Alterations made by the legislation of 1925. The prevailing practice, by which the legal fee simple was conveyed to a mortgagee, presented a difficult problem to the draftsmen of the 1925 legislation. How were they to bring it into line with the principles that they intended to introduce ?

The corner-stone of their policy was that the legal fee simple should always be vested in its true owner and that he should be able to convey it free from equitable interests. In the eyes of the law the true owner is the mortgagor. Yet, all that he held before 1926 was an equitable interest, and unless some alteration were made there could be no question of his ability to

---

[1] *Supra*, pp. 597 *et seq.*
[2] *Supra*, pp. 449 *et seq.*
[3] *Infra*, pp. 649–52, 684–6.

convey any kind of legal estate during the continuance of the mortgage.

On the other hand it was important to protect the mortgagee in the enjoyment of certain valuable advantages that he derived from his legal ownership. Pre-eminent among these was the priority which, by virtue of the legal fee simple, he obtained over other mortgages created in the same land, for these were necessarily equitable in nature. Moreover, his possession of the title deeds enabled him to control the actions of the mortgagor in his dealings with the land. He also enjoyed the right to take actual possession of the land, and therefore to grant leases ; and lastly, when he exercised his power of sale on failure by the mortgagor to repay the loan, he was able to vest the legal estate in the purchaser.[1]

The solution contained in the Law of Property Act 1925 is to revert to the old fifteenth-century method of effecting mortgages by means of a lease for a term of years. *Law of mortgages now re-cast*

Mortgages by which the legal fee simple is vested in the mortgagee are prohibited, and a mortgagee who requires a legal estate instead of a mere equitable interest is compelled to take either a long term of years or a newly invented interest called a *charge by deed expressed to be by way of legal mortgage*. Thus in the first case both parties have legal estates :

the mortgagee has a legal term of years absolute, and

the mortgagor has a reversionary and legal fee simple, subject to the mortgagee's term ;

while in the case of a charge by way of legal mortgage the mortgagee has the same protection powers and remedies as if he had taken a legal term of years.

In this way the principle that the legal fee simple should always remain vested in the true owner has been maintained. The mortgagor is owner at law as well as in equity, and the mortgagee has only a right *in alieno solo*. The charge by way of legal mortgage at last provides a method which reflects the reality of the transaction and goes some way towards rebutting Maitland's description of a mortgage deed as one long *suppressio veri* and *suggestio falsi*.[2] We should also notice two important consequences of the change made by the 1925 legislation. First, the mortgagor's retention of the legal estate means that any second and subsequent mortgages which he creates may be legal. And secondly, the rights of the parties remain unchanged, and in particular, the mortgagor's equity of redemption is still of importance. This, as before 1926, is an equitable proprietary interest and is in value equal to the value of the land less the amount of the debt secured by the mortgage. The mortgagor

---

[1] (1925), 60 *L. J. News*, 91 (J. M. Lightwood).

[2] Maitland *Equity*, p. 182. For a precedent of a mortgage deed, see *infra*, p. 643.

retains that interest and keeps a legal estate as well. On the other hand, the mortgagee retains all his remedies, and, for instance, may sell and convey the fee simple, if the mortgagor defaults in his obligations.[1]

SECTION II. METHODS OF CREATING MORTGAGES AFTER 1925

SUMMARY

(1) LEGAL MORTGAGES
(A) BY LEASE

A *legal* mortgage of an estate *in fee simple* must be effected by either—

Legal mortgages to be effected by lease or legal charge.

1. a demise for a term of years absolute, subject to a provision (called a provision for cesser) that the term shall cease if repayment is made on a fixed day ; or

2. a charge by deed expressed to be by way of legal mortgage.[2]

Length of lease. To confine our attention for the moment to the former method, the Act does not state for what period the lease must be made, but it enacts that if any person in future attempts to create a mortgage by the old method of a transfer of the fee simple, the conveyance shall operate as a lease of the land for 3000 years, without impeachment for waste, but subject to cesser on redemption.[3] There is, of course, no obligation for a mortgage term to be granted for so long a period as this.

Subsequent mortgages. If it is desired to create further *legal* mortgages in the same land, the mortgagor may lease the land to each mortgagee after the first for a term which is usually at least one day longer than the term limited to the immediately preceding mortgagee.[4] If, for

---

[1] *Infra*, p. 669.
[2] L.P.A. 1925, s. 85 (1).
[3] *Ibid.*, s. 85 (2).
[4] *Ibid.*, s. 85 (2) (b).

instance, the mortgagor raises money first from A., then from B. and then from C. on the security of Blackacre, there may be

a lease to A. for 3000 years,

a lease to B. for 3000 years and one day (subject to A.'s term), and

a lease to C. for 3000 years and two days (subject to the terms of A. and B.).

The effect in such a case is, as we have seen,[1] that the second and all subsequent mortgagees now take legal interests in the land instead of mere equitable interests as formerly.

Subsequent mortgages now legal.

At first sight the possession by B. of a term of 3000 years and one day, subject to a prior term of 3000 years, does not seem of much value, but when the first term ceases on redemption, B. acquires the first right to the land for the residue of the term; and moreover he always has the right, after giving adequate notice, to pay to A. what A. lent to the mortgagor, and thus to succeed to A.'s position. In such a case B. remains entitled to hold the land under the lease until the advances made both by A. and by himself have been paid.

The following is a precedent of a mortgage deed [2] :—

Parties.

THIS MORTGAGE is made the first day of January 1975 between A. of etc. (hereinafter called the borrower) of the one part and B. of etc. (hereinafter called the lender) of the other part.

Recital of title of borrower.

Whereas the borrower is the estate owner in respect of the fee simple absolute in possession of the property described in the schedule hereto free from incumbrances.

Recital of agreement to lend.

And whereas the lender has agreed to lend to the borrower the sum of £5000 upon having the repayment thereof together with interest thereon secured in manner hereinafter appearing.

NOW THIS DEED WITNESSETH as follows:

Covenant for payment of principal and interest.

1. In consideration of the sum of £5000 now paid by the lender to the borrower (the receipt of which sum the borrower hereby acknowledges) the borrower hereby covenants with the lender that he will pay to the lender on the first day of July next the sum of £5000 with interest thereon from the date hereof at the rate of £11 per cent.

---

[1] *Supra*, p. 641.
[2] Adapted from *Encyclopædia of Forms and Precedents* (4th Edn.), vol. 14. p. 166.

per annum and if the said sum (hereinafter called the principal money) or any part thereof shall not be paid on the said date will at the date aforesaid pay to the lender (as well after as before any judgment) interest on the principal sum or such part thereof as shall from time to time remain owing by equal half yearly payments on the first of July and first of January in each year.

Demise of mortgaged property.

2. For the consideration aforesaid the borrower as beneficial owner hereby demises to the lender all the property specified in the schedule hereto TO HOLD the same unto the lender for the term of 3000 years from the date hereof without impeachment of waste subject to the provision for cesser hereinafter contained.

Proviso for cesser.

3. Provided that if the borrower shall on the first day of July next pay to the lender the principal sum with interest thereon from the date hereof at the rate aforesaid the term hereby created shall cease.

Covenants by borrower.

4. The borrower hereby further covenants with the lender
[Here follow covenants by the borrower to insure and repair buildings etc.]

In Witness etc.

Schedule

Position of the parties to a legal mortgage of the fee simple.

The obvious effect of such a deed is that the mortgagor remains seised in fee simple, while the mortgagee acquires a legal term of years that entitles him, if he so desires, to take possession of the land. Outwardly, indeed, he appears to acquire a term that will necessarily last for 3000 years unless the capital sum is paid on July 1st, 1975. Such, of course, is not the true position, for the equity of redemption that arises after that date entitles the mortgagor to procure the cessation of the term by the repayment in full of all that is due by way of principal and interest.

Mortgage of leaseholds.

Where the mortgagor has a term of years only. The next question to examine is how a mortgage is made when the mortgagor holds, not the fee simple, but a term of years. Again, the only possible methods of creating a legal mortgage are by a lease (in this case a sub-lease) for a term of years absolute, or by a legal charge.[1]

---

[1] L.P.A. 1925, s. 86 (1).

Confining ourselves for the moment to a sub-lease,[1] let us suppose that Mortgage by
way of
sub-lease.

A., the owner in fee simple, has leased his land to T. for 99 years, and T. wishes to mortgage his tenancy, which has still 70 years to run, to L. as security for an advance. The Act provides that T. may sublet the premises to L. for a period which must be less by at least one day than the term he himself holds.[2] He will therefore grant a sub-lease for, say, 69 years and 355 days, subject to a proviso that the title of L. shall cease on the repayment of the loan by T.

If T. later wishes to borrow more money from S. on the same premises, he must grant him another sub-lease for a period longer by one day than that of L.; in fact, however many later mortgagees there may be, they will each take a term one day longer than the immediately preceding term.[3]

The case, then, works out as follows :

A. is entitled to the reversion in fee simple ;

L. is sub-tenant for 69 years and 355 days;

S. subject to the tenancy of L., is sub-tenant for 69 years and 356 days ;

T. (the mortgagor), subject to the two sub-tenancies, is tenant for 70 years.

If L. chooses to take possession, he can do so, and can remain in possession until paid off either by T. (the mortgagor) or by S. If L. is paid off by T., then S. possesses the same rights until he is paid off by T. If L. is paid off by S. the latter can take possession and hold it until the advances made both by L. and by himself have been paid.

If L. sells, as he has a statutory right to do,[4] his conveyance to the purchaser will pass not only his mortgage term of 69 years and 355 days, but also the whole term of 70 years held by the mortgagor, and it will thus extinguish the mortgage terms held by S. and any later lender.[5]

Thus, the interest of a subsequent mortgagee, although it amounts to a legal estate, is a somewhat precarious security, since it will be destroyed if a prior mortgagee exercises his statutory

---

[1] For a precedent see *Encyclopædia of Forms and Precedents* (4th Edn), vol. 14. pp. 421–2.
[2] L.P.A. 1925, s. 86 (1).
[3] *Ibid.*, s. 86 (2).
[4] *Infra,* p. 669.
[5] L.P.A. 1925, s. 89 (1), *infra,* p. 670.

power of sale or obtains a foreclosure decree.[1]   The only remedy then left is to sue the mortgagor upon the personal covenant.

Abolition of mortgage by assignment of term.   The alternative method before 1926 of creating a mortgage by an assignment of the entire residue of the term to the mortgagee is prohibited, and any purported assignment intended to be by way of mortgage necessarily operates as a sub-lease for a term of years absolute, subject to cesser on redemption.[2]

Meaning of sub-mortgage.   **Sub-Mortgages.**   A mortgage term, whether created by lease or sub-lease, is available as a security to the mortgagee if he himself wishes to raise a loan.

> For example, the mortgagee, B., has lent £10,000 to A. and has taken a lease of A's fee simple as security.   If he now requires £1,000 for his immediate use, it may be inconvenient to enforce his rights against A. and to demand repayment in full of £10,000, for perhaps at the moment there is no suitable investment for £9000.   Again, the danger of calling upon A. for £1000 is that he, not having the funds, may be compelled to borrow £10,000 from a third party, X., and to transfer the mortgage to the latter.[3]   B., however, may sub-mortgage his own security to C. in return for a loan of £1000. This is effected by an assignment to C. of the mortgage debt (*i.e.* the right to receive £10,000) and by the grant to him of a sub-lease for a period shorter than his own mortgage term, but subject to a right of redemption in B. on payment of £1000.[4]   Since a mortgage debt is a chose in action, C. should protect himself by giving written notice to A. of its assignment.[5]

The effect of this transaction is to put C. in the position of B.[6]

Thus, the statutory power of sale is not exercisable by B. during the existence of the sub-mortgage,[7] and, therefore, if A defaults in the repayment of the £10,000, C. may sell the land by virtue of the original mortgage and transfer a title to the purchaser free from the mortgage and sub-mortgage.   Out of the purchase money, he will retain £1000, pay £9000 to B. and give any surplus to A.

Alternatively, if B. defaults in the repayment of £1000, C. may exercise the statutory power of sale incidental to the sub-mortgage.   In this case he transfers to the purchaser the mortgage

---

[1] L.P.A. 1925, s. 89 (2) ; *infra*, p. 673.   Fisher and Lightwood, *Law of Mortgage* (8th Edn.), pp. 134–5.

[2] *Ibid.*, s. 86 (2); *Grangeside Properties, Ltd.* v. *Collingwood's Securities, Ltd.*, [1964] 1. W. L. R. 139, [1964] 1 All E. R. 143.

[3] See Elphinstone, *Introduction to Conveyancing* (7th Edn.), p. 290.

[4] L.P.A. 1925, s. 86 (3); 1st Sched., Part VII, para. 4.

[5] *Ibid.*, s. 136 ; *infra*, pp. 711–3.   [6] *Ibid.*, s. 88 (5).

[7] Said to be doubtful in *Cruse* v. *Nowell* (1856), 25 L. J. Ch. 709.

debt together with the original mortgage term, but of course leaves A.'s equity of redemption intact. After retaining £1000, he will pay any surplus to B.[1]

(B) By a Legal Charge.

The Law of Property Act 1925 provides that a legal mortgage may also be created by

" a charge by deed expressed to be by way of legal mortgage." [2]

Charges have been utilized for a long time as a means of affording security to lenders, but hitherto they have for the most part been less efficacious than legal mortgages. If, for instance, a borrower agrees in writing that his land shall stand charged with the payment of £500, the lender, or chargee, obtains a mere equitable interest which does not entitle him either to recover possession or to grant leases, and which before 1926 also exposed him to the risk of being postponed to a later lender who acquired a legal mortgage in the land.

But, presumably in the pursuit of simplicity, the legislature in 1925 invented a new species of charge which operates to pass a legal interest to the chargee, though it does not convey to him a legal term of years. A short precedent of such a charge, which in practice is expanded so as to contain further appropriate covenants by the borrower,[3] is furnished by the Law of Property Act 1925.[4]

THIS LEGAL CHARGE is made the First day of January, 1975, between A. of the one part and B. of the other part.

Form of charge.

WHEREAS A. is seised of the hereditaments hereby charged and described in the schedule hereto for an estate in fee simple in possession free from incumbrances ;

NOW IN CONSIDERATION of the sum of £5000 now paid by B. to A. (the receipt whereof A. doth hereby acknowledge) this Deed witnesseth as follows :

1. A. hereby covenants with B. to pay on the first day of July next the sum of £5000 with interest thereon at the rate of £11 per cent. per annum.

2 A. as beneficial owner hereby charges by way of legal mortgage All and Singular the property mentioned in the Schedule hereto with the payment to B. of the principal money, interest and other money hereby covenanted to be paid by A.

---

[1] For a precedent see *Encyclopædia of Forms and Precedents* (4th Edn.), vol. 14. pp. 777–8.

[2] L.P.A. 1925, s. 85.

[3] For fuller precedents, see *Encyclopædia of Forms and Precedents* (4th Edn.), vol. 14. pp. 170–84, 413–9.

[4] Sched. 5, Form No. 1.

The Act does not vest a term of years in the mortgagee,[1] but it
provides that he shall have "the same protection, powers and
remedies" as if he had taken a lease of a fee simple or a sub-lease
of demised premises.[2]   In other words, he is in exactly the same
position as if the relationship of landlord and tenant existed between him and the mortgagor.[3]

If, for instance, A. has charged his term of years in favour
of B. and later commits a breach of a covenant contained in
the lease by reason of which his landlord starts proceedings
for the enforcement of his right of re-entry under a forfeiture
clause, B. is entitled to claim relief under section 146 of the
Law of Property Act 1925.[4]

This method of creating a mortgage has steadily gained popularity
since its introduction, and at the present day is adopted by most,
though not all,[5] practitioners in preference to the long lease.   Its
defect is that it does not contain the proviso for cesser that always
figures in the mortgage by demise.   This proviso corresponds to
the old proviso for redemption, the importance of which lay in fixing the date at which the mortgagor's right to redeem and the
mortgagee's right to foreclose came into being.   In the mortgage
given above on page 643, for instance, the property can neither be
redeemed by the mortgagor nor foreclosed by the mortgagee before
July 1st, 1975,[6] and although the right of a legal *chargee* to foreclose
probably arises by implication at the date fixed in the covenant for
repayment, provided that the mortgagor makes default, yet the
matter cannot be regarded as settled until it has been judicially
decided.   It is safer, therefore, to amplify the statutory form by the
insertion of a proviso for redemption or discharge in addition to
the covenant for repayment.

There are, however, two advantages that may justly be claimed
for the legal charge as compared with the demise.

First, the legal charge is as appropriate for leaseholds as it is
for freeholds, and therefore it provides a simple method of
executing a compound mortgage which relates to both
these different interests.

---

[1] *Weg Motors, Ltd.* v. *Hales*, [1962] Ch. 49; [1961] 3 All E. R. 181; *Cumberland Court (Brighton), Ltd.* v. *Taylor*, [1964] Ch. 29 ; [1963] 2 All E. R. 536 ;
Edwards v. *Marshall-Lee* (1975), 119 Sol. Jo. 506.
[2] L.P.A. 1925, s. 87 (1).
[3] *Regent Oil Co., Ltd.* v. *J. A. Gregory (Hatch End), Ltd.*, [1966] Ch. 402, at
p. 431 ; [1965] 3 All E. R. 673, at p. 681 ; M. & B. p. 588.
[4] *Grand Junction Co., Ltd.* v. *Bates*, [1954] 2 Q. B. 160; [1954] 2 All E. R.
358; *Church Commissioners for England* v. *Ve-Ri-Best Manufacturing Co. Ltd.*,
[1957] 1 Q. B. 238; [1956] 3 All E. R. 777.   See also p. 442, *supra*.
[5] See the remarks in *Prideaux's Forms and Precedents in Conveyancing* (24th
Edn.), vol. 2. pp. 337–8, and compare them with *ibid.*, 25th Edn., vol. 2,
p. 342 ; see Report of Committee on Enforcement of Judgment Debts, 1969
(Cmnd. 3909), para. 1347.
[6] *Williams* v. *Morgan*, [1906] 1 Ch. 804 ; *Kreglinger* v. *New Patagonia Meat
and Cold Storage Co., Ltd.*, [1914] A. C. 25, at p. 48.

Secondly, a mortgagor with a leasehold interest who holds his term on condition that he will not sub-lease without the consent of his landlord, must clearly obtain this consent if his mortgage takes the form of a sub-demise,[1] but a legal charge, since it does not create an actual legal estate, is presumably not a breach of a covenant against underletting.[2]

If the legal chargee desires to create a sub-mortgage, he cannot do so by means of a sub-lease, since he himself holds no term of years. He must, therefore, assign the mortgage debt to the sub-mortgagee subject to a right of redemption.

Sub-mortgage.

Mortgages to several persons. If land is mortgaged to two or more persons the mortgage term vests in the mortgagees, or the first four of them, as joint tenants, and, failing a contrary intention expressed in the deed, they hold it in the same way as if the money belonged to them on a joint account.[3] This, as we have seen,[4] enables the surviving mortgagees to give a good discharge for the money, but the conversion into a joint tenancy is not allowed to prejudice the beneficial interests of the mortgagees in the principal and interest. Thus they are entitled to dispose of their shares in the money, and to hold the trustees liable to account for the income.[5]

Mortgages to tenants in common.

(2) EQUITABLE MORTGAGES.

The statutory provisions that have been noticed so far apply only to a case in which it is desired to create a legal mortgage, and do not affect equitable mortgages and charges.[6] It always has been, and still is, possible to confer upon a lender a mere equitable right over the land by way of security, instead of passing a legal estate to him.

Equitable mortgages still permissible.

The commonest examples of equitable mortgages prior to the Act were those which followed a legal mortgage in the same land, but, as we have seen, second and subsequent mortgages may now be created by a long lease or by a charge so as to give each lender a legal estate or interest. The following forms of equitable mortgages, however, still remain:—

(A) CONTRACT TO CREATE A LEGAL MORTGAGE.

Equity looks on that as done which ought to be done, and therefore if A. agrees that, in consideration of money advanced, he will execute a legal mortgage in favour of B., an equitable

Effect of contract to grant a mortgage.

---

[1] *Matthews* v. *Smallwood*, [1910] 1 Ch. 777.
[2] *Grand Junction Co., Ltd.* v. *Bates*, [1954] 2 Q. B. 160, at p. 168; [1954] 2 All E. R. 385, at p. 388, *per* UPJOHN, J.
[3] L.P.A. 1925, s. 34 (2), proviso.
[4] *Supra*, p. 213.
[5] L.P.A. 1925, s. 102.
[6] *Ibid.*, s. 117 (1).

mortgage is created in favour of B., and he can enforce the execution of a legal mortgage by suing in equity for specific performance.[1] But such a contract does not have this effect unless the money has been actually advanced, for a contract to make a loan, whether under seal or not, can never be specifically enforced by either party.[2] The only remedy is the recovery of damages. As a mortgage of land is an interest in land within the meaning of section 40 of the Law of Property Act 1925, the contract is not specifically enforceable unless it is evidenced by a sufficient memorandum or supported by an act of part performance.[3]

The result of a successful suit is that B. obtains a legal term for 3000 years, and can then pursue all the statutory remedies open to a legal mortgagee.[4]

Furthermore, an imperfect legal mortgage, as, for instance, where A. purports to create a legal mortgage in writing, may be treated by equity as if it were a contract to create a legal mortgage with similar consequences.

(B) Deposit of Title Deeds.

Effect of deposit of deeds.

Although a mortgage is an interest in land, and therefore not enforceable in the absence of a written memorandum or an act of part performance, it has been held, since the case of *Russel* v. *Russel*[5] in 1783, that an equitable mortgage is created by the delivery to the lender of the title deeds relating to the borrower's land, provided that it is intended to treat the land as security.

In this particular case there need be no memorandum, since the deposit ranks as an act of part performance,[6] and the deposit alone is treated as constituting a contract to execute a legal mortgage.[7] An actual deposit, though essential, is not in itself sufficient. The depositee must go further, and prove by parol or by written evidence that the deposit was intended to be by way of security,[8] for the mere deposit by a customer of his deeds with a bank will not, for instance, constitute the bank an equitable mortgagee in respect of an overdraft.

In practice, however, the borrower usually signs a memorandum under seal contemporaneously with the delivery of the deeds, for a memorandum under seal makes the transaction a mortgage by deed within the meaning of the Law of Property Act

---

[1] *Tebb* v. *Hodge* (1869), L. R. 5 C. P. 73.

[2] *Sichel* v. *Mosenthal* (1862), 30 Beav. 371.

[3] *Ex parte Leathes* (1833), 3 Deac. & C. 112. As to what constitutes a memorandum or an act of part performance, see *supra*, pp. 115 *et seq.*

[4] *Infra*, pp. 668 *et seq.*

[5] (1783), 1 Bro. C. C. 269. The right to create this kind of equitable mortgage is saved by L.P.A. 1925, s. 13.

[6] *Bank of N.S.W.* v. *O'Connor* (1889), 14 App. Cas. 273, at p. 282.

[7] *Carter* v. *Wake* (1877), 4 Ch. D. 605, at p. 606 ; Jessel, M.R.

[8] *Dixon* v. *Muckleston* (1872), L. R. 8 Ch. 155. See *Re Wallis and Simonds (Builders) Ltd.*, [1974] 1 W. L. R. 391 ; [1974] 1 All E. R. 561.

1925, and entitles the equitable mortgagee to exercise all the powers, including the power of sale, given by the Act.[1] But since an equitable mortgagee cannot convey the legal estate to a purchaser, it is usual to insert a power of attorney or a declaration of trust, or both, in the memorandum, so as to enable the mortgagee to deal with the legal estate.[2]

(C) MORTGAGE OF AN EQUITABLE INTEREST

A mortgage of an equitable interest, such as a life interest arising under a settlement, or a contract for a lease,[3] is itself necessarily equitable. The method of creation corresponds to that employed before 1926 in the case of a legal mortgage of the fee simple, namely, the entire equitable interest is assigned to the mortgagee, subject to a proviso for reassignment on redemption.[4]

The assignment, if not made by will, must be in writing signed by the mortgagor or by his agent thereunto lawfully authorized in writing,[5] and the mortgagee should protect himself by giving written notice of it to the owner of the legal estate.[6]

(D) EQUITABLE CHARGES

Another form of equitable security, differing in respect of the remedies it confers from the three forms already described, is the equitable charge. This arises where, without any transfer of, or agreement to transfer, ownership or possession, property is appropriated to the discharge of a debt or some other obligation.[7] *Description of a charge.*

In one case[8] KINDERSLEY, V.-C., said:—

" With regard to what are called equitable mortgages, my notion is this. Suppose a man signed a written contract, by which he simply agreed that he thereby charged his real estate with £500 to A., what would be the effect of it?

It would be no agreement to give a legal mortgage, but a security by which he equitably charged his lands with payment of a sum of money, and the mode of enforcing it would be by coming into a court of equity to have the money raised by sale or mortgage ; that would be the effect of such a simple charge. It is the same thing as if a testator devised an estate to A. charged with the payment of a sum of money to B. B.'s right is not to foreclose A., but to have his charge raised by sale or mortgage of the lands.... But the thing would be distinctly an equitable charge, and not a

---

[1] *Infra*, pp. 668 *et seq.*
[2] *Encyclopædia of Forms and Precedents* (4th Edn.), vol. 14. p. 614.
[3] *Rust* v. *Goodale*, [1957] Ch. 33 ; [1956] 3 All E. R. 373.
[4] Waldock, *Law of Mortgages* (2nd Edn.), pp. 136–9.
[5] L.P.A. 1925, s. 53 (1) (c).
[6] *Ibid.*, s. 137 (1).
[7] *London County and Westminster Bank* v. *Tompkins*, [1918] 1 K. B. 515, 528.
[8] *Matthews* v. *Goodday* (1861), 31 L. J. Ch. 282, at pp. 282–3.

mortgage nor an agreement to give one. On the other hand the party might agree that, having borrowed a sum of money, he would give a legal mortgage whenever called upon. That agreement might be enforced according to its terms, and the court would decree a legal mortgage to be given, and would also foreclose the mortgage, unless the money was paid."

Summary
of forms
of mortages The remedies of an equitable chargee will be considered later.[1]

If we now glance back at the different kinds of mortgages, we shall find that they may be either legal or equitable, and that the same land may be subjected both to several legal and to several equitable mortgages. For instance the tenant in fee simple of Blackacre may have created the following mortgages upon his land in the subjoined order :

A lease of 500 years to A.
A lease of 500 years and one day to B.
A written agreement charging the land in favour of C.
A lease of 500 years and two days to D.

The first mortgagee, A., may demand the title deeds relating to the property,[2] and in practice usually does so. This is one of the ways of ensuring that subsequent mortgagees are put on inquiry as to the existence of a prior mortgage. As we shall see later, failure to enforce this right may entail serious consequences.[3] If A. does obtain the deeds, then B. and D. are called *puisne mortgagees*, since they have acquired legal estates, but have not obtained possession of the deeds.[4] On the other hand, C. is called a *general equitable chargee*. A general equitable charge is statutorily defined as any equitable charge (with a few exceptions)

" which (a) is not secured by a deposit of documents relating to the legal estate affected ; and (b) does not arise or affect an interest arising under a trust for sale or a settlement ; and (c) is not included in any other class of land charge. "[5]

The puisne mortgages of B. and D. and the general equitable charge of C. are registrable as land charges under the Land Charges Act 1972, and, as we shall see, registration is of crucial importance in determining the priorities of mortgages.[6]

SECTION III. POSITION AND RIGHTS OF THE MORTGAGOR

SUMMARY

---

[1] *Infra*, p. 684. [2] *Infra*, p. 680. [3] *Infra*, pp. 688 *et seq.*
[4] L.C.A. 1972, s. 2 (4), Class C (i).
[5] *Ibid.*, s. 2 (4), Class C (iii). [6] *Infra*, pp. 698 *et seq.*

(1) THE EQUITY OF REDEMPTION

(A) Its Nature

Introductory Note. A mortgagor, as we have seen, is the owner of the equity of redemption.[1] This is fundamental to the law of mortgages. It arises in the case of every conveyance or other transaction relating to property, whether styled a mortgage or not, in which the true intention of the parties is that the subject-matter shall be security for a debt or other obligation. Outwardly a transaction may wear the appearance of an absolute conveyance ; it may even be deliberately couched in language calculated to give that appearance, yet evidence is admissible to disclose the true intention of the parties.[2] A transaction, for instance, which takes the form of a sale by A. to B., with a right in B. of re-purchase upon payment of a given sum on a day certain may or may not be a mortgage. It is a matter of intention.

> " The question always is—was the original transaction a *bona fide* sale with a contract for repurchase, or was it a mortgage under the form of a sale." [3]

If it was the former, there is no right in B. to redeem the property after the contract date.

What particularly concerns us here, however, is to notice that equity, in order to ensure that a transaction intended to be by way of mortgage shall afford nothing more than security to the lender, has laid down two important rules concerning, first, the inviolability of the right of redemption; and secondly, the limits within which collateral advantages may be reserved to a mortgagee.

Let us consider these rules separately.

(i) The right of redemption is inviolable. Since the object of a mortgage is merely to provide the mortgagee with a security, any provision which directly or indirectly prevents the recovery by the mortgagor of his property upon performance of the obligation for which the security was created, is repugnant to the very nature of the transaction and therefore void, for when performance is completed there is no longer any need or justification for the retention of the security.

> " Now," said ROMER, J., " there is a principle which I will accept without any qualification, ... that on a mortgage you cannot, by contract between the mortgagor and mortgagee, clog,

Marginal notes:
- *Test that determines redeemability.*
- *Right of redemption must not be fettered.*
- *Any clog on equity of redemption is void.*

---

[1] *Supra,* pp. 638–9.

[2] " No mortgage by any artificial words can be altered, unless by subsequent agreement, " *Jason* v. *Eyres* (1681), 2 Cas. in Ch. 33.

[3] *Williams* v. *Owen* (1840), 5 My. & Cr. 303, 306, *per* Lord COTTENHAM.

as it is termed, the equity of redemption so as to prevent the mortgagor from redeeming on payment of principal, interest and costs.''[1]

Once a mortgage always a mortgage.

This principle is generally expressed in the aphorism, *once a mortgage always a mortgage*,[2] and the most obvious example of its infringement is a provision which leaves the mortgagor with nothing more than an illusory right of redemption. In *Fairclough v. Swan Brewery Co., Ltd.*,[3] for instance :

A mortgage of a term of twenty years contained a clause postponing the contractual right of redemption for nineteen years and forty-six weeks.

This provision for redemption rendered the property substantially irredeemable, and it was held that the mortgagor was entitled to redeem at an earlier date.[4]

Further, the courts refuse to countenance any provision which unduly restricts, though it does not altogether prevent, the right of redemption. Each of the following cases exemplifies an agreement that was held void as being inconsistent with or repugnant to the true nature of a mortgage transaction.

An agreement that redemption should be available to the mortgagor and *the heirs of his body*, and not to anyone else.[5]

An agreement which renders part of the mortgaged property absolutely irredeemable.[6]

A covenant by the mortgagor that the mortgagee, if he so desired, should be entitled to a conveyance of so much of the mortgaged estate as should equal the value of the loan at twenty years purchase.[7]

---

[1] *Biggs* v. *Hoddinott*, [1898], 2 Ch. 307, at p. 314.
[2] *Samuel* v. *Jarrah Timber and Wood Paving Corpn., Ltd.*, [1904] A. C. 323, at p. 329.
[3] [1912] A. C. 565; M. & B. p. 597.
[4] This decision of the P.C., is in conflict with the decision of the Court of Appeal in *Santley* v. *Wilde*, [1899] 2 Ch. 474 ; M. & B. p. 595. A 10 year lease in a theatre was mortgaged by the tenant and the deed provided that the mortgagee should receive *during the whole of the remainder of the term* a third of the net profits derived from sub-leases made by the mortgagor. This provision was held to be binding upon the mortgagor, even though he was ready and willing to pay principal, interest and costs in full. Yet, in effect, it made the mortgage irredeemable. It meant that the mortgagor, despite payment of principal, interest and costs, could never recover the term in its former condition, since it would remain charged with the payment to the mortgagee of the profits. See the opinions to this effect of Lord MACNAGHTEN and Lord DAVEY in *Noakes & Co., Ltd.* v. *Rice*, [1902] A. C. 24, 31–2, 34. In *Knightsbridge Estates Trust, Ltd.* v. *Byrne*, [1939] 1 Ch. 441, 456–7, the C.A. cited *Fairclough* v. *Swan Brewery Co., Ltd.*, in support of the above rule, and ignored *Santley* v. *Wilde, supra.* See too M. & B., pp. 594–5.
[5] *Howard* v. *Harris* (1681), 1 Vern. 33 ; *Salt* v. *Marquess of Northampton*, [1892] A. C. 1.
[6] *Davis* v. *Symons*, [1934] 1 Ch. 442.
[7] *Jennings* v. *Ward* (1705), 2 Vern. 520, as explained in *Biggs* v. *Hoddinott*, [1898] 2 Ch. 307, at pp. 315, 323.

A covenant that if the borrower died before his father the subject-matter of the mortgage should belong absolutely to the mortgagee.[1]

An option to purchase the mortgaged property given to the lender upon the creation [2] or the assignment [3] of the mortgage. Such an option, however, is valid if it is given by a subsequent and independent transaction, even though the only consideration is the release of the mortgagor from his obligation to pay the original loan.[4]

An important question is whether the postponement for a considerable period of the contractual right to redeem is objectionable as being an unreasonable interference with the rights of the mortgagor. If a mortgage is in essence a mere security, it is arguable that a clause which prolongs the security after the mortgagor is ready and willing to pay all that is due, is one that ought not to be upheld, even though it was accepted by him without objection at the time of the loan. The question was much canvassed by the Court of Appeal in *Knightsbridge Estates Trust, Ltd.* v. *Byrne,*[5] where the facts were as follows :—

Right to redeem may be postponed.

> The Knightsbridge Company had mortgaged their property, consisting of 75 houses, eight shops and a block of flats, to the Prudential Assurance Company in return for a loan of £300,000 at 6½ *per cent.* The loan was liable to be called in at any time, and the mortgagors, desiring to obtain a reduction in the rate of interest and also to spread the repayment of the principal sum over a long term of years, transferred the mortgage to the Royal Liver Friendly Society. This mortgage was for £310,000 at 5¼ *per cent.*, and at the suggestion of the mortgagors it was agreed that the loan should be repaid in forty years by half-yearly instalments. The mortgagees agreed not to call the money in before the end of this period, provided that the instalments were punctually paid. A few years later the mortgagors sued for a declaration that they were entitled, on giving the usual six months' notice, to redeem the mortgage upon payment of principal, interest and costs.

It was argued for the mortgagors that this suspension for forty years of the contractual right to redeem their property was unreasonable and therefore void. The Court of Appeal, however, upheld the suspension and denied that reasonableness, whether in respect of time or in·other respects, is the true criterion of validity in such a case. A contract freely entered into after due deliberation by parties dealing with each other at arms' length is not lightly to be interfered with. A court of equity, indeed, is

---

[1] *Salt* v. *Marquess of Northampton*, [1892] A. C. 1.

[2] *Samuel* v. *Jarrah Timber and Wood Paving Corpn., Ltd.*, [1904] A. C. 323 ; M. & B. p. 591. For a searching criticism of this scholastic attitude, see (1944), 60 L. Q. R. at p. 191 (G. L. Williams).

[3] *Lewis* v. *Frank Love, Ltd.*, [1961] 1 W. L. R. 261 ; [1961] 1 All E. R. 446 ; M. & B. p. 593.

[4] *Reeve* v. *Lisle*, [1902] A. C. 461.

[5] [1939] Ch. 441 ; [1938] 4 All E. R. 618; M. & B. p. 598.

vigilant in its support of the principle that " redemption is of the very nature and essence of a mortgage," [1] but none the less it does not attempt to reform mortgage transactions. The rule, in short, is that a provision postponing the contractual date for redemption is not void unless

it renders redemption illusory, as in *Fairclough* v. *Swan Brewery Co., Ltd.*,[2] or

it is a device to fetter the right of redemption as in *Davis* v. *Symons*,[3] or

it is in fact oppressive or unconscionable.[4]

Doctrine of restraint of trade applicable to mortgages.   A mortgage, however, is subject to the common law doctrine that invalidates any contract in restraint of trade which places an unreasonable restriction upon the freedom of a man to pursue his trade or profession.[5]   It may happen, therefore, that a postponement of the right of redemption which is not *per se* oppressive may nevertheless become so if it is accompanied by an excessive restraint upon the mortgagor's business activities.   This was the position, for instance, where a garage was mortgaged to suppliers of motor fuels, and the mortgagors covenanted that they would not exercise their right of redemption for twenty-one years and, during the same period, would not buy or sell any fuel other than that supplied by the mortgagees.[6]

(ii) Equitable rules concerning collateral advantages.

A collateral advantage means something that is granted to the mortgagee in addition to the return of his loan with interest, as for instance where a publican mortgagor agrees that for a given number of years he will sell no beer on the premises except that which is brewed by the mortgagee.

Modern tendency to uphold collateral advantages.   The question whether the reservation of such an advantage is valid is rendered difficult by a number of apparently irreconcilable decisions stretching back for more than a century.   Indeed, the

---

[1] *Noakes & Co., Ltd.* v. *Rice*, [1902] A. C. 24, at p. 30, *per* Lord MACNAGHTEN.
[2] [1912] A. C. 565 ; M. & B. p. 597'; *supra*, p. 654.
[3] [1934] Ch. 442, as explained in the *Knightsbridge Case*, [1939] Ch. 441, at p. 462 ; [1938] 4 All E. R. 618, at p. 629.
[4] *Knightsbridge Estates Trust, Ltd.* v. *Byrne*, [1939] Ch. 441, at p. 457 ; [1938] 4 All E. R. 618, at p. 626 ; on appeal, [1940] A. C. 613 ; [1940] 2 All E. R. 401, the House of Lords decided the case on an entirely different ground, namely that the mortgage was a valid debenture under the Companies Act, 1929, s. 74 (now 1948, s. 89) and expressed no opinion upon whether the Court of Appeal had laid down the correct rule as to the validity of a suspension of the contractual date for redemption.   There is no reason to doubt its correctness, though earlier cases had more than suggested that the appropriate test was reasonableness; see for example, *Talbot* v. *Braddill* (1683), 1 Vern. 183; *Teevan* v. *Smith* (1882), 20 Ch. D. 724, 729; *Morgan* v. *Jeffreys*, [1910] 1 Ch. 620.   See Consumer Credit Act 1974, ss. 94, 173 (1) ; *infra*, p. 718.
[5] *Esso Petroleum Co., Ltd.* v. *Harper's Garage (Stourport), Ltd.*, [1968] A.C. 269 ; [1967] 1 All E. R. 699 ; *Re Petrol Filling Station, Vauxhall Bridge Road* (1969), 20 P. & C. R. 1 ; M. & B. p. 617 ; *Texaco, Ltd.* v. *Mulberry Filling Station, Ltd.*, [1972] 1 W. L. R. 814 ; [1972] 1 All E. R. 513.   See Cheshire and Fifoot, *Law of Contract* (8th Edn.), pp. 357 *et seq.* ; Heydon, *Restraint of Trade Doctrine* (1971), Chaps. 3, 9.   [6] *Ibid.*

case law will be unintelligible unless it is realized that the attitude of the courts towards the matter has changed materially in the course of the last hundred years, and that reliance can no longer be placed upon many of the older decisions. Lord HALDANE, in a reference to one of the more modern cases,[1] said :

"In the 17th and 18th centuries a Court of Equity could hardly have so decided, and the judgment illustrates the elastic character of equity jurisdiction and the power of equity judges to mould the rules which they apply in accordance with the exigencies of the time."[2]

In early days the judges frowned upon any attempt by a mortgagee to reap some additional advantage, as is shown by a remark of the Master of the Rolls in 1705 that " a man shall not have interest for his money on a mortgage, and a collateral advantage besides for the loan of it."[3]   In modern times a more realistic and favourable note has been struck, and for this change of heart probably the most significant reason is that at the present day a mortgagor can scarcely be regarded as in need of special protection.   In the eye of the novelist, no doubt, he is an impoverished debtor on the brink of ruin, unable to resist the demands of the rapacious lender, and it is perhaps true that the Court of Chancery in its more paternal days tended to take a somewhat similar view of his predicament.   In fact, however, the parties to a modern mortgage may be hard-headed business men well able to protect their own interests, and in these days, when so much stress is laid upon the sanctity of contracts, it is difficult to appreciate why one of them should be allowed to disregard a bargain freely made, simply because he happens to be a mortgagor.   Such maxims as " Once a mortgage, always a mortgage " and " A mortgage cannot be made irredeemable," undoubtedly express an important principle, but to apply them in an unbending and inflexible fashion so as to upset an ordinary commercial transaction would be out of keeping with the times.

Reasons for changed attitude.

Despite the judicial uncertainties of the past, the modern law on the subject is perfectly clear, though its application to particular cases may be a difficult matter.   It can be summarized quite shortly.

Modern rule stated.

A contract that grants a collateral advantage to a mortgagee is valid and enforceable unless it is oppressive and unconscionable or unless it is calculated to prevent or unduly to hamper redemption.[4]

---

[1] *Biggs* v. *Hoddinott*, [1898] 2 Ch. 307 ; M. & B. p. 604.
[2] *Kreglinger* v. *New Patagonia Meat and Cold Storage Co., Ltd.*, [1914] A. C. 25, at p. 38.
[3] *Jennings* v. *Ward* (1705), 2 Vern. 520.
[4] *Biggs* v. *Hoddinott, supra.*

First, if a contract is oppressive or unconscionable, which is a pure question of fact, it is void not so much because of its association with a mortgage, but because of the general principle of public policy that a contract shall not be used as an engine of oppression. It has repeatedly been affirmed that the courts will set aside " any oppressive bargain, or any advantage exacted from a man under grievous necessity and want of money," [1] and instances are not wanting of where this principle has been applied to a mortgage transaction.[2]   In fact, if the mortgagee stands in a fiduciary relationship to the mortgagor, as for instance where he is his trustee, solicitor or spiritual adviser, the burden is on him to prove the fairness of the transaction if it is challenged on the ground of undue influence or unconscionable conduct.[3]

Secondly, a provision is void if its effect is to render either the contractual or the equitable right of redemption virtually inoperative.   If it prejudices the contractual right of redemption it is inconsistent with the intention of the parties.   If it prejudices the right of the mortgagor to recover his property after the contractual date has passed, it is void as being a clog on the equity of redemption, for anything is stigmatized as a clog which " prevents the mortgagor from getting back his property free of any fetter when it is redeemed." [4]   Such will be the position if the obligation imposed upon him by the provision renders the recovery of his property unprofitable, hazardous or economically and substantially less valuable.   This was the position in *Noakes*

& Co. Ltd. v. Rice.[5]

---

[1] *Barrett* v. *Hartley* (1866), L. R. 2 Eq. 789, at p. 795, *per* Stuart, V.-C.

[2] *James* v. *Kerr* (1889), 40 Ch. D. 449.   *Cf. Horwood* v. *Millar's Timber and Trading Co.,* [1917] 1 K. B. 305.   *Cityland and Property (Holdings), Ltd.* v. *Dabrah,* [1968] Ch. 166 ; [1967] 2 All E. R. 639.

[3] Waldock, *The Law of Mortgages* (2nd Edn.), chapter viii, and cases there cited.

[4] *Knightsbridge Estates Trust, Ltd.* v. *Byrne,* [1939] Ch. 441, at p. 448; [1938] 4 All E. R. 618, at p. 623, *per* Greene, M.R.   In the view of Lindley, L.J., the application of the rule depends upon whether the mortgage deed provides that there shall be no redemption until the collateral advantage has been fully implemented, or whether it first allows redemption upon payment of principal, interest and costs, and then expresses the collateral advantage in a super-added clause.   In the first case he insists that the mortgagor cannot redeem until he has satisfied his own contractual obligations, including his obligation to allow the collateral advantage to operate.   " When you get a security for a debt or obligation, that security can be redeemed the moment the debt or obligation is paid or performed, *but on no other terms* " ; *Santley* v. *Wilde,* [1899] 2 Ch. 474, at p. 475.   It is doubtful, however, whether the distinction is helpful in the present connection, for, if it is to be adopted, the validity of a collateral advantage will apparently depend upon the drafting of the mortgage deed, not upon the substantial merits of the case.   As against this, however, it may be argued that if the advantage is deliberately and consciously made part of the security, then this is a business transaction that ought to be upheld.

[5] [1902] A. C. 24 ; M. & B. p. 605.   See also *Morgan* v. *Jeffreys,* [1910] 1 Ch. 620.   The discussions in these two cases could now be justified on the ground that the tie imposed upon the publican was void as being in restraint of trade ; see *Esso Petroleum Co., Ltd.* v. *Harper's Garage (Stourport), Ltd., supra,* p. 640.

The tenant of a public-house, under a lease which had 26 years to run, mortgaged the premises as security for a loan and covenanted that *during the remainder of the term* he would not sell any malt liquors except those provided by the mortgagees. Three years later he claimed a declaration that he should be released from the covenant upon payment of all moneys due under the mortgage.

It was held by the House of Lords, affirming the decisions of the two lower courts, that he was entitled to the release he claimed. It was clear that the benefit of redemption would be to a great extent nullified if the mortgagor were to remain bound by the covenant. His right of redemption was hampered in the sense that after attainment of the object for which the security was created he would not be master in his own house—he would not recover his property as it was before the mortgage. "The public-house, which was free when mortgaged, would have been tied to the mortgagee when redeemed."[1] The covenant was in fact inconsistent with the express proviso for redemption, and was also a clog upon the equity.

Biggs v. *Hoddinott*,[2] however, serves as a reminder that the application of the general rule must depend upon the view that the court takes of the facts. In that case :

> A. mortgaged his hotel to B., a brewer, in return for an advance of £7654, and agreed that during the continuance of the mortgage he would sell no other beer than that supplied by B. It was mutually agreed that the mortgage should not be redeemable, nor should the loan be repayable, for five years.

The claim of A., made two years later, that he was entitled to procure beer elsewhere upon repayment of the loan, was dismissed. It was held that the bargain, which was to cease with redemption, was advantageous to both parties and must remain in force. It in no way hampered the right of redemption.

The position is further illustrated by *Bradley* v. *Carritt*.[3]

> In that case the defendant, who owned shares which gave him a controlling interest in a tea company, mortgaged them to the plaintiff, a tea-broker, and in further consideration for the loan entered into the following contract :
>
> > " I agree ... to use my best endeavours as a shareholder to secure that you or any firm of brokers of which you for the time being shall be a partner shall *always hereafter* have the sale of the company's teas as broker, and in the case of any of the company's teas being sold otherwise than through you or your firm, I personally agree to pay you or your firm the amount of the commission which you or your firm would have earned if the teas had been sold through you or your firm."

Biggs v. *Hoddinott.*

Bradley v. *Carritt.*

---

[1] *Bradley* v. *Carritt*, [1903] A. C. 253, at pp. 277–8, *per* Lord LINDLEY.
[2] [1898] 2 Ch. 307 ; M. & B. p. 604 ; approved by the House of Lords in *Noakes & Co. Ltd.* v. *Rice, supra.*
[3] [1903] A. C. 253 ; M. & B. p. 608.

The plaintiff was appointed broker; but the defendant repaid the loan, redeemed his shares and transferred them to another mortgagee, X., who succeeded in ousting the plaintiff from his appointment.

The House of Lords, reversing the court of first instance and the Court of Appeal, held that the agreement set out above was void, and that the defendant was not liable for its breach.   Lord LINDLEY and Lord SHAND, however, dissented.   What weighed with the majority, was that if the defendant were to remain liable for payment of commission the shares would have far less value after redemption than they had before the mortgage.   The only likely purchasers of shares of that particular kind were tea brokers, whose sole object in buying would be to acquire the privilege of selling the company's tea.   After redemption, therefore, the shares would be more or less frozen assets in the hands of the mortgagor, since, unless he showed great vigilance, their sale would almost certainly result in his being liable to the plaintiff for loss of brokerage ; they gave him a controlling interest in the tea company, and it was only by retaining them that he could ensure the continued employment of the plaintiff as broker.   The agreement was, therefore, said to be repugnant both to the contractual right of redemption and to the equity.

Kreglinger v. New Patagonia Meat and Cold Storage Co. Ltd.

The House of Lords came to a different conclusion in *Kreglinger* v. *New Patagonia Meat and Cold Storage Co., Ltd.*,[1] where the facts were as follows :

A firm of woolbrokers lent £10,000 to a company which carried on business as meat preservers, the agreement being that the company might pay off the loan at any time by giving a month's notice. The loan was secured, not by an ordinary mortgage, but by an analogous security called a floating charge.[2]   It was agreed that for five years from the date of the loan the company would not sell sheepskins to any person other than the lenders, so long as the latter were willing to pay the full market price.   It was also agreed that the lenders would not demand repayment before five years had elapsed.   The loan was repaid within two and a half years. The point that fell to be decided was whether the option on the sheepskins was enforceable by the lenders after repayment of the loan.

The House held unanimously that the lenders were entitled to an injunction restraining the company from selling skins to third parties during the remainder of the five years.   While it was true that the company would not be as free in the conduct of their business after repayment of the loan as they were before the grant of the charge, the House of Lords was of opinion that the

---

[1] [1914] A. C. 25; M. & B. p. 609.

[2] This, though a charge upon the assets for the time being, does not prevent a company from dealing with its property in the ordinary course of business, but it does so when the chargee takes steps, such as by the appointment of a receiver, to crystallize the security.   For the characteristics of the charge, see *Re Yorkshire Woolcombers Association, Ltd.*, [1903] 2 Ch. 284, at p. 295, *per* ROMER, J.

agreement was a reasonable one that ought to be upheld. For Viscount HALDANE, L.C., the matter was one of construction :[1]

> "The question in the present case is whether the right to redeem has been interfered with. And this must ... depend on the answer to a question which is primarily one of fact. What was the true character of the transaction? Did the appellants make a bargain such that the right to redeem was cut down, or did they simply stipulate for a collateral undertaking, outside and clear of the mortgage, which would give them an exclusive option of purchase of the sheepskins of the respondents? The question is in my opinion not whether the two contracts were made at the same moment and evidenced by the same instrument, but whether they were in substance a single and undivided contract or two distinct contracts. ... If your Lordships arrive at the conclusion that the agreement for an option to purchase the respondents' sheepskins was not in substance a fetter on the exercise of their right to redeem, but was in the nature of a collateral bargain the entering into which was a preliminary and separable condition of the loan, the decided cases cease to present any great difficulty."

And their Lordships so concluded. This approach provides the court with a much needed flexibility in the area of collateral advantages and enables it to adapt the earlier strict rules to modern circumstances.

Bradley v. *Carritt* thus represents the high-water mark of the conception of a mortgage as an onerous obligation imposed upon a necessitous borrower, in whose favour the court should therefore intervene.[2] The *Kreglinger Case*, on the other hand, reveals a judicial appreciation of a mortgage as a transaction freely concluded by business men without colour of oppression, which should therefore form no exception to the maxim *pacta sunt servanda*. This is a more realistic and reasonable approach, and one more compatible with the business conditions of the twentieth century.

The mortgagor may, however, be a private individual who is borrowing money to finance the purchase of a house. If he mortgages the house to a building society,[3] then he enjoys the added protection of the provisions of the Building Societies Acts.[4] Whether or not the mortgagee is a building society, the court will be astute to invalidate any provision which is oppressive and unconscionable.[5]

Thus in *Cityland and Property (Holdings) Ltd.* v. *Dabrah*,[6] the mortgagor who was buying his house and " obviously of limited

---

[1] At p. 39: *Re Petrol Filling Station, Vauxhall Bridge Road* (1969), 20 P. & C. R. 1 ; M. & B. p. 617.

[2] Waldock, *Law of Mortgages* (2nd Edn.), chap. viii.

[3] In *Pettitt* v. *Pettitt*, [1970] A. C. 777, at p. 824 ; [1969] 2 All E. R. 385 ; Lord DIPLOCK referred to " a real-property-mortgaged-to-a-building-society-owning democracy. "

[4] 1874–1962. See *infra*, p. 717.

[5] See also Consumer Credit Act 1974, ss. 137–40 ; *infra*, p. 718.

[6] [1968] Ch. 166 : [1967] 2 All E. R. 639. On this type of mortgage see Annual Report of Committee on Enforcement of Judgment Debts (1969 Cmnd. 3909), paras. 1355–1358.

means " undertook to pay a premium or bonus which represented either no less than 57% of the amount of the loan or interest at 19%. GOFF, J., stressed that this was not a " bargain between two large trading concerns " and held that the mortgagor was entitled to redeem by paying the capital sum borrowed with reasonable interest fixed by the court.

(B) ENFORCEMENT OF THE EQUITY OF REDEMPTION

The right of redemption is lost if any one of the following events occurs :—

> The release of the right by the mortgagor to the mortgagee ; the lapse of time under the Limitation Act 1939; the sale of the land by the mortgagee under his statutory power; or a foreclosure decree obtained by the mortgagee.

The last two methods are discussed later.[1]

Release of equity of redemption. Although a provision in the mortgage deed itself giving the mortgagee an option to purchase the land is void as being a clog on the equity,[2] there is nothing to prevent the mortgagor from getting rid of the debt by releasing the equity of redemption to him, provided that it is the result of an independent bargain made subsequently to the mortgage deed.

As regards lapse of time it is enacted that :—

Limitation Act 1939.
> " When a mortgagee of land has been in possession of any of the mortgaged land for a period of twelve years, no action to redeem the land of which the mortgagee has been so in possession shall thereafter be brought by the mortgagor or any person claiming through him." [3]

If, however, the mortgagee in possession either receives any sum in respect of principal or interest or signs an acknowledgment of the mortgagor's title, an action to redeem the land may be brought at any time before the expiration of twelve years after the last payment or acknowledgment.[4] An acknowledgment given after the mortgagee has been in possession for twelve years, without receiving a payment in respect of principal or interest, is ineffective.[5]

Enlargement of the term into a fee simple. When a mortgagee has obtained a title to the land free from the mortgage by remaining in possession for twelve years he may by deed enlarge the term of years into a fee simple under the Law of Property Act 1925.[6]

---

[1] *Infra*, p. 669 (sale); p. 673 (foreclosure).
[2] *Supra*, p. 655.
[3] Limitation Act 1939, s. 12, replacing Real Property Limitation Act 1874, s. 7.
[4] *Ibid.*, ss. 23 (3), 24 (1).   [5] *Ibid.*, s. 16.
[6] L.P.A. 1925, ss. 88 (3) ; 153. *Supra*, p. 462.

When, as in the ordinary case, a mortgagee does not take possession of the land, the mortgagor can redeem regardless of the lapse of time.

Presuming that the mortgagor has not lost his right to redeem the security, he is entitled, under the contract contained in the mortgage deed, to tender the exact amount due,[1] and to claim redemption on the date fixed for repayment. This date is not usually, however, meant to be taken seriously, and if it has elapsed, the mortgagor must give either six months' notice or six months' interest before he can redeem.[2] If a notice so given is not followed by repayment upon the date notified, he must give a fresh notice of a reasonable length.[3] Where, however, the mortgage is merely temporary, as for instance in the case of an equitable mortgage by deposit of title deeds, the mortgagee is not entitled to six months notice or interest in lieu. The mortgagor must give him a reasonable time, though it may be short, to look up the deeds.[4]

Redemption by mortgagor.

Before January 1st, 1926, a reconveyance by the mortgagee was necessary to revest the legal estate in the mortgagor upon redemption, but now, when redemption has been effected, there is no need for the mortgagee to execute a deed surrendering the term. A receipt written at the foot of the mortgage deed will be sufficient to extinguish the mortgage, provided that it states the name of the person who pays the money and is executed by the person in whom the mortgage is vested. In the ordinary case of a mortgage by demise this receipt effects a surrender of the term and merges it in the reversion held by the mortgagor.[5] If a person, such as a second mortgagee, to whom the immediate equity of redemption does not belong, pays the money that is due, the benefit of the mortgage passes to him by virtue of the receipt,[6] and thus his incumbrance is kept alive. But of course where there are two mortgages of the same land and the mortgagor pays off the first, the receipt does not transfer the first mortgage term to him so as to enable him to keep it alive against the second mortgagee.[7] Moreover, it is enacted that a mortgage term shall, after repayment of the money, become a satisfied term, and shall cease.[8]

Reconveyance by endorsed receipt.

---

[1] In an action for redemption the mortgagor must pay all that is due in respect of principal and interest, including interest which is statute-barred. *Holmes* v. *Cowcher*, [1970] 1 W. L. R. 834 ; [1970] 1 All E. R. 1224.
[2] *Cromwell Property Investment Co.* v. *Western and Toovey*, [1934] Ch. 322.
[3] *Ibid.*
[4] *Fitzgerald's Trustee* v. *Mellersh*, [1892] 1 Ch. 385, *per* CHITTY, J.
[5] L.P.A. 1925, s. 115 (1). A building society may use either a reconveyance or a special statutory receipt. Building Societies Act 1962, s. 37, Sched. 6.
[6] *Ibid.*, s. 115; (2) *Cumberland Court (Brighton), Ltd.* v. *Taylor*, [1964] Ch. 29; [1963] 2 All E. R. 536.
[7] *Ibid.*, s. 115 (3). *Otter* v. *Lord Vaux* (1856), 6 De G. M. & G. 638 ; *Parkash* v. *Irani Finance, Ltd.*, [1970] Ch. 101 ; [1969] 1 All E. R. 930.
[8] *Ibid.*, s. 116. *Edwards* v. *Marshall-Lee* (1975), 119 Sol. Jo. 506.

Disposal of deeds by mortgagee.

It is the duty of a mortgagee, upon receiving repayment of the loan, to deliver the title deeds to the person who has the best right to them, *i.e.* the mortgagor if there is only one incumbrance, or the next mortgagee if the land has been subjected to more incumbrances than one.[1] A mortgagee will not, however, incur liability to a later mortgagee for delivering the deeds to the mortgagor, unless he has actual notice of the later mortgage.[2] Mere registration of a mortgage as a land charge[3] does not in this case constitute notice, but nevertheless he is for several reasons well advised to search at the Registry before handing over the deeds to the mortgagor.[4]

Sale in lieu of redemption.

The mortgagor may commence proceedings to enforce redemption, and if he is successful, an order will be made directing the mortgagee to surrender or give a statutory receipt upon receiving payment within six months. But where such proceedings are taken, the mortgagor may have a judgment for sale instead of for redemption, and the court may, on the request either of the mortgagor or of the mortgagee, and despite the dissent of the other party, direct a sale on such terms as it thinks fit.[5]

Transfer of mortgage.

Finally, upon payment of the amount due, a mortgagor is entitled to require the mortgagee to transfer the debt and the property to a third person, and the mortgagee unless he is or has been in possession, is bound to comply.[6] This is the procedure adopted where a third person pays the amount of the loan to the mortgagee, and then himself assumes the position of mortgagee.

(C) Effect of Death of Mortgagor

Land remains liable to debt.

On the death of a mortgagor the equity of redemption goes through his personal representatives to the persons entitled on intestacy if he dies without leaving a will, and to his devisee if he leaves a will. Under the law as it existed prior to 1854, such an heir or devisee was entitled to have the mortgage debt paid out of the personal estate of the deceased, and to take the property free from the mortgage burden, but, in accordance with the general principle that he who has the benefit ought to have the burden, this rule was reversed by the Real Estate Charges Acts of 1854, 1867 and 1877. These statutes have now been repealed, although their general tenor is retained, and it is enacted that property, whether land or not, which at the time of the owner's death is charged with the payment of money, whether by way of legal

---

[1] *Re Magneta Time Co., Ltd.* (1915), 84 L. J. Ch. 814.
[2] L.P.A. 1925, s. 96 (2), as amended by L.P.(A.)A. 1926, Sched.
[3] *Infra,* p. 741.
[4] See (1926), 61 *L. J. News.* pp. 431, 471, 488, 519 (T. Cyprian Williams).
[5] L.P.A. 1925, s. 91.
[6] *Ibid.*, s. 95. The reason for the exception is that a mortgagee, having once been in possession, remains liable to account for the profits that the transferee has, or ought to have, received after the transfer. He should, therefore, never transfer the security without an order of the court; *Hall* v. *Heward* (1886), 32 Ch. D. 430, at p. 435.

mortgage, equitable charge or otherwise, shall, as between the different persons claiming through the deceased, be primarily liable for the payment of the charge.[1]   This rule is not to apply, however, if the deceased has expressed a contrary intention by will, deed or other document, but such intention must be clear and unambiguous, and is not to be implied merely because the deceased has directed that his debts are to be paid out of his personal estate or his residuary estate.[2]

(2) RIGHTS OF A MORTGAGOR WHO REMAINS IN POSSESSION

In the eyes of equity the mortgagor remains the true beneficial owner of the property, and as long as he remains in possession he is entitled to appropriate the rents and profits to his own use without any liability to account for them, even though he may be in default in the payment of interest.   As we shall see, the mortgagee has the right to enter into possession of the land, independently of any default on the part of the mortgagor,[3] but in normal circumstances the mortgagor remains in possession. Provided that the mortgagee has not given notice of his intention to take possession or to enter into receipt of the rents and profits, the mortgagor in possession may sue in his own name for the recovery of possession and for the rents and profits.   He may bring an action to prevent, or recover damages for, any trespass or other wrong done to the land.[4] *Mortgagor usually retains possession.*

Where a mortgagor retained possession, it was formerly a common practice to include in the mortgage deed a clause by which he *attorned* to the mortgagee, i.e. acknowledged that he held the land as a tenant at will or from year to year of the mortgagee.   The chief advantages were that it enabled the mortgagee to pursue the remedies available to a landlord for the recovery of arrears of rent, and also to obtain a summary judgment for possession if the need arose. *Attornment.*

These two advantages, however, no longer exist, for the mortgagee cannot distrain upon the premises for arrears unless the attornment clause has been registered as a bill of sale;[5] and a summary judgment is available to him independently of attornment.[6]   Nevertheless, an attornment clause is not altogether superfluous, for it enables a covenant by a mortgagor which touches

---

[1] A.E.A. 1925, s. 35 (1).
[2] *Ibid.*, s. 35 (1), (2).   *Re Neeld*, [1962] Ch. 643 ; [1962] 2 All E. R. 335. *Re Wakefield*, [1943] 2 All E. R. 29.
[3] *Infra*, p. 676.
[4] L.P.A. 1925, s. 98.
[5] *Re Willis, ex parte Kennedy* (1888), 21 Q. B. D. 384.
[6] R.S.C. Ord. 14, r. 1 (2), Ord. 88.   See generally (1969), 22 *C. L. P.*, pp. 143–6 (E. C. Ryder).

and concerns the land to be enforced against his successors in title.[1]

A mortgagor, *while in actual possession* is given the following statutory powers:—

(A) Right to Grant Valid Leases

Leasing power at common law.

At common law a mortgagor is entitled to grant a lease binding between him and the lessee, and his power in this respect has not been affected by statute.[2] But if granted without the concurrence of the mortgagee[3] it confers only a precarious title upon the lessee, since the paramount title of the mortgagee may be asserted against both him and the mortgagor.[4]

Statutory leasing powers.

The Conveyancing Act 1881 expanded the power of the mortgagor in this particular by allowing him to grant leases for limited periods which would be binding upon the mortgagee. The present position is governed by the Law of Property Act 1925, which confers upon a mortgagor *in possession* a statutory right to grant the following leases that will be binding upon all incumbrancers:—

1. Agricultural or occupation leases for any term not exceeding 21 years, or, if the mortgage was made on or after January 1st, 1926, for any term not exceeding 50 years.

2. Building leases, either for 99 or for 999 years, according as the mortgage was made before or after January 1st, 1926.[5]

Essentials of lease.

Such a lease must be made to take effect in possession not later than twelve months after its date ; it must reserve the best rent that can reasonably be obtained, and no fine must be taken[6] ; it must contain a condition of re-entry in the event of rent being in arrears for 30 days,[7] and the mortgagor is bound to deliver to the mortgagee within one month a counterpart of the lease executed by the lessee.[8]

---

[1] *Regent Oil Co., Ltd.* v. *J. A. Gregory (Hatch End), Ltd.,* [1966] Ch. 403 ; [1965] 3 All E. R. 673, where the covenant was included in a charge by way of legal mortgage. But since the relationship between the parties is in effect that of landlord and tenant, would not the covenant run even in the absence of attornment?; see (1966), 82 *L. Q. R.,* 21 (P.V.B.).

[2] *Iron Trades Employers' Insurance Association* v. *Union Land and House Investors, Ltd.,* [1937] Ch. 313 ; [1937] 1 All E. R. 481.

[3] The mortgage deed itself may confer leasing powers within defined limits upon the mortgagor ; L.P.A. 1925, s. 99 (14).

[4] *Corbett* v. *Plowden* (1884), 25 Ch. D. 678, at p. 681, *per* Lord Selborne, L.C.

[5] L.P.A. 1925, s. 99 (1), (3).

[6] *Ibid.,* s. 99, (5), (6). See, for example, *Rust* v. *Goodale,* [1957] Ch. 33, 39; [1956] 3 All E. R. 373, 376, where the consideration for a sub-lease was an immediate payment of £2,260 and a rent of £5.

[7] *Ibid.,* s. 99 (7). It is doubtful whether this requirement must be satisfied in the case of an oral tenancy ; *Pawson* v. *Revell,* [1958] 2 Q. B. 360 ; [1958] 3 All E. R. 233. *Rhodes* v. *Dalby,* [1971] 1 W. L. R. 1325, at pp. 1331–2.

[8] *Ibid.,* s. 99 (11). But not in the case of an oral tenancy. *Rhodes* v. *Dalby, supra.* A lease which fails to comply with one or more of these requirements may be validated under s. 152, *supra,* p. 282. See, *e.g., Pawson* v. *Revell, supra.*

Thus,

when a mortgagor makes a lease to A. for 50 years, the effect is that the mortgagee, though he holds a long term of years, is not entitled to actual possession during the continuance of A.'s term ; but if he is driven to pursue his remedies, he is entitled to receipt of the rent paid by A.

These statutory powers of leasing may be, and in practice frequently are, excluded or abridged by the mortgage deed,[1] but no such exclusion or abridgement is allowed in the case of a mortgage of agricultural land made after March 1st, 1948.[2]

If a mortgagor in possession grants a lease which does not satisfy the provisions of the Law of Property Act 1925 or the terms of the mortgage deed, the lease may be binding on both the mortgagor and the tenant under the doctrine of estoppel.[3] Thus the mortgagor may sue or distrain for the rent.[4] The mortgagee, however, is not bound by the lease. As between the lessee and the mortgagee and his successors in title the lease granted by the mortgagor is void.[5] The mortgagee has an option. He may either treat the lessee as a trespasser or accept him as his own tenant.[6] If, for instance, he demands that the rent be paid direct to him instead of to the mortgagor, the original tenancy is destroyed and replaced by a yearly tenancy between the mortgagee and the lessee.[7] Moreover, the acceptance of rent without any such demand raises the implication of a yearly tenancy. This implication, however, does not arise merely because the mortgagee, being aware of the lease, allows the tenant to remain in possession.[8]

Effect of unauthorised lease.

If a mortgagee refuses to recognize an unauthorized lease, the tenant may redeem the mortgage and thus secure himself against eviction.[9]

(B) RIGHT TO ACCEPT SURRENDERS OF LEASES

Although the statutory powers just mentioned enable a mortgagor to grant a lease out of the mortgagee's term, yet the effect of such a lease is to vest the reversion thereon in the mortgagee, and without the latter's concurrence it would normally be impossible for

Statutory power to accept surrenders of leases.

---

[1] L.P.A. 1925, s. 99 (13).
[2] Agricultural Holdings Act, 1948, 7th Sched., para. 2 (1) ; see *Pawson v. Revell*, [1958] 2 Q. B. 360 ; [1958] 3 All E. R. 233 ; *Rhodes v. Dalby*, [1971] 1 W. L. R. 1325.
[3] *Cuthbertson v. Irving* (1860), 6 H. & N. 135 ; *Church of England Building Society v. Piskor*, [1954] Ch. 553 ; [1954] 2 All E. R. 85. *Supra*, p. 404.
[4] *Trent v. Hunt* (1853), 9 Exch. 14.
[5] *Rust v. Goodale*, [1957] Ch. 33 ; [1956] 3 All E. R. 373 ; *Cf. Lever Finance, Ltd. v. Needleman's Trustee*, [1956] Ch. 375 ; [1956] 2 All E. R. 378 (mortgagee's assignee estopped from asserting invalidity of lease).
[6] *Stroud Building Society v. Delamont*, [1960] W. L. R. 431, at p. 434 ; [1960] 1 All E. R. 749 ; *Chatsworth Properties, Ltd. v. Effiom*, [1971] 1 W. L. R. 144 ; [1971] 1 All E. R. 604.
[7] *Taylor v. Ellis*, [1960] Ch. 368, at pp. 375–6 ; [1960] 1 All E. R. 549.
[8] *Ibid.*
[9] *Tarn v. Turner* (1888), 39 Ch. D. 456.

a mortgagor to accept a surrender of an existing lease with a view to the grant of a new one.[1] The Law of Property Act 1925, therefore, authorizes a mortgagor to accept a surrender of any lease, if, and only if, his object in doing so is to grant a new lease that falls within his statutory powers.[2] Such a surrender, however, is not valid unless a new lease is granted within one month, for a period not shorter than the unexpired term of the surrendered lease, and at a rent not less than the old rent.[3]

A subsequent mortgagee who exercises the statutory powers of leasing and of accepting surrenders exercises them in his capacity as mortgagee and not because he derives his title from the mortgagor.[4] There is therefore, for instance, no obligation on him to deliver a counterpart of the lease to the mortgagor.[5]

SECTION IV. RIGHTS OF THE MORTGAGEE

(1) *RIGHTS OF LEGAL MORTGAGEES*

SUMMARY

We now come to the remedies which are available to a legal mortgagee for enforcing the payment of what is due to him under the mortgage. They may be divided into those which do and those which do not involve the realization of the mortgaged property.

---

[1] *Robbins* v. *Whyte*, [1906] 1 K. B. 125.
[2] L.P.A. 1925, s. 100 (1).
[3] *Ibid.*, s. 100 (5).
[4] *Ibid.* ss. 99 (18), 100 (12).
[5] *Cf. Robbins* v. *Whyte, supra.*

(A) REMEDIES WHICH INVOLVE REALIZATION OF THE MORTGAGED PROPERTY

(1) SALE

As soon as the mortgage money has become due, that is, as soon as the date fixed for repayment has passed, the legal mortgagee or chargee has a statutory power, which may be varied or extended by the parties or excluded altogether,[1] to sell the mortgaged property *provided that the mortgage has been made by deed*.[2] If the money secured by the mortgage is payable by instalments, the power of sale arises as soon as an instalment is due and unpaid.[3]

When statutory power of sale arises.

Although the power of sale arises as soon as the mortgage money becomes due, it nevertheless does not become exercisable until *one* of the following events has occurred :—

When exercisable.

1. Until notice requiring payment of the mortgage money has been served on the mortgagor, and default has been made in payment of the money, or part thereof, for three months after such service.[4]

    This notice, which must be in writing,[5] may demand payment either immediately or at the end of three months, and if it is drafted in the latter form, the mortgagee need not wait for a further three months before selling, but can exercise his power after the lapse of three months from the service of notice.[6]

    If there are more mortgages than one, the notice should also be served upon the later mortgagees.

2. Until some interest is in arrear and remains unpaid for two months after becoming due.[7]

3. Until there has been a breach of some provision (other than the covenant to pay the loan and interest) which is contained either in the mortgage deed or in the Law of Property Act 1925, and which imposes an obligation upon the mortgagor.[8]

    For instance, if the mortgagor has broken a covenant to keep the premises in repair, the mortgagee can exercise his power of sale immediately, despite the fact that no interest is in arrear and that he has not demanded repayment of the loan.

Sections 101–107 of the Law of Property Act 1925 contain detailed provisions dealing with the power of sale.[9] The mortgagee

---

[1] *Alliance Building Society* v. *Shave*, [1952] Ch. 581 ; [1952] 1 All E. R. 1033.
[2] L.P.A. 1925, s. 101 (1) (i).
[3] *Payne* v. *Cardiff R.D.C.*, [1932] 1 K. B. 241.
[4] L.P.A. 1925, s. 103 (i).   [5] *Ibid.*, s. 196.
[6] *Barker* v. *Illingworth*, [1908] 2 Ch. 20.
[7] L.P.A. 1925, s. 103 (ii).
[8] *Ibid.*, s. 103 (iii).
[9] See Consumer Credit Act 1974, s. 126 ; *infra*, p. 719.

may sell the mortgaged property, or any part thereof, either subject to prior charges or not, and either together or in lots, by public auction or by private contract. He may sell the land either with or apart from the minerals, and may impose either on the sold or on the unsold part of the mortgaged land such conditions or restrictive covenants as seem desirable.[1]

Equity of redemption extinguished.

Effect of sale. If a mortgagee realizes his security by exercising the statutory power of sale, the effect is to extinguish the mortgagor's equity of redemption. It is, however, the contract to sell and not the subsequent conveyance that represents the effective exercise of the mortgagee's power ; and, providing that there is no impropriety in the sale, the mortgagor's equity is extinguished as soon as the contract of sale is made.[2]

Fee simple passes to purchaser.

A mortgagee, although he holds only a term of years or a charge by way of legal mortgage, is given express statutory power to vest the fee simple in the purchaser. The conveyance may be made in the name of the mortgagor as estate owner, and it operates to pass his legal fee simple to the purchaser and to extinguish the mortgage terms vested both in the selling mortgagee and in any subsequent mortgagees.[3] If the person exercising the power of sale is not the first mortgagee, then the purchaser takes the fee simple subject to prior mortgages.

Realization of mortgages of leaseholds.

Where a term of years has been mortgaged by a sub-lease, the effect of a sale by the mortgagee is to convey to the purchaser both the mortgage sub-term and the residue of the term vested in the mortgagor.[4] The sub-term is extinguished, since it merges in the mortgagor's reversion which thus passes to the purchaser. The conveyance, however, does not have this effect if the mortgage term does not comprise the whole of the land included in the mortgagor's term, unless the rent and the covenants have been apportioned, or unless the land excluded from the mortgage term bears a rent of no money value.[5] The acquisition of the reversion by the purchaser results in his becoming liable, in his capacity as assignee, upon the covenants contained in the lease from the lessor to the mortgagor. The Act, therefore, provides that if the leave of the court is obtained the sub-term alone may be conveyed to the purchaser to the exclusion of the mortgagor's reversion.[6]

---

[1] L.P.A. 1925, s. 101 (2). This section, however, only applies to mortgage deeds executed after December 31st, 1911.

[2] *Lord Waring* v. *London and Manchester Assurance Co., Ltd.*, [1935] Ch. 310 ; M. & B. p. 632 ; *Property and Bloodstock Ltd.* v. *Emerton*, [1968] Ch. 94 ; [1967] 3 All E. R. 321. For the effect of a contract of sale by the mortgagor upon the powers of the mortgagee, see *Duke* v. *Robson*, [1973] 1 W. L. R. 267 ; [1973] 1 All E. R. 481.

[3] L.P.A. 1925, s. 88 (1) ; 113. [4] *Ibid.*, s. 89 (1).

[5] *Ibid.*, s. 89 (6). " Apportionment " includes an equitable apportionment, *i.e.* one made without the consent of the lessor ; L.P.(A.)A. 1926, Sched., amending L.P.A. 1925, s. 89.

[6] *Ibid.*, s. 89 (1) (*a*).

The above provisions also apply where the owner of a charge by way of legal mortgage exercises his power of sale.

It is clear, therefore, that there is no difficulty in transferring to a purchaser a valid legal title to the whole interest vested in the mortgagor. Such a purchaser takes the estate freed from all estates, interests and rights to which the mortgage has priority;[1] but if he buys from a second mortgagee he will take the fee simple subject to the term vested in the first mortgagee, and he will himself be deprived of the fee simple if such a first mortgagee exercises his powers of sale or foreclosure. A sale which is made in the professed exercise of the statutory power of sale (and after December 31st, 1925, every sale made by a mortgagee is deemed so to have been made unless a contrary intention appears) cannot be impeached on the ground that no case has arisen to authorize the sale, or that the power has been improperly exercised. If either of these facts is proved, then the injured person has his remedy against the mortgagee who exercised the power, not against the purchaser.[2]

A purchaser is thus only concerned to see that the power of sale has arisen, and this he can discover merely by examining the mortgage deed. He need not satisfy himself that the power of sale has become exercisable or that it has been properly exercised. If, however, he " becomes aware . . . of any facts showing that the power of sale is not exercisable, or that there is some impropriety in the sale, then, in my judgment, he gets no good title on taking the conveyance." [3]

Position of purchaser from a mortgagee.

The money received from a purchaser is held by the mortgagee, after any prior mortgages have been paid off, on trust :—

Application of purchase money.

First, to pay all expenses incidental to the sale,

Secondly, to pay to himself the principal, interest and costs due under the mortgage, and

Thirdly, to pay the surplus, if any, to the person entitled to the mortgaged property.[4] The words " person entitled to the mortgaged property " include subsequent mortgagees, and the rule is that where there are several mortgagees interested in the same land, a prior mortgagee holds any surplus proceeds on trust for those later mortgagees of whose incumbrances he has notice.[5] Registration as a land charge now constitutes notice,[6] and therefore if he pays the surplus to the mortgagor he is liable to that extent

---

[1] L.P.A. 1925, s. 104 (1).

[2] *Ibid.*, s. 104 (2), (3).

[3] *Lord Waring* v. *London and Manchester Co. Ltd.* [1935] Ch. 310, at p. 318, *per* CROSSMAN, J. : see *Jenkins* v. *Jones* (1860), 2 Giff. 99 ; *Selwyn* v. *Garfit* (1888), 38 Ch. D. 273 ; *Bailey* v. *Barnes*, [1894] 1 Ch. 25.

[4] L.P.A. 1925, s. 105 ; replacing Conveyancing Act 1881, s. 21 (3). *Weld-Blundell* v. *Synott*, [1940] 2 K. B. 107 ; [1940] 2 All E. R. 580.

[5] *Thorne* v. *Heard and Marsh*, [1895] A. C. 495.

[6] L.P.A. 1925, s. 198 (1) as amended by Local Land Charges Act 1975, s. 17, Sched. 1. *Infra*, p. 744.

to the next mortgagee whose mortgage has been registered.[1] In case of doubt he may pay the money into court.[2]

If, however, the right of redemption of a mortgagor and of persons claiming through him has been extinguished under the Limitation Act 1939 (by reason of the mortgagee having been in possession for 12 years without receiving any sum in respect of principal or interest and without acknowledging the title of the mortgagor), a subsequent mortgagee is not a " person entitled to the mortgaged property." Since the title which he claims through the mortgagor is extinguished, his interest has ceased. Therefore, if the mortgagee sells under his statutory power, he is entitled to retain the whole proceeds, although they may exceed the amount due to him for principal and interest. [3]

Mortgagee not a trustee of power of sale.

Duty of mortgagee excercising power of sale. A mortgagee who exercises his power of sale is not in other respects a trustee for the mortgagor,[4] and in the absence of fraud, provided that he acts prudently and obtains a fair price and, above all, sells only after the statutory essentials have been satisfied, the sale will not be impeached by the court on the ground that his motive was dishonest. JESSEL, M.R., in *Nash* v. *Eads* [5] said :—

> " The mortgagee was not a trustee of the power of sale for the mortgagor, and if he was entitled to exercise the power the court could not look into his motives for so doing. If he had the right to sell on the 1st of June and he then said, ' the mortgagor is a member of an old county family, and I don't wish to turn him out of his property and will not sell it at present, ' and then on the 1st of July he said, ' I have had a quarrel with the mortgagor and he has insulted me ; I will show him no more mercy but will sell him up at once. '—if all this was proved, the court could not restrain the mortgagee from exercising his power of sale, except on the terms of payment of the mortgage debt. . . . Of course, there were some limits to the powers of the mortgagee. He, like a pledgee, must conduct the sale properly, and must sell at a fair value, and he could not sell to himself. But he was not bound to abstain from selling because he was not in urgent want of his money, or because he had a spite against the mortgagor ''

Thus the mortgagee can allow the whole of the money due from the purchaser to remain on loan secured on the very property

---

[1] *West London Commercial Bank* v. *Reliance Building Society* (1884), 27 Ch. D. 187, 29 Ch. D. 954. *Re Thomson's Mortgage Trusts*, [1920] 1 Ch. 508. Distinguish the mortgagee's duty with regard to delivery of the title deeds after redemption, for which purpose registration of a later mortgage does not constitute notice ; *supra,* p. 664.

[2] T.A. 1925, s. 63.

[3] *Young* v. *Clarey*. [1948] Ch. 191 ; [1948] 1 All E. R. 197.

[4] *Warner* v. *Jacob* (1882), 20 Ch D. 220 ; *Lord Waring* v. *London & Manchester Assurance Co., Ltd.,* [1935] Ch. 310 ; M. & B. p. 632.

[5] (1880), 25 Sol. Jo. 95.

sold,[1] but he cannot sell to himself either alone[2] or with others, nor to a trustee for himself, nor to anyone employed by him to conduct the sale. Such a sale is no sale at all, even though the price fixed is the full value of the property.[3]

Further the mortgagee can sell when he likes, "even though the market is likely to improve if he holds his hand and the result of an immediate sale may be that instead of yielding a surplus for the mortgagor the purchase price is only sufficient to discharge the mortgage debt and the interest owing on it."[4] If, however, he acts in good faith and the purchase price is lower than would have been the case due to his negligence or that of his agent, then he must account to the mortgagor for the difference between that price and the true market value.[5]

(2) FORECLOSURE

Method and Procedure. Foreclosure is a judicial procedure[6] by which the mortgagee acquires the land for himself freed from the mortgagor's equity of redemption. We have seen that Equity regards the mortgagor's right to redeem the property as inviolable, and that, despite the lapse of the contractual right to redeem, it forbids the mortgagee to appropriate the legal fee simple without making an application to the court. Until the time fixed in the deed for repayment of the loan has arrived, no question of foreclosure can arise, but as soon as that date has passed and the equitable right to redeem has superseded the contractual right, the mortgagee can bring an action in the Chancery Division praying that the mortgagor shall either pay what is due or be foreclosed, that is, deprived altogether of his right to redeem. *[Foreclosure action.]*

If the mortgagor does not pay, the court issues what is called an order for *foreclosure nisi*, the effect of which is that the mortgagor loses his property unless he pays upon a certain date (generally six months later) specified by the Master's certificate. The judgment orders that an account shall be taken of what is *[Order nisi.]*

---

[1] *Belton* v. *Bass, Ratcliff and Gretton, Ltd.*, [1922] 2 Ch. 449.

[2] *Williams* v. *Wellingborough Borough Council* [1975] 1 W. L. R. 1327.

[3] *Farrar* v. *Farrars, Ltd.* (1888), 40 Ch. D. 395, at p. 409, and authorities cited by LINDLEY, L.J.

[4] *Cuckmere Brick Co. Ltd.* v. *Mutual Finance Ltd.*, [1971] Ch. 949, at p. 969 ; [1971] 2 All E. R. 633, *per* CROSS, L.J.

[5] *Cuckmere Brick Co., Ltd.* v. *Mutual Finance Ltd., supra* (failure to mention planning permission for flats in advertisement for sale of land by auction) ; *Palmer* v. *Barclays Bank, Ltd.* (1972), 23 P. & C. R. 30 ; *Waltham Forest London Borough* v. *Webb* (1974), 232 Estates Gazette 461 ; *Johnson* v. *Ribbins* (1975), 235 Estates Gazette 757. A building society must take reasonable care to ensure that the price is the best price which can reasonably be obtained. Building Societies Act 1962, s. 36 ; *Reliance Permanent Building Society* v. *Harwood-Stamper*, [1944] Ch. 362 ; [1944] 2 All E. R. 75.

[6] See generally Fisher and Lightwood, *Law of Mortgage* (8th Edn.), chaps. 20 and 21. There appears to be a revival in its popularity as a remedy. Report of Committee on Enforcement of Judgment Debts 1969 (Cmnd. 1309), para. 1360.

due to the plaintiff for principal, interest and costs, and directs
that if this amount is paid within six months, the mortgage
term shall be surrendered to the defendant, but that if default
in payment is made, the defendant shall stand absolutely de-
barred and foreclosed of and from all right, title, interest and
equity of redemption in and to the mortgaged premises. The
mortgagee then proves in Chambers what is due to him for
principal, interest and costs, and the Master draws up a certificate

Order absolute. of what is due and fixes a day and an hour for repayment (usually
six months therefrom). On that day the mortgagee attends, and
waits for the mortgagor, and if the latter does not appear, an
affidavit is sworn in proof of non-payment either prior to or at the
appointed time, and a motion is made for *foreclosure absolute.*

Effect of Foreclosure Order. The effect of the order
absolute is to vest the fee simple absolute (or other the whole
estate of the mortgagor) in the mortgagee, and to extinguish his
mortgage term and all subsequent mortgage terms.[1]

The rights of prior mortgagees are not affected. If there are
more mortgagees than one interested in the same land, an order

" Foreclose down ". absolute obtained by the first mortgagee forecloses all subsequent
incumbrancers, while if (say) the second mortgagee obtains such
an order, its effect is to foreclose the third and later mortgagees,
but to leave untouched the rights of the first mortgagee. The
rule is " foreclose down." [2]

Where there are in this way several mortgagees and the first
brings an action for foreclosure, not only the mortgagor, but also
each of the subsequent mortgagees must be given an opportunity
to redeem, and the ordinary practice is to direct in the order *nisi*
that any of the subsequent incumbrancers may repay the amount
due to the first man on the date appointed.[3] If subsequent
mortgagees are not made parties they are not foreclosed.

Sale in lieu of fore- closure. The court has statutory jurisdiction in a foreclosure action to
order a sale instead of a foreclosure on the request of the mortgagee
or mortgagor, or of any person interested in the mortgage money
or the equity of redemption, notwithstanding the dissent of any
other person.[4]

---

[1] L.P.A. 1925, ss. 88 (2), 89 (2).

[2] From this must be distinguished the maxim "Redeem up, foreclose down."
This applies where there are several mortgagees and in a redemption action
one of them seeks to redeem a prior mortgage. Thus, if there are five mortgagees and the fourth seeks to redeem the second mortgage, he must redeem
up i.e. redeem the third as well as the second, and foreclose down i.e. foreclose
the fifth mortgage and the mortgagor. The first mortgage is unaffected.
Waldock, *Law of Mortgages* (2nd Edn.), p. 337.

[3] If subsequent mortgagees request that they may be granted successive
periods for repayment, an order to that effect is generally issued ; *Platt* v.
Mendel (1884), 27 Ch. D. 246.

[4] L.P.A. 1925, s. 91 (2) ; *Silsby* v. *Holliman*, [1955] Ch. 552 ; [1955] 2 All
E. R. 373.

An action for foreclosure is an action to recover land,[1] and must therefore be brought within twelve years from the date upon which the right of recovery accrues.[2] The right accrues at the date fixed for payment of the principal,[3] but there is a fresh accrual, and the twelve years begin to run again, from any payment of principal or interest by the mortgagor or from a written acknowledgment by him of the mortgagee's title.[4]

Right of foreclosure barred by lapse of time.

Revival of Equity of Redemption. But it must not be thought that a foreclosure absolute irrevocably passes the mortgagor's interest to the mortgagee, although it appears on the surface to do so, for there are certain circumstances in which the foreclosure may be re-opened and the equity of redemption revived. This re-opening takes place if the mortgagee, after obtaining an order absolute, proceeds to sue on the personal covenant;[5] but in addition to this case the court has a discretion to re-open a foreclosure if such relief appears in the special circumstances of the case to be due to the mortgagor. Moreover, the foreclosure may be re-opened against one who has purchased the estate from the mortgagee. It is impossible to lay down a general rule as to when the relief will be granted, for everything turns upon the particular circumstances of each case.

Foreclosure may be re-opened.

In *Campbell* v. *Holyland*,[6] JESSEL, M.R., enumerated those factors which might influence the court in re-opening the foreclosure : the promptness of the mortgagor's application, his failure to redeem being due to an accident which prevented him from raising the money, the difference between the value of the property and the loan,[7] and any special value which the property had to the parties. Further the court may still re-open the foreclosure, even if the mortgagee has sold the property after the foreclosure absolute ; as, for example, where a purchaser bought the property within twenty-four hours after the order and with notice of the fact that it was of much greater value than the amount of the mortgage debt.[8]

---

[1] Limitation Act, 1939, s. 18 (4).
[2] *Ibid.*, s. 4 (3).
[3] *Purnell* v. *Roche*, [1927] 2 Ch. 142 ; *Lewis* v. *Plunkett*, [1937] Ch. 306 ; [1937] 1 All E. R. 530.
[4] Limitation Act, 1939, s. 23 ; *Harlock* v. *Ashberry* (1882), 19 Ch. D. 539.
[5] *Perry* v. *Barker* (1806), 13 Ves. 198.
[6] (1877), 7 Ch. D. 166, at pp. 172–5; M. & B. p. 639.
[7] *Lancashire and Yorkshire Reversionary Interest Co., Ltd.* v. *Crowe* (1970), 114 Sol. Jo. 435 (foreclosure decree made absolute in respect of mortgage of reversionary interest, and re-opened after the interest fell into possession on death of the tenant for life. The sum due was £3,000, and the fund £6,100.)
[8] *Campbell* v. *Holyland, supra.*

(B) REMEDIES WHICH DO NOT INVOLVE
REALIZATION OF THE MORTGAGED PROPERTY

(1) ACTION ON THE PERSONAL COVENANT

Personal
remedy.

A mortgage deed contains an express covenant whereby the mortgagor covenants to repay the principal sum on a definite date, and meanwhile to pay interest at a certain rate per cent. The moment that date has passed, the mortgagee can sue on this personal covenant for the recovery of the principal sum and any interest that may be in arrear, and can have the judgment satisfied out of any property belonging to the mortgagor, though it is not comprised in the mortgage. Further, the mortgagor remains liable on the covenant to the mortgagee, even though he has transferred his interest in the mortgaged property.[1] He usually takes a covenant of indemnity from the transferee.[2]

Effect of
Limitation
Act 1939

An action to recover the principal sum is barred unless it is brought within twelve years from the date when the right to receive the money accrued.[3] This date is that which is fixed by the mortgage deed for repayment, but on each occasion that some part of the principal or interest is paid or a written acknowledgment of his liability to pay is given by the mortgagor, the period of twelve years begins to run afresh.[4] In the case of interest, only six years' arrears are recoverable.[5] Once the mortgagee's right to recover the principal sum is statute barred, he loses his status as a mortgagee. He can no longer sue for possession or for foreclosure, nor can he redeem a prior mortgage.[6]

(2) ENTRY INTO POSSESSION

Right to take
possession.

A legal mortgagee has the right to enter into possession of the mortgaged property. As HARMAN, J., said;

> " The right of the mortgagee to possession in the absence of some contract has nothing to do with default on the part of the mortgagor. The mortgagee may go into possession before the ink is dry on the mortgage unless there is something in the contract, express or by implication,[7] whereby he has contracted himself out of that right. He has the right because he has a legal term of years in the property."[8]

---

[1] *Kinnaird* v. *Trollope* (1888), 39 Ch. D. 636.
[2] A transferee for value is under an implied obligation to indemnify ; *Bridgman* v. *Daw* (1891), 40 W. R. 253.
[3] Limitation Act 1939, s. 18 (1).   [4] *Ibid.*, s. 23 (3) ; 24 (1)
[5] *Ibid.*, s. 18 (5).
[6] *Cotterell* v. *Price*, [1960] 1 W. L. R. 1097 ; [1960] 3 All E. R. 315.
[7] See *Esso Petroleum Co., Ltd.* v. *Alstonbridge Properties, Ltd.*, [1975] 1 W. L. R. 1474, at p. 1484 ; [1975] 3 All E. R. 358.
[8] *Four-Maids, Ltd.* v. *Dudley Marshall (Properties), Ltd.*, [1957] Ch. 317 at p. 320 ; [1957] 2 All E. R. 35 ; M. & B. p. 624. See Report of the Committee on the Enforcement of Judgment Debts 1969 (Cmnd. 3909), pp. 355 *et seq.*

If a mortgagee seeks possession he will usually take proceedings in the Chancery Division or the County Court.[1] Unless the mortgagee agrees, the court has no jurisdiction to decline the order or to adjourn the hearing. But it may adjourn the application for a short time to enable the mortgagor to pay off the whole of the mortgage debt.[2] Where, however, a mortgagee brings an action for possession of a dwelling-house,[3] wide discretionary powers are given to the court by statute.[4] The court may adjourn the proceedings, or suspend[5] or postpone the possession order " if it appears that the mortgagor is likely within a reasonable period to pay any sums due under the mortgage or to remedy a default consisting of a breach of any other obligation " under the mortgage.[6] Where the mortgagor is entitled to pay the principal sum by instalments, the court may treat as sums due only those instalments which are actually in arrear, even if the mortgage makes the whole of the balance outstanding payable on any default by the mortgagor.[7] But the court may only exercise its discretion, if the mortgagor is likely to be able within a reasonable period also to pay any further instalments then due.[8]

It is not usual for a mortgagee, despite his legal right, to enter into possession of the mortgaged property, unless he wishes to do so as a preliminary to exercising his statutory power of sale. It is important for him to do this so that he can offer vacant possession to a purchaser.[9]

It is, in theory at least, possible for a mortgagee to enter into possession to ensure the payment of interest, but a formidable deterrent to this course is the strict supervision which equity exercises over a mortgagee in possession. The rule is that he must

Relief of mortgagor.

Liability of mortgagee to account strictly

---

[1] R.S.C. Ord. 88 : County Courts Act 1959, s. 48 (1) as amended by A.J.A. 1973, s. 6 Sched. 2, gives jurisdiction to the County Court where the rateable value does not exceed £1,000. See also Consumer Credit Act 1974, s. 126, *infra* p. 719.

[2] *Birmingham Citizens Permanent Building Society* v. *Caunt*, [1962] Ch. 883 ; [1962] 1 All E. R. 163. See Rudden and Moseley *Mortgages*, pp. 61–4.

[3] The fact that part of it is used for business purposes does not prevent a house from being a dwelling-house (s. 39 (2)).

[4] A.J.A. 1970, s. 37. If the land is outside Greater London or the County Palatine of Lancaster, and if a County Court has jurisdiction (*supra*, note 1) the action must be brought in the County Court (s. 37). See *Mornington Permanent Building Society* v. *Ghai* (1975), 119 Sol. Jo. 592.

[5] *Royal Trust Co. of Canada* v. *Markham* [1975] 1 W. L. R. 1416.

[6] A.J.A. 1970, s. 36.

[7] Administration of Justice Act 1973, s. 8 (1) ; reversing the effect of *Halifax Building Society* v. *Clark*, [1973] Ch. 307 ; [1973] 2 All E. R. 33. But the grant of the statutory discretion was unnecessary. *First Middlesbrough Trading and Mortgage Co., Ltd.* v. *Cunningham* (1974), 28 P. & C. R. 69. See (1973) 37 Conv. (N.S.) 213, (1974) 38 Conv. (N.S.) 1.

[8] *Ibid.*, s. 8 (2). In instalment mortgages, the discretionary powers extend to foreclosure actions, whether or not possession is claimed in the same proceedings, s. 8 (3). See *Lord Marples of Wallasey* v. *Holmes* (1975), 119 Sol. Jo. 866.

[9] See HARMAN, J., in *Four-Maids, Ltd.* v. *Dudley Marshall (Properties), Ltd.*, *supra*, at p. 321 ; and *Hughes* v. *Waite* [1957] 1. W. L. R. 713 at p. 715 ; [1957] 1 All E. R. 603.

get no advantage out of the mortgage beyond the payment of principal, interest and costs, and he is made to account not only for what he has actually received, but also for what he might have received but for his own wilful default or neglect.[1]   Thus he is liable for voluntary waste, and again if he allows property to remain vacant which might have been let, he is personally liable to pay an occupation rent.[2]   Thus in *White* v. *City of London Brewery Co.*[3]

> Mortgagees, who happened to be brewers, took possession of the mortgaged premises and leased them to a tenant, subject to a restriction that he should take his supply of beer entirely from them. It was held that they must account for the additional rent that they would have received had they let the premises as a " free," instead of a " tied," house.

(3) APPOINTMENT OF A RECEIVER.

Object of appointing receiver.

We have seen that, owing to the strict supervision that the court exercises over a mortgagee, it is undesirable for him to take possession of the land, but, on the other hand, there are cases where it is essential that he should be able to intercept the rents and the profits, and employ them in keeping down the interest. The mortgaged property may have been leased by the mortgagor to third parties under his statutory powers or the property may consist not of land but of a rent-charge, so that there is an annual sum which can be prevented from reaching the mortgagor and can be set against interest. In such cases the most effective procedure is to appoint a receiver of the income of the property.

Statutory power to appoint receiver.

The mortgage deed may contain special provisions with regard to this matter, and in some cases, as for instance where the property is already let to tenants, it is not uncommon to appoint a receiver from the moment when the mortgage is created.   But apart from this a mortgagee has a statutory power of appointing a receiver in the case of every mortgage created by deed,[4] even though he has already gone into possession before the appointment.[5] The appointment and removal of a receiver must be effected in writing.[6]

When exercisable.

Although this statutory power arises as soon as the mortgage money has become due, it cannot be exercised until one of those

---

[1] *Chaplin* v. *Young* (1864), 33 Beav. 330 ; *White* v. *City of London Brewery Co.* (1889), 42 Ch. D. 237, at p. 243.

[2] *Gaskell* v. *Gosling* (1896), 1 Q. B. 669, at p. 691.

[3] (1889), 42 Ch. D. 237; M. & B. p. 627.

[4] L.P.A. 1925, s. 101 (1) (iii).

[5] *Refuge Assurance Co., Ltd.* v. *Pearlberg*, [1938] Ch. 687 ; [1938] 3 All E. R. 231.

[6] L.P.A. 1925, ss. 109 (1) (5).

three events that qualify a mortgagee to exercise his power of sale has occurred.[1]

The advantage of such an appointment from the mortgagee's point of view is that the receiver is deemed to be the agent of the mortgagor, and that the sole responsibility for his acts and defaults falls on the latter.[2] The receiver is not entitled to grant leases without the sanction of the court,[3] but he has power to recover the income of the property by action or distress or otherwise,[4] and to give effectual receipts, and he is bound to apply any money received by him in the following order[5] :—

1. In discharge of rents, taxes, rates and outgoings.

2. In keeping down payments that rank before the mortgage.

3. In paying his own commission, fire and other insurances, and the cost of repairs.

4. In payment of the mortgage interest.

5. In discharging the principal sum if so directed by the mortgagee. A breach of this direction renders him liable to an action for an account.[6]

Any residue that remains must be paid to the mortgagor.

Concurrence and cumulation of remedies. These five remedies available to a legal mortgagee are numerous and varied. They may all be pursued concurrently as soon as the mortgagor is in default, so that, for instance, the mortgagee at one and the same time may sue upon the personal covenant and begin foreclosure proceedings. They are also cumulative. Thus if the mortgagee exercises his power of sale and the purchase price is less than the mortgage debt, he may sue the mortgagor for the balance on the covenant to pay.[7] Foreclosure, however, puts an end to other remedies; a mortgagee who has foreclosed can only sue on the covenant to pay if he is prepared to reopen the foreclosure.[8] *(margin note: Comprehensive nature of remedies.)*

(C) FURTHER RIGHTS OF LEGAL MORTGAGEES

(1) GRANT AND ACCEPTANCE OF SURRENDER OF LEASES

If a mortgagee takes possession of the land with a view to utilizing the profits in satisfaction of the money due to him, he is authorized by statute to grant leases, and to accept surrenders of *(margin note: Leasing and timber powers.)*

---

[1] L. P. A. 1925, s. 109 (1), *supra*, p. 669.
[2] *Ibid.*, s. 109 (2). See *Chatsworth Properties, Ltd.* v. *Effiom*, [1971] 1 W. L. R. 144 ; [1971] 1 All E. R. 604.
[3] *Re Cripps*, [1946] Ch. 265.   [5] *Ibid.*, s. 109 (8).
[4] L.P.A. 1925, s. 109 (3).
[6] *Leicester Permanent Building Society* v. *Butt*, [1943] Ch. 308 ; [1943] 2 All E. R. 523.
[7] *Rudge* v. *Richens* (1873), L. R. 8 C. P. 358 ; *Gordon Grant & Co., Ltd.* v. *Boos*, [1926] A.C. 781.
[8] *Perry* v. *Barker* (1806), 13 Ves. 198.

leases, within the limits made applicable to a mortgagor who is in actual possession.[1]   He is also permitted, where the mortgage is made by deed, to cut and sell timber and other trees if they are ripe for cutting and are not planted for shelter or ornament.[2]

(2) INSURANCE OF THE MORTGAGED PROPERTY

When mortgagee may insure.

Where a mortgage is made by deed, the mortgagee has statutory authority to insure the property against loss or damage by fire, and to charge the premiums on the mortgaged property.[3] But the amount of the insurance must not exceed the amount specified in the mortgage deed, or, if no amount is specified, must not exceed two-thirds of the sum it would take to restore the premises in the event of their total destruction.   Moreover, the mortgagee does not possess this statutory right where the mortgage deed contains a declaration that no insurance is required, or where an insurance is kept up by the mortgagor according to the mortgage deed, or where that deed contains no provision and the mortgagor himself insures up to the statutory amount.[4]   Insurance money, when received, may be applied at the instance of the mortgagee in the discharge of the mortgage debt.[5]

(3) POSSESSION OF THE TITLE DEEDS

A legal mortgagee takes a lease or, if he is a chargee, is in the same position as if he had done so, and the ordinary rule is that a leaseholder is not entitled to hold title deeds appertaining to the fee simple of the lessor.   But, since the continued possession of the deeds by the mortgagor involves considerable risk to one who has advanced money on the security of the land, it is enacted that a first mortgagee shall have the same right to possession of documents as if his security included the fee simple.[6]

(4) TACKING OF FURTHER ADVANCES

We shall see later that a mortgagee who makes a further loan to the mortgagor is allowed, in certain circumstances, to demand that both loans shall be paid out of the land in priority to loans made by other mortgagees, although the latter may have taken their securities before the date of such further loan.[7]

(5) CONSOLIDATION

Description of right.

Consolidation is the right of a person who holds two or more mortgages granted by the same mortgagor on different properties

---

[1] L.P.A. 1925, ss. 99 (2), 100 (2) ; *supra*, p. 666.
[2] *Ibid.*, s. 101 (1) (iv).
[3] *Ibid.*, s. 101 (1) (ii).
[4] *Ibid.*, s. 108 (1), (2).
[5] *Ibid.*, s. 108 (4).
[6] *Ibid.*, ss. 85 (1), 86 (1).
[7] *Infra*, pp. 693 ; 708.

to refuse in certain circumstances to be redeemed as to one, unless he is also redeemed as to the other or others.[1]

The mortgages in actual fact are quite separate, having been given on different properties and perhaps at different times, but none the less the mortgagee is allowed in certain cases to consolidate them and treat them as one. The right is based upon the doctrine that *he who comes to equity must do equity* ; for a mortgagor who is seeking to redeem is in truth asking a favour in the sense that he is petitioning equity for the restoration of his property after the date fixed by the mortgage deed for redemption has passed, and this being so, he must himself be prepared to act equitably.

Suppose, for instance,

> that A. has mortgaged Blackacre to B. for £5000 and White-acre to B. for £5000. If Blackacre diminishes, while White-acre appreciates, in value, it is unethical that A. should be allowed to redeem the latter unless he is also prepared to repay the loan of £5000 on Blackacre. In such a case B. can insist that both properties shall be treated as one and redeemed together.

This example illustrates the primary meaning and the simplest application of consolidation, but the doctrine has been developed further and extended to cases where the mortgages were originally made *to* different mortgagees. In such a case if the mortgages ultimately become vested in one person, that is, in one mortgagee, he possesses the right of consolidation.[2] Thus, if— *Extension of right to consolidate.*

> A. mortgages W. to B.,
> A. mortgages X. and Y. to C.,
> B. and C. transfer their mortgages to D.,

A. cannot redeem any one of the properties W., X., Y., unless, if called upon, he pays the amount due on the other two.

But consolidation extends even further than this, and applies to a case where the person who is entitled to redeem is not the original mortgagor, but a transferee of one or more of the equities. There are two different cases to be considered, since the law differs according as the equities of redemption have all become united in one person, or have become separated so that the person claiming to redeem, that is, the person against

---

[1] *Jennings* v. *Jordan* (1881), 6 App. Cas. 698, 700 ; White and Tudor, *Leading Cases in Equity* (9th Edn.), vol. ii. p. 129. For a criticism of the doctrine see Waldock, *Law of Mortgages* (2nd Edn.), pp. 293–5. As to whether the right amounts to a general equitable change within L.C.A. 1972, s. 2 (4), Class C (iii), see (1948) 92 Sol. Jo. 736 ; Wolstenholme and Cherry, vol. 1, p. 189.

[2] *Vini* v. *Padgett* (1858), 2 De G. & J. 611 ; *Pledge* v. *White*, [1896] A. C. 187.

whom the doctrine of consolidation is invoked, is not the owner of all the equities.

Application of doctrine where all equities transferred to one person.

1. If a person acquires the equities upon all the properties, whether as heir, trustee in bankruptcy, purchaser or second mortgagee, the mortgages can in all cases be consolidated against him, even though the mortgage terms did not become vested in one mortgagee until after the person seeking to redeem had obtained the equities.

> An illustration may elucidate this statement [1] :
> 1968 A. mortgages U. and V. to B.
> 1970 A. mortgages W. to C.
> 1971 A. mortgages X., Y., and Z. to D.
> 1973 A. sells the *equities* on U., V., W., X., Y., and Z. to F.
> 1975 E. acquires all the mortgages from B., C., and D.
>
> Here all the mortgages are vested in one person, E. and, although he knew, when he bought out B., C., and D., that the equities were not vested in the original mortgagor, he can require F. to redeem all the properties or none.

As Lord DAVEY said in *Pledge* v. *White* [2] :—

> " It appears to me, my Lords, that an assignee of two or more equities of redemption from one mortgagor stands in a widely different position from the assignee of one equity only. He knows, or has the opportunity of knowing, what are the mortgages subject to which he has purchased the property, and he knows they may become united by transfer in one hand. If the doctrine of consolidation be once admitted it appears to me not unreasonable to hold that a person in such a position occupies the place of the mortgagor or assignor to him towards the holders of the mortgages, subject to which he has purchased. . . . "

Application of doctrine when equities separated.

2. Turning now to the case where the equities are separated and do not all pass to one person, it will be as well, before stating the general principle, to present an illustration showing how the purchaser of a single equity of redemption may find himself saddled with the burden of redeeming other mortgages of whose very existence he was unaware.

Thus :

> If at different times A. mortgages X., Y., and Z. to B., and then later transfers the fee simple of X. to C., who gives full value and knows nothing of the other two properties which have been mortgaged, C., on tendering the amount of the loan due on X., may be unable under the doctrine of consolidation to redeem X. unless he also pays what is due on Y. and Z.

---

[1] *Pledge* v. *White, supra* ; M. & B. p. 643.
[2] [1896] A. C. 187, at p. 198.

Where the mortgage transactions entered into by the original mortgagor are many, and where dealings have taken place both in the equities and in the mortgages, the question whether in any particular case consolidation is enforceable appears at first sight to be both difficult and complicated. But all difficulty disappears if attention is paid to the cardinal rule. This rule covers all cases of separation of equities, and clearly defines the limits within which consolidation is applicable. It may be stated in this way :

> Consolidation is allowed only if, at the date when redemption is sought, all the mortgages, having originally been made by one mortgagor, are vested in one mortgagee and all the equities are vested in one person, or if, *after these two things have once happened, the equities of redemption have become separated.*[1]

Test for application of doctrine.

If all the mortgages are in one hand and all the equities in another, it is clear that the right of consolidation exists against the mortgagor. It is equally clear that, *once this right has been established in respect of all the properties*, a transferee of one or more of the equities cannot stand in a better position than the mortgagor from whom he took the transfer. The principle of law involved here is that a person who buys an equity of redemption from a mortgagor takes it subject to all liabilities to which it was subject at the time of the sale ; one of these is the liability to have certain other mortgages consolidated with it, provided, however, that the consolidation was enforceable against that particular equity *at the time of the purchase.*[2] In the words of Lord SELBORNE :—

> " The purchaser of an equity of redemption must take it as it stood at the time of his purchase, subject to all other equities which then affected it in the hands of his vendor, of which the right of the mortgagee to consolidate his charge on that particular property with other charges *then* held by him on other property at the same time redeemable under the same mortgagor was one."[3]

But on no principle of law would it be justifiable to hold the purchaser of an interest bound by equities which were not enforceable against that interest at the time of its sale. It follows from this that the assignee of an equity does not become subject to consolidation in respect of mortgages created *after* the sale to him, nor in respect of mortgages which, though created before that date, became united in one mortgagee afterwards.[4]

---

[1] *Pledge* v. *White*, [1896] A. C. 187, at p. 198, *per* Lord DAVEY.
[2] *Cummins* v. *Fletcher* (1880), 14 Ch. D. 699, at p. 712.
[3] *Jennings* v. *Jordan* (1881), 6 App. Cas. 698, at p. 701.
[4] *Harter* v. *Colman* (1882), 19 Ch. D. 630.

Suppose, for instance, that the following transactions successively occur :

> A. mortgages X. to B.,
> A. mortgages Y. to B.,
> A. sells the equity of redemption in Y. to C ,
> A. mortgages Z. to B.[1]

When C. seeks to redeem his own property Y., he can be
compelled by B. to redeem X., because, at the time when he
bought his equity, the equities on X. and Y. were vested in
one person, and the mortgages were vested in one person.
But he cannot be compelled to redeem Z., for the mortgage on
it was created only after the sale of the equity on Y. to C., so
that the right to have Z. consolidated with X. and Y. obviously
did not exist at that time.

The holder of an equity of redemption who is compelled under
the doctrine of consolidation to redeem some other mortgage
steps into the shoes of the mortgagee, and can demand payment
from the mortgagor in respect of the mortgage he has had to
redeem.

Mortgages must be *by* same person.   No right to consolidation arises if the mortgages were
originally made *by* different mortgagors, even though the equities
subsequently become united in one hand.[2]

Reservation of right to consolidate.   The right of consolidation does not exist as a matter of course,
but only where it is expressly reserved in the various deeds
or in one of them. When the right is not so reserved, it is enacted
that [3] :—

> "A mortgagor seeking to redeem any one mortgage is entitled to
> do so without paying any money due under any separate mortgage
> made by him, or by any person through whom he claims, solely on
> property other than that comprised in the mortgage which he seeks
> to redeem."

This is a re-enactment of the Conveyancing Act 1881, and
it does not apply where all the mortgages were made before
January 1st, 1882. In mortgages made before that date the right
of consolidation existed as a matter of course.

(2) *RIGHTS OF EQUITABLE MORTGAGEES*

Twofold division of equitable mortgages.   The remedies of an equitable mortgagee vary according as the
security is a mortgage in the strict sense, namely,

---

[1] *Hughes* v. *Britannia Permanent Benefit Building Society*, [1906] 2 Ch. 607 ;
M. & B. p. 646.

[2] *Sharp* v. *Rickards*, [1909] 1 Ch. 109.

[3] L.P.A. 1925, s. 93.

a contract to create a legal mortgage,
a deposit of title deeds,
a mortgage of an equitable interest,[1]

or is a mere charge upon property.[2] We will take these two classes separately.

If the mortgage falls within the first class the general principle is that the remedies available to the lender correspond as nearly as possible with those available to a legal mortgagee.

Thus the primary remedy of foreclosure applies where a deposit of title deeds with the lender has been accompanied by an agreement by the borrower to give a legal mortgage if required to do so[3]; and the same is true where there has been a deposit without any memorandum, since the law considers that the deposit is evidence of a contract to create a legal mortgage.[4] When such an equitable mortgagee takes foreclosure proceedings to enforce his security the decree of the court declares that the deposit operated as a mortgage, that in default of payment the mortgagor is trustee of the legal estate for the mortgagee and that he must convey that estate to him.[5]

Foreclosure.

The general rule is that foreclosure and not sale is the proper remedy for an equitable mortgagee.[6] But if the mortgage is made in a form which entitles him to require the execution of a mortgage containing a power of sale, he can exercise the statutory power of sale which is given by the Law of Property Act 1925.[7] This statutory power, however, is exercisable only when the mortgage is made by deed, and therefore the proper course is for an equitable mortgagee not to be content with a mere deposit or with a deposit supported by a written memorandum, but to take a memorandum under seal. If this is done he can sell the property subject to the conditions specified by the Act. The memorandum should also give the mortgagee a power of attorney authorizing him, upon exercising the power of sale, to convey the mortgaged property in the name of the mortgagor to the purchaser. This enables the mortgagee, though only an equitable incumbrancer, to convey the legal estate in the property to the purchaser.[8] The same result may be achieved by inserting in the memorandum a declaration of trust, stating that the mortgagor holds the legal estate on trust for the mortgagee and empowering him to appoint someone, including himself, as trustee

Sale.

---

[1] *Supra*, pp. 649–51. [2] *Supra*, p. 651.
[3] *York Union Banking Co.* v. *Artley* (1879), 11 Ch. D. 205.
[4] *Backhouse* v. *Charlton* (1878), 8 Ch. D. 444; *Carter* v. *Wake* (1877), 4 Ch. D 605.
[5] *Marshall* v. *Shrewsbury* (1875), 10 Ch. App. 250, at p. 254.
[6] *James* v. *James* (1873), L. R. 16 Eq. 153.
[7] S. 101 (1) (i), *supra*, p. 669.
[8] *Re White Rose Cottage*, [1965] Ch. 940; [1965] 1 All E. R. 11; M. & B. p. 636.

in place of the mortgagor.   The mortgagee can thus vest the legal estate in himself or the purchaser.

Again, the statutory power of the court to order a sale instead of foreclosure, which we have already noticed, is exercisable in favour of an equitable mortgagee even though he has taken a mere deposit of deeds without a memorandum.[1]

Appointment of receiver.   If an equitable mortgage is created by deed, the statutory power of appointing a receiver is available to the mortgagee,[2] but in the absence of a deed the appointment must be made by the court.[3]

Possession.   An equitable mortgagee is not entitled to take possession of the land unless the right to do so has been expressly reserved[4] or unless the court makes an order to that effect.   Though this is the prevalent view, it has been argued with considerable force that it is justified neither on principle nor on the authorities.[5]

An equitable mortgagee can sue the mortgagor personally for recovery of the money lent.

Finally, where an equitable mortgage is created by deposit of title deeds, the mortgagee has the right to retain the deeds under the mortgage until he is paid, but he has no separate legal lien.[6]

Equitable charge.   The second class of equitable security is the charge, which involves no transfer of a legal or equitable interest to the lender, but entitles him to have the debt discharged out of the land.   His sole remedies in this respect are to have the charge satisfied by the sale of the land or by the appointment of a receiver under the direction of the court.   He has no right to take possession of the land nor may he foreclose.   In the words of Lord HATHERLEY:—

> "Although some of the authorities appear to conflict with each other, it seems, on the whole, to be settled that if there is a charge *simpliciter*, and not a mortgage, or an agreement for a mortgage, then the right of the parties having such a charge is a sale and not foreclosure."[7]

From a mere equitable charge, must be distinguished the charge by deed expressed to be by way of legal mortgage introduced by the legislation of 1925, for as we have seen such a chargee has the same remedies as if he held a term of years absolute.[8]

---

[1] L.P.A. 1925, s. 91.
[2] *Ibid.*, s. 101 (1) (ii) ; *supra*, p. 678.
[3] *Meaden* v. *Sealey* (1849), 6 Hare, 620.
[4] *Finck* v. *Tranter*, [1905] 1 K. B. 427, 429 ; *Barclays Bank, Ltd.* v. *Bird*, [1954] Ch. 284, at p. 280 ; [1954] 1 All E. R. 449, at p. 452.
[5] (1955), 71 *L. Q. R.*, 204 (H. W. R. Wade).
[6] *Re Molton Finance Ltd.*, [1968] Ch. 325 ; [1967] 3 All E. R. 843.   See also *Capital Finance Co., Ltd.* v. *Stokes*, [1969] 1 Ch. 261, at p. 278 ; [1968] 3 All E. R. 625 ; *Burston Finance, Ltd.* v. *Speirway, Ltd.*, [1974] 1 W. L. R. 1648 ; [1974] 3 All E. R. 735.
[7] *Tennant* v. *Trenchard* (1869), L. R. 4 Ch. 537, at p. 542 ; *Re Owen*, [1894] 3 Ch. 220.
[8] *Supra*, p. 648.

SECTION V. PRIORITY OF MORTGAGES[1]

Introductory Note. If two or more mortgagees have advanced money on the security of the same land and if the land is of insufficient value when realized to satisfy the claims of all, it is vital to know in what order they are entitled to be paid out of the land. The mortgagor has, let us say, granted separate and successive mortgages on Blackacre to A., B., C. and D. Owing to unforeseen circumstances Blackacre has depreciated in value and its sale will produce sufficient money to repay only one or perhaps two of the mortgagees the amount of their advances. This does not mean that mortgagees who fail to get satisfaction out of the land are remediless, for they can of course sue the mortgagor on his personal covenant, but since his other property may be of little value it will be their object to proceed against the land if the law allows them to do so. A knowledge of the former rules that governed this matter, although they were substantially affected by the legislation of 1925, is essential to an understanding of the modern law on this subject ; and, as we shall see, there are situations in which they may still be applicable.[2]

Rules for order of payment to mortgagees.

(1) PRIORITY OF MORTGAGES BEFORE 1926

(A) THE PRIORITY OF THE LEGAL MORTGAGEE OF LAND

To understand the order in which mortgages ranked for repayment out of the land before 1926 we must recall that under the practice then prevailing it was usual in the case of a mortgage of the fee simple to convey the legal estate in fee simple to the mortgagee. There might be several mortgages of Blackacre, but there could be only one *legal* mortgage, and all the others, whether created before or after the legal mortgage, were necessarily equitable in nature.

Where equities are equal the law prevails.

The fundamental rule before 1926, based upon the maxim " where the equities are equal the law prevails," was that the mortgagee who held the legal estate ranked, for the purpose of obtaining satisfaction out of the land, before all other mortgagees of whose securities he had no notice at the time when he made his advance.[3] Equity respected the legal title, and it was a rule without exception that a court of equity took away from a purchaser for value without notice nothing that he had honestly acquired.[4] Lord HARDWICKE said :—

---

[1] For a closely reasoned study see (1940), *C. L. J.* 243 (R. E. Megarry) ; Waldock, *Law of Mortgages* (2nd Edn.), pp. 381–435.
[2] *Infra,* pp. 704 *et seq.*
[3] *Plumb* v. *Fluitt* (1791), 2 Anst. 432.
[4] *Heath* v. *Crealock* (1874), 10 Ch. App. 22, at p. 33.

"As courts of equity break in upon the common law, where necessity and conscience require it, still they allow superior force and strength to a legal title to estates ; and therefore where there is a legal title and equity on one side, this court never thought fit that by reason of a prior equity against a man, who had a legal title, that man should be hurt, and this by reason of that force this court necessarily and rightly allows to the common law and to legal titles." [1]

If therefore a mortgagor granted an equitable mortgage to A and later conveyed the legal estate to B by way of mortgage, the latter had the best right to the land provided that, when he made his own advance, he had no notice of the earlier mortgage to A. The onus lay on him to prove this affirmatively. [2]   B., the legal mortgagee, had an even stronger case against mortgagees who obtained their securities at a date *later* than his own, for not only did he alone hold the legal title, but having acquired it first in order of time he could invoke the maxim *qui prior est tempore potior est jure.*

This rule giving priority to the legal mortgagee, however, applied only where the equities were equal, *i.e.* where the legal mortgagee had as good a moral right as the equitable mortgagees, and in the following cases he was displaced in favour of equitable mortgagees :—

Cases where equities not equal.

(a) **Where the Legal Mortgagee had notice of an Earlier Mortgage.**   If, at the time when he advanced his money, the legal mortgagee had actual or constructive notice of an earlier incumbrance, he was postponed to the earlier incumbrancer.   A legal mortgagee who failed to investigate his mortgagor's title according to the usual practice or who abstained from investigation altogether, was affected with notice of, and therefore postponed to, any earlier mortgage that he would have discovered had he followed the customary practice. [3]

(b) **Where the Legal Mortgagee was negligent with regard to the Title Deeds.**   The obvious duty of a person who acquires a legal estate is to obtain and to keep possession of the title deeds, or, if for some reason this is impossible, to make inquiries for them.   Title deeds are the symbol of ownership, and if they are not produced by a mortgagor the suspicion naturally arises that they have been utilized by him in order to vest some right in a third person, and that he is deliberately concealing this transaction from the mortgagee.

There are two indiscretions in this connection that a mortgagee may commit, namely, failure to obtain the deeds

---

[1] *Wortley* v. *Birkhead* (1754), 2 Ves. Sen. 571, at p. 574.
[2] *A.-G.* v. *Biphosphated Guano Co.* (1879), 11 Ch. D. 327.
[3] *Berwick & Co.* v. *Price*, [1905] 1 Ch. 632.

at the time of the transaction, and failure to retain deeds of which he has once had possession.

It was well established before 1926 that a legal mortgagee who made no inquiries whatever for the deeds must be postponed to a prior equitable incumbrancer who had already secured them, and even to a later innocent incumbrancer who was more diligent in getting them into his custody.[1] On the other hand, if he made inquiry and yet failed to obtain them, it depended upon the circumstances whether he was postponed to an earlier equitable incumbrancer in whose possession they were. Postponement was not an automatic result of failure to obtain possession, for it was always held that in addition there must have been some degree of negligence. The cases show a growing severity against the legal mortgagee. At first it was laid down that he must not be postponed unless he had been guilty of fraud in the transaction under which he acquired the legal estate, or unless he had shown such wilful negligence as to indicate complicity in the fraud.[2] But a new rule more favourable to an earlier equitable mortgagee was pronounced by the Court of Appeal in 1899 in the case of *Oliver* v. *Hinton*.[3] This may be stated in the words of LINDLEY, L.J. :

(i) Postponement owing to failure to obtain deeds.

Degree of negligence necessary to postpone.

> " To deprive a purchaser for value[4] without notice of a prior incumbrance of the protection of the legal estate it is not, in my opinion, essential that he should have been guilty of fraud ; it is sufficient that he has been guilty of such gross negligence as would render it unjust to deprive the prior incumbrancer of his priority."[5]

The case related to a purchaser of a legal estate, but the result would have been the same had the person who acquired the legal estate been a mortgagee. The facts were as follows :

> A., the owner of the legal estate, deposited the title deeds with X. as security for advances to the value of £400 made by the latter. Some two years later A. conveyed the legal estate to the purchaser, P., in consideration of £320. P. inquired about the deeds, but was told that they could not be delivered as they related also to some other property. This

---

[1] *Walker* v. *Linom*, [1907] 2 Ch. 104 ; M. & B. p. 656.

[2] *Hunt* v. *Elmes* (1860), 2 De F. & J. 578 ; *Ratcliffe* v. *Barnard* (1870), L. R. 6 Ch. 652 ; (1871), 6 Ch. App. 652 ; see *Hudston* v. *Viney*, [1921] 1 Ch. 98, 103-4 ; *Northern Counties of England Fire Insurance Co.* v. *Whipp* (1884), 26 Ch. D. 482 ; M. & B. p. 652.

[3] [1899] 2 Ch. 264 ; M. & B. p. 650.

[4] This includes a mortgagee.

[5] It would have been simpler to apply the doctrine of the bona fide purchaser for value without notice and to postpone the later legal mortgagee unless he satisfies that test. See ROMER, J., at first instance in *Oliver* v. *Hinton*, [1899] 2 Ch. 264, at p. 268 ; and PARKER, J., in *Walker* v. *Linom*, [1907] 2 Ch. 104, at p. 114 ; M. & B. p. 656.

answer was accepted, and A. was not even asked to produce the deeds for inspection. It was held that P., though entirely innocent of fraud or of any complicity in fraud, must be postponed to X.

Epithets such as " gross " are unreliable guides, and the rule as stated by the Court of Appeal left open in each case the question whether the requisite degree of negligence had been shown, but the expression " gross negligence " was described in a later case as meaning something more than mere carelessness. EVE, J., said [1] :—

> " It must at least be carelessness of so aggravated a nature as to amount to the neglect of precautions which the ordinary reasonable man would have observed and to indicate an attitude of mental indifference to obvious risks."

Postponement to earlier incumbrancers.

If, therefore, a mortgagee had inquired for the title deeds and had been given a reasonable excuse for their non-delivery, he would not be postponed to an earlier equitable mortgagee. An extreme case is, perhaps, *Hewitt* v. *Loosemore*,[2] where the defendant, who had taken a legal mortgage of a leasehold interest from a solicitor by way of assignment, failed to obtain possession of the lease, which, as a matter of fact, had already been deposited with the plaintiff. Part of the answer made by the defendant to the bill which the plaintiff brought against him was as follows :—

> " The defendant . . . was a farmer and unacquainted with legal forms ; but upon the said indenture of assignment being handed to him as aforesaid, he inquired of [the mortgagor] whether the lease of the premises ought not to be delivered to him as well ; when [the mortgagor] replied that it should, but that, as he was rather busy then, he would look for it and give it to the defendant when he next came to market."

It was held that in the circumstances the plaintiff had failed to make out a sufficient case for postponing the defendant.

Postponement to later incumbrancers.

Likewise failure to obtain the deeds might entail postponement of a legal mortgagee to a *later* equitable incumbrancer. Again, however, nothing short of gross negligence was sufficient to produce this result. Thus in *Grierson* v. *National Provincial Bank of England Ltd.*[3] :

> A mortgagor, having already deposited the deeds with a bank as security for a loan, executed a legal mortgage in favour of the plaintiff. The plaintiff had actual notice of this earlier equitable mortgage, but he neither informed the bank of his legal mortgage, nor instructed them to deliver the deeds to him should the mortgagor repay their loan. The mortgagor later paid off the bank, obtained the deeds and deposited

---

[1] *Hudston* v. *Viney*, [1921] 1 Ch. 98, 104.
[2] (1851), 9 Hare, 449 ; M. & B. p. 649. See also *Agra Bank Ltd.* v. *Barry* (1874), L. R. 7 H. L. 135.   [3] [1913] 2 Ch. 18.

them with the defendant as security for an advance. The defendant was ignorant of the plaintiff's legal mortgage.

It was held that the plaintiff had not been sufficiently negligent to justify his postponement to the defendant.

It was also the case under the old law that the conduct of the legal mortgagee in dealing with the title deeds *after* he had obtained them might be such as to justify his postponement to subsequent equitable mortgagees.

(ii) Post-
ponement
due to
subsequent
negligence.

In the first place the principle of *Oliver* v. *Hinton* applied, and any conduct on the part of the legal mortgagee in relation to the deeds which would have made it inequitable for him to claim priority over an earlier equitable mortgagee was sufficient to postpone him to a subsequent mortgage the creation of which was due entirely to his own conduct.[1] There need not have been fraudulent conduct, but there must have been gross negligence. Thus in a leading case [2] the priority of the legal mortgagee was not displaced where:

> A company took a legal mortgage from its manager, and the manager, having stolen the deeds from a safe to which he had access, used them to create another mortgage in favour of an innocent person.

The following remarks were passed by the court upon the arguments that had been advanced in favour of postponement:

> " The case was argued as if the legal owner of land owed a duty to all other of Her Majesty's subjects to keep his title deeds secure; as if title deeds were in the eye of the law analogous to fierce dogs or destructive elements, where from the nature of the thing the courts have implied a general duty of safe custody."[3]

In the second place a legal mortgagee was postponed if he constituted the mortgagor his agent with authority to raise more money on the security of the land. This postponement occurred for instance where the mortgagor, having been entrusted with the deeds for the purpose of obtaining a further loan of a given amount, procured one of a greater amount without disclosing to the lender the existence of the first mortgage. In such a case the legal mortgagee was postponed on the ground that, having enabled the mortgagor to represent himself as unincumbered owner, he was estopped from asserting that the actual authority had been exceeded.[4]

---

[1] *Walker* v. *Linom*, [1907] 2 Ch. 104, at p. 114 ; *Northern Counties of England Fire Insurance Co.* v. *Whipp* (1884), 26 Ch. D. 482 ; M. & B. p. 652. *Cf Re King's Settlement*, [1931] 2 Ch. 294.

[2] *Northern Counties, etc.* v. *Whipp, supra.*

[3] *Northern Counties of England Fire Insurance Co.* v. *Whipp, supra,* at p. 493.

[4] *Perry Herrick* v. *Attwood* (1857), 2 De G. & J. 21 ; M. & B. p. 653 ; *Northern Counties of England Fire Insurance Co.* v. *Whipp, supra,* at p. 493 ; *Brocklesby* v. *Temperance, etc., Society,* [1895] A. C. 173.

(B) Priority as between Equitable Mortgagees of Land

Qui prior est tempore potior est jure.

Where the legal estate was outstanding and a conflict arose between incumbrancers who all held equitable mortgages, the rule was that the several mortgagees must be paid according to their priority of time, *qui prior est tempore potior est jure.*[1]

If, therefore, a mortgagor subjected his land to equitable charges first in favour of A. and then in favour of B., or if, after granting a legal mortgage to X., he made subsequent mortgages first to A. and then to B., A. had the prior right as against B. to receive payment out of the land. He had a better and superior equity because it was an earlier equity. This rule was based upon the principle that:

" An owner of property, dealing honestly with it, cannot confer upon another a greater interest in that property than he himself has."[2]

All that the mortgagor had to dispose of when he had once made a legal mortgage was the equitable interest, and it had long been the rule that:

" Every conveyance of an equitable interest is an innocent conveyance, that is to say, the grant of a person entitled merely in equity passes only that which he is justly entitled to, and no more."[3]

Priority of time not always decisive.

The rule that priority of time gave the better right to payment might, however, be excluded in two cases:

First, where the equities were in other respects not equal.

Secondly, where the doctrine of tacking operated.

Postponement due to negligence.

Equities not equal. In a contest between equitable claimants, the court had to be satisfied that the party with the earlier equity had acted in such a way as to justify his retention of priority over the later incumbrancer.[4] Thus, he lost the protection that was normally due to him if his negligent failure to obtain or to retain the title deeds had misled the later mortgagee into believing that no earlier equity existed. The question as to what degree of negligence sufficed to produce this result scarcely admits of a dogmatic answer, for the judges expressed varying opinions, and one view was that the priority of an equitable mortgage was more easily displaced than that of a legal mortgage.[5] No decision has been found, however, in which the negligence held sufficient to postpone

---

[1] *Brace* v. *Duchess of Marlborough* (1728), 2 P. Wms. 491, at p. 495; *Willoughby* v. *Willoughby* (1756), 1 Term Rep. 773.

[2] *West* v. *Williams*, [1899] 1 Ch. 132, at p. 143; *per* Lindley, M.R.

[3] *Phillips* v. *Phillips* (1862), 4 De G. F. & J. 208, at p. 215, *per* Lord Westbury.

[4] *National Provincial Bank of England* v. *Jackson* (1886), 33 Ch. D. 1, at p. 13, *per* Cotton, L.J.

[5] *Taylor* v. *Russell*, [1891] 1 Ch. 1, at p. 17; [1892] A. C. 244, at p. 262.

an equitable mortgagee would not also have defeated a legal mortgagee.[1] In the case before 1926 of a legal mortgage to A., followed by equitable mortgages to B. and C., the question could arise only exceptionally, since A. would normally hold the deeds, but it would arise in an acute form if the only transactions effected by the mortgagor were of an equitable nature. In this connection two rules at least were definitely established :

First, if an incumbrancer was entitled to have the deeds as part of his security but did not insist upon his right, he was postponed to a later equitable incumbrancer who obtained them without notice of the earlier equity. This occurred in *Farrand* v. *Yorkshire Banking Co.*,[2] where the facts were these : **Failure to obtain deeds.**

> The mortgagor agreed to deposit the deeds relating to the mortgaged property with A., but the deposit was never made. A year later he handed the deeds to a bank with which he had made a similar agreement.

It was held that A. must be postponed, for it was entirely due to his inactivity that the bank had been defrauded into advancing a second loan.

Secondly, if an equitable incumbrancer obtained the deeds but later delivered them to the mortgagor, he was postponed to a later lender to whom they had been delivered as security.[3] **Failure to retain deeds.**

> " It is an elementary principle," said KINDERSLEY, V.-C., that a party coming into equity in such a case is bound to show that he has not been guilty of such a degree of neglect as to enable another party so to deal with that which was the plaintiff's right, as to induce an innocent party to assume that he was dealing with his own." [4]

Tacking. The general rule that equitable mortgagees ranked for payment according to the dates at which they took their mortgages was also liable to be displaced by the operation of the doctrine of tacking, or " the creditor's *tabula in naufragio* " (" the plank in the shipwreck ").[5] This doctrine, which is founded on technical and justly suspected reasoning, is an example of the superiority attached by courts of law and of equity to the legal estate. Equitable owners who were equally meritorious in regard to honesty of dealing might compete for the legal estate, and the one who succeeded in obtaining it won the right to rank before an earlier equitable mortgagee despite the maxim *qui prior est tempore potior est jure*. The reason was that, having obtained **Doctrine of tacking.**

---

1 See the discussion in Waldock, *Law of Mortgages* (2nd Edn.), pp. 397–8.
2 (1888), 40 Ch. D. 182.
3 *Waldron* v. *Sloper* (1852), 1 Drew. 193.
4 *Waldron* v. *Sloper* (1852), 1 Drew. 193, at p. 200.
5 *Brace* v. *Duchess of Marlborough* (1728), 2 P. Wms. 491.

the legal estate, he could take advantage of that other and more potent maxim " where equities are equal, the legal title prevails."[1]

There were two distinct branches of tacking under the old law, and we must consider these separately.

(i) Where equitable mortgagee acquired the legal estate.

1. The first form consisted of joining an equitable mortgage to the legal mortgage in order to squeeze out and gain priority over an intermediate mortgage. If a legal mortgage to A. was followed by equitable mortgages first to B. and secondly to C., then C. would gain priority of payment over B. if he paid off A. and took a conveyance of his legal estate. C. now had the prior right to recover from the land not only the amount which A. had advanced on the first mortgage, but also the amount which C. himself had advanced to the mortgagor. But he could not tack his own advance to the legal estate and squeeze out B. unless he had an equal equity with B.; and the equities were not equal unless, *at the time when he made his advance*, he was without notice that B. had made an earlier advance.

(ii) Where the legal mortgagee made a further advance.

2. The second form of tacking was available only to a *legal* mortgagee who had made a further advance. It was not available to equitable mortgagees before 1926. If a legal mortgagee, subsequently to his original loan, made a further advance to the mortgagor without *at that time* having notice of equitable mortgages created after the legal mortgage, he could, by virtue of his ownership of the legal estate, tack the second to the first advance and recover the whole amount due to him in priority to all other incumbrancers.[2]

If, for instance :

> The mortgagor made a legal mortgage to A. for £2000, a second mortgage to B., a third mortgage to C., and then a further mortgage to A. for £500, A. was entitled to be paid £2500 out of the land before B. and C. received anything.

Notice excluded tacking.

But this right did not avail the legal mortgagee if, at the time when he made his further advance, he knew that other persons had already lent money on the security of the land. Thus in *Freeman v. Laing* [3] :

> Three trustees advanced money jointly on a legal mortgage of land and subsequently made a further advance. At the time of this second advance one alone of the trustees had notice

---

[1] *Bailey* v. *Barnes*, [1894] 1 Ch. 25, at p. 36, *per* LINDLEY, L.J.
[2] *Brace* v. *Duchess of Marlborough* (1728), 2 P. Wms. 491.
[3] [1899] 2 Ch. 355.

of an intermediate mortgage. It was held that the successors in title of the trustees could not tack the second loan to the first, for since each of them was individually entitled to the entire security, notice to one was notice to all.

An important application of this rule, that notice excluded the right to tack, occurred where land was mortgaged by way of security not only for the original loan, but also for such future advances as might be made. A mortgagee likes to know that he can have recourse to the land in respect of any money he may advance later, and when such further loans are contemplated it has always been customary to provide expressly in the deed that they, equally with the original loan, shall be secured by the land. But it was laid down in *Hopkinson* v. *Rolt*[1] that, notwithstanding such an express provision, the right to tack was excluded by notice of other incumbrances. This principle was carried further by the case of *West* v. *Williams*[2] and made applicable where the legal mortgagee had not (as in *Hopkinson* v. *Rolt*) taken security merely for such further advances as he might *voluntarily* make, but had entered into a binding covenant to make further advances upon the security of the land, if called upon to do so. The fact that he was under a contractual obligation to increase his original loan did not entitle him to priority in respect of a further advance made with notice of a later incumbrance.

The doctrine of tacking was abolished in 1874 by the Vendor and Purchaser Act, but as this prejudiced the ability of mortgagors to obtain further advances from first mortgagees, it was restored by the Land Transfer Act of 1875.

(C) Priority between Assignees and Mortgagees of an Equitable Interest in Pure Personalty

Priority between mortgagees of pure personalty has been governed since 1823 by the rule in *Dearle* v. *Hall*.[3] This rule, which is of greater importance now than formerly because of its extension by the Law of Property Act 1925, applied whenever successive mortgages or assignments were made of an equitable interest in pure personalty, as distinct from an interest, whether legal or equitable, in freeholds or leaseholds. To make the rule applicable, the mortgagor or assignor must have had an equitable interest in a debt or fund and he must have made two or more successive assignments of that subject matter in favour of different persons.[4] It is chiefly remarkable as being a departure from the

The Rule in *Dearle* v. *Hall*.

---

[1] (1861), 9 H. L. C. 514.   [2] [1899] 1 Ch. 132.
[3] (1823), 3 Russ. 1; M. & B. p. 659.
[4] *B. S. Lyle Ltd.* v. *Rosher*, [1959] 1 W. L. R. 8, at pp. 16, 19 ; [1958] 3 All E. R. 597, at pp. 603, 605.

fundamental principle that equities are entitled to rank according to the order of time in which they have been created.

The rule laid down that as between mortgagees or assignees of an equitable interest in pure personalty (*i.e.* excluding leaseholds, but including an interest under a trust for sale[1]) priority depended upon the order in which notice of the mortgages or assignments was received[2] by the legal owner of the personalty (*i.e.* in most cases by the trustees). However, a later mortgagee or assignee, who had actual or constructive notice of a prior mortgage or assignment at the time when he lent his money, could not gain priority by giving notice first.[3] The head-note to the report of *Dearle* v. *Hall* makes the general position clear :

> "A person having a beneficial interest in a sum of money invested in the names of trustees, assigns it for valuable consideration to A., but no notice of the assignment is given to the trustees ; afterwards, the same person proposes to sell his interest to B., and B., having made inquiry of the trustees as to the nature of the vendor's title, and the amount of his interest, and receiving no intimation of the existence of any prior incumbrance, completes the purchase, and gives the trustees notice : B. has a better equity than A. to the possession of the fund, and the assignment to B., though posterior in date, is to be preferred to the assignment to A."

Thus in equitable mortgages of personalty notice to the trustees supplants order of time as the determining factor in the question of priorities.

Principle
of the rule.

Although the principle upon which *Dearle* v. *Hall* was decided has been obscured by later cases, it would appear to be simply this, that in order to perfect his title a mortgagee of equitable personalty must do that which in equity is the nearest approach to the delivery of a personal chattel.[4] PLUMER, M.R., explained this as follows[5]:—

> "They say, that they were not bound to give notice to the trustees, for that notice does not form part of the necessary conveyance of an equitable interest. I admit, that, if you mean to rely on contract with the individual, you do not need to give notice ; from the moment of the contract, he, with whom you are dealing, is personally bound. But if you mean to go further, and to make your right attach upon the thing which is the subject of the contract, it is necessary to give notice ; and, unless notice is given, you do not do that which is essential in all cases of transfer of personal property. The law of England has always been, that personal property passes by delivery of possession ; and it is possession which determines the apparent ownership. If, therefore, an individual, who in the way of purchase or mortgage contracts

---

[1] *Lee* v. *Howlett* (1856), 2 K. & J. 531 ; *infra*, p. 698.
[2] *Calisher* v. *Forbes* (1871), 7 Ch. App. 109.
[3] *Spencer* v. *Clarke* (1878), 9 Ch. D. 137 ; *Re Holmes* (1885), 29 Ch. D. 786.
[4] *Meux* v. *Bell* (1841), Hare, 73, 85 ; *Foster* v. *Cockerell* (1835), 3 Cl. & Fin. 456, at p. 476 ; but see Lord MACNAGHTEN, *Ward* v. *Duncombe*, [1893] A. C. 369, at pp. 392–3.
[5] *Dearle* v. *Hall* (1823), 3 Russ. 1, at p. 22.

with another for the transfer of his interest, does not divest the vendor or mortgagor of possession, but permits him to remain the ostensible owner as before, he must take the consequences which may ensue from such a mode of dealing."

It is in fact the duty of an assignee or mortgagee to affect the conscience of the trustees, for by doing so he acquires a better equity than a prior mortgagee who has failed to act likewise, and where one of two innocent parties must suffer through the fraud of the mortgagor, it certainly should not be the one who has done all in his power to prevent any fraudulent dealing. But this consideration was lost sight of in later years, and instead of the principle being that priority should depend upon the diligence of the claimants in perfecting their title, it was gradually made dependent upon the bare fact of notice, it being held that it was immaterial whether notice was given with the deliberate intention of completing the title or whether it was purely informal or even accidental.[1] The following will serve to illustrate this fact and, at the same time, to state the main rules that have grown up in the application of *Dearle* v. *Hall*.

Rule extended by judicial interpretation

(*a*) **The Notice may be informal.** It is not necessary, in order to gain priority, that a mortgagee should give express notice to the trustees with the intention of doing all that is possible to perfect his title. In fact it is not necessary that *he* should give notice at all, provided that the trustees have notice. It is enough if he can prove that the mind of the trustee has in some way been brought to an intelligent apprehension of the existence of the incumbrance, so that a reasonable man or an ordinary man of business would regulate his conduct by that knowledge in the execution of the trust.[2] Thus, notice which a trustee obtained from reading a newspaper has been held to be sufficient,[3] and in a later case it was held that where a trustee *before* his appointment acquired knowledge of an incumbrance on the trust estate in such a way that when appointed he would normally act on the information, the priority thereby attached to the incumbrance was not displaced by an express formal notice given after his appointment by another incumbrancer.[4]

Nature of the notice.

(*b*) **Effect of notice not given to *all* the Trustees.** The course which a diligent mortgagee should pursue is to give notice to each trustee, for a failure to do so may cause his postponement to a later mortgagee who has been more careful. The two principles relevant to the situation are,

---

[1] See (1895), 11 *L. Q. R.* 337. (E. C. C. Firth).
[2] *Lloyd* v. *Banks* (1868), L. R. 3 Ch. 488, at p. 490 ; *per* Lord CAIRNS.
[3] *Lloyd* v. *Banks, supra.*
[4] *Ipswich Permanent Money Club, Ltd.* v. *Arthy*, [1920] 2 Ch. 257.

first, that a notice given to one alone of several trustees is effective against later mortgages created while that one trustee remains in office, but is ineffective against mortgages created after he vacates office [1] ; secondly, that a notice to all existing trustees remains effective even after they have vacated office. The result may be appreciated from three examples.

1. A., B. and C. are the trustees. Mortgagee, X., notifies A. only. A later mortgagee, Y. notifies A., B. and C. A. dies.
     X. ranks before Y., for when Y. took his mortgage X.'s notice to A. was still effective. [2]
2. A., B. and C. are the trustees. Mortgagee X. notifies A. only. A. dies. A later mortgagee, Y., notifies B. and C.
     Y. ranks before X., since the effectiveness of X.'s notice ceased with the death of the one person to whom he gave it. [3]
3. A., B. and C. are the trustees. Mortgagee, X., notifies A., B. and C. A., B. and C. retire in favour of D., E. and F., who are not informed of X.'s mortgage. A later mortgagee, Y., notifies D., E. and F.
     X. ranks before Y. [4]

Limits of
rule in
Dearle v.
Hall.

We must finally observe that before 1926 the rule in *Dearle* v. *Hall* was restricted to the assignment of choses in action, of which an equitable interest in pure personalty is an example, and to assignments of such interests in real estate as could reach the hands of the assignor only in the shape of money, as for instance a beneficial interest given to him by a trust for sale. [5] The rule did not apply to mortgages or assignments of equitable interests in *land*, whether freehold or leasehold. Thus in a case where

a testator, having bequeathed a leasehold interest to trustees, charged it with the payment of an annuity of £45 to his daughter, and the daughter mortgaged the annuity first to A. and then to B., it was held that A. had the prior claim against the land, although B. alone had given notice to the trustees. [6]

Having thus reviewed the rules which obtained before the legislation of 1925, we are in a position to examine the existing law governing the priorities between mortgages in general.

(2) PRIORITY OF MORTGAGES AFTER 1925

General
design of
the 1925
legislation
concerning
priority.

Introductory Note. The Law of Property Act 1925 and the Land Charges Act 1925[7] introduced a new system for the determination of priorities. The apparent design of this is to fix

---

[1] *Smith* v. *Smith* (1833), 2 Cr. & M. 231.
[2] *Ward* v. *Duncombe,* [1893] A. C. 369.
[3] *Timson* v. *Ramsbottom* (1837), 2 Keen, 35 ; *Re Phillip's Trusts,* [1903] 1 Ch. 183.
[4] *Re Wasdale,* [1899] 1 Ch. 163.
[5] *Lee* v. *Howlett* (1856), 2 K. & J. 531 ; *Re Wasdale, supra* ; *Ward* v. *Duncombe, supra.*
[6] *Wiltshire* v. *Rabbits* (1844), 14 Sim. 76.
[7] Now replaced by L.C.A. 1972.

the priority of a mortgage according to the time of its creation, provided that the mortgagee has taken steps to render the completion of the transaction easily ascertainable by persons who later have dealings with the mortgagor.[1] There are three ways of doing this which vary with the circumstances.

First, by obtaining possession of the title deeds. This will put a later mortgagee upon inquiry and will normally affect him with notice of the earlier incumbrance.

Secondly, if possession of the deeds is unobtainable and if the property given as security is a *legal* estate, by recording the mortgage, whether legal or equitable, in a public register.

Thirdly, if the property given as security is an *equitable* interest in land or pure personalty, by notifying the mortgage to the owner of the legal interest, thereby putting it on record.

Such is the design in outline, but it is not fully worked out by the Acts and we shall see that certain doubts and complexities remain.

The modern rules vary not with the nature of the mortgage as under the old law, but with the nature of the mortgaged property, and we must therefore consider

Scheme of present account.

first, legal and equitable mortgages of a *legal estate* ; and

secondly, mortgages of an *equitable interest*, whether in land or in personalty.

(A) Priority as between Legal and Equitable Mortgagees of a Legal Estate

We have seen that before 1926 a legal mortgagee who had not been guilty of gross negligence in respect of the title deeds enjoyed priority over the other mortgagees (necessarily equitable) of the same land of which he had no notice. It is obvious that the introduction of the new method of creating mortgages, under which there may be several *legal* mortgages and not one only as before 1926, precluded the retention of the old rule that the legal estate as such gave priority. Some substitute had to be found. The other rule of the pre-1926 law, that equitable mortgages ranked according to the order of their creation, could scarcely be made universally applicable, since it would render it difficult for a mortgagee to ascertain by inquiry the true state of the mortgagor's commitments. The Acts of 1925, therefore, attempted to introduce a new scheme, the *motif* of which apparently was that priorities should depend upon the order of registration,

Why the law was changed by legislation.

---

[1] Waldock, *Law of Mortgages* (2nd Edn.), pp. 409–10.

though whether in the actual result registration is as important as it was intended to be is, perhaps, a little doubtful.

Relevant statutory provisions.

It is necessary to set out the relevant statutory provisions in order that the matter may be viewed in the right perspective.

The Law of Property Act 1925, in section 97, provides as follows :

> " Every mortgage affecting ~ legal estate in land made after the commencement of this Act, v iether legal or equitable (not being a mortgage protected by the deposit of documents relating to the legal estate affected) shall r ..k according to its date of registration as a land charge pursuant to the Land Charges Act, 1925."[1]

Registration of mortgages constitutes notice.

The same statute, in section 198 (1), provides that registration shall constitute notice :

> " The registration of any instrument or matter under the Land Charges Act 1972 or any local land charges register shall be deemed to constitute actual notice of such instrument or matter, and of the fact of such registration, to all persons and for all purposes connected with the land affected, as from the date of registration or other pre-scribed date and so long as the registration continues in force."[2]

What mortgages are registrable.

The Land Charges Act 1972 contains two relevant sections. Section 2[3] specifies the two kinds of mortgages that are regis-trable,[4] namely :

(a) Puisne mortgage.

(a) " Puisne mortgages," *i.e.* a *legal* mortgage which is not protected by a deposit of documents relating to the legal estate affected (Class C (i)).

(b) General equitable charge.

(b) " General equitable charges," *i.e.* any equitable charge which is not secured by a deposit of documents relating to the legal estate affected, does not arise, or affect an interest arising, under a trust for sale or a settlement, and is not included in any other class of land charge (Class C (iii)).

Effect of non-regis-tration.

The Land Charges Act 1972 finally states what the effect shall be of a failure to register.   Section 4 (5)[4] provides that a Class C land charge created or arising after 1925 shall :—

> " be void as against a purchaser of the land charged with it, or of any interest in such land, unless the land charge is registered in the appropriate register before the completion of the purchase."

Section 17 (1) defines " purchaser " as

> " any person (including a mortgagee or lessee) who, for valuable consideration, takes any interest in land or in a charge on land."

Priority notice.

A mortgagee, X., does not pay the amount of the loan until the transaction has been completed by the execution of the deed. There is, therefore, a danger that after he has searched the register another mortgage of the same land may have been registered in favour of Y., the effect of which will be to render X.'s mortgage

---

[1] Or L.C.A. 1972.   See L.C.A. 1972, s. 18 (6).
[2] As amended by Local Land Charges Act 1975, s. 17, Sched. 1.
[3] S. 2 (4), Class C (i), (iii), replacing L.C.A. 1925, s. 10 (1).
[4] For registration of charges created by companies see *infra*, p. 749.
[5] Replacing L.C.A. 1925, s. 13 (2).

at the moment of its completion void against Y. X. is, therefore, allowed to protect himself by registering a *priority notice*, giving notice of his contemplated mortgage.[1]

One outstanding feature, then, of this legislation is that no mortgage, legal or equitable, under which the mortgagee obtains the title deeds, is capable of registration. The principal reason for this exclusion is to avoid the inconvenience that would arise if the efficacy of temporary advances that are so frequently made against a deposit of deeds were to be affected by a failure to register. Section 2, however, provides in the next paragraph that an estate contract shall be registrable as a land charge Class C (iv). An estate contract is a contract by an estate owner to convey or create a legal estate. The normal example is a contract for the sale of a legal fee simple or for the grant of a term of years absolute, but it also includes a contract to create a legal mortgage, *i.e.* to grant a mortgage term. Further, it would seem to include the equitable mortgage that arises from a deposit of title deeds, for as we have already seen the deposit constitutes an implicit agreement to create a legal mortgage. It has therefore been suggested that an express agreement, accompanied by the title deeds, to create a legal mortgage, and a deposit of title deeds by way of security, are registrable as estate contracts, in spite of the fact that because accompanied by the deeds they are excluded from registration by the paragraph which deals specifically with mortgages.[2] It is submitted, however, that the correctness of this view is at least doubtful. If the sub-section which explicitly defines what mortgages shall be registrable deliberately excludes those that are accompanied by a deposit of documents, it seems inconsistent to permit their registration in their other capacity as estate contracts. The result of doing so would be to render void against a subsequent incumbrancer an unregistered mortgage to which the sub-section concerned with mortgages denies the possibility of registration. Moreover, to put this construction upon the statute would prejudice the commercial practice by which deeds are deposited with bankers to secure a temporary loan, for the result of invalidating against later lenders an arrangement that is often only transient would be to discourage a convenient business transaction. The question can scarcely be answered with assurance until it has come before the courts, and meanwhile the following account is based on the assumption that a mortgage accompanied by a deposit of the deeds is not registrable.

A mortgage accompanied by the deeds is not registrable.

---

[1] L.C.A. 1972, s. 11 ; for details, see *infra*, p. 746.

[2] (1940), *C. L. J.*, at pp. 250–1 (R. E. Megarry) ; (1962), 26 *Conv.* (N. S.), pp. 446–449 (R. G. Rowley). Williams, *Contract of Sale of Land*, p. 247 ; Fisher and Lightwood, *Law of Mortgage* (8th Edn.), p. 46 ; Waldock, pp. 425–8.

Priorities where no mortgagee obtains the deed.

The question of priorities seems comparatively simple to determine against the legislative background if we confine ourselves to a series of mortgage transactions *none of which is accompanied by a delivery of the title deeds.* It depends upon a combination of section 97 of the Law of Property Act 1925 and section 4 (5) of the Land Charges Act 1972, but it would appear that the latter is the dominating enactment. The decisive factor, in other words, is that a registrable mortgage is void against a later mortgage unless it is registered before completion of the latter transaction.[1] Suppose that :

A. takes a mortgage without the title deeds on May 1st.
B. takes a mortgage without the title deeds on May 10th.
A. registers on May 11th.
B. registers on May 20th.
C. takes a mortgage without the deeds on May 30th and registers.

The order in which the parties rank, whether their mortgages are legal or equitable, is B.–A.–C., for A.'s mortgage, though created before B.'s was created and registered before B.'s was registered, was nevertheless not registered upon completion of the second mortgage. It is therefore void under section 4 (5) as against B. It is not of course void as against C., since its registration was effected before completion of C.'s mortgage on May 30th. Moreover, by virtue of section 198 (1) of the Law of Property Act, C. has, but B. has not, statutory notice of A.'s mortgage.

Priority of registration not in itself sufficient.

It is arguable that in accordance with section 97 of the Law of Property Act A. should rank before B. since he was the first to register, but it is difficult to agree that a void charge can be revivified and given precedence over the very charge in relation to which its invalidity has been declared by statute. There can be no renascence of what is void. One of the main objects of registration is to enable a mortgagee to discover the state of the mortgagor's title, but if he is to be displaced by a registration effected after it has been certified to him by the Registrar that no prior charge stands in his way, the object will certainly be frustrated.[2] The truth appears to be that there was a lack of co-ordination in the drafting of this section 97 and section 13 (2) of the Land Charges Act 1925 (now replaced by section 4 (5) of the Land Charges Act 1972).

Subrogation sometimes necessary to determine priorities.

In the example given above priority is not difficult to determine, but this is by no means always true. Suppose, for instance, that, after a mortgage has been granted to X. who takes possession

---

[1] But for another view, see (1950), 13 *M. L. R.*, pp. 534–5 (A. D. Hargreaves).

[2] For a discussion of the question, see (1940), *C. L. J.*, pp. 255–6 (R. E. Megarry).

of the title deeds, further mortgages of the same land are given in the following order :

A puisne mortgage to A. on May 1st to secure £1000.
A general equitable charge to B. on May 10th to secure £1000.
A puisne mortgage to C. on May 20th to secure £2000.

    A. registers on May 11th.
    C. registers on May 20th.
    B.'s charge is not registered.

We know that A.'s mortgage is statutorily void against B., and that B.'s mortgage is void against C., but at first sight it seems impossible to arrange all three claimants in order of priority. An objection can be raised to every possible permutation. For instance, the order is not A.–B.–C., for though A. ranks before C. he must be postponed to B. ; neither is it B.–A.–C., for C. is to be preferred to B. though not to A. ; neither is it A.–C.–B., since A. must rank after B. If such a case were to arise the court would presumably be driven to base its decision upon the doctrine of subrogation.[1] Subrogation is the process by which one creditor is substituted for another creditor when both have claims against the same debtor.[2] The relevant factors in its application to the present example are that:

    B. ranks before A.,
    A. ranks before C., and
    C. ranks before B.,

so that any starting point is as arbitrary as any other in this *circulus inextricabilis*. But a solution may be found by transferring to C. the right of B. to be paid £1000 before A. C. is subrogated to B., *but only to the extent to which B. has priority over A.* The actual order of payment will therefore be as follows :

    (i) C. is entitled to a first payment of £1000.

This is the £1000 that is due to B. in priority to A.

    (ii) A. is entitled to the next payment of £1000.

Theoretically, at any rate, A. suffers no injury. His claim is not sustainable until £1000 has been paid out of the land, and it is no concern of his whether that sum is paid to B. or to C.

    (iii) C. is entitled to the next payment of £1000.

This represents the remainder of C's. advance, the whole of which is payable before that of B.

    (iv) B. is entitled to £1000 if the proceeds arising from the sale of the land are sufficient.

---

[1] *Benham* v. *Keane* (1861), 1 John. & H. 685, at pp. 710–12 ; *Re Wyatt*, [1892] 1 Ch. 188, at pp. 208–9 ; M. & B. p. 667 ; *cf. Re Weniger's Policy*, [1910] 2 Ch. 291.
[2] White and Tudor's *Leading Cases in Equity* (9th Edn.), vol. i. pp. 147 *et seq.*

If the sums advanced were £1000 by A., £1000 by B. and £600 by C., the order would be this :

> (i) C. : £600.
> (ii) B. : £400.
> (iii) A. : £1000.
> (iv) B. : £600.[1]

Subrogation scarcely provides a satisfactory solution.

However, it cannot be said that the doctrine of subrogation provides more than a rough and ready method of solving the difficulty. It cannot escape the criticism of being arbitrary, for it is not obvious why the subrogation should begin with one claimant rather than with another. In the example just given the process might equally well start with B. rather than with C. Neither is the justice of the solution obvious. In the first example, B. gets nothing until £2000 has been paid to C. and £1000 to A., and yet he has a prior right to A.

Where the value of the land is insufficient to satisfy all the mortgages in full, it might be more just to admit the inextricable circle and to decree a payment *pari passu*, *i.e.*, a division of the proceeds among the various claimants in proportion to the respective amounts of their advances.

Priorities where one mortgage protected by the deeds.

We must now consider the question of priorities where one of the competing mortgages is accompanied by the title deeds, which is, of course, the usual case. The chief problem here is : What is the significance of excluding such a mortgage from the list of registrable incumbrances ? Is the implication that in all cases a person who obtains possession of the deeds ranks first ? Presumably not, for it must never be forgotten that the governing principles which obtained under the old law were not expressly altered by the legislation of 1925. These principles were that:

A legal was preferred to an equitable mortgage ; mortgages ranked in the order of their creation, subject to the preference given to the legal mortgage ; but either of these principles might be displaced by negligent conduct with reference to the deeds.

---

[1] A similar problem may arise under *Dearle* v. *Hall* (*supra*, p. 695). See, for instance, the illustration given by Fry, L.J., in *Re Wyatt*, [1892] 1 Ch. at pp. 208–9 ; M. & B. p. 662. There are two trustees of a fund, X. and Y. The first incumbrancer, A., notifies X. only ; the second incumbrancer, B., notifies X. and Y. ; X. then dies and the third incumbrancer, C., notifies the surviving trustee, Y. Here A. ranks before B. (*Ward* v. *Duncombe, supra*, p. 698) ; B. before C. (*ibid.*) ; C. before A., for A.'s notice is nullified as against incumbrances created after X.'s death (*Timson* v. *Ramsbottom, supra*, p. 698). Therefore, says Fry, L.J. : "The fund would be distributed as follows : First, to the third incumbrancer to the extent of the claim of the first. Secondly, to the second incumbrancer. Thirdly, to the third incumbrancer to the extent to which he might remain unpaid after the money he had received whilst standing in the shoes of the first incumbrancer ; see *Benham* v. *Keane* (1861), 1 John. & H. 685, where a similar problem was similarly solved." See generally (1968) 32 Conv. (N.S.) 325 (W. A. Lee) ; 71 Yale L. J. 53 (G. Gilmore).

The pre-1926 law, therefore, cannot be ignored altogether, though obviously its application is materially affected by the introduction of the system of registration. Another difficulty is the uncertainty of the statutory expression "protected by a deposit of documents," for a mortgagee may be entitled to this protection if he receives only some of the deeds relating to the legal estate, honestly and reasonably believing that he has received all.[1] Thus a contest may arise between two mortgagees, both of whom are protected by a deposit of documents and neither of whom, because of the deposit, has registered his incumbrance.[2]

The following account of the general question is based upon two hypothetical cases, first, that the mortgage with the deposit of deeds comes first in order of date, secondly that it comes later.[3]

(a) First mortgagee acquires the deeds.

Let us suppose that :

A. takes a mortgage protected by the title deeds ;
B. takes a later mortgage, necessarily without the deeds.

Example of a mortgage by deposit followed by second mortgage.

We require to ascertain whether the order is A.–B., but to do this it is necessary, having regard to the principles of the pre-1926 law which are still to a large extent relevant, to consider the problem according as the parties obtain legal or equitable mortgages.

(i) *A.'s mortgage is legal, B.'s is equitable*

Under the pre-1926 law, as we have seen,[4] the rule in such a case as this was that, by force of the legal estate and also by virtue of the maxim *qui prior est tempore potior est jure*, A. ranked first, unless his subsequent negligence with regard to the deeds, as for instance by handing them back to the mortgagor, justified his postponement to B. These rules of the pre-1926 law, which specify the limits within which conduct with regard to deeds causes loss of priority, still hold good, for section 13 of the Law of Property Act 1925 provides that :

First mortgage legal, second equitable.

"This Act shall not prejudicially affect the right or interest of any person arising out of or consequent on the possession by him of any documents relating to a legal estate in land, nor affect any question arising out of or consequent upon any omission to obtain or any other absence of possession by any person of any documents relating to a legal estate in land."

---

[1] *Ratcliffe* v. *Barnard* (1871), 6 Ch. App. 652 ; *Dixon* v. *Muckleston* (1872), 8 Ch. App. 155.

[2] For a discussion of this particular case, see (1940), *C. L. J.*, pp. 249–2 53 (R. E. Megarry).

[3] See the valuable series of articles in (1933), 76 *L. J. News*, pp. 83–4, 95, 106–7, 122–3, 131–3 R. L. Bignell and C. H. H. Wilss.

[4] *Supra*, pp. 687 *et seq.*

Presuming that this section is linked to the Land Charges Act by section 97 quoted above,[1] it seems clear that the ranking of A. and B. still depends upon precisely the same considerations as before 1926.   A. will rank first unless his fraud or subsequent negligence justifies his postponement.

(ii) *The mortgages both of A and of B are legal*

Both mort-
gages legal.

The position could not arise before 1926, when only one legal mortgage of the fee simple was possible.   There seems no doubt, however, that A. ranks first, since he has the earlier legal estate and also possession of the deeds, though of course if he negligently parts with the deeds and thereby causes the deception of B., he may as in the last case lose his priority.

(iii) *A.'s mortgage is equitable, B.'s is legal*

First mort-
gage equit-
able, second
legal.

This position arises, for instance, where a mortgage by deposit of deeds is made to A., and later a legal charge is granted to B. Before 1926, B., as the holder of the legal estate, ranked first, unless he had failed to inquire for the deeds or had rested content with an unreasonable excuse for their non-production, or unless he had notice of A.'s equitable mortgage at the time when he took his own.   The question now arises—what constitutes notice of A.'s mortgage?   Certainly not registration, for a mortgagee with the deeds cannot register.   The answer is contained in section 199 (1) (ii) of the Law of Property Act 1925.   It provides that a purchaser, including a mortgagee,[2] shall not be prejudicially affected by notice of any instrument or matter which is incapable of registration under the Land Charges Act unless :

What con-
stitutes
notice of
non-regis-
trable
mortgage.

" (*a*) it is within his own knowledge, or would have come to his knowledge if such inquiries and inspections had been made as ought reasonably to have been made by him ; or

(*b*) in the same transaction with respect to which a question of notice to the purchaser arises, it has come to the knowledge of his counsel, as such, or of his solicitor or other agent, as such, or would have come to the knowledge of his solicitor or other agent, as such, if such inquiries and inspections had been made as ought reasonably to have been made by the solicitor or other agent."

In other words, the old doctrine of actual or constructive notice is still in force with regard to mortgages that are incapable of registration.   Again, there is nothing in the legislation of 1925 which deprives the owner of the legal estate of that pre-eminent position which he has always enjoyed.

It would seem, therefore, that in the majority of circumstances B. will rank second, for he will have actual notice of A.'s mortgage

---

[1] *Supra*, p. 700, *sed quaere.*
[2] L.P.A. 1925, s. 205 (1) (xxi).

if he inquires for the deeds, and constructive notice if he makes no inquiry. Presumably, however, a case like *Hewitt* v. *Loosemore* [1] would still be decided as it was before 1926.

(iv) *The mortgages both of A. and of B. are equitable*

In this case there has been a deposit of the deeds with A. followed by a general equitable charge in favour of B. When there was a contest under the pre-1926 law between equitable incumbrancers, it was the maxim *qui prior est tempore potior est jure* that prevailed. In the circumstances that we are now considering A. would have ranked first, unless, by a voluntary redelivery of the deeds to the mortgagor, he had negligently allowed a fraud to be perpetrated on B.[2] There is nothing in the modern legislation to upset the old law, and there is little doubt that the maxim *qui prior est tempore potior est jure* is still applicable.[3]

Both mortgages equitable.

(b) First mortgagee does not acquire the deeds.

Let us suppose that the following transactions occur :

    A. takes a puisne mortgage.
    B. takes a later mortgage, either legal or equitable, and also obtains possession of the deeds.

Example of mortgage without deeds followed by mortgage with deeds.

It is perfectly clear that if A. has registered his mortgage before the completion of B.'s, he will rank first, since section 97 of the Law of Property Act provides that his mortgage shall rank according to its date of registration, and furthermore section 198 provides that registration under the Land Charges Act shall constitute notice to all persons and for all purposes connected with the land affected. If, however, it was due to A.'s gross negligence that he failed to obtain the deeds, it is conceivable, but scarcely probable, that despite registration he might, by virtue of section 13 of the Law of Property Act 1925,[4] be postponed to B. in accordance with the principles of the old law.[5]

Where the first mortgage is legal.

It seems equally clear that if A. has failed to register his mortgage before the transaction with B. is completed, he will in all circumstances be postponed to B. This follows from the enactment that a registrable mortgage shall be void against a purchaser of the land charged, unless it is registered before completion of the purchase.[6] It may be argued, however, that, if A. inquired for the deeds in the first place and received a reasonable excuse for their non-delivery, his legal estate, as under the old law,

---

[1] *Supra*, p. 690   [2] *Supra*, p. 692.
[3] *Cf. Beddoes* v. *Shaw*, [1937] 1 Ch. 81 ; [1936] 2 All E. R. 1108.
[4] *Supra*, p. 705.
[5] (1940), *C. L. J.*, p. 259 (R. E. Megarry).
[6] L.C.A. 1972, s. 4 (5).

will still give him priority by virtue of section 13 of the Law of Property Act.[1]

This seems doubtful. Not only is the mortgage rendered absolutely void against B., but it may also be said that A. has been negligent in not taking advantage of the protection that registration would have afforded him.

Where the first mortgage is equitable.

If the facts are altered slightly and we suppose that

A. takes a general equitable charge, and
B. takes a mortgage, either legal or equitable, also obtaining possession of the deeds,

it would seem that the same result ensues. If the charge is registered, A. ranks first, otherwise B. will be preferred.

Partial abolition of tacking.

Tacking. The doctrine of tacking has been materially affected by the Law of Property Act 1925.[2] One branch of that doctrine has been abolished, the other has been retained. The first branch, which under the pre-1926 law[3] comprised the right of a later mortgagee to buy in the legal estate from the first incumbrancer and to squeeze out an intermediate mortgage, has been abolished.[4] The second branch has been retained, for it is important that a mortgagee should be at liberty to tack further advances to his first loan. In fact, the preservation of this right is essential where a bank takes a mortgage from a client as security for his current account, since a further advance is made whenever his cheque is honoured. It is therefore enacted that in certain cases, which will be given in a moment,

Further advances may be tacked.

" a prior mortgagee shall have a right to make further advances to rank in priority to subsequent mortgages (whether legal or equitable)."[5]

Circumstances in which further advances may be tacked.

It will be noticed that this enactment does not confine the right to the first mortgagee or to a legal mortgagee, but grants it to any " prior " mortgagee, legal or equitable, against every later mortgagee. But it is only in the three following cases that the right may be exercised :

(*a*) **When Later Mortgagees agree.**[6] This is an obvious and not an unusual case. After mortgages of Blackacre have been granted to A., B. and C., the mortgagor may seek a further advance from B. on the same security. B. will

---

[1] *Supra*, pp. 688–91.   (1926), 61 *L. J. News*, 398 (J. M. Lightwood), cited and considered, (1933), 76 *L. J. News*, at p. 132.
[2] S. 94.   See (1958) 22 Conv. (N.S.) 44 (R. G. Rowley).
[3] *Supra*, p. 693.
[4] L.P.A. 1925, s. 94 (3).
[5] *Ibid.* s. 94 (1).
[6] L.P.A. 1925, s. 94 (1) (*a*).

rank for payment of both his loans before C. if he makes an arrangement to that effect with C. before advancing further money. C. is not likely to agree unless the land is sufficient cover for all the money with which it is charged.

(b) When there is no Notice of Later Mortgages.[1]

A mortgagee who has no notice of subsequent mortgages at the time when he makes his further advances may claim priority for both his loans over subsequent mortgagees. This is the same rule as applied before 1926,[2] with this important difference, however, that registration of a later mortgage as a land charge is deemed to constitute *actual* notice of that mortgage.[3] A mortgagee therefore who contemplates a further advance should not make it until he has ascertained by a search at the Land Registry that no later mortgages have been made.

There is, however, an important exception to this rule that the mere registration of a mortgage will prevent a prior mortgagee from tacking later advances. It is enacted that in the case of a mortgage made expressly for securing, | Two cases in which registration is not notice.

(a) a current account, or
(b) other further advances,

the mere registration of a subsequent mortgage shall not constitute notice sufficient to deprive the earlier mortgagee of his right to tack. In those two cases the rule is that :

> " A mortgagee shall not be deemed to have notice of a mortgage merely by reason that it was registered as a land charge, if it was not so registered at the time when the original mortgage was created or when the last search (if any) by or on behalf of the mortgagee was made, whichever last happened."[4]

Thus registration of a subsequent mortgage constitutes actual notice of that mortgage to a prior incumbrancer and necessarily displaces his right to tack, except where the prior mortgage was taken not merely as security for the original loan, but as security either for the original loan and further advances or for a current account. In either of these cases registration will be notice only if it was in being when the prior mortgage was created (which might of course be before any money was actually advanced by the prior mortgagee, as often happens where a current account is secured), or when the prior mortgagee last made a search at the Land Registry. Failing registration at one of these dates a prior mortgagee will not be deprived of the right to tack unless,

---

[1] L. P. A. 1925, s. 94 (1) (b).   [2] *Supra*, p. 694.
[3] L.P.A. 1925, s. 198 (1), as amended by Local Land Charges Act 1975, s. 17, Sched. 1.
[4] *Ibid.*, s. 94 (2), as amended by L.P.(A.)A. 1926, Sched.

at the time of the further advance, he had notice, in the old sense of actual or constructive notice, of the later mortgage.

This exception to the rule that registration is equivalent to actual notice has been made in the interest of bankers, for were the rule unqualified it would be impracticable to take a mortgage as security for a current account. An illustration will make this clear.

> If A. mortgages his land to a bank in order to secure an overdraft which at the time of the mortgage is £3000, and if he subsequently grants a mortgage of the same land to B., notice of which is given to the bank, the rule as laid down in *Hopkinson* v. *Rolt* [1] is that the bank obtains priority only for the amount due from the mortgagor at the time when the second mortgage to B. was made. If the overdraft at that moment is £4000, then £4000 is the amount with which the land is charged in favour of the bank. When, moreover, A. from time to time pays sums into his account, and the overdraft is thus reduced below £4000, only the reduced amount is recoverable under the mortgage;[2] and although, after notice of the second mortgage, the actual overdraft may be increased as a result of drawings out, the payments or further advances by the bank in respect of these drawings cannot be tacked to the loan as it stood at the time when notice of the second mortgage was received.[3] To fix the mortgage at £4000 is equitable if the bank has actual notice of the second mortgage, but it would make this side of banking business impossible if mere registration constituted notice, for it would be unsafe to honour the customer's cheques unless on each occasion a search were made at the Land Registry.

Two practical results emerge from this legislation. First, a mortgage will generally provide expressly that the land shall be security for further advances, since this will enable a further advance to be made without a search at the Land Registry; secondly, a mortgagee who searches and discovers the existence of a prior mortgage expressly made to secure a current account or further advances will be careful to notify his mortgage to the prior mortgagee.

(c) When the Mortgage imposes an *Obligation* on the Mortgagee to make Further Advances.

When the provision in the prior mortgage is not that the land shall be security for any further advances which *may* be made, as in the case (*b*) just considered, but that the mortgagee shall be bound to make further advances if called upon to do so, the new rule is [4] that the doctrine of tacking shall apply to such advances notwithstanding the fact that at the time of making them the prior mortgagee had notice of a later mortgage.

---

[1] (1861), 9 H. L. C. 514 ; *supra*, p. 695.
[2] *Clayton's Case* (1816), 1 Mer. 572.
[3] *Deeley* v. *Lloyds Bank*, [1910] 1 Ch. 648 ; [1912] A. C. 756.
[4] L.P.A. 1925, s. 94 (1) (*c*).

The law as laid down in *West* v. *Williams* [1] is therefore reversed.

(B) PRIORITY AS BETWEEN MORTGAGEES OF AN EQUITABLE INTEREST IN LAND OR PERSONALTY

We have already seen that under the old law the priority as between mortgagees of an equitable interest in pure personalty depended, in accordance with the rule in *Dearle* v. *Hall*, upon the order in which the trustees had received notice from the mortgagees, but that this principle did not apply to mortgages of freeholds or of leaseholds.[2] The innovation made by the 1925 legislation is the extension of the rule in *Dearle* v. *Hall* to mortgages of *all* equitable interests, realty being put on the same footing as personalty. This assimilation is accomplished by the following enactment [3] :

> " The law applicable to dealings with equitable things in action which regulates the priority of competing interests therein, shall, as respects dealings with equitable interests in land, capital money, and securities representing capital money effected after the commencement of this Act, apply to and regulate the priority of competing interests therein."

Statutory extension of Dearle v. Hall.

This extension of the rule to all mortgages and assignments of equitable interests in freeholds and leaseholds is of especial importance owing to the increased number of interests that are necessarily equitable since 1925. Thus, the purchaser or mortgagee of an interest arising under a strict settlement, such as a life interest, an entailed interest or any species of future interest, must protect himself by giving the necessary notice. In effect the priority of mortgages of equitable beneficial interests under strict settlements and trusts for sale is now determined by the same rule.

The rules that existed before 1926 with regard to the nature of the notice still hold good,[4] subject to one exception. This is that a notice given otherwise than in writing in respect of any dealing with an equitable interest in real or personal property shall not affect the priority of competing claims of purchasers or mortgagees.[5]

New rules regarding notice.

The Law of Property Act 1925 contains the following rules with regard to the persons upon whom the written notice must be served :

Persons to whom notice must be given.

(1) Where the equitable interest is in settled land or capital money.[6]

Where dealings take place with such an interest, notice must be given to the *trustees of the settlement*. If the

---

[1] [1899] 1 Ch. 132 ; *supra*, p. 695.
[2] *Supra*, pp. 696; 698.
[3] L.P.A. 1925, s. 137 (1).
[4] *Supra*, pp. 697–8.
[5] L.P.A. 1925, s. 137 (3).
[6] *Ibid.*, s. 137 (2) (i).

interest in question has been created by a derivative settlement (*i.e.* one by which an interest already settled is re-settled), then notice must be given to the trustees of the derivative settlement.

(2) Where the equitable interest is in land held on trust for sale.

In this case notice must be given to the *trustees* for sale.[1]

(3) Where the equitable interest is neither (1) nor (2).[2]

If, for instance, the subject of the transaction is a life annuity charged on land by a tenant in fee simple, it is provided that notice shall be given to the *estate owner*.

It will be remembered that certain complexities had arisen under the old law with regard to a notice served on a single trustee.[3] The proper course, which, however, is not always adopted, is to serve the notice on each of the trustees and to take a receipt from each, and it is perhaps regrettable that the Act has not made this practice compulsory. No statutory direction has, however, been given, and it therefore appears that in this regard the old decisions continue to represent the law.[4]

To meet any difficulty that may arise in identifying the appropriate person to receive notice, the Act provides that where

Notice by way of endorsed memorandum.

(*a*) the trustees are not persons to whom a valid notice can be given ; or

(*b*) there are no trustees ; or

(*c*) for any other reason a valid notice cannot be served, or cannot be served without unreasonable cost or delay,

the assignee may require that a memorandum of the transaction be endorsed on, or permanently annexed to, the instrument which creates the trust.[5] Such a memorandum, as respects priorities, operates in like manner as if a written notice had been given to trustees. Thus if the land in which the equitable interest exists is subject to a strict settlement, the memorandum will be annexed to the trust instrument ; if it is land belonging to an owner who has died intestate, the memorandum will be annexed to the letters of administration. The objection to a memorandum of this nature is that trust instruments may become overladen with endorsements of charges and assignments. Therefore an alternative method of registering a notice has been provided.[6] It is provided that a settlor when drafting a settlement, or the court at a later date, may nominate a trust corporation to whom notice of dealings affecting real or personal property may be given. Where such a nomination has been made, notice of any dealings

Notice to nominated trust corporation.

---

[1] L.P.A. 1925, s. 137 (2) (ii).
[2] *Ibid.*, s. 137 (2) (iii).   [3] *Supra*, p. 698.
[4] See (1925), 60 *L. J. News* 264 (J. M. Lightwood) ; Wolstenholme and Cherry (13th Edn.), vol. 1, p. 246.
[5] L.P.A. 1925, s. 137 (4).   [6] *Ibid.*, s. 138.

with the equitable interest must be given to the trust corporation, and if given to the trustees must be transmitted by them to the corporation. A notice which is not received by the corporation has no effect on priorities.

The object of the rule in *Dearle* v. *Hall* is to enable a person to discover by inquiries addressed to the trustees whether the owner of an equitable interest has created any earlier incumbrances. But this object was not always attained under the old law, for since, in the language of LINDLEY, L.J., " it is no part of the duty of a trustee to assist his *cestui que trust* in selling or mortgaging his beneficial interest and in squandering or anticipating his fortune,"[1] it was held that a trustee owed no greater duty to a person who was proposing to deal with a *cestui que trust*.[2]

Right to production of notice.

Thus a trustee might refuse to answer inquiries, and even if he gave an answer that contained wrong information, he was not liable for the consequences unless he had been guilty of fraud or had made such a clear and categorical statement that he was estopped from denying its truth.[3] A prospective assignee, however, is given at least this advantage by the Act, that he may demand production of any written notice that has been served on the trustees or their predecessors.[4]

SECTION VI. REGISTERED LAND

A mortgage of registered land[5] may be created (i) by registered charge (ii) by unregistered mortgage and (iii) by deposit of the land or charge certificate.

(i) A registered charge is a legal interest which must be created by deed. It may be made by a charge by way of legal mortgage, or it may contain, in the case of freehold land, an express demise, and, in the case of leasehold land, an express sub-demise.[6] Otherwise, it will, subject to any contrary provision in the charge,[7] take effect as a charge by way of legal mortgage.[8] In registered land it is not necessary to use the words " by way of legal mortgage " in order to create a legal charge.[9] The land must be described by reference to the register or in some other way that will enable the land to be identified without reference

Registered charge.

---

[1] *Low* v. *Bouverie*, [1891] 3 Ch. 82, at p. 99.
[2] *Burrows* v. *Lock* (1805), 10 Ves. 470.   [3] *Ibid.*
[4] L.P.A. 1925, s. 137 (8).
[5] See generally Ruoff and Roper, chap. 25 ; Fisher and Lightwood, *Law of Mortgage* (8th Edn.), chap. 3 ; Barnsley, *Conveyancing Law and Practice*, pp. 418–23.
[6] L.R.A. 1925, ss. 27 (1), (2).
[7] *Ibid.*, s. 27 (1).
[8] *Ibid.*, s. 25. An equitable charge is not registrable under this section. *Re White Rose Cottage*, [1965] Ch. 940, at p. 949, *per* Lord DENNING, M.R.
[9] *Cityland and Property (Holdings), Ltd.* v. *Dabrah*, [1968] Ch. 166 ; [1967] 2 All E. R. 639.

to any other document.   A registered charge must not refer to any other interest or charge which (a) would have priority over it and is not registered or protected in the register and (b) is not an overriding interest.

The charge is completed by the registrar entering on the charges register the chargee as proprietor of the charge.[1]   A legal estate does not arise until the charge is registered.[2]   A charge certificate is then issued to the chargee, the land certificate being deposited at the registry until the charge is cancelled.[3]

Power of chargee.

Subject to any entry on the register or provision in the charge to the contrary, the proprietor of a charge has all the powers conferred by law on the owner of a legal mortgage.[4]   Thus he may enter into possession, foreclose and sell.   Upon foreclosure the proprietor of the charge is registered as proprietor of the land, and the charge and all incumbrances and entries inferior to it are cancelled.   In the same way, a sale will be completed by registration which will transfer the legal estate to the purchaser, once again cancelling the charge and all incumbrances and entries inferior to it.   It appears that a right to consolidate may be reserved as in the case of unregistered land.[5]

Covenants are implied, subject to any entry on the register or provision in the charge to the contrary, on the part of the proprietor of the land to pay principal and interest and, where the charge is created on a leasehold, to pay rent, observe covenants and conditions and to indemnify the proprietor of the charge.[6]

Priorities of charges.

Registered charges rank for priority according to the order in which they are entered on the register, not according to the order in which they are created, unless an entry on the register or a provision in the charge provides otherwise.[7]   As regards tacking, section 94 of the Law of Property Act 1925 does not apply to

Tacking.

registered land.[8]   Tacking is only possible (a) if the registered proprietor is under an obligation to make further advances or (b) where a registered charge is made for securing further advances. In this case the Registrar must, before making any entry in the register which would prejudicially affect the priority of any further advances, give notice by registered post to the proprietor of the charge, who may tack any advances made by him up to the time when he receives or ought to have received the notice in due course of post.[9]   In case (a) any subsequent registered charge takes

---

[1] L.R.A. 1925, s. 26 (1).
[2] *Grace Rymer Investments, Ltd.* v. *Waite*, [1958] Ch. 831 ; [1958] 2 All E. R. 777; M. & B. p. 673.
[3] L.R.A. 1925, ss. 63, 65 ; L.R.R. 1925, r. 262.
[4] *Ibid.*, s. 34 ; L.R.R. 1925, r. 140.
[5] Ruoff and Roper, pp. 549–52.
[6] L.R.A. 1925, s. 28 ; L.R.R. 1925, r. 140.
[7] *Ibid.*, s. 29 ; L.R.R. 1925, r. 140.   Priority of certain statutory charges may depend on the order of creation *e.g.* Housing Act 1957, s. 15 (1).
[8] *Supra*, p. 709.
[9] L.R.A. 1925, s. 30 (1) (3), added by L.P.(A.)A. 1926, s. 5.

effect subject to any further advance made pursuant to the obligation.

The discharge of a registered charge can only be effected by notification of the cessation of the charge on the register.[1] The provisions of the Law of Property Act 1925 relating to the discharge of a mortgage of unregistered land do not apply to registered land.[2] There is a prescribed form of discharge, but the Registrar may accept any other proof of satisfaction of a charge which he deems sufficient.[3]

Discharge.

(ii) A proprietor of registered land may mortgage the land in the same way as if it were unregistered, and the mortgage so created may be protected by a " mortgage caution " in the proprietorship register.[4] This form of mortgage is very rarely employed, for it has no advantages over the registered charge and several disadvantages.[5]

Unregistered mortgage.

Puisne mortgages and general equitable charges which in unregistered land are capable of registration as land charges under the Land Charges Act 1972,[6] may be protected by notice under section 49 of the Land Registration Act 1925, if the land certificate can be produced,[7] or is on deposit at the Land Registry.[8]

(iii) The proprietor of registered land or of a registered charge may create a lien by deposit of the land or charge certificate respectively.[9] The lien is similar to a mortgage by deposit of title deeds of unregistered land, and takes effect subject to overriding interests, registered interests and any entries then upon the register. The mortgagee by deposit should give written notice of the deposit to the Registrar, who will enter on the charges register a notice that will operate as a caution.[10] Notices of deposit are often used, especially by banks. The protection they give is threefold ; the depositee being in possession of the land certificate can prevent any dealing for which its production is required ; purchasers will have notice of the depositee's rights, and the notice

Deposit of land or charge certificate.

---

[1] L.R.A. 1925, s. 35 ; L.R.R. 1925, rr. 151, 267.
[2] L.P.A. 1925, s. 115 (10) ; *supra*, p. 663.
[3] L.R.R. 1925, r. 151.
[4] L.R.A. 1925, s. 106 ; L.R.R. 1925, r. 223.
[5] See Ruoff and Roper, pp. 193, 554 ; Curtis and Ruoff, *Registered Conveyancing* (2nd Edn.), pp. 592–6. [6] *Supra*, p. 700.
[7] L.R.A. 1925, ss. 64, 65. An ordinary caution against dealings may also be lodged to protect any charge when the land certificate cannot be produced or is not on deposit at the Land Registry. A caution gives scant protection ; see L.R.A. 1925, ss. 53–6.
[8] It may also have been deposited because of the existence of a prior registered charge.
[9] L.R.A. 1925, s. 66 ; *Re White Rose Cottage*, [1965] Ch. 490 ; [1965] 1 All E. R. 11 ; M. & B. p. 129 (equitable mortgage protected by notice of deposit has priority to subsequent equitable charge protected by caution). See (1966), C. L. P. 26 (E. C. Ryder). See also *Barclays Bank, Ltd.* v. *Taylor*, [1974] Ch. 137 ; [1973] 1 All E. R. 752.
[10] L.R.R. 1925, r. 239. A lien may also be created by giving a notice of intention to deposit. L.R.R. 1925, rr. 240, 241.

operates as a caution.[1]   It would appear, however, that the deposit of the land certificate alone is sufficient to give notice to a purchaser.[2]   Nevertheless, registration of a notice of deposit would provide greater protection.

Lodging of cautions and inhibitions governs priority of equitable interests.

Priority of mortgages of equitable interests.   It will be recalled that, in unregistered land, priorities of mortgages or assignments of equitable interests are governed by the rule in *Dearle* v. *Hall* as extended by the Law of Property Act 1925.[3] In registered land, such priorities are in some cases governed by special rules and not by the receipt of notice by trustees.   A mortgagee or other assignee of certain equitable interests may lodge a " priority inhibition " (used in the case of an absolute assignment) or a " priority caution " (used in all other cases). Priorities between assignees and incumbrancers of such interests are determined by the order in which these inhibitions and cautions are lodged.   They are entered in the " Minor Interests Index," a misleading name, for it is not a register of minor interests at all but a register of " dealings with minor interests, which do not affect the powers of disposition of the proprietor."[4]

The Minor Interests Index is of very little importance.[5]   It suffices to state here that it is a completely separate entity from the register of title and is of no concern to a person dealing with the legal estate in the land or charge concerned ; and further it is applicable solely to priorities between assignees and incumbrancers of life interests, remainders, reversions and executory interests in registered land held under a settlement or trust for sale or in a debt secured by a registered charge.

An entry on the Index takes the place of notice to the trustees under the rule in *Dearle* v. *Hall*, or, in the absence of trustees, of an endorsed memorandum under section 137 of the Law of Property Act 1925, or of notice to a trust corporation nominated under section 138.[6]   The latter section applies as though the Registrar were so nominated.[7]   But a priority caution or inhibition once lodged differs in an important respect from notice given to trustees in the case of unregistered land, for a mortgagee who protects himself by an entry will obtain priority over an earlier unprotected mortgage, even if he knows of its existence.

---

[1] *Infra*, p. 781.
[2] *Barclays Bank, Ltd.* v. *Taylor, supra*.
[3] Ss. 137, 138, *supra*, pp. 711 *et seq*.
[4] L.R.R.1925, r. 11 (1).   See L.R.A. 1925, s. 102; L.R.R. 1925, r. 229.
[5] See Ruoff and Roper, pp. 135-9.   Law Commission Working Paper No. 37 (1971) Part C recommends the abolition of the Index.   Only 17 inspections were made between 1959 and 1970.
[6] *Supra*, pp. 711-3.
[7] L.R.R. 1925, r. 229 (5).

SECTION VII. TYPES OF MORTGAGE

Finally, we must notice in broad outline two special types of mortgage.

(1) BUILDING SOCIETY MORTGAGES[1]

Building societies are a special kind of mortgagee and have for many years been the main source of finance for the purchase of houses in owner-occupation.   They are societies formed for raising, by the subscription of the members, a fund for making advances to members out of the funds of the society upon security by way of mortgage of land.[2]   The principal Act regulating such societies is the Building Societies Act 1962.   The general method of operation is to borrow money from the general public at interest and then to lend that money at interest by making advances to house purchasers on the security of their houses.   The mortgage is usually an instalment mortgage, that is to say, it is paid off by monthly payments at a rate which covers payment of interest and repayment of capital, so that the capital is paid off over an agreed period of time, for example, thirty years.

The general law of mortgage applies to these transactions. The main difference between a building society mortgage and any other is that the mortgagor is a member of a society, and, accordingly, the rules of the society will be incorporated in the mortgage. The rules usually require the mortgagor to obey the rules of the society and reserve the right to increase the rate of interest after giving notice to the mortgagor.   Another important difference is that there are statutory limits on the lending powers of a building society.   It may not advance money by way of second mortgage, unless the prior mortgage is in favour of the society.[3]   And the right of a society to lend members more than £20,000 is restricted.[4]

Finally, we have already noticed that a building society, when selling as a mortgagee, must take reasonable care to ensure that the price is the best price which can reasonably be obtained.[5]

---

[1] See Wurtzburg and Mills, *Building Society Law* (13th Edn. 1970) ; Waldock, chap. 4 ; Fisher and Lightwood, pp. 157–61 ; (1974) 118 Sol. Jo. 744, 768, 785, 803, 841 ; (1975) 125 N. L. J. 1149 (W. A. Greene).

[2] Building Societies Act 1962, s. 1 (1).   The primary object is to assist the members in obtaining a small freehold or leasehold property.   See preamble to Building Societies Act 1836.

[3] *Ibid.*, s. 32.

[4] *Ibid.*, ss. 21, 22.   Building Societies (Special Advances) Order 1975 (S.I. 1975 No. 1205).

[5] *Ibid.*, s. 36 ; *supra*, p. 673, n. 5.

(2) CONSUMER CREDIT AGREEMENTS

The Consumer Credit Act 1974[1] establishes a comprehensive code which regulates the supply of credit not exceeding £5,000 to an individual.[2]   It includes provisions on advertising and canvassing ; the licensing of credit and hire businesses ; all aspects of the agreement ; and judicial control over its enforcement.

To come within the Act, a mortgage must constitute a regulated consumer agreement, that is to say, a personal credit agreement by which a creditor provides a debtor with a credit not exceeding £5,000.[3]   There are, however, exempt agreements,[4] of which the most important are loans made by a building society or local authority for house purchase.   Banks are not exempt.   We can only notice in very general terms the main areas where the ordinary law of mortgage is affected.

(A) Creation.   If the formalities prescribed by the Act are not complied with,[5] section 65 provides that an agreement which is " improperly-executed " can be enforced against the debtor on an order of the court[6] only.

(B) Rights of the Mortgagor.   The most far-reaching provision for the protection of the mortgagor is the power given to the court to " re-open " a credit agreement if the credit bargain is extortionate.[7]   This power extends to all credit bargains, whether regulated, exempt or above the £5,000 limit, other than those in which the debtor is a body corporate.   A credit bargain is extortionate if the payments to be made under it are " grossly extortionate " or if it " otherwise grossly contravenes the ordinary principles of fair dealing. "   The court is required to take into account interest rates prevailing when the bargain was made ; factors in relation to the debtor, such as his age, experience and business capacity, and the degree to which he was under financial pressure when he made the bargain ; and the degree of risk accepted by the creditor.   The court has wide discretion " to do justice between the parties ".

Under section 94, the debtor under a regulated agreement has the right, on giving notice to the creditor, to redeem prematurely

---

[1] The Act is not yet in operation.   It will be supplemented by a mass of subordinate legislation.   See Guest and Lloyd, *Consumer Credit Act* 1974 ; Goode, *Consumer Credit Act* 1974 ; (1975) 34 C. L. J. 79 (R. M. Goode) ; (1975) 39 Conv. (N.S.) 94 (J. E. Adams).
[2] This includes sole traders and partnerships, s. 189 (1).
[3] S. 8.
[4] S. 14.
[5] Part V of the Act.   See also s. 105.
[6] The County Court has exclusive jurisdiction, s. 141 (1).   See also s. 127.
[7] Ss. 137–40, *cf. Cityland and Property (Holdings), Ltd.* v. *Dabrah,* [1968] Ch. 166 ; [1967] 2 All E. R. 639, *supra,* p. 661.

at any time. Any provision in the agreement which limits his rights in this respect is void.[1] It would seem that if a provision to postpone the contractural right to redeem were included in a regulated agreement it would be void.[2]

(C) **Rights of the Mortgagee.** Consonant with the object of the Act, these are curtailed. A security cannot be enforced by reason of any breach of a regulated agreement by the debtor, until the creditor has served a notice under section 87. This is similar to, but not identical with, the notice required by section 146 of the Law of Property Act 1925 in the case of the forfeiture of a lease.[3] Further, a land mortgage securing a regulated agreement is enforceable by an order of the court only.[4] This is a most important provision, since a mortgagee cannot exercise his rights of taking possession and of sale without such an order. If, however, he sells without an order, it would seem that he can pass a good title to the purchaser.[5]

Finally, under section 113, a creditor shall not derive from the enforcement of the security any greater benefit than he would obtain from enforcement of a regulated agreement, if the security were not provided. This would seem to deny the mortgagee the full benefit of foreclosure.[6]

---

[1] S. 173 (1).
[2] *Knightsbridge Estates Trust, Ltd.* v. *Byrne*, [1939] Ch. 441 ; [1938] 4 All E. R. 618 ; *supra*, p. 655.
[3] *Supra*, p. 442.
[4] S. 126. For the orders which the court can make, see Part IX of the Act.
[5] S. 177 (2).
[6] *Supra*, p. 674. 39 Conv. (N.S.) 94, at p. 108.

BOOK III

THE TRANSFER AND EXTINCTION OF ESTATES AND INTERESTS

SUMMARY

PAGE

PART 1

INTRODUCTORY NOTE

It may be said that what we have described so far is the law at rest. Our attention has been directed to the actual rights that can be enjoyed in land. We have taken each estate and interest that is capable of subsisting, either at law or in equity, and have explained by what methods it may be brought into existence and what incidents are applicable to it when it exists. It now remains to treat of the law in motion, that is, to show how estates and interests, once validly created, may be transferred and dealt with generally, and how they may be extinguished.

The principal function of conveyancers as regards real property is to draft appropriate instruments for creating or transferring the landed interests already described, and in connection with this task, to ensure that the person who makes the transfer has an estate or interest that is sufficient to justify the transaction contemplated. Thus, in the case of a conveyance by way of sale of the fee simple, it is essential to see that the vendor has, as the result of conveyances and acts in the law extending over a number of years, acquired a fee simple estate and is therefore in a position to pass that estate to the purchaser. This preliminary inquiry is known as investigation of title. Again, where the task in question is to draft a will, it is essential to remember, for example, that whatever the testator may desire, it is useless to frame a limitation that offends the rule against perpetuities.

Some of the instruments by which estates and interests may be dealt with have already been described and need little further mention, but it is well to notice that though it is usual to regard conveyancing as the transfer of rights in property from one person to another, yet frequently an instrument creates rather than transfers a right, as for instance, in the case of the creation of a trust or the grant of a mortgage or a lease. Furthermore, all transfers are not necessarily effected by an instrument, but may operate independently of the person whose interest is primarily affected, as for instance, where land passes to a trustee in bankruptcy on the adjudication of its owner as bankrupt.

Transfer. The first point that requires discussion is transfer, which falls naturally into transfer *inter vivos* and transfer upon death.

Transfer *inter vivos* may be either (A) by act of parties, or (B) by act in the law, *i.e.* either due to the deliberate intention of the estate owner or in spite of his intention.

(A) The principal occasions of voluntary transfer by act of parties arise when the land is sold or settled, and also where an entailed interest is converted into a fee simple absolute by a disentailing assurance.

The main object of the next three chapters, which deal with transfer by act of parties, is to discuss the conveyance of a legal fee simple by way of sale. The general scheme is to show, first, the practice that conveyancers adopt in effecting a conveyance of the legal estate; secondly, the effect of the conveyance upon the third party rights.

In the second respect we encounter a difficulty, since not only the details of the conveyance, but more especially its effect upon third party rights, vary with the status of the vendor. We must recall that the legal estate in the entirety of every piece of land is necessarily vested in an *estate owner*. An estate owner is the owner of a legal estate. Every legal estate must have an estate owner. Blackacre may have been subjected to a trust, a settlement or a mortgage; it may have been devised to a number of beneficiaries, either in succession or in common; it may have been charged with a variety of incumbrances; but in each case the fee simple absolute in possession is necessarily vested in one person or in a number of persons jointly. Further, every conveyance of the legal estate must be made by the estate owner except where a mortgagee under his power of sale conveys the legal fee simple that is vested in the mortgagor, and even in this case the conveyance may be made in the name of the mortgagor. The possible estate owners are the following :—

Beneficial owners.
Personal representatives.
Trustees for sale.
Tenants for life and statutory owners.
Mortgagors and mortgagees.
Bare trustees.[1]

The plan adopted in the following three chapters, therefore, is to begin with a description of a sale by a beneficial owner, *i.e.* a person entitled to the whole

---

[1] For definition of bare trustee, see *supra*, p. 102, note 3.

ownership for his own benefit, and then to notice any variation from the law applicable to this transaction that is peculiar to the other estate owners. The main chapter is the first which deals with the beneficial owner, since it contains a general account of the proof and investigation of title that under the system of unregistered conveyancing is necessary in all cases irrespective of the character of the vendor. This is followed by an account of the different method that must be adopted where the title to the land is registered under the Land Registration Act 1925. The second chapter treats of personal representatives, for their position raises matters that have not been discussed in the preceding pages. The remaining estate owners—tenants for life, statutory owners, trustees for sale and mortgagors—are grouped together in the third chapter, for to deal with them *in extenso* would involve a considerable repetition.

(B) Involuntary transfer by operation of law arises where the owner of an estate or interest is

Involuntary transfer.

(i) sued to judgment for non-payment of a debt, or

(ii) made bankrupt, or

(iii) dies insolvent,

in each of which cases his land is liable to be seized in satisfaction of the debts.

Turning to transfer on death, testacy and intestacy are dealt with in Part IV.

Transfer on death.

The next subject of discussion in Part V is the extinguishment of estates and interests. Under the modern law a right to land may be extinguished by

Extinction of estates and interests.

1. forfeiture,

2. lapse of time, or

3. merger.

1. Forfeiture may operate where, for instance, land is leased to a tenant with a condition for forfeiture on non-payment of rent, or where an interest is subjected to a condition subsequent, but, these cases having already been considered, the subject of forfeiture will be omitted from the following pages.

2. Lapse of time causes the extinguishment of an interest whose owner remains out of possession, either of the land or of its profits, for the appropriate period designated by the Limitation Act 1939.

3. Where a smaller interest and a larger interest in the same land become united in one person, the doctrine of merger, subject to certain conditions, operates to extinguish the smaller interest.

The discussion of extinction, therefore, is confined to lapse of time and merger.

Finally attention is given to those special persons, such as infants and mental patients, for whom the law has prescribed special rules with respect both to the holding and to the transfer of interests in land.

BOOK III

THE TRANSFER AND EXTINCTION OF ESTATES AND INTERESTS

PART II

TRANSFER *INTER VIVOS* BY ESTATE OWNERS

SUMMARY

CHAPTER I

BENEFICIAL OWNERS: THE SALE
OF LAND[1]

SUMMARY

---

[1] See generally *Emmet on Title* (15th Edn.) ; Farrand, *Contract and Conveyance* (2nd Edn.) ; Gibson's *Conveyancing* (20th Edn.) ; Barnsley, *Conveyancing Law and Practice.*

SECTION I.   UNREGISTERED CONVEYANCING
(A) INVESTIGATION OF TITLE

SUMMARY

(1) INTRODUCTORY NOTE

A vendor and a purchaser of land generally desire that a binding[1] contract should be concluded at the earliest possible moment, subject to the purchaser's right to rescind if the vendor cannot show a good unincumbered title.   Accordingly the purchaser usually does not investigate the vendor's title before contract.[2]   Once a binding contract has been made, however, the procedure to be followed depends upon whether the contract relates to registered or unregistered land.   If the land is unregistered,

Delivery of abstract.   1. The vendor is bound to show a good title to the interest that he has contracted to sell, and to this end and with a view to simplifying the purchaser's task, he must at his own expense deliver to the purchaser an abstract of title, that is, a summary of all the documents, such as wills and deeds of conveyance, that have dealt with the interest during the period for which his ownership has to be proved, and of all the

---

[1] For the creation, enforceability and effect of a contact of sale, see *supra*, pp. 112 *et seq.*

[2] For inquiries which are usually made before contract see Law Commission Report on " Subject to Contract " Agreements (Law Com. No. 65, 1975) pp. 4, 9–13 ; *Emmet on Title* (16th Edn.), pp. 1 *et seq.* ; (1970), 120 *New L. J.* 610, 630 ; (1973) 123 N. L. J. 1032 (J. E. Adams).

events, such as deaths, that have affected the devolution of the ownership during that period. The period is either the 15 years fixed by statute, or that which is prescribed by a special stipulation in the contract of sale, though, as we shall see, the period will be longer than the statutory 15 years if a good root of title cannot otherwise be shown.

2. The vendor then verifies the abstract by producing evidence of the accuracy of the statements that he has made in the course of setting out his title. After this the purchaser's solicitor, at the expense of the purchaser, peruses the abstract, requisitions (*i.e.* addresses inquiries to) the vendor about any defects he may observe, satisfies himself that the property described in the contract is identical with that which has been dealt with in the documents abstracted, calls for evidence (such as death certificates) of events material to the title, and finally advises the purchaser whether he must or can with safety accept the title offered.

Perusal of abstract.

3. The vendor is then obliged to convey the property free from incumbrances, to execute a deed of conveyance and to hand over to the purchaser all the title deeds relating to the property. The expense of preparing the deed of conveyance falls upon the purchaser.

Conveyance.

The exact obligations of a vendor may, as we have said, be either specified or unspecified. If they are unspecified, and so left to be implied by law, the vendor is said to sell under an *open contract*. We will now proceed to state the rights and obligations of the parties, first where the contract is open, secondly where it contains the special stipulations generally found in practice.

(2) UNDER AN OPEN CONTRACT

The rights and the duties of the parties under an open contract are as follows :—

(i) DUTY OF VENDOR TO SHOW TITLE FOR 15 YEARS[1]

Since the obligation of the vendor is to convey to the purchaser the interest that he has agreed to sell, free from incumbrances and competing interests, it follows that he must disclose and verify the state of his title to the land. Save in the rare case where he has been invested with an absolute title by Act of Parliament, he can scarcely show that he is entitled to an interest good against the whole world, for, however long he and his predecessors may

Possession is evidence of title.

---

[1] Barnsley, *Conveyancing Law and Practice*, pp. 245–59.

have possessed and administered the land, the existence of some adverse claimant, such as a remainderman or reversioner, is always a possibility.   But possession is *prima facie* evidence of seisin in fee and if he shows that he and his predecessors have been in possession for a considerable time, the existence of an earlier and therefore better title is at least improbable.   On this assumption, the practical rule was ultimately evolved that proof of the exercise of acts of ownership over the land by the vendor and his predecessors for a period of not less than sixty years was *prima facie* evidence of his right to convey what he had agreed to sell. " It is a technical rule among conveyancers to approve a possession of sixty years, as a good title to a fee simple." [1]   This period was statutorily reduced to forty years in 1874, [2] to thirty years in 1925, [3] and to fifteen years in 1969. [4]

Necessity to explain origin of possession.
Enjoyment for this period, however, is not conclusive evidence of a good title, and if it appears from the information supplied by the vendor or if it can be shown *ab extra* that the title falls short of what is required by the contract, the purchaser is not bound to complete.   Possession by the vendor is no doubt evidence of seisin in fee, but nevertheless he must show its origin, for though it is probably attributable to his position as tenant in fee, there is always the possibility that he is a mere tenant for life or years. As Lord Erskine once said : " No person in his senses would take an offer of a purchase from a man, merely because he stood upon the ground." [5]   Even the rule under the Limitation Act 1939, that a person's title to land is extinguished after twelve years' adverse possession by a disseisor, [6] does not in itself enable a disseisor to show a good title by proving possession in himself for even fifteen years, since possession for the statutory period does not bar the rights of remaindermen and reversioners entitled to the land upon the determination of the disseisee's interest.   He must go further and show what persons were entitled to the land when he took possession and prove that their claims have been barred by his continuance in possession. [6]

Evidence of title usually documentary.
The usual way, therefore, in which the vendor proves his title is to produce the deeds or other documents by which the land has been disposed of in the past in order to show that the interest which he has agreed to sell has devolved upon him.   Thus, in the normal case the evidence of his title is documentary and is set out in the abstract of title that he delivers to the purchaser.   This abstract must start with what is called a *good root of title*, *i.e.* a document which deals with the legal estate in the land, which is valid without

---

[1] *Barnwell* v. *Harris* (1809), 1 Taunt. 430, at p. 432, *per* Heath, J.
[2] Vendor and Purchaser Act 1874, s. 1.
[3] L.P.A. 1925, s. 44 (1).   [4] L.P.A. 1969, s. 23.
[5] *Hiern* v. *Mill* (1806), 13 Ves. 114, at p. 122.
[6] *Games* v. *Bonnor* (1884), 54 L. J. 517 ; *Scott* v. *Nixon* (1843), 3 Dr. & War. 388 (Ireland). *Infra*, pp. 883 *et seq.*

requiring a reference to any earlier document, which adequately identifies the land, and which contains nothing to cast doubts on the title of the disposing party.

Thus a conveyance by way of sale or of legal mortgage[1] effected at least 15 years ago is a perfect root of title, since it may be presumed that the alienee was satisfied at that time with the state of the alienor's title, and if the intervening dispositions have been satisfactory, the present purchaser will obviously acquire a good title. A *general*, as distinct from a *specific*, devise of land is not a good root of title, since it does not identify the property and therefore does not show that the will passed the ownership of the same land as the vendor has now agreed to sell.

The obligation to begin the abstract with a good root of title may, of course, necessitate going back to some document more than fifteen years old. NORTH, J., in one case said :—

> " And when I say a [15] years' title, I mean a title deduced for [15] years, and for so much longer as it is necessary to go back in order to arrive at a point at which the title can properly commence. The title cannot commence *in nubibus* at the exact point of time which is represented by 365 days multiplied by [15]. It must commence at or before the [15] years with something which is in itself . . . a proper root of title."[2]

There are a few cases in which the period for which title must be shown is longer than fifteen years.[3] Thus,

(a) where an advowson is sold, title must be shown for at least 100 years with a list of presentations during that period ;[4]

(b) upon the sale of a leasehold, an abstract or copy of the lease, however old, must be produced with proof of dealings with the lease from a disposition at least 15 years old,[5] but the purchaser is not entitled to call for the title to the reversion ;[6]

(c) if the subject-matter of the sale is a reversionary interest, an abstract of the instrument which created the interest must be produced, with proof of 15 years title back from the date of purchase.

---

[1] Even though a post-1925 mortgage does not take effect as a conveyance of the fee simple, *supra*, p. 641. Barnsley, *Conveyancing Law and Practice*, p. 256.

[2] *Re Cox and Neve's Contract*, [1891] 2 Ch. 109, at p. 118.

[3] L.P.A. 1925, s. 44 (1). See *Emmet on Title* (16th Edn.), p. 120.

[4] Benefices Act 1898, s. 1 ; Benefices Act 1898 (Amendment) Measure 1923 ; Dart, *Vendors and Purchasers of Real Estate* (8th Edn.), vol. i. p. 292.

[5] *Frend* v. *Buckley* (1870), L. R. 5 Q. B. 213 ; *Williams* v. *Spargo*, [1893] W. N. 100.

[6] L.P.A. 1925, s. 44 (2), (3), (4).

(ii) Duty of Vendor to Abstract and Produce Documents[1]

The vendor must at his own expense abstract and, if under his own control, produce the document which forms the root of his title, and all subsequent documents that affect the legal estate. In addition he must state and prove all facts that have affected the legal estate in the last 15 years.

But there are certain things that must not be abstracted, and certain titles and documents that cannot be called for.

(a) Certain equitable interests not to be abstracted.

Overreached equities not to be abstracted.

Under the old law a purchaser who took a conveyance of the legal estate was bound by any equitable interests affecting that estate of which he had notice. If, for instance,

the abstract showed that the legal estate was held by the vendor as trustee, then, provided that he was not an express trustee for sale, the equitable interests were *ipso facto* notified to the purchaser. It was necessary for the vendor to abstract the title to the equitable interests, and to obtain the concurrence of the beneficiaries in the conveyance.

But, as we have seen, one of the chief objects of the legislation of 1925 was to enable a purchaser to acquire the legal estate from the estate owner without being required to concern himself with equitable interests enforceable against the land. In general pursuance of this idea the Law of Property Act 1925 provides that in certain cases it shall not be proper to mention equitable interests in the abstract. It does not exclude all such interests, but only those that are overreached by the conveyance. What these are will be stated below.[2] The sub-section in question is as follows [3]:—

" Where title is shown to a legal estate in land, it shall be deemed not necessary or proper to include in the abstract of title an instrument relating only to interests or powers which will be overreached by the conveyance of the estate to which title is being shown ; but nothing in this Part of this Act affects the liability of any person to disclose an equitable interest or power which will not be so overreached, or to furnish an abstract of any instrument creating or affecting the same."

Thus, to take a simple illustration, when a tenant for life contracts to sell settled land, he is not required to abstract the equitable interests of the beneficiaries.

---

[1] Barnsley, *Conveyancing Law and Practice*, pp. 255–68, 273–8.
[2] *Infra*, pp. 792–3 ; 796–7.
[3] L.P.A. 1925, s. 10 (1).

(b) Freehold title not to be abstracted on sale of lease-hold. If the subject-matter of the sale is a term of years, the vendor is bound, as we have seen, to abstract and produce the lease under which he holds the land ; but it is enacted that in an open contract he shall not be required to prove the title to the freehold.[1] This latter rule applies where a fee simple owner agrees to *grant* a lease.

Thus :

> If A. is fee simple owner of the land, and if he agrees to grant a lease to B. for 99 years, B. is not entitled to call for proof of A.'s title to the fee simple, unless he has inserted an express stipulation to that effect in the contract. Again, if B. agrees later to sell his lease to C., the latter is precluded from calling for the title of A.

Similar rules apply to an agreement to sell a leasehold interest that is derived out of a leasehold interest, or to an agreement to grant such a lease.[2] If, for example :

> A. leases to B. and B. underleases to C., and C. agrees to sell his underlease to D., then D. is entitled to production of the underlease,[3] but he cannot call for the lease to B.

These rules were formerly contained in the Vendor and Purchaser Act 1874, and the Conveyancing Act 1881, and it was held under those statutes that, failing their express exclusion by the contract, a lessee or a purchaser of a term of years was bound by equities affecting the legal estate that would have come to his notice had he expressly required the freehold title to be disclosed. This was decided in *Patman* v. *Harland.*[4]

> In that case the plaintiff sold land to A. subject to a restrictive covenant. A. sold to B., and B. leased part of the land to the defendant, who committed a breach of the covenant. The defendant had no knowledge of the existence of the restrictive covenant, and, in an action brought against her for an injunction, it was argued that, as in an open contract she was debarred by the statute from inquiring into the title to the freehold out of which her lease was derived, she had no notice, actual or constructive, of the restrictive covenant, and therefore was not liable for its breach.

This argument was rejected by the Court of Appeal.

It is now, however, provided that, in contracts made after 1925, a person who, under the above rules, is not entitled to call for the title to the freehold or the leasehold reversion shall

Marginal notes:
Contents of abstract when leasehold assigned.

Liability of assignee to equities.

Patman v. *Harland.*

Abolition of rule in *Patman* v. *Harland.*

---

[1] *Ibid.*, s. 44 (2).   [2] *Ibid.*, s. 44 (3), (4).
[3] *Gosling* v. *Woolf*, [1893] 1 Q. B. 39.
[4] (1881), 17 Ch. D. 353 ; M. & B. p. 413. See (1950), 56 *L. Q. R.* 361 (D. W. Logan).

not be deemed to be affected with notice of any matter or thing of which, if he had contracted that such title should be furnished, he might have had notice.[1] The doctrine of *Patman* v. *Harland* is therefore abolished in cases where a purchaser of a leasehold interest has no right to call for the freehold title, though, in the case of registered land, it still applies to incumbrances which are entered in the register.[2] This statutory alteration operates, therefore, to the detriment of the owner of the equity, but the alteration is subject to the qualification that the lessee remains bound by any incumbrances that have been registered under the Land Charges Act 1972.[3]

There is also a more general enactment to the effect that a purchaser shall not be deemed to have notice of any matter or thing of which, if he had investigated the title prior to the beginning of the 15 years' period, he might have had notice, unless he actually makes the investigation.[4]

Purchaser in this·connexion means one who acquires an interest for money or money's worth, and includes a lessee and a mortgagee.[5] The expression *money's worth* excludes the consideration of marriage.

(iii) OBLIGATION OF PURCHASER TO BEAR THE COST OF PRODUCING CERTAIN DOCUMENTS

In general vendor bears cost.

We have seen that one of the duties of a vendor is to produce a perfect abstract of title ; it is incidental to this that he must produce at his own expense the documents which go to prove the title. If these are not in his possession, he must arrange for the production of those dated after the period of 15 years began in so far as they are material.[6] But as regards the expense of producing documents, the rule varies according as they are in the possession of the vendor or not.

Where purchaser bears cost.

At common law a vendor was bound to bear the cost of producing documents whether in his own possession or not, but the Conveyancing Act 1881 provided that the expenses of the production and of the inspection of documents *not in the vendor's possession*, the expenses of all journeys incidental thereto, and the expenses of procuring all evidences and information not in the vendor's possession should be borne by the purchaser.[7]

---

[1] L.P.A. 1925, s. 44 (5).

[2] *White* v. *Bijou Mansions, Ltd.*, [1937] Ch. 610.

[3] *Ibid.*, at p. 619. See *Shears* v. *Wells*, [1936] 1 All E. R. 832 ; M. & B. p. 295 ; (1956), *C. L. J.* pp. 230–4 (H. W. R. Wade).

[4] L.P.A. 1925, s. 44 (8).

[5] *Ibid.*, s. 205 (1) (xxi).

[6] *Re Stamford, etc., and Knight's Contract*, [1900] 1 Ch. 287.

[7] S. 3 (6).

It was held under this section that where the vendor had mortgaged his property, the purchaser must pay the mortgagee's solicitor a fee for producing the deeds relating to the property.[1] This was a harsh application of the rule, and therefore the Law of Property Act 1925, while re-enacting the provisions of the Conveyancing Act, expressly provides that the expense of producing deeds which are in the possession of the vendor's *mortgagee or trustee* shall fall upon the vendor.[2] If, however, the mortgagee retains possession of a document, the purchaser must pay for any copy which he desires to have.

(iv) Obligation of Purchaser to examine the Abstract at his own expense

The perusal of the abstract is carried out by the purchaser's solicitor, whose duty it is to advise whether the vendor has shown a good title to the exact interest that he has agreed to sell. The solicitor must satisfy himself that the abstract exhibits an ordered sequence of all the documents and events which have disposed of or affected the interest during the last 15 years, and if he observes defects or omissions, he must requisition the vendor on the matter. He must compare the abstract with the original deeds which are produced by the vendor's solicitor, and put in requisitions on points of discrepancy. *Perusal of abstract.*

The solicitor must, for instance, require proper evidence of facts which affect the interest, ascertain that the abstracted documents bear stamps of the proper value, and inquire concerning the existence of tenancies and easements.

Search of Registers. One of the first essentials in the investigation of an abstract of title is that a purchaser should search for incumbrances and equitable interests which affect the land to be sold, and which may have been registered by their owners in a public register. This will be seen to be of great importance when we come to examine whether the purchaser of a legal estate takes the estate free from equitable interests charged thereon. There are two registers to be noticed, namely, *Registration of incumbrances.*

1. a central register[3] kept by the Land Charges Department of the Land Registry at Plymouth, and

2. the various local land charges registers kept in London by each London borough or the City of London, and elsewhere by each district council.[4]

---

[1] *Re Willett and Argenti* (1889), 60 L. T. 735.
[2] L.P.A. 1925, s. 45 (4).
[3] C day for computerization of the index was September 9th, 1974. The registers themselves are in book form.
[4] Local Land Charges Act 1975, s 3 (1) ; *infra*, p. 748.

Under the Land Charges Act 1972, the Registrar of the Land Registry keeps five separate Registers,[1] namely,

(1) a register of pending actions ;
(2) a register of annuities ;
(3) a register of writs and orders affecting land ;
(4) a register of deeds of arrangement affecting land ; and
(5) a register of land charges.[2]

We will take these registers separately, and notice what kind of right or interest in land may be registered in each.

Actions relating to land.

(i) **Register of pending actions.** It is obviously impossible to bring an action relating to land to a successful termination if alienation *pendente lite* is permissible, and therefore, in order that a plaintiff may not lose the fruits of his action, the law provides him with the means of protecting himself. This is afforded by the right to register a pending land action, *i.e.* any action, information or proceeding which is pending in court, and which relates to land or to any interest in, or charge on, land.[3]

Petition in bankruptcy.

Again, if a creditor wishes to make his debtor's property available for distribution among creditors generally, he may register in the same register the petition in bankruptcy which is the first step in setting bankruptcy proceedings in motion.[4]

Effect of failure to register.

If a pending action (*i.e.* either an action relating to land or a petition in bankruptcy) is registered, the registration remains effective for five years, but it may be renewed for successive periods of five years.[5] A purchaser for value (which word includes a mortgagee or lessee) of any interest in the land takes free from an *unregistered* pending action unless he has express, as distinct from constructive, notice of it.[6] In the case of an unregistered bankruptcy petition, however, this protection avails him only if he is a purchaser of a *legal* estate in good faith for money or money's worth,[7] without notice of an available act of bankruptcy.[8]

---

[1] L.C.A. 1972, s. 1. The historical order of the registers, as set out in L.C.A. 1925, s. 1 (1) has been followed. The new order is land charges, pending actions, writs and orders, deeds of arrangement and annuities. See generally Barnsley, *Conveyancing Law and Practice*, chap. 14. On the history of registration see *Ministry of Housing and Local Government* v. *Sharp*, [1970] 2 Q. B. 223, at pp. 280 *et seq.* ; [1970] 1 All E. R. 1009, *per* Cross, L.J.

[2] *Ibid.*, s. 1 (1).

[3] *Ibid.*, s. 5 (1) ; see *Taylor* v. *Taylor* [1968] 1. W. L. R. 378 ; [1968] 1 All E. R. 843 ; *Calgary and Edmonton Land Co., Ltd.* v. *Dobinson*, [1974] Ch. 102 [1974] 1 All E. R. 484.

[4] L.C.A. 1972, s. 5 (1).

[5] *Ibid.*, s. 8.

[6] *Ibid.*, s 5 (7).

[7] *Ibid.*, ss. 5 (8), 6 (5).

[8] An act which has occurred within three months before the presentation of a petition. Bankruptcy Act 1914, ss. 1, 4 (1)(c), 167 ; *infra*, p. 807.

(ii) **Register of annuities.** Under the old law annuities or Annuities.
rentcharges did not affect purchasers of the land upon
which they were charged unless they were registered
in the Register of Annuities.   No annuity can be entered in
this Register after 1925, and it will be closed as soon as the
annuities registered before January 1, 1926, have been worked
off.[1]

Annuities, being interests for life merely, are necessarily
equitable in nature after 1925, and they may now be registered
as *general equitable charges* in the Register of Land Charges,
provided that they do not arise under a settlement or a trust
for sale.[2]

(iii) **Register of writs and orders affecting land.** Writs and
Any writ or order affecting land issued by a court for the Orders.
purpose of enforcing a judgment,[3] any order which appoints
a receiver or sequestrator of land, and any receiving order in
bankruptcy, whether it is known to affect land or not, is void
against a purchaser for value of the land unless it is registered.[4]
The registration remains effective for five years, but it may
be renewed for successive periods of five years.[5]

A receiving order is an order of the Bankruptcy Court Receiving
placing the debtor's property under the control of the court Order.
through its officer, the official receiver, and it is practically
equivalent to a decision that the debtor is to be adjudged
bankrupt.   It is enacted that an unregistered receiving order
is to be void only against a purchaser of a legal estate in
good faith, for money or money's worth and without notice
of an available act of bankruptcy.[6]

(iv) **Register of deeds of arrangement affecting land.** Arrange-
An insolvent debtor sometimes comes to an arrangement ments with
with the general body of his creditors whereby, although he creditors.
does not pay his debts in full, he obtains a release from the
claims of the creditors.   As a rule the debtor either com-
pounds with his creditors, or assigns his property to a trustee
for distribution among the creditors.

If such an arrangement is reduced to writing, it is called
a deed of arrangement whether it is made under seal or not.[7]
It is enacted that such an arrangement shall be void against
a purchaser for value of the debtor's land unless it is registered

---

[1] L.C.A. 1972, s. 1 (4), Sched. 1.
[2] *Ibid.*, s. 2 (4), Class C (iii), *infra*, p. 741.
[3] *Infra*, pp. 803–6.
[4] L.C.A. 1972, ss. 6 (1), (4).
[5] *Ibid.*, s. 8.
[6] *Ibid.*, s. 6 (5).   For receiving order, see *infra*, p. 807.
[7] Deeds of Arrangement Act 1914, s. 1.

Land charges.

in the above Register. Registration ceases to have any effect after five years unless it is renewed.[1]

(v) **Register of land charges.** The term *land charge* is comprehensive ; it includes a number of different rights and interests affecting land. The Land Charges Act 1925, which made considerable additions to this part of the law, divided land charges into five classes, denominated A, B, C, D, and E ; a further Class F was added by the Matrimonial Homes Act 1967.[2] The whole has now been consolidated in the Land Charges Act 1972.[3]

Class A[4]

Class A.

This comprises a rent or a sum of money which is charged upon land, *pursuant to the application of some person,* under the provisions of any Act of Parliament, and with the object of securing money which has been spent on the land under the provisions of such Act. It also comprises a rent or a sum of money charged upon land in accordance with certain sections in, for example,

the Land Drainage Act 1930,[5]
the Agricultural Holdings Act 1948,[6]
the Tithe Annuities Apportionment Act 1921[7] and the Tithe Acts 1918[8] and 1936[9]
the Landlord and Tenant Act 1927.[10]

Thus, if a tenant for life has to pay compensation to an outgoing agricultural tenant, he may obtain an order charging the holding with the repayment of the amount, and may have the charge registered. A land charge of this class is void against a purchaser unless it is registered before the completion of the purchase.[11]

Class B[12]

Class B.

This comprises a charge on land (not being a local land charge) of any of the kinds described in Class A, provided that it has not been created " pursuant to the application of any person," and is imposed automatically by statute.

---

[1] L.C.A. 1972, s. 7.
[2] The fifth class, E, comprises annuities created before 1926 and not registered in the Register of Annuities. This register, as we have seen, was closed to new entries as from January 1, 1926, but annuitants who omitted to register before that date may register under Class E.
[3] See Land Charges Rules 1974 (S. I. 1974 No. 1286).
[4] L.C.A. 1972, s. 2 (2), Class A.
[5] S. 9 (5).   [6] Ss. 72, 73, 74, 82.   [7] S. 1.   [8] S. 30 (1).
[9] Ss. 4 (2), 6 (1).
[10] S. 12, Sched. 1, para. 7, as amended by Landlord and Tenant Act 1954, s. 45 and Sched. 7, Pt. I. For other examples, see L.C.A. 1972, s. 2, Sched. 2.
[11] L.C.A. 1972, s. 4 (2).
[12] *Ibid.*, s. 2 (3), as amended by Local Land Charges Act 1975, s. 19, Sched. 2, Class B.

An example is a charge on property recovered or preserved for an assisted litigant arising under the Legal Aid Act 1974, in respect of unpaid contributions to the legal aid fund.[1]

Charges of this class, however, are not important as regards searches in the Land Registry, because they mostly arise under the Public Health Act 1936, and being in the majority of cases of a local nature (as, for instance, those arising in respect of paving expenses) they are *local land charges* and must therefore be registered locally.[2]

Failure to register such a charge (not being a local land charge) at the Land Registry renders it void as against a purchaser for valuable consideration of the land or of any interest therein

   (i) if it arises after December 31st, 1925, and has not been registered ;

   (ii) if it arose before that date and has not been registered within a year from the first conveyance of the charge made after December 31st, 1925.[3]

Class C[4]

This class is important in that it creates a system of registration of mortgages of land, and provides for the registration of estate contracts. It comprises four different land charges (not being local land charges), namely :— Class C.

(i) **A puisne mortgage.** This is a *legal* mortgage not protected by a deposit of documents relating to the legal estate affected.

(ii) **A limited owner's charge.** This is an equitable charge acquired under any statute by a tenant for life or statutory owner by discharging capital transfer tax or other liabilities, and to which special priority is given by the statute. Thus a charge may arise under the Finance Act 1975,[5] in favour of a tenant for life who pays capital transfer tax in respect of the estate out of which his life interest is carved.

(iii) **A general equitable charge.** This is a comprehensive expression that includes all equitable charges that are not assigned to a class of their own (such as estate contracts), and which do not arise or affect an interest

---

[1] S. 9.
[2] *Infra*, p. 748.
[3] L.C.A. 1972, ss. 4 (5), (7).
[4] *Ibid.*, s. 2 (4), Class C, as amended by Local Land Charges Act 1975, s. 17 (1) (b).
[5] *Ibid.*, s. 2 (4), as amended by F.A. 1975, s. 52, Sched. 12, para 18 (2). See *supra*, p. 205.

arising under a trust for sale or a settlement. In particular it includes an equitable mortgage of a legal estate which is not secured by a deposit of the title deeds, but it also comprises a rentcharge for life and a vendor's lien for unpaid purchase money.[1] To be registrable, the charge must be on land, and not for instance upon the purchase money that will arise from the sale of land.[2]

(iv) **An estate contract.** This is the only item included within Class C which is not in the nature of a mortgage. It is defined as being[3]

> " a contract by an estate owner or by a person entitled at the date of the contract to have a legal estate conveyed to him to convey or create a legal estate, including a contract conferring either expressly or by statutory implication a valid option of purchase, a right of pre-emption[4] or any other like right."[5]

This in practice means a contract for the sale of a legal fee simple, a contract for the grant of a term of years absolute,[6] or an option to acquire either of these interests.[7] We have already seen that the effect of such a contract is to confer an equitable interest upon the intending purchaser or tenant.[8] The effect of the Land Charges Act is to make it capable of registration whether it is written or oral.[9]

---

[1] See *Uziell-Hamilton* v. *Keen* (1971), 22 P. & C. R. 655.
[2] *Georgiades* v *Edward Wolfe & Co., Ltd.,* [1965] Ch. 487 ; [1964] 3 All E. R. 433.
[3] L.C.A. 1972, s. 2 (4), Class C. (iv).
[4] *First National Securities* v. *Chiltern District Council,* [1975] 1 W. L. R. 1075 ; [1975] 2 All E. R. 786.
[5] *Shiloh Spinners, Ltd.* v. *Harding,* [1973] A. C. 691, at p. 719
[6] *Sharp* v. *Coates,* [1949] 1 K. B. 285; [1948] 3 All E. R. 871. (Contract by estate owner to convey an estate greater than he was entitled to at the time of the contract.) It also includes a contract by which A. agrees with B. to create a legal estate in favour of such third person as B. may nominate, *Turley* v. *Mackay,* [1944] Ch. 37 ; [1943] 3 All E. R. 1 ; but not a contract by which A agrees that B has the power to accept offers to purchase made by third persons, *Thomas* v. *Rose,* [1968] 1 W. L. R. 1797 ; [1968] 3 All E. R. 765.
[7] *Beesly* v. *Hallwood Estates Ltd.,* [1960] 1 W. L. R. 549; [1960] 2 All E. R. 314. BUCKLEY, J., was able to reach this decision despite the difficulty that the statutory definition pre-supposes a contract, and yet an option is not a contract but a standing offer which the offeree may or may not convert into a contract. The decision was affirmed on another point, [1961] Ch. 105; [1961] 1 All E. R. 90. A notice to treat served under a compulsory purchase order is not a contract, though it may lead to one, and therefore is not registrable; *Capital Investments, Ltd.* v. *Wednesfield U.D.C.,* [1965] Ch. 774; [1964] 1 All E. R. 655. *Cf.* Leasehold Reform Act 1967, s. 5 (5) (notice given by tenant of his desire to acquire the freehold or an extended lease registrable as estate contract).
[8] *Supra,* p. 125.
[9] *Universal Permanent Building Society* v. *Cooke,* [1952] Ch. 95, at p. 104 ; [1951] 2 All E. R. 893, at p. 898. See *Barrett* v. *Hilton Developments, Ltd.,* [1975] Ch. 237 ; [1974] 3 All E. R. 944 (registration against the name of a person who has contracted to purchase land is not sufficient).

Class D[1]

This comprises the three following different land charges (not being local land charges) :—

(i) **A charge for capital transfer tax.** The Comissioners of Inland Revenue may register a charge on the occasion of the transfer of land which gives rise to the liability for tax under the Finance Act 1975.[2]

(ii) **A restrictive covenant.** This has already been described,[3] and the only remark needed here is that restrictive covenants made between a lessor and a lessee are expressly excluded, and are not capable of registration.

(iii) **An equitable easement.** This is defined as[4]

> " any easement right or privilege over or affecting land created or arising on or after 1st January 1926, and being merely an equitable interest."

Thus, an easement held for some smaller interest than a fee simple absolute in possession or for a term of years absolute, or an easement that has been informally created, satisfies this definition and is therefore registrable.

The three charges in this Class D are not registrable unless they have arisen after 1925.

Class F[5]

This is the right of occupation of a dwelling house given to a spouse by the Matrimonial Homes Act 1967.

The effect of a failure to register the land charges comprised in Classes C, D, and F is as follows :

Puisne mortgages,
Limited owners' charges,
General equitable charges
Spouse's right of occupation

are void against

any purchaser for valuable consideration of the land charged therewith or of *any interest* in such land, unless registered

---

[1] L.C.A. 1972, s. 2 (5), as amended by Local Land Charges Act 1975, s. 17 (1) (*b*), Class D.

[2] L.C.A. 1972, s. 2 (5), Class D (i), as amended by F.A. 1975, s. 52 Sched. 12, para 18 (3). See F.A. 1975, s. 19, Sched. 4, para 21, and *supra*, pp. 124 *et seq.*

[3] *Supra*, pp. 605 *et seq.*

[4] For a discussion of this Class see *Shiloh Spinners, Ltd.* v. *Harding*, [1973] A. C. 691 ; [1973] 1 All E. R. 90 ; M. & B. p. 34 (equitable right of re-entry on breach of contract not registrable as Class D (iii) land charge) and, *supra*, pp. 103 ; *infra*, p. 748.

[5] See *supra*, p. 233. For Class E see, *supra*, p. 740, note 2.

before completion of the purchase.[1] " Purchaser " means any person, including a mortgagee or lessee, who takes any interest in land for valuable consideration.[2] " Valuable consideration " includes marriage, but does not include a nominal consideration in money.[3]

It will be seen from the words italicized that a purchaser even of an equitable interest in the land affected takes free from these charges if unregistered, irrespectively of whether he has actual notice or not.

Estate contracts,
Charges for capital transfer tax.
Restrictive covenants,
Equitable easements

are void against

a purchaser of the *legal estate* in the land for *money or money's worth* unless registered before completion of the purchase.[4]

It therefore follows that these four charges, even if unregistered, bind a purchaser of an equitable interest whether he has notice or not.[5] Again, a purchaser even of a legal estate whose title is supported only by a marriage consideration, cannot rely upon the omission to register.

Subject to this distinction, the general effect of the non-registration of an interest that is registrable as a land charge is that it is void against a purchaser for value of any interest in the land. Furthermore, it is immaterial that the purchaser has actual knowledge of the unregistered interest,[6] and this is so even if the land is conveyed to him expressly subject to it.[7]

Effect of registration.
We must now turn to the effect of registration and its mechanics. The effect is contained in section 198 (1) of the Law of Property Act 1925 :—

" The registration of any instrument or matter in any register kept under the Land Charges Act 1972 or any local land charges register shall be deemed to constitute actual notice of such instrument or matter, and of the fact of such registration, to all persons and for

---

[1] L.C.A. 1972, s. 4 (5), (8).
[2] *Ibid.*, s. 17 (1).
[3] *Cf.* L.P.A. 1925, s. 205 (1) (xxi).
[4] L.C.A. 1972, s. 4 (6), as amended by F.A. 1975, s. 52, Sched. 12, para. 18 (5).   In the case of Class D (i) a purchaser means " a purchaser in good faith for consideration in money or money's worth other than a nominal consideration ". *Ibid.*, s. 51 (1).
[5] *McCarthy and Stone, Ltd.* v. *Julian S. Hodge & Co., Ltd.*, [1971] 1 W. L. R. 1547 ; [1971] 2 All E. R. 973 ; M. & B. p. 49 (unregistered estate contract held to have priority over subsequent equitable mortgage).
[6] L.P.A. 1925, s. 199 (1) (i).
[7] *Hollington Bros., Ltd.* v. *Rhodes*, [1951] 2 T. L. R. 691 ; M. & B. p. 45. L.P.A. 1925, s. 199 (1) (i).   An unregistered interest is not always void and unenforceable owing to lack of registration (*e.g.* a pending land action L.C.A. 1972, s. 7) and in such case a purchaser with express notice is bound.

all purposes connected with the land affected, as from the date of
registration . . . and so long as the registration continues in force." [1]

As we have seen,[2] this makes a substantial inroad on the doctrine of the bona fide purchaser for value without notice : that
doctrine no longer operates in respect of land charges which are
registrable.

It is important to notice that land charges affecting unregistered
land are registered, not against the burdened *land,* as is the case
with registered land, but against the *name* of the estate owner of
the land at the time when the land charge was created.[3]   If,
therefore, a purchaser desires to make a complete search at the
Land Registry, he will have to discover the names of every owner
of a legal estate in the land since January 1st, 1926.[4]   Even
though this may be impossible, he will nevertheless be bound by a
registered land charge. This causes difficulty to a purchaser and
has led to recent statutory intervention.[5]

*Land
charges
registered
against
name of
estate
owner.*

**1. Land charge discovered between contract and com-
pletion.**   As we have seen, a purchaser does not normally investigate the vendor's title before contract.[6]   In *Re Forsey and
Hollebone's Contract,*[7] EVE, J., took the view that by virtue of
section 198 of the Law of Property Act 1925, a purchaser has notice
at the date of the contract of land charges which are then on the
register, whether he knows of them or not.   The difficulty for a
purchaser under an open contract[8] is that at the pre-contract
stage he will not normally know the names of all the estate owners,
and so he may be compelled to take a conveyance of the land
subject to registered land charges which he cannot discover.
Section 24 of the Law of Property Act 1969 amends the law so as
to ensure that in respect of contracts entered into after January 1st,
1970, *as against the vendor,* a purchaser will only be deemed to
have notice of those registered land charges of which he has actual
or imputed knowledge at the date of the contract.[9]   Consequently,
a purchaser will no longer be prevented from rescinding the
contract on the ground of an undisclosed land charge merely

*Law of
Property
Act 1969.*

---

[1] As amended by Local Land Charges Act 1975, s. 17, Sched. 1.   For an
exception in the case of tacking see L.P.A. 1925, s. 198 (2), *supra,* p. 708.   See
also s. 96 (2), as amended by L.P.A.A. 1926, Sched.   *Supra,* p. 664.

[2] *Supra,* p. 103.

[3] L.C.A. 1972, ss. 3 (1), 17 (1).   On the mechanics of the register see *Oak
Co-operative Building Society* v. *Blackburn,* [1968] Ch. 730 at p. 741, *per*
RUSSELL, L.J.

[4] Since January 1st, 1889 in respect of Class A land charges.

[5] L.P.A. 1969, ss. 24, 25.   See generally Report of the Committee on Land
Charges 1956 (Cmd. 9825) ; Law Commission Report on Land Charges affecting
unregistered land 1969, (Law Com. No. 18) : (1970), 34 *Conv.* (N.S.) 4 (F. R.
Crane).

[6] *Supra,* p. 730.   [7] [1927] 2 Ch. 379.

[8] See Law Society's Conditions of Sale (1953 Edn.), Condition 20 (3) for an
appropriate condition to avoid the consequences of the rule.

[9] The parties must not contract out of the section.   L.P.A. 1969, s. 24 (2).
It does not apply to local land charges, nor to registered land, s. 24 (1), (3).

because it has been registered.   The owner of the registered land charge, however, remains protected : here registration still constitutes notice to all the world.

2. " Old land charge " discovered after completion.

In this case a purchaser, who has carried out a full and proper investigation of title, may discover after completion that he is bound by land charges registered before the commencement of the vendor's title.   He can, of course, stipulate for a list of all estate owners since January 1st, 1926,[1] but this may be impracticable. The risk that he may be caught by an " old land charge " is increased by the reduction of the minimum period of investigation of title to 15 years.

The Law of Property Act 1969 preserves the validity of the registered land charge against the purchaser, but provides that where he has suffered loss as a result of its existence he is entitled to compensation.[2]   This is payable if (a) his purchase was completed after January 1st, 1970, (b) he purchased without actual or imputed knowledge of the land charge and (c) the charge was registered against the name of a person who did not appear as an estate owner in the relevant title.[3]   Relevant title means either the statutory period of 15 years under an open contract, or the period of title in fact contracted for, whichever is the longer.[4]

3. Land charge discovered after grant or assignment of lease.

As we have seen, in the case of an open contract for the grant or assignment of a lease or underlease, the lessee or assignee is not entitled to call for the superior reversionary titles.[5] He may, however, be bound by registered land charges affecting those titles, even though he is unable to discover the names of the estate owners which are concealed in those titles.   The Law of Property Act 1969 makes no change : the Law Commission is considering the matter in the context of the rule that the reversionary titles may not be called for.[6]

Priority notices.

The fact that a charge cannot be registered until it has actually been created occasioned some difficulty after the Land Charges Act 1925 came into operation.   The provision of the Act that a charge on land, such as a restrictive covenant, shall be void against a subsequent purchaser of the legal estate for money or money's worth unless it is registered before *completion* of that purchase, produces an *impasse* in certain cases, for it is sometimes impossible to effect

---

[1] And perhaps should where he purchases land for development. See (1969), 113 Sol. Jo. 930 (S. M. Cretney).
[2] S. 25 This does not apply to local land charges.
[3] S. 25 (1) payable by the Chief Land Registrar out of public funds.
[4] S. 25 (10).
[5] *Supra*, p. 735.
[6] Law Com. (1969 No. 18), para. 37.

registration before completion.   A common example of this arises where

> X. agrees to sell Blackacre to Y. and takes a restrictive covenant from Y.   Y., being unable to find the whole of the purchase money, arranges to mortgage Blackacre to Z.   The conveyance from X. to Y. which creates the restrictive covenant, and the mortgage from Y. to Z. are in practice completed at the same time, so that it is practically impossible for X. to register his restrictive covenant before it is rendered void under the Act by the completion of the purchase in favour of Z.

The Law of Property (Amendment) Act 1926[1] removed this difficulty by providing that any person *intending* to apply for the registration of any *contemplated* charge may register notice of his intention at the Land Registry.   This notice, which is called a *priority notice*, must be given at least fifteen days before the registration is to take effect.[2]   When the contemplated charge is actually created and later registered, then, provided that it is registered within thirty days after the priority notice, it takes effect as if registration had been secured at the very moment of its creation.[3]

Although a purchaser may search in a register himself, it is usual to obtain an official search.[4]   Upon receipt of such a requisition (as it is called) the registrar, after making the search, issues an official certificate, which is conclusive in favour of the purchaser.[5]   If another charge is registered by a third person between the time when the certificate is issued and the time when the purchase is completed by the certificate holder, the registration does not affect the latter, provided that he completes his purchase within fifteen days of the issue of the certificate.[6]

Official searches.

---

[1] S. 4 (1) ; now L.C.A. 1972, s. 11 (1).
[2] L.C.A. 1972, s. 11 (3), (6).   Days when the registry is not open to the public are excluded.
[3] *Ibid.*, s. 11 (3).
[4] See Ruoff, *Searching Without Tears* (1974) ; H.M. Land Registry, *Computerised Land Charges Department* (1974) ; (1974) 118 Sol. Jo. 692 (T. B. F. Ruoff).
[5] L.C.A. 1972, s. 10 (4).   To be effective registration must be in the correct full name of the estate owner.   If it is not, a clear certificate as a result of an official search against the correct name will not bind a purchaser.   " But if there be registration in what may fairly be described as a version of the full names of the vendor, albeit not a version which is bound to be discovered on a search in the correct full names, we would not hold it a nullity against someone who does not search at all, or who (as here) searches in the wrong name." *Oak Co-operative Building Society* v. *Blackburn*, [1968] Ch. 730, at p. 743 ; [1968] 2 All E. R. 117, *per* RUSSELL, L.J.   See too *Du Sautoy* v. *Symes*, [1967] Ch. 1146 ; [1967] 1 All E. R. 25.   On liability where an erroneous certificate is issued see *Ministry of Housing and Local Government* v. *Sharp*, [1970] 2 Q. B. 223 ; [1970] 1 All E. R. 1009 ; *Coats Patons (Retail), Ltd.,* v. *Birmingham Corp.* (1971), 69 L. G. R. 356 ; *Diligent Finance Co., Ltd.* v. *Alleyne* (1971), 23 P. & C. R. 346 ; L.C.A. 1972, s. 10 (6).
[6] *Ibid.*, s. 11 (5) (*b*).

Summary of position as regards registration of land charges. In unregistered conveyancing the Land Charges Act 1972 thus plays a major part in enabling a purchaser to discover whether certain rights bind the land or not. The effect of the Act is automatic : if a registrable interest is registered, it binds ; if not, in general a purchaser for value of any interest in the land takes free from it. Many of the risks which arise to him from the doctrine of constructive notice have thus been mitigated, but there is still a residual category of equitable interests which are neither registrable nor over-reachable and will therefore bind a purchaser unless he is a bona fide purchaser for value of the legal estate without notice.[1]

Further the difficulties which are inherent in a system of registration based on a names register are themselves mitigated by the Law of Property Act 1969.

The importance of the Land Charges register will eventually decline as the system of registration of title under the Land Registration Act 1925 is extended throughout the country. But its importance will continue for a long time to come.[2] Many freehold and leasehold titles will remain unregistered, since, as we have seen,[3] compulsory registration of title occurs only on the first conveyance of the freehold, or on the grant or first assignment of a long lease, and short leases are incapable of registration.

Finally we must mention two registers which are kept in addition to those at the Land Registry.

(i) Local Land Charges Registers

Local Land Charges Registers. These are maintained under the Local Land Charges Act 1975[4] by all district councils in England and Wales, and also by London boroughs and the Common Council of the City of London.[5] They differ from those kept at the Land Registry in that the charges are registered against the land and not against the name of the estate owner; they relate both to registered and to unregistered land[6] and are of a public rather than a private nature.[7] Local land charges are a heterogeneous collection[8] and include charges for securing

---

[1] *Supra*, p. 103.

[2] In 1974–1975 there were 307,238 fresh registrations, rectifications and renewals. In the same period there were 3,536,548 official searches (number of names), and 445,969 official searches (limited to insolvency of named persons); and 68,708 personal searches. See Report on H.M. Land Registry 1974–1975, para. 30. [3] *Supra*, p. 107.

[4] This replaces L.C.A. 1925, s. 15 and other sections set out in L.C.A. 1972, s. 18, Sched. 4. See Law Commission Report on Local Land Charges 1974 (Law Com. No. 62). Garner, *Local Land Charges* (7th Edn.) ; (1975) L. G. C. 592 (J. F. Garner) ; Barnsley, pp. 157–73. The Act is to come into force on a day to be appointed, s. 20 (3).

[5] Local Land Charges Act 1975, s. 3. This includes the Inner Temple and the Middle Temple, s. 3 (4).

[6] *Infra*, p. 775.

[7] For an exception see the notice under the Rights of Light Act 1959, s. 2, *supra*, p. 552.

[8] Local Land Charges Act 1975, ss. 1, 2. A condition or limitation subject to which planning permission is granted is now excluded, s. 2 (*e*). *Infra*, p. 941.

money recoverable by local authorities under public health legislation, and prohibitions of or restrictions on the user of land imposed by a local authority, Minister of the Crown or a government department.

The Act has made a significant change in the effect of the non-registration of a local land charge.   Section 10 provides that failure to register such a charge in the local land charges register shall not affect the enforcement of the charge, but that a purchaser[1] shall be entitled to compensation for any loss suffered by him by reason that the charge was not registered, or was not shown as registered by an official search certificate.[2]   This follows a recommendation by the Law Commission that the overwhelming majority of local land charges are created in the public interest, and that it is usually inappropriate that lack of registration or non-disclosure in an official certificate of search should affect their enforceability.[3]

(ii) Companies Register

This is a register maintained under the Companies Act 1948 of land charges created by a company for securing money.   Registration on this register of a charge created by a company before 1970 or so created at any time as a floating charge, is sufficient in place of registration in the Land Charges Register and has the same effect.   A charge created by a company on or after January 1st, 1970, other than a floating charge, must be registered at the Land Charges Registry if it is to bind a purchaser.[4]   If it is to bind creditors and liquidators it must also be registered in the Companies Register within twenty-one days of its creation.[5]

Companies Register.

(v) DUTY OF VENDOR TO CONVEY THE IDENTICAL PROPERTY THAT HE HAS AGREED TO SELL

The vendor must prove that the property which he is able to convey is substantially the same in nature, situation and quantity as that which he has agreed to sell, and it is advisable, when a contract for the sale of land is drafted, to obtain a description of the land from the " parcels " clause of the last conveyance.[6]

Distinction between trifling and material variation.

---

[1] Local Land Charges Act 1975, s. 10 (3) (*a*) defines a purchaser as a person who, for valuable consideration, acquires any interest in land or the proceeds of sale of land ; and this includes a lessee or mortgagee.

[2] Under L.C.A. 1925, s. 15, a local land charge was void against a purchaser for money or money's worth of a legal estate in the land affected, unless registered before completion of the purchase.

[3] Law Commission Report, *supra*, para. 90.   See also paras. 52–4.

[4] L.C.A. 1972, s. 3 (7), (8).

[5] Companies Act 1948, s. 95.   See *Capital Finance Co., Ltd.* v. *Stokes*, [1969] 1 Ch. 261 ; [1968] 3 All E. R. 625.

[6] Williams, *Vendor and Purchaser* (4th Edn.), p. 36 ; for the " parcels " clause," see *infra*, pp. 761 ; 764.

If, in the case of an open contract, the property is not identical in quantity or quality with that agreed to be sold, the vendor cannot compel enforcement of the contract subject to compensation, unless the difference is insignificant and his conduct has been honest.[1]

> " If a vendor sues and is in a position to convey substantially what the purchaser has contracted to get, the court will decree specific performance with compensation for any small and immaterial deficiency, provided that the vendor has not, by misrepresentation or otherwise, disentitled himself to his remedy."[2]

Thus, if a contract for sale is made, and investigation of the title shows that the property is subject to restrictive covenants, the vendor cannot force the title on the purchaser subject to compensation,[3] but he can do so, for example, if the sole mistake is that a right of common attached to the land extends only to sheep instead of being, as represented, unlimited.[4]

A purchaser, on the other hand, is in a more favourable position, for as a general rule he is allowed to take all that he can get, and to subject the vendor to a proportionate diminution of the purchase-money.   But specific performance will not be decreed at the suit of the purchaser if the property which the vendor is in a position to convey is entirely different from that which he agreed to sell, or if the difference is one for which it is impossible to fix pecuniary compensation, or if the effect of decreeing specific performance would be to cause injustice to third parties.[5]

(vi) DUTY OF THE PURCHASER TO COMPLETE THE CONTRACT

Completion.   After the purchaser has investigated the abstract, it is his duty either to accept or to reject the title offered to him.   If he takes the latter course, the parties are left to their remedies as specified above.[6]   If, however, the purchaser is satisfied with the title, then the contract must be completed at once.   Completion of a contract means that the purchaser must at his own expense prepare a proper deed of conveyance which is effectual to pass the interest to be sold and which contains the usual covenants for title by the vendor.   He must also tender the price that he has agreed to pay.   On the vendor's side completion involves the execution of the conveyance and the delivery of possession of the land to the purchaser.[7]

---

[1] *Cox* v. *Coventon* (1862), 31 Beav. 378 ; *Re Arnold* (1880), 14 Ch. D. 270, 279 ; *supra*, p. 132.
[2] *Rutherford* v. *Acton-Adams*, [1915] A. C. 866, at pp. 869–70.
[3] *Cf. Rudd* v. *Lascelles*, [1900] 1 Ch. 815.
[4] *Howland* v. *Norris* (1784), 1 Cox, Eq. Cas. 59.
[5] *Willmott* v. *Barber* (1880), 15 Ch. D. 96.
[6] *Supra*, pp. 129 *et seq.*
[7] Williams, *Vendor and Purchaser* (4th Edn.), p. 37.

(vii) Duty of Vendor to Deliver the Title Deeds[1]

The vendor must deliver to the purchaser all title deeds which relate solely to the property sold, though he may retain such documents where he retains any part of the land to which they relate, or where the document consists of a trust instrument creating a trust that is still subsisting.[2] Where the documents which are necessary to show a good title remain in the vendor's possession, or where their custody belongs to some person other than the vendor, it is the vendor's duty to give a written acknowledgment of the purchaser's right to their production and to delivery of copies and a written undertaking for their safe custody. The effect of such an acknowledgment is that the purchaser, or persons claiming under him, can, at their own expense, demand to see the documents, or claim to be furnished with copies.[3]

(viii) Duty to Deliver Vacant Possession

Lastly, it is an implicit term of a contract of sale that vacant possession shall be given to the purchaser on completion.[4] Therefore a refusal by the purchaser to complete is justified if the land is subject to an unexpired tenancy, or if it has been lawfully requisitioned by a public authority.[5]

(3) CONDITIONS OF SALE UNDER CONTRACTS CONTAINING SPECIAL STIPULATIONS

We have now described in bare outline the nature of the parties' obligations under an open contract. Land, however, is not usually sold in this manner. As we have seen,[6] if the contract is by correspondence, statutory conditions apply ; and, in practice, it is usual for the parties to regulate their rights and duties by *special conditions* in the contract of sale. A professionally drawn contract will generally incorporate the terms of either the Law Society's Contract and Conditions of Sale or the National Conditions of Sale with variations to meet the particular case.[7] Reference

Special conditions.

---

[1] As to the right to possession of title deeds, see *Clayton* v. *Clayton*, [1930] 2 Ch. 12.

[2] L.P.A. 1925, s. 45 (9).

[3] *Ibid.*, s. 64.

[4] *Cook* v. *Taylor*, [1942] Ch. 349 ; [1942] 2 All E. R. 85. See Farrand, *Contract and Conveyance* (2nd Edn.), pp. 232–7.

[5] *Cook* v. *Taylor, supra* ; *James Macara, Ltd.* v. *Barclay*, [1945] K. B. 148 ; [1944] 2 All E. R. 589 ; dist. *Re Winslow Hall Estates Co. and United Glass Bottle Manufacturers, Ltd.'s Contract* [1941] Ch. 503 ; [1941] 3 All E. R. 124 ; *Hillingdon Estates Co.* v. *Stonefield Estates, Ltd.*, [1952] Ch. 627 ; [1952] 1 All E. R. 853.

[6] *Supra*, p. 113.

[7] The latest editions are 1973 Revision and 18th Edn. (1969) respectively. See *supra*, pp. 113–4.

must be made to the standard textbooks on conveyancing for full treatment.[1]

Matters which are commonly the subject of special conditions are

the root of title and the length of title (although this will be less important as a result of the Law of Property Act 1969)[2]

the date upon which possession is to be given, and the consequences if default is made ;

interest to be payable by the purchaser on the purchase price, if the sale is not completed on the stipulated date ;

the restriction of the purchaser's remedies for minor misdescriptions ;

and planning matters.

(B) THE CONVEYANCE
SUMMARY

(1) NECESSITY FOR A DEED

Deed of grant not universal till 1845.

Forms of Alienation. The appropriate form at the present day for the conveyance of any interest in land is a deed of grant, but this form, though always required for the transfer of incorporeal hereditaments, was not extended to freehold estates in possession until 1845. Before that date the distinction drawn by the law was that freehold estates in possession *lay in livery, i.e.* were transferable by delivery of possession, and that incorporeal interests *lay in grant, i.e.* must be conveyed by deed of grant.[3] The Real Property Act of 1845, however, provided that all corporeal hereditaments should, as regards the conveyance of the immediate freehold thereof, be deemed to lie in grant as well as in livery. This Act did not, however, abolish the old forms of conveyance, and although it led to the general use of a deed of grant as a means of transferring all kinds of landed interests, there were still occasions upon which such forms as the feoffment and the bargain and sale were used.

Real Property Act 1845.

---

[1] Wilkinson, *Standard Conditions of Sale of Land* (2nd Edn. 1974) ; *Emmet on Title* (16th Edn.), pp. 54–69 and passim ; Gibson's *Conveyancing* (20th Edn.), pp. 125–48 ; Farrand, *Contract and Conveyance* (2nd Edn.), pp. 73–83.

[2] *Supra*, p. 731.

[3] For the history of the forms of alienation, see Holdsworth, *History of English Law*, vol. iii. pp. 217–46 ; vol. vii. pp. 357–62. See *supra*, p. 50, note 1.

The Law of Property Act 1925 simplified practice by providing that [1] :

" All lands and all interests therein lie in grant and are incapable of being conveyed by livery or livery and seisin, or by feoffment, or by bargain and sale ; and a conveyance of an interest in land may operate to pass the possession or right to possession thereof, without actual entry, but subject to all prior rights thereto."

This section, which shows that a grant is the usual method of conveying any interest in land, is followed by another which provides that all conveyances of land, or of any interest therein, are void for the purpose of conveying or creating a legal estate unless they are made by deed.[2] This enactment, if unqualified, would cause inconvenience in certain cases, and it is therefore subject to exceptions. These are as follows[3] :—

1. **Assents by personal representatives.** The land of a deceased person vests in his personal representatives for the purposes of administration, and any devises he may have made are suspended until the administration is completed.[4] Upon such completion the land does not pass automatically to a devisee, but only when the assent of the personal representatives has been given. It is enacted that an assent to the vesting of a legal estate shall be *in writing*, signed by the personal representatives, and shall name the person in whose favour it is given and shall operate to vest in that person the legal estate to which it relates. An assent not in writing or not in favour of a named person is ineffectual to pass a legal estate.[5] An implied assent, *i.e.* one inferred from conduct, may be effective to pass a title to equitable interests or to *choses in action* and personal chattels.[6]

2. **Disclaimers by a trustee in bankruptcy.** When any part of the estate of a bankrupt consists of land which is burdened with onerous covenants and is therefore unsaleable, the trustee in bankruptcy may, by writing, disclaim the property. Such a disclaimer operates to determine the rights and the liabilities of the bankrupt in respect of the property, but it does not affect the rights of third parties. The court may, on the application of any person who is interested in the disclaimed property, make an order vesting the property in

---

[1] L.P.A. 1925, s. 51 (1).
[2] *Ibid.*, s. 52 (1).
[3] *Ibid.*, s. 52 (2).   [4] *Infra*, pp. 784 *et seq*.
[5] A.E.A. 1925, s. 36 (1), (4).
[6] *Re Hodge*, [1940] Ch. 260. *Re King's Will Trusts*, [1964] Ch. 542 ; [1964] 1 All E. R. 833 ; (1964), 28 *Conv.* (N.S.) 298 (J. F. Garner) ; Farrand, *Contract and Conveyance* (2nd Edn.), 111–19 ; Barnsley, *Conveyancing Law and Practice*, pp. 290–1.

him, and the effect of such an order is that the property vests in that person without any conveyance.[1]

Parol leases. 3. **Leases for a term not exceeding three years.**[2]

Vesting orders of the court. 4. **Vesting orders of the Court.** A vesting order is an order made by the court which may operate to vest, convey or create a legal estate in the same way as if a conveyance had been executed by the estate owner.[3] If, for instance,

> an equitable chargee applies for a sale of the land, the court may make an order vesting the land for a legal estate in the purchaser.[4]

Express surrender requires deed. 5. **Surrenders by operation of law.** *Surrender* is not an instrument, but means that the owner of a smaller estate yields up that estate to the person who is entitled in reversion or remainder to the larger estate in the same lands, as for instance, where the tenant for life of Blackacre surrenders his life interest to the person who is entitled to the fee simple in the land. In such a case the life interest is merged in the fee simple.

Surrenders are either express or implied and when implied they are said to arise by operation of law.

No deed in implied surrender. An express surrender is void at law unless it is made by deed, but an implied surrender is effectual without any formality.[5]

6. **Conveyances taking effect by operation of law.**[6] Examples of these are grants of probate or of letters of administration and adjudications in bankruptcy.

7. **Receipts not required to be under seal.** We have already seen that the legal estate of a mortgagee is re-vested in the mortgagor upon redemption not by a reconveyance under seal, but by an endorsed receipt.[7]

Finally we must consider the formalities necessary for the creation of a trust and for the disposition of an equitable interest. In neither case is a deed required.

Early Law. 1. **Creation of a Trust.** There are very few rules restricting the mode in which a trust must be created. The trust is the successor of the old use, and for the raising of a use no formalities were

---

[1] Bankruptcy Act 1914, s. 54, *infra*, p. 809.
[2] L.P.A. 1925, s. 54(2), *supra*, p. 390.
[3] *Ibid.*, s. 9.
[4] *Ibid.*, s. 90.   [5] *Supra*, p. 461.
[6] L.P.A. 1925, s. 52 (2) (g).   [7] *Supra*, p. 663.

necessary.   Spoken words were as effectual as written instruments, and according to the preamble to the Statute of Uses bare signs and gestures seem to have been sufficient.   The one guiding principle was that effect should be given to the intention of the settlor, no matter how it had been indicated by him.   So in general is it with the modern trust.

A trust may be created either by an instrument *inter vivos* or by will.

Summary of modern law.

If it is created *inter vivos* and if it relates to land, it must conform to the Law of Property Act 1925, which requires a writing.[1]

Inter vivos trusts.

If it is created by will, then, whether it relates to real or to personal property, the instrument of creation must be made in accordance with the Wills Act 1837, which prescribes the manner in which all wills must be made.[2]

Testamentary trusts.

If neither the Law of Property Act 1925 nor the Wills Act 1837 applies, if, that is to say, the trust relates neither to freeholds nor to leaseholds, and if it is not contained in a will, it may be created by word of mouth or by some other indication of intention, and without any kind of formality.   A clear oral declaration by the owner of pure personalty that he is a trustee of that property for another person constitutes a valid trust and can be enforced by the volunteer in whose favour it was declared.[3]

Trusts of pure personalty.

But it was found in the case of land that parol declarations of trusts led to disputes and inconveniences, and therefore the Statute of Frauds in 1677 required for the first time that the creation of a trust of real estate should be manifested and proved by some writing signed by the settlor.[4]   This provision has now been re-enacted by section 53 (1) (*b*) of the Law of Property Act 1925 in the following words :—

Trusts of land.

> " A declaration of trust respecting any land or any interest therein must be manifested and proved by some writing signed by some person who is able to declare such trust or by his will."

Formalities under Law of Property Act 1925.

There are several points that should be noticed about this enactment.   Thus it is confined to land and does not interfere with the rule that a trust of pure personalty may be constituted by an oral declaration.

It does not require a deed, but only a writing, and even so it does not require that the trust should have been declared by writing in the first place.   The statute uses the words " manifested and proved," and it is sufficient if the trust can be proved

---

[1] S. 53 (1) (*b*) *infra*.
[2] *Infra*, pp. 837 et seq.
[3] *Jones* v. *Lock* (1865), L. R. 1 Ch. App. 25.
[4] S. 7.

by some writing signed by the settlor no matter what the date of the writing may have been.[1]

The writing is to be signed by " some person who is able to declare such trust," that is, the person who is the owner of the property in respect to which the trust is declared.[2]   No provision is made for signature by an agent.

The statutory provisions apply only to express trusts, and not to resulting, implied or constructive trusts.[3]

2. Disposition of Equitable Interest.   Section 53 (1) (*c*) of the Law of Property Act 1925 provides that

" a disposition of an equitable interest or trust subsisting at the time of the disposition must be in writing signed by the person disposing of the same, or by his agent thereunto lawfully authorized in writing or by will."

In this context the word " disposition " must be given the wide meaning that it bears in normal usage, and therefore, for instance, an oral direction by a beneficiary to trustees to hold an equitable interest upon new trusts is a disposition that is ineffective for want of writing.[4]

(2) THE GENERAL NATURE OF A DEED[5]

Form of deed.

Signing, sealing, and delivery.   It is difficult to give an exact definition of a deed.   In general, however, a deed of grant is a written instrument, which is signed, sealed and delivered by the grantor as his act, and in which he expresses an intention to pass an interest to the grantee.   Before 1926 it was a moot question whether it was necessary for a deed to be signed, though in practice it has always been customary for all parties to append their signatures.   But signing is now essential in the case of an individual,[6] for it is enacted that where an *individual* executes a

Signature essential.

---

[1] *Rochefoucauld* v. *Boustead*, [1897] 1 Ch. 196. at p. 206.

[2] *Tierney* v. *Wood* (1854), 19 Beav. 330.

[3] L.P.A. 1925, s. 53 (2). ; *Hodgson* v. *Marks*, [1971] Ch. 892 ; [1971] 2 All E. R. 684.   See Hanbury, *Modern Equity*, pp. 98–102.

[4] *Grey* v. *I. R. Comrs.*, [1960] A.C. 1 ; [1959] 3 All E. R. 603 ; *Oughtred* v. *I. R. Comrs.*, [1960] A.C. 206 ; [1959] 3 All E. R. 673 ; *Vandervell* v. *I. R. Comrs.* [1967] 2 A. C. 291 ; [1967] 1 All E. R. 1.   *Re Tyler*, [1967] 1 W. L. R. 1269 ; [1967] 3 All E. R. 389.   *Re Danish Bacon Co., Ltd. Staff Pension Fund Trusts*, [1971] 1 W. L. R. 248 ; [1971] 1 All E. R. 486 ; *Re Vandervell's Trusts* (No. 2), [1974] Ch. 269 ; [1974] 1 All E. R. 47.

[5] See generally Barnsley, *Conveyancing Law and Practice*, pp. 381–9.

[6] Deeds executed by a corporation must be executed according to the special regulations, if any, prescribed by its constitution.   A company incorporated under the Companies Act 1948 is in this particular governed by the articles of association.   But in order to relieve a purchaser from the obligation of ascertaining whether such regulations have been observed, L.P.A. 1925, s. 74 (1), provides that a deed executed after 1925 shall be deemed to have been duly executed by a corporation aggregate if its seal be affixed thereto in the presence of and attested by its clerk, secretary, or other permanent officer or his deputy, and a member of the board of directors, council or other governing body of the corporation.   *D'Silva* v. *Lister House Development, Ltd.* [1971] Ch. 17 ; [1970] 1 All E. R. 858 ; (1973) 89 L.Q.R. 14 (M. J. Albery).

deed after 1925, he shall either sign or place his mark upon the same, and sealing alone shall not be deemed sufficient.[1] To satisfy the requirement of sealing, it is sufficient if a party signs the document with the intention of executing it as a deed, provided that it bears wax, or a wafer or some other indication of a seal.[2]

Signing and sealing a deed are ineffectual to pass the interest to the grantee without delivery. This does not mean a mere physical delivery, but a delivery accompanied by words or conduct signifying the grantor's intention to be bound by the provisions in the deed. The most apt and expressive mode of acknowledging this liability is for the grantor to hand the deed over, saying, " I deliver this as my deed," but any other words or acts that show an undoubted acknowledgment of immediate liability will suffice.[3] A physical delivery, however, unaccompanied by this express or implied acknowledgment, is insufficient, so that if, for instance,

Delivery.

> the grantor signs and seals the deed and then delivers it to his solicitor to be dealt with according to instructions to be given later, it does not operate as an immediate grant of the interest.

Escrow. There are, therefore, two kinds of delivery recognized by the law in this connection, one absolute and the other conditional.[4] If a document is delivered, either to a party to it or to a stranger,[5] with an intimation, express or implied, that it is not to become effective until some condition has been performed, it is called an escrow. In such a case the deed is inoperative until the condition is performed, but upon performance it takes effect as a deed without further delivery, and relates back to the time when it was delivered as an escrow.[6] A delivery of a deed as an escrow is a final delivery in the sense that it cannot be withdrawn by the grantor before the grantee has had an opportunity to decide whether to fufil the condition or not. A deed delivered subject to a condition and subject to such a right of withdrawal is not an escrow, but merely an undelivered deed.[7] A common example of delivery as an escrow occurs where a vendor executes a deed of conveyance and gives it to his solicitor for transference to the purchaser upon payment by the latter of the purchase money.

Conditional delivery.

---

[1] L.P.A. 1925, s. 73.
[2] *Stromdale and Ball, Ltd.* v. *Burden,* [1952] Ch. 223 ; [1952] 1 All E. R. 59.
[3] *Xenos* v. *Wickham* (1866), L. R. 2 H. L. 296, at p. 312.
[4] *Foundling Hospital* v. *Crane,* [1911] 2 K. B. 367, at p. 377.
[5] *London Freehold and Leasehold Property Co.* v. *Baron Suffield,* [1897] 2 Ch. 608, at pp. 621–2.
[6] *Vincent* v. *Premo Enterprises (Voucher Sales), Ltd.,* [1969] 2 Q. B. 609 ; [1969] 2 All E. R. 941.
[7] *Beesly* v. *Hallwood Estates, Ltd.,* [1961] Ch. 105; [1960] 1 All E. R. 90; *Windsor Refrigerator Co., Ltd.* v. *Branch Nominees Ltd.,* [1961] Ch. 88; [1960] 2 All E. R. 568; reversed on a different point, [1961] Ch. 375; [1961] 1 All E. R. 277 ; *D'Silva* v. *Lister House Development, Ltd. supra.*

If the sale is not completed in due course, the vendor is released, and the solicitor has no authority to hand over the conveyance.[1]

Witness not essential.
Attestation. Signing, sealing and due delivery are, then, essential to constitute a valid deed. Strictly speaking, attestation is not necessary, but it is the invariable practice for parties to execute deeds in the presence of a witness,[2] and to add a statement that the deed has been signed, sealed and delivered in the presence of the witness, who himself signs.

Indentures.
Deeds poll and indentures. Deeds are either deeds poll or indentures. A deed poll is one which is executed by a party of one part, an indenture is a deed (such as a conveyance by way of sale) to which there are parties of two or more parts.

In ancient days, when deeds were more concise than they are at present, it was usual, when they were made between two parties, to write two copies on the same parchment with some words written in the middle through which the parchment was cut in acute angles or indentations.[3] These two parts were called " counterparts," and, when put together so that the indentations fitted into each other, constituted the complete deed. Hence the name " indenture." (Counterparts are not nowadays written on the same parchment, but that which is executed by the grantor of an interest is called the *original*, while that which is executed by the party to whom the interest passes—for example, a lessee— is called the *counterpart*.[4]) The custom of indenting deeds gradually died out, and all that the term " indenture " now indicates is that the deed in question involves parties of more than one part. Despite the provision of the Real Property Act 1845 that a deed should have the effect of an indenture although not actually indented, it remained customary to introduce every deed which involved more than one party by the expression *This Indenture*. But even this survival has now gone, for it is enacted [5] that any deed may be described according to the nature of the transaction to be effected, so that now the introductory words are

" This Trust Deed,"
" This Legal Charge,"
" This Conveyance,"
" This Lease,"

or a similar appropriate expression.

A deed poll is so called because, unlike an indenture, it was formerly polled (or cut even) at the top.

---

[1] *Kingston v. Ambrian Investment Co., Ltd.* [1975] 1 W. L. R. 161 ; [1975] 1 All E. R. 120 ; *Glessing v. Green*, [1975] 1 W. L. R. 863 ; [1975] 2 All E. R. 696.
[2] Norton, *A Treatise on Deeds* (2nd Edn.), p. 24.
[3] Blackstone, vol. ii. p. 295.
[4] Elphinstone, *Introduction to Conveyancing* (7th Edn.), p. 60.
[5] L.P.A. 1925, s. 57.

Conveyance by a person to himself. It is sometimes necessary that an interest shall be conveyed by the grantor to himself jointly with another person, as for instance where a surviving trustee desires to vest the legal estate in himself and a new trustee. At common law this could not be done by one deed, for the effect of a grant by A. to A. and B. was to vest the whole estate in B. The only solution was that A. should convey to X., who would then convey to A. and B., though an alternative method became available, and in fact general, under the doctrine of uses, for if A. conveyed to X. *to the use* of himself and B., the effect of the Statute of Uses was to vest an immediate legal estate in A. and B. jointly. It has been possible, however, since August 1859 in the case of leaseholds, and since 1881 in the case of freeholds, for a person to convey land to himself jointly with another person by a direct deed of grant, and as the Statute of Uses has been repealed, this is now the only method.[1]

Conveyance to oneself and to another.

There are also occasions when it is necessary that a person should convey land to himself (as, for example, where personal representatives assent to the land vesting in themselves as trustees for sale).[2] Although, in the example given, the design could be effected in a direct manner under statutory provisions, it remained generally true, prior to 1926, that a conveyance by a person to himself required a grant to uses. It is now provided, however, that

Conveyance to oneself.

" a person may convey land to or vest land in himself." [3]

This, however, does not enable an owner to grant a tenancy to himself, for a lease, though it falls within the statutory definition of a "conveyance" and no doubt vests a legal estate in the lessee, is essentially a contractual transaction. At the lowest it creates a number of implied obligations and liabilities, a situation that is impossible where only one person is involved. A man cannot contract with himself.[4]

Grant by two persons to one of themselves.

Two or more persons (whether trustees or personal representatives or not) may convey any property vested in themselves to any one or more of themselves, though if the conveyance amounts to a breach of trust, it is liable to be set aside.[5]

(3) THE MODERN FORM OF A DEED OF CONVEYANCE ON SALE

It will perhaps elucidate the subject if we now set out a simple deed of conveyance, and state and explain the effect of each of its

---

[1] L.P.A., 1925, s. 72 (1), (2) ; replacing L.P.(A.)A. 1859, s. 21, and Conveyancing Act 1881, s. 50.
[2] *Re King's Will Trusts,* [1964] Ch. 542 : [1964] 1 All E. R. 833.
[3] L.P.A. 1925, s. 72 (3).
[4] *Rye* v. *Rye,* [1962] A. C. 496 ; [1962] 1 All E. R. 146 ; M. & B. p. 384.
[5] L.P.A. 1925, s. 72 (4).

parts. The following is a precedent of a conveyance executed by the owner of a fee simple absolute. The words which form part of the deed are put in heavier type in order to distinguish them from what is added by way of comment or explanation.

Parties.	**THIS CONVEYANCE is made the 1st day of January 1975 BETWEEN ADAM SMITH of Balliol College, Oxford, Gentleman (hereinafter called the vendor) of the one part, AND WILLIAM BLACKSTONE of All Souls College, Oxford, Knight (hereinafter called the purchaser) of the other part.**

All parties whose intentions are expressed later in the deed must be mentioned, and there are said to be parties of as many " parts " as there are different intentions expressed. Smith intends to transfer the land and receive the purchase money, Blackstone intends to transfer the money and receive the land, and therefore they are parties of different parts. If Smith and Robinson were selling as trustees for sale, they would be parties of one part.[1]

Recitals.	**WHEREAS the vendor is seised of the hereditaments intended to be hereby conveyed for an estate in fee simple absolute in possession free from incumbrances and has agreed to sell the same to the purchaser for the sum of £50,000 ;**

Recitals.

Recitals are not a necessary part of a deed, but they are generally inserted in order to indicate the purpose of the deed in which they are contained, and to state the past history of the property conveyed.[2]

Narrative recitals.

Narrative recitals are those which show the nature of the interest that is being transferred, and if the vendor is seised in fee simple (as in our example), they merely state that fact. On the other hand, where a mortgagee sells under his statutory power, the recitals must state that the mortgage was made, and that the mortgage loan remains owing. Again, if it is not obvious why certain persons are parties to the deed, the explanation will be given in the recitals. Thus a conveyance by personal representatives will recite the will, the appointment of the vendors as executors, the death of the testator and the grant of probate.

---

[1] Elphinstone, *Introduction to Conveyancing* (7th Edn.), pp. 61–2.
[2] See Farrand, *Contract and Conveyance* (2nd Edn.), pp. 307 *et seq.*

Introductory recitals are inserted in order to explain the object of the deed—that is, in our example, the transfer from Smith to Blackstone of a fee simple absolute.

Owing to the doctrine of estoppel, great care is necessary in the framing of recitals. Any recital which is precise and un-ambiguous, and which is clearly intended to bind the person by whom it is made, estops him and all persons claiming through him from denying the truth of the statement.   Thus a recital that the vendor is seised in fee simple raises an estoppel. If this statement is untrue, but the vendor at a later date actually acquires the fee simple from the true owner, he is estopped from denying that he was owner at the time of the sale, and the fee simple passes to the purchaser under the doctrine of feeding the estoppel.[1]

The recitals are followed by what is called the *testatum*, which comprises the *operative part* of the deed, *i.e.* the part by which the object is actually effected.

<table>
<tr><td>Testa-
tum.</td><td>**NOW THIS DEED WITNESSETH that in consideration of the sum of £50,000 paid to the vendor by the purchaser (the receipt of which sum the vendor hereby acknowledges) the VENDOR AS BENEFICIAL OWNER**</td></tr>
<tr><td>Opera-
tive
words.</td><td>**HEREBY CONVEYS unto the pur-chaser**</td></tr>
<tr><td>Parcels.</td><td>**ALL and singular the hereditaments known as Blackacre and situate at Kidlington in the County of Oxford and containing 24 acres 2 roods or thereabouts.**</td></tr>
</table>

A deed is not void for want of consideration, but it is the invariable practice to state the amount of the purchase money and the fact of its receipt, because the amount of stamp duty payable thereby becomes ascertainable, while a receipt so inserted in the body of a deed is a sufficient discharge to the purchaser without any further receipt being indorsed on the deed.[2] Again, such a receipt is sufficient evidence to a subsequent purchaser of the payment, provided that he has no notice that the money was not actually paid.[3]

The words " Beneficial Owner." The effect of using the expression " beneficial owner " requires explanation. In former days a deed of conveyance ran to considerable length since it usually contained elaborate covenants for title, the object of which

---

[1] *Supra*, p. 404.   [2] L.P.A. 1925, s. 67.   [3] *Ibid.*, s. 68.

was to render the vendor liable in covenant if a flaw were later discovered in his title. Although titles were traditionally investigated with such care that a purchaser would seldom need to enforce this contractual liability, it was usual before 1882 to set out the appropriate undertakings at length[1], a practice which, while it militated against simplicity and brevity, increased the profits of solicitors, whose remuneration in those days depended upon the length of the documents they prepared. Since 1881, however, covenants for title need not be expressly stated. If the appropriate words designated by statute[2] are used (and the appropriate words vary according as the grantor conveys freeholds or assigns leaseholds for valuable consideration, or by way of settlement, or as trustee and so on), the effect is that certain covenants for title, also designated by the Act,[3] are implied.

Implied covenants.

The appropriate words for raising these covenants upon sale of land are " beneficial owner." If the conveyance is for valuable consideration, and if the vendor " conveys and is expressed to convey as beneficial owner," and if in fact he possesses that status,[4] the effect is that the four following covenants are implied:—

1. **Covenant that vendor has a good right to convey.**
   This means that the vendor has full power to convey the interest which he has agreed to sell. Hence, if he has agreed to sell 84 acres, and it happens that 150 feet of this area have been acquired by adverse possessors under the Limitation Act,[5] he will be liable under the implied covenant to lose the difference between the value of the property he agreed to sell and that of the property which he is entitled to convey.

2. **Covenant that purchaser shall have quiet enjoyment.**
   A physical interference with the enjoyment of the land, as, for instance, the exercise of a right of way lawfully acquired by a stranger from the vendor prior to the sale, constitutes a breach of the covenant, though of course in such a case the existence of the easement also constitutes a breach of the covenant that the vendor has a right to convey.

   The object of implying this covenant in addition to the covenant that the vendor has a good right to convey is that the Limitation Act begins to run from the date of the deed in the

---

[1] See (1962), 26 *Conv.* (N. S.) 45 (M. J. Russell).
[2] L.P.A. 1925, s. 76.
[3] *Ibid.*, Sched. 2. See generally Farrand, *Contract and Conveyance*, (2nd Edn.) pp. 327 *et seq.* ; Barnsley, *Conveyancing Law and Practice*, chap. 24 ; (1968) 32 Conv. (N.S.) 123 ; (1970) 34 Conv. (N.S.) 178 (M. J. Russell).
[4] *Fay* v. *Miller, Wilkins & Co.*, [1941] Ch. 360 at p. 362; [1941] 2 All E. R. 18 at p. 23; *Pilkington* v. *Wood*, [1953] Ch. 770, at p. 777; [1953] 2 All E. R. 810, at p. 813 ; *Re Robertson's Application*, [1969] 1 All E. R. 257, at p. 258.
[5] *Eastwood* v. *Ashton*, [1915] A. C. 900.

latter case, since that is the time at which the breach occurs, but from the date of the interference in the case of a covenant for quiet enjoyment.

3. **Covenant that the property is free from incumbrances.** This means that the property is free from all estates, incumbrances, claims and demands other than those to which the conveyance is expressly made subject.

4. **Covenant for further assurance.** This obliges the vendor to execute assurances and to do everything that is right and possible in order to perfect the conveyance.

It should be noted that the undertakings which have been set out are not four independent and separate covenants, but parts of one entire contract. They are not absolute, but qualified, since they extend only to the acts and omissions[1] of the vendor and those claiming through him and to the acts and omissions of persons through whom he claims, except those from whom he has taken the property for a money consideration. Thus, a vendor who himself purchased the land for value from X. on a previous occasion is not liable under the covenant for quiet enjoyment if X. disturbs the possession of the ultimate purchaser.[2] *Qualified nature of implied covenants.*

The covenants implied by the Act may be varied or extended. The different covenants that are implied when the conveyance is by a mortgagor, settlor, trustee, mortgagee[3] and so on, are set out in the second schedule to the Law of Property Act 1925.

We will now turn to the *operative words* of the conveyance. In old deeds, instead of using the single word *convey*, it was customary *per majorem cautelam* to employ a much more extensive series of words, such as *grant, bargain, sell, aliene, convey, release and confirm.* Since the Real Property Act 1845, however, which enacted that all corporeal hereditaments should lie in grant, the word *grant* alone has been sufficient to transfer both corporeal and incorporeal interests. This is, however, not essential,[4] and *convey* is the word adopted in the various forms of instrument given in the Law of Property Act 1925. *Operative words.*

It sometimes happens that the recitals are inconsistent with the operative words. In this case the law has been judicially stated as follows [5] : *Discrepancy between recitals and operative words.*

" If the recitals are clear and the operative part is ambiguous, the recitals govern the construction. If the recitals are ambiguous, and

---

[1] See (1967), 31 *Conv.* (N.S.) 268 (M. J. Russell).
[2] *David* v. *Sabin*, [1893] 1 Ch. 523; *Stoney* v. *Eastbourne R.D.C.*, [1927] 1 Ch. 367. " Purchase for value " in this context does not include a conveyance in consideration of marriage; L.P.A. 1925, Sched. 2, Part I.
[3] See (1964), 28 *Conv.* (N.S.) 205 (A. M. Prichard).
[4] L.P.A. 1925, s. 51 (2).
[5] *Ex parte Dawes* (1886), 17 Q. B. D. 275, at p. 286, *per* Lord ESHER; *Re Sassoon,* [1933] Ch. 858 ; affd, [1935] A. C. 96.

the operative part is clear, the operative part must prevail. If both the recitals and the operative part are clear, but they are inconsistent with each other, the operative part is to be preferred."

"General words" now implied.

The Parcels Clause. The operative words are followed by the *parcels clause*,[1] the object of which is to give a physical description of the property sold : this may be accompanied by a plan, to which reference is made in the clause. A grant operates to pass the rights incidental to the land, such as easements and profits which have become attached thereto. But since rights such as *quasi*-easements which have not become legally appurtenant to the land would not pass without special mention, it was usual, prior to 1882, to insert *general words*, which were framed widely enough to include all rights actually enjoyed by the vendor in respect of the land. Since 1881, however, unless a contrary intention is expressed, such *general words* are implied in every conveyance.[2] Thus a conveyance of land now operates, by virtue of the Law of Property Act 1925, to convey all buildings, erections, fixtures, commons, hedges, ditches, fences, ways, waters, watercourses, liberties, privileges, easements, rights and advantages whatsoever, appertaining or reputed to appertain to the land or any part thereof. An equally wide implication is raised with regard to rights appertaining to buildings.[3]

Grantor's whole interest passes.

"All Estate Clause." It was also usual before 1882 to add what was called an *all estate clause* with the object of ensuring that the entire interest of the grantor should be transferred. This was as a matter of fact quite ineffective to transfer anything that would not pass automatically, and it is now omitted in reliance on the enactment that, unless a contrary intention is expressed, every conveyance is effectual to pass all the estate, right, title, interest, claim, and demand which the conveying parties respectively have in, to, or on the property.[4]

Proceeding now with the precedent, we next arrive at the *habendum clause*.

Haben- **To hold unto the purchaser in fee**
dum. **simple.**

The object of this is to define the extent of the interest taken by the purchaser.

Finally come the *testimonium*, which states that the parties have signed and sealed the deed in witness of what it contains, and the *attestation clause*.

---

[1] See generally Farrand, *Contract and Conveyance* (2nd Edn.), pp. 353 *et seq.* ; Barnsley. *Conveyancing Law and Practice*, pp. 461 *et seq.*
[2] L.P.A. 1925, s. 62.
[3] *Ibid.*, s. 62 (2) ; *supra*, pp. 530–2. [4] *Ibid.*, s. 63.

Testi-
monium.

In witness whereof the said parties hereto have hereunto set their respective hands and seals the day and year first above written.

Attesta-
tion
Clause.

Signed sealed and delivered by the vendor in the presence of John Roe of 200 St. Aldates Oxford solicitor.   ADAM SMITH   (Seal)

The whole precedent, then, stands as follows :—

Parties.

THIS CONVEYANCE is made the 1st day of January 1975 BETWEEN ADAM SMITH of Balliol College, Oxford, Gentleman, (hereinafter called the vendor) of the one part, AND WILLIAM BLACKSTONE of All Souls College, Oxford, Knight (hereinafter called the purchaser) of the other part.

Recitals.

WHEREAS the vendor is seised of the hereditaments intended to be hereby conveyed for an estate in fee simple absolute in possession free from incumbrances and has agreed to sell the same to the purchaser for the sum of £50,000;

Testa-
tum.

NOW THIS DEED WITNESSETH that in consideration of the sum of £50,000 paid to the vendor by the purchaser (the receipt of which sum the vendor hereby acknowledges) the VENDOR AS BENEFICIAL OWNER

Opera-
tive
words.

HEREBY CONVEYS unto the purchaser

Parcels.

ALL and singular the hereditaments known as Blackacre and situate at Kidlington in the County of Oxford and containing 24 acres 2 roods or thereabouts,

Haben-
dum.

To hold unto the purchaser in fee simple.

	In witness whereof the said parties
Testi-	hereto have hereunto set their re-
monium.	spective hands and seals the day and
	year first above written.

Attesta-	Signed sealed and delivered by the	
tion	vendor in the presence of John Roe	Adam
clause.	of 200 St. Aldates Oxford solicitor.	Smith

SECTION II. REGISTERED CONVEYANCING

SUMMARY

(1) THE MACHINERY OF TRANSFER INTER VIVOS

Duties of vendor.   The preliminary enquiries and the contract of sale follow the pattern of unregistered conveyancing, but the investigation of the title is radically different. No longer does the vendor need to trace the history of the transactions in which the estate has been involved, for the register is conclusive on the question of ownership. The register is, however, private and the vendor must give the purchaser authority to inspect it and, in lieu of an abstract of title, supply him with a copy of the entries and of any filed plans and copies or abstracts of any documents noted on the register. The register is, however, not conclusive as to third party rights and a vendor is therefore required to provide a purchaser with copies, abstracts and evidence of all rights and interests appurtenant to the registered land, as to which the register is not conclusive.[1]

Requisitions and searches.   Requisitions on title follow the usual form but where the title is absolute or good leasehold, they are limited to overriding interests and other matters in respect of which the register is not conclusive. Possessory or qualified titles will require more careful investigation.[2] Searches must be made of local land charges registers, for local land charges are overriding interests. But it will not be necessary to search the register of land charges under the Land Charges Act 1972, as third party rights which would appear there if the land were unregistered will appear on the register under the Land Registration Act 1925. The main

---

[1] L.R.A. 1925, s. 110.
[2] For a detailed treatment of requisitions, see Ruoff and Roper, pp. 345–6.

search will therefore be of the register itself. This may be undertaken either personally or by an official search. The official search has a considerable advantage, for once a purchaser has applied for an official search, any entry made thereafter during a priority period of, in effect, fifteen working days is postponed to the purchaser's application to register his transfer, provided that he delivers this application to the registry in the proper form before the end of the priority period.[1]

The transfer must be on one of the forms set out in the Rules. It will be deemed to contain the general words implied by section 62 of the Law of Property Act 1925, so far as they are appropriate.[2] The usual covenants for title may be incorporated by inserting the appropriate words whereby a person is expressed to convey " as beneficial owner ", " as settlor ", " as trustee ", etc., as the case may be.[3] The transfer must be by deed in the same way as a conveyance under the Law of Property Act 1925, stamped with the appropriate Inland Revenue Stamp, and sent to the registry together with the Land Certificate. Registration of the transferee's name completes the transfer and terminates the legal ownership of the transferor.[4]

Form of transfer.

The simplicity of the form of transfer inter vivos is shown from the reproduction below of the form authorised by the Land Registry for the transfer of the whole of a parcel of freehold or leasehold land. It has been completed with the details of the sale of the fee simple of Blackacre similar to those set out in the precedent of the conveyance under the unregistered system on page 765.

H.M. LAND REGISTRY
LAND REGISTRATION ACTS 1925 to 1971

TRANSFER OF WHOLE *(Freehold or Leasehold)*
(Rule 98 or 115, Land Registration Rules 1925)

Administrative Area   OXFORDSHIRE
District or London Borough   CHERWELL

---

[1] Land Registration (Official Searches) Rules 1969. The priority period may be extended once only for a further period of 14 working days after the initial period (rr. 6 and 7). See Barnsley, *Conveyancing Law and Practice*, pp. 356–9, *Smith* v. *Morrison*, [1974] 1 W. L. R. 659 ; [1974] 1 All E. R. 957.

[2] L.R.A. 1925, ss. 19 (3), 22 (3) ; *supra*, p. 530. See also Ruoff and Roper, pp. 103–4.

[3] L.R.A. 1925, s 38 (2) : L.R.R. 1925, r. 76. See Ruoff and Roper, pp. 306 *et seq.* Farrand, *Contract and Conveyance* (2nd Edn.), pp. 346–53 ; Barnsley, *op cit.*, pp. 346–53. *Hissett* v. *Reading Roofing Co., Ltd.*, [1969] 1 W. L. R. 1757 ; [1970] 1 All E. R. 122 ; (1970), 34 *Conv.* (N.S.) 128 (F. R. Crane).

[4] Registration takes effect as from the day on which a completed application is delivered: L.R.R. 1925, r. 83.

Title number   ON 00001

Property   BLACKACRE, KIDLINGTON

Date   1 January 1975   In consideration of   Fifty
thousand

pounds (£50,000) *the receipt whereof is hereby acknowledged*

I,   ADAM SMITH, of BALLIOL COLLEGE,
OXFORD, GENTLEMAN

as beneficial owner hereby transfer to:

> WILLIAM BLACKSTONE, OF ALL SOULS
> COLLEGE, OXFORD, KNIGHT

the land comprised in the title above mentioned

Signed, sealed and delivered by the said ⎫
    Adam Smith   ⎬   ADAM SMITH   (Seal)
in the presence of   ⎭

Name   John Roe

Address   200 St. Aldates Oxford

Description or occupation   Solicitor

(2) THE TITLE

We have already seen that there are four different classes of title which may be entered on the proprietorship register; absolute, qualified, possessory and good leasehold. We have already described the absolute title, which is available for both freeholds and leaseholds.[1] " Possessory titles are granted in less than one in a hundred applications for first registration in compulsory areas. Qualified titles are virtually unknown. Good leasehold titles are common." [2]

Good
leasehold
title.
The good leasehold title is only available for leaseholds. Where, as frequently happens, a leaseholder cannot produce the title to the reversion, he may be registered as the owner of a good leasehold title. The title to the leasehold interest only is investigated and guaranteed by the Land Registry. This is the same as with an absolute title, with the important exception that " registration does not affect or prejudice the enforcement of any estate, right or interest affecting or in derogation of the title of the lessor to grant the lease ".[3] The guarantee is of course similarly limited.

[1] *Supra*, pp. 108–9.
[2] Ruoff, p. 45.
[3] L.R.A. 1925, s. 10.

Possessory titles usually arise out of claims by squatters, and also occasionally where a documentary title is lodged, which is too weak for a better kind of title but not deserving of outright rejection. Possessory titles are mainly freeholds, although possessory leaseholds do exist. The guarantee is a limited one, as the registration does not affect or prejudice the enforcement of any estate, right or interest adverse to or in derogation of the title of the first proprietor and subsisting or capable of arising at the time of the first registration.[1] In the case of a freehold or leasehold interest registered with a possessory title the guarantee covers, therefore, only dealings which take place after the registration and does not extend to the title prior to registration.

Possessory title.

Where an application is made to register a freehold with an absolute title and the Registrar comes to the conclusion on the examination of title that it can be established only for a limited period or subject to certain reservations, he may, at the applicant's request, register a qualified title. This title may except from the effect of registration any estate, right or interest arising before a specified date, or arising under a specified instrument, or otherwise described in the register, and has the same effect as an absolute title save for the estate, right or interest excepted.[2] A qualified title may also be registered at the applicant's request in respect of a leasehold when the examination of the title either of the lessor to the reversion, or of the lessee to the leasehold interest, discloses similar problems to those described above. It has the same effect as a good leasehold or absolute title as the case may be, subject to the exception of the specified interests.[3]

Qualified title.

The Act provides for the conversion of inferior titles to absolute or good leasehold titles, and of good leasehold into absolute.[4] Possessory titles, if for no other reason than the effect of the Limitation Act, cannot remain so permanently. For example, the Registrar, after due enquiry, must convert possessory titles of freehold land to absolute where the title has been registered for fifteen years, and possessory titles of leasehold to good leasehold where registered for ten years, but he must be satisfied that the proprietor is in possession.[5] The Registrar also has under section 77 an option to convert into absolute (or good leasehold) titles in other cases as set out therein, as well as a very important power to convert good leasehold to absolute leasehold titles if the applicant furnishes evidence as to the reversionary title (including in appropriate cases the mere existence of a registered reversionary title).[6]

Conversion of titles.

---

[1] L.R.A. 1925, ss. 6 and 11.
[2] *Ibid.*, s. 7.
[3] *Ibid.*, s. 12.
[4] *Ibid.*, s. 77.
[5] *Ibid.*, s. 77(3)(b).
[6] For a full discussion see Ruoff and Roper, pp. 278–84.

(3) RECTIFICATION AND INDEMNITY[1]

Rectification
of register.

Under section 82 of the Land Registration Act 1925, the register may be rectified, *inter alia*, when an entry has been obtained by fraud,[2] when a legal estate has been registered in the name of a person who if the land had not been registered would not have been the estate owner,[3] or when, because of any error or omission in the register it would be just to rectify it.[4] In *Chowood, Ltd.* v. *Lyall* (*No.* 2), for example, the register was rectified in favour of a squatter who had acquired title by adverse possession to part of the land registered in the name of the proprietor.[5] The section, however, protects a *proprietor in possession* by providing that rectification may only take place against him if :

(*a*) it is to give effect to an overriding interest, or

(*b*) he is a party or privy, or has caused or substantially contributed by his act, neglect or default to the fraud, mistake or omission which needs to be rectified,[6] or

(*c*) the immediate disposition to him was void, or the disposition to any person through whom he claims otherwise than for value was void, or

(*d*) for any other reason, it would be unjust not to rectify against him.[7]

The principle which emerges is that a *purchaser* who buys registered land and remains in *possession* of it is guaranteed his possession, and rectification will not be ordered against him except to give effect to an overriding interest. If, however, he has contributed to the error, rectification may be ordered against him. An applicant for registration will be regarded as having contributed to a mistaken registration if, however innocently, the

---

[1] See (1971), 35 *Conv.* (N.S.) 390 (T. Ruoff and P. Meehan) ; (1968), 84 *L. Q. R.* 528 (S. M. Cretney and G. Dworkin) ; Ruoff and Roper, pp. 827 *et seq.* ; Farrand, *Contract and Conveyance* (2nd Edn.), pp. 209–20 ; Barnsley, *Conveyancing Law and Practice*, pp. 60–73 ; Law Commission, Working Paper No. 45 (1972), pp. 36–74.
[2] *Re Leighton's Conveyance*, [1936] 1 All E. R. 667 ; affirmed [1937] Ch. 149 (fraudulent misrepresentation and undue influence).
[3] *Chowood, Ltd.* v. *Lyall* (*No. 2*), [1930] 2 Ch. 156 ; *Re 139 High Street, Deptford*, [1951] Ch. 884 ; [1951] 1 All E. R. 950 ; M. & B. p. 137 (land erroneously included on first registration in title of neighbouring proprietor).
[4] *Re Dances Way, West Town, Hayling Island*, [1962] Ch. 490 ; [1962] 2 All E. R. 42 (notice of adverse easement cancelled).
[5] [1930] 2 Ch. 156.
[6] *Re 139 High Street, Deptford, supra*, following *Chowood, Ltd.* v. *Lyall* (*No. 2*), [1930] 2 Ch. 156 ; *Claridge* v. *Tingey, Re Sea View Gardens*, [1967] 1 W. L. R 134 ; [1966] 3 All E. R. 935 ; M. & B. p. 139 ; (1968) 84 L. Q. R. 528, at pp. 541–5.
[7] *Epps* v. *Esso Petroleum Co. Ltd.* [1973] 1 W. L. R. 1071 ; [1973] 2 All E. R. 465 ; M. & B. p. 141.

description of the property in an application leads to other property being included in the area of which the applicant is eventually registered as first proprietor.[1]   There is an overriding discretionary element in the jurisdiction, however, and rectification may not be ordered in favour of an owner who has stood by and has watched a defendant build on the land before intervening.[2]

A right of indemnity is available under section 83 to anyone   Right of suffering loss by reason of: indemnity.

(a)   any rectification of the register,

(b)   an error or omission on the register which is not rectified,

(c)   the loss or destruction of any document lodged at the registry for inspection or safe custody, or an error in any official search.

Apart from (c), compensation is paid only when someone *suffers loss by reason of* a rectification, or of a mistake that has been made on the register, which is not to be rectified.   Hence, when a purchaser bought registered land on part of which, unknown to the purchaser, a squatter had already established a title by adverse possession and rectification was ordered (because the right was an overriding interest), the purchaser was unable to obtain an indemnity because his loss was not "by reason of the rectification" but had resulted from the purchase itself,[3] *i.e.* because he had purchased land from a vendor against whom a squatter had already obtained title so that the rectification made him no worse off than before.   If, however, a proprietor of registered land claims in good faith under a disposition which is forged and the register is rectified against him, he is deemed to have suffered loss by reason of the rectification.[4]   But compensation is never payable if

" the applicant or a person from whom he derives title (otherwise than under a disposition for valuable consideration which is registered or protected on the register) has caused or substantially contributed to the loss by fraud or lack of proper care."[5]

A macabre example of a refusal to rectify leading to a true owner being given indemnity is provided by the case of the acid bath murderer, Haigh.[6]   Haigh forged the signature of a registered proprietor, was registered in his name and then, in that name,

---

[1] For criticism, see Law Commission Working Paper No. 45 (1972), pp. 80–1.

[2] *Claridge* v. *Tingey, Re Sea View Gardens, supra,* at pp. 141 and 941, respectively, *per* PENNYCUICK, J.

[3] *Re Chowood's Registered Land,* [1933] Ch. 574 ; M. & B. p. 139 ; applied in *Re Boyle's Claim,* [1961] 1 W. L. R. 339 ; [1961] 1 All E. R. 620.

[4] L. R. A. s. 83 (4).

[5] S. 83 (5) (a) as amended by Land Registration and Land Charges Act 1971, s. 3, with effect from July 27, 1971.

[6] Recounted in Ruoff and Roper, p. 852.

sold to an innocent purchaser for value. Rectification was not ordered as the purchaser was in possession. But the personal representatives of the real proprietor were compensated in full.

(4) OVERRIDING INTERESTS[1]

Definition of overriding interests.

Overriding interests are defined and listed in the Land Registration Act 1925. By section 3 (xvi), unless the context otherwise requires,

" Overriding interests " mean all the incumbrances, interests, rights, and powers not entered on the register but subject to which registered dispositions are by this Act to take effect...

By section 70 (1)

All registered land shall, unless...the contrary is expressed on the register, be deemed to be subject to such of the following overriding interests as may be for the time being subsisting in reference thereto...

and then follows a list, to which additions have been made by later enactments.[2]

(a) Rights of common,[3] drainage rights, customary rights (until extinguished), public rights, profits à prendre, rights of sheepwalk, rights of way, watercourses, rights of water, and other easements not being equitable easements required to be protected by notice on the register.

Under this paragraph all easements and profits are overriding interests except apparently equitable easements.[4] Equitable easements should be protected by notice or caution on the register of the servient title.

(b) Liability to repair highways by reason of tenure, quit-rents, crown rents, heriots, and other rents and charges (until extinguished) having their origin in tenure:

(c) Liability to repair the chancel of any church ;[5]

(d) Liability in respect of embankments, and sea and river walls ;

---

[1] See Ruoff and Roper, chap 6 ; Wolstenholme and Cherry, vol. 6, pp. 63–67 ; Farrand, *Contract and Conveyance* (2nd Edn.), pp. 184–209 ; Barnsley, *Conveyancing Law and Practice*, pp. 63–7 ; Law Commission Working Paper, No. 37 (1971).
[2] *Infra*, p. 776.
[3] By the Commons Registration Act 1965, s.1(1), no rights of common over land which is capable of registration under that Act can be registered under the Land Registration Acts.
[4] Farrand, pp. 180–90. *Poster* v. *Slough Estates, Ltd.*, [1969] 1 Ch. 495, at at p. 507 ; [1968] 3 All E. R. 257 ; M. & B. p. 504 ; *supra*, p. 588 ; (1969), 33 *Conv.* (N.S.) 135 (P. Jackson) ; *Payne* v. *Adnams*, [1971] C. L. Y. 6486.
[5] Now under consideration by the Law Commission, Sixth Annual Report, 1970–1971 (Law Com. No. 47) para. 27.

(*e*) Land tax,[1] tithe rentcharge,[2] payments in lieu of tithe, and charges or annuities payable for the redemption of tithe rentcharges ;

(*f*) Subject to the provisions of this Act, rights acquired or in course of being acquired under the Limitation Acts;

As we shall see,[3] when the limitation period has run, the estate of the registered proprietor is not extinguished, as it is under the system of unregistered conveyancing : instead, he holds the land adversely possessed on trust for the adverse possessor.

(*g*) The rights of every person in actual occupation of the land or in receipt of the rents and profits thereof, save where enquiry is made of such person and the rights are not disclosed ;[4]

This is an important paragraph which shows that the legisla- Section ture accepted a compromise in respect of its replacement of the 70(1)(*g*). old doctrine of notice by the system of registration. A purchaser should inspect the premises, and he should ask anyone in occupation on what grounds he is there. He will thereby be able to discover the rights and interests of persons in occupation, and it seemed right therefore to subject a purchaser to those rights and interests rather than to let him disregard them because someone had failed to enter them on the register. Some of these rights may, however, be capable of being protected by notice or caution on the register of the title affected, and if they are, notices or cautions should be applied for by the person entitled. In short, the general policy of the Land Registration Act 1925 is that all claims rights and interests should be protected by entry on the register as far as possible. This special exception of paragraph (*g*) is made in the case of the rights of a person in actual occupation. The purchaser should get to know what these rights are, and, on balance, it is better that he should take subject to them, even at the expense of the doctrine of completeness of the register. As we have seen,[5] a contract for the sale or lease[6] of registered land should be protected by notice or caution as a minor interest, but if the purchaser or lessee is let into occupation before formal transfer *and* there is no note on the register of his interest, the mere fact of his occupation turns his minor interest into an overriding one.[7] The paragraph is not confined to the single

---

[1] Extinguished by Finance Act 1963, s. 68.

[2] Extinguished and replaced by tithe redemption annuities ; Tithe Act 1936, s. 13(11) ; Finance Act 1962, s. 32.

[3] *Infra*, p. 908.

[4] See *per* Lord DENNING in *Strand Securities, Ltd.* v. *Caswell* [1956] Ch. 958 at pp. 979–81 ; *supra*, p. 110, and *per* RUSSELL, L. J., at p. 984.

[5] *Supra*, pp. 511–2.

[6] A contract for the grant of a lease (for 21 years or less) is not an over-riding interest under L.R.A. 1925, s. 70 (1) (*k*), as there has been no " grant " ; *City Permanent Building Society* v. *Miller*, [1952] Ch. 840 ; [1952] 2 All E. R. 621. S. 3 (x), taken by itself, is misleading on this point.

[7] *Woolwich Equitable Building Society* v. *Marshall*, [1952] Ch. 1; [1951] 2 All E. R. 769; *Mornington Permanent Building Society* v. *Kenway*, [1953] Ch. 382; [1953] 1 All E. R. 951.

right to occupy, for it extends to the *rights of those in* occupation, which includes an option to purchase the freehold contained in a lease[1] and an unpaid vendor's lien where the vendor remains in occupation under a lease back by the purchaser.[2]   Furthermore a person who has a right to the fee simple in equity against the registered proprietor may have an overriding interest under this paragraph if he is in occupation.   Thus in *Hodgson* v. *Marks*,[3]

> Mrs. H. an elderly widow, voluntarily transferred the registered title to her house to E., who was her lodger.   She intended that the house, though it was in E.'s name, should remain hers, and she continued to reside there.   E. then sold it to M. who became the registered proprietor and executed a mortgage in favour of a building society.   Mrs. H. claimed that E. held the house as a bare trustee for her, that she was entitled to the beneficial interest in it, and that M. and his mortgagee took subject to her rights " as a person in actual occupation " when M. became the registered proprietor.

The Court of Appeal held that Mrs. H. was " in actual occupation " within the meaning of paragraph (*g*) and ordered rectification of the register in her favour as M. had not made any enquiries of Mrs. H. prior to registration of the transfer to him.[4]

Paragraph (*g*), as we have seen, carries the doctrine of *Hunt* v. *Luck* forward into registered land.   It may, however, be wider than the rule in two ways.   First it protects not only the rights of every person in actual occupation of the land, but also those of every person in receipt of the rents and profits thereof.[5]   Secondly, " the paragraph is not qualified by any requirement about enquiry of an occupier as to his rights being reasonable (i.e. for constructive notice)."[6]   In *Hodgson* v. *Marks*, RUSSELL, L.J. was

> " prepared, for the purposes of this case, to assume (without necessarily accepting) that section 70 (1) (*g*) ... is designed only to apply to a case in which the occupation is such, in point of fact, as would in the case of unregistered land affect a person with constructive notice of the rights of the occupier."[7]

It is uncertain whether the rule in *Hunt* v. *Luck* applies where a person is in possession of unregistered land together with the vendor.[8]   In the case of registered land, however, the Court of Appeal adopted a literal construction of paragraph (*g*), and held

---

[1] *Webb* v. *Pollmount, Ltd.*, [1966] Ch. 584 ; [1966] 1 All E. R. 481 ; M. & B. p. 111.

[2] *London and Cheshire Insurance Co., Ltd.* v. *Laplagrene Property Co., Ltd.*, [1971] Ch. 499 ; [1971] 1 All E. R. 766. M. & B. p. 120.

[3] [1971] Ch. 892 ; [1971] 2 All E. R. 684 ; M. & B. p. 116.

[4] See (1971), 35 *Conv.* (N.S.) 255, 268–76 (I. Leeming) : Law Commission Published Working Paper No. 37 (1971), paras. 56–77.

[5] See *Strand Securities, Ltd.* v. *Caswell*, [1965] Ch. 958 ; [1965] 1 All E. R. 820 ; M. & B. p. 114.

[6] *Emmet on Title* (16th Edn), p. 188 ; (1973) 36 M. L. R. 25 (R. H. Maudsley).

[7] At p. 932.   The occupation must have some degree of permanence. *Epps* v. *Esso Petroleum Co., Ltd.*, [1973] 1 W. L. R. 1071 ; [1973] 2 All E. R. 465.

[8] *Supra*, p. 67.

that Mrs. H., who was in actual occupation of the house together with E., the vendor, was protected.[1]   Further, it must be emphasized that it is the rights of the occupier and not the occupation itself that are crucial.   As RUSSELL, L.J. put it[2] :—

> " It seems to me that section 70 in all its parts is dealing with rights in reference to land which have the quality of being capable of enduring through different ownerships of the land, according to normal conceptions of title to real property.... It is the rights of such a person which constitute the overriding interest and must be examined, not his occupation."

Thus the deserted wife in occupation of the matrimonial home has no right affecting property entitling her to claim an overriding interest,[3] while the owner of an option to purchase a freehold contained in a lease has, since it "affects the reversion . . . and subsists in reference to the registered land".[4]

Finally, it should be noted that a spouse's rights of occupation under the Matrimonial Homes Act 1967 and the rights of a tenant arising from a notice under the Leasehold Reform Act 1967 of his desire to acquire the freehold or an extended lease are declared by statute *not* to be overriding interests.[5]   Both these rights should be protected by entry of a notice or a caution on the register of the title affected.

> (*h*) In the case of a possessory, qualified, or good leasehold title,[6] all estates, rights, interests, and powers excepted from the effect of registration.

These three classes of title may be converted[7] and on a conversion this overriding interest determines to the extent resulting from the conversion.

> (*i*) Rights under local land charges unless and until registered or protected on the register in the prescribed manner.[8]

This is a very important category of overriding interests.   Local land charges have the same meaning as they have in the Local Land Charges Act 1975 and that Act applies to both unregistered and registered land.   A purchaser must therefore search in the local authority's register whether or not the land is registered.

---

[1] At pp. 934–5 ; *cf. Caunce* v. *Caunce* [1969] 1 W. L. R. 286 ; [1969] 1 All E. R. 722 ; M. & B. p. 221.

[2] *National Provincial Bank, Ltd.* v. *Hastings Car Mart, Ltd.*, [1964] Ch. 665, at p. 696 ; [1964] 3 All E. R. 93 ; a dissenting judgment which was upheld (with special reference to this passage) in the House of Lords : [1965] A.C. 1175, at pp. 1226, 1228, 1240 and 1261–2.

[3] *National Provincial Bank, Ltd.* v. *Ainsworth*, [1965] A. C. 1175 ; [1965] 2 All E. R. 472 ; M. & B. p. 110.

[4] *Webb* v. *Pollmount*, [1966] Ch. 584, at pp. 595–6, 597–9 ; [1966] 1 All E. R. 481, at p. 485, and pp. 486–7, per UNGOED-THOMAS, J.

[5] Matrimonial Homes Act 1967, s. 2(7) ; Leasehold Reform Act 1967, s. 5(5). See *supra*, pp. 233 and 491.

[6] *Supra*, p. 768.   [7] L.R.A. 1925, s. 77 ; *supra*, p. 769.

[8] *I.e.* on the register at the Land Registry.

The Registrar comments as follows on the failure to require the entry of all local land charges on the register at the Land Registry.

> " Just as it would be impracticable to set out a summary of the material facts relating to them on the deeds and documents used in unregistered conveyancing, so there is at present no machinery devised for entering them on the register of title at the Land Registry. Even if the necessary machinery were to be set up it would involve an enormous expenditure of manpower and of public money."[1]

(*j*) Rights of fishing and sporting, seignorial and manorial rights of all descriptions (until extinguished), and franchises.

(*k*) Leases for any term or interest not exceeding twenty-one years, granted at a rent without taking a fine.

This paragraph does not include a contract for the grant of a lease for 21 years or less, as there has been no grant.[2]

In addition, the following overriding interests have been added by later enactments :

1. Title redemption annuities ;[3]
2. All coal and mines of coal and associated interests and ancillary rights which are vested in the National Coal Board ;[4]
3. Rights, privileges and appurtenances appertaining or reputed to appertain to land or demised, occupied or enjoyed therewith or reputed or known as part or parcel of or appurtenant thereto, which adversely affect registered land.[5]

Criticism of overriding interests.

The effect of overriding interests is, as we have seen, to bind a transferee from a registered proprietor, whether he knows about them or not. They thus detract from the principle that the register should be a mirror of the title, and so it is important that they should be able to justify their existence as a separate category within the system of registered conveyancing. A balance has to be struck between the protection of the person enjoying the interest and the inconvenience to a purchaser. Sympathy for the latter leads to a plea for as complete an abolition of the category as is feasible.

Criticism of overriding interests must, however, be tempered by four considerations. Firstly, the category cannot be abandoned completely, however desirable it is that the register should be a complete mirror of the title. It is impossible to enter on the register rights arising under the Limitation Act 1939, or easements and profits being acquired by prescription. Secondly, as we have

---

[1] Ruoff and Roper, 114. A local land charge to secure money must be registered as a registered charge at the Land Registry before it can be entered against registered land : L.R.A. 1925, s. 59(2).

[2] *Supra*, p. 773, note 6. Paragraph (*l*) specifies certain rights to mines and minerals existing before 1926.

[3] Tithe Act 1936, s. 13(11).

[4] Coal Act 1938, s. 41 ; Coal Industry Nationalisation Act 1946, ss. 5, 8, Sched. 1.

[5] L.R.R. 1925, r. 258.

seen, the legislature has decided as a matter of policy that protection should be accorded to the rights of a person in actual occupation, even if he has failed to register his interests. This is most desirable in those situations when the holder of the right might not consult a solicitor and therefore be unaware of the need for entry on the register, *e.g.* a contract for a lease. This is the opposite to the Draconian policy of the Land Charges Act 1972 for unregistered conveyancing. " The rule for registered land is much more reasonable, for possession is the strongest possible title to security."[1] Thirdly, it is impracticable to require the registration of all short tenancies. Fourthly, overriding interests appear frequently on the register, and if they do they are not regarded as overriding.[2] The Registrar has a mandatory duty to enter a notice on first registration of " any easement, right, privilege, or benefit created by an instrument " which appears on the title and adversely affects the land.[3] He also has a discretion to enter on the register a notice that the land is free or subject to certain overriding interests.[4] As the Registrar writes :—

> " The plain fact is... that there are mandatory provisions requiring most overriding interests to be entered on the register, which operate either on first registration,[5] or on a dealing with registered land,[6] or at any time on proof of their being furnished,[7] and so ensure that, save for squatters' rights,[8] which cannot be recorded, or rights of occupiers or lessees, which are discoverable, under the rule in *Hunt* v. *Luck*,[9] from a proper inspection and inquiry, or local land charges which obviously must be recorded locally,[10] they are all entered on the register.[11]"

(5) MINOR INTERESTS

Minor interests are defined by section 3 (xv) Land Registration Act 1925 as follows :— *Definition of minor interests.*

> " Minor interests " mean the interests not capable of being disposed of or created by registered dispositions and capable of being overridden (whether or not a purchaser has notice thereof) by the proprietors unless protected as provided by this Act, and all

---

[1] (1956) C. L. J. 228 (H. W. R. Wade). *Cf.* Law Commission Working Paper No. 37 (1971), para. 20.
[2] *Webb* v. *Pollmount, Ltd.*, [1966] Ch. 584, at p. 594 ; [1966] 1 All E. R. 481, *per* UNGOED-THOMAS, J. L.R.A. 1925, s. 3 (xvi).
[3] L.R.A. 1925, s. 70 (2). *Re Dances Way, West Town, Hayling Island*, [1962] Ch. 490, at p. 508, per DIPLOCK, L.J. *Supra*, p. 586.
[4] *Ibid.*, s. 70(1), (3). L.R.R. 1925, rr. 194, 197, 198, 250, 252, 254.
[5] *Ibid.*, s. 70(2).
[6] *Ibid.*, ss. 19(2), 22(2).
[7] *Ibid.*, s. 70(3). This is in fact discretionary only.
[8] *Ibid.*, s. 70(1)(*f*).
[9] [1902] 1 Ch. 428.
[10] L.R.A. 1925, s 70 (1) (*i*). See *supra*, p. 775.
[11] (1969), 32 *M. L. R.*, at p. 129 (T. B. F. Ruoff). There is, on general principle, a duty to declare any overriding interest that is not obvious.

rights and interests which are not registered or protected on the register and are not overriding interests, and include:—

(*a*) in the case of land held on trust for sale, all interests and powers which are under the Law of Property Act, 1925, capable of being overridden by the trustees for sale, whether or not such interests and powers are so protected; and

(*b*) in the case of settled land, all interests and powers which are under the Settled Land Act, 1925, and the Law of Property Act, 1925, or either of them, capable of being overridden by the tenant for life or statutory owner, whether or not such interests and powers are so protected as aforesaid."

This definition is complex, by being both exclusionary and inclusionary in its terms, and must be read in conjunction with section 2 of the Land Registration Act 1925. Once it is laid down in that section that the only estates which can be registered are " estates capable of subsisting as legal estates ", then it follows that they must be excluded from the definition of minor interests and that " all other interests in registered land (except overriding interests...) shall take effect in equity as minor interests." Minor interests therefore are a residual category of interests within the system of registered land.

The definition prefaces the two classes (a) and (b) with the word " include ". There is thus no finite list as there is in unregistered land. Any interest, right or claim may be entered on the register in the appropriate manner, but the validity of the entry may be challenged later.

There are two main classes of minor interests :

(a) those which are capable of being overridden by registered dispositions for valuable consideration, whether or not they are protected by an entry on the register. This class includes those interests which are overreachable under the Law of Property Act 1925, and the Settled Land Act 1925, in unregistered conveyancing. i.e. the equitable interests of beneficiaries under a trust for sale or a strict settlement.

(b) All other minor interests. The most important examples in this class are those interests which in unregistered conveyancing are registrable as land charges under the Land Charges Act 1972.[1] Interests in this class must be protected by an entry on the register, if they are not to be overridden by a registered disposition for valuable consideration. Furthermore, as in unregistered conveyancing actual notice of what should be protected in the register, but is not so protected, is immaterial.[2]

---

[1] The provisions of the Land Charges Act 1972 are excluded from registered conveyancing, L.R.A. 1925, s. 59. For a chart showing the registration machinery which replaces that of the Land Charges Act, see Ruoff and Roper, p. 127 ; M. & B. pp. 127–9.

[2] *Hodges* v. *Jones*, [1935] Ch. 657, at p. 671, *per* Luxmore, J.   L.R.A. 1925, s. 59 (6), as amended by F.A. 1975, s. 52, Sched. 12, para. 5.   *De Lusignan* v. *Johnson* (1973), 230 Estates Gazette 499.

It is important to notice that in neither class will interests be overridden by any disposition made without valuable consideration, and in this case, it is immaterial whether or not they have been entered on the register.[1]

Minor interests may be protected on the register in four different ways, namely, by the entry of a notice, a restriction, a caution or an inhibition.[2]

Protection of minor interests.

(a) Notice

A notice may be entered on the charges register[3] to protect any of a number of lesser interests and rights affecting the land.[4] It will only protect an interest that is valid and effective independently of the register for, unlike registration of title, a notice is incapable of converting an invalid interest into a potentially valid one.   Nor does entry of a covenant guarantee that it will run with land.[5]   A notice may also be entered of a *claim* to a right or interest.[6]   A notice of such a claim includes notice of claim to rights appurtenant to a title as well as to those binding it.   It is sometimes used to indicate that the proprietor of a title claims an appurtenant right, the title to which can neither be guaranteed nor rejected out of hand.   But subject to these reservations, entry by way of a notice gives protection to and information about important rights adverse to land like easements,[7] covenants, long leases[8] and estate contracts.   Noting of adverse interests is quite separate, of course, from the *registration* of leaseholds and of the *benefit* of easements in the property register ; though there will frequently be cross references.   For instance, registration of a lease will always be accompanied by a note of it on the title out of which it is carved.[9]

Notice.

---

[1] L.R.A. 1925, ss. 20(4), 23 (5).

[2] See generally (1958), 22 *Conv.* (N.S.) 14 (F. R. Crane); (1953), 17 *Conv.* (N.S.) 105 (T.B.F. Ruoff). For mortgages see *supra*, pp. 713 *et seq.*

[3] L.R.R. 1925, r. 7.

[4] L.R.A. 1925, ss. 52, 59, and L.R.R. 1925, r. 190. For the residual character of notices, see particularly s. 49 (1).

[5] *Cator* v. *Newton and Bates*, [1940] 1 K. B. 415; [1939] 4 All E. R. 457; L.R.A. 1925, s. 52. *Supra*, p. 622.

[6] L.R.A. 1925, s. 52 (2).

[7] The Registrar must enter on the register all adverse easements shown to exist in the documents produced at the time of first registration: s. 70 (2). Thereafter, adverse easements may be entered by him, in his discretion: L.R.R. r. 41 (1).   See generally *Re Dances Way, West Town, Hayling Island*, [1962] Ch. 490 ; [1962] 2 All E. R. 42.

[8] Leases for 21 years or less granted at a rent without taking a fine are overriding interests and, despite the generous wording of L.R.A. 1925 s. 70 (3), never appear on the register, but are protected only as overriding interests. See L.R.A. 1925, ss. 19 (2), 48 (1). Generally on the subject of leases and under-leases, see *Strand Securities, Ltd.* v. *Caswell*, [1965] Ch. 958, [1965] 1 All E. R. 820. *Supra*, pp. 509 *et seq.*

[9] Lease includes underlease: s. 3 (x). Accordingly, underleases are properly noted on the title of the head-lease.

Notice in the register has, in general, the same function that registration in the Land Charges Register has in unregistered conveyancing. Subsequent dispositions of the land are subject to those interests capable of affecting a transferee as are the subject of a notice, while *purchasers* for valuable consideration take free of interests requiring a notice for protection if they are not so protected,[1] unless they are also overriding interests, or are protected in some other way, *e.g.* by caution.

The availability of protection by way of a notice does not exclude protection under other parts of the registration machinery. Thus, an option in a lease to purchase the freehold can both be protected by a notice and, independently of the register, may constitute an overriding interest[2]; again, a deposit of a land certificate as security for a loan can be the subject of protection in several different ways.[3]

A notice is a particularly good method of protecting an interest or right, as, assuming the right or interest itself to be valid, all dispositions by the proprietor of the land take effect subject to the right or interest (unless it is capable of being overridden by the disposition independently of the Land Registration Act 1925).[4] The weakness of a notice lies in that, in order to secure its entry, the applicant must, except in the case of a notice of a lease at a rent without taking a fine, lodge the Land Certificate of the title concerned,[5] unless it is already deposited at the Land Registry because of the existence of a prior registered charge.[6] Notices thus can usually be entered only with the co-operation of the owner of the land affected.

(b) Restriction

Restriction.

A restriction is an entry which prevents dealings in registered land until certain specified conditions or requirements have been complied with.[7] Its object is thus to record, on the proprietorship register,[8] any impediment to the proprietor's freedom of disposal.

---

[1] L.R.A. 1925, ss. 20, 23, 48, 50, 52 (1), 101; *White* v. *Bijou Mansions,* [1937] Ch. 610; [1937] 3 All E. R. 269. Ss. 20, 23 and 101 refer to " valuable consideration", and nowhere is there the reference that one would expect to s. 3 (xxi), defining "purchaser" as *bona fide* purchaser for value. See also *Jones* v. *Lipman,* [1962] 1 W. L. R. 832; [1962] 1 All E. R. 442.

[2] *Webb* v. *Pollmount, Ltd.* [1966] Ch. 584 [1966] 1 All E. R. 481 ; M. & B. p. 133, interpreting L.R.A. 1925, s. 59 (1). Again, L.R.A. 1925, s. 48 makes provision for notice, on the superior title, of leases that do not constitute overriding interests *as such* (i.e., leases for more than 21 years or leases not granted at a rent or leases taking a fine), but in fact most lessees and lessors can claim the protection given to an overriding interest under s. 70 (1) (*g*) : see *supra,* p. 773.

[3] *Re White Rose Cottage,* [1965] Ch. 940 ; M. & B. p. 129, especially *per* Lord DENNING, M.R., at pp. 949–50. *Supra,* pp. 713.

[4] L.R.A. 1925, s. 52(1).

[5] *Ibid.,* s. 64 (1) (c) as amended by F.A. 1975, s. 52 ; Sched. 12, para. 5.

[6] *Ibid.,* s. 65.   [7] *Ibid.,* s. 58.

[8] L.R.R. 1925, r. 6.   Or on the charges register when interests in a registered charge are to be protected.

A restriction can in effect only be entered on the register with the concurrence of the proprietor or at the instance of the Registrar and, once entered, no transaction will be permitted except in conformity with its terms, although the Registrar must not enter any restriction which he considers to be " unreasonable or calculated to cause inconvenience ". As we have seen,[1] restrictions at the instance of the Registrar are employed *inter alia* to give effect to strict settlements and trusts for sale of registered land and the entry of such restrictions is obligatory.   The rules on the production of the land certificate are the same as in the case of notices.

(c) Caution

A caution against dealings, unlike a notice or a restriction, is a hostile act, and is used to protect interests in land (or a charge) registered in the name of another person.   Production of the land or charge certificate is not necessary, nor is the concurrence of the proprietor of the land or charge.   If the caution is against the land, it is entered in the proprietorship register ; if against the charge, in the charges register.[2]   Cautions can be " warned off " by the registered proprietor, in which case notice is served by the Registrar on the cautioner, and if the cautioner consents or does not object within the time specified in the notice, the caution is cancelled.   If the cautioner objects, and cannot resolve his objection by agreement with the registered proprietor, the dispute is adjudicated on by the Registrar or the court.[3]

If the caution is not " warned off " or withdrawn by the cautioner, it remains on the register, and the Registrar may not register any dealing or notice of deposit affecting the land (or the charge, if the caution is against the charge) until he has served notice on the cautioner.   After such notice has been served, it operates as though it were a "warning-off " notice.

In order to protect an interest in land not yet registered, a caution against first registration may be lodged.   The Registrar will serve notice on the cautioner, who may then oppose the application for first registration in manner similar to that in which a cautioner against dealings may oppose the registration of a dealing or notice of deposit.

(marginal notes) Caution against dealings.

Caution against first registration.

---

[1] *Supra*, pp. 196, 203.   [2] L.R.R. 1925, rr. 6, 7.

[3] For the court's exercise of its jurisdiction to order the vacation of cautions, see *Rawlplug Co., Ltd.* v. *Kamvale Properties, Ltd.* (1969), 20 P. & C. R. 32 ; *Calgary and Edmonton Land Co., Ltd.* v. *Discount Bank (Overseas) Ltd.*, [1971] 1 W. L. R. 81 ; [1971] 1 All E. R. 551 ; *Clearbrook Property Holdings, Ltd.* v. *Verrier*, [1974] 1 W. L. R. 243 ; [1973] 3 All E. R. 614 ; *Tiverton Estates, Ltd.* v. *Wearwell*, [1975] Ch. 146 ; [1974] 1 All E. R. 209 ; *Lester* v. *Burgess* (1973), 26 P. & C. R. 536 ; *Calgary and Edmonton Land Co., Ltd.* v. *Dobinson*, [1974] Ch. 102 ; [1974] 1 All E. R. 484 ; *Norman* v. *Hardy*, [1974] 1 W. L. R. 1048 ; [1974] 1 All E. R. 1170 ; (1974) 38 Conv. (N.S.) 208 (F. R. Crane) ; *Price Bros. (Somerford) Ltd.* v. *J. Kelly Homes (Stoke-on-Trent) Ltd.*, [1975] 1 W. L. R. 1512.

The provisions of the Acts and Rules relating to cautions against dealings and against first registration are complex,[1] but the following observations may be made :

(i) Cautions give no priority or protection other than a right to object. The objection may or may not succeed. A caution against dealings is thus much inferior to a notice, and should therefore be applied for only where application for a notice will fail because the land certificate is not available for lodging, or is not already on deposit.

(ii) If there is no successful objection to a caution against dealings, it seems that a purchaser takes subject to an interest which is protected by the entry.[2] But the entry does not affect priorities as between two competing equitable interests. Apart from statutory provision,[3] a caution does not give a later equitable interest priority over an earlier one. Thus in *Barclays Bank, Ltd.* v. *Taylor*,[4] an equitable mortgage by deposit of the land certificate, even if it was not itself protected by a notice of the deposit.[5] was held by the Court of Appeal to have priority over a subsequent estate contract which was protected by a caution. As RUSSELL, L.J. said : [6]

> " We ask ourselves what provision is there in the Act which reverses the ordinary rule that as between equities ... priority is governed by the time sequence? " After answering this question in the negative, his Lordship continued : " The caution lodged on behalf of the purchasers had no effect whatever by itself on priorities : it simply conferred on the cautioners the right to be given notice of any dealing proposed to be registered. "

(iii) A caution against dealings will not be accepted by the Registrar if the cautioner's interest is already registered or protected by a notice or restriction, unless the Registrar specifically consents.[7]

(iv) The cautioner's interest, unless it is in a charge, must be in " land ". This includes an interest under a trust for sale of the land.[8]

---

[1] For a full discussion see Ruoff and Roper, chaps. 14 and 36.
[2] *Parkash* v. *Irani Finance, Ltd.*, [1970] Ch. 101 ; [1969] 1 All E. R. 930 ; M. & B. p. 131.
[3] L.R.A. 1925, s. 102 (2), *supra*, p. 716.
[4] [1974] Ch. 137 ; [1973] 1 All E. R. 752 ; M. & B. p. 674 ; (1973) 89 L. Q. R. 170 (P. V. B.) ; See also (1971) 35 Conv. (N.S.) 100, 168 ; (1974) 124 N. L. J. 634 (S. Robinson).
[5] For the creation of mortgages in registered land, see *supra*, pp. 713 *et seq.*
[6] At p. 146.
[7] L.R.A. 1925, s. 54.
[8] *Elias* v. *Mitchell*, [1972] Ch. 652 ; [1972] 2 All E. R. 153 (equitable tenant in common under trust for sale). See, however, Ruoff and Roper, pp. 768–70 and Wontner's *Guide to Land Registry Practice* (12th Edn.), p. 138.

(v) If a person lodges a caution without reasonable cause, he is liable to pay compensation to those who have sustained damage as a result.[1]

(vi) In addition to cautions against dealings and against first registration, cautions against the conversion of a registered title to a higher class can be lodged. This form of caution is extremely rare.[2]

(d) Inhibition

An inhibition is also hostile, and is entered on the application of a person interested.[3] Such an entry prevents any dealings with the registered land, either generally or for a given time or until the occurrence of a specified event. This is an extreme step to take and should be considered only in exceptional circumstances, as, for instance, where it is suspected that there has been or is likely to be a fraudulent dealing. Inhibitions are very rarely encountered, except for the bankruptcy inhibition automatically entered by the Registrar.[4]

Inhibition.

---

[1] L.R.A. 1925, s. 56 (3) ; *Clearbrook* v. *Property Holdings, Ltd.* v. *Verrier, supra.*
[2] See Ruoff and Roper, pp. 96–7, 281, 770.
[3] L.R.A. 1925, s. 57. The court, or the Registrar, must agree to its entry.
[4] *Ibid.*, s. 61. *Infra*, p. 815.

CHAPTER II

PERSONAL REPRESENTATIVES

Functions of personal representatives. The next class of estate owner consists of personal representatives, *i.e.* the persons, whether executors or administrators, to whom the property of a deceased owner passes. The functions and powers of those persons are described later,[1] but certain matters must be anticipated. Broadly speaking, all the property of a deceased person, real as well as personal, with the exception of life interests, joint tenancies and entailed interests unless disposed of by the deceased's will, becomes vested in his personal representatives. Their duties are to pay the debts of the deceased and all expenses and dues arising on his death out of the property, and then to distribute the residue among the beneficiaries under the will or among those entitled in the case of intestacy. Both at common law and by statute they have exceedingly wide powers of disposition over the property.[2]

They have the powers of trustees for sale. Thus a conveyance by personal representatives of the legal estate may become necessary in two types of cases ; first where, in order to raise money for the payment of debts, they convey to a purchaser in the ordinary course of administration ; secondly, where they transfer the land to a beneficiary. Amongst the powers of disposal conferred upon them are included :

> " All the powers, discretions and duties conferred or imposed by law on trustees holding land upon an effectual trust for sale (including power to overreach equitable interests and powers as if the same affected the proceeds of sale)."[3]

Transfer to beneficiary effected by assent. The transfer of land to a beneficiary is effected in practice, not by a conveyance by deed, but by an *assent, i.e.* a document in writing that operates to vest the estate or interest in the person entitled.[4] Prior to 1926 an assent was valid if it was oral or even if it could be inferred from conduct,[5] but, as we have already seen, this is no longer true where the interest to be transferred is a *legal estate*.[6]

---

[1] *Infra*, pp. 843 *et seq.*
[2] *Infra*, p. 845.
[3] A.E.A. 1925, s. 39 (1) (ii).
[4] *Ibid.*, s. 36 (1), (2).
[5] *E.g., Wise* v. *Whitburn*, [1924] 1 Ch. 460.
[6] *Supra*, p. 753.

The beneficiary, in order to protect himself against a later conveyance of the same land by the personal representative, usually requires that notice of the assent be endorsed on the probate copy of the will or letters of administration, *i.e.* on the official documents which certify that the representative is entitled to act as such.[1] Even so, a beneficiary in whose favour an assent has been made is not secure, for an unpaid creditor of the deceased may enforce payment by following the property into the hands of a devisee, except one who takes in consideration of money or marriage.[2] When this course is taken, the court, notwithstanding the assent, may declare a beneficiary to be a trustee of the land for a creditor, or may order a sale or other transaction to be carried out in order to satisfy the rights of the persons interested, or may make a vesting order with a view to the execution of a conveyance.[3]

The statutory provision that personal representatives shall have the overreaching powers of trustees holding land " upon an effectual trust for sale," [4] shows that the overreaching effect of their conveyance is normally that of a conveyance made by ordinary trustees for sale,[5] and also, if the occasion arises, that of a conveyance made by approved trustees under an *ad hoc* trust for sale.[6] Thus, even equities charged on the land prior to the death of the deceased may be overreached. No approval by the court is necessary; neither is it necessary, as it is in the case of trustees for sale, that there should be at least two personal representatives.[7]

The assent plays an important part when the beneficiary in whose favour it has been made conveys the legal estate to a purchaser, since it acts as a "curtain" to keep the equities off the title. The Administration of Estates Act 1925[8] provides that the assent shall, in favour of a purchaser for money or money's worth, be sufficient evidence that the beneficiary is entitled to have the legal estate conveyed to him, unless notice of a previous assent or conveyance has been endorsed on the probate copy or letters of administration. It has been held, however, that an assent will not avail a purchaser if his investigation of title discloses that the person in whose favour it was given was not entitled to the legal estate.[9] The first duty, then, of the purchaser is to inspect the probate copy, for in the normal case he will find there an endorsement of an assent in favour of the beneficiary. Thus, the last two links in the title made by a beneficiary are the probate copy or letters of administration and the assent. The assent is a transfer of the legal title, showing its passing from the deceased through the personal representative to the beneficiary : it then operates as a " curtain " in

Marginal notes:

Notice of assent should be endorsed on the probate.

Right of creditors to follow property.

Overreaching powers of personal representatives.

Conveyance by beneficiary in whose favour an assent has been made.

---

[1] A.E.A. 1925, s. 36 (5).
[2] *Ibid.*, s. 38 (1); *Salih* v. *Atchi*, [1961] A. C. 778.
[3] A.E.A. 1925, s. 38 (2).   [4] *Ibid.*, s. 39 (1) (i), (ii).
[5] *Infra*, pp. 796–7.   [6] *Infra* pp. 797–9.
[7] L.P.A. 1925, s. 27 (2).   [8] S. 36 (7), (11).
[9] *Re Duce and Boots Cash Chemists (Southern), Ltd's Contract*, [1937] Ch. 642.

the sense that the purchaser need not investigate the will (which operates only in equity) in order to ascertain whether the assent has been given in favour of the proper beneficiary. The beneficial interests under a will, like those arising under a settlement or a trust for sale, are thus kept off the title to land, the legal estate in which has passed to a beneficiary by virtue of an assent.

Conveyance by personal representatives to a purchaser. Another section of the Act comes into play when the personal representatives themselves convey to a purchaser. The danger here is that the legal estate may already have been passed to a beneficiary under the will, but it is provided that a written statement by a personal representative that he has not given or made an assent or conveyance in respect of a legal estate, shall, in favour of a purchaser for money or money's worth, be sufficient evidence that no previous assent or conveyance has been given, unless notice of such has been endorsed on the probate or administration.[1] A purchaser who obtains this written statement acquires a good title to the legal estate, subject, however, to one exception, for it is provided that the statement shall not be conclusive against an earlier purchaser for money or money's worth who has taken a conveyance either from the personal representative or from a beneficiary in whose favour an assent has been given. If, therefore, A. takes a conveyance for value of a legal estate from a personal representative without having the fact endorsed on the probate, and B. later takes a conveyance from the personal representative of the same estate, relying upon the written but untrue statement that no previous conveyance has been made, it would seem that B. obtains no protection from the statute.

Validity of conveyance not affected by revocation of probate. The revocation of the probate or administration after a conveyance has been made by a personal representative does not affect the title of the purchaser.[2] If, for instance, probate of a will dated 1973 is granted to an executor, A., and subsequently a different will dated 1975 is discovered, the grant of probate to A. will be revoked and a new one made to the executor appointed by the 1975 will. All conveyances, however, of any interest in real or personal estate made by A. *virtute officii* in favour of a purchaser remain valid.

Special grants of probate in respect of settled land. As we shall see, general personal representatives give way to special personal representatives in respect of property which the deceased held as tenant for life under a settlement.[3] In such a case, after paying taxes due on the death the special exe-

---

[1] A.E.A. 1925, s. 36 (6) (11).
[2] *Ibid.*, s. 37; confirming *Hewson* v. *Shelley*, [1914] 2 Ch. 13. "Purchaser" means a lessee, mortgagee or other person who in good faith acquires an interest in property for valuable consideration, s. 55 (1) (xviii).
[3] *Infra*, p. 790.

cutors or administrators execute a vesting assent by which they transfer the legal estate to the next tenant for life. The vesting assent and the special probate or letters of administration, since they are documents passing the legal estate, will appear on the title if the tenant for life subsequently exercises his power of sale.

It has been held, however, in *Re Bridgett and Hayes' Contract*,[1] that if the settlement ceases on the death of the tenant for life there is no necessity for a special grant of probate or administration. In that case,

Special grant necessary only where settlement continues.

> By a will which took effect before 1926 land was devised to A. for life, and if (as happened) she should die without leaving children, to trustees upon trust for sale.

> A. died in 1926 and a general grant of probate of her will was made to the executor, X. X. made a contract to sell the land.

It was held that a special grant of probate to the trustees was unnecessary, and that X. could make a good title to the land under his general grant.

The statute requires a special grant of probate in the case of " settled land." " Settled land," however, means land which continues to be settled after the death of the testator. In the instant case the land ceased to be settled on the death of A. and became subject to a trust for sale. The provisions relating to special grants do not apply to trusts for sale. Therefore, the land was vested in X., to whom a general grant of A.'s property had been made, and X., by virtue of his executorship under the grant, could make title.

Personal representatives of a sole registered proprietor or of the survivor of two or more joint proprietors are entitled to be registered as proprietors in place of the deceased proprietor on the production to the Registrar of the grant of probate or letters of administration.[2] There is, however, an alternative procedure which is more frequently adopted, for the personal representatives need not themselves be registered but may have the land transferred direct to the devisee, legatee or purchaser, who will be registered in place of the deceased proprietor on production of the instrument of assent or transfer together with the grant of probate or letters of administration.[3] Although this latter alternative procedure saves some trouble, it is undesirable, as, pending the lodging of the transfer or assent, the register is necessarily kept out of date, and notice served by the Land Registry on the deceased proprietor could well go astray.

Registered land.

---

[1] [1928] Ch. 163 ; M. & B. p. 275 ; followed in : *In the Estate of Bordass,* [1929] P. 107 ; *In the Estate of Birch,* [1929] P. 164.
[2] L.R.A. 1925, s. 41 : L.R.R. 1925, r. 168.
[3] *Ibid.,* s. 37 ; L.R.R. 1925, r. 170.

Rule 170 (5) of the Land Registration Rules 1925, dealing with transfer or assent by personal representatives[1] provides that

> " it shall not be the duty of the Registrar nor shall he be entitled to consider or to call for any information concerning the reason why any transfer is made, or as to the terms of the will, and, whether he has notice or not of its contents, he shall be entitled to assume that the personal representative is acting (whether by transfer, assent or appropriation or vesting assent) correctly and within his powers."

This rule shows the extent to which the curtain principle applies to registered land.

---

[1] Assents must be in Form 57 in the case of land settled by the deceased's will, and in Form 56 in all other cases. Transfers by personal representatives are in the usual form of transfer. L.R.R. 1925, r. 170 (2),(3).

CHAPTER III

TENANTS FOR LIFE AND STATUTORY OWNERS, TRUSTEES FOR SALE, MORTGAGORS

SUMMARY

SECTION I. TENANTS FOR LIFE AND STATUTORY OWNERS

In the earlier part of the book we discussed the evolution and framework of the strict settlement.[1] On the conveyancing side three further topics require consideration in more detail.

The vesting of the legal estate in each new tenant for life as and when he becomes entitled to possession ; the termination of the settlement ; and the statutory simplification of a conveyance of settled land.

(A) VESTING OF LEGAL ESTATE

The scheme of the Act, as we have already noticed, is that the legal estate shall be vested from time to time in each new tenant for life as and when he becomes entitled to possession. Let us take the different circumstances that may arise and observe how this procedure operates.

Procedure on cessation of life interest.

---

[1] *Supra,* pp. 71 *et seq.,* 165 *et seq.*

(*a*) Death of tenant for life.

Let us suppose that under a settlement lands stand limited to H. for life and then, after certain interests in favour of the other members of H.'s family, to his son, S., for life. When H. dies the legal estate devolves upon his special personal representatives, *i.e.* the trustees of the settlement, and not upon his general personal representatives whose task it is to administer his non-settled property.[1] Upon the death of H. the special personal representatives come under an obligation to convey the legal estate to S. This may be done either by a vesting deed or by a vesting assent, which contains the particulars set out above at page 171.[2]

(*b*) Infant tenant for life reaches full age.

An infant cannot be an estate owner,[3] and if he becomes entitled to a tenancy for life under a settlement the statutory powers are exercisable by the trustees, to whom, in their capacity as *statutory owners*,[4] the legal estate must be conveyed. It is their duty, however, upon the attainment by the infant of his majority, to convey the legal estate to him by a vesting deed or a vesting assent.[5]

(*c*) Tenant for life deprived of his statutory powers.

Where for example there is a limitation to A. for life with a limitation over to X. and Y. on *protective trusts* (*i.e.* trusts which give certain powers to X. and Y. if A. becomes bankrupt or attempts to part with his life interest in favour of his creditors),[6] A. is bound to convey the legal estate to X. and Y. as statutory owners upon the occurrence of an event bringing the trusts into operation.[7]

(*d*) Person of full age becoming absolutely entitled.

If a person of full age becomes absolutely entitled to the land, *e.g.* where there is a limitation to A. for life with remainder to X. in fee simple and A. dies, the settlement comes to an end and the land is no longer settled. There is no room for *special* personal representatives and the legal estate must be conveyed by A.'s general personal representatives to X., the absolute owner.[8]

(B) TERMINATION OF SETTLEMENT

Termination of settlement.

A settlement comes to an end if all equitable interests have ceased and if there can be no further occasion to exercise the

---

[1] A.E.A. s. 22 (1) ; *infra*, pp. 816 ; 842 *et seq.*
[2] S.L.A. 1925, s. 7 (1), 1st Sched., Form No. 5.
[3] *Infra*, p. 916.
[4] *Supra*, p. 176. Wide powers of management are conferred by S.L.A. 1925, s. 102 upon the trustees during a minority, see *infra*, pp. 921–2.
[5] S.L.A., 1925, s. 7 (2), (3) ; s. 19 (3).
[6] *Supra*, p. 364.
[7] S.L.A. 1925, s. 7 (4).
[8] *Ibid.*, s. 7 (5) *Re Bridgett and Hayes' Contract*, [1928] Ch, 163 ; M. & B. p. 275, *supra*, p. 787 ; *In the Estate of Bordass*, [1929] P. 107.

statutory powers, provided that the person entitled to the legal estate is of full age.[1] When this occurs it is essential that the person beneficially entitled should be fortified by a document showing his right to deal freely with the land, and it is therefore provided that he may require the trustees to execute a *deed of discharge* declaring that the land is free from the trusts.[2] The termination of a settlement, however, most frequently occurs on the death of a tenant for life, as for example when he dies leaving no widow, but an only son who bars the entail limited to him by the settlement. In this case there is no need for a deed of discharge. It is sufficient if the personal representatives of the tenant for life vest the legal estate in the son by an absolute vesting assent, *i.e.* one which does not nominate trustees.[3]

(C) SIMPLIFICATION OF CONVEYANCING

Taking the normal case, and presuming that the legal estate has been vested in the tenant for life by virtue of a vesting deed, it is worth our while to notice how the sale of the settled land to a purchaser is expedited and simplified, as compared with the practice prevailing before 1926. The main object of reducing the rights of the various beneficiaries to the status of equitable interests is to keep those rights off the title to the legal estate and to relieve a purchaser from the responsibility of seeing that they are not prejudiced by the sale. The fate of the equitable interests is to be no concern of the purchaser. His one concern is that the title to the *legal* estate shall be proved. He must, therefore, investigate the title down to the first vesting deed, *i.e.* he must require the vendor to prove that the person who purported to vest the legal estate in the estate owner by the principal vesting deed was entitled to do so, though of course if land remains settled for a generation or two the time will come when title is made by the production of a series of vesting deeds or assents. But the former practice of abstracting the beneficial limitations is forbidden. The trust instrument is not disclosed; it is not allowed to appear on the title; and with a few exceptions [4] the purchaser is not entitled to call for it or to make it the subject of interrogatories. Moreover, once satisfied that the vesting deed was executed by a party competent to execute it, " a purchaser of a legal estate in settled land " must take it at its face value and make the following assumptions :—

> That the estate owner named in the vesting deed is the tenant for life and entitled to exercise the statutory powers.

Position of purchaser from life tenant.

---

[1] S.L.A. 1925, s. 3 ; L.P.(A.)A. 1926 ; Sched.
[2] *Ibid.*, s. 17 (1).
[3] *Ibid.*, s. 110 (5).
[4] *Ibid.*, s. 110 (2) (*a*), (*b*), (*c*), (*d*). For example, where a settlement *inter vivos* has not been created by the proper method or where there is a pre-1926 settlement, whether made *inter vivos* or by will. See *Emmet on Title* (16th Edn.), pp. 689 *et seq.*

That the trustees named in the deed are the properly constituted trustees.

That the statements contained in the deed in accordance with the requirements of the Settled Land Act 1925 are correct.

That a later deed appointing new trustees is correct.[1]

This is a distinct simplification of the practice that obtained before 1926. Before that date, as we have seen,[2] a purchaser was compelled to investigate the whole settlement, including resettlements, so as to satisfy himself that the land was settled land within the meaning of the Settled Land Act 1882, that the vendor was tenant for life within the same meaning, and that there were proper trustees of the settlement. But all these facts are now certified by the vesting deed, for this short document guarantees the fundamentals concerning which enquiries had formerly to be made. The purchaser is secure in taking a conveyance of the legal estate from the person by whom the vesting deed asserts that this estate is held ; he can presume, in reliance on the same deed, that the Settled Land Act powers apply to the property ; and, provided that he pays the purchase money to the certified trustees,[3] he can ignore the equitable rights of the beneficiaries.

Interests that are overreached by conveyance of settled land. In other words, the conveyance by the tenant for life overreaches the equitable interests of the beneficiaries and also certain other interests, *i.e.*, makes them enforceable against the money in the hands of the trustees, and no longer against the land. More precisely, the position in this respect is as follows :—

The conveyance by the tenant for life passes to the purchaser a title to the legal estate discharged from the following :—

(i) All legal or equitable estates, interests and charges arising *under* the settlement.[4]

(ii) Limited owner's charges,[5] general equitable charges [6] and certain annuities.[7]

These three interests are overreached even though they have been registered as land charges and even though they were created prior to the settlement.[8] The reason is that they lose nothing in value or protection by their conversion into claims against the purchase money.

---

[1] S.L.A. 1925, s. 110 (2) ; but the proviso to the section contains exceptions.   [2] *Supra*, pp. 79–80.
[3] *Infra*, p. 793.   [4] S.L.A. 1925, s. 72 (2).
[5] *Supra*, p. 741.   [6] *Supra*, p. 741.
[7] *I.e.*, under L.C.A. 1972, s. 1 (4), Sched. 1.   " Annuity " is here limited to annuities for one or more life or lives created after April 25th, 1855, and before January 1st, 1926. The register in which they might formerly have been entered was closed as from January 1st, 1926. All annuities created after 1925 are registrable as general equitable charges.
[8] S.L.A. 1925, s. 72 (3) ; see (1934), 77 *L. J. News*, 3, 21, 39, 57 (J. M. L.).

On the other hand the conveyance by the tenant for life does not overreach the following :— *Interests that are not overreached.*

(i) Legal estates and charges by way of legal mortgage having priority to the settlement.[1]

(ii) Legal estates and charges by way of legal mortgage to secure money which has been actually raised before the date of the conveyance.[2]

An example is a mortgage created before the conveyance by which money has been raised for the payment of portions.

(iii) Terms of years, easements and profits granted for money or money's worth under the settlement.[3]

(iv) Estate contracts, restrictive covenants and equitable easements created after 1925,[4] if registered as land charges.[5]

(v) Restrictive covenants and equitable easements created before 1926, but only if the purchaser has actual or constructive notice of them.[6]

(vi) Estate contracts created before 1926 if the purchaser has actual or constructive notice of them, or if they are capable of registration and have been registered. Such a contract becomes capable of registration upon its assignment after 1925. [7]

For the overreaching provisions to apply, it is essential that upon a sale of the land by the tenant for life or the statutory owner, the purchase money is paid either to the trustees or into court ; [8] moreover, except where the trusteeship is held by a trust corporation,[9] there must be at least two trustees to whom this payment is made.[10] *Purchase money paid to trustees, not to tenant for life.*

---

[1] S.L.A. 1925, s. 72 (2) (i).

[2] *Ibid.*, s. 72 (2) (ii). See *Re Mundy and Roper's Contract*, [1899] 1 Ch. 275, at p. 289, *per* CHITTY, L.J.

[3] *Ibid.* s. 72 (2) (iii) (a).

[4] *Supra*, pp. 742, 743.

[5] S.L.A. 1925, s. 72 (2) (iii) (a), (b).   [6] *Supra*, p. 743.

[7] L.C.A. 1972, s. 4 (7).   [8] S.L.A. 1925, s. 18 (1) (b).

[9] *Ibid.*, s. 117 (1) (xxx). " Trust corporation " means, " The Public Trustee or a corporation either appointed by the court in any particular case to be a trustee or entitled by rules made under sub-s. (3) of s. 4 of the Public Trustee Act 1906, to act as custodian trustee ". Corporations which are entitled under the Public Trustee Rules 1912 r. 30 as substituted by the Public Trustee (Custodian Trustee) Rules 1975 r. 2 (S.I. 1975 No. 1189), include any corporation which (i) is constituted under the law of the United Kingdom or of any other Member State of the European Economic Community ; and (ii) is empowered by its constitution to undertake trust business in England and Wales ; (iii) has one or more places of business in the United Kingdom ; and (iv) being a registered company has a capital (in stock or shares) for the time being issued of not less than £250,000 (or its equivalent in the currency of the state where the company is registered), of which not less than £100,000 (or its equivalent) has been paid up in cash. This definition is extended by L.P.(A.)A. 1926, s. 3, to include *inter alios* a trustee in bankruptcy, the Treasury Solicitor and the Official Solicitor.

[10] *Ibid.*, s. 18 (1) (c).

Faulty Conveyances. If the machinery of the Settled Land
Act 1925 is observed, then not only is conveyancing simplified in
favour of a purchaser, but also adequate protection is accorded
to the beneficial interests of the settlement. We have seen how
the Act makes provision for failure to use the machinery at all,[1]
and we must now consider some of the problems that arise where
the statutory machinery is used but nevertheless mistakes occur
in its use.

In the first place, section 5 (3) of the Settled Land Act 1925
provides that a vesting deed shall not be invalidated by reason only
of any error in any of the statements or particulars required to be
contained in it. This must be read in conjunction with section
110 (2) which, as we have seen,[2] provides that a purchaser of a
legal estate in settled land shall not be entitled to call for the trust
instrument, but, instead, must assume that certain particulars
stated in the vesting deed are true. There are, however, exceptional cases in which a purchaser must examine the trust instrument and satisfy himself that the statements in the vesting deed
are true. In these cases, of course, section 5 (3) will not avail
him.

In the second place a purchaser may take a conveyance of
settled land under the mistaken impression that the vendor is still
a tenant for life, whereas in fact he is no longer so. What is the
position if a testator leaves Blackacre by will to W., his widow, for
her life or until re-marriage, remainder to X. in fee simple; W.
then re-marries and, as tenant for life, purports to sell Blackacre
to Y. who pays the purchase money to the trustees of the settlement? It is probable that Y. obtains the legal estate from W.,
but the question then arises whether he can rely on section 110 (2)
and defeat a claim to the legal fee simple by X. To do this Y.
must show that he is " a purchaser of a legal estate in the settled
land " and he can only do this if " settled land " means " land
which appears to be settled land but is not."[3]

The converse situation, where a purchaser takes a conveyance
from a vendor under the mistaken impression that the vendor is
an absolute owner in fee simple when he is in fact a tenant for life
of settled land, however, has been the subject of two inconsistent
judicial decisions at first instance. The solution to this problem
depends on how far reliance can be placed on section 110 (1),
which reads as follows :

> " On a sale, exchange, lease, mortgage, charge, or other disposi-
> tion, a purchaser dealing in good faith with a tenant for life or
> statutory owner shall, as against all parties entitled under the
> settlement, be conclusively taken to have given the best price,
> consideration, or rent, as the case may require, that could reasonably

---

[1] *Supra*, pp. 173–4.
[2] *Supra*, pp. 791–2.
[3] For the problem and its detailed analysis see Megarry and Wade, *Law
of Real Property* (4th Edn.), p. 307 ; M. & B. p. 278.

be obtained by the tenant for life or statutory owner, and to have complied with all the requisitions of this Act."

In *Weston* v. *Henshaw*,[1] X., a tenant for life, suppressed the settlement and purported to grant a legal mortgage to Y. as security for advances made to him personally, professing to be absolute and beneficial owner of the fee simple. The question was whether the mortgage to Y. was void against the beneficiaries under the settlement. DANCKWERTS, J., held that the mortgage was void because it was not a transaction authorised under section 18 (1) (a). He rejected an argument that Y. was protected under section 110 (1); admittedly Y. was in good faith and had complied with all the requirements of the Act, but nevertheless the section could only be relied upon where Y. knows X. to be a tenant for life and deals with him on that footing.

In *Re Morgan's Lease*,[2] however, UNGOED-THOMAS, J., took the opposite view.

" There is, in the section, no express provision limiting its benefit to a purchaser who knows that the person with whom he is dealing is a tenant for life. On its face it reads as free of limitation and as applicable to a person without such knowledge as to a person who has it. There is a limitation, namely that the purchaser must act in good faith ; but that limitation reads as applicable to a purchaser with such knowledge as without. Thus my conclusion is that section 110 applies whether or not the purchaser knows that the other party to the transaction is tenant for life."[3]

This interpretation of section 110 (1) seems preferable. *Weston* v. *Henshaw* appears to be the only decision in unregistered land which is an exception to the immunity of the purchaser for value of the legal estate without notice.[4]

SECTION II. TRUSTEES FOR SALE

The definition of a trust for sale and the powers of the trustees for sale have already been discussed.[5] It remains to consider the investigation of title when the land is sold and the overreaching effect of the conveyance to the purchaser. *Proof of title and overreaching.*

Proof of title. What has been said above about the proof and investigation of title in the case of a sale by a person beneficially entitled in his own right to a fee simple estate applies equally to trustees for sale.[6] Failing a special stipulation, they must show by reference to a good root of title at least fifteen years old that the creator of the trust was entitled to vest the legal *Statutory protection of purchasers.*

---

[1] [1950] Ch. 510; M. & B. p. 245.
[2] [1972] Ch. 1 ; [1971] 2 All E. R. 235 ; M. & B. p. 246.
[3] At p. 1510; *Mogridge* v. *Clapp*, [1892] 3 Ch. 382.
[4] See (1971) 87 L. Q. R. 338 (D. W. Elliott; (1973) 36 M. L. R. at p. 28 (R. H. Maudsley).
[5] *Supra*, pp. 197–202.
[6] *Supra*, pp. 730 *et seq.*

estate in them. There are, however, certain statutory provisions designed to protect the purchaser and to facilitate dealings with the land. We have already noticed those that relate to the postponement of sale[1] and the requirement of consents. [2]

Duration
of trust
for sale.

If the beneficiaries are all of full age and have become absolutely entitled under the limitations of the settlement, they may terminate the trust and direct the trustees not to sell the land. Theoretically, this confronts a purchaser with a difficulty, for how does he know that such a direction has not been given to the trustees ? It is, therefore, enacted that, so far as regards the safety and protection of the purchaser, the trust is to be deemed to be subsisting until the land has been conveyed to, or under the direction of, the persons interested in the proceeds of sale.[3] In other words, the purchaser is safe in taking a conveyance from the trustees until the beneficiaries, being absolutely entitled and of full age, have terminated the trust by taking a conveyance to themselves.[4]

Equities
arising under
the trust
over-
reached.

Overreaching. As we have already seen, a virtue long possessed by the trust for sale is that upon the sale of the land the equitable interests of the beneficiaries are kept off the title to the legal estate and are not disclosed to the purchaser.[5] The conveyance by the trustees overreaches the beneficial interests that arise *under* the trust for sale. By the equitable doctrine of conversion the beneficial interests are in the proceeds of sale from the moment that the trust for sale comes into operation ; by the conveyance the interests are transferred from notional to actual money. To be more precise, the purchaser acquires a title to the legal estate, unaffected by the trusts that have been declared of the proceeds of sale and of the rents and profits until sale, even though the trusts have been declared by the same instrument as that which creates the trust for sale.[6] He does not enjoy this immunity, however, unless he pays the purchase money to at least two trustees or to a trust corporation, if one has been appointed.[7]

In *Caunce* v. *Caunce*,[8] for example, W., a wife, had contributed to the purchase price of the matrimonial home. In breach of an agreement that the property should be vested in both W. and H., her husband, as joint tenants at law, it was conveyed to H. alone in fee simple. The effect of this was that both H. and W. became

---

[1] *Supra*, p. 200.   [2] *Supra*, p. 201.
[3] L.P.A. 1925, s. 23 ; re-enacting Conveyancing Act 1911, s. 10.
[4] For a difficulty in joint tenancy, see *supra*, p. 228.
[5] *Supra*, pp. 82–3.
[6] L.P.A. 1925, s. 27 (1) ; T.A. 1925, s. 14 (1) ; *supra*, p. 82. Although it is better to execute two deeds on the creation of a trust for sale, there is no necessity for this.
[7] *Ibid.*, s. 27 (2). For a definition of trust corporation see L.P.A. 1925, s. 205 (1) (xxviii), as extended by L.P.(A)A. 1926, s. 3. *Supra*, p. 793.
[8] [1969] 1 W. L. R. 286 ; [1969] 1 All E. R. 722 ; M. & B. p. 221.

beneficially entitled and the property was subject to a statutory trust for sale under the Law of Property Act 1925.[1] H. then, without W.'s knowledge, purported to act as sole beneficial owner and charged the property to a bank by way of legal mortgage. The question was whether the bank took subject to or free from W.'s equitable interest. It was clear that the bank could not overreach it, because it had paid the mortgage money to only one trustee, H. It was, however, held that the bank took free, as a bona fide purchaser for value of the legal estate without notice.[2]

The extent of overreaching in the case of a trust for sale would appear to be less than that accorded to a purchaser from a tenant for life under the Settled Land Act 1925.[3] There is no power to overreach any interests which arise prior to the trust for sale.[4]

SECTION III. APPROVED TRUSTEES

The overreaching effect of a conveyance either by trustees for sale or by a tenant for life under a settlement is limited in the sense that it does not extend to equitable interests that were in existence before the creation of the trust or settlement.[5]

Ad hoc trust for sale.

> If, for instance, a fee simple owner charges his land with the payment of a sum of money, and later subjects it to a trust for sale, the normal rule is that a purchaser from the trustees takes the legal estate burdened by the equitable charge.

The Law of Property Act 1925, however, introduced what is variously called an *ad hoc*, or a *special* or an *approved* trust for sale which enables the trustees to overreach even prior interests.[6] Whether it is of this special nature depends entirely upon the character of the trustees. They must be either,

> " (a) two or more individuals approved or appointed by the court or the successors in office of the individuals so approved or appointed ; or
> (b) a trust corporation." [7]

An alternative open to an estate owner whose land is already subject to an equitable interest is to create an *ad hoc* settlement

Ad hoc settlement.

---

[1] L.P.A. 1925, s. 35, *supra*, p. 223.
[2] *Supra*, p. 103, note 3. See M. & B. pp. 221-2. *Cf.* the position under S.L.A. 1925 ; *Weston* v. *Henshaw*, [1950] Ch. 510 ; *Re Morgan's Lease*, [1972] Ch. 1 ; [1971] 2 All E. R. 235 ; *supra*, p. 795.
[3] *Supra*, p. 792.
[4] Apart from the creation of an *ad hoc* trust for sale. See *Emmet on Title* (16th Edn.), pp. 177-8 ; Megarry & Wade, *Law of Real Property* (4th Edn.), p. 377, n. 56 citing *Re Ryder and Steadman's Contract*, [1927] 2 Ch. 62, at p. 82.
[5] Except in three cases under S.L.A. 1925, s. 72 (2), (3). *Supra*, p. 792.
[6] L.P.A. 1925, s. 2 (2).
[7] Defined *supra*, p. 793, note 9.

under the Settled Land Act. If he executes a vesting deed, declaring the legal estate to be vested in him upon trust to give effect to equitable interests to which it is subject, and if at the same time he names as trustees either a trust corporation or two persons appointed or approved by the court,[1] the result is that the land becomes settled land and he acquires the statutory powers of a tenant for life, including the power of sale.[2]

Operation of ad hoc assurances.   The *ad hoc* trust for sale and the *ad hoc* settlement are similar in their effects. The land will be conveyed by the estate owner— by the trustees in the one case, by the tenant for life in the other—and, though the equitable charge will be overreached by the conveyance to the purchaser, it will be the duty of the trustees to see that it is paid out of the proceeds of sale to which it has now become attached.

Over-reaching effect of conveyance under ad hoc trust or settlement.   Neither device, however, is of great practical use, for the number of equitable interests capable of being overreached is severely limited. It is enacted that a conveyance, whether under the trust for sale or under the settlement, shall not affect the following interests.[3]

(i) Equitable interests protected by a deposit of documents, relating to the legal estate affected *e.g.*, where title deeds are deposited with a bank to secure an overdraft.

(ii) Certain equitable interests that cannot be represented in terms of money, namely,

(*a*) restrictive covenants ;
(*b*) equitable easements ;
(*c*) estate contracts.[4]

These three interests, however, if created after 1925, will be void as against a purchaser of the legal estate for money or money's worth, unless they are registered under the Land Charges Act 1972. If they were created before 1926, they do not bind a purchaser unless he has actual or constructive notice of them.[5]

(iii) Any equitable interest that has been registered in accordance with the Land Charges Act 1972,[6] *except*

(*a*) certain annuities ; [7]
(*b*) limited owner's charges; [8] and
(*c*) general equitable charges.[9]

---

[1] S.L.A. 1925, s. 21.   [2] *Ibid.*, s. 21 (1) (*a*).
[3] L.P.A. 1925, s. 2 (3) ; S.L.A. 1925, s. 21 (2).
[4] *Supra*, pp. 742–3.
[5] L.P.A. 1925, s. 2 (5).
[6] *Supra*, p. 738.
[7] *I.e.*, annuities created and registered before 1926 ; *supra*, p. 739.
[8] *Supra*, p. 741.
[9] *Supra*, p. 741.

Registration of these three interests does not prevent them from being overreached, since they are adequately protected if enforceable against the money instead of against the land.

Thus, if land held by a beneficial owner in his own right, *i.e.*, land that is subject neither to a trust for sale nor a settlement, is burdened with the payment of, for instance, a general equitable charge which impedes the transfer of an absolute title to a purchaser, there are four possible methods of clearing off the incumbrance, namely : Methods by which legal estate may be cleared of equities.

(*a*) The creation of an *ad hoc* trust for sale.

(*b*) The creation of an *ad hoc* settlement.

(*c*) A conveyance of the land to the purchaser by the beneficial owner with the concurrence of the incumbrancer.

(*d*) An application for leave to pay into Court a sum of money in discharge of the incumbrance.[1]

SECTION IV.   MORTGAGORS AND MORTGAGEES

It will be recalled that in a mortgage of a legal fee simple, the mortgagor remains the estate owner of the legal fee simple, but nevertheless the mortgagee is entitled by virtue of his power of sale to convey it to a purchaser.[2] Mortgagors and mortgagees.

The rules concerning proof of title by a beneficial owner apply to a sale by a mortgagee. He must satisfy the purchaser in the usual manner that the legal estate is vested in the mortgagor. The purchaser, however, although he must investigate the title to the legal estate, is not concerned to inquire whether a case has arisen to authorize the sale or whether notice has been given by the mortgagee to the mortgagor.[3] Proof of title.

---

[1] L.P.A. 1925, s. 50.
[2] *Supra*, pp. 641–2.   [3] *Supra*, p. 671.

BOOK III

THE TRANSFER AND EXTINCTION OF ESTATES AND INTERESTS

PART III

TRANSFER BY OPERATION OF LAW

SUMMARY

Note. The land of a debtor, equally with his personal property, is liable to be seized at the instance of a creditor in satisfaction of unpaid debts. If we omit the case in which land has been expressly mortgaged by way of security for a loan, there are three different situations in which land may be taken from an owner for the benefit of his creditor or creditors : (*a*) where he is sued to judgment in respect of a debt, and thus becomes a judgment debtor ; (*b*) where he is made bankrupt ; and (*c*) where he dies and his property passes to his personal representatives for the purposes of administration. We will take these cases separately.

CHAPTER I

TRANSFER AS A RESULT OF EXECUTION AGAINST LAND BELONGING TO A JUDGMENT DEBTOR

History. At common law, in all actions where judgment for money alone was obtained, the creditor was entitled to seize the goods and chattels of the debtor (including chattels real) and the growing profits of the land, but not the land itself ; for just as the original feudal law forbade the alienation of feuds, so also did it forbid them to be incumbered with debts. The writ under which the goods and chattels were seized was, and still is, called the writ of *fieri facias*, " from the words in it where the sheriff is commanded, *quod fieri faciat de bonis*, that he cause to be made of the goods and chattels of the defendant the sum or debt recovered." [1] When the power of alienation became available to feudal landowners, the rule that feuds could not be incumbered with debts still remained, with the result that a creditor could seize only the rents and profits of the land, and he lost even this right if the debtor conveyed his land to a stranger.

To remedy this it was enacted in 1285 by the Statute Westminster II that a judgment creditor should be allowed to choose between two courses. He might either have execution upon the goods of the debtor by the writ of *fieri facias*, or have a writ of *elegit* by virtue of which *half* the land of the debtor and all his chattels with the exception of his oxen and the beasts of the plough, were seized and held till the debt was paid. [2] In pursuance of this statute a new writ was invented called a writ of *elegit* because, when a creditor chose this method, the entry on the roll was *quod elegit sibi executionem fieri de omnibus catallis et medietate*

Originally no remedy against freehold.

Origin of elegit.

Available for half of land.

---

[1] Blackstone, vol. iii. p. 417. The writ of *levari facias* was available where the sheriff was directed to levy the debt out of the goods and profits of the land. Holdsworth, *History of English Law*, vol. viii. p. 230.

[2] 13 Edw. I, c. 18. Holdsworth, *History of English Law*, vol. iii. p. 131. This was an extension of an earlier rule obtaining under the laws of the Jewry by which a Jewish creditor was entitled to take his debt from the chattels or from the lands of his debtor : Lincoln, *The Legal Background to the Starrs*, p. 54.

terrae. The effect of the statute was that a judgment recovered in a court of record became a charge upon the debtor's freehold estates, since it enabled a creditor to seize one-half of the debtor's lands and tenements.[1] Such a judgment, when followed by the issue of the writ, operated to transfer a definite interest in the land, called a tenancy by *elegit*, to the judgment creditor, who moreover could pursue his remedy against the land even though it had meanwhile come into the hands of a purchaser or of the heir of the debtor.

In 1838, however, it was provided by the Judgments Act that it should be lawful for the sheriff to whom any writ of *elegit* was directed to take *all* the lands, tenements and hereditaments of the debtor.[2] The operation of the writ was thereafter confined to land, so that a creditor who chose to proceed against chattels sued out a *fi. fa.*, while if he chose to seize freeholds, he sued out an *elegit*.[3] Leaseholds might be seized and sold under a *fi. fa.* or under an *elegit*, but it was usual to proceed under a *fi. fa.*, not under an *elegit*, for when once the latter had been executed, it was not possible to obtain another writ of execution : Available for whole land.

" And though he takes but an acre of land in execution, yet it is held a satisfaction of the debt, be it never so great, because it may in time come out of it."[4]

The Modern Law. The writ of *elegit* was abolished by the Administration of Justice Act 1956, as from January 1st, 1957,[5] and a judgment creditor may now apply to the court either for a charging order under the Act or for the appointment of a receiver by way of equitable execution, though he may indeed pursue both these remedies. Remedies now available.

The High Court or a County Court, having given judgment for the payment of money to a person, is empowered by the Act to impose a charge on the land of the debtor or upon any interest that he may hold in land[6] for the purpose of securing payment of the amount adjudged to be due.[7] Such a charge has the same effect and is enforceable in the same manner as an equitable charge created (1) Charging order.

---

[1] Cruise, *Digest*, Tit. xiv. ss. 1, 17–19.   [2] S. 11.
[3] The seizure of goods under a writ of *elegit* was prohibited by the Bankruptcy Act 1883, s. 146 (1).
[4] Bacon, *Abridgement of the Law* (7th Edn.), vol. 3. p. 393.
[5] S. 34 (1) ; S. I. 1956 No. 1979.·
[6] This does not include the individual interest of one of several beneficiaries under a trust for sale. *Irani Finance Ltd.* v. *Singh*, [1971] Ch. 59 ; [1969] 3 All E. R. 1455 ; but *cf. National Westminster Bank, Ltd.* v. *Allen*, [1971] 2 Q. B. 718 ; [1971] 3 All E. R. 201 ; (1971), 121 *New L. J.* 724 (S. M. Cretney). See Law Commission Working Paper No. 46 (1972) Charging Orders on Land, which recommends, *inter alia*, that a judgment creditor should be able to obtain such a charge, but the charge should operate as security only and not carry a right to apply for the sale of the land.
[7] *Ibid.*, s. 35 (1) ; County Courts Act 1959, s. 141.

by the debtor himself,[1] *i.e.* it entitles the creditor to apply for the sale of the land or for the appointment of a receiver.[2]

Registration of the order.
In the case of unregistered land the order is registrable as an order affecting land within the meaning of the Land Charges Act 1972,[3] and if not registered is void against a purchaser of the land for valuable consideration.[4] If the order is so registered, a later order appointing a receiver, whether made in proceedings to enforce the charge or by way of equitable execution, will bind a purchaser even though not itself registered.[5]   Where the land is registered, the order may be protected by a notice or a caution, and if not so protected, will similarly be void against a purchaser.[6]

(2) Appointment of receiver by way of equitable execution.
Courts of equity from an early period were prepared to aid a creditor who was unable to reach the land of his debtor under the common law writ of *elegit*, as for instance where the debtor was entitled to an equity of redemption or to an interest limited by a trust under which he was not the sole beneficiary.   Despite the abolition of the writ of *elegit*, this equitable jurisdiction continues in full force and it is made effective, as it always has been, by the appointment of a receiver with a direction to him to realize the interest of the judgment debtor in the land and to apply the proceeds in satisfaction of the debt.[7]

The Administration of Justice Act 1956, however, has enlarged the jurisdiction by providing that the power of the High Court or of a County Court to appoint a receiver by way of equitable jurisdiction shall extend to all legal estates and interests in land.[8]   This power of the court is additional to its power to appoint a receiver in proceedings to enforce a charging order and is exercisable whether or not such an order has been made.[9]   The order by which the appointment is made is registrable under the Land Charges Act 1972.[10]

---

[1] Administration of Justice Act 1956, s. 35 (3).
[2] *Supra,* p. 686.
[3] L.C.A. 1972, s. 6 (1). *Supra,* p. 739.
[4] *Ibid.,* ss. 6 (4) ; 17 (1).
[5] Administration of Justice Act 1956, s. 36 (3).
[6] L.R.A. 1925, ss. 49 (1), 59 (1).   Ruoff and Roper, pp. 554–5.
[7] Ashburner, *Principles of Equity* (2nd Edn.), p. 354.
[8] S. 36 (1).   County Courts Act 1959, s. 142.
[9] *Ibid.,* s. 36 (3).   [10] L.C.A. 1972, s. 6 (1) (*b*).

CHAPTER II

TRANSFER OF LAND BELONGING TO A BANKRUPT DEBTOR[1]

Bankruptcy procedure. After a debtor has committed an act of bankruptcy as defined by the Bankruptcy Act 1914,[2] either he or his creditors may present a bankruptcy petition to the court requesting that a *receiving order* be made for the protection of his estate. The effect of such an order is not to make him bankrupt, but to place his property under the control of the official receiver. If no arrangement for the discharge of his liabilities is accepted by the creditors, an *adjudication order* is made by the court, whereupon the debtor is rendered bankrupt, and his property vests in the trustee in bankruptcy appointed by the creditors.

Receiving order followed by adjudication order.

The certificate of the Department of Trade and Industry confirming the trustee's appointment is deemed to be a conveyance from the debtor to the trustee, and the general rule is that all the property which was formerly vested in the debtor as beneficial owner is transferred to the trustee in bankruptcy for distribution among the creditors. But we must observe, and this is an important rule of law, that it is not merely the property which was owned by the debtor at the date of the adjudication, or even at the date of the receiving order, that is transferred to the trustee, but also the property which he had at the *commencement of the bankruptcy*. This commencement is earlier than either the receiving order or the adjudication. The bankruptcy is deemed by statute to relate back to, and to commence at, the time when the act of bankruptcy was committed upon which the receiving order has been made. If more than one act has been committed, the bankruptcy commences at the *first* act, provided that it occurred not more than three months before the presentation of the bankruptcy petition.[3] An act of bankruptcy ceases to be available after three months.

Commencement of bankruptcy.

Property of debtor at commencement of bankruptcy. Having thus fixed the moment at which the bankruptcy is deemed

Property that passes to trustee.

---

[1] See generally *Williams on Bankruptcy* (18th Edn. 1968).
[2] There are eight available acts of bankruptcy, of which one is a notice by a debtor that he has suspended payment of his debts.
[3] Bankruptcy Act 1914, s. 37 (1).

to begin, the Act provides that with certain exceptions[1] there shall pass to the trustee,

> (a) all such property as may belong to or be vested in the bankrupt *at the commencement of the bankruptcy*, or may be acquired by or devolve on him before his discharge ; and
>
> (b) the capacity to exercise and to take proceedings for exercising all such powers in or over or in respect of property as might have been exercised by the bankrupt for his own benefit at the commencement of his bankruptcy or before his discharge, except the right of nomination to a vacant ecclesiastical benefice.[2]

Examples of interests in land which pass.

The following illustrations show the comprehensive nature of these statutory provisions.

General power.

1. A general power of appointment is property within the meaning of the Act, and if such power is exercisable by deed as distinct from will, it can be exercised by the trustee in bankruptcy during the lifetime of the debtor for the benefit of the creditors.[3]

Entailed interest.

2. If the bankrupt is entitled to an entailed interest, the trustee in bankruptcy may bar the entail, and dispose of the land for the benefit of the creditors.[4]

Future interest.

3. Again, if property is settled upon a tenant for life, and then upon such of his children as may be living at his death, the future interest of a child who becomes bankrupt before the tenant for life's death passes to the trustee in bankruptcy.[5]

On the other hand, an interest in land determinable upon the debtor's bankruptcy does not pass to the trustee. We have already seen [6] that although a person may not settle his own property upon himself *until he becomes bankrupt*, yet he may so settle it upon another person. In the same way a lease may provide that the tenancy shall be forfeited if the tenant becomes bankrupt, and the effect of this is that, subject to the provisions of the Law of Property Act 1925,[7] the term does not pass to the trustee upon the bankruptcy of the tenant.

---

[1] (i) personal earnings so far as they are necessary for the support of the bankrupt and his family ; (ii) interests limited by third parties and made defeasible upon bankruptcy (*supra*, pp. 372–3) ; (iii) rights of action in respect of bodily or personal injury ; (iv) rights under contracts of insurance (Third Parties (Rights against Insurers) Act 1930, s. 1 (v) property held by the bankrupt on trust for any other person ; (vi) the tools of his trade and the necessary wearing apparel and bedding of himself and his family up to the value of £20.

[2] Bankruptcy Act 1914, s. 38.

[3] *Nichols* v. *Nixey* (1885), 29 Ch. D. 1005.

[4] Bankruptcy Act 1914, s. 55 (5).

[5] *Higden* v. *Williamson* (1731), 3 P. Wms. 132.

[6] *Supra*, pp. 372–3.   [7] S. 146 (9), (10). *Supra*, pp. 447–9.

The trustee in bankruptcy stands with regard to the property which passes to him in the same position in which the debtor would have stood had he not become bankrupt. The broad general principle is that the trustee takes all the property, but takes it subject to all the liabilities which affected it while it was in the debtor's hands,[1] so that if, for instance, the property is mortgaged, the trustee takes only the equity of redemption, and if the property consists of a term of years, he is liable to pay rent and to observe the covenants contained in the lease.

Position of trustee as regards the land.

He may, however, disclaim a lease within twelve months of his appointment if in his opinion it is burdened with onerous covenants.[2] Normally, this presents no difficulty and inflicts no hardship, for the term is surrendered to the landlord by operation of law. But the case is different if there has been a sub-lease. At common law, if the lease disappears, the sub-lease disappears also, the branch falls with the tree,[3] but as the intention of the legislature is to allow disclaimer with the least possible injury to third parties, the Act contains a provision designed to protect the rights of third parties and particularly of sub-tenants.[4] It allows the court to vest a disclaimed leasehold interest in any person who is interested therein, as, for instance, a mortgagee or a sub-tenant, but it can do so only upon the terms of making that person

Disclaimer of lease.

(1) subject to the same liabilities and obligations as affected the bankrupt at the date when the bankruptcy petition was filed ; or

(2) if the court thinks fit, subject only to the same liabilities and obligations as would have existed if the lease had been assigned to the mortgagee or the sub-tenant at that date.[5]

The advantages of the second clause are that the person in whom the interest is vested becomes liable only for breaches of covenant which occur after the date of the bankruptcy petition, and he may also escape from liability for future breaches by assigning the lease to a third party. It has been said that the court should exercise its discretion in favour of imposing condition (2) if the result will be to place the sub-lessee in no better position and the lessor in no worse position than if there had been no disclaimer.[6]

---

[1] *Re Garrud* (1881), 16 Ch. D. 522, at p. 531, *per* JAMES, L.J. ; *Bendall v. McWhirter,* [1952] 2 Q. B. 466, 487; [1952] 1 All E. R. 1307, 1317, *per* ROMER, L.J.

[2] Bankruptcy Act 1914, s. 54 (1). A similar power is exercisable by the liquidator of a company (Companies Act 1948, s. 323). In certain cases the leave of the court must first be obtained ; Bankruptcy Rules 1952, r. 278, made under Bankruptcy Act 1914, s. 54 (3).

[3] *Re Carter and Ellis,* [1905] 1 K. B. 735, at p. 743, *per* VAUGHAN WILLIAMS, L.J.

[4] *Re Holmes,* [1908] 2 K. B. 812, at p. 815; *per* JELF, J.

[5] Bankruptcy Act 1914, s. 54 (6).

[6] *Re Carter and Ellis,* [1905] 1 K. B. 735, at p. 747.

After-acquired Property. There is an important distinction between property belonging to the bankrupt at the commencement of the bankruptcy and property acquired by him afterwards.

Over the former he has no right of disposition whatsoever, but, by the rule in *Cohen* v. *Mitchell*,[1] if he completes a disposition of the after-acquired property in favour of a person dealing with him *bona fide* and for value before the trustee intervenes, the disposition is unimpeachable.

It should be noticed that the property as soon as acquired vests immediately in the trustee and not in the bankrupt, who has only a right to possession until the trustee intervenes to exercise his right. All that the rule means is that the ownership of the trustee is liable to be defeated if he fails to intervene before its disposition by the bankrupt is completed.[2]

The fact that the alienee has notice of the bankruptcy does not constitute lack of *bona fides*, since, so far as he knows, the trustee may have authorized the transaction.

Position of Third Parties.—The rule that the title of the trustee relates back to the commencement of the bankruptcy seriously affects transactions occurring in the interval between an available act of bankruptcy and the order of adjudication. If the trustee is entitled to all that was in the apparent ownership of the bankrupt during this interval, is a conveyance of land made in favour of a third party after the commission of an act of bankruptcy to be upset ? The general principle is clear and has been stated in these words :

" Nothing is more firmly established in bankruptcy law than that a man who has committed an act of bankruptcy is not entitled to deal with his estate."[3]

It follows from this that every disposition of property made by a man after the commission of an act of bankruptcy is void against the trustee, and the property is recoverable by him from the

person to whom it has been conveyed.[4] This principle, however, is subject to the following statutory modifications.

(i) Conveyances for value

Any conveyance or assignment made by the bankrupt for valuable consideration is valid, provided that it takes place before the date of the receiving order, and that the alienee has no notice at the time of the conveyance of an available act of bankruptcy.[5]

---

[1] (1890), 25 Q. B. 262. For the extension of the rule to realty see Bankruptcy Act 1914, s. 47.

[2] *Re Pascoe*, [1944] Ch. 219 ; [1944] 1 All E. R. 281.

[3] *Ponsford, Baker & Co.* v. *Union of London and Smith's Bank, Ltd.*, [1906] 2 Ch. 444, at p. 452, *per* Fletcher Moulton, L.J.

[4] *Ibid.*   [5] Bankruptcy Act 1914, s. 45.

In the case of unregistered land, the Land Charges Act 1972 affects the question of notice. If a bankruptcy petition or a receiving order is registered, the title of the purchaser is void against the trustee, since registration constitutes notice. If neither is registered, then a purchaser for money or money's worth is protected unless he had notice at the time of conveyance of an available act of bankruptcy.[1]

(ii) Executions completed by judgment creditors

A judgment creditor who issues execution against the land of a debtor, is entitled to the *benefit of the execution, i.e.* to a prior right to be paid in full out of the land,[2] provided that he *completes the execution*, as for example by procuring the appointment of a receiver, before the date of the receiving order *and* before notice of the presentation of any bankruptcy petition or of the commission of an act of bankruptcy by the debtor.[3] Hence, if a receiving order is made or if a petition or act of bankruptcy becomes known to the judgment creditor before completion of the execution, he loses the fruits of his diligence and the land becomes divisible among the general body of creditors.

Completed executions.

(iii) Distress levied by a landlord

A landlord may distrain for rent due from a bankrupt tenant, but if he levies the distress after the commencement of the bankruptcy he can recover only six months' rent accrued due prior to the date of the adjudication order.[4] There is no limit in the case of rent accruing due *after* adjudication, so that if the trustee takes possession and does not disclaim the lease, the remedy of distress is available to the landlord for rent actually due.[5]

Distress for six months' rent.

Transactions voidable by the Trustee. A trustee is permitted to set aside certain transactions that have taken place even before the commencement of a bankruptcy. These are as follows :

Transactions voidable by trustee.

(i) Voluntary Settlements

In order to prevent a debtor from transferring property to relatives to the detriment of his creditors, section 42 of the Bankruptcy Act 1914[6] provides that a voluntary settlement shall be void against the trustee.

Voluntary settlements.

(*a*) if the settlor becomes bankrupt within two years after the date of the settlement ; or

---

[1] L.C.A. 1972, ss. 5, 6. For registered land, see *infra*, p. 815.
[2] *Re Andrew*, [1937] Ch. 122 ; [1936] 3 All E. R. 450.
[3] Bankruptcy Act 1914, s. 40 (1).   [4] *Ibid.*, s. 35 (1).
[5] *Ibid.*, s. 35 (2). Distress cannot be levied for rent payable in advance.
[6] See generally Pettit, *Equity and the Law of Trusts* (3rd Edn.), pp. 145–52.

(b) if the settlor becomes bankrupt within ten years after the date of the settlement, unless the beneficiaries can prove that the settlor at the date of the settlement was able to pay all his debts without the aid of the settled property, and also that his interest passed to the trustees of the settlement on its execution.[1]

A settlement is said to be " voluntary " if it is not made for money or for money's worth, or in consideration of a *future* marriage.   Normally, if a man settles property acquired by him **Meaning of "voluntary" settlement.** *after* his marriage in right of his wife he is deemed to make a voluntary settlement, but for the purposes of the present rule this particular form of settlement is expressly regarded as having been made for valuable consideration.   In the result, therefore, the following transactions are unaffected by section 42 :

First, a transfer to a purchaser or incumbrancer in good faith and for valuable consideration.   "Purchaser" in this context means a purchaser in the commercial sense, *i.e.*, one who furnishes the debtor with consideration in replacement of the property extracted from his creditors.[2]

Secondly, a settlement made before and in consideration of marriage, unless the intention of the parties is to defeat creditors.[3]

Thirdly, a settlement made in favour of the wife or children if the property has accrued to the settlor after the marriage in right of the wife, as for example where he acquires property under his wife's intestacy.[4]

The Act provides that a settlement falling within the above provisions shall be *void* " against the trustee in bankruptcy." These words mean, not that the settlement is void generally, but **The settlement is voidable, not void.** that it becomes voidable at the instance of the trustee *if bankruptcy supervenes*.[5]   It follows from this that if the beneficiary under the settlement transfers the settled property for value before the commencement of the bankruptcy, the title of the transferee cannot be avoided.[6]   Moreover, a disposition made after the commencement of bankruptcy but before intervention by the trustee is unassailable if the transferee for value had no notice of an available act of bankruptcy.[7]   If duly avoided, a settlement is void only to the extent necessary to pay the debts and cost of the bankruptcy.

---

[1] Bankruptcy Act 1914, s. 42 (1).   For the purposes of this section, "settlement" includes any conveyance or transfer of property, s. 42 (4).

[2] *Re A Debtor*, [1965] 1 W. L. R. 1498 ; [1965] 3 All E. R. 453 ; *Re Densham*, [1975] 1 W. L. R. 1519 ; [1975] 3 All E. R. 726 ; *Re Windle*, [1975] 1 W. L. R. 1628 ; [1975] 3 All E. R. 987.

[3] *Columbine* v. *Penhall* (1853), 1 Sm. & G. 228.

[4] Bankruptcy Act 1914, s. 42 (1) ; *Re Bower Williams*, [1927] 1 Ch. 441.

[5] *Re Carter and Kenderdine's Contract*, [1897] 1 Ch. 776.

[6] *Re Carter and Kenderdine's Contract, supra* ; *Re Vansittart*, [1893] 2 Q. B. 377.

[7] *Re Hart*, [1912] 3 K. B. 6.

Section 42 operates where the settlor becomes bankrupt, and therefore it does not apply where he dies insolvent and the court orders that his estate shall be administered according to the law of bankruptcy. In such a case he has never been adjudicated bankrupt.[1]

(ii) Conveyances in Fraud of Creditors

It was provided in 1571 by the Statute 13 Eliz. c. 5 (and this is a statute which applied generally and not merely to a case of supervening bankruptcy) that any alienation of real or personal property made with the intention of delaying, hindering or defrauding creditors should be void as against such creditors. The statute, however, contained an exception in favour of purchasers for valuable consideration who had no notice that the grantor was actuated by a fraudulent intention.

Conveyances in fraud of creditors voidable.

The Statute of Elizabeth has now been re-enacted in a modern form by section 172 of the Law of Property Act 1925 :[2]

> " (1) Save as provided in this section, every conveyance of property, made whether before or after the commencement of this Act, with intent to defraud creditors, shall be voidable at the instance of any person thereby prejudiced.
>
> (3) This section does not extend to any estate or interest in property conveyed for valuable consideration and in good faith or upon good consideration and in good faith to any person not having, at the time of the conveyance, notice of the intent to defraud creditors."

It will be noticed that a person who takes an estate or interest in good faith will be protected if the conveyance to him was supported either by valuable or by good consideration. Good consideration arises where a person conveys land to someone to whom he is supposed to bear natural love and affection, as for instance to his children, brothers, sisters, nephews and nieces. The rule under 13 Eliz. c. 5 was that a conveyance which was supported by good, as distinguished from valuable, consideration could be set aside in favour of creditors, notwithstanding that the grantee took in good faith,[3] but the intention of the legislature in the Act of 1925 apparently is to reverse this rule.[4]

This enactment must be distinguished from section 42 of the Bankruptcy Act, for since it is of general application and in no way dependent upon the bankruptcy of the alienor it may be invoked

---

[1] *Re Gould*, (1887), 19 Q. B. D. 92.
[2] See generally Pettit, *Equity and the Law of Trusts* (3rd Edn.) pp. 136–44.
[3] *Twyne's Case* (1602), Smith's *Leading Cases*, vol. i. p. 1.
[4] HARMAN, J., however, in *Re Eichholz*, [1959] Ch. 708, at pp. 725–6 ; [1959] 1 All E. R. 166, took the view that the Act of 1925 is a consolidating statute that *prima facie* is not to be construed as making any substantial alteration in the pre-existing law. But see (1959), 75 *L. Q. R.* 307 (R. E. M.). *Lloyds Bank, Ltd.* v. *Marcan*, [1973] 1 W. L. R. 339, at p. 344, *per* PENNYCUICK, V-C. ; *supra*, p. 9, n. 2.

if an order for the administration of his estate in bankruptcy is made after his death.[1]

What must be proved in order to set aside an alienation under the statute varies according as the alienee is a voluntary alienee or a purchaser for good or valuable consideration. A voluntary conveyance is voidable if its necessary effect is to defeat creditors, although a fraudulent intention cannot actually be proved.[2] Thus a voluntary conveyance made by a man upon the eve of starting a hazardous business, which is likely to embarrass him financially, is voidable upon his subsequent insolvency, even though he could have paid his debts in full at the time of the conveyance.[3] In such cases the onus of disproving a fraudulent intent lies upon the alienee.

On the other hand, a conveyance made for valuable or good consideration is not voidable unless it is proved,

First, that the grantor was actuated by a fraudulent intention[4] and, secondly, that the grantee was aware of that fraudulent intention, not necessarily that he actively participated in the fraud.[5]

With regard to the first matter, the court, in each particular case, must determine what was the true object of the conveyance. If, for instance, a trader, sorely pressed by creditors, forms a company and sells the whole of his property to it, receiving in return all or nearly all the shares, the almost irresistible inference is that he intends to delay and hinder his creditors.[6]

Nevertheless, it is not the intent of the statute to prevent honest dealings between one person and another, even though the result may be to hinder creditors. Thus in one case[7]:

J. granted by deed of gift a farmhouse in trust for her daughters, in consideration of which they covenanted to pay the debts

" incurred by J. up to the date of the deed in connection with the working and management of the farm."

J. had no other property. The plaintiff, to whom J. owed a debt having no connection with the farm, brought an action to have the conveyance set aside. He failed because it represented a perfectly honest family arrangement, whereby the daughters undertook to pay part of their mother's debts, in consideration of which they were to take immediately property which in all probability they would have received on her death.

In this case it will be noticed that the conveyance was founded

---

[1] *Re Eichholz*, [1959] Ch. 708 ; [1959] 1 All E. R. 166. See (1959) 22 M. L. R. 423 (P. M. Bromley).

[2] *Freeman* v. *Pope* (1870), 5 Ch. App. 538 ; *Re Eichholz, supra.*

[3] *Mackay* v. *Douglas* (1872), L. R. 14 Eq. 106 ; *Re Butterworth,* (1882), 19 Ch. D. 588.

[4] *Lloyds Bank, Ltd.* v. *Marcan*, [1973] 1 W. L. R. 1387, at p. 1392, *per* CAIRNS, L.J.

[5] *Re Fasey*, [1923] 2 Ch. 1.

[6] *Re Fasey, supra.*   [7] *Re Johnson* (1881), 20 Ch. D. 389.

partly upon good consideration and partly upon valuable consideration. The former consisted of the relationship of the grantees to the grantor, and the latter of the agreement to pay the mother's debts. In the then state of the law the relationship alone (*i.e.* good consideration) would not have sufficed to protect the interest granted to the daughters, but presumably, in view of the alteration introduced by the Act of 1925 which has already been mentioned, that interest could not now be defeated under the statute even though there were no promise to pay debts.[1]

It is provided that the enactment shall not affect the operation of a disentailing assurance.[2] Thus a resettlement of property which has been preceded by a disentailment is not voidable.

Resettlement not voidable.

Registered Land.[3] If a registered proprietor is adjudicated bankrupt, his estate vests in his trustee in bankruptcy who may be registered in his place.[4] At the earlier stages, creditors are protected by a creditors' notice and a bankruptcy inhibition. As soon as practicable after a bankruptcy petition has been registered at the Land Registry, the Registrar will enter a creditors' notice against the title of any registered land or charge which appears to be affected. This prevents the land or charge from being dealt with free from the creditors' claims, except in proper cases such as a sale by a prior registered chargee or by the trustee in bankruptcy. The bankruptcy inhibition is entered on the proprietorship register when a receiving order is made, and this ensures that, except in proper cases, no dealing with the registered land can take place until the trustee in bankruptcy is registered as proprietor.

Registered land.

If no creditors' notice and no bankruptcy inhibition are entered on the register, section 61 (6) of the Land Registration Act 1925 sets out the circumstances in which the title of the trustee in bankruptcy will be void as against a purchaser :—

" Where under a disposition to a purchaser in good faith for money or money's worth such purchaser is registered as proprietor of an estate or a charge, then, notwithstanding that an available act of bankruptcy has been committed by the person making the disposition, the title of his trustee in bankruptcy acquired after the commencement of this Act shall, as from the date of such disposition, be void as against such purchaser unless at the date of such disposition, either a creditors' notice or a bankruptcy inhibition has been registered, but a purchaser who, at the date of the execution of the registered disposition, has notice of an available act of bankruptcy, or of the receiving order, or adjudication, shall not be deemed to take in good faith.[5]

Nothing in this section shall impose on a purchaser a liability to make any search under the Land Charges Act 1925."[6]

---

[1] But see *supra*, p. 813, note 4.   [2] L.P.A. 1925, s. 172 (2).
[3] See generally Ruoff and Roper, chap. 31.
[4] L.R.A. 1925, ss. 42 (1), 61 (5). L.R.R. 1925, rr. 174–7. Until the appointment of a trustee, the official receiver is entitled to be registered.
[5] *Ibid.*, s. 61 ; L.R.R. 1925, rr. 179, 180.   [6] See Ruoff and Roper, pp. 655–8.

CHAPTER III

TRANSFER OF THE LAND OF A DECEASED DEBTOR

Assets.

Introductory Note. Property which belongs to a person for an interest not ceasing with his life is transferred upon his death to his personal representatives,[1] and it becomes liable for the payment of his debts. Property which thus becomes available for creditors is called assets, and the phrase *administration of assets* is employed to indicate the obligation of the personal representatives to pay the funeral and testamentary expenses and the debts of the deceased out of the property, before distributing the residue among those who are beneficially entitled.

Personalty as assets in case of a will.

History—Personalty. Originally, whether property was assets varied according as it was personalty or realty.

In the earliest days of English Law a man's personal property was apparently divided into three parts, one of which went to his heirs, another to his wife, while the third was at his own disposal, but by imperceptible degrees the rights of the wife and the children disappeared, and a man became entitled to bequeath his personal property as he liked.[2]

Bequeathed personalty did not pass directly to the donees under the will, but vested first in the executors and became in their hands assets for the payment of debts.

Personalty as assets in case of intestacy.

If a man neglected to make a will, his property could in the earliest times be seized by the king, but as it was thought that the clergy, being supposedly of better conscience than laymen, were more fitted to make a disposition that would bring repose to the soul of the deceased, the king allowed the bishop of a diocese to seize the personalty of one who had died intestate. The bishop was expected to use the property for pious purposes, his only liability being to God, but as the result of this freedom from control was that the clergy arrogated to themselves one-third of the property

---

[1] *Infra*, pp. 820 *et seq.*   [2] Blackstone, vol. ii. pp. 492–3.

and generally omitted to pay the debts of the deceased, it was enacted by the Statute Westminster II that the bishop should be bound to pay those debts so far as the goods extended, just as executors were bound where the deceased had left a will. But as the clergy were still enabled to appropriate anything that was left after payment of debts, it was finally provided that in case of intestacy the bishop should depute the nearest and most lawful friends of the deceased to administer his goods, and that such administrators should be on the same footing as executors appointed by will.[1] So it is true to say that from an early date the personal property of a deceased person, including both chattels personal and chattels real, passed to his personal representatives and became in their hands answerable for his debts.

History—Realty. The case stood differently, however, with realty. At common law, before the Statute of Wills 1540, the fee simple estate of a deceased person passed directly to his heir, and, after a will of lands was permitted, passed directly to his devisee if he had exercised his testamentary power. Whether he died testate or intestate, his land did not go to his personal representatives, and whether it went to the heir-at-law or to a devisee, it did not constitute assets for the payment of debts. *(Land originally not assets.)*

There were, however, three cases in which a fee simple estate was liable to the creditors of the deceased. Debts due to the Crown and debts due to *judgment* creditors were enforceable against the land notwithstanding the death of the owner, and thirdly, if the fee simple tenant had in his lifetime covenanted by deed for himself and his heirs to pay a sum of money, the creditor (called a *specialty creditor*) could make the heir liable for the debt to the extent of the land which had descended to him. But this privilege of the specialty creditor was not at first enforceable against an equitable fee simple, and it was strictly limited to a right of action against the *heir* of the deceased, so that the creditor was defrauded of his money if the deceased devised his land to a stranger. These two defects were later remedied, for the Statute of Frauds in 1677 made equitable fees simple liable equally with legal estates, and in 1691 the Statute of Fraudulent Devises[2] provided that a devisee should be liable in the same way as an heir for the specialty debts of his testator. Real estate which in this manner became liable in the hands of an heir or devisee for specialty debts was called " assets by descent." *(Exceptions.)*

The result of the common law treatment as thus modified by statute was, then, that specialty creditors had a remedy against the fee simple estates of a deceased owner, while simple contract creditors had not.

---

[1] Blackstone, vol. ii. pp. 295–6 ; *Hewson* v. *Shelley*, [1914] 2 Ch. 13, at pp. 38–9.
[2] 3 Will. & Mar. c. 14.

An estate tail was not liable for payment of debts, for unless it was barred by the tenant during his life it descended to the appropriate heir freed from the obligations of the deceased.

Estates *pur autre vie* were not liable for the debts of a deceased owner, whether they passed to a general or to a special occupant.[1] The Statute of Frauds, however, which allowed a tenant *pur autre vie* to devise his interest, enacted that if there was no devise, the interest should be assets by descent in the hands of the heir to the same extent as if it were a fee simple; and if there was a devise, it should go to the personal representatives and be assets in their hands.

Intervention of equity. Such were the rules at common law, but in certain cases equity stepped in and afforded simple contract creditors a remedy against the land. We have seen that personal representatives had no power over real estate, since it passed directly to the heir or the devisee, but if a testator gave his executors a power of sale over his land for the purpose of paying his debts, equity treated the land to which the power related as being **Equitable assets.** *equitable assets.* Land became available in this way for payment of debts if a testator gave his executors an express power of sale for that purpose, or if he gave them merely an implied power of sale (as for instance by the creation of a general charge of debts upon his real estate), or if he devised his land to the executors upon trust to sell and pay debts out of the proceeds.

Again, acting on the view that assets must be confined to property actually owned by the deceased, common law refused to include in this category property over which he had a power of appointment.[2] In the case of a general power, however, equity permitted proceedings in Chancery to be taken in order to make the appointed property available for payment of debts. The appointee became a trustee for creditors.[3]

Administration of Estates Act 1833. Such was the position with regard to assets when the Administration of Estates Act 1833 was passed, except that an Act passed in 1807 had already provided that the land of a deceased *trader* should be liable in equity for the payment of his debts, whether specialty or simple contract. The Act of 1833 provided that any estate or interest in lands which the deceased owner had not charged with, or devised subject to, the payment of debts should be assets to be administered in courts of equity for the payment both of specialty and of simple contract debts. Simple contract creditors thus obtained a remedy against land, even where a testator had omitted to make express provision for the payment of their debts, but the Act of 1833 still favoured specialty creditors to

---

[1] *Supra*, p. 266, note 1.

[2] *Lord Townshend* v. *Windham* (1750), 2 Ves. Sen. 1, at pp. 10–11 ; *O'Grady* v. *Wilmot*, [1916] 2 A. C. 231.

[3] *O'Grady* v. *Wilmot*, at pp. 246–8, *per* Lord Buckmaster.

the extent of allowing them, if the heirs of the debtor were bound, to be paid the full amount of the debts due to them before any creditors by simple contract, or creditors by specialty in which the heirs were not bound, received satisfaction for any part of their demands. This priority was, however, removed by Hinde Palmer's Act 1869,[1] which provided that all creditors, as well specialty as simple contract creditors, should be treated as standing in equal degree.

The distinction that existed between legal and equitable assets did not depend upon whether the property was legal or equitable in nature (for instance, an equitable fee simple was legal assets for specialty debts), but upon whether the remedy lay at law or in equity. If a creditor could make property available for the payment of debts by suing at common law, the property was legal assets, but if he was compelled to take proceedings in equity, the property was equitable assets.[2] Distinction between legal and equitable assets.

Thus equitable assets included land charged or devised for payment of debts, land which was made available under the Administration of Estates Act 1833, and personal estate in respect to which the testator had exercised a general power of appointment. Legal assets were themselves divided into *real* assets and *personal* assets. Real assets consisted of property which was held by an heir or a devisee, and for the recovery of which a creditor could maintain an action : personal assets consisted of the personal property which devolved upon the executor or the administrator *virtute officii*.

Land Transfer Act 1897. The Land Transfer Act 1897 placed the law upon an entirely new basis and abolished most of the old distinctions. Establishment of real representation.

We have seen that under the old law, while personal property passed to the personal representatives and became in their hands liable to the payment of debts, real property went straight to the heir or the devisee. Personal property constituted legal assets ; real property constituted legal assets if it had been made subject to a specialty in which heirs were bound, but equitable assets if it was made available by proceedings in Chancery under the Administration of Estates Act 1833. The object of the first part of the Land Transfer Act 1897 was to simplify and improve the machinery for the administration of *real* assets without disturbing the ultimate rights of the beneficiaries. It effected this by providing that those persons who already had control over the personal property should also have control over the real estate.[3] The Act, in other words, established a *real* representative,

---

[1] A.E.A. 1869
[2] *Cook* v. *Gregson* (1856), 3 Drew, 547.
[3] *Re Williams*, [1904] 1 Ch. 52 ; *Re Vickerstaff*, [1906] 1 Ch. 762.

Land now
assets.

who was always the same person as the personal representative. It enacted that the real estate of persons dying after 1897 should, notwithstanding any testamentary disposition, devolve to and become vested in the personal representatives as if it were a chattel real. The personal representatives were given the same powers and duties with respect to the realty as if it had been personalty; and, as regards administration of assets, it was enacted that the real estate should be administered in the same manner and should be subject to the same liabilities for debts as if it were personal estate.

Before this Act was passed, if a deceased person had charged his debts on his real estate, the executors had power to raise the necessary money by a sale of the land ; where the deceased either died intestate or made no provision in his will for the payment of debts, the creditors, in order to make his land available, were obliged to bring an administration action in the Chancery Division to which the heir or the devisee, as well as the executors, had to be made parties. But after the Act was passed (*i.e.* in the case of any person dying after December 31, 1897), the land of a deceased person could in all cases be made available for the payment of debts without the necessity for any proceedings.

The following interests, however, were excepted from the operation of the Act :

1. real estate which some other person had a right to take by survivorship (joint tenancy) ;

2. land of copyhold tenure or customary freehold ;

3. estates tail.

What
property
now assets.

Administration of Estates Act 1925. The first part of the Land Transfer Act 1897 was re-enacted, with a number of amendments, by the Administration of Estates Act 1925.

The first section provides that real estate to which a deceased person was entitled for an interest not ceasing on his death is to devolve, like chattels real, on his personal representative, *i.e.* on the executor in the case of a will, and on the administrator when the deceased dies intestate.[1] The expression *real estate* includes a variety of interests. Thus land with respect to which the deceased has by his will exercised a general power of appointment is to pass to the personal representatives as if it had belonged to the testator.[2] Again, and this is a striking innovation, an entailed interest which a testator has disposed of by will is to vest in the personal representatives.[3] If, however, he dies without making any such disposition, and without having barred the entail, his interest ceases on his death, and therefore does

---

[1] A.E.A. 1925, s. 1 (1).   [2] *Ibid.*, s. 3 (2).   [3] *Ibid.*, s. 3 (3).

not pass to the personal representatives.[1] *Real estate* includes chattels real, land in possession, remainder or reversion, and every interest in or over land to which a deceased person was entitled at the time of his death ; also real estate held on trust (including settled land) or held by way of mortgage or security.[2] It does not include an interest under a joint tenancy where another person survives the deceased,[3] nor the interest of a corporator sole in the corporation property.[4]

As regards administration of assets, section 32 of the Administration of Estates Act 1925 declares what property shall be available for the payment of debts :—

" (1) The real and personal estate, whether legal or equitable, of a deceased person, to the extent of his beneficial interest therein, and the real and personal estate of which a deceased person in pursuance of any general power (including the statutory power to dispose of entailed interests) disposes by his will, are assets for payment of his debts (whether by specialty or simple contract) and liabilities, and any disposition by will inconsistent with this enactment is void as against the creditors, and the court shall, if necessary, administer the property for the purpose of the payment of the debts and liabilities . . .

(2) If any person to whom any such beneficial interest devolves or is given, or in whom any such interest vests, disposes thereof in good faith before an action is brought or process is sued out against him, he shall be personally liable for the value of the interest so disposed of by him, but that interest shall not be liable to be taken in execution in the action or under the process." *Administration of assets.*

Thus broadly speaking, all the property of a deceased person is now available in the hands of the personal representatives for the payment of debts, and the distinction between legal and equitable assets is obsolete.

Procedure. There are three methods by which an estate may be administered.

(i) **Administration by the personal representatives out of court.** If this method is adopted, as is usually the case, the personal representatives themselves undertake the task of satisfying the debts of the deceased out of the assets.

(ii) **Administration in court.** The Chancery Division of the High Court has jurisdiction[5], upon an action for administration being brought by the personal representatives or by a creditor or a beneficiary, to order that the estate shall be admini- *Modes of administration.*

---

[1] A.E.A. 1925, s. 3 (3).   [2] *Ibid.*, s. 3 (1).
[3] *Ibid.*, s. 3 (4).   [4] *Ibid.*, s. 3 (5).
[5] County Courts have concurrent jurisdiction where the estate does not exceed in amount or value £5,000. County Courts Act 1959, s. 52 (1), as amended by Administration of Justice Act 1969, s. 5. The County Court may also have jurisdiction by agreement between the parties irrespective of the amount or value. *Ibid.*, s. 53.

stered in court. This is the method that is adopted where some dispute has arisen between the interested parties or where a point of law requires decision, as, for instance, if the conduct of the executors is contested by the creditors or beneficiaries, or if a claimant's right to a legacy is questioned.

(iii) **Administration of an insolvent estate in court.** An estate is insolvent if it is not sufficient to satisfy all personal and testamentary expenses and debts. In such a case a petition, praying for an order that the estate be administered according to the law of bankruptcy, may be presented either by the personal representatives or by any creditor who would have been entitled to present the petition had the deceased been still alive.[1] The order, if made, is equivalent to an adjudication order.[2]

Ranking of creditors and beneficiaries. Two important matters, which may conveniently be called *priority of creditors* and *priority of beneficiaries*, arise in connection with the administration of assets. If an estate is solvent the question of priority of creditors obviously does not arise, for all will be paid in full ; but in the case of insolvency it is essential to know whether all creditors rank *pari passu* or whether some have a prior right of payment to others. The question of priority of beneficiaries may arise when the estate is solvent, *i.e.* if it is sufficient to satisfy all the creditors but not all the legatees and devisees. Here, since some of the beneficiaries must suffer in the sense that some of them must surrender their beneficial interests to satisfy the creditors, it is essential to have fixed rules that determine which of the beneficial interests must be taken first. In other words, there must be an *order of application of assets*.

Rules as to payment of debts where estate insolvent. **Priority of Creditors.** The law before 1926 with regard to the order in which creditors were paid out of an insolvent estate was unnecessarily difficult, for it varied according as administration was effected in or out of court, and according to the nature of the assets, whether legal or equitable. These old rules, however, may happily be allowed to fall into oblivion, for it was enacted by the Administration of Estates Act 1925[3] Bankruptcy rules prevail. that no matter what may be the mode of administration the bankruptcy rules that regulate the order of payment of creditors shall prevail.

The bankruptcy order is as follows :

Subject to the payment of funeral and testamentary expenses the following debts have priority [4] :

(i) Property belonging to a friendly society which was in the possession of the deceased as an officer of the society.[5]

---

[1] Bankrupty Act 1914, s. 130.   [2] *Supra,* p. 807.
[3] S. 34 (1) ; 1st Sched., Part I.   [4] Bankruptcy Act 1914, s. 33 (9).
[5] Friendly Societies Act 1896, s. 35 (1).

(ii) Property belonging to a trustee savings bank which was in the possession of the deceased as an officer of the bank. [1]

Subject to the above, the following classes of debts are entitled to preferential payment :

(a) Local rates due from the deceased at the date of his death, having become due within twelve months before that time. [2]

(b) Assessed taxes, property or income tax assessed on the deceased up to the 5th of April next before his death, but not exceeding one year's assessment. [3]

(c) Wages or salary not exceeding £200 of any clerk or servant in respect of services rendered during four months before the death of the deceased. [4]

(d) Wages not exceeding £200 of any labourer or workman in respect of services rendered during four months before the death of the deceased. [5]

(e) Contributions payable by the deceased under the National Insurance (Industrial Injuries) Act 1965, or the National Insurance Act 1965 in respect of employed contributors or employed persons [6] during the twelve months before his death.

(f) Accrued holiday remuneration payable to an employee on the termination of his employment with the deceased. [7]

(g) General betting duty, [8] gaming licence duty, [9] bingo duty [10] value added tax [11] or car tax [12] due from the deceased at the date of his death, having become due within twelve months before that time.

These seven preferential debts rank equally between themselves.

Subject to the above all debts are paid *pari passu* except that the following three classes are deferred and rank last for payment :

(i) Money lent by the husband of the deceased for the purposes of her trade or business. [13]

(ii) Money lent by the wife of the deceased for the purposes of his trade or business. [14]

(iii) A loan bearing interest which was to vary with the profits made by the deceased in his business. [15]

---

[1] Trustee Savings Banks Act 1969, s. 72.
[2] Bankruptcy Act 1914, s. 33 (1) (a), (5).
[3] These include capital gains and corporation tax. F.A. 1965, s. 45 (12), Sched. 10, Part II, para 15 (1).
[4] Bankruptcy Act, 1914, s. 33 (1) (b), (5) ; Companies Act 1947, ss. 91 (1), (4)–(6) (b), 115 (1) ; Companies Act 1948, Scheds. 16, 17.
[5] Bankruptcy Act 1914, s. 33 (1) (c), (5) ; Companies Act 1947, ss. 91 (1), (2), (4), (6) (b), 115 (1), (6) ; Companies Act 1948, Scheds. 16, 17.
[6] Bankruptcy Act 1941, s. 33 (1) (f), (5) ; National Insurance (Industrial Injuries) Act 1965, s. 87 (2) ; National Insurance Act 1965, ss. 61, 117 (2).
[7] Companies Act 1947, ss. 91 (5), 6 (a), 115 (1), (6) ; Companies Act 1948, Scheds. 16, 17.
[8] Betting and Gaming Duties Act 1972, s. 1.
[9] *Ibid.*, s. 13.
[10] *Ibid.*, s. 17.
[11] F.A. 1972, s. 41 (1) (a), 2 (a).
[12] *Ibid.*, s. 52, Sched. 7, para. 18.
[13] Bankruptcy Act 1914, s. 36 (1).
[14] *Ibid.*, s. 36 (2).
[15] *Ibid.*, s. 33 (9).

(iv) Money due to the seller of the goodwill of a business in respect of a share of the profits which the deceased contracted to pay when buying the business.[1]

Rights of secured creditors.

A secured creditor, *i.e.* one who holds a mortgage, charge or lien upon the property of the deceased, occupies a stronger position than unsecured creditors, for since he holds a definite interest in the property he is unaffected by the amount of assets or the number or class of other creditors. He may either[2]

> realize his security and prove in the bankruptcy for the balance of the principal and interest ; or
> surrender the security and prove for the whole debt ; or
> without realization or surrender, put a valuation upon his security and prove for the balance after deducting the assessed value.

Right of preference.

In respect of the estates of persons dying before January 1st, 1972, there were two rights possessed by a personal representative, namely his right of preference and his right of retainer, which if exercised disturbed the normal order of payment of debts.

Right of retainer.

The right of preference entitled a personal representative to pay one creditor before he paid another of equal degree with himself.

Further, as a personal representative cannot sue himself, it had been the rule that, as against creditors of equal degree, he could take sufficient assets to satisfy a debt that was due to him from the deceased. He was entitled in other words, to prefer himself.[3]

These rights of preference and retainer were inconsistent with the principle of the Bankruptcy Act 1914 under which all creditors of the same degree are paid *pari passu*. In 1970 the Law Commission said that " it is highly anomalous for a person in a fiduciary position to have rights of that sort."[4] They were abolished

Administration of Estates Act 1971.

by the Administration of Estates Act 1971 in relation to the estates of persons dying after 1971, subject to a proviso that a personal representative who reasonably and in good faith pays a debt to any creditor (including himself) at a time when he has no reason to believe that the estate is insolvent is not liable to account to any creditor of the same degree as the creditor who has been paid if it subsequently appears that the estate is insolvent.[5]

Order of application of assets where estate is solvent.

Priority of beneficiaries. As we have seen, if an estate, though sufficient to pay the debts in full, is insufficient to pay all the legatees and other beneficiaries, some of the beneficiaries must suffer, and it thus becomes imperative to have definite

---

[1] Partnership Act 1890, s. 3.
[2] Bankruptcy Act 1914, Sched. 2, paras. 10–12, 17.
[3] A.E.A. 1925, s. 34 (2).
[4] Law Commission Report on Administration Bonds, etc., 1970 (Law Com. No. 31), paras. 5, 7–9.
[5] Ss. 10, 12 (6), 14 (2). This proviso does not apply to a creditor-administrator who pays his own debts before those of other creditors. S. 10 (2).

rules prescribing which of them must forfeit their gifts in order that the creditors may be paid. If, for example, the residuary personalty is taken first, the result is to benefit the specific legatees and the devisees, including the residuary devisee, at the expense of the residuary legatee. The outstanding feature of the order prevailing before 1926 was that residuary personalty had to be taken first. Property comprised in a residuary devise came sixth on the list. The old rules, however, have been abolished, and the following new order of the application of assets in the case of a solvent estate was introduced by the Administration of Estates Act 1925.[1]

(1) Property undisposed of by will, subject to retention thereout of a fund sufficient to meet pecuniary legacies.

Property is " undisposed of by will" not only in the rare case where the testator fails to dispose of some specific part of the estate, but also where a gift lapses owing to the death of the donee before the testator or for some other reason, such as the attestation of the will by the beneficiary. Thus in effect the primary fund for the payment of debts is no longer the residuary personalty, but property, real or personal, that has lapsed. It may be a devise of land,[2] or a share of income[3] or of residue.[4]

We may perhaps venture upon an example in order to illustrate the difference between the old order of application and the new. Suppose, for instance, that a testator, who at the time of his death owes debts to the amount of £2000, leaves a will containing the following gifts : — The new order illustrated.

(a) Pecuniary legacies to the amount of £3000.
(b) A specific devise.
(c) Several specific bequests.
(d) A residuary bequest to X., and a residuary devise to Y.

Let us further suppose that Y. predeceases the testator, and that therefore his share of the residue lapses.

On these facts, under the law as it stood before 1926, the general rule that the primary fund for the payment of debts was the residuary personalty would have operated to reduce by £2000 X.'s share of the estate. Under the new rule, however, the land comprised in the residuary devise to Y., as being property undisposed of by the will, constitutes the primary fund.

---

[1] S. 34 (3) ; 1st Sched. Part II. See generally Mellows, *Law of Succession* (2nd Edn. 1973) pp. 523–33 ; Snell's *Principles of Equity* (27th Edn.) pp. 316–21.
[2] *Re Atkinson*, [1930] 1 Ch. 47 ; *Re Martin*, [1955] Ch. 698 ; [1955] 1 All E. R. 865.
[3] *Re Tong*, [1931] 1 Ch. 202.
[4] *Re Lamb*, [1929] 1 Ch. 722 ; *Re Worthington*, [1933] Ch. 771 ; *Re Sanger*, [1939] Ch. 238 ; [1938] 4 All E. R. 417 ; *Re Harland-Peck*, [1941] Ch. 182 ; [1940] 4 All E. R. 347 ; *Re Midgley*, [1955] Ch. 576 ; [1955] 2 All E. R. 625.

This is held by the executors upon trust for sale and out of the proceeds, first to set aside £3000 to meet the pecuniary legacies,[1] then to pay the debts, and finally to distribute the balance among the persons entitled under the rules that govern distribution upon intestacy. Thus X. occupies a better position than he would have done before 1926.

(2) Property not specifically devised or bequeathed but included in a residuary gift, subject to the retention thereout of a fund sufficient to meet pecuniary legacies, so far as not provided for as aforesaid.[2]

Thus property, whether realty or personalty, comprised in a residuary gift, is taken after undisposed of property. Before 1926, as we have seen, residuary personalty came first, but a residuary devise was treated as a specific devise and came sixth in the list, ranking with specific bequests. So, under this new rule, if there had been no lapse in the example given above, the pecuniary legacies and the debts would have been satisfied at the expense of X. and Y. equally.[3]

(3) Property specifically appropriated or devised or bequeathed for the payment of debts.

It seems a little curious that property which has deliberately been earmarked as a fund for the payment of debts should not be used first. The same principle, however, obtained before 1926, when realty devised in trust for the payment of debts ranked second in the list after residuary personalty, and it was generally justified by the observation that since a man does not normally realize property for the payment of debts if he has sufficient cash in his possession, it is only consistent to adopt the same course after his death.

(4) Property charged with, or devised or bequeathed subject to a charge for the payment of debts.

(5) The fund, if any, retained to meet pecuniary legacies.

(6) Property specifically devised or bequeathed, rateably according to value.

If, for instance, there is a devise of Blackacre to X., of Whiteacre to Y. and a bequest of a diamond ring to Z., and debts to the amount of £900 are still due after exhaustion of the properties enumerated (1) to (5) above, the rule is that X., Y. and Z. must

---

[1] *Re Anstead*, [1943] 1 Ch. 161 ; [1943] 1 All E. R. 522.
[2] *Re Wilson*, [1967] Ch. 53 ; [1966] 2 All E. R. 867.
[3] This would seem to be so despite *Re Thompson*, [1936] Ch. 676 ; [1936] 2 All E. R. 141 ; *Re Rowe*, [1941] Ch. 343 ; [1941] 2 All E. R. 330 ; *Re Anstead, supra.*

contribute *pro rata* and *pari passu*. To ascertain the amount of the contributions it is necessary to discover " the value to the testator "[1] of each property. Thus if the value of Blackacre is £1500, of Whiteacre £1200 and of the ring £300, each of the donees must contribute 3–10ths, *i.e.* X., £450 ; Y., £360 ; and Z., £90.

(7) Property appointed by will under a general power, including the statutory power to dispose of entailed interests, rateably according to value.

This rule, which obtained also under the old law, is confined to property subject to a *general* power, and does not apply unless the power has been actually exercised.

The final observation to make is that the order set out above may be varied by the will of the deceased.[2] If the testator indicates with sufficient clearness that some particular property shall constitute the primary fund for payment, as for instance where he creates a mixed fund for the purpose, his intention must be followed.[3] Thus in *Re Petty* : *(Statutory order may be varied by testator.)*

> The testator devised and bequeathed his real and personal estate upon trust for sale and conversion, and after directing that debts should be paid out of the mixed fund, he gave half of it to his wife and half to two daughters. His wife predeceased him.

It will be seen that the lapsed share of the wife constituted the primary fund for payment under the statutory order, but it was held that since the debts had clearly been thrown rateably on the mixed fund they must be paid out of it and not primarily out of the lapsed half. The same result ensues if the will provides that " subject to the payment of funeral and testamentary expenses, debts and legacies " the residue shall pass to two persons, one of whom predeceases the testator.[4]

---

[1] *Re John*, [1933] Ch. 370, at p. 372, *per* FARWELL, J. ; *Re Cohen*, [1960] Ch. 179 ; [1959] 3 All E. R. 740 (probate value, not later sale price taken).
[2] A.E.A. 1925, 1st Sched., Part II, para. 8.
[3] *Re Petty*, [1929] 1 Ch. 726 ; *Re Kempthorne*, [1930] 1 Ch. 268 ; *Re Atkinson*, [1930] 1 Ch. 47 ; *Re Littlewood*, [1931] 1 Ch. 443 ; *Re Ridley*, [1950] Ch. 415 ; [1950] 2 All E. R. 1 ; *Re Meldrum's Will Trusts*, [1952] Ch. 208 ; [1952] 1 All E. R. 274 ; *Re Berrey's Will Trusts*, [1959] 1 W. L. R. 30 ; [1959] 1 All E. R. 15.
[4] *Re Harland-Peck*, [1941] Ch. 182 ; [1940] 4 All E. R. 347 ; and see *Re James*, [1947] Ch. 256 ; [1947] 1 All E. R. 402.

BOOK III

THE TRANSFER AND EXTINCTION OF ESTATES AND INTERESTS

PART IV

TRANSFER ON DEATH

SUMMARY

CHAPTER I

TESTACY[1]

SUMMARY

SECTION I. GENERAL NATURE OF A WILL

Will of Lands. A will is a declaration made by a testator, Nature of
in the form required by law, of what he desires to be done after his a will.
death. It may define his desires with regard to several matters,
such as the manner in which his funeral shall be conducted, the
appointment of guardians for his children and the like, but we are
concerned to examine a will only in so far as it operates as a disposition of property. There is a palpable distinction between a
will and a deed. As BACON, V.-C., said [2] :—

---

[1] See generally *Jarman on Wills* (8th Edn.) ; *Theobald on Wills* (13th Edn.) ;
Williams and Mortimer on Executors, Administrators and Probate ; Mellows,
The Law of Succession (2nd Edn.).
[2] *Olivant* v. *Wright* (1878), 9 Ch. D. 646, at p. 650.

" A deed is a contract by which the owner of property gives a certain destination to it then and thenceforth for ever, and he parts with all his power over it.   A will is an instrument which is not to take effect till the death of the testator."

Distin-
guished
from
settlement.

Thus a settlement, created *inter vivos*, is an instrument by which a settlor may make a disposition of beneficial interests to persons by way of succession.   Unless expressly stated to the contrary, this is irrevocable.   A will, on the other hand, is always revocable notwithstanding the strongest expressions to the contrary that it may contain.

Thus, if a person makes a disposition by will in fulfilment of an agreement to leave certain property to another, the power of revocation remains open to him, though if the contract is made for consideration and is, in the case of land, evidenced by a memorandum in writing under section 40 of the Law of Property Act 1925, he or his executors will be liable for breach of contract.   If he puts such testamentary disposition out of his power by conveying the property in his lifetime to a third person, he is, personally and at once, liable in damages ; if he dies possessed of the property, but without having made the disposition he agreed to make, the court, although it does not set the will aside, may order the property to be conveyed to the promisee.[1]

A will is
ambulatory.

So a will has no effect, either upon the testator's property or in any other regard, until death, but when that event occurs the will takes effect as a disposition of property.   Its essential characteristic is that it is ambulatory, a fact which is clear if we again contrast the case of a settlement.   The effect upon the beneficial enjoyment by A. is exactly the same where A. devises Blackacre to B. in fee as where he settles it upon himself for life with remainder to B. in fee, but in the former case B. is entitled to nothing until the death of A., while in the latter he immediately becomes entitled to a vested interest in remainder.[2]

Before 1837
will of
realty
did not
speak from
testator's
death.

A devise of land before the Wills Act 1837 was treated very differently from a bequest of personalty.   It was regarded as a species of posthumous conveyance, and therefore acquired several attributes of a conveyance.   Thus, since it is impossible for a man to convey what he has not got, every devise was necessarily specific, *i.e.*, it was capable of passing only specific property owned by the testator at the time of the will.   It did not pass land that he acquired later, or land that he disposed of after the will, notwithstanding that he later re-acquired it.   Even a residuary devise was specific.

---

[1] *Synge* v. *Synge*, [1894] 1 Q. B. 466.
[2] *Jarman on Wills* (8th Edn.), p. 26.

Hence, if T., seised of Blackacre and Whiteacre, devised Blackacre to A. and the residue of his land to B., and the gift of Blackacre failed owing to the death of A. before T., Blackacre did not pass to B., for the gift to him of the residue was nothing more than a gift of the specific Whiteacre under the denomination " residue." [1]

On the other hand, it was well established that a bequest of personalty included all the personalty belonging to the testator at the time of his death. It spoke from his death, not from its execution.

Real estate, however, was put on the same footing as personalty in this respect by the following section of the Wills Act 1837.

> " Every will shall be construed, with reference to the real estate and personal estate comprised in it, to speak and take effect as if it had been executed immediately before the death of the testator, unless a contrary intention shall appear by the will." [2]

Alteration by Wills Act 1837.

A further section provides that a residuary devise shall include devises that have lapsed or become void.[3]

Consequently, if the subject-matter of a devise is described generically, it may be increased or diminished after the will is made, and whether the testator has parted with land that he owned at the time of the will or has acquired more land subsequently, his devise will pass what he actually owns at his death. Thus a will is ambulatory in the sense that it may pass property coming to the testator after its execution.

Although, strictly speaking, a will consists of all the properly executed writings in which a person has expressed his intentions, it is usual to contrast it with a codicil. A codicil is part of a person's will, and must be executed in precisely the same manner, but whereas the will is the principal, the codicil is the accessory instrument. It is in effect a supplementary instrument by which a testator alters or adds to his will.

Codicil.

Provision for family and dependants.—In most European countries testamentary freedom has been restricted by the rule that the members of a testator's family are entitled to a definite proportion of his estate. A similar rule obtained in England in early days with regard to wills of personalty, but it has long disappeared and for many years an English testator has been free to confer a princely endowment upon a prostitute or a charity and to leave his family penniless.[4] In 1938, however, the Inheritance (Family Provision) Act introduced a new principle by empowering the court to vary a will at the instance of the testator's surviving spouse and children.

Inheritance (Provision for Family and Dependants) Act 1975.

---

[1] Hayes, *Introduction to Conveyancing*, vol. i. pp. 343–4 ; on the subject generally see Digby, *History of the Law of Real Property*, p. 385.

[2] S. 24.   [3] S. 25.

[4] In the case of the fee simple and the estate tail, a widow might be fortunate enough to obtain her third by way of dower, but in practice she was generally deprived of this by the device of uses to bar dower and since 1833 she has in this respect been entirely in her husband's power, *infra*, pp. 870.

In 1952 the Act was extended to cases of intestacy,[1] and in 1958 a former spouse of the deceased was first given the right to apply for provision from the deceased's estate.[2] In 1975 this piecemeal legislation was repealed, and a single code enacted to empower the court to make provision from the estate of a deceased person for his or her family and dependants. The Inheritance (Provision for Family and Dependants) Act 1975[3] applies to any person dying domiciled in England and Wales[4] on or after April 1st, 1976.[5]

Applicants for provision. The Act enables the court to modify either the will or the rules of distribution on intestacy, if it is satisfied that reasonable financial provision has not been made for one of the following persons set out in section (1).

(*a*) the wife or husband of the deceased ;[6]
(*b*) a former wife or former husband of the deceased who has not remarried ;[7]
(*c*) a child of the deceased ;
(*d*) any person (not being a child of the deceased) who, in the case of any marriage to which the deceased was at any time a party, was treated by the deceased as a child of the family in relation to that marriage ;
(*e*) any person (not being a person included in the foregoing paragraphs of this subsection) who immediately before the death of the deceased was being maintained, either wholly or partly, by the deceased.

Child includes an illegitimate child and a child *en ventre sa mère*[8] and a person is treated as maintained by the deceased, if the latter, otherwise than for full valuable consideration, was making a substantial contribution in money or money's worth towards the reasonable needs of that person.[9]

Court orders. If the court is satisfied, on an application being made to it, that the will of the deceased or the law relating to intestacy, or the com-

---

[1] Intestates' Estates Act 1952. It was further amended by the Family Provision Act 1966, the Family Law Reform Act 1969, and the Law Reform (Miscellaneous Provisions) Act 1970.
[2] Matrimonial Causes (Property and Maintenance) Act 1958, ss. 3–6. These provisions were replaced by Matrimonial Causes Act 1965, ss. 26–8, which were amended by the statutes in n. 1 and also by the Divorce Reform Act 1969 and the Matrimonial Proceedings and Property Act 1970.
[3] See Law Commission Family Law Second Report on Family Property: Family Provision on Death (Law Com. No. 61, 1974). For the earlier legislation, see Wolstenholme and Cherry, vol. 5.
[4] For criticism of this limitation, see (1946) L. Q. R. 170, 178–9 (J. H. C. Morris). See also Law Com. No. 61, paras. 258–62.
[5] Inheritance (Provision for Family and Dependants) Act 1975, ss. 1 (1), 27 (3).
[6] Including a person who in good faith entered into a void marriage with the deceased (which was not dissolved or annulled during the deceased's lifetime) and who did not enter into a later marriage during the deceased's lifetime, s. 25 (4).
[7] Including a spouse who is judicially separated from the deceased at the date of death.
[8] Inheritance (Provision for Family and Dependants) Act 1975, s. 25 (1).
[9] *Ibid.*, s. 1 (3).

bination of the will and that law, does not make reasonable financial provision for the applicant, it may make an order for such provision to be made out of the net estate.[1] The court may make an order for periodical payments, or for a lump sum,[2] or for both. It may also make an order for the transfer or settlement of any property; for the acquisition of property for the applicant or for settlement for his benefit ; and for the variation of marriage settlements. The court has wide powers to allocate the burden of the award between beneficiaries.[3]

If it appears that the applicant is in immediate need of financial assistance but that it is not yet possible to determine what order should be made, and if there is available property to meet the need of the applicant, the court may make an interim order for the payment to him of such sums and at such intervals as appear reasonable.[4]

Interim orders.

An application for an order must be made within six months from the date on which representation is first taken out, but the court may permit a later application.[5]

Limit of time for application.

The court has power to vary any order made for periodical payments,[6] but orders for lump sum payments or for transfer of property are final and not subject to later variation.[7]

Variation of orders.

The court also has power to make an order concerning the deceased's severable share of any property of which he was a beneficial joint tenant immediately before his death. It may order that it shall be treated as part of the net estate to such extent as appears to be just in all the circumstances.[8] In the absence of this power, the court would be unable to make an order for provision out of such property, since on the death of one joint tenant the beneficial ownership is held by the surviving joint tenant.[9] This is important where husband and wife are beneficial joint tenants of the matrimonial home.[10] Further the Act gives the court important powers to counter evasion of its provisions. Where the deceased makes an *inter vivos* disposition less than six years before his death, otherwise than for full valuable consideration being given by the donee, and with the intention of defeating an application for financial provision under the Act, the court may order the

Power to counter evasion.

---

[1] *Ibid.*, s. 2. See also ss. 8, 9, 10.
[2] This may be made payable by instalments. *Ibid.*, s. 7 (1).
[3] *Ibid.*, s. 2 (4).
[4] *Ibid.*, s. 5.
[5] *Ibid.*, s. 4. See *Re Ruttie*, [1970] 1 W. L. R. 89 ; [1969] 3 All E. R. 1633. See also s. 9 (1).
[6] *Ibid.*, s. 6.
[7] Except in the case of instalments, when the amount, number and date of payments may be varied. *Ibid.*, s. 7 (2).
[8] *Ibid.*, s. 9.
[9] *Supra*, p. 212.
[10] *Supra*, p. 231.

donee to provide property or money from which a claim for provision may be satisfied.[1] Similar provisions apply, *mutatis mutandis*, where the deceased enters at any time into a contract to leave property by will, or undertakes that his personal representatives will transfer property out of his estate.[2]

Reasonable financial provision.

Finally we must consider how the court exercises its discretion in deciding whether " reasonable financial provision " has been made for an applicant by the deceased's will or by the rules of intestacy, and, if not, what order should be made.

The Act draws a new distinction between an applicant who is a surviving spouse and all other applicants. In the case of the former, reasonable financial provision means

> " such financial provision as it would be reasonable in all the circumstances of the case for a husband or wife to receive, whether or not that provision is required for his or her maintenance " ;

and, for other applicants, it is confined to securing reasonable provision for their maintenance.[3] The test is thus not subjective but objective. It is not whether the deceased stands convicted of unreasonableness, but whether the provision in fact made is reasonable.[4]

Guidelines for exercise of discretion.

Section 3 of the Act sets out guidelines to which the court should have regard in determining applications for financial provision. It must consider the following matters, based on facts known to it at the date of the hearing; the financial resources and needs of the applicant, of any other applicant and of any beneficiary of the estate ; any obligations and responsibilities of the deceased to any applicant or beneficiary ; the size and nature of the net estate ; any physical or mental disability of any applicant or beneficiary ; and " any other matter, including the conduct of the applicant or any other person, which in the circumstances of the case the court may consider relevant ". Special matters to be considered where the applicant is a surviving or a former spouse are the age of the applicant and the duration of the marriage ; the contribution made by the applicant to the welfare of the family of the deceased ; and, in the case of a surviving spouse, the provision which the applicant might reasonably have expected to receive if, when the deceased died, the marriage had been ended by divorce, and not by death.[5]

---

[1] Inheritance (Provision for Family and Dependants) Act 1975, ss. 10, 12, 13.

[2] *Ibid.*, ss. 11, 12, 13. Ss. 10 and 11 do not apply to dispositions or contracts made before April 1st, 1976, s. 11 (6).

[3] *Ibid.*, s. 1 (2).

[4] *Re Goodwin*, [1969] 1 Ch. 283, at p. 288, *per* MEGARRY, J. ; *Millward* v. *Shenton*, [1972] 1 W. L. R. 711 ; [1972] 2 All E. R. 1025 (1938 Act) ; *Re Shanahan* [1973] Fam. 1 ; [1971] 3 All E. R. 873 (1965 Act).

[5] Inheritance (Provision for Family and Dependants) Act 1975, s. 3 (2). For special matters in connexion with other categories of applicant, see s. 3 (3) (4).

SECTION II. IN WHAT FORM A WILL MUST BE MADE

The formalities essential to the creation of a valid will are prescribed by the Wills Act 1837 in the following words :—

" No will shall be valid unless it shall be in writing and executed in manner hereinafter mentioned; (that is to say), it shall be signed at the foot or end thereof by the testator, or by some other person in his presence and by his direction; and such signature shall be made or acknowledged by the testator in the presence of two or more witnesses present at the same time, and such witnesses shall attest and shall subscribe the will in the presence of the testator, but no form of attestation shall be necessary."

The essentials, then, are these :

1. writing,
2. signature of the testator, either made or acknowledged in the presence of the witnesses, and
3. attestation by the witnesses.

Signature. The testator must sign the will either by writing his name at its end in the normal fashion or by adding some mark or phrase intended to represent his name. Thus, the signature may be represented, for instance, by a rubber stamp or by the impress of an ink-smudged thumb,[1] or by some such phrase as " your loving mother."[2] Alternatively he may procure some person to sign on his behalf in his presence and under his direction.

The Act of 1837 required that the signature should be *at the foot or end* of the will, but as the courts construed this strictly and refused to admit a signature unless it was so placed that nothing could be written between it and the last words of the will, the law was altered by the Wills Act Amendment Act 1852. This provides that a signature shall be valid if it is

" so placed at or after, or following, or under, or beside, or opposite to the end of the will, that it shall be apparent on the face of the will that the testator intended to give effect by such his signature to the writing signed as his will."[3]

On the other hand, the Act provides that no disposition underneath or following the signature shall be valid. The courts have put a liberal construction upon this enactment. They admit a signature, even though written in the margin, if they are satisfied

---

[1] *In the Estate of Finn* (1936), 53 T.L.R. 153. See *In the Goods of Chalcraft*, [1948] P. 222 ; [1948] 1 All E. R. 700 (testatrix too ill to write more than " E. Chal " ; held valid) ; *cf. Re Colling*, [1972] 1 W. L. R. 1440 ; [1972] 3 All E. R. 729.

[2] *In the Estate of Cook*, [1960] 1 W. L. R. 353 ; [1960] 1 All E. R. 689.

[3] S. 1. *In the Estate of Little*, [1960] 1 W. L. R. 495 ; [1960] 1 All E. R. 387.

that the whole document was written before signature, and that the dispositive part of the document may fairly be read as preceding and leading up to the part containing the signature.[1] But they refuse to regard a document as part of a will, unless it was attached to the signed portion of the will at the time of signature. Thus, two separate papers, one of which is signed by the testator, the other by the witnesses, will not be admitted to probate,[2] though the reverse is the case if they are both fastened together.[3] Again, merely to sign the envelope in which the will is contained is not sufficient.[4]

No form of attestation necessary.

Attestation. The testator must sign, or acknowledge his signature, in the simultaneous presence of the witnesses, *i.e.* both the witnesses must be present at the moment of signature or acknowledgment,[5] and finally they must attest and subscribe the will in the presence of the testator. If the testator has signed his name in more places than one, the attestation will not be effective unless the witnesses attest the operative signature, *i.e.* the one that comes at the foot or end of the will.[6] Although not specifically required by the statute, the usual practice is for the witnesses to attest in the presence of each other and to record the fact in the following attestation clause, which records that all the statutory requirements have been observed :—

Usual form.

" Signed by the said testator as his last will in the presence of us, present at the same time, who in his presence and at his request and in the presence of each other have hereunto subscribed our names as witnesses."

If this clause is omitted, probate will not be granted unless it is proved by an affidavit of one of the witnesses or by some other satisfactory evidence that the statutory requirements have been observed.[7] Such evidence, however, is not conclusive.[8]

---

[1] *In the Estate of Mabel Amy Long*, [1936] P. 166 ; [1936] 1 All E. R. 435 ; *Re Stalman* (1931), 145 L. T. 339 ; contrast *In the Goods of Mary Moorhouse Smith*, [1931] P. 225 ; *In the Estate of Roberts*, [1934] P. 102 ; *In the Goods of Hornby*, [1946] P. 171 ; [1946] 2 All E. R. 150 ; dist. *Re Harris*, [1952] P. 319 ; [1952] 2 All E. R. 409 ; *Re Beadle*, [1974] 1 W. L. R. 417; [1974] 1 All E. R. 493.

[2] *In the Goods of J. Hatton* (1881), 6 P. D. 204. In a later case LANGTON, J., departed from the rule where a holograph will signed by the witnesses only was placed in an envelope signed by the testator ; *In the Goods of Mann*, [1942] P. 146 ; [1942] 2 All E. R. 193. See the Senior Registrar's *Practice Direction*, [1953] 1 W. L. R. 689, dealing with the case where a will, extending to two pages, is signed only at the foot of the first page.

[3] *In the Goods of Horsford* (1874), L. R. 3 P. & D. 211.

[4] *In the Estate of Bean*, [1944] P. 83 ; [1944] 2 All E. R. 348. *Cf. In the Goods of Mann, supra.* See also *Re Beadle*, [1974] 1 W. L. R. 417 ; [1974] 1 All E. R. 493.

[5] *Re Groffman*, [1969] 1 W. L. R. 733 ; [1969] 2 All E. R. 108 ; *Re Colling*, [1972] 1 W. L. R. 1440 ; [1972] 3 All E. R. 729.

[6] *In the Estate of Bercovitz*, [1961] 1 W. L. R. 892 ; [1961] 2 All E. R. 481.

[7] Non-Contentious Probate Rules, 1954 r. 10 ; *Re Selby-Bigge*, [1950] 1 All E. R. 1009. A blind person is incapable of witnessing a will, *In the Estate of Charles Gibson*, [1949] P. 434 ; [1949] 2 All E. R. 90.

[8] *Vere-Wardale*, [1949] P. 395 ; [1949] 2 All E. R. 250.

The Wills Act 1837 also provides that if any beneficial interest is given to a witness or to the spouse of a witness who is married at the time of the attestation, the attestation is valid and effective, but the gift is void.[1] An attesting witness is not excluded as a beneficiary under this enactment unless he is interested under the will at the time of attestation. He may retain any benefit that accrues to him later.[2] Again, the gift to him is void only if it is contained in the very document that he has attested, not, for instance, where he is a beneficiary under a secret trust,[3] nor where his attestation is confined to a codicil that merely confirms the will under which he claims.[4]

Effect of gift to a witness.

The Wills Act 1968 modifies the law in one respect. Where a testator dies after May 30th, 1968, the attestation by a beneficiary or his or her spouse shall be disregarded if the will is duly executed without his attestation ; that is to say, where there are at least two witnesses who are not themselves beneficiaries as well.

Wills Act 1968.

Privileged Wills of Soldiers, Sailors and Airmen.— At common law no particular form was required for wills, which in the case of pure personalty might even be nuncupative. This was altered by the Statute of Frauds, which, besides placing such restrictions upon the nuncupative will that it fell into disuse, required a will of *land* to be in writing and attested by three or four credible witnesses. It provided, however, in section 22 that soldiers' wills with regard to their " movables, wages and personal estates " might still be made in the informal manner hitherto recognized as sufficient.

Statute of Frauds.

This indulgence was continued by section eleven of the Wills Act 1837, which provided that

Wills Act 1837.

" Any soldier being in actual military service or any mariner or sea-
" man being at sea,"

might dispose of his *personal estate* (an expression which has been held to include personal property over which there is a general or special power of appointment),[5] as he might have done before the passing of the Act. Such a will is privileged in the sense that the usual statutory formalities are not essential for its making or its revocation,[6] and it is valid even though the testator is under the

---

[1] S. 15. Under the previous law the effect of such a gift was to invalidate the will, unless there were sufficient other witnesses who were not beneficiaries. S. 15 does not apply to the privileged will described in the following paragraph, *Re Limond*, [1915] 2 Ch. 240.

[2] *Re Royce's Will Trusts*, [1959] Ch. 626 ; [1959] 3 All E. R. 278.

[3] *Re Young*, [1951] Ch. 344 ; [1950] 2 All E. R. 1040. As to secret trusts, see Hansbury's *Modern Equity* (9th Edn.), ch. 8.

[4] *Re Trotter*, [1899] 1 Ch. 764.

[5] *Re Chichester's (Earl) Will Trusts*, [1946] Ch. 289 ; [1946] 1 All E. R. 722.

[6] *In the Estate of Gossage*, [1921] P. 194 ; Family Law Reform Act 1969, s. 3 (4).

age of 18 years.[1]   But for spoken words to constitute a nuncupative will, they must have been intended by the deceased to operate
as a disposition of his property.   They must not merely inform his
hearers of what he proposes to do,[2] but must be intended to guide
them in carrying out his wishes.[3]

Two classes
of privileged
testators.

The Wills (Soldiers and Sailors) Act 1918 extended the privilege by providing that it should apply to wills of realty in England
or Ireland[4] and that the expression " soldier " should include a
member of the Air Force.[5]   In the result there are two classes of
privileged testators :—

> First, any soldier or airman who is *in actual military
> service* at the time of making his will, or any member of the
> naval or marine forces of the Crown who at that time " is so
> circumstanced that if he were a soldier he would be *in actual
> military service* within the meaning of " the Wills Act 1837,
> s. 11.[6]
>
> Secondly, any member of the naval or marine forces of
> the Crown or any member of the merchant marine who is *at
> sea* at the time of making his will.

The difficulty experienced by the courts has been to determine
the meaning of the two expressions *in actual military service*[7] and
at sea.

Meaning of
in actual
military
service.

The statutory privilege has existed for over 250 years and it is
not surprising that with the gradual change in the nature of war
the courts, in construing the expression " in actual military
service," have at different times laid the emphasis upon different
factors.   Until comparatively recent times, the instinct of the
courts was to construe the expression in the light of Roman law
from which the rule in the Statute of Frauds had admittedly been
copied.[8]   An English soldier was not to be privileged unless a
Roman legionary, placed in like circumstances, would have been
regarded as *in expeditione*.   According to this test, which has now,
however, been discarded,[9] the will of a soldier made while he was
quartered in barracks even in time of war would not be privileged.[10]
In the first half of the nineteenth century, the Ecclesiastical
Courts, which had exclusive jurisdiction in probate until 1857,

---

[1] Wills (Soldiers & Sailors) Act 1918, s. 1, confirming *Re Wernher*, [1918]
2 Ch. 82 ; Family Law Reform Act 1969, s. 3 (1).
[2] *In the Estate of Knibbs*, [1962] 1 W. L. R. 852 ; [1962] 2 All E. R. 829 ;
(" if anything ever happens to me, Iris will get anything I have got ").
[3] *Re Stable*, [1919] P. 7.   (" if anything happens to me, and I stop a bullet,
everything of mine will be yours ") ; *In the Goods of Spicer*, [1949] P. 441 ;
[1949] 2 All E. R. 659.
[4] S. 3.   [5] S. 5 (2).   [6] *Ibid.*, s. 2.
[7] See (1949), 12 *M.L.R.* 183 (D. C. Potter).
[8] The eminent civilian, Sir Leoline Jenkins, was responsible for it.
[9] *Re Booth*, [1926] P. 118, 136 ; *Re Wingham*, [1949] P. 187 ; [1948] 2
All E. R. 908.
[10] *Drummond* v. *Parish* (1843), 3 Curt. 522.

further insisted that the testator should be *inops consilii* at the time of making the will, and on this ground it was held in one case that the privilege did not apply to an officer stationed in Bombay, whose unit had been ordered to proceed to attack the citadel of Joadhpore and who made his will two days before setting out.[1]

In the course of the Boer War and of the First World War the conception of actual military service was broadened in the sense that emphasis was now laid upon whether the testator had taken some active step towards engaging in hostilities, as for example by going into barracks preparatory to being drafted to the seat of war.[2] The decisions during the Second World War went further in the same direction and showed so marked a tendency to extend the class of privileged testators as to evoke the criticism that the mere wearing of uniform in time of war is equivalent to being in actual military service.[3] The authorities, indeed, seem to justify the statement that

> not only the fighting troops, but also men and women, such as doctors, nurses and chaplains, who are "actually serving with the armed forces in connexion with military operations which are or have been taking place or are believed to be imminent" are in actual military service within the meaning of the Wills Act.[4]

The statute is satisfied in that respect, for instance, if at the time of making the will and while war is impending or in progress, the testator or testatrix is an airman undergoing training in Saskatchewan,[5] an artillery officer under orders to rejoin his battery just before the outbreak of war,[6] a soldier quartered at a camp in England though not under orders to proceed to the scene of fighting,[7] a member of the Women's Auxiliary Air Force in charge of a depot in Gloucestershire,[8] a person on duty as a member of the Home Guard,[9] or a serviceman under 21 of the British Army of the Rhine stationed in Germany nine years after the cessation of hostilities.[10]

A mariner in the Royal Navy or in the merchant service, though not in actual military service, is entitled to the statutory privilege even in time of peace, subject to the condition that he is *at sea* at the time of making his will. The expression "*at sea*" has been liberally construed and is considerably wider than "on the sea."[11] Thus the condition was held to be satisfied where at

Meaning of at sea.

---

[1] *Bowles* v. *Jackson* (1854), 1 Spinks 294.
[2] *In the Goods of Hiscock,* [1901] P. 78.
[3] (1949), 12 *M.L.R.* p. 188. (D. C. Potter)
[4] *Re Wingham,* [1949] P. 187; [1948] 2 All E. R. 912, at pp. 196, 913 respectively, *per* DENNING, L.J.
[5] *Re Wingham, supra.*
[6] *In the Estate of Rippon,* [1943] P. 61; [1943] 1 All E. R. 676.
[7] *In the Estate of Spark,* [1941] P. 115; [1941] 2 All E. R. 782.
[8] *In the Estate of Rowson,* [1944] 2 All E. R. 36.
[9] *Blyth* v. *Lord Advocate,* [1945] A. C. 32; [1944] 2 All E. R. 375.
[10] *In the Estate of Colman,* [1958] 1 W. L. R. 457; [1958] 2 All E. R. 35.
[11] The authorities are fully discussed in *In the Estate of Newland,* [1952] P. 71; [1952] 1 All E. R. 841.

the critical moment the testator was the mate of a gunnery vessel permanently moored in Portsmouth Harbour,[1] a woman living in lodgings until the next sailing of the *Lusitania* on which she was employed as a typist,[2] an officer of a tanker under orders to rejoin his ship at Sunderland within the next three days.[3]

Lost wills.

Lost Will. The contents of a private document must, if possible, be proved by primary evidence, that is, by production of the document itself, but they may be proved by secondary evidence, as for instance by oral testimony, when the document has been lost. Such extrinsic evidence is admissible in the case of a will that has been lost or destroyed *sine animo revocandi*.[4]

" Declarations, written or oral, made by a testator, both before and after the execution of his will, are, in the event of its loss, admissible as secondary evidence of its contents. The contents of a lost will may be proved by the evidence of a single witness, though interested, whose veracity and competency are unimpeached. When the contents of a lost will are not completely proved, probate will be granted to the extent to which they are proved."[5]

The standard of proof required is the ordinary standard of proof in civil cases, namely, a reasonable balance of probabilities, and not proof beyond all reasonable doubt.[6]

SECTION III. PERSONAL REPRESENTATIVES AND THEIR DUTIES AND POWERS
(1) APPOINTMENT OF EXECUTORS

Classes of personal representatives.

We have already seen that the property of a testator does not go directly to the beneficiaries under the will, but devolves upon his personal representatives for the purposes of administration. Personal representatives are either executors or administrators. An executor is a person who is appointed by the testator for the purpose of carrying the provisions of his will into effect. If no such appointment is made, or if the appointment fails, for instance, by the death, renunciation, infancy or lunacy of the executor, the court makes a grant of administration *cum testamento annexo*.[7] The order of priority of right to such a grant is based on the beneficial claims under the will, the residuary legatee having the first right.[8]

---

[1] *In the Goods of M'Murdo* (1868), L. R. 1 P. & D. 540.
[2] *In the Goods of Sarah Hale*, [1915] 2 I. R. 362.
[3] *In the Estate of Wilson*, [1952] P. 92 ; [1952] 1 All E. R. 852 ; *In the Estate of Newland*, [1952] P. 71 ; [1952] 1 All E. R. 841.
[4] *Re Webb*, [1964] 1 W. L. R. 509 ; [1964] 2 All E. R. 91.
[5] Taken verbatim from the headnote to *Sugden* v. *Lord St. Leonards*. (1876), L. R. 1 P. D. 154. See too Civil Evidence Act 1968, s. 2.
[6] *Re Wipperman*, [1955] P. 59 ; [1913] 1 All E. R. 764, *per* Pearce, J. explaining a dictum of Lord Herschell in *Woodward* v. *Goulstone* (1886), 11 App. Cas. 469) ; *Re Yelland* (1975), *Times*, April 1st. *Cf. In the Estate of Macgillivray*, [1946] 2 All E. R. 301.
[7] Supreme Court of Judicature (Consolidation) Act 1925, s. 166.
[8] Non-Contentious Probate Rules 1954, s. 19.

If a last surviving executor proves the will of X., and dies testate without having completed his office, then *his* executor steps into his place and becomes the executor of X.

" An executor of a sole or last surviving executor of a testator is the executor of that testator."[1]

But if such last surviving executor dies intestate, his administrator does not become the executor of the will of X.,[2] and in such a case it is necessary for the court to appoint another person to administer such property as is still unadministered. This is called administration *de bonis non*.

While any legal proceeding that concerns the validity of a will is pending, the court may appoint an administrator *pendente lite*, who has all the powers of a general administrator except that he cannot distribute the residue among those entitled.[3]

(2) THEIR DUTY TO OBTAIN PROBATE

The first duty of an executor is to prove the will in court. The jurisdiction to grant and revoke probates, which was formerly vested in the ecclesiastical courts, was transferred in 1858 to the Court of Probate.[4]   When the Supreme Court of Judicature was set up under the Judicature Act 1873, the jurisdiction was vested in the Probate, Divorce and Admiralty Division of the High Court of Justice.   Under the redistribution of business among the divisions of the High Court on October 1st, 1971, by the Administration of Justice Act 1970, this division was renamed the Family Division.   Non-contentious or common form probate business remains with the Family Division, and all other probate business is assigned to the Chancery Division.[5] *Jurisdiction to grant probate.*

The proof of a will may be either in common or in solemn form.

1. Probate in common form is granted, not by the court itself, but by the principal registry of the Family Division in London or by a district probate registry, and such a grant has effect over the estate of the deceased in all parts of England.[6]   The executor must swear an oath before a Commissioner of Oaths, in which he states his belief that the instrument he submits for probate is the true and last will of the testator, and in which he declares the gross value of the real and personal *Probate in common form.*

---

[1] A.E.A., 1925, s. 7 (1).   [2] *Ibid.*, s. 7 (3).
[3] Supreme Court of Judicature (Consolidation) Act 1925, s. 163.
[4] Court of Probate Act 1857.
[5] Administration of Justice Act 1970, s. 1 (1), (4).
[6] Supreme Court of Judicature (Consolidation) Act 1925, s. 151 (1).   In the case of small estates, where the value of the net estate is less than £1,000 and that of the gross estate less than £3,000 an application for grant of representation may be made through an authorized officer of customs and excise ; Small Estates (Representation) Act 1961, s. 1 (1).   As to cases where property may be disposed of on death without representation see Administration of Estates (Small Payments) Act 1965.

estate. If the will is correct in form and contains the attestation clause which has been given above, probate is granted on the oath of the executor alone.[1]

Will altered after execution.

Any obliteration, interlineation or other alteration made *after* the execution of a will is not admitted to probate unless it has been signed by the testator and duly attested.[2]   Moreover, the onus is on those who will benefit by the alteration to prove that it was made before execution.[3]   If there has been no signature and attestation to the alteration, probate is granted of the will as it stood before the alteration, provided that the original words are still *apparent*.[4]   In this event the original words remain in force contrary to the obvious intention of the testator. If, however, they are not apparent, probate is granted with the altered part of the will left blank.

Words are " apparent " if they can be read by looking at the will itself, however elaborate may be the devices used and however skilful the eye of the reader.[5]   But they are not apparent if their elucidation requires the creation of a new document, as for example, by taking an infra-red photograph.[6]

Probate in solemn form.

2. Proof in solemn form, which is an action before the court in the Chancery Division, is necessary where the validity of the will is doubtful, or where there is a likelihood that it may be opposed.   The action may be brought by the executor, a person who contests the will, or a " person interested," *i.e.*, a widow or widower, a legatee or devisee and the persons who would be entitled to take on intestacy.   A creditor is not a " person interested."

Title of executor.

A will, after it has been proved, is kept in the Registry of the court, and a copy, together with a certificate that the will has been proved, is given to the executor.   The copy and the certificate are called the probate of the will, and they are conclusive as to the validity both of the testamentary dispositions and of the right of the executor to perform his duties.   But an executor derives his title from the will and not from the grant of probate, and therefore the general rule is that he may do all such things and perform all such duties upon the death of the deceased as fall within the province of an executor.[7]

---

[1] *Supra*, p. 838.   [2] Wills Act 1837, s. 21.
[3] *In the Estate of Oates*, [1946] 2 All E. R. 735.   *In the Estate of Campbell*, [1954] 1 W. L. R. 516 ; [1954] 1 All E. R. 448.
[4] Wills Act 1837, s. 21.
[5] *Ffinch* v. *Combe*, [1894] P. 191.
[6] *In the Goods of Itter*, [1950] P. 130 ; [1950] 1 All E. R. 68.
[7] He cannot obtain relief from the court without first proving his title by obtaining a grant of probate.   *Chetty* v. *Chetty*, [1916] 1 A. C. 603 ; *Re Crowhurst Park*, [1974] 1 W. L. R. 583 ; [1974] 1 All E. R. 991.

If a person without obtaining a grant of probate takes upon himself to meddle with the property of a deceased person in such a way as to indicate that he assumes the rights of an executor, he is said to be an executor *de son tort*.[1] Section 28 of the Administration of Estates Act 1925 provides that if any person, to the defrauding of creditors or without full valuable consideration, obtains, receives or holds any real or personal estate of a deceased person or releases any debt due to the estate, he shall be liable as an executor *de son tort* to the extent of the estate in his hands or of the debt released, after deducting

Executor de son tort.

1. any debt for valuable consideration and without fraud due to him from the deceased, and

2. any payment made by him which might properly be made by a personal representative.

(3) THEIR DUTY TO ADMINISTER THE ESTATE

It is not within the scope of this book to give an exhaustive account of an executor's duties, and only a *résumé* will be attempted.

An executor should make an inventory and account of the real and personal estate of the deceased, and he may be compelled, upon an application to the court by a person interested in the estate of the testator, to exhibit the inventory on oath.[2]

Inventory.

His next duty is to collect all the estate of the deceased, to realize investments which it is undesirable to keep, to recover loans which are protected merely by personal security, to call in money lent on mortgage if it is required for some testamentary purpose. For these purposes all causes of action vested in the deceased survive to the personal representative, except in the cases of defamation and the action of a master for the loss of his servant's services.[3]

Realization of estate.

Having collected and obtained control over the assets, the executor must next pay the debts of the deceased. We have already seen what his duty is in this respect. In order that this may be effectually performed, the Administration of Estates Act 1925, after providing that the real as well as the personal estate of the deceased shall vest in the personal representatives, enacts that they shall have the same power to dispose of and deal with

Power to dispose of estate in order to pay debts

---

[1] An executor named in the will who intermeddles before probate is not a a wrongdoer. *Sykes* v. *Sykes* (1870), L. R. 5 C. P. 113, at p. 117, *per* Bovill, C. J. He may pay debts and legacies, but he will not enjoy the statutory protection afforded to an executor who is acting under a grant of probate. A.E.A. 1925, s. 27.

[2] A.E.A. 1925, s. 25, as replaced by A.E.A. 1971, s. 9.

[3] Law Reform (Miscellaneous Provisions) Act 1934, s. 1, as amended by Law Reform (Miscellaneous Provisions) Act 1970, ss. 4, 5.

the land as they formerly possessed in respect of personal property.[1] Personal representatives always had complete power of alienation over personal property, and since the Land Transfer Act 1897 they have been in the same position as regards land.

Thus they can sell, mortgage or partition the land,[2] and they are now empowered by statute to grant a lease for a term of years absolute (with or without impeachment of waste) to trustees upon trust for raising any sum of money for which the land is liable, and also to grant a rentcharge for giving effect to any annual sum for which the land is liable.

Disposition of land.

But a sale of land by executors differs, in its method, from a sale of personalty. One executor may sell pure personalty without the concurrence of his co-executors, but it is enacted that a conveyance of land shall not be made without the concurrence of all the proving executors, unless an order of the court is obtained.[3]

Representatives are trustees for sale.

In order that personal representatives may have full powers of management while they are dealing with the property of the deceased, it is provided that in addition to having power to raise money by mortgage they shall be in the position of trustees for sale as regards both the ability to overreach equitable interests and the right to exercise the powers conferred by statute upon trustees for sale.[4] These powers are those which are conferred upon a tenant for life under the Settled Land Act 1925, in addition to the powers given by the Trustee Act 1925, and the Law of Property Act 1925.[5]

Distribution of estate.

After the debts have been paid, the duty of the executor is to distribute the residue among those persons who are beneficially entitled under the will. Before he does this, however, he should protect himself against claims of which he may not be aware by publishing advertisements in accordance with the directions of the Trustee Act 1925.[6] This provides that with a view to the conveyance of real or personal property to beneficiaries either trustees or personal representatives may give notice by advertisement in the *Gazette* and in a newspaper circulating in the district where the land is situated, requiring persons to give particulars of any claim they may have against the estate of the deceased. At the expiration of the time fixed by the notice (which must not be less than two months) the personal representatives may convey the property to the beneficiaries, and they are not liable to any person of whose claim they had no notice at the time of the conveyance.

Protection by means of advertisement.

---

[1] S. 2. [2] *Re Kemnal and Still's Contract*, [1923] 1 Ch. 293.
[3] A.E.A. 1925, s. 2 (2). See *Fountain Forestry, Ltd.* v. *Edwards*, [1975] Ch. 1 ; [1974] 2 All E. R. 280 as to contracts by a single personal representative.
[4] *Ibid.*, s. 39. [5] L.P.A. 1925, s. 28.
[6] T.A. 1925, s. 27 ; as amended by L.P.(A.)A. 1926, Sched.

But the creditors may follow the property even after it has Right to follow property. been conveyed to beneficiaries. Notwithstanding such a conveyance, a creditor or other person interested in the property may apply to the court, and the court may declare a beneficiary to be a trustee of the land for the creditor, or may order a different conveyance to be made or may make a vesting order.[1] This power to follow the property does not, however, exist where the conveyance is made not to a beneficiary, but to a purchaser in the ordinary way of administration.[2] In such a case the purchaser receives ample protection.[3] Thus all conveyances of *any interest* in real or personal property made to a purchaser, either by an executor who has proved the will or by the administrator of a person who has died intestate, are valid notwithstanding a subsequent revocation or variation of the probate or administration.[4]

SECTION IV.   PARTICULAR RULES

SUMMARY

(1) FAILURE OF GIFTS BY LAPSE

A lapse occurs where the donee predeceases the testator, and a *Commorientes.* preliminary point to notice is that it may be difficult to decide whether this has been the sequence of events if both have been the victims of a common calamity, as for instance where they have both been killed in the same motor car accident. The common law rule in such a case is that the representatives of the donee who claims under the will must prove that in fact he survived the testator. Otherwise the claim fails.[5] This rule was altered by the following section of the Law of Property Act 1925.[6]

> " In all cases where, after the commencement of this Act, two or more persons have died in circumstances rendering it uncertain which of them survived the other or others, such deaths shall (subject to any order of the court), for all purposes affecting the title to property, be presumed to have occurred in order of seniority, and accordingly the younger shall be deemed to have survived the elder.[7]

---

[1] A.E.A. 1925, s. 38.
[2] *Ibid.*, s. 38.
[3] *Ibid.*, s. 36 (6), (7), (8).
[4] *Ibid.*, s. 37. extending *Hewson* v. *Shelley*, [1914] 2 Ch. 13.
[5] *Wing* v. *Angrave* (1860), 8 H. L. Cas. 183.
[6] S. 184.
[7] For its modification as between spouses if one of them dies intestate, see I.E.A. 1952, s. 1 (4), *infra*, p. 872. For the capital transfer tax implications, see F.A. 1975, s. 22 (9). Wheatcroft and Hewson, *Capital Transfer Tax*, para. 4–07 ; (1976) 120 Sol. Jo. 71 (S. M. Cretney).

It was thought that this section had finally solved the question, but in *Hickman* v. *Peacey*,[1] where four persons had been killed by the explosion of a bomb, it was contended that the common law rule still prevailed if the deaths were simultaneous. If, it was argued, two persons have died simultaneously, it is not " uncertain which of them survived the other." For the section to apply the deaths must have been consecutive. This argument, which *inter alia* ignores the virtual impossibility of two human beings ceasing to breathe at exactly the same moment of time, was rejected by a bare majority of the House of Lords, and the simple rule laid down that

> unless it is possible to say for certain which of the persons died first, the younger is presumed to have survived.

In other words, the section is not excluded unless there is clear evidence that one person survived the other.[2] In one case, for instance, a man aged twenty-nine, left all his property to his wife, aged twenty-six, with a gift over to his nephew in the event of her death "preceding or coinciding" with his own. A month later the husband and wife set sail on a ship which sank with all on board, only one body being found. It was held that the words "coinciding with" were not intended to denote two deaths occurring on the same occasion from the same cause, but two deaths coincident in point of time, *i.e.* so close to each other that the normal man would describe them as simultaneous. There was no evidence as to the order of their occurrence, and therefore the wife was presumed to have survived her husband.[3]

Meaning of lapse.

Once it is proved that the donee under a will died before the testator, the rule is that the gift lapses and ceases to take effect.[4] This is so despite the addition to the gift of words of limitation such as to the donee and his heirs or to him and his executors.[5] It is usual to provide against the event, but to render this effective something more is required than a mere declaration that the gift shall not lapse. There must be a further gift limited to take effect upon the premature death of the first donee, as for example by a provision that

> " the devise to A. shall not lapse if he predeceases the testator but shall take effect in favour of his eldest surviving son." [6]

Two cases where no lapse.

The Wills Act 1837 provides that no lapse shall occur in the following two cases, unless there is a contrary intention :

---

[1] [1945] A. C. 304 ; [1945] 2 All E. R. 215.
[2] *Re Bate*, [1947] 2 All E. R. 418.
[3] *Re Rowland*, [1963] Ch. 1 ; [1962] 2 All E. R. 837 (Lord Denning, M.R., dissenting) ; (1963) 26 *M. L. R.* 353 (Michael Albery).
[4] For the explanation, see *Re Harvey's Estate*, [1893] 1 Ch. 567, at p. 570.
[5] *Elliott* v. *Davenport* (1705), 1 P. Wms. 83 ; *Browne* v. *Hope* (1872), L. R. 14 Eq. 343.
[6] *Re Greenwood*, [1912] 1 Ch. 392 ; *Re Ladd*, [1932] 2 Ch. 219.

1. **Gift of Entailed Interest.** Where a person, to whom realty or personalty has been left by will in tail, dies in the lifetime of the testator leaving issue capable of inheriting under the entail, and any such issue shall be living at the death of the testator, the gift does not lapse, but takes effect *as if the death of such person had happened immediately after the testator's death.*[1]

2. **Gift to Testator's Issue.** A devise or bequest to the child or other issue of the testator for an interest not determinable at or before the death of the donee does not lapse if the donee predeceases the testator *leaving issue alive at the testator's death,* but takes effect *as if the death of the donee had happened immediately after the testator's death.*[2]

The second exception does not apply where the gift to the issue of the testator is a class gift, for the essence of such a gift is that it is made to a fluctuating class of objects who are to be ascertained at the death of the testator.[3]   Hence, if there is a devise to the children of A., or to the children of A. equally, the entire property vests in those children who survive the testator irrespective of prior deaths.[4]   Nor does the exception apply to an appointment by will under a special power.[5] *{margin: Class gifts.}*

The Act, it will be noticed, fictitiously prolongs the life of the donee until immediately after the death of the testator.   The sole purpose of this, however, is to amplify the preceding words and to leave no manner of doubt that the gift is to be effective despite the premature death in fact of the donee.   His life is not deemed to have been prolonged for any other purpose.   The estate that he himself may have left is, indeed, posthumously increased by virtue of his ancestor's will, but this increase falls to be administered with the rest of his estate according to the circumstances as they existed at the time of his actual death.[6]   The significance of this may be seen from a hypothetical case : *{margin: Operation of the statutory exceptions.}*

> The testator, T., devises Blackacre to his son, X., in fee simple.   X. predeceases T. but is survived by his own son Y.

In this case, if X. died intestate, the ascertainment of the persons entitled to the additional property, Blackacre, will depend upon the circumstances existing at the time of his death, not at the moment immediately after T.'s death.   If X. left a will disposing of his residuary estate to Z., Blackacre will fall into the residue.[7]

---

[1] Wills Act 1837, s. 32 ; L.P.A. 1925, s. 130 (1).

[2] *Ibid.*, s. 33.   Issue includes legitimated issue, *Re Brodie*, [1967] Ch. 818; [1967] 2 All E. R. 97 ; and where the testator dies after 1969, illegitimate issue. Family Law Reform Act 1969, s. 16.

[3] *Supra*, p. 326.

[4] *Olney* v. *Bates* (1855), 3 Drew, 319 ; *Re Harvey's Estate*, [1893] 1 Ch. 567.

[5] *Holyland* v. *Lewin* (1884), 26 Ch. D. 266.   Cf. *Eccles* v. *Cheyne* (1856), 2 K. & J. 676 (general power).

[6] *Re Basioli*, [1953] Ch. 367 ; [1953] 1 All E. R. 301 ; where all the authorities are collected.

[7] *Johnson* v. *Johnson* (1843), 3 Hare, 157.

for, although the survival of Y. prevents the lapse of the gift, there is no provision that what has been given to X. shall pass beneficially to Y. Y. will only take, however, if he is entitled under X.'s will or intestacy. Again, since Blackacre is deemed to have belonged to X. at his death, it follows that it will vest in his trustee in bankruptcy if he died a bankrupt.[1]

Destination of lapsed property.

Where neither of the exceptions applies, the destination of lapsed property depends upon whether the will contains a residuary gift. If so, the property passes to the residuary devisee or legatee according as it is realty or personalty [2]; otherwise it enures for the benefit of those persons entitled on intestacy.

(2) EFFECT OF A GENERAL DEVISE OF LAND

A devise of land is either specific or general.

General devise includes leaseholds.

A specific devise is a gift by will of a particular part of the testator's real estate and identified by a sufficient description, as for instance a gift of " my farm Blackacre " or of " all my lands in the parish of X."

A general devise is a gift of land which does not specify any particular part, but is couched in generic terms, as for instance a gift of " all my freehold lands."

The rule before the Wills Act 1837 was that if a testator had both freeholds and leaseholds and made a devise of all his " land," the devise operated to pass only the freeholds.[3] If, however, he had leaseholds only, then they passed under the general gift. This rule was altered by that Act, which provides that a devise of land described in a general manner shall be construed to include the leasehold as well as the freehold interests unless a contrary intention appears in the will.[4] This enactment does not apply to entailed interests, which, despite the power of testamentary disposition given by the Law of Property Act 1925 to a tenant in tail in possession, are not caught by a general devise.[5]

General devise includes land subject to general power.

Power of Appointment. Similarly, the rule before the Wills Act 1837 was that a general devise of land did not operate to pass land over which the testator had a power of appointment, unless he had no land other than that which was subject to the power.[6] This rule was altered by section 27, which provides that a general devise of land shall include estates over which a testator has " power to appoint in any manner he may think proper," and shall operate as an execution of such power, unless a contrary

---

[1] *Re Pearson*, [1920] 1 Ch. 247.
[2] Wills Act 1837, s. 25.
[3] Carson, *Real Property Statutes* (3rd Edn.), p. 526.
[4] Wills Act 1837, s. 26.
[5] *Supra*, p. 262.
[6] Hawkins and Ryder, *Construction of Wills*, pp. 27 *et seq.*

intention shall appear by the will.[1]   A similar rule is prescribed
for a general bequest of personalty.   The Act, it will be noticed,
does not refer to a general as distinct from a special power, but to
one which the donee may exercise without restriction.   The power
vested in the testator may not be " special " in the sense that it is
exercisable in favour only of defined objects,[2] yet, if it in any
manner limits his choice, as where it is exercisable in favour of
any person in the world except himself[3] or his wife,[4] he cannot
be described as entitled to appoint " in any manner he may think
proper," and therefore section 27 is inapplicable.

It is a difficult question in practice to decide whether a general
gift operates as an exercise of a special power of appointment.   It
is no doubt true

Special powers on different footing.

> " that in order to exercise a special power there must be a sufficient
> expression or indication of intention in the will or other instrument
> alleged to exercise it ; and that either a reference to the power or a
> reference to the property subject to the power constitutes in general
> a sufficient indication for the purpose " [5]

but the problem is to determine whether the testator's language is
sufficiently precise where he has referred neither to the power nor
to its subject-matter.[6]

(3) EFFECT OF A GIFT OVER ON FAILURE OF ISSUE

The natural meaning of a devise of realty

> " to A., but if he shall die without issue, then to B.,"

is that A. is to take a fee simple, which, if he has no children or
other issue *at the time of his death*, is to go over to B.   Before 1837,
however, the courts construed such expressions as

Former construction of such gifts.

> " die without issue," or
> " die without leaving issue,"

as meaning an indefinite failure of issue, *i.e.*, that the estate given
to A. was to endure until his issue failed, no matter how long it
might be before the failure occurred.   The effect of this construction was that A. took an estate tail by implication, with remainder

---

[1] Wills Act 1837, s. 27 ; *Re Thirlwell*, [1958] Ch. 146 ; [1957] 3 All E. R. 465.
[2] *Supra*, pp. 275–6.
[3] *Re Park*, [1932] 1 Ch. 580 ; *Re Jones*, [1945] Ch. 105.
[4] *Re Byron's Settlement*, [1891] 3 Ch. 474 ; dist. *Re Harvey*, [1950] 1 All E. R.
491 ; where the excepted appointee did not and could not exist.
[5] *Re Ackerley*, [1913] 1 Ch. 510, at p. 515, *per* SARGANT, J., adapting
similar language used by BUCKLEY, J., in *Re Weston's Settlement*, [1906] 2 Ch.
620, 624.
[6] See *Re Knight*, [1957] Ch. 441 ; [1957] 2 All E. R. 252, and cases there
cited.

to B. and his heirs.[1] A. could, therefore, bar the entail and so defeat both his issue and the remaindermen.

Alteration by Wills Act 1837.

In order, therefore, to assimilate the legal and the natural meaning of the expression it was provided by the Wills Act 1837 that the words " die without issue " or " die without leaving issue," or any other words which import a failure of the issue of a person either at his death or at some indefinite time, shall be construed to mean a want or failure in his lifetime, and not an indefinite failure.[2]

The effect of this enactment, which applies to gifts both of realty and personalty, if taken alone, is that in the example given above B. becomes entitled to take the fee simple if A. dies leaving no issue.   But as this would mean that A. could never know during his lifetime whether the fee simple given to him by the will was absolute or not, because of the possibility that his existing children might predecease him and so entitle B. to take, further statutory alterations have been made.

Alteration by Conveyancing Act 1882.

The Conveyancing Act, 1882,[3] enacted in the case of instruments coming into operation after December 31, 1882, that where there is a person entitled to land for an estate in fee, or for a term of years absolute, or for term of life *with an executory limitation over on failure of his issue* whether within a specified time or not, such executory limitation shall be void and become incapable of taking effect as soon as there is living any issue who has attained the age of 21 years.   It will be noticed that this enactment applies only to land and that its operation is restricted to the interests specifically mentioned.   It is still the governing enactment with regard to instruments coming into operation

Alteration by Law of Property Act 1925.

between December 31, 1882, and December 31, 1925.   But in furtherance of the general principle of assimilation it is now enacted for instruments coming into operation after December 31, 1925, that where there is a person entitled to

"(a) an equitable interest in land for an estate in fee simple or for any less interest not being an entailed interest, or

(b) any interest in *other property*, not being an entailed interest,"

a gift over on failure of issue shall be void as soon as there is living any issue who has attained the age of 18 years.[4]   This rule applies to deeds as well as to wills, and to all interests in property, whether real or personal, with the exception of entailed interests. The reason for excepting an entailed interest is that the gift over can, in any event, be defeated by disentailment.   The reason for confining the rule to an *equitable* fee simple is that, under the

---

[1] A similar gift of personalty was construed to give A. the absolute ownership, since personalty was not entailable before 1926.

[2] Wills Act 1837, s. 29.   [3] S. 10.

[4] L.P.A. 1925, s. 134, as amended by Family Law Reform Act 1969, s. 1 (3), Sched. 1.

modern law, a fee simple subject to a gift over cannot subsist as a legal estate, but is necessarily equitable.[1]

SECTION V. CONSTRUCTION OF WILLS

The duty of a court which is called upon to construe a will is first to discover what was the intention of the testator as expressed by his will, and then to give effect to that intention. The fundamental rule to which all others must bend is that the intention of a testator must be obeyed, however informal the language may be by which it has been expressed [2]; but, though this principle has been asserted with vehemence from the earliest times, and has on various occasions been referred to as *the pole star, the sovereign guide*, and *the cardinal rule*, it is important to remember that in ascertaining intention the court considers the writing alone. It does not indulge in conjecture. It attributes to the written words their ordinary grammatical meaning, it gives to technical words, such as " heir," their technical meaning, and does not allow itself to be influenced by the probability that such could not have been the meaning intended by the testator.[3] For one thing, the facts known to the testator may not be before the court [4]; for another, it would be futile to require a will to be in writing if the clearly written wishes of the testator were to be open to revision after his death.

Effect must be given to testator's intention.

Consequently, parol evidence is in general inadmissible to contradict, add to or vary what he wrote.[5] There are, however, exceptions to this principle.

Thus, if it is clear on the face of the will that he has not accurately or completely expressed his intention, the court will add words, provided that no person applying common sense can have any doubt what in fact he intended.[6] Similarly, it will omit words which have come in by inadvertence or misunderstanding, if their omission gives effect to the intention of the testator.[7]

Exceptionally court will add or omit words.

Again, the words used by a testator refer to facts and circumstances within his knowledge concerning his property and the persons mentioned in his will, and therefore it would often be

Parol evidence sometimes admissible.

---

[1] L.P.A. 1925, s. 1 (1), (3). The land, being subject to a gift over, becomes settled land.

[2] A statutory exception to this rule has been made by L.P.A. 1925, s. 130, which provides that an entailed interest can be created only by formal words of limitation ; *supra*, pp. 249–50.

[3] *Boyes* v. *Cook* (1880), 14 Ch. D. 53.

[4] *Ralph* v. *Carrick* (1879), 11 Ch. D. 873, 878.

[5] *Earl of Newburgh* v. *Countess of Newburgh* (1820), 5 Madd. 364.

[6] *Re Whitrick*, [1957] 1 W. L. R. 884 ; [1957] 2 All E. R. 467 ; and authorities there cited.

[7] *Re Morris*, [1971] P. 62 ; [1970] 1 All E. R. 1057 ; *Re Phelan*, [1972] Fam. 33.

impossible to fulfil his intention unless parol evidence were admissible. " You may place yourself, so to speak, in the testator's armchair, and consider the circumstances by which he was surrounded when he made his will to assist you in arriving at his intention."[1] As has been said: "When seated there, however, the court is not entitled to make a fresh will for the testator merely because it strongly suspects that he did not mean what he has plainly said."[2] In other words, "the function of a court of construction is not to declare the actual subjective intention of the testator, but the objective intention as expressed in his language."[3]

> " Thus if a testator devises the house he lives in, or his farm called Blackacre, or the lands which he purchased of A., parol evidence must be adduced to show what house was occupied by the testator, what farm is called Blackacre, or what lands were purchased of A., such evidence being essential for the purpose of ascertaining the actual subject of disposition. The distinction obviously is that, though evidence *dehors* the will is not admissible to show that the testator used his terms of description in any peculiar or extraordinary sense yet it may be adduced to ascertain what the description properly comprehends."[4]

Other cases where parol evidence is admitted for the same reason occur where a testator uses nicknames in the will, or expressions which, though bearing a definite meaning in ordinary language, are used in a peculiar sense by persons of the class to which the testator belonged or in the locality where he dwelt. [5]

Equivocation. Further, parol evidence is admissible to explain an equivocation. The word *equivocation* in this connection means that although the devise is on the face of it perfect and intelligible, yet an ambiguity arises making it hard to determine which of two persons or things the testator meant to denote, since the words of the will point equally well to either. An early instance of such a latent ambiguity was where, [6]

> a testator devised one house to George Gord the son of George Gord, a second to George Gord the son of John Gord, and a third to " George Gord the son of Gord." It was held that evidence of the testator's declarations were admissible to show that he intended by this last description to indicate George Gord the son of George Gord.

Limits to admissibility of extrinsic evidence. But although extrinsic evidence is admissible in such cases, it is never admitted to prove that words which are perfectly clear in themselves were intended by the testator to bear some different meaning. If a will bears a definite construction it cannot have another and a different construction imposed upon it by extrinsic

---

[1] *Boyes* v. *Cook* (1880), 14 Ch. D. 53, at p. 56, *per* JAMES, L.J.
[2] *Perrin* v. *Morgan*, [1943] A. C. 399, at p. 420; *per* Lord ROMER; [1943] I All E. R. 187.
[3] (1963), 26 *M.L.R.*, p. 357 (Michael Albery).
[4] Jarman (8th Edn.), p. 522.   [5] *Ibid.*, p. 515.
[6] *Doe d. Gord* v. *Needs* (1836), 2 M. & W. 129 ; *Re Jackson*, [1933] Ch. 237. But see *Re Mayo*, [1901] I Ch. 404.

evidence, for there is a fundamental distinction between evidence which is simply explanatory of the words of a will and evidence which is designed to prove intention itself as an independent fact.[1] This was explained by Lord CAVE in the following manner [2] :—

"No doubt a court, called upon to construe a will, is entitled to know the facts which the testator knew, and to use that knowledge for the purpose of resolving doubts as to the identity of persons or things mentioned in the will, or of assigning a meaning to expressions which otherwise would have no adequate or intelligible sense....

But it is quite another thing to say that when a testator has used an unambiguous expression such as '*my brothers and sisters*', extrinsic evidence can be adduced to show that he must have intended the expression to refer to brothers and sisters already born. That would be to use the facts, not as evidence of identity, but as evidence of intention ; and such a use of them would be contrary to settled principles of construction."

The identification of donees may give rise to further **problems**. Thus, where the donee is referred to as the wife of X. and she is married at the date of the will, the wife in existence at that date is prima facie intended to take, and not any subsequent wife. If, however, the testator confirmed the will by codicil after the death of X.'s wife, a subsequent wife of X. may take,[3] the effect of the codicil being " to bring the will down to the date of the codicil and effect the same disposition of the testator's will as if the testator had at that date made a new will."[4]

Gift to spouse of another.

Where there is a gift to a class, *e.g.* to the children of X., certain rules of construction have been established for the ascertainment of the class.[5] The object of the rules, which are sometimes known as the rule in *Andrews* v. *Partington*,[6] is to enable the donees to know their shares and the executors to distribute the estate at the earliest possible moment.[7] We have already seen their operation in the context of the rule against perpetuities,[8] but it is important to understand that their primary purpose is to facilitate the distribution of the estate and that it is only incidentally that they may save a gift from invalidity under that rule. Thus, in the case of a gift to the children of X. prima facie all those in existence at the death of the testator take, so that those who predecease the testator and those who are born after his death are excluded. If,

Gift to class.

---

[1] *Re Grainger*, [1900] 2 Ch. 756, 763–4, *per* RIGBY, L.J. ; reversed *sub nom. Higgins* v. *Dawson*, [1902] A. C. 1, 10.

[2] *Ward* v. *Van der Loeff*, [1924] A. C. 653, 663–4.

[3] *Re Hardyman*, [1925] Ch. 287.

[4] *Re Fraser*, [1904] 1 Ch. 726 *per* STIRLING, L.J.

[5] For a full and valuable account of the technical class-closing rules see (1954), 70 *L. Q. R.* 61 (J. H. C. Morris) : Morris and Leach, *The Rule against Perpetuities* (2nd Edn. 1962, and Supplement, 1964), pp. 109 *et seq.* ; (1958), *C.L.J.* 39 (S. J. Bailey) ; *Theobald on Wills* (13th Edn.), chap. 30.

[6] (1791). 3 Bro. C. C. 401.

[7] The rules apply to all forms of property, and to settlements as well as to wills.

[8] *Supra*, pp. 327–9.

however, no child of A. is alive at the testator's death the class remains open and all after-born children will be included.[1] Further, where there is a gift to X. for life, then to such of X.'s children who shall attain the age of 21, the class closes at the death of X., or when the eldest child becomes 21, whichever event happens last.[2] If, however, there are no children alive when X. dies, the class closes when the eldest child becomes 21, and after-born children are excluded.[3] Finally, it must be noticed that these rules are rules of construction only. They may be excluded by the testator's express direction or where they are inconsistent with the context of his will, and it seems that the courts are becoming less reluctant to find that inconsistency.[4]

Finally, we may notice that legislation has changed the long established rule of construction that " the description ' child,' ' son,' ' issue,' every word of that species must be taken prima facie to mean legitimate child, son or issue."[5]

Section 15 of the Family Law Reform Act 1969 provides that in the case of dispositions made after 1969 reference to any child or other relation shall, unless a contrary intention appears, include a reference to any illegitimate child and to any person related through an illegitimate person. Likewise by the Legitimacy Act of 1926 a child may include a child born illegitimate but legitimated by the subsequent marriage of the parents before the testator's death.[6] In the case of adopted children, where a will is made after 1949 or confirmed after April 1, 1959, and the adoption order precedes the death of the testator, the adopted children are treated as children of the adopter for the purposes of dispositions of property, unless a contrary intention appears.[7] The Children Act 1975 extends the definitions to include children adopted *after* the testator's death, where the testator dies on or after January 1st, 1976 ; and, similarly, in the case of legitimated children.[8] Thus, where T dies, leaving property to all the children of X whenever born,[9] a child adopted by X in 1977, or legitimated by his parents' subsequent marriage in 1977, will take if T dies in 1976, but not if T died in 1975.

---

[1] *Weld* v. *Bradbury* (1715), 2 Vern. 705 ; *Re Ransome*, [1957] Ch. 348, at p. 359, *per* Upjohn, J.

[2] *Re Emmet's Estate* (1880), 13 Ch. D. 484.

[3] *Re Bleckly*, [1951] Ch. 740 ; [1951] 1 All E. R. 1064.

[4] See the cases cited *supra*, p. 327, n. 6.

[5] *Wilkinson* v. *Adam* (1813), 1 Ves & B. 422, *per* Lord Eldon, L.C.

[6] S. 3.

[7] Adoption Act 1958, ss. 16 (2), 17 (2), 59, Sched. 5, para. 4. *Re Jones' Will Trusts*, [1965] Ch. 1124 ; [1965] 2 All E. R. 828.

[8] S. 8, Sched. 1, paras. 1 (5), 3 (1), 5 (1), 12 (1) (3). See (1976) 126 New L.J. 7 (S. M. Cretney).

[9] Thus excluding the class-closing rules. *Re Edmondson's Will Trusts*, [1972] 1 W. L. R. 183 ; [1972] 1 All E. R. 444 ; *supra*, pp. 327, 855.

Law Reform

In 1973 the Law Reform Committee[1] considered that the rules of construction of wills were too rigid. It unanimously recommended that no change should be made in the existing law under which the court has no power to make a will for the testator, and that, as long as there is no legitimate dispute about its meaning, the will which he has signed should be the only effective expression of his dispositive intention.[2] The majority of the committee recommended that all extrinsic evidence bearing on interpretation should be admissible, except for direct evidence of the testator's dispositive intention.[3] A minority would include the latter as well.[4]

Law Reform Committee Report 1973.

The Committee further recommended that the equitable doctrine of rectification should apply to wills within six months of their being proved. It would be available where there is a demonstrable clerical error, and where the testator's instructions have been misunderstood.[5]

SECTION VI. REVOCATION OF WILLS

A will is revoked in any of the following ways :—

(1) Subsequent Marriage of a Testator. Marriage, since it raises a moral obligation to provide for the new family, requires a reconsideration of any testamentary gifts that may have already been made by either party. At common law, subsequent marriage revoked the will of a woman, but not that of a man, since in any event his wife was adequately provided for under the law of dower.

Marriage now revokes will.

It is enacted, however, by the Wills Act 1837 that a will made by a man or a woman shall be revoked by his or her marriage.[6] There are two exceptions to this rule.

Exceptions.

> The first derives from the postulate that it is useless to invalidate a prior will if in the result no benefit will accrue to the testator's family. The Act, therefore, provides that the testamentary exercise of a power of appointment shall not be revoked by the testator's subsequent marriage unless the property if unappointed would go to his heir, executor, administrator or the persons entitled on intestacy.[7]
>
> Secondly, the Law of Property Act 1925 provides[8] that a will expressed to be made *in contemplation of marriage* shall

---

[1] Nineteenth Report (1973 Cmnd. 5301).   [2] Paras. 35–8, 65 (4).
[3] Paras. 46–54, 65 (6).   [4] Paras. 46, 55–9, 65 (7).
[5] Paras. 19–21, 25, 65 (1–3). See *Re Reynette-James* [1975] 3 All E. R. 1037 at p. 1043, *per* TEMPLEMAN, J.
[6] Wills Act 1837, s. 18.
[7] S. 18 ; *In the Goods of Gilligan*, [1950] P. 32. See A.E.A. 1925, s. 50 (1), *infra*, p. 871.   [8] S. 177 (1).

not be revoked by the solemnization of the marriage contemplated.[1] To escape revocation, however, the will must be expressed to be made in contemplation of marriage to a particular person, and moreover it must be followed by the solemnization of that marriage.[2]

The will must contain an expression which sufficiently shows that the will as a whole[3] was made in contemplation of the particular marriage solemnized. This may be in express terms, but the section is satisfied if the will as a whole is made in favour of " my fiancée " X,[4] or, probably, of " my wife " Y.[5]

(2) Later Will or Codicil.

A will may be revoked by a later will or codicil, provided that the later instrument observes the formalities required by law for the execution of a valid will.[6]

Express revocation.

A will or a codicil may revoke a prior will either by an express clause of revocation or by disposing of property in a manner inconsistent with a previous devise. The first method requires no comment, except that there is no technical rule as to the words necessary to operate as a revocation or as to the extent of the revocation, the question being simply one of intention.[7] The usual practice is, however, for a testator to use the simple formula:—

> " I hereby revoke all former wills, codicils and testamentary instruments made by me, and declare this to be my last will."

Implied revocation.

As regards a later disposition of property inconsistent with one made in a prior will, we must note that the mere use of the words " last will " does not necessarily revoke a former will.[8] A will may consist of several independent instruments executed at different times, and where a testator expresses his intention in several instruments without having executed an express clause of revocation, the earlier instruments are revoked by implication in so far, but only in so far, as they are inconsistent with the later ones.

> " The mere fact of making a subsequent testamentary paper does not work a total revocation of a prior one, unless the latter expressly or in effect revoke the former, or the two be incapable of standing together ; for though it be a maxim . . . that no man can die with two testaments, yet any number of instruments, whatever be their relative date, or in whatever form they may be (so as they be all clearly

---

[1] *Pilot* v. *Gainfort*, [1931] P. 103.

[2] *Sallis* v. *Jones*, [1936] P. 43 ; *In the Estate of Langston*, [1953] P. 100 ; [1953] 1 All E. R. 928.

[3] And not merely parts of it. *Re Coleman*, [1975] 2 W. L. R. 213 ; [1975] 1 All E. R. 675.

[4] *In the Estate of Langston*, *supra* ; *Re Coleman*, *supra*, where the authorities are reviewed by MEGARRY, J. See also (1975) 39 Conv. (N.S.) 121 (R. J. Edwards and B. F. J. Langstaff).

[5] *Pilot* v. *Gainfort*, [1931] P. 103 ; criticised in *Re Coleman*, *supra*.

[6] Wills Act 1837, s. 20.

[7] *Cotterell* v. *Cotterell* (1872), 2 P. & D. 397, at p. 399. *Lowthorpe-Lutwidge* v. *Lowthorpe-Lutwidge*, [1935] P. 151.

[8] *Simpson* v. *Foxon*, [1907] P. 54.

testamentary), may be admitted to probate, as together containing the last will of the deceased."[1]

If, for instance,

a testator, having devised Blackacre to A. in fee, by a subsequent will devises it to B. in fee, the former devise is obviously revoked ; but if he devises Blackacre to C. in fee and then, by codicil, devises it to the first son of D. who shall attain the age of 21 years, the first devise is revoked only to the extent necessary to give effect to the executory interest, so that C. will take the fee simple until the son of D. attains the required age.[2]

But if a subsequent and inconsistent gift, which, if valid, would override a prior gift, fails by reason of the rule against perpetuities or for any other reason, it does not operate as a revocation unless an independent and clear intention to revoke is expressed.[3]   This is known as the doctrine of dependent relative revocation.   " The revocation is relative to the new gift, and if the gift fails the revocation fails also, unless the testator clearly shows in the later instrument that he intends in any event to revoke the earlier will."[4]   In other words, the revocation of the prior gift is conditional on the effectiveness of its substitute.   This doctrine applies even where there is an express clause of revocation in the later instrument, for at bottom the question is always one of intention, but in this case a heavy burden lies upon those who allege that what was expressly prescribed was intended to be conditional upon the validity of the substituted gift.[5]

Doctrine of
dependent
relative
revocation.

If the court is satisfied that such was the testator's intention, it may in certain circumstances spell one composite will out of the two that he has executed. This solution was reached on the following facts:

By the earlier will the testatrix appointed X. executor, made certain bequests and left the residue of her estate to X. absolutely.   By the later will, she revoked all previous wills, appointed X. executor, made certain bequests which were entirely inconsistent with those contained in the earlier will, and then left the residuary clause incomplete so that in fact the residue was undisposed of.

---

[1] *Williams on Executors and Administrators* (5th Edn.), p. 140, adopted *Lemage* v. *Goodban* (1865), 1 P. & D. 57, 62 ; *Re Plant*, [1952] Ch. 298 ; [1952] 1 All E. R. 78 n. See Williams & Mortimer, *Executors, Administrators and Probate*, p. 186.

[2] *Duffield* v. *Duffield* (1829), 1 Dow and Cl. 268. *Cf. Re Baker*, [1929] 1 Ch. 668. *Re Pearson*, [1963], 1 W. L. R. 1358 ; [1963] 3 All E. R. 763.

[3] *Ward* v. *Van der Loeff*, [1924] A. C. 653. *Re Robinson*, [1930] 2 Ch. 332; *Re Hawksley's Settlement*, [1934] Ch. 384, at pp. 400–1. *In the Estate of Hope Brown*, [1942] P. 136 ; [1942] 2 All E. R. 176.

[4] *Ward* v. *Van der Loeff*, [1924] A. C. at p. 656, in argument. See (1955), 71 L. Q. R. 374 (F. H. Newark).

[5] *Re Murray*, [1956] 1 W. L. R. 605 ; [1956] 2 All E. R. 353.

It was held that she had inserted the revocation clause in the mistaken belief that she had disposed of the whole of her estate, and that therefore the later will, omitting the revocation clause, and the earlier will, omitting the bequests, must both be admitted to probate as together constituting the true last will of the testatrix.[1]

The Wills Act 1837 provides that revocation may be effected not only by a later will or codicil duly executed, but also by *some writing* declaring an intention to revoke " a will. A writing, however, is ineffectual to cause revocation unless it is executed in accordance with the formalities prescribed by the Act.[2]

Two elements necessary.

(3) **Destruction** *animo revocandi.* The Wills Act 1837 provides that a will may be revoked [3]

> " by the burning, tearing, or otherwise destroying the same by the testator, or by some person in his presence and by his direction, with the intention of revoking the same."

Physical destruction.

It will be seen that two distinct things must occur if a will is to be revoked by destruction. There must be the physical act of destruction and the mental act of the intention to revoke.

> " All the destroying in the world without intention will not revoke a will, nor all the intention in the world without destroying : there must be the two." [4]

Again, the act of destruction, if not carried out by the testator, must be carried out in his presence by some person acting under his direction.[5] Destruction without intention, intention without destruction, destruction with intention but carried out in the absence of the testator, none of these is operative to produce revocation.

Thus in one case, a testator drew his pen through parts of his will, wrote on the back of it " this will is revoked " and threw it into the waste-paper basket. A servant later rescued it and placed it on the table where it was found seven years later at the testator's death. The will was admitted to probate. It had not been revoked by a signed and attested writing, neither had it been physically destroyed. Indeed, had the servant burnt the contents of the basket, there would have been no destruction within the meaning of the Act.[6] If the testator destroys part of a will, that part only will be revoked,[7] unless the mutilation is such as to raise an inference that it was done *animo revocardi* of the whole will.[8]

---

[1] *In the Estate of Cocke,* [1960] 1 W. L. R. 491 ; [1960] 2 All E. R. 289.
[2] Wills Act 1837, s. 20.   [3] *Ibid.*
[4] *Cheese* v. *Lovejoy* (1877), 2 P. D. 251, 253.
[5] *In the Goods of Dadds* (1857), Dea. and Sw. 290.
[6] *Cheese* v. *Lovejoy, supra.*
[7] *In the Goods of John Woodward* (1871), L. R. 2 P. & D. 206 (seven or eight lines excised from will written on seven sheets) ; *Re Everest,* [1975] Fam. 44 ; [1975] 1 All E. R. 672 (lower half of first page cut away).
[8] *Leonard* v. *Leonard,* [1902] P. 243 (first two out of five sheets destroyed).

The physical act of destruction is in itself inconclusive, and it may be necessary to show whether it was accompanied by the *animus revocandi* or not. For this purpose extrinsic evidence is admissible. Thus, if a testator has destroyed a will in a fit of drunkenness[1] or of insanity[2] or under the mistaken impression that it is useless,[3] parol evidence of his declarations, his capacity or his conduct may be adduced in order to show that the necessary intention to revoke was wanting. *Intention to revoke.*

The doctrine of dependent relative revocation operates where the act of destruction is conditional upon an assumption that is in fact false,[4] as for example that a new will is valid;[5] that the effect is to revive a former will;[6] or that the beneficiary under the destroyed will is entitled to equal benefits if the testator dies intestate.[7] *Doctrine of dependent relative revocation.*

" If the truth of a particular fact is a condition of the destruction, and the fact turns out not to be true, there is no revocation."

These strict rules concerning revocation do not apply to the privileged will of the soldier, sailor or airman. For instance, a soldier before proceeding to South Africa on active service left his will with his fiancée, but in consequence of certain statements made as to her conduct wrote from that country instructing her to hand the will to his sister, which she did.   Later, in accordance with his written request, the sister burnt the will and it was held that this was a sufficient revocation notwithstanding that the destruction did not take place in the testator's presence.[8] *Revocation by soldiers, sailors and airmen.*

Revival of Will.   It is provided by the Wills Act 1837 that a will which has been revoked cannot be revived unless the testator re-executes it with the proper formalities, or unless he executes a codicil showing an intention to revive the will.[9] The object of this enactment was to abolish implied revivals, for under the law prior to 1838 a revoked will was presumed to be revived if the will which effected the revocation was itself later revoked. Now, however, the intention to revive the revoked will must appear on the face of the later instrument, either by express words referring to a will as revoked and importing an intention to revive the same, or by some expression conveying to the mind of the court with reasonable certainty the existence of the intention.[10] *Intention to revive.*

---

[1] *In the Goods of Brassington,* [1901] P. 1.
[2] *In the Goods of Hine,* [1893] P. 282.
[3] *Beardsley* v. *Lacey* (1897), 78 L. T. 25 ; *In the Estate of Southerden,* [1925] P. 177.
[4] *Re Feis,* [1964] Ch. 106 ; [1963] 3 All E. R. 303.
[5] *Onions* v. *Tyrer* (1716), 1 P. Wms. 343, 345.
[6] *Powell* v. *Powell* (1866), L. R. 1 P. & D. 209; *In the Estate of Bridgewater,* [1965] 1 W. L. R. 416 ; [1965] 1 All E. R. 717.
[7] *In the Estate of Southerden,* [1925] P. 177. See *Re Jones* (1976), 120 Sol. Jo. 1, 10.
[8] *In the Estate of Gossage,* [1921] P. 194.   [9] Wills Act 1837, s. 22.
[10] *In the Goods of Steele* (1868), L. R. 1 P. & D. 575 ; *Goldie* v. *Adam,* [1938] P. 85 ; [1938] 1 All E. R. 586 ; *In the Estate of Davis,* [1952] P. 279 ; [1952] 2 All E. R. 509 ; *Re Pearson,* [1963] 1 W. L. R. 1358 ; [1963] 3 All E. R. 763.

CHAPTER II

INTESTACY[1]

SUMMARY

SECTION I. APPOINTMENT OF THE ADMINIS-TRATOR AND HIS GENERAL POWERS

Grant of
adminis-
tration.

When a person dies testate having appointed executors in his will, the estate is administered, as we have seen, by the executors. If, however, he dies intestate, or, though testate, fails to appoint executors, it is necessary to make application to the court for the appointment of personal representatives. When the court does this, it is said to grant administration, or more fully, to grant letters of administration, and the personal representative to whom the grant is made is called an administrator.

The property of the deceased, both real and personal, passes to an administrator upon his appointment by the court to the same extent as it passes to an executor, but in the interval between the death of the deceased and the appointment of an administrator both the real and personal estate of the deceased vests in the Probate Judge *i.e.* the President of the Family Division of the High Court until administration is granted.[2]

---

[1] See generally Williams and Mortimer, *Executors, Administrators and Probate.*

[2] A.E.A. 1925, s. 9, 55 (xv), as amended by Administration of Justice Act 1970, s. 1, Sched. 2, para. 5.

Who may be appointed Administrators. The first question that requires consideration is this : To what persons will the court grant letters of administration? The matter lies within its discretion, but the Judicature Act 1925,[1] as amended by the Administration of Justice Act 1928,[2] contains somewhat detailed provisions for the guidance of the court in the exercise of its discretion.

After prescribing in general that the court shall have regard to the rights of all persons interested in the real and personal estate or the proceeds of sale thereof, the Act provides that where the deceased died wholly intestate as to his real and personal estate, administration shall, unless by reason of the insolvency of the estate or other special circumstances the court thinks it expedient to grant administration to some other person, be granted to some one or more persons interested in the residuary estate of the deceased, if they make an application for the purpose.[3]

Where land has been settled by the intestate in his lifetime, administration thereof must be granted to the trustees of the settlement if they are willing to act.[4] Representation is not to be granted to more than four persons in regard to the same property, and if any beneficiary is an infant, administration must be granted either to a trust corporation (with or without an individual) or to not less than two individuals.[5]

The court may limit its grant in any way it considers to be proper. For instance, it may grant representation in respect of the realty separately from the personality, or in respect of a trust estate alone, or in respect of the realty alone if there is no personal estate.[6]

The Administration of Estates Act 1971[7] provides that as a condition of granting letters of administration one or more sureties may be required to enter into a guarantee[8] for the due performance

---

[1] S. 162.   [2] S. 9.

[3] It is now provided by the Non-Contentious Probate Rules 1954, r. 21, as amended by S.I. 1969 No. 1689, and S.I. 1971 No. 1977, that the order in priority of rights to a grant of administration shall be as follows :—(1) Husband or wife ; (2) children or other issue of deceased taking *per stirpes* ; (3) father or mother ; (4) brothers and sisters of the whole blood, or the issue of the whole blood taking *per stirpes* ; (5) brothers and sisters of the half blood, or the issue of deceased brothers and sisters of the half blood taking *per stirpes* ; (6) grandparents ; (7) uncles and aunts of the whole blood, or the issue of deceased uncles and aunts of the whole blood taking *per stirpes* ; (8) uncles and aunts of the half blood, or the issue of deceased uncles and aunts of the half blood taking *per stirpes* ; (9) the Crown ; (10) creditors. As to the discretion of the Court to grant administration to some other person, see *In the Goods of Edwards-Taylor*, [1951] P. 24.

[4] Supreme Court of Judicature (Consolidation) Act 1925. s. 162 (1) (*a*).

[5] *Ibid.*, s. 160.   [6] *Ibid.*, s. 155.

[7] Following the recommendations of Law Commission Administration Bonds, etc. 1970 (Law Com. No. 31), paras. 3–4, 10–17. Until 1973 an administration bond was required.

[8] Supreme Court of Judicature (Consolidation) Act 1925, s. 167, as replaced by A.E.A. 1971, s. 8.

of the administrator's duties.[1]   Probate rules, however, have been made to limit this requirement to those cases in which the creditors or beneficiaries need special protection.   The limit of the surety's liability under the guarantee will normally be the gross value of the estate.[2]

Title of an Administrator.   An administrator, unlike an executor, derives his title solely from the grant of letters, and until he receives the grant he is not entitled to deal with the estate of the deceased.   But in order that no wrong may go without a remedy, it has been the rule from the earliest times that the administrator's title upon his appointment relates back to the death of the intestate, so that he may maintain trespass or trover against a wrongdoer who has interfered with the estate of the deceased between the death and the grant of administration.[3] Although this rule is more often of importance in the case of goods, it applies equally to wrongs committed against land.[4]

The death of an administrator before the administration has begun or been completed necessitates the appointment of another person, for the office does not devolve on death as does that of an executor.[5]

Relation back of administrator's title.

Powers of an Administrator.   An administrator, as we have said, has the same powers with regard to the administration of the estate as are possessed by executors, but a new departure was made by the Administration of Estates Act 1925, by vesting in him a statutory trust for sale.   This is required because the property of the intestate is usually distributable in shares among the beneficial successors, and it has the added advantage of enabling the administrator to make an overreaching conveyance of land.   It is expressly enacted that upon the death of a person intestate his real and personal estate shall be held by his personal representatives

Administrator holds on trust for sale.

" (a) as to the real estate upon trust to sell the same ; and
   (b) as to the personal estate upon trust to call in sell and convert
       into money such part thereof as may not consist of
       money."[6]

The administrator, however, has full power to postpone the sale for such period as he may think proper.   He is not to sell any reversionary interest until it falls into possession unless there is some special reason to justify the sale, neither is he to sell personal chattels unless they are required for purposes of administration

---

[1] A.E.A. 1925, s. 25, as replaced by A.E.A. 1971, s. 9, *supra*, p. 845.
[2] Non-Contentious Probate Rules 1954, r. 38, as replaced by Non-Contentious Probate (Amendment) Rules 1971, r. 8.
[3] *Tharpe* v. *Stallwood* (1843), 12 L. J. (N.S.) C. P. 241.
[4] *In the Goods of Pryse*, [1904] P. 301.   [5] *Supra*, pp. 842-3.
[6] A.E.A. 1925, s. 33 (1).

owing to a deficiency of other assets, or unless there is some other special reason for the sale.[1]

Personal chattels mean

" carriages, horses,[2] stable furniture and effects (not used for business purposes),[3] motor cars and accessories (not used for business purposes), garden effects, domestic animals, plate, plated articles, linen, china, glass, books, pictures, prints, furniture,[4] jewellery,[5] articles of household or personal use[6] or ornament, musical and scientific instruments and apparatus, wines, liquors and consumable stores, but do not include any chattels used at the death of the intestate for business purposes nor money or securities for money."[7]

The administrator must use the money arising from the sale, and also any ready money that the intestate may have left, in discharging the funeral, testamentary and administration expenses, and the debts due from the estate.[8] During the minority of any person beneficially entitled and pending the final distribution of the estate the administrator may invest in authorised securities[9] so much of the money as is not required for the payment of debts.[10] *Residuary estate of intestate.*

After all the debts have been paid, the residue of the money arising from sale and any investments which may have been made, and any property which may have been retained unsold, are together called *the residuary estate of the intestate*.[11] It is this estate that is distributed among the persons who are entitled to succeed to the property of the intestate.

SECTION II. DISTRIBUTION OF THE RESIDUARY ESTATE OF THE INTESTATE

SUMMARY

---

[1] *Ibid.*
[2] *Re Hutchinson*, [1955] Ch. 255 ; [1955] 1 All E. R. 689.
[3] For meaning of " business " see *Re Ogilby*, [1943] Ch. 288 ; [1942] 1 All E. R. 524.
[4] *Re Crispin's Will Trusts*, [1975] Ch. 245 ; [1974] 3 All E. R. 772 (long case and bracket clocks).
[5] *Re Whitby*, [1944] Ch. 210 ; [1944] 1 All E. R. 299.
[6] *Re Reynolds' Will Trusts*, [1966] 1 W. L. R. 19 ; [1965] 3 All E. R. 686 (stamp collection kept as a hobby) ; (1966), 82 *L. Q. R.* 18 (R. E. M.) ; *cf. Re Collin's Will Trusts*, [1971] 1 W. L. R. 37 ; [1971] 1 All E. R. 283 ; *Re Chaplin*, [1950] Ch. 507 ; [1950] 2 All E. R. 155 (small yacht used for family purposes). *Re Crispin's Will Trusts, supra* (clocks and watches worth £50,000).
[7] A.E.A. 1925, s. 55 (1) (x).
[8] *Ibid.*, s. 33 (2).
[9] See Trustee Investments Act 1961, which greatly increased the range of investments previously authorised by the Trustee Act 1925.
[10] A.E.A. 1925, s. 33 (3).   [11] *Ibid.*, s. 33 (4).

(1) INTRODUCTORY NOTE

Rules of
descent now
changed.

Assimilation of Real to Personal Property. A far-reaching reform of the law governing the beneficial distribution of the property of an intestate dying after 1925 was effected by the Administration of Estates Act 1925. Before 1926 the destination of the property varied according as it consisted of freehold estates of inheritance or of leaseholds and chattels personal. The rules of descent relating to the fee simple and the fee tail depended partly upon the common law and partly upon statute ; the rules by which leaseholds and chattels personal were distributed depended entirely upon statutes, the chief of which were the Statutes of Distribution of 1670 and 1685. The Administration of Estates Act 1925, however, abolished the law of descent so far as it related to the fee simple, and introduced a new scheme of distribution which applies both to realty and to personality. This scheme is not the same as that laid down for chattels by the Statutes of Distribution. Those statutes have been swept away,

Four reasons why knowledge of old rules still essential.

and a fresh start has been made. Unfortunately, however, there are four reasons why conveyancers must still acquaint themselves with the canons of descent in respect of the fee simple that prevailed before 1926.

Old titles.

The investigation of title upon the sale of land may disclose the intestacy of a former owner. The vendor or some predecessor in title may have claimed the estate as heir of that intestate, and it will therefore be necessary for the purchaser to ascertain who was entitled under the old rules to succeed to the estate, and to satisfy himself that the right person did succeed.

Entailed interests.

Secondly, the persons who are entitled to succeed to an entailed interest which has neither been barred nor devised by its owner must be ascertained according to the old rules of descent.[1]

Heirs taking by purchase.

Thirdly, the Law of Property Act 1925 provides as follows [2] :—

> A limitation of real or personal property in favour of the heir, either general or special, of a deceased person which, if limited in respect of freehold land before the commencement of this Act, would have conferred on the heir an estate in the land by purchase, shall operate to confer a corresponding *equitable* interest in the property on the person who would, *if the general law in force immediately before such commencement had remained unaffected*, have answered the description of the heir, either general or special, of the deceased in respect of his freehold land, either at the death of the deceased or at the time named in the limitation, as the case may require.

---

[1] *Supra*, pp. 243-4.
[2] L.P.A. 1925, s. 132.

The object of this provision is clear. A testator who has no wish to die intestate, yet who desires that his land shall go to the person who will be his heir-at-law, may make a will devising his land to his heir. The effect of this is that the heir, when ascertained according to the rules of intestate succession, takes the land as devisee, *i.e.* as a purchaser and not by title of descent.[1] A will in these terms before 1926 was convenient and reasonable, for in every case but one the heir was a single person. The legislation of 1925, however, abolished heirship except for entailed interests, and introduced a system under which the fee simple is sold and the proceeds distributed among near relatives. The effect of the present enactment is, therefore, that a testator who is so minded may still devise land to his heir, and that if he does so the devisee shall be ascertained according to the old law of descent. When ascertained he takes the fee simple in the case of inheritable freeholds, and the absolute ownership of personalty.

Fourthly, it is provided that in certain cases the property of a person suffering from mental disorder, within the meaning of the Mental Health Act 1959 who dies intestate shall descend according to the old rules.[2]

Mental patient's property.

(2) THE DESCENT OF THE FEE SIMPLE BEFORE 1926

Rule 1. Descent must be traced from the last purchaser.[3] We have seen in dealing with entailed interests[4] that this rule obliges us to look for the heir of the person who last took the land otherwise than by descent, escheat, partition or enclosure; in other words, by act of parties, not by operation of law. This rule persisted till 1926, save only for a modification in 1859 by the Law of Property Amendment Act[5] which provided that if there are no heirs of the last purchaser, the descent shall be traced from the person who was last *entitled* to the land, although he may not have been a *purchaser*. If, for instance,

Meaning of " purchaser."

a purchaser dies intestate leaving a widow and one son, but no other relative, the son becomes *entitled* by descent to take the land. If the son dies intestate and a bachelor, the land would, apart from this statutory rule, escheat to the Crown. But since the statute permits the heir of the person last

---

[1] Inheritance Act 1833, ss. 3, 4.
[2] A.E.A. 1925, s. 51 (2), as amended by the Mental Health Act 1959, Sched. 8. See *Re Gates*, [1930] 1 Ch. 199; *Re Sirett*, [1969] 1 W. L. R. 60 [1968] 3 All E. R. 186.
[3] Inheritance Act 1833, ss. 1, 2.   [4] *Supra*. p. 243.   [5] S. 19.

entitled (that is, the son) to take, the land may go to the son's mother, because, although she is not of the blood of her husband, the last purchaser, she *is* of the blood of the son.[1]

Priority of males.

Rule 2. Males have a prior right to females. The fee simple passes in the first place to the lineal descendants of the purchaser, and the male are preferred to the female descendants.

Primogeniture and coparcenary.

Rule 3. Primogeniture. Under the rule of primogeniture, the eldest male takes to the exclusion of all other males in equal degree. Females in equal degree, however, take equally as coparceners. If, for instance, the intestate dies leaving two sons and two daughters, the eldest son takes the whole of the land If, however, there are no male descendants, then the female descendants who are in equal degree share the land equally as coparceners.[2]

Representation.

Rule 4. Representation. The lineal descendants of the purchaser represent him in that they stand in the same place as he himself would have done. Thus the lineal descendants of a deceased child who, had he lived, would have been heir, stand in the place of that child. If, for instance, the purchaser has two sons and dies leaving his younger son alone alive, the estate will pass to the eldest son of his deceased elder son and not to his living younger son.

Ancestral line.

Rule 5. Lineal ancestors take after lineal descendants.[3] The rule prior to the Inheritance Act 1833 was that a fief could not ascend, but that Act provides that if there are no lineal descendants of the purchaser, or if they have all failed, the estate shall go to the nearest lineal ancestor.

Male paternal ancestors.

Rule 6. The paternal ancestors are preferred to the maternal.[4] The effect of this rule and the preceding one is that if there are no lineal descendants of the purchaser, the land will go to the nearest male ancestor or, if he is dead leaving issue, then to the issue representing the ancestor under rule 4. Thus the nearest lineal ancestor is the father of the intestate, or, if the father is dead, the eldest son of the father. A father therefore is a nearer heir than a brother. But in searching for the heir among the paternal ancestors and their issue, the rule is that preference must be given to the whole blood as against the half blood.[5]

Half blood on male side.

Before the Inheritance Act 1833 the half blood were excluded altogether, but that Act provided that where the common

---

[1] And see *Bradley* v. *McAtamney*, [1936] N. I. 74.
[2] This rule was varied by the local customs of gavelkind and borough-English ; *supra*, p. 18.
[3] Inheritance Act 1833, s. 6.   [4] *Ibid.*, ss. 7, 8.
[5] *Ibid.*, s. 9.

ancestor is a male (*i.e.* where a man has married two wives), a relative by half blood ranks next after a relative in the same degree of the whole blood and his or her issue. If, for instance,

> the father of a purchaser who dies without descendants married Emma and had by her the purchaser and a sister Julia, and then married Arabella, by whom he had John, the effect of the statutory rule is that, while Julia and her issue take first, the estate passes to John if they fail.

If the purchaser's father is dead and the father's issue non-existent or extinct, recourse is next had to the father's father and his issue, and so on up through the male *paternal* ancestors ; and when the males in this class are exhausted they are followed by the females.

If there is no reasonable likelihood of ascertaining that there are descendants from the male paternal ancestors still alive, then[1] the next persons who are entitled, and who must be sought for, are the female paternal ancestors and their descendants.[2] But the search for the heir within this class is not the same as in the case of the male paternal ancestors. We have seen that after the purchaser's descendants are exhausted, we go to the male paternal ancestors, and that we start with the father and work upwards. In other words, we go from the father to the grandfather and then to the great-grandfather and so on. But the Inheritance Act provides that in dealing with the female paternal ancestors we start with the mother of the remotest male *paternal* ancestor known and her descendants.

Female paternal ancestors.

> Suppose, for instance, that the purchaser's father, grand-father and great-grandfather are dead, and their descendants extinct. The next person whose descendants are entitled is the great-great-grandfather. If, however, he is not known, then we take the last paternal ancestor who *is* known, *i.e.* the great-grandfather, and look for the descendants of his mother.

That is the meaning of the enactment that[3]

> " Where there shall be a failure of male paternal ancestors of the person from whom the descent is to be traced and their descendants, the mother of his more remote male paternal ancestor, or her descendants, shall be the heir or heirs of such person, in preference to the mother of a less remote male paternal ancestor, or her descendants."

---

[1] *Greaves* v. *Greenwood* (1877), 2 Ex. D. 289.
[2] Inheritance Act 1833, s. 7.
[3] *Ibid.*, s. 8. For this curious rule, said to be justified by feudal principles, but which has given rise to no decision, see Blackstone, vol. ii. p. 238.

If there are no descendants of the great-grandfather's mother, the next persons entitled are the descendants of the grandfather's mother, then the grandmother and her descendants, and lastly the mother and her descendants.

Male and female maternal ancestors. Having exhausted the male and female paternal ancestors, the next step is to start with the mother and work up the male and down the female line, as in the case of the father.

When the person entitled to succeed is a female ancestor who is dead, the estate will descend to her issue as representing her.

If, for instance,

> the only ancestor with issue is the purchaser's mother, and she is dead having left a child by another husband than the father of the purchaser, that child will be entitled to take. The child, of course, is a relative of the half blood to the purchaser.

We have seen that where the common ancestor is a male, the relatives of the half blood take after the relatives of the same degree of the whole blood. Where, however, as in the present case, the common ancestor is a female, *i.e.* where the purchaser's *mother* has married twice, it is enacted that the relatives of the half blood shall take next after the female ancestor.[1]

Curtesy. **Curtesy and Dower.** It must be remembered that the above rules of descent were subject, under the old law, to the respective rights of a surviving husband and a surviving wife. If a wife died intestate, the husband was entitled, in certain circumstances, to an estate by the curtesy in her freeholds of inheritance. This species of estate has already been discussed.[2]

Dower. Similarly, when a husband died having at some time been solely seised of a fee simple or an estate tail, his surviving wife became entitled by way of dower to a life estate in one-third of the land.[3] In order to establish this right, however, she must have been able to show

> 1. that issue capable of inheriting the land *might* have been born, and
>
> 2. that she had not been expressly deprived of the right to her third.

1. As regards the first point, she must have shown that she herself might have had a child capable of inheriting the land out of which she claimed dower. Thus:

> if land was settled on a husband and his heirs begotten on the body of X., X. was dowable even though the

---

[1] Inheritance Act 1833, s. 9.
[2] *Supra*, p. 244.
[3] For the customary rule in gavelkind see, *supra*, p. 18.

husband died childless ; but if X. died and the husband married Y., the latter had no claim to dower, for she could never have had children capable of inheriting the land in accordance with the terms of the original limitation.

2. As to the second point, the rule after the Dower Act 1833 was that a husband could deprive his wife either expressly or by implication of her right to dower, and the law was that no such right existed if the husband had disposed of the estate by deed or will;[1] if he expressly stated in a deed or will that she was not to have dower;[2] if he devised to her other land out of which she was not dowable;[3] or if, as for instance under a settlement, she accepted a jointure. Thus in effect it was only where a husband died intestate actually seised of an unbarred interest in tail or of a fee simple estate that a question of dower arose.

(3) THE MODERN RULES OF DISTRIBUTION

The Administration of Estates Act 1925 prepared the way for new rules of distribution by abolishing with regard to the real and personal estate of persons dying on or after January 1, 1926, all the former rules of descent and distribution. Moreover, it abolished the husband's curtesy, the widow's dower, and all customary modes of descent, such as gavelkind and borough-English, that formerly obtained in any part of the country. Escheat, whether to the Crown or to a mesne lord,[4] was also abolished and replaced by the right of the Crown to take all undistributed property as *bona vacantia*.[5]

Abolition of old rules.

On the death of a person intestate, his estate, as we have seen, is held by his personal representatives upon trust

(*a*) to sell the real estate, and

(*b*) to sell such part of the personal estate as does not consist of money,

with power to postpone the sale for so long as may seem fit.[6]

The Act then provided that the residuary estate (*i.e.* the residue, after payment of debts, of the proceeds of sale and any investments

---

[1] Dower Act 1833, s. 4.

[2] *Ibid.*, s. 6.

[3] *Ibid.*, s. 7.

[4] See *Re Lowe's Will Trusts*, [1973] 1 W. L. R. 882 ; [1973] 2 All E. R. 1136.

[5] A.E.A. 1925, s. 45. Certain of the old rules, of course, still apply to the entailed interest, *supra*, p. 244. Curtesy is still possible in the case of an entailed interest not disposed of by will.

[6] *Ibid.*, s. 33 (1) ; *supra*, p. 864.

by which they are represented, including any part of the estate still unsold) [1] should be distributed according to certain rules which varied according as the intestate left or did not leave a surviving spouse.   Where a surviving spouse is left, however, these rules have been radically altered by the Intestates' Estates Act 1952, as amended by the Family Provision Act 1966 and the Family Provision (Intestate Succession) Order 1972. [2]   In 1969 the Family Law Reform Act amended the law with respect to illegitimate children.   The present position where the intestate died after June 30th, 1972 is as follows.

Surviving spouse.

1. **Where the Intestate leaves a Surviving Spouse.**—If it is uncertain which spouse survived the other the statutory rule that the younger spouse survived the elder [3] does not apply.   The estate of each is distributed separately. [4]   If a spouse dies intestate after a decree of judicial separation and whilst the separation is still continuing, his or her estate devolves as if the other spouse were dead. [5]

Intestate leaves issue.

(1) *If the intestate also leaves issue*, the surviving spouse takes

(*a*) all the personal chattels absolutely, [6]

(*b*) a fixed net sum of £15,000 [7] (or such larger sum as may from time to time be fixed by the Lord Chancellor), with interest thereon at the rate of 4 per cent. from the date of death ; [8]

(*c*) a life interest in half of the residuary estate.

The other half of the residuary estate and the reversion on the life interest is held upon the statutory trusts for the issue. [9]

No issue, but a parent or brother or sister.

(2) *If the intestate leaves no issue, but leaves one or more of the following*, namely, a parent, a brother or sister of the whole blood or issue of such brother or sister, the surviving spouse takes :—

(*a*) the personal chattels absolutely ;

(*b*) £40,000 [10] (or such larger sum as may from time to time be fixed by the Lord Chancellor), with interest at 4 per cent. from the date of death ;

---

[1] A.E.A. 1925, s. 33 (4).   [2] S.I. 1972 No. 916.
[3] *Supra*, p. 847.   [4] A.E.A. 1925, s. 46 (3), added by I.E.A. 1952.
[5] Matrimonial Causes Act 1973, s. 18 (2), replacing Matrimonial Proceedings and Property Act 1970, s. 40.
[6] For definition, see *supra*, p. 865.
[7] Family Provision (Intestate Succession) Order 1972, *supra*, r. 2 (a).
[8] A.E.A. 1925, s. 46 (1) (i), as amended by I.E.A. 1952, s. 1 and by Family Provision Act 1966, s. 1 (1) (*a*).
[9] A.E.A. 1925, s. 46 (1) (i), as amended by I.E.A. 1952, s. 1 (2), and Family Provision Act 1966, s. 1.   For the rights of the issue, see *infra*, pp. 877–8.
[10] Family Provision (Intestate Succession) Order 1972 *supra*, r. 2 (b).

(*c*) one-half of the residuary estate absolutely.

The other half of the residue goes to the parents absolutely or, if there is no surviving parent, to the brothers and sisters or their issue upon the statutory trusts.[1]

(3) *If the intestate leaves no issue, no parents, and no brothers or sisters of the whole blood or their issue*, the surviving spouse takes the whole residuary estate absolutely to the exclusion of all other relatives.[2] Thus where there is a surviving spouse, the brothers and sisters of the half-blood are entirely excluded.

No issue, parents or brothers and sisters.

We have seen that where the intestate leaves issue, the surviving spouse takes a life interest in one-half of what is left of the estate after deduction of the personal chattels and £15,000. The existence of this life interest precludes a final distribution of the estate, and in most cases the survivor prefers to receive a lump sum. The Act, therefore, provides that if the surviving spouse so elects the personal representatives must redeem the life interest by paying its capital value to the tenant for life.[3] Thus the initiative lies with the surviving spouse, but the election must be made within twelve months from the date on which representation is first taken out, unless the court extends the period on the ground that it will operate unfairly.[4] Once made, it cannot be revoked without the consent of the personal representatives.[5] Owing to the difficulty of valuing reversionary interests, it is provided that a demand for redemption can be made only in respect of property to which the intestate was entitled in possession.[6]

Redemption of life interest.

The Administration of Estates Act 1925 empowers a personal representative to appropriate any part of the estate of the deceased in its actual condition or state of investment in or towards satisfaction of any share or interest in the estate to which a beneficiary may be entitled.[7] Thus, for example, an investment held by the intestate at the time of his death may be allocated to his widow in part satisfaction of her right to £15,000. The consent of any beneficiary who is absolutely and beneficially entitled in possession must first be obtained.[8]

Rights of surviving spouse as respects the matrimonial home.

This power of appropriation has been extended to include the matrimonial home. The Intestates' Estates Act 1952 provides that

> where the residuary estate comprises an interest in a dwelling-house in which the *surviving* husband or wife was resident at the time of the intestate's death, the surviving spouse may *require* the personal

---

[1] A.E.A. 1925, s. 46 (1) (i), as amended by I.E.A. 1952, s. 1 and by Family Provision Act 1966, s. 1 (i) (*a*).

[2] *Ibid.*, as substituted by I.E.A. 1952, s. 1 (2).

[3] *Ibid.*, s. 47A added by I.E.A. 1952, Sched. 1. For rules upon which the capital value must be calculated, see s. 47A (2).

[4] *Ibid.*, s. 47 A (5).   [5] *Ibid.*, s. 47 A (6).

[6] *Ibid.*, s. 47 A (3).

[7] *Ibid.*, s. 41.

[8] *Ibid.*, s. 41 (1) (ii) (*a*).

representative to appropriate the house in or towards satisfaction of any *absolute* interest of the survivor in the estate.[1]

This right is personal to the survivor and is not exercisable after his or her death.[2] If the house is worth more than the interest to which the survivor is entitled, it may be appropriated upon payment in cash of the balance.[3]

Meaning of " dwelling-house."

The expression " dwelling-house " includes part of a building that at the time of the intestate's death was used as a separate dwelling.[4] In the following four cases, however, the right of the survivor is not enforceable unless an application is made to the court and the court is satisfied that the appropriation is not likely to diminish the value of assets in the residuary estate (other than the interest in the dwelling-house) or to make them more difficult to dispose of, namely where—

(*a*) the dwelling-house is part of a building the whole of which is comprised in the residuary estate ; or

(*b*) the dwelling-house is held with agricultural land, an interest in which is comprised in the residuary estate ; or

(*c*) the whole or part of the dwelling-house was used as a hotel or lodging-house at the time of the intestate's death ; or

(*d*) part of it was at the time used for purposes other than domestic purposes,[5] at the time of the intestate's death.

There is no right to the appropriation if the house was held by the intestate on a lease due to end within two years of his or her death or on a lease, such as one from year to year, that the landlord can determine by a notice given within two years after the death.[6]

Time within which claim must be made.

The right must be claimed within twelve months after representation has first been taken out[7] and it must be exercised by a written notification to the personal representatives, or, where there are two or more representatives of whom one is the claimant, to all of them.[8] During this period of twelve months the house may not be sold without the written consent of the surviving spouse, unless there is an insufficiency of assets for the payment of debts.[9]

---

[1] I.E.A. 1952, 2nd Sched., para. 1 (1). Although this power of appropriation is exercisable only in satisfaction of an " absolute interest," the latter expression includes a life interest which the survivor has elected to have redeemed, *ibid.*, para. 1 (4). The date for valuation is that of appropriation, not death. *Re Collins*, [1975] 1 W. L. R. 309 ; [1975] 1 All E. R. 321.

[2] *Ibid.*, para. 3 (1) (*b*).

[3] *Ibid.*, para. 5 (2).

[4] *Ibid.*, para. 1 (5).

[5] *Ibid.*, para. 2.

[6] *Ibid.*, para. 1 (2).

[7] *Ibid.*, para. 3 (1) (*a*).

[8] *Ibid.*, 2nd Sched., para. 3 (1) (*c*).

[9] *Ibid.*, para. 4 (1).

If a sale is effected in violation of this prohibition, however, no right against the purchaser is conferred upon the surviving spouse.[1]

The requirement of a written notice to the representative is expressly excluded where the surviving spouse is the sole personal representative, for a person can scarcely demand of himself that he shall effect a certain transaction for his own benefit.[2] Unfortunately, however, it is not clear whether a surviving spouse who is also the sole personal representative can exercise this right of appropriation under the Act of 1952. It may be that his only course is to proceed under section 41 of the Administration of Estates Act 1925.[3]

2. **Where the intestate leaves no surviving spouse.** The rules for the distribution of the residuary estate in this event are laid down by the Administration of Estates Act 1925, and are unaffected by the Act of 1952. *No surviving spouse.*

They prescribe that the estate shall be distributed among the relatives of the deceased according to the following scheme :—

(1) If the intestate leaves issue the residuary estate is held on the *statutory trusts* for the issue.[4]

The word " issue " means the lineal descendants of the intestate. Under this rule the beneficiaries are the surviving children and the descendants of children who predeceased the intestate. Such descendants represent the deceased child and take among themselves the exact share that the child would have taken had he survived the intestate. This taking by representation is called taking *per stirpes*—according to the roots. *Doctrine of representation.*

" All the branches inherit the same share that their root, whom they represent, would have done."[5]

If, for instance, the intestate is survived by two children and by four grandchildren, the offspring of a daughter who predeceased him, the children each take one-third of the estate and the remaining third is divisible equally between the four grandchildren.

(2) If the intestate leaves no issue but is survived by a parent or parents, his father and mother take the whole estate absolutely in equal shares.[6] If only one parent survives, that parent takes absolutely.[7]

---

[1] I.E.A. 1952, para. 4 (5).   [2] *Ibid.*, para. 3 (1) (*c*).
[3] *Supra*, p. 873; see (1952), 16 *Conv.* (N.S.), pp. 417–419 (G. B. Graham).
[4] A.E.A. 1925, s. 46 (1) (ii).
[5] Blackstone, vol. ii. p. 217.
[6] A.E.A. 1925, s. 46 (1) (iii).
[7] *Ibid.*, s. 46 (1) (iv).

(3) If the intestate leaves no issue or parent, the following persons " living at the death of the intestate " are entitled in the following order [1]:—

   (a) His brothers and sisters of the whole blood, on the statutory trusts ; failing these

   (b) his brothers and sisters of the half-blood, on the statutory trusts ; failing these

   (c) his grandparents, if more than one, in equal shares ; failing these

   (d) his uncles and aunts of the whole blood, on the statutory trusts ; failing these

   (e) his uncles and aunts of the half-blood, on the statutory trusts.

If the deceased leaves none of the relatives just enumerated and no issue or surviving spouse, his estate belongs to the Crown or to the Duchy of Lancaster or Duke of Cornwall, as the case may be, as *bona vacantia* and in lieu of any right to escheat.

The Crown may however, provide out of the estate for dependants of the intestate, whether kindred or not, and other persons for whom he might reasonably have been expected to make provision.[2]

Representation. The words " living at the death of the intestate " in the opening statement of the enumeration do not exclude the issue of a brother, sister, uncle or aunt who predeceased him, for under the doctrine of representation they take the share that their parent would have taken had he survived the intestate.[3]

Distant relatives excluded. The list of beneficiaries, it will be noticed, does not include distant relatives. Since the oldest ancestor entitled is the grandparent, the claimant must at least have descended from him or her, and it follows that the most remote relative entitled to a share is a first cousin and his issue, *i.e.* first cousins once, twice or further removed. Thus, second cousins are excluded.

Capacity to take. **Capacity to take under an intestacy.** In addition to legitimate relations the following may take under these provisions :

Adopted. (a) Adopted children are deemed to be the children of their adopting and not their natural parents ; and members of the adopting family may take under the intestacy of an adopted child.[4]

---

[1] A.E.A. 1925, s. 46 (1) (v). See *Re Scott*, [1975] 1 W. L. R. 1260 ; [1975] 2 All E. R. 1033.

[2] See generally Ing, *Bona Vacantia* (1971), chap. 10.

[3] A.E.A. 1925, ss. 47 (1) (i) ; 47 (3).

[4] Children Act 1975, s. 8, Sched. 1, paras. 3, 1 (5), 5 (1) (3). In the case of intestacies occurring before January 1st, 1976, similar provision was made by Adoption Act 1958, ss. 16 (1), 17 (1), 59, Sched. 5.

(b) Similarly where a child is legitimated by the subsequent Legitimated.
marriage of his or her parents under the Legitimacy Acts 1926
and 1959, the rules of distribution apply as if the child had been
born legitimate.[1]

(c) The Family Law Reform Act 1969[2] provides that, where Illegitimate.
death occurs after 1969, an illegitimate child shall be entitled to
share in the intestacy of both his parents equally with their
legitimate issue. Both parents are equally entitled to share in
his intestacy. On the other hand the Act does not abolish the
distinction between legitimate and illegitimate birth for the purposes of intestacy. An illegitimate child may not take under the
intestacy of collaterals or of ancestors more remote than parents.
Nor may any person take under the intestacy of an illegitimate if
he dies without leaving issue, a surviving spouse or either parent.
For the purposes of distribution an illegitimate child is presumed
not to have been survived by his father, unless the contrary is
shown.

The statutory trusts. Whenever the property is distri- The
butable among a class of persons the members of which may be statutory
indefinite in number and some of them under age, the Act provides trusts.
that it shall be held for them on the *statutory trusts*.[3] This is so
in the case of issue, brothers, sisters, uncles and aunts, but not in
the case of parents or grandparents.

The statutory trusts for the issue mean that the property is Statutory
held in trust in equal shares for the children of the intestate alive trusts for
at his death who attain the age of eighteen or who, whether male the issue.
or female, marry under that age. Thus the children take *per
capita*. But if a child predeceases the intestate leaving issue alive
at the death of the intestate, such issue as attain eighteen or marry
represent their parent and take his share *per stirpes*.[4]

The result is that an infant, whether a child or more remote Position
issue, takes only a contingent share that will not vest until marriage during
or the attainment of majority. In the meantime, however, the of a
personal representatives may, at their sole discretion, apply the beneficiary.
whole or part of the income of the property to which the infant
is contingently entitled for or towards his maintenance, education
or benefit.[5] They may also apply the capital for his advancement
or benefit[6] to an amount not exceeding one-half of his presumptive

---

[1] Children Act 1975, s. 8, Sched. 1, paras. 12 (2), (3). In the case of intestacies occurring before January 1st, 1976, see Legitimacy Act 1926, ss. 3 (1)
(a), 4.
[2] S. 14. It does not apply to or affect the right of any person to take any
entailed property. S. 14 (5). Children Act 1975, s. 8, Sched. 1, para. 17.
[3] Unfortunately the same expression is used by L.P.A. 1925, in the entirely
different context of tenancies in common and joint tenancies, see *supra*, p. 223.
[4] A.E.A. 1925, s. 47 (1), as amended by Family Law Reform Act 1969,
s. 3 (2). When the intestate dies before 1970, the age remains twenty-one.
[5] A.E.A. 1925, s. 47 (1) (ii) ; T.A. 1925, s. 31 (1).
[6] *Pilkington* v. *I. R. Comrs.*, [1964] A.C. 612 ; [1962] 3 All E. R. 622.

share, but this must be brought into account when he becomes entitled to a vested interest at his majority or marriage.[1] Subject to the exercise of these powers, the personal representatives must accumulate the income at compound interest and hold the accumulation in trust for the infant.[2] The personal representatives may also permit any infant contingently entitled to have the use and enjoyment of any personal chattels in such manner and subject to such conditions (if any) as they may consider reasonable, and without being liable to account for any consequential loss.[3]

Statutory trusts illustrated. The operation of the statutory trusts may be elucidated by a simple illustration. Suppose the following facts :—

The intestate had four sons, A. to D. At his death,

A. and B. are alive.

C. is dead, but he is survived by two children, C.ᵃ and C.ᵇ both over 18 years of age.

D. and his son D.ᵃ are dead, but D.ᵃ left two daughters D.ᵇ and D.ᶜ who are alive at the intestate's death, but are still infants and unmarried.

The residuary estate, therefore, is divided into fourths. A. and B. each take one-fourth ; C.ᵃ and C.ᵇ represent their father, C., and share equally the fourth that would have accrued to him had he lived ; the infants, D.ᵇ and D.ᶜ, being issue of D., are equally, but contingently, entitled to the remaining fourth part. If one of them dies in infancy and still unmarried, her share passes to her sister. While their shares remain contingent, the income may be spent on their maintenance or education and up to one-half of the capital may be employed for their advancement or benefit.

Advancement to child deducted from his share under the intestacy.

Advancement to remoter issue not deducted.

Hotchpot.—The distribution of the property among the issue, however, is subject to what is called the *hotchpot rule*, which is designed to ensure equality of distribution. The rule, failing a contrary intention, is that any money or property which the intestate in his lifetime has paid to or settled on, or covenanted to pay to or settle on, a child, either by way of advancement or in view of marriage, shall be brought into account and deducted from the share which is payable to that child or to that child's issue under the intestacy.[4] If the advance was made directly to a grandchild (or remoter issue) it is not taken into account if that grandchild becomes entitled to share in the intestacy as representing his deceased parent.

---

[1] T.A. 1925, s. 32 (1).
[2] *Ibid.*, s. 31 (2).
[3] A.E.A. 1925, s. 47 (1) (iv), as added by I.E.A. 1952, s. 4 and 1st Sched.
[4] *Ibid.*, s. 47 (1) (iii). See (1961), 25 *Conv.* (N.S.) 469 (J. T. Farrand).

No absolute test can be laid down as to what constitutes an advancement for the purposes of the rule, but its broad meaning is a gift intended to make a permanent provision for the child—an intention that is more readily inferred if the sum is substantial and if it has been paid at an early stage in the life of the child.[1] It does not include casual payments or money given to relieve a child from some temporary embarrassment. Jessel, M.R., dealt with the matter in these words :— Meaning of advance-
ment.

> " I have always understood that an advancement by way of portion is something given by the parent to establish the child in life, or to make what is called a provision for him. . . . You may make the provision by way of marriage portion on the marriage of the child. You may make it on putting him into a profession or business in a variety of ways ; you may pay for a commission, you may buy him the goodwill of a business and give him stock in trade ; all these things I understand to be portions or provisions. Again, if in the absence of evidence you find a father giving a large sum to a child in one payment, there is a presumption that that is intended to start him in life or make a provision for him ; but if a small sum is so given you may require evidence to show the purpose." [2]

In the case from which these words are quoted it was held that the payment of the admission fee to an Inn of Court was an advancement, but that the price of an outfit and the passage money of a military officer who was going with his regiment to India, the payment of debts incurred by an officer in the army, and sums given to a clergyman towards his housekeeping expenses were not advancements.

The statutory trusts for brothers, sisters, uncles and aunts are the same as those applicable to issue, except that the hotchpot rule is excluded.[3] Statutory trusts for classes other than issue.

> If, for instance, the intestate dies unmarried leaving no parents, but survived by a brother and a nephew, the son of a deceased brother, his estate will be divided equally between these two survivors, and any advancement that he may have made in his lifetime to his deceased brother will not be deducted from the nephew's share.

Partial Intestacy.—The above rules apply to a case of partial intestacy, which occurs where a person leaves a will disposing only of part of his property. In these circumstances the property that is undisposed of is distributed among the persons in the manner and order applicable to a case of total intestacy. There is a distinction, however, between a total and partial in- Application of hotchpot rule to partial intestacy.

---

[1] *Re Hayward*, [1957] Ch. 528 ; [1957] 2 All E. R. 474 ; (1957) 73 L. Q. R. 21, 302 (R. E. M.) ; *Hardy* v. *Shaw* [1975] 2 W. L. R. 1002 ; [1975] 2 All E. R. 1052.

[2] *Taylor* v. *Taylor* (1875), L. R. 20 Eq. 155, 157.

[3] A.E.A. 1925, s. 47 (3) ; added by I.E.A. 1952, Sch. I. For the interpretation of s. 47 (5), see *Re Lockwood*, [1958] Ch. 231 ; [1957] 3 All E. R. 520.

testacy with regard to the hotchpot rule.   The position is this :—

First, the value of any beneficial interest, other than a bequest of chattels, left by the will to the surviving spouse must be set off against the sum of £15,000 or £40,000 (as the case may be)[1] payable to that spouse under the partial intestacy.[2]

Secondly, children must account for beneficial interests given to them by the will as well as for advancements made to them in the lifetime of the deceased.[3]

Thirdly, remoter issue must account for beneficial interests left to them by the will and for advancements made to children through whom they claim, but not for advancements made to them personally by the deceased in his lifetime.[4]

The term "beneficial interest" includes a life or a lesser interest[5] and also an interest given by the testamentary exercise of a general power of appointment, but not of a special power.[6]

---

[1] *Supra*, pp. 872–3.
[2] A.E.A. 1925, s. 49 (1) (*aa*) added by I.E.A. 1952, s. 3 (2).
[3] *Ibid.*, s. 49 (1) (*a*).
[4] *Ibid.*, s. 47 (1) (iii) ; 49 (1) (*a*).
[5] *Re Young*, [1951] Ch. 185 ; *Re Morton*, [1956] Ch. 644 ; [1956] 2 All E. R. 259.   *Re Grover's Will Trusts*, [1971] Ch. 168 ; [1970] 1 All E. R. 1185.   See also *Re Bowen-Buscarlet's Will Trusts*, [1972] Ch. 463 ; [1971] 3 All E. R. 636, (1973) 26 C. L. P. 208 (E. C. Ryder).
[6] A.E.A. 1925, s. 49, added by I.E.A. 1952, s. 3 (3).

BOOK III

THE TRANSFER AND EXTINCTION OF ESTATES AND INTERESTS

PART V

EXTINCTION OF ESTATES AND INTERESTS

SUMMARY

CHAPTER I

EXTINCTION UNDER THE STATUTES OF LIMITATIONS

SUMMARY

SECTION I.   INTRODUCTORY NOTE

Most systems of law have realized the necessity of fixing some   Necessity
definite period of time within which persons who have been unlaw- for Statutes
fully dispossessed of their land must pursue their claims.   It of Limita-
is, no doubt, an injustice that after this period has elapsed the tions.
wrongdoer should be allowed to retain the land against the person
whom he has ousted, but it would be an even greater injustice
to the world at large if the latter were allowed after any interval
of time, however long, to commence proceedings for recovery of

possession.   If A., having ejected B., is allowed to remain in long and undisturbed possession of the land, the impression will grow that his title is superior to B.'s, and the public should be allowed to deal safely with him on that footing.   As Lord ST. LEONARDS remarked[1]:

> " All statutes of limitation have for their object the prevention of the rearing up of claims at great distances of time when evidences are lost ;   and in all well-regulated countries the quieting of possession is held an important point of policy."

Operation of English statutes is negative.

The effect of a person remaining in possession of the land of another for the period of time fixed by law varies in different countries and in different ages.   Thus the effect of *usucapio* in Roman Law was to confer a positive title to the land upon a person who had remained in possession for a certain time.   Under the Statutes of Limitation which were in force in England prior to 1833 the effect of remaining in possession for the prescribed period was to bar only the remedy of the person dispossessed, not his right.   His *title* remained intact, and if he came lawfully into possession of the land again, his title might prevail against the possessor.[2]   Under the statutes that have been in force since 1833[3] the effect of remaining in possession for the statutory period of twelve years is still merely negative, but now in the sense that the right as well as the remedy of the person dispossessed is extinguished.   The *usucapio* of Roman Law exemplified what is sometimes called acquisitive prescription in the sense that possession of another's land for a given period conferred a positive title upon the occupier, or squatter as he is familiarly described, but English law has never adopted this theory in its treatment of corporeal hereditaments and chattels, though it has done so in the case of easements and profits.

The modern Acts.

The English law relating to the period within which an action for the recovery of land must be brought was recast and simplified by the Real Property Limitation Act of 1833, and was finally consolidated and amended by the Limitation Act 1939.   Originally the period was fixed at the discretion of individual judges.   Later, certain dates (such as the first coronation of Henry II) were chosen from time to time by the legislature.   Then in 1623 the Limitation Act introduced the modern principle that actions must be brought within a fixed number of years.   But even so the state of the law was unsatisfactory owing to the variety of remedies that lay for the recovery of land, and to the fact that the period of limitation varied according to the nature of the remedy adopted.   An account of the old law must, however,

---

[1] *Dundee Harbour Trustees* v. *Dougall* (1852), 1 Macq. 317.   See too *R. B. Policies at Lloyd's* v. *Butler*, [1950] 1 K. B. 76 at p. 81 ;   [1949] 2 All E. R. 226, at p. 229.

[2] Lightwood, *Possession of Land*, p. 153.

[3] Real Property Limitation Act 1833 ;   Real Property Limitation Act 1874 ;   Limitation Act 1939.

be sought in works on legal history.[1]   We will confine ourselves to describing the law as it has been established by the Limitation Act 1939.[2]

SECTION II. PERIOD OF LIMITATION FOR ACTIONS TO RECOVER LAND

The Act has retained the old law by enacting that no action shall be brought to recover any land after the expiration of twelve years from the date on which the *right of action accrued* to the plaintiff, or to the person through whom he claims.[3]   This limitation applies to a foreclosure action.[4] {Normal period : twelve years.}

" Land " is defined in wide terms.   It includes[5] :

> " corporeal hereditaments, tithes[6] (except tithes belonging to a spiritual or eleemosynary corporation sole), and rentcharges, and any legal or equitable estate or interest therein, including an interest in the proceeds of the sale of land held upon trust for sale, but save as aforesaid does not include any incorporeal hereditament."

It will be observed that although land held upon trust for sale is deemed to be money under the doctrine of conversion,[7] yet the interests of the beneficiaries in the proceeds of sale are regarded as interests in land for the purposes of limitation.

There are certain exceptional cases in which the ordinary period of twelve years is increased. {Exceptions.}

Actions by the Crown.—The Crown Suits Act 1769, generally called the *Nullum Tempus Act*, altered the ancient rule that Statutes of Limitations do not bind the Crown and prescribed a period of sixty years in the case of an action to recover land.   This period is now reduced to thirty years,[8] and there is a general provision that the " Act shall apply to proceedings by or " against the Crown in like manner as it applies to proceedings " between subjects." [9]   An action to recover land brought *against* the Crown, however, is subject to the twelve years' period. {Actions by Crown : thirty years.}

Action by Corporation Sole.   An action to recover land by a spiritual or an eleemosynary corporation sole, such as a bishop, dean or master of a hospital, must be brought within {Actions by corporation sole : thirty years.}

---

[1] See especially Hayes, *Introduction to Conveyancing*, vol. i. pp. 222 *et seq.* ; Holdsworth, *History of English Law*, vol. iv. p. 484 ; vol. vii. pp. 29 *et seq.* ; Simpson, *Introduction to History of Land Law*, pp. 141–5.

[2] See generally Preston and Newsom, *Limitation of Actions* (3rd Edn.).

[3] Limitation Act 1939, s. 4 (3).   An appointee under a special power is not deemed to claim through the appointor, s. 31 (4).

[4] *Ibid.*, s. 18 (4).   [5] *Ibid.*, s. 31 (1).

[6] This means uncommuted tithes, not tithe rentcharge.   These, though rare, are occasionally found.

[7] *Supra*, p. 81.

[8] Limitation Act 1939, s. 4 (1).   It remains 60 years where foreshore is owned by the Crown.

[9] *Ibid.*, s. 30 (1).   This applies to proceedings by or against the Duke of Cornwall or the Duchy of Lancaster.

thirty years after the date on which the right of action accrued to the corporation or to the person through whom the corporation claims.[1] The ordinary period of twelve years applies in the case of a corporation aggregate, such as one of the colleges of Oxford or Cambridge.

Meaning of
" claiming
through
a person ". In the case of the Crown or a spiritual or eleemosynary corporation the position with regard to *claiming through a person* may be illustrated by examples :

> The Crown purchases from X. in 1970 land which is in the wrongful possession of a third party.

If a right of action to recover the land from the wrongful possessor accrued to X. more than twelve years before 1970, X.'s title is extinguished and the Crown acquires nothing. If, however, X.'s right of action accrued less than twelve years before 1970, say in 1965, then the Crown can sue the wrongdoer at any time within thirty years after 1965.[2]

The reverse case arises where a person claims through the Crown or a corporation sole after a cause of action has already accrued, as for example where,

> in 1970 the Crown conveys to X. land which has been in the wrongful possession of W. P. since 1950.

The statutory rule here is that X.'s remedy against W. P. is barred either thirty years after 1950, when the cause of action accrued to the Crown, or twelve years after the cause of action accrued to himself, *whichever period expires first*.[3] The cause of action accrued to X. by virtue of the conveyance of 1970, but nevertheless his remedy is barred in 1980.

Advowsons. No patron may bring an action to enforce a right to present to or bestow any ecclesiastical benefice after the period during which three successive incumbencies have been held adversely to the right, or sixty years of adverse possession, whichever is the longer, with a maximum of one hundred years.[4]

SECTION III. THE DATE FROM WHICH TIME BEGINS TO RUN

SUMMARY

		PAGE
(A) Present interests		889
(B) Future interests		892
(C) Forfeiture or breach of condition		893
(D) Settled land and land held on trust		893
(E) Tenancies		896

---

[1] Limitation Act 1939, s. 4 (2). The former period was two successive incumbencies plus six years after a third incumbent had been appointed, *or* sixty years, whichever was the longer period ; Real Property Limitation Act 1833, s. 29.

[2] *Ibid.*, s. 4 (1), (2).   [3] *Ibid.*, s. 4 (3) proviso.

[4] *Ibid.*, s. 14.

Time begins to run against a plaintiff only from the date on which the right of action accrued to him or to the person through whom he claims. In the case of land, as distinct from other cases such as contract or tort, the Act lays down specific rules fixing the date at which in varying circumstances this accrual occurs. It deals separately with present interests, future interests, settled land, land held on trust for sale, tenancies and forfeiture or breach of condition.

Before dealing with these different cases, however, it is necessary to notice an overriding provision of the greatest importance. This is that time does not begin to run from the specified dates unless there is some person in adverse possession of the land. It does not run merely because the land is vacant.[1] There must be both absence of possession by the plaintiff and adverse possession by the defendant.

This rule, founded on the obvious reason that a right of action cannot accure unless there is somebody against whom it can be asserted, was well established after the Real Property Limitation Act 1833, in the case where an *actual possessor* left possession vacant, though there was some doubt whether it applied where the land of a deceased owner remained vacant owing to the failure of the person entitled thereto to take possession. All doubts are now dispelled, for each statutory rule fixing the date at which the right of action accrues is subject to the overriding condition that there must be some person in possession of the land in whose favour time can run. This condition is enacted in the following words [2]:

> " No right of action to recover land shall be deemed to accrue unless the land is in the possession of some person in whose favour

Marginal notes: Time runs from accrual of right of action. Time does not run unless land occupied by adverse possessor.

---

[1] *M'Donnell* v. *M'Kinty* (1847), 10 I. L. R. 514 ; *Smith* v. *Lloyd* (1854), 9 Exch. 562.

[2] Limitation Act 1939, s. 10 (1). "Adverse possession " bore a technical meaning before the Real Property Limitation Act 1833. Before that date wrongful possession did not ripen into a claim to bar the owner's remedy unless there had been ouster of the seisin in one of five ways (for which see Carson, *Real Property Statutes*, notes to R.P.L.A. 1833, s. 2). Moreover, possession where possible was referred to a lawful title, and there were several cases where possession obviously held without title was held not to be "adverse." For instance, possession of a younger brother was possession of the heir ; possession of one co-parcener, joint tenant or tenant in common was the possession of all, unless an intention to claim the whole was expressed ; tenant for years continued to hold for lessor after the lease ended ; if a squatter was entitled to an interest in the land less in extent than that which he claimed under the statute, his possession was referred to his lawful title ; see *Lightwood on Possession*, pp. 159 *et seq.* Lord St. Leonards described the effect of the 1833 Act in these words : " It is perfectly settled that adverse possession is no longer necessary in the sense in which it was formerly used, but that mere possession may be and is sufficient under many circumstances to give a title adversely " : *Ely (Dean)* v. *Bliss* (1852), 2 De G. M. & G. at pp. 476–7. The effect of the Act was " to substitute for a period of adverse possession in the old sense a simple period of time calculated from the accrual of the right of action " : Preston and Newsom, *Limitation of Actions* (3rd Edn.), p. 87. So " adverse possession " is now a useful expression to describe the possession of those

the period of limitation can run (hereafter in this section referred to as adverse possession), and where ... any such right of action is deemed to accrue on a certain date and no person is in adverse possession on that date, the right of action shall not be deemed to accrue unless and until adverse possession is taken of the land." [1]

Successive adverse possessors.

This general principle may be illustrated by the case where the adverse possessor (let us call him X.) fails for one reason or another to occupy for the full period of twelve years. In this connection there are four possible situations which must be considered separately.

(*a*) Successor of deceased adverse possessor.

(*a*) X. dies or transfers his interest to another person before the lapse of twelve years.

The principle obtaining here is that since possession is *prima facie* evidence of seisin in fee, X. holds a transmissible interest in the land. The time during which he has possessed is available to his successor in title, and therefore a purchaser or devisee who immediately follows him into possession and holds for the remainder of the twelve years acquires as good a right to the land as if he himself had been in possession for the whole period.[2]

(*b*) Adverse possessor leaves land vacant.

(*b*) Possession is abandoned by X. and is not retaken by another person.

After this abandonment the dispossessed person is in the same position as if he had never been deprived of possession by X. There is no one whom he can now sue. There is no need for him to perform some act or ceremony in order to rehabilitate himself. The former possession of X., as Lord MACNAGHTEN said, is not available to "some casual interloper or lucky vagrant."[3] This rule is now confirmed by section 10 (2) of the Limitation Act 1939 :—

" Where a right of action to recover land has accrued and thereafter, before the right is barred, the land ceases to be in adverse possession, the right of action shall no longer be deemed to have accrued and no fresh right of action shall be deemed to accrue unless and until the land is again taken into adverse possession."

(*c*) Land left vacant by one adverse possessor is taken by another.

(*c*) Possession is abandoned by X. and *after an interval of time* is taken by Y.

---

against whom a right of action has accrued to the owner.   See generally, Smith's *Leading Cases* (12th Edn.), vol. ii. pp. 667 *et seq.*; *Lightwood on Possession*, pp. 159 *et seq.*, pp. 180–1, Holdsworth, *History of English Law*, vol. vii. pp. 69–72, 78–9.   See *Paradise Beach and Transportation Co., Ltd.* v. *Price-Robinson*, [1968] A. C. 1072 ; [1968] 1 All E. R. 530.

[1] *Moses* v. *Lovegrove*, [1953] 2 Q. B. 533 ; [1952] 1 All E. R. 1279.   The mere fact that the premises become subject to the Rent Acts, so that possession cannot be recovered without a court order, does not prevent the tenant's possession from being adverse.   See too *Hughes* v. *Griffin*, [1969] 1 W. L. R. 23 ; [1969] 1 All E. R. 460.

[2] *Asher* v. *Whitlock* (1865), L. R. 1 Q. B. 1; M. & B. p. 161.

[3] *Trustees, Executors and Agency Co., Ltd.* v. *Short* (1888), 13 App. Cas. 793, at p. 798; explained by PARKER, J., in *Samuel Johnson and Sons, Ltd.* v. *Brock*, [1907] 2 Ch. 533, 538 ; (1956), 19 *M. L. R.* p. 22, note 11 (A. D. Hargreaves).

It follows from what was said by Lord MACNAGHTEN and from what is now enacted, that in this case the time during which X. has occupied is not available to Y., for during a distinct and definite period there was no person against whom the person ousted by X. could bring an action for the recovery of the land. Y. is not a successor in title of X., and his intrusion causes a fresh right of action to accrue in favour of the person dispossessed by X.

(*d*) X. loses possession and is followed by a succession of trespassers each claiming adversely to the others.

(*d*) Continuous adverse possession by several persons.

Here there is no distinct interval of time during which the possession is vacant. X., for instance, ejects V., Y. ejects X., Z. ejects Y., and is in actual possession when the statutory period of twelve years has run from the time of V.'s ejectment. Who is entitled to succeed in an action to recover the land ? [1] Objection may be taken to the title of each of these persons, for V. has been out of possession for more than twelve years, and yet none of the trespassers has been in possession for that period. Nevertheless, V. is barred.

"A *continuous* adverse possession for the statutory period, though by a succession of persons not claiming under one another, does, in my opinion, bar the true owner." [2]

As for the trespassers, something might be said by the moralist for the earliest possessor, also for the one who has possessed for the longest period, and again for the latest possessor,[3] but it is clear that these conflicting claims must be decided in accordance with the general principle that possession is evidence of title.[4] X., while in possession, is ejected by Y. His possession, therefore, entitles him to recover the land from the wrongdoer, Y. If he takes no proceedings, then Y., upon being ejected by Z., may recover upon the strength of his existing possession.

"Possession being once admitted to be a root of title, every possession must create a title which, as against all subsequent intruders, has all the incidents and advantages of a true title." [5]

We are now in a position to deal with the accrual of the cause of action in the different cases described by the statute.

(A) PRESENT INTERESTS

Time does not begin to run against a person in present possession of land until possession has been taken by another person. The Act states the rule in this way [6] :

Accrual at dispossession or discontinuance.

"Where the person bringing an action to recover land, or some person though whom he claims, has been in possession thereof, and

---

[1] See Pollock and Wright, *Possession in the Common Law*, pp. 95 *et seq.* Lightwood, *Possession of Land*, pp. 275 *et seq.*

[2] *Willis* v. *Earl Howe*, [1893] 2 Ch. 545, at p. 553, *per* KAY, L.J.

[3] *Dixon* v. *Gayfere* (*No.* 1) (1853), 17 Beav. 421, at p. 430 *per* Lord ROMILLY.

[4] *Asher* v. *Whitlock* (1865), L. R. 1 Q. B. 1, at p. 6 ; approved, *Perry* v. *Clissold*, [1907] A. C. 73 ; Pollock and Wright, *op. cit.*, p. 98.

[5] Pollock and Wright, *op. cit.*, p. 95. [6] S. 5 (1).

has while entitled thereto been *dispossessed* or *discontinued his possession*, the right of action shall be deemed to have accrued on the date of the dispossession or discontinuance."

This language is not altogether happy, for, unless the true meaning of " discontinuance " is appreciated, it might be thought that a mere abandonment of possession is sufficient to set time running.[1]   This is not so, however, for the factor common to dispossession and discontinuance is entry upon the land by a stranger.

> " The difference," said FRY, J., " between dispossession and the discontinuance of possession might be expressed in this way : the one is where a person comes in and drives out the others from possession, the other case is where the person in possession goes out and is followed in by others." [2]

What constitutes adverse possession.

Dispossession. The question whether a person has been dispossessed so as to set time running against him does not always admit of a ready answer.   Some cases, of course, may be obvious, as for instance where a stranger occupies the house of another or encloses and cultivates a strip of his neighbour's land.[3]   In a doubtful case, however, the acts claimed to constitute possession, whether by the plaintiff or the defendant, must be considered relatively to the nature of the land.[4]   Regard must be had, in other words, both to the kind of enjoyment that is possible and to the intention of the owner.   The mere fact that X. has interfered in some way with the land of A. is not enough to show adverse possession in him ; he must go further and prove some act which is inconsistent with the form of enjoyment that is available to, or intended by, A.   If the act of interference precludes A. from exploiting the land in the manner he intended, there is dispossession, otherwise not.   The leading case on the subject is *Leigh* v. *Jack*,[5] where the facts were these :

> In 1854 the plaintiff conveyed to the defendant a plot of land on the south side of a strip of land which it was intended to make into a street.   In 1872 the defendant took a conveyance of the land to the north of the strip.   The strip was never dedicated by the plaintiff to the public as a highway, and the defendant used it for various pur-

---

[1] Preston and Newsom, *Limitation of Actions* (3rd Edn.), p. 99.   See *Techild Ltd.* v. *Chamberlain* (1969), 20 P. & C. R. 633.

[2] *Rains* v. *Buxton* (1880), 14 Ch. D. 537, 539–40.

[3] *Marshall* v. *Taylor*, [1895] 1 Ch. 641.   " It must be a very exceptional case in which enclosure . . . will not demonstrate the relevant adverse possession required for a possessory title."   *George Wimpey & Co., Ltd.* v. *Sohn*, [1967] Ch. 487, at p. 512 ; [1966] 1 All E. R. 232, *per* RUSSELL, L.J.   And that case illustrates the exception.   Cultivation without fencing may, however, amount to adverse possession.   *Seddon* v. *Smith* (1877), 36 L. T. 168.

[4] Preston and Newsom, *op. cit.*, pp. 102–3.

[5] (1879), 5 Ex. D. 264 ; M. & B. p. 150 ; followed in *Littledale* v. *Liverpool College*, [1900] 1 Ch. 19 ; *Williams Brothers Direct Supply, Ltd.* v. *Raftery*, [1958] 1 Q. B. 159 ; [1957] 3 All E. R. 593 ; *George Wimpey & Co., Ltd.* **v.** *Sohn, supra* ; *West Bank Estates, Ltd.* v. *Arthur*, [1967] 1 A. C. 665 ; *Bligh* v. *Martin*, [1968] 1 W. L. R. 804 ; [1968] 1 All E. R. 1157 ; *Wallis's Cayton Bay Holiday Camp, Ltd.* v. *Shell-Mex and B.P., Ltd.*, [1975] Q. B. 94 ; [1974] 3 All E. R. 575 ; (1975) 39 Conv. (N.S.) 57 (F. R. Crane).

poses connected with his own property. For instance, from 1854 he regularly encumbered it with materials used at his factory so as to close it to all except pedestrians; in 1865 he enclosed an oblong portion of it; and in 1872 he fenced in the ends. Within a few years of the action the plaintiff had repaired the fence.

It was held that the plaintiff had not lost his title to the land. His intention was to dedicate it to the use of the public, and therefore his failure to exploit it for his own advantage was consistent with that intention and therefore did not constitute a discontinuance of possession. Neither had he been dispossessed by the acts of the defendant, for these were not inconsistent with the ultimate use of the land as a public way. They were not done *animo possidendi*, *i.e.* with the intention of excluding the plaintiff and all other persons.

Deceased person in possession at death. When A., the person entitled to land, dies while still in possession, and a stranger seizes possession after his death, time begins to run from the date of his death, not from the wrongful seizure, against those who claim under his will or upon his intestacy.[1] The same rule applies to a rentcharge created by will or taking effect upon death.[2]

Failure to acquire possession on death.

Grant of present interest. Where an interest in possession has been granted to A., or where the land has been charged in his favour with the payment of a rentcharge, and he has not taken possession or has not received the rent, time begins to run against him from the date of the grant.[3]

Failure to acquire possession under a grant.

So far as a rentcharge is concerned this rule meets the case where the chargor has never made a payment of the money due.

Rentcharge.

Where, however, he wrongfully makes payment to a stranger,[4] the statutory rule is that time shall begin to run against the chargee from "the date of the last receipt of rent" by him.[5] The result of this is to reduce the limitation period of twelve years, for normally a right of action would accrue and time would begin to run, not from the last receipt of rent, but from the date when the rent again became due.

If, for example, the rent is payable annually on September 29, and payment is duly made on that date in 1974, no *right of action or of distraint* accrues until September 29, 1975.

Nevertheless time begins to run under the statute on September 29, 1974, so that in effect the period of limitation is reduced to eleven years.[6]

---

[1] Limitation Act 1939, s. 5 (2), replacing Real Property Limitation Act 1833, s. 3, second branch.
[2] *Ibid.*
[3] *Ibid.*, s. 5 (3), replacing Real Property Limitation Act, s. 3, third branch.
[4] See generally Preston and Newsom, *Limitation of Actions* (3rd Edn.), pp 118 *et seq.*
[5] Limitation Act 1939, s. 31 (6).
[6] *Owen* v. *De Beauvoir* (1847), 16 M. & W. 547.

(B) FUTURE INTERESTS

Accrual
depends
upon
whether
preceding
owner
continues
in possession.

The date upon which time begins to run against the owner of a future interest depends upon whether the person entitled to the preceding estate was in possession when it came to an end. Suppose, for instance, that there is a

grant to A. for life, remainder to B. in fee simple,

and that B. fails to take possession on the death of A. In such a case the statute enacts alternative rules.

(i) If A. dies while still possessed of the land, B.'s right of action accrues upon the determination of the life interest, *i.e.* he must sue within twelve years from the death of A.[1]

(ii) If A. is not in possession at death, *e.g.* where he has been dispossessed by a stranger, B. has the longer of two alternative periods within which he may bring his action, namely, twelve years from the time when the cause of action accrued to A., or six years from the death of A.[2]

This second rule does not apply where the preceding estate is a term of years absolute.[3] Thus time does not begin to run against a landlord until the lease determines, even though the tenant may have been ejected before that date.[4]

Future
interests
expectant
upon
entailed
interest.

Neither rule applies to an interest limited after an entailed interest which is capable of being barred by the tenant in tail.[5] In this case the remainderman " claims through " the tenant in tail, so that if time has commenced running against the latter it continues to run against the remainderman, and does not start afresh upon the determination of the entail.

Settlement
made by
person
against
whom time
is already
running.

Future interests created by a settlor after time has commenced to run against him are subject to a different rule. The second case given above contemplates that *after* the settlement in favour of B. has been made, a right of action accrues to A., the owner of the preceding estate, against an adverse possessor. In those circumstances, as we have seen, B. may recover the land within six years from the death of A., though it may be more than twelve years since A. was wrongfully dispossessed. But if time once begins to run against a settlor, no *subsequent* alteration in his title, *e.g.* by the later creation of future interests, will prevent the bar from operating after the lapse of twelve years. The persons deriving title from the settlor cannot be in a better position than he is.[6]

---

[1] Limitation Act 1939, s. 6 (1).

[2] *Ibid.*, s. 6 (2). The corresponding periods are thirty years and twelve years where the Crown or a spiritual or eleemosynary corporation is entitled to the future interest. [3] *Ibid.*

[4] *Infra*, p. 896.

[5] Limitation Act 1939, s. 6 (3). [6] *Ibid.*, s. 6 (4).

" Thus, if A., seised in fee in possession, were dispossessed by B., and were afterwards to settle the estate upon C. for life, remainder to D. in fee, the time would run from the dispossession, in the same manner as if no such settlement had been made."[1]

Where a person is entitled to successive interests in land, one present the other future, the general principle is that, if his present interest is barred, the bar shall extend also to his future right.[2] Thus if land stands limited,

One person entitled to successive interests.

to A. for life, remainder to B. for life, remainder to A. in fee simple,

and A. is dispossessed for twelve years, he and those claiming under him lose the right to recover both the life interest and the fee simple in remainder. The right to recover the fee simple, however, is not barred if, to quote the words of the Act, " possession has been recovered by a person entitled to an intermediate estate or interest." [3]

If, for instance, in the example just given, B. were to recover possession after A. had been dispossessed for twelve years, a right of recovery in respect of the fee simple would accrue to A., and those claiming under him, upon the death of B.

(C) FORFEITURE OR BREACH OF CONDITION

A right of action to recover land by virtue of a forfeiture or breach of condition accrues on the date on which the forfeiture was incurred or the condition broken. If, however, a reversioner or remainderman fails to take advantage of the forfeiture or breach of condition he still retains the right of recovery that accrues to him when his estate falls into possession.[4]

Time runs from breach of condition.

" So if A., lessee for years, subject to a condition of re-entry, breaks the condition, the time runs against the reversioner in respect of his right of entry for the breach from its occurrence ; but a bar to such right of entry will not affect his right to enter on the expiration of the lease by effluxion of time."[5]

(D) SETTLED LAND AND LAND HELD ON TRUST

Equitable interests in land, such as a life interest under a settlement and equitable interests in the proceeds of sale of land held upon trust for sale, are " land " within the meaning of the Limitation Act 1939.[6] In general, the provisions of the Act apply to these interests in like manner as they apply to legal estates, and the right to sue for the recovery of the

Application of the statute to equitable interests.

---

1 Hayes, *Introduction to Conveyancing*, vol. i. p. 257.
2 Limitation Act 1939, s. 6 (5).
3 *Ibid.*, replacing Real Property Limitation Act 1833, s. 20.
4 *Ibid.*, s. 8, replacing Real Property Limitation Act 1833, s. 3, fifth branch, and s. 4.
5 Hayes, *Introduction to Conveyancing*, vol. i. p. 252.
6 Limitation Act 1939, s. 31 (1).

land is deemed to accrue to the person entitled in possession on the date on which it would accrue if his interest were a legal estate.[1] Where such equitable interests exist the legal estate will, according to the circumstances, be vested in a tenant for life or statutory owner, or in personal representatives or in trustees for sale, all of whom are trustees for the purposes of the Act.[2]

There are two circumstances in which the beneficiaries entitled to the equitable interests may be affected by wrongful possession.

(i) the trustee in possession may disregard the rights of the beneficiaries.

(ii) a stranger may seize possession and hold it adversely to the beneficiaries.

Statute does not run in favour of trustee.

The first case raises no difficulty, for a trustee cannot obtain a title to the land by adverse possession against the beneficiaries. It is expressly enacted that no period of limitation shall apply to an action brought by a beneficiary,

> (a) in respect of any fraud or fraudulent breach of trust to which the trustee was a party or privy ; or
>
> (b) *to recover from the trustee trust property or the proceeds thereof in the possession of the trustee* or previously received by the trustee and converted to his use.[3]

Thus, if a person, who is in possession of land as trustee for A. and B., pays the whole of the profits to A., time does not run against B.[4] Even a notional receipt of property may come within this enactment. Thus, a trustee who remains in occupation of trust land for his own benefit is deemed to have received profits belonging to the beneficiaries, since in the circumstances he is chargeable with an occupation rent. Therefore, he can never escape liability for payment of this by pleading lapse of time, unless, indeed, under the equitable doctrine of laches, a beneficiary has been so tardy in bringing his action that it would be practically unjust to grant him relief.[5]

Effect upon tenancies in common.

The statutory provision (b) has an important effect upon tenancies in common. Where land is limited to A. and B. as tenants in common in fee, the beneficiaries become, as we have seen,[6] joint tenants and trustees of the legal estate upon trust to sell the land and to give effect to their own beneficial interests. If, therefore, A. appropriates the whole of the rents and profits to himself for many years, he does not acquire a title against B.,

---

[1] Limitation Act 1939, s. 7 (1).
[2] *Ibid.*, s. 31 (1).
[3] *Ibid.*, s. 19 (1).
[4] *Knight* v. *Bowyer* (1858), 2 De G. & J. 421 ; see Preston and Newsom, *Limitation of Actions* (3rd Edn.), pp. 148, 169.
[5] *Re Howlett*, [1949] Ch. 767 ; [1949] 2 All E. R. 490.
[6] *Supra*, p. 222.

for, since the land is in his possession as trustee, time does not run in his favour.[1]

Where the claim is not comprised in classes (*a*) and (*b*), as for instance where it concerns an unauthorized investment, the beneficiary must sue the trustee within six years from the accrual of his cause of action.[2]

As regards (ii), that is to say, where a stranger seizes possession, the rule stated above, that the statutory provisions apply to equitable interests as well as to legal estates, if it stood alone, would mean that twelve years' possession held by the stranger adversely to the trustee would extinguish the legal estate and bar the remedy of the beneficiaries. This, however, is not so. It is provided by another section that [3] :

> Where possession of land has been held for twelve years adversely to the trustee (*i.e.* adversely to a tenant for life or statutory owner of settled land, or to trustees for sale), the legal estate shall not be extinguished so long as the right of a beneficiary to recover the land has not accrued or has not been barred.

Thus the legal estate is not extinguished until the right of action of the *beneficiary* is barred. There is a further provision that a statutory owner or a trustee may sue for the recovery of the land on behalf of a beneficiary whose title to the equitable interest has not been barred.[4] By way of illustration :

> Suppose that land is settled upon A. for life with remainder to B. in fee simple, and that a stranger seizes the land in A's. lifetime and remains in adverse possession for twelve years.

In these circumstances the *beneficial* life interest of A. is extinguished, with the result that the adverse possessor acquires an equitable interest *pur autre vie*. Nevertheless the *legal fee simple*, held by A. under the provisions of the Settled Land Act 1925, remains intact, and therefore B., as the owner of a future interest, will be able to enforce his right of action when it accrues to him upon the death of A. When that event occurs, the representatives of A., upon whom his legal fee simple devolves, may recover the land on behalf of B. [5]

The only case remaining for consideration is where a *beneficiary* claims title by virtue of adverse possession for twelve years. Under the law as it stood before 1940 such a person, although he was ordinarily regarded as tenant at will of the trustee, acquired a title by twelve years' possession if he occupied the land to the

Marginal notes:

Time does not run against trustee until beneficiary is barred.

Time does not run against trustee in favour of beneficiary.

---

[1] *Re Landi*, [1939] Ch. 828 ; *Re Milking Pail Farm Trusts*, [1940] Ch. 996 ; Preston and Newsom, *Limitation of Actions* (3rd Edn.), pp. 149–51. See (1941), 57 *L. Q. R.* 26 (R. E. M.); (1971) 35 Conv. (N.S.) 6 (G. Battersby).
[2] Limitation Act 1939, s. 19 (2).
[3] *Ibid.*, s. 7 (2), (3).   [4] *Ibid.*, s. 7 (4).
[5] See generally Preston and Newsom, *op. cit.*, pp. 143–6.

exclusion of the trustees and the other beneficiaries.[1] Now, however, his possession cannot be adverse to these persons, for it is enacted that during his occupation of the land time shall not run against a tenant for life, statutory owner, trustee or beneficiary.[2]

(E) TENANCIES

Lessor's right against tenant accrues at end of lease.

Recovery of possession from the tenant. The right of action of a lessor to recover the land from the tenant accrues when the lease determines by effluxion of time.[3] He must, therefore, sue within twelve years from this date. The mere fact that he has received no rent for many years does not affect his right to recover the land within this period.[4]

Lessor's right to enforce a forfeiture.

If the lease contains a clause providing for the forfeiture of the premises upon non-payment of the rent, and if the rent is not paid within the stipulated period, the landlord acquires by virtue of this clause a right to recover the land during the continuance of the tenancy.[5] This right accrues to him, as we have seen, when the forfeiture is incurred,[6] but the fact that he fails to enforce it does not affect his right to recover the land within twelve years after the determination of the term. Moreover, his failure to enforce one forfeiture does not prejudice him with regard to the future. A fresh right of re-entry accrues to him on each occasion that the tenant defaults in payment.[7]

Rights of lessor and tenant against stranger.

Recovery of possession from a stranger. If a stranger enters upon land which is held by lease, time begins to run in his favour against the *tenant* from the moment when the latter is dispossessed ; but it does not begin to run against the *landlord* until the end of the lease, for it is only then that the landlord's right of action arises. The landlord must sue within the next twelve years, even though the existing lease is renewed in favour of the lessee while the stranger is still in possession.[8]

Time runs against lessor from adverse receipt of rent.

But since the receipt of rent is the only fact that symbolizes the landlord's title to the land, and since an adverse receipt by a stranger is really tantamount to dispossession, it is enacted that [9]:

> Where any person is in possession of land by virtue of a *written lease*, under which a yearly rent of not less than *twenty shillings* is reserved, and the rent is received by some person wrongfully claim-

---

[1] *Burroughs* v. *M'Creight* (1844), 1 Jo. & Lat. 200 (Ireland).

[2] Limitation Act 1939, s. 7 (5). But see Preston and Newsom, *Limitation of Actions* (3rd Edn.), p. 148.

[3] *Ibid.*, s. 6 (1).

[4] *Doe d. Davy* v. *Oxenham* (1840), 7 M. & W. 131.

[5] *Supra*, pp. 435–6.

[6] *Supra*, p. 893.

[7] *Barratt* v. *Richardson and Cresswell*, [1930] 1 K. B. 686.

[8] *Ecclesiastical Commissioners of England and Wales* v. *Rowe* (1880), 5 App. Cas. 736.

[9] Limitation Act 1939, s. 9 (3) ; re-enacting Real Property Limitation Act 1833, s. 9

ing to be entitled to the reversion, the landlord's right of action shall be deemed to have accrued at the time of the first wrongful receipt of rent, and not at the date of the determination of the lease.

Thus, if the rent is wrongfully received by a stranger for twelve years, both the right of action and the title of the landlord are irretrievably barred, but if before the twelve years have elapsed rent is once more received by him, his right of action revives.[1] If the lease is not in writing or if the annual rent is less than twenty shillings, adverse receipt of the rent does not set time running against the landlord.

Tenancies at will and from year to year have received special treatment.

1. **Tenancy at will.** Time begins to run against the lessor in either of two events. Time runs from determina-

First, from the determination of the tenancy.[2] The landlord may determine the tenancy either by demanding possession or by exercising some act of ownership on the land which is inconsistent with the right of the tenant. tion or from end of first year.

Secondly, in the absence of determination, time begins to run against the lessor at the end of one year from the beginning of the tenancy.[3] The object of this enactment is to make the possession of the tenant adverse at an early date, for otherwise he might remain in occupation for an indefinite period, making no payment and giving no acknowledgment of the lessor's title, without ever being able to acquire a valid and transferable title.

If, therefore, the lessor does nothing that constitutes a positive determination, his title is extinguished in thirteen years from the commencement of the tenancy, though a written and signed acknowledgment of his title given by the tenant before the expiration of thirteen years, will revive his cause of action.[4] Similarly, the determination of the old tenancy and the creation of a new one before the expiration of the thirteen years, will cause time to run afresh.[5] The payment of rent by the tenant does not *per se* prevent time running against the landlord, but if it is payable on a yearly basis the tenancy is converted into one from year to year.

These rules are confined to a tenancy at will properly so called. If, for instance, A. is given exclusive occupation of the land of B. for an indefinite period and the circumstances show that all that is intended is that he shall have a personal privilege with no interest in the land, he is not a tenant at will, but a licensee, and time does not run against B. under the Act.[6] Licence distin-guished from tenancy.

---

[1] Limitation Act 1939, ss. 16, 23 (4).
[2] *Ibid.*, s. 9 (1).
[3] *Ibid.*
[4] *Ibid.*, ss. 23 (1) ; 24 (1).
[5] *Doe d. Groves* v. *Groves* (1847), 10 Q. B. 486.
[6] *Cobb* v. *Lane*, [1952] 1 All E. R. 1199 ; *Hughes* v. *Griffin*, [1969] 1 W. L. R. 23 ; [1969] 1 All E. R. 460 ; *Heslop* v. *Burns*, [1974] 1 W. L. R. 1241 ; [1974] 3 All E. R. 406 ; M. & B. p. 371. *Supra*, pp. 399–401.

In the case of a tenancy at sufferance, time runs from the beginning of the tenancy.

Oral lease.

2. **Tenancy from year to year.**   In the case of a tenancy from year to year or other period *without a lease in writing*,[1] the right of the lessor to recover the land accrues either at the end of the first of such years or other period, or at the last receipt of rent, whichever shall last occur.[2]   If the tenant remains in possession without paying rent for twelve years after the right of action has arisen, and without giving a written acknowledgment of the lessor's title, the cause of action is effectually barred,[3] and a subsequent acknowledgment or payment of rent does not start time running afresh.[4]

Written lease.

If the lease is in writing the present rule does not apply, and the lessor's right of action accrues when he determines the tenancy by notice to quit.

Certain equitable claims subject to no statutory bar.

The doctrine of laches.   Despite the general rule that the provisions of the Limitation Act apply to equitable interests in land,[5] there are certain cases in which an equitable claim is unaffected by the statutory bars just discussed.   Thus, as we have seen, a claim by a beneficiary to recover trust property retained by a trustee or to recover damages from a fraudulent trustee is subject to no period of limitation.[6]   Again, the statutory bars do not apply to any claim for specific performance, an injunction or other equitable relief, except in so far as they may be applied by analogy to the Act.[7]

Effect of the equitable doctrine of laches.

Nevertheless, whenever a plaintiff seeks to enforce an equitable right to which no statute of limitation applies or to obtain a form of relief unknown to the common law, courts of equity have always required him to prosecute his claim with due diligence.   In pursuance of the maxim—*vigilantibus non dormientibus aequitas solverit*—they discourage what is called *laches*, a word that signifies the negligent failure of a plaintiff to take proceedings for the enforcement of his claim within a reasonable time after he has become aware of his rights.[8]   But the application of the doctrine of laches has always depended upon whether or not the suit in equity corresponds to an action at law that is within a statute of limitation.

If the equitable claim is substantially similar to a legal right

---

[1] The possession by the tenant of a rent book does not convert an oral into a written lease, *Moses* v. *Lovegrove*, [1953] 2 Q. B. 533 ; [1952] 1 All E. R. 1279.

[2] Limitation Act, 1939, s. 9 (2) ; re-enacting Real Property Limitation Act 1833, s. 8 ; *Re Jolly*, [1900] 2 Ch. 616, 619.

[3] *Hayward* v. *Challoner*, [1968] 1 Q. B. 107 ; [1967] 3 All E. R. 122 ; M. & B. p. 155.

[4] *Nicholson* v. *England*, [1926] 2 K. B. 93.

[5] Limitation Act 1939, s. 7 (1).

[6] *Ibid.*, s. 19 (1); *supra*, p. 894.   [7] *Ibid.*, s. 2 (7).

[8] For a detailed discussion, see Brunyate, *Limitation of Actions in Equity*, pp. 185 *et seq.* ; Preston and Newsom, *Limitation of Actions* (3rd Edn.), pp. 256–64 ; *Snell's Principles of Equity* (27th Edn.), pp. 33–6.

that is subject to a statutory bar, the courts act by analogy to the statute and enforce the same bar upon the equitable right of action.[1] Thus an action by a widow for the assignment to her of specific land in satisfaction of her right to dower, which lay in Chancery before the abolition of dower, would fail unless she started proceedings within the statutory period prescribed for an action of ejectment.[2] The court, however, will not adopt the analogous statutory bar if the equitable claim has been deliberately omitted from the Act as a matter of policy. Relevant examples are the right of a mortgagor to redeem a mortgage of personalty,[3] or of a beneficiary to recover trust property retained by a trustee.

(1) Effect where corresponding remedy at common law.

This principle of analogous application is now of much diminished importance, for the legislation of the 19th century, fortified by the Limitation Act 1939, has imposed a statutory bar upon most equitable claims.

If there is no corresponding claim or remedy at common law, or if, despite such correspondence, the equitable claim has been omitted from the statutory limitation as a matter of policy, equity applies its own test of unreasonable delay. Mere delay is seldom sufficient to constitute laches. It must be considered in the light of the circumstances.

(2) Effect where no corresponding remedy at law.

> " A defence based on staleness of demand renders it necessary to consider the time which has elapsed and the balance of justice and injustice in affording or refusing relief." [4]

At bottom, the enquiry is whether the reasonable inference from the delay and the attendant circumstances is that the plaintiff has acquiesced in the violation of his right, once it has become known to him, and thereby has in effect waived his claim against the defendant.[5] A further factor is whether the defendant has altered his position to his prejudice in the belief that the claim has been abandoned.[6]

Such will be the nature of the enquiry if laches is pleaded as a defence to an action by a beneficiary to recover property retained by a trustee ; by a mortgagor, to redeem a mortgage of pure personalty ;[7] or by a mortgagee to foreclose an equitable mortgage of an advowson.[8]

---

[1] *Knox* v. *Gye* (1872), L. R. 5 H. L. 656, at p. 674, *per* Lord WESTBURY.

[2] *Williams* v. *Thomas*, [1909] 1 Ch. 713.

[3] Waldock, *Law of Mortgages* (2nd Edn.), p. 199. An action to foreclose a mortgage of personalty is barred by the Limitation Act after twelve years, but not an action to redeem such a mortgage.

[4] *Re Sharpe*, [1892] 1 Ch. 154, at p. 168, *per* LINDLEY, L.J.

[5] See *Lindsay Petroleum Co.* v. *Hurd* (1874), L. R. 5 P. C. 221, at p. 239; approved in *Erlanger* v. *New Sombrero Phosphate Co.* (1878), 3 App. Cas. 1218, at p. 1279.

[6] *Allcard* v. *Skinner* (1887), 36 Ch. D. 145, at p. 192, *per* BOWEN, L.J.

[7] *Weld* v. *Petre*, [1929] 1 Ch. 33.

[8] *Brooks* v. *Muckleston*, [1909] 2 Ch. 519. Such an action of foreclosure is subject to no statutory bar, since an advowson, an incorporeal interest, is not "land" within the meaning of the Limitation Act 1939. Distinguish an action to enforce an advowson which is barred after the expiration of the relevant period prescribed by the Limitation Act 1939, s. 14. *Supra*, p. 886.

Doctrine of
laches still
enforced.

This doctrine of laches, which is of ancient origin, is preserved by the following provision of the Limitation Act 1939:

> " Nothing in this Act shall affect any equitable jurisdiction to refuse relief on the ground of acquiescence or otherwise."[1]

SECTION IV. THE NATURE OF THE TITLE ACQUIRED UNDER THE STATUTE

It is necessary to consider what effect the expiration of the statutory period produces upon the title to the land.

What is the effect upon the legal position, first, of the person dispossessed, secondly of the person who has held adverse possession for twelve years ?

Remedy
and title of
former
owner
extinguished.

When time has run against a claimant, the effect in every case, no matter whether his claim is founded on tort, breach of contract, dispossession of land or some other wrong, is to bar his *remedy*. As a general rule, however, his *right* is not barred. He is precluded by the extinction of his remedy from a resort to legal proceedings, but he is free to enforce his still existent right by any other method that may be available. Before 1833 this was the effect of adverse possession of land for the required period, but the Real Property Limitation Act of that year provided that at the end of the statutory period the right, as well as the remedy, of the dispossessed owner should be extinguished.[2] This rule is retained by the Limitation Act 1939 in a section which runs as follows [3]:

> " At the expiration of the period prescribed by this Act for any person to bring an action to recover land (including a redemption action) or an action to enforce an advowson, the title of that person to the land or advowson shall be extinguished."

Two
exceptions.
(i) Settled
land.

There are, however, two exceptions.

First, in the case of settled land and land held on trust for sale, as we have already seen, the title of the trustee to the legal estate is not extinguished until all the beneficiaries have been barred.[4]

(ii) Regis-
tered land.

Secondly, where a person registered as owner under the Land Registration Act 1925 is dispossessed for twelve years, his title is not forthwith extinguished, but he is deemed to hold the land upon trust for the adverse possessor.[5] The register may be rectified in favour of the latter if he makes application to that end, but no rectification will prejudice any other person interested in the land whose right has not been extinguished by lapse of time.[6]

In considering the extent to which the *status quo ante* of the parties is affected by the statutory extinguishment of the right of

---

[1] S. 29.   [2] S. 34.
[3] S. 16. S. 3 (2) has now extended the rule to conversion and detinue of chattels.
[4] *Supra*, p. 895.   [5] L.R.A. 1925, s. 75 (1).
[6] *Ibid.*, s. 75 (2), (3) ; *infra*, p. 908.

action, we will deal first with the former possessor and then with the
squatter.

What the dispossessed person loses. The dispossessed
person and those who claim through him lose the title to possession
that he could previously have enforced against the squatter. To
that extent, his title is finally destroyed and there is no method by
which it can be revived, not even by a written acknowledgment
given by the squatter.[1]

But the restricted effect of the extinguishment must be realized.
It extinguishes nothing more than the title of the dispossessed
against the squatter.[2] Thus, the dispossession of a lessee does not
destroy his lease. His title against the lessor remains good, so that,
for instance, he is entitled to resume possession if the land is vacated by the squatter. Likewise, the lessor remains entitled to sue
the lessee on the covenants or indeed to re-enter the land for a
forfeiture committed by the squatter if the lease contains a proviso
for forefeiture.[3]

A fortiori, the titles of third parties who have enforceable interests in the land, such as those entitled to the benefit of a
restrictive covenant, are unaffected by the adverse possession of
the land, for no remedy accrues to them until *their* rights have been
infringed.[4]

[Margin note: Title of dispossessed person against squatter alone extinguished.]

What the squatter acquires. It follows from what
has been said, that the sole, though substantial, privilege acquired
by a squatter is immunity from interference by the person dispossessed. In other words, the statutory effect of twelve years'
adverse possession is merely negative; not, as Baron PARKE once
said, "to make a parliamentary conveyance to the person in
possession."[5] This judicial heresy has long been exploded and it
is now recognised that:

[Margin note: Squatter acquires the right not to be disturbed by dispossessed person.]

> " we must not confound the negative effect of the statute with the
> positive effect of a conveyance." [6]

There is no transfer, statutory or otherwise, to the squatter of
the very title held by the dispossessed person.

[Margin note: The effect of the Limitation Act is merely negative.]

> " He is not at any stage of his possession a successor to the title of the
> man he has dispossessed. He comes in and remains in always by
> right of possession, which in due course becomes incapable of
> disturbance as time exhausts the one or more periods allowed by
> statute for successful intervention. His title, therefore, is never
> derived through but arises always in spite of the dispossessed
> owner." [7]

---

[1] *Nicholson* v. *England*, [1926] 2 K. B. 93.
[2] *Fairweather* v. *St. Marylebone Property Co., Ltd.*, [1963] A. C. 510, at
p. 539; [1962] 2 All E. R. 288, *per* Lord RADCLIFFE.
[3] *Ibid.*, at p. 545, *per* Lord DENNING.
[4] *Re Nisbet and Potts' Contract*, [1905] 1 Ch. 391 ; M. & B. p. 168 ; *supra*,
pp. 603–4.
[5] *Doe d. Jukes* v. *Sumner* (1845), 14 M. & W. 39, at p. 42.
[6] Hayes, *Introduction to Conveyancing*, vol. i, p. 269.
[7] *Fairweather* v. *St. Marylebone Property Co., Ltd.*, [1963] A. C. 510, at
p. 535; [1962] 2 All E. R. 288, *per* Lord RADCLIFFE.

Thus if a man ejects a tenant for years and remains in possession for the statutory period, he cannot be sued for breach of a repairing covenant contained in the lease, for there has been no transfer to him of the tenant's estate.[1] Again, any right enjoyed by the dispossessed person that is based upon an implied grant, such as a way of necessity, will not avail an adverse possessor, for the doctrine of implication cannot be imported into a statutory provision that is purely negative.[2]

Negative effect illustrated by dispossession of a lessee.

The decision of the House of Lords in *Fairweather* v. *St. Marylebone Property Co., Ltd.*,[3] is a further illustration of the rule that there is no transfer to a squatter of an interest commensurate with that held by the person dispossessed. The facts relevant to the present enquiry may be stated in a much simplified form as follows:

> A house and garden containing a shed were leased by X. to Y. for 99 years. The shed was occupied by a neighbour, Z., for more than twelve years adversely to Y. While the lease was still running, Y. surrendered it to the freeholder, X.
>
> The question was whether X., *qua* freeholder, could resume possession immediately or whether he had no such right until the lease determined by effluxion of time.

The majority of the House of Lords, overruling *Walter* v. *Yalden*,[4] gave judgment for X. Despite the title acquired by the squatter against Y. the lessee, the relationship between X. and Y. still continued with all its implications, including the right of Y. to retain possession as against X. By surrendering the lease, Y. had abandoned the right to possession, with the result that his tenancy had merged in the freehold and had disappeared. Therefore, the landlord could recover the shed on the strength of his own right to immediate possession of the freehold.[5]

The earlier decision of *Taylor* v. *Twinberrow*[6] was approved. In that case, the facts were in effect as follows:

> X., a yearly tenant, allowed Y. to occupy a cottage for more than thirteen years as a tenant at will. X. then bought the fee simple, with the result that the yearly tenancy was determined by its merger in the freehold. It was argued that the title acquired by Y. was commensurate with that lost by X.

---

[1] *Tichborne* v. *Weir* (1892), 67 L. T. 735; M. & B. p. 167; *supra*, p. 460.

[2] *Wilkes* v. *Greenway* (1890), 6 T. L. R. 449; similarly in registered land *Palace Court Garages (Hampstead), Ltd.* v. *Steiner* (1958), 108 Law Jo. 274.

[3] [1963] A. C. 510; [1962] 2 All E. R. 288; M. & B. p. 163.

[4] [1902] 2 K. B. 304.

[5] Lord Morris dissented. He took the view that the tenant could not surrender what he had not himself got, namely, a right to immediate possession. *Nemo dat quod non habet.* For a criticism of the decision, see (1962), 78 L. Q. R., 541 (H. W. R. Wade). For a discussion of the difficulty of terminology in this context see (1964), 80 L. Q. R. 63 (Bernard Rudden). See also (1973) 37 Conv. (N.S.) 85 (J. A. Omotola).

[6] [1930] 2 K. B. 16.

and that therefore he was entitled to the half a year's notice to quit appropriate to a yearly tenancy.

This argument was fallacious. All that the squatter had acquired was a title to possession indefeasible by the yearly tenant. With the disappearance of the yearly tenancy, the former yearly tenant had become the freeholder, and as such ne had an immediate right to recover possession.

One effect of these decisions is that the lessor and lessee can combine to defeat the squatter. If the lessor accepts a surrender of the term, he is then able to grant a new lease to the tenant.[1]

Nevertheless, despite the negative operation of the Limitation Act, the title to possession acquired by a squatter against the person dispossessed may ultimately ripen into a title to the fee simple.

Adverse title may ripen into absolute title to fee simple.

" Whenever you find a person in possession of property, that possession is *prima facie* evidence of ownership in fee, and that *prima facie* evidence becomes absolute when once you have extinguished the right of every other person to challenge it." [2]

In other words, a squatter, though a wrongdoer, acquires by virtue of his possession a new independent title to the fee simple which prevails against all persons except those who can rely on an earlier and therefore a better title. Moreover, it is a title that will prevail against those with better titles if they fail to assert their rights within the period prescribed by the Limitation Act. Thus, a title originally defeasible may in course of time become indefeasible.[3]

For instance,

X. dispossesses W., the fee simple owner of Blackacre, and remains in possession for eight years when he himself is dispossessed by Y.

As between X. and Y., X.'s is the earlier and therefore the stronger title of the two, but he must assert it against the weaker within the statutory period. If Y. is allowed to remain in possession for twelve years without being challenged either by W. or X., his title to possession of the fee simple becomes indefeasible. It rests on the infirmity of the right of others to eject him.[4]

Again, if some lesser title than that to the fee simple is destroyed, as when a tenant for years is ejected, the squatter may still be challenged by the landlord, the freeholder. So, if the lease terminates by effluxion of time or becomes forfeitable for breach

---

[1] *Fairweather* v. *St. Marylebone Property Co., Ltd.*, [1963] A. C. 510, at p. 547; *per* Lord DENNING; [1962] 2 All E. R. 288.
[2] *Re Atkinson and Horsell's Contract*, [1912] 2 Ch. 1, at p. 9.
[3] *St. Marylebone Property Co., Ltd.* v. *Fairweather*, [1962] 1 Q. B. 498, at p. 513; *per* HOLROYD PEARCE, L.J.; [1961] 3 All E. R. 560.
[4] Darby and Bosanquet, *Statutes of Limitation* (2nd Edn.), p. 493, adopted by BOWEN, L.J., in *Tichborne* v. *Weir* (1892), 67 L. T. 735.

of condition,[1] the freeholder's right to recover possession accrues and prevails over that of the squatter. Relatively to the tenant, the squatter's right is the stronger; relatively to the freeholder, it is the weaker. But if the freeholder does not pursue his remedy within six years from the end of the lease, the squatter's title to the fee simple becomes indefeasible.

Proof of title. A consequence of the negative effect of the Limitation Act 1939 is that as between vendor and purchaser a title based on adverse possession alone for the limitation period or longer is not necessarily a good title. The claims of a reversioner or a remainderman may have yet to be extinguished[2]; the reversion may be on a 99 year lease; the remainderman's interest may not vest in possession for over 100 years.[3] But if a vendor can establish that the flaw in an otherwise good title is one that can be cured by the running of time in his favour under the Act, he can force a purchaser to take the title.[4] Proof that rival claims have been extinguished by the lapse of time may be very difficult, and in practice a purchaser often agrees to accept an imperfect title.[5]

SECTION V. CIRCUMSTANCES IN WHICH THE STATUTORY PERIOD IS EXTENDED

In three cases, namely,

1. where the person entitled to recover land is under a disability ;
2. where there has been fraud or fraudulent concealment of a cause of action, and
3. where a person seeks relief from the consequences of a mistake,

the period of twelve years within which an action must normally be brought is lengthened.

Persons under a disability.

1. **Disability.** A person is deemed to be under a disability for the purposes of the Act while he is an infant or of unsound mind.[6]

---

[1] *Tickner* v. *Buzzacott*, [1965] Ch. 426; [1965] 1 All E. R. 131.
[2] Limitation Act 1939, s. 6.
[3] *Cadell* v. *Palmer* (1833), Cl. & Fin. 372: vesting postponed for over 100 years (note to *Re Villar*. [1928] Ch, 471, 478).
[4] *Re Atkinson's and Horsell's Contract*, [1912] 2 Ch. 1; *Re Spencer and Hauser's Contract*, [1928] Ch. 598; distinguished in *George Wimpey & Co., Ltd.* v. *Sohn*, [1967], Ch. 487; [1966] 1 All E.R. 232.
[5] M. & B. p. 148.
[6] Limitation Act 1939, s. 31 (2), as amended by Statute Law Repeals Act 1969, s. 1, sched., Part VII, and s. 31 (3) as amended by Mental Health Act 1959, Sched. 7, Part I. *Kirby* v. *Leather*, [1965] 2 Q. B. 367 ; [1965] 2 All E. R. 441. If a cause of action arose before January 1, 1970, the change from 21 to 18 years for the age of majority does not affect the time for bringing actions. Family Law Reform Act 1969, s. 1 (4), Sched. 3, para. 8.

If, on the date when a right of action for the recovery of land accrues, the person to whom it has accrued is under a disability, the action may be brought at any time within six years from the removal of the disability or from his death, whichever event first occurs, notwithstanding that the period of limitation has expired.[1] No action, however, to recover land or money charged on land may be brought after the expiration of thirty years from the date on which the right accrued.[2] A disability which begins *after* the accrual of a right of action does not prevent time from continuing to run against the disabled person.[3]

Six years from cessation of disability or from death.

If before the cessation of one disability another one supervenes, time does not begin to run until both have ceased.[4] For instance :

Successive disabilities.

A. dispossesses B., an infant six years of age. When fifteen years old B. becomes of unsound mind, and is still in this state upon the attainment of his majority. Time does not begin to run until he recovers his sanity.

If the person entitled to the right of action dies while still under a disability, his successor in title must sue within six years even though he himself is under a disability.[5]

2. Fraud or fraudulent concealment of right of action. Section 26 of the Limitation Act 1939 provides that where :

Right accrues on discovery of fraud.

" (a) the action is based upon the fraud of the defendant or his agent or of any person through whom he claims or his agent, or

(b) the right of action is concealed by the fraud of any such person as aforesaid."

time shall not begin to run until the plaintiff has discovered, or could with reasonable diligence have discovered the fraud.[6] There is, however, a saving clause which provides that the enactment shall not enable a person to recover the land from a purchaser for valuable consideration who was not a party to the fraud, and who at the time of the purchase did not know and had no reason to believe that a fraud had been committed.

Wrongfully to enter land without the knowledge of the owner does not constitute concealed fraud.[7] The fraud contemplated by the statute is not restricted to what common law regards as deceit, but " is used in the equitable sense to denote conduct by the defendant or his agent such that it would be ' against conscience ' for him to avail himself of the lapse of time ".[8] At any rate, it

Meaning of " concealed fraud."

---

[1] Limitation Act 1939, s. 22 (1).
[2] *Ibid.*, s. 22 (1) (c). [3] *Ibid.*, s. 22 (1).
[4] *Borrows* v. *Ellison* (1871), L. R. 6 Exch. 128.
[5] Limitation Act, 1939, s. 22 (1) (b).
[6] See *Eddis* v. *Chichester Constable*, [1969] 2 Ch. 345 ; [1969] 2 All E. R. 912.
[7] *Rains* v. *Buxton* (1880), 14 Ch. D. 537.
[8] *Applegate* v. *Moss*, [1971] 1 Q. B. 406, at p. 413 ; [1971] 1 All E. R. 747, *per* Lord DENNING ; *Clark* v. *Woor* ; [1965] 1 W. L. R. 650, 654 ; [1965] 2 All E. R. 352, at p. 356 ; *King* v. *Victor Parsons & Co.*, [1973] 1 W. L. R. 29, at p. 33 ; [1973] 1 All E. R. 206.

clearly covers a case in the context of adverse possession where a person, knowing that the land belongs to X., conceals from X. the circumstances which confer the right upon him, and thus enables himself to enter and hold.[1] Examples are the destruction of title deeds,[2] the intentional concealment of a voluntary conveyance to the plaintiff,[3] the passing off of a bastard as the eldest legitimate son,[4] the procuring a conveyance from a person of unsound mind,[5] and where a builder covers up what he knows to be rubbishy foundations and does not tell the owner anything about it.[6]

Right accrues upon discovery of mistake.

3. **Mistake.** Similar provisions apply " where the action is for relief from the consequences of a mistake."[7] The relief, however, is only available " where the mistake is an essential ingredient of the cause of action,"[8] as for instance where the action is to recover money paid under a mistake. There is no general rule that a mistake prevents time from running under the Act.

SECTION VI. THE METHODS BY WHICH TIME MAY BE PREVENTED FROM RUNNING

Assertion by owner of his right.

Time which has begun to run under the Act is stopped, either when the owner asserts his right or when his right is admitted by the adverse possessor.

Assertion of right occurs when the owner takes legal proceedings or makes an effective entry into the land. The old rule was that a merely formal entry was sufficient to vest possession in the true owner and to prevent time from running against him. Such a nominal entry, even though it was secret, entitled him to bring an action within a year afterwards, and as it was possible to make such an entry every year, in this case called *continual claim*, the title to land might be in doubt for longer than the period of limitation. It was therefore provided by the Real Property Limitation Act 1833,[9] in a section which has been repeated in the Limitation Act 1939,[10] that a person shall not be deemed to have been in possession merely because he has made an entry on the land. He must either make a peaceable and effective entry, or sue for the recovery of the land.

Admission of owner's right.

An admission of the right of the person entitled occurs where the adverse possessor acknowledges the right, or, if the right is to the payment of money, where he makes a part payment.

---

[1] *Petre* v. *Petre* (1853), 1 Drew. 371 at p. 397, *per* KINDERSLEY, V.-C.
[2] *Lawrance* v. *Lord Norreys* (1890), 15 App. Cas. 210.
[3] *Re McCallum*, [1901] 1 Ch. 143.
[4] *Vane* v. *Vane* (1873), 8 Ch. App. 383.
[5] *Lewis* v. *Thomas* (1843), 3 Hare, 26.
[6] *Applegate* v. *Moss*, [1971] 1 Q. B. 406 ; [1971] 1 All E. R. 747 ; *King* v. *Victor Parsons & Co.*, [1973] 1 W. L. R. 29 ; [1973] 1 All E. R. 206.
[7] Limitation Act 1939, s. 26 (c).
[8] *Phillips-Higgins* v. *Harper*, [1954] 1 Q. B. 411, at p. 419 ; [1954] 1 All E. R. 116, *per* PEARSON, J.
[9] Ss. 10, 11.   [10] S. 13.

Acknowledgment. Where a right of action to recover land or an advowson or to foreclose a mortgage has already accrued to X. and his title is later acknowledged by the person in possession, his right shall be deemed to have accrued on and not before the date of the acknowledgment.[1] The effect is that the owner's right of action recommences, not only against the person who makes the admission, but also against all later possessors, and remains effective until there has been adverse possession for a further period of twelve years.[2] An acknowledgment, however, has no effect if it is given after the period of limitation has run its full course.[3]

Every acknowledgment must be in writing and signed by the person by whom it is made.[4] It must be made to the person whose title or claim is being acknowledged or to his agent.[5] Any written statement is sufficient that implicitly recognizes the title of the person to whom it is made, as for instance an offer by a squatter to purchase the land from the freeholder;[6] or a request for further time within which to pay made by the possessor of land in response to a demand for rent.[7]

Part payment. If, after a right of foreclosure or other cause of action has accrued to a mortgagee, the possessor of the land or the person liable for the mortgage debt makes any payment of principal or interest, there is a fresh accrual of the right of action from the date of payment.[8]

Where a right of action has accrued to recover any debt or other liquidated pecuniary claim, as for instance rent due under a lease, and the person liable acknowledges the claim or makes any payment in respect thereof, the right is deemed to accrue on and not before the date of the acknowledgment or last payment.[9] A payment of part only of rent does not, however, enable the remainder then due to be recovered more than six years after it became due.[10]

An acknowledgment to be effective for this purpose must admit the existence of the debt, but it need not state its precise amount, provided that this is ascertainable by extrinsic evidence.[11]

Persons bound by acknowledgment and part payment. There is a distinction between acknowledgment and part payment with regard to the persons upon whom they are binding

Marginal notes:
Acknowledgment.

Acknowledgment must be in writing and signed.

Part payment: foreclosure action.

Part payment and acknowledgment: rent.

Part payment binds more persons than an acknowledgment.

---

[1] Limitation Act 1939, s. 23 (1).   [2] *Ibid.*, s. 25 (1).
[3] *Sanders* v. *Sanders* (1881), 19 Ch. D. 373.
[4] Limitation Act 1939, s. 24 (1).   [5] *Ibid.*, s. 24 (2).
[6] *Edginton* v. *Clark*, [1964] 1 Q. B. 367; [1963] 3 All E. R. 468.
[7] *Fursdon* v. *Clogg* (1842), 10 M. & W. 257.
[8] Limitation Act 1939, s. 23 (1) (*b*).
[9] *Ibid.*, s. 23 (4).
[10] *Ibid.*, proviso.
[11] *Dungate* v. *Dungate*, [1965] 1 W. L. R. 1477 ; [1965] 3 All E. R. 393, explaining *Good* v. *Parry*, [1963] 2 Q. B. 418; [1963] 2 All E. R. 59.

An acknowledgment binds only the acknowledgor and his successors,[1] *i.e.* persons who claim through him, such as a trustee in bankruptcy or an executor.[2]   A part payment of a debt or other liquidated money claim, on the other hand, binds all persons liable in respect thereof,[3] for since they derive advantage from the payment it is only just that they should share the disadvantage of a fresh accrual of a right of action to the creditor.   Thus a part payment of rent by a tenant revives the landlord's right of action against a surety.[4]

Acknow-
ledgment
and part
payment
after
period
has run.

We have already seen that in the case of an action to recover land an acknowledgment given *after* the period of limitation has run is ineffective.   The reason is that, since the right as well as the remedy is barred, there is nothing left to acknowledge.   In other cases, however, where the remedy alone is barred, the established principle is that an acknowledgment or part payment is effective though given after the period has elapsed.   The Limitation Act 1939 preserves this rule but restricts the binding effect of either form of admission to the person who makes the acknowledgment or part payment and his successors.[5]   There is, however, a particular case in which a " successor " is not bound, *i.e.* where the tenant for life of land, which is mortgaged or charged with the payment of money, makes an acknowledgment or a part payment to the creditor after the period has elapsed. In this case the admission of liability, though binding on the tenant for life, does not bind the remainderman.[6]

SECTION VII.   REGISTERED LAND

The Limitation Act 1939 applies to registered land, and a title to a registered estate may be acquired by adverse possession.[7] There is, however, one important difference which springs from the mechanics of registration.   When a squatter acquires a legal title to unregistered land by adverse possession, the former owner's estate is automatically extinguished.   With registered land, however, there is no automatic extinction of the proprietor's title but it is deemed to be held by the proprietor on trust for the squatter, though without prejudice to the rights of any other person interested in the land whose estate or interest is not extinguished by the Act of 1939.   Anyone claiming to have acquired a title to registered land under the Limitation Act may apply to be registered as proprietor and he may be registered with an absolute, good leasehold, qualified or possessory title, as the case may be, but

---

[1] Limitation Act 1939, s. 25 (5).
[2] *Ibid.*, s. 25 (8).   [3] *Ibid.*, s. 25 (6)
[4] *Re Powers* (1885), 30 Ch. D. 291 ; *Re Frisby* (1889), 43 Ch. D. 106.
[5] S. 25 (5), (6).   [6] S. 25 (5) proviso, (6) proviso.
[7] See generally Ruoff and Roper, pp. 687 *et seq.*

his estate will be a completely new one and the registration will be treated as that of a first proprietor.[1]

Rights acquired or in course of being acquired under the Limitation Acts are overriding interests,[2] and therefore a registered purchaser for value can never be in a better position than his predecessor in title and must take subject to the rights of the squatter.[3] The purchaser's registered title even if absolute may be rectified in favour of the squatter,[4] but the purchaser will not be entitled to an indemnity, as he has only lost thereby a valueless asset *i.e.* a title barred by adverse possession on the part of the squatter.[5]

---

[1] L.R.A. 1925, s. 75 ; *St. Marylebone Property Co., Ltd.* v. *Fairweather*, [1963] A. C. 510, at pp. 541, 548 ; [1962] 2 All E. R. 288.
[2] *Ibid.*, s. 70 (1) (*f*) ; *Bridges* v. *Mees*, [1957] Ch. 475 ; [1957] 2 All E. R. 577.
[3] *Bridges* v. *Mees, supra.*
[4] *Chowood* v. *Lyall (No. 2)*, [1930] 2 Ch. 156.
[5] See *Re Chowood's Registered Land*, [1933] Ch. 574 ; M. & B. p. 139.

CHAPTER II

MERGER

The term *merger* means that, where a lesser and a greater
estate in the same land come together and vest, without any intermediate estate, in the same person and in the same right, the
lesser is immediately annihilated by operation of law.   It is said
to be " merged," *i.e.* sunk or drowned, in the greater estate.[1]

For example :

> If land is limited to A. for life, remainder to B. in fee
> simple, merger will result from any event which produces
> the union in one person of the life interest and the re-
> mainder in fee.   Thus if A. conveys his life interest to
> B., or if B. conveys his remainder to A., there is in each
> case a merger.   Again, a term of years may merge in a life
> interest, and an estate *pur autre vie* may merge in the
> interest held by a tenant for his own life.

At common law the doctrine of merger has nothing to do with
the intention of the parties, and provided that certain essentials
are satisfied, the effect is automatically to annihilate the smaller
estate.

The essentials are that the estates shall unite in the same
person without any intervening estate, and that the person in whom
they unite shall hold them both in the same right.

To illustrate the first essential, if A., who is tenant for life, with
remainder to B. for life, remainder to C. in fee, purchases and
takes a conveyance of C.'s fee, the intervening life interest of B.,
since it is vested, excludes the possibility of merger.

As regards the second essential, if an executor takes, under the
Administration of Estates Act 1925, a term of years which belonged
to the testator, and then purchases the reversion in fee on his own
behalf, the term which the executor holds for the purposes of

---

[1] Blackstone, vol. ii. p. 177; Cruise. *Digest* Tit. xxxix. s. 1

administration does not merge in the fee which he owns beneficially.[1]

Entailed interests. The exception to the doctrine of No merger
of entailed
merger at common law is that an entailed interest does not merge interest.
in the fee simple in reversion or remainder, for the intention of the
Statute *De Donis* is that such an interest shall descend to the issue
of the tenant in tail. If, for instance, where lands are limited to A.
in tail, remainder to B. in fee simple, A. were able by a purchase of
the reversion in fee to extinguish his entailed interest under the
doctrine of merger, a simple method of defeating the issue would
be thrown open. It has therefore been the rule since the sixteenth
century that in such a case no merger results.[2]

One effect of the common law doctrine was that the merger of Effect of
merger of
a term of years in the reversion destroyed the covenants contained term of
in any sub-lease that had been carved out of the term. years.

> Suppose, for instance, that A., seised in fee, leased the land to T.
> who sub-leased it to S. If T. were to surrender his interest to
> A., the covenants contained in the sub-lease would become un-
> enforceable, since the reversion to which they were formerly attached
> no longer existed.[3]

To remedy this, it was enacted in effect by the Real Property
Act 1845,[4] in a section reproduced in the Law of Property Act
1925,[5] that where the reversion on a lease is destroyed by surrender
or merger, the next vested interest in the land shall be deemed to
be the reversion for the purpose of preserving the incidents and
obligations of the defunct reversion.

> Thus, in the example given above, the covenants entered into
> between T. and S. are enforceable by and against A. and S.
> respectively.

View of Equity. Equity has taken a different view of merger. Merger in
At common law merger results automatically from the union of equity.
two estates in the circumstances we have mentioned, and intention
does not affect the result. But Equity looks to the intention and
to the duties of the parties. If an intention is expressly declared
to the effect that the lesser estate shall be kept alive, there is no
difficulty;[6] but even in the absence of such an express declaration
Equity will presume an intention against merger if it is clearly
advantageous to the person in whom the estates are united, or if
it is consistent with his duty, that the lesser interest shall not be
destroyed.[7] This view now prevails, for it was enacted by the
Judicature Act 1873 that there should be no merger by operation

---

[1] *Chambers* v. *Kingham* (1878), 10 Ch. D. 743.
[2] *Wiscot's Case* (1599), 2 Co. Rep. 60b, 61a.
[3] *Webb* v. *Russell* (1789), 3 Term Rep. 393.
[4] S. 9. [5] S. 139.
[6] *Golden Lion Hotel (Hunstanton), Ltd.* v. *Carter*, [1965] 1 W. L. R. 1189 ;
[1965] 3 All E. R. 506.
[7] *Ingle* v. *Vaughan Jenkins*, [1900] 2 Ch. 368 ; *Re Fletcher*, [1917] 1 Ch. 330.

of law of any estate the beneficial interest in which would not be deemed to be merged or extinguished in equity.[1]

In *Snow* v. *Boycott*, for instance,[2]

land was limited to A. for life, remainder to B. for life. A., being too old to manage the property, conveyed the land to B. for the rest of her life to the use that B. should pay her £400 a year out of the profits. The effect of this was that an estate *pur autre vie* and an estate for his own life vested in B., so that at common law the estate *pur autre vie* was destroyed by merger. B. died in the lifetime of A., and the question arose whether A.'s life estate had been destroyed so as to let in the estates which were limited to take effect after B.'s life estate. It was held that there was no merger *in equity*, and therefore no such destruction, for the parties could not have intended to create an interest *pur autre vie* in order that it should be immediately swallowed up in an existing life interest and thereby lost.

In another case :

X., the first tenant for life under a settlement, agreed to let three acres of the land for 99 years to Y., the second tenant for life, at an annual ground rent of £9, in consideration that Y. would erect thereon a house at a cost of £1,500. After the house had been erected, X. died, with the result that at common law Y's term of years was merged in the life interest to which he now became entitled.

On the death of Y., the remainderman contended that Y's executor was prevented by this merger from claiming any further leasehold interest in the land. The contention failed. The court's one concern is the benefit of the person in whom the two interests unite, and in the instant circumstances it was obviously to the advantage of Y. that the term of years should be kept separate from the life interest.[3]

---

[1] S. 25 (4) ; reproduced in L.P.A. 1925, s. 185.
[2] [1892] 3 Ch. 110.
[3] *Ingle* v. *Vaughan Jenkins*, [1900] 2 Ch. 368.

BOOK III

THE TRANSFER AND EXTINCTION OF ESTATES AND INTERESTS

PART VI

INCAPACITIES AND DISABILITIES WITH REGARD TO THE HOLDING AND TRANSFER OF ESTATES AND INTERESTS

SUMMARY

CHAPTER I

INFANTS

SUMMARY

SECTION I. INTRODUCTORY NOTE

An infant[1] is a person, whether male or female, who has not What is full
attained full age.   After January 1st, 1970, a person attains full age age.
at the first moment of the eighteenth anniversary of his birth.[2]

---

   [1] Or a minor.   Family Law Reform Act 1969, s. 12.
   [2] Persons of 18 or over, but under 21 attained full age on that date.   *Ibid.*,
ss. 1 (1), 9.   See Report of the Committee on the Age of Majority (the Latey
Report) 1967 (Cmnd. 3342).   (1970), 120 *New L. J.* 144 (S. M. Cretney).
S. 1 (2) provides that for the " construction of ' full age,' ' infant,' ' infancy,'
' minor,' ' minority ' and similar expressions " in any statutory provision,
whenever passed or made, the references shall be deemed to be references to the
age of majority as amended by the Act.   Where, however, a statutory
provision refers to a specified age, s. 1 (3), Sched. 1, sets out those statutes in
which references to 21 are changed to 18.   S. 1 (4), Sched. 2 excepts certain

Hitherto the age of majority had been the first moment of the day preceding the twenty-first anniversary.[1]

Our task in the present chapter is to deal with three aspects of infancy, namely :

    1. the acquisition by an infant of interests in land ;
    2. the alienation by an infant of interests in land ; and
    3. the management of an infant's property.

SECTION II. ACQUISITION BY AN INFANT OF INTERESTS IN LAND

Infant cannot be estate owner. In accordance with the fundamental principle of the legislation of 1925, an infant can never hold a *legal estate* in land.[2] He cannot be an estate owner.[3] This restriction, which is imposed in the interests of a simplified system of conveyancing, does not mean that he cannot hold and enjoy beneficially an equitable interest[3] and there is nothing to prevent land being transferred to him by way of gift, sale or settlement. In such a case, the statutory policy is to treat the land as settled land, and during the infancy to vest the legal estate in trustees whose identity will depend upon whether the infant comes to his interest as grantee, devisee, heir on intestacy, beneficiary under a settlement, mortgagee, or trustee of the land for the benefit of another person.

(A) GRANT *INTER VIVOS* TO AN INFANT

Grant operates as contract to settle. It is enacted that a conveyance of a legal estate in land to an infant alone, or to two or more persons jointly, both or all of whom are infants, for his or their own benefit, shall operate only as an agreement for valuable consideration to execute a settlement in his or their favour.[4] This means that the grantor must as soon as possible execute a principal vesting deed and a trust instrument,[5] meanwhile holding the land in trust for the infant. In this case, however, the legal estate will be transferred by the vesting deed not to the infant as tenant for life, but to the trustees when they are appointed, who then become the " statutory owners."[6]

---

statutes from s. 1 (2) *e.g.* the Regency Acts 1937–1953, Representation of the People Act 1969. For changes in fiscal legislation, see F.A. 1969, s. 16 and in the age of franchise Representation of the People Act 1969. In the case of private transactions the Act is not retrospective *e.g.* " to X on attaining his majority," if made in a will or settlement before 1970, X takes at 21 ; if made after 1969, X takes at 18.

[1] See Latey Report, paras. 37–42. *Re Shurey*, [1918] 1 Ch. 263.
[2] L.P.A. 1925, s. 1 (6).
[3] *Ibid.*, s. 19 (1) ; S.L.A. 1925, ss. 26 (6), 27 (2).
[4] *Ibid.*, s. 19 (1) ; S.L.A. 1925, s. 27 (1). This is registrable as an estate contract under L.C.A. 1972. *Supra*, p. 742.
[5] *Supra*, pp. 170 *et seq.*
[6] *Supra*, p. 176.

If a legal estate is conveyed to an infant jointly with one or more other persons of full age, the person or persons of full age take the legal estate on trust for sale.[1] In this case the persons of full age hold upon the *statutory trusts* applicable to a joint tenancy, *i.e.* upon trust to sell the land and to hold the proceeds and the profits until sale for the benefit of themselves and the infant.[2] If, however, life interests are given, there is a settlement and the adults are tenants for life under the Settled Land Act 1925.[3]

Grant to infant jointly with adult.

(B) DEVISE TO AN INFANT

In the case of a devise to an infant the legal estate vests at first in the personal representatives of the deceased by virtue of the Administration of Estates Act 1925, but in considering the ultimate destination of the legal estate we must distinguish between a devise of an absolute interest, and a devise by way of settlement in which trustees of the settlement have been appointed.

Representatives take legal estate.

Where the land is devised to the infant for an estate in fee simple or for a term of years absolute, or where it is settled upon him for life and no trustees are appointed, the personal representatives can retain the land until the infant attains his majority, and until that time they possess all the powers of a tenant for life under a settlement,[4] and also the powers of trustees for sale.[5] If, however, they do not desire to retain the land, they may appoint trustees to be trustees of the land for the purposes of the Settled Land Act and for the purposes of the statutory provisions relating to the management of land during a minority.[6]

Where the land is devised by way of settlement to an infant for a limited interest and the testator has appointed trustees of the settlement, the Act directs that the personal representatives shall, when their administration duties are completed, transfer the legal estate to the trustees if they are required to do so.[7]

(C) DESCENT OF LAND TO AN INFANT

In the case of deaths occurring after 1925 it is impossible for an infant to become entitled to a fee simple estate by descent. The rules of primogeniture do not apply and the residuary estate of the intestate, as we have seen,[8] is held by the administrator upon trust to sell and to divide the proceeds among the relatives entitled under the Administration of Estates Act 1925. If an infant is the sole relative so entitled, he will become entitled absolutely to the fee simple when he either marries or attains his majority.

Fee simple estate.

---

[1] L.P.A. 1925, s. 19 (2).
[2] *Ibid.*, s. 35.
[3] S. 19 (3).
[4] S.L.A. 1925, s. 26 (1).
[5] A.E.A. 1925, s. 39 (1).
[6] *Ibid.*, s. 42.
[7] S.L.A. 1925, ss. 6, 26.
[8] *Supra*, pp. 871 *et seq.*

But as we have seen, an infant cannot hold a legal estate in land, and therefore, the land remains settled land until he attains his majority.[1]

Entailed interests.

The old law of descent, however, still applies to the entailed interest, but if the heir is an infant the legal estate must be vested in the trustees of the settlement until he attains his majority. If money is required during his minority for his maintenance, education or benefit, the court if necessary may make an order under the Trustee Act 1925,[2] appointing a person to execute a disentailing assurance which will bar the issue and remaindermen as completely as if it were effected by the infant after attaining his majority.[3]

(D) SETTLEMENT OF LAND IN FAVOUR OF AN INFANT

Two methods of effecting settlement.

A person who desires to settle land in favour of an infant has an alternative, for he may create either a settlement under the Settled Land Act 1925 or a trust for sale.

In the case of a settlement, the statutory powers of a tenant for life and the trustees of a settlement, together with any additional powers that may be conferred by the settlement, become exercisable by the trustees,[4] who, in their capacity as " statutory owners,"[5] are entitled to have the legal estate transferred to them by a vesting deed. If the settlor adopts the method of a trust for sale, the trustees not only obtain the legal estate but they also possess all the statutory powers under the Settled Land Act 1925, so long as the land remains unsold.[6]

Infant tenant for life.

If a tenant for life under an existing settlement is succeeded by an infant tenant for life, the latter is not entitled to the legal estate until he attains his majority. In the meantime the legal estate and the statutory powers will be held by the trustees of the settlement.[7]

Infant becoming absolutely entitled.

Where an infant becomes absolutely entitled under a settlement, as, for example, where there is a grant or a devise

> to A. for life, remainder to B (an infant) in fee simple, and A. dies during the minority of B.,

the settlement continues until B. attains his majority,[8] the legal estate in the meantime being vested in the trustees of the settlement. In a case such as this, statutory provision is made to meet the contingency of the infant dying under age, for it is enacted that unless he marries before reaching his majority he shall be

---

[1] A.E.A. 1925, s. 47, *supra*, p. 877.
[2] T.A. 1925, s. 53.
[3] *Re Gower's Settlement*, [1934] Ch. 365.
[4] S.L.A. s. 26 (1) (*b*).   [5] *Ibid.*, s. 117 (1) (**xxvi**).
[6] L.P.A. 1925, s. 28 (1).
[7] S.L.A. 1925, s. 26 (1).
[8] *Ibid.*, s. 3 (*b*).

deemed to have had an entailed interest at the time of his death.[1]
In other words, the fee simple of the infant B., in the above example,
though potentially absolute,[2] is cut down to an entail until he
marries or reaches eighteen.   Therefore, if he is an unmarried
infant at his death, the estate will revert to the settlor if the settlement was by deed, or will pass to the residuary devisee in the case
of a testamentary settlement, for an infant cannot make a valid
will, and if unmarried cannot have heirs capable of taking the
estate tail.   It is better that there should be this reversion to the
settlor, rather than that the estate should enure for the benefit
of some distant relative of the infant, which would be the result
if he were to die owning an absolute interest.

(E) MORTGAGE TO AN INFANT

It is expressly enacted that a legal estate cannot be conveyed to
an infant by way of mortgage.   A grant of a legal mortgage of
land to an infant merely operates as an agreement for valuable
consideration that the grantor will execute a proper conveyance
when the infant attains full age, and that in the meantime he will
hold the beneficial interest on trust for the infant.[3]   If, however,
the conveyance is made to the infant and to another person of full
age, it operates as if the infant had not been named, though of
course his beneficial interest is not prejudiced.[4]

Mortgage operates as contract to convey.

(F) CONVEYANCE TO AN INFANT AS TRUSTEE

An infant cannot be appointed a trustee.[5]   A conveyance
which purports to convey land to an infant as trustee does not
transfer the legal estate, but operates as a declaration of trust in
favour of the beneficiaries designated.[6]   In such a case the person
who is empowered by the trust instrument to appoint new trustees
may make a new appointment,[7] or, if there is no such person, the
court may do so.[8]

Infant cannot be trustee.

We have already seen that the legal estate cannot pass to an
infant who is appointed executor by the will of a testator.[9]

SECTION III.   ACQUISITION AND ALIENATION OF EQUITABLE INTERESTS IN LAND BY AN INFANT

An equitable interest, as distinct from a legal estate, may be
effectively transferred to an infant, but since the ownership of an
interest in land may occasionally prove to be more of a burden

Conveyance to infant voidable.

---

[1] A.E.A. 1925, s. 51 (3).
[2] *Re Taylor*, [1931] 2 Ch. 243, at p. 246.
[3] L.P.A. 1925, s. 19 (6).   The infant's interest is registrable as an estate
contract under L.C.A. 1972.   *Supra*, p. 742.
[4] *Ibid.*, s. 19 (6).
[5] *Ibid.*, s. 20.
[6] *Ibid.*, s. 19 (4).
[7] T.A. 1925, s. 36.
[8] *Ibid.*, s. 41.
[9] Supreme Court of Judicature (Consolidation) Act 1925, s. 165.   Nor can
an infant be an administrator.   *In the Goods of Manuel* (1849), 13 Jur. 664.

than a benefit, especially in the case of a leasehold containing onerous covenants, the long established rule is that the transfer is voidable at the option of the infant, either on attaining his majority or within a reasonable time thereafter.   In the event of his death his personal representatives may exercise the same power within a reasonable time.[1]   But repudiation must not be unduly delayed.   Thus where an infant bought land at a price payable by instalments, and continued to pay them for some time after he reached full age, it was held that his procrastination had defeated his right of avoidance and that he must pay the instalments which remained due.[2]

Conveyance by infant voidable.

An infant cannot make an irrevocable disposition of his interest, for the rule is that any disposition is voidable and can be repudiated by him during his minority or within a reasonable time after he attains full age.[3]   So the disability is not absolute. It goes no further than is necessary for the protection of the infant. It leaves him the power to act during infancy, but in order that he may have protection, it permits him to avoid the transaction when he comes of age if he finds it right and proper to do so.[4] The tendency of the courts, however, is to regard very slight acts, such as the receipt of rent in the case of a lease, as amounting to a ratification of the conveyance.[5]

Wills of infants.

An infant cannot make a will, either of real or of personal property,[6] unless he is a person entitled to the privileges granted by the Wills Act 1837, and Wills (Soldiers and Sailors) Act 1918.[7]

Settlements by infants.

In accordance with the principle applicable to alienation in general, a settlement made by an infant in contemplation of marriage is voidable, but it becomes binding upon him or her unless it is repudiated within a reasonable time after the attainment of majority.[8]   The reasonable time is calculated from the attainment of majority, and not, as was once thought, from the moment when the property falls into possession.[9]   If, for instance,

> an infant settles a reversionary interest, consisting of a fee simple estate which will come to him on the death of his

---

[1] Blackstone, vol. ii. p. 292 ;   *North Western Rly. Co.* v. *McMichael* (1850), 5 Ex. 114, 123.

[2] *Whittingham* v. *Murdy* (1889), 60 L. T. 956.

[3] Co. Litt., 171b.   The Infant Settlements Act 1855, which enabled a male infant over 20 and a female infant over 17 to make a binding marriage settlement of property with the consent of the Chancery Division, was repealed by the Family Law Reform Act 1969, s. 11 (a) as from January 1, 1970, " except in relation to anything done before " that date.

[4] *Burnaby* v. *Equitable Reversionary Interest Society* (1885), 28 Ch. D. 416, 424.

[5] *Slator* v. *Brady* (1863), 14 Ir. C. L. R. 61.

[6] Wills Act 1837, s. 7.

[7] *Ibid.*, s. 11 ;   Wills (Soldiers and Sailors) Act 1918, s. 3 (1) ;   *supra*, pp. 839–42.

[8] *Edwards* v. *Carter*, [1893] A. C. 360.

[9] *Carnell* v. *Harrison*, [1916] 1 Ch. 328.

mother, he will lose his right to repudiate unless he takes the necessary steps soon after he reaches full age, notwithstanding that it may be many years before possession of the land becomes available by the death of his mother.

His ignorance of the right of repudiation does not absolve him from the obligation to take steps within a reasonable time.[1]

SECTION IV. MANAGEMENT OF AN INFANT'S PROPERTY

Land to which an infant is beneficially entitled, either absolutely or as tenant for life, is, as we have seen, deemed to be settled land. This involves the existence of trustees, and wide powers of management have been conferred upon them by statute. Thus they have all the ordinary powers conferred on a tenant for life and upon settlement trustees by the Settled Land Act 1925.[2] They may enter into and continue in possession of the land on behalf of the infant, and if they do, they are directed to manage or superintend the management of the land, with full power, *inter alia* :

Powers of trustees.

1. to fell timber in the usual course for sale or for repairs ;
2. to erect, pull down, rebuild and repair buildings ;
3. to work mines which have usually been worked ;
4. to drain or otherwise improve the land ;
5. to deal generally with the land in a proper and due course of management.[3]

These powers are also exercisable, subject to any prior interests or charges, where an infant is contingently entitled to land.[4]

As regards the use which must be made of surplus income during the minority, it is provided[5] that the trustees may, at their sole discretion, apply a reasonable part of the income of the property for the maintenance, education or benefit of the infant, notwithstanding that some other fund may be applicable to those purposes, or that some other person, such as a parent, may be legally bound to provide for the infant's maintenance or education. But in deciding whether income shall be used for such purposes, the trustees must have regard to the age and requirements of the infant and to the circumstances of the case in general. In particular they must, in spite of the latitude allowed them, take into account whether some other fund may be used for the purpose.

Application of surplus income.

The residue of the income is to be accumulated by way of compound interest, and the accumulations are to be paid over to

---

1 *Carnell* v. *Harrison*, [1916] 1 Ch. 328.
2 S.L.A. 1925, s. 26 ; *supra*, pp. 177 *et seq.* ; 200.
3 *Ibid.*, s. 102.   4 *Ibid.*, s. 102 (5).
5 Trustee Act 1925, s. 31 (1).

the infant when he attains eighteen years or marries under that age, provided that his interest is vested.[1]   If the infant has a merely contingent interest, or if he dies under eighteen years of age and without having married, the accumulations must be added to capital.[2]   Where land to which an infant is entitled is subject to a trust for sale, the trustees are empowered to use the capital to an amount not exceeding one-half of his presumptive or vested share for his advancement or benefit.[3]

SECTION V.   REGISTERED LAND

As with unregistered land, an infant cannot be an estate owner,[4] and, consequently, he cannot be registered as a proprietor.[5]   If he is so registered, the register may be rectified,[6] so as to give effect to the legal position as it would be in unregistered conveyancing,[7] and until rectification has been effected, the position can be safeguarded by entering a restriction to prevent all dealings with the land.

Section 111 of the Land Registration Act 1925 provides that no purported disposition in favour of an infant, whether by deed or will, shall entitle the infant to be registered as proprietor until he attains full age, but in the meantime shall operate only as a declaration binding on the proprietor or personal representative that the registered land is to be held on trust to give effect to minor interests in favour of the infant corresponding, as nearly as may be, with the interests which the disposition purports to transfer or create.   The disposition or a copy or extract from it must be deposited at the Land Registry and must unless and until the tenants for life, statutory owners, personal representatives or trustees for sale are registered as proprietors, be protected by means of a restriction or otherwise on the register.   If a disposition is made to an infant jointly with another person of full age, that person will, during the minority, be entitled to be registered as proprietor and the infant may not be registered until he attains full age.   The beneficial interest of the infant should be protected by the entry of an appropriate restriction.

---

[1] Reduced from 21 years by Family Law Reform Act 1969, s. 1, Sched. 3, para. 5, in respect of dispositions coming into effect after 1969.
[2] Trustee Act 1925, s. 31 (2).
[3] *Ibid.*, s. 32.
[4] L.R.A. 1925, s. 3 (iv).   See generally Ruoff and Roper, pp. 158–9, 394–6.
[5] *Ibid.*, s. 2 (1).
[6] *Ibid.*, s. 82 (1) (*g*).
[7] Ruoff and Roper, p. 159.

CHAPTER II

MARRIED WOMEN

History. Married women have at last emerged from that bondage which formerly characterized their status. The history of their proprietary disabilities forms an illuminating chapter in the growth of English law. At common law husband and wife were one person. The general result of this merger of the wife's status in that of her husband was that he became absolute owner of her personal chattels, he might dispose of her leaseholds and take the proceeds, and he had the sole right of controlling and managing her freehold estates. If she predeceased him, he became absolutely entitled to any personal property of which she died possessed, and to a life estate by curtesy in her freehold estates of inheritance provided that a child had been born.[1] Again, a man could not make a grant to his wife directly or enter into a covenant with her, for to allow either of these things would have been to suppose her separate existence. In short, the effect of marriage at common law was to make a man complete master of his wife's property and to deprive her of contractual capacity.

Gradually, however, and quite apart from legislation, wives were placed by the courts of equity in an even more favourable position than men or unmarried women, a result that was due to the invention by the Court of Chancery of the doctrine of *equitable separate estate*. If property was given to a married woman by words which indicated either expressly or by implication that she was to enjoy it *for her sole and separate use*, equity removed that property from the control of the husband by regarding him as a trustee, and conferred upon the wife full powers of enjoyment and disposition. But equity went even further than this, for, perceiving the danger that a husband might over-persuade his wife to sell her separate property and hand the proceeds to him, it permitted the insertion in marriage settlements of what was known as a *restraint upon anticipation*. The effect of such a restraint was that a woman, while possessing full enjoyment of the income, was prevented during her coverture from

---

[1] *Supra*, p. 244.

alienating or charging the corpus of the property.   She could devise, but could not sell or mortgage it.

Statutory
separate
property.

The next step in the emancipation of married women came with the enactment from 1870 onwards of various Married Women's Property Acts.[1]   The principle of these was not to let the existence of separate property depend upon the intention of the donor, but to provide that in all cases property of married women should be separate property.   Thus the intervention of the court of equity was no longer needed, for all property belonging to a married woman became her *statutory separate property* over which she had sole control and power of disposition.

Woman's
proprietary
rights now
unaffected
by marriage.

The final stage in the emancipation of married women came with the Law Reform (Married Women and Tortfeasors) Act 1935.   This provides that so far as concerns the acquisition, holding and disposition of any property a married woman shall be in the same position as if she were a *feme sole*.   This Act also forbade the imposition of restraints upon anticipation after 1935, while preserving those already in existence, but in 1949 all restrictions upon anticipation or alienation, whether already imposed or not, were totally abolished.[2]   Thus in future any restriction which it is proposed to place upon the enjoyment of property by a married woman must take the form of a protective trust, which is the only form of restriction applicable to a man or a *feme sole*.[3]

Married
Women's
Property
Act 1964.

The position of a married woman has, indeed, been improved in a more positive sense by a statute which entitles her to a half share in any property acquired out of money given to her for household expenses.[4]

---

[1] See Dicey, *Law and Opinion in England* (2nd Edn.), pp. 371–395.
[2] Married Women (Restraint upon Anticipation) Act 1949.
[3] *Supra*, p. 364.
[4] Married Women's Property Act 1964, s. 1.   See Bromley, *Family Law* (4th Edn.), pp. 362–3.   For the rights of one spouse in the matrimonial home owned by the other spouse, see *supra*, pp. 231–5.

CHAPTER III

PERSONS SUFFERING FROM MENTAL DISORDER

The law relating to mentally incompetent persons, originally styled " lunatics " by the legislature, then " persons of unsound mind " and now " mental patients," has been codified and radically altered by the Mental Health Act 1959. There is no longer any distinction between lunatics *so found* and lunatics *not so found*, for the former practice under which, after a formal inquiry (" inquisition "), a patient could be declared to be of unsound mind and the management of his property be entrusted to a person called a " committee " has been abolished. Moreover, there are no longer different categories of patients, but only one, namely, a person who is suffering from " mental disorder " as defined by the Act.[1] The jurisdiction relating to the property of a patient is vested in the Lord Chancellor and three judges of the Chancery Division, called " nominated judges ", whose functions are also exercisable by the Master, Deputy Master or a nominated officer of the Court of Protection.[2] When exercising the statutory powers of management, such a person is referred to as " the judge. "[3]

This jurisdiction is exercisable where, after considering medical evidence, the judge is satisfied that a person is incapable by reason of mental disorder of managing and administering his property and affairs,[4] though in a case of emergency the judge may exercise his powers pending the determination of mental incapacity.[5] The jurisdiction is very wide.

Mental Health Act 1959.

Wide powers of management vested in the judge.

> " The general scheme of the new code is to confer on the judge a wide power in general terms to do anything expedient for the benefit of the patient or members of his family or other persons for whom he might be expected to provide, followed by certain express powers which are to be without prejudice to the overriding general power. In fact, it is difficult to think of any power which the judge would want to exercise which is not to be found in the specific powers."[6]

---

[1] Mental Health Act 1959, s. 4.
[2] This is not in fact a court, but an office of the Supreme Court.
[3] *Ibid.*, s. 100, 119 (1).
[4] *Ibid.*, s. 101.
[5] *Ibid.*, s. 104.
[6] (1960), 23 *M. L. R.* 421, 423 (Raymond Jennings).

Thus, in pursuance of his specific powers, the judge may make such orders as he thinks fit for the sale, exchange, charging, lease or other disposition of the patient's property,[1] and for the acquisition, settlement, or gift of any property.[2] Further the judge has power to direct or authorize the execution of a will or codicil, provided that the patient is of full age and the judge has reason to believe that the patient is incapable of making a valid will himself.[3]

Appointment of a receiver.

The judge may also appoint as receiver a specified person or the holder of a specified office and may authorize him to do all such things in relation to the property of a patient as he himself is empowered to do by the Act.[4]

Preservation of interests in property disposed of.

The paramount consideration of the judge in his exercise of these powers is the interest of the patient, even though this may mean changing the nature of his property to the detriment of those who would otherwise have been entitled to it on his death. The Act, therefore, includes provisions designed to preserve the interests of such persons. It provides in effect that where the patient's property has been disposed of by sale, exchange, charging or other disposition or where money has been spent on the purchase of property, then the proprietary rights of the persons entitled under his will or intestacy shall attach to that property in its new form. If the property was real property, any property representing it shall so long as it remains part of his estate be treated as real property.[5]

Conveyances of legal estate.

As regards conveyances of property, it is enacted that when a legal estate in land (whether settled or not) is vested in a person suffering from mental disorder, the judge may order his receiver or some other authorized person to make all requisite dispositions for conveying or creating a legal estate on his behalf.[6] Again, if land is vested in such a person on trust for sale, a new trustee must be appointed in his place.[7]

Intestacy in case of freehold held before 1926.

As regards the descent of land on intestacy, the rule under the Administration of Estates Act 1925 is that where a person of unsound mind was alive on 1st January, 1926 and was before that date entitled to a beneficial interest in freehold property, such interest shall in the event of his intestacy descend according to the old

---

[1] Mental Health Act 1959, s. 103 (1) (*b*).

[2] *Ibid.*, s. 103 (1) (*c*), (*d*). See *e.g. Re D.M.L.*, [1965] Ch. 1133 ; [1965] 2 All E. R. 129 ; *Re L.(W.J.G.)*, [1966] Ch. 135 ; [1965] 3 All E. R. 865 ; *Re C.M.G.*, [1970] Ch. 574 ; [1970] 2 All E. R. 740. A settlement made by a settlor when compos mentis may be varied under the Variation of Trusts Act 1958. *Re C.L.*, [1969] 1 Ch. 587 ; [1968] 1 All E. R. 1104.

[3] *Ibid.*, s. 103 (1) (*dd*), added by Administration of Justice Act 1969, s. 17 ; (1970) 34 Conv. (N.S.) 150 (D. G. Hunt and M. E. Reed). *Re H.M.F.* [1975] 3 W. L. R. 395 ; [1975] 2 All E. R. 795.

[4] *Ibid.*, s. 105 (1).

[5] *Ibid.*, s. 107 (1).

[6] L.P.A. 1925, s. 22 (1), as substituted by Mental Health Act 1959, s. 149 (1), Sched. 7, Part 1.

[7] *Ibid.*

canons of descent applicable to freeholds of inheritance before 1926.[1]

Where the proprietor of registered land or a registered charge is suffering from mental disorder, his receiver may exercise, in the name and behalf of the patient, all the powers which he could have exercised for himself if free from disability. In practice no restriction is entered on the register, unless the receiver expressly asks for one, or is himself registered as the proprietor.[2]

Registered land.

Finally we must notice that, once a receiver has been appointed, the patient loses all legal capacity to exercise any powers of disposition *inter vivos* over his property. Any attempted disposition is void.[3] He can, however, make a will during a lucid interval.[4] If no receiver is appointed, a disposition made during mental incapacity is voidable at the instance of the person making it, if the other party knows of the incapacity.[5]

Patient's incapacity.

The Law Commission is considering the law and practice governing powers of attorney and other forms of agency in relation to the mental incapacity of the principal.[6]

---

[1] A.E.A. 1925, s. 51 (2). *Supra*, p. 867. See *Re Gates*, [1930] 1 Ch. 199 ; *Re Sirett*, [1969] 1 W. L. R. 60 ; [1968] 3 All E. R. 186.

[2] L.R.A. 1925, s. 111 (5), as amended by Mental Health Act 1959, s. 149 (1), Sched. 7. See Ruoff and Roper, pp. 160–1.

[3] *Re Walker*, [1905] 1 Ch. 160 ; *Re Marshall*, [1920] 1 Ch. 284. No change was made in the rules by the Mental Health Act 1959.

[4] *In the Estate of Walker* (1912), 28 T.L.R. 466.

[5] *Molton* v. *Camroux* (1849), 4 Exch. 17 ; *Beaver* v. *M'Donnell* (1854), 9 Exch. 309 ; *Imperial Loan Co.* v. *Stone*, [1892] 1 Q. B. 599.

[6] Tenth Annual Report 1974–1975 (Law Com. No. 71).

CHAPTER IV

CORPORATIONS

Nature of corporations. **Necessity for incorporation.** One of the reasons for the existence of corporations is the principle of law that rights of property can be vested only in definite persons. It frequently occurs that a body of persons desires to hold and enjoy land, but apart from the case where a fluctuating class of persons acquires rights in the nature of easements by the method known as custom,[1] there are only two methods by which effect can be given to the desire. Either the land must be vested in trustees upon trust to hold and manage the land for the benefit of the proposed beneficiaries, or else the indefinite body of persons must be turned into a definite, though artificial, person called a corporation ; and this must be done by Royal Charter or by the authority of Parliament, whether in a special statute or by incorporation under the Companies Act 1948. The effect of this latter method is that the corporation becomes in the eye of the law a separate person, distinct from the members of which it is formed, and capable of acquiring, holding and alienating land.

Effect of incorporation. Thus the modern limited liability company is not, like a partnership, a mere collection or aggregate of the shareholders, but is a metaphysical entity, a legal *persona* with many of the rights and powers of a human person.

Classifications. **Classifications of Corporations.** Corporations may be classified in several ways. The main classification is into aggregate and sole.

Corporations aggregate. A corporation aggregate is a collection of several persons who are united together into one body and who are followed by a perpetual succession of members, so that the corporation is capable of existing for ever.[2] Examples are:

> the head and fellows of a college,
> the dean and chapter of a cathedral,
> the mayor and corporation of a city,
> a limited liability company incorporated under the Companies
>   Act 1948, and national corporations, such as the B.B.C. and
>   and the British Railways Board.

---

[1] *Supra,* pp. 571 *et seq.*   [2] Blackstone, vol. i. p. 469.

A corporation sole consists of a single person occupying a particular office and each and several of the persons in perpetuity who succeed him in that office, as, for instance, the vicar of a parish, the Secretary of State for the Environment and the Public Trustee. *Corporations sole.*

Another division of corporations is into ecclesiastical and lay.

Ecclesiastical corporations are those which exist for upholding religion and perpetuating the rights of the Church, such as bishops, parsons, and deans and chapters, and the abbot and monks of an earlier age. *Ecclesiastical corporations.*

Lay corporations may be either trading or non-trading corporations. *Lay corporations.*

Trading corporations are those which have been incorporated by charter, by special Act of Parliament or under the provisions of the Companies Act 1948, and whose main object is trade. *Trading.*

Non-trading corporations are those which have no concern with commerce, but which exist either for the better government of a town or district, such as urban district councils and municipal corporations, or for eleemosynary purposes, such as St. Thomas's Hospital and the colleges of Oxford and Cambridge. *Non-trading.*

A corporation can in general exist only if it has been formed under the authority of the State, and the two methods of creation in use at the present day are by charter from the Crown or by the authority of Parliament. If, for instance, a town wishes to become a borough, application must be made for a charter ; while persons who wish to form themselves into a trading corporation must either secure the passing of a private Act of Parliament or take advantage of the Companies Act 1948, which contains provisions enabling companies to be formed without the necessity of a special statute. *Methods of creation.*

But in addition to those that are incorporated by charter or by statute, corporations may also exist by common law and prescription.

Examples of common law corporations are a parson, a bishop, and the Crown. Corporations by prescription are those which have existed so long that the law presumes that they received from the Crown a grant or charter that has been lost.[1]

Doctrine of *Ultra Vires*. Statutory corporations are subject to the *ultra vires* doctrine. At common law a corporation that has been created by charter has power to deal with its property and to bind itself by contract to the same extent as a private person, and even if the charter imposes some direction which would have the effect of limiting its natural capacity, the legal power of the corporation is not affected, though the direction may be enforced by the Attorney-General.[2] *Ultra vires doctrine.*

---

[1] *Re Free Fishermen of Faversham* (1887), 36 Ch. D. 329, *supra*, p. 575.
[2] *Baroness Wenlock* v. *River Dee Co.* (1887), 36 Ch. D. 674, at p. 684 ; BOWEN, L.J.

But the case of a statutory corporation is very different. Such a body exists for certain purposes which are defined in the statute to which it owes its origin, and the powers of a statutory corporation are limited to those which are reasonably necessary to the realization of the purposes for which it is incorporated. The corporation possesses its own constitution (called, in the case of a trading company, the memorandum of association), which has statutory effect. Anything that the constitution authorizes, either expressly or by implication, can be done, but what is not so authorized is *ultra vires* and cannot be done.[1]

Capacity to deal with land. Corporations, whether aggregate or sole, have the same capacity as natural persons to acquire, hold and dispose of land. Where land is registered and the powers of alienation are limited in a way that would affect a purchaser if it were unregistered, an entry, usually in the form of a restriction, must be made on the register.[2]

Abolition of certain technicalities.

The Law of Property Act 1925 has removed certain conveyancing difficulties. There were rules at common law that leaseholds could not be granted to a corporation *sole* in such a way as to make them vest in the successive holders of the office ; and that a grant of land to a corporation sole made at a time when the office was vacant was void. If leaseholds were granted to a parson *qua* parson, and he died before the term had run out, his personal representatives and not his successor in the office became entitled to the residue of the lease.[3]

It is now, however, enacted [4] that where any property or *any interest* therein is or has been vested in a corporation sole, whether before or after 1926, it shall pass to the successors from time to time of such corporation. Again, it is enacted [5] that where property is granted to a corporation sole during a vacancy of the office, or to a corporation aggregate during a vacancy of the headship, the property shall, notwithstanding such vacancy, vest in the successor of the corporation sole, or in the corporation aggregate, as the case may be.

Words of limitation.

Again, the rule formerly was that, unless a grant was made to a corporation sole *and his successors*, the grant operated to confer a life estate upon the actual holder of the office in his natural capacity ; but now, as we have already seen, a conveyance of freehold land to a corporation sole by his corporate designation even without the word "successors" passes to the corporation the fee simple or other the whole interest which the grantor has power

[1] See Cheshire and Fifoot, *Law of Contract* (8th Edn.), pp. 411–14. For the effect on the doctrine of the European Communities Act 1972, s. 9 (1), see (1973) 32 C. L. J. 1. (J. G. Collier and L. S. Sealy.)

[2] L.R.R. 1925, r. 123 (4). See generally Ruoff and Roper, pp. 443 *et seq.*

[3] Co. Litt., 46b.

[4] L.P.A. 1925, s. 180 (1).

[5] *Ibid.*, s. 180 (2).

to convey in such land, unless a contrary intention appears in the conveyance.[1]

The rule at common law is that when a corporation is dissolved, any land which it may have held does not escheat to the Crown, but reverts to the original donor,[2] but after 1925 when a legal estate determines for this reason, the court is empowered to vest a corresponding estate in the person who would have been entitled to the estate had it not determined.[3] This power is apparently meant to be used when the corporation has been holding land as a trustee.

Dissolution of corporation.

Until January 1st, 1961, when the Charities Act 1960 came into force, the long established rule was that no land could be assured to or for the benefit of, or acquired by or on behalf of, any corporation unless the corporation was authorized, either by some statute or by a licence from the Crown, to hold land. If land was transferred by way of gift, sale, mortgage, settlement or devise to a corporation which had no such authority, the land was liable to be forfeited to the Crown.[4] The explanation of this disability lies far back in history and is to be found in the exigencies of the feudal system.[5]

Repeal of law of mortmain.

With the progress of time the restrictions imposed by the Mortmain and Charitable Uses Act 1891 had become of little significance, for the vast majority of corporations were for one reason or another exempt from the necessity to obtain a licence from the Crown. The subject, however, requires no further elaboration, for the Act was repealed by the Charities Act 1960,[6] and thus the law of mortmain is now defunct.

---

[1] *Supra*, p. 153.
[2] Co. Litt., 13*b* ; Blackstone, vol. i. pp. 484–5 ; *Hastings Corpn.* v. *Letton.* [1908] 1 K. B. 378 ; *Re Woking U.D.C.*, [1914] 1 Ch. 300, at p. 310.
[3] L.P.A. 1925, s. 181.
[4] Mortmain and Charitable Uses Act 1888, s. 1.
[5] See Simpson, *Introduction to the History of Land Law*, pp. 50–3, 172.
[6] S. 38.

CHAPTER V

CHARITIES

Abolition of
restrictions
upon
charitable
gifts of
land. **Assurances of land to a charity.** The right of a charity to acquire land was until recently severely restricted by the Mortmain and Charitable Uses Acts of 1888 and 1891, which dealt separately with assurances *inter vivos* and devises. Subject to many exceptions, the statutory rule broadly speaking was that an assurance of land *inter vivos* was void unless it was irrevocable and gave the charity the right to take immediate possession; and, if not made for valuable consideration, unless it was executed at least twelve months before the death of the alienor.

On the other hand, charitable devises, which generally speaking were not permitted until 1891, were declared to be valid by the Act of that year, subject however to the proviso that the land must be sold within one year from the testator's death unless the High Court or the Charity Commissioners decided otherwise.[1]

These restrictions, however, have now disappeared with the repeal of the Acts of 1888 and 1891 by the Charities Act 1960.[2]

Restriction
on charities
dealing with
their land. **Alienation of land by a charity.** All land which is vested in trustees for charitable, ecclesiastical or public purposes is deemed to be settled land under the Settled Land Act 1925, and the trustees have all the powers conferred by that Act on a tenant for life and on the trustees of the settlement, subject to obtaining any consents or orders required apart from the Act.[3] The land does, not, however, become settled land for all purposes ; for instance, a conveyance to a charity does not have to be made by a vesting deed and a trust instrument, and a sole trustee may receive capital money if the trust deed for the charity allows him to do so.[4]

These wide powers are subject to important restrictions. The freedom of charities to alienate or deal with their land has long been restricted by a series of Charitable Trusts Acts and now by the Charities Act 1960. The latter, replacing the former statutes, provides that no property forming part of the permanent

---

[1] Mortmain and Charitable Uses Act 1891, s. 5.   [2] S. 38.
[3] S.L.A. 1925, s. 29, as amended by Charities Act 1960, Sched. 7.
[4] *Re Boots and Southend-on-Sea Co.'s Contract*, [1927] 1 Ch. 579.

endowment[1] of a charity shall, without an order of the court or of the Charity Commissioners be mortgaged or charged by way of security for the repayment of money borrowed, nor, in the case of land in England or Wales, be sold, leased or otherwise disposed of.[2] Similar restrictions apply to land which is or has at any time been occupied for the purposes of a charity, even though it does not form part of the permanent endowment ; but if a transaction in respect of such land is entered into without the required order, it will nevertheless be valid in favour of a person who in good faith acquires an interest in or charge on the land for money or money's worth.[3] An order, however, is not required for a charity to grant a lease for a term ending not more than twenty-two years after it is granted, provided that it is not granted wholly or partly in consideration of a fine.[4]

These restrictions upon alienation do not affect " exempt charities," a list of which is given in the Act.[5] The list includes, *inter alia*, the universities of Oxford, Cambridge, London and Durham; the colleges and halls in Oxford, Cambridge and Durham; any university or similar institution declared by an Order in Council to be an exempt charity,[6] the British Museum and the Church Commissioners. *(margin: Exempt charities.)*

Registered land. In the case of registered land, the managing trustees of the charity, or, if there are no managing trustees and the land is vested in a corporation, the corporation, will be the registered proprietors, unless the legal estate is vested in the Official Custodian for Charities,[7] who will then be registered as proprietor, notwithstanding that the powers of disposition are vested in the managing trustees.[8] Further, if consent is required for dealing with the land, then a restriction must be entered on the register.[9] It is upon the Registrar " that the responsibility falls for reproducing on the register the facts of ownership and the limitations on the power of disposition which exist in the case of charity land."[10] *(margin: Registered land.)*

---

[1] *I.e.* property held subject to a restriction on the expenditure of capital. Charities Act 1960, s. 45 (3).

[2] Charities Act 1960, s. 29 (1).

[3] *Ibid.*, s. 29 (2).

[4] *Ibid.*, s. 29 (3) (*b*).

[5] *Ibid.*, s. 29 (4); Sched. 2.

[6] Further universities were added by Exempt Charities Orders 1962 (S.I. No. 1343), 1965 (S.I. No. 1715), 1966 (S.I. No. 1460), 1967 (S.I. No. 821), and 1969 (S.I. No. 1496) (The Open University).

[7] A public official in whom the property of a charity may be vested as a custodian trustee. Charities Act 1960, ss. 3, 17 (1).

[8] L.R.A. 1925, s. 98 ; L.R.R. 1925, r. 60.

[9] L.R.R. 1925, rr. 123 (2), 124.

[10] Ruoff and Roper, p. 420. See generally chap. 21. Purchasers of registered charity land need to see that the terms of any restriction on the register have been complied with, but if they do this it is not incumbent on them to give the registered title of a charity the same complex and detailed consideration that they would in the case of unregistered charity land.

BOOK IV

PLANNING LAW

SUMMARY

SECTION I. PLANNING CONTROL[1]

(1) PRIVATE PLANNING CONTROL

The aims of " planning control " are not identical with those of " planning ". Planning control is negative, and consists of being able to prevent changes on land which are for some reason thought to be objectionable. Planning is positive and consists of devising projects for the improvement of land from the standpoint of amenity and convenience, though not necessarily of profit. Both sets of aims are essentially subjective, and will perhaps be tolerable only if a sufficient measure of agreement about them exists among the public at large or the people who will be affected in any particular case. *Aims of planning and of planning control.*

The fact that Parliament has enacted the planning legislation now in force suggests that what those Acts contain is sufficiently acceptable to public opinion, even though many individuals may think otherwise. But it must be remembered that common law and equity have also developed a body of law relevant to the objectives of both " planning " and of " planning control ". There is the positive development of land which all owners and occupiers may carry out within the framework and protection of the law— the building and engineering projects, the mining and quarrying and other forms of land exploitation, which give us our present towns and villages, farms and factories—subject to the familiar restraints on activities which unjustifiably affect other persons either directly or indirectly. There are also those obligations by which the use and development of land is regulated between private owners, or public bodies acting in the same way as private owners, namely building and letting schemes comprising restrictive and leasehold covenants.[2] *Planning in private land law.*

The objectives of private planning and control by these methods are fundamentally the same as the objectives of public planning and control, but the decisions are taken largely with private ends in view, not public ones. This is very natural. The spacious squares and crescents might please the public, but these were *Limitations of private planning.*

---

[1] See generally *Encyclopaedia of the Law of Town and Country Planning*; Heap, *An Outline of Planning Law* (6th Edn. 1973) ; McCauslan, *Land, Law and Planning* (1975) ; Telling, *Planning Law and Procedure* (4th Edn. 1973).
[2] And to a lesser extent reciprocal positive freehold covenants and also easements. *Supra*, pp. 596 ; 623.

intended primarily to please the prospective residents who would be induced to buy or rent them. Many matters of public interest might not be dealt with completely or at all : sanitation and new main roads, prevention or removal of slums, containment of industry and commerce, preservation of the countryside and open space. The conclusion drawn from this, perhaps grudgingly, was that a body of *public* land law must be brought into existence beside the already developed body of private land law concerned with these objectives, and that it could only be achieved by statute. The immense variety of private local acts, the general acts governing public health and housing, waterworks and tramways and innumerable other public matters affecting land, which Parliament enacted during the nineteenth century, dealt in detail with specific kinds of land use. A generalized procedure for acquiring land for these various purposes, with recourse to compulsion if necessary,

Origins of public planning.

was evolved at the same time. Eventually it came to be accepted that there should be a generalized public control of land use as well. The first planning statute was passed in 1909,[1] though it only applied to " town " planning, and planning on the fringes of existing towns at that. Planning control, which was still potential rather than actual, later came to be extended more generally over towns, and then over the countryside also.[2] Finally, in 1943, the general extent of control became actual instead of potential and the modern planning era opened.[3]

Private planning in law is as extensive as ever it was, and the development of case law means that in theory and principle it is still growing.[4] In effect, what we now have are two general planning systems in law : one private, one public. The latter, however, seems to have stolen much of the thunder once belonging to the former, and with it this chapter is concerned.

(2) THE PUBLIC PLANNING SYSTEM

Planning statutes.

Until recently the principal planning statute was the Town and Country Planning Act 1962, which consolidated most of the previous

---

[1] Housing, Town Planning, etc. Act 1909.

[2] Hence " town *and country* " planning, though it might be thought less cumbersome to speak now simply of " planning ", or " land planning ". Under T.C.P.A. 1932 it depended largely on the initiative of local authorities whether or not a " planning scheme " would be devised in each particular case.

[3] Town and Country Planning (Interim Development) Act 1943. " Interim development " was originally development of any land begun *between* the decision to prepare a planning scheme and its coming into force : this needed official approval if it were to rank for compensation in the event of being overridden later by the requirements of the plan. The Act of 1943 applied this control everywhere.

[4] The unwary developer who thinks that because he has a planning permission he can ignore a restrictive covenant may receive a shock. But L.P.A. 1969, s. 28, requires the Lands Tribunal to " take into account the development plan and any declared or ascertainable pattern for the grant or refusal of planning permissions " when deciding whether a restrictive covenant should be discharged or modified, *supra*, p. 618. For development plans see *infra*, p. 939.

statutes, particularly the Town and Country Planning Acts of 1947, 1954 and 1959. It was altered in its turn by the Town and Country Planning Act 1968 ; and both have now been combined into a new consolidating Act, the Town and Country Planning Act 1971. Some other recent statutes have also contributed to planning law, including the Control of Office and Industrial Development Act 1965, the Civic Amenities Act 1967 and a small and highly technical Town and Country Planning Act 1963[1] ; and a number of their provisions are in the Town and Country Planning Act 1971.

Planning control is administered by a system of authorities, central and local. The central authority is now the Department of the Environment.[2] The Secretary of State for the Environment does not usually administer planning control directly ; but appeals are made to him from decisions of local planning authorities and he has the power to " call in " applications from them for decision at first instance.[3] A mass of statutory detail, including some matters of fundamental importance, is contained in subordinate legislation, the Acts having entrusted him with wide powers of making orders and regulations. He also has default powers[4] and exercises a co-ordinating function by issuing circulars which give guidance and advice to local planning authorities.

Central and local control.

Detailed administration is the task of the local planning authorities, which are county and district councils.[5] The former are " county planning authorities ", concerned chiefly with " strategic " matters ; the latter are " district planning authorities ", concerned normally with the routine business of planning control.

These authorities must not make their decisions at random. They are required to make, and constantly revise, " development plans " for their area ; and planning decisions should always be made with the appropriate development plan in mind even if for sound reasons they deviate from it.[6] The old system of develop-

Development plans.

---

[1] Dealing with marginal or " existing use " development : see *infra*, p. 972. There is also the Caravan Sites and Control of Development Act 1960.

[2] Successor to the Ministry of Town and Country Planning, whose existence was begun by the Minister of Town and Country Planning Act 1943, the Ministry of Local Government and Planning (1951) and the Ministry of Housing and Local Government (1951–1970). The duty of the Department was one of " securing consistency and continuity in the framing and execution of a national policy with respect to the use and development of land throughout England and Wales " (1943 Act, s. 1, repealed by the Secretary of State for the Environment Order 1970 (S.I. 1970 No. 1681), and not replaced). There are separate statutes for planning control in Scotland and Northern Ireland.

[3] See *infra*, p. 949.

[4] T.C.P.A. 1971, s. 276.

[5] Local Government Act 1972, ss. 182–3 and Sched. 16. In Greater London both the G.L.C. and the London boroughs including the City Corporation have planning powers (T.C.P.A. 1971, ss. 5, 19 and Sched. 3).

[6] T.C.P.A. 1971, s. 29 (1), requires local planning authorities to " have regard to the provisions of the development plan, so far as material to the application " for planning permission in any particular case.

ment plans has now been " frozen ", while a new system, introduced by Part I of the 1968 Act, is gradually being brought into use. The old system was discredited by its delays, which were caused by the requirement that the Minister must approve all plans, in every detail, before they could become effective.[1]

Structure and local plans.

The new system is to consist of two kinds of plan. First comes the structure plan, to formulate " policy and general proposals ".[2] The county planning authority must make it in draft and submit it to the Secretary of State ; and there must be publicity, to enable objectors to make representations to him, which he will deal with by causing " a person or persons appointed by him for the purpose to hold an examination in public of such matters affecting his consideration of the plan as he considers ought to be so examined. "[3] Second come the local plans, which may provide in detail for any part of the area covered by the structure plan. They are not normally to be submitted to the Secretary of State (in order to reduce delay), and the local planning authorities must themselves deal with representations from objectors.[4] Any parts of an authority's area which need to be generally replanned are to be specified in the structure plan as " action areas " and given their own local plans.[5]

The essence of any plan is a written statement. A local plan " shall consist of a map " as well ; but detailed scale maps are to be avoided in structure plans.[6] The pre-requisite for all these plans is a survey, which it is " the duty of the local planning authority to institute . . . in so far as they have not already done so ".[7]

Purpose of development plans.

The legal effect of development plans is largely indirect, in that their main function is to guide authorities in making policy decisions. There are exceptions to this, notably the requirement to consider development plans when compulsory purchase compensation is claimed on the basis that it includes " development value ",[8] and also the right to serve certain kinds of " blight notice ".[9]

---

[1] T.C.P.A. 1962, Part II. The delays are now longer than before.

[2] T.C.P.A. 1971, ss. 7–10.

[3] *Ibid.*, s. 9 (3), as substituted by the T.C.P. (Amendment) Act 1972, s. 3 (1). Ss. 1 and 2 of the latter Act also inserted ss. 10A and 10B into the T.C.P.A. 1971, making provision for joint plans and withdrawal of plans.

[4] *Ibid.*, ss. 11–15. District planning authorities will normally prepare local plans, but subject to " development plan schemes " made by each county planning authority to co-ordinate these activities (T.C.P.A. 1971, s. 10C, inserted by the Local Government Act 1972, s. 183 (2)).

[5] " Action areas " will broadly replace the old-style " comprehensive development areas, " ss. 7 (5) and 11 (6) ; local plans for them must be prepared " as soon as practicable after the approval of the (structure) plan ", and their re-planning will normally involve compulsory purchase : see *infra*, p. 969.

[6] T.C.P.A. 1971, ss. 7 (3), (6) ; 11 (3).

[7] *Ibid.*, s. 6. Planning staffs of local authorities continually review the state of development of their areas.

[8] The point is decided in many cases by seeing how the land is " zoned " in the current plan. See *infra*, p. 966.

[9] The occasion for a " blight notice " in many cases is an indication in the current plan that land will be required for some project of public development—

A brief mention may be made here of registers which local planning authorities are required to keep for public inspection. In addition to registers of local land charges, which include various orders, agreements and notices relevant to planning and compulsory purchase,[1] there are registers kept specifically for planning. Thus there are registers of planning applications, of applications for consent to display advertisements and of caravan site licences ; and there are also lists of buildings of special architectural or historic interest.[2] Prospective purchasers and their solicitors should always consult these registers and lists in appropriate circumstances, just as they normally apply for an official search of the local land charges registers.

Registers and lists.

(3) PLANNING AND THE COURTS

Planning disputes most commonly arise between local planning authorities and developers, or between acquiring authorities and owners ; and the rules of planning law, like practically all law, are framed with the basic purpose of giving guidance towards the settlement of disputes. If the assessment of compensation is in issue the dispute should be settled by the Lands Tribunal,[3] but if not the Secretary of State should normally settle it. But any dispute may have to be settled by the courts if it turns on a point of law.

The best way to understand the theory which underlies the system is to add, to the two judicial elements of law and fact, a third element, policy.[4] The Secretary of State is entitled to reach a decision on a general basis of law, fact and policy, or any of them ; but his paramount concern, as the central planning authority, is with policy, so long as he ascertains the facts and complies with the law. Indeed he is normally empowered to substitute his own policy decision purely and simply for that of the local planning authority. Thus an " appeal " to the Secretary of State is to be understood in an administrative rather than a judicial sense.[5]

Law, fact and policy.

However, even statutory branches of law are developed by judicial interpretation, and there is a constant flow of planning

---

roads being the most notorious example. See *infra*, p. 970. The current plan may have legal consequences in relation to claims for planning compensation (see *infra*, p. 974) that may be rejected as premature: T.C.P.A. 1971, s. 147 (4) (*a*)), and in relation to mineral working (*ibid.*, s. 265).

[1] *E.g.* enforcement notices, revocation and discontinuance orders, planning agreements, tree preservation orders, notices of compulsory purchase orders if general vesting declarations are to be made, planning compensation notices, and agreements under the Housing Act 1974, s. 126 (*infra*, p. 947, n. 2).

[2] T.C.P.A. 1971, ss. 34, 54 ; Caravan Sites and Control of Development Act 1960, s. 25 ; Town and Country Planning (Control of Advertisements) Regulations 1969, (S.I. No. 1532), reg. 31 ; Community Land Act 1975, s. 46 (*infra*).

[3] See *infra*, pp. 961, 973, 974.

[4] Usually referred to by the courts as " discretion," to indicate that it lies outside their control so long as its exercise is *intra vires*.

[5] See *Stringer* v. *Minister of Housing and Local Government*, [1970] 1 W.L.R. 128 ; [1971] 1 All E. R. 65.

cases into the law reports. These cases come before the courts whenever a dispute throws up a pure issue of law which the parties are prepared to pursue separately from disputes of fact or policy. The courts interpret the statutes, in principle and in detail, as confining them to such issues, and it is submitted that this is entirely right. The public authorities are inevitably the experts on policy, subject to Parliament and the electorate. The courts are the experts on the law.[1]

In one case, where it was alleged that a purported planning permission was invalid, the court said, " the validity of the so-called permission being a matter completely outside the jurisdiction of the Minister, there could be no conceivable reason for the [developers] not being able, if they so desired, to proceed in the courts for a declaration as to the validity of the permission ".[2] Again, a court will sometimes say, for example, " . . . the ground . . . stated by the Minister is not a valid ground at all and accordingly in my judgment this decision will have to be quashed " ;[3] or, " the Minister erred in law . . . In my judgment this case must go back to the Minister with the opinion of this court ".[4] On the other hand the courts frequently speak in terms like these: " Having come to the conclusion that it is impossible to say that the Minister erred in law, I would dismiss the appeal ".[5] But the courts must not alter a decision on policy grounds, even if they regard a policy decision as " surprising ".[6]

Restrictions on recourse to the courts.

There are stringent restrictions on recourse to the courts in planning cases. Many, but not all, decisions of the Secretary of State (as distinct from those of other authorities) can only be challenged by application within six weeks to the High Court ; and even so the court can only quash such decisions on the ground that they are " not within the powers of [the relevant Act], or that the interests of the applicant have been substantially prejudiced " by some procedural default.[7]

The restriction on recourse to the courts only applies to disputes over the *content* of a decision, that is to say a dispute which assumes

---

[1] *Certiorari* will lie to quash a decision of a planning authority for " error of law on the face of the record " : *R.* v. *Hillingdon London Borough Council, Ex parte Royco Homes, Ltd.* [1974] Q. B. 720 ; [1974] 2 All E. R. 643.
[2] *Edgwarebury Park Investments, Ltd.* v. *Minister of Housing and Local Government*, [1963] 2 Q. B. 408, at p. 417 ; [1963] 1 All E. R. 124, *per* Lord Parker, C.J. This hint concerning actions for a declaration is a valuable one.
[3] *R.* v. *Minister of Housing and Local Government, ex parte Chichester Rural District Council* [1960] 1 W.L.R. 587, at p. 589 ; [1960] 2 All E. R. 407, *per* Lord Parker, C.J. See *infra*, p. 969, n. 6.
[4] *Birmingham Corpn.* v. *Minister of Housing and Local Government and Habib Ullah*, [1964] 1 Q. B. 178, at p. 190, [1963] 3 All E. R. 668, *per* Lord Parker, C.J.
[5] *Cheshire County Council* v. *Woodward*, [1962] 2 Q. B. 126, at p. 135 ; [1962] 1 All E. R. 517, per Lord Parker, C.J.
[6] *Bendles Motors, Ltd.* v. *Bristol Corpn.*, [1963] 1 W. L. R. 247 at p. 252; [1963] 1 All E. R. 578, *per* Lord Parker, C.J.
[7] See, *e.g.* T.C.P.A. 1971, ss. 242, 245 ; Acquisition of Land (Authorization Procedure) Act 1946, 1st Sched., para 15.

that a contested decision of an authority, whether or not its content is bad in law, is inherently valid. The right to challenge the existence of a decision on the ground that it is invalid and so a nullity seems not to be restricted ; and it is submitted that this is a most desirable distinction to draw. If it were otherwise " the court must accept and could not even inquire whether a purported determination was a forged or inaccurate order . . . ", which would be absurd. " A more reasonable and logical construction is that . . . Parliament meant a real determination, not a purported determination ".[1] Again, " the courts' supervisory duty is to see that [the authority] makes the authorised inquiry according to natural justice and arrives at a decision, whether right or wrong . . . they will not intervene merely because it has or may have come to the wrong answer, provided that this is an answer that lies within its jurisdiction ".[2]

The reference to " natural justice " leads to the next point, that the Secretary of State's decisions, taken remotely from each locality concerned, are usually reached on the basis of first granting a hearing to objectors. Many of the statutory provisions require him to " afford . . . an opportunity of appearing before, and being heard by, a person appointed by the Secretary of State for the purpose "[3] (*i.e.* an inspector) to objectors, appellants, claimants or " persons aggrieved ". It is settled that such proceedings must not be conducted in defiance of " natural justice ", which comes down to two basic rules, namely that the person presiding must not be biased and that both sides are given a proper hearing on the points at issue.[4] A proceeding of this kind, although held as part of an *administrative* process, is often said to be " quasi-judicial " even though the rest of the process is not ; so that the final decision emerging from that process can be quashed by the courts if " natural justice " is not observed. The quashing will be on an issue of law, never of fact or policy.

[margin note: Natural justice. *]*

Recently some of these inquiries have been subjected to safeguards additional to the rules of " natural justice ". These are planning appeal inquiries[5] and compulsory purchase order inquiries. The various sets of Inquiries Procedure Rules[6] govern-

[margin note: Inquiries Procedure Rules. *]*

---

[1] *Anisminic, Ltd.* v. *Foreign Compensation Commission,* [1969] 2 A. C. 147, at p. 199 ; [1969] 1 All E. R. 208, at p. 237, *per* Lord PEARCE.
[2] *Ibid.,* at p. 195. The decision questioned in this case was a determination by the Foreign Compensation Commission which, as provided by the Foreign Compensation Act 1950, s. 4 (4), " shall not be called in question in any court of law ". This is not a planning case, but the underlying principle is fully relevant to planning law.
[3] See, *e.g.* T.C.P.A. 1971, ss. 35 (5), 36 (4), 45 (3), 51 (6), 182 (3).
[4] See *R.* v. *Sussex Justices, Ex parte McCarthy,* [1924] 1 K. B. 256, for the first rule (" Justice should not only be done, but should manifestly and undoubtedly be seen to be done ") ; and *Errington* v. *Minister of Health,* [1935] 1 K. B. 249, for the second rule. See Jackson, *Natural Justice.*
[5] On applications, but not on enforcement. See *infra,* pp. 949, 952.
[6] See Town and Country Planning Appeals (Determination by Appointed Persons) (Inquiries Procedure) Rules 1974 (S.I. No. 420) ; Town and Country

ing these inquiries prescribe time limits, and what notice shall be given to the parties concerned, and above all that there shall be written submissions made in advance by the authority stating the contentions on which they intend to rely. Another important provision is that, although the Secretary of State has full discretion to make his eventual decision, so that he may reject any or all of the recommendations made by the inspector in his report, nevertheless he must hear any further representations if he should disagree on any finding of fact (not policy) or consider any new issues or evidence of fact ; and in the latter two cases he must re-open the inquiry if asked to do so.[1]

(4) THE NATURE OF DEVELOPMENT

Definition
of "develop-
ment".

The definition of " development " is the basic concept of planning law. Section 22 (1) of the 1971 Act defines it as meaning " the carrying out of building, engineering, mining or other operations in, on, over or under land, or the making of any material change in the use of any buildings or other land ". Thus there will be development either if an " operation " is carried out, or if a "material change of use " is brought about. Often a project involves development because there will be one or more operations and a material change of use as well.[2]

Use
Classes.

Section 22 lists specific matters which either are or are not " development ". The latter include " in the case of buildings or other land which are used for a purpose of any class specified in an order made by the Minister under this section, the use thereof for any other purpose of the same class ".[3] Thus we have the Town and Country Planning (Use Classes) Order 1972,[4] which lists eighteen " use classes " ; and any change within a " use class " is not development at all,[5] or in other words not " material ".

Planning (Inquiries Procedure) Rules 1974 (S.I. No. 419) ; Compulsory Purchase by Local Authorities (Inquiries Procedure) Rules 1962 (S.I. No. 1424); Compulsory Purchase by Ministers (Inquiries Procedure) Rules 1967 (S.I. No. 720) ; Pipe-Lines (Inquiries Procedure) Rules 1967 (S.I. No. 1769).
    [1] One or two requirements govern conduct of the inquiry itself, but by and large the inspector is not bound by rules of evidence and procedure which must be observed in court. Disagreement on policy is not of course disagreement on fact : see *Lord Luke of Pavenham* v. *Minister of Housing and Local Government*, [1968] 1 Q. B. 172 ; [1967] 2 All E. R. 1066. Where issues wider than those of pure planning are at stake, the Secretary of State may replace an ordinary inquiry by a "planning inquiry commission", which will involve a more elaborate procedure altogether. See T.C.P.A. 1971, ss. 47–9.
    [2] *E.g.* if a field used for agriculture is developed by building a house on it. For expansion of a building below ground, see T.C.P.A. 1971, s. 22 (2) (*a*). For interpretation generally, see *ibid.*, s. 290.
    [3] T.C.P.A. 1971, s. 22 (2) (*f*).
    [4] S.I. 1972, No. 1385 ; M. & B. p. 781.
    [5] Except under a planning permission granted subject to a condition that no change of use occurs, even within the same use class : see *Kingston-upon-Thames Royal London Borough Council* v. *Secretary of State for the Environment*, [1973] 1 W.L.R. 1549 ; [1974] 1 All E. R. 193.

Whether any work amounts to an " operation " or whether any "Fact and change of use is " material " is a " question of fact and degree "[1] degree." in the circumstances of each particular case. Building a model village as a permanent structure has been held to involve an " operation "[2] but not placing a mobile hopper and conveyor in a coal-merchant's yard.[3] Placing an egg-vending machine on the roadside of a farm has been held to involve a material change of use;[4] but not altering part of a railway station yard from a coal depot to a transit depot for crated motor vehicles.[5] In all four cases the court merely declined to invalidate a finding already made. The burden of proof, in other words, rests heavily on that party who alleges that a finding in relation to development is *ultra vires*.

Ownership of land, or of things placed on land, is irrelevant to Special planning except in special circumstances :[6] what matters is the aspects of nature of what is done on or to the land. Some ancillary questions ment. which may be relevant are : (i) actual area involved ;[7] (ii) whether there are multiple uses on a given area of land and whether these are of equal importance,[8] or are major and minor uses,[9] or are confined to separate parts of the premises,[10] or are intermittent, alternating or recurring.[11] Three especially teasing questions are, whether

---

[1] Per GLYN-JONES, J., in *Marshall* v. *Nottingham Corpn.* [1960] I W. L. R. 707 ; [1960] I All E. R. 659, quoted by Lord PARKER, C.J., in *East Barnet Urban District Council* v. *British Transport Commission*, [1962] 2 Q. B. 484, at p. 491 ; [1961] 3 All E. R. 878. To use land for agriculture or forestry does not constitute development, regardless of any change in use which may be involved ; this includes buildings occupied with such land : T.C.P.A. 1971, s. 22 (2) (e). Breeding and training horses for show-jumping is not "agriculture" (*Belmont Farm, Ltd.* v. *Minister of Housing and Local Government* (1962), 13 P. & C. R. 417) which is defined in s. 290 of the 1971 Act.
[2] *Buckinghamshire County Council* v. *Callingham*, [1952] 2 Q. B. 515 ; [1952] I All E. R. 1166.
[3] *Cheshire County Council* v. *Woodward*, [1962] 2 Q. B. 126 ; [1962] I All E. R. 517; M. & B. p. 784.
[4] *Hidderley* v. *Warwickshire County Council* (1963), 14 P. & C. R. 134. (So has a change from bed-sitters to hotel accommodation, see *Mayflower Cambridge* v. *Secretary of State for the Environment* (1975), 30 P. & C. R. 28.)
[5] *East Barnet Urban District Council* v. *British Transport Commission*, [1962] 2 Q. B. 484 ; [1961] 3 All E. R. 878; M. & B. p. 785.
[6] See (1960), J.P.L., p. 436. Also irrelevant is the question whether a public body or a private firm is carrying out a particular use of premises : *Rael-Brook, Ltd.* v. *Minister of Housing and Local Government*, [1967] 2 Q. B. 65 ; [1967] I All E. R. 262.
[7] The relevant " planning unit " is normally the total area of land occupied, e.g. the house with its curtilage, as distinct from merely the conservatory built onto the house, in *Wood* v. *Secretary of State for the Environment*, [1973] I W.L.R. 707 ; [1973] 2 All E. R. 404 ; M. & B. p. 787.
[8] *Marshall* v. *Nottingham Corpn.*, [1960] I W. L. R. 707 ; [1960] I All E. R. 659.
[9] *Mansi* v. *Elstree Rural District Council* (1964), 16 P. & C. R. 153 ; *Vickers-Armstrong, Ltd.* v. *Central Land Board* (1957), 9 P. & C. R. 33.
[10] *Hartnell* v. *Minister of Housing and Local Government*, [1965] A. C. 1134; [1965] I All E. R. 490.
[11] *Webber* v. *Minister of Housing and Local Government*, [1968] I W.L.R. 29; [1967] 3 All E. R. 981; M. & B. p. 789.

demolition is an " operation ",[1] and whether the abandonment
or the intensification of a use is a " material change ".[2]

(5) CONTROL OF DEVELOPMENT

Planning
permission
and
develop-
ment
orders.

Section 23 of the 1971 Act states that planning permission is
" required " for carrying out development (subject to certain
special exceptions).[3]   Section 24 empowers the Secretary of State
to make " development orders," for the purpose (among others)
of actually granting permission, on a general and automatic basis,
for certain forms of development.   The Town and Country
Planning General Development Order 1973.[4] widely known as the
" G.D.O.", gives such permission for twenty-three classes of development which it carefully specifies.   Apart from this there are
other sections in the 1971 Act under which planning permission
is " deemed " to be granted.[5]

Outline
applica-
tions.

The G.D.O. prescribes the procedure for making applications
to the local planning authority for planning permission.   If a
building is to be erected, an application may be made for " outline "
permission, which means for approval in principle.   If this is
refused no time and expense need be wasted on detailed plans.   If
it is granted, separate application will need to be made for details
to be approved—" reserved matters ".[6]

How to
apply for
planning
permission.

Any person may apply for planning permission ; but an applicant who owns neither a freehold nor a leasehold in all the land
affected (normally a prospective purchaser) must notify all freeholders, leaseholders with ten years or more to run, and farm tenants,
either directly or, if that is not possible, by local press publicity.[7]
There are also certain classes of controversial development which
must be publicised.[8]   The persons notified by these methods may

---

[1] *Coleshill and District Investment Co. Ltd.* v. *Minister of Housing and Local
Government,* [1969] 1 W.L.R. 746 ; [1969] 2 All E. R. 525.
[2] Abandonment by itself is hardly likely to be held to constitute development, but *resumption* of use after abandonment is another matter.   See
Hartley v. *Minister of Housing and Local Government,* [1970] 1 Q. B. 413 ; [1969]
3 All E. R. 1658 ; and *Fyson* v. *Buckinghamshire County Council,* [1958]
1 W.L.R. 634 ;   [1958] 2 All E.R. 286. For intensification, see *Birmingham
Corpn.* v. *Minister of Housing and Local Government,* [1964] 1 Q. B. 178 ; [1963]
3 All E. R. 668; M. & B. p. 787.
[3] Omitted here for reasons of space.   They relate to temporary and intermittent uses, and lack of use, dating back to 1948, and also to resumption of
uses after temporary planning permissions or enforcement notices.   The
resumed use may itself be lawful—i.e. not subject to enforcement procedure
(even if only for the reason that it is protected by lapse of time) : see *L.T.S.S.
Print and Supply Services, Ltd.* v. *Hackney London Borough Council,* [1975]
1 W. L. R. 138 ; [1975] 1 All E. R. 374.   But even this is not essential : see
W. T. Lamb & Sons, Ltd. v. *Secretary of State for the Environment,* [1975]
2 All E. R. 1117.
[4] S.I. 1973, No. 31 (amended by S.I. 1973, No. 273 and S.I. 1974, No. 418).
[5] See ss. 40 and 64.
[6] G.D.O. article 5.
[7] T.C.P.A. 1971, s. 27.   G.D.O. article 9.
[8] *Ibid.,* s. 26.   G.D.O. article 8.

" make representations " which the authority must take into account.

A more tentative approach may be made by a prospective developer who is not certain whether his project amounts to " development " at all, by requesting the authority (in writing) to " determine that question ".[1] Again, it is possible for " a person interested in land " to make an agreement with the authority (enforceable against him or persons deriving title under him) regulating development of that land on a more general basis than for a normal planning permission.[2]

On receiving an application the local planning authority must consult other authorities and government departments, as appropriate, and " have regard to the provisions of the development plan ".[3] Within two months they must notify their decision to the applicant.[4] They may grant permission[5] unconditionally, or " subject to such conditions as they think fit", or refuse it.[6] The possibility that a project could be regulated under some other statutory procedure does not preclude a refusal of planning permission, even if that other procedure might carry with it a right to compensation.[7]

Planning conditions are subject to a test of validity both in

Determinations and agreements.

Grant or refusal of planning permission.

Conditional planning permissions.

---

[1] And also to say if an application for planning permission " is required ", *ibid.*, s. 53. Appeal lies to the Secretary of State, and thence, on a point of law, to the High Court (*ibid.*, s. 247).

[2] T.C.P.A. 1971, s. 52. Restrictions binding on an owner under such an agreement run with the land to bind his successors even though they do not benefit any land of the local planning authority as covenantees. Housing Act 1974, s. 126, empowers local authorities to enter into *positive* agreements for the development of land, also binding on successors.

[3] *Ibid.*, ss. 25, 29, 31. G.D.O., articles 7, 11–14. To " have regard to " the development plan does not mean that there is any duty to conform strictly with its details : *Enfield London Borough* v. *Secretary of State for the Environment* (1974), 233 Estates Gazette 53.

[4] G.D.O., article 7, para 3.

[5] A person with the benefit of a planning permission has the choice either to make use of it or to continue as before. If he chooses the former he cannot complain of being made to forgo the latter. In *Petticoat Lane Rentals, Ltd.* v. *Secretary of State for the Environment*, [1971] 1 W. L. R. 1112 ; [1971] 2 All E. R. 793 ; M. & B. p. 792, permission was given, and acted on, to build upon a derelict site. An attempt to continue the previous use of the site for market trading (the new building being raised on pillars) was held to be a breach of planning control. Planning permissions may be retrospective (T.C.P.A. 1971, s. 32). For the suspension of permissions under the Community Land Act 1975, ss. 19–22, see *infra*.

[6] T.C.P.A. 1971, s. 29 (1) (*a*), (*b*). Reasons must be given for refusals or conditional grants of planning permission : G.D.O., article 7, para. 4 (*a*). Decisions will be communicated by officials, who must not exceed their authority. But they have an implied authority to allow trivial variations of permission : *Lever Finance, Ltd.* v. *Westminster (City) London Borough Council*, [1971] 1 Q. B. 222 ; [1970] 3 All E. R. 496; M. & B. p. 794. Moreover, an authority may be estopped from denying a permission given in excess of an officer's powers, though not if the recipient suffers no detriment from the denial : *Norfolk County Council* v. *Secretary of State for the Environment*, [1973] 1 W. L. R. 1400 ; [1973] 3 All E. R. 673.

[7] *Westminster Bank Ltd.* v. *Beverley Borough Council*, [1971] A.C. 508 ; [1970] 1 All E. R. 734. And see T.C.P.A. 1971, s. 289.

principle and in detail. That is to say they must " fairly and reasonably relate to the permitted development "[1] and they must be reasonable in respect of their detailed terms. A condition that cottages to be built must only be occupied by " persons whose employment or latest employment is or was employment in agriculture " seems to have satisfied both tests.[2] A condition that a project of industrial development on a site next to a dangerously congested main road must include the provision of a special access road, and that this access road should be made available to members of the public visiting adjoining premises, seems to have satisfied the first test but not the second.[3]

Time limits for development. Conditions which may be valid include those which require a new use to cease after a stated time. These are referred to as " limitations" and they give effect to temporary planning permissions ;[4] apart from them permissions are normally permanent and " enure for the benefit of the land ".[5] Other time conditions, which are so frequent as to be virtually standard-form conditions, specify the time within which development must take place, or at least begin. There is a statutory three-year deadline in " outline " permissions for seeking approval for all detail or " reserved matters ",[6] followed by a two-year deadline for starting development after final approval ; alternatively there is an overall five-year deadline for starting development, if longer,[7] as well as a five-year deadline for starting development under ordinary as distinct from " outline " permissions.[8] The authority, however, can vary any of these periods. There is, moreover, an additional control, by " completion notice ". Where any of the above deadlines applies and development has duly begun in the time specified but has not been completed in that time, the local planning autho-

---

[1] *Pyx Granite Co., Ltd.* v. *Minister of Housing and Local Government*, [1958] 1 Q. B. 554, at p. 572 ; [1958] 1 All E. R. 625, *per* Lord DENNING.
[2] *Fawcett Properties, Ltd.* v. *Buckinghamshire County Council*, [1961] A. C. 636 ; [1960] 3 All E. R. 503; M. & B. p. 797.
[3] *Hall and Co., Ltd.* v. *Shoreham Urban District Council*, [1964] 1 W.L.R. 240 ; [1964] 1 All E. R. 1. If an invalidated condition is trivial the planning permission will survive shorn of it, but if it is not trivial the permission falls with it : *Kent County Council* v. *Kingsway Investments (Kent) Ltd.*, [1971] A.C. 72 ; [1970] 1 All E. R., 70, *per* Lord MORRIS OF BORTH-Y-GEST. Yet this question would seem to be one of planning policy, not law, and should therefore be remitted to the appropriate authority to decide. Planning permissions, however conditional, ought to be regarded *as a whole*. An altered permission is a different permission, except perhaps in respect of trivial variations (see *Lever Finance, Ltd.* v. *Westminster (City) London Borough Council*, [1971] 1 Q. B. 222 ; [1970] 3 All E. R. 496). The court may remit a case to a planning authority (see *Birmingham Corpn.* v. *Minister of Housing and Local Government*, [1964] 1 Q. B. 178 ; [1963] 3 All E. R. 668).
[4] T.C.P.A. 1971, s. 30.
[5] *Ibid.*, s. 33 (1).
[6] Thus in cases of " outline " permissions applicants may submit as many detailed proposals in respect of the " reserved matters " as they wish, so long as they do so within the three-year period (*per* Lord DENNING, M.R., in *Kingsway Investments, Ltd.* v. *Kent County Council*, [1969] 1 All E. R. 601, at p. 607).
[7] T.C.P.A. 1971, s. 42.
[8] *Ibid.*, s. 41.

rity may serve a " completion notice ", subject to confirmation by the Secretary of State (with or without amendments) specifying a time, not less than a year, by which development must be complete or else the permission " will cease to have effect ".[1]

If he so wishes, the Secretary of State may direct that a planning application be " called in " (as it is usually termed), that is referred to him instead of being decided by the local planning authority.[2] Such cases, however, are as rare as appeals are frequent. Appeals to the Secretary of State against a refusal of permission, or a grant made subject to conditions, or a failure to give any decision within the appropriate time-limit, must be made in writing within six months of the adverse decision or of the expiry of the time-limit.[3] He may allow or dismiss the appeal or reverse or vary any part of the permission, and his decision is as free as if he were deciding at first instance. The procedure is now governed by statutory rules, which have already been discussed, and a hearing must be given if it is asked for.[4]

The Secretary of State's decision on an appeal, or that made by an inspector on his behalf, is " final " and cannot be challenged in a court except in the circumstances described earlier.[5]

Planning permission can be revoked or modified.[6] The authorities which do this must pay compensation for any abortive expenditure and for any depreciation in relation to development value which, having come into existence by virtue of the permission, disappears because of the revocation or modification. Revocation or modification orders must be confirmed by the Secretary of State[6] except in uncontested cases.[7] If permission is given automatically by the G.D.O. it may *in effect* be revoked or modified, if by an " article 4 direction " under the G.D.O. it is partly or wholly withdrawn and a specific application is then made which is refused or only granted subject to conditions.[8]

---

[1] T.C.P.A. 1971, s. 44.

[2] *Ibid.*, s. 35. G.D.O. article 15. The proposed development will probably be controversial, as at the Monico Café site in Piccadilly Circus.

[3] *Ibid.*, ss. 36–7. G.D.O. article 16. The time-limit of 2 or 3 months (see *supra*, p. 947) is merely to facilitate appeals ; it is not mandatory, and a decision given later (there are many such) will not be automatically invalidated : *James* v. *Secretary of State for Wales*, [1968] A. C. 409 ; [1966] 3 All E. R. 964.

[4] The inspector, who presides over the hearing or inquiry afforded in connection with a decision to be made by the Secretary of State, may be allowed in prescribed cases to make the decision himself instead of merely reporting back : T.C.P.A. 1971, 9th Sched. This may make for quicker results in routine cases. See Town and Country Planning (Determination of Appeals by Appointed Persons) (Prescribed Classes) Regulations 1972 (S.I. No. 1652).

[5] See *supra*, p. 942.

[6] T.C.P.A. 1971, s. 45. The recipient is entitled to prior notice and a hearing.

[7] *Ibid.*, s. 46.

[8] G.D.O., article 4. The Secretary of State must normally make or confirm the direction ; but there is no provision for any prior notice or hearing. Or the development order itself might be partly or wholly withdrawn. For compensation see *infra*, p. 973 : T.C.P.A. 1971, ss. 164–5.

In so far as authorized development has actually taken place, even if only in part, revocation or modification orders and " article 4 directions " are ineffective. To put an end to any actual development or " established use " of land (except of course where it is the necessary consequence of acting on a planning permission that this should happen) requires a discontinuance order, which must be confirmed by the Secretary of State *a fortiori*.[1] Compensation must be paid for loss of development value and abortive expenditure and also the cost of removal or demolition.[2] As compliance involves physical action there is also an enforcement procedure in cases of recalcitrance, similar in essentials to ordinary enforcement of planning control.[3]

Finally, a brief mention may be made of the methods by which certain particular kinds of development are controlled : first, industrial and office development, and second, development by public authorities.

Control of industrial and office development.

Industrial and office development, which like development in general may occur by means of operations or material changes of use, each need in many cases a grant of permission from the Secretary of State as well as planning permission, and need it in advance. Minor cases are exempt from this additional control, and exemption is based on floor-space. What is obtained from the Secretary of State is an " industrial development certificate " or an " office development permit " respectively.[4] Office control, however, only applies to the " metropolitan region " and certain other urban areas specially designated, and will end in 1977 unless extended.[5] There is no right of appeal or other redress if an I.D.C. or an O.D.P. is refused, or granted subject to restrictions (governing the mode of applying for planning permission) or conditions (governing the development itself).[6]

Development by public authorities.

Public authorities are subject to planning control with certain reservations. The most far-reaching concerns the Crown, to which planning control does not apply at all, though as a matter of practice the relevant government departments do normally consult

---

[1] T.C.P.A. 1971, s. 51. The recipient is entitled to prior notice and a hearing. An " article 4 direction " was held to be ineffective when permitted development under the G.D.O. had been carried out in *Cole* v. *Somerset County Council*, [1957] 1 Q. B. 23 ; [1956] 3 All E. R. 531.

[2] *Ibid.*, s. 170. See *infra*, p. 973.

[3] *Ibid.*, s. 108. For ordinary enforcement procedure see *infra*, pp. 951-4.

[4] *Ibid.*, ss. 66-86 ; for mixed office and industrial use see s. 76.

[5] *Ibid.*, s. 86 as amended by the T.C.P. (Amendment) Act 1972 s. 5. The " metropolitan region " is most of south-east England.

[6] When considering an application for an I.D.C. or an O.D.P. the Secretary of State must have regard to " the proper distribution of industry " and " the better distribution of employment " respectively. (T.C.P.A. 1971, ss. 67 (1), (3), 74 (3)). For the effect of I.D.C. control on planning compensation and purchase notices (*infra*, pp. 969-74), see T.C.P.A. 1971, ss. 72, 151, 169 (5), 191 (2).

local planning authorities when proposing to develop land.[1] Ordinary local authorities, however, have no such immunity, except that when any project which involves expenditure requires the approval of a government department such approval may also be expressed to confer " deemed " planning permission, with or without conditions, if needed.[2] This rule applies to " statutory undertakers " as well, that is the nationalized industries and public utility authorities ; but with them there is also another factor, the difference between their " operational " and non-operational land (the latter being offices, houses, investment property and any other land which is not the site of their operating functions). " Operational " land has the benefit of one or two special rules in planning law, for example in regard to compensation for restrictions on development.[3] As for local *planning* authorities, separate regulations are prescribed, whereby they are " deemed " to have planning permission from the Secretary of State (unless he requires a specific application) for any development they carry out in accordance with their own development plan ; but they must normally apply to him specifically if they wish to go against the plan.[4]

(6) BREACH OF PLANNING CONTROL

It is not a criminal offence to develop land without planning permission. If this happens the local planning authority should first consider whether it would be " expedient " to impose sanctions, " having regard to the development plan and to any other material considerations."[5] If it would, they may serve an " enforcement notice " on the owner and occupier of the land.[6] It must specify the " breach of planning control " complained of and the steps[7] required to remedy it, and also two time-limits, namely a period of at least twenty-eight days before the notice takes effect followed by the period allowed for compliance.[8]

Enforcement notices.

---

[1] T.C.P.A. 1971 does not provide for the Crown to be bound, and so the Crown needs no planning permission : *Ministry of Agriculture, Fisheries and Food* v. *Jenkins*, [1963] 2 Q. B. 317 ; [1963] 2 All E. R., 147 ; but agreements with local planning authorities may be made, subject to the approval of the Treasury, concerning the use of Crown Land. Crown tenants, etc., are subject to planning control in certain respects: see T.C.P.A. 1971, s. 266–8.

[2] *Ibid.*, s. 40.

[3] *Ibid.*, Part XI.

[4] *Ibid.*, s. 270 ; Town and Country Planning General Regulations 1974 (S.I. No. 596). See *Gregory* v. *Camden London Borough Council*, [1966] 1 W. L. R. 899 ; [1966] 2 All E. R. 196.

[5] *Ibid.*, s. 87 (1). It would be vindictive to impose sanctions for unauthorized development *if* permission would have been granted in response to a proper application.

[6] *Ibid.*, s. 87 (1), (4). Caravan dwellers may be " occupiers " : *Stevens* v. *Bromley London Borough Council*, [1972] Ch. 400 ; [1972] 1 All E. R. 712.

[7] The authority have a reasonable discretion over these : see *Iddenden* v. *Secretary of State for the Environment*, [1972] 1 W. L. R. 1433 ; [1972] 3 All E. R. 883.

[8] *Ibid.*, s. 87 (6)–(8). See *Burgess* v. *Jarvis and Sevenoaks Rural District Council*, [1952] 2 Q. B. 41 ; [1952] 1 All All E. R. 592.

" Breach of planning control " occurs when development takes place either without the necessary permission or in disregard of conditions or limitations contained in a permission.[1]

There is also what amounts to a limitation period, in that the " breach of planning control " must have occurred after 1963 ; and if it comprises either a *change of use* to a single dwelling-house or any kind of operation the time limit for serving an enforcement notice is restricted to four years.[2]

Stop notices.

The period specified in the notice before it takes effect is intended to allow for making an appeal, and the notice is " of no effect " while any appeal is going forward.[3] This of course may encourage a recalcitrant developer to press on with his activities in the meantime. The local planning authority is therefore given the additional power, during this period, to serve a " stop notice " prohibiting specified *operations* on the land in question, being the same or " substantially the same operations " as those " alleged in the enforcement notice to constitute a breach of planning control"[4]

Enforcement appeals.

Appeal may be made against an enforcement notice by the recipient " or any other person having an interest in the land " within the time specified before it is to take effect.[5] It must be made in writing to the Secretary of State, and may be on one or more of seven specified grounds :[6] (*a*) permission ought to be granted or a condition or limitation ought to be discharged ; (*b*) there has been no " breach of planning control " ; (*c*) the alleged breach occurred more than four years ago, where that limit applies;

---

[1] T.C.P.A. 1971, s. 87 (2).

[2] *Ibid.*, s. 87 (1), (3).

[3] *Ibid.*, s. 88 (1), (3). A notice may be withdrawn before it " takes effect " : *Ibid.*, s. 87 (9).

[4] *Ibid.*, ss. 90. A stop notice must take effect on a specified date three to fourteen days ahead. Contravention is an offence punishable by a fine up to £400 in summary proceedings or without a specified limit on indictment; and continuance after conviction is a further offence punishable by a fine up to £50 a day in summary proceedings or without a specified limit on indictment. But a stop notice may in effect turn out to be unjustified, and the authority will be liable then to pay compensation for loss caused thereby : T.C.P.A. 1971, s. 177.

[5] *Ibid.*, s. 88. The burden of proof lies on the appellant : *Nelsovil, Ltd.* v. *Minister of Housing and Local Government,* [1962] 1 W. L. R. 404 ; [1962] 1 All E. R. 423. Ss. 94 and 95 enact that conclusive proof that there has been no breach of planning control may be achieved by means of an " established use certificate," relating to a use of land begun before 1964 (and continuous thereafter) either without a planning permission or in contravention of one, or a use begun since 1963 (and continuous thereafter) which did not need one. This procedure only applies to current uses, and does not apply to use as a single dwelling house. The certificate is conclusive in an appeal to the Secretary of State under s. 88 against any enforcement notice served after it has been issued. Application is made to the local planning authority ; and there may be " called in " applications and appeals to the Secretary of State, whose decision is " final " (see *supra*, pp. 942, 949).

[6] Although the notice of appeal must be given within the time specified, the grounds of appeal may be notified later : *Howard* v. *Secretary of State for the Environment,* [1973] Q. B. 481 ; [1974] 1 All E. R. 644.

(*d*) the alleged breach occurred before 1964 ; (*e*) the enforcement notice was not served on the proper parties ; (*f*) the specified steps for compliance are excessive ; (*g*) the specified time for compliance is too short.   The Secretary of State must arrange a hearing or inquiry before an inspector, if either side requires it ; and he may uphold, vary or quash the enforcement notice and also grant planning permission if appropriate.   He may " correct any informality, defect or error " in the notice if " satisfied " that it is " not material ", and may disregard a failure to serve it on a proper party if neither that party nor the appellant has been " substantially prejudiced ".   Judicial comment on all this is as follows : " an enforcement notice is no longer to be defeated on technical grounds. The Minister . . . can correct errors so long as, having regard to the merits of the case, the correction can be made without injustice. No informality, defect or error is a material one unless it is such as to produce injustice ".   That was said in the course of a judgment in which it was held to be at most an immaterial misrecital for an enforcement notice to allege development " without permission " when in fact a brief temporary permission existed under the G.D.O. " The notice was plain enough and nobody was deceived by it."[1]

Further appeal from the Secretary of State's decision on an enforcement notice lies to the High Court on a point of law.[2] But apart from these appeals as a general rule anyone may challenge the validity of an enforcement notice in legal proceedings.   It is, however, provided that no such challenge shall be made on grounds (*b*), (*c*), (*d*) or (*e*) above, otherwise than by appeal to the Secretary of State.[3]   One obvious possibility of challenge is in defence to a prosecution, since although a breach of planning control is not a criminal offence the breach of an enforcement notice is.[4]   There is a distinction between prosecution for failure to carry out works other than discontinuance of a use, when it is specially provided that an owner who has transferred his interest to a subsequent owner can bring the latter before the court, and prosecution for failure to discontinue a use or to comply with any condition or limitation, when the accused is given the right to challenge the enforcement notice even on grounds (*b*), (*c*), (*d*) or (*e*) above.[5] *Enforcement and the Courts.*

In addition to prosecution after failure to comply with an effective enforcement notice within the time specified in it, the *Enforcement default powers.*

---

[1] *Miller-Mead* v. *Minister of Housing and Local Government,* [1963] 2 Q. B. 196, at p. 221 ; [1963] 1 All E. R. 459, *per* Lord DENNING; M. & B. p. 814.

[2] T.C.P.A. 1971, s. 246.

[3] *Ibid.,* s. 243 (1) (*a*).

[4] *Ibid.,* s. 89.   The penalty on conviction is a fine up to £400 in summary proceedings or without a specified limit on indictment ; and continuance after conviction is a further offence punishable by a fine up to £50 a day in summary proceedings or without a specified limit on indictment.

[5] Provided that it was not served on him, and his interest in the land dates back before such service, and he could not reasonably have known of it : T.C.P.A. 1971, s. 243 (2).   See s. 89 (2), (3) for bringing a subsequent owner before the court.

authority also have the power, after that time, to enter on the land and carry out the steps prescribed by the notice, other than discontinuance of any use, and recover from the owner the net cost reasonably so incurred. He may in turn recover from the true culprit, if different, his reasonable expenditure on compliance.[1]

(7) PRESERVATION OF AMENITY

What is meant by "amenity."

The other major aim of planning law apart from the control of development is the protection of amenity. Both aims are closely linked in practice ; but the basic concepts are distinct. There is no statutory definition of amenity, but it "appears to mean pleasant circumstances, features, advantages " ;[2] and the standpoint seems to be that of the general public rather than of particular persons.

The subject matter of the provisions governing amenity comprises trees, buildings of special interest, advertisements, caravan sites and unsightly land.

Trees.

To grow or cut trees is not of itself development.[3] But local planning authorities are specifically empowered, " in the interests of amenity ", to make " tree preservation orders " for specified " trees, groups of trees or woodlands ", restricting interference with the trees except with the consent of the local planning authority. Dangerous trees, however, may be cut if necessary. There are also provisions governing replanting.[4] Unauthorized interference with any protected tree calculated to destroy it is a criminal offence.[5]

A T.P.O. must first be confirmed by the Secretary of State, with or without modifications, unless it is not contested ; also in an emergency such confirmation may be dispensed with for up to six months.[6] Regulations are prescribed governing the procedure for making T.P.O.s, and their content. Standard provisions in T.P.O.s lay down essentially the same procedure for applying

---

[1] T.C.P.A. 1971, s. 91. A subsequent planning permission will cause an enforcement notice to lapse ; but mere compliance with the notice will not, because of the possibility that offending development may recur after compliance : *ibid.* ss. 92–3.

[2] *Re Ellis and Ruislip-Northwood Urban District Council*, [1920] 1 K. B. 343, at p. 370 ; *per* SCRUTTON, L.J.

[3] Either might be part of a " material " change of use, and conditions in planning permissions commonly require the preservation or planting of trees. T.C.P.A. 1971, s. 59, requires " the imposition of conditions, for the preservation or planting of trees ", in planning permissions, as far as is reasonably possible.

[4] *Ibid.*, ss. 60, 62. Control from the standpoint of commercial timber production is imposed by the Forestry Act 1967.

[5] Punishable on summary conviction by a fine up to £400, or twice the value of the tree, whichever is the greater : T.C.P.A. 1971, s. 102 ; as amended by the Town and Country Amenities Act 1974, ss. 8, 10. But if the offence is " otherwise " (i.e. less destructive) the maximum fine is £200. Continuance after conviction in any case is a further offence punishable by a fine up to £5 a day. " Radical " injury counts as destruction : *Barnet London Borough Council* v. *Eastern Electricity Board*, [1973] 1 W. L. R. 430 ; [1973] 2 All E. R. 319. M. & B. p. 817.

[6] T.C.P.A., ss. 60 (4), (5), 61.

for consents to interfere with protected trees as exists for applying for planning permissions.[1]

" Amenity " is not expressly mentioned in relation to buildings of special interest. Section 277 of the Act of 1971, however, refers to " areas of special architectural or historic interest the character or appearance of which it is desirable to preserve or enhance ", and requires local planning authorities to determine where such areas exist and designate them as " Conservation Areas ". When one of these areas has been designated, " special attention shall be paid to the desirability of preserving or enhancing its character or appearance " by exercising appropriate powers under the Act of 1971, and also by publicizing planning applications for development which in the authority's opinion would affect that character or appearance.[2]

The phrase " special architectural or historic interest " applies chiefly to buildings, although trees and other objects may affect their character and appearance. The Secretary of State has the duty of compiling or approving lists of such buildings, after suitable consultations, and supplying local authorities with copies of the lists relating to their areas. Such authorities must notify owners and occupiers of buildings included in (or removed from) these lists.[3] The Secretary of State may, when considering any building for inclusion in a list, take into account the relationship of its exterior with any group of buildings to which it belongs and also " the desirability of preserving . . . a man-made object or structure fixed to the building or forming part of the land and comprised within the curtilage of the building ".[4] If a building is not " listed " the local planning authority may give it temporary protection by a " building preservation notice " while they try to persuade the Secretary of State to list it.[5]

Except when for the time being a " listed building " is an ecclesiastical building used for ecclesiastical purposes,[6] or an ancient monument, (when no doubt it will be adequately protected by either Church or State) it is a criminal offence to cause such a

---

[1] Town and Country Planning (Tree Preservation Order) Regulations 1969 (S.I. No. 17), which contain a " Model " T.P.O.

[2] T.C.P.A. 1971, s. 277 (8), in the form substituted by the Town and Country Amenities Act 1974, s. 1. See also ss. 277A and 277B, enacted by the same Act, which respectively prohibit demolition generally in a conservation area without a listed building consent and impose on local planning authorities a duty to formulate and publicise proposals for enhancing conservation areas.

[3] *Ibid.*, s. 54 (1), (4), (7), (10). Ancient monuments, however, have a special code of protection under the Ancient Monuments Act 1931 and the Historic Buildings and Ancient Monuments Act 1953, the effect of which is shown in *Hoveringham Gravels, Ltd.* v. *Secretary of State for the Environment*, [1975] Q. B. 754 ; [1975] 2 All E. R. 931.

[4] *Ibid.*, s. 54 (2).

[5] *Ibid.*, s. 58. If they fail, they may have to pay compensation : s. 173.

[7] This exemption ceases to apply in cases of impending demolition : see *A.-G.* v. *Howard United Reformed Church Trustees, Bedford*, [1975] Q. B. 41 ; [1975] 3 All E. R. 273.

building to be demolished, or altered " in any manner which would affect its character as a building of special architectural or historic interest ", without first obtaining and complying with a " listed building consent " from the local planning authority or the Secretary of State, unless works have to be done as a matter of urgency. A consent may be granted subject to conditions, contravention of which is also a criminal offence.[1] A planning permission which expressly specifies works involving interference with a listed building operates as a consent and may include conditions requiring works for preserving, restoring or reconstructing the building so far as is practicable.[2]

The procedure for applying for listed building consents, and for appeals and revocations, is laid down on lines very similar to the procedure in ordinary cases of planning permission for development ; and so is the procedure for listed building enforcement notices and purchase notices.[3] Compensation is payable for restrictions on consent to works not amounting to development.[4] If an owner fails to keep a listed building in proper repair, a county council or other local authority or the Secretary of State may first serve a " repairs notice " and, if this is not complied with after two months, may then compulsorily purchase the property.[5]

Advertisements.

Control of the display of advertisements is provided for, in the interests of amenity and safety, but not censorship.[6] The details of this control are laid down in regulations.[7] The use of any land for the display of advertisements requires in general an application to the local planning authority for consent, which in normal cases is for periods of five years. Appeal lies to the Secretary of State. There are several categories of display in which consent is " deemed " to be given, including the majority of advertisements of a routine nature and purpose ; but " areas of

---

[1] T.C.P.A. 1971, ss. 55-6. The penalty on conviction for either offence is imprisonment up to three months or a fine up to £250, or both, in summary proceedings, and imprisonment up to twelve months or a fine without a specified limit, or both, on indictment ; and the fine should be fixed in the light of any financial benefit enjoyed by the offender. If an owner does or permits deliberate damage to a listed building without a consent, that is also a criminal offence punishable summarily by a fine up to £100 ; and continuance after conviction is a further offence punishable summarily by a fine up to £20 a day (s. 57).
[2] *Ibid.*, s. 56 (2), (3), (4).
[3] *Ibid.*, 11th Sched., ss. 56 (6), 96-100, 190. For planning compensation generally see *infra*, pp. 971-4. For purchase notices see *infra*, p. 969.
[4] *Ibid.*, ss. 171-2.
[5] *Ibid.*, ss. 114-7. If the owner does comply with the repairs notice he may apply to the magistrates to stay compulsory purchase proceedings, (s. 114 (6)). But if he has deliberately allowed the building to become derelict not only will the compulsory purchase take place but he will be entitled only to " minimum compensation," excluding any element of value whatever in respect of the possibility of demolition or alteration. For compulsory purchase of land generally, see *infra*, p. 959.
[6] *Ibid.*, s. 63.
[7] Town and Country Planning (Control of Advertisements) Regulations 1969 (S.I. No. 1532).

special control " may be declared where restrictions are greater. If however the authority " consider it expedient to do so in the interests of amenity or public safety " they may serve a " discontinuance notice " to terminate the " deemed " consent of most kinds of advertisement enjoying such consent ; but there is a right of appeal to the Secretary of State. Contravention of the regulations is a criminal offence.[1] Consent under the regulations is " deemed " to convey planning permission also, should any development be involved.[2]

The control of caravan sites, in the context of planning law, may be regarded as a question of amenity, even though " amenity " is only referred to very incidentally in the legislation. The purpose of control is, in detail, very much a question of public health, and there is authority for the view that control for purposes of public health must not be exercised for purposes of amenity.[3] But there can be little doubt in practice that although control is concerned with health and safety on the caravan site itself it preserves amenity for the neighbourhood of the site.

Caravan sites.

Until 1960 disputes over the establishment of caravan sites were largely ordinary planning disputes, turning on the question of whether there was a " material " change of use in a given case and so development requiring planning permission.[4] Since 1960 the question of development still arises, and planning permission must still be sought for it ; but the detailed control of the use of the site is governed by a system of " site licences ", obtainable from the local authority.[5] " There are two authorities which have power to control caravan sites. On the one hand, there is the planning authority . . . On the other hand, there is the site authority . . . The planning authority ought to direct their attention to matters in *outline*, leaving the site authority to deal with all matters of *detail*. Thus the planning authority should ask themselves this broad question : Ought this field to be used as a caravan site at all ? If " Yes ", they should grant planning permission for it, without

---

[1] Punishable summarily by a fine up to £100. Continuance after conviction is a further offence punishable by a fine up to £5 a day : T.C.P.A. 1971, s. 109. *Prima facie* the owner of the land or the vendor of the goods advertised will be liable : see *John* v. *Reveille Newspapers, Ltd.* (1955), 5 P. & C. R. 95.

[2] T.C.P.A. 1971, s. 64. See also s. 176 for compensation payable in certain special cases.

[3] *Pilling* v. *Abergele Urban District Council*, [1950] 1 K. B. 636 ; [1950] 1 All E. R. 76.

[4] " Intensification " of the use of land for caravans by means of a gradual increase in numbers was one problem : *Guildford Rural District Council* v. *Fortescue*, [1959] 2 Q. B. 112 ; [1959] 2 All E. R. 111. Seasonal change of use is a problem which has come to a head more recently : *Webber* v. *Minister of Housing and Local Government*, [1968] 1 W. L. R. 29 ; [1967] 3 All E. R. 981; M. & B. p. 789. For movement of caravans from one field to the next, see *Morel* v. *Dudley*, (1961) 178 E. G. 335. For the availability of an injunction as the ultimate deterrent, at the suit of the Attorney-General, see *A.-G.* v. *Bastow*, [1957] 1 Q. B. 514 ; [1957] 1 All E. R. 497.

[5] Caravan Sites and Control of Development Act 1960, s. 3.

going into details as to number of caravans and the like, or imposing any conditions in that regard ". Nevertheless—" Many considerations relate both to planning and to site . . . In all these matters there is a large overlap, where a condition can properly be based both on planning considerations and also on site considerations ".[1]

Site licences and conditions.

It is the " occupier " of land who must apply for a site licence, which must be granted if the applicant has the benefit of a specific planning permission, and withheld if he has not ; and it must last as long as that permission lasts, perpetually in a normal case.[2] The practical question, therefore, is what conditions a site licence shall contain. They are " such conditions as the authority may think it necessary or desirable to impose ", with particular reference to six main kinds of purpose.[3] Appeal may be made to a magistrates' court against the imposition of any conditions, or a decision or refusal to vary them at any time after imposition, on the ground that as imposed or varied they are " unduly burdensome."[4]

There are several categories of use of land for caravans which are exempted from control, and also additional powers conferred on local authorities in special cases.[5]

Unsightly land.

Finally there is the question of unsightly land : neglected sites, rubbish dumps and the like. Local planning authorities are empowered to deal with " any garden vacant site or other open land " whose condition is such that " the amenity of any part of their area, or of any adjoining area, is seriously injured " thereby. A notice is served on the owner and occupier specifying steps to be taken to remedy the state of the land. As with enforcement notices, two time limits must also be specified : a period (of twenty-eight days or more) before the notice takes effect, and the time for compliance.[6]

---

[1] *Esdell Caravan Parks, Ltd.* v. *Hemel Hempstead Rural District Council*, [1966] Q. B. 895, at p. 922; [1965] 3 All E. R. 737; *per* Lord DENNING, M.R.; M. & B. p. 823. It follows that a condition in a site licence based solely on planning considerations is *ultra vires*.

[2] Caravan Sites (etc.) Act 1960, s. 4. For the meaning of " occupier " and " caravan site " see s. 1 (3), (4). Use of land as a caravan site without a site licence is an offence (s. 1 (1), (2)) unless the local authority have failed to grant one within 2 months (ss. 3 (4), (6)). Contravention of the terms of a licence is also an offence, punishable on the third occasion by revoking the licence (s. 9). For transfer of licences to new owners, see s. 10.

[3] *Ibid.*, s. 5. The list of purposes is not exhaustive, but any terms unconnected with health, safety or amenity will amost certainly be *ultra vires* : *Mixnam's Properties, Ltd.* v. *Chertsey Urban District Council*, [1965] A.C. 735 ; [1964] 2 All E. R. 627. Agreements between owners and occupiers of such sites are now regulated by the Mobile Homes Act 1975.

[4] *Ibid.*, ss. 7, 8. See also Ministry of Housing and Local Government Circular No. 42/1960 for " Model Standards for Caravan Sites ".

[5] *Ibid.*, 1st Sched., and ss. 23, 24.

[6] T.C.P.A. 1971, s. 65. The " condition " of land is not to be regarded in isolation from its use : *Britt* v. *Buckinghamshire County Council*, [1964] 1 Q. B. 77 ; [1963] 2 All E. R., 175. Failure to comply is a summary offence punishable by a fine up to £50 : *ibid.*, s. 104. The enforcement and appeal procedure is similar to the general enforcement notice procedure (*supra*, p. 951).

Appeal lies, at any time before the notice takes effect, to a magistrates' court on any of the following grounds : (*a*) the condition of the land is not injurious to amenity ; (*b*) the condition of the land reasonably results from a use or operation not contravening planning control ; (*c*) the land is not of a kind to which such a notice applies ;[1] (*d*) the specified steps for compliance are excessive ; (*e*) the specified time for compliance is too short. The magistrates may uphold, quash or vary the notice, and " correct any informality, defect or error " if it is not material.[2]

SECTION II. COMPULSORY PURCHASE, COMPENSATION AND BETTERMENT[3]

(1) BACKGROUND OF COMPULSORY PURCHASE

Compulsory purchase of land is considerably older than planning control. In the eighteenth century it commonly took the form of inclosures, whereby various owners' rights in land were transformed compulsorily, either by redistribution or by expropriation, the compulsion being sanctioned by statute. Such statutes were private local Acts, and these specified the actual land to be dealt with in each case. Vast numbers of such Acts, at great expense, were procured during the century 1750–1850, differing (on the whole) only in respect of the particular land to which they related.

Early forms of compulsory purchase.

In the early nineteenth century similar local initiatives brought about the promotion, by municipal corporations or other groups of persons, of various forms of public works and " improvements " such as water-works and gas-works. At the same time canal and railway undertakings were being promoted. The result was another stream of private local Acts for these purposes.

Eventually the idea dawned that a general statute could be passed to standardize the repetitive grant of powers, and the Lands Clauses Consolidation Act 1845 duly provided a procedural code for compulsory purchase and compensation, though not for the actual choice of land required. It became customary for

Procedure standardized.

---

[1] For a site to which s. 65 did not apply, see *Stephens* v. *Cuckfield Rural District Council*, [1960] 2 Q. B. 373 ; [1960] 2 All E. R. 716.

[2] T.C.P.A. 1971, s. 105. There is a further right of appeal to the Crown Court (s. 106). The notice is suspended while an appeal is going forward.

The authority may also, in default of compliance with an effective notice within the specified period, enter on the land and carry out the steps prescribed by it and recover the net cost reasonably so incurred from the owner. The owner or occupier may recover from the true culprit, if different from themselves, their reasonable expenditure on compliance (s. 107). Powers of control over dumping of refuse and abandonment of vehicles are given to local authorities by the Civic Amenities Act 1967, Part III.

[3] See generally *Encyclopædia of the Law of Compulsory Purchase and Compensation* ; Davies, *Compulsory Purchase and Compensation* (2nd Edn. 1975).

statutes to authorize compulsory purchase on the basis that particular land was to be selected when required and the necessary authorization for its compulsory purchase given by a " provisional order ", made by a Minister on the acquiring body's behalf and submitted to Parliament (with a batch of other such orders) in a Provisional Order Bill.[1] In the twentieth century the " compulsory purchase order " was devised instead, the difference being that for this submission to Parliament is not normally necessary.[2]

The development of the law governing compensation is quite recent. Until the first world war Parliament assumed that compensation was solely a question of evidence (expert or otherwise)[3] and left the courts to evolve the rules necessary to settle disputes. But eventually, in the Acquisition of Land (Assessment of Compensation) Act 1919, Parliament devised its own set of rules for assessment of the " market value" of land. Later still, the introduction of planning control gave rise to difficulties in deciding whether " market value " should comprise any " development value " over and above " existing use value " in particular cases, and the statutory rules governing " market value " had to be made more elaborate as a result.

Compulsory purchase statutes.

The position now is that compulsory purchase of land normally brings into play four main sets of statutory provisions, as follows. First, there is the authorizing Act. No longer is this normally a private local Act, but instead in most cases a public general Act authorizing a public body or class of public bodies (*e.g.* county councils)[4] to carry out some specified function, and going on to state (*a*) whether such a body may acquire land for the purpose, (*b*) whether they may buy it compulsorily, (*c*) whether they may obtain power to do this by compulsory purchase order specifying the land required, and (*d*) if so what procedure is to be followed when

---

[1] Procedure could be separately prescribed by each Act, but was later largely standardized ; it is now rarely used.

[2] Compulsory purchase orders must sometimes be laid before each House of Parliament before they come into effect, though this does not involve the sequence of stages needed for legislation and is therefore not the same as " provisional order " procedure. See Statutory Orders (Special Procedure) Acts 1945 and 1965 for this " special parliamentary procedure ", as it is called. The Acquisition of Land (Authorization Procedure) Act 1946 prescribes several cases where this procedure has to be used, namely in taking local authority land, land of statutory undertakers acquired " for the purposes of their undertaking ", and various kinds of open space and National Trust land, ancient monuments and the like (s. 1 (2) and 1st Sched. Part III).

[3] Elaborate provisions for assessment *procedure* (not principles) were laid down in Land Clauses Consolidation Act 1845, ss. 22–68.

[4] The typical acquiring authority nowadays is often a local authority ; but government departments and " statutory undertakers " are also acquiring authorities in many circumstances. As for *disposal* of land (sale, lease, exchange, appropriation to a different purpose) see Local Government Act 1972, ss. 120–3 ; T.C.P.A. 1959, ss. 23, 26 ; *London and Westcliff Properties, Ltd.* v. *Minister of Housing and Local Government,* [1961] 1 W. L. R. 519 ; [1961] 1 All E. R. 610.

making the C.P.O. There is now a standardized procedure laid down by the Acquisition of Land (Authorization Procedure) Act 1946, though alternative procedures are occasionally specified instead.[1] Second, therefore, is the Act of 1946 (or such alternative code as the authorizing Act may prescribe), which governs the making of the C.P.O. ; and it may be said that the great majority of acquisitions are made under that Act. Third is the Compulsory Purchase Act 1965, which has to all intents and purposes replaced the Act of 1845 and governs the actual procedure for acquisition after the C.P.O. has sanctioned it.[2] Fourth is the Land Compensation Act 1961, which contains the current rules for assessing compensation in so far as it relates directly to land values.

Disputes over compulsory purchase fall broadly into two main cases, depending on whether or not they relate to the assessment of compensation. If they do (and also in one or two special cases to be mentioned below) they must be brought before the Lands Tribunal, a specialized body staffed by valuers and lawyers. Otherwise they should normally be brought before the High Court. Appeal lies to the Court of Appeal not only from the High Court but also from the Lands Tribunal (though on a point of law only, by way of case stated, and within six weeks of the Tribunal's decision).[3]

Lands Tribunal and the Courts.

(2) COMPULSORY PURCHASE PROCEDURE

Any acquiring authority who are empowered by the appropriate authorizing Act to select and acquire compulsorily the particular land they need by C.P.O. procedure must normally make the C.P.O. in accordance with the procedure laid down in the 1946 Act. This involves making the order in draft, and submitting it to a " confirming authority ", which will be the appropriate Minister or Secretary of State unless of course he himself is acquiring the land. In all cases there must be prior press publicity and notification to the owners and occupiers of the land, and the hearing of objections by an inspector from the Ministry or Department concerned. Statutory inquiries procedure rules for hearings and inquiries are in force, closely parallel with those discussed above in relation to planning appeals.[4] The order may be confirmed, with or without modifications, or rejected. If confirmed

Compulsory purchase orders.

---

[1] For new towns, see New Towns Act 1965, 3rd and 4th Scheds. For slum clearance, see Housing Act 1957, 3rd and 4th Scheds. The basic procedure is the same in these as in Acquisition of Land (Authorisation Procedure) Act but there are various differences of detail.

[2] In most cases the statutes which apply to the various stages of a compulsory purchase will be public general Acts, and particular land will be mentioned not in them but in the C.P.O.s and other procedural instruments made under them. See also T.C.P.A. 1968, Scheds. 3 and 3A.

[3] Lands Tribunal Act 1949, s. 3 (4) ; Rules of Supreme Court (Revision) 1965, Sched. 1, Ord. 61.

[4] *Supra*, p. 943, note 6. And see *Sunley Homes* v. *Secretary of State for the Environment*, [1975] J. P. L. 151 (facts distinguished from opinions).

it takes effect when the acquiring authority publish a notice in similar manner to the notice of the draft order and serve it on the owners and occupiers concerned. The order cannot be challenged (except presumably on the ground of invalidity) apart from the standard procedure for appeal to the High Court within six weeks on the ground of *ultra vires* or a procedural defect substantially prejudicing the appellant.[1]

Notices to treat. The C.P.O. will lapse, in relation to any of the land comprised in it, unless it is acted on within three years.[2] When the authority wish to act on the order they must serve such a notice on the persons with interests in the land to be acquired, requiring them to submit details of their interests and their claims for compensation.[3] When the compensation is agreed in each case, it and the notice to treat together amount to an enforceable contract for the sale of the land.[4] This is then subject to completion by the execution of a conveyance in the same way as a private land transaction.

General vesting declarations. There is, however, an alternative procedure at the authority's option whereby the two stages comprising respectively the notice to treat and the conveyance are telescoped into one stage. This is the " general vesting declaration ". The authority must notify the owners and occupiers concerned, in the same notice as that which states that the C.P.O. is in force (or a separate, later notice), that they intend to proceed in this manner by making a vesting declaration not less than two months ahead. This, when made, will by unilateral action vest the title to the land in the authority at a date not less than twenty-eight days after notification to the owners concerned ; and it will by and large have the same consequences as if a notice to treat were served.[5]

Interests acquired. Freeholds and leaseholds, both legal and equitable,[6] are capable of compulsory acquisition. Leasehold tenancies with a year or

---

[1] 1946 Act, s. 1 and 1st Sched. On this, *cf.*, *supra*, p. 943, notes 1, 2. For examples of *ultra vires* orders, see *London and Westcliff Properties, Ltd.* v. *Minister of Housing and Local Government*, [1961] 1 W. L. R. 519 ; [1961] 1 All E. R. 610 (urban redevelopment), and *Webb* v. *Minister of Housing and Local Government*, [1965] 1 W. L. R. 755 ; [1965] 2 All E. R. 193 (coast protection). See 35 *Conv.* (N.S.) 316 (K. Davies.)

[2] C.P.A. 1965, s. 4. This is taken to mean that a " notice to treat " must be served within that period : see *Grice* v. *Dudley Corpn.*, [1958] Ch. 329 ; [1957] 2 All E. R. 673.

[3] C.P.A. 1965, s. 5. Details should be submitted, or negotiations begun, within 21 days : *ibid.*, s. 6.

[4] *Simpson's Motor Sales (London), Ltd.* v. *Hendon Corpn.*, [1964] A.C. 1088 ; [1963] 2 All E. R. 484; M. & B. p. 829.

[5] T.C.P.A. 1968, s. 30, Scheds. 3, 3A. The notice which states that this procedure is to be used must be registered as a local land charge. The procedure will not affect leasehold tenants with a year or less to run, including periodic tenants, nor those with such longer periods to run as may be specified by the acquiring authority ; though notices to treat may subsequently be served.

[6] " Land " is usually defined in the appropriate authorizing Act. Equitable freeholds and leaseholds include estate contracts, under which the benefit has already passed to the purchaser : *Hillingdon Estates Co.* v. *Stonefield Estates Ltd.*, [1952] Ch. 627 ; [1952] 1 All E. R. 853. Options are included in the rule : *Oppenheimer* v. *Minister of Transport*, [1942] 1 K. B. 242 ; [1941] 3 All E. R. 485. The same applies to equitable leases : *Blamires* v. *Bradford Corpn.*,

less to run, including periodic tenancies, are not subject to acquisition and compensation but allowed to run out, after due service of notice to quit if necessary ; although if the authority desires possession in a hurry they can take it subject to payment of compensation for the loss caused.[1] An authority cannot normally, without clear statutory authorisation, take rights over land in the limited form of an easement or other right less than full possession (even a stratum of land beneath the surface).[2] But if they acquire a dominant tenement they acquire the easements appurtenant to it, as in private conveyancing ; and if they acquire a servient tenement they either allow the easements and other servitudes over it to subsist without interference or else pay compensation for " injurious affection " to the dominant land if they do so interfere.[3]

If part only of an owner's land is to be acquired, this is "severance". The owner of "any house, building or manufactory" or of "a park or garden belonging to a house" can require the authority to take all or none ; but the authority can counter this by saying that to take part only will not cause any "material detriment", and any such dispute is to be settled by the Lands Tribunal.[4] Similar rules now apply to farms.[5] Partial acquisitions.

Unjustifiable delay by the authority after service of a notice to treat may amount to abandonment of the acquisition.[6] As for Delay and entry.

[1964] Ch. 585 ; [1964] 2 All E. R. 603. In this context, failure to register the estate contract as a land charge is immaterial (*ibid.*). An authority can acquire freeholds and leave leaseholds, or even *vice versa* : but see *London and Westcliff Properties, Ltd.* v. *Minister of Housing and Local Government*, [1961] 1 W. L. R. 519 ; [1961] 1 All E. R. 610.

[1] C.P.A. 1965, s. 20 ; *Newham London Borough Council* v. *Benjamin*, [1968] 1 W. L. R. 694 ; [1968] 1 All E. R. 1195. This procedure applies whether notices to treat or general vesting declarations are being used for the interests in reversion.

[2] This was in issue when a compulsory purchase order for part of the Centre Point building in London was quashed, in *Sovmots Investment, Ltd.* v. *Secretary of State for the Environment*, [1976] 2 W. L. R. 73.

[3] This is " injurious affection arising on land not taken from the claimant " : see *infra*, p. 967. See *e.g. Eagle* v. *Charing Cross Rail Co.* (1867), L. R. 2 C. P. 638, (easement of light) and *Re Simeon and Isle of Wight Rural District Council*, [1937] Ch. 525 ; [1937] 3 All E. R. 149. (restrictive covenant not to interfere with percolating water). For a case where a stratum of land beneath the surface was taken, see *City and South London Rail Co.* v. *United Parishes of St. Mary Woolnoth and St. Mary Woolchurch Haw*, [1905] A. C. 1. The same principle seems to be applicable in cases of appropriation of land, as well as acquisition : *Dowty Boulton Paul, Ltd.* v. *Wolverhampton Corpn.* (*No.* 2), [1973] 2 W. L. R. 618 ; [1973] 2 All E. R. 491. But see *Earl of Leicester* v. *Wells-next-the-Sea U.D.C.*, [1973] Ch. 110 ; [1972] 3 All E. R. 77.

[4] C.P.A. 1965, s. 8 (1), and Land Compensation Act 1973, s. 58. The right to make the acquiring authority take all the land in such a case seems to apply even if the C.P.O. itself relates only to the part of the land the authority require (see *Genders* v. *London County Council*, [1915] 1 Ch. 1). T.C.P.A. 1968, Sched. 3A, added by Land Commission (Dissolution) Act 1971, applies similar rules to vesting declarations. On the meaning of "material detriment", see *Ravenseft Properties, Ltd.* v. *London Borough of Hillingdon*, (1968), 20 P. & C. R. 483 ; M. & B. p. 832.

[5] Land Compensation Act 1973, ss. 53–7. The test is whether the rest of the farm unit cannot be reasonably farmed even with any other available land.

[6] *Grice* v. *Dudley Corpn.*, [1958] Ch. 329; [1957] 2 All E. R. 673. But delay was held not to amount to abandonment in *Simpson's Motor Sales*

making actual entry on the land, the authority is not normally entitled to do this until completion and the payment of compensation, unless they first serve a " notice of entry " ; and entry before payment of compensation entitles an owner to receive interest on the compensation to be paid.[1]

Agreements and third party rights.

Many acquisitions by authorities are made by agreement.[2] Obligations owed to third parties, as in restrictive covenants, do not normally involve the expropriated owner in liability, and the third party should seek his remedy against the authority if there is any breach in such a case.[3]   On the other hand an owner must not increase the authority's liability to compensation by creating new tenancies and other rights in the land or carrying out works on it after service of the notice to treat, which are " not reasonably necessary."[4]

(3) COMPULSORY PURCHASE COMPENSATION

The acquiring authority must compensate the expropriated owner for the land taken, by way of purchase price, and for any depreciation of land retained by him, as well as for " all damage directly consequent on the taking ".[5]

"Market value."

The basis of compensation for the taking or depreciation of land is " market value ", namely " the amount which the land *if sold in the open market by a willing seller* might be expected to realize ".   " Special suitability or adaptability " of the land which depends solely on " a purpose to which it could be applied only in pursuance of statutory powers, or for which there is no market apart from the special needs of a particular purchaser or the requirements of any authority possessing compulsory purchase powers ", must be disregarded.[6]   There must be no addition to nor deduction

---

(*London*), *Ltd.* v. *Hendon Corpn.*, [1964] A. C. 1088 ; [1963] 2 All E. R. 484 ; M. & B. p. 829 the owners themselves being at least partly responsible for it.

[1] C.P.A. 1965, s. 11 (1). Where a general vesting declaration is used notices of entry are not needed, but interest must still be paid in respect of advance entry. For interest, see Land Compensation Act 1961, s. 32.

[2] Authorities are usually wise to obtain a C.P.O. first, in case negotiations break down. Agreement does not abrogate the *ultra vires* rule ; such acquisitions are still governed by the appropriate authorizing Act. The selling owner may himself be vulnerable in law, if he is in the position of a trustee, and may, therefore, apply to the Lands Tribunal to certify that a sale by agreement is " at the best price that can reasonably be obtained " (Land Compensation Act 1961, s. 35).

[3] See *Baily* v. *De Crespigny* (1869), L. R. 4 Q. B. 180. But see *Matthey* v. *Curling*, [1922] 2 A. C. 180.

[4] 1946 Act, 2nd Sched., para. 8. Assignments, however, are in order, *Cardiff Corpn.* v. *Cook*, [1923] 2 Ch. 115.

[5] *Harvey* v. *Crawley Development Corpn.*, [1957] 1 Q. B. 485, at p. 492, [1957] 1 All E. R. 504 ; M. & B. p. 842, *per* DENNING, L.J.

[6] Land Compensation Act 1961, s. 5. For " sitting tenants " see *Lambe* v. *Secretary of State for War*, [1955] 2 Q. B. 612 ; [1955] 2 All E. R. 386. Business and farm tenants are to be compensated on expropriation on the footing that the value of their statutory security of tenure is to be taken into account ; and this is reflected also in their landlords' compensation (Land Compensation Act 1973, ss. 47–8).

from market value purely on the ground that the purchase is compulsory, nor any addition specifically on account of the project to be carried out by the acquiring authority.[1] An increase in the value of adjoining land of the owner not taken by the authority, if it results from the compulsory acquisition, must be " set off " against compensation.[2]

Special situations are, however, catered for. If the property acquired comprises dwellings " unfit for habitation ", then normally it is only the market value of the *site* which is to be taken into account.[3] And if the property has been developed and used for a purpose which has no effective market value, such as a church, then the Lands Tribunal may order that compensation " be assessed on the basis of the reasonable cost of equivalent reinstatement ", if " satisfied that reinstatement in some other place is bona fide intended."[4]

Special cases.

These intricate legal rules are intended for the guidance of valuers rather than lawyers. Valuers engaged in the assessment of the compensation are required, subject to such guidance, to reach a figure which will put the expropriated owner in a position as near as reasonably possible to that in which he would find himself if there had been no compulsory acquisition and he has sold his land in an ordinary private sale.[5]

Market value, however, has in any case two distinct main elements : " existing use value " and " prospective development value ".[6] Since development is not lawful without planning permission, the absence of permission will inhibit purchasers from

Market demand and planning control.

---

[1] Land Compensation Act 1961, ss. 5, 9 ; *Pointe Gourde Quarrying and Transport Co., Ltd.* v. *Sub-Intendent of Crown Lands*, [1947] A. C. 565 ; *Wilson* v. *Liverpool Corpn.*, [1971] 1 W. L. R. 302 ; [1971] 1 All E. R. 628. The so-called " *Pointe Gourde* rule ", however, cannot always be reconciled with the " willing seller " rule which is the true basis for assessing compensation.

[2] *Ibid.*, s. 7. There must be no purely notional additions to or reductions from the price of the land taken, on the assumption that it might *not* have been taken, which are attributable to the authority's development to be carried out on the rest of the land taken, if that is unlikely to have been carried out in circumstances other than those of the acquisition itself : *ibid*, s. 6 : See also s. 8, and *Davy* v. *Leeds Corpn.*, [1965] 1 W. L. R. 445 ; [1965] 1 All E. R. 753.

[3] Housing Act 1957, s. 59 and 2nd Sched. Land Compensation Act 1961 s. 10 and 2nd Sched. ; Housing (Slum Clearance Compensation) Act 1965 ; Housing Act 1969, Part V.

[4] Land Compensation Act 1961, s. 5, rule 5 ; *Birmingham Corpn.* v. *West Midland Baptist (Trust) Association (Inc.)*. [1970] A. C. 874 ; [1969] 3 All E. R. 172 ; *Zoar Independent Church Trustees* v. *Rochester Corporation*, [1975] Q. B. 246, [1974] 3 All E. R. 5.

[5] " . . . . the sum to be ascertained is in essence one sum, namely, the proper price or compensation payable in all the circumstances of the case ". *Horn* v. *Sunderland Corpn.*, [1941] 2 K. B. 26, at p. 34 ; [1941] 1 All E. R. 480, *per* GREENE, M.R. For purchases by agreement see *supra*, p. 964, note 2.

[6] The latter is *not* the cost of development : any actual development carried out will add yet another item to the eventual total cost of land. " Prospective development value " is what is added to " existing use value " when, for example a field becomes available, and is in demand, as a building plot, but no physical steps whatever have yet been taken to carry out building works on it.

paying any amount over and above " existing use " value, whether the land is built on or vacant in its present state of development. Before the days of planning control, " prospective development value " over and above " existing use value " depended on market demand. It must not be forgotten that this is still true. " It is not planning permission by itself which increases value. It is planning permission coupled with demand ".[1]

Assessing the existence of demand is essentially a question of valuers' expert evidence ; though of course the Lands Tribunal is better qualified than a court to pronounce on such evidence. Assessing the availability of planning permission, however, calls for special statutory rules, because there are many cases where planning permission is refused purely because proposed development, which is otherwise acceptable, is ruled out by the impending compulsory purchase, which in turn will often be for the purpose of a public works project with little or no market value.

Planning assumptions. " Assumptions as to planning permission " are therefore authorized by statute. The most useful of these turn on the allocation or " zoning " in the current development plan of areas of land which include the owner's property for uses which command a lucrative development value : residential, commercial or industrial. There may be a range of such uses.[2] But permission can only be assumed if it is also reasonable to do so in relation to the particular circumstances of the land itself.[3] If the development plan does not " zone " the land in this way the owner (or the authority) can apply to the local planning authority for a " certificate of appropriate alternative development " in relation to the particular circumstances of the land. Appeal lies to the Secretary of State ; and from him in turn lies the usual limited right of appeal within six weeks to the High Court.[4]

Severance and injurious affection. In addition to purchase price compensation there is compensation for depreciation of land retained. This is usually termed " severance " if it relates to the *pro rata* reduction in value of the land retained over and above its reduction in size.[5] If, however,

---

[1] *Camrose (Viscount)* v. *Basingstoke Corpn.*, [1966] 1 W. L. R. 1100, at p. 1106 ; [1966] 3 All E. R. 161, *per* Lord Denning, M.R. ; M & B. p. 837. See also *Myers* v. *Milton Keynes Development Corpn.*, [1974] 1 W. L. R. 696 ; [1974] 2 All E. R. 1096. But see now Community Land Act 1975, s. 25 (*infra*).

[2] See Land Compensation Act 1961, ss. 14–16, for details and *Provincial Properties (London), Ltd.* v. *Caterham and Warlingham U.D.C.*, [1972] 1 Q. B. 453 ; [1972] 1 All E. R. 60 ; M. & B. p. 835.

[3] A strip merely wide enough for a road could not reasonably be the subject of planning permission to build houses, notwithstanding that the surrounding area had been " zoned " for housing. See *Jelson, Ltd.* v. *Minister of Housing and Local Government,* [1970] 1 Q. B. 243 ; [1969] 3 All E. R. 147 ; *Margate Corpn.* v. *Devotwill Investments, Ltd.*, [1970] 3 All E. R. 864.

[4] Land Compensation Act 1961, ss. 17–22. See *Jelson's* Case, *supra*.

[5] As a result of that reduction (*i.e.* taking part of the owner's land and leaving part). See *Holt* v. *Gas Light and Coke Co.* (1872), L. R. 7 Q. B. 728 ; *Palmer and Harvey, Ltd.* v. *Ipswich Corpn.*, (1953), 4 P. & C. R. 5. But note that C.P.A. 1965, s. 7, speaks of " severing . . . or *otherwise* injuriously affecting . . . " " Injurious affection " is in fact the Victorian term for " depreciation ", in which sense it strictly *includes* " severance ".

it refers to depreciation caused by what is done on the land taken, it is termed " injurious affection ".[1] The latter is closely analogous to damages in tort for private nuisance,[2] though it may well include loss not compensatable in tort.[3] But if what is done goes beyond what is authorized by the statutory powers of the acquiring authority, then it will in any case be unlawful and so compensatable (if at all) in tort and not as " injurious affection ".[4]

It is also possible to obtain compensation for " injurious affection " when no land has been acquired from the claimant. Here it is necessary to prove four things : (*a*) the loss is caused by acts authorised by statute, (*b*) it would be actionable at common law if it were not so authorized, (*c*) it is strictly a depreciation in land value, and (*d*) it arises from the carrying out of works on the compulsorily acquired land and not from its subsequent use.[5] But depreciation caused by the *use* of public works, including highways and aerodromes, is in many cases now compensatable under Part I of the Land Compensation Act 1973, if attributable to " physical factors. "[6] The claim period is from one to three years after the use begins. *[side note: Injurious affection when no land is taken from the claimant.]*

Another head of compensation is " disturbance ", which is not strictly land value but " must . . . refer to the fact of having to vacate the premises ".[7] Thus it may include the loss of business profits and goodwill, removal expenses and the cost of acquiring new premises.[8] It has been held that to claim for " disturbance " *[side note: Disturbance.]*

---

[1] The depreciation need not be caused *entirely* by what is done on the land taken as distinct from other land, provided that it is at least *partly* so caused (Land Compensation Act 1973, s. 44).

[2] Land " retained " by an owner may be considered for severance or injurious affection compensation even if not immediately contiguous with the land taken (*Cowper Essex* v. *Acton Local Board* (1889), 14 App. Cas. 153) and even if enjoyed under a different interest, such as an option (*Oppenheimer* v. *Minister of Transport*, [1942] 1 K. B. 242 ; [1941] 3 All E. R. 485).

[3] *E.g.*, loss of privacy : *Duke of Buccleuch* v. *Metropolitan Board of Works* (1872), L. R. 5 H. L. 418. The depreciation must be compensated in full as a straightforward matter of valuation.

[4] Including where the authority " have statutory powers which they . . . exercise in a manner hurtful to third parties " when they could have done so " in a manner innocuous to third parties ", this being a perverse choice amounting to negligence : *Lagan Navigation Co.* v. *Lambeg Bleaching, etc., Co.*, [1927] A. C. 226 (*per* Lord ATKINSON). Stopping up a highway does not, *per se*, normally give a right to compensation : see *Jolliffe* v. *Exeter Corpn.*, [1967] 1 W. L. R. 993 ; [1967] 2 All E. R. 1099.

[5] *Metropolitan Board of Works* v. *McCarthy* (1874), L. R. 7 H. L. 243. See also *Ricket* v. *Metropolitan Rail, Co.* (1867), L. R. 2 H. L. 175, and *Argyle Motors (Birkenhead), Ltd.* v. *Birkenhead Corpn.*, [1975] A. C. 99 ; [1974] 1 All E. R. 201.

[6] These are : noise, vibration, smell, fumes, smoke, artificial lighting, and solid or liquid discharge.

[7] *Lee* v. *Minister of Transport*, [1966] 1 Q. B. 111, at p. 122 ; [1965] 2 All E. R. 986, *per* DAVIES, L.J. But it is regarded as part of the price of the land.

[8] *Harvey* v. *Crawley Development Corpn.*, [1957] 1 Q. B. 485 ; [1957] 1 All E. R. 504 ; M. & B. p. 842. The additional capital cost of buying dearer property, however, is " value for money ", and not compensatable. It is not the same as compensation on the basis of " equivalent reinstatement ". See the judgment of DENNING, L.J. The cost of preparing the compensation claim itself may be included in the claim (*London County Council* v. *Tobin*, [1959] 1

an owner must forego " prospective development value " in his purchase price compensation ; that is to say his " true loss " is whichever is the higher : " existing use " plus " prospective development " or " existing use " plus " disturbance ".[1]

Since disturbance *compensation* is (illogically) supposed to be an integral part of land value it is not payable where the acquiring body, having expropriated the landlord, displace a short-term tenant by *notice to quit*. In such cases the Land Compensation Act 1973[2] provides for " disturbance payments " (removal expenses, business losses) by the acquiring body to the tenant.[3]

Assess-
ment of
compensa-
tion.

A claimant " must once for all make one claim for all damages which can be reasonably foreseen ".[4] The date of the notice to treat fixes the interests which may be acquired, but not compensation, which must be assessed as at the time of making the assessment, or of taking possession (if earlier), or of the beginning of " equivalent reinstatement ".[5]

(4) COMPULSORY PURCHASE IN PLANNING

Acquisition
"for
planning
purposes".

The planning statutes are themselves the authorizing Acts for certain kinds of compulsory purchase of land. Thus they authorize acquisition " in connection with development and for other planning purposes ".[6] This means " to secure the treatment as a

W. L. R. 354 ; [1959] 1 All E. R. 649) but as " any other matter ", not " disturbance " (*Lee* v. *Minister of Transport, supra*; Land Compensation Act 1961, s. 5, rule (6). On goodwill, see Land Compensation Act 1973, s. 46.

[1] *Horn* v. *Sunderland Corpn.* [1941] 2 K. B. 26 ; [1941] 1 All E. R. 480; M. & B. p. 842. In a private sale to a developer a vendor would expect to sacrifice all the profits arising from the existing use in order to secure the additional value which the prospect of development would put on to the market price of the land. But even a vendor selling purely at the " existing use " value would not expect to get his removal expenses paid by the purchaser ; so to this extent " disturbance " compensation may be a bonus.

[2] Ss. 37–8. See also ss. 29–33 (" home loss payments "), ss. 34–6 (" farm loss payments ") and ss. 39–43 (rehousing displaced residents).

[3] Except farm tenants (but see ss. 59, 61). Farm and business tenants enjoying statutory security of tenure have compensation rights against their *landlords*.

[4] *Chamberlain* v. *West End of London, etc., Rail. Co.* (1863), 2 B. & S. 617, *per* ERLE, C. J. If compensation is not agreed within 21 days of service of the notice to treat (or the general vesting declaration : see *supra*, p. 962, note 5) the dispute is referrable to the Lands Tribunal: C.P.A. 1965, s. 6. Unreasonable delay in submitting a claim will lead to an order to pay the authority's costs incurred through the delay ; and if either side refuses an unconditional offer by the other, which is then kept secret (a " sealed offer ") and turns out to be more favourable than the Tribunal's award, the costs of the other side incurred through the delay thereby caused will also have to be paid : Land Compensation Act 1961, s. 4. See *Pepys* v. *London Transport Executive*, [1975] 1 W. L. R. 234 ; [1975] 1 All E. R. 748.

[5] *Birmingham Corpn.* v. *West Midland Baptist (Trust) Association (Inc.)*, [1970] A. C. 874 ; [1969] 3 All E. R. 172. For advance payments, see Land Compensation Act 1973, s. 52.

[6] See T.C.P.A. 1971, s. 112. " Planning purposes " is not defined. Acquisition of land " for planning purposes " can perhaps be said to occur also under *e.g.* New Towns Act 1965, Town Development Act 1952, National Parks and Access to the Countryside Act 1949, Countryside Act 1968, and Land Compensation Act 1973, Part II.

whole, by development, redevelopment or improvement, or partly by one and partly by another method ", either of the land itself or of adjoining land ; or to relocate population or industry or to replace open space ; or " to acquire the land immediately for a purpose which it is necessary to achieve, in the interests of the proper planning of an area in which the land is situated ".[1] Local authorities in general have this power, subject to the standard compulsory purchase procedure. They can themselves develop land so acquired, but not without the Secretary of State's consent. More usually they dispose of the land to private developers, " in such manner and subject to such conditions as may appear to them to be expedient ".[2]

Another aspect of compulsory purchase in planning is " inverse compulsory purchase ", of which there are two species : purchase notices and " blight notices ". The owners supply the compulsion in these cases, not the acquiring authorities.[3] A purchase notice is served in consequence of an adverse planning decision ; but a blight notice is served in consequence of adverse planning proposals.

Compulsory purchase instigated by owners.

If planning permission is in a particular case refused, or granted subject to conditions, so that as a result " the land has become incapable of reasonably beneficial use in its existing state ", then an owner may serve a purchase notice on the local borough or district council.[4] If the council are unwilling to accept it they must normally refer it to the Secretary of State who must then exercise his own judgment as to whether the notice is justifiable and ought to be upheld.[5] He must not uphold it merely on the ground that " the land in its existing state and with its existing permissions is substantially less useful to the server ", since that is true of nearly all planning refusals.[6] The land must in fact be virtually useless to justify a purchase notice.

Purchase notices.

---

[1] T.C.P.A. 1971, s. 112 (1) (*a*)–(*d*) ; and see s. 7 (5) : " action areas "— *cf. supra*, p. 940. See *infra*, p. 974, for " community land ".

[2] *Ibid.*, ss. 122–4. This is what happens to bring about " urban renewal ", meaning town-centre redevelopment in most cases. " Action areas " will normally be prescribed for such " positive planning " in future (see note 1, *supra*).

[3] *Ibid.*, Part IX. No. C.P.O. is required, and an effective notice is the equivalent of a notice to treat, so that all that remains to do is to assess the compensation by the usual procedure : *ibid.*, ss. 181 (2), 186 (2), 196 (1). Compensation for purchase notices will largely be concerned with prospective development value, for " blight " notices with existing use value, though not exclusively so in either case.

[4] *Ibid.*, s. 180. For revocation and discontinuance orders, etc., see ss. 188–191.

[5] *Ibid.*, ss. 181–6. Certain more specialized courses are also open to him.

[6] *R.* v. *Minister of Housing and Local Government, ex parte Chichester Rural District Council*, [1960] 1 W. L. R. 587 ; [1960] 2 All E. R. 407 ; M. & B. p. 849. But see T.C.P.A. 1971, s. 184 (reversing *Adams and Wade, Ltd.* v. *Minister of Housing and Local Government* (1965), 18 P. & C. R. 60). For the meaning of " owner ", see *London Corpn.* v. *Cusack-Smith*, [1955] A. C. 337 ; [1955] 1 All E. R. 302, and T.C.P.A. 1971, s. 290.

A " blight notice " is served on a prospective acquiring authority.[1] There are four principal requirements : (1) the proposal affecting the owner's land must be within one of the " specified descriptions " ; (2) the server must be an owner-occupier (or his mortgagee) with an interest " qualified for protection " ; (3) he must have made genuine but unsuccessful attempts to sell for a reasonable price on the open market ; and (4) the authority must in fact intend to acquire the land. Within two months the authority concerned may serve a counter-notice alleging that any of the above requirements has not been met.[2] The claimant then has two more months in which to refer the dispute to the Lands Tribunal, before whom the burden of proof is on the authority if they deny an intention to inquire any or all of the land but on the claimant in other cases.[3]

The " specified descriptions " are as follows. The land must be indicated as being required for the functions of a public[4] body in a local plan or, failing that, in a structure plan or, failing that, indicated in any development plan as required for a highway ; or as land in or beside the line of a trunk or special road,[5] or sufficiently indicated in writing by the Secretary of State to the local planning authority as required for such a road, or selected for a highway by a resolution of a local highway authority ; or as land covered by a C.P.O. which has not yet been acted upon, or else subject to compulsory purchase by virtue of a special enactment.[6]

To be " qualified for protection " it is necessary to be (a) a freeholder or a leaseholder with three years to run,[7] as well as (b) a resident owner-occupier of a dwelling or the owner-occupier either of an " agricultural unit " or of other premises (with an annual value, in the latter case, not exceeding a prescribed limit).[8]

---

[1] T.C.P.A. 1971, s. 193. See also s. 205 (" the government department, local authority or other body by whom . . . the land is liable to be acquired ").

[2] *Ibid.*, s. 194. In some cases the authority need only show an intention not to acquire for 15 years.

[3] *Ibid.*, s. 195. See *Bolton Corpn.* v. *Owen*, [1962] 1 Q. B. 470 ; [1962] 1 All E. R. 101 ; M. & B. p. 853.

[4] Land " zoned " for housing in a development plan is *not* thereby indicated as required for the local council as housing authority, since at that stage the question is still open whether private housing development may be permitted there : *Bolton Corpn.* v. *Owen*, *supra*.

[5] As indicated in an operative scheme or order under the Highways Acts 1959 to 1971. The Highway Act 1971 introduces other special cases.

[6] T.C.P.A. 1971, s. 192. This complex list covers many, but not all, of the circumstances in which owners are likely to complain that the marketability of their land is " blighted ". It has been increased by the Land Compensation Act 1973, ss. 68–76. The underlying common basis is the likelihood of eventual public acquisition, the " blight " being the intervening delay.

[7] *Ibid.*, s. 203 (4).

[8] *Ibid.*, s. 192 (2)–(4) ; Town and Country Planning (Limit of Annual Value) Order 1973, S.I. No. 425 (which prescribes £2,250). See *Essex County Council* v. *Essex Incorporated Congregational Church Union*, [1963] A.C. 808 ; [1963] 1 All E. R. 326. If a farm is only within the " specified descriptions " as to part of its area, the rest can be included in the blight notice provided that it is not reasonably capable of being farmed on its own or with any other available land (Land Compensation Act 1973, ss. 79–81).

The period of actual occupation must have been for six months immediately before serving the blight notice or before leaving the premises unoccupied for not more than twelve months before serving the notice.[1] A mortgagee of a person " qualified for protection " may also serve a blight notice provided that his power of sale has arisen, and he is given an extra six months in which to do so.[2]

(5) BETTERMENT AND PLANNING COMPENSATION

In discussing " market value " compensation above, " existing use value " was distinguished from " prospective development value ", and the latter shown to depend on there being both market demand and planning permission for development. " Prospective development value " is synonymous with " betterment " in its current meaning, although formerly " betterment " seems to have meant the increase in the *overall* market value of land by reason of beneficial public works on other land nearby. Either way, the meaning is a purely financial one.

New and old meanings of " betterment ".

The switch in meaning was the result of the Uthwatt Report of 1942.[3] The new meaning has held the field since then, and with it has arisen the view that " betterment," unlike " existing use " value or the actual cost of development, has not been earned by the owner who realizes it. In a sense only the community as a whole can be said to have " earned " the prospective development value of land.

If " betterment " accrues, therefore, is the community entitled to take all or any of it ? The Town and Country Planning Act 1947 went on the assumption that the community was entitled to take all of it, since it could not thenceforth come into existence without a planning permission. The Act imposed a " development charge " which appropriated to a new government body, the Central Land Board, all " betterment " (*i.e.* development value) accruing as the result of any grant of planning permission. At the same time it was decided that all owners to whom such betterment had already accrued by the time of the Act's commencement should receive once-for-all compensation for the loss of it.[4] This was to have been paid in 1953 out of a special £300 million fund ; but as from 1952 development charges were abolished and the compensation proposals halted.[5] The " established claims " on the fund, however,

Development charges.

---

[1] T.C.P.A. 1971, s. 203 (1)–(3).
[2] *Ibid.*, s. 201.
[3] Final Report of the Expert Committee on Compensation and Betterment, 1942, (Cmd. 6386).
[4] T.C.P.A. 1947, Part VI. The compensation was to be " once-for-all ", but development charges would be imposed every time permission was granted. Commencement occurred on July 1, 1948, the " appointed day ".
[5] T.C.P.A. 1953.

were soon to be made use of in a peculiar manner, as will be explained below.[1]

Betterment levy.

The Land Commission Act 1967 reimposed a charge on betterment, this time called " betterment levy " and restricted initially to 40 per cent.[2]   A successor to the Central Land Board, termed the Land Commission, was set up to collect it.   The Land Commission was abolished in 1971 ; but " betterment " continued to be taxed, as a capital gain, and in 1974 this capital gain became treated for tax purposes as if it were income.[3]

Loss of development value.

The converse of appropriating " betterment " to the community is awarding compensation to owners who are deprived of it by the community, not in the sense that market demand is prevented from arising for the development of particular land but in the sense that development itself is prevented by planning restrictions.   It might be thought that, as a principle of State policy, it would be logical to decide either that if there is 100 per cent betterment levy there should be no planning compensation, or that there should be 100 per cent compensation if there is no levy.   In practice the policy applied has not been so simple, nor so logical.

Varieties of restriction on development.

To begin with, the statutes require two main distinctions to be drawn : first, between (a) restrictions on development imposed at the outset by a refusal (or conditional grant) of planning permission and (b) restrictions imposed as an afterthought by revocation or modification of permission already granted ; and second, between (a) " new " development and (b) development which is marginal to existing use.   The latter type of development consists of certain categories set out in the Eighth Schedule to the Town and Country Planning Act 1971,[4] and " marginal " or " existing use " development is a convenient name for it.   " New development " is, by definition, such development as is not listed in that schedule.[5]

---

[1] See *infra*, p. 973.

[2] Land Commission Act 1967, ss. 27–8 ; Betterment Levy (Prescribed Rate) Order 1967, S.I. No. 544.

[3] Land Commission (Dissolution) Act 1971 ; Finance Act 1971, s. 55 ; Finance Act 1974, s. 38. The White Paper, " Development Land Tax ". (Cmnd. 619) published in August 1975 proposes that " betterment " be taxed in a way very similar to betterment levy, but under the name " development land tax " and at the rate of 80%.   Under the Community Land Act 1975 (*infra*, p. 974) " development land " is to be acquired by local authorities (with some exemptions) at *current use* value, and disposed of at *market* value, which will transfer much of the available " betterment " to public authorities without invoking taxation procedures at all (provided that there is still a market for disposals).

[4] The categories in question are modified by the 18th schedule and also by certain provisions in sections 168, 169, 180 and 278.   The main ones are rebuilding and alteration of buildings and extensions of uses within property, with a narrow limit on the extent of any increase involved (in some cases 10% of floor area and of cubic capacity ; in other cases no increase at all).

[5] T.C.P.A. 1971, s. 22 (5).   It must be emphasized that this distinction between " new " and " marginal " development is *relevant solely to compensation* and has nothing directly to do with planning permissions.   But there are one or two categories of " marginal " development whose limits coincide, in a rough and ready way, with categories of " permitted development " under the

Restrictions on development imposed by way of revocation, modification or discontinuance orders, since they are in effect regarded as interference with the enjoyment of development value previously conceded to an owner by the grant of planning permission, are fully compensatable—by the local planning authority.[1] Restrictions on development imposed at the outset—*i.e.* because the original application for permission is itself refused, or granted subject to conditions—are also fully compensatable, by the local planning authority, but only if the restricted development is " marginal " development.[2]

Restrictions imposed at the outset on applications to carry out " new " development are only exceptionally compensatable ; though when they are the compensation is payable by the Secretary of State. The underlying principle is peculiar. It will be remembered how the payment of compensation for expropriation of development values was held in suspended animation after 1952 when development charges were abolished. The Town and Country Planning Act 1954 enacted that rights to the benefit of " established claims " to that compensation, termed " claim holdings ", were to be adapted to a new purpose. They would be transformed into a passport to future compensation for restrictions imposed at the outset on " new " development, in certain specific cases.[3]

The " claim holding ", which was a chose in action, was converted into a right in land and renamed the " unexpended balance of established development value ", or " U.X.B.".[4] From 1955 onwards the sum (if any) certified by the Secretary of State as the

---

G.D.O. (see *supra*, p. 946), notably certain extensions, not exceeding 10%, to houses and some other buildings.

[1] T.C.P.A. 1971, ss. 164–5, 170. See *supra*, p. 949. An example can be seen in *Blow* v. *Norfolk County Council*, [1967] 1 W. L. R. 1280 ; [1966], 3 All E. R. 579 (discontinuance order). For tree preservation orders and certain special cases of advertisements, see T.C.P.A. 1971, ss. 174–6. See also *Bollans* v. *Surrey County Council* (1968), 20 P. & C. R., 745 (tree preservation). For listed buildings and building preservation notices see T.C.P.A. 1971, ss. 171–3 (*supra*, p. 955, note 5 ; p. 956, note 4.

[2] Except the first two of the eight categories prescribed for that development, where the only remedy is to serve a purchase notice : T.C.P.A. 1971, s. 169. (For I.D.C. control see *supra*, p. 950, note 6). In all these cases of full compensation payable by the local planning authority it is provided that the " market value " rules laid down in Land Compensation Act 1961, s. 5 (see *supra*, p. 964) " shall, so far as applicable and subject to any necessary modifications, have effect [as for compulsory purchase] " : T.C.P.A. 1971, s. 178. Disputes are to be referred to the Lands Tribunal (*ibid.*, s. 179), with the usual limited right of appeal to the Court of Appeal (see *supra*, p. 961).

[3] In other words, he who wants X, let him have Y ; and he who wants Y, should have asked for X in the first place. Claims had been assessed in relation to loss of development potential as it existed for land in 1948. Yet the amounts then settled are now arbitrarily applied to limit compensation for *restrictions*, large or small, imposed at any time in the foreseeable future.

[4] After first making a deduction from the amount of the claim for any compensation payable under the Act retrospectively for loss of development value before 1955, and an addition to the remainder (if any) of $\frac{1}{8}$ as a notional accrual of interest. See now T.C.P.A. 1971, ss. 134–9.

U.X.B. for particular land represents the limit up to which (and no further) compensation is payable by him for depreciation caused by restrictions at the outset on " new " development.[1] Moreover there are several categories of restriction which do not qualify for this compensation, so it is of limited application.[2]

Exhaustion of right to compensation ; and liability to repay compensation. The U.X.B., then, is used up by the payment of this kind of planning compensation, which, as far as it goes, is a way of realizing the development value of land. Other ways, which also use up the U.X.B., include the receipt of compulsory purchase compensation and the actual carrying out of " new " development.[3] Compensation over £20 is repayable to the Secretary of State if permission is later granted for certain substantial kinds of development.[4] This also applies where the original compensation was paid for a revocation or modification order ; but, since in such a case the local planning authority would have paid it, the Secretary of State, who receives the repayment, must pass it on to that authority. For this reason he is empowered to contribute to revocation or modification compensation to the extent that U.X.B. compensation would have been payable had the restrictions been imposed in response to the original planning application ; and if he has done this he is entitled to retain that amount out of any repayment made to him in such circumstances.[5]

(6) COMMUNITY LAND

Public control of development land. The Community Land Act 1975[6] has various subsidiary objectives but two main ones to which most attention should be devoted. These are: (i) to bring the supply of land available for development substantially under public control; and (ii) to transfer prospective development value in land (sometimes known as " betterment ") for the most part into public ownership. This

---

[1] T.C.P.A. 1971, ss. 145–6, 152–7. Disputes go to the Lands Tribunal (s. 156), with the usual limited right of appeal to the Court of Appeal (see *supra*, p. 961).

[2] *Ibid.*, ss. 147–9. For I.D.C. control, see *supra*, p. 950, note 6. For the power of the Secretary of State to alter an adverse decision to avoid paying compensation, and the claimant's power to modify his claim as a result, see *ibid.*, ss. 38–9, 155.

[3] *Ibid.*, ss. 140–4.

[4] *Ibid.*, ss. 158–161. See the kinds of development specified in s. 159 (2). Compensation over £20 must be registered as a local land charge, on notification by the Secretary of State. Failure to disclose an entry in the register on an official search, means that repayment cannot be demanded for a subsequent owner. In *Minister of Housing and Local Government* v. *Sharp*, [1970] 2 Q. B. 223 ; [1970] 1 All E. R. 1009, C. A. held that the Minister could recover damages in tort for negligence, when failure to disclose a compensation notice prevented him from enforcing repayment of compensation from a purchasing developer.

[5] *Ibid.*, ss. 166–8. The government pay a contribution to the local planning authority, who make payment to the owner, who pays it (by a reduction in purchase price) to a successor, who on getting permission to develop pay it back to the government, who deduct the contribution and pay the balance to the local planning authority.

[6] The Act received the Royal Assent on November 12th, 1975. See (1975) 119 Sol. Jo. pp. 803, 820, 838, 857 and (1976) 120 Sol. Jo., pp. 4, 23 (R. N. D. Hamilton).

in fact amounts to two aspects of the same objective, which is to make the initiation of and profit from land development throughout Great Britain a public rather than a private matter.

The carrying out of the functions considered necessary to achieve these objectives is, in England and Scotland, a task assigned to " authorities ". These are local authorities generally, that is to say county and district councils, together with new town corporations, National Park planning boards and (if necessary) joint boards specially constituted by the Secretary of State for the Environment (or for Scotland). In Wales, on the other hand, there is a Land Authority for Wales to discharge these duties comprehensively.[1] The central government, in the form of the Secretary of State, is to exercise general co-ordination and control in the customary manner by making regulations and orders and by authorising compulsory acquisition of land ; he also has certain more particular duties, where the scheme of the Act so requires, and these will be touched on below.

Since development land is the subject-matter of these provisions, it is important to note first that " development " is defined in exactly the same way as in the main planning enactments.[2] But " development land " is a subjective concept, namely land which in the opinion of a local authority is suitable for " relevant development ".[3] The latter term is of crucial importance. It means[4] *all* development (as defined above) *except* : (i) such kinds as shall be specified in regulations to be made by the Secretary of State ; (ii) such as consists exclusively of the building of a single dwelling-house ; (iii) "exempt development", which means development in a form permissible under a *general* development order or in the form of agricultural and forestry operations not involving the building of dwellings.[5] Thus " development " is for the purposes of the new Act divided into two kinds, " relevant development " and " excepted development "; and " exempt development " is one subdivision of the latter.

The sequence of dates on which various stages of the main scheme of the Act come into effect is somewhat obliquely prescribed, and can only be ascertained by tracing the different procedures concerned through the Act and seeing whether each of them presupposes the prior operation of any other. The following pattern emerges.

The first step to be taken under the Act is the preparation in England and Scotland of a " land acquisition and management scheme "[6] for each *county* area, by all the authorities in that area

Sequence of starting dates—(1).

---

[1] See Part II of the Act (ss. 8–14) and Sched. 3 for the Authority's constitution and finances.
[2] See *supra*, p. 944, and T.C.P. (Scotland) Act 1972, s. 19.
[3] Community Land Act 1975, s. 3 (1).
[4] *Ibid.*, s. 3 (2).
[5] *Ibid.*, Sched. 1. For development orders, see *supra.*, p. 946.
[6] *Ibid.*, s. 16.

acting jointly, immediately from the date of the Royal Assent (or, truth to tell, before). This scheme must contemplate the acquisition of land by any of those authorities in order to dispose of it to developers in due course or else develop it themselves. Clearly the county councils (including the Greater London Council) must take most of the initiative ; indeed " community land " policies can be said to operate primarily on a county basis in England and Scotland alike.

Any further progress then depends absolutely on the Secretary of State. This is not because he is to receive a copy of each scheme[1] but because his issue of regulations specifying " excepted development " (other than single dwelling-houses, and " exempt development ") is an absolute pre-requisite for the knowledge by any person whatsoever of what constitutes " relevant development ". When the meaning of the latter has been made known in this way it will be possible for authorities to undertake their assessment of what land constitutes " development land " suitable for such development.[2] This in turn is the pre-requisite for carrying out the duty which the Act imposes on all authorities in Great Britain as from the " first appointed day ", which is to be specified in an order by the Secretary of State.[3] The duty is as follows. Every authority must " have regard to the desirability— (a) of bringing development land into public ownership, and of developing that land themselves or of making it available for development by others, and (b) of securing the proper planning of their area ".[4]

Sequence of starting dates—(2).

The duty just mentioned is a duty to consider acquisitions, not a duty to acquire. The latter duty does indeed arise, but not until the Secretary of State makes an order having that effect; and no such order can come into force until the " first appointed day ".[5] An order of this kind is not general in its effect but particular to the area (or part of the area) of a specified authority. Not only that, but it must also specify the kinds of " relevant development " to which it applies, termed " designated relevant development ". The date on which any such order comes into force is referred to as the " relevant date " ; and the Secretary of State must keep a public register of these orders.[6] Thus there may be any number of " relevant dates ", even for one local authority area, each one giving rise to a separate duty to acquire. All the authorities whose areas come wholly or partly under one of these orders are then subjected to that duty, which is " to arrange between them for all land which is needed for the purposes

---

[1] Community Land Act 1975, Sched. 5 (which also empowers him to revise schemes, and if necessary make them himself).
[2] *Ibid.*, s. 3 (1). For draft regulations, see *infra*, p. 980.
[3] *Ibid.*, s. 7.
[4] *Ibid.*, s. 17. These duties are amplified in Sched. 6.
[5] *Ibid.*, s. 18 (*infra.*, p. 980).
[6] *Ibid.*, Sched. 2, Part II.

of designated relevant development to be acquired by one of those authorities ", having regard to " any relevant land acquisition and management scheme ",[1] except for land wholly owned by public authorities and land not needed for ten years.

These " relevant dates " are in turn a pre-requisite for the final procedural stage under the Act, namely the " second appointed day ". This must not occur until *every part* of Great Britain is the subject of one or more " relevant dates " having the consequence that *all* " relevant development " has been " designated ".[2] It too must be specified in an order by the Secretary of State ; and it marks the stage at which the " community land " system will be (so to speak) fully in operation. The basic sequence of stages is therefore as follows : Royal Assent—land acquisition and management schemes (other than in Wales)— " relevant development "—first appointed day—" relevant dates " —second appointed day.

The acquisition of development land in accordance with these procedures may occur by agreement or by compulsory purchase, the latter being conducted under the normal statutory procedure and authorised by the Secretary of State.[3] Adjoining land needed for works to facilitate the use of the development land may be acquired as well. There is also a power to appropriate land already held for other purposes ; but acquisition and appropriation are alike unlawful before the " first appointed day ". The management of land acquired is a matter to be prescribed in each " land acquisition and management scheme ". The Land Authority for Wales " shall have the general function of managing and turning to account land acquired by them under this Act ".[4]

There are also provisions which empower authorities to pass a resolution declaring any part of their area a " disposal notification area " at a date not less than three months ahead, in which any person intending to dispose privately of a freehold, or a leasehold with seven years to run, must first notify them. They may serve a counter-notice within four weeks stating if they themselves mean to acquire the land or any part of it ; and, unless they say they do not, the land is then eligible for the service of a " blight notice' ". These areas cannot be constituted before the " first appointed day ".[5]

In order to prevent private owners from carrying out " relevant development " until the authorities for the area have decided against, or been prevented from, acquiring the land, the Act provides for the suspension of planning permissions.[6] It states

Land acquisition and management.

Suspension of planning permissions.

---

[1] Community Land Act 1975, s. 16, *supra*, p. 975.
[2] *Ibid.*, s. 7.   For the purpose of the second appointed day, see *infra*, p. 978.
[3] *Ibid.*, s. 15 (subject to detailed modifications set out in Sched. 4).
[4] *Ibid.*, s. 14.
[5] *Ibid.*, ss. 23–4 and Sched. 8.   For " blight notices ", see *supra*, p. 970.
[6] *Ibid.*, ss. 19–22.

that planning permissions granted *after* any " relevant date " for
the kinds of " relevant development " which are " designated " as
from that date are suspended indefinitely unless the development
covered by the permission : (i) is to be carried out by or for an
authority on land in which no other public or charitable body
owns a freehold or a leasehold with seven years to run ; or (ii)
is to be carried out on land for which the Secretary of State refuses
to confirm a compulsory purchase order, declaring at the same
time that there is to be no suspension ; or (iii) is approved by any
authority for land in which a freehold or a leasehold with seven
years to run has been obtained from them and no other such
interest is held by a public or charitable body.[1]

A planning permission already granted *before* the " relevant
date " in question is suspended *temporarily*, provided that the
application for it was made *after* the " first appointed day ",
until the authorities tell the owner or developer that they either
do or do not intend to buy the land. When they buy it, or
abandon their power to buy it, the suspension ends. If they
abandon their power to buy the land the period of abandonment
lasts for five years. If they give notice of intention not to buy,
the period of abandonment begins then ; but if they give notice
of intention to buy, the period of abandonment will begin one
year thereafter (or after notice of appeal from a refusal of permission) unless by that time notice of the making of a compulsory
purchase order is published, whereupon they have one year in
which to serve notice to treat on all persons owning freeholds or
leaseholds with seven years to run.[2]

This system of temporary suspension also applies where
application for planning permission is made *before* the " first
appointed day ", but only if the owner elects to have it applied.[3]
No suspension applies to permissions granted on or before September 12th, 1974.

Reduction
of com-
pulsory
purchase
compensa-
tion.

The purpose of the " second appointed day "[4] is to bring in a
general lowering of compulsory purchase compensation. Prospective development value will on the whole be excluded from it
and thus transferred to the " community " (in the guise of the
acquiring authority). This presupposes that there will continue
to be a market, since the point is that the exclusion should not
apply when public bodies dispose of development land ; but it
may be that prospective development value will disappear from
the market altogether. The Act provides that, where notice to
treat is served after the " second appointed day ", it shall no
longer be assumed that planning permission is available for

---

[1] Community Land Act, 1975, s. 21.
[2] *Ibid.*, s. 20, and Sched. 7. For the acquisition of land, see *ibid.*, s. 15,
supra, p. 977. For notices to treat, see *supra*, p. 962.
[3] *Ibid.*, s. 19.
[4] *Ibid.*, s. 7, *supra*, p. 977.

development other than the limited kinds listed in Schedule 8 of the Town and Country Planning Act 1971 ; and any actual permissions are to be disregarded if they are in suspense.[1] Transactions between public bodies will be subject to special rules.[2] There will be special hardship tribunals, set up under regulations to be made by the Secretary of State, to authorise additional payments where particular circumstances justify this.[3]

There is a more immediate change in compensation, at any rate in wording, where claimants rely on " certificates of appropriate alternative development ". Such claimants must now assert that assumed planning permission covers development which " would be appropriate for the land in question " ; and instead of the words " might reasonably have been expected to be granted " there are substituted the words " would have been granted " in regard to such permission. It may be that this will be effective to reduce chances of obtaining development value ; but this is by no means certain.[4]

The rest of Parts V and VI of the Act relate to reserve powers and other ancillary matters, such as the keeping by authorities of accounts in respect of " community land " transactions,[5] and extending the power of the Crown to acquire " public service land ".[6] " Special parliamentary procedure " is no longer to apply to compulsory acquisitions of land from local authorities and statutory undertakers.[7] An additional section is inserted into the Local Government Act 1972 prohibiting the disposal by " principal councils " of freeholds, and leaseholds with seven years to run, without the Secretary of State's consent.[8] The latter is empowered to make regulations for the keeping by local authorities of public registers of " their acquisitions, holdings and disposals of land ".[9] *Supplemental provisions.*

Finally a brief mention may be made of Part IV of the Act,[10] which empowers the Secretary of State compulsorily to purchase buildings in which 5,000 square metres or more of office floor space exist of which 75% remains unoccupied for two years after construction or conversion (temporary occupations during this *Acquisition of empty offices.*

---

[1] Community Land Act 1975, s. 25. For T.C.P.A. 1971, Sched. 8, see *supra*, p. 972, n. 4. The corresponding provisions for Scotland are in the T.C.P. (Scotland) Act 1972, Sched. 6. Special relaxations of these rules apply to land held for charitable purposes.

[2] *Ibid.*, s. 26.

[3] *Ibid.*, s. 27.

[4] *Ibid.*, s. 47 and Sched. 9. See *supra*, p. 966. The change took effect on December 12th, 1975.

[5] *Ibid.*, ss. 43–4

[6] *Ibid.*, s. 37.

[7] *Ibid.*, s. 41.

[8] *Ibid.*, s. 42. The additional section is 123A (the corresponding provision for Scotland being the Local Government (Scotland) Act 1973, s. 74A). " Principal councils " are county and district councils.

[9] *Ibid.*, s. 46. For other registers kept by local authorities, see *supra*, p. 941.

[10] *Ibid.*, ss. 28–36.

period for less than six months are disregarded). For compensation in these cases the *lower* amount is to be taken of values current at the date of : (a) completion of the accommodation, (b) acquisition. For lesser interests such as leases, reversions, mortgages, or interests in part only of the property, the proportionate value payable is to be ascertained by reference to prices current : (a) at the date of completion of the accommodation, when establishing the total value of the unencumbered legal freehold, but (b) at the date of assessment (or taking possession, if earlier), when establishing the relevant proportion of the value ; but this is not to operate to the detriment of a mortgagee. The Secretary of State may by notice specify the date when the accommodation is deemed to have been completed, subject to a right of appeal to the county court. Property " unoccupied " for rating purposes is to be regarded as " unoccupied " for the purposes of the 1975 Act also.

Categories of " excepted development ".
The " first appointed day " under the Community Land Act is likely to be April 6th, 1976. The same day has also been proposed for the coming into force of regulations to specify the categories of " excepted development " (other than " exempt development " and the construction of single dwelling-houses) without which it will not be possible to recognise what projects will amount to " relevant development " within the meaning of the Act. The draft Community Land (Excepted Development) Regulations 1976, published in January 1976, set out thirteen classes of " excepted development ", as follows :

Class 1. Development for which there is a planning permission dating back to September 12th, 1974.

Class 2. Development substantially comprising the building of dwellings or industrial buildings on land of which the freehold has been held continuously since September 12th, 1974 by a builder or developer of residential or industrial property (or a succession of such persons) provided that one of the authorities for the area has received from the current freeholder a notice, in a prescribed form, of this continuous ownership, not later than 21 days after service or publication before October 5th, 1976 of the latest notice of a planning application for such development (or, if there is no such notice, not later than the application itself), and in any case not later than October 5th, 1976.

Class 3. The erection of any number of industrial buildings where either the freehold or a leasehold with seven years to run has been held by an industrial undertaking (or a succession of them) continuously since September 12th, 1974.

Class 4. The erection of industrial buildings with an aggregate gross floor-space not exceeding 1,500 square metres.

Class 5. The erection of other kinds of buildings with an aggregate gross floor-space not exceeding 1,000 square metres.

Class 6. The erection of farm buildings.

Class 7. The rebuilding or alteration of buildings either currently in existence or destroyed within the previous ten years where the gross floor-space is not increased beyond ten per cent.

Class 8. Development on freehold land owned by the Scottish or Welsh Development Agency.

Class 9. Development appropriate to operational land of statutory undertakers.

Class 10. Development excluded from the permission granted by a general development order solely by reason of a condition imposed by permission granted in some other form.

Class 11. Development not involving the erection of a building, and not envisaging the subsequent erection of a building, if the latter would involve " relevant development ".

Classes 12 and 13. Combinations of development in the foregoing categories, but not so as to exceed the prescribed limits on floor-space.

(7) DEVELOPMENT LAND TAX

On February 27th, 1976, the Development Land Tax Bill was introduced into the House of Commons. Tax is to be charged " in respect of the realisation of the development value of land in the United Kingdom " (cl. 1), as from a date to be declared by order, known as the "appointed day", when it will take the place of development gains tax (cl. 34). There will be " realised development value " on a disposal of land (cl. 4) or on a deemed disposal " immediately before a project of material development is begun " (cl. 2). " Material development " is any development other than that permitted under a general development order (cl. 7(7)), or listed in Schedule 4, Part II (being various marginal categories of limited importance).

Development land tax.

Local authorities, and certain other bodies such as the Commission for the New Towns, are to be exempt. The first £10,000 of value will be exempt in each financial year. Thereafter the first £150,000 of value will be chargeable to tax at $66\frac{2}{3}$ per cent, until March 31st, 1979. Subject to this, the rate will be 80 per cent (cl. 1, 11–13),

The exempt bodies referred to above, and government departments, will buy land net of tax whenever the price includes development value (cl. 38); and this means that tax will be collected by those bodies and not by the Board of Inland Revenue in such cases. Other details are omitted here for reasons of space.

INDEX

A

[1]

Index

DEFINITIONS, STATUTORY AND NON-STATUTORY—*continued*
coparceners, 219
corporation aggregate, 154
        sole, 153
corporeal hereditaments, 137
covenant, 456
determinable fee, 149
          interest, 362
development, 944
easements, 515
engineering operations, 944
estate contract, 128
estovers, 269
fair wear and tear, 416
fee simple, 148
        absolute, 149
        in possession, 151
feudalism, 10
fixtures, 138
half a year, 465
hereditaments, 137
immediate binding trust for sale, 198
inclosure, 569
incorporeal hereditaments, 137
infant, 915
interest in land, 98
issue, 252
joint tenancy, 211
land, 137
lapse, 848
lease not exceeding three years, 390
limitation, 367
merger, 410
mortgage, 637
mortgagee, 637
mortgagor, 637
open contract, 113
power, 272
praedial servitude, 514
privity of estate, 457
profit à prendre, 515, 558
public policy, 374
purchase, 253n
purchaser, 243
remainder, 244, 300
rent service, 428
rentcharge, 625
seisin, 29
service tenant, 470
servitude, 514
settlement, 167
shifting use, 74
specific performance, 131
springing use, 74
statutory life, 348
        owner, 176
sub-mortgage, 647
subrogation, 702
subsidiary vesting deed, 171
tenant at sufferance, 401
    by the curtesy, 244
    for life, 174
    pur autre vie, 265
term of years, 382
        absolute, 382
timber, 268
trust, 197
    for sale, 197
trustee securities, 192
vested interests, 293
vesting deed, 170
voluntary settlement, 811
waste, 267
wear and tear, 416
DEPENDANTS' MAINTENANCE. *See* FAMILY PROVISION.

[11]

[12]

[17]

Index

LIGHT,
    easement of. *See* EASEMENT.
LIMITATION,
    condition distinguished, 367
    meaning, 367
    words of. *See under* WORDS.
LIMITATION OF ACTIONS,
    accrual, date of, breach of condition, 893
                equitable interests, 893
                equity of redemption, 662
                forfeiture, 893
                fraud, in case of, 905
                future interests, 892
                mistake, in case of, 906
                present interests, 889
                tenancies, 896
                        at will, 897
                        from year to year, 898
    acknowledgement, effect, 907
                person bound by, 907
    assertion of right, 906
    breach of condition, for, 893
    corporation sole, action by, 885
    Crown, actions by, 885
    dispossession, interference with, 890
    disseisor, estate acquired, 903
            title, 903
    foreclosure, 673
    fraudulent concealment, in case of, 905
    future interests, 892
                created while time running, 892
                expectant on entailed interests, 892
    " good possessory title," 901
    laches, doctrine of, 898
    limitation period, 885, 886
                commencement. *See* accrual, *supra.*
                expiration, effect, 900
                extension, 904
    mistake, effect, 906
    mortgages, 669, 675
    necessity for, 883, 884
    negative operation, 884
    part payment, effect, 907
    possession, adverse, effect, 900
                meaning, 887
                necessity for, 887
                what constitutes, 890
        failure to acquire on death, 891
                under grant, 891
    possessors, adverse, restrictive covenants binding on, 603
                successive, 888
                title transferred to, 900
    present interests, 889
    redemption of mortgages, 662
    registered land, 900, 908
    rent, action to recover, 434
    rentcharge, to recover, 891
    right as well as remedy barred, 900
        of action, accrual, date of, 889
    settled land, 900
    statutes, necessity for, 884
              negative effect, 901, 902
    successive interests, one person entitled to, 893
    tenancies, 896
            at will, 897
            from year to year, 898
    tenant, against, 896
    tenants in common, between, 894
    trustee, against, 894
        by, 895
LIMITED OWNER'S CHARGE
    registration, 741
LOCAL COURTS,
    establishment, 12

[31]

[34]

[35]

[43]

Index

RESTRICTIVE COVENANT—*continued*
  equitable assignees bound by—*continued*
    doctrine—*continued*
      dominant land, annexation to, effect, 608
        whole, 607
          or part, 608
        ascertainable, must be, 600
        covenant must touch, 601
        effect where none, 600
        part, affecting, 608
        purchaser of part, whether passing to, 608
          whether benefit passes with, 605
      general nature, 597
      limits on assignment, 610–611
      notice, originally based on, 598
      origin, 597
      schemes of development, 612–615. *And .see* BUILDING
    interests, as, 70, 602   [SCHEME
  extinction, 617
  Halsall v. *Brizell*, doctrine of, 596
  indemnity covenants, chain of, 595
  Law Commission Report on, 621
  lease, in, common law, enforceability at, 595
  lease, long, enlargement into freehold, 596
  modification, 617
  negative, equitable doctrine applies, 597, 600
  occupiers, binding on, 603
  overreaching, not liable to, 793
  positive, equitable doctrine does not apply to, 600
  registered land, 621
  registration as land charge, 605, 743
  running with land in equity. *See* equitable doctrine, *supra.*
  successors in title, meaning, 609
  Tulk v. *Moxhay*, doctrine of, 597
  underlessees bound by, 603
  unity of seisin, covenant discharged by, 620
  void against purchaser, 605, 743
  whether binding, statutory power to declare, 620
RETAINER,
  right of, 824
REVERSION,
  covenant, benefit of, runs with, 454
    lease in writing where, 455
    burden of, running with, 456
  merger in. *See* MERGER.
  remainder distinguished, 295
  severed part of, owner's rights, 457
  title to, 733
REVERSIONARY LEASES, 382, 386
RIGHT,
  writ of, 29
RIGHTS OF WAY,
  easements, are, 523
  grant, implied, 538
  necessity, way of, 533, 534
  non-user, 557
RIPARIAN OWNERS,
  rights, 157, 158, 159
RIVER,
  beds, rights in, 157
  fishing rights, 160, 161
  public rights, 159
  riparian owners' rights, 157, 158, 159
ROMAN EMPIRE,
  break up, 10
ROMAN LAW,
  dominium in, 32, 36
ROOT OF TITLE,
  possession as, 31
  seisin is, 29

S.

SAILORS,
  privileged wills, 841
    revocation, 861

[44]

[45]

[52]